SOCIAL AND POLITICAL PHILOSOPHY
Contemporary Readings

BARUCH A. BRODY

Rice University and Baylor College of Medicine

GEORGE SHER

Rice University

HARCOURT BRACE COLLEGE PUBLISHERS

Fort Worth   Philadelphia   San Diego   New York   Orlando   Austin   San Antonio
Toronto   Montreal   London   Sydney   Tokyo

Publisher	Earl McPeek
Acquisitions Editor	David C. Tatom
Project Editor	Claudia Gravier
Art Director	Burl Sloan
Production Manager	Diane Gray

ISBN: 0-15-503746-3
Library of Congress Catalog Card Number: 98–86565

Address for Orders
Harcourt Brace College Publishers
6277 Sea Harbor Drive
Orlando, FL 32887-6777
1-800-782-4479

Address for Editorial Correspondence
Harcourt Brace College Publishers
301 Commerce Street, Suite 3700
Fort Worth, TX 76102

Web Site Address
http://www.hbcollege.com

Printed in the United States of America

8 9 0 1 2 3 4 5 6 7   039   9 8 7 6 5 4 3 2 1

Harcourt Brace College Publishers

PREFACE

To most people, the prevailing political, legal, and economic institutions are simply unquestioned elements of our existence—the background against which life is lived. However, unlike other crucial background facts—our mortality, the need for food and shelter, the finitude of the available resources—the organization of society is not immutable. Social institutions are human constructs that can be changed. But before we can sensibly ask whether a given institution should be changed, we must understand its purpose and justification and before we can do that, we must reflect more broadly on what kind of society we want and what the moral constraints on institutions are. The branch of philosophy that carries out such reflection is social and political philosophy, and the problems it addresses are the subject matter of this anthology.

Social and Political Philosophy: Contemporary Readings seeks to present these problems in a systematic and organized fashion. When initially planning the book, we began by mapping out the main problems of the discipline and the main approaches to each problem, and only afterwards proceeded to ask who the best representative of each approach might be. The result is an anthology with more structure than any other of which we are aware.

We begin with a division between political philosophy, focusing on the state as the fundamental political institution, and social philosophy, focusing on social ideals and their implementation in social institutions. Within the first part of the text we consider the legitimate functions of the state, the process of decision making in the state, and the relations between states and larger and smaller communities. Within the second part, we consider a variety of social ideals (for example, justice, equality, and liberty) and ways of implementing them in such institutions as education, the family, and the criminal justice system.

To aid the student, we have included an introduction to each of the major sections of each part of the book. When we were constructing our map of the main problems of the discipline, we tried to survey as wide an area as possible, and the book's range of topics is correspondingly broad. Although it contains many readings on such central and familiar issues as political obligation, democracy, rights, and justice, it also contains a good deal of material on less widely discussed issues—exploitation, commodification, secession, multiculturalism, education, and the family, to name just a few. Moreover, within each topic, we have tried to find selections representing each major approach. These selections were chosen on the basis of their philosophical merit and their accessibility. Because we wanted to make available the most recent developments on the subject and because the work that is being done today is characterized by a high degree of rigor and insight, the vast majority of the selections have been drawn from contemporary or near-contemporary works. The only exceptions are selections by Jeremy Bentham, John Stuart Mill, and Henry Sidgwick—three earlier utilitarians whose lucid and eloquent formulations of important positions remain unsurpassed.

We are pleased to acknowledge the assistance of two able Rice University graduate students whose efforts made the editing process much easier and more enjoyable. In the book's early stages, when we were sifting through the literature trying to decide what to include, Maureen Kelley contributed both abundant energy and many good ideas. In the later stages, when the book was actually being assembled, Amy Rowland handled many thankless but vital tasks with calm efficiency. Early reviewers for the textbook development process included John Arthur, Binghamton University; Marcia Baron, University of Illinois at Champaign-Urbana; Lawrence Becker, College of William & Mary; Alan Buchanan, University of Wisconsin; Ann Davis, University of Colorado; Daniel Farrell, Ohio State University; Leslie Francis, University of Utah; Fred Miller, Bowling Green University; William Nelson, University of Houston; and Alan Wertheimer, University of Vermont. Thanks also to those who helped us work through the publication process: David Tatom, Pam Hatley, Cathlynn Richard, Mike Norris, Claudia Gravier, Burl Sloan, and Diane Gray.

Putting this book together has proven to be a valuable experience for us. We having learned a lot and will be quite content if those who use the book end up learning as much.

Baruch A. Brody
George Sher

TABLE OF CONTENTS

PART III: Is There an Obligation to Obey the Law?

SECTION TWO:
DECISION MAKING IN THE STATE

PART IV: Justifications of Majoritarian Decision Making

PART V: Forms of Majoritarian Decision Making

PART VI: Constitutional Limits on Majoritarian Decision Making

SECTION THREE:
BEYOND THE STATE

PART VII: National Self-Determination and Secession

PART VIII: Cosmopolitanism, Multiculturalism, and Community

SOCIAL PHILOSOPHY

SECTION FOUR:
SOCIAL IDEALS

PART IX: Justice

PART X: Equality

PART XI: Liberty, Rights, Property and Self-Ownership

SECTION FIVE:
SOCIAL INSTITUTIONS

Part XII: Education

PART XIII: The Family

PART XIV: Punishment

POLITICAL PHILOSOPHY

ONE

THE THEORY OF THE STATE

Government profoundly affects each citizen's life. What we can buy and sell, what we can do with what we own, how we can resolve our disagreements— these and virtually all other aspects of each persons's life are regulated by an omnipresent legal system. We are, to be sure, not always burdened by the law's requirements. As long as we are independently inclined to do what the law dictates, we can operate quite happily within its constraints. Still, burdensome or not, those constraints are always there, and they are always backed by the state's irresistible power. If we do not obey them willingly, we will generally do so unwillingly.

Can an institution so powerful and so pervasive be justified? If so, what are its functions or purposes? Are there limits on what it may legitimately do? And, if we can get away with disobedience, why should we obey its laws? Taken together, these questions constitute *the problem of political authority,* and they are the topic of this book's first section.

One answer to the question "What purpose(s) does the state serve?" is that contemporary states serve *no* legitimate purpose. This view is called *philosophical anarchism,* and it is defended in the book's opening selection by A. John Simmons. Anarchism is not an option that we usually take seriously; when we consider it at all, most of us tend to think vaguely of bearded bomb-throwers in long coats. However, according to Simmons, philosophical anarchism is a direct consequence of a view that many *do* take seriously—namely, that as long as we violate no one else's rights, we are not obligated (and may not be forced) to do anything we have not *agreed* to do. This voluntarist principle, Simmons argues, renders all governments illegitimate because the requisite agreements to obey the law have simply not been forthcoming. However, Simmons also argues that philosophical anarchism does not imply that anyone may engage in anarchic behavior: even if our government is illegitimate, we may, and often do, have compelling moral and prudential reasons to do what its laws require.

Like John Simmons, Robert Nozick takes anarchism seriously; but unlike Simmons, Nozick does not think we are forced to accept it. Instead, Nozick argues in reading 2 that if all people have "natural rights" of the sort described by the British philosopher John Locke—not coincidentally, the same rights that Simmons thinks we have—then governments can develop through a sequence of legitimate steps. In Locke's view, each person has a right to enforce his (other) rights. Because each individual has only a limited amount of strength, Nozick argues that people who did not live under a government—people in a "state of nature"—would have strong incentives to form protective coalitions. Given the dynamics of the situation, each geographical territory would eventually come to be dominated by a single such coalition. These dominant "protective associations" would enjoy *de facto* monopolies on force and would be morally obligated to protect even non-members. These are just the features that distinguish governments, therefore each dominant protective association would in effect *be* a minimal state.

Given his Lockean starting point, it is not surprising that Nozick thinks the legitimate functions of government are restricted to protecting citizens from force, fraud, and other violations of their rights. But other philosophers begin from different starting points, and their views of the state's function are correspondingly more expansive. One alternative view, advanced by the influential nineteenth-century utilitarian Henry Sidgwick in reading 3, is that the basic aim of government is not to protect people's rights, but rather to maximize their well-being. This view, Sidgwick thinks, is not only philosophically defensible, but also provides the best explanation of many actual political arrangements. It explains, for example, why we have laws that protect people from physical harm and damage to their property—the sorts of laws that Nozick endorses— but also why the law protects natural resources, prevents monopolies, and sometimes takes steps that equalize wealth.

Others understand the aims of government more expansively yet. One important view, defended by Robert George in reading 4, is that in addition to protecting people's rights and promoting their welfare, governments ought to try to improve their citizens' characters. In developing this view, George takes a position that is similar, but not identical, to that of Aristotle. Like Aristotle, George argues that reason alone cannot motivate everyone to do the right thing; and like Aristotle too, he argues that coercion can provide valuable supplementary motives, and that because the law is impersonal, its use of force is unlikely to elicit undue resentment. However, unlike Aristotle, George believes that there is no single best way for humans to live. He thus maintains that instead of channelling all citizens down a single path, governments can at best "proscribe only the fairly small number of acts and practices that are incompatible with any morally good life."

Although the authors discussed so far disagree about *what* functions government ought to serve, they agree that all legitimate governments ought to serve the *same* functions. However, according to Michael Walzer (reading 5), this is true only in a qualified sense. Although Walzer concedes that every legitimate government should try to satisfy needs and protect rights, he insists that the content of these needs and rights are understood very differently by different cultures. For example, the ancient Athenians thought that public provision should be made for religion but not for education, while among us, precisely the opposite understanding holds. In Walzer's view, there is no objective standpoint from which one such judgment can be discovered to be right and another wrong. These are decisions that can only be made by a society's members, and participation in making them is itself an important social good. Thus, according to Walzer, "the common life is simultaneously the prerequisite of provision and one of its products."

To what degree does the state's function impose *limits* on what it may legitimately do? That depends, it seems, on which theory of the state's function one adopts. On a view like Nozick's, the very rights that governments exist to protect also prohibit them from interfering with their citizens' lives in any more extensive ways. However, on other accounts, the relation between the state's function and its limits are not this close.

Consider, for example, the utilitarian approach. If we hold, as Sidgwick did, that the state's primary aim is to promote the welfare of its citizens, then we seem committed to the view that paternalistic laws—that is, laws that interfere with people's liberty for their own good—are often justified. But Sidgwick did not believe this, and neither did the earlier utilitarian, John Stuart Mill. In Mill's famous tract *On Liberty,* a part of which appears as selection 6, he argued on utilitarian grounds that the only basis on which government or society may legitimately interfere with an individual's freedom is to prevent that person from harming others. This means, in particular, that the state may not interfere with a person's liberty either to prevent him from harming himself or to induce him to live a better life. Mill defended his "harm principle" both on the grounds that each individual knows his own interest best and cares about it most and on the grounds that each of us benefits immensely by being exposed to the greatest possible variety of "experiments in living."

More than a century after it was articulated, Mill's harm principle remains a benchmark of liberal thought. However, in reading 7, Joel Feinberg argues that in addition to preventing harm to others, there is a further (though far less weighty) rationale for using the state's power to interfere with citizens' liberty. Such interference may also be justified if it will prevent activities that are extremely offensive to others. This rationale must of course be used with care; for as Mill noted, "there is no parity between the feeling of a person for his own opinion, and the feeling of another who is offended at his holding it." Nevertheless, according to Feinberg, "there are [some] human experiences that are harmless in themselves yet so unpleasant that we can rightly demand legal protection from them even at the cost of other persons' liberties." In an extraordinary piece of philosophical writing—surely one of the funniest ever published—Feinberg makes his case by regaling the reader with thirty-one incidents of highly offensive behavior on a public bus.

According to Feinberg, whether the state should prohibit a particular kind of offensive behavior depends, among other things, on "the ease with which unwilling witnesses can avoid the offensive displays." By this criterion, the publication and distribution of pornography probably should not be entirely banned. But another rationale for prohibiting pornography, originally advanced by Catherine MacKinnon and summarized in reading 8 by Rae Langton, is that certain forms of it contribute to a pattern of degradation and subordination of women. This pattern is said to render women systematically vulnerable to battery, rape, and various other injuries. Whether suppressing pornography for this reason is consistent with Mill's harm principle is left for the reader to consider.

Whatever else is true, governments may seem to overstep their bounds when they prohibit harmless consensual commercial transactions. But, for two distinct reasons, some have argued that governments sometimes should do just that. One reason for limiting what people may buy and sell is that certain crucial aspects of human experience would be distorted or devalued if they could be traded in the marketplace. Thus, some argue that prostitution should remain illegal because human sexuality must not be treated as a commodity, and that surrogate motherhood should be banned because human beings should not be bought or sold. Both claims are examined sympathetically by Margaret Radin in reading 9, while the second is discussed more critically by Richard Arneson in reading 10. A second reason for prohibiting harmless consensual transactions, including surrogate motherhood—namely, that such actions can wrongfully exploit one of the parties—is analyzed and criticized by Alan Wertheimer in reading 11.

As we saw, the harm principle prohibits interference with liberty to prevent citizens from harming themselves or to induce them to live better lives. But both forms of interference have also had defenders. In reading 12, John Kleinig discusses two arguments for paternalism. The first argument, which trades on the fact that individuals are often poor judges of their own interests, is said to be objectionable because it "denies a person's status as an agent, as a source of reasons for action to whom respect is due." However, the second, which appeals to the fact that people are sometimes mistaken even about what is required by *their own* central values or projects, is indeed said to justify paternalism in some cases. And, in reading 13, George Sher argues that the state may legitimately try to induce its citizens to live good lives—a view that is closely related to Robert George's claim that governments should try to improve their citizens' characters. Against Sher's view, some object that no way of living can be objectively valuable unless it is chosen *because of* its value, and that agents cannot choose ways of living because of their value if their choices are responses to incentives or threats. However, in response, Sher points out that even if someone initially engages in an activity for reasons unrelated to its value, he may, simply through engaging in it, eventually come to appreciate its merits. If he does, he may then indeed end up choosing it precisely because of its value.

So far, we have considered only questions about how governments should treat their citizens. However, it is one thing to say that a law has been legitimately enacted, and quite another to say that citizens are obligated to obey it.

Of course, many laws, such as those that prohibit murder and rape, forbid conduct that is wrong in itself. But is the wrongness of such conduct the *only* reason to obey these laws, or do we also have independent reasons? And what reason do we have to obey laws such as tax and traffic codes, which require actions that would otherwise *not* be obligatory? To answer these questions, we must ascertain whether, and if so why, there is a general obligation to obey the law.

Because one relatively unproblematic way of incurring an obligation to do something is to agree to do it, some philosophers have sought to ground an obligation to obey the law in some form of tacit consent. Along these lines, Harry Beran argues in reading 14 that citizens in effect agree to obey the state's laws when they (a) remain within the territory where the laws apply, (b) do not band together with others to secede, and (c) do not publicly renounce their membership in the state. To the standard objection that remaining within a state's territory cannot count as consent if one lacks the resources to leave, Beran responds by making a distinction between coercion, which does invalidate consent, and poverty and ignorance, which, in his view, do not.

Might we be obligated to obey the law for reasons other than consent? In particular, might we become obligated simply by accepting or receiving benefits? There are, in general, two ways of making the case: first, by arguing that we have an obligation of fairness to those whose sacrifices made the benefits possible, and, second, by arguing that we owe a debt of gratitude to the institution that provides them. In the next three readings, these answers are considered in some detail.

The first answer rests on what is often referred to as *the principle of fairness*. This principle, originally articulated by H. L. A. Hart, is summarized in reading 15 by Robert Nozick as follows: "When a number of persons engage in a just, mutually advantageous, cooperative venture according to rules and thus restrain their liberty in ways necessary to yield advantages for all, those who have submitted to these restrictions have a right to similar acquiescence on the part of those who have benefited from their submission." By presenting a series of imaginative examples, Nozick tries to convince the reader that receiving benefits from a cooperative scheme to which one has not agreed does not obligate one to support the scheme. But in reading 16, Richard Arneson responds that Nozick has run together several different types of case. Even if the non-voluntary receipt of benefits does not *always* create obligations of fairness, Arneson argues that it does create them when the benefits are collective in the sense that all must enjoy them if anyone does, and when certain other conditions are satisfied.

The second way of arguing that the non-voluntary receipt of benefits creates an obligation to obey the law is to construe that obligation as one of *gratitude*. Although such arguments have a long history—one can be found in Plato's dialogue *Crito*—they have been criticized on various grounds. For example, it has been objected that gratitude can be owed only to individuals, that many actions that benefit us do not call for requital, and that even if the state's benefits do call for requital, it is not clear why obedience to law is the form it should take. But according to A. D. M. Walker (reading 17), these objections either are not directed at the strongest version of the gratitude argument or else can be met. Walker contends that the argument's strongest version takes the debt of gratitude to be owed not to any abstract political institution but to one's fellow citizens considered collectively. He contends, as well, that to think in terms of requital is to confuse gratitude with fairness and that the relevant obligation is "not to act in ways incompatible with the attitudes which constitute the core of the grateful response." This obligation, he thinks, is violated when citizens disobey the law because their disobedience ungratefully damages the state's interests.

A final approach to obedience to law is suggested by Rolf Sartorius in reading 18. As a utilitarian, Sartorius rejects all attempts to defend a general obligation to obey the law: he specifically criticizes both the tacit consent and the fairness argument. However, even though Sartorius rejects these arguments, he accepts the claim that "a viable political association must in the normal case rest upon a generally shared expectation on the part of most of its members that most duly enacted laws will be obeyed." To account for these expectations, he lists various considerations that generally support the utility of obedience to law. These include both the fact that the laws generally operate in beneficial ways and our inability reliably to identify the cases in which disobedience would produce more utility than obedience. When these conditions are believed to prevail, most citizens will act just as they would if they *did* acknowledge an obligation to obey the law; and if they do, then our inability to justify such an obligation will not matter at all.

PART

I

FUNCTIONS AND PURPOSES OF LEGITIMATE STATES

1.
Philosophical Anarchism

A. JOHN SIMMONS

Serious political voluntarism commits us to the acceptance of philosophical anarchism.* Since Lockean political philosophy is *essentially* voluntarist, in my view, this means that Lockeans must also accept philosophical anarchism. And because I believe political voluntarism to be the correct view to take on its subject (a claim supported in part by the rejection of nonvoluntarist fairness theory outlined above),[1] I believe as well that Lockean political philosophy is on secure ground in its commitment to this form of anarchism. Lest this seem a depressing conclusion, however, I will suggest below that Lockean anarchism in fact entails a view of our actual political lives that is free of many dramatically counterintuitive implications, implications that might force us to reassess the arguments that lead us to that view.[2]

It might seem, of course, that Lockean philosophical anarchism could hardly be a more counterintuitive position. For Lockean anarchism might seem to imply both that (a) all existing governments are morally equal (since all are equally illegitimate or nonauthoritative, equally lacking "political power" over their subjects), and (b) residents of existing "communities" may do as they please, lacking any political obligations to obey valid law in their societies or support the other institutions of government that preserve public order and supply vital goods. A position that had those consequences would, indeed, be sufficiently odd to make reasonable persons question the arguments that led to it. But Lockean anarchism in fact implies neither of these counterintuitive claims.[3]

---

* Simmons defines voluntarism as the view that "political relationships among persons are morally legitimate only when they are the product of voluntary, willing, morally significant acts by all parties." Philosophical anarchism is the view that "there are no morally legitimate states; few (if any) citizens in existing political societies have political obligations."—eds.

[1] More precisely . . . , I think Locke is correct in claiming that each person is born to natural freedom (i.e., to *moral* freedom from political obligation and the de jure authority of others). And I think that only political voluntarism is consistent with acceptance of the natural freedom of persons. The only political obligations we have are those we have voluntarily assumed, at least for the cases of polities even remotely like our own. I take my arguments in *Moral Principles and Political Obligations* (Princeton: Princeton University Press, 1979) to be support for these claims, and to establish that *nonvoluntarist* accounts of political obligation (such as those utilizing a principle of utility, a principle of gratitude, or natural duties of justice or allegiance) are uniformly unsuccessful when applied to modern political communities.

[2] As examples of those who disagree with me here, arguing that the consequences of philosophical anarchism *are* damningly counterintuitive, see Michael Lessnoff, *Social Contract* (Atlantic Highlands: Humanities Press, 1986), and Thomas Senor, "What if There Are No Political Obligations? A Reply to A. J. Simmons," *Philosophy & Public Affairs* (Summer 1987).

[3] For a fuller defense of several of the claims argued immediately below, see my *Moral Principles and Political Obligations,* chapter 8.

First, of course, from the mere fact that all existing governments or societies are illegitimate (in the sense in which a Lockean must use that term), it in no way follows that they are all morally equal. Governments may do more or less good, for their "subjects" and for others, and they may do more or less harm. They may violate the rights of persons more or less regularly, systematically, and seriously. They may be more or less merciful, responsive, beneficent, efficient, and wise. In short, governments may still, within the Lockean anarchist model, be properly said to exemplify to varying degrees all of the virtues and vices that we normally associate with governments.

Nothing in Lockean anarchism prevents us from ranking governments morally, as better or worse, in just the ways that we are normally inclined to do. We may even say that good governments are those that most deserve our free consent, those that it would be most reasonable for people to *make* legitimate (in existing or modified form) by the free contract (consent) and trust that establish the political relationship. The one thing we must *not* say, according to Lockean anarchism, is that good governments are, by virtue of those qualities that make them good, therefore legitimate, or that they therefore wield genuinely political power. Good governments, however extensive their virtues, cannot obtain over free people (without their consent) "the right to command and be obeyed." And to the extent that good (but still illegitimate) governments, albeit with the best of intentions, utilize ("nonpolitical") force in violation of the rights of free persons, they act (prima facie) wrongly.

Second, the fact that most residents of existing societies must be understood not to have political obligations, on the Lockean anarchist view, in no way implies that these persons may act however they please. All persons have basic, natural moral duties to one another . . .—duties not to harm others in their lives, liberty, health, limb, or goods. . . . Even with no general obligation to obey the law, then, individuals in existing societies still have duties to refrain from those actions that in all legal systems constitute the most serious crimes (e.g., murder, assault, rape, theft, fraud). Similarly, I have argued that Lockeans (and others) ought to accept some positive duties and rights—that is, duties to aid those in need and to extend their surplus wealth to the poor.[4] This implies, of course, that even if legal duties in this realm (where they exist) have no moral force, persons are still morally bound to care for one another in certain ways. They may even choose to (or, in hard cases, need to) discharge such duties by supporting salient cooperative efforts to help those in need, possibly including efforts by (their own or other) governments. And where others are abiding by innocent laws or conventions, and my violation of those rules would endanger them, I am bound not to violate those rules—even though the rules have *in themselves* no force with respect to me, and even though the behavior to which I am bound is not *naturally* obligatory. Thus, if others follow the convention of driving their vehicles on the right (and in so doing violate no right of mine), I must not knowingly endanger them by driving on the left, for I am morally forbidden to deliberately harm the innocent. This is true even if I am not a party

---

[4] See my *Lockean Theory of Rights* (Princeton: Princeton University Press, 1982), chapter 6.

to their practices and even though driving on the left is not naturally (i.e., in all times and places) immoral. The natural law prohibition on harming others extends itself to cases where their choices (e.g., innocent convention-following) or other (e.g., medical) developments make other persons vulnerable to harm in ways that are not natural or typical.

Lockean anarchism, then, insists that persons in existing societies are by no means free to do as they please, but rather that they have a wide range of moral duties that will overlap considerably (i.e., require the same conduct as) their nonbinding legal duties. And in most societies these moral duties overlap the most central and important legal duties, prohibiting physical harming and most serious disruption of others' lives. Further, however, even where persons owe no natural moral duties to others, there can still be additional moral reasons not to interfere with or upset the innocent plans or arrangements of others.[5] Even if I do not count as harming you by upsetting your plans (and so am entitled to upset them), it would plainly be malicious to do so gratuitously. We are not morally obligated to act, nor ought we to act, just whenever we have a right to do so.[6] Indeed, simple decency demands that we not press others to secure our unimportant rights, where doing so will result in no substantial gain for us and serious cost for others. We have, in short, good moral reason, even if no moral duty, to practice the virtues of patience, courtesy, consideration, and so on, toward others. Again, Lockean anarchism does not advocate insensitive or destructive conduct.

It is easy to see, then, that Lockean philosophical anarchism does not have the direct and profoundly counterintuitive consequences that we considered initially. But we can see already as well several ways in which Lockean anarchism pushes us to substantially revise our thinking about ordinary "political" life. While we live in structured societies with laws and governments, we are not "subject" to those laws or governments, bound to obey them. We cannot act on the general presumption that obedience is obligatory, advisable, or even morally permissible. We must, rather, view legal requirements and the governments that make them with a certain skepticism,[7] with a (in my view healthy) focus on their actual moral standing. Our obligations to comply with laws (i.e., to act in the ways they require) have nothing to do with any special bond to the community whose laws they are, but only with the specific content of the laws. The same laws, imposed in some other similar country, would call for compliance by us in the same ways and for the same reasons.[8] We are bound to act toward our colleagues, our governors, and members of other societies all as fellow residents in a highly socialized state of nature, one in which we all are

---

[5] See *Moral Principles and Political Obligations*, 193–94, and my "The Anarchist Position: A Reply to Klosko and Senor," *Philosophy and Public Affairs* (Summer 1987): 278.

[6] See *Lockean Theory of Rights*, pp. 119–20.

[7] Leslie Green, *The Authority of the State* (Oxford: Oxford University Press, 1988), pp. 254–255.

[8] That is, those laws whose point is territorially limited (e.g., specific traffic laws) will call for compliance when we are in the relevant territory, while those whose point is universal (e.g., laws forbidding murder) will call for compliance regardless of which country enacts them.

surrounded by many people with false beliefs about their rights and duties with respect to us.

The extent to which existing governments should be complied with, disobeyed, or resisted (and the respects in which such conduct is optional) is, of course, in part just a function of the specific character of the government in question. But the content of each person's natural rights provides a set of basic guidelines, as a common background for all such considerations. According to Lockean moral and political philosophy . . . , each person is born to a broad right of self-government, which includes the right to be free of coercive interference by others (except to prevent or in response to wrongdoing), the right to act in pursuit of "innocent delights" and to advance one's own and others' well-being (within the limits set by others' equal rights), and the powers to make property, to alienate or acquire rights by contract or promise, and so on. Each person also has the right to punish others who act immorally (up to the limits set by natural law) and to secure just reparation for injuries done them.[9] Free residents of existing societies may, of course, have alienated or forfeited some (or all) of these rights or acquired others in private activities, transactions, or interactions. But we must otherwise think of ourselves and others as (at least for the most part) possessors of this basic set of natural moral rights.

Viewed in this light, it is easy to see in what areas typical existing governments most often wrong (i.e., violate the rights of) those who reside within their territories. For (to simplify substantially) the most familiar types of (restrictive) laws imposed and enforced by governments can be divided into five categories: (1) those that prohibit acts that wrongly harm (including those that wrongly fail to benefit) others—that is, acts that are naturally immoral or *mala in se;* (2) those that impose systems of coordination on morally permissible activities, in order to prevent unintended harm (as in traffic laws); (3) those that prohibit private conduct that is harmless (and thus not forbidden by natural morality), but which is for other reasons deemed wrong or unnatural; (4) those that require or forbid acts in order to protect the government or the state (as in laws prohibiting treason or requiring military service); (5) those that require payments (or which permit seizures of property) to finance or facilitate government operations, provision of public benefits, and the like.

Of these five categories, it seems clear that governments will most often be justified in enforcing laws in the first two. For while it is true that the residents of existing states still possess their natural rights to punish moral wrongdoers, those who govern and administer the law are also persons possessing this right. When states punish those who harm others, officials of the state may in fact be justifiably exercising their natural rights to do so.[10] States may not demand that

---

[9] For a fuller account of these basic rights, see *Lockean Theory of Rights,* especially chapter 2.

[10] Provided, of course, that their punishments are just in kind and amount. States invariably act wrongly in prohibiting private citizens (or outsiders) from exercising *their* equal rights to punish (i.e., in seizing a monopoly on force); but this wrong is usually not a very serious one. For reasonable persons will not wish to compete for the right to punish (possibly dangerous) wrongdoers, at least if the state is punishing immorality efficiently and fairly.

we *obey* their laws; but they may legitimately punish us for doing what is in fact contrary to law, when our so acting also breaches a moral duty.

In categories (3)–(5), however, governments routinely wrong those against whom their laws are enforced. No one may interfere with harmless, morally innocent activities (as the law does in category [3]). Nor does an illegitimate government have the right to force free people to protect it or the territories it claims (by enforcing laws in category [4]). If persons cannot be brought to voluntarily uphold a government or defend a territory (or to freely consent to do so in the future), the state is not entitled to insist that it continue to exist.[11] Good governments may merit our support, but they are not entitled to require it (without our free consent). And even the best governments wrong us in many ways (as the present argument is in part designed to show). Finally, governments may not demand or seize payment to support their operations or programs (by using laws in category [5]) from those who never authorized such activities. Even the state's enforcement of laws in categories (1) and (2), although possibly a permissible activity, is not an activity for which the state may demand payment. For governments were never authorized to be the sole enforcers of natural morality, nor did typical residents ever consent to pay for this. Payment from another may only be required in order to enforce a right (e.g., to repair a wrong or secure what has been promised). Only in the very rare instance when a government program provides the *only* way for an individual to do his or her moral duty can the government legitimately require participation and payment.[12]

Lockean anarchism maintains that existing governments regularly and systematically wrong their "citizens," no matter how many good qualities (some of) these governments may otherwise display. Good governments limit this wrongdoing by, for instance, minimizing the number of laws in category (3), making military service voluntary, taxing citizens as little as possible, and so on. And good governments often act in ignorance of any wrongdoing and with the intention (and sometimes the effect) of benefiting persons within and without their societies. But even good governments still wrong us, still violate our rights.

How shall we view this wrongdoing in assessing our moral positions? Those of us who live under good governments (to whose authority we never consented) are not, of course, in precisely the situation of any of the persons discussed in chapter 6—that is, we are not members of an originally legitimate community who are now being wronged by the society's breach of its legitimating contract or by the government's breach of its trust. We never contracted

---

[11] Robert Paul Wolff. *In Defense of Anarchism* (New York: Harper & Row, 1970), p. 80.

[12] This claim, with others in this paragraph, is in fact slightly too strong. Governments may sometimes act justifiably even when they violate individual rights. For rights may conflict and other morally relevant factors (such as dramatic utilities) may need to be considered. Moral justification is not a simple matter of respecting rights. Governments may, then, sometimes be justified in coercing individuals, even where they lack the right to do so (and even where they violate the rights of others in the process). But coercion on the massive scale necessary to the enforcement of laws in categories (3)–(5) is unlikely to be defensible except in circumstances of serious crisis.

with those around us or entrusted any government with our rights. Neither, however, are we in . . . a state of war with our governments. For while our governments have used against us "force without right," we have seen . . . that such a wrong is not in fact sufficient to originate a state of war (Locke's own claims to the contrary notwithstanding). Most of our governments (or at least most of those whose legitimacy might seriously have been maintained) have not conspired or acted to deprive us of our lives or freedom, and so have not made war upon us. . . . Rather, most of us in the "free world" are in Lockean terms just persons in the state of nature (simpliciter), subjected by our governments to a variety of (usually) relatively minor, but frighteningly regular, wrongful acts and policies. Illegitimate governments need not be warmakers. They can be quite benign, even progressive or responsive. They can govern the sorts of societies to which residence *would* give consent, if only residents were offered a clear choice situation. They can also, of course, be the sorts of governments we are entitled (or even obligated) to oppose with all means at our disposal. Most often in the "free world," however, they are merely bumbling and inefficient, sometimes well-intentioned, sometimes moved by personal or partisan concerns, occasionally oppressive or tyrannical, and still somehow able to do a reasonable amount of good.

Should those of us living under such governments, then, just obey our moderately good laws and support our moderately good polities? Or should we pursue some alternative course? Here we do well to attend to the Lockean position on justified *individual* resistance, even though that position was framed primarily for those who began in a consensual political relationship (as we did not). For while "the majority" has no moral standing in the state of nature (there being no "people" there on whose behalf they may decide), individuals (such as ourselves) whose rights are violated by de facto governments or societies are in much the same moral situation as individuals who are *returned* to the state of nature by a previously legitimate government's or society's violation of their rights (with this exception: that a contract is breached in the latter case, but not in the former). And . . . we saw what Lockean political philosophy must say about such individuals. Individuals have the right to resist and repair violations of their rights and to recruit others who are entitled to assist them in this, regardless of whether the individuals live within or without political society. And in the state of nature (but not in political society) they may resist, repair, and punish even nonsystematic, nondeliberate violations. In thus enforcing our rights, we are limited only by the requirements that we avoid infringing the more pressing rights of others and avoid causing dramatic social harm (or preventing the accomplishment of dramatic social good).

When we confront a moderately good (but still illegitimate) legal system and government, then, we must weigh the importance of the rights it violates against the consequences of our various possible strategies. If the government is a good one, its violations of our rights would need to be very serious indeed (which will be unusual under a good government) for us to be justified in doing anything that will cause it to be unable to function effectively. For it will likely be doing significant good and preventing significant harm. And while we have no contractual duty to resist wrongs done to others (as we would toward fellow members of a legitimate polity) . . . we have a natural moral duty to aid those in need, as far at least as we comfortably can (and perhaps farther). This duty may require us to in certain ways support the efforts of governments (if only by refraining from disabling them) when they assist those in need. Finally, of course, unless a government's violation of our rights is very serious, the acts we will be morally entitled to perform (in order to justly resist, punish, and repair those wrongs) will be anyway unlikely to be violent or destructive enough to cause serious disruption of a government's functions. For we are not at war with such governments as I am considering here. These moral facts, plus considerations of simple prudence (i.e., our interest in avoiding legal punishment), seem to dictate that moderately good governments, which violate our rights only in the ways such governments typically do, ought not to be resisted in ways that threaten to destroy them or to replace them with distinctly inferior alternatives. Lockean anarchism acknowledges that there can be strong moral reasons for supporting, or at least not actively resisting, even (certain) illegitimate governments. In this regard again, Lockean anarchism is not dramatically counterintuitive in its implications. It is only philosophically, not practically anarchic.

In the face of the wrongs done us by moderately good existing governments, of course, it will still usually be morally permissible to simply disobey those laws that are wrongly enforced against us, and it will be reasonable to do so as far as it remains possible to avoid detection or serious legal consequences. For simple individual disobedience almost never has dramatic social consequences. And it remains permissible, even if almost never prudent, to attempt to forcibly secure just compensation for the wrongs done us. It will usually be best to press for public recognition of these wrongs, sometimes even by conspicuous disobedience, within the legal frameworks offered in our society. To disobey conspicuously and pursue legal remedies is not to acknowledge the legitimacy of those frameworks (as the proponent of civil disobedience insists we must do); it is rather only to take action that is well within morally permissible limits in the context of illegitimate, but virtually unavoidable, legal mechanisms.

What we certainly have good reason to do is to press by legal means for those changes in our political arrangements that will permit the establishment of genuinely voluntary political societies. Thus, changes that would clarify the resident's choice situation, expand membership options, reduce the cost of membership, facilitate internal or external emigration, and so on, would all go far toward making the choice between membership and its alternatives adequately informed and fully voluntary. Such changes would help to secure the natural right of self-government to which each of us is born, a right that includes the privilege of genuine freedom in the choice of political (or nonpolitical) forms of life. Although Locke . . . may have been wrong in claiming that life in the state of nature is always precarious and unstable (our lives in *this* state of nature are not, for instance, as he described them), he was surely right at least in maintaining that life in a free, consensual polity is *morally* preferable to life in even a stable, structured society built on force and acquiescence.

It would be foolish to pretend that many actual societies are likely to change or emerge in the ways Lockean political philosophy prescribes. In the world of illegitimate states that will continue, moral persons must cast off their childhood lessons in good citizenship, and proceed by selectively supporting or opposing their governments' actions and policies solely according to the particular moral standing of each governmental move. Even if we find that we can seldom justify or bear the consequences of active disobedience or substantial opposition, we can at least lobby for the elimination of those laws that interfere with harmless choices, impose needless regimentation of behavior and lifestyle, limit personal liberty without securing important social benefits. For any movement in such directions, as we have seen, will at least help to reduce the violation of basic personal rights.

Even when Lockean political philosophy directs us to obey the laws and support the government (of, say, a moderately good but still illegitimate state), and so tells us to do what common intuition prescribes, however, it still forces us to view our conduct in a new light. Lockean philosophical anarchism demands of us that we be more thoughtful about and more sensitive to the particular moral issues in our lives. For we can no longer just appeal to a general presumption of governmental legitimacy of political obligation, viewing it as overriding or outweighing more specific questions about the moral merits or defects of the individual laws, actions, or policies of our governments. We must confront directly and balance carefully the effects of such laws or policies on the performance of our natural duties and the exercise of our natural rights. Perhaps many of us have preferred to avoid the burden of these concerns. Perhaps in our complacency we have assisted the progress of political unfreedom and helped to further popularize the comfortable myth of easy legitimacy. If so, we have, in Locke's words, "done the truth and the public wrong." We owe both, as well as ourselves, a better effort.

2.
The Minimal State
ROBERT NOZICK

POLITICAL PHILOSOPHY

The fundamental question of political philosophy, one that precedes questions about how the state should be organized, is whether there should be any state at all. Why not have anarchy? Since anarchist theory, if tenable, undercuts the whole subject of *political* philosophy, it is appropriate to begin political philosophy with an examination of its major theoretical alternative. Those who consider anarchism not an unattractive doctrine will think it possible that political philosophy *ends* here as well. Others impatiently will await what is to come afterwards. Yet, as we shall see, archists and anarchists alike, those who spring gingerly from the starting point as well as those reluctantly argued away from it, can agree that beginning the subject of political philosophy with state-of-nature theory has an *explanatory* purpose. (Such a purpose is absent when epistemology is begun with an attempt to refute the skeptic.)

Which anarchic situation should we investigate to answer the question of why not anarchy? Perhaps the one that would exist if the actual political situation didn't, while no other possible political one did. But apart from the gratuitous assumption that everyone everywhere would be in the same nonstate boat and the enormous unmanageability of pursuing that counterfactual to arrive at a particular situation, that situation would lack fundamental theoretical interest. To be sure, if that nonstate situation were sufficiently awful, there would be a reason to refrain from dismantling or destroying a particular state and replacing it with none, now.

It would be more promising to focus upon a fundamental abstract description that would encompass all situations of interest, including "where we would now be if." Were this description awful enough, the state would come out as a preferred alternative, viewed as affectionately as a trip to the dentist. Such awful descriptions rarely convince, and not merely because they fail to cheer. The subjects of psychology and sociology are far too feeble to support generalizing so pessimistically across all societies and persons, especially since the argument depends upon *not* making *such* pessimistic assumptions about how the *state* operates. Of course, people know something of how actual states have operated, and they differ in their views. Given the enormous importance of the choice between the state and anarchy, caution might suggest one use the "minimax" criterion, and focus upon a pessimistic estimate of the nonstate situation: the state would be compared with the most pessimistically described Hobbesian state of nature. But in using the minimax criterion, the Hobbesian situation should be compared with the most pessimistically described possible state, including *future* ones. Such a comparison, surely, the worst state of nature would win. Those who view the state as an abomination will not find minimax very compelling, especially since it seems one could always bring back the state if that came to seem desirable. The "maximax" criterion, on the other hand, would proceed on the most optimistic assumptions about how things would work out—Godwin, if you like that sort of thing. But imprudent optimism also lacks conviction. Indeed, no proposed decision criterion for choice under uncertainty carries conviction here, nor does maximizing expected utility on the basis of such frail probabilities.

More to the point, especially for deciding what goals one should try to achieve, would be to focus upon a nonstate situation in which people generally satisfy moral constraints and generally act as they ought. Such an assumption is not wildly optimistic; it does not assume that all people act exactly as they should. Yet this state-of-nature situation is the best anarchic situation one reasonably could hope for. Hence investigating its nature and defects is of crucial importance to deciding whether there should be a state rather than anarchy. If one could show that the state would be superior even to this most favored situation of anarchy, the best that realistically can be hoped for, or would arise by a process involving no morally impermissible steps, or would be an improvement if it arose, this would provide a rationale for the state's existence; it would justify the state.[1]

This investigation will raise the question of whether all the actions persons must do to set up and operate a state are themselves morally permissible. Some anarchists have claimed not merely that we would be better off without a state, but that any state necessarily violates people's moral rights and hence is intrinsically immoral. Our starting point then, though nonpolitical, is by intention far from nonmoral. Moral philosophy sets the background for, and boundaries of, political philosophy. What persons may and may not do to one another limits what they may do through the apparatus of a state, or do to establish such an apparatus. The moral prohibitions it is permissible to enforce are the source of whatever legitimacy the state's fundamental coercive power has. (Fundamental coercive power is power not resting upon any consent of the person to whom it is applied.) This provides a primary arena of state activity, perhaps the only legitimate arena. Furthermore, to the extent moral philosophy is unclear and gives rise to disagreements in people's moral judgments, it also sets problems which one might think could be appropriately handled in the political arena.

• • •

THE STATE OF NATURE

Individuals in Locke's state of nature are in "a state of perfect freedom to order their actions and dispose of their possessions and persons as they think fit,

---

[1] This contrasts with a theory that presents a state's arising from a state of nature by a natural and inevitable process of *deterioration,* rather as medical theory presents aging or dying. Such a theory would not "justify" the state, though it might resign us to its existence.

within the bounds of the law of nature, without asking leave or dependency upon the will of any other man" (sect. 4).[2] The bounds of the law of nature require that "no one ought to harm another in his life, health, liberty, or possessions" (sect. 6). Some persons transgress these bounds, "invading others' rights and . . . doing hurt to one another," and in response people may defend themselves or others against such invaders of rights (chap. 3). The injured party and his agents may recover from the offender "so much as may make satisfaction for the harm he has suffered" (sect. 10); "everyone has a right to punish the transgressors of that law to such a degree as may hinder its violation" (sect. 7); each person may, and may only "retribute to [a criminal] so far as calm reason and conscience dictate, what is proportionate to his transgression, which is so much as may serve for reparation and restraint" (sect. 8).

There are "inconveniences of the state of nature" for which, says Locke, "I easily grant that civil government is the proper remedy" (sect. 13). To understand precisely what civil government remedies, we must do more than repeat Locke's list of the inconveniences of the state of nature. We also must consider what arrangements might be made within a state of nature to deal with these inconveniences—to avoid them or to make them less likely to arise or to make them less serious on the occasions when they do arise. Only after the full resources of the state of nature are brought into play, namely all those voluntary arrangements and agreements persons might reach acting within their rights, and only after the effects of these are estimated, will we be in a position to see how serious are the inconveniences that yet remain to be remedied by the state, and to estimate whether the remedy is worse than the disease.[3]

In a state of nature, the understood natural law may not provide for every contingency in a proper fashion (see sections 159 and 160 where Locke makes this point about legal systems, but contrast section 124), and men who judge in their own case will always give themselves the benefit of the doubt and assume that they are in the right. They will overestimate the amount of harm or damage they have suffered, and passions will lead them to attempt to punish others more than proportionately and to exact excessive compensation

---

[2] John Locke, *Two Treatises of Government*, 2nd ed., ed. Peter Laslett (New York: Cambridge University Press, 1967). Unless otherwise specified, all references are to the *Second Treatise.*

[3] Proudhon has given us a description of the *state's* domestic "inconveniences." "To be GOVERNED is to be watched, inspected, spied upon, directed, law-driven, numbered, regulated, enrolled, indoctrinated, preached at, controlled, checked, estimated, valued, censured, commanded, by creatures who have neither the right nor the wisdom nor the virtue to do so. To be GOVERNED is to be at every operation, at every transaction noted, registered, counted, taxed, stamped, measured, numbered, assessed, licensed, authorized, admonished, prevented, forbidden, reformed, corrected, punished. It is, under pretext of public utility, and in the name of the general interest, to be placed under contribution, drilled, fleeced, exploited, monopolized, extorted from, squeezed, hoaxed, robbed; then, at the slightest resistance, the first word of complaint, to be repressed, fined, vilified, harassed, hunted down, abused, clubbed, disarmed, bound, choked, imprisoned, judged, condemned, shot, deported, sacrificed, sold, betrayed; and to crown all, mocked, ridiculed, derided, outraged, dishonored. That is government; that is its justice; that is its morality." P. J. Proudhon, *General Idea of the Revolution in the Nineteenth Century,* trans. John Beverly Robinson (London: Freedom Press, 1923), pp. 293–294, with some alterations from Benjamin Tucker's translation in *Instead of a Book* (New York, 1893), p. 26.

(sects. 13, 124, 125). Thus private and personal enforcement of one's rights (including those rights that are violated when one is excessively punished) leads to feuds, to an endless series of acts of retaliation and exactions of compensation. And there is no firm way to *settle* such a dispute, to *end* it and to have both parties know it is ended. Even if one party *says* he'll stop his acts of retaliation, the other can rest secure only if he knows the first still does not feel entitled to gain recompense or to exact retribution, and therefore entitled to try when a promising occasion presents itself. Any method a single individual might use in an attempt irrevocably to bind himself into ending his part in a feud would offer insufficient assurance to the other party; tacit agreements to stop also would be unstable.[4] Such feelings of being mutually wronged can occur even with the clearest right and with joint agreement on the facts of each person's conduct; all the more is there opportunity for such retaliatory battle when the facts or the rights are to some extent unclear. Also, in a state of nature a person may lack the power to enforce his rights; he may be unable to punish or exact compensation from a stronger adversary who has violated them (sects. 123, 126).

PROTECTIVE ASSOCIATIONS

How might one deal with these troubles within a state of nature? Let us begin with the last. In a state of nature an individual may himself enforce his rights, defend himself, exact compensation, and punish (or at least try his best to do so). Others may join with him in his defense, at his call.[5] They may join with him to repulse an attacker or to go after an aggressor because they are public spirited, or because they are his friends, or because he has helped them in the past, or because they wish him to help them in the future, or in exchange for something. Groups of individuals may form mutual-protection associations: all will answer the call of any member for defense or for the enforcement of his rights. In union there is strength. Two inconveniences attend such simple mutual-protection associations: (1) everyone is always on call to serve a protective function (and how shall it be decided who shall answer the call for those protective functions that do not require the services of all members?); and (2) any member may call out his associates by saying his rights are being, or have been, violated. Protective associations will not want to be at the beck and call of their cantankerous or paranoid members, not to mention those of their members who might attempt, under the guise of self-defense, to use the association to violate the rights of others. Difficulties will also arise if two different members of the same association are in dispute, each calling upon his fellow members to come to his aid.

---

[4] On the difficulties of binding oneself into a position, and on tacit agreements, see Thomas Schelling's *The Strategy of Conflict* (Cambridge, Mass.: Harvard University Press, 1960).

[5] Others may punish, without his call . . .

A mutual-protection association might attempt to deal with conflict among its own members by a policy of nonintervention. But this policy would bring discord within the association and might lead to the formation of subgroups who might fight among themselves and thus cause the breakup of the association. This policy would also encourage potential aggressors to join as many mutual-protection associations as possible in order to gain immunity from retaliatory or defensive action, thus placing a great burden on the adequacy of the initial screening procedure of the association. Thus protective associations (almost all of those that will survive which people will join) will not follow a policy of nonintervention: they will use some procedure to determine how to act when some members claim that other members have violated their rights. Many arbitrary procedures can be imagined (for example, act on the side of that member who complains first), but most persons will want to join associations that follow some procedure to find out which claimant is correct. When a member of the association is in conflict with nonmembers, the association also will want to determine in some fashion who is in the right, if only to avoid constant and costly involvement in each member's quarrels, whether just or unjust. The inconvenience of everyone's being on call, whatever their activity at the moment or inclinations or comparative advantage, can be handled in the usual manner by division of labor and exchange. Some people will be *hired* to perform protective functions, and some entrepreneurs will go into the business of selling protective services. Different sorts of protective policies would be offered, at different prices, for those who may desire more extensive or elaborate protection.

An individual might make more particular arrangements or commitments short of turning over to a private protective agency all functions of detection, apprehension, judicial determination of guilt, punishment, and exaction of compensation. Mindful of the dangers of being the judge in his own case, he might turn the decision as to whether he has indeed been wronged, and to what extent, to some other neutral or less involved party. In order for the occurrence of the social effect of justice's being seen to be done, such a party would have to be generally respected and thought to be neutral and upright. Both parties to a dispute may so attempt to safeguard themselves against the appearance of partiality, and both might even agree upon the *same* person as the judge between them, and agree to abide by his decision. (Or there might be a specified process through which one of the parties dissatisfied with the decision could appeal it.) But, for obvious reasons, there will be strong tendencies for the above-mentioned functions to converge in the same agent or agency.

People sometimes now do take their disputes outside of the state's legal system to other judges or courts they have chosen, for example, to religious courts.[6] If all parties to a dispute find some activities of the state or its legal system so repellent that they want nothing to do with it, they might agree to forms

---

[6] See I. B. Singer, *In My Father's Court* (New York: Farrar, Strauss, and Giroux, 1966); for a recent "counterculture" example see *WIN Magazine* (November 1, 1971): pp. 11–17.

of arbitration or judgment outside the apparatus of the state. People tend to forget the possibilities of acting independently of the state. (Similarly, persons who want to be paternalistically regulated forget the possibilities of contracting into particular limitations on their own behavior or appointing a given paternalistic supervisory board over themselves. Instead, they swallow the exact pattern of restrictions a legislature happens to pass. Is there really someone who, searching for a group of wise and sensitive persons to regulate him for his own good, would choose that group of people who constitute the membership of both houses of Congress?) Diverse forms of judicial adjudication, differing from the particular package the state provides, certainly could be developed. Nor do the costs of developing and choosing these account for people's use of the state form. For it would be easy to have a large number of preset packages which parties could select. Presumably what drives people to use the state's system of justice is the issue of ultimate enforcement. Only the state can enforce a judgment against the will of one of the parties. For the state does not *allow* anyone else to enforce another system's judgment. So in any dispute in which both parties cannot agree upon a method of settlement, or in any dispute in which one party does not trust another to abide by the decision (if the other contracts to forfeit something of enormous value if he doesn't abide by the decision, by what agency is *that* contract to be enforced?), the parties who wish their claims put into effect will have no recourse permitted by the state's legal system other than to use that very legal system. This may present persons greatly opposed to a given state system with particularly poignant and painful choices. (If the state's legal system enforces the results of certain arbitration procedures, people may come to agree—supposing they abide by this agreement—without any actual direct contact with what they perceive to be officers or institutions of the state. But this holds as well if they sign a contract that is enforced only by the state.)

Will protective agencies *require* that their clients renounce exercising their right of private retaliation if they have been wronged by nonclients of the agency? Such retaliation may well lead to counterretaliation by another agency or individual, and a protective agency would not wish *at that late stage* to get drawn into the messy affair by having to defend its client against the counter-retaliation. Protective agencies would refuse to protect against counterretaliation unless they had first given permission for the retaliation. (Though might they not merely charge much more for the more extensive protection policy that provides such coverage?) The protective agencies need not even require that as part of his agreement with the agency, a client renounce, by contract, his right of private enforcement of justice against its *other clients*. The agency need only refuse a client C, who privately enforces his rights against other clients, any protection against counterretaliation upon him by these other clients. This is similar to what occurs if C acts against a nonclient. The additional fact that C acts upon a client of the agency means that the agency will act toward C as it would toward any nonclient who privately enforced his rights upon any one of its clients. This reduces intra-agency private enforcement of rights to minuscule levels.

THE DOMINANT PROTECTIVE ASSOCIATION

Initially, several different protective associations or companies will offer their services in the same geographical area. What will occur when there is a conflict between clients of different agencies? Things are relatively simple if the agencies reach the same decision about the disposition of the case. (Though each might want to exact the penalty.) But what happens if they reach different decisions as to the merits of the case, and one agency attempts to protect its client while the other is attempting to punish him or make him pay compensation? Only three possibilities are worth considering:

1. In such situations the forces of the two agencies do battle. One of the agencies always wins such battles. Since the clients of the losing agency are ill protected in conflicts with clients of the winning agency, they leave their agency to do business with the winner.[7]
2. One agency has its power centered in one geographical area, the other in another. Each wins the battles fought close to its center of power, with some gradient being established.[8] People who deal with one agency but live under the power of the other either move closer to their own agency's home headquarters or shift their patronage to the other protective agency. (The border is about as conflictful as one between states.)

In neither of these two cases does there remain very much geographical interspersal. Only one protective agency operates over a given geographical area.

3. The two agencies fight evenly and often. They win and lose about equally, and their interspersed members have frequent dealings and disputes with each other. Or perhaps without fighting or after only a few skirmishes the agencies realize that such battling will occur continually in the absence of preventive measures. In any case, to avoid frequent, costly, and wasteful battles the two agencies, perhaps through their executives, agree to resolve peacefully those cases about which they reach differing judgments. They agree to set up, and abide by the decisions of, some third judge or court to which they can turn when their respective judgments differ. (Or they might establish rules determining which agency has jurisdiction under which circumstances.)[9] Thus emerges a system of appeals courts and agreed upon rules about jurisdiction and the conflict of laws. Though different agencies operate, there is one unified federal judicial system of which they all are components.

---

[7] Exercise for the reader: describe how the considerations discussed here and below lead to each geographical area having one agency or a federal structure of agencies dominant within it, even if initially the area contains a group of agencies over which "wins almost all the battles with" is a connected relation and a *nontransitive* one.

[8] See Kenneth R. Boulding, *Conflict and Defense* (New York: Harper, 1962), chap. 12.

[9] For an indication of the complexity of such a body of rules, see American Law Institute, *Conflict of Laws; Second Restatement of the Law,* Proposed Official Draft, 1967–1969.

In each of these cases, almost all the persons in a geographical area are under some common system that judges between their competing claims and *enforces* their rights. Out of anarchy, pressed by spontaneous groupings, mutual-protection associations, division of labor, market pressures, economies of scale, and rational self-interest there arises something very much resembling a minimal state or a group of geographically distinct minimal states. Why is this market different from all other markets? Why would a virtual monopoly arise in this market without the government intervention that elsewhere creates and maintains it? [10] The worth of the product purchased, protection against others, is *relative:* it depends upon how strong the others are. Yet unlike other goods that are comparatively evaluated, maximal competing protective services cannot coexist; the nature of the service brings different agencies not only into competition for customers' patronage, but also into violent conflict with each other. Also, since the worth of the less than maximal product declines disproportionately with the number who purchase the maximal product, customers will not stably settle for the lesser good, and competing companies are caught in a declining spiral. Hence the three possibilities we have listed.

Our story above assumes that each of the agencies attempts in good faith to act within the limits of Locke's law of nature.[11] But one "protective association" might aggress against other persons. Relative to Locke's law of nature, it would be an outlaw agency. What actual counterweights would there be to its power? (What actual counterweights are there to the power of a state?) Other agencies might unite to act against it. People might refuse to deal with the outlaw agency's clients, boycotting them to reduce the probability of the agency's intervening in their own affairs. This might make it more difficult for the outlaw agency to get clients; but this boycott will seem an effective tool only on very optimistic assumptions about what cannot be kept secret, and about the costs to an individual of partial boycott as compared to the benefits of receiving the more extensive coverage offered by an "outlaw" agency. If the "outlaw" agency simply is an *open* aggressor, pillaging, plundering, and extorting under no plausible claim of justice, it will have a harder time than states. For the state's claim to legitimacy induces its citizens to believe they have some duty to obey its edicts, pay its taxes, fight its battles, and so on; and so some persons cooperate with it voluntarily. An openly aggressive agency could not depend upon, and would not receive, any such voluntary cooperation, since persons would view themselves simply as its victims rather than as its citizens.

• • •

---

[10] See Yale Brozen, "Is Government the Source of Monopoly?" *The Intercollegiate Review,* 5, no. 2 (1968–69), 67–78; Fritz Machlup, *The Political Economy of Monopoly* (Baltimore: Johns Hopkins Press, 1952).

[11] Locke assumed that the preponderant majority, though not all, of the persons living in the state of nature would accept the law of nature. See Richard Ashcroft, "Locke's State of Nature," *American Political Science Review,* (September 1968): 898–915, especially part I.

THE MINIMAL STATE AND THE ULTRAMINIMAL STATE

The night-watchman state of classical liberal theory, limited to the functions of protecting all its citizens against violence, theft, and fraud, and to the enforcement of contracts, and so on, appears to be redistributive.[12] We can imagine at least one social arrangement intermediate between the scheme of private protective associations and the night-watchman state. Since the night-watchman state is often called a minimal state, we shall call this other arrangement the *ultraminimal state*. An ultraminimal state maintains a monopoly over all use of force except that necessary in immediate self-defense, and so excludes private (or agency) retaliation for wrong and exaction of compensation; but it provides protection and enforcement services *only* to those who purchase its protection and enforcement policies. People who don't buy a protection contract from the monopoly don't get protected. The minimal (night-watchman) state is equivalent to the ultraminimal state conjoined with a (clearly redistributive) Friedmanesque voucher plan, financed from tax revenues.[13] Under this plan all people, or some (for example, those in need), are given tax-funded vouchers that can be used only for their purchase of a protection policy from the ultraminimal state.

Since the night-watchman state appears redistributive to the extent that it compels some people to pay for the protection of others, its proponents must explain why this redistributive function of the state is unique. If some redistribution is legitimate in order to protect everyone, why is redistribution not legitimate for other attractive and desirable purposes as well? What rationale specifically selects protective services as the sole subject of legitimate redistributive activities? A rationale, once found, may show that this provision of protective services is *not* redistributive. More precisely, the term "redistributive" applies to types of *reasons* for an arrangement, rather than to an arrangement itself. We might elliptically call an arrangement "redistributive" if its major (only possible) supporting reasons are themselves redistributive. ("Paternalistic" functions similarly.) Finding compelling nonredistributive reasons would cause us to drop this label. Whether we say an institution that takes money from some and gives it to others is redistributive will depend upon *why* we think it does so. Returning stolen money or compensating for violations of rights are *not* redistributive reasons. I have spoken until now of the night-watchman state's *appearing* to be redistributive, to leave open the possibility that nonredistributive types of reasons might be found to justify the provision of protective services for some by others. . . .

A proponent of the ultraminimal state may seem to occupy an inconsistent position, even though he avoids the question of what makes protection uniquely

---

[12] Here and in the next section I draw upon and amplify my discussion of these issues in footnote 4 of "On the Randian Argument," *The Personalist* (Spring 1971).

[13] Milton Friedman, *Capitalism and Freedom* (Chicago: University of Chicago Press, 1962), chap. 6. Friedman's school vouchers, of course, allow a choice about who is to supply the product, and so differ from the protection vouchers imagined here [See reading 61—eds.]

suitable for redistributive provision. Greatly concerned to protect rights against violation, he makes this the sole legitimate function of the state; and he protests that all other functions are illegitimate because they themselves involve the violation of rights. Since he accords paramount place to the protection and non-violation of rights, how can he support the ultraminimal state, which would seem to leave some persons' rights unprotected or ill protected? How can he support this *in the name of* the nonviolation of rights?

THE INDIVIDUALIST ANARCHIST

We have surveyed the important issues underlying the view that moral side constraints limit how people may behave to each other, and we may return now to the private protection scheme. A system of private protection, even when one protective agency is dominant in a geographical territory, appears to fall short of a state. It apparently does not provide protection for everyone in its territory, as does a state, and it apparently does not possess or claim the sort of monopoly over the use of force necessary to a state. In our earlier terminology, it apparently does not constitute a minimal state, and it apparently does not even constitute an ultraminimal state.

These very ways in which the dominant protective agency or association in a territory apparently falls short of being a state provide the focus of the individualist anarchist's complaint *against* the state. For he holds that when the state monopolizes the use of force in a territory and punishes others who violate its monopoly, and when the state provides protection for everyone by forcing some to purchase protection for others, it violates moral side constraints on how individuals may be treated. Hence, he concludes, the state itself is intrinsically immoral. The state grants that under some circumstances it is legitimate to punish persons who violate the rights of others, for it itself does so. How then does it arrogate to itself the right to forbid private exaction of justice by other nonaggressive individuals whose rights have been violated? *What* right does the private exacter of justice violate that is not violated also by the state when it punishes? When a group of persons constitute themselves as the state and begin to punish, *and forbid others from doing likewise,* is there some right these others would violate that they themselves do not? By what right, then, can the state and its officials claim a unique right (a privilege) with regard to force and enforce this monopoly? If the private exacter of justice violates no one's rights, then punishing him for his actions (actions state officials also perform) violates his rights and hence violates moral side constraints. Monopolizing the use of force then, on this view, is itself immoral, as is redistribution through the compulsory tax apparatus of the state. Peaceful individuals minding their own business are not violating the rights of others. It does not constitute a violation of someone's rights to refrain from purchasing something for him (that you have not entered specifically into an obligation to buy). Hence, so the argument continues, when the state threatens someone with punishment if he does not contribute to the protection of another, it violates (and its officials violate) his rights. In threatening him with something that would be a violation of his rights if done by a private citizen, they violate moral constraints.

To get to something recognizable as a state we must show (1) how an ultra-minimal state arises out of the system of private protective associations; and (2) how the ultraminimal state is transformed into the minimal state, how it gives rise to that "redistribution" for the general provision of protective services that constitutes it as the minimal state. To show that the minimal state is morally legitimate, to show it is not immoral itself, we must show also that these transitions in (1) and (2) *each* are morally legitimate. We argue that the first transition, from a system of private protective agencies to an ultraminimal state, will occur by an invisible-hand process in a morally permissible way that violates no one's rights. Secondly, we argue that the transition from an ultra-minimal state to a minimal state morally must occur. It would be morally im-permissible for persons to maintain the monopoly in the ultraminimal state without providing protective services for all, even if this requires specific "re-distribution." The operators of the ultraminimal state are morally obligated to produce the minimal state.

● ● ●

THE DE FACTO MONOPOLY

The tradition of theorizing about the state . . . has a state claiming a monopoly on the use of force. Has any monopoly element yet entered our account of the dominant protective agency? *Everyone* may defend himself against unknown or unreliable procedures and may punish those who use or attempt to use such procedures against him. As its client's agent, the protective association has the right to do this for its clients. It grants that every individual, including those *not* affiliated with the association, has this right. So far, no monopoly is claimed. To be sure, there is a universal element in the content of the claim: the right to pass on *anyone's* procedure. But it does not claim to be the sole possessor of this right; everyone has it. Since no claim is made that there is some right which it and only it has, no monopoly is claimed. With regard to its own clients, how-ever, it applies and enforces these rights which it grants that everyone has. It deems its own procedures reliable and fair. There will be a strong tendency for it to deem all other procedures, or even the "same" procedures run by others, either unreliable or unfair. But we need not suppose it excludes *every* other pro-cedure. Everyone has the right to defend against procedures that are in fact not, or not known to be, both reliable and fair. Since the dominant protective asso-ciation judges its own procedures to be both reliable and fair, and believes this to be generally known, it will not allow anyone to defend against *them*: that is, it will punish anyone who does so. The dominant protective association will act freely on its own understanding of the situation, whereas no one else will be able to do so with impunity. Although no monopoly is claimed, the dominant agency does occupy a unique position by virtue of its power. It, and it alone, enforces prohibitions on others' procedures of justice, as it sees fit. It does not claim the right to prohibit others arbitrarily; it claims only the right to prohibit anyone's using actually defective procedures on its clients. But when it sees itself as acting against actually defective procedures, others may see it as acting against what it thinks are defective procedures. It alone will act freely against what it thinks are defective procedures, whatever anyone else thinks. As the most powerful applier of principles which it grants everyone the right to apply *correctly,* it enforces its will, which, from the inside, it thinks *is* correct. From its strength stems its actual position as the ultimate enforcer and the ultimate judge with regard to its own clients. Claiming only the universal right to act correctly, it acts correctly by its own lights. It alone is in a position to act solely by its own lights.

Does this unique position constitute a monopoly? There is no right the dominant protective association claims uniquely to possess. But its strength leads it to be the unique agent acting across the board to enforce a particular right. It is not merely that it *happens* to be the only exerciser of a right it grants that all possess; the nature of the right is such that once a dominant power emerges, it alone will actually exercise that right. For the right includes the right to stop others from wrongfully exercising the right, and only the dominant power will be able to exercise this right against all others. Here, if anywhere, is the place for applying some notion of a *de facto* monopoly: a monopoly that is not *de jure* because it is not the result of some unique grant of exclusive right while others are excluded from exercising a similar privilege. Other protective agencies, to be sure, can enter the market and attempt to wean customers away from the dominant protective agency. They can attempt to replace it as the dominant one. But being the already dominant protective agency gives an agency a significant market advantage in the competition for clients. The dominant agency can offer its customers a guarantee that no other agencies can match: "Only those procedures *we* deem appropriate will be used on our customers."

The dominant protective agency's domain does *not* extend to quarrels of nonclients *among themselves.* If one independent is about to use his procedure of justice upon another independent, then presumably the protective association would have no right to intervene. It would have the right we all do to intervene to aid an unwilling victim whose rights are threatened. But since it may not intervene on paternalistic grounds, the protective association would have no proper business interfering if both independents were satisfied with *their* procedure of justice. This does not show that the dominant protective association is not a state. A state, too, could abstain from disputes where all concerned parties chose to opt out of the state's apparatus. (Though it is more difficult for people to opt out of the state in a limited way, by choosing some other procedure for settling a particular quarrel of theirs. For that procedure's settlement, and their reactions to it, might involve areas that not all parties concerned have removed voluntarily from the state's concern.) And shouldn't (and mustn't) each state allow that option to its citizens?

PROTECTING OTHERS

If the protective agency deems the independents' procedures for enforcing their own rights insufficiently reliable or fair when applied to its clients, it will prohibit the independents from such self-help enforcement. The grounds for this prohibition are that the self-help enforcement imposes risks of danger on its clients. Since the prohibition makes it impossible for the independents credibly to threaten to punish clients who violate their rights, it makes them unable to protect themselves from harm and seriously disadvantages the independents in their daily activities and life. Yet it is perfectly possible that the independents' activities including self-help enforcement could proceed without anyone's rights being violated (leaving aside the question of procedural rights). According to our principle of compensation . . . , in these circumstances those persons promulgating and benefiting from the prohibition must compensate those disadvantaged by it. The clients of the protective agency, then, must compensate the independents for the disadvantages imposed upon them by being prohibited self-help enforcement of their own rights against the agency's clients. Undoubtedly, the least expensive way to compensate the independents would be to *supply* them with protective services to cover those situations of conflict with the paying customers of the protective agency. This will be less expensive than leaving them unprotected against violations of their rights (by not punishing any client who does so) and then attempting to pay them afterwards to cover their losses through having (and being in a position in which they were exposed to having) their rights violated. If it were *not* less expensive, then instead of buying protective services, people would save their money and use it to cover their losses, perhaps by jointly pooling their money in an insurance scheme.

Must the members of the protective agency *pay* for protective services (vis-à-vis its clients) for the independents? Can they insist that the independents purchase the services themselves? After all, using self-help procedures would not have been without costs for the independent. The principle of compensation does not require those who prohibit an epileptic from driving to pay his full cost of taxis, chauffeurs, and so on. If the epileptic were allowed to run his own automobile, this too would have its costs: money for the car, insurance, gasoline, repair bills, and aggravation. In compensating for disadvantages imposed, the prohibitors need pay only an amount sufficient to compensate for the disadvantages of the prohibition *minus* an amount representing the costs the prohibited party would have borne were it not for the prohibition. The prohibitors needn't pay the complete costs of taxis; they must pay only the amount which when combined with the costs to the prohibited party of running his own private automobile is sufficient for taxis. They may find it less expensive to compensate in kind for the disadvantages they impose than to supply monetary compensation; they may engage in some activity that removes or partially lessens the disadvantages, compensating in money only for the net disadvantages remaining.

If the prohibitor pays to the person prohibited monetary compensation equal to an amount that covers the disadvantages imposed *minus* the costs of the activity where it permitted, this amount may be insufficient to enable the prohibited party to overcome the disadvantages. If his costs in performing the prohibited action would have been monetary, he can combine the compensation payment with this money unspent and purchase the equivalent service. But if his costs would not have been directly monetary but involve energy, time, and the like, as in the case of the independent's self-help enforcement of rights, then this monetary payment of the difference will not by itself enable the prohibited party to overcome the disadvantage by purchasing the equivalent of what he is prohibited. If the independent has other financial resources he can use without disadvantaging himself, then this payment of the difference will suffice to leave the prohibited party undisadvantaged. But *if* the independent has no such other financial resources, a protective agency may *not* pay him an amount *less* than the cost of its least expensive protective policy, and so leave him only the alternatives of being defenseless against the wrongs of its clients or having to work in the cash market to earn sufficient funds to total the premium on a policy. For this financially pressed prohibited individual, the agency must make up the difference between the *monetary* costs to him of the unprohibited activity and the amount necessary to purchase an overcoming or counterbalancing of the disadvantage imposed. The prohibitor must completely supply enough, in money or in kind, to overcome the disadvantages. No compensation need be provided to someone who would not be disadvantaged by buying protection for himself. For those of scanter resources, to whom the unprohibited activity had no monetary costs, the agency must provide the difference between the resources they can spare without disadvantage and the cost of protection. For someone for whom it had some monetary costs, the prohibitor must supply the additional monetary amount (over and above what they can spare without disadvantage) necessary to overcome the disadvantages. If the prohibitors compensate in kind, they may *charge* the financially pressed prohibited party for this, up to the monetary costs to him of his unprohibited activity provided this amount is not greater than the price of the good.[14] As the only effective supplier, the dominant protective agency must offer in compensation the difference between its own fee and monetary costs to this prohibited party of self-help enforcement. It almost always will receive this amount back in partial payment for the purchase of a protection policy. It goes without saying that these dealings and prohibitions apply only to those using unreliable or unfair enforcement procedures.

Thus the dominant protective agency must supply the independents—that is, everyone it prohibits from self-help enforcement against its clients on the grounds that their procedures of enforcement are unreliable or unfair—with protective services against its clients; it may have to provide some persons services for a fee that is less than the price of these services. These persons may, of course, choose to refuse to pay the fee and so do without these compensatory services. If the dominant protective agency provides protective services in this

---

[14] May the prohibitors charge the prohibited party for the other costs to him of performing the activity were it unprohibited, such as time, energy, and so on?

way for independents, won't this lead people to leave the agency in order to receive its services without paying? Not to any great extent, since compensation
is paid only to those who would be disadvantaged by purchasing protection for
themselves, and only in the amount that will equal the cost of an unfancy policy when added to the sum of the monetary costs of self-help protection plus
whatever amount the person comfortably could pay. Furthermore, the agency
protects these independents it compensates only against its own paying clients
on whom the independents are forbidden to use self-help enforcement. The
more free riders there are, the more desirable it is to be a client always protected
by the agency. This factor, along with the others, acts to reduce the number of
free riders and to move the equilibrium toward almost universal participation.

THE STATE

We set ourselves the task . . . of showing that the dominant protective association within a territory satisfied two crucial necessary conditions for being a state:
that it had the requisite sort of monopoly over the use of force in the territory,
and that it protected the rights of everyone in the territory, even if this universal protection could be provided only in a "redistributive" fashion. These very
crucial facets of the state constituted the subject of the individualist anarchists'
condemnation of the state as immoral. We also set ourselves the task of showing that these monopoly and redistributive elements were themselves morally legitimate, of showing that the transition from a state of nature to an ultraminimal
state (the monopoly element) was morally legitimate and violated no one's
rights and that the transition from an ultraminimal to a minimal state (the "redistributive" element) also was morally legitimate and violated no one's rights.

A protective agency dominant in a territory does satisfy the two crucial necessary conditions for being a state. It is the only generally effective enforcer of
a prohibition on others' using unreliable enforcement procedures (calling them
as it sees them), and it oversees these procedures. And the agency protects those
nonclients in its territory whom it prohibits from using self-help enforcement
procedures on its clients, in their dealings with its clients, even if such protection must be financed (in apparent redistributive fashion) by its clients. It is
morally required to do this by the principle of compensation, which requires
those who act in self-protection in order to increase their own security to compensate those they prohibit from doing risky acts which might actually have
turned out to be harmless[15] for the disadvantages imposed upon them.

We noted . . . that whether the provision of protective services for some by
others was "redistributive" would depend upon the reasons for it. We now see
that such provision need not be redistributive since it can be justified on other
than redistributive grounds, namely, those provided in the principle of compensation. (Recall that "redistributive" applies to reasons for a practice or institution, and only elliptically and derivatively to the institution itself.) To sharpen

---

[15] Here, as at all other places in this essay, "harm" refers only to border crossings.

this point, we can imagine that protective agencies offer two types of protection policies: those protecting clients against risky private enforcement of justice and those not doing so but protecting only against theft, assault, and so forth (provided these are not done in the course of private enforcement of justice). Since it is only with regard to those with the first type of policy that others are prohibited from privately enforcing justice, only they will be required to compensate the persons prohibited private enforcement for the disadvantages imposed upon them. The holders of only the second type of policy will not have to pay for the protection of others, there being nothing they have to compensate these others for. Since the reasons for wanting to be protected against private enforcement of justice are compelling, almost all who purchase protection will purchase this type of protection, despite its extra costs, and therefore will be involved in providing protection for the independents.

We have discharged our task of explaining how a state would arise from a state of nature without anyone's rights being violated. The moral objections of the individualist anarchist to the minimal state are overcome. It is not an unjust imposition of a monopoly; the *de facto* monopoly grows by an invisible-hand process and *by morally permissible means,* without anyone's rights being violated and without any claims being made to a special right that others do not possess. And requiring the clients of the *de facto* monopoly to pay for the protection of those they prohibit from self-help enforcement against them, far from being immoral, is morally required by the principle of compensation.

• • •

THE INVISIBLE-HAND EXPLANATION OF THE STATE

Have we provided an invisible-hand explanation . . . of the state's arising within a state of nature; have we given an invisible-hand explanation of the state? The *rights* possessed by the state are already possessed by each individual in a state of nature. These rights, since they are already contained whole in the explanatory parts, are *not* provided an invisible-hand explanation. Nor have we provided an invisible-hand explanation of how the state acquires rights unique to it. This is unfortunate; for since the state has no special rights, there is nothing of that sort to be explained.

We have explained how, without anyone having this in mind, the self-interested and rational actions of persons in a Lockean state of nature will lead to single protective agencies dominant over geographical territories; each territory will have either one dominant agency or a number of agencies federally affiliated so as to constitute, in essence, one. And we have explained how, without claiming to possess any rights uniquely, a protective agency dominant in a territory will occupy a unique position. Though each person has a right to act correctly to prohibit others from violating rights (including the right not to be punished unless shown to deserve it), only the dominant protective association will be able, without sanction, to enforce correctness as it sees it. Its power makes it the arbiter of correctness; *it* determines what, for purposes of punishment, counts as a breach of correctness. Our explanation does not assume or claim that might makes right. But might does make enforced prohibitions, even if no one thinks the mighty have a *special* entitlement to have realized in the world their own view of which prohibitions are correctly enforced.

Our explanation of this *de facto* monopoly is an invisible-hand explanation. If the state is an institution (1) that has the right to enforce rights, prohibit dangerous private enforcement of justice, pass upon such private procedures, and so forth, and (2) that effectively is the *sole wielder* within a geographical territory of the right in (1), then by offering an invisible-hand explanation of (2), though not of (1), we have partially explained in invisible-hand fashion the existence of the state. More precisely, we have partially explained in invisible-hand fashion the existence of the *ultraminimal* state. What is the explanation of how a *minimal* state arises? The dominant protective association with the monopoly element is morally required to compensate for the disadvantages it imposes upon those it prohibits from self-help activities against its clients. However, it actually might fail to provide this compensation. Those operating an ultraminimal state are morally required to transform it into a minimal state, but they might choose not to do so. We have assumed that generally people will do what they are morally required to do. Explaining how a state could arise from a state of nature without violating anyone's rights refutes the principled objections of the anarchist. But one would feel more confidence if an explanation of how a state *would* arise from a state of nature also specified reasons why an ultraminimal state would be transformed into a minimal one, in addition to moral reasons, if it specified incentives for providing the compensation or the causes of its being provided in addition to people's desire to do what they ought. We should note that even in the event than no nonmoral incentives or causes are found to be sufficient for the transition from an ultraminimal to a minimal state, and the explanation continues to lean heavily upon people's moral motivations, it does not specify people's objective as that of establishing a state. Instead, persons view themselves as providing particular other persons with compensation for particular prohibitions they have imposed upon them. The explanation remains an invisible-hand one.

3.
Utility and Government

HENRY SIDGWICK

THE GENERAL PRINCIPLES OF LEGISLATION

§ 2. What then are the principles on which the laws defining the primary civil rights of private members of a civilized community should be constructed, or the criteria by which the goodness or badness of any actual body of such laws should be tested? In answering this question, I do not seek, as I said in my first chapter, to propound and establish any new principles, not recognized in ordinary political thought and discussion; my aim is merely to render somewhat more precise in conception the principles that I find commonly recognized, and to make their application to particular cases as clear and consistent as possible.

In the first place, we are all agreed that laws ought to be just or not unjust:[1] and by this we do not merely mean that they ought to be justly *administered*— i.e. that the general rules of law ought to be impartially applied without "respect of persons" to the particular cases brought before the courts for judgment—but we mean also that these general rules themselves ought to be framed so as to avoid injustice. But when I try to give a definite signification to this principle, the only signification I can find which would really carry with it universal agreement is, that all *arbitrary* inequality is to be excluded: that persons in similar circumstances are to be treated similarly; and that, so far as different classes of persons receive different treatment from the legislator, such differences should not be due to any personal favor or disfavor with which the classes in question are regarded by him. This agreement therefore gives no positive guidance as to the plan on which our impartially framed laws are to be constructed: it does not enable us to say how far and on what grounds persons in different circumstances are to be treated differently.

I think, however, that we may go a step further, and claim general—if not universal—assent for the principle that the true standard and criterion by which right legislation is to be distinguished from wrong is conduciveness to the general "good" or "welfare." And probably the great majority of persons would agree to interpret the "good" or "welfare" of the community to mean, in the last analysis, the happiness of the individual human beings who compose the community; provided that we take into account not only the human beings who are actually living but those who are to live hereafter. This, at any rate, is my own view. Accordingly, throughout this treatise I shall take the happiness of the persons affected as the ultimate end and standard of right and wrong in determining the functions and constitution of government.

---

[1] I say "or not unjust," because it would be commonly recognized that there is an ideal justice which we cannot hope to realize in the legal relations of the members of any actual community. But we shall certainly agree in holding that laws ought not to be unjust.

I draw special attention to the inclusion of posterity in my statement of the ultimate end of legislation: because it appears to me that whatever force there is in the arguments urged[2] against the view that the end of government is the happiness of the individuals governed, depends on the conception of these individuals as present, actually existing, members of the particular community in question. I fully concede that there are crises of national life in which it is the duty of the present generation of citizens, the actually living human beings who compose any political community, to make important sacrifices of personal happiness for the "good" or "welfare of their country," and that this good or welfare cannot be completely analyzed into private happiness of the individuals who make the sacrifices. I should add that there are cases in which it is the duty of the members of one political society to make sacrifices for the good or welfare of other sections of the human race. But I hold that if this good is not chimerical and illusory, it must mean the happiness of *some* individual human beings: if not of those living now, at any rate of those who are to live hereafter. And I have tried in vain to obtain from any writer who rejects this view, any other definite conception of the "good of the State."[3]

If it is urged[4] that there are many most important sources of the happiness of human beings with which government has little or nothing to do, and which it will only make a mistake if it tries to control—art, literature, and for the most part industry—the answer is, that it appears from this very argument that the limits of government interferences in these departments are capable of being determined on utilitarian principles; for the argument is that interference beyond those limits will be demonstrably the reverse of useful—will be *not* conducive to the general happiness.

§ 3. We have thus arrived at the utilitarian doctrine that the ultimate criterion of the goodness of law, and of the actions of government generally, is their tendency to increase the general happiness. The difficult question how far, if at all, the interests of any one community are to be postponed by its government to the interests of other sections of humanity is one that it will become necessary to deal with at a later stage; but we are hardly called upon to consider it when we are discussing the internal functions of government—the principles of its action in relation to the governed. The happiness then of the governed community will be assumed as the ultimate end of legislation, throughout the nine chapters that follow.[5] But even the acceptance of this principle gets us very little way towards a system of legislation: since we find it admitted equally by persons differing profoundly in their political aims and tendencies. . . . Hence,

---

[2] *E.g.* by Johan Caspar Bluntschli. *Theory of State* (translated), Book v. [Freeport, N.Y., Books for Libraries Press, 1971—eds.]

[3] *E.g.* Bluntschli, *l.c.* (Book v. ch. iv.) speaks of "devolopment of a people's natural gifts" and the "perfecting of a people's life;" but I know no criterion for determining wherein the perfection of life consists and for distinguishing the right development of natural gifts from the wrong development, if the utilitarian criterion be rejected.

[4] As by Bluntschli, *l.c.*, Book v. ch. iii. §2.

[5] Except so far as the pain of inferior animals is also taken into account, in legislation prohibiting cruelty to animals.

when we have agreed to take general happiness as the ultimate end, the most important part of our work still remains to be done: we have to establish or assume some subordinate principle or principles, capable of more precise application, relating to the best means for attaining by legislation the end of Maximum Happiness.

Now when we consider the different ways in which the happiness of individuals may be promoted by laws, the most fundamental distinctions appear to be two.

I. In the first place, legal control may be exercised in the interest of the person controlled, or of other persons: the government may either aim at making each of the individuals to whom its commands are addressed promote his own happiness better than he would without interference, or it may aim at making his conduct more conducive to the happiness of others. So far as the former is the avowed aim of government, its control resembles that properly exercised by a father over his children: accordingly this kind of governmental interference is commonly spoken of as "paternal;" and I shall adopt this as the most convenient name for it. The term is used with more or less sarcasm, because such interference—as applied to sane adults—is commonly regarded as being in general undesirable in modern civilized communities. The grounds for this opinion are chiefly these: (1) that men, on the average, are more likely to know what is for their own interest than government is, and to have a keener concern for promoting it, so that, even supposing paternal legislation would be generally obeyed, its direct effects are likely to be on the whole mischievous—taking into account the annoyance caused by coercion; and (2) that, even if its direct effects are beneficial, its indirect effects in the way of weakening the self-reliance and energy of individuals, and depriving them of the salutary lessons of experience, are likely to outweigh the benefit; while (3) such laws are specially liable to evasion, since, in cases where they are felt to be coercive, there will usually be no private individuals who feel directly interested in the effectiveness of the coercion—the persons whom the laws are primarily designed to benefit being the very persons who require to be coerced. It is further held that, even if any little good were done by this kind of legislation, it would not be worth the expense entailed by it both of money and of the energies of statesmen needed for other functions; and finally, that there is a serious political danger in the increase of the power and influence of government that would be involved in a consistent application of the "paternal" principle. I shall consider hereafter how far these arguments are valid to the complete exclusion of this principle; at present it is enough to say that neither in current political reasoning nor in the actual facts of legislation is anything more than a very subordinate place now ever allowed or claimed for its application. We are all agreed that, in the main, the coercion of law is and ought to be applied to adult individuals in the interest primarily of other persons.

II. But here a second fundamental distinction suggests itself. The services which an individual is legally bound to render to others may be positive or negative; they may consist in doing useful acts, or in forbearing to do mischievous acts. Now there is no doubt that the constant rendering of re-ciprocal positive services is indispensable to the production of the greatest attainable happiness for the human beings who compose a modern civilized community; all agree, indeed, that such exchange of services has continually to become more complex and elaborate, if we are to realize the economic ad-vantages of that development of industry which the progress of the arts con-tinually renders possible. And most of us would readily accept, as a moral ideal, what I may call *ethical* as contrasted with *political* socialism; that is, the doctrine that the services which men have to render to others should be rendered, as far as possible, with a genuine regard to the interests of others: that, as J. S. Mill, after Comte, lays down, "every person who lives by any useful work should be habituated to regard himself, not as an individual working for his private benefit, but as a public functionary," working for the benefit of society; and should regard "his wages of whatever sort . . . as the provision made by society to enable him to carry on his labor." But it is widely held that it is the business of the moralist and the preacher, not of the legislator, to aim at producing in the community this habit of thought and feeling; and that it will be on the whole conducive to the general good to leave the terms of positive social co-operation—except so far as it is needed to prevent aggression—to be settled by private agreement among the per-sons co-operating. It is held, in short, that what one sane adult is legally com-pelled to render to others should be merely the negative service of non-interference, except so far as he has voluntarily undertaken to render positive services; provided that we include in the notion of non-interference the obligation of remedying or compensating for mischief intentionally or carelessly caused by his acts—or preventing mischief that would otherwise result from some previous act. This principle for determining the nature and limits of governmental interferences is currently known as "Individualism," and I shall refer to it by this name; the requirement that one sane adult, apart from contract or claim to reparation, shall contribute positively by money or services to the support of others I shall call "socialistic." I shall also ap-ply this term to any limitation on the freedom of action of individuals in the interest of the community at large, that is not required to prevent interfer-ence with other individuals, or for the protection of the community against the aggression of foreigners.

The legislation of modern civilized communities then, is, in the main, framed on an Individualistic basis; and an important school of political thinkers are of opinion that the coercive interference of government should be strictly limited to the application of this principle. I propose, accordingly, in subsequent chap-ters, to trace in outline the chief characteristics of the system of Law that would result from the consistent application of the Individualistic principle to the actual conditions of human life in society.

• • •

INDIVIDUALISM AND THE INDIVIDUALISTIC MINIMUM

§ 1. In this and the four following chapters I propose to work out in some detail what I may call the "Individualistic minimum" of governmental interference: that is, the distribution of legal rights and obligations among private persons that results from applying the Individualistic principle, as strictly as seems practically possible, to the actual conditions of human life in society. But before I proceed to this examination, it ought to be noted that some Individualists view this principle in a light fundamentally different from that in which I have regarded it in the preceding chapter. They hold the realization of freedom or mutual non-interference to be not merely desirable as most conducive to human happiness, but absolutely desirable as the ultimate end of law and of all governmental interference: an ideal good which would be degraded if it were sought merely as a means of obtaining pleasure and avoiding pain. This opinion, however, may I think be shown to be inconsistent with the common sense of mankind, as expressed in actual legislation, and even with the practical doctrines—when they descend to particulars— of the thinkers who profess to hold it. For the kind of laws which Individualists generally agree to recommend may be shown to require for their justification a utilitarian interpretation of the individualistic principle: that is, they require us to conceive, as the general aim of law and government, not the prevention among the governed of mutual interference with freedom in the ordinary sense, but the prevention of mutual interference with each one's pursuit of happiness for himself and his family. And I think that the attempt to show this, under each of the chief heads of individualistic legislation, will be the best way of clearing up our general conception of the individualistic principle; while at the same time it will afford a convenient opportunity of surveying the whole range of the subject before we proceed to consider it in detail.

Let us begin by examining the usage of the words "Freedom," or "Liberty"—which I take to be synonymous. When employed without qualification "freedom" signifies primarily the absence of physical coercion or confinement: A is clearly not a free agent if B moves his limbs, and he is not free if he cannot get out of a building because B has locked the door. But in another part of its meaning—which from our present point of view is more important—"freedom" is opposed not to physical constraint, but to the moral restraint placed on inclination by the fear of painful consequences resulting from the action of other human beings. There is, however, some disagreement as to the extent of this latter meaning: it is disputed whether the moral restraint that impairs my freedom may be caused by fear of any other man's action or only by fear of *governmental* action. The latter view was taken by Hobbes, who regarded the "state of nature"—that is, of no government—as a state of unlimited liberty, though also one of intense mutual fear. But this view is paradoxical: it seems absurd to say that it is contrary to liberty to be restrained by dread of the magistrate, and not contrary to liberty to be similarly or more painfully restrained by dread of the lawless violence of a neighbor: we should generally agree with Paley that not only happiness but liberty is less in the Hobbist state of nature than in a well-ordered political society. If it be granted, then, that my liberty is impaired by the restraint on volition caused by fear of the acts of human beings generally, the statement sometimes made that "every law is contrary to liberty" is misleading, though in a sense true: since the diminution of liberty caused by the fear of legal penalties may be more than balanced by the simultaneous diminution of private coercion. It may be fairly said that the end of government is to promote liberty, so far as governmental coercion prevents worse coercion by private individuals.

We have, however, to observe that freedom is sometimes attributed to the citizens of a state, not because the governmental coercion applied to them is restricted to the prevention of private coercion, but because it is exercised with the consent of a majority of the citizens in question. Indeed, the notion of "liberty" in this sense—which may be distinguished as "constitutional liberty"—has had a very prominent place in political discussion. I do not wish to discard this use of the term altogether: but I think it is liable to be misleading. It may be fairly affirmed that a *body* of persons is "free"—in the ordinary sense—when the only rules restraining them are in accordance with the corporate will of the body: but it is only in a very peculiar sense—liable to collide markedly with the ordinary meaning of the term—that "freedom" can be therefore affirmed of every *member* of the body. It is obvious that my inclinations may be restrained to any extent, and in the most annoying way, under a government of which the supreme control is vested in the mass of the citizens, if I have the misfortune to belong to the minority of this body: while, again, it is quite conceivable that under a despotic government I may be subject to no further coercion than is necessary to prevent worse coercion by private persons. Accordingly, when I speak without qualification of freedom as belonging to individuals, I shall not mean constitutional freedom, but civil freedom as above defined—in absence of physical and moral coercion.

It is certainly conceivable that the maintenance of "equal freedom" in this sense should be taken as the ultimate and sole end of legislation, and of governmental interference generally. But in fact, as I have said, all governments and most Individualists practically go beyond this, and aim at protecting the governed from pain—and loss or diminution of their means of gratifying their desires—caused by the action of other human beings. In so doing, I maintain they adopt by implication a utilitarian view of the mutual interference that law ought to prevent—even while expressly disavowing the utilitarian criterion.

§ 2. Let us proceed to particulars: and take first the class of rights which Blackstone distinguishes as "Personal Rights." We find that under this head all civilized systems of law aim at securing the personal *safety* of individuals no less than their personal *liberty;* i.e. they seek to prevent the infliction of physical injury or pain—even serious physical discomfort that can hardly be called pain—as well as the imposition of constraint. No doubt physical injury or pain usually involves a kind of constraint; since the injured man, even if not physically disabled, is prevented from doing what he likes by the fear of the recurrence of the injury. This is an important reason for preventing physical injury, and the main reason for making the mere threat of inflicting such injury a legal offence: but it would be absurd to maintain that assault and battery are prohibited solely on account of their tending to produce subsequent alarm in the person assaulted and battered sufficient to have a coercive effect on his conduct: all would admit that they ought to be prevented, even if such coercive effect did not follow. Hence common sense clearly requires us to understand the non-interference, which such prohibition secures, to include not only non-interference with Freedom but non-interference with Happiness.

This is still more obviously true as regards the interference with physical comfort, prohibited under the head of nuisances; and I think it is also true of the attacks on reputation, which all civilized nations aim at preventing by law. No doubt such attacks may be a form of moral coercion: but it is not thought that my right to be protected against calumny depends on the question whether my action has been or is likely to be modified by the unmerited dislike and contempt which the calumny has caused. Again, the defamation of A by B undoubtedly tends to impair A's ability to gratify his desires, by rendering it difficult for him to obtain the co-operation of others. But it palpably strains the common notion of freedom to say that A is less free merely because other people will not do what he wants them to do. And as B's freedom is directly and palpably diminished if he is prohibited from saying what he thinks of A, the restraints of the law of libel can hardly be justified if freedom—in any ordinary sense—and not happiness, be taken as the ultimate criterion.

Again, Individualists—and legislators generally—agree that where law has not succeeded in preventing injury to person or reputation, it ought generally to enforce on the wrongdoer pecuniary compensation for the mischief, unless the injury is one that does not admit of being repaired;—so as to bring about a condition of things approximating as far as possible to what would have existed had there been no injury. From the point of view of utilitarian individualism this duty is clear; but if freedom be taken as an absolute end, it is difficult to show how the loss of freedom can properly be compensated by money. For if it be said that the richer man, as such, enjoys more freedom than the poorer, the fundamental aim of Individualism—to secure by law equal freedom to all—seems to transform itself into the fundamental aim of extreme Socialism, to secure equal *wealth* to all.

This leads us naturally to consider the application of the individualistic principle in the department of law which is concerned with the protection of property. The Individualistic minimum of governmental interference is commonly stated to include "protection of property" as well as of "person": and it is obvious that we are bound to prevent any interference by one man with the property of another, if we suppose private property already instituted; since in fact, the legal institution of private property *means* the prohibition of such interference. But the institution itself can hardly be justified by the general principle of Individualism, if we take freedom—in the ordinary sense—as an ultimate end, without any regard to utility; it would rather seem that the end would be most completely realised by preventing A from thwarting B's actual use of material things, without going so far as to support B in the permanent exclusion of other men from the enjoyment of things that he has once used. The case is different if we interpret the principle in a utilitarian sense. From this point of view the protection of exclusive use is obviously required in order that individuals may have adequate inducement to labor in adapting matter to the satisfaction of their needs and desires. The natural reward of labor is the full enjoyment of the utility resulting from it; without the prospect of this natural reward—or of some adequate substitute for it—we could not expect much of the labor to be performed. Hence, from the point of view of utilitarian Individualism, the law ought clearly to aim at securing each individual from the interference of others with his enjoyment of the results of his labor: and, in fact, the provision of this security is often simply stated as the end by reference to which private property is to be justified.

It ought, however, to be observed that this principle does not directly justify the appropriation of material things in their original or unlabored condition: and if, on the utilitarian ground above given, A is held to interfere with B by using matter to which B has applied his labor, it cannot be denied that B's claim to exclude A from this matter involves some interference with A, if it appreciably restricts A's power of adapting matter to the satisfaction of his needs and desires. Still, I conceive that private property may be clearly justified on the individualistic principle—taken in a utilitarian sense—so far as it can be shown either (1) that the thing appropriated would not practically have been available for human use, if the appropriator had not labored in seeking for it; or (2) that his appropriation does not materially diminish the opportunities open to other persons of obtaining similar things, owing to the natural abundance of such opportunities. On one or other of these grounds it is easy to justify the appropriation such things as fish caught in the open sea, or wild animals, plants, or even minerals, found in large tracts of uncultivated country. And it has been maintained by Locke and others, that in the "beginning and first peopling of the great common of the world" the appropriation of land was similarly justifiable, "since there was still enough and as good left, and more than the yet unprovided could use." But however true this may have been in a primitive condition of human society, it seems evident that social development has long since deprived this justification of any validity; and now, at any rate, the individuals who have not inherited land do not find "enough and as good" within their reach. Accordingly, in the case of land, the principle of mutual non-interference is, I conceive, only applicable in a limited and qualified manner. And, in fact, when the question of regulating the appropriation of land has been practically presented to modern states in a simple form[6]—for instance, in relation to land as yet unappropriated, in a newly colonised country—it has not commonly been held that individuals desirous of using such land, for agricultural or other purposes, have a right to claim the exclusive use of as much land as they may find it convenient to occupy. The question how such land is to be allotted I shall consider more in detail in the next chapter. Here I am chiefly concerned to

---

[6] That is, in a form not complicated by the consideration of established rights of private property, which could not justly be abolished without compensation. . . .

point out that Absolute Individualism supplies no method of dealing with its difficulties.

So far I have tacitly assumed that the labor necessary to adapt matter to human uses can be sufficiently encouraged by appropriating to the laborer the thing so adapted. There is, however, another case of property, of considerable importance in modern civilized communities, where quite peculiar obligations have to be imposed on non-owners: I mean the case of "patents" and "copyrights," by which the exclusive use of certain products of intellectual labor is secured to the producers or to their grantees. Here, from the nature of the labor, the only way of securing its results to the laborer is by prohibiting other members of the community from imitating them. At the same time, such an interference with the freedom of action of the persons prohibited is difficult to justify from the point of view of absolute individualism; since it cannot be shown that this prohibition of imitation tends to secure the persons concerned from physical or moral coercion. But it certainly tends to secure the greatest possible independent production of utility, assuming that the results that would be attained by imitation are such as the imitators could not possibly have arrived at independently. On this assumption, indeed, property in the results of intellectual labor, protected by patents and copyrights, is *more* simply justifiable on the (utilitarian) principle of mutual non-interference, than property in material things: just because the labor is not "mixed" with matter. To what extent the assumption is in different cases legitimate I shall consider in the next chapter.

• • •

SOCIALIST LEGISLATION

. . . When the question is whether Government should coerce individuals in their own interest, it is argument enough on the negative side, if it be granted that, in the matter under discussion, men may be expected in the long run to discover and aim at their own interests better than Government will do this for them—from their better opportunities of learning what conduces to their own welfare, or from their keener and more sustained concern for the attainment of this; while, further, this habit of self-help will give not only knowledge, but also self-reliance, activity, enterprise.

But, granting all this to be true, it by no means follows that an aggregate of persons, seeking each his private interest intelligently, with the least possible restraint, is therefore certain to realise the greatest attainable happiness for the aggregate. It is, indeed, obvious that if the mode of action on the part of any one such individual which is really most conducive to his own interest diverges from that which is most conducive to the interest of all, then the more completely he is left free to pursue the former end, and the more skill he shows in the pursuit, the more certain it is that he will not promote the latter in the highest attainable degree. Hence, to complete theoretical argument for *laissez faire,* we require, besides the psychological proposition that every one can best take care of his own interest, to establish the sociological proposition that the common welfare is best attained by each pursuing exclusively his own welfare and that of his family[7] in a thoroughly alert and intelligent manner.

Now this latter proposition has been maintained, in a broad and general way, by the main tradition of what is called "orthodox political economy," since its emergence in France in the middle of the eighteenth century. The argument may be briefly stated thus: Consumers generally—i.e. the members of the community generally, in their character as consumers—seeking each his own interest intelligently, will cause an effectual demand for different kinds of products and services, in proportion to their utility to society; while producers generally, seeking each his own interest intelligently, will be led to supply this demand in the most economic way, each one training himself or being trained by his parents for the most useful—and therefore best rewarded—services for which he is adapted. Any excess of any class of products or services will be rapidly corrected by a fall in the price offered for them; and similarly any deficiency will be rapidly made up by the stimulus of a rise. And the more keenly and persistently each individual—whether as consumer or producer—pursues his private interest, the more certain will be the natural punishment of inertia or misdirected effort anywhere, and the more complete consequently will be the adaptation of social efforts to the satisfaction of social needs.

Now no one who, under the guidance of Adam Smith and his successors, has reflected seriously on the economic side of social life can doubt that the motive of self-interest does work powerfully and continually in the manner above indicated; and the difficulty of finding any substitute for it, either as an impulsive or as a regulating force, constitutes the chief reason for rejecting all large schemes for reconstructing social order on some other than its present individualistic basis. The socialistic interference for which, in the present chapter, I propose to offer a theoretical justification is here only recommended as a supplementary and subordinate element in a system mainly individualistic. At the same time, I think it important to show by general reasoning that—even as applied to a society of "economic men"—the sociological argument above given is palpably inadequate to establish the practical conclusion based on it by the more extreme advocates of the "system of natural liberty."

With a view to methodical clearness, it is convenient to begin by granting the assumption—tacitly made in the general economic argument that I have just given—that the higher market value of products and services consumed by the rich, as compared with those consumed by the poor, represents a correspondingly higher degree of utility to society. I shall presently point out how paradoxical this supposition is: but for formal clearness of discussion it is as well to begin by making it; since even on this supposition it can, I think, be shown that there are several distinct cases in which, under a strictly individualistic system of governmental interference, the individual's interest has no tendency—or no

---

[7] So far as the interests of children are concerned, we require the further assumption that they can be safely left to the care of parents until the children are able to provide for themselves: but for simplicity I omit this point here.

sufficient tendency—to prompt him to the course of action most conducive to the common interest.

§ 2. In the first place, it should be observed that the argument above given, even if fully granted, would only justify appropriation to the laborer, and free exchange of the utilities produced by labor; it affords no direct justification for the appropriation of natural resources, which private property in material things inevitably involves. Hence, so far as this appropriation of natural resources restricts other men's opportunities of applying labor productively, the appropriation, as we have seen, is of doubtful legitimacy, from the point of view of the strictest individualism. It must, therefore, be regarded as theoretically subject to limitation or regulation, in the interest of the whole aggregate of individuals concerned. How far this limitation and regulation should go must be determined by experience in different departments: but it may be laid down generally that it is the duty of Government as representing the community to prevent the bounties of nature from being wasted by the unrestricted pursuit of private interest. Thus, for instance, Government may properly interfere to protect mines and fisheries from wasteful exhaustion, and save rare and useful species of plants from extermination; and, when necessary, may undertake or control the management of natural watercourses, with a view both to irrigation and to the supply of motive power. And I conceive that measures of a much more sweeping kind in the same direction—including even the complete abolition of private property in land—are theoretically defensible on the basis of individualism; they have, indeed, received the support of thoroughgoing advocates of this doctrine.

Secondly, individuals may not be able—at all, or without inconvenience practically deterrent—to remunerate themselves by the sale of utilities which it is for the general interest that they should render to society. This may be either because the utility is from its nature incapable of being appropriated, or because—though undeniably important from the point of view of the community—its value to any individual is too uncertain and remote to render it worth purchasing on grounds of private interest. An example of the former is furnished by forests: since no private landowner who maintains a forest can, by free exchange, exact any return for such benefit as he may confer on the community by its favorable influence on climate in moderating and equalizing rainfall. The other case may be illustrated by scientific investigation generally; since most of the advances made in scientific knowledge, even though they may be ultimately the source of important material benefits to man's estate, would hardly remunerate the investigator if treated as marketable commodities, and only communicated to private individuals who were willing to pay for them.

Even where the inconvenience of selling a commodity would not be deterrent, the waste of time and labor that the process would involve may be so great as to render it on the whole a more profitable arrangement for the community to provide the commodity out of public funds. For instance, no one doubts that it would be inexpedient to leave bridges in towns generally to be provided by private enterprise and paid by tolls.

We have also to take account of waste of time and trouble in forming business connections, which seems an inevitable incident of a competitive organization of business. Definite items of this economic loss are expressed in the sums spent on advertisements, and in the promotion of joint-stock companies. But to these we have to add the much larger though less definite waste of labor spent in rendering services of comparatively small utility, by traders who have not yet established a business connection, or who are slowly losing business through the pressure of competition or of industrial change; and the similar waste in the case of professional services of all kinds.

Again, there is an important class of cases in which the individuals have an adequate motive for rendering *some* service to society, but not for rendering as much service as it is in their power to render. These are cases in which competition is excluded by natural or artificial monopoly of the production or sale of a commodity. For the interest of the monopolist of any ware is liable to conflict very materially with the interest of the community; since the demand for a monopolized commodity is often of such a nature that a greater total profit can be obtained from the sale of a smaller quantity, owing to the extent to which the price would fall if the supply were increased. The importance of this case, it may be observed, tends to increase as the opportunities for monopoly grow with the growth of civilization: partly from the increasing advantages of industry on a large scale, partly from the increasing ease with which combination among the members of any class of producers is brought about and maintained.[8]

Combination resulting in monopoly may, as I have just shown, be a source of economic loss to the community. On the other hand, there are cases in which combined action or abstinence on the part of a whole class of producers is required to realise a certain utility, either at all or in the most economical way: and in such cases the intervention of Government, though not the only method of securing the result, is likely to be the most effective method. If, indeed, we could assume that *all* the persons concerned will act in the most intelligent way, the matter might be left to voluntary association; but in any community of human beings that we can hope to see, the most we can expect is that the great majority of any industrial class will be adequately enlightened, vigilant, and careful, in protecting their own interests: and where the efforts and sacrifices of a great majority might be rendered useless by the neglect of one or two individuals, it would be dangerous to trust to voluntary association. The protection of land below the sea-level against floods, or of useful animals and plants against infectious disease, are cases of this kind which we already noticed.

And the ground for governmental interference is still stronger if the very fact of a combination among the great majority of an industrial class to attain a given result materially increases the inducement for individuals to stand aloof

---

[8]   It is noteworthy that economic arguments to prove the advantage of "free competition" commonly assume that the notion of free competition excludes monopoly resulting from combination: and yet the governmental interference needed to repress such combination is manifestly contrary to Individualism as a political principle,—so far at least as the combination is the result of perfectly uncoerced choice on the part of the persons combining.

from the combination. Thus, if it were ever so clearly the interest of shop-keepers to close their shops on Sundays or other holidays, provided the closing were universal, it would still be very difficult to effect the result by purely voluntary combination; since the closing of a great number of shops would obviously tend to throw custom into the hands of the few who kept their shops open.

Even where the need of uniformity is not imperative, voluntary combination is likely to be found inadequate for the attainment of results of public importance, if the interest of any individual in such results is indirect and uncertain;—as may easily be the case even though the public interest is plain and undeniable.

Finally, there are certain kinds of utility which Government, in a well-ordered modern community, is peculiarly adapted to provide. Thus, being financially more stable than private individuals and companies, it can give completer security to creditors; and is thus specially adapted to undertake banking and insurance for the poor, and to bear the responsibilities of a paper currency for the community generally. So again, it enjoys special facilities for collecting and diffusing useful statistical information,—a point of growing importance in modern communities.

§ 3. I have said enough to show that, even in the more or less ideal society of intelligent persons which is contemplated in the traditional argument for *laissez faire,* there is no reason to suppose that a purely individualistic organization of industry would be the most effective and economical. And the reasons above given largely explain and justify the extent to which in modern States the provision of utilities—other than security from wrong—is undertaken by Government in the name of the community, or subjected to special governmental regulations, instead of being left to private enterprise; on the ground that the interests of the whole community will be better promoted by this arrangement.

• • •

§ 6. Let us now turn to consider how far the action of government should be directed to the end which would be commonly called "socialistic" in a narrower sense than that in which I have so far used the term—the diminution of the marked inequalities in income which form so striking a feature of modern civilized societies. Here, first, it should be observed that some effect of this kind tends to be produced by any successful assumption of industrial functions by Government: since the most marked inequalities of private wealth are due—directly or indirectly—to the unequal distribution of capital (including land); and any successful extension of the industrial functions of Government tends to increase the stock of capital owned by the community, and reduce the field of employment for private capital. Accordingly, a main aim of current Socialism in its extremest form—we may distinguish is as Collectivism—is to substitute common for private ownership, and governmental for private management, of the instruments of production in all important departments of industry: so that the payment of interest on industrial capital may cease and "labor receive its full reward." Such a scheme has much attraction for thoughtful and sympathetic persons; not only from its tendency to equalize wealth, but also from the possibilities it holds out of saving the waste and avoiding the unmerited hardships incident to the present competitive organization of business; and of substituting industrial peace, mutual service, and a general diffusion of public spirit, for the present conflict of classes and selfish struggles of individuals.

In discussing this scheme from the point of view of general theory, it will be well not to complicate the issue by supposing the change to be introduced suddenly or with violence: we may suppose it to take place gradually, with due regard to the rights of existing proprietors of the instruments of production. As so considered, the question of its expediency primarily turns on a comparison of governmental management of business with private competitive management: and it is reasonable to suppose further that, before the final transition to Collectivism takes place, our experience of the qualifications of Government for carrying on different kinds of industry will have been materially increased by partial extensions of its sphere of action. It is, I think, quite conceivable that, through improvements in the organization and working of governmental departments, aided by watchful and intelligent public criticism—together with a rise in the general level of public spirit throughout society—the results of the comparison above mentioned will at some future time be more favorable to governmental management than they have hitherto been. At present, a wide experience would seem in most cases to support strongly the judgment of the overwhelming majority of political economists in favor of private competitive management of industry carried on under ordinary conditions: as securing an intensity of energy and vigilance, an eager inventiveness in turning new knowledge and new opportunities to account, a freedom and flexibility in adapting industrial methods to new needs and conditions, a salutary continual expurgation of indolence and unthrift, which public management cannot be expected to rival in the present state of social morality, and for the loss of which it cannot compensate, except under specially favorable conditions. We may therefore infer that—leaving out of account the disturbances of the transition—the realization of the Collectivist idea at the present time or in the proximate future would arrest industrial progress; and that the comparative equality in incomes which it would bring about would be an equality in poverty:—even supposing population not to increase at a greater rate than at present, as it must be expected to do if work and adequate sustenance were secured to all members of the community, unless measures of a novel and startling kind were taken to prevent the increase.

A full discussion, however, of Collectivism, including a critical exposition of the economic arguments urged in favor of it, would be out of place here: it falls more properly within the sphere of Political Economy. But there is an important part of the work actually undertaken by modern governments which must be admitted to be "socialistic" in the narrower sense of the word: that is, which has for its main object—I will not say "the equalisation of wealth," as that would suggest an aim to which the means used are wholly disproportionate, but—the mitigation of the harshest inequalities in the present distribution of incomes. The most obvious examples of this are to be found in the large expenditure incurred in various forms for the relief of the indigent; but I conceive that a part at least of the expenditure on education which modern states generally agree to regard as desirable has been undertaken on this ground, and requires this for its justification. And there is a strong drift of opinion at the present time in favor of further legislation in this direction. I propose, therefore—without considering in detail the adaptation of means to ends in particular measures of this kind, or the special dangers and drawbacks attending them—to point out certain general considerations which must to some extent govern our estimate of the expediency of all such schemes.

In the first place, it seems to me indubitable that the attainment of greater equality in the distribution of the means and opportunities of enjoyment is in itself a desirable thing, if only it can be attained without any material sacrifice of the advantages of freedom. I cannot accept the assumption—so far granted for the sake of simplifying the discussion—that the utility to the community of services rendered to the rich may be measured by their market value: I conceive, on the contrary, that the support of common sense may be claimed for Bentham's view, that any given quantum of wealth is generally likely to be less useful to its owner, the greater the total of private wealth of which it forms a part. It is an accepted economic principle—illustrated by the general effect of an increase of supply on the price of any article—that the utility of a given quantum of any particular commodity to its possessor tends to be diminished, in proportion as the total amount of the commodity in his possession is increased; and Bentham's proposition is merely an extension of this principle to the aggregate of commodities which we call wealth.

There are, no doubt, counterbalancing considerations which ought not to be overlooked. Any great equalization of wealth would probably diminish the accumulation of capital, on which the progress of industry depends; and would deteriorate the administration of the capital accumulated; since the most economic organization of industry, under existing conditions, requires capital in large masses under single management, and the management of borrowed or joint-stock capital is likely to be, on the average, inferior to that of capital owned by the manager. Moreover, the effective maintenance and progress of intellectual culture—which is a necessary condition of its effective diffusion—seems to require the existence of a numerous group of persons enjoying complete leisure and the means of ample expenditure; since the disinterested curiosity that is the mainspring of the advance of knowledge, and the refinement of taste that leads to the development of art, can hardly find free play and the fostering influence of sympathy except within such a group, although they may be found in a high degree in individuals outside it.

Still, after allowing all weight to such arguments as these, I cannot doubt that at least a removal of the extreme inequalities, found in the present distribution of wealth and leisure, would be desirable, if it could be brought about without any material repression of the free development of individual energy and enterprise, which the individualistic system aims at securing. When from this point of view we examine the various legislative measures which have a "Socialistic" aspect—in the narrower sense of appearing to aim at a diminution of inequalities of wealth—we find that they differ very markedly in the manner and degree in which they come into conflict with the principle of Individualism. Some of these measures must be admitted to diminish the inducements to industry and thrift, without any counterbalancing tendency to stimulate labor by enlarging its opportunities; they simply and nakedly take the produce of those who have labored successfully to supply the needs of those who have labored unsuccessfully or not at all. I am afraid that the English system of poor relief—though it has many merits that ought not to be undervalued or lightly lost—must be admitted to have this fundamental defect. Others again involve restrictions on freedom that are frankly and uncompromisingly anti-individualistic; to this class belongs the proposal to fix by law a maximum length of day's labor for adults—so far as this prevents any individual laborer from rendering the amount of service to society which he and his employer agree in thinking it their common interest that he should render.[9] But there are other measures designed for the benefit of the poor which do not come under either of these heads; measures of which the primary aim is not to redistribute compulsorily the produce of labor, but to equalize the opportunities of obtaining wealth by productive labor, without any restriction on the freedom of adults. State aid to emigration is an example of this class, and a part at least of the expenditure on education must be held to belong to it. Now measures of this kind, however Socialistic, are not in their primary aim opposed to Individualism; since we obviously increase instead of diminishing the stimulus to self-help and energetic enterprise by placing a man in a position to gain more than he could otherwise have done by the exercise of these qualities. In fact, in the general reasoning by which political economists have tried to prove that *laissez faire* supplies the greatest possible stimulus to the development of useful qualities, equality of opportunity has often been tacitly assumed—or at least, the loss to the community arising from the restricted opportunities of large masses has been tacitly overlooked. So far as the community, acting through its government, can equalize opportunities, without doing harm in any other way, such interference actually gives greater scope for the admitted advantages of the individualistic system to be attained.

"But," it may be said, "this equalization of opportunities—as e.g. by State aid to education or to emigration—inevitably costs money and usually a good deal of money, which has to be raised by taxation; and thus in its taxational aspect it comes to be opposed to the individualistic principle, though it may not be so in its primary aim. A portion of A's income has to be taken to enable B

---

[9] Such a measure may be justified—on the principle applied in justifying a compulsory weekly holiday—if the excess of daily labor prevented is injurious to the laborer's efficiency, so that the average effectiveness of a day's labor might be expected not to be materially diminished by the restriction. But so far as the admitted effect of the measure is to diminish materially the amount of the daily service rendered by the laborer to society, I think that no government ought to take the responsiblity of causing the consequent loss of wealth to individuals and to the community as a whole.

to labor under better conditions, and in this way that absolute security to the fruits of the individual's labor, at which individualism aims, is inevitably impaired."

This argument, however, ignores the fact—pointed out in a previous chapter[10]—that the institution of private property as actually existing goes beyond what the individualistic theory justifies. Its general aim is to appropriate the results of labor to the laborer, but in realizing this aim it has inevitably appropriated natural resources to an extent which, in any fully peopled country, has entirely discarded Locke's condition of "leaving enough and as good for others." In any such country, therefore, the propertied classes are in the position of encroaching on the opportunities of the unpropertied in a manner which—however defensible as the only practicable method of securing the results of labor—yet renders a demand for compensation justifiable from the most strictly individualistic point of view. It would seem that such compensation may fitly be given by well directed outlay, tending either to increase the efficiency and mobility of labor, or to bring within the reach of all members of a civilized society some share of the culture which we agree in regarding as the most valuable result of civilization: and in so far as this is done without such heavy taxation as materially diminishes the stimulus to industry and thrift of the persons taxed, this expenditure of public money, however justly it may be called Socialistic, appears to be none the less defensible as the best method of approximating to the ideal of Individualistic justice.

[10] See Chap. V. § 2.

4.

Government and Character

ROBERT GEORGE

No one deserves more credit (or blame) than Aristotle for shaping the central tradition's ideas about justice and political morality. Centuries before the liberal assault on the tradition got into full swing, Aristotle himself anticipated, criticized, and firmly rejected what has become the defining doctrine of mainstream contemporary liberalism, namely, the belief that the law of a political community (*polis*) should be merely "(in the phrase of the Sophist Lycophron) 'a guarantor of men's rights against one another'—instead of being as it should be, a rule of life such as will make the members of a polis good and just." [1] Aristotle's argument in his *Politics* was that:

> any polis which is truly so called, and is not merely one in name, must devote itself to the end of encouraging goodness. Otherwise a political association sinks into a mere alliance, which only differs in space [i.e. in the contiguity of its members] from other forms of alliance where the members live at a distance from one another . . . a polis is not an association for residence on a common site, or for the sake of preventing mutual injustice and easing exchange. There are indeed conditions which must be present before a polis can exist; but the presence of all these conditions is not enough, in itself, to constitute a polis. What constitutes a polis is an association of households and clans in a good life, for the sake of attaining a perfect and self-sufficing existence. . . . It is therefore for the sake of good actions, and not for the sake of social life, that political associations must be considered to exist. [2]

Making men moral, Aristotle supposed, is a—if not *the*—central purpose of any genuine political community. Why?

To answer that question, we must turn to Aristotle's writing on moral goodness and virtue. Near the end of the *Nicomachean Ethics,* he pointedly asks why sound moral arguments are not in and of themselves sufficient to lead men away from vice and toward virtue. Having provided, at least in outline, a philosophical account of "the virtues, and also friendship and pleasure," Aristotle suggests the need for the project he undertakes in his *Politics,* observing that:

> while [moral arguments] seem to have power to encourage and stimulate the generous-minded among our youth, and to make a character which is gently

---

[1] *Pol.* iii. 5. 1280^{b}; quotations are from the translation by Ernest Barker, in *The Politics of Aristotle* (Oxford: Clarendon Press, 1946). Barker's use of the term "rights" here is somewhat anachronistic; the modern use of the term is foreign to Greek and Roman thought, and Aristotle's quotation from Lycophron would be more exactly rendered "guarantor of reciprocal justice."

[2] Ibid.

born, and a true lover of what is noble, ready to be possessed by virtue, they are not able to encourage the *many* to nobility and goodness.[3]

Why not? Are "the many" too stupid to understand moral arguments? People obviously differ in native intelligence; and it is plausible to think that only a minority of people have the intellectual capacity to follow the most subtle and complex philosophical arguments. Is it the case that, when it comes to the power of moral arguments to encourage and stimulate people to nobility and goodness, the difference between "the many" for whom the arguments are insufficient, and the few for whom they are virtually all that is needed, is one in native intelligence?

No. While Aristotle suggests that "the many" and "the few" differ by nature, the relevant difference, as he sees it, is not, or at least not fundamentally, a difference in raw intellectual capacity to follow philosophical argumentation. Rather, it is from the start a difference in *character*. The problem with "the many" is that:

> these do not by nature obey the sense of shame, but only fear, and do not abstain from bad acts because of their baseness but through fear of punishment; living by passion they pursue their own pleasures and the means to them, and avoid the opposite pains, and have not even a conception of what is noble and truly pleasant, since they have never tasted it.[4]

Is virtue, then, unattainable by "the many"? Is the average person, "living by passion," and lacking "a character which is gently born, and a true lover of what is noble," simply incapable of living virtuously? Aristotle indeed concludes that moral argument is futile with such people. It is pointless to argue with them. Argument can merely inform people of the right thing to do; it cannot motivate them to do it. Thus argument is sufficient only for the already "generous-minded" few who have been blessed by nature with a character "ready to be possessed by virtue." Nevertheless, Aristotle holds that other means may dispose those whose character is not "gently born" to attain some measure of moral goodness:

> It is hard if not impossible, to remove by argument the traits that have long since been incorporated in the character; and perhaps we must be content if, when all the influences by which we are thought to become good are present, we get some tincture of virtue.[5]

What are these "influences by which we are thought to become good"? How can "the many" be brought under them? Plainly Aristotle supposes that character is, by and large, given by nature. Of nature's part in making men good, he says that it "evidently does not depend on us, but as a result of some divine causes is present in those who are truly fortunate." Nevertheless, he maintains

---

[3] *Nic. Eth.* x. 9. 1179ᵇ; quotations are from the translation by W. D. Ross in *The Basic Works of Aristotle* (New York: Random House, 1941).

[4] Ibid.

[5] Ibid.

that the character of the average person is not completely fixed by nature; it can be improved, if only slightly, by good influences. These influences can supply a bit (though apparently not much) of what nature has left out of the character of the average person, thus making it possible for him to "get some tincture of virtue."

Inasmuch, however, as the average person is moved by passion and not by reason, what is needed to prepare him for virtue is not argument, but coercion. "In general," Aristotle says, "passion seems to yield not to argument but to force." [6] Therefore, if "the many" are to have even the small measure of moral goodness of which they are capable, they must be forbidden from doing what is morally wrong and required to do what morality requires; and these commands must be backed by threats of punishment. If people have passionate motives (e.g. love of pleasure) for doing what is morally bad, they must be presented with more powerful countervailing passionate motives (e.g. fear of pain) not to do it. While people motivated by love of what is morally good can be expected to do the right thing *because* it is the right thing (once they understand it to be the right thing), people motivated by passion cannot be expected to do the right thing when they have a passionate motive not to do it and no more powerful countervailing passionate motive to do it. They can be expected to do what is right only when their passionate motives for doing so are more powerful than any competing passionate motives for not doing so. A lively fear of a sufficient punishment typically provides the countervailing motive needed to get the average person to do what is right and avoid doing what is wrong.

Building thus on an analysis of character and its formation, Aristotle develops his view of the role of law in providing the influences necessary to make men moral. Here again I shall let Aristotle speak for himself:

> But it is difficult to get from youth up a right training for virtue if one has not been brought up under right laws; for to live temperately and hardily is not pleasant to most people, especially when they are young. For this reason their nurture and occupations should be fixed by law; for they will not be painful when they have become customary. But it is surely not enough that when they are young they should get the right nurture and attention; since they must, even when the are grown up, practise and be habituated to them, we shall need laws for this as well, and generally speaking to cover the whole of life; for most people obey necessity rather than argument, and punishments rather than the sense of what is noble. [7]

Apparently referring to the teaching of Plato, he goes on to observe that:

> This is why some think that legislators ought to stimulate men to virtue and urge them forward by the motive of the noble, on the assumption that those who have been well advanced by the formation of habits will attend to such

---

[6] Ibid.

[7] Ibid. x. 9. 1179^b–1180^a.

influences; and that punishments and penalties should be imposed on those who disobey and are of inferior nature, while the incurably bad should be completely banished. A good man . . . will submit to argument, while a bad man, whose desire is for pleasure, is corrected by pain like a beast of burden. This is, too, why they say the pains inflicted should be those that are most opposed to the pleasures men love.[8]

It may seem from these passages that Aristotle has missed an elementary point about moral goodness, namely, that coercing people to do the right thing, even when it is successful, does not make them morally better; it does nothing more than produce external conformity to moral norms. Morality, however, is above all an internal matter, a matter of rectitude in choosing: one becomes morally good precisely, and only, by doing the right thing *for the right reason.* In other words, morality, unlike knowledge, or beauty, or even skillful performance, is a reflexive good, namely, a good that is (and can only be) realized in *choosing* uprightly, reasonably, well; a good into whose very definition *choice* enters.[9] A coerced choice, however, does not adopt the good and the reason which might have shaped the chosen option; instead one adopts that option for the sake of avoiding pain, harm, or loss to oneself. So, someone is not "just and noble" for doing merely out of fear of punishment something that would truly be just and noble if done for the sake of what is good and right. If the legal enforcement of moral obligations does nothing more for the masses than present them with subrational motives for outward conformity with what morality requires, it does nothing toward making men moral.

Aristotle's point, however, is not that moral good is realized whenever the law produces in people outward behavior that conforms with what morality requires, even if that behavior is purely the product of fear of punishment. Rather, his point is that, given the natural tendency of the majority of people to act on passionate motives in preference to reason (i.e. love of the good), the law must first settle people down if it is to help them to gain some appreciation of the good, some grasp of the intrinsic value of morally upright choosing, some control by their reason of their passions. Mere arguments will not do the job, "for he who lives as passion directs will not hear argument that dissuades him, nor understand it if he does."[10] It is precisely inasmuch as the average man is given to passions that, "like a beast of burden," he must be governed by fear of punishment. The law must combat his emotional motives for wrongdoing with countervailing emotional motives. Once the law is successful in calming his passions and habituating him to doing what is right and avoiding what is wrong, he—unlike a brute animal—may gain some intelligent, reasonable, and reflective control of his passion. Even the average person may then learn to

---

[8] Ibid. x. 9. 1180ᵃ. Cf. Plato's analyses in *Laws,* 722 D. ff., and *Protagoras,* 325 A.

[9] By such a choice, one *adopts* the good inherent in the right reasons that shaped the option one thus chooses. One determines and integrates one's character, to a greater or lesser degree, around that good and that reason for acting.

[10] *Nic. Eth.* x. 9. 1179ᵇ.

appreciate the good a little, and, in choosing for the sake of the good, become morally better.[11]

Someone might object to Aristotle's claim that legal coercion can help put people into shape to appreciate the value of moral uprightness by settling them down and habituating them to virtue, on the ground that the more likely effect of such coercion is to instill resentment in people, and even incline them to rebellion. Here, too, Aristotle has an answer. "While people hate *men* who oppose their impulses, even if they oppose them rightly, the law in its ordaining of what is good is not burdensome." [12] What he appears to have in mind here is that, while resentment and rebellion can be expected where one person brings coercion to bear against another in an effort to prevent him from doing something morally wrong, people will accept coercion more readily when an immoral act is prohibited *generally,* that is, throughout a society, and by the *impersonal* force of the law.

Why, though, does Aristotle suppose that immoral acts must be prohibited by *public* authority as opposed to the authority of the head of the household or family? His argument is that:

> the paternal command . . . has not the required force or compulsive power (nor in general has the command of one man, unless he be king or something similar), but the law has compulsive power, while it is at the same time a rule proceeding from a sort of practical wisdom and reason.[13]

It is, once again, the generality of legal prohibition that makes the difference. People, notably including children, are formed not only in households, but in neighborhoods, and wider communities. Parents can prohibit a certain act, but their likelihood of success in enforcing the prohibition, and transmitting to their children a genuine grasp of the wrongness of the prohibited act, will be lessened to the extent that others more or less freely perform the act.

For example, parents can forbid their teenage sons to look at pornographic magazines; if, however, other boys with whom they have contact are freely circulating such material, it will be difficult for the parents to enforce their prohibition. Moreover, the boys whose parents have forbidden them to have pornography are likely to experience that prohibition as more onerous to the extent of their knowledge that other boys are free to indulge their taste for pornography. They are more likely to feel resentment, and to rebel, when they are being deprived of a freedom that others enjoy. Whatever authority parents have over their own children, they lack the authority to deprive other people in the community, or other people's children, of the legal liberty to perform immoral acts; only public officials possess authority of that kind. If, however,

---

[11] Much later in the tradition, Aristotle's view is echoed by Kant: "Man must be trained, so as to become domesticated and virtuous later on. The coercion of government and education make him supple, flexible and obedient to the laws; then reason will rule" *Gesammelte Schriften,* xv. 522–3 (Prussian Academy edn., 1923); quoted from the translation by G. Kelly, in *Idealism, Politics and History* (London: Cambridge University Press, 1969).

[12] *Nic. Eth.* x. 9. 1180ᵃ.

[13] Ibid.

public authorities fail to combat certain vices, the impact of widespread immorality on the community's moral environment is likely to make the task of parents who rightly forbid their own children from, say, indulging in pornography, extremely difficult.

Nevertheless, Aristotle argues that where the *polis* is failing to do its job, other institutions, including households, should do what they can to prevent immorality.

> Now it is best that there should be a public and proper care for such matters; but if they are neglected by the community it would seem right for each man to help his children and friends towards virtue, and that they should have the power, or at least the will, to do this.[14]

Indeed, he seems to recognize that the kind of moral formation that goes on in families, whatever its limitations, has certain advantages in the formation of moral character.

> For as in cities laws and prevailing types of character have force, so in households do the injunctions and habits of the father, and these have even more because of the tie of blood and the benefits he confers; for the children start with a natural affection and disposition to obey. Further, private education has an advantage over public; for while in general rest and abstinence from food are good for a man in a fever, for a particular man they may not be. . . . It would seem, then, that the detail is worked out with more precision if the control is private; for each person is more likely to get what suits his case.[15]

In short, families, unlike political authorities, can deal with individuals as individuals, taking into account their distinctive needs and circumstances. So, Aristotle finally implies, making men moral is not a task for the *polis* alone: political communities should do what they can to encourage virtue and prevent vice, while other institutions should do what they can to complement the work of the *polis*.[16]

• • •

The idea that public morality is a public good, and that immoral acts—even between consenting adults—can therefore do public harm, has not been refuted by liberal critics of the central tradition. On the contrary, the idea is vindicated by the experiences of modern cultures which have premised their law on its denial. The institutions of marriage and the family have plainly been weakened in cultures in which large numbers of people have come to understand

---

[14] Ibid.

[15] *Nic. Eth.* x. 9. p. 1180^{b}

[16] Aristotle's view of the matter appears to be unstable, however, for in *Pol.* i. 1. 1252^{b} 13–30 he assumes that the household or family is merely an association for the sake of life, while the *polis* is an association for the sake of the good life; and, in *Pol.* viii. 1. 1337^{a}23–32, he concludes that education is the responsibility of the *polis* and not (or at least not primarily) the responsibility of parents.

themselves as "satisfaction seekers" who, if they happen to desire it, may resort more or less freely to promiscuity, pornographic fantasies, prostitution, and drugs. Of course, recognition of the public consequences of putatively private vice does not mean that liberalism is wrong to be critical of morals legislation. For, as we shall see in later chapters, contemporary liberals make a variety of moral arguments against such legislation that do not depend on the propositions that public morality is not a public good or that private immorality cannot do public harm. It does mean, however, that a crucial premiss of the tradition's case against moral *laissez-faire* remains unshaken: societies have reason to care about what might be called their "moral ecology."

The tradition, as embodied in the sorts of laws and public policies to which orthodox liberalism objects, has not followed Aristotle and Aquinas in every detail. It has come to give greater room to freedom, and to be more circumspect in the use of the law's coercive power, than Aristotle and Aquinas would have thought necessary or appropriate. I shall argue that, where the tradition has developed in these ways, it has been right to do so. Although Aristotle and Aquinas were correct in supposing that the law may justly and appropriately seek to combat vice and encourage virtue, and while the whole tradition, including Aristotle and Aquinas, is superior to liberalism in allowing, in principle at least, for the quasi-paternalistic (and, in some cases, even the paternalistic) and educative use of the law to forbid certain immoralities, their analyses of these questions were flawed in various ways. And, indeed, there are certain respects, especially those touching upon religious liberty, in which the influence of liberalism on the tradition has been salutary.

While ancient and medieval life was not without diversity, Isaiah Berlin is probably correct to criticize the tradition for failing to understand the diversity of basic forms of good and the range of valid pluralism.[17] Aristotle, for example, plainly failed to allow room in his ethical and political theory for the diversity of irreducible human goods which, considered as providing basic reasons for action and options for choice, are the bases for a vast range of valuable, but mutually incompatible, choices, commitments, and plans and ways of life. And he lacked anything like a good argument for his view that there must be a single superior way of life, or a uniquely highest life for those capable of it; nor did he provide anything approaching a plausible theory of where those not capable of what he believed to be the highest life fit into a society that treats that way of life as the best.

Without adopting the relativistic view which sees the good as so radically diverse that whatever people happen to want is good, we can and should recognize a multiplicity of basic human goods and a multiplicity of ways that different people (and communities) can pursue and organize instantiations of those goods in living valuable and morally upright lives. Our recognition of (non-relativistic) value pluralism opens up something that Aristotle never clearly saw: people are not simply disposed by nature (and/or culture) well or

---

[17] This theme runs through Berlin's essays in *The Crooked Timber of Humanity* (London: John Murray, 1990).

badly, they dispose themselves, and can dispose themselves, well or badly, in a vast variety of ways. Human beings put their lives together in different ways by making different choices and commitments based on different values that provide different reasons for choice and action. There is no single pattern anyone can identify as the proper model of a human life, not because there is no such thing as good and bad, but because there are many goods. Moreover, people are fulfilled in part by deliberating and choosing for themselves a pattern of their own. Practical reasoning is not merely a human capacity; it is itself a fundamental aspect of human well-being and fulfillment: a basic dimension of the human good consists precisely in bringing reason to bear in deliberating and choosing among competing valuable possibilities, commitments, and ways of life.[18]

Lacking an appreciation of the diversity of basic human goods, and thus the diversity of valuable ways of life ordinarily available to people, Aristotle wrongly supposed that people have preordained stations in life, and that the wise legislator who is concerned to promote virtue will therefore have the job of slotting people into their proper stations and seeing to it that each person fulfills the duties of his particular station. Working from an implausibly limited and hierarchical view of human good, Aristotle failed to perceive that persons, as loci of human goods and of rational capacity for self-determination by free choices, are *equal in dignity,* however unequal they are in ability, intelligence, and other gifts: hence his élitism, not to mention his notorious doctrine of "natural slaves." [19]

Aristotelian élitism is a fundamental and gross error, which is itself rooted in a failure to appreciate the diversity of basic human goods that fulfill the persons in and by whom they are instantiated and realized. It is this diversity that confounds every attempt to identify a "highest" or "best" life to which those who are by nature suited to that life (and are thus the "highest" or "best" examples of human beings) should aspire. In any event, whatever may have been the case in Aristotle's Athens, legislators in modern representative democracies are unlikely to be morally superior to the people who elect them. One might even argue that, given what it takes to achieve public office, the average legislator today is likely to be generally less strict in the observance of certain moral norms than the average voter.

At the same time, there is in normal circumstances no reason to suppose, as Aristotle did, that the great mass of people are incapable of being reasonable

---

[18] See John Finnis, *Natural Law and Natural Rights* (Oxford: Clarendon Press, 1980), 88–9.

[19] For a proper understanding of this doctrine, see W. W. Fortenbaugh "Aristotle on Slaves and Women," in J. Barnes, M. Schofield, and R. Sorabji (eds.), *Articles on Aristotle,* ii (London: Duckworth, 1975). Also see Daniel N. Robinson's exceptionally valuable analysis in *Aristotle's Psychology* (New York: Columbia University Press, 1989). It is worth noting here that Professor Robinson, whose penetrating and meticulous scholarship I greatly admire, has proposed an interpretation of Aristotle's eudaimonism that goes far toward the sort of *pluralistic* perfectionism that I myself defend. Interpreted in this way, I find Aristotle's practical philosophy considerably less objectionable. As Professor Robinson points out, however, there are certain "unavoidable differences in the interpretation of Aristotle's subtle and sometimes inconsistent treatises" (ibid., p. xi).

and need to be governed by fear. Nor is there any reason to believe in the existence of a moral élite whose members need only understand moral truth in order to live up to its demands. The fact is that all rational human beings are capable of understanding moral reasons; yet all require guidance, support, and assistance from others. All are susceptible to moral failure, even serious moral failure; and all are capable of benefiting from a milieu which is more or less free from powerful inducements to vice. All require freedom if they are to flourish; but unlimited freedom is the enemy, not the friend, of everyone's well-being.

Once we have brought into focus the diversity of human goods, it becomes clear that legislators concerned to uphold morality cannot prohibit all that much. At most, they can legitimately proscribe only the fairly small number of acts and practices that are incompatible with any morally good life. Paternalism is strictly limited by the diversity of goods whose recognition makes nonsense of the idea of assigning people to "natural" or "appropriate" stations in life. Of course, there are morally valuable institutions, such as marriage, which, while not morally obligatory for everyone, are nevertheless worthy of protection. To defend such institutions from forces and developments in a society that may threaten them, legislators will need to understand their nature, value, and vulnerability. It will be complicated, then, for legislators to design laws that protect institutions such as marriage. To ban an act such as adultery on the ground of its intrinsic immorality is fairly straightforward (if difficult to enforce); to design just and good laws pertaining to marital break-up, divorce, and the care of children, however, is not so simple.

5.
Membership and Community
MICHAEL WALZER

MEMBERSHIP AND NEED

Membership is important because of what the members of a political community owe to one another and to no one else, or to no one else in the same degree. And the first thing they owe is the communal provision of security and welfare. This claim might be reversed: communal provision is important because it teaches us the value of membership. If we did not provide for one another, if we recognized no distinction between members and strangers, we would have no reason to form and maintain political communities. "How shall men love their country," Rousseau asked, "if it is nothing more for them than for strangers, and bestows on them only that which it can refuse to none?"[1] Rousseau believed that citizens ought to love their country and therefore that their country ought to give them particular reasons to do so. Membership (like kinship) is a special relation. It's not enough to say, as Edmund Burke did, that "to make us love our country, our country ought to be lovely."[2] The crucial thing is that it be lovely for us—though we always hope that it will be lovely for others (we also love its reflected loveliness).

Political community for the sake of provision, provision for the sake of community: the process works both ways, and that is perhaps its crucial feature. Philosophers and political theorists have been too quick to turn it into a simple calculation. Indeed, we are rationalists of everyday life; we come together, we sign the social contract or reiterate the signing of it, in order to provide for our needs. And we value the contract insofar as those needs are met. But one of our needs is community itself: culture, religion, and politics. It is only under the aegis of these three that all the other things we need become *socially recognized needs,* take on historical and determinate form. The social contract is an agreement to reach decisions together about what goods are necessary to our common life, and then to provide those goods for one another. The signers owe one another more than mutual aid, for that they owe or can owe to anyone. They owe mutual provision of all those things for the sake of which they have separated themselves from mankind as a whole and joined forces in a particular community. *Amour social* is one of those things; but though it is a distributed good—often unevenly distributed—it arises only in the course of other distributions (and of the political choices that the other distributions require).

[1] Jean Jacques Rousseau, " A Discourse on Political Economy," in *The Social Contract and Discourses,* trans. G. D. H. Cole (New York, 1950), pp. 302–3.
[2] Edmund Burke, *Reflections on the French Revolution* (London, 1910), p. 75.

Mutual provision breeds mutuality. So the common life is simultaneously the prerequisite of provision and one of its products.

Men and women come together because they literally cannot live apart. But they can live together in many different ways. Their survival and then their well-being require a common effort: against the wrath of the gods, the hostility of other people, the indifference and malevolence of nature (famine, flood, fire, and disease), the brief transit of a human life. Not army camps alone, as David Hume wrote, but temples, storehouses, irrigation works, and burial grounds are the true mothers of cities.[3] As the list suggests, origins are not singular in character. Cities differ from one another, partly because of the natural environments in which they are built and the immediate dangers their builders encounter, partly because of the conceptions of social goods that the builders hold. They recognize but also create one another's needs and so give a particular shape to what I will call the "sphere of security and welfare." The sphere itself is as old as the oldest human community. Indeed, one might say that the original community is a sphere of security and welfare, a system of communal provision, distorted, no doubt, by gross inequalities of strength and cunning. But the system has, in any case, no natural form. Different experiences and different conceptions lead to different patterns of provision. Though there are some goods that are needed absolutely, there is no good such that once we see it, we know how it stands vis-à-vis all other goods and how much of it we owe to one another. The nature of a need is not self-evident.

Communal provision is both general and particular. It is general whenever public funds are spent so as to benefit all or most of the members without any distribution to individuals. It is particular whenever goods are actually handed over to all or any of the members.[4] Water, for example, is one of "the bare requirements of civil life," and the building of reservoirs is a form of general provision.[5] But the delivery of water to one rather than to another neighborhood (where, say, the wealthier citizens live) is particular. The securing of the food supply is general; the distribution of food to widows and orphans is particular. Public health is most often general, the care of the sick, most often particular. Sometimes the criteria for general and particular provision will differ radically. The building of temples and the organization of religious services is an example of general provision designed to meet the needs of the community as a whole, but communion with the gods may be allowed only to particularly meritorious

---

[3]   Cf. David Hume, *A Treatise of Human Nature*, bk. III, part II, chap. 8.

[4]   I don't mean to reiterate here the technical distinction that economists make between public and private goods. General provision is always public, at least on the less stringent definitions of that term (which specify only that public goods are those that can't be provided to some and not to other members of the community). So are most forms of particular provision, for even goods delivered to individuals generate non-exclusive benefits for the community as a whole. Scholarships to orphans, for example, are private to the orphans, public to the community of citizens within which the orphans will one day work and vote. But public goods of this latter sort, which depend upon prior distributions to particular persons or groups, have been controversial in many societies, and I have designed my categories so as to enable me to examine them closely.

[5]   The quotation is from the Greek geographer Pausanias, in George Rosen, *A History of Public Health* (New York, 1958), p. 41.

members (or it may be sought privately in secret or in nonconformist sects). The system of justice is a general good, meeting common needs; but the actual distribution of rewards and punishments may serve the particular needs of a ruling class, or it may be organized, as we commonly think it should be, to give to individuals what they individually deserve. Simone Weil has argued that, with regard to justice, need operates at both the general and the particular levels, since criminals need to be punished.[6] But that is an idiosyncratic use of the word *need*. More likely, the punishment of criminals is something only the rest of us need. But need does operate both generally and particularly for other goods: health care is an obvious example that I will later consider in some detail.

Despite the inherent forcefulness of the word, needs are elusive. People don't just have needs, they have ideas about their needs; they have priorities, they have degrees of need; and these priorities and degrees are related not only to their human nature but also to their history and culture. Since resources are always scarce, hard choices have to be made. I suspect that these can only be political choices. They are subject to a certain philosophical elucidation, but the idea of need and the commitment to communal provision do not by themselves yield any clear determination of priorities or degrees. Clearly we can't meet, and we don't have to meet, every need to the same degree or any need to the ultimate degree. The ancient Athenians, for example, provided public baths and gymnasiums for the citizens but never provided anything remotely resembling unemployment insurance or social security. They made a choice about how to spend public funds, a choice shaped presumably by their understanding of what the common life required. It would be hard to argue that they made a mistake. I suppose there are notions of need that would yield such a conclusion, but these would not be notions acceptable to—they might not even be comprehensible to—the Athenians themselves.

The question of degree suggests even more clearly the importance of political choice and the irrelevance of any merely philosophical stipulation. Needs are not only elusive; they are also expansive. In the phrase of the contemporary philosopher Charles Fried, needs are voracious; they eat up resources.[7] But it would be wrong to suggest that therefore need cannot be a distributive principle. It is, rather, a principle subject to political limitation; and the limits (within limits) can be arbitrary, fixed by some temporary coalition interests or majority of voters. Consider the case of physical security in a modern American city. We could provide absolute security, eliminate every source of violence except domestic violence, if we put a street light every ten yards and stationed a policeman every thirty yards throughout the city. But that would be very expensive, and so we settle for something less. How much less can only be decided politically.[8] One can imagine the sort of things that would figure in the debates.

---

[6] Simone Weil, *The Need for Roots*, trans. Arthur Wills (Boston, 1955), p. 21.

[7] Charles Fried, *Right and Wrong* (Cambridge, Mass., 1978), p. 122.

[8] And should be decided politically: that is what democratic political arrangements are for. Any philosophical effort to stipulate in detail the rights or the entitlements of individuals would radically constrain the scope of democratic decision making I have argued this point elsewhere.

Above all, I think, there would be a certain understanding—more or less widely shared, controversial only at the margins—of what constitutes "enough" security or of what level of insecurity is simply intolerable. The decision would also be affected by other factors: alternate needs, the state of the economy, the agitation of the policemen's union, and so on. But whatever decision is ultimately reached, for whatever reasons, security is provided because the citizens need it. And because, at some level, they all need it, the criterion of need remains a critical standard (as we shall see) even though it cannot determine priority and degree.

THE EXTENT OF PROVISION

Distributive justice in the sphere of welfare and security has a twofold meaning: it refers, first, to the recognition of need and, second, to the recognition of membership. Goods must be provided to needy members because of their neediness, but they must also be provided in such a way as to sustain their membership. It's not the case, however, that members have a claim on any specific set of goods. Welfare rights are fixed only when a community adopts some program of mutual provision. There are strong arguments to be made that, under given historical conditions, such-and-such a program should be adopted. But these are not arguments about individual rights; they are arguments about the character of a particular political community. No one's rights were violated because the Athenians did not allocate public funds for the education of children. Perhaps they believed, and perhaps they were right, that the public life of the city was education enough.

The right that members can legitimately claim is of a more general sort. It undoubtedly includes some version of the Hobbesian right to life, some claim on communal resources for bare subsistence. No community can allow its members to starve to death when there is food available to feed them; no government can stand passively by at such a time—not if it claims to be a government of or by or for the community. The indifference of Britain's rulers during the Irish potato famine in the 1840s is a sure sign that Ireland was a colony, a conquered land, no real part of Great Britain.[9] This is not to justify the indifference—one has obligations to colonies and to conquered peoples—but only to suggest that the Irish would have been better served by a government, virtually any government, of their own. Perhaps Burke came closest to describing the fundamental right that is at stake here when he wrote: "Government is a contrivance of human wisdom to provide for human wants. Men have a right that these wants should be provided for by this wisdom."[10] It only has to be said that the wisdom in question is the wisdom not of a ruling class, as Burke seems to have thought, but of the community as a whole. Only its culture, its

---

[9] For an account of the famine and the British response, see C. B. Woodham-Smith, *The Great Hunger: Ireland 1845—1849* (London, 1962).

[10] Burke, *French Revolution* [2], p. 57.

character, its common understandings can define the "wants" that are to be provided for. But culture, character, and common understandings are not givens; they don't operate automatically; at any particular moment, the citizens must argue about the extent of mutual provision.

They argue about the meaning of the social contract, the original and reiterated conception of the sphere of security and welfare. This is not a hypothetical or an ideal contract of the sort John Rawls has described. Rational men and women in the original position, deprived of all particular knowledge of their social standing and cultural understanding, would probably opt, as Rawls has argued, for an equal distribution of whatever goods they were told they needed.[11] But this formula doesn't help very much in determining what choices people will make, or what choices they should make, once they know who and where they are. In a world of particular cultures, competing conceptions of the good, scarce resources, elusive and expansive needs, there isn't going to be a single formula, universally applicable. There isn't going to be a single, universally approved path that carries us from a notion like, say, "fair shares" to a comprehensive list of the goods to which that notion applies. Fair shares of what?

Justice, tranquility, defense, welfare, and liberty: that is the list provided by the United States Constitution. One could construe it as an exhaustive list, but the terms are vague; they provide at best a starting point for public debate. The standard appeal in that debate is to a larger idea: the Burkeian general right, which takes on determinate force only under determinate conditions and requires different sorts of provision in different times and places. The idea is simply that we have come together, shaped a community, in order to cope with difficulties and dangers that we could not cope with alone. And so whenever we find ourselves confronted with difficulties and dangers of that sort, we look for communal assistance. As the balance of individual and collective capacity changes, so the kinds of assistance that are looked for change, too.

The history of public health in the West might usefully be told in these terms. Some minimal provision is very old, as the Greek and Jewish examples suggest; the measures adopted were a function of the community's sense of danger and the extent of its medical knowledge. Over the years, living arrangements on a larger scale bred new dangers, and scientific advance generated a new sense of danger and a new awareness of the possibilities of coping. And then groups of citizens pressed for a wider program of communal provision, exploiting the new science to reduce the risks of urban life. That, they might rightly say, is what the community is for. A similar argument can be made in the case of social security. The very success of general provision in the field of public health has greatly extended the span of a normal human life and then also the span of years during which men and women are unable to support themselves, during which they are physically but most often not socially, politically, or morally incapacitated. Once again, support for the disabled is one of the oldest and most common forms of particular provision. But now it is required on a much larger

[11] John Rawls, *A Theory of Justice* (Cambridge, Mass., 1971), part I, chaps. 2 and 3.

scale than ever before. Families are overwhelmed by the costs of old age and look for help to the political community. Exactly what ought to be done will be a matter of dispute. Words like *health, danger, science,* even *old age,* have very different meanings in different cultures; no external specification is possible. But this is not to say that it won't be clear enough to the people involved that something—some particular set of things—ought to be done.

Perhaps these examples are too easy. Disease is a general threat; old age, a general prospect. Not so unemployment and poverty, which probably lie beyond the ken of many well-to-do people. The poor can always be isolated, locked into ghettos, blamed and punished for their own misfortune. At this point, it might be said, provision can no longer be defended by invoking anything like the "meaning" of the social contract. But let us look more closely at the easy cases; for, in fact, they involve all the difficulties of the difficult ones. Public health and social security invite us to think of the political community, in T. H. Marshall's phrase, as a "mutual benefit club." [12] All provision is reciprocal; the members take turns providing and being provided for, much as Aristotle's citizens take turns ruling and being ruled. This is a happy picture, and one that is readily understandable in contractualist terms. It is not only the case that rational agents, knowing nothing of their specific situation, would agree to these two forms of provision; the real agents, the ordinary citizens, of every modern democracy have in fact agreed to them. The two are, or so it appears, equally in the interests of hypothetical and of actual people. Coercion is only necessary in practice because some minority of actual people don't understand, or don't consistently understand, their real interests. Only the reckless and the improvident need to be forced to contribute—and it can always be said of them that they joined in the social contract precisely in order to protect themselves against their own recklessness and improvidence. In fact, however, the reasons for coercion go much deeper than this; the political community is something more than a mutual benefit club; and the extent of communal provision in any given case—what it is and what it should be—is determined by conceptions of need that are more problematic than the argument thus far suggests.

Consider again the case of public health. No communal provision is possible here without the constraint of a wide range of activities profitable to individual members of the community but threatening to some larger number. Even something so simple, for example, as the provision of uncontaminated milk to large urban populations requires extensive public control; and control is a political achievement, the result (in the United States) of bitter struggles, over many years, in one city after another.[13] When the farmers or the middlemen of the dairy industry defended free enterprise, they were certainly acting rationally in their own interests. The same thing can be said of other entrepreneurs who defend themselves against the constraints of inspection, regulation, and en-

[12] T. H. Marshall, *Class, Citizenship, and Social Development* (Garden City, New York, 1965), p. 298.

[13] See Judith Walzer Leavitt, *The Healthiest City: Milwaukee and the Politics of Health Reform* (Princeton, 1982), chap. 5.

forcement. Public activities of these sorts may be of the highest value to the rest of us; they are not of the highest value to all of us. Though I have taken public health as an example of general provision, it is provided only at the expense of some members of the community. Moreover, it benefits most the most vulnerable of the others: thus, the special importance of the building code for those who live in crowded tenements and of anti-pollution laws for those who live in the immediate vicinity of factory smokestacks or water drains. Social security, too, benefits the most vulnerable members, even if, for reasons I have already suggested, the actual payments are the same for everyone. For the well-to-do can, or many of them think they can, help themselves even in time of trouble and would much prefer not to be forced to help anyone else. The truth is that every serious effort at communal provision (insofar as the income of the community derives from the wealth of its members) is redistributive in character.[14] The benefits it provides are not, strictly speaking, mutual.

Once again, rational agents ignorant of their own social standing would agree to such a redistribution. But they would agree too easily, and their agreement doesn't help us understand what sort of a redistribution is required: How much? For what purposes? In practice, redistribution is a political matter, and the coercion it involves is foreshadowed by the conflicts that rage over its character and extent. Every particular measure is pushed through by some coalition of particular interests. But the ultimate appeal in these conflicts is not to the particular interests, not even to a public interest conceived as their sum, but to collective values, shared understandings of membership, health, food and shelter, work and leisure. The conflicts themselves are often focused, at least overtly, on questions of fact; the understandings are assumed. Thus the entrepreneurs of the dairy industry denied as long as they could the connection between contaminated milk and tuberculosis. But once that connection was established, it was difficult for them to deny that milk should be inspected: *caveat emptor* was not, in such a case, a plausible doctrine. Similarly, in the debates over old-age pensions in Great Britain, politicians mostly agreed on the traditional British value of self-help but disagreed sharply about whether self-help was still possible through the established working-class friendly societies. These were real mutual-benefit clubs organized on a strictly voluntary basis, but they seemed about to be overwhelmed by the growing numbers of the aged. It became increasingly apparent that the members simply did not have the resources to protect themselves and one another from poverty in old age. And few British politicians were prepared to say that they should be left unprotected.[15]

Here, then, is a more precise account of the social contract: it is an agreement to redistribute the resources of the members in accordance with some shared understanding of their needs, subject to ongoing political determination

---

[14] See the careful discussion in Harold L. Wilensky, *The Welfare State and Equality* (Berkeley, 1975), pp. 87–96.

[15] P. H. J. H. Gosden, *Self-Help: Voluntary Associations in the Nineteenth Century* (London, 1973), chap. 9.

in detail. The contract is a moral bond. It connects the strong and the weak, the lucky and the unlucky, the rich and the poor, creating a union that transcends all differences of interest, drawing its strength from history, culture, religion, language, and so on. Arguments about communal provision are, at the deepest level, interpretations of that union. The closer and more inclusive it is, the wider the recognition of needs, the greater the number of social goods that are drawn into the sphere of security and welfare.[16] I don't doubt that many political communities have redistributed resources on very different principles, not in accordance with the needs of the members generally but in accordance with the power of the wellborn or the wealthy. But that, as Rousseau suggested in his *Discourse on Inequality,* makes a fraud of the social contract.[17] In any community, where resources are taken away from the poor and given to the rich, the rights of the poor are being violated. The wisdom of the community is not engaged in providing for their wants. Political debate about the nature of those wants will have to be repressed, else the fraud will quickly be exposed. When all the members share in the business of interpreting the social contract, the result will be a more or less extensive system of communal provision. If all states are in principle welfare states, democracies are most likely to be welfare states in practice. Even the imitation of democracy breeds welfarism, as in the "people's democracies," where the state protects the people against every disaster except those that it inflicts on them itself.

So democratic citizens argue among themselves and opt for many different sorts of security and welfare, extending far beyond my "easy" examples of public health and old-age pensions. The category of socially recognized needs is open-ended. For the people's sense of what they need encompasses not only life itself but also the good life, and the appropriate balance between these two is itself a matter of dispute. The Athenian drama and the Jewish academies were both financed with money that could have been spent on housing, say, or on medicine. But drama and education were taken by Greeks and Jews to be not merely enhancements of the common life but vital aspects of communal welfare. I want to stress again that these are not judgments that can easily be called incorrect.

---

[16] See, for example, Harry Eckstein's discussion of conceptions of community and welfare policies in *Norway: Division and Cohesion in Democracy: A Study of Norway* (Princeton, 1966), pp. 85–87.

[17] Rousseau, *Social Contract* [1], pp. 250–52.

PART

II

THE LIMITS OF LEGITIMATE STATE ACTION

6.

The Harm Principle

JOHN STUART MILL

The object of this essay is to assert one very simple principle, as entitled to govern absolutely the dealings of society with the individual in the way of compulsion and control, whether the means used be physical force in the form of legal penalties or the moral coercion of public opinion. That principle is that the sole end for which mankind are warranted, individually or collectively, in interfering with the liberty of action of any of their number is self-protection. That the only purpose for which power can be rightfully exercised over any member of a civilized community, against his will, is to prevent harm to others. His own good, either physical or moral, is not a sufficient warrant. He cannot rightfully be compelled to do or forbear because it will be better for him to do so, because it will make him happier, because, in the opinions of others, to do so would be wise or even right. These are good reasons for remonstrating with him, or reasoning with him, or persuading him, or entreating him, but not for compelling him or visiting him with any evil in case he do otherwise. To justify that, the conduct from which it is desired to deter him must be calculated to produce evil to someone else. The only part of the conduct of anyone for which he is amenable to society is that which concerns others. In the part which merely concerns himself, his independence is, of right, absolute. Over himself, over his own body and mind, the individual is sovereign.

It is, perhaps, hardly necessary to say that this doctrine is meant to apply only to human beings in the maturity of their faculties. We are not speaking of children or of young persons below the age which the law may fix as that of manhood or womanhood. Those who are still in a state to require being taken care of by others must be protected against their own actions as well as against external injury. For the same reason we may leave out of consideration those backward states of society in which the race itself may be considered as in its nonage. The early difficulties in the way of spontaneous progress are so great that there is seldom any choice of means for overcoming them; and a ruler full of the spirit of improvement is warranted in the use of any expedients that will attain an end perhaps otherwise unattainable. Despotism is a legitimate mode of government in dealing with barbarians, provided the end be their improvement and the means justified by actually effecting that end. Liberty, as a principle, has no application to any state of things anterior to the time when mankind have become capable of being improved by free and equal discussion. Until then, there is nothing for them but implicit obedience to an Akbar or a Charlemagne, if they are so fortunate as to find one. But as soon as mankind have attained the capacity of being guided to their own improvement by conviction or persuasion (a period long since reached in all nations with whom we need here concern ourselves), compulsion, either in the direct form or in that of pains and penalties for noncompliance, is no longer admissible as a means to their own good, and justifiable only for the security of others.

It is proper to state that I forego any advantage which could be derived to my argument from the idea of abstract right as a thing independent of utility. I regard utility as the ultimate appeal on all ethical questions; but it must be utility in the largest sense, grounded on the permanent interests of man as a progressive being. Those interests, I contend, authorize the subjection of individual spontaneity to external control only in respect to those actions of each which concern the interest of other people. If anyone does an act hurtful to others, there is a *prima facie* case for punishing him by law or, where legal penalties are not safely applicable, by general disapprobation. There are also many positive acts for the benefit of others which he may rightfully be compelled to perform, such as to give evidence in a court of justice, to bear his fair share in the common defense or in any other joint work necessary to the interest of the society of which he enjoys the protection, and to perform certain acts of individual beneficence, such as saving a fellow creature's life or interposing to protect the defenseless against ill usage—things which whenever it is obviously a man's duty to do he may rightfully be made responsible to society for not doing. A person may cause evil to others not only by his actions but by his inaction, and in either can he is justly accountable to them for the injury. The latter case, it is true, requires a much more cautious exercise of compulsion than the former. To make anyone answerable for doing evil to others is the rule; to make him answerable for not preventing evil is, comparatively speaking, the exception. Yet there are many cases clear enough and grave enough to justify that exception. In all things which regard the external relations of the individual, he is *de jure* amenable to those whose interests are concerned, and, if need be, to society as their protector. There are often good reasons for not holding him to the responsibility; but these reasons must arise from the special expediencies of the case: either because it is a kind of case in which he is on the whole likely to act better when left to his own discretion than when controlled in any way in which society have it in their power to control him; or because the attempt to exercise control would produce other evils, greater than those which it would prevent. When such reasons as these preclude the enforcement of responsibility, the conscience of the agent himself should step into the vacant judgment seat and protect those interests of others which have no external protection; judging himself all the more rigidly, because the case does not admit of his being made accountable to the judgment of his fellow creatures.

But there is a sphere of action in which society, as distinguished from the individual, has, if any, only an indirect interest: comprehending all that portion of a person's life and conduct which affects only himself or, if it also affects others, only with their free, voluntary, and undeceived consent and participation. When I say only himself, I mean directly and in the first instance; for whatever affects himself may affect others through himself; and the objection which may be grounded on this contingency will receive consideration in the sequel. This, then, is the appropriate region of human liberty. It comprises, first, the inward domain of consciousness, demanding liberty of conscience in the most comprehensive sense, liberty of thought and feeling, absolute freedom of opinion and sentiment on all subjects, practical or speculative, scientific, moral, or theological. The liberty of expressing and publishing opinions may seem to fall under a different principle, since it belongs to that part of the conduct of an individual which concerns other people, but, being almost of as much importance as the liberty of thought itself and resting in great part on the same reasons, is practically inseparable from it. Secondly, the principle requires liberty of tastes and pursuits, of framing the plan of our life to suit our own character, of doing as we like, subject to such consequences as may follow, without impediment from our fellow creatures, so long as what we do does not harm them, even though they should think our conduct foolish, perverse, or wrong. Thirdly, from this liberty of each individual follows the liberty, within the same limits, of combination among individuals; freedom to unite for any purpose not involving harm to others: the persons combining being supposed to be of full age and not forced or deceived.

• • •

OF THE LIBERTY OF THOUGHT AND DISCUSSION

The time, it is to be hoped, is gone by when any defense would be necessary of the "liberty of the press" as one of the securities against corrupt or tyrannical government. No argument, we may suppose, can now be needed against permitting a legislature or an executive, not identified in interest with the people, to prescribe opinions to them and determine what doctrines or what arguments they shall be allowed to hear. This aspect of the question, besides, has been so often and so triumphantly enforced by preceding writers that it needs not be specially insisted on in this place. Though the law of England, on the subject of the press, is as servile to this day as it was in the time of the Tudors, there is little danger of its being actually put in force against political discussion except during some temporary panic when fear of insurrection drives ministers and judges from their propriety; and, speaking generally, it is not, in constitutional countries, to be apprehended that the government, whether completely responsible to the people or not, will often attempt to control the expression of opinion, except when in doing so it makes itself the organ of the general intolerance of the public. Let us suppose, therefore, that the government is entirely at one with the people, and never thinks of exerting any power of coercion unless in agreement with what it conceives to be their voice.

But I deny the right of the people to exercise such coercion, either by themselves or by their government. The power itself is illegitimate. The best government has no more title to it than the worst. It is as noxious, or more noxious, when exerted in accordance with public opinion than when in opposition to it. If all mankind minus one were of one opinion, mankind would be no more justified in silencing that one person than he, if he had the power, would be justified in silencing mankind. Were an opinion a personal possession of no value except to the owner, if to be obstructed in the enjoyment of it were simply a private injury, it would make some difference whether the injury was inflicted only on a few persons or on many. But the peculiar evil of silencing the expression of an opinion is that it is robbing the human race, posterity as well as the existing generation—those who dissent from the opinion, still more than those who hold it. If the opinion is right, they are deprived of the opportunity of exchanging error for truth; if wrong, they lose, what is almost as great a benefit, the clearer perception and livelier impression of truth produced by its collision with error.

It is necessary to consider separately these two hypotheses, each of which has a distinct branch of the argument corresponding to it. We can never be sure that the opinion we are endeavoring to stifle is a false opinion; and if we were sure, stifling it would be an evil still.

First, the opinion which it is attempted to suppress by authority may possibly be true. Those who desire to suppress it, of course, deny its truth; but they are not infallible. They have no authority to decide the question for all mankind and exclude every other person from the means of judging. To refuse a hearing to an opinion because they are sure that it is false is to assume that *their* certainty is the same thing as *absolute* certainty. All silencing of discussion is an assumption of infallibility. Its condemnation may be allowed to rest on this common argument, not the worse for being common.

Unfortunately for the good sense of mankind, the fact of their fallibility is far from carrying the weight in their practical judgment which is always allowed to it in theory; for while everyone well knows himself to be fallible, few think it necessary to take any precautions against their own fallibility, or admit the supposition that any opinion of which they feel very certain may be one of the examples of the error to which they acknowledge themselves to be liable. Absolute princes, or others who are accustomed to unlimited deference, usually feel this complete confidence in their own opinions on nearly all subjects. People more happily situated, who sometimes hear their opinions disputed and are not wholly unused to be set right when they are wrong, place the same unbounded reliance only on such of their opinions as are shared by all who surround them, or to whom they habitually defer; for in proportion to a man's want of confidence in his own solitary judgment does he usually repose, with implicit trust, on the infallibility of "the world" in general. And the world, to each individual, means the part of it with which he comes in contact: his party, his sect, his church, his class of society; the man may be called, by comparison, almost liberal and large-minded to whom it means anything so comprehensive as his own country or his own age. Nor is his faith in this collective authority at all shaken by his being aware that other ages, countries, sects, churches, classes, and parties have thought, and even now think, the exact reverse. He devolves upon his own world the responsibility of being in the right against the dissentient worlds of other people; and it never troubles him that mere accident has decided which of these numerous worlds is the object of his reliance, and that the same causes which make him a churchman in London would have made him a Buddhist or a Confucian in Peking. Yet it is as evident in itself, as

any amount of argument can make it, that ages are no more infallible than individuals—every age having held many opinions which subsequent ages have
deemed not only false but absurd; and it is as certain that many opinions, now
general, will be rejected by future ages, as it is that many, once general, are rejected by the present.

The objection likely to be made to this argument would probably take some
such form as the following. There is no greater assumption of infallibility in
forbidding the propagation of error than in any other thing which is done by
public authority on its own judgment and responsibility. Judgment is given to
men that they may use it. Because it may be used erroneously, are men to be
told that they ought not to use it at all? To prohibit what they think pernicious
is not claiming exemption from error, but fulfilling the duty incumbent on
them, although fallible, of acting on their conscientious conviction. If we were
never to act on our opinions, because those opinions may be wrong, we should
leave all our interests uncared for, and all our duties unperformed. An objection which applies to all conduct can be no valid objection to any conduct in
particular. It is the duty of governments, and of individuals, to form the truest
opinions they can; to form them carefully, and never impose them upon others
unless they are quite sure of being right. But when they are sure (such reason-
ers may say), it is not conscientiousness but cowardice to shrink from acting on
their opinions and allow doctrines which they honestly think dangerous to the
welfare of mankind, either in this life or in another, to be scattered abroad without restraint, because other people, in less enlightened times, have persecuted
opinions now believed to be true. Let us take care, it may be said, not to make
the same mistake; but governments and nations have made mistakes in other
things which are not denied to be fit subjects for the exercise of authority: they
have laid on bad taxes, made unjust wars. Ought we therefore to lay on no
taxes and, under whatever provocation, make no wars? Men and governments
must act to the best of their ability. There is no such thing as absolute certainty,
but there is assurance sufficient for the purposes of human life. We may, and
must, assume our opinion to be true for the guidance of our own conduct; and
it is assuming no more when we forbid bad men to pervert society by the propagation of opinions which we regard as false and pernicious.

I answer, that it is assuming very much more. There is the greatest difference
between presuming an opinion to be true because, with every opportunity for
contesting it, it has not been refuted, and assuming its truth for the purpose of
not permitting its refutation. Complete liberty of contradicting and disproving
our opinion is the very condition which justifies us in assuming its truth for purposes of action; and on no other terms can a being with human faculties have
any rational assurance of being right.

When we consider either the history of opinion or the ordinary conduct of
human life, to what is it to be ascribed that the one and the other are no worse
than they are? Not certainly to the inherent force of the human understanding,
for on any matter not self-evident there are ninety-nine persons totally incapable of judging of it for one who is capable; and the capacity of the hun-
dredth person is only comparative, for the majority of the eminent men of every
past generation held many opinions now known to be erroneous, and did or

approved numerous things which no one will now justify. Why is it, then, that there is on the whole a preponderance among mankind of rational opinions and rational conduct? If there really is this preponderance—which there must be unless human affairs are, and have always been, in an almost desperate state—it is owing to a quality of the human mind, the source of everything respectable in man either as an intellectual or as a moral being, namely, that his errors are corrigible. He is capable of rectifying his mistakes by discussion and experience. Not by experience alone. There must be discussion to show how experience is to be interpreted. Wrong opinions and practices gradually yield to fact and argument; but facts and arguments, to produce any effect on the mind, must be brought before it. Very few facts are able to tell their own story, without comments to bring out their meaning. The whole strength and value, then, of human judgment depending on the one property, that it can be set right when it is wrong, reliance can be placed on it only when the means of setting it right are kept constantly at hand. In the case of any person whose judgment is really deserving of confidence, how has it become so? Because he has kept his mind open to criticism of his opinions and conduct. Because it has been his practice to listen to all that could be said against him; to profit by as much of it as was just, and to expound to himself, and upon occasion to others, the fallacy of what was fallacious. Because he has felt that the only way in which a human being can make some approach to knowing the whole of a subject is by hearing what can be said about it by persons of every variety of opinion, and studying all modes in which it can be looked at by every character of mind. No wise man ever acquired his wisdom in any mode but this; nor is it in the nature of human intellect to become wise in any other manner. The steady habit of correcting and completing his own opinion by collating it with those of others, so far from causing doubt and hesitation in carrying it into practice, is the only stable foundation for a just reliance on it; for, being cognizant of all that can, at least obviously, be said against him, and having taken up his position against all gainsayers—knowing that he has sought for objections and difficulties instead of avoiding them, and has shut out no light which can be thrown upon the subject from any quarter—he has a right to think his judgment better than that of any person, or any multitude, who have not gone through a similar process.

• • •

Let us now pass to the second division of the argument, and dismissing the supposition that any of the received opinions may be false, let us assume them to be true and examine into the worth of the manner in which they are likely to be held when their truth is not freely and openly canvassed. However unwillingly a person who has a strong opinion may admit the possibility that his opinion may be false, he ought to be moved by the consideration that, however true it may be, if it is not fully, frequently, and fearlessly discussed, it will be held as a dead dogma, not a living truth.

There is a class of persons (happily not quite so numerous as formerly) who think it enough if a person assents undoubtingly to what they think true, though he has no knowledge whatever of the grounds of the opinion and could not make a tenable defense of it against the most superficial objections. Such persons, if they can once get their creed taught from authority, naturally think that no good, and some harm, comes of its being allowed to be questioned. Where their influence prevails, they make it nearly impossible for the received opinion to be rejected wisely and considerately, though it may still be rejected rashly and ignorantly; for to shut out discussion entirely is seldom possible, and when it once gets in, beliefs not grounded on conviction are apt to give way before the slightest semblance of an argument. Waiving, however, this possibility—assuming that the true opinion abides in the mind, but abides as a prejudice, a belief independent of, and proof against, argument—this is not the way in which truth ought to be held by a rational being. This is not knowing the truth. Truth, thus held, is but one superstition the more, accidentally clinging to the words which enunciate a truth.

If the intellect and judgment of mankind ought to be cultivated, a thing which Protestants at least do not deny, on what can these faculties be more appropriately exercised by anyone than on the things which concern him so much that it is considered necessary for him to hold opinions on them? If the cultivation of the understanding consists in one thing more than in another, it is surely in learning the grounds of one's own opinions. Whatever people believe, on subjects on which it is of the first importance to believe rightly, they ought to be able to defend against at least the common objections. But, someone may say, "Let them be *taught* the grounds of their opinions. It does not follow that opinions must be merely parroted because they are never heard controverted. Persons who learn geometry do not simply commit the theorems to memory, but understand and learn likewise the demonstrations; and it would be absurd to say that they remain ignorant of the grounds of geometrical truths because they never hear anyone deny and attempt to disprove them." Undoubtedly; and such teaching suffices on a subject like mathematics, where there is nothing at all to be said on the wrong side of the question. The peculiarity of the evidence of mathematical truths is that all the argument is on one side. There are no objections, and no answers to objections. But on every subject on which difference of opinion is possible, the truth depends on a balance to be struck between two sets of conflicting reasons. Even in natural philosophy, there is always some other explanation possible of the same facts; some geocentric theory instead of heliocentric, some phlogiston instead of oxygen; and it has to be shown why that other theory cannot be the true one; and until this is shown, and until we know how it is shown, we do not understand the grounds of our opinion. But when we turn to subjects infinitely more complicated, to morals, religion, politics, social relations, and the business of life, three-fourths of the arguments for every disputed opinion consist in dispelling the appearances which favor some opinion different from it. The greatest orator, save one, of antiquity, has left it on record that he always studied his adversary's case with as great, if not still greater, intensity than even his own. What Cicero practiced as the means of forensic success requires to be imitated by all who study any subject in order to arrive at the truth. He who knows only his own side of the case knows little of that. His reasons may be good, and no one may have been able to refute them. But if he is equally unable to refute the reasons on the opposite side, if he does not so much as know what they are, he has no ground for preferring either opinion. The rational position for him would be suspension of judgment, and unless he contents himself with that, he is either led by authority or adopts, like the generality of the world, the side to which he feels most inclination. Nor is it enough that he should hear the arguments of adversaries from his own teachers, presented as they state them, and accompanied by what they offer as refutations. That is not the way to do justice to the arguments or bring them into real contact with his own mind. He must be able to hear them from persons who actually believe them, who defend them in earnest and do their very utmost for them. He must know them in their most plausible and persuasive form; he must feel the whole force of the difficulty which the true view of the subject has to encounter and dispose of, else he will never really possess himself of the portion of truth which meets and removes that difficulty. Ninety-nine in a hundred of what are called educated men are in this condition, even of those who can argue fluently for their opinions. Their conclusion may be true, but it might be false for anything they know; they have never thrown themselves into the mental position of those who think differently from them, and considered what such persons may have to say; and, consequently, they do not, in any proper sense of the word, know the doctrine which they themselves profess. . . .

We have now recognized the necessity to the mental well-being of mankind (on which all their other well-being depends) of freedom of opinion, and freedom of the expression of opinion, on four distinct grounds, which we will now briefly recapitulate:

First, if any opinion is compelled to silence, that opinion may, for aught we can certainly know, be true. To deny this is to assume our own infallibility.

Secondly, though the silenced opinion be an error, it may, and very commonly does, contain a portion of truth; and since the general or prevailing opinion on any subject is rarely or never the whole truth, it is only by the collision of adverse opinions that the remainder of the truth has any chance of being supplied.

Thirdly, even if the received opinion be not only true, but the whole truth; unless it is suffered to be, and actually is, vigorously and earnestly contested, it will, by most of those who receive it, be held in the manner of a prejudice, with little comprehension or feeling of its rational grounds. And not only this, but, fourthly, the meaning of the doctrine itself will be in danger of being lost or enfeebled, and deprived of its vital effect on the character and conduct; the dogma becoming a mere formal profession, inefficacious for good, but cumbering the ground and preventing the growth of any real and heartfelt conviction from reason or personal experience.

• • •

OF INDIVIDUALITY, AS ONE OF THE ELEMENTS
OF WELL BEING

Such being the reasons which make it imperative that human beings should be free to form opinions and to express their opinions without reserve; and such the baneful consequences to the intellectual, and through that to the moral nature of man, unless this liberty is either conceded or asserted in spite of prohibition; let us next examine whether the same reasons do not require that men should be free to act upon their opinions—to carry these out in their lives without hindrance, either physical or moral, from their fellow men, so long as it is at their own risk and peril. This last proviso is of course indispensable. No one pretends that actions should be as free as opinions. On the contrary, even opinions lose their immunity when the circumstances in which they are expressed are such as to constitute their expression a positive instigation to some mischievous act. An opinion that corn dealers are starvers of the poor, or that private property is robbery, ought to be unmolested when simply circulated through the press, but may justly incur punishment when delivered orally to an excited mob assembled before the house of a corn dealer, or when handed about among the same mob in the form of a placard. Acts, of whatever kind, which without justifiable cause do harm to others may be, and in the more important cases absolutely require to be, controlled by the unfavorable sentiments, and, when needful, by the active interference of mankind. The liberty of the individual must he thus far limited; he must not make himself a nuisance to other people. But if he refrains from molesting others in what concerns them, and merely acts according to his own inclination nd judgment in things which concern himself, the same reasons which show that opinion should be free prove also that he should be allowed, without molestation, to carry his opinions into practice at his own cost. That mankind are not infallible; that their truths, for the most part, are only half-truths; that unity of opinion, unless resulting from the fullest and freest comparison of opposite opinions, is not desirable, and diversity not an evil, but a good, until mankind are much more capable than at present of recognizing all sides of the truth, are principles applicable to men's modes of action not less than to their opinions. As it is useful that while mankind are imperfect there should be different opinions, so it is that there should be different experiments of living; that free scope should be given to varieties of character, short of injury to others; and that the worth of different modes of life should be proved practically, when anyone thinks fit to try them. It is desirable, in short, that in things which do not primarily concern others individuality should assert itself. Where not the person's own character but the traditions or customs of other people are the rule of conduct, there is wanting one of the principal ingredients of human happiness, and quite the chief ingredient of individual and social progress.

• • •

Having said that the individuality is the same thing with development, and that it is only the cultivation of individuality which produces, or can produce, well-developed human beings, I might here close the argument; for what more or better can be said of any condition of human affairs than that it brings human beings themselves nearer to the best thing they can be? Or what worse can be said of any obstruction to good than that it prevents this? Doubtless, however, these considerations will not suffice to convince those who most need convincing; and it is necessary further to show that these developed human beings are of some use to the undeveloped—to point out to those who do not desire liberty, and would not avail themselves of it, that they may be in some intelligible manner rewarded for allowing other people to make use of it without hindrance.

In the first place, then, I would suggest that they might possibly learn something from them. It will not be denied by anybody that originality is a valuable element in human affairs. There is always need of persons not only to discover new truths and point out when what were once truths are true no longer, but also to commence new practices and set the example of more enlightened conduct and better taste and sense in human life. This cannot well be gainsaid by anybody who does not believe that the world has already attained perfection in all its ways and practices. It is true that this benefit is not capable of being rendered by everybody alike; there are but few persons, in comparison with the whole of mankind, whose experiments, if adopted by others, would be likely to be any improvement on established practice. But these few are the salt of the earth; without them, human life would become a stagnant pool. Not only is it they who introduce good things which did not before exist; it is they who keep the life in those which already exist. If there were nothing new to be done, would human intellect cease to be necessary? Would it be a reason why those who do the old things should forget why they are done, and do them like cattle, not like human beings? There is only too great a tendency in the best beliefs and practices to degenerate into the mechanical; and unless there were a succession of persons whose ever-recurring originality prevents the grounds of those beliefs and practices from becoming merely traditional, such dead matter would not resist the smallest shock from anything really alive, and there would be no reason why civilization should not die out, as in the Byzantine Empire. . . .

I have said that it is important to give the freest scope possible to uncustomary things, in order that it may in time appear which of these are fit to be converted into customs. But independence of action and disregard of custom are not solely deserving of encouragement for the chance they afford that better modes of action, and customs more worthy of general adoption, may be struck out; nor is it only persons of decided mental superiority who have a just claim to carry on their lives in their own way. There is no reason that all human existence should be constructed on some one or some small number of patterns. If a person possesses any tolerable amount of common sense and experience, his own mode of laying out his existence is the best, not because it is the best in itself, but because it is his own mode. Human beings are not like sheep; and even sheep are not undistinguishably alike. A man cannot get a coat or a pair of boots to fit him unless they are either made to his measure or he has a whole warehouseful to choose from; and is it easier to fit him with a life than with a coat, or are human beings more like one another in their whole physical and spiritual conformation than in the shape of their feet? If it were only that people have diversities of taste, that is reason enough for not attempting to shape them all after one model. But different persons also require different conditions for their spiritual development; and can no more exist healthily in the same moral than all the variety of plants can in the same physical, atmosphere and climate. The same things which are helps to one person toward the cultivation of his higher nature are hindrances to another. The same mode of life is a healthy excitement to one, keeping all his faculties of action and enjoyment in their best order, while to another it is a distracting burden which suspends or crushes all internal life. Such are the differences among human beings in their sources of pleasure, their susceptibilities of pain, and the operation on them of different physical and moral agencies that, unless there is a corresponding diversity in their modes of life, they neither obtain their fair share of happiness, nor grow up to the mental, moral, and aesthetic stature of which their nature is capable. . . .

It would be a great misunderstanding of this doctrine to suppose that it is one of selfish indifference, which pretends that human beings have no business with each other's conduct in life, and that they should not concern themselves about the well-doing or well-being of one another, unless their own interest is involved. Instead of any diminution, there is need of a great increase of disinterested exertion to promote the good of others. But disinterested benevolence can find other instruments to persuade people to their good than whips and scourges, either of the literal or the metaphorical sort. I am the last person to undervalue the self-regarding virtues: they are only second in importance, if even second, to the social. It is equally the business of education to cultivate both. But even education works by conviction and persuasion as well as by compulsion, and it is by the former only that, when the period of education it passed, the self-regarding virtues should be inculcated. Human beings owe to each other help to distinguish the better from the worse, and encouragement to choose the former and avoid the latter. They should be forever stimulating each other to increased exercise of their higher faculties, and increased direction of their feelings and aims towards wise instead of foolish, elevating instead of degrading, objects and contemplations. But neither one person, nor any number of persons, is warranted in saying to another human creature of ripe years, that he shall not do with his life for his own benefit what he chooses to do with it. He is the person most interested in his own well-being; the interest which any other person, except in cases of strong personal attachment, can have in it, is trifling, compared with that which he himself has; the interest which society has in him individually (except as to his conduct to others) is fractional, and altogether indirect; while with respect to his own feelings and circumstances, the most ordinary man or woman has means of knowledge immeasurably surpassing those that can be possessed by anyone else. The interference of society to overrule his judgment and purposes in what only regards himself must be grounded on general presumptions; which may be altogether wrong, and even if right, are as likely as not to be misapplied to individual cases, by persons no better acquainted with the circumstances of such cases than those are who look at them merely from without. In this department, therefore, of human affairs, individuality has its proper field of action. In the conduct of human beings towards one another it is necessary that general rules should for the most part be observed, in order that people may know what they have to expect; but in each person's own concerns his individual spontaneity is entitled to free exercise. Considerations to aid his judgment, exhortations to strengthen his will, may be offered to him, even obtruded on him, by others; but he himself is the final judge. All errors which he is likely to commit against advice and warning are far outweighed by the evil of allowing others to constrain him to what they deem his good. . . .

The distinction here pointed out between the part of a person's life which concerns only himself, and that which concerns others, many persons will refuse to admit. How (it may be asked) can any part of the conduct of a member of society be a matter of indifference to the other members? No person is an entirely isolated being; it is impossible for a person to do anything seriously or permanently hurtful to himself, without mischief reaching at least to his near connections, and often far beyond them. If he injures his property, he does harm to those who directly or indirectly derived support from it, and usually diminishes, by a greater or less amount, the general resources of the community. If he deteriorates his bodily or mental faculties, he not only brings evil upon all who depended on him for any portion of their happiness, but disqualifies himself for rendering the services which he owes to his fellow-creatures generally; perhaps becomes a burden on their affection or benevolence; and if such conduct were very frequent, hardly an offense that is committed would detract more from the general sum of good. Finally, if by his vices or follies a person does no direct harm to others, he is nevertheless (it may be said) injurious by his example; and ought to be compelled to control himself, for the sake of those whom the sight or knowledge of his conduct might corrupt or mislead.

And even (it will be added) if the consequences of misconduct could be confined to the vicious or thoughtless individual, ought society to abandon to their own guidance those who are manifestly unfit for it? If protection against themselves is confessedly due to children and persons under age, is not society equally bound to afford it to persons of mature years who are equally incapable of self-government? If gambling, or drunkenness, or incontinence, or idleness, or uncleanliness, are as injurious to happiness, and as great a hindrance to improvement, as many or most of the acts prohibited by law, why (it may be asked) should not law, so far as is consistent with practicability and social convenience, endeavor to repress these also? And as a supplement to the unavoidable imperfections of law, ought not opinion at least to organize a powerful police against these vices, and visit rigidly with social penalties those who are known to practice them? There is no question here (it may be said) about restricting individuality, or impeding the trial of new and original experiments in living. The only things it is sought to prevent are things which have been tried and condemned from the beginning of the world until now; things which experience has shown not to be useful or suitable to any person's individuality. There must be some length of time and amount of experience after which a moral or prudential truth may be regarded as established: and it is merely desired to prevent generation after generation from falling over the same precipice which has been fatal to their predecessors.

I fully admit that the mischief which a person does to himself may seriously affect, both through their sympathies and their interests, those nearly connected with him and, in a minor degree, society at large. When, by conduct of this sort, a person is led to violate a distinct and assignable obligation to any other person or persons, the case is taken out of the self-regarding class, and becomes amenable to moral disapprobation in the proper sense of the term. If, for example, a man, through intemperance or extravagance, becomes unable to pay his debts, or, having undertaken the moral responsibility of a family, becomes from the same cause incapable of supporting or educating them, he is deservedly reprobated, and might be justly punished; but it is for the breach of duty to his family or creditors, not for the extravagance. If the resources which ought to have been devoted to them, had been diverted from them for the most prudent investment, the moral culpability would have been the same. George Barnwell murdered his uncle to get money for his mistress, but if he had done it to set himself up in business, he would equally have been hanged. Again, in the frequent case of a man who causes grief to his family by addiction to bad habits, he deserves reproach for his unkindness or ingratitude; but so he may for cultivating habits not in themselves vicious, if they are painful to those with whom he passes his life, or who from personal ties are dependent on him for their comfort. Whoever fails in the consideration generally due to the interest and feelings of others, not being compelled by some more imperative duty, or justified by allowable self-preference, is a subject of moral disapprobation for that failure, but not for the cause of it, nor for the errors, merely personal to himself, which may have remotely led to it. In like manner, when a person disables himself, by conduct purely self-regarding, from the performance of some definite duty incumbent on him to the public, he is guilty of a social offense. No person ought to be punished simply for being drunk; but a soldier or a policeman should be punished for being drunk on duty. Whenever, in short, there is a definite damage, or a definite risk of damage, either to an individual or to the public, the case is taken out of the province of liberty, and placed in that of morality or law. . . .

But the strongest of all the arguments against the interference of the public with purely personal conduct is that, when it does interfere, the odds are that it interferes wrongly, and in the wrong place. On questions of social morality, of duty to others, the opinion of the public, that is, of an overruling majority, though often wrong, is likely to be still oftener right; because on such questions they are only required to judge of their own interests; of the manner in which some mode of conduct, if allowed to be practiced, would affect themselves. But the opinion of a similar majority, imposed as a law on the minority, on questions of self-regarding conduct, is quite as likely to be wrong as right; for in these cases public opinion means, at the best, some people's opinion of what is good or bad for other people; while very often it does not even mean that; the public, with the most perfect indifference, passing over the pleasure or convenience of those whose conduct they censure, and considering only their own preference. There are many who consider as an injury to themselves any conduct which they have a distaste for, and resent it as an outrage to their feelings; as a religious bigot, when charged with disregarding the religious feelings of others, has been known to retort that they disregard his feelings, by persisting in their abominable worship or creed. But there is no parity between the feeling of a person for his own opinion, and the feeling of another who is offended at his holding it; no more than between the desire of a thief to take a purse, and the desire of the right owner to keep it. And a person's taste is as much his own peculiar concern as his opinion or his purse. It is easy for anyone to imagine an ideal public which leaves the freedom and choice of individuals in all uncertain matters undisturbed, and only requires them to abstain from modes of conduct which universal experience has condemned. But where has there been seen a public which set any such limit to its censorship? or when does the public trouble itself about universal experience? In its interferences with personal conduct it is seldom thinking of anything but the enormity of acting or feeling differently from itself; and this standard of judgment, thinly disguised, is held up to mankind as the dictate of religion and philosophy, by nine-tenths of all moralists and speculative writers. These teach that things are right because they are right; because we feel them to be so. They tell us to search in our own minds and hearts for laws of conduct binding on ourselves and on all others. What can the poor public do but apply these instructions, and make their own personal feelings of good and evil, if they are tolerably unanimous in them, obligatory on all the world?

7.

The Offense Principle

JOEL FEINBERG

I. OFFENSIVE NUISANCES

1. Disclaimers: the relative triviality of mere offense

Passing annoyance, disappointment, disgust, embarrassment, and various other disliked conditions such as fear, anxiety, and minor ("harmless") aches and pains, are not in themselves necessarily harmful. Consequently, no matter how the harm principle is mediated, it will not certify as legitimate those interferences with the liberty of some citizens that are made for the sole purpose of preventing such unpleasant states in others. For convenience I will use the word "offense" to cover the whole miscellany of universally disliked mental states . . . and not merely that species of the wider genus that are offensive in a strict and proper sense. If the law is justified, then, in using its coercive methods to protect people from mere offense, it must be by virtue of a separate and distinct legitimizing principle, which we can label "the offense principle" and formulate as follows: *It is always a good reason in support of a proposed criminal prohibition that it would probably be an effective way of preventing serious offense (as opposed to injury or harm) to persons other than the actor, and that it is probably a necessary means to that end* (i.e., there is probably no other means that is equally effective at no greater cost to the other values). The principle asserts, in effect, that the prevention of offensive conduct is properly the state's business.

Like the word "harm," the word "offense" has both a general and a specifically normative sense, the former including in its reference any or all of a miscellany of disliked mental states (disgust, shame, hurt, anxiety, etc.), and the latter referring to those states only when caused by the wrongful (right-violating) conduct of others. Only the latter sense—wrongful offense—is intended in the offense principle as we shall understand it. In this respect there is a parallel with the harm principle. We can also use the verb "to offend" meaning "to cause another to experience a mental state of a universally disliked kind (e.g., disgust, shame). The offense principle then cites the need to prevent some people from *wrongfully offending* (offending and wronging) others as a reason for coercive legislation. Finally, the word "offense" in the strict and proper sense it bears in ordinary language is specific in a different way. Whereas "offense" in the sense of the offense principle specifies an objective condition—the unpleasant mental state must be caused by conduct that really is wrongful—"offense" in the strict sense of ordinary language specifies a subjective condition—the offending act must be taken by the offended person to wrong him whether in fact it does or not. In the strict and narrow sense, I am offended (or "take offense") when (a) I suffer a disliked state, and (b) I attribute that state to the wrongful conduct of another, and (c) I *resent* the other for his role in causing me to be in the state. The sense of grievance against the other or resentment of him for wronging me in this way is a phenomenological component of the unpleasant experience itself, an element that actually reenforces and magnifies its unpleasantness. If I am disgusted by the sight of a hospital patient's bloody wounds, the experience is one of that miscellany of disliked states I call "offended states of mind in the broad sense," but I can hardly resent the poor fellow for his innocent role in causing me to suffer that state of mind, and indeed there may be nobody to resent, in which case I do not "take offense," which is to say I am not offended in the strict and narrow sense.

The offense principle requires that the disliked state of mind (offense in the broad sense) be produced wrongfully by another party, but not that it be an offense in the strict sense of ordinary language. The victim may not know, or may not care, that another has wrongfully caused his unease, and therefore his unpleasant state of mind will not contain the element of resentment, and thus will not be offense in the strict sense. The offense principle as we shall interpret it then applies to offended states in either the broad or the strict sense—that is either with or without resentment—when these states are in fact wrongfully produced in violation of the offended party's rights. It is necessary that there be a wrong, but not that the victim *feel* wronged. And there will always be a wrong whenever an offended state (in the generic sense) is produced in another without justification or excuse.

Since I shall be defending a highly restricted version of the offense principle in this chapter, I should begin with some important disclaimers. To begin with, *offense it surely a less serious thing than harm.* That comparative value judgment seems to me self-evident, yet not simply true by definition. It is possible to deny it without contradiction if only because offense is not strictly commensurable with harm. It is a misconception to think of offenses as occupying the lower part of the same scale as harms; rather offenses are a different sort of thing altogether, with a scale all of their own. Yet most people after reflection will probably acknowledge that a person is not treated as badly, other things being equal, when he is merely offended as when he is harmed. We may (at most) be inclined to rank extreme offenses as greater wrongs to their victims than trifling harms, but perhaps that is because they may become so offensive as to be actually harmful, in a minor sort of way. (At any rate the comparison of extreme offense with minor harm is the only place controversy could reasonably arise over the relative seriousness of offenses and harms.) Continued extreme offense . . . can *cause* harm to a person who becomes emotionally upset over the offense, to the neglect of his real interests. But the offended mental state in itself is not a condition of harm. From the moral point of view, considered in its own nature (apart from possible causal linkages to harmful consequences), it is a relatively trivial thing.

It follows from this evident but unprovable truth that the law should not treat offenses as if they were as serious, by and large, as harms. It should not, for example, attempt to control offensiveness by the criminal law when other modes of regulation can do the job as efficiently and economically. For the control of uncommon and transitory forms of offensiveness, for example, reliance can be placed on individual suits for injunctions, or by court orders initiated by police to cease and desist on pain of penalty, or by licensing procedures that depend on administrative suspension of license as a sanction. These alternatives would not entirely dispense with the need for punishment (which is almost always a disproportionately greater evil to the offender than offended mental states are to his "victims"), but punishment would be reserved as a back-up threat, not inflicted for offending others so much as for defying authority by persisting in prohibited conduct. . . . It may well be that the ordinary criminal law need not concern itself at all with defining crimes of offensiveness, even though offensiveness is the sort of evil it could in principle be used legitimately to combat. It is more likely, however, that for various practical reasons, reliance on injunctions, administrative orders, and license withdrawals would be insufficient to control *all* properly prohibitable offensive conduct. In some cases, we can know very well in advance that conduct of a certain kind will offend; that is, we don't have to wait for the particular circumstances to decide the question. Moreover, in some cases there will not be time to get an injunction or administrative hearing. By the time that sort of relief is forthcoming, the annoyance has come and gone, and the offense, such as it is, already committed.

Even if there must be defined crimes with specified penalties for purely offensive conduct, however, the penalties should be light ones: more often fines than imprisonment, but when imprisonment, it should be measured in days rather than months or years. Where crimes are divided into the categories of misdemeanor and felony, purely offensive crimes should always be misdemeanors, never felonies. Where penal codes follow the American Law Institute model[1] in dividing offenses into felonies, misdemeanors, petty misdemeanors, and "violations,"[2] harmlessly offensive conduct at its worst should be a petty misdemeanor, but typically only a violation—a status it would share with traffic and parking violations, various illegal sales, and unintentional violations of health or safety codes. When a given crime is both harmful and offensive the punishment can properly be severe, but legislators and judges should make it clear that the severity of the punishment is primarily a function of the harmfulness (or dangerousness) of the criminal act, not a reaction to its offensiveness. The state should punish a very harmful or dangerous but only routinely offensive crime much more severely than a crime that is greatly offensive but harmful or dangerous only to a minor degree.

• • •

---

[1]   American Law Institute, *Model Penal Code, Proposed Official Draft* (Philadelphia, 1962), Section 1.04.

[2]   An offense is said to constitute a violation, as opposed to any kind of crime, if no other sentence than a fine, or fine and forfeiture, or other civil penalty is authorized upon conviction by the law defining the offense, and conviction gives rise to no disability or legal disadvantage based on conviction of criminal offense. (Section 1.04, pt. 5.)

3. A ride on the bus

There is a limit to the power of abstract reasoning to settle questions of moral legitimacy. The question raised by this chapter is whether there are any human experiences that are harmless in themselves yet so unpleasant that we can rightly demand legal protection from them even at the cost of other persons' liberties. The best way to deal with that question at the start is to engage our imaginations in the inquiry, consider hypothetically the most offensive experiences we can imagine, and then sort them into groups in an effort to isolate the kernel of the offense in each category. Accordingly, this section will consist of a number of vividly sketched imaginary tales, and the reader is asked to project himself into each story and determine as best he can what his reaction would be. In each story the reader should think of himself as a passenger on a normally crowded public bus on his way to work or to some important appointment in circumstances such that if he is forced to leave the bus prematurely, he will not only have to pay another fare to get where he is going, but he will probably be late, to his own disadvantage. If he is not exactly a captive on the bus, then, he would nevertheless be greatly inconvenienced if he had to leave the bus before it reached his destination. In each story, another passenger, or group of passengers, gets on the bus, and proceeds to cause, by their characteristics or their conduct, great offense to you. The stories form six clusters corresponding to the kind of offense caused.

A. *Affronts to the senses*
   Story 1. A passenger who obviously hasn't bathed in more than a month sits down next to you. He reeks of a barely tolerable stench. There is hardly room to stand elsewhere on the bus and all other seats are occupied.
   Story 2. A passenger wearing a shirt of violently clashing orange and crimson sits down directly in your forward line of vision. You must keep your eyes down to avoid looking at him.
   Story 3. A passenger sits down next to you, pulls a slate tablet from his brief case, and proceeds to scratch his fingernails loudly across the slate, sending a chill up your spine and making your teeth clench. You politely ask him to stop, but he refuses.
   Story 4. A passenger elsewhere in the bus turns on a portable radio to maximum volume. The sounds it emits are mostly screeches, whistles, and static, but occasionally some electronically amplified rock and roll music blares through.
B. *Disgust and revulsion*
   Story 5. This is much like story 1 except that the malodorous passenger in the neighboring seat continually scratches, drools, coughs, farts, and belches.
   Story 6. A group of passengers enters the bus and shares a seating compartment with you. They spread a table cloth over their laps and proceed to eat a picnic lunch that consists of live insects, fish heads, and pickled sex organs of lamb, veal, and pork, smothered in garlic and onions. Their table manners leave almost everything to be desired.

Story 7. Things get worse and worse. The itinerant picnickers practice gluttony in the ancient Roman manner, gorging until satiation and then vomiting on to their table cloth. Their practice, however, is a novel departure from the ancient custom in that they eat their own and one another's vomit along with the remaining food.

Story 8. A coprophagic sequel to story 7.

Story 9. At some point during the trip the passenger at one's side quite openly and nonchalantly changes her sanitary napkin and drops the old one into the aisle.

C. *Shock to moral, religious, or patriotic sensibilities*

Story 10. A group of mourners carrying a coffin enters the bus and share a seating compartment with you. Although they are all dressed in black their demeanor is by no means funereal. In fact they seem more angry than sorrowful, and refer to the deceased as "the old bastard," and "the bloody corpse." At one point they rip open the coffin with hammers and proceed to smash the corpse's face with a series of hard hammer blows.

Story 11. A strapping youth enters the bus and takes a seat directly in your line of vision. He is wearing a T-shirt with a cartoon across his chest of Christ on the cross. Underneath the picture appear the words "Hang in there, baby!"

Story 12. After taking the seat next to you a passenger produces a bundle wrapped in a large American flag. The bundle contains, among other things, his lunch, which he proceeds to eat. Then he spits into the star-spangled corner of the flag and uses it first to clean his mouth and then to blow his nose. Then he uses the main striped part of the flag to shine his shoes.

D. *Shame, embarrassment (including vicarious embarrassment), and anxiety*

Story 13. The passenger who takes the seat directly across from you is entirely naked. On one version of the story, he or she is the same sex as you; on the other version of the story, he or she is the opposite sex.

Story 14. The passenger in the previous story proceeds to masturbate quietly in his or her seat.

Story 15. A man and woman, more or less fully clothed to start, take two seats directly in front of you, and then begin to kiss, hug, pet, and fondle one another to the accompaniment of loud sighs and groans of pleasure. They continue these activities throughout the trip.

Story 16. The couple of the previous story, shortly before the bus reaches their destination, engage in acts of mutual masturbation, with quite audible instructions to each other and other sound effects.

Story 17. A variant of the previous story which climaxes in an act of coitus, somewhat acrobatically performed as required by the crowded circumstances.

Story 18. The seat directly in front of you is occupied by a youth (of either sex) wearing a T-shirt with a lurid picture of a copulating couple across his or her chest.

Story 19. A variant of the previous story in which the couple depicted is recognizable (in virtue of conventional representations) as Jesus and Mary.

Story 20. The couple in stories 15–17 perform a variety of sadomasochistic sex acts with appropriate verbal communications ("Oh, that hurts so sweet! Hit me again! Scratch me! Publicly humiliate me!").

Story 21. The two seats in front of you are occupied by male homosexuals. They flirt and tease at first, then kiss and hug, and finally perform mutual fellatio to climax.

Story 22. This time the homosexuals are both female and they perform cunnilingus.

Story 23. A passenger with a dog takes an aisle seat at your side. He or she keeps the dog calm at first by petting it in a familiar and normal way, but then petting gives way to hugging, and gradually goes beyond the merely affectionate to the unmistakably erotic, culminating finally with oral contact with the canine genitals.

E. *Annoyance, boredom, frustration*

Story 24. A neighboring passenger keeps a portable radio at a reasonably low volume, and the sounds it emits are by no means offensive to the senses. Nor is the content of the program offensive to the sensibilities. It is, however, a low quality "talk show" which you find intensely boring, and there is no possible way for you to disengage your attention.

Story 25. The two seats to your left are occupied by two persons who put on a boring "talk show" of their own. There is no way you can avoid hearing every animated word of their inane conversation, no way your mind can roam to its own thoughts, problems, and reveries.

Story 26. The passenger at your side is a friendly bloke, garrulous and officious. You quickly tire of his conversation and beg leave to read your newspaper, but he persists in his chatter despite repeated requests to desist. The bus is crowded and there are no other empty seats.

F. *Fear, resentment, humiliation, anger* (from empty threats, insults, mockery, flaunting, or taunting)

Story 27. A passenger seated next to you reaches into a military kit and pulls out a "hand grenade" (actually only a realistic toy), and fondles and juggles it throughout the trip to the accompaniment of menacing leers and snorts. Then he pulls out a (rubber) knife and "stabs" himself and others repeatedly to peals of maniacal laughter. He turns out to be harmless enough. His whole intent was to put others in apprehension of harm.

Story 28. A passenger sits next to you wearing a black arm band with a large white swastika on it.

Story 29. A passenger enters the bus straight from a dispersed street rally. He carries a banner with a large and abusive caricature of the Pope and an anti-Catholic slogan. (You are a loyal and pious Catholic.)

Story 30. Variants of the above. The banner displays a picture of a black according to some standard offensive stereotype (Step 'n Fetchit, Uncle Tom, etc.) with an insulting caption, or a picture of a sneering, sniveling, hook-nosed Fagin or Shylock, with a scurrilous anti-Jewish caption, or a similar offensive denunciation or lampooning of groups called "Spicks," "Dagos," "Polacks", etc.

Story 31. Still another variant. A counter-demonstrator leaves a feminist rally to enter the bus. He carries a banner with an offensive caricature of a female and the message, in large red letters: "Keep the bitches barefoot and pregnant."

4. The modes and meaning of "offense"

I have tried to make a number of different points by telling these bloodcurdling tales: that there are at least six distinguishable classes of offended states that can be caused by the blamable conduct of others; that to suffer such experiences, at least in their extreme forms, is an evil; but that to the normal person (like the reader) such experiences, unpleasant as they are, do not cause or constitute harm. It is very important that the reader put himself on the bus and imagine his own reactions, for no amount of abstract argument can convince him otherwise that the represented experiences are in principle of a kind that the state can legitimately make its business to prevent.

• • •

It should be clear at this point that despite the miscellaneous character of "offended states" they have some important characteristics in common. They are at the very least unpleasant to the one who suffers them, though the mode of displeasure varies from case to case. With the exception of irritations to the senses, and only some of these, they are complex states whose unpleasantness is in part a function of the tension between conflicting elements. And, most importantly from the legislative point of view, they are nuisances, making it difficult for one to enjoy one's work or leisure in a locality which one cannot reasonably be expected to leave in the circumstances. In extreme cases, the offending conduct commandeers one's attention from the outside, forcing one to relinquish control of one's inner state, and drop what one was doing in order to cope, when it is greatly inconvenient to do so.

5. The relation between offense and privacy

In what manner, if any, do the offensive people on the bus violate the privacy of their fellow passengers? The word "privacy" may seem clear enough in ordinary discourse, but its ever more frequent use in law courts and legislatures has caused increasing bewilderment and controversy. Privacy as a legal category came into American law less than a century ago. Its first appearance was in the law of torts, where it served to protect persons from misappropriation of their names or pictures for commercial purposes, and then was gradually extended to include protection of persons from embarrassing publicity, from being put in a false light by the public attribution of beliefs they do not hold, and most importantly, from unwarranted intrusion into their personal affairs by such means as wire tapping, electronic surveillance, shadowing, and peeping. The moral rights to be free of these various evils are certainly genuine ones, and the evils themselves, genuine evils. These rights, moreover, had not been adequately protected by the common law before the "right to privacy" was invented or discovered. But they have an irreducibly heterogeneous character summarizable in a unitary way only by such an imprecise phrase as "the right to be let alone."

Soon it became popular to designate still other legal protections under the same flexible rubric. The old privilege of confidentiality protecting certain special relationships is now considered a special case of privacy.[3] In torts, the right to privacy came to encompass not only the right not to be known about in certain ways by others, but also the right to avoid "seeing and hearing what others say,"[4] apparently on the ground that "it may be as distasteful to suffer the intrusions of a garrulous and unwelcome guest as to discover an eavesdropper or peeper."[5] In constitutional law, the Supreme Court has come to discover a miscellany of "penumbral rights" of privacy against governmental action that impose limits even on otherwise valid legislation, including a right to marital privacy which is violated by a state statute prohibiting the sale of contraceptives even to married couples.[6] The tendency to apply the one concept "privacy" to such a motley collection of rights has alarmed many commentators who fear that so plastic and expansive a concept will obfuscate legal analysis. "Given this disparity of central issues," wrote Paul Freund, "privacy becomes too greedy a legal concept."[7]

Many or most of the disparate legal uses of the idea of privacy, however, can be grouped in one or the other of two families of sense. Elizabeth Beardsley has put the distinction well: "Alleged violations [of privacy] seem to fall into two major categories: conduct by which one person *A* restricts the power of another person *B* to determine for himself whether or not he will perform an act *X* or undergo an experience *E,* and conduct by which one person *A* acquires or discloses information about *B* which *B* does not wish to have known or disclosed."[8] Beardsley labels the right to privacy violated in the former case, the right to *autonomy,* and that violated in the latter case, the right to *selective disclosure.* Window peeping, secret shadowing or photographing, wire tapping, publishing of intimate conversation, intercepted correspondence, candid photo-

---

[3] Paul A. Freund, "Privacy: One Concept or Many?," in *Nomos XIII: Privacy,* ed. J. R. Pennock and J. W. Chapman (New York: Atherton Press, 1971), p. 102.

[4] Fowler V. Harper and Fleming James, Jr., *The Law of Torts* (Boston: Little, Brown, and Co., 1956), vol. I. p. 681.

[5] *Loc. cit.*

[6] *Griswold v. Connecticut,* 381 U.S. 479 (1965).

[7] Freund, *op. cit.* (footnote 3), p. 192. See also Hyman Gross, "Privacy and Autonomy" in the same volume, pp. 169–81.

[8] Elizabeth L. Beardsley, "Privacy, Autonomy and Selective Disclosure," in *Nomos XIII: Privacy,* ed. J. R. Pennock and J. W. Chapman (New York: Atherton Press, 1971), p. 56. Letter variables revised to accord with the convention of this book.

graphs, and the like, all violate a person's privacy in the sense that they invade his right not to be observed or known about in certain ways without his consent. Nothing like that kind of wrong is committed by the offensive passengers on the bus against their fellow travelers, so we can put that notion of privacy aside. A typical violation of privacy in the sense of autonomy occurs when unwanted noises obtrude upon one's experience restricting one's power to determine for oneself "whether one will do X, or undergo E, or not." "Noise removes [one's] power to choose effectively between sound and silence, or between one sound and another, as features of [one's] immediate experience." [9] The offensive passengers clearly *do* violate their neighbors' privacy in this sense (autonomy) not only when they are noisy, but also when they are disgusting, shocking, embarrassing, boring, threatening, and enraging, for in each case, they deprive the unwilling spectators of the power to determine for themselves whether or not to undergo a certain experience. No passenger, moreover, would decide, if the choice were left to him, to undergo experiences of these offensively unpleasant kinds. Each must spend the whole bus trip coping with feelings induced in himself from the outside when he would much prefer, presumably, to be doing something else. In being made to experience and be occupied in certain ways by outsiders, and having had no choice in the matter whatever, the captive passengers suffer a violation of their autonomy (assuming that the "boundaries" of the autonomous realm do not shrink to the vanishing point when they enter the public world).

We can agree with Beardsley that "selective disclosure" and "autonomy" are two different kinds of things commonly called "privacy," while insisting that they are not without a common element that explains why the word "privacy" is commonly applied to both. They are, in short, two species of the genus "privacy" rather than two distinct senses of the word "privacy." The root idea in the generic concept of privacy is that of a privileged territory or domain in which an individual person has the exclusive authority of determining whether another may enter, and if so, when and for how long, and under what conditions. . . . Within this area, the individual person is—pick your metaphor— boss, sovereign, owner. The area includes not only the land and buildings he owns and occupies, but his special relationships with spouse, attorney, or priest, and his own mental states or "inner sanctum." His rightful control over his "inner property" is violated when another learns and/or reveals its secret contents without his consent, for he should be the one who decides what is to be known of them and by whom. His will alone reigns supreme over them. But his sovereignty or ownership is also violated when others obtrude their own sounds, and shapes, and affairs upon his "territory" without his consent, for within the privileged area, he has the sole right to determine what he is to experience, insofar as these matters are rightfully subject to his control. [10] When

---

[9] *Ibid.*, p. 58.

[10] And they cannot be reasonably expected to be very much subject to his control. As Beardsley notes:

> Of course sounds which (like thunder) are not produced by the intentional acts of human beings, or which (like subway clatter) could reasonably have been predicted by X to be part of an

he is forced to experience loud or grating sensations, disgusting or enraging activities while on his privileged ground, something like a property right has been violated,[11] and violated in a manner similar to that of "private nuisance." The legislative problem of determining when offensive conduct is a public or criminal nuisance could with equal accuracy be expressed as a problem about determining the extent of personal privacy or autonomy. The former way of describing the matter (in terms of "nuisance") lends itself naturally to talk of *balancing* (the independent value or reasonableness of the offending conduct against the degree of seriousness of the offense caused) whereas the latter way (in terms of "privacy") lends itself naturally to talk of drawing *boundaries* between the various private domains of persons, and between the private domain of any given person and the public world. The metaphors are different; the actual modes of reasoning are the same.

II. MEDIATING THE OFFENSE PRINCIPLE

1. On the scales: the seriousness of the offense

The case for the legitimacy of the criminal law's concern with "mere offensiveness even in the absence of harm or danger, must in the end rest on the intuitive force of the examples given, most of which have been made as extreme as possible and depicted with uncompromising vividness. Offensiveness produces unpleasant experiences and causes annoying inconveniences, both of which are surely evils, though not as great evils as actual harms. Unlike certain other evils, however, offenses and harms are done to persons. They have determinate victims with genuine grievances and a right to complain against determinate wrongdoers about the way in which they have been treated. . . . Those facts, it seems to me, constitute as good reasons as one could expect to find for the legitimacy in principle of legal interference, even though in a given case, or even in all given cases, there are stronger countervailing reasons of a practical kind.

There are abundant reasons, however, for being extremely cautious in applying the offense principle. People take offense—perfectly genuine offense—at many socially useful or even necessary activities, from commercial advertisement to inane chatter. Moreover, bigoted prejudices of a very widespread kind (e.g., against interracial couples strolling hand in hand down the main street of a town in the deep South) can lead onlookers to be disgusted and shocked, even "morally" repelled, by perfectly innocent activities, and we should be loath to permit their groundless repugnance to outweigh the innocence of the offending

---

environment into which X has chosen to enter, or which (like the roar of compressed air drills and *perhaps* like some recorded music) have a redeeming social utility, have come to be accepted: questions about "violations of privacy" are often not so much as thought of, as far as most of the din of modern life is concerned." (Beardsley, *op. cit.,* p. 58.)

[11] This point is well appreciated by Ernest Van den Haag in his "On Privacy" in *Nomos XIII: Privacy,* ed. J. R. Pennock and J. W. Chapman (New York: Atherton Press, 1971), pp. 150ff. One should point out that *if* the analogy to landed property rights is perfect, then even an unconsented-to intrusion of delightful and appreciated sounds and activities into the private domain is a technical violation of privacy on the model of trespass.

conduct. For these and similar reasons, the offense principle must be formulated in a very precise way, and supplemented by appropriate standards or mediating maxims, so as not to open the door to wholesale and intuitively unwarranted legal interference.

As formulated so far, the offense principle commits us only to the view that when public conduct causes offense to someone, the fact of that offense is relevant to the permissibility of the conduct in question. A relevant consideration, of course, can be outweighed by relevant reasons on the other side, and there always is another side, namely that of the offending actor's own interests. Hence conscientious legislators can no more escape the necessity of balancing conflicting considerations when they consider prohibiting offensive conduct than they can escape interest-balancing in the application of the harm principle. Following the model of nuisance law, they will have to weigh, in each main category and context of offensiveness, the seriousness of the offense caused to unwilling witnesses against the reasonableness of the offender's conduct. The seriousness of the offensiveness would be determined by (1) the intensity and durability of the repugnance produced, and the extent to which repugnance could be anticipated to be the general reaction of strangers to the conduct displayed or represented (conduct offensive only to persons with an abnormal susceptibility to offense would not count as *very* offensive); (2) the case with which unwilling witnesses can avoid the offensive displays; and (3) whether or not the witnesses have willingly assumed the risk of being offended either through curiosity or the anticipation of pleasure. (The maxim *Volenti non fit injuria* applies to offense as well as to harm.) We can refer to these norms, in order, as "the extent of offense standard," "the reasonable avoidability standard," and "the *Volenti* standard."

These factors would be weighed as a group against the reasonableness of the offending party's conduct as determined by (1) its personal importance to the actors themselves and its social value generally, remembering always the enormous social utility of unhampered expression (in those cases where expression is involved); (2) the availability of alternative times and places where the conduct in question would cause less offense; (3) the extent, if any, to which the offense is caused with spiteful motives. In addition, the legislature would examine the prior established character of various neighborhoods, and consider establishing licensed zones in areas where the conduct in question is known to be already prevalent, so that people inclined to be offended are not likely to stumble on it to their surprise.

• • •

III. PROFOUND OFFENSE

7. The Nazis in Skokie

Profound offense is never more worthy of respect than when it results from brandishing the symbols of race hatred and genocide. The attempt of an American Nazi Party to demonstrate in the 60% Jewish community of Skokie, Illinois in 1977 was a rare pure case of symbolic conduct of just that kind, and has since become a kind of symbol of the category ("Skokie-type cases"). The case became legally complex and difficult, ironically, because of its very purity. Political expression is almost categorically defended by the First Amendment, and no one can validly prevent the public advocacy (in appropriate time, place, and manner) of any political opinions no matter how odious. But the small group of American Nazis planned no political advocacy in Skokie. Their avowed purpose was to march in the Village parks without giving speeches and without distributing literature, but dressed in authentic stormtroopers' uniforms, wearing swastikas, and carrying taunting signs. Free expression of opinion, a preemptive constitutional value, was not obviously involved. Rather the point was deliberately and maliciously to affront the sensibilities of the Jews in Skokie (including from 5,000 to 7,000 aged survivors of Nazi death camps), to insult them, lacerate their feelings, and indirectly threaten them. Surely if they had carried banners emblazoned only with the words "Jews are scum," they could not have been described as advocating a political program or entering an "opinion" in "the marketplace of ideas." Only some speech acts are acts of advocacy, or assertions of belief; others are pure menacing insult, no less and no more.[12] The Nazi demonstration was to have been very close to the pure insult extreme.[13]

One of the holocaust survivors in Skokie had witnessed the death of his mother during the Second World War, when fifty German troopers, presumably attired in brown shirts, boots, and swastika armbands, threw her and fifty other women down a well and buried them alive in gravel. The other survivors had all suffered similar experiences. Now their village was to be the scene of a celebration of Hitler's birthday by jack-booted youths in the same Nazi uniforms. The American Nazis had deliberately sought them out; their "message" was not primarily for non-Jews. Who could blame the anxious residents of Skokie for interpreting that "message" thus: "You escaped us before, you dirty Jew, but we are coming and we will get you"?[14] This seems a much more natural interpretation of the "symbolic behavior" of the uniformed demonstrators than that of the Illinois Supreme Court in 1978, when it struck down the prohibitive injunction of a lower court. Addressing only the somewhat narrower question of whether an injunction against display of the swastika violated First Amendment rights, it wrote: "The display of the swastika, as offensive to the principles of a free nation as the memories it recalls may be, is symbolic

---

[12] As must be apparent to the reader by now, the concept of an *insult* (or "affront") is central to the discussion of much "profound offense." . . . One of the functions of obscene words is to express insults. . . . But not all insults involve obscene words and not all obscene words occur in insults. The concept of insulting is of much more general importance.

[13] The ostensible occasion of the demonstration that became the main subject of subsequent court hearings was to protest a Skokie Park District requirement that the Nazis post a $350,000 insurance policy as a condition for a permit to use the Skokie parks. The placards and banners to be displayed contained only such slogans as "Free Speech for the White Man" and "Free Speech for White America." The "pure insult" was conveyed through the symbolism of the swastika and the Nazi uniforms.

[14] Letter to the editor, *The Nation,* May 6, 1978 from Gilbert Gordon, Senior Attorney to the Village of Skokie.

political speech intended to convey to the public the beliefs of those who display it." That is almost as absurd as saying that a nose thumbing, or a giving of "the finger," or a raspberry jeer is a form of "political speech," or that "Death to the Niggers!" is the expression of a political opinion.

The Nazi demonstration without question would have produced "offended states of mind" of great intensity in almost any Skokie resident forced to witness it. Equally clearly, the offense would be of the profound variety since the planned affront was to values held sacred by those singled out as targets. But since the Nazis announced the demonstration well in advance, it could be easily avoided by all who wished to avoid it, in most cases with but minimal inconvenience. Even those who would have to endure some inconvenience to escape witnessing the spectacle, for example a mother who could not take her children to the park that afternoon, could complain only of a minor nuisance, since with so much notice, nearly as satisfactory alternative arrangements could be made. The main complainants then would be those who stayed at home or at work, and found that physical separation from the witnessed event was no bar to their experiencing intolerably severe emotions. The offense derived from bare knowledge that the demonstration was taking place in Skokie was an experience that could have been shared at the time equally intensely and equally profoundly by a Jew in New York, Los Angeles, or Tel Aviv. That offense would be a complex mental state, compounded of moral indignation and disapproval, resentment (offense in the strict sense), and perhaps some rage or despair. But insofar as the moral elements predominate, there will be little sense of *personal* grievance involved, and even less of a case, objectively speaking, that the person in question was himself wronged. It is not a necessary truth that we are personally wronged by everything at which we are morally outraged. Insofar as there is a sense of personal grievance in the non-witnessing Skokie Jew, it would no doubt be directed at the nuisance he suffered in having to avoid the area of the Village Hall and adjacent public parks. That element in the experience, however, is not "profound."

Despite the intense aversion felt by the offended parties, there was not an exceptionally weighty case for legal interference with the Nazis, given the relative ease by which their malicious and spiteful insults could be avoided. But the scales would tip the other way if their behavior became more frequent, for the constant need to avoid public places at certain times can become a major nuisance quickly. Even more to the point, if the Nazis, at unpredictable intervals, freely mingled with the throngs in shopping malls or on public sidewalks while wearing swastika armbands and stormtrooper uniforms, then they would clearly cross the line of public nuisance. Practically speaking, the best remedies for those nuisances that consist of group affronts are administrative—cease and desist orders, withheld permits, and injunctions, with criminal penalties reserved only as back-up sanctions. But without such measures, the whole public world would become as unpleasant for some as the revolting public bus . . . and equally inescapable.

8.

Pornography and the Oppression of Women

RAE LANGTON

The purpose of this section is to review briefly a certain feminist civil rights argument about pornography, in the hope of showing how the question is transformed once it is placed in a civil rights context.

• • •

The reader should be aware that the argument reviewed in this section is one of a variety of feminist responses, many of which disagree with both the analysis and the course of action advocated by this one.[1]

In contrast to the argument discussed in Dworkin's paper on the topic, this feminist argument against pornography sets aside questions about "morality" and focuses instead on the civil status of women. The argument has been put very forcefully by Catherine MacKinnon,[2] who has written widely on the subject, and who was involved in the drafting of the Indianapolis ordnance. In that ordinance pornography is defined as a civil rights violation:[3] "We define

---

[1] For MacKinnon's view see Catherine MacKinnon, *Feminism Unmodified* (Cambridge, Mass.: Harvard University Press, 1987), esp. "Francis Biddle's Sister: Pornography, Civil Rights and Speech," pp. 163–97.

For a range of views other than MacKinnon's, see, e.g., Gail Chester and Julienne Dickey, eds., *Feminism and Censorship: The Current Debate* (Bridport, Eng.: Prism Press, 1988); Nan D. Hunter and Sylvia A. Law, "Brief Amici Curiae of Feminist Anti-Censorship Taskforce, et al.," in *American Booksellers, Inc. v. Hudnut*, 771 F 2d 323 (1985); Andrea Dworkin, *Pornography: Men Possessing Women* (London: The Women's Press, 1981); Varda Burstyn, ed., *Women Against Censorship* (Vancouver: Douglas and MacIntyre, 1985); and Edward Donnerstein, Daniel Linz, and Steven Penrod, *The Question of Pornography: Research Findings and Policy Implications* (New York: Free Press, London Collier Macmillan, 1987), chaps. 7, 8.

[2] See MacKinnon, *Feminism Unmodified*, esp. "Francis Biddle's Sister." There are many important aspects of MacKinnon's argument that I do not take time to consider in any detail here—for example, the claim that pornography constitutes a form of subordination (which has been considered by Melinda Vadas in "A First Look at the Pornography/Civil Rights Ordinance: Could Pornography Be the Subordination of Women?" *Journal of Philosophy* [1987]: 487–511), and the claim (in answer to the champions of free speech) that pornography silences women, preventing women's exercise of free speech. The latter claim, if developed, might lead to an argument of a rather different kind, which saw the issue as presenting a conflict, not between liberty and equality, but between the liberty of men and the liberty of women.

[3] It should be noted that the ordinance made pornography civilly actionable, rather than a criminal offense. The definition used here is one that raises many difficult legal and philosophical questions in its own right, but I am afraid that such questions, while admittedly important, lie beyond the scope of this paper. A further question related to definitional problems is that of the "slippery slope," a question that rightly concerned Dworkin (and the Williams Committee) and again deserves more attention than I give it here. While the "slippery slope" problem raises many difficulties, one should not, I take it, assume that it is insoluble; I proceed on the assumption that the problem is not so daunting that it rules out the possibility of discussion.

pornography as the graphic sexually explicit subordination of women through pictures or words that also includes women dehumanized as sexual objects, things, or commodities; enjoying pain or humiliation or rape; being tied up, cut up, mutilated, bruised, or physically hurt; in postures of sexual submission or servility or display: reduced to body parts, penetrated by objects or animals, or presented in scenarios of degradation, injury, torture; shown as filthy or inferior: bleeding, bruised or hurt in a context which makes these conditions sexual."[4] The ordinance distinguished pornography from erotica, taking erotica to be sexually explicit material other than that covered by the above definition. It should be emphasized that according to this argument, and in contrast to "moralistic" arguments, there is nothing wrong whatsoever with materials that are simply sexually arousing and explicit: the focus of concern lies elsewhere.[5] Insofar as the ordinance is not concerned with explicit material per se, it departs of course from a more traditional or popular conception that simply equates pornography with the sexually explicit, a conception I take Dworkin to have been using. Pornography as defined above is a subset, though, of pornography as it is popularly conceived, and Dworkin's remarks about the relevance of his own argument to the "radical feminist" case[6] indicate that he views pornographers as having a right to this kind of pornography as well.

The distinctive feature of the MacKinnon argument is that it views pornography—as defined in the ordinance—as having implications for sexual equality: pornography is seen as a practice that contributes to the subordinate status of women, just as certain other practices (segregation among them) contribute to the subordinate status of blacks. The argument seeks to establish at least two things: one is that women do not, as a matter of fact, currently have equal status; and the other is that pornography does, as a matter of fact, contribute significantly to the continuing subordinate position of women.

The first claim is, I think, not very controversial, and a cursory glance at sociological facts about the distribution of income and power should be enough to confirm it. One dimension to the inequality is the economic; women earn

---

[4] MacKinnon, "Francis Biddle's Sister," p. 176.

[5] To give the reader some idea of the kind of pornography that might be covered by the above definition. I offer the following description of a relatively soft-core example, which appeared on the cover of an issue of *Hustler:* "The photograph is captioned 'Beaver Hunters.' Two white men, dressed as hunters, sit in a black Jeep. The Jeep occupies almost the whole frame of the picture. The two men carry rifles. The rifles extend above the frame of the photograph into the white space surrounding it. The men and the Jeep face into the camera. Tied onto the hood of the black Jeep is a white woman. She is tied with thick rope. She is spread-eagle. Her pubic hair and crotch are the dead center of the car hood and the photograph. Her head is turned to one side, tied down by rope that is pulled taut across her neck, extended to and wrapped several times around her wrists, tied around the rearview mirrors of the Jeep, brought back across her arms, crisscrossed under her breasts and over her thighs, drawn down and wrapped around the bumper of the Jeep, tied around her ankles. . . . The text under the photograph reads: 'Western sportsmen report beaver hunting was particularly good throughout the Rocky Mountain Region during the past season. These two hunters easily bagged their limit in the high country. They told HUSTLER that they stuffed and mounted their trophy as soon as they got her home.'" (Description given in Andrea Dworkin, *Pornography: Men Possessing Women*, pp. 25–26).

[6] Ronald Dworkin, *A Matter of Principle* (Cambridge, Mass.: Harvard University Press, 1985), p. 1.

substantially less than men, and a disproportionate number of women live in poverty.[7] A further dimension to the inequality is to be found in the scale of the sexual abuse, including but not confined to rape, that women suffer and that men, as a rule, do not.[8] The advent of feminism has brought with it a new and more acute awareness of the conditions of women, says MacKinnon. I will let her continue:

> Rape, battery, sexual harassment, forced prostitution, and the sexual abuse of children emerge as common and systematic. . . . Sexual harassment of women by men is common in workplaces and educational institutions. Based on reports in one study of the federal workplace, up to 85 percent of women will experience it, many in physical forms. Between a quarter and a third of women are battered in their homes by men. Thirty-eight percent of little girls are sexually molested inside or outside the family. . . . We find that rape happens to women in all contexts, from the family, including rape of girls and babies, to students and women in the workplace, on the streets, at home, in their own bedrooms, by men they do not know and by men they do know, by men they are married to, men they have had a social conversation with, and, least often, men they have never seen before. Overwhelmingly, rape is something men do or attempt to do to women (44 percent of American women according to a recent study) at some point in our lives.[9]

What is different about MacKinnon's approach to facts like these is that she sees sexual violence not simply as "crime" (as Dworkin seemed apt to do), but rather as a dimension to the inequality of the sexes, and one that calls for an explanation. These things are done to women; they are not, by and large, done to men. To call such violence simply "crime," says MacKinnon, without remarking upon the interesting fact that the perpetrators are nearly always members of one class of citizens, and the victims members of another, would be to disguise its systematically discriminatory nature.

Turning now to the second claim, the feminist argument can be seen as offering a hypothesis about the explanation for this pattern of sexual abuse: part

---

[7] "What women do is seen as not worth much, or what is not worth much is seen as something for women to do," comments MacKinnon about women's pay, which at the time of her writing was 59 cents to the man's dollar ("Francis Biddle's Sister," p. 171). According to more recent figures, women in the United States who work full time now earn 66 cents to the man's dollar and constitute more than 60 percent of adults living below the federal poverty line (Claudia Wallis, "Onward Women!" *Time*, 4 December 1989, 85).

[8] This is not, of course, to say that it is only women who suffer sexual abuse, or to underrate the extent of the sexual violence suffered by children of both sexes, or by men in prisons. It is only to say that, as a pervasive phenomenon, sexual violence seems to be directed mainly against women.

[9] MacKinnon, "Francis Biddle's Sister," p. 169. (I have taken some liberties with the order of these passages.) MacKinnon cites a formidable array of studies in support of these claims; the constraints of space dictate that I cannot reproduce all of her sources here, so I refer the reader to the notes in her work (*Feminism Unmodified*, pp. 277–79). Joel Feinberg cites 1980 FBI Uniform Crime statistics, according to which "a twelve-year-old girl in the United States has one chance in three of being raped in her lifetime" (*Offense to Others* [New York: Oxford University Press, 1985], p. 149).

of the explanation lies in the fact that certain kinds of pornography help to form and propagate certain views about women and sexuality. Such pornography is said to work as a kind of propaganda, which both expresses a certain view about women and sexuality and perpetuates that view; it "sexualizes rape, battery, sexual harassment, prostitution, and child sexual abuse, it thereby celebrates, promotes, authorizes and legitimizes them." [10] To back up this claim, a substantial amount of empirical evidence was cited by those supporting the ordinance (in the form of both social science studies and testimony of people whose lives had been directly affected by pornography) which pointed to the conclusion that pornography influences behavior and attitudes, and does so in ways that undermine both the well-being of women and sexual equality.[11] In the light of evidence of this kind, the Indianapolis City Council issued the following findings:

> Pornography is a discriminatory practice based on sex which denies women equal opportunities in society. Pornography is central in creating and maintaining sex as a basis for discrimination. Pornography is a systematic practice of exploitation and subordination based on sex which differentially harms women. The bigotry and contempt it promotes, with the acts of aggression it fosters, harm women's opportunities for equality of rights in employment, education, access to and use of public accommodations, and acquisition of real property; promote rape, battery, child abuse, kidnapping and prostitution and inhibit just enforcement of laws against such acts; and contribute significantly to restricting women in particular from full exercise of citizenship and participation in public life.[12]

The case was viewed by the district court as presenting a conflict between First Amendment guarantees of free speech and the Fourteenth Amendment

---

[10] MacKinnon, "Francis Biddle's Sister," pp. 171–72.

[11] The question of what is involved in making a causal claim of this kind is an important one. No one is claiming, of course, that there is a simple link; one can agree with Feinberg that "pornography does not cause normal decent chaps, through a single exposure, to metamorphoze into rapists" (*Offense to Others,* p. 153). For an interesting discussion of the notions of causality that bear on questions of this kind, see Frederick Schauer, "Causation Theory and the Causes of Sexual Violence," *American Bar Foundation Research Journal* 1987, no. 4 (Fall 1987): 737–70. Questions about the empirical evidence are also important, and deserve more attention than I can give them here, but in brief: The social science studies seem to suggest that pornography, especially some kinds of violent pornography, can increase aggression against women in certain circumstances, and that it can change attitudes in the following ways. Subjects who are exposed to it can become more likely to view women as inferior, more disposed to accept "rape myths" (e.g., that women enjoy rape), more callous about sexual violence, more likely to view rape victims as deserving of their treatment, and more likely to say that they would themselves rape if they could get away with it. The personal testimony cited at the original Minneapolis Public Hearings (with reference to an ordinance nearly identical to that passed at Indianapolis, which did not, however, become law) included, among other things, testimony of women who had been victims of "copycat" rapes inspired by pornography. See the transcript of the 1983 Minneapolis Public Hearings, published as *Pornography and Sexual Violence: Evidence of the Links* (London: Everywoman, 1988): see also Eva Feder Kittav, "The Greater Danger—Pornography, Social Science and Women's Rights. Reply to Brannigan and Goldenberg, *Social Epistemology* 2 (1988): 117–33; for a more comprehensive discussion of the social science evidence, see Donnerstein et al., *The Question of Pornography.*

[12] *American Booksellers, Inc. v. Hudnut,* 598 F. Supp. 1327 (S.D. Ind. 1984) (hereafter *Hudnut*).

right to be free from sex-based discrimination.[13] The ordinance would survive constitutional scrutiny only if the state's interest in sex-based equality were "so compelling as to be fundamental," for "only then can it be deemed to outweigh interest of free speech."[14] And the court concluded, as a matter of law, that the state's interest in sex-based equality was not so compelling.[15]

It is worth noting that the empirical findings were not disputed; in fact, when the case went to the court of appeals, Judge Frank Easterbrook went so far as to say, "We accept the premises of this legislation. Depictions of subordination tend to perpetuate subordination. The subordinate status of women in turn leads to affront and lower pay at work, insult and injury at home, battery and rape on the streets." His conclusion, however, is that "this simply demonstrates the power of pornography as speech."[16]

[13] *Hudnut* 1327.

[14] *Hudnut* 1316. The case also raised constitutional problems in connection with the "due process" requirements of the Fifth and Fourteenth Amendments. The ordinance was judged to be vague and to establish prior restraint of speech, and would therefore have been unconstitutional on those grounds alone.

[15] *Hudnut* 1326.

[16] 771 F 2d 329 (7th Cir. 1985).

9.

Prostitution, Surrogacy, and Commodification

MARGARET RADIN

UNIVERSAL COMMODIFICATION

Our investigation of contested commodification must begin with an understanding of the archetype in which commodification is uncontested. As an archetype, universal commodification is oversimplified, a caricature. It is my attempt to gather together and boil down fragments that are part of a certain way of thinking and of talking. The archetype is useful for analysis, although it does not—and could not[1]—fully describe the complexities of the real world or real people. I present here a more or less intuitive overview of its contours, which can serve as a basis of exploration. . . .

The archetype of universal commodification presents a one-dimensional world of value. From the perspective of universal commodification, all things desired or valued—from personal attributes to good government—are commodities. Anything that some people are willing to sell and that others are willing to buy can and should in principle be the subject of free market exchange. All social interactions are conceived of as free market exchanges. For example, when John gives his bicycle to Mary, he exchanges the bicycle, which he values at $100, for a feeling of generosity, which he values at $150. In the terms of universal commodification, the person is conceived of as both a commodity-holder and a commodity-trader. The person is a commodity-holder: universal commodification describes in monetary terms all things of value to the person—including personal attributes, relationships, and religious and philosophical commitments. In the framework of universal commodification, the functions of government, wisdom, a healthful environment, and the right to bear children are all commodities. The person is also a commodity-trader: all these things are assumed in principle to be alienable; they are capable of being exchanged for money; and freedom is defined as free trade of all things.

In universal commodification, the value of a commodity (from the social point of view) is defined as its exchange value, often referred to as market value, when it is traded in a laissez-faire market—or hypothetically traded in a hypothetical laissez-faire market. Valuation in terms of dollars implies that all commodities are fungible and commensurable—capable of being reduced to money without changing in value, and completely interchangeable with every

---

[1] Indeed, there is a conceptual difficulty with universal commodification that at least shows that it cannot exist in the real world and probably not hypothetically without contradiction.

other commodity in terms of exchange value. (Commensurability is central to commodification, and I return to it below.)

Universal commodification takes into account that people may value their commodities "subjectively" at a sum other than the market price, but the value is still assumed to be a price. From the individual point of view, the value of a commodity is defined as either the sum of money the holder will accept in order to relinquish it, or the sum of money the potential holder will pay in order to acquire it. The simplest version of universal commodification tends to presume that individual value is equivalent to exchange value. When possible divergence is acknowledged, exchange value is often called "objective" value and individual value is often called "subjective" value.[2]

Most legal academics are familiar with this economistic conception of life, because "law and economics" has been a prominent intellectual paradigm in law school teaching since the 1970s. Many of the writings of Gary Becker and of Judge Richard Posner, formerly a law professor, call readily to mind the archetype of universal commodification.

In his discussion of the criteria for an appropriate property regime in *Economic Analysis of Law*, Posner assumes that everything people value is (or should be) ownable and salable.[3] Posner's criteria are "universality," "exclusivity," and "transferability." He argues that "if every valuable (meaning scarce as well as desired) resource were owned by someone (universality), if ownership connoted the unqualified power to exclude everybody else from using the resource (exclusivity) as well as to use it oneself, and if ownership rights were freely transferable, or as lawyers say alienable (transferability), value would be maximized."[4] The only limitation Posner places on this claim that everything valuable should be alienable property is that it must be qualified by the costs of implementing such a system.

These arguments may seem abstract, but Posner and Becker show the depth (and courage) of their convictions by applying this analysis to people's desire for, and relationships with, children. In a 1978 article coauthored with Elisabeth Landes, Posner explored the advantages of a free market in babies. He considered "the possibility of taking some tentative and reversible steps toward a free baby market in order to determine experimentally the social costs and benefits of using the market in this area."[5] He speculated that the poor may actually do better in a free baby market than under present adoption law, because "[p]eople who might flunk the agencies' criteria on economic grounds might,

---

[2] Even when a difference between "objective" and "subjective" value is recognized, universal commodification tends to presume that the two measures of "subjective" value are equivalent. The possible divergence between what an entitled holder would demand to relinquish something and what an unentitled potential holder would pay to acquire it is sometimes called by critics "the offer-asking problem." See C. Edwin Baker, "The Ideology of the Economic Analysis of Law," 5 *Philosophy and Public Affairs* 3, 32–41 (1975); Duncan Kennedy, "Cost-Benefit Analysis of Entitlement Problems: A Critique," 33 *Stanford Law Review* 387, 401–421 (1981).

[3] See Richard A. Posner, *Economic Analysis of Law* (Boston: Little, Brown, 1992), pp. 31–35.

[4] Id. at 34.

[5] Elisabeth M. Landes and Richard A. Posner, "The Economics of the Baby Shortage," 7 *Journal of Legal Studies* 323, 347 (1978); see also Posner, *Economic Analysis of Law* at 150–154.

in a free market with low prices, be able to adopt children, just as poor people are able to buy color television sets."[6]

Gary Becker, like Posner, unflinchingly employs the market model to analyze the desire for children. In straightforwardly speaking of children as a commodity, Posner and Becker are using the vocabulary I call market rhetoric. In doing so they extend the market, metaphorically at least, beyond what we are conventionally comfortable with. But how close do they come to the archetype of universal commodification? Do they want to extend the market to everything?

Yes, insofar as they adhere to characteristic neoclassical economic methodology, particularly as that methodology is applied by practitioners of law and economics. The methodology universalizes the market, both literally (to the extent possible, absent market failure) and metaphorically. The tendency toward universalization of metaphorical markets can be seen, for example, in Posner's definition of "value" in terms of money[7] and in his conception of justice as a good with a price.[8]

Many practitioners of law and economics define economics globally. In Posner's words, it is "the science of rational choice" in a world of scarce resources. Its task is "to explore the implications of assuming that man is a rational maximizer of his ends in life, his satisfactions—what we shall call his 'self-interest.'"[9] Unlike many other practitioners of the genre, Posner goes all the way; he applies his analysis to human sexuality. In *Sex and Reason,* he argues that sexual orientation and behavior can be explained in terms of the "reason" of economics: sexual actors are simply seeking to satisfy their preferences in such a way as to achieve the largest difference between benefits and costs.[10]

---

[6] Posner, *Economic Analysis of Law* at 154. After publishing the article in which these remarks first appeared, Posner said, however, that he "did not advocate a free market in babies"; Richard A. Posner, "Mischaracterized Views," 69 *Judicature* 321 (1986).

[7] Posner, *Economic Analysis Law* at 12–13. See also Richard A. Posner, *The Economics Of Justice* 115 (1981), defending wealth maximization as "the criterion for judging whether acts and institutions are just or good."

[8] Posner, *Economic Analysis of Law* at 27; see also id. at 266 (stating that the threat of liability promised by "corrective justice" is a "kind of price"). Lest it appear that Becker and Posner occupy the entire field, for other applications of economic analysis to spheres that are not conventionally considered economic, see, for example, Margaret F. Brinig, "Rings and Promises," 6 *Journal of Law, Economics and Organizations* 203 (1990); Lloyd Cohen, "Marriage, Divorce, and Quasi-Rents; or, 'I Gave Him the Best Years of My Life,'" 16 *Journal of Legal Studies* 267 (1987); Martin Zelder, "The Economic Analysis of the Effect of No-Fault Divorce Law on the Divorce Rate," 22 *Harvard Journal of Law & Public Policy* 241 (1993); Paula England and George Farkas, *Households, Employment and Gender* (1986). Legal academics and policy analysts will recognize how pervasive the rhetoric of economic analysis is even where practitioners do not mean to embrace its deeper implications.

[9] Posner, *Economic Analysis of Law* at 3; note also idem, *The Economics of Justice* at 1–5 (defending the application of economics to all fields of human activity).

[10] Richard A. Posner, *Sex and Reason* (Cambridge, MA: Harvard University Press, 1992). For lively responses to *Sex and Reason* setting forth objections to conceiving of sexuality in this way, see, among others, Gillian K. Hadfield, "Flirting with Science: Richard Posner on the Biomechanics of Sexual Man," 106 *Harvard Law Review* 479 (1992); Martha Nussbaum, "'Only Grey Matter?' Richard Posner's Cost-Benefit Analysis of Sex," 59 *University of Chicago Law Review* 1689 (1992).

Universal commodification, in conceiving of the person as a commodity-trader, implies a certain view of human freedom. Market trading and its outcomes represent individual freedom and the ideal for individuals and society. Unrestricted choice about what goods to trade represents individual freedom, and maximizing individual gains from trade represents the individual's ideal. In keeping with its conception of the person as a commodity-trader, universal commodification also implies a certain view of political life. All social and political interactions are conceived of as exchanges for monetizable gains. Politics reduces to "rent seeking" by logrolling selfish individuals or groups, in which those individuals or groups vie to capture social wealth for themselves. The social ideal reduces to efficiency.[11]

Efficiency is pursued through the market methodology of cost-benefit analysis. Cost-benefit analysis evaluates human actions and social outcomes in terms of actual or hypothetical gains from trade, measured in money. In seeking efficiency through market methodology, universal commodification posits the laissez-faire market as the rule. Laissez-faire is presumptively efficient because it is a system of voluntary transfers. In the framework of universal commodification, voluntary transfers are presumed to maximize gains from trade, and all human interactions are characterizable as trades. Because freedom is defined as free choices of the person seen as trader, laissez-faire also presumptively expresses freedom.

The presumptive efficiency and presumptive freedom of laissez-faire suggest that the philosophical commitments of theorists whose views evoke universal commodification may be either utilitarian or libertarian. Many (probably most) law-and-economics theorists are utilitarians.[12] Some theorists whose views tend toward universal commodification see themselves as libertarians. If their reasoning is pressed, though, the ethic that drives their analysis seems to be wealth or welfare maximization.[13]

Later I will be exploring the philosophical implications of commodification—its theories of freedom, personhood, and politics—in more detail. For

[11] Proponents of law and economics often note that they do not endorse the view that efficiency equals justice, because an efficient state (however efficiency is defined) is always efficient relative to an initial wealth distribution, and the initial distribution may be unjust. See, for example, Posner, *Economic Analysis of Law* at 14. But many of them ignore their caveat. See id. at 27, stating that efficiency is "perhaps the most common" meaning of "justice."

[12] See, for example, Robert C. Ellickson, "Adverse Possession and Perpetuities Law: Two Dents in the Libertarian Model of Property Rights," 64 *Washington University Law Quarterly* 723, 737 (1986) (finding, with approval, that "the deep structure of property law has traditionally been . . . transaction-cost utilitarianism"); idem, Round Table Discussion, "Time, Property Rights, and the Common Law," 64 *Washington University Law Quarterly* 793, 796 (1986) (suspecting that "most of us" law-and-economics scholars are utilitarians at bottom).

[13] See, for example, James M. Buchanan, *The Limits of Liberty: Between Anarchy and Leviathan* (1975); Richard Epstein, *Takings: Private Property and the Power of Eminent Domain* 331–350 (1985). Epstein seems to have undergone an odyssey from libertarianism to utilitarianism, passing through a stage in which he tried to embrace both at once. The utilitarian consequentialist commitment to rest rightness on prediction is, in my view, ultimately at odds with the libertarian deontological commitment to preexisting and immutable natural property rights. See Margaret Jane Radin, "Problems for the Theory of Absolute Property Rights," in *Reinterpreting Property* (Chicago: University of Chicago Press, 1993), 98–119.

now, it is worth noting that the archetype I characterize as universal commodification is different from mere consequentialism or mere utilitarianism.

Consequentialism is a very broad label for the idea of identifying right and wrong by results; of course it is possible to do this without making monetization or market trading central to the scheme. Although some utilitarians may endorse universal commodification, others do not go all the way to its theoretical pure form, in which all values can be expressed in dollars. Amartya Sen, a prominent economist and social theorist, defines individual and aggregate social value as welfare maximization without supposing utility to be intrinsically characterizable in money terms and without supposing interpersonal comparisons to be possible.[14] This type of utilitarianism diverges to some extent from the characteristic reductionism of the market metaphor: that all values may be translated into—reduced to—money and readily (numerically) compared. . . .[15]

Finally, as I will discuss in more detail later, universal commodification implies extreme objectification. Commodities are socially constructed as objects separate from the self and social relations. Universal commodification assimilates personal attributes, relations, and desired states of affairs to the realm of objects by assuming that all human attributes are possessions bearing a value characterizable in money terms, and by implying that all these possessions can and should be separable from persons to be exchanged through the free market.

• • •

Payment in exchange for sexual intercourse and payment in exchange for relinquishing a child for adoption are nodal cases of contested commodification. They express the double bind for women especially clearly. They implicate issues of race and class. They show how our culture stubbornly insists on conceiving of the person as a moral agent, as a subject distinct from a world of objects, yet how at the same time our culture persistently commodifies and objectifies.

Social policy decisions about these practices, which have become focal mirrors for the crosscurrents of our culture, cannot help but symbolize how we view ourselves now, and how we envision our future. In pursuit of our vision of the future we might see certain changes as desirable for our culture as a whole. But policy decisions are made piecemeal, and our vision of what the whole is, and should be, keeps changing as those piecemeal decisions are made. It is in this context that we try to make incremental changes for the better, as we see the better. Our vision of the whole is always implicated.

[14] See generally Amartya K. Sen, *Inequality Reexamined* (Cambridge, MA: Harvard University Press, 1992); idem, *Choice, Welfare, and Measurement* (Cambridge, MA: MIT Press, 1982).

[15] Thus, economists who accept the possibility of judgments calculating Kaldor-Hicks efficiency are closer to universal commodification than those who do not. Kaldor-Hicks efficiency is the state of affairs obtaining when all winners" (from any particular course of action) *could* compensate all "losers" and still have the action register a net gain. The compensation need not be carried out. In order for the comparison to be made at all, though, we need to assume that the "losers" value their dollars the same way the "winners" do, or at least in some functional relationship that can be definitely ascertained. See, for example, Posner, *Economic Analysis of Law* at 13–16.

In fact any decision, including the decision to avoid decision (the decision to privilege the status quo), gets made in the context of our entire situation, whether or not we explicitly recognize its larger context. As a pragmatist, I can't claim that explicit recognition of larger cultural context is always useful or important, regardless of the practice to be evaluated. It depends on the practice and the circumstances. But explicit recognition of the symbolic meaning of the practices targeted for discussion here, in light of the surrounding cultural institutions and practices, is indeed useful and important. As we decide what to do about them, for now (for we may well need to decide again, later, in different circumstances), we should try explicitly to make whatever sense we can of the cultural/conceptual crosscurrents pervading commodification and the general issue of objectification.

PROSTITUTION

Start with the traditional ideal of sexual interaction as equal nonmonetized sharing. In an ideal theory of justice, we might hold that the "good" commodified sexuality ought not to exist: that sexual activity should be market-inalienable. But considerations of nonideal justice might tell us that prohibiting sale of sexual services in order to preserve sexuality as nonmonetized sharing is not justified under current circumstances. One reason to say this is that sex is already commodified. Legalized prostitution has existed in many places, and there has always been a large black market of which everyone is well aware. Those who purchase prostitutes' services are often not prosecuted, at least in traditional male-female prostitution.[16] This practice tolerates commodification of sexuality, at least by the purchasers.[17]

Moreover, in our nonideal world, market-inalienability—especially if enforced through criminalization of sales—may cause harm to ideals of personhood instead of maintaining them, primarily because it exacerbates the double bind. Poor women who believe that they must sell their sexual services in order to survive are subject to moral opprobrium, disease, arrest, and violence. The ideal of sexual sharing is related to identity and contextuality, but the identity of those who sell is undermined by criminalization and powerlessness, and their contextuality, their ability to develop and maintain relationships, is stunted in these circumstances.

[16] I am confining the present discussion to traditional male-female prostitution because I am considering a set of would-be commodities that women would control. Gay male prostitution is an important separate topic requiring an analysis of its own.

[17] For various views on prostitution, see, for example, Debra Satz, "Markets in Women's Sexual Labor," 106 *Ethics* 63 (1995); Stephen J. Schnably, "Property and Pragmatism: A Critique of Radin's Theory of Property and Personhood," 45 *Stanford Law Review* 347, 359–360 (1993); Robin L. West, "Legitimating the Illegitimate: A Comment on 'Beyond Rape,'" 93 *Columbia Law Review* 1442, 1449 (1993); Lars O. Ericsson, "Charges against Prostitution: An Attempt at a Philosophical Assessment," 90 *Ethics* 335, 337–357 (1980); Carole Pateman, "Defending Prostitution: Charges against Ericsson," 93 *Ethics* 561, 563 (1983); Alison M. Jaggar, "Prostitution," in *The Philosophy of Sex* (ed. Alan Soble, Totowa, NJ: Littlefield, Adams, 1980); David A. J. Richards, "Commercial Sex and the Rights of the Person: A Moral Argument for the Decriminalization of Prostitution," 127 *University of Pennsylvania Law Review* 1195 (1979).

Despite the double bind and the harms of the black market to prostitutes, fear of a domino effect—the discourse contagion of market rhetoric—might be thought to warrant market-inalienability as an effort to ward off conceiving of all sexuality as commodified. To this suggestion many people would protest that the known availability of commodified sex does not by itself render non-commodified sexual interactions impossible or even more difficult. They would say that the prevalence of ideals of interpersonal sexual sharing despite the widespread association of sex and money,[18] is proof that the domino effect in rhetoric is not to be feared.

But we must evaluate the seriousness of the risk if commodification proceeds. What if sex were fully and openly commodified? Suppose newspapers, radio, TV, and billboards advertised sexual services as imaginatively and vividly as they advertise computer services, health clubs, or soft drinks. Suppose the sexual partner of your choice could be ordered through a catalog, or through a large brokerage firm that has an 800 number, or at a trade show, or in a local showroom. Suppose the business of recruiting suppliers of sexual services was carried on in the same way as corporate headhunting or training of word-processing operators.

If sex were openly commodified in this way, its commodification would be reflected in everyone's discourse about sex, and in particular about women's sexuality. New terms would emerge for particular gradations of sexual market value. New discussions would be heard of particular abilities or qualities in terms of their market value. With this change in discourse, when it became pervasive enough, would come a change in everyone's experience, because experience is discourse dependent. The open market might render an understanding of women (and perhaps everyone) in terms of sexual dollar value impossible to avoid. It might make the ideal of nonmonetized sharing impossible. Thus, the argument for noncommodification of sexuality based on the domino effect, in its strongest form, is that we do not wish to unleash market forces onto the shaping of our discourse regarding sexuality and hence onto our very conception of sexuality and our sexual feelings.

This domino argument assumes that nonmonetized equal-sharing relationships are the norm or are at least attainable. That assumption is now contested. Some feminists, notably Catharine MacKinnon, argue that male-female sexual relationships that actually instantiate the ideal of equal sharing are under current social circumstances rare or even impossible.[19] According to this view, moreover, women are oppressed by this ideal because they try to understand their relationships with men in light of it, and conceal from themselves the truth

[18] See, for example, Scott Altman," (Com)modifying Experience," 65 *Southern California Law Review* 293 (1991).

[19] See, for example, Catharine MacKinnon, *Feminism Unmodified: Discourses on Life and Law* (1987); idem, "Feminism, Marxism, Method, and the State: Toward Feminist Jurisprudence," 8 *Signs: Journal of Women in Culture and Society* 635 (1983); idem, "Feminism, Marxism, Method, and the State: An Agenda for Theory," 7 *Signs: Journal of Women in Culture and Society* 515 (1982); Rhonda Gottlieb, "The Political Economy of Sexuality," 16 *Review of Radical Political Economics* 143 (1984); Catharine Wells (formerly Hantzis), "Is Gender Justice a Completed Agenda?" 100 *Harvard Law Review* 690 (1987).

about their own condition. They try to understand what they are doing as giving, as equal sharing, while their sexuality is actually being taken from them. If we believe that women are deceived (and deceiving themselves) in this way, attempted noncommodification in the name of the ideal may be futile or even counterproductive. Noncommodification under current circumstances is part of the social structure that perpetuates false consciousness about the current role of the ideal.

Some feminists also argue that many male-female sexual relationships are (unequal) economic bargains, not a context in which equal sharing occurs.[20] If that is true, attempted noncommodification of sexuality means that prostitutes are being singled out for punishment for something pervasive in women's condition. They are being singled out because their class or race forecloses more socially accepted forms of sexual bargaining. This situation returns us to the double bind.

Perhaps the best way to characterize the present situation is to say that women's sexuality is incompletely commodified, perhaps both in the sense that it is a contested concept and in the sense that its meaning is internally plural. Many sexual relationships may have both market and nonmarket aspects: relationships may be entered into and sustained partly for economic reasons and partly for the interpersonal sharing that is part of our ideal of human flourishing. Under current circumstances the ideal misleads us into thinking that unequal relationships are really equal. Yet because the ideal of equal sharing is part of a conception of human personhood to which we remain deeply committed, it seems that the way out of such ideological bondage is not to abandon the ideal, but rather to pursue it in ways that are not harmful under these nonideal circumstances. Market-inalienability (attempted noncommodification) seems harmful as it is practiced in our world. Yet complete commodification, if any credence is given to the feared domino effect, may foreclose out conception of sexuality entirely.

---

[20] See, for example, Alison M. Jaggar, *Feminist Politics and Human Nature* (Totowa, NJ: Rowman & Allanheld, 1983); Patricia A. Roos, *Gender and Work* (Albany: State University of New York Press, 1985), 119–154; Gayle Rubin, "The Traffic in Women: Notes on the 'Political Economy' of Sex," in *Toward an Anthropology of Women* (ed. Rayna R. Reiter, New York: Monthly Review Press, 1985), 157. Insistence on continued noncommodification of homemaker services of a wife is also problematic. The context of current sexual politics makes both commodification and noncommodification seem generally disempowering to women. Assimilation to the market paradigm seems defeating for personhood, relationships, and political identity, but given economic and cultural realities, so does continued insistence on a realm of nonmarket interpersonal sharing. On the history of this debate, see Reva Siegel, "Home as Work: The First Women's Rights Claims concerning Wives' Household Labor, 1850–1880," 103 *Yale Law Journal* 1073 (1994). The additional argument that the commodity form of a thing might drive out the noncommodified version of the 'same' thing does not seem at present a great threat to nonmarketized homemaker services. A domestic services market (though not one that is in full bloom) does coexist with a parallel class of unpaid providers. It does not appear that, as a result, we have implicitly come to think of homemaker services in market rhetoric. And if we had—here is the double bind again—many women would be better off at divorce, when money is all that is left at stake. See Lenore J. Weitzman, *The Divorce Revolution* (New York: Free Press, 1985), 323–401, describing the disastrous economic consequences to women and children of the present system of divorce.

So perhaps the best policy solution, for now, is a regime of regulation expressing incomplete commodification. The issue becomes how to structure an incomplete commodification that takes account of our nonideal world yet does not foreclose progress to a better world of more nearly equal power (and less susceptibility to the domino effect of market rhetoric). In my opinion, we should now decriminalize the sale of sexual services. We should not subject poor women to the degradation and danger of the black market nor force them into other methods of earning money that seem to them less desirable than selling their bodies. At the same time, in order to check the domino effect, I believe we should prohibit the free-market entrepreneurship that would otherwise accompany decriminalization and could operate to create an organized market in sexual services. Such regulation would include, for example, such deviations from laissez-faire as banning brokerage (pimping) and worker training (recruitment).

In structuring a regulatory regime expressing incomplete commodification for sexual activity, an important issue is whether contracts to sell sexual services should be enforced. The usual reason given for precluding specific performance of personal service agreements is that forcing performance smacks of slavery. If sexual service contracts were to be specifically performed, persons would be forced to yield their bodily integrity and freedom. This is commodification of the person. Suppose, then, that we decide to preclude specific performance but allow a damage remedy. Enforceable contracts might make the "goods" command higher prices. Prostitutes might welcome such an arrangement; it might be on the procommodification side of the double bind. The other side is that having to pay damages for deciding not to engage in sex with someone seems very harmful to the ideal of sexuality as integral to personhood. Moreover, it seems that determining the amount of damages due is tantamount to complete commodification. Granting a damage remedy requires an official entity to place a dollar value on the "goods"; commodification is thus officially imposed.

In this context both specific performance and damages seem to go all the way to complete commodification. Thus, we should continue to make prostitution contracts unenforceable, denying the most important factor of commodification—enforceable free contract. We could either provide for restitution if the woman reneges or let losses lie. If we let losses lie, we preclude any increased domino effect that official governmental (court) pronouncements about commodified sexuality might cause. But letting losses lie would also allow men to take and not pay when women are ignorant or powerless enough to fail to collect in advance. Similar two-edged results are reached by the doctrine of nonenforcement of illegal contracts, under which contracts to render sexual services are currently unenforceable because of the illegality of prostitution.

An incomplete commodification regime for prostitution might also include banning advertising. Trying to keep commodification of sexuality out of our discourse by banning advertising does have the symbolic effect of failing to legitimate the sales we allow, and hence it may fail to alleviate significantly the social disapproval suffered by those who sell sexual services. It also adds "information costs" to their "product," and thus fails to yield them as great a "return" as would the full-blown market. But these nonideal effects must be borne if we really accept that extensive permeation of our discourse by commodification-talk would alter sexuality in a way that we are unwilling to countenance.

BABY-SELLING

Just as some women wish to sell their sexual services, some wish to sell their children. Is a regulatory regime expressing incomplete commodification also now warranted for baby-selling? In my opinion, the answer is no, but the issues are very complex.

Let me start with the general issue of selling babies to would-be parents. If our regime were to allow would-be parents to approach a woman of their choice and commission a pregnancy for a fee, with the woman releasing the baby to them at birth, we would no doubt characterize this regime as one in which babies are being produced for sale. I refer to this scenario as "commissioned adoption." A regime allowing commissioned adoption would provide for a full-blown market in babies. The supply of newborn babies for sale would be related primarily to the demand of the would-be parents who wanted to buy them; that is, the quantity of children supplied would depend on the prices would-be parents would pay and how many would be willing to buy children at a given offering price.

If our regime were to allow would-be parents to approach a woman who is already pregnant, or who has already given birth, and for a fee have her release the baby to them, we would also characterize this regime as one in which babies are sold, though not one in which babies are being produced for sale. I refer to this scenario as "paid adoption of 'unwanted' children." This regime would not be a full-blown market in babies, because the supply of newborn babies for sale would not be related primarily to the demand of the would-be parents who wanted to buy them. Instead, supply would probably be related primarily to access to birth control information and education, and to cultural characteristics having to do with sexuality and permissibility of abortion. Of course, this regime could approach a black-market version of a commissioned adoption regime, because some women might conceive babies without any prearranged purchaser but hoping to put them up for sale.

As far as I know, no jurisdiction permits paid adoption of "unwanted" children; it is universally prohibited as baby-selling. (Many jurisdictions permit the birth mother to be paid expenses, and this arrangement creates a gray market.) A fortiori, no jurisdiction permits commissioned adoption. Our status quo "official" social regime—and the "official" regime is the one that has the most symbolic cultural significance—bans the exchange of children for money. That cultural significance makes troubling even the market rhetoric I have been using in these paragraphs.

Like relationships of sexual sharing, parent-child relationships are closely connected with personhood, particularly with personal identity and contextuality, and the interest of would-be parents is a strong one. Moreover, poor women caught in the double bind raise the issue of freedom: they may wish to sell a baby on the black market, as they may wish to sell sexual services, perhaps to try to provide adequately for other children or family members.[21] But the double bind is not the only problem of freedom implicated in baby-selling. Under a market regime, prostitutes may be choosing to sell their sexuality, but babies are not choosing for themselves that under current nonideal circumstances they are better off as commodities. If we permit babies to be sold, we commodify not only the mother's (and father's) babymaking capacities—which might be analogous to commodifying sexuality—but also the baby herself.

When the baby becomes a commodity, all of her personal attributes—sex, eye color, predicted I.Q., predicted height, and the like—become commodified as well. Hence, as Gary Becker says, there would be "superior" and "inferior" babies, with the market for the latter likened to that for "lemons." [22] As a result, boy babies might be "worth" more than girl babies; white babies might be "worth" more than nonwhite babies.[23] Commodifying babies leads us to conceive of potentially all personal attributes in market rhetoric, not merely those of sexuality. Moreover, to conceive of infants in market rhetoric is likewise to conceive of the people they will become in market rhetoric, and this might well create in those people a commodified self-conception.

Hence, the domino theory has a deep intuitive appeal when we think about the sale of babies. Yet perhaps we are being too pessimistic about our "nature" as market actors if we succumb to it. Maybe the fact that we do not now value babies in monetary terms suggests that we would not do so even if our official regime allowed babies to be sold. Maybe. Perhaps babies could be incompletely commodified, valued by the participants in the interaction in a nonmarket way, even though money changed hands. Perhaps. Although this outcome is theoretically possible . . . , it seems risky to commit ourselves to this optimistic view in our nonideal world.

---

[21] See generally Elaine Landau, *Black Market Adoption and the Sale of Children* (New York: F. Watts, 1990); Nancy C. Baker, *Babyselling: The Scandal of Black-Market Adoptions* (New York: Vanguard Press, 1978), and id. at 43, suggesting that most birth mothers who give up babies for adoption on the black market are 13-to-14-year-old girls. In the past decade, the black market for children has become an international problem. Whites from wealthy nations are buying babies from poor non-whites in less developed countries. In these transactions the problem of the double bind is especially evident. Babies are sold for thousands of dollars (anywhere from $7,000 to $20,000), but mothers receive only a tiny portion of the sale price after the commissions of intermediaries are extracted. See Holly C. Kennard, "Curtailing the Sale and Trafficking of Children: A Discussion of the Hague Conference Convention in Respect of Intercountry Adoptions," 14 *University of Pennsylvania Journal of International Business Law* 623 (1994); Kristina Wilken, "Controlling Improper Financial Gain in International Adoptions," 2 *Duke Journal of Gender Law and Policy* 85 (1995). See also Lisa Swenarski, "In Honduras, a Black Market for Babies," *Christian Science Monitor,* May 13, 1993, p. 12.

[22] See Gary S. Becker, *A Treatise on the Family* (2nd. ed., Cambridge, MA: Harvard University Press, 1991), 140–141.

[23] See, e.g., Harry D. Krause, *Family Law* (St. Paul, MN: West Publishing Co., 1996), stating that "in 1984, the 'black market' price for a healthy white infant was reported to be $50,000." Contrast this with figures for nonwhite babies in note 21 above.

If a free-market baby industry were to come into being, with all of its accompanying paraphernalia, how could any of us, even those who did not produce infants for sale, avoid measuring the dollar value of our children? How could our children avoid being preoccupied with measuring their own dollar value? This measurement makes our discourse about ourselves (when we are children) and about our children (when we are parents) like our discourse about cars.[24]

Perhaps we should separately evaluate the risk in the cases of selling "unwanted" babies and selling babies commissioned for adoption or otherwise "produced" for sale. The risk of complete commodification may be greater if we officially sanction bringing babies into the world for purposes of sale than if we sanction accepting money once they are already born. Such a distinction would probably be quite difficult to enforce, however, because nothing prevents a would-be seller from declaring any child to be "unwanted." Permitting the sale of any babies (any kind of paid adoption) is perhaps tantamount to permitting the production of them for sale (commissioned adoption).

I suspect that an intuitive grasp of the injury to personhood involved in commodification of human beings is the reason many people lump baby-selling together with slavery.[25] But this intuition can be misleading. Selling a baby, whose personal development requires caretaking, to people who want to act as the caretakers is not the same thing as selling a baby or an adult to people who want to act only as users of her capacities. Moreover, if the reason for our aversion to baby-selling is that we believe it is like slavery, then it is unclear why we do not prohibit baby-giving (release of a child for adoption) on the ground that enslavement is not permitted even without consideration. Perhaps most important, we might say that respect for persons prohibits slavery but may require adoption. There might be cases in which only adoptive parents will treat the child as a person, or in the manner appropriate to becoming a person.

But this answer is still somewhat unsatisfactory. It does not tell us whether biological parents who are financially and psychologically capable of raising a child in a manner we deem proper nevertheless may give up the child for adoption, for what we would consider less than compelling reasons. If parents are

---

[24] As Lewis Hyde recounts: "In 1980 a New Jersey couple tried to exchange their baby for a secondhand Corvette worth $8,800. The used-car dealer (who had been tempted into the deal after the loss of his own family in a fire) later told the newspapers why he changed his mind: 'My first impression was to swap the car for the kid. I knew moments later that it would be wrong—not so much wrong for me or the expense of it, but what would this baby do when he's not a baby anymore? How could this boy cope with life knowing he was traded for a car?'" Lewis Hyde, *The Gift: Imagination and the Erotic Life of Property* (New York: Random House, 1983), 96n.

[25] It is sometimes argued that baby-selling violates the Thirteenth Amendment. See, for example, Angela R. Holder, "Surrogate Motherhood: Babies for Fun and Profit," 12 *Law, Medicine and Health Care* 115 (1984); Anita L. Allen, "Surrogacy, Slavery, and the Ownership of Life," 13 *Harvard Journal of Law and Public Policy* 139, 147–148 (1990) ("One strains to see female liberation in a practice that pays so little, capitalizes on the traditionally female virtues of self-sacrifice and care-taking, and enables men to have biologically related children without the burden of marriage"); idem, "Privacy, Surrogacy, and the *Baby M* Case," 76 *Georgetown Law Journal* 1759 (1988). For a summary of various arguments leveled against baby-selling, see Robert S. Prichard, "A Market for Babies?" 34 *University of Toronto Law Journal* 341 (1984).

morally entitled to give up a child even if the child could have (in some sense) been raised properly by them,[26] our aversion to slavery does not explain why infants are subject only to market-inalienability. There must be another reason why baby-giving is unobjectionable.

Baby-giving is unobjectionable, I think, because we do not fear relinquishment of children unless it is accompanied by—understood in terms of, structured by—market rhetoric. Relinquishing a child may be seen as admirable altruism. Some people who give up children for adoption do so with pain, but with the belief that the child will have a better life with someone else who needs and wants her, and that they are contributing immeasurably to the adoptive parents' lives as well as to the child's. Baby-selling might undermine this belief because if wealth determined who gets a child, we would know that the adoptive parents valued the child as much as a Volvo but not as much as a Mercedes. If an explicit sum of money entered into the birth parent's decision to give the child up, then she would not as readily place the altruistic interpretation on her own motives. Again, however, if babies could be seen as incompletely commodified, in the sense of coexistent commodified and noncommodified internal rhetorical structures, the altruism might coexist with sales.

The objection to market rhetoric as the discursive construction of the relinquishment of a child may be part of a moral prohibition on market treatment of any babies, regardless of whether nonmonetized treatment of other children would remain possible. To the extent that we condemn baby-selling even in the absence of any domino effect, we are saying that this "good" simply should not exist. Conceiving of any child in market rhetoric wrongs personhood. To the extent the objection to baby-selling is not (or is not only) to the very idea of this "good" (marketed children), it stems from a fear that the nonmarket version of human beings themselves will become impossible because of the power of market discourse (the domino effect).

---

[26] But perhaps we should prophylactically decline to trust any parents wishing to give a child away for "frivolous" reasons to raise a child adequately if forced to keep her.

10.

In Defense of Surrogacy

RICHARD ARNESON

The intrusion of market relations into the decision to become a parent is said to have a symbolic significance that threatens to erode the idea that persons are to be prized and respected for their intrinsic humanity, not valued at their market price. Radin and Alexander Capron write, "a market in reproductive services would have adverse effects on all persons, not simply on those who choose to enter that market. All personal attributes of ourselves as well as our children (sex, eye color, predicted IQ and athletic ability, and so forth) would be given a dollar value by the market, whether or not we wanted to regard ourselves and our progeny in these terms."[1]

This is a serious concern, not to be dismissed lightly. Capron and Radin are asserting (1) that we all have a stake in maintaining social norms that function as barriers to regarding persons as fungible commodities and (2) that this concern is a good reason legally to prohibit commercial surrogacy. My claim will be that we can go a long way toward agreeing with (1) without accepting (2).

There is no denying that many of us intuitively find the practice of attaching price tags to persons and aspects of persons to be repulsive. Commercial surrogacy aside, one can point to other social norms whose purpose is to insulate children from direct tagging by market price. For example, John Roemer has observed that a social norm appears to be in force in the field of education that prohibits a school from directly charging its students varying prices tailored to estimates of their individual teachability.[2] (To some extent talent-based scholarships offered by private schools achieve a very rough and indirect approximation to such price discrimination.) Obviously the costs of educating a child vary according to his particular traits, but allowing schools to charge a different price for the "same" education for different children would be too close to tolerating price tags on individual children—hence the social norm. The fear that commercial surrogacy would induce a commonly known price list for desired traits in children so that each child could compute what his parents might have paid for him is similar in kind to distaste for the pricing of individual children in an educational market.

However, there are reasons to doubt that a suitably regulated market in adoption and gestational services would allow market pricing to run amok. First, notice that the social norm against explicit pricing of individual children's educations is maintained without apparent legal coercion, at least in the private

---

[1] A. M. Capron and M. J. Radin, "Choosing Family Law over Contract Law as a Paradigm for Surrogate Motherhood," *Law, Medicine, and Health Care* 16 (1988): 36.

[2] John E. Roemer, "Providing Equal Educational Opportunity: Public vs. Voucher Schools," *Social Philosophy and Policy* 9 (1992): 291–309.

school arena. Second, even if commercial surrogacy and a limited market in adoption services are accepted, the overwhelming majority of children will continue to be raised by natural parents whose initial relation to their child is not mediated by surrogacy or adoption. Market trading in parental rights and duties will take place at the margin, not at the center, of childbearing practices. Moreover, the revulsion many of us feel in response to imaginary scenarios involving something uncomfortably close to explicit pricing of children will tend to inhibit such explicit pricing. In a somewhat similar way, there are now in contemporary societies marketlike dating practices and what economists would call "shadow pricing" of individual attributes in the quasi market for romantic mates and marriage partners.[3] Such practices coexist with social norms that work to prevent the spread of explicit economic markets in this domain. The tendency of the market to encompass ever-wider areas of social life in the absence of legal barriers to its spread is just that—a tendency, not a law of nature.[4] Third, state regulation of commercial surrogacy and adoption services could be adapted to the goal of shrouding the pricing of individual attributes if a threat of inordinately explicit pricing on a wide scale was perceived.

Perhaps most important, the fear that decriminalizing commercial surrogacy will promote market pricing of children's attributes assumes that the surrogacies in question are partial surrogacies. However, in the long run, as medical technology improves, one would expect partial surrogacy to be eclipsed by full surrogacy. But with full surrogacy the pricing of the gestational services provided by the surrogate does not even implicitly involve pricing of children's attributes. So perhaps any movement toward commodification of the sort that spurs the strongest concern will be a short-lived phenomenon. Full surrogacy leaves intact the threat of commodification of women's childbearing labor but lessens the threat of commodification of children.

Another, closely related fear expressed by opponents of commercial surrogacy is that the more persons are legitimately conceived, in some respects, as commodities, the less gripping will be the norm that each person is individually precious, has rights that should be respected, and is owed reasonable opportunities to live a good life. Once made explicit, this fear appears misplaced. We are used to the idea that market evaluation of people's labor power is fully compatible with regarding persons as nonfungible in other ways. Thomas Hobbes stated bluntly, "The *value,* or WORTH of a man, is as of all other things, his Price; that is to say, so much as would be given for the use of his Power."[5] But

---

[3] Gary Van Gorp, John Stempfle, and David Olson, "Dating Attitudes, Expectations, and Physical Attractiveness" (unpublished manuscript), cited in Eliot Aronson, *The Social Animal* (New York: W. H. Freeman, 1984), p. 418. See also Gary S. Becker, "A Theory of Marriage," in his *The Economic Approach to Human Behavior* (Chicago and London: University of Chicago Press, 1976), pp. 205–50.

[4] This point is made by Eric Mack, "Dominos and the Fear of Commodification," in *NOMOS XXXI: Markets and Justice,* ed. John W. Chapman and J. Roland Pennock (New York: New York University Press, 1989), pp. 198–225.

[5] Thomas Hobbes, *Leviathan,* ed. C. B. MacPherson (1651; Harmondsworth, Middlesex, Eng.: Penguin Books, 1968). Pt. 1. chap. 10, p. 151.

the history of market economies shows that a fine-grained appreciation of the differential value of people's labor power is fully compatible with an entrenched (if sometimes embattled) popular belief that all these people are endowed with certain basic rights that ought to be respected and that they are in that sense all of equal worth.

When new social practices strike us as bizarre or make us feel uncomfortable, we are tempted to place undue reliance on purely speculative harms that our fancy associates with the new and disturbing practices. Such speculative claims that the freedom to experiment with the new practices would do grave harm should be treated with caution. We should recall Lord Brougham's confidence in 1838 that a proposed parliamentary bill allowing mothers to visit their children living with their legally separated fathers could "ruin half the families in the kingdom." Lord Brougham cautioned that it would be "dangerous . . . to tamper" with the "delicate" structure of contemporaneous family law.[6] With hindsight, the dangers that some discern today from changing the symbolism of family relations by permitting commercial surrogacy may be seen to have no firmer foundation in reality than Lord Brougham's conservative fears.

Similarly, it is pure speculation to suggest that market pricing bound up with commercial surrogacy, which might result in a higher price for blond, blue-eyed babies than for others, would tend to decrease people's willingness to accord proper respect to the individual rights of all persons or to believe that the proper goal of governmental policy is the good of all citizens regardless of race, creed, ethnic origin, or the market price of their labor power.

Finally, suppose that giving legal legitimacy to commercial surrogacy would in fact cause a widespread increase in the market pricing of individual traits and that this effect would be per se undesirable. We still would need some way of deciding how undesirable this effect would be and of determining how to weigh this loss together with other moral costs and benefits. Welfarist consequentialism modified by varying degrees of egalitarian weighting provides ways of making these determinations. To pick out one unique way, one would have to determine the appropriate stringency of egalitarian weighting. Evidently some way is needed—the argument against commercial surrogacy must go beyond merely pointing to a possible undesirable effect.

In this connection it is important to note that there are very obvious, considerable, and morally uncontroversial benefits that would accrue from a policy of permitting commercial surrogacy and tolerating an expanded market in adoption services. Many couples want their own children but are infertile. Besides heterosexual married couples, one should count infertile lesbian and gay couples. If the cause of the infertility is the inability of either member of the couple to become pregnant or to carry a fetus to term, surrogacy can help. In other cases, a woman who wishes to have a child may find that pregnancy is

---

[6] Cited from the English parliamentary debate in Frances E. Olsen, "The Family and the Market: A Study of Ideology and Legal Reform," *Harvard Law Review* 96 (1983): 1507.

unduly medically risky for her.[7] Nonstandard procreative techniques ranging from artificial insemination by donor (AID) to various surrogacy arrangements (in which the surrogate is either the genetic and gestational mother or only the latter) can provide a close substitute for having a child of one's own. This desire for one's own child is undeniably very important to many childless persons. There should be a strong legal and moral presumption in favor of permitting arrangements that enable this desire to be satisfied. A solid showing of significant harm to nonconsenting parties could overturn this presumption, as could a solid paternalistic argument to the effect that commercial surrogate mothers (or conceivably the commissioning parties) would be bringing about severe harm to themselves, in a significant number of cases, despite their willingness to engage in this contractual arrangement. I do not see even the vague outline of any such arguments in the literature assessing the practice of commercial surrogacy.

Some advocates of prohibition of surrogacy have made claims that suggest that the desires of nonchildbearing individuals who seek surrogacy arrangements are morally suspect, so that the satisfaction of these desires should be discounted in the formation of public policy. Some have speculated that the patriarchal desire of males to carry on their genetic line is the major impetus toward surrogacy. As Radin puts it, "paid surrogacy within the current gender structure may symbolize that women are fungible baby-makers for men whose seed must be carried on."[8] In a similar vein, some have observed that those who have recourse to commercial surrogacy could have sought to become adoptive parents but decided against this option. Perhaps such attempts to circumvent the adoption system should raise the suspicion that some of those who seek surrogacy would not be judged fit parents by an adoption agency or are motivated by the untoward desire not to become the parents of a child (perhaps of another race) that they could get through adoption procedures. This last point suggests the claim that surrogacy offers no genuine good to prospective parents that is not already available to them through the adoption system. But if surrogacy is not needed to benefit prospective parents, then even the speculative suspicion that surrogacy might create social harm might suffice to warrant legal prohibition.

This argument fails on two counts: (1) adoption is not available for many would-be parents who should be deemed fit to assume the parenting role and (2) even if adoption were available, for many would-be parents an adopted child is not a close substitute for a child to whom they are genetically related. Adoption laws vary from country to country and, within the United States, from state to state, but everywhere the procedures are restrictive, particularly those followed by public adoption agencies. Waiting lists are long, and one can

---

[7] Of course, the legal availability of surrogacy could also permit women who wish to have children to avoid pregnancy for reasons of convenience. But if this were deemed unacceptable, surrogacy for reasons of "mere convenience" could be legally prohibited. One can support a legal policy of permitting commercial surrogacy without supporting a laissez-faire unregulated market in surrogacy services.

[8] Margaret Jane Radin, "Market-Inalienability," *Harvard Law Review* 100 (1987), p. 1937.

expect a time lag of several years between initiation and completion of an adoption procedure. The alternative of privately arranged adoption is costly and only quasi-legal in some jurisdictions. It is easier to obtain an older child through adoption, but most would-be adoptive parents would prefer a new baby. In many areas Anglo couples can adopt more quickly if they are willing to adopt a non-Anglo child, but in a racist society in which positive affirmation of one's racial identity is an important mode of coping among members of minority races, reluctance to cross racial lines when adopting is understandable, though unfortunate. Moreover, if the existence of a surplus of nonwhite children available for adoption is a reason to limit surrogacy arrangements, why is it not also a good reason to restrict normal childbearing by fertile individuals, who could choose to adopt instead of bearing their own children just as nonfertile individuals could adopt instead of engaging in surrogacy? I raise this question not in order to suggest restricting the freedom to bear children in the standard way but in order to challenge the bias against nonstandard procreative techniques and the motives of those who would opt to use them.

An adopted child is for many individuals and couples not a close substitute for a child to whom one is genetically related. The enormous investment by many couples in medical procedures to enhance their fertility suggests the depth of this concern (though of course it does not establish that the concern is reasonable). I postulate that much of this concern reflects the simple desire that the child one raises bear traits that run in one's family, and I think the burden of proof should be on those who would impugn the innocence of this desire to have a child of one's own, a child who carries one's genes. Moreover, it is not unreasonable for would-be parents to surmise that such a genetic relation facilitates bonding and enhances the relationship between parent figure and child.[9] There is yet a further potential advantage of surrogacy over adoption from the commissioning couple's point of view. The contractual negotiations and the screening of potential surrogate mothers by the agency and the would-be parents give the couple some assurance that the child they hope to raise will be well cared for in the womb. The adoption process rarely if ever generates this sort of assurance. So many morally innocent and understandable motives can prompt the desire for commercial surrogacy that it is idle to speculate about possible suspect motives.

Moreover, whatever one believes oneself entitled to infer about the retrograde patriarchal aspirations of a man who wishes to have a child by a commercial surrogacy arrangement, one should remember that in the typical surrogacy arrangement the would-be parents include a woman who wishes to raise a child as her own but is unable to undergo pregnancy or can do so only

---

[9] A recent survey of statistical patterns in family homicides provides suggestive evidence on this point. The authors appeal to a wide range of studies showing that people are less likely to kill genetic relatives than genetically unrelated family members or others living in the same household. For example, in the United States, if you are a child living with one or more stepparents you are one hundred times more likely to die of child abuse than if you are a child living with both of your genetic parents. See Martin Daly and Margo Wilson, "Evolutionary Social Psychology and Family Homicide," *Science* 242 (1988): 519–23.

at excessive risk. Unless we hold that biology is destiny, we ought to respect this desire to be a parent even though one is biologically ill-equipped for pregnancy. Although I know of no empirical work that directly addresses the issue, I believe it is unreasonable to suppose that in the typical couple seeking surrogacy the male is the prime mover and the female is passively acquiescing to male desires. After all, "many different kinds of evidence suggest that *on average* women feel a stronger desire for children than men do and a greater concern for their welfare after they are born." [10]

[10] Victor R. Fuchs, *Women's Quest for Economic Equality* (Cambridge, Mass.: Harvard University Press, 1988), p. 4.

11.
Surrogacy and Exploitation
ALAN WERTHEIMER

I. INTRODUCTION

Commercial surrogacy has been criticized on many fronts.[1] It has been argued that surrogacy is baby-selling, that it is harmful to the children born to surrogates, that it is harmful to all children, whose sense of security is undermined by the practice, and that it is harmful to women as a class.[2] Another line of argument maintains that surrogacy involves the wrongful "commodification" of persons or relationships, or that it violates the Kantian maxim that persons should never be treated merely as means but always as ends-in-themselves.[3]

In addition to these (and other) arguments, it is frequently alleged that surrogacy exploits the surrogate mothers and that such exploitation is grounds for prohibiting commercial surrogacy.[4] I say "alleged" not to prejudge the coherence or validity of such claims, but because they have typically been advanced without much analysis or argument. Instead, it is simply said that surrogacy is

---

[1] Two points about terminology. First, because it is in widespread use, I shall use the term "surrogate mother," even though she is typically the genetic and gestational mother and thus not a "surrogate." Second, although it is important to distinguish between commercial and noncommercial (unpaid) surrogacy, I shall drop the adjective "commercial" in what follows except in those places where I want to draw the distinction.

[2] For an argument that focuses on the effects of surrogacy on women as a class, see Debra Satz, "Markets in Women's Reproductive Labor," *Philosophy & Public Affairs* 21, no. 2 (Spring 1992): 107—31. Here is one specific way in which women might be affected: the legitimation of surrogacy might impose psychic costs on poor women who would then have to treat the decision not to be a surrogate as a constant lost opportunity to earn additional income for their family. See Henry Hansmann, "The Economics and Ethics of Markets for Human Organs," *Journal of Health Politics, Policy and Law* 14 (1989): 57–85.

[3] Elizabeth S. Anderson. "Is Women's Labor a Commodity?" *Philosophy & Public Affairs* 19, no. 1 (Winter 1990): 71–92. For a critique of this view, see Richard J. Arneson, "Commodification and Commercial Surrogacy," *Philosophy & Public Affairs* 21, no. 2 (Spring 1992): 132–64.

[4] "Once money enters into the arrangement [the] possibilities of exploitation are everywhere." Peter Singer and Deane Wells. *The Reproductive Revolution* (New York: Oxford University Press, 1984), p. 125. "One of the most serious charges against surrogate motherhood contracts is that they exploit women." Martha Field, *Surrogate Motherhood* (Cambridge, Mass.: Harvard University Press, 1989), p. 25. "The prohibition on payments may be understood as protecting . . . women—especially poor, single women—from being exploited . . . paid 'breeding stock.'" Alexander Capron and Margaret J. Radin, " Choosing Family Law Over Contract Law as a Paradigm for Surrogate Motherhood," in *Surrogate Motherhood,* ed. Larry Goslin (Bloomington: Indiana University Press, 1990), p. 62. "But the core reality of surrogate motherhood is that it is both classist and sexist: a method to obtain children genetically related to white males by exploiting poor women." George J. Annas "Fairy Tales Surrogate Mothers Tell," in *Surrogate Motherhood,* ed. Gostin, p. 43. "[Even in] compelling medical circumstances the danger of exploitation of one human being by another appears . . . to outweigh the potential benefits in almost every case." Mary Warnock, *A Question of Life: The Warnock Report on Human Fertilisation and Embryology* (Oxford, Blackwell, 1985), p. 46.

exploitative, as if the meaning, validity, and moral force of these claims were self-evident. They are not.

In this article I will consider two related questions about surrogacy and exploitation: (1) Is surrogacy exploitative? (2) If surrogacy is exploitative, what is the moral force of this exploitation? Briefly stated, I shall argue that whether surrogacy is exploitative depends on whether exploitation must be *harmful* to the exploited party or whether (as I think) there can be mutually advantageous exploitation. It also depends on some facts about surrogacy about which we have little reliable evidence and on our philosophical view on what *counts* as a harm to the surrogate. Our answer to the second question will turn in part on the account of exploitation we invoke in answering the first question and in part on the way in which we resolve some other questions about the justification of state interference. I shall suggest, however, that if surrogacy is a form of voluntary and mutually advantageous exploitation, then there is a strong presumption that surrogacy contracts should be permitted and even enforceable, although that presumption may be overridden on other grounds.

II. EXPLOITATION

Although there is no canonical (non-Marxist) account of exploitation, we typically say that A wrongfully exploits B when A takes unfair advantage of B.[5] Now the notion of an "unfair advantage" seems to reflect two dimensions of an exploitative transaction, what I shall refer to as the dimension of *value* and the dimension of *choice*.[6] With respect to the dimension of value, it seems that A must benefit from the transaction, for A would not *exploit* B if A were to *abuse* B without benefiting from the abuse. In addition, A exploits B only when the transaction is harmful or unfair to B. With respect to the dimension of choice, we typically say that A exploits B only when B's choice is somehow compromised, even if, as I believe, exploitation does not require that B's choice be strictly involuntary.[7] It appears that exploitation requires at least *some* defect in choice, because A does not exploit B when B makes an entirely voluntary and altruistic transfer of disproportionate value to A.

Now some have argued that exploitation must always be harmful to the exploitee and that a transaction cannot be exploitative unless the exploitee is coerced (or perhaps defrauded).[8] I see no reason to put either constraint on what counts as exploitation, at least at the outset. Indeed, if exploitation were always harmful, it would be a less interesting phenomenon, for it would be much more

[5] I say *wrongfully* exploits because there are perfectly standard senses of "exploit" and "exploitation" that are morally neutral, as when we say, "A exploits his talents to the fullest extent."

[6] I shall confine myself to exploitative transactions; there may be forms of wrongful exploitation that do not involve transactions at all.

[7] Joel Feinberg, *Harmless Wrongdoing* (New York: Oxford University Press, 1988), p. 179.

[8] Stephen Munzer, for example, writes that "persons are exploited if (1) others secure a benefit by (2) using them as a tool or resource so as (3) to cause them serious harm." *A Theory of Property* (Cambridge: Cambridge University Press, 1990), p. 171.

obvious why it is wrong and its moral force would be much less in doubt. Following Feinberg, I think it best to begin with a broad account of exploitation, one that allows for the possibility of mutually advantageous and voluntary exploitation.[9]

Given these two dimensions of exploitation, to say that the surrogate is exploited seems to imply some defect in the values exchanged. On one view, surrogacy is exploitative because the intended parents gain from the transaction while the surrogate is—on balance—harmed.[10] Call this *harmful exploitation*. On a second view, the surrogate gains from the transaction but in a way that is unfair to her, perhaps because the intended parents gain much more than the surrogate. Call this *mutually advantageous exploitation*. Third, it may be argued that surrogacy is exploitative because the intended parents gain from a transaction that is fundamentally immoral, perhaps because the relationship involves an exchange of radically incommensurate values, or because the transaction wrongly commodifies procreational labor. For want of a better term, call this *moralistic exploitation*. Now it is not clear, at this point, why incommensurability or commodification should be taken to involve exploitation. But since the link between commodification and exploitation has been made in the literature and because I think there is a way in which it might be sustained, I shall try to see what moralistic exploitation might involve.

• • •

V. THE MORAL FORCE OF EXPLOITATION

A. General Remarks

Suppose that we come to the view that surrogacy is typically exploitative. What follows? It depends. It depends, in part, on whether surrogacy is a case of harmful exploitation, moralistic exploitation, or mutually advantageous exploitation. If surrogacy is a case of harmful exploitation, we need to ask whether paternalistic restrictions would be justified, although here our task will be relatively easy, particularly if we have reason to doubt the voluntariness of the surrogate's decision. If surrogacy is a case of moralistic exploitation, we need to ask whether restrictions can be justified on grounds of moral paternalism. And that would be at least somewhat harder. Note, however, that if we are prepared to restrict exploitative transactions when they are harmful (nonmorally or morally), it is not clear what role the exploitation is playing in the justification of the restriction. So things also depend on whether exploitation has any independent moral force in the absence of harm.

We are in a better position to consider the latter issue if we focus on mutually advantageous exploitation. If consenting adults should be able to engage in

[9] See Feinberg, *Harmless Wrongdoing*, pp. 176ff.

[10] The surrogate is encouraged "to make a grave self-sacrifice to the broker's and adoptive couple's advantage" (Anderson, "Is Women's Labor a Commodity?" p. 87).

mutually advantageous transactions in the absence of compelling reasons to the contrary, then it does not follow that just because it is wrong for A to exploit B, we should prohibit A from exploiting B. If exploitation is to serve as an independent basis for social restraints (even if it is not a dispositive basis), we would need to explain how the exploitativeness of a transaction justifies preventing someone from engaging in a transaction from which she benefits, particularly if prohibition is the only viable option.

B. Reducing Exploitation

But prohibition may not be the only viable option. Suppose that surrogacy would be less exploitative (or nonexploitative) if the compensation were higher or the contract terms were somewhat different. Might this justify societal intervention?

It might. Unlike some other contexts of alleged exploitation, I see no reason to believe that surrogacy presents a general problem of inequality of bargaining power. In principle, the potential surrogate may be in a very strong negotiating position—the intended parents may desire the services of the surrogate at least as much as she desires the money. If this is so, then why don't surrogates receive greater compensation? I suspect that the market for surrogate mothers may be relatively thin, in part because surrogacy is viewed with such moral skepticism. Information and competition are low. And unlike many other bargaining contexts, in which bargainers believe they can legitimately press for a better deal, social norms may suggest that it is inappropriate for a surrogate to hold out for a higher wage. As a result, it is entirely possible that the terms contained in surrogacy contracts are much closer to the reservation price of the surrogate than to the reservation price of the intended parents.[11] Somewhat ironically, then, the widespread acceptance of the moral norms to which the critics of surrogacy often appeal may contribute to its exploitativeness.

If I am right, potential surrogates may face a collective action problem. Left to their own devices, most potential surrogates might be able to negotiate an agreement that is less desirable than would be negotiated if all were permitted only to negotiate more favorable agreements.[12] It is entirely possible that most of the surrogacy agreements that would occur at a $10,000 fee would also occur at a $50,000 fee if the government were to establish that as the minimum compensation level. Some agreements would not occur. Some intended parents would be unwilling or unable to pay the higher price, but many would. We would then face a problem of moral trade-offs. We would need to weigh the moral importance of reducing the exploitation of those who would be helped by this form of minimum wage legislation as opposed to those who would be hurt, that is, those who are excluded from the market because people refuse to purchase their services for the higher mandated price.

---

[11] A seller's reservation price is the lower price that she would accept. A buyer's reservation price is the highest price that he is prepared to pay.

[12] I am bracketing regulations of the nonprice terms of surrogacy contracts, but the argument would apply there as well.

Yet the latter point highlights a moral consideration that many critics of surrogacy have chosen to ignore. Any restrictions that discourage surrogacy arrangements hurt those who would have benefited from such arrangements and arguably also interfere with their autonomy. If we are to respect the autonomy of potential surrogates, it is important that we not automatically apply the moral principles that define our conception of an ideal world to the situations we find in our actual, nonideal world.[13] As Magaret Radin has argued, even if "market-inalienability would protect all things important to personhood" in an ideal world, it may be morally preferable to allow the commodification of procreational labor in our actual world.[14]

C. Autonomy

So the question arises whether considerations of autonomy would preclude using exploitation as grounds for restricting mutually advantageous and voluntary surrogacy arrangements. Not surprisingly, I do not have a theory of autonomy to offer. I do want to argue that two strategies—one conceptual, one legal—that have been advanced as solutions to this problem are less than fully satisfactory.

The *conceptual* strategy maintains that since a woman's "true" freedom or autonomy is violated by surrogacy contracts, the prohibition of such contracts does not constitute a violation of her freedom or autonomy.[15] In slightly different terms, it is said that if we adopt a "positive" rather than a "negative" conception of freedom, treating a woman's procreative labor as inalienable is not, in fact, a restriction of her overall freedom.[16]

I do not want to deny that there is something to the notion of positive freedom or to the values it attempts to capture (for those values may be better captured by other terms). But even if we say that "true" freedom includes proper self-development, and if we think that surrogacy "would detract from the ideal of human flourishing that society should seek to foster," it remains an open question whether the right to choose not to be positively or truly free is a crucial dimension of one's autonomy.[17]

If we are tied to a maximizing notion of freedom in which we aggregate the total package of negative and positive freedoms, then we may promote a

---

[13] For the distinction between ideal theory and nonideal theory, see John Rawls, *A Theory of Justice* (Cambridge, Mass: Harvard University Press, 1971), pp. 8ff.

[14] Margaret Radin. "Market-Inalienability." *Harvard Law Review* 100 (1987): 1903. Radin adds, "If we think respect for persons warrants prohibiting a mother from selling something personal to obtain food for her starving children, we do not respect her personhood more by forcing her to let them starve instead" (pp. 1910–11).

[15] As Elizabeth Anderson puts it, prohibiting surrogacy contracts does not violate the autonomy of women because "the content of the surrogate contract itself compromises the autonomy of surrogate mothers" ("Is Women's Labor a Commodity?" p. 91).

[16] "If we adopt a positive view of liberty that includes proper self-development as necessary for freedom, then inalienabilities needed to foster that development will be seen as freedom-enhancing rather than as impositions of unwanted restraints on our desire to transact in the markets" (Radin, "Market-Inalienability," p. 1899)

[17] Capron and Radin. "Choosing Family Law Over Contract Law," p. 64.

woman's overall freedom by limiting her freedom to serve as a surrogate. But we may not be tied to a maximizing view. We may think that one should be free not to maximize one's freedom. Even if Mill is right to claim that one should not be free to sell oneself into *slavery,* it is less clear that—as a general matter—"the principle of freedom cannot require that he should be free not to be free."[18] And this is particularly so when it involves one's freedom to alienate one's *positive* freedom. Referring to a value as positive *freedom* does not suffice to show that the same reasons that would count against the alienation of one's negative freedom (as in slavery) also apply with comparable force to the alienation of positive freedom. Moreover, even if, as Anderson argues, surrogacy "takes advantage of motivations—such as self-effacing 'altruism'—which women have formed under social conditions inconsistent with genuine autonomy," there remains the question whether respect for a woman's autonomy also requires that we respect her choices given that these motivations are her motivations.[19] Consider people who altruistically donate to their religion or church on a weekly basis. We certainly do not think that we can justifiably prevent religious organizations from soliciting or accepting such donations just because we (even rightly) believe that the motivations that give rise to those donations may have been formed under social conditions inconsistent with genuine autonomy.[20]

A popular *legal* strategy for solving the autonomy problem is not to prohibit surrogacy through the criminal law, but to "make the arrangement performable or not at the option of the mother."[21] On this view, it is one thing if the surrogate wants to consummate the transaction; it is quite another if the surrogate irrevocably commits herself to surrendering the child in advance. It might be thought that this would give us the best of both worlds: it would permit women to enter into surrogacy arrangements, thereby preserving their freedom to do so, but would refuse to enforce surrogacy contracts, thereby preserving their freedom to keep the child if they so wish.[22]

It is entirely possible that the "unenforceable contract" solution is the preferred public policy.[23] But it does not resolve the autonomy problem. There are two related ways in which it fails to do so. First, it fails to acknowledge that the ability to enter into a *binding* agreement is a crucial dimension of one's

---

[18] John Stuart Mill. *On Liberty,* chap. 5.

[19] Anderson. "Is Women's Labor a Commodity?" p. 91.

[20] I have in mind "normal" contributions to "normal" religious organizations, not contributions that are clearly the product of fraud. Interestingly, to the extent that surrogacy takes advantage of altruistic preferences, it does not represent a problem of commodification. After all, it is one thing to maintain that surrogacy does not represent a "gift" relation, and another thing to assume that it does, but that women have been involuntarily socialized into giving such gifts.

[21] Field. *Surrogate Motherhood.* p. 78.

[22] "One attractive feature of this solution is that it helps avoid resolution of the debate, which is currently dividing feminists, about whether surrogacy exploits women or liberates them. It recognizes the truth of both positions. Surrogacy is still available when the surrogate mother desires ultimately to carry out the contract . . . But it avoids one of the most troubling features—a contract severing the maternal bond when the mother is unwilling to relinquish her child" (ibid).

[23] See Michael Trebilcock and Rosemin Keshvani, "The Role of Private Ordering in Family Law: A Law and Economics Perspective," *University of Toronto Law Journal* 41 (1991) 533–99.

autonomy. If B wants to enter into a surrogacy arrangement with A, but A will not do so unless B's agreement is enforceable, a decision not to enforce such agreements constrains B's ability to make a decision she prefers—a justifiable restraint, perhaps, but a restraint nonetheless.

Second, it may be argued that in trying to protect a woman from having to surrender a child against her strong maternal desires, we are refusing to treat her as an autonomous and responsible person.[24] Even if it is true that many surrogates ultimately come to regret their decision and might benefit from a more protective public policy, to deny them the capacity to enter into an enforceable agreement "is to exclude women from full-fledged membership in human society."[25] Whether or not this line of argument is ultimately decisive, and it is entirely possible that it is not, it suggests that the unenforceable contract solution does not fully protect the autonomy of potential surrogates.

D. Justice

Finally, I wish to consider a set of arguments for prohibiting mutually advantageous but exploitative surrogacy arrangements that appeals to considerations of justice, which is, after all, the gravamen of our concern with exploitation. These arguments assert that surrogacy is wrongfully exploitative because it (and this is not entirely clear) derives from or symbolizes or reinforces or creates inequalities in class or gender.[26] There are at least three different lines of justice-based arguments that we might consider.

First, it might be argued that we should prevent transactions that instantiate unjust distributions even if, given the unjust background conditions, the transactions are beneficial to all concerned. On this view, injustice is "a free-floating evil"—it is wrong to allow unjust transactions to occur, even when (as contrasted with the world in which they do not occur) these particular transactions are not bad for anyone.[27] Thomas Nagel puts it this way: "Inequality, even if it harms no one, counts as something bad in itself . . . [and] this may provide a reason to reject a Pareto-superior alternative because the inequality it permits is too great to be outweighed by other advantages."[28]

---

[24] "Her state of mind at the moment of agreement is not to be taken seriously because it is subject to change during the performance of her undertaking, due to the nature of pregnancy. The insinuation is that it is unreasonable to expect her to keep her promise because her faculty of reason is suspended by the emotional facets of her biological constituency." Carmel Shalev, *Birth Power* (New Haven: Yale University Press, 1989). p. 121.

[25] Ibid., p. 122.

[26] "Distributive justice requires that society's benefits and burdens be distributed fairly among different social classes. . . . Since women who are less well off will almost always be the ones to serve as surrogates for wealthier or professional women, the distribution is not fair" (Ruth Macklin, "Is There Anything Wrong with Surrogate Motherhood?" in *Surrogate Motherhood,* ed. Gostin, p. 147). "Surrogate motherhood is a method to obtain children genetically related to white males by exploiting poor women . . . it subverts any principled notion of economic fairness and justice, and undermines our commitment to equality" (Annas, "Fairy Tales," p. 43).

[27] Feinberg, *Harmless Wrongdoing.* p. 18.

[28] Thomas Nagel. *Equality and Partiality* (New York: Oxford University Press, 1991), p. 107. It is not clear whether Nagel's claim is meant to apply to particular practices such as surrogacy or only to what Rawls calls the "basic structure of society."

Now I do not think it necessarily irrational or immoral for an individual to refuse to participate in a transaction that will improve her welfare on the grounds that the transaction derives from or instantiates unjust inequalities. But the question is not whether an individual can reasonably refuse to participate in an unjust but beneficial transaction, but whether society can justifiably prevent someone from participating in a beneficial transaction because it is unjust.

If injustice is to have independent moral weight (apart from its effect on people's welfare) in justifying social restraints—and it is at least somewhat difficult to see why it should—the extent of that moral weight is not clear. Indeed, after suggesting that inequality is bad even when it works to the benefit of the worse-off, Nagel himself quickly adds that this unfairness may be overridden by "countervailing factors," including benefits to the worse-off. And thus we cannot assume that the intrinsic badness of inequality would justify the prohibition of surrogacy.

A second justice-based argument focuses on the *relational* dimension of surrogacy. It is one thing, it might be said, if the rich can buy material goods that the poor cannot; it is quite another if the rich can purchase this highly personal service *from* the poor. The problem is not that surrogacy results in different "holdings," but that surrogacy involves highly asymmetrical and unjust personal relations. Relational inequality is a serious matter, and it must be included in any "all things considered" assessment of whether a woman would be benefited or harmed by entering into a surrogacy transaction. But if, when appropriate weight is given to these considerations, a woman can plausibly maintain that she would benefit by such an arrangement, it is hard to see why such relations should be prohibited on account of justice—if the welfare of the potential surrogate is the focus of our concern.

And that gives rise to a third line of argument, one that focuses not on the interests of the (potential) surrogates themselves, but on the interests of third parties. This general line of argument can take many forms. Here I mention two. First, surrogacy may negatively affect the interests of women as a group. It is, for example, often argued that pornography exploits *all* women because it reduces their perceived value as persons, whether or not it is particularly exploitative with respect to those who are paid for their services. Similarly, it may be argued that surrogacy is principally exploitative with respect to all (or many) women, because surrogacy reinforces inequalities of gender.[29]

Second, it may be argued that society has a general interest in restricting exploitative transactions. That argument begins from the observation that fairness matters to people. People will refuse to engage in transactions they believe to be unfair even if they stand to gain from the transaction. *Homo economicus* to the contrary notwithstanding, buyers will often refuse to pay an "exorbitant" price for some good even though the price is lower than their reservation price and no lower price is available.[30] Nor is this irrational, even from a

---

[29] As Debra Satz puts it, "[surrogacy] contracts will turn women's labor into something that is used and controlled by others and will reinforce gender stereotypes that have been used to justify the unequal treatment of women" ("Markets in Women's Reproductive Labor," pp. 123–24).

[30] Daniel Kahneman, Jack L. Knetsch, and Richard Thaler. "Fairness and the Assumptions of Economics," *Journal of Business* 59 (1986): 285–300.

self-interested perspective. For one is a more effective bargainer if others believe that one cares about fairness, and others may be more likely to believe that one cares about fairness if one really *does* care about fairness.[31] If principles of fair division are important personal, social, and cultural goods, then the prohibition of mutually advantageous exploitative agreements can be understood as one way that society signals its commitment to principles of fair division, thus increasing the probability that the agreements that do occur will not be unfair.

I want to make three points about the preceding line of argument. First, if we argue that surrogacy should be prohibited by shifting our attention from surrogacy's effect on surrogates to surrogacy's effect on third parties, then we have, in effect, conceded that the (mutually advantageous) exploitation of surrogate mothers does not, in itself, justify its prohibition. And that is of some importance. Second, even if the prohibition of surrogacy has egalitarian consequences, we would be imposing a burden on one class of women (those who would be benefited by serving as surrogates) in order to benefit a larger class of women. In effect, we would be treating potential surrogates "merely as a means" to bring about a desirable social change rather than treating them as ends-in-themselves. And thus the same Kantian considerations that motivate much opposition to surrogacy may themselves be raised against its prohibition. This is not a decisive objection to the prohibition of surrogacy. We are often justified in imposing costs on some persons in order to realize gains to other (present or future) persons.[32] But when the costs are incurred in the present and the gains are to realized only in the future, we should be reasonably confident that such gains will be realized.

That brings me to the third point, namely, that we have no reason to think that the prohibition of surrogacy actually has egalitarian consequences or that surrogacy causally reinforces, perpetuates, or worsens (as contrasted with "symbolizing") social inequalities. It is plausible to suppose that the legitimation of surrogacy will have inegalitarian effects, but it is equally plausible that it will not. It is arguable that the legitimation of commercial surrogacy will *empower* women in their relations with men.[33] And it is arguable that prohibiting surrogacy might simply shield our eyes from the background inequalities from which it derives, while allowing surrogacy would forcefully bring those inequalities to our attention and motivate us to change them. Suppressing mutually advantageous exploitative relationships may be akin to removing the homeless from public places; we may feel better, but the problem persists.

[31] See Robert Frank, *Passions Within Reason* (New York: Norton, 1988), p. 168.

[32] The Editors of *Philosophy & Public Affairs* suggest that if allowing surrogacy has harmful effects on nonsurrogate women, then there is a comparable moral problem in *allowing* surrogacy. And this might be so. But there does seem to be a distinction between the direct costs that preventing surrogacy would impose on those who wish to serve as surrogates and the very *indirect* and diffuse harms that allowing surrogacy imposes on other women. We do not want to say that allowing *every* preventable harm treats those who are harmed as means. I am reluctant to say that if a 65-mph speed limit results in more deaths than a 55-mph speed limit, a 65-mph speed limit treats those additional deaths as "means."

[33] See Shalev, *Birth Power*.

12.

Two Arguments for State Paternalism

JOHN KLEINIG

Of the various objections to paternalism, . . . [one of] the most powerful relates to what is regarded as its insulting, demeaning, or degrading character. By appearing to dismiss the capacity of an other to determine and choose for him- or herself what to do with his or her life, the paternalist undermines the other's individuality, effectively making him or her a means to ends of the paternalist's making, rather than being recognized as the source of his or her own ends.

Yet despite this powerful criticism, paternalism has not been without defenders, including some within the liberal tradition. Absolute opposition to all paternalism, even to all strong paternalism, is seen as a doctrinaire and uncompassionate overreaction, contrary to our humanitarian impulses and good sense. Paternalists, after all, are not generally or at least obviously out to advance their own interests, except in so far as they have the interests of others as one of their interests. And that would appear to be a morally commendable interest. Moreover, those toward whom they act paternalistically often seem petty, careless, silly, or stubborn in their preference for risky or nonbeneficial courses of action, allowing themselves to be actuated by reasons altogether insufficient for or unworthy of a rational being.

There is another factor that has contributed significantly to the attractiveness of what, within liberalism, tends to be seen as paternalism. This is the sense of connectedness between individuals. "None of us lives unto himself"; "No man is an island"; "Self and other exist in mutual interdependence"; and so on, are assertions that call into question the liberal dichotomy between the harm principle and the principle of paternalism. To the extent that recent liberal theory has moved in the direction of a greater communitarianism and communitarian doctrines of various kinds have engaged the modern imagination, what is condemned as paternalistic by some liberals is advocated by others as a proper recognition of our interdependence. . . .[1]

In this chapter I will examine first those arguments that might be described as moving paternalism toward a new patriarchalism or, alternatively, toward subsuming it under the harm principle. Various consequentialist arguments for paternalism are then considered, followed by arguments that endeavor to give greater weight to the Argument from Oppression of Individuality (or Disrespect for Persons). One argument, the Argument from Personal Integrity, I judge to provide a valid but not necessarily sufficient reason for strong paternalism, though clearly its force needs to be carefully circumscribed. Factors bearing on the latter are considered at the end of the chapter.

[1] T. H. Green. "Liberal Legislation and Freedom of Contract." In *The Political Theory of T. H. Green: Selected Writings*, ed. John R. Rodman. (New York: Appleton-Century-Crofts, 1964).

CONSEQUENTIALIST ARGUMENTS FOR PATERNALISM

It is probably no accident that liberalism has been closely associated with consequentialism. The Enlightenment belief in and commitment to progress sat more comfortably with "forward-looking" theories of ethics and politics than traditionalist and natural law theories, and, for some writers at least, utilitarianism, when cashed out in terms of pleasure and pain, harmonized with the demands of a dominant empiricism. But there are many varieties of consequentialism, some monistic, others pluralistic, some clearly distinguishable from deontological theories, others not obviously so. Not surprisingly, they show some variation in the standing given to freedom, and hence to paternalism. Several variants repay attention.

The Argument from the Instrumentality of Freedom

According to one version of the Argument from Paternalistic Distance . . . there is some ultimate value (or set of values) that is likely to be realized more effectively and fully if individuals are permitted to order their own lives as they see fit, without interference by others. Maximum plausibility is given to this position if the ultimate value or end is some "mental state," such as the satisfaction of desire, or, on certain accounts, pleasure or happiness. In such cases, we can presume that the person concerned will have a greater commitment to the realization of this end than others and, moreover, will be in a privileged position with respect to the choices most conducive to it. The rebuttable nature of this presumption provides the room needed for the Argument from the Instrumentality of Freedom.

Despite the interest that people have in their well-being, there is ample evidence that they are often poor judges of it. Some of the reasons for this stem from a lack of motivation—the failure to keep long-term goals and remote effects consistently before their eyes; some stem from defects in knowledge or rationality—an inadequate appreciation of subtleties, hasty and ill-considered inferences, culpable ignorance, and so forth. For all the talk of our being "rational animals," we show a disturbing capacity for irrationality, which, though under our control, is not removed simply by correction. . . .[2] It is not that such claims about our irrationality are especially controversial, for they are not. It is rather that, individually, we do not make very good use of the powers that we have. The value of wearing a seat belt when traveling in a car is clear when the statistics are considered, yet a large proportion of drivers and travelers neglect to avail themselves of them, unless compelled to do so. "Belt-up" campaigns have been remarkably ineffective in producing long-term changes to habits, even where people are persuaded of the value of belts. There is always a tendency to rationalize, to make an exception of oneself, without there being any good reason for doing so.

---

[2] Stephen P. Stich. "Could Man Be an Irrational Animal: Some Notes on the Epistemology of Rationality." *Synthese* 64 (July 1985): 115–134.

It is not too difficult to spell out cases of this kind, and where we can do so, there would seem to be strong consequentialist grounds for limiting liberty. True, we would need to take into account the distuility of coercive measures, though on the other side there would be the misery avoided and most probably the gratitude of those whose lives had been saved from serious injury or loss as a result.

An argument of this kind is likely to attract two kinds of replies. The first kind of reply is that the calculation of utilities is arguably much more complex and uncertain than I have made it appear. This kind of response is outlined and criticized by Rolf Sartorius. . . .[3] Defending Mill against the simple criticism that a utilitarian defence of liberty can hardly justify total opposition to paternalism, Sartorius suggests that Mill is to be understood as being absolutely opposed only to paternalistic legislation. In individual cases, paternalistic interference might indeed maximize utility, but this cannot be concluded so far as paternalistic laws are concerned, because of the problems involved in providing and applying criteria for identifying those classes of behavior in which the benefits of intervention would outweigh the evils.

We might reasonably question Sartorius's interpretation of Mill. Although he is correct to see that translating what is permissible at an individual level into public policy complicates the utilitarian picture, we have no reason to think that Mill was utilizing this when opposing paternalism. His opposition is much more general. Moreover, as Sartorius himself goes on to argue, it would still amount to no more than a strong presumptive argument against paternalistic legislation. Legislators ought to be extremely cautious about introducing such legislation; even so, occasions for it may be indicated:

> There are instances in which it is empirically demonstrable that people will act against their own interests if not coerced into acting otherwise; thus statutes making compulsory the wearing of protective helmets by motorcycle-riders, and others prohibiting swimming after dark at unguarded beaches. Where identifiable classes of individuals can be shown to be likely to manifest choice behavior inconsistent with their preferences as those preferences can be unproblematically attributed to them, the odds may change in favor of interfering with their personal liberty, if necessary, in order to protect them against themselves. Mill's principle can and should be modified accordingly. . . .[4]

In making this rejoinder, Sartorius appears to slide from a "mental state" to an "ideal" utilitarian position, for he points out that the paternalistic imposition must be in line with individuals preferences "as these preferences can be unproblematically attributed to them." How can this be if coercion is required? We shouldn't need to be coerced into acting on our preferences! Two responses might be suggested. First, we could distinguish, with Sartorius, between stable

[3] Rolf Sartorius. *Individual Conduct and Social Norms: A Utilitarian Account of Social Union and the Rule of Law.* (Encino, CA: Dickenson), Chapter 8.

[4] Ibid., p. 157.

preferences and choice behavior, or, perhaps, between settled and temporary or passing preferences. Second, we could identify certain "objective" interests as essential to the execution of preferences, whatever those preferences may be. . . .[5] Though neither of these moves would be unproblematic, they provide an explanation of how, on "mental state" utilitarian grounds, it might be possible to justify a limited measure of paternalism. Where the utilitarianism is of an "ideal" kind, the epistemological difficulties may not appear so pressing, for the claim to a privileged access to one's good is not so easily sustained.

The second kind of reply to this consequentialist argument for paternalism takes up and questions the assumption that freedom is simply an instrumental value. Freedom, it may be claimed, is not merely a means to the satisfaction of our preferences, but is itself a source of satisfaction—a major one at that. . . .[6] Paternalistic interferences therefore, even if they help to achieve some of the ends to which freedom is normally a means, will nevertheless frustrate one important end, freedom of choice.

But, as stated, this does not pose an insuperable problem for the consequentialist case. For, though the abrogation of freedom can represent a real loss, it may be counterbalanced by satisfactions not otherwise securable. Should it be claimed that the freedom to choose is one of our most important sources of satisfaction, perhaps even the most important, this may still not be decisive in cases where the freedom lost is small and the other ends secured are substantial. After all, it is not as though the person who is paternalistically imposed upon loses all freedom. The only freedom lost would be that which would have led to the closing off of other important sources of satisfaction.

The contours of this instrumental account of freedom and the space it provides for a limited measure of paternalism can be appreciated more easily by reference to Joel Feinberg's discussion of liberty as an *interest*. . . .[7] Three kinds or levels of interest are distinguished. First and foremost is a welfare interest in freedom, an interest in that level of liberty necessary to sustain personal life. Unless we are permitted a certain freedom with respect to our thoughts, tastes, and choices, we will not be able to express those characteristics that distinguish genuinely human life, nor be able to relate to each other in a truly personal way. Like the inhabitants of *Brave New World,* we will be "programmed" to respond, think, and act in certain ways, devoid of creative and self-critical capacities, incapable of taking real responsibility for what we do, whether as achievement or failure—beyond praise and blame. We might, of course, like robots, be able to accomplish valuable tasks but, also like robots, credit would lie with the programmer rather than its executor. And we might, like the inhabitants of *Brave New World,* be susceptible to feelings of pleasure and pain, but the "happiness" or "unhappiness" associated with such capacities would not be recognizably human. We identify with John the Savage rather than the

[5] Phillipa Foot. "Moral Beliefs." *Proceedings of the Aristotelian Society* 59: 83–104.

[6] Op cit., p. 152.

[7] Joel Feinberg. *Rights, Justice, and the Bounds of Liberty.* (Princeton: Princeton University Press, 1980), p. 30–44.

Director, or, in more Millian terms, with Socrates dissatisfied rather than the pig satisfied. Understood as a welfare interest, liberty is clearly of enormous instrumental value, and encroachments on it will be exceedingly difficult, if not impossible, to justify. Enforced slavery of a very limiting kind, the sort of possibilities for genetic and social manipulation speculated on in *Brave New World,* and the omnipresent monitoring, coerciveness, and reconstructive character of Newspeak in Orwell's *Nineteen Eighty-Four* are meant to illustrate the effects of the welfare interest in freedom denied.

But it is not obvious that all strong paternalism would amount to a denial of our welfare interest in liberty. If paternalistic interventions are limited to negating only those choices that would severely limit or destroy our capacity to make rational choices, a case based on our welfare interest in liberty, though strong, would not be compelling.

The interest in liberty is not confined to our welfare needs. Feinberg distinguishes two further interests, a security and an accumulative interest, that extend beyond the minimum threshold required to satisfy our welfare interest.

Many of us believe it important, once we have developed our capacities and established an identity and life-plan, to be able nevertheless to accommodate unexpected contingencies or even changes of interest. Life is not so secure that, once we have set ourselves on a particular course, it will not be interrupted or diverted; moreover, with the progress, development, and unfolding of our capacities and perhaps the discovery of new talents, we may find that the course upon which we originally embarked, or the persons we at one time believed ourselves to be, will change in significant ways. We will want the freedom to respond productively to such contingencies. Unlike our welfare interest in freedom, this security interest may never be resorted to. It may be like money put aside for the rainy day that never comes. Nevertheless, as Feinberg observes, it is of some importance to us that it is there and known to be there. Life is much too unpredictable to dispense with it, and even if it were, happily, more predictable in certain respects, we would still not want to 'lock ourselves into' routines and pursuits that allowed for no shifts of interest or developments of talent.

But for all that, the security interest in liberty is not of such centrality that it would be unreasonable to sacrifice at least some part of it to other interests. If Arthur's security interest in freedom (represented, let us say, by the $50,000 he has saved) is all but expropriated in order that he may undergo a life-saving operation that will enable him to continue in the occupations in which he is presently engaged, he has not been too badly done by. Considered as a security interest, his liberty was not likely to be so important as to make such a trade-off unreasonable.

Unlike the welfare and security interests in liberty, the accumulative interest is noninstrumental. It involves a desire for liberty as an end, liberty for its own sake. Like Jonathan Livingston Seagull, one may get a sense of uplift, of euphoric exultation, from the contemplation of one's liberty, an urge to preserve and expand it, as a precious and self-sustaining pursuit.

The accumulative interest in freedom has some claim to our recognition, but its claims are markedly weaker than those of the welfare and security interests.

Certainly a person could become so engrossed in the enterprise of expanding his or her options that the accumulation of options came to assume the character of a welfare interest, but this would not seem to be typical. Most of us can do with fewer options than we presently have without being substantially affected. We value our liberty but do not feel we have to cling to every bit of it. If some of our options are foregone to improve our health or safety, the balance may well lie in favor of health or safety. Of course, matters are never quite as simple as this, but in general terms at least, there would seem to be less against paternalism where the interest in liberty is an accumulative one.

• • •

What is surely the most serious difficulty confronting . . . the Argument from . . . the Instrumentality of Freedom is its failure to come to terms with the special claims of the Argument from the Oppression of Individuality, or its Kantian counterpart, the Argument from Disrespect for Persons. What paternalism does, even when motivated by a concern for freedom-protection/maximization, is to undermine individuality. A person is made to act in a way that no longer reflects his or her own judgement and choice, but the determinations of an other. With respect to his or her well-being, the individual is treated as if lacking in the capacity for rational choice. In a more Kantian mode, paternalism denies a person's status as an agent, as a source of reasons for action to whom respect is due. While others may dislike or object to the individual's choices, considering them stupid, self-destructive, or freedom-diminishing, it is not for them to interfere, not for them to superimpose their own judgements. Failure to observe this constraints is, in effect, to "depersonalize" the person, to ignore his or her standing as an end and not merely the instrument of others' evaluations and determinations.

The point of these objections is not blunted by the comparatively small "sacrifice" of freedom involved and the potentially large gains to be made. A consequentialist "calculus" may work strongly in favor of intervention. The point is that people are dispossessed of their choices, are made subservient to others' determinations, and not treated as a source of evaluations and determinations. Admittedly, their choices may not be as good as the choices of others, but this is not the point, which is that the choices be *their* choices. Joel Feinberg gets close to the heart of the objection when he writes that

> When a mature adult has a conflict between getting what he wants and having his options left open in the future, we are bound by our respect for his autonomy not to force his present choice in order to protect his future "liberty". His present autonomy takes precedence even over his probable future good, and he may use it as he will, even at the expense of the future self he will one day become. Children are different. Respect for the child's future autonomy, as an adult, often requires preventing his free choice now. Thus the future self does not have as much moral weight in our treatment of adults as it does with children. Perhaps it should weigh as much with adults pondering their *own* decisions as it does with adults governing their own children. In the self-regarding case, the future self exerts itself in the form of a claim to prudence,

but prudence cannot rightly be imposed from the outside on an autonomous adult. . . .[8]

To treat an adult paternalistically is tantamount to treating that adult as one who is still normatively a child, as yet incapable of prudence. It is the implied insult in this that consequentialists overlook or fail to appreciate when arguing for paternalism, albeit on freedom-maximizing grounds.

We might, in conclusion, question whether consequentialist attempts at justification are really concerned with paternalism. As we earlier characterized them, impositions are paternalistic to the extent that they are designed to secure a person's good, as an end. But it is not someone's good, as an end, that constitutes the focus of much consequentialism. It is a more general, impersonal end, such as happiness or freedom which is the end, and to which a particular person's good is the means or in which it is at best an ingredient. Where this is so, consequentialist arguments fail to offer a motivation appropriate to paternalism. Although they suggest reasons for imposing on individuals for their own good, it is not, in the very nature of the case, *their* good *as an end* that is sought. Of course, consequentialism may be individualized, so that the happiness or freedom which it is proposed to maximize is the happiness or freedom of the individual who is imposed on. But in such cases we may wonder about the 'purity' of the consequentialism. . . .[9]

THE ARGUMENT FROM PERSONAL INTEGRITY

I have already foreshadowed some of the factors that bear on this last, and I believe most promising, argument for paternalism. It seeks to accommodate the attractive features of other arguments we have considered while avoiding their defects.

To see how it does this, we need to go back to the conception of human nature that informs liberal theory. What we find is not a single, fixed blueprint, intended as a pattern for all development, but something far more complex and varied. Within certain broad limits, we differ from each other in our capacities, and even when our capacities are similar, they are likely to differ in their potential for development. Even for any particular individual there is no single developmental path. Most of us possess more capacities than we can possibly

---

[8] Joel Feinberg, "The Child's Right to an Open Future," in *Whose Child? Children's Rights, Parental Authority, and State Power,* eds. William Aiken and Hugh LaFollette. (Totowa, N.J.: Littlefield, Ado & Co., 1980). p. 127–128. and Stanley Benn. "Benevolent Interference and Respect for Persons: Comments on Papers by John Kleinig, Cathy Lowy, and Robert Young. *Bulletin of the Australian Society of Legal Philosophy* 21 (December): 99–112.

   Benn states: "Assuredly, valuing a person and concern for his continuance as a rational chooser can be a reason for action of forbearance; but it is a different one from respect: that looks to his future, this is exhausted altogether in recognizing his present moral status. My claim is that where considerations of respect for that present status block interference, concern for his future, even his future as a person, will not license it" (1981, p. 107).

[9] John Stuart Mill. *On Liberty,* in *Collected Works of John Stuart Mill,* ed. John M. Robson, vol. 18: *Essays on Politics and Society.* (Toronto: University of Toronto Press, 1977), p. 224.

develop, or develop to their fullest extent, and so the formation of a life-plan is not a simple matter of "letting nature take its course," but rather an ongoing enterprise requiring deliberation, experimentation, and accommodation. The human individual does not come into the world a fully formed personality, but a bundle of undeveloped and uncoordinated capacities. We acquire a specific personality, a specific identity, through learning. This is not to be conceived on the model of a jigsaw puzzle, in which the variously shaped pieces are fitted together into a predetermined whole. It is more like the construction of a coherent and cohesive unity out of a large assortment of blocks, some of which are identical, but many of which differ in shape, color, or texture. For each of us, there is a somewhat different assortment from which to work.

In our early years, we lack the ability to form these blocks into complex, coordinated structures. Our hands need to be held or steadied and guided. But as we gain better control over our movements, as we come to appreciate what might be involved in shaping a unified configuration and acquire an interest in its realization, as our confidence increases and our imagination is stimulated, we are able to build using our own initiative, creating a structure that has "our own stamp" upon it. Building is a lifetime process, though it is quite likely that the general shape will become evident after several years. Obviously, how it ends up will depend partly on the adequacy of our early training, partly on the numbers and kind of blocks available to us, and partly on our building environment. Although some people manage to create complex yet tightly integrated and stable structures, most of us find ourselves with something less coherent and cohesive. Although we have arrived at a stage in our development where responsibility for the structure of purposes, attitudes, interests, beliefs, desires, values, and so on that constitute our identity and life-plans devolves upon us, our "ownership" of some of these elements may be equivocal or a matter of embarrassment or regret. Our lives do not always display the cohesion and maturity of purpose that exemplifies the liberal ideal of individuality, but instead manifest a carelessness, unreflectiveness, short-sightedness, or foolishness that not only does us no credit but also represents a departure from some of our own more permanent and central commitments and dispositions. That is characteristic of the self-regarding vices, and most of us are prey to some. On many occasions, the consequences of such lapses and deviations will not be serious, and we must wear them as best we can. But sometimes because of our actions, consequences of a more catastrophic kind may become inevitable or considerably more probable, consequences that would be quite disproportionate to the conduct's value for us. This we may fail to appreciate, not because we are incapable of it, but because of our lack of discipline, our impulsiveness, or our tendency to rationalize the risks involved. It would not take much to act more prudently, yet we are inclined to negligence.

It is against this background that the Argument from Personal Integrity operates. Where our conduct or choices place our more permanent, stable, and central projects in jeopardy, and where what comes to expression in this conduct or these choices manifests aspects of our personality that do not rank highly in our constellation of desires, dispositions, etc., benevolent interference will constitute no violation of integrity. Indeed, if anything, it helps to preserve it. Though it acknowledges the liberal ideal of individuality, it works with a more differentiated and less abstract conception of the self than is customary in liberal thinking. Not only do we have a diversity of aims, preferences, wants, and so on, but they vary in the status we accord them so far as our core identity and life-plans are concerned. We can differentiate passing and settled desires, major and minor projects, central and peripheral concerns, valued and disvalued habits and dispositions. Our conduct and choices may reflect any of these, though not necessarily in a way that matches their ranking in our hierarchy of values and concerns. The settled may give way to the passing, the major to the minor, the central to the peripheral, the valued to the disvalued. The argument in question maintains that where a course of conduct would, in response to some peripheral or lowly ranked tendency, threaten disproportionate disruption to highly ranked concerns, paternalistic grounds for intervention have a legitimate place. Strong, no less than weak, paternalism may thus find a toe hold.

So much for the argument's general outline. We can flesh it out by considering some of the objections it is likely to attract. For a start, adherents of the Argument from Oppression of Individuality will want to complain that it flies in the face of the very ends it proclaims. To interfere with a person's voluntary conduct for paternalistic reasons is to supplant that person's own judgment, it is to set his evaluations and determinations at naught, to treat him merely as an instrument, a vehicle for the paternalist's altruism, and not as a project-maker in his own right. So it will be claimed. But in this form the charge is somewhat unfair. From the fact that the paternalist has an interest in the other's interests, it does not follow that the other's interests are being made subservient to the interests of the paternalist. For the paternalist may be motivated and directed by a concern for the *other's* relatively permanent and highly ranked projects, and not by his or her own conception of what would be in the other's best interest.

A defender of the Argument from Oppression of Individuality is not likely to be convinced by this disclaimer, for it will be rejoined that by intervening the paternalist *is* thwarting at least *one* of the other's projects, the one that is believed to be jeopardizing the rest. This can be admitted. But it will be counterclaimed that in interfering the paternalist is doing no more than reflecting a tension that already exists between the other's projects, in which the pursuit of one is placing the others at risk. Further, it will be insisted that the direction taken by the intervention accords with the other's ordering (even if not present choice) of projects. There is, therefore, no violation of integrity or life-plans. The paternalist is neither determining what ends are constitutive of the other's good nor ranking those ends, but giving them effect in the face of certain character failings. Although the person interfered with can be held responsible for such failings, preventing them from having their worst effects does not violate that person's integrity. The paternalism here is not moralistic. No alien values are imported

• • •

Now the kinds of character deficiencies of which I have been speaking in out-lining the Argument from Personal Integrity represent a falling short of full vol-untariness in the comparative sense, but do not (necessarily) divest one of responsibility in the absolute sense. More often they render us objects of legit-imate criticism. If, through carelessness or weakness of will, we come to grief, it might properly be said that we have only ourselves to blame. The respon-sibility is ours; the deficiency explains but does not excuse. Certainly we may become objects of others' sympathy rather than condemnation if the conse-quences of our shortcomings are very serious, but this is because the conse-quences are out of all proportion to the failing. Even though they have only themselves to blame, there is something callous about saying of motorcyclists who kill themselves or suffer massive injuries through not wearing a helmet that it "served them right."

In suggesting that paternalistic intervention might be justified where, as a re-sult of some character deficiency, a person places his or her life-plans in jeop-ardy, it is not my intention to imply that grounds for paternalistic intervention would exist only rarely. All too often the carelessness or impulsiveness that jeopardizes a person's projects has gained a firm albeit somewhat unwelcome foothold in a person's character, and may display itself with some frequency. This does not mean that a strong ground for paternalism exists in every case, for it is often better, so far as the person's own development is concerned, that he or she bears the cost of failure to bring projects to completion. But some-times the consequences of failure may be so serious that something stronger than persuasion might be called for. The student who is strongly tempted, just before his or her final exams, to "throw it in," may need to be "sat upon" rather than simply advised and pleaded with. If we know, as we may, that the failure to go through with the exams would be a source of serious and continuing re-gret and considerable personal loss, something stronger than rational pressure may reasonably be called for.

This, no doubt, will trouble the antipaternalist. Why not accept people as they are with all their complexities and internal tensions, regretting the mess they sometimes make of their lives but not intruding to the point of liberty-diminishing interference? Does it really show respect for their integrity, their in-dividuality, if only part of their person is permitted to express itself? These are serious questions, and a defender of the Argument from Personal Integrity can-not brush them aside. There is a cost involved in strong paternalism—the pa-ternalist takes a moral risk, and the demand for justification is an especially strong one. But it may be met. For the person who is interfered with, the proper response may be gratitude rather than resentment or forgiveness—a recogni-tion that the intrusion expressed a sympathetic identification with his or her core aims and attitudes rather than officious intermeddling or disguised ma-nipulation. While it is true that respect for a person's integrity or individuality must allow for the fragile complexity that this sometimes involves, it needs also to recognize the hierarchy of values through which this complexity is mediated. It is one thing to interfere with a person whose twin ambitions are excellence as a philosopher and mountain climber; it is another to interfere with a person whose philosophical (or mountain-climbing!) ambitions are put at unnecessary risk because he or she can't be bothered to put on a seat belt. It is cases of the latter rather than former sort that fall within the purview of the Argument from Personal Integrity.

Nevertheless, as I have stated, there is some cost involved, just because a constraint has been placed on voluntary conduct. It would be a better world were such paternalism not necessary, just as it would be a better world were punishment not sometimes called for. Paternalism is not something to evangelistic about. It is not a substitute for persuasion and education, but a strategy of last resort. Like punishment, it is something that, though justified, we would like to see less of, something there are strong moral reasons for seeking to eliminate the need for. However, provided that it is limited to those character deficiencies, and those expressions of them, that place at unnecessary risk the aims and activities that are intimately connected with our self-identity, its use can be justified.

But there is still more to be said on the antipaternalist side. It may be granted that paternalism can accord with a person's settled and long-term interests and thus not undermine individuality. Nevertheless, the person interfered with may feel peculiarly put out by the imposition: "Who do you think you are?" "By virtue of what right or authority do you decide what I shall do?" "What is your standing, such that you can impose on me?" "What business is it of yours?" "What has it got to do with you?" Just as the person who deserves to be punished may feel offended that some particular person should take it into his or her hands to inflict it, a similar offense may be felt by the person on whom some paternalistic constraint is placed.

There are weak and strong versions of this objection. According to the weak version, the issue is one of the precise relationship between the paternalist and paternalized. Where there is some sort of close relationship between them—as in friendship—there has been an acknowledgment of goodwill and concern. Even though paternalistic intrusions have not been written into such relationships in the form of prior consent, they might nevertheless constitute an acceptable expression of the values embodied in the relationship. It is one thing for one's wife to take a paternalistic interest in one's diet[10] . . . , it is another for a stranger, however well-meaning, to do so. In the first case, a relationship has been entered into, and a certain complex of values realized thereby; if the intrusion undermines those values or disrupts them too much, the relationship may be weakened or terminated. This is a risk that the paternalistic party must take. In the second case, there are no bonds of affection to sustain and give redeeming significance to the interference, no inbuilt sanctions that would discriminate it from officious intermeddling, and if the paternalistic agent is as powerful as the state, there may be no escape or redress.

The weak version demands, but does not preclude the possibility of, standing. However, it severely circumscribes it. Friends, lovers, and those to whom

---

[10] Douglas Neil Husak. "Paternalism and Autonomy," *Philosophy & Public Affairs* 10 (Winter) 1981: 45.

one stands in a fiduciary relationship may be morally positioned to take such risks; strangers will not. The situation of the state is morally ambiguous, and our understanding may be dependent on both circumstance and background understanding. Those of a Bosanquetian bent may grant it standing[11] . . . ; those possessing a more individualistic metaphysics may see the state as little more than an alien other. To choose between these (and various other) positions would take us too far afield, though perhaps that is not the most helpful way to think about the issue. In so far as the state is seen as a locus of both authority and power, its standing may be ineliminably ambiguous.

The strong version denies the possibility of standing, except where consent has been given. Whatever the wisdom or benefit of intervention, strong paternalism is seen as an inexcusable (though not necessarily unforgivable) moral trespass, an unjustified violation of individual rights. On this view, the standing that is acquired by virtue of the capacity to determine and pursue one's own good is like that acquired when the title to a piece of land passes into one's hands: there is a boundary that may not be crossed save by invitation of the title holder. So long as the property is not used in a manner detrimental to others' interest, the boundary acts as a "side constraint" [12] . . . on their conduct. This standing does not operate simply as a consideration to be taken into account by others, to be weighed or played off against, and perhaps overridden by, other considerations, such as beneficence, but it functions as a restriction on their reach. It is part of what it is to be a person in a world of persons that entry into this sphere may be made only with consent. The paternalist is to be charged with confusing a legitimate concern for others (which may lead to and justify admonition or remonstration) with a respect for their sovereignty (which limits the expression of concern to conduct falling short of imposition).

It is, however, one thing to assert individual sovereignty, with its implication that enforced benevolence would be morally *ultra vires*. It is another to establish this role for it. It is one thing to assert that this sovereignty is warranted in virtue of the individual's capacity to make his or her own choices, and that this is in *no way* contingent on what is chosen (so long as it is self-regarding). It is another thing to explain why *no* exceptions are endurable. Is it part of the very meaning of "sovereignty"? In that case, why does the capacity for self-development demand sovereignty over self? Is it because choices have a value in their own right? Dworkin suggests as much, when interpreting Mill: "To be able to choose is a good that is independent of the wisdom of what is chosen" . . .[13] But if that is so, the capacity to make one's own choice does not generate a side constraint on the conduct of others, but functions simply as an independent value, possibly to be outweighed by the unwisdom of what is chosen. Antipaternalists have wanted it to carry more weight than that—to see it

[11] Bernard Bosanquet. *The Philosophical Theory of the State.* (London: Macmillan, 1899), p. 186–7.

[12] Robert Nozick. *Anarchy, State, and Utopia.* (London: Blackwell, 1974), Chapter 3.

[13] Gerald Dworkin. "Paternalism" in *Morality and the Law,* ed. Richard Wasserstrom. (Belmont, CA: Wadsworth, 1971), p. 117.

as not just a value but a principle, constituting a framework within which the balancing or trading off of values can take place. But can the standing this demands for individual choice be sustained?

There is a very important insight informing the strong account of standing. It is that morality is not chiefly concerned with the realization or maximization of values or something of that sort, but with the quality of relationship that exists between persons, whether individually or collectively. A "morality" that takes as its fundamental commitment the maximization of utility or value views the individuals who are bearers or creators of that utility or value as essentially anonymous, potentially replaceable instruments in its realization. They are no longer personalized individuals, and the relations they bear to each other are not judged in terms of the quality they have as relations between persons, but in terms of the utility or value realized. The individual persons vanish, to be replaced by some value, which, it so happens, requires as the precondition for its realization its origination (for the most part) in free choice.

The standing that one has in virtue of the capacity to make one's own choices thus reflects a profoundly *moral* attitude. It recognizes the fundamental concern that morality has with personal relationships. Yet even so, it is not obvious that the demands of autarchy/autonomy constitute a strict *side* constraint. For what is it that one respects when one respects the individuality of an other? Is it any and every free choice, or is it those free choices that manifest the other's established and valued concerns—the other's integrity? It is not to voluntary choices as such that liberalism is committed, but to the persons who express themselves in their choices. Where choices having marginal significance to a person's settled life-plans and values threaten serious disruption to their realization, we do not violate their integrity in interfering with them. This, admittedly, is a risky business, for, as we have already observed, people are generally better placed to know what accords with their own conception of good and their voluntary choices provide strong evidence that what they are doing will further it. Nevertheless, the evidence is not decisive, and risking unjustifiable offense may be called for. Relationships without risk are likely to be relationships without moral depth.

I have argued that proponents of the Arguments from Oppression of Individuality and Disrespect for Persons tend to see the individual too monochromatically. We can add a further dimension to this criticism by reflecting on the "ontology" of the individual person. There is a tendency for defenders of these arguments to see people in terms of their immediate presentation, and to abstract expressed desires from the individual of whom they are an expression. There is a tendency to give full sovereignty to the present free decision, no matter how badly it sits with the individual's other pursuits, ideals, beliefs, and plans. But individuals are continuants—existents who persist through time, having a past and future as well as a present. This is not simply a function of their physiology but of their personal life, which does not (usually) focus exclusively on the present, but reaches backward and forward in expectations, ongoing projects, life-plans, and so on. Recognition of the individuality of others, then, is not some respect for bare voluntary choices or rational choosers in an abstract sense, but for continuants whose capacities have found concrete expression in ongoing projects, life-plans, etc., and who in day-to-day decision-making can be expected to work within the framework they provide. But as we know, sometimes to our continuing regret, we are often disposed to act in ways that are perilous to the projects and plans that are partially constitutive of our identity. Where this is so, paternalism may not be violative of integrity.

It is a corollary of the Argument from Personal Integrity that any impositions it sanctions will be relatively minor. . . . Though they will impede or even prevent the risk-taking activity, they will not interfere with the individual's significant pursuits. It is for this reason that seat belt and safety helmet legislation has found considerable support. . . . But . . . we need to be careful when making claims of this kind. Whether a restriction is trivial is not independent of the beliefs, purposes, temperament, life-plans, etc. of the person interfered with. What is seen as a minor inconvenience by one person may be seen as a major intrusion by another. For most English people, the requirement to wear a safety helmet when travelling on a motorcycle was at worst a nuisance, but for the local Sikh population it was viewed as a serious encroachment on religious freedom. Hence Mill's comment, in relation to the person who, after warning, still chooses to cross the unsafe bridge, that "no one but the person himself can judge of the sufficiency of the motive that may prompt him to incur the risk" . . .[14] Though Mill overstates the point, it provides a salutary warning against the assumption that judgments of triviality can be made without regard to people's life-plans. What may be said in favor of seat belt and safety helmet legislation is that they are unlikely to provide a substantial impediment to most people's pursuits, and that where they do, it should be possible to make legislative provision for this.

One interesting consequence of the Argument from Personal Integrity is that the ardent antipaternalist may be spared its paternalistic conclusion. If it is of great importance to a person that his or her liberty be maximized, then any paternalistic imposition will be experienced as a gross intrusion, not because of what it directly requires or prohibits, but because it violates a central commitment. With such a person it may not be legitimate to do more than remonstrate.

---

[14] Mill, p. 294.

13.
Government and Good Lives
GEORGE SHER

IV

Let us now turn to the value-of-autonomy argument itself. At least in broad outline, that argument is very familiar. Bruce Ackerman, who characterizes it as one of "several weighty arguments in support of neutrality,"[1] summarizes it this way:

> Even if you don't think you need to experiment, you may adopt a conception of the good that gives a central place to autonomous deliberation and deny that it is possible to *force* a person to be good. On this view, the intrusion of non-Neutral argument into power talk will seem self-defeating at best— since it threatens to divert people from the true means of cultivating a truly good life.[2]

In a similar vein, David A. J. Richards first postulates "a general right of personal autonomy,"[3] but then goes on to write that "[t]he neutrality, in Dworkin's sense, of this right, among a wide number of visions of the good life, arises from its source in the value of autonomy."[4] And while Mill tends to present the case against government interference in people's lives as resting on the value of individuality rather than autonomy, similar reasoning can be extracted from various passages in *On Liberty*.[5]

Familiar though it is, however, the idea that governments can always promote the most value by allowing citizens to exercise their own autonomy is extremely puzzling. Perhaps the most obvious problem is that even if autonomy has great value, it hardly follows (and is almost certainly false) that autonomy is the *only* thing with value. Indeed, on the account of autonomy just defended—an agent acts autonomously when he acts in response to reasons provided by his situation—the claim that nothing except autonomy has value *must* be false. It must be false because an agent cannot respond to a reason for pursuing X unless there *is* a reason for him to pursue X, and there cannot be such

---

[1] Bruce Ackerman, *Social Justice in the Liberal State* (New Haven: Yale University Press, 1980), p. 11

[2] Ibid.

[3] David A. J. Richards, "Human Rights and Moral Ideals: An Essay on the Moral Theory of Liberalism," *Social Theory and Practice* 5, 3–4 (1980), p. 474.

[4] Ibid.

[5] Here I have in mind not only some of what Mill says about individuality in Chapter 3 of *On Liberty*—see for example, his remarks about Calvinism—but also his emphasis in Chapter 2 on the importance of understanding the grounds for one's beliefs.

a reason unless his pursuing or attaining X either has intrinsic value or has acquired value from its relation to something else.[6] Because one cannot respond to a reason unless there is some value that gives rise to that reason, it is inconsistent to hold both that autonomy is responsiveness to reasons and that autonomy is the only thing with value.

Yet if autonomy is *not* the only thing with value—if it is only one good thing among others—then exactly how can its value justify neutralism? Even if promoting other values invariably undermines autonomy, why must governments always resolve the dilemma in autonomy's favor? If governments or their agents have well-grounded beliefs that citizens' lives are improved by close and committed family relationships, or that the breakdown of public civility is a bad thing, why shouldn't they promote public civility or the family even at the cost of sacrificing some autonomy? Or, again, why shouldn't they sacrifice some autonomy to promote such values as high culture or communal solidarity? There actually are two cases to consider, since either the value of autonomy is commensurable with these other values or it is not. But if the values are not commensurable, then nothing follows about how governments should choose between autonomy and other values; while if they are commensurable, then the conclusion seems to be that governments should *not* promote autonomy if they can do more good by promoting other values. Either way, the inference from the value of autonomy to neutralism appears to fail.[7]

Is there any way to rescue it short of retreating to the untenable view that autonomy is the only thing with value? One possibility, suggested by Ackerman, is that it is "not necessary for autonomy to be the only good thing; it suffices for it to be the best thing that there is."[8] Here Ackerman's thought appears to be that if autonomy is better than anything else—as he believes it to be—then governments can never reasonably promote other values at its expense. Yet even if autonomy *is* the best thing there is, the amount of value a government can produce by promoting it may still be smaller than the amount of value that can be produced by promoting more of something less valuable. Thus, to rule out the possibility of trade-offs, the value of autonomy must be prior in some stronger sense.

Can a stronger priority claim be made out? Although I know of no neutralist who has squarely addressed this question, one possibility, at least, seems worth exploring. This is the suggestion that autonomy is *internally* connected to the other values that appear to call for trade-offs—that, in other words, the value of superior ways of life resides not merely in (say) their intrinsic nature, but rather in their being chosen *because* of that nature. On this account, the values of family, culture, community, and the rest will not be competitors to autonomy, but rather will presuppose it; for lives involving close family ties,

---

[6] Here I assume, of course, that the case is not one in which *duty* supplies a reason to pursue X.

[7] Hurka notices this problem in "Why Value Autonomy?" *Social Theory and Practice*, Vol. 13, No. 3 (Fall 1987), p. 377.

[8] Ackerman, *Social Justice in the Liberal State,* p. 368.

culture, and community will be valuable only when (or only to the extent that) they are adopted *for the reasons provided by their value.*

Is this suggestion coherent? At first glance, it may seem not to be; for it asserts both that whether a way of life is valuable depends on whether it is autonomously chosen and that whether a way of life is autonomously chosen depends on whether it has independent value. Given this circularity, we may seem unable to make determinations of either autonomy or value. Yet despite initial appearances, the circularity need not be vicious. To tame it, we need only say, first, that when we call a way of life independently valuable, what we mean is that it *would* have actual value if it were chosen autonomously and, second, that choosing it autonomously is choosing it precisely because one recognizes this potentiality. To mark this complication, I shall henceforth speak not simply of responding to value but of responding to (potential) value.

Like the idea that autonomy is responsiveness to reasons, the idea that only autonomously chosen ways of life have value is not new. Although Lawrence Haworth does not recognize the complication just discussed, he plainly implies that at least some values presuppose autonomy when he writes:

> What is there to value in a community of shared values when the members of the community are automata? The fact of sharing or of being mutually devoted to a transcendent or collective good commands respect only to the extent that the members of the community participate autonomously—to the extent that each, by joining with the rest in a collective pursuit, is living his own life, pursuing his (procedurally) own conception of the good.[9]

Will Kymlicka makes the same point in more general terms when he writes that "no life goes better by being led from the outside according to values the person doesn't endorse. My life only gets better if I'm leading it from the inside, according to my beliefs about value."[10] Moreover, the view we are considering—that some ways of life are better than others, but that even the (potentially) best lack value if not chosen for the right reasons—is the exact structural analogue of Kant's famous view that some sorts of actions are morally better than others, but that even the (potentially) best lack moral value if not performed for the right reasons.

This view immediately opens up new possibilities. If only autonomously chosen activities can have value, then any government that tries to increase the value of its citizens' activities at the expense of their autonomy will merely destroy the conditions under which their activities can *be* valuable. Because of this, a person's activities will always lack value when his government has induced him to pursue them nonautonomously; but they will *not* always lack

---

[9] Lawrence Haworth, *Autonomy: An Essay in Philosophical Psychology and Ethics* (New Haven: Yale University Press, 1986), p. 208. For a similar suggestion, see Hurka, "Why Value Autonomy?" p. 378.

[10] Will Kymlicka, *Liberalism, Community and Culture* (Oxford: Oxford University Press, 1989), p. 12.

value when his government has *not* induced him to pursue them nonautonomously. Under these conditions, one's chances of living a valuable life may indeed be best if one's government interferes least with one's autonomy.[11]

It should now be clear why the value-of-autonomy argument must treat autonomy as responsiveness to reasons. We just saw that that argument will not succeed if there can be trade-offs between autonomy and other values. We saw, as well, that the only way to rule out such trade-offs is to hold that no activity can have value unless it is chosen on the basis *of* its (potential) value. Since this way of saving the argument equates being chosen autonomously with being chosen on the basis of (potential) value, it in effect presupposes a responsiveness-to-reasons account of autonomy. Of course, the reasons provided by an activity's (potential) value need not exhaust the reasons for engaging in it, so this version of the responsiveness-to-reasons account does not exactly match the one developed earlier. Still, as long as the current version also requires that the reasons provided by (potential) value exceed a certain level of strength, it can be viewed as an especially stringent variant of the original.

The harder question, of course, is whether it is *true* that only autonomously chosen activities can have value. Certainly that premise is not universally accepted. Against it, some would maintain that there is value even (or especially) in unquestioning obedience to (divine or human) authority. Others would insist that certain specific ways of behaving—for example, premarital chastity and marital fidelity—are best no matter *what* the agent's reasons. Of course, the mere fact of disagreement settles nothing, since it may be the dissenters who are mistaken; but right or wrong, their view does not seem absurd. Thus, the premise that only autonomously chosen activities have value is itself in need of defense.

V

Fortunately, we need not decide whether it can be defended; for the argument from the value of autonomy—or, as we now might more accurately call it, the argument from autonomy's contribution *to* value—breaks down decisively at another point. To succeed, that argument must presuppose not merely that only autonomously chosen activities have value, but also that when governments try to induce citizens to choose valuable activities, the resulting choices never *are* autonomous. Yet whatever we say about the first premise, the second is clearly false.

---

[11] As David Christensen has pointed out to me, the reasoning of this paragraph presupposes that autonomy is an all-or-nothing matter. If instead autonomy is a matter of degree, then even policies that do diminish autonomy may increase people's chances of living valuable lives. In particular, this will be possible whenever (1) a policy does not undermine a person's autonomy enough to prevent his choices from actualizing any (potential) value, and (2) it leads him to choose activities that are much more (potentially) valuable than any alternatives. This rejoinder is significant because responsiveness to reasons (and hence, on my account, autonomy) does seem to be a matter of degree. However, in the discussion to follow, I shall forgo this objection in favor of others.

In the remainder of this chapter, I shall argue this point in some detail. First, though, I must specify more precisely what needs to be shown. . . . A government can promote (what it considers) a valuable form of life in at least four ways. It can (1) threaten to punish those who reject that form of life; (2) offer citizens incentives to accept it; (3) nonrationally cause them to acquire a preference for it; or (4) create institutions or social forms that make the favored way of life possible or enable it to flourish. Because the most interesting version of neutralism forbids all four methods of promoting good lives, we could block the current argument for that version merely by showing that *one* of those methods can issue in autonomous choices. But if we showed only this much, we would leave open the possibility of invoking autonomy's contribution to value to establish a weaker version of neutralism. To foreclose this possibility, I shall try to show that *all four* methods of promoting valuable lives can issue in autonomous choices.

Consider, first, policies aimed at nonrationally causing citizens to acquire or retain preferences for (what the policy makers consider) good lives. Although their actual rationales are no doubt mixed, many current policies appear to have this aim among others. These policies encompass the use of "directive" techniques of moral education, including exhortation, reward, punishment, and personal example, to cause students to acquire desirable habits and preferences. They also include employing the techniques of advertising to instill an aversion to drug use and other unwholesome activities; encouraging writers to portray women in nonstereotyped ways; hiring workers who are positive "role models" for persons with low aspirations; making work a condition of public assistance to alter the habits of recipients; and trying to reform criminals by incarcerating them. To simplify the discussion, I shall simply assume that some such policies do nonrationally cause people to acquire new preferences. Granting this, the question is whether those preferences can issue in autonomous choices.

Given our analysis of autonomy, the answer may at first seem to be a clear no. For suppose a government's policies do nonrationally cause a citizen C to prefer a way of life W; and suppose, further, that C's choice of W is motivated by the preference that is thus caused. Because that preference is, by hypothesis, not a response to any reason for preferring W, C's choice of W must also not be a response to any such reason. However, according to our account of autonomy, an autonomous choice just *is* a choice that is made in response to good reason. Hence, it may seem to follow immediately that nonrational conditioning cannot issue in autonomous choices.

I shall explain shortly what I take to be wrong with this argument. First, though, I want to discuss briefly a response that we should *not* make. We saw earlier that even if neither being married nor being single has any inherent value, the fact that X wants to marry Y can itself give X a good reason to marry Y. We saw, further, that if X does choose to marry Y for this reason, X's choice can indeed be autonomous. But if so, then it may seem that C's choice of W can similarly qualify as autonomous; for even if C's preference for W is not *grounded* in a good reason to adopt W, that preference itself may *provide* C with such a reason. If it does, then C's choice of W will indeed be grounded in a good reason and, hence, will be made autonomously, as long as C chooses W in response to the reason that is thus provided.

The problem with this rejoinder is that it ignores the special requirements imposed by the current context. Because our aim is to find out whether C's choice of W can actualize W's (potential) value, our question is not merely whether C's choice of W is autonomous in the sense of being a response to *some* sufficiently strong reason. Instead, it is whether C's choice of W satisfies the more stringent requirement of being a response to a sufficiently strong reason *that is provided by W's potential value*. Of course, the mere fact that C's immediate reason is his preference for W does not show that C is *not* responding to W's (potential) value; for many preferences are themselves grounded in deeper reasons. But because C's preference for W has by hypothesis been nonrationally instilled, that cannot be the case here. Hence, for present purposes, C's choice of W must indeed be nonautonomous.

This, I think, is (one of) the grain(s) of truth in the widely held view that nonrationally influencing people's preferences undermines their autonomy. But although the point is not insubstantial, it falls far short of establishing that governments can not induce their citizens to live valuable lives by nonrationally influencing their preferences. To establish that, one would have to show not merely that C's *initial* choice of W is nonautonomous, but also that its lack of autonomy infects any *further* choices to which it leads. Yet even if C does choose W nonautonomously at t_1, his resulting later choice(s) of W may surely have a different status. Precisely *by* living the life he was nonrationally caused to prefer, C may become increasingly aware of the value-based reasons for living that way. He may come to appreciate W's (potential) value "from the inside." By putting C in a position to do this, his choosing W at t_1 may enable him to respond at t_2 to the reasons provided by W's (potential) value. If at t_2 C does choose W on the basis, then C's nonrational conditioning *will* have led him to choose W in a way that actualizes its (potential) value.

This is far more than a bare logical possibility. We have all known students who were first influenced to take up a subject by a respected teacher, but who later made it their life's work because they recognized its beauty or depth, or because they were challenged by its puzzles. We also know people who at first acted truthfully and fairly to avoid punishment or to please their parents, but who now act in these ways because they recognize the interests of others. In these and many other cases, the agent's behavior eventually acquires whatever value his initial failure to respond to the appropriate reasons may have caused it to lack. Even if the later behavior is overdetermined—even if either the original nonrationally acquired preference *or* the agent's new appreciation of reasons would now be sufficient to motivate it—there is no reason to deny that it has value.[12] And the same holds, mutatis mutandis, of the behavior of citizens who have come to appreciate the reasons for continuing to live in the ways that they were nonrationally caused to prefer.

[12] For pertinent discussion, see George Sher and William J. Bennett, "Moral Education and Indoctrination," *Journal of Philosophy* 79, 11 (November 1982), pp. 665–77.

Thus, nonrationally induced preferences can indeed lead individuals to make choices that are autonomous enough to actualize the (potential) value of what is chosen. But what, next, of *incentives* to adopt (potentially) valuable ways of life? Although incentives are less widely regarded as threats to autonomy than conditioning, they too provide reasons for choosing that are unconnected to the (potential) value of what is chosen. Hence, choices motivated by incentives must also lack the autonomy that (we are assuming) is alone capable of actualizing (potential) value. Indeed, in one respect, incentives are actually *more* inimical to autonomy than nonrational conditioning; for while preferences instilled by conditioning can generally coexist with the appreciation of (potential) value, incentives are apt to divert attention from the (potential) value of what they make attractive. In this way, incentives can actively prevent agents from responding to (potential) value.[13]

Here again, however, an influence that does not at first lead someone to choose something for the right reasons may in the longer run do precisely that. Like choices based on nonrationally conditioned preferences, choices that are directed at incentives, and hence are unconnected to the (potential) value of what is chosen, may themselves put agents in a position to appreciate that (potential) value "from the inside." If as a result an agent subsequently does respond to an activity's (potential) value, the incentive *will* indirectly have led him to choose it autonomously. Moreover, while incentives admittedly can divert attention from value-based reasons, they can also cancel the effects of counter-incentives that otherwise would themselves divert attention from such reasons. For example, by subsidizing artistic projects, a government can reduce the need for artists to undertake commercial ventures, and thus can free them to respond to more purely aesthetic considerations.

Our third method of promoting valuable activities—the creation and sustenance of valuable options—may seen even less threatening to autonomy. Unlike its predecessors, this method does not seem even to diminish anyone's *present* ability to respond to value-based reasons. Instead, when governments codify and enforce what they consider potentially valuable types of arrangements—when, for example, they extend official approval and protection to monogamous but not polygamous marriages—they appear only to enrich the array of value-based reasons to which their citizens may respond. Hence, this method of promoting valuable activities may seem entirely unproblematical.

But on closer inspection, the issue is not this simple; for, as Jeremy Waldron has argued, "[t]he decision to favor one type of relationship with a legal framework but not another artificially distorts people's estimate of which sort of relationship is morally preferable."[14] To make this estimate without distortion,

---

[13] Compare Jeremy Waldron: "The trouble with a perfectionist tax is that it provides a reason for refraining from an activity that is not one of what I have called 'the merits' of the case. A subsidy would be objectionable on similar grounds if it were so substantial as to provide a positive inducement to an activity thought to be noble. We would then worry because people were responding, not to the nobility of the activity, but to the bribe that was being offered for pursuing it" (Waldron, "Autonomy and Perfectionism in Raz's *Morality of Freedom*," *Southern California Law Review* 62 [1989], p. 1147).

[14] Ibid., p. 1151.

[E]veryone who chooses to live with another and to make a life together has to contemplate the possibility that things may go wrong. The relationship may break up or one of the partners may die, and then property and financial entanglements will have to be sorted out. One of the partners may fall ill. . . . Even if things do not go wrong, they may be complicated. A child may be born, and questions will then arise about who should take care of it and make decisions about its future.[15]

Thus, to choose monogamy autonomously, one must do so (at least partly) because it generates fewer complications than polygamy. However, in sanctioning monogamous but not polygamous marriages, "[t]he government has decided on the basis of its estimate of these factors to distort the matter by making it *even easier* for monogamous couples to sort these problems out than for polygamists."[16] By thus making it more difficult to respond to monogamy's true measure of (potential) value, a government does reduce the chances that its citizens will choose it autonomously.

Although I doubt that monogamy's (potential) value has much to do with the relative ease with which monogamists can "sort out problems," Waldron may be right to say that governments that recognize only monogamous marriages provide what amount to artificial incentives to choose monogamy over polygamy. But even if he is right, this will hardly save the case for neutralism. The reason, of course, is that in that case, the same considerations that showed that *incentives* can induce citizens to respond to (potential) value will also show this about the state's attempts to create new options. Thus, even if this third method of inducing citizens to live good lives is no less threatening to autonomy than the first two, it is at least no more threatening either.

VI

I have now discussed three of the four ways in which governments can use their power to promote the good. The fourth way—the use of threats and force—will be considered shortly. However, before I turn to it, I must consider the objection that even if the first three methods sometimes do lead citizens to choose the good autonomously, they do not do so often enough to tip the balance against neutralism.

This objection trades on two concessions that were made earlier. I conceded above that only *some* of the persons who are induced by nonrational conditioning or incentives to adopt (potentially) valuable ways of life will eventually respond to their (potential) value. I conceded, as well, that the choices that stem more immediately from nonrationally conditioned preferences and incentives are *not* autonomous in the relevant sense. But given these concessions, can't a neutralist still insist that many people's lives will have more value if their government does *not* try to shape their preferences or provide them with incentives?

[15] Ibid.
[16] Ibid.

And, hence, isn't the consequentialist case for rejecting neutralism inconclusive at best?

I think, in fact, that this suggestion badly underestimates our ability to make reasonable predictions. While not all incentives or nonrationally induced preferences are equally likely to increase an agent's later responsiveness to (potential) value, we can say a good deal about the conditions under which these effects are likely. Where those conditions are met, there is every reason to believe that the agent's later choices will actualize enough (potential) value to outweigh any earlier losses.

But this is not the main problem with the current suggestion. A further (and in my view more decisive) difficulty is that no government can *avoid* either nonrationally shaping its citizens' preferences or providing them with incentives. Even if governments do not try to produce these effects, they are bound to occur as unintended consequences of many political arrangements—including, importantly, many arrangements that are adopted for quite different reasons. It was, indeed, precisely this sort of fact that led us to interpret neutralism as ruling out not all political arrangements with value-promoting *effects,* but rather all political reasoning that *appeals to* such effects. By taking neutralism to forbid only the adoption of political arrangements *because* they will issue in preferences or incentives that favor certain ways of life, we can acknowledge that all political arrangements will have such effects without concluding that it is impossible to be a neutralist.

But the same considerations that compelled this reinterpretation now suggest that if a government knows which ways of living are (potentially) best, it can definitely increase overall value through the judicious use of conditioning and incentives. The reason, in brief, is that if all political arrangements do nonrationally shape preferences and provide incentives, a government will not *further* diminish autonomy simply by producing these effects intentionally. It will only further diminish autonomy if it shapes preferences or provides incentives in ways that undermine responsiveness to reasons more than it would be undermined in any event. Thus, if a government makes no effort to promote value by conditioning preferences and providing incentives, the result will be no gain in autonomy, but only a lessening in the number of citizens who live in the ways that the government considers (potentially) valuable. Since by hypothesis those ways of life *are* (potentially) valuable, this means that fewer citizens will be put in a position to appreciate their (potential) value from the inside, and hence that fewer citizens will eventually respond to it. Thus, the ultimate effect of neutralism will be to prevent at least some citizens from living valuable lives.[17]

---

[17] In making this argument, I assume that however much conditioning interferes with autonomy, it does leave room for at least some autonomous choices. Some thinkers, such as B. F. Skinner, reject this assumption; see, for example, Skinner, *Beyond Freedom and Dignity* (New York: Knopf, 1971). If a neutralist followed Skinner in rejecting it but retained the premise that only autonomously chosen lives have value, he could recast his argument by inferring, first, that all attempts to promote valuable ways of life are doomed and, second, that any available funds should be spent in pursuit of more achievable aims. But in addition to invoking (what I take to be) an extremely implausible premise, this move would transform what began as an appeal to the value of autonomy into an appeal to its impossibility. This would entirely fail to capture the argument's original intent.

VII

Far from ruling out all four methods of promoting valuable ways of life, autonomy's contribution to value has been found to be compatible with at least three. But we have yet to consider its bearing on what many regard as the core thesis of neutralism. This, of course, is the thesis that governments should never us force (or threats of force) to promote ways of life they consider valuable, or to deter behavior that does not harm others but is viewed as ignoble, base, or degraded. A prohibition against such "legal moralism" is sometimes regarded as the sole consequence of the appeal to autonomy's (contribution to) value, and is always regarded as its most important consequences.

It is not hard to see why. Although threats do not so much undermine responsiveness to reasons as alter the reasons to which agents can respond, threats resemble incentives and conditioned preferences in that none of the choices that they motivate are grounded in the (potential) value of what is chosen. Hence, no such choices can be autonomous in the sense that concerns us. Moreover, in addition to being just as destructive to autonomy as the other methods, the use of force is much easier for governments to avoid. While eliminating one form of conditioning only opens the way for others, and while removing one incentive may only make others more attractive, a government that decriminalizes one class of acts need not compensate by criminalizing another. Although every government needs some criminal justice system, governments may punish their citizens for wider or narrower ranges of activities. Hence, if a government does not pass laws against (what it considers) base, ignoble, or degrading behavior, it will genuinely reduce the number or reasons that compete with the reasons provided by (potential) value.

In view of this, it is not surprising that the second premise of the argument designed to ground neutralism in autonomy's contribution to value—the premise that government efforts to promote good lives do not lead to autonomous choices—is most often couched in terms of threats or force.[18] Thus construed, the premise asserts that it is either useless or self-defeating for a government to force its citizens to lead good lives because any activity that is undertaken to avoid punishment is *ex hypothesi* not undertaken because of its (potential) value. Yet while this version of the premise may be less decisively false than its predecessors, it is vulnerable to essentially the same reply: that even if a choice is not itself a response to (potential) value, it may contribute to further choices that *are* responses to (potential) value.

Before I elaborate the reply as it applies to threats and coercion, it may again be helpful to introduce some examples. Many laws forbid or seriously restrict activities that do not harm others in any straightforward way. These activities

---

[18] To cite just one example, Will Kymlicka seems mainly concerned with threats and force when he writes that "[s]ince lives have to be led from the inside, someone's essential interest in leading a life that is in fact good is not advanced when society penalizes, or discriminates against, the projects that she, on reflection, believes are most valuable for her" (Kymlicka, "Rawls on Teleology and Deontology," *Philosophy and Public Affairs* 17, 3 [Summer 198], p. 186). Kymlicka suggests that similar claims are attributable to Mill, Rawls, Nozick, and Ronald Dworkin (ibid., p. 187 n. 20).

include, among others, copulating in public places, defecating in public, using profane language on television or radio, selling bodily organs, selling babies, gambling, and using narcotic drugs. Although some of the laws clearly have non-perfectionist aims—human waste endangers health, gambling and narcotics are said to attract organized crime[19]—they also appear to be informed by a widely shared vision of what sorts of lives are decent and worthy. Although the notion of decency can easily seem quaint or even priggish, I believe . . . that it represents a deep and significant evaluative category. I believe, too, that it is a notion that few persons, either in our own age or in others, would altogether wish to discard. And while I have already conceded that anyone who is deterred by laws against the cited activities is not responding to the (potential) value of a decent and worthy life, it is not hard to see how the laws can make eventual responses to that (potential) value more likely.

For, first, if an agent avoids narcotic drugs, he will obviously not become addicted. Thus, even if his choice is not autonomous, it will protect his later capacity to respond to (potential) value—including, but not restricted to, the (potential) value of a drug-free life. If his behavior provides an example to others, or reduces the peer pressure on them, the choice that he made in order to avoid punishment may also help to protect *their* capacity to respond to (potential) value. Similarly, if an agent is in danger of becoming a compulsive gambler, his nonautonomous decision not to gamble may protect his later capacity to respond to (potential) value. By attaching penalties to such autonomy-threatening behavior, the law acknowledges that disvaluable as well as valuable activities can be most attractive "from the inside."

This, however, is not the main point; for although any activity can become a habit, most disvaluable behavior is neither especially addictive nor especially destructive of one's general capacity to respond to value. But even when the general capacity remains intact, repeated exposure to disvaluable activities can reduce one's sensitivity to specific kinds of value or disvalue. Hence, an even more important rationale for laws against disvaluable behavior is that those laws create and sustain the conditions under which such sensitivity can thrive.

This, I think, is the most significant effect of laws that attach penalties to coarse and licentious activities. Where such activities abound, it becomes difficult even to envision, much less to see the appeal of, the richer but subtler possibilities of a more refined sensibility. But by creating an environment in which (at least outward) decency and civility prevail, the law can inscribe a measure of these qualities in the public culture. Moreover, since there is no clear boundary between the public culture and our inner lives, all citizens can thereby be made acquainted with the texture of decent, civil lives and the possibilities these afford. Assuming that decency and civility really are (potentially) valuable, all citizens will thus be put in a better position to appreciate their (potential) value and, hence, to choose them for the right reasons. And, al-

---

[19] Of course, in resoponse to this justification, it can be replied that gambling and narcotices attract organized crime precisely because they are illegal; for discussion, see Ethan A. Nadelmann, "The Case for Legalization," *Public Interest* 92 (Summer 1988), pp. 3–31.

though I think the argument is less promising, a similar case can be made that prohibiting the sale of bodily organs curtails commercialism while increasing responsiveness to the demands of altruism.[20]

Of course, none of this shows (or is intended to show) that governments should criminalize any major part of the behavior that most citizens consider disvaluable. Even if we assume, unrealistically, that the majority's unreflective judgments are usually correct, some disfavored activities—watching and reading pornography are standard examples—may become less rather than more attractive with repetition. These may best be allowed to extinguish or stabilize themselves. Others, such as gambling, become addictive to comparatively few. Still others, such as disapproved sexual behavior, are detectable only through massive invasions of privacy, or are preventable only by laws that are so intrusive as to elicit strong resentment. A person who is forced to curtail his sexual proclivities, or to endure religious prohibitions he does not accept, is more apt to despise than to internalize his society's way of life. Hence, threatening him with punishment is unlikely to increase the value of what he subsequently chooses.

Yet these facts demand not that governments altogether avoid using the criminal law to promote valuable choices, but only that they temper its use with good judgment. They suggest that before any government uses force to encourage the better or suppress the worse, it must ask both how successful the effort is likely to be and whether any expected gains are important enough to warrant overriding the general presumption in favor of liberty and noninterference. If there are no deeper objections, a government that wishes its citizens to live the best possible lives must neither use coercion indiscriminately nor withhold it altogether, but must consider each occasion on its merits.

---

[20] See Richard Titmuss, *The Gift Relationship* (New York: Random House, Pantheon Books, 1971). For an interesting exchange on Titmuss's book, see Kenneth J. Arrow, "Gifts and Exchanges," *Philosophy and Public Affairs* 1, 4 (Summer 1972), pp. 343–62, and Peter Singer, "Altruism and Commerce," *Philosophy and Public Affairs* 2, 3 (Spring 1973), pp. 312–20.

III

IS THERE AN OBLIGATION TO OBEY THE LAW?

14.

Political Obligation and Consent

HARRY BERAN

I

The consent theory of political obligation and authority (the Consent Theory below) is much more plausible than its many critics have realized. However, its plausibility can only be appreciated if the precise and limited scope of the theory within a complete theory of reasons for political obedience is recognized. These are the two claims I will try to substantiate in this paper.

To understand the scope of the Consent Theory let us note the following characteristics of political obligation and political authority.

1. To have political authority is for someone, A, to be in authority over some others, B and C; and for A to have authority over B and C is necessarily for A to have the right to make demands (in certain areas of conduct) on B and C and for the latter to have an obligation to meet these demands. The right of A to make these demands and B's and C's obligation to meet them are the correlatives. Hence, if a state has political authority, the right to govern, then there must be someone who has a correlative obligation. It is this particular obligation of the citizens to obey the state, the correlative of political authority, to which I refer by the term "political obligation." Since political obligation and political authority are correlatives, whatever is the logical basis of one must also be the logical basis of the other. When I speak, below, of a political authority relationship, I will be referring to the two correlatives which make it up.

2. One can distinguish between conclusive reasons for doing something and a (not necessarily conclusive) reason for doing it. To be under political obligation is for there to be a (not necessarily conclusive) reason for obeying the state. This must be so since it is possible to be under political obligation and yet to be morally justified in disobeying the state. Two sorts of cases are worth mentioning. One is morally justified civil disobedience, that is, disobedience of a law because it is morally objectionable. For unlike rebellion, which typically involves a denial that one is under political obligation, civil disobedience typically does not involve such a denial but rather the assertion that there are moral reasons for disobeying the state which override one's political obligation. The other sort of case is disobedience of a law which is not morally objectionable. Even if one is under political obligation one may be morally justified in breaking such a law, say the law against theft, if this is necessary for the sake of a greater good, say, saving a child from starvation. Since political obligation and political authority are correlatives, a state's

having political authority is also only a (not necessarily conclusive) reason for obeying it.[1]

3. "Political obligation" refers not just to any reason for obeying the state but to one specific reason: that reason which is logically related both to political obligation and its correlative, political authority. If I promise my mother to obey state S then there is a reason for my obeying it and, moreover, I am under an obligation to obey it. But clearly this obligation has nothing to do with political obligation, since my promising my mother to obey state S does not give it authority to govern me.

From the above three points the scope of the Consent Theory can be understood. Within a theory of reasons for political obedience the Consent Theory distinguishes between obeying a state because it stands in an authority to its members and obeying it for other reasons. The Consent Theory merely claims that consent is a necessary condition for there being an authority relationship between a state and its members (and possibly also a sufficient condition, but this stronger claim cannot be considered in this paper). It does not claim that consent is either a necessary or a sufficient condition for there being conclusive reasons for obeying the state. The Consent Theory can deny this since the existence of a political authority relationship is neither a sufficient condition for the existence of conclusive reasons for political obedience (as has been shown already) nor a necessary condition for the existence of such reasons (as will be shown in Section II).

II

Recognition of the precise scope of the Consent Theory resolves some of the traditional disputes about the theory. However, before I can demonstrate this, I have to make some further preliminary points.

I must grant that, in using the term "political obligation" to refer to that obligation which is the correlative of political authority, I am using it in a narrower sense than that in which some others have used it. Still, this is surely one proper sense of "political obligation" and, moreover, an important one, since the authority relationship between a state and its members is an important

---

[1] Within the field of moral reasons for action the distinction between a reason for action and conclusive reason for action has been marked since W. D. Ross by speaking of a prima facie obligation or ought (a reason for action) and an actual obligation or ought (conclusive reason for action). In "Ought, Obligation, and Duty" (*Australasian Journal of Philosophy* 50 [1972]: 207–21), I argued for the view that this way of making the distinction is unnecessary and confused. I claimed there that the "prima facie/actual" terminology is unnecessary, since the distinction between a reason for action and conclusive reason for action is already embodied in ordinary language through obligation statements always having the former force and (unqualified) ought statements always having the latter force. Throughout this article I will use "obligation" with the force of a reason for action and "ought" with the force of a conclusive reason for action. However, the arguments which follow merely depend on the distinction between a reason for action and a conclusive reason for action itself, not on the terminology used to mark the distinction.

political phenomenon. Also, it is a sense of "political obligation" which suits my aim in this paper, which is to find a sense of "political obligation" and of "consent" such that it can plausibly be claimed that consent is (at least) a necessary condition of political obligation.

What do I mean by "consent" in the Consent Theory? Consent consists in acceptance of membership in a state by each person who is under political obligation.[2] For in accepting membership in an association, be it a state or some other association, one agrees to obey the rules of that association; and in agreeing to obey the rules of the state, one puts oneself under an obligation to obey its rules and gives it authority to govern. Naturalized citizens explicitly agree to obey the state in the naturalization ceremony. Native-born citizens implicitly agree to obey when they cease to be political minors and accept adult status, that is, full membership, in the state.[3] I wish this model of consent as acceptance of membership in an association to be taken quite literally. There is at least one other kind of association where a particularly important obligation to obey the association's rules rests on implicit acceptance of membership: namely, churches. Very plausibly the obligation of Anglicans to obey the rules of their church is based on their acceptance of membership in the Church of England. Most members of the Anglican church are baptized into it, and hence become members of it, as infants; but such members' obligation to obey the church as adults can hardly be grounded in infant baptism or confirmation at the age of twelve and, therefore, most plausibly, is grounded in implicit (continuing) acceptance of membership at the age when such acceptance can be morally binding.

Agreeing to do something is either a form of promising or something analogous to promising; and promissory obligations are moral obligations. Hence agreeing to do X, like promising to do X, gives rise to a moral obligation to do X. So the Consent Theory subsumes political obligation and the right involved in political authority under moral obligation and moral right, that is, the kind of moral obligation and moral right which arise out of a promise. Since consenting and agreeing to do something are either forms of promising or analogous to promising, I do not, in this article, distinguish between consenting, agreeing, and promising to do something.

Recognition of the precise and limited scope of the Consent Theory makes possible convincing replies to some of the traditional objections to the Consent Theory.

---

[2] Some Consent Theorists identify consent with participation in democratic elections. I have tried to show that this identification is untenable in "Political Obligation and Democracy," *Australasian Journal of Philosophy* 54 (1976): 250–54.

[3] The distinction between two sorts of members of the state, political minors and full members, is well recognized. The following are among the more important differences between political minors and adults. The former do not have the legal right to hold political office; they have neither the legal right nor the obligation to take part in the selection of governments; they do not have the legal right to leave the state without the permission of their legal guardian; they cannot sue— their "next friend" has to do it on their behalf—nor be sued, and if a criminal action is brought against them it is heard in a children's court; they cannot serve on juries; and they are legally compelled to do many things, e.g., to go to school, which adults are not compelled to do.

H. A. Prichard, Margaret MacDonald, T. D. Weldon, J. C. Rees, and Thomas MacPherson have all claimed that classical political philosophy rests on a mistake.[4] Their argument for this claim runs roughly thus: The problem of political obligation—Why should I or anyone obey the state?—is the fundamental problem of political philosophy. Classical philosophy assumed that there is a single answer to this question, for example, that the state has the consent of its members or that it promotes the general good. But there is no single answer to this question, for reasons why one should obey (or disobey) the law depend on the circumstances of particular cases. Deeply committed democrats may (rightly) think they ought to obey a dictator if this is the least evil possible under certain circumstances; and they may (also rightly) think they are not morally required to obey a genuinely democratic government which refuses, for no sufficient reasons, to let them leave the country. As MacDonald puts it "there is no general criterion" of political obligation (no "sole justification for accepting any or every law") "but an indefinite set of vaguely shifting criteria, different for different times and circumstances. . . ." She adds, "No general criterion of all right actions can be supplied. Similarly, the answer to 'Why should I obey *any* law, acknowledge the authority of *any* State or support *any* Government?' is that this is a senseless question." [5]

As a criticism of the Consent Theory this objection is misconceived. For the Consent Theory distinguishes between authoritative and nonauthoritative states and merely claims that consent is (at least) a necessary condition for a state being authoritative and, therefore, that consent is a necessary condition for the members of a state being under political obligation. Thus while the Consent Theory does propose a criterion for any state being authoritative, it does not propose to answer the question, Why should I obey *any* law . . . or support *any* government? The Consent Theory is quite consistent with MacDonald's claim that the answer to the last question cannot be given in terms of necessary and sufficient conditions, without, however, being committed to this claim.

It may be thought that a state which does not have authority to govern cannot be morally justified in exercising political power. But this is not so. A group of people cannot have *authority* to govern without the consent of the governed, but they may be morally justified in exercising *power* without consent. According to the Consent Theory this must be at least logically possible. For one of the starting points of this theory is the claim that not just any moral reason for obeying the state constitutes a political authority relationship (cf. Section I). Hence there may be reasons for obeying the state other than the reason which is involved in the existence of a political authority relationship; and these reasons may sometimes be conclusive.

---

[4] See H. A. Prichard, "Green's Principles of Political Obligation," in *Moral Obligation,* ed. H. A. Prichard (Oxford, 1968); Margaret MacDonald, "The Language of Political Theory," in *Logic and Language,* ed. Anthony Flew, 1st ser. (Oxford, 1963), pp. 167–86; T. D. Weldon, *The Vocabulary of Politics* (London, 1953), p. 96; J. C. Rees, "The Limitations of Political Theory," *Political Studies* 2 (1954): 242–57; Thomas MacPherson, *Political Obligation* (London, 1967).

[5] MacDonald, pp. 183–86; the last quotation is from p. 183.

Let me illustrate this through an example. According to classical Marxism there will be a dictatorship of the proletariat between the overthrow of capitalism and the withering away of the state; this is thought to be necessary, *inter alia,* to prevent a counterrevolution by the expropriated capitalists. According to Leninism this dictatorship may be exercised by the vanguard of the proletariat, that is, by the leaders of the Communist party; in other words a dictatorship by a small minority of the population. If such a dictatorship did not have the support of the people it would not be an authoritative government; however, if such a dictatorship really were a necessary condition for the creation of a just society of free and unalienated human beings, it would perhaps be morally justified despite its lack of authority.

The plausibility of Hume's objection to the "unnecessary shuffle" [6] (see "Of the Original Contract") [7] also depends on a failure to recognize the precise scope of the Consent Theory. Consent Theorists, Hume claims, ask:

1. Why are we bound to obey our government?

and answer: Because

2. We have promised to obey our government, and
3. We are bound to keep our promises.

Hume challenges this argument by asking:

4. Why should we keep our word?

and answering: Because

5. It is necessary for civilized life.

But, Hume continues, 5 is in itself a sufficient answer to 1; so there is no need to derive 1 from 3 by means of a highly speculative act of promising. In fact, Hume claims, 1 and 3 are principles which "stand precisely on the same foundations"; both obligations, that to obey one's government and that to keep one's promises, are established by their necessity for civilized life.

Hume does not establish his conclusion. Married people have an obligation to love and support each other because they promise to do so in the marriage ceremony. I hope no one would want to challenge this "consent theory or marital obligation" on the ground that marital obligation can be derived directly from the necessity of the family for civilized life. No one should be swayed by such a challenge, since it tried to make do with one answer to two distinct questions:

Why do we have the institution of marriage?

Why do individuals A and B have certain marital obligations to each other? The answer to the first question may well be that the institution of the family is

---

[6] "Locke's doctrine represents, for Hume, an unnecessary shuffle; one might as well appeal directly to utility" (John Rawls, *A Theory of Justice* [Cambridge, Mass., 1971], p. 32; cf. Anthony Quinton, ed., *Political Philosophy* [Oxford, 1967], p. 12).

[7] Hume, "Of the Original Contract," in *Hume's Ethical Writings,* ed., Alasdair MacIntyre (New York, 1965), pp. 255–73, esp. 267–69.

necessary for civilized life. But this answer cannot explain why two particular individuals have certain marital obligations to each other. The answer to this question is that they have promised to love and support each other.

Similarly, it may well be the case that we have the institution of the state because of its utility—because the state is necessary for civilized life. But, on the face of it, the utility of the state cannot in itself explain why a particular state stands in an authority relation to some particular individuals. Hence, both the question of utility (Is the state worth having?) and the question of fidelity (Do the members of a particular state owe it obedience?) have to be asked and answered. And just as A's marital obligations to a certain woman cannot be explained directly in terms of the utility of the institution of marriage, so A's political obligation to a certain state cannot be explained directly in terms of the utility of the state.

Hume simply assumes that political obligation, unlike marital obligation, can be explained directly in terms of the utility of the state. Thus he assumes, but does not show, that there is no need to distinguish between a state's authority relationship to its members as a reason for obedience and other possible reasons for obedience. Hence Hume has not shown that the admittedly speculative appeal to an act of promising is an unnecessary shuffle.

III

Even if it is granted that recognition of the limited scope of the Consent Theory shows that the above objections to it are misconceived, there are further well-known objections which may be regarded as fatal to the Consent Theory even as now understood. To these objections I now turn.

S. I. Benn and R. S. Peters argue thus:

> . . . if consent is a *necessary* condition for political obligation, it would deny a government any rightful authority over anyone who dissented from the basic principles of the constitution. Force used against Communists in a liberal democracy, or against liberals in a "people's democracy," would alike be naked aggression, for the law authorizing it would not be *their* law. In this form, no one who chose to contract out could be legitimately coerced.
>
> And is it reasonable to assume that all members of a state subscribe to its constitution? In the 1946 referendum, eight million Frenchmen voted against the constitution of the Fourth Republic, and a further eight million did not vote at all. In what sense, then, did they consent to it? Some may have rejected even the majority principle.[8]

This objection does not get a grip on the version of the Consent Theory I defend. I identify consent with acceptance of membership in the state; and one can (continue to) accept membership in a state although one votes against a constitution or abstains from a referendum on a constitution.

---

[8] S. I. Benn and R. S. Peters, *Social Principles and the Democratic State* (London, 1969), p. 322.

One must distinguish between the statements "A *agrees with* the constitution" and "A *agrees to obey* the constitution." The second statement can be true, though the first is false. But why would those who vote against a constitution yet agree to obey it? Well perhaps because they would rather (continue to) be members of a particular state, though it has a constitution with which they disagree, than not to be members of that state at all. After all, what true Frenchman, though he be a communist and given that he cannot have a Communist France now, would not rather live in Capitalist France than Communist Russia!

But perhaps some of those who dissent from the constitution do not wish to agree to obey it. There are three ways in which they can avoid agreeing to obey the constitution: secession, migration, or a public declaration that they are not accepting membership in the state in whose territory they are living. I will discuss each option in turn.

It is true, these days, that a repressed or disenchanted minority cannot found a new state of their own liking or an anarchist community by migrating to hitherto unoccupied territory. But they can, and I am inclined to think they have a moral right to, found a new state or an anarchist community by secession. The number of new independent communities which can be founded by discovering unoccupied territory is necessarily limited; but that which can be founded by secession is, for all practical purposes, not. Politically speaking, new Americas can always be found *within* America.

The claim that there is a moral right to secession is congenial to the Consent Theory. The claim needs, nevertheless, to be supported by argument. However, instead of supplying such an argument now, I will merely note that secession is a topic completely neglected by contemporary philosophers. Hence I am not making a claim against which there exist arguments in the literature (or otherwise known to me). Despite Katanga, Biafra, Rhodesia, Northern Ireland, and Bangla Desh—not to mention Scottish and Welsh Nationalists, French Canadians, Spanish Basques, and Croatian Yugoslavs—there does not seem to be a single recent philosophical contribution to the problem of the justification of secession. Nor have the major classical political philosophers had much to say on the topic.

Migration, as a way of avoiding political obligation to a particular state, raises some well-known objections. Hume put one of them thus: "Should it be said, that, by living under the dominion of a prince, which one might leave, every individual has given a tacit consent to his authority, and promised him obedience; it may be answered, that such an implied consent can only have place, where one imagines, that the matter depends on his choice. . . . [But] can we seriously say, that a poor peasant . . has a free choice to leave his country, when he knows no foreign language or manners, and lives from day to day, by the small wages he acquires?" [9]

I take the point of the objection to be that if the peasant cannot leave his state then his putative implicit agreement to obey is not made freely and, therefore, cannot create a promissory obligation. Hence the Consent Theory is committed

[9] "Of the Original Contract," p. 263.

to the implausible claim that the peasant is not under political obligation simply because he is too poor and ignorant to leave his state.

Well, is the peasant in a position, despite his predicament, to make a morally binding promise to obey the state? H. L. A. Hart has made extremely plausible the view that the serious[10] utterance of "I promise to do X" counts as a morally binding promise, provided none of certain defeating conditions are present.[11] Some of the more important conditions which defeat a claim that a morally binding promise has been made are deception, mental incapacity, coercion or undue influence, and unfair bargaining position. The claim that "free choice" is a necessary condition for the creation of a promissory obligation can be regarded as a compendious way of claiming that a promissory obligation is created only if none of the defeating conditions hold.

The Consent Theory is committed to the view that one's agreement to obey the state does not create an obligation if there obtains one or more of the conditions which defeat the claim that a promissory obligation has been created. But there is nothing in the peasant's predicament that defeats the claim that his acceptance of membership in the state counts as putting himself under a promissory obligation to obey. Not even the coercion defense applies: P is coerced by A to do X only if P's doing X is (partly) brought about by A threatening P, or a third party, with harm unless P does X. But Hume's peasant is prevented from leaving his state not by any threat of harm by the state should he attempt to leave, but by his ignorance and poverty. He accepts membership in the state not because of the state's threat of harm should he do otherwise, but because of his poverty and ignorance.

In general, it simply does not follow from one's being unable to leave a state that there is present one or more of the conditions which prevent one's promise to obey that state from creating an obligation.[12]

What if a government did coerce citizens into staying within its territory? Would this be a case where the citizens are no longer under political obligation? Hume did not think so; he wrote: "And did a prince observe, that many of his subjects were seized with a frenzy of migrating to foreign countries, he would doubtless, with great reason and justice, restrain them, in order to prevent the depopulation of his kingdom. Would he forfeit the allegiance of all his subjects, by so wise and reasonable a law? Yet the freedom of their choice is surely, in

---

[10] By this qualification I mean to exclude such "nonserious" utterances of the promising formula as in play acting, telling jokes, philosophical examples, etc.

[11] See "The Ascription of Responsibility and Rights," in Flew, ed., pp. 145–66. I have to make three remarks on my use of Hart's work. (1) Hart deals with the question, What conditions must hold for a legal contract to exist? But, clearly, his arguments also apply, *mutatis mutandis,* to the question, What conditions must hold for a morally binding promise (i.e., a promise which creates an obligation) to exist? (2) The list, which I have given, of conditions which prevent the serious utterance of the promising formula from creating a promissory obligation is not complete. It may not even be possible to state the conditions exhaustively once and for all. I must leave it to the reader to consider possible defeating conditions not listed. (3) The creation of a promissory obligation through an implicit or tacit promise depends just as much on the absence of defeating conditions as does that through an explicit promise. I can see no good reason for doubting this view.

[12] A similar argument can be found in M. D. Bayle's article "A Concept of Coercion," in *Coercion,* ed. J. R. Pennock and J. W. Chapman (Chicago/New York, 1972), pp. 27–28.

that case, ravished for them." [13] Unlike the case of the poor, ignorant peasant, now it *is* the government which has "ravished free choice," not circumstances for which the government is not responsible.

The trouble with this objection lies in our knowing a "prince" whose subjects were seized with a frenzy of migrating to foreign countries. To make this frenzy ineffective he built a wall across the main escape route from his "kingdom" and put sharpshooters on it with orders to shoot anyone who tried to get over it. I do think this "prince" has forfeited the right to the allegiance of those of the people in his "kingdom" who stay in it out of fear of being killed if they try to leave without permission. These people are obliged to stay under his rule, but they are not under political obligation.

According to the United Nations Universal Declaration of Human Rights, people have the moral right to leave their country permanently and to change their nationality and should have the corresponding legal rights. Now, if people are forcibly denied the exercise of the moral right to leave the state of which they are citizens, then surely it is not implausible to claim that they cease to be under political obligation. Or at least it is not implausible to claim this, provided that they have not put themselves under some special obligation which they cannot fulfill if they leave, that they have not broken the law and not yet met the penalty, and that their leaving is compatible with the government fulfilling its constitutional functions.

Political minors present a further problem for the claim that one can escape political obligation through migration. Assume there is an authoritative state. It would seem plausible that the adolescent as well as the adult members of this state are under political obligation. Assume further that there is some age, say fourteen, at which adolescents, while sufficiently mature to be under an obligation to obey the law, are not sufficiently mature to choose their place of residence; hence they would not have the moral or legal right to emigrate without their parents' consent; hence they could be coerced to remain in a state without ceasing to be under political obligation. It seems that these political minors are under political obligation without anything having created that obligation that can plausibly be regarded as morally binding consent.

This objection forces a qualification on the Consent Theory. Some philosophers distinguish between logically primary and logically secondary cases falling under a concept. D. M. Armstrong offers this definition of "logically secondary:" "Let it be given that there is a class of things of the sort X, and a sub-class of X: the class of things Y. Y's are then logically secondary instances of X if, and only if, (i) it is logically possible that there should be no Y's and yet there still be X's; but (ii) it is logically impossible that Y's should be the only X's which exist." [14]

If this definition of "logically secondary" is tenable then the political obligation of political minors is a logically secondary instance of political obligation. For it is logically impossible for all the members of the class "persons who

---

[13] "Of the Original Contract," p. 264.

[14] D. M. Armstrong, *Belief, Truth, and Knowledge* (Cambridge, 1973), p. 28.

are under political obligation to state S" to be political minors; if this were so there could not be a state S (though there could be a society S not politically organized) since, by definition, political minors cannot fill the positions which must be filled for a state to exist. On the other hand, it is logically possible that this class should consist of full members only.

So, the claim that consent is a necessary condition of political obligation and authority has to be qualified thus: consent is a necessary condition of political obligation and authority in logically primary cases. This qualification is to be understood as required whenever I claim that consent is a necessary condition of political obligation and authority.

Let me now deal with a difficulty which brings us back to the importance of recognizing the precise and limited scope of the Consent Theory. The version of the Consent Theory which I defend relies on the notion of implicit consent. But nothing A does in situation S can count as A's implicit consent to do X, unless it is in fact possible for A in S to do something that would count as refusing to agree to do X. For implicit consent to do X simply consists in the absence of explicit refusal to agree to do it in a context which gives such absence of (explicit) refusal the significance of (implicit) consent. Hence, I must grant that at least persons who are unable to leave their state, for example, Hume's poor ignorant peasant, can avoid political obligation by, say, declaring publicly and to the appropriate officials that they are not accepting membership in the state. I do grant this, but subject to the following remarks. If some people neither agree to obey the state, nor emigrate, nor secede, then though they would not be under political obligation, the state may well be justified in banishing them to a "Dissenters' Territory" (i.e., a no-man's land created by an adjustment of existing borders) where those who do not agree to obey the state may live.

If the state does not banish them then they would indeed live within its territory, yet not be under political obligation.[15] Needless to say, they would still be morally required to act in accordance with the law in many cases because of moral reasons for doing what is legally required which are independent of the existence of the law. One is not morally justified in killing people just because one is not under political obligation not to do so.

While the admission just made again reveals the limited scope of the Consent Theory, this limited scope does not trivialize it. Let P be someone who lives in a given state but is not under political obligation to it. What difference does this absence of political obligation make to the justification of political action? If one is under political obligation then there is a (not necessarily conclusive) reason for obeying the law. Hence there is one reason for obeying the law, for those who are under political obligation, which does not hold for P. Hence P

---

[15] I refer the reader who thinks I have lost touch with reality to the seven children of the Breton Nationalist couple M. and Mme. Manrot Le Goarnic (see *Guardian* [December 14, 1974]). The French government refuses to admit their existence since they were given Breton first names, which is contrary to French law. Hence, they are not listed on government records, their parents have never been able to claim social security allowances for them, they have no identity papers, and the eldest boy has been refused a driver's license. The *Guardian* adds, "But—in theory—they will not be asked to pay taxes."

may be morally justified in disobeying the law in some cases where those who are under political obligation would not be. For example, assume that there is a law against doing X and there are no moral reasons for or against doing X independent of the possible political obligation to do X. (Regrettably states do sometimes ban actions which are not morally wrong.) Then those who are under political obligation have a moral reason against doing X, no moral reasons for doing X, and, therefore, ought, morally speaking, not to do X. On the other hand, P is not under political obligation, and, therefore, it is morally indifferent whether P does X or not.

One further objection has to be considered. The Consent Theory claims that what creates the political obligation of native-born citizens is their acceptance of full membership in the state when they cease to be political minors. This acceptance of full membership in the state is what counts as their implicit agreement to obey it. In other words, staying in the state when one gets the legal right to leave counts as implicit agreement to obey it. Now surely ordinary people are not aware that their remaining within a state when they cease to be political minors counts as their implicit agreement to obey. But if they are not aware of this, then this act cannot give rise to an obligation. For if one does not know that doing W counts as agreeing to do X, then although one does W does not thereby make a morally binding agreement to do X—the claim that one has created an obligation to do X can be defeated by an epistemological defense. So according to the Consent Theory only those few who hold this theory are under political obligation!

This is a very persuasive objection, but it is not conclusive. Adults in contemporary states with universal education do know the following propositions.

1. In remaining within the territory of a state when one comes of age one accepts full membership in it.
2. In accepting membership in a rule-governed association (in the absence of coercion, deception, etc.,) one puts oneself under an obligation to obey its rules.
3. The state is a rule-governed association.

From 1–3 it follows that

4. In remaining within the territory of a state when one comes of age (in the absence of coercion, deception, etc.) one puts oneself under an obligation to obey its rules.

Now either citizens make the inference to 4 or they do not. If they do, then the key premise of the present objection is false. If they do not, it may yet be true that they are under political obligation and that this obligation rests on their acceptance of membership in the state when they come of age. For ignorance that doing W counts as agreeing to do X is only a conclusive defense against the claim that one has agreed to do X if such ignorance is not negligent. If one's ignorance that doing W counts as agreeing to do X is negligent then one's doing W may count as a morally binding agreement despite one's ignorance. Now may one not be negligent in not making the inference from propositions 1, 2, and 3 to proposition 4 when one assumes full adult status, including the legal right to leave the state? It may well be negligent, since people should consider what moral significance there is in their new status and their new rights. So, even if there are some citizens who do not make the inference to proposition 4, this ignorance may not defeat the claim that in accepting full membership of a state when they come of age they put themselves under political obligation.

IV

I have tried to defend the claim that consent is a necessary condition of political obligation and authority; but I have done so without asserting that this condition has in fact held for the majority of the members of any state that has ever existed.

Such caution was not due to timidity but to a desire to separate the theory of political obligation and authority from an application of the theory to particular cases. The agreement to obey the state only gives rise to political obligation if it is free from the conditions which defeat an agreement's giving rise to an obligation, for example, if the agreement is due neither to coercion nor deception. At least two things are necessary for an application of this theory to particular cases. First, what absence of coercion and deception (as well as the other defeating conditions) amounts to would have to be specified much more clearly than I have done in this paper. Second, much empirical information on how much coercion and deception exist in a particular state would have to be available to make it possible to say whether that state has the uncoerced and undeceived consent of the governed.

I cannot attempt to apply the Consent Theory to particular states now beyond noting obvious differences between, for example, Australia and the USSR. Australian citizens are virtually never prevented by their governments from exercising their legal right to leave Australia permanently, and there seems to be very little political censorship by the government. Citizens of the USSR who wish to leave Russia permanently are usually prevented from doing so (except for Jews, many of whom have recently been permitted to leave), and there is a very high level of political censorship in Russia.[16] Hence, even from an armchair, there must be much greater doubt about the extent of uncoerced and undeceived consent by the governed in Russia than in Australia.

---

[16] According to the *Australian* of January 15, 1973, a list of subjects that Russian publications are not permitted to publish has recently been published in the journal *Index*, published by Writers and Scholars International and edited by Michael Scammell. Among the banned subjects are the earnings of government and Communist party officials, comparisons between the earnings of Soviet families and the cost of goods in the shops, rising living standards in noncommunist countries, and food shortages in Russia.

15.
The Principle of Fairness

ROBERT NOZICK

A principle suggested by Herbert Hart, which (following John Rawls) we shall call the *principle of fairness,* would be of service here if it were adequate. This principle holds that when a number of persons engage in a just, mutually advantageous, cooperative venture according to rules and thus restrain their liberty in ways necessary to yield advantages for all, those who have submitted to these restrictions have a right to similar acquiescence on the part of those who have benefited from their submission.[1] Acceptance of benefits (even when this is not a giving of express or tacit undertaking to cooperate) is enough, according to this principle, to bind one.

• • •

The principle of fairness, as we stated it following Hart and Rawls, is objectionable and unacceptable. Suppose some of the people in your neighborhood (there are 364 other adults) have found a public address system and decide to institute a system of public entertainment. They post a list of names, one for each day, yours among them. On his assigned day (one can easily switch days) a person is to run the public address system, play records over it, give news bulletins, tell amusing stories he has heard, and so on. After 138 days on which each person has done his part, your day arrives. Are you obligated to take your turn? You *have* benefited from it, occasionally opening your windows to listen, enjoying some music or chuckling at someone's funny story. The other people *have* put themselves out. But must you answer the call when it is your turn to do so? As it stands, surely not. Though you benefit from the arrangement, you may know all along that 364 days of entertainment supplied by others will not be worth your giving up *one* day. You would rather not have any of it and not give up a day than have it all and spend one of your days at it. Given these preferences, how can it be that you are required to participate when your scheduled time comes? It would be nice to have philosophy readings on the radio to which one could tune in at any time, perhaps late at night when tired. But it may not be nice enough for you to want to give up one whole day of your own as a reader on the program. Whatever you want, can others create an obligation for

---

[1] Herbert Hart, "Are There Any Natural Rights?" *Philosophical Review,* 1955: John Rawls, *A Theory of Justice* (Cambridge, Mass.: Harvard University Press, 1971), sect. 18. My statement of the principle stays close to Rawls'. The argument Rawls offers for this principle constitutes an argument only for the narrower principle of fidelity (bona fide promises are to be kept). Though if there were no way to avoid "can't get started" difficulties about the principle of fidelity (p. 349) other than by appealing to the principle of fairness, it *would* be an argument for the principle of fairness.

you to do so by going ahead and starting the program themselves? In this case you can choose to forgo the benefit by not turning on the radio; in other cases the benefits may be unavoidable. If each day a different person on your street sweeps the entire street, must you do so when your time comes? Even if you don't care that much about a clean street? Must you imagine dirt as you traverse the street, so as not to benefit as a free rider? Must you refrain from turning on the radio to hear the philosophy readings? Must you mow your front lawn as often as your neighbors mow theirs?

At the very least one wants to build into the principle of fairness the condition that the benefits to a person from the actions of the others are greater than the costs to him of doing his share. How are we to imagine this? Is the condition satisfied if you do enjoy the daily broadcasts over the PA system in your neighborhood but would prefer a day off hiking, rather than hearing these broadcasts all year? For you to be obligated to give up your day to broadcast mustn't it be true, at least, that there is nothing you could do with a day (with that day, with the increment in any other day by shifting some activities to that day) which you would prefer to hearing broadcasts for the year? If the only way to get the broadcasts was to spend the day participating in the arrangement, in order for the condition that the benefits outweigh the costs to be satisfied, you would have to be willing to spend it on the broadcasts rather than to gain *any* other available thing.

If the principle of fairness were modified so as to contain this very strong condition, it still would be objectionable. The benefits might only barely be worth the costs to you of doing your share, yet others might benefit from *this* institution much more than you do; they all treasure listening to the public broadcasts. As the person least benefited by the practice, are you obligated to do an equal amount for it? Or perhaps you would prefer that all cooperated in *another* venture, limiting their conduct and making sacrifices for it. It is true, *given* that they are not following your plan (and thus limiting what other options are available to you), that the benefits of their venture *are* worth to you the costs of your cooperation. However, you do not wish to cooperate, as part of your plan to focus their attention on your alternative proposal which they have ignored or not given, in your view at least, its proper due. (You want them, for example, to read the Talmud on the radio instead of the philosophy they are reading.) By lending the institution (their institution) the support of your co-operating in it, you will only make it harder to change or alter.[2]

On the face of it, enforcing the principle of fairness is objectionable. You may not decide to give me something, for example a book, and then grab money from me to pay for it, even if I have nothing better to spend the money on. You have, if anything, even less reason to demand payment if your activity that gives me the books also benefits you; suppose that your best way of getting

---

[2] I have skirted making the institution one that you didn't get a fair say in setting up or deciding its nature, for here Rawls would object that it doesn't satisfy his two principles of justice. Though Rawls does not require that every microinstitution satisfy his two principles of justice, but only the basic structure of the society, he seems to hold that a microinstitution must satisfy these two principles if it is to give rise to obligations under the principle of fairness.

exercise is by throwing books into people's houses, or that some other activity of yours thrusts books into people's houses as an unavoidable side effect. Nor are things changed if your inability to collect money or payments for the books which unavoidably spill over into others' houses makes it inadvisable or too expensive for you to carry on the activity with this side effect. One cannot, whatever one's purposes, just act so as to give people benefits and then demand (or seize) payment. Nor can a group of persons do this. If you may not charge and collect for benefits you bestow without prior agreement, you certainly may not do so for benefits whose bestowal costs you nothing, and most certainly people need not repay you for costless-to-provide benefits which yet *others* provided them. So the fact that we partially are "social products" in that we benefit from current patterns and forms created by the multitudinous actions of a long string of long-forgotten people, forms which include institutions, ways of doing things, and language (whose social nature may involve our current use depending upon Wittgensteinian matching of the speech of others), does not create in us a general floating debt which the current society can collect and use as it will.

Perhaps a modified principle of fairness can be stated which would be free from these and similar difficulties. What seems certain is that any such principle, if possible, would be so complex and involuted that one could not combine it with a special principle legitimating *enforcement* within a state of nature of the obligations that have arisen under it. Hence, even if the principle could be formulated so that it was no longer open to objection, it would not serve to obviate the need for other persons' *consenting* to cooperate and limit their own activities.

16.
The Principle of Fairness and Free-Rider Problems

RICHARD J. ARNESON

In a celebrated essay, H. L. A. Hart briefly calls attention to a situation he calls "mutual restriction" and claims that "political obligation is intelligible" only once it is understood exactly how this situation gives rise to obligation.[1] To clarify this matter Hart proposes a principle of mutual restriction: ". . . when a number of persons conduct any joint enterprise according to rules and thus restrict their liberty, those who have submitted to these restrictions when required have a right to a similar submission from those who have benefited by their submission." According to Hart, the rights of the rule followers here entail a corresponding obligation on the part of the beneficiaries. This principle has been taken over by John Rawls, renamed the "principle of fairness," and reformulated as follows: ". . . when a number of persons engage in a just, mutually advantageous, cooperative venture according to rules and thus restrain their liberty in ways necessary to yield advantages for all, those who have submitted to these restrictions have a right to similar acquiescence on the part of those who have benefited from their submission."[2] One of the more promising minor achievements of Robert Nozick's *Anarchy, State, and Utopia* is its vigorous polemic against this principle. Nozick writes, "The principle of fairness, as we stated it following Hart and Rawls, is objectionable and unacceptable."[3] As we shall see, some of Nozick's criticisms are well taken, but they appear to motivate revision of the principle rather than its abandonment. Nozick, however, leaps from his criticisms to the conclusion that no reformulation of the principle of fairness would obviate the need for actual individual consent to social requirements before those requirements can rightly be deemed obligations binding on that individual and enforceable by others. Others have endorsed Nozick's leap.[4] Since Hart at any rate proposed the principle in order to correct the tendency of the social contract theorists to assimilate all sources of obligation to voluntary consent of the sort found in promise making, Nozick's

[1] H. L. A. Hart, "Are There Any Natural Rights?" *Philosophical Review* 64 (1955): 175–91; see esp. p. 185.

[2] John Rawls, *A Theory of Justice* (Cambridge, Mass.: Harvard University Press, 1971), pp. 108–14. The formulation quoted in the text follows the suggested phrasing of Robert Nozick, *Anarchy, State, and Utopia* (New York: Basic Books, 1974), p. 90.

[3] Nozick, p. 93.

[4] Frank Miller and Rolf Sartorius, "Population Policy and Public Goods," *Philosophy and Public Affairs* 8 (1979): 148–74; see esp. pp. 165–67; A. John Simmons, "The Principle of Fair Play," *Philosophy and Public Affairs* 8 (1979): 307–37 (this is a shortened and revised version of chap. 5 of his *Moral Principles and Political Obligations* [Princeton, N.J.: Princeton University Press, 1980]).

conclusion jettisons the project of explaining and justifying political obligation by tracing its origin to mutuality of restriction.

The present article salvages this project.

• • •

It will be useful to state in summary form the main objections to which the principle of fairness as quoted above appears to be liable:

1. The principle incorrectly allows that if some persons organize a cooperative scheme that demands a certain contribution from each beneficiary of the scheme, each beneficiary is obligated to make this assigned contribution, even if the cost to him of making the contribution (including the opportunity cost) exceeds the benefit he gains from the scheme.
2. The principle incorrectly allows that an ongoing cooperative scheme that distributes benefits unevenly among individuals can impose on individuals an obligation to make an equal contribution toward the scheme, even though one beneficiary benefits greatly from the scheme while another receives benefits that barely exceed the cost of his contribution.
3. The principle incorrectly allows that a person may be obligated to contribute to a particular scheme, even though he has disinterested, conscientious reasons for opposing the scheme and is working to gain recognition for a substitute scheme.
4. It is not in general true that one acquires the right to coerce somebody by bestowing some benefit on him and then demanding reciprocal payment. "You may not decide to give something, for example a book, and then grab money from me to pay for it, even if I have nothing better to spend the money on," Nozick observes. "You have, if anything, even less reason to demand payment if your activity that gives me the book also benefits you; suppose that your best way of getting exercise is by throwing books into people's houses, or that some other activity of yours thrusts books into people's houses as an unavoidable side effect. . . . One cannot, whatever one's purposes, just act so as to give people benefits and then demand (or seize) payment. Nor can a group of persons do this." [5]

This list is a motley. One might quibble that the term "just" inserted into Rawls's formulation of the principle rules out at least objections 1–3. More fundamentally, 1–3 do not seem to strike at the core idea of the principle but only against the principle construed as generating reasons for ascribing obligations that no counterconsideration could ever override. In contrast, objection 4 urges that satisfaction of the terms of the principle of fairness gives no reason at all to hold that a person is under an obligation as specified by the principle. In what follows I concentrate my attention on 4. I simply assume that 1 through 3 are roughly correct; and, when I attempt a revised statement of the principle of fairness, the revisions accommodate these points.

---

[5] Nozick, p. 95.

Taking a cue from Nozick's mention of a book as a benefit whose distribution one might regulate by the principle of fairness, we concede straightaway that the principle is plausible only if its application is restricted to particular types of benefits. There is a distinction between gift and exchange which the unrevised principle threatens to collapse. Consider a neighborhood gift-giving association. According to the rules of the association, whenever a resident of the neighborhood has a birthday the other residents are all bound to contribute toward the purchase of a nice present for him. The members of the association cite Hart's principle when a justification is demanded for their forcing residents of the neighborhood to comply with the rules of the organization. But by showering me with gifts you do not succeed in creating an obligation on my part to lavish gifts on you or your friends in return. The members of a neighborhood gift-giving club who initially include me on their list of recipients can simply cross my name off the list, excluding me from future gifts, when I fail to contribute my assigned share to the birthday celebrations of others. The others are free to carry on the scheme without my participation. In such circumstances the idea of mutuality of restriction has no proper application.

Some, but not all, benefits are appropriately regulated by the principle of fairness. Which ones? A start here is to distinguish private from public goods. For a given group of persons, a good is public according to the degree to which it exhibits three features: (1) a unit of the good consumed by one person leaves none the less available for others (jointness), (2) if anyone is consuming the good it is unfeasible[6] to prevent anybody else from consuming the good (nonexcludability), and (3) all members of the group must consume the same quantity of it. The logical relations among the three features are that 3 entails 2 but 2 does not entail 3, and 1 and 2 are quite independent of one another. A television broadcast signal that can be received by any TV set, when TV sets are as common as mud, exhibits 1 but not 2 or 3. A scrambled television signal that can be received only by a TV set equipped with a special unscrambling device, not easily copied, exhibits 1 and 2 but not 3. National defense for those residing in a geographically unified nation is a stock example of a good for which 1, 2, and 3 all hold to a high degree. It will prove handy to introduce two more labels: we will say a good characterized by 2 is a *collective* good, and a good characterized by 3 will be referred to as a *pure public* good.

Notice that, once a pure public good is supplied to a group of persons, there cannot really be any voluntary acceptance or enjoyment of the benefit by individual consumers. One cannot voluntarily accept a good one cannot voluntarily reject. A person can choose not to watch a television program broadcast over the airwaves, but he cannot opt out of the security that a system of national defense provides—at least not in the present state of warfare technology. Of course, a person made uncomfortable by his enjoyment of national security could choose to emigrate to a remote land with no provision for national

---

[6] "Unfeasible" here is to be understood as straddling "impossible" and "extremely costly." There is a vast economic literature on public goods; most of it concerned with analyzing the required conditions for efficiently supplying such goods.

security, but declining to shoulder the immense costs of emigration does not render one's acceptance of national security truly voluntary.[7] It is also true that people form plans and projects whose success is contingent upon the continued supply of pure public goods such as national defense or safety from epidemic disease, but forming such projects and relying on the continued supply of pure public goods do not count as voluntary acceptance either.

The Hart and Rawls formulations of the principle of fairness assert that those who submit to the rules of cooperative enterprises have a right to similar submission from those who have benefited from their cooperation. In these formulations, the wording does not settle whether a person can qualify as benefiting from a cooperative enterprise without having voluntarily accepted those benefits. In explicating the principle, Rawls does make it plain that he understands "benefited" to mean "voluntarily benefited," but his reason is a matter of definition: he restricts the term "obligation" to refer only to moral requirements that arise from voluntary action undertaken by the person who thereby binds himself. Hart leaves the matter undecided. Textual exegesis aside, it is clear that the principle of fairness cannot fulfill the philosophical ambitions assigned to it by Hart unless it is interpreted as regulating schemes that distribute pure public goods. Hart announced that his principle can help elucidate the character of a range of obligations, including political obligation, which the social contract theorists had tried unsuccessfully to assimilate to the class of obligations deliberately undertaken via promises and contracts. Several of the goods standardly supplied by state authority—for example, military defense, police protection, and the rule of law—are such that all citizens within a given territory must consume pretty much the same amount of them. For practical purposes, significant variety in consumption levels is ruled out. Yet it is in virtue of providing such goods that governments acquire legitimate authority over their citizens; neither Hobbes nor Locke would say a citizen is obligated to obey a government that fails to establish minimal conditions of personal security. Hence any principle such as Hart's that is offered to explain the nature of political obligation, if it is to be interpreted sympathetically, must be taken as intended to apply to those paradigm cases of political obligation.

Further examples will trace out in more detail the limited, tenuous connection between voluntary acceptance of benefits and the generation of obligations under the principle of fairness. Recall the neighborhood gift-giving association. Presented with a gift from the associated neighbors, one has the option to accept or reject. But voluntary receipt of such gifts from the association, even as mediated by its rules, does not generate obligations in the recipient. Even if the rules are common knowledge, and they state unequivocally that acceptance of a gift is tantamount to pledging that one will contribute to future gifts for others, one can always cancel the implied pledge by announcing beforehand that one's acceptance of a gift in this case is *not* to be understood as tacit acceptance of an obligation. Once again the key feature seems to be excludability. In these

---

[7] For the sense of "voluntary" invoked here, see H. L. A. Hart and A. M. Honoré, *Causation in the Law* (Oxford: Clarendon Press, 1959), pp. 38–41.

circumstances the members of the gift-giving association are still free to exclude this open noncontributor from the benefits. If they do choose to give him a gift anyway, they are doing just that: bestowing a gift and not imposing an obligation.

There are also cases in which nonexcludability prevails and yet voluntary acceptance of benefits does not incur obligation. Consider a case in which a cooperative scheme supplies a collective good—perhaps a plane is hired to write pleasant sayings in the sky—but the scheme is ill-advised (i.e., total costs are greater than total benefits) or significantly unfair in its distribution of the burdens of cooperation. In either of these circumstances, the scheme does not generate genuine obligation. The individual consumer can decide whether or not to enjoy the good here supplied; he can avert his eyes and refrain from peeking at the skywriting (to simplify, let us stipulate that this aversion of eyes involves no inconvenience). Yet it is plausible to hold that in these circumstances the consumer is at liberty to enjoy the collective good without placing himself under obligation to those who ill-advisedly or unfairly supply it. Enjoying the skywriting boosts one's own happiness by a jot and lowers no one else's. If consumption of collective benefits from ill-advised and unfair schemes generated individual obligation to contribute to the scheme, then persons who are simply trying to minimize the losses in happiness from a botched project would willy-nilly generate obligations in themselves to continue support of the scheme.

Where nonexcludability prevails, the scheme is worth its costs, and the division of burdens is fair, yet the good supplied is not a pure public good, voluntary acceptance of the benefits of the scheme by the individual will generally be sufficient to place him under obligation.

So far I have urged several claims about how features of public goods affect our understanding of the scope of the principle of fairness. Where pure public goods are supplied, voluntary acceptance of benefits is impossible and so unnecessary to generate obligations according to the principle of fairness. Mere receipt of benefits may suffice to obligate. Where goods are characterized by jointness, but it is feasible to single out any desired person and exclude him from consumption, even voluntary acceptance of benefits may be insufficient to obligate. Where exclusion of anybody from consumption is unfeasible but individuals may choose whether to engage in consumption—that is to say, where the benefits of cooperation are collective but not pure public—voluntary acceptance of benefits is generally sufficient to generate obligation, provided the cooperative scheme is fair and not ill-advised. So far this is all just counter-assertion against Nozick's assertion. My strategy has been to render the principle of fairness less controversial by revising it so that dubious implications no longer follow from it. This retrenching permits a response to Nozick's challenges quoted under 4 above: while it is not in general true that bestowing a benefit on somebody places the beneficiary under an obligation, the circumstance that collective goods are in the offing creates a special situation. A group of individuals cooperating to supply a collective good cannot supply themselves without allowing all other individuals for whom the good is collective to consume some of the good if they choose. If the cooperators may not enforce collection of a charge amounting to a fair price from all consumers, they must either add private incentives to the scheme so that each beneficiary is induced to contribute his fair share of the cost, or forgo the collective benefit altogether, or allow free riders to enjoy the benefit of the scheme without helping defray its cost. The first of these alternatives is often unfeasible and the latter two are often morally repugnant.

Public goods are ubiquitous, but in many cases the benefits they supply are small change that is insufficient to justify imposition of coercion. A handsomely dressed man or woman walking down the street supplies a public good to those in the vicinity who relish the sight of a fashionable pedestrian. But cooperatively organized fashionable dressers cannot claim the right to enforce a charge against ogling pedestrians, because the value supplied is less than the disvalue of enforced collection of costs. When I was very young my mother and I, along with other neighbors, gathered near the local railroad tracks to watch the mid-morning freight train roll by, but we would have scoffed at the idea of the railroad charging us for this sight. Neither the people watchers nor the freight watchers in these examples are free riders.

Free-rider conduct as I shall understand it emerges when the following conditions hold:

a) A number of persons have established an ongoing cooperative scheme supplying a benefit B that is collective with respect to the members of a group G.

b) For each member of G the benefits of B are greater than the cost to him of contributing a fair share of the costs of supplying B (including the cost of such coercion as may be required to sustain the scheme).[8]

c) The actual ongoing scheme distributes the cost of supplying B to all beneficiaries in a manner such that the payment requested of each individual beneficiary is fair. In particular, no beneficiary who has a disinterested motive for not contributing to the scheme for supplying B is required to contribute.[9]

d) It is unfeasible that the cooperative scheme be arranged so that private benefits are supplied to each beneficiary of B in sufficient quantity to induce all beneficiaries to contribute their fair share of the costs of the scheme.[10]

e) Each member of G finds his assigned fair share of the costs of supplying B to be burdensome or to involve disutility.

f) The choice by any individual member of G whether to contribute to the co-operative scheme supplying B or not is independent of the choice of every other member. That is, no member's choice is made under the expectation

---

[8] The costs of coercion will include the harms imposed on each person who suffers coercion under the scheme, as well as the costs of paying for a coercing agency.

[9] This requirement is intended to ensure that the principle of fairness will not lay obligations upon those who are genuinely conscientious objectors to the scheme for supplying public goods. My understanding of the requirement is that, in order to have a disinterested motive, the beliefs which give rise to the motive cannot be acquired or sustained in a culpably irrational fashion.

[10] The rationale of d is simply that, if one can secure the needed public good in a fair manner and without coercion, one should not resort to coercion.

that it will influence any other member's choice.[11]

g) No single member of G will derive such great benefits from B that it is to his advantage to contribute the entire cost of supplying B in the absence of contributions by others. Nor will any coalition of a few members of G find it possible to divide the costs of B among the members of the coalition so that each member of the coalition will find the benefits of B to him outweigh the cost to him of contributing toward the supply of B according to the terms of the coalition. A large number of persons must contribute toward the supply of B if the benefits each receives are to overbalance the cost of each one's contribution.

When conditions *a–g* hold, each person who benefits from the cooperative scheme supplying B can correctly reason as follows: either other persons will contribute sufficient amounts to assure continued provision of B, or they will not. In either case, the individual is better off if he does not contribute. (The razor-edge possibility that the individual's personal contribution might make the difference between success and failure of the scheme has a probability so low that it can be ignored in the individual's calculation of what to do.) If this reasoning induces an individual not to contribute, he counts as a free rider.

Free-rider reasoning contrasts with two other closely related rationales for individual refusal to contribute to mutual benefit schemes supplying collective benefits. The *nervous cooperator* desires to contribute his assigned fair share of the costs of supplying B, provided that enough other persons also contribute to keep the scheme viable. He fears that other individuals will fail to contribute to the required extent, that the scheme will collapse, and that B will not be supplied regardless of his own contribution. Accordingly he declines to contribute. The *reluctant cooperator* desires to contribute his assigned fair share of the costs of supplying B, provided that all others (or almost all others) also contribute their fair share. He fears that in fact it will not be the case that all or almost all individuals will contribute their assigned fair share. In this situation, if he contributes he will be assisting the provision of the fruits of cooperation to people who do not contribute their fair share. Accordingly, he declines to contribute. The nervous cooperator does not want to waste resources in support of a lost cause, and the reluctant cooperator is unwilling to allow himself to be, as he thinks, exploited by free riders. What crucially distinguishes the nervous cooperator and the reluctant cooperator from the free rider is that the desire to benefit from the cooperative behavior of others without paying one's fair share of cooperation forms no part of the motivation which induces the former two types to refuse to contribute, while just this desire does loom large in the reasoning of the free rider. While the conduct of each of these types may threaten the stability of cooperative enterprises, the nervous and reluctant cooperators do not seem blameworthy.

---

[11] No single individual's decision is expected to influence the decisions of others, but note that this is compatible with individuals basing their choices on expectations about what the aggregate of others will decide.

Where free-rider conduct is possible, there obligations arise, under the principle of fairness, prohibiting such conduct. Borrowing pertinent provisions from *a* to *g* above, we may state a revised principle of fairness: where a scheme of cooperation is established that supplies a collective benefit that is worth its cost to each recipient, where the burdens of cooperation are fairly divided, where it is unfeasible to attract voluntary compliance to the scheme via supplementary private benefits, and where the collective benefit is either voluntarily accepted or such that voluntary acceptance of it is impossible, those who contribute their assigned fair share of the costs of the scheme have a right, against the remaining beneficiaries, that they should also pay their fair share. A moral obligation to contribute attaches to all beneficiaries in these circumstances, and it is legitimate to employ minimal coercion as needed to secure compliance with this obligation (so long as the cost of coercion does not tip the balance of costs and benefits adversely). This revised formulation preserves the root insight that accepting or even simply receiving the benefits of a cooperative scheme can sometimes obligate an individual to contribute to the support of the scheme, even though the individual has not actually consented to it. The principle of fairness thus streamlines social contract theory by eliminating that theory's awkward dependence on dubious accounts of tacit consent.

17.

Political Obligation and the Argument from Gratitude

A. D. M. WALKER

. . . Political obligation, I shall argue, can be seen as an obligation of gratitude: our obligation to comply with the law is grounded in considerations of gratitude for benefits received from the state. This, I realize, is a claim few will be disposed to regard with favor. The argument from gratitude has never enjoyed philosophical popularity. First sketched in Plato's *Crito,* it does not figure in the writings of the classical political philosophers of the seventeenth and eighteenth centuries. It appears to be endorsed by Mill in *On Liberty,* and in the present century has attracted a handful of adherents, of whom the best known is probably Sir David Ross. But within the last decade it has received detailed critical scrutiny on a number of occasions, and each time been pronounced radically defective.[1] The argument's widespread lack of appeal, however, probably owes less to a sober examination of its supposed defects than to a deeper revulsion at the very idea of basing political obligation on considerations of gratitude. Some perhaps think that if political obligation is a matter of gratitude we are bound to accede to the demands of the state in an uncritical and childlike way, and are led by this thought to have no truck with an argument which seems to legitimize so deplorably supine an attitude to authority. Others may feel that, like the argument from prescription, it requires special prior assumptions of a religious or metaphysical kind and commits its advocates to a mystical or Hegelian reverence for the state.[2]

There is no denying the melancholy history of the argument from gratitude. But nonetheless I wish to argue that the argument *does* represent a defensible response to the problem of political obligation. My basic point will be that discussion of the argument has been vitiated by misunderstanding, prejudice, and an imperfect grasp of the nature of gratitude. As a result, only the less plausible versions of the argument have been considered, and while the objections

---

[1] See Plato, *Crito* 48b–52d; J. S. Mill, *On Liberty* (London: Collins, 1979), chap. IV. p. 205; W. D. Ross, *The Right and the Good* (Oxford: Oxford University Press, 1930), p. 27; Plamenatz, *Consent, Freedom and Political Obligation* 2d ed. (Oxford: Oxford University Press, 1967), p. 24; A. C. Ewing, *The Individual, the State and World Government* (London: Macmillan, 1947), p. 218. Recent discussions of the argument are to be found in A. D. Woozley, *Law and Obedience* (London: Duckworth, 1979), chap. 4. John Simmons, *Moral Principles and Political Obligations* (Princeton: Princeton University Press, 1979), chap. VII; M. B. E. Smith, "Is There a Prima Facie Obligation to Obey the Law?" *Yale Law Journal* 82 (1973), esp. pp. 953–54.

[2] Cf. Nannerl O. Henry on the argument from prescription in "Political Obligation and Collective Goods," in *Political and Legal Obligations,* Nomos XII, ed. J. R. Pennock and J. W. Chapman (New York: New York University Press, 1970), p. 265.

advanced against them are often well founded, they neglect the possibility of restating the argument in a more powerful form that would evade their force.

I

At least two versions of the argument from gratitude are to be found in the literature. The first has its prototype in Plato's *Crito* and appeals to an analogy between a citizen's relationship to the state and a child's to its parents.[3] It compares the benefits citizens receive from the state with the benefits children receive form their parents in the course of their upbringing, and argues that as a child owes obedience to its parents, the citizen has an analogous obligation of gratitude to comply with the law. This version of the argument need not detain us. Quite apart from the many points of dissimilarity between political and familial relationships, which weaken the analogy, a crucial flaw in the argument is its assumption that a child's obligation to obey its parents is *an obligation of gratitude*. Even if we concede that children have obligations of gratitude to their parents and also have an obligation to obey them, it is unclear that the latter is a particular instance of the former. And if a child's obligation to obey its parents is not an obligation of gratitude, the appeal to the relationship between parents and children does nothing to show that among any obligations of gratitude a citizen may have to the state, there will be, specifically, an obligation to obey the law.

The second version of the argument needs to be considered at greater length. It dispenses with the analogy between political and familial relationships and seeks to derive a citizen's obligation to comply with the law from a general principle of gratitude. The brief remarks in Ross and Plamenatz suggest that they would have developed the argument along those lines, and it is in this form that the argument has received careful scrutiny in A. J. Simmons's recent discussion.[4] As discussed by Simmons, the argument appears to rest on the idea that the receipt of a benefit puts one under an obligation to requite one's benefactor, to confer on him a benefit in return for the benefit one has received from him. It is this principle of requital or reciprocation that the argument applies to the relationship between citizen and state to establish the fact of political obligation. In outline the argument runs as follows:

(1) The person who receives benefits from X has an obligation to requite or make a suitable return to X. (Let us call this the "principle of requital.")
(2) Every citizen has received benefits from the state.
(3) Every citizen has an obligation to make a suitable return to the state.
(4) Compliance with the law is a suitable return.
(5) Every citizen has an obligation to comply with the laws of his state.

---

[3] This version of the argument is discussed in Woozley, *Law and Obedience*, esp. pp. 64–70, and Simmons, *Moral Principles and Political Obligations*, pp. 160–62.

[4] See Ross, *The Right and the Good*, p. 27; Plamenatz, *Consent, Freedom and Political Obligation*, p. 24; Simmons, *Moral Principles and Political Obligations*, chap. VII.

Simmons rightly challenges this version of the argument. First, its foundation is insecure. As it stands, step 1, which states the principle of requital, is false. The mere receipt of benefits does not put one under an obligation of requital or reciprocation; the person who receives benefits from another does not always have an obligation to requite his benefactor, but only in certain circumstances. So if we are to defend the argument, we need to modify step 1 by restricting the application of the principle of requital to those circumstances in which beneficiaries genuinely have an obligation to requite their benefactors. Simmons himself clarifies five conditions which he claims must be satisfied before the recipient of a benefit has an obligation of requital—the chief of these being (1) that "the benefit must be granted by means of some special effort or sacrifice" and (2) that "the benefit must not be granted unintentionally, involuntarily, or for disqualifying reasons" (such as reasons of self-interest or malice). But all this merely shifts the difficulty to a different point in the argument. For whether or not we accept every detail of Simmons's implicit reformulation of the principle of requital, it looks as if the benefits citizens receive from the state will not meet all the conditions laid down by this new version of the principle as necessary for the existence of an obligation of requital. In other words, the problem will now be step 2: if we modify step 2 in line with the necessary modifications to step 1, what step 2 asserts will be false.[5]

Simmons's second objection focuses on step 4. Even if, as step 3 asserts, citizens have an obligation of gratitude to make a suitable return to the state, it still has to be shown that compliance with the law constitutes a suitable return. That it does is not self-evident. And even if this could be shown, it would not be enough. For what seems needed at step 4 to complete the argument is the premise that compliance with the law is not merely *a suitable,* but *the uniquely suitable,* return. Without this stronger premise it may be argued that there is some other, equally suitable return and that the citizen who has made that return, having discharged his obligation of gratitude to the state, has no further obligation of gratitude to comply with the law.[6]

Finally, to add a comment of my own, this version of the argument is in fact even more seriously defective than Simmons supposes. The fundamental problem is that it does not take sufficient account of the existence of different kinds of obligations of gratitude, and in consequence states the basic principle to which it appeals in a vague and confused way. The truth is that the principle of requital, however qualified, does not focus unambiguously on any genuine obligation of gratitude. In this connection it is worth remembering that Simmons typically regards obligations of gratitude as a matter of compensation or repayment. He occasionally refers to obligations that it would be strained to characterize in these terms, but apparently without recognizing the significance of the fact. And he abandons his discussion of the content of obligations

[5] See Simmons, *Moral Principles and Political Obligations,* pp. 169–79, 187–90. The quotations summarizing Simmons's first and second conditions are taken from p. 178.

[6] See ibid., pp. 185–87; and cf. Smith, "Is There a Prima Facie Obligation to Obey the Law?" pp. 953–54.

of gratitude without reaching any definite conclusions.[7] He has, I suspect, little interest in the matter because he thinks that whatever kinds of obligation may be distinguished, none will provide a secure foundation for the argument from gratitude. I shall argue that the grateful response comprises a number of different obligations and that while we cannot base political obligation on a beneficiary's obligation to requite or compensate his benefactor, arguments based on *other* obligations of gratitude have a better prospect of success. Before developing these thoughts, though, I must deal with a difficulty which seems to threaten any version of the argument from gratitude.

II

Since the state is the source of the benefits to which the argument from gratitude appeals, and the resultant obligation of gratitude is an obligation owed to the state, proponents of the argument must assume it makes sense to be grateful not only to individual persons, but also to institutions. This assumption is, I am sure, the source of much hostility to the argument, it being widely held that gratitude to institutions or even groups of persons is impossible[8]—unless perhaps an exotic metaphysics allows us to conceive of social entities as superpersons. This difficulty requires immediate attention if my strategy is to stand any chance of success.

Like many contemporary philosophers,[9] I take the state to be a kind of association. I see it as a collection of individuals organized for the achievement of certain aims within a legal and political framework, and I understand claims about the state as claims about individuals or groups of individuals insofar as they play a part within this framework. Thus in speaking of political obligation as an obligation of gratitude owed to the state, I mean that the obligation is owed to one's fellow citizens collectively. Two aspects of this position deserve emphasis. First, the state is not to be identified with the government. Acceptance of the argument from gratitude does not commit us to viewing political obligation, in the manner of Socrates, as essentially a relationship between "rulers" and their subjects. The obligation is owed by citizens to their fellow citizens collectively rather than to the government. Second, the conception of the state as an association of individuals, whatever its problems, manifestly does not depend on exotic metaphysical assumptions. If the argument from gratitude has a mystical flavor, its source is not here.

Now, some may think that I have already said enough to dispose of the objection that gratitude to institutions is an impossibility. For if the state is no more than an association of individuals, and the obligation to comply with the law is owed to our fellow citizens collectively, is not the objection *irrelevant* to

[7] See Simmons, *Moral Principles and Political Obligations*, pp. 164–69.

[8] See ibid., pp. 187–89.

[9] See, e.g., the account in D. D. Raphael, *Problems of Political Philosophy* (London: Macmillan, 1976), pp. 39–53.

the argument from gratitude? Our fellow citizens are surely not an institution. I have considerable sympathy with this line of thought, but nonetheless it seems unwise to dismiss the objection quite so quickly. After all, might it not be counterargued with some plausibility that if our fellow citizens viewed collectively are the state, it follows, since the state *is* an institution, that our obligation to comply with the law *is* owed to an institution? And in any case, as I mentioned earlier, even the possibility that gratitude may be owed to a group of individuals collectively is sometimes held to be problematic. It will be better, I think, to proceed more slowly and consider in its own right the claim that gratitude to institutions is impossible.

I shall offer two arguments against this claim: first, that ordinary thought recognizes the possibility of gratitude to institutions, so gratitude of this kind is at least not as strange or exceptional as some philosophers would have us believe; and second, that the reasons commonly given for believing that institutions cannot be a legitimate focus of gratitude are easily countered. I should also add that my own account of gratitude, presented in the next section, has no difficulty in accommodating gratitude to institutions. But naturally at this stage I cannot develop this point.

Let me begin my first line of argument with some examples: the patient who donates a sum of money to the hospital in which she received treatment, perhaps many years before, and the former pupil or former student who gives something as a gift to his old school or university. These individuals will say that they have been helped or benefited by the institution, and that the donation or gift is given out of gratitude or to express their gratitude. Nor, I should add, do they merely *feel grateful* to the institution without thinking they have any obligations to it. Sometimes this may be so. But if, say, the institution were in financial difficulty or threatened with closure, they might well see themselves as under an obligation to contribute to an appeal: they would insist, and rightly, that they owed it to the institution to do what they could to ensure its survival. All this is familiar enough. Cynics may attribute it to a mixture of sentimentality of the part of the donors and self-interest on the part of the recipient institutions. But why should the cynics always be right? And even if they were, it would still be a significant fact that someone who was not actually grateful to an institution could at least represent himself or herself as being grateful to it.

Certainly by themselves these examples do not take us very far. They merely invite the stock response that the persons in question are really grateful not to an institution but to particular individuals within it, and that to describe them as grateful to the institution is to speak loosely and improperly.[10] But this response, I believe, is inadequate. Even if the grateful patient and grateful pupil are grateful to specific persons within the relevant institutions, it does not follow from this that they are grateful to these persons *and not to the institutions*. And it is, after all, to the institutions, and not to particular persons within them, that the gifts are given. Further, the suggestion that if we are to speak accurately we must always describe individuals as grateful to persons, never to

[10] See Simmons, *Moral Principles and Political Obligations*, p. 188.

institutions, rides roughshod over a vital distinction. Must we not distinguish between the person who loathes his old school and all it stands for but feels gratitude towards a particular master who befriended him, and the very different person who, while having no recollections of special kindness from any particular master, thinks that his schooldays were the happiest days of his life? Against the background of these and similar possibilities the description of someone as grateful to an institution seems sometimes precisely the right description of him.

But, our objector may persist, even when the former pupil cannot fix on any particular master or masters to whom he is grateful (so that we are inclined to say that he is grateful to the school), he must still be *primarily* or *basically* grateful to individual persons. His gratitude to the school rests on—that is, has arisen by association, transference, or some other process out of—gratitude to certain individuals (whom perhaps he can no longer identify). Gratitude to institutions must always be derivative in this way from gratitude to individuals. This claim too, however, need not disturb us. For one thing, it implicitly acknowledges the genuineness of gratitude to institutions. In insisting that gratitude to institutions is derivative, it concedes that gratitude to institutions is a genuine possibility. So even if the claim were true, it would pose no threat to the argument from gratitude. But the claim is not obviously true. While gratitude to an institution may *sometimes* be derivative from gratitude to persons within the institution—as when the patient who appreciates the dedication of the staff who nursed her in the intensive care unit is grateful to the hospital when she is, basically, grateful to these particular members of its staff—the reverse process also appears to be a possibility. What of the person who has been in hospital many times, perhaps without ever encountering conspicuous concern or kindness from the hospital staff, but who one day happens to reflect on the extent to which she has benefited from her treatment over the years? Could she not feel grateful to the hospital for the totality of these benefits, and grateful derivatively to particular doctors and nurses as members of this beneficent institution? What does seem to be true is that if one is grateful to an institution, one's gratitude presupposes activity by some person or persons associated with the institution. (This would be a simple consequence of the truth that an institution cannot benefit or help us except through the activities of its members.) It would be easy to confuse this point with the rather different one that gratitude to an institution presupposes *gratitude* to a person or persons associated with the institution, and to take the truth of the former for the truth of the latter. Needless to say, the fact that gratitude to an institution presupposes activity on the part of its members raises no difficulty for the argument from gratitude.

Ordinary thought, then, recognizes the possibility of gratitude to institutions, and philosophically inspired attempts to dispose of or reinterpret familiar examples of this possibility do not succeed. Further—to turn now, more briefly, to my second line of argument—the objections commonly advanced against the possibility of gratitude to institutions are easily met. Take the objection that we cannot be grateful to an institution because gratitude is appropriate only when benefits are conferred from a particular motive, and institutions cannot have motives.[11] Well, certainly an institution cannot have motives; but institutions do have something *analogous* to motives. We can speak of the *purpose* or *function* of an institution, of the *policies* which guide its operations, and of the *reasons* why it produces whatever benefits it produces. We can distinguish between the *intended* and the *unintended* benefits that result from the operations of an institution, and draw distinctions, similar to those we draw in the case of benefits conferred by individuals, between someone's benefiting from an institution which exists to benefit him, his benefiting incidentally from the operations of an institution, his receiving benefits which are intended ultimately to further the interests of the institution, and so on.

Gratitude to institutions is a fascinating topic in its own right, and deserves more attention than I can give it here. I do not pretend to have exhausted the topic, but I do think that I have established a prima facie case for the possibility of gratitude to institutions that permits us to proceed with our exploration of the argument from gratitude.

III

Since previous discussions of the argument from gratitude have been flawed by an imperfect grasp of the nature of gratitude, I shall preface my own attempt to find a satisfactory version of the argument with some general remarks about the notion. I shall not offer much by way of defending this account of gratitude: I hope its constituent elements will seem persuasive without argument.[12]

The core of the grateful response is a set of *attitudes*.[13] We cannot understand what gratitude requires in the sphere of action without first understanding the attitudes grateful individuals are presumed to have. Gratitude, as the appropriate response to benefits received through the agency of a benefactor, involves attitudes both towards the benefit and towards the benefactor: we must properly *appreciate* the benefit and have *goodwill* and *respect* for our benefactor. The notions of appreciation, goodwill, and respect are themselves vague and could do with further scrutiny—I shall say more below about goodwill—but our first priority must be to consider how these attitudes are related to the requirements of gratitude in the sphere of action. The fundamental point here is that the attitudes which form the basis of the grateful response generate constraints on action in two different ways. The grateful person must, on the one hand, demonstrate or make clear to his benefactor that he has the appropriate attitudes and, on the other, not act in ways incompatible with his possession of these attitudes. It is vital to keep these different types of obligation

---

[11] See ibid., pp. 189–90.

[12] The best account of gratitude with which I am familiar is Aquinas, *Summa Theologiae* IIaIIae, qq 106 7. I have discussed some of the points I make in this section in "Gratefulness and Gratitude," *Proceedings of the Aristotelian Society* 81 (1980–81).

[13] This point is well argued in Fred Berger, "Gratitude," *Ethics* 85 (1974–75).

distinct. What gratitude requires on the first count is essentially declarative. In discharging an obligation of this type the grateful person seeks to communicate to his benefactor that he has certain attitudes: he acts not just because he is grateful but to show his benefactor that he is. Hence what he does may have a largely symbolic significance, and his purpose is typically achieved once and for all by a single expression of thanks or token or gesture of appreciation. By contrast, what gratitude requires on the second count is not essentially declarative. When, for example, a grateful person hears that his benefactor has fallen on hard times and is moved by goodwill to come to his aid, he acts not because he wishes to *show* that he has goodwill, but because he *has* goodwill—he may even act in secret and conceal his identity from his benefactor. The benefit he confers is substantial rather than symbolic, and is not naturally described as a token or gesture of gratitude. Further, the requirements of gratitude on this second count cannot be met once and for all. For example, what the grateful person is committed to by the goodwill he has for his benefactor depends upon the circumstances: having helped his benefactor on one occasion, he is not then free of obligation, because circumstances may arise in which goodwill requires him to give help again.

All this is only a sketch, but it will suffice. The main point I wish to draw from it seems uncontentious: there are different kinds of obligations of gratitude. We have distinguished obligations to demonstrate our gratitude from obligations not to act in ways incompatible with the attitudes which make up the core of the grateful response. But we can also distinguish obligations of gratitude in terms of the different attitudes underlying them: some arise out of goodwill, others out of respect, and so on. A proper awareness of this variety is essential if we are to develop a satisfactory version of the argument from gratitude.

It is equally clear, I think, that gratitude is not a species of fairness. Quite apart from the point that a grasp of the appropriate attitudes is fundamental for an understanding of gratitude in a way that is not for fairness, it is plain that the *content* of obligations of gratitude is often such that they cannot plausibly be thought of as obligations of fairness. What gratitude requires cannot always be seen as, say, a matter of reciprocity or of conformity to a practice in which both beneficiary and benefactor are participants. Further, even when the content of an obligation of gratitude might allow us to view it as an obligation of fairness, the grateful person cannot be motivated to fulfill the obligation by considerations of fairness. If he acts well towards his benefactor only because he thinks that fairness requires this, or because he wishes to reward or compensate his benefactor, we shall be inclined to say that despite first appearances we do not after all have a case of gratitude. Appeals to gratitude, then, are not appeals to fairness, and the argument from gratitude is not a species of the argument from fairness.

All this puts us in a better position to appreciate my point that discussions of the argument from gratitude have been hampered by an imperfect grasp of the nature of gratitude. If (with Simmons) we base the argument on an obligation of requital, we leave it obscure what obligation of gratitude this is meant to be. And if we then clarify the obligation (as Simmons does) in terms of compensation or repayment, it seems no longer to be an obligation of gratitude at all. True, at least one recent discussion does fare better than Simmons's in this respect. The version of the argument discussed by M. B. E. Smith appeals unequivocally to the obligation to show or display our gratitude to a benefactor. But even Smith does not recognize the variety of obligations of gratitude, and in dismissing this version of the argument he overlooks the possibility of a version which appeals not to an obligation to demonstrate our gratitude, but to an obligation not to act in ways incompatible with the attitudes which constitute the core of the grateful response. It is this possibility I shall explore in what follows.

IV

Gratitude requires appreciation of the benefits we receive together with goodwill and respect for our benefactors. Now, it may well be possible to base a persuasive version of the argument from gratitude on the requirements of appreciation or respect, but our best chance of success, I believe, lies with an argument based on the requirements of goodwill—an argument that appeals to our obligation not to act in ways that betray lack of goodwill for a benefactor.

Let me first indicate, very roughly, the content of this obligation. Goodwill for a benefactor may involve other constraints on our actions besides those I list; some of the constraints I list may be as much requirements of respect as requirements of goodwill; and a longer account would have to offer more detailed formulations of the several constraints. But for the moment none of this matters. My immediate purpose is simply to give a preliminary view of the different ways of developing the argument from gratitude in terms of the requirement of goodwill. With these provisos, it seems safe to say that goodwill for a benefactor requires one

(a) to help him if he is in need or distress and one can do so at no great cost to oneself;
(b) to comply with his reasonable requests;
(c) to avoid harming him or acting contrary to his interests; and
(d) to respect his rights.

Violation of any of these requirements would seem prima facie to license a charge of ingratitude.

Clearly, however, an adequate version of the argument from gratitude must be based on a principle which is not only true or acceptable, but meets certain other criteria as well. First, the principle must satisfy the criterion of *relevance*. It must be relevant to, or bear on, the issue of a citizen's compliance with the law. We must be able to see compliance with the law as an instance of the kind of action which the principle asserts to be required by considerations of gratitude. Second, as a response to the traditional problem of political obligation, the argument from gratitude must be an independent argument. If it can persuade us that we have an obligation to comply with the law only by pre-supposing another argument which can already persuade us of this, we would do better to jettison the argument from gratitude in favor of this other, more fundamental argument. An adequate version of the argument must therefore appeal to a principle which meets the criterion of *independence*. The actions required by the principle must be actions whose obligatoriness in the name of gratitude does not depend on their being already obligatory for some other reason.

Judged by these criteria, principles (a), (b), and (d) appear unlikely to yield adequate versions of the argument. Principles (a) and (b) do not seem to meet the criterion of relevance. It seems intolerably strained to represent the citizen who complies with the law either as helping a benefactor in need or as meeting a benefactor's reasonable request: his compliance with the law does not rescue the state from any kind of grave misfortune, and the state does not *request* but *demands* his compliance. Principle (d), on the other hand, runs afoul of the criterion of independence. We have a general obligation to respect the rights of others, even if the violation of a benefactor's rights is peculiarly reprehensible. An argument based on (d) will not count as an independent argument, since the appeal to (d) presupposes that the state already has a right to its citizens' compliance with the law, in which case the problem of political obligation has already been solved.

Principle (c), that one has an obligation to avoid harming one's benefactor or acting contrary to his interests, may look at first as unpromising as principles (a), (b), and (d). But a little reflection shows that this is not so. Admittedly, *some* of the actions proscribed by (c) (for example, the infliction of physical harm on a benefactor) may owe their proscription on grounds of ingratitude to their already being proscribed by some other obligation. But this is not true of all the actions that come within the scope of the principle. It is not true, conspicuously, of some of the actions that involve damage to a benefactor's interests rather than physical harm to him. We do have a particular obligation of gratitude to be mindful of our benefactors' interests, to take care not to damage them, and to give them a special weight in our deliberations. Most of us, for example, do not scruple in casual conversation to pass on gossip about mutual acquaintances; nor do we, I believe, have any general obligation to abstain from gossip. If, however, the gossip concerns someone who has given me a great deal of help, I *do* feel myself under an obligation not to retail it: I have an obligation to protect my benefactor's reputation, and passing on the gossip is incompatible with the regard I should have for his interests. Again, as a member of a committee, I may feel an obligation not to vote for a proposal which would significantly damage my benefactor's interests. Doubtless this obligation will almost always be outweighed by my duty, as a member of the committee, to some wider good; but even so, I shall apologize to my benefactor for having acted in a way that adversely affects his interests—a fact which surely suggests the existence of an obligation that has been overridden. Rather differently, I may feel an obligation not to put myself in competition with a benefactor, and take care to avoid situations in which I can succeed only at his expense.

We do indeed, it seems, have an obligation of gratitude not to damage our bene-factors' interests, and the obligatoriness of the actions required under this rubric does not, in general, depend on their being already obligatory for an-other reason. Thus a version of the argument from gratitude that appeals to principle (c) can meet the criterion of independence.

But what of the criterion of relevance? Is principle (c) relevant to the prob-lem of political obligation? Does a citizen's compliance with the law fall within the scope of principle (c), so that noncompliance with the law can be argued on this ground to be in violation of an obligation of gratitude? If citizens are beneficiaries of the state—a matter to which I shall return below—it seems that this question must be answered affirmatively. In general, noncompliance with the law damages the interests of the state. It is manifestly in the state's interests that its citizens should be law-abiding; indeed without a fair measure of com-pliance with the law no state could function or survive. This does not mean that it is in the state's interests that its citizens should comply with every law, how-ever pointless, misconceived, or unjust, or that their compliance should ever be slavish or uncritical. On the contrary, the interests of the state may sometimes be advanced if bad legislation is opposed or disregarded, and in these circum-stances the argument from gratitude will demand not compliance, but non-compliance with the law. Once we have allowed for these points, however, we can hardly deny that it is in the state's interests for its citizens to respect the law and that this respect will involve general compliance with the law.

Ignoring for the moment, then, the ways in which its various premises stand in need of qualification, we can summarize the new version of the argument from gratitude as follows:

(1) The person who benefits from X has an obligation of gratitude not to act contrary to X's interests.
(2) Every citizen has received benefits from the state.
(3) Every citizen has an obligation of gratitude not to act in ways that are con-trary to the state's interests.
(4) Noncompliance with the law is contrary to the state's interests.
(5) Every citizen has an obligation of gratitude to comply with the law.

V

This version of the argument from gratitude may still not seem especially at-tractive, but in this section I shall try to improve its chances of acceptance by showing that the objections most likely to be brought against it do not succeed. I shall begin with two objections which apply specifically to this version of the argument, and then consider some other objections which have a wider application.

The first objection concedes that it is in the state's interests that its citizens should comply with the law but holds that typically noncompliance does not fall within the scope of principle (c) because it is not motivated by ill will

towards the state. If the law is broken in the course of revolutionary or sedi-
tious activity or because an individual wishes to revenge himself on the authorities, noncompliance may have this kind of motivation. But these cases are
atypical: usually the lawbreaker acts out of self-interest and harbors no particular ill will towards the state. Hence in the typical case noncompliance with the
law cannot be said to contravene principle (c) or violate the associated obligation of gratitude which a citizen may owe to the state.

The facts to which this objection appeals cannot be disputed; what is open
to dispute is whether they justify the objection. I have claimed that gratitude requires a measure of goodwill towards a benefactor, and that the person who
acts in a way that is contrary to his benefactor's interests lacks that goodwill.
But lack of goodwill does not entail positive ill will. The possession of ill will is
but one way of lacking goodwill: indifference, absence of concern, and want of
consideration may all, as much as ill will, betray lack of goodwill for a person.
So actions can show a lack of goodwill without being motivated by ill will; and
the fact that lawbreakers typically act from motives of self-interest does *not*
mean that their contravention of the law cannot betray a lack of goodwill towards the state and violate principle (c).

The second objection challenges what the first concedes. It maintains that
while general noncompliance with the law may be contrary to the state's interests, it does not follow that individual acts of noncompliance are. Particular
breaches of the law, it insists, are not contrary to the interests of the state. The
idea is not that sometimes, in the case of bad laws, the state's interests may positively require noncompliance, but that most particular failures to comply with
the law have no effect on the state's interests. As a rule, it is wildly implausible
to attribute disastrous consequences to individual acts of noncompliance: few
individual acts of this kind are even remotely likely to destroy the state or the
legal system, whether by setting an example to others, by causing a loss of
confidence in the rule of law, or in some other way.[14] Most breaches of the law
thus "make no difference" to the state and cannot violate any obligation citizens may have to avoid actions contrary to the state's interests.

This objection, too, is easily answered. First of all, just as damage to a person's interests need not involve a threat to his existence—his interests may be
harmed without his life being even remotely in danger—so what poses no
threat to the state's existence may still in some other way be contrary to its interests—and in this connection we should not forget that typically a breach of
the law is at least *likely* to have *some* undesirable consequences for the state. Of
course, this point does not take us very far; it merely exposes the core of the objection, which is that these undesirable consequences of particular breaches of
the law either are too trivial to qualify as damage to the state's interests or, if
they do so qualify, constitute damage so slight as to be negligible. But clearly,
if this is the objection, it assumes that when we consider the bearing of acts of
noncompliance with the law on the state's interests we must take into account
only the effects of each particular act in isolation. It is therefore an adequate

---

[14] See, e.g., Woozley, *Law and Obedience*, pp. 112ff.

reply to point out that this assumption is at least dubious. Many philosophers, and among them many consequentialists, have denied that the moral significance of an action is determined by its effects alone in isolation from the effects of other similar actions. In particular, Derek Parfit has recently shown that when acts have very small or imperceptible effects, we can sometimes reach strongly counterintuitive conclusions if we look only at the consequences of each act on its own; in these circumstances, he argues, we must look at the consequences of what we collectively do.[15] Thus in considering whether acts of noncompliance with the law damage the state's interests we are certainly not obliged, as the present objection assumes, to confine our attention to the consequences of each act in isolation. There is no denying that collectively the activities of lawbreakers inflict severe damage on vital interests of the state. In the light of Parfit's arguments we might appeal to this fact and claim that each act of noncompliance with the law contravenes principle (c) because all of them taken together cause significant damage to the state's interests.

So far we have focused on the *distinctive* features of my version of the argument from gratitude, and have neglected those features which it shares with all versions of the argument. In particular, we have not considered its assumption that citizens receive benefits from the state, and are as a result under an obligation of gratitude to it. This assumption we must now examine.

That citizens under all but the most ineffectual or barbarous of governments receive significant benefits from the states to which they belong seems undeniable. This is not to say that the state is the source of all or even most of the goods we enjoy: that would be a grotesque exaggeration. Nor do we all receive the same benefits from the state or benefit to the same degree: especially between citizens of different states there may be great variations in the nature and extent of these benefits. Such variations within and between states would imply that the resultant obligation of gratitude does not always have the same weight or stringency. But this is a consequence I am happy to accept. (By the same token, citizens who receive no significant benefits from the state will fall outside the scope of the argument. But again this is no objection: do we really want to say that anyone in this unfortunate situation has a general obligation to comply with the law?) Moreover, the fact that citizens receive significant benefits from the state does not mean that they cannot suffer harm or injustice at its hands, or that, overall, they might not fare better as citizens of another state or outside the jurisdiction of any state. These considerations, the truth of which will sometimes be very difficult to assess, are undoubtedly relevant to the issue of our obligation to comply with the law. But they are best handled as possible grounds for distinct lines of argument whose conclusions we must then weigh against that of the argument from gratitude in order to settle whether, all things considered, in a particular case a citizen should comply with the law.

If the argument from gratitude is to succeed, however, we must establish not only that citizens receive benefits from the state but that these benefits place

---

[15] See Derek Parfit, *Reasons and Persons* (Oxford: Oxford University Press, 1984), chap. 3, esp. pp. 75–82.

them under an obligation of gratitude. Recent discussions tend to take much too restrictive a view of the circumstances in which a grateful response is appropriate. Simmons, for example, as I have said, lays down five conditions which must be met before the receipt of a benefit can give rise to an obligation of gratitude, the chief of these being (1) that "the benefit must be granted by means of some special effort or sacrifice" and (2) that "the benefit must not be granted unintentionally, involuntarily, or for disqualifying reasons." He then argues that the benefits citizens receive from the state do not meet these conditions and that, if only for this reason, the argument from gratitude must fail.[16] But should we accept Simmons's account? Is he not simply mistaken to hold that benefits call for gratitude only if they involve special effort or sacrifice on the part of a benefactor? If I am about to drown when a strong swimmer already in the water notices my plight, swims over, and rescues me, without any special effort or sacrifice on his part, do I owe him no gratitude? Would gratitude in these circumstances be inappropriate? Again, so far as motivation is concerned, while I may be under no obligation to the person who benefits me inadvertently or entirely out of self-interest, we must not inflate this point and claim that only benefits motivated purely by goodwill require gratitude. We should allow that obligations of gratitude *are* generated when benefits are the result of mixed motives and conferred from a mixture of self-interest and goodwill. If so, we can accept that there is *some* truth even in a Thrasymachean view of the state, while still holding that the benefits citizens receive from the state give rise to obligations of gratitude. Only if these benefits were provided *solely* by way of advancing the interests of the authorities or a particular class would the argument from gratitude collapse. (But then if we thought Thrasymachus's view represented the whole truth about the state, we would hardly want to say that citizens have any obligation to comply with the law.) In sum, provided we take a tolerably realistic view of the way the state operates and bear in mind what was said in Section II in response to the claim that gratitude to institutions is impossible, we appear to have no good reason for denying that the benefits citizens receive from the state can generate obligations of gratitude.

This may be challenged, finally, by those who believe that gratitude to the state is ruled out by the fact of taxation. Taxes, it will be said, are the price citizens pay for the benefits they receive from the state: the relationship between citizen and state resembles a commercial relationship, and no more in the one case than in the other is there a place for gratitude. This objection can be quickly disposed of. First, we may challenge its easy assumption that gratitude never has a place in commercial relationships. Second, we must surely reject the idea that the relationship of citizen to state is akin to a commercial relationship. For one thing, the state, unlike a commercial institution, is a redistributive agency. There is no direct relationship between the taxes one pays and the benefits one receives, many of the benefits provided by the state being available even to those who pay no taxes at all. Third, the objection seems to equate the state with the authorities or the government: it represents taxation as the price

---

[16] See note 5 above.

paid collectively by citizens for the benefits supplied by the government. Hence what it would exclude, if successful, is the possibility of an obligation of gratitude owed by citizens to the government. But this is not what I have sought to establish. In my view political obligation as an obligation of gratitude to the state is an obligation which each citizen owes to his fellow citizens collectively.

VI

Sections IV and V present what I believe is a strong case for my version of the argument from gratitude. More can be said in its defense, but I prefer to conclude with a number of more general points which I hope will place my enterprise in a favorable light and supply a motive for tackling whatever other difficulties are thought still to lie in its way.

First, the claim made by my version of the argument is a limited one. Although it seeks in the spirit of traditional answers to the problem of political obligation to establish a general obligation to comply with the law, this obligation is only, in Ross's phrase, a prima facie obligation, and I have said nothing about its weight or stringency, save to remark that it will vary with the nature and extent of the benefits a citizen receives. My version of the argument, then, unlike the Socratic version in the *Crito,* allows that our obligation of gratitude to comply with the law may sometimes be overridden by other, weightier obligations and does not involve us in any extravagant commitments.

Second, considerations of gratitude can provide a congenial framework for reflection on other issues in political philosophy. As we have seen, the considerations to which my version of the argument from gratitude appeals would justify *noncompliance* with the law in certain circumstances. It looks therefore as if they could supply the foundation for a theory of civil disobedience.[17] Further, since the motivation of the benefits we receive bears on the appropriateness of a grateful response to them, the argument from gratitude forces us to consider the spirit in which the state provides benefits for its citizens and calls for scrutiny of, among other things, the intentions and motives of the authorities and others who play a special part in the provision of these benefits. I have stressed, however, that gratitude involves several different attitudes and a variety of distinct obligations. My attempt to deal with the problem of political obligation has drawn on only one element in the grateful response. But is it not reasonable to hope that other elements in the grateful response will prove relevant to other aspects of political life? And if so, shall we not be even better placed to answer the complaint (mentioned at the beginning of this article) that the traditional problem of political obligation unnaturally isolates the issue of compliance with the law from our other political responsibilities?

[17] In this respect my version of the argument from gratitude fares better than the argument from consent. As Hanna Pitkin has observed, though the argument from consent may sometimes *permit* noncompliance with the law, it seems to have no place for an *obligation* not to comply with the law. See Pitkin, "Obligation and Consent," in *Philosophy, Politics, and Society,* ser. IV, ed. P. Laslett, W. G. Runelman, and Q. Skinner (Oxford: Blackwell, 1979), pp. 66–67.

Lastly, it is a commonplace that different answers to the problem of political obligation invite different views of the nature of political communities. As Simmons points out, the argument from fair play is more attractive than the argument from consent insofar as it portrays citizens as standing "in a cooperative relationship to their fellows," whereas the argument from consent represents them as standing "in an adversary relationship with the government." [18] The argument from gratitude seems even more attractive in this respect than the argument from fair play: it suggests a view of political communities as communities whose members are, or should be, bound to one another by ties of goodwill and respect. But this, it may be said, so far from being an attractive feature of the argument, is its fundamental weakness. Its conception of the political community as one whose members are bound to one another by what Aristotle would call "civic friendship" may fit the "face-to-face" society of the Greek *polis,* but has no place in the modern nation state. This claim, I believe, is false; but the issue it raises is, as Aristotle himself would doubtless have agreed, more appropriately discussed elsewhere. For the present I must be content to let the fate of the argument from gratitude depend on the satisfactory resolution of this larger issue.

[18] See Simmons, *Moral Principles and Political Obligations,* p. 116.

18.
Utility and Obedience to Law
ROLF E. SARTORIUS

1. POLITICAL OBLIGATION

The bonds of social union should not be cemented by force alone, even in those rare instances where this is possible. The ideal of an infallible political decision-making process is in practice unattainable. The only alternative to political anarchy which traditional theory recognizes would identify the ties of political association with the general recognition of a moral obligation to obey the law as such, regardless of the intrinsic merits of what it prescribes or of the likelihood of legal sanctions being applied in the case of disobedience. A political association is on this view at bottom a moral union resting upon common recognition of mutual moral obligations. The members of a political community on this view can have secure expectations that most laws will be obeyed by most men to the extent that they believe that their fellow citizens are inclined to recognize and honor their moral obligations.

Arguments for the existence of an obligation to obey the law as such fall into three chief categories: (1) Those which invoke some sort of a generalization principle; (2) Those which would reduce the obligation to obey the law to a promissory obligation by way of the notion of tacit consent; (3) Those that rely upon a principle of fair play. I shall comment but briefly upon each of these three arguments in turn.

The generalization argument implies that since the consequences of everyone's disobeying the law would obviously be disastrous, any given individual has a prima facie obligation to obey any given law. As was seen earlier . . . , the appropriate reply to the rhetorical question "What would happen if everyone did that?" is simply "Did *what?*" Any conscientious law violator who believed himself justified in violating a particular law would surely not view himself as thereby endorsing indiscriminate disobedience to laws in general, nor would he be oblivious to the importance of considering how his act of disobedience would *in fact* be likely to influence the behavior of others. If, as a matter of fact, a particular act of law violation would be likely to lead to widespread disobedience to laws in general, the act-utilitarian must surely take this into account. But if the generalization principle permits him to do so, and also permits him to treat as relevant the (much more probable) fact that his act of disobedience is *not* likely to influence the behavior of others, then it is indistinguishable from the act-utilitarian principle itself. On the other hand, if the generalization principle does not permit a consideration of how others are actually behaving or are in fact likely to behave, then it has . . . absurd consequences.

The notion that the citizens of a state may under certain conditions be taken to have given their consent to obey any valid law, whatever its content and regardless of the consequences of obeying it, has had the most widespread philosophical appeal. Indeed, it would seem that social contract theory has even become part of the folk wisdom in the United States, complete with the traditional claim that continued voluntary residence constitutes tacit consent— thus contemporary dissenters confronted with bumper stickers reading "America—Love It Or Leave It." At the time of the present writing, official political rhetoric has become equally sophisticated.

The standard objection to social contract theory seems to me to be conclusive: In order for there to be a (promissory) obligation to obey the law, there must be some act or acts which can be understood as representing full and free consent to do so. Express consent is rare, and even where it is present—as perhaps with naturalized citizens required to take an oath of allegiance—its voluntary character is suspect. It is thus that the contract theorist must rely upon the notion of tacit consent—some sign of agreement other than the written or the spoken word. Continued residence is the favorite candidate, but it is only by the wildest stretch of the philosophical imagination that it could be taken typically to be fully voluntary. For the average citizen of the modern nation state, to pack up and leave the country of one's birth and native language—to abandon one's friends, family, employment and cultural ties—is simply not a live option. And even if it were, what—according to the argument of the contract theorist—would be the plight of one who did not wish to incur an obligation to obey the laws of *any* state? Must such an individual spend his life on a raft in international waters?

A further objection to contract theory, on my view, is this: Even if one had promised to obey the law, this would not create a prima facie obligation of obedience to law which was absolute with respect to considerations of utility . . . it would still be open to the individual citizen to decide each case of obedience or disobedience on its (utilitarian) merits. The only difference that an express or tacit promise to obey the law would make is that it would create expectations the disappointment of which would be a disutility, as well as bring into play considerations concerning the likelihood of incurring the social sanctions associated with the conventional norm that one ought to keep one's promises.

The principle of fair play is this: If one has voluntarily accepted the benefits which accrue from others doing their share by way of contributing what is required of them by the rules of a just scheme of mutual cooperation, then one has a duty to do one's share when it comes one's turn. Failing to assume one's share of the burdens while accepting the benefits which come from others doing so is to be a freeloader; it is to take unfair advantage of those whose compliance with the rules of the practice render freeloading possible.

The principle of fair play has often been claimed to lie at the foundation of a prima facie duty to obey the law; one benefits from others obeying laws which one approves of but with which they disagree, one therefore has a duty to obey those laws that others approve of (if they are valid according to the relevant constitutional criteria) even though one neither approves of them nor benefits from their existence. Although the fair play principle is typically understood to leave open the possibility that other moral considerations might in the final analysis justify disobedience to law, direct utilitarian considerations are not taken to be among them. The argument applying the general principle of fair play to political obligation is found in Plato's *Crito,* and was developed at some length by John Rawls in his "Justice as Fairness."

There is an interesting connection between the principle of fair play and the generalization argument: where the former is applicable, so must be the latter. For an individual can have a duty of fair play only if he comes under the rules of a social practice *general compliance* with which produces the *benefits* which he has accepted. If *everyone* failed to do his duty as required by the rules, the practice would collapse, with the *undesirable* consequence that the benefits which are produced by it would be lost.

The fair play principle turns out to be subject to some of the same objections as is the generalization argument. In particular: Even though substantial benefits to himself or others might follow from an individual failing to assume the burdens which a given practice requires him to shoulder, and in spite of the fact that his deviation from the rules of the practice would not cause others to act similarly, he is said to have a duty to conform which cannot be overridden by a direct consideration of consequences. This view seems to me rightly described as involving what Smart has called "rule worship," and it involves the further absurdity that one would be under a duty to comply with the rules of a joint scheme of cooperation due to the acceptance of past benefits even though others generally were no longer complying. As with the generalization principle, much of the plausibility which the principle of fair play may initially seem to have stems in large part from the implicit but totally unwarranted assumption that a given act of rule violation is likely to have the consequence of causing others to act in a similar way.

Some form of a general principle of fair play does, I suspect, have the status of a conventional moral rule. The paradigm cases of its application are small group activities in which participation is clearly voluntary and the possibility of withdrawing from the activity remains a live option for all or most participants, while its frequent exercise would in fact eventually bring the activity to an end. Children playing a ball game and taking turns rotating between desirable and undesirable positions is a good example. If after pitching for three innings Johnny declines to take his turn in left field, perhaps lamely offering the excuse that it is time for his dinner, he is with good reason likely to be met with the charge of "not playing fair."

As applied to political duty or obligation, though, the argument in terms of fair play suffers from the same difficulty as does the contract theorist's argument in terms of tacit consent. It relies upon *voluntary* participation and acceptance of benefits, which, as even Rawls is now prepared to admit, "is difficult to find . . . in the case of the political system into which we are born and begin our lives." [1]

---

[1] John Rawls, *A Theory of Justice* (Cambridge, Mass.: Harvard University Press, 1971), p. 337. Rawls now argues that there is a natural duty to support just institutions in general, and a duty of obedience to law as a way of supporting a just constitution in particular, which is absolute with respect to considerations of utility and which does not rest upon any form of tacit or express consent.

As with contract theory, then, two replies are to be made to the argument that one has an obligation to obey the law based upon a principle concerning what fair play requires by way of mutual cooperation under a just constitution. First, a necessary condition for the application of the principle—fully voluntary participation—is lacking. Secondly, even if the principle were applicable, the intended result—an obligation or duty to obey the law that was absolute with respect to considerations of utility—would not follow. For the principle of fair play has at best the status of a conventional moral norm. . . . Although it was seen that such norms do bar direct appeals to utility in one sense—that having to do with the conditions under which the social sanction will be triggered, they do not generate prima facie obligations of the kind which prevent each case from being decided on its merits upon the basis of a direct consideration of utilitarian consequences.

The germ of truth contained in traditional theories of political obligation seems to me to be this: A viable political association must in the normal case rest upon a generally shared expectation on the part of most of its members that most duly enacted laws will be obeyed, and that most judicial decisions, even those that are legally and morally controversial, will be voluntarily complied with. I shall now turn to an account, in act-utilitarian terms, of the possible genesis of such expectations.

2. THE UTILITY OF OBEDIENCE TO LAW

Under certain all too familiar conditions, morality might demand rebellion and revolution, rather than support of the existing legal regime. Under other circumstances, especially within minority groups the members of which are the victims rather than the beneficiaries of the forms of conduct which the law requires, there might be a strong moral presumption in favor of disobedience, particularly with respect to certain kinds of laws. I mention this—the obvious—here only to serve as a reminder that it is only under certain conditions that there is anything for the act-utilitarian or anyone else to explain, that is, the character of the legitimate assumption that there is some kind of a presumption in favor of obedience to law.

• • •

There is much to be learned from Hobbes. Indeed, the core of my account of individual conduct and social norms can be viewed as resulting from the substitution of (at least moderately) benevolent men for selfish men in the Hobbesian model. As did Hume, Hobbes understood that it could be fully rational for individuals guided by a consequentialist choice principle to deliberately create institutions which would restructure the sets of considerations of consequences of which they in the future would have to take account. Although each individual retains the original autonomy of judgment which permits him to decide each case on its merits, his behavior will be directed into channels which it would not otherwise take because each, in conjunction with others, has acted in a manner which effects the eligibility of future candidates for action. A system of laws backed by coercive sanctions has served as our paradigm case.

Although I have followed Hobbes in conceding the significance of psychological egoism, I have not given it the central place that he did. Benevolence also operates as a strong motive, and it could well become stronger than the motive of self-interest in an affluent society (where no individual would ever have to choose between satisfying his own most basic needs and those of others) of act-utilitarians. And even within a society of men motivated solely by considerations of benevolence, I have argued that other sources of fallibility of judgment would exist which, unless corrected, would produce a socially intolerable level of mistaken attempts to identify exceptions to generally reliable rules of thumb. In those instances in which the exceptions to a generally reliable rule of thumb cannot be reliably identified, there are good reasons for giving them the status of legal norms backed by sanctions, thus rendering attempts to identify exceptions to them less likely to appear as optimistic on act-utilitarian grounds.

The legal sanction thus need not be viewed by the citizen as the imposition of an alien coercive force from above, but rather may be understood by him as representing the operation of institutions which he and others have the very best of reasons to support. There is power, and there is power. The utilitarian must reject the notion that there is a distinction to be made between legitimate and illegitimate forms of its use insofar as this distinction implies that there is a prima facie obligation to obey those having "legitimate" power or authority. But the utilitarian surely can make a distinction between those political institutions which are worthy of support on consequentialist grounds and those which are not. Where the members of a political association view themselves as mutually supporting a structure of legal norms backed by sanctions the existence of which is seen as a positive social benefit, strong ties of community are bound to exist, and individuals are likely to be quite secure in their expectation that most men will voluntarily comply with the law. To borrow Kantian terminology my use of which within an act-utilitarian framework hopefully will not be misleading: The members of a political association view one another as autonomous moral agents subject to laws that they have set unto themselves, and upon whose mutual cooperation the continued stability of their legal and political institutions depends.

Act-utilitarians would of course not seek to give social norms the status of anything *more* than rules of thumb unless they were convinced that they were *at least* generally reliable guides to conduct. Although I have argued that what I called "the reflection principle" . . . may break down, and thus that the very best law that might be enacted might on occasion be justifiably disobeyed, this is by no means to deny that the paramount concern of the members of a political community must be to assure that only the best laws possible are enacted and enforced. In light of the curious notions of political society which have found such widespread appeal, it is clear that the obvious has been lost sight of: The firmest foundation for a stable polity is simply a shared belief among its members that most laws are good, that most men will understand this, and are moral enough in most instances therefore to voluntarily obey them. When political rhetoric begins to concentrate on reasons for obedience which are far removed from such considerations, whether they be quite real (the rubber truncheons and gas grenades of the protectors of law and order), or philosophical fictions (an obligation to obey the law as such, whatever its content and regardless of the consequences of obedience), it is a sure sign that the bonds of political union are in the process of disintegrating.

Plato and Rousseau understood all of this quite well, and although we may not share their faith in the possibility of providing institutional guarantees that only good laws will be enacted, the act-utilitarian must recognize that it is a contingent question whether or not it would be rational to defer to the judgments of a class of putative experts on certain matters. Indeed, the crucial question is not whether or not one ought to recognize expertise of the sort which leads one to conclude that one must have been mistaken if one finds oneself in disagreement with the experts. It is rather this: Is it possible to identify experts who are reliable enough to warrant transferring to them considerable institutional power to make and enforce political decisions, and whose institutional role it is rational to support even when considerable doubts exist as to the wisdom of particular decisions which they reach? Where such an institutional transfer of political power is reasonable, as I believe it is in the case of the judiciary, common knowledge that this is so will provide a basis for the shared conviction that it may sometimes be necessary to obey the law simply to avoid the damage which would otherwise result to a valuable social institution. (But the question of likely institutional effects is, of course, an empirical one.) A further element in the bonds of political union, in other words, is the common conviction among the members of a community that their political and legal institutions—imperfect as they may be—are good enough to be worthy of continued support.

When they are present to a sufficient degree, as they often are, the factors considered above provide sufficient grounds for members of a political community to expect that most laws will be obeyed by most men most of the time. Not only will they have such expectations; they will arrange their affairs and make their future plans on the basis of them. The disappointment of these expectations, the interference with those arrangements, the frustration of such plans—all are disutilities associated with disobedience to law of which the act-utilitarian can and must take account. The situation, in short, is *as if* men had promised to obey the law, or recognized some other basis for an obligation to do so, such as considerations of fair play. The purpose of traditional theories of obligation, in other words, is to explain how it is that obedience to law could be generally relied upon, as it admittedly must be, within a stable political community. What we have seen is that this may be explained without positing any principle of obligation independent of the act-utilitarian principle itself.

A final concession may be made to the traditional view that there is a prima facie obligation to obey the law as such, independent of, and absolute with respect to, considerations of utility. It is this: Where things are as they should be with respect to institutional forms and the wise and moral use of political power, the presumption that any given law ought to be obeyed may be so strong as to warrant the members of a society of act-utilitarians giving the principle that one ought to obey the law the status of a conventional moral norm. Whether or not this is so is, of course, a contingent matter, and . . . such a conventional norm may be supported by one who retains the right to deviate from it on direct utilitarian grounds.

TWO

DECISION MAKING IN THE STATE

Virtually all Americans believe that governmental decisions should reflect the will of the governed; and virtually all believe, too, that the will of the governed is best expressed through a system of majoritarian decision making. Because there is so much consensus about the desirability of democracy—because we encounter so few champions of monarchy or dictatorship—we may be tempted to suppose that there is little here to discuss.

Yet just because democracy is so seldom challenged, we can easily lose sight of both its advantages and its difficulties. And, in fact, a moment's thought reveals much about democracy that is problematic. There are hard questions about its justification, its best form, and its proper limits.

Perhaps the most obvious question, and certainly the most fundamental, is why we should favor democracy at all. Broadly speaking, there are two main types of answer. To defend a system of majoritarian decision making, someone might argue either that such a system is likely to produce the best decisions or that it is the best way of *reaching* decisions. If someone takes the first approach, he is focusing on the results of the democratic process, while if someone takes the second, he is focusing on the process itself.

Before anyone can argue that democracy yields the best decisions, he must offer an account of what makes one decision better than another; and one standard that is often mentioned is the principle of utility. As we saw in Section 1, this principle tells us to maximize happiness or the satisfaction of desire. In reading 19, Jonathan Riley defends democracy on utilitarian grounds.

According to Riley, democracy and utilitarianism are internally related. More specifically, democracy is what we get when we try to apply the principle of utility without being able to compare the happiness, or utility, of different people. Democracy occupies this status because even if we cannot make such "interpersonal utility comparisons," we can at least establish how highly each person would *rank* any given outcome by asking him to choose between it and various others. Thus, to determine which course of action has the highest aggregate ranking, we need only give each person an equal voice, or vote, and then select the course of action that gains the most support. This means that utilitarians are committed to democracy if—as many believe—interpersonal utility comparisons are impossible. By extension, utilitarians may be committed to democracy even if interpersonal utility comparisons *are* possible; for the principle of utility itself forbids such comparisons when the costs of making them outweigh the benefits.

In reading 20, John Stuart Mill offers a very different kind of utilitarian defense of democracy. Unlike Riley, who focuses on the utility of democratic *decisions,* Mill stresses the utility of wide participation in the democratic *process.* Such participation, he argues, has a highly salutary effect on the character of citizens. Whereas dictatorship fosters passivity, democracy calls forth various active and cooperative virtues. It encourages initiative, fosters cooperation, compels us to look beyond our private concerns, imposes practical discipline, and provides an education in a variety of subjects. Because this argument appeals to the results of participating in the democratic process, Mill's justification of democracy incorporates elements of both the process- and the results-oriented approaches.

By contrast, other justifications are more purely process-oriented. For example, in reading 21, Peter Jones defends majority rule on the grounds that it is the *fairest* method of reaching decisions in many types of associations, including political ones. Democracy is the fairest method because it gives each member of an association an equal say in determining what it will decide and do. Having an equal say is important because each member usually has an equal interest in what the association decides.

By thus stressing democracy's fairness, Jones expresses a thought that appeals to many. But Jones maintains that this justification only succeeds when a democracy contains no stable groups that are consistently outvoted. For when a democracy does contain such a "persistent minority," the interests of its members are not satisfied in proportion to their numbers. Even if the minority makes up (say) a third of the population, its interest will not win out a third of the time. This, Jones says, gives the members of persistent minorities "a reason to complain in terms of the very principle of equality that underlies democracy."

In the end, the way we defend democracy will depend on our conception of the political process; and in reading 22, Jon Elster distinguishes three such conceptions. According to the first, voting is a way of advancing pre-existing preferences—the same ones that guide an individual's economic choices—and political decisions are therefore a means of reconciling such preferences. On the second account, voting is part of a larger process that also includes public debate and discussion—a process in which political agents seek not to advance their private interests, but to arrive at rational agreement about which policies are best. On the third account, political activity is neither a means of advancing private aims nor a vehicle for rational dialogue, but is rather something that is valuable in itself. Although Elster criticizes all three approaches, his own sympathies clearly lie with the second.

So far, we have taken "democracy" to mean simply "any political system whose important decisions are determined by majority vote." But many different structures can be democratic in this sense, so a further important question is which form of democracy is best. The next six readings explore this question.

One answer, advanced in reading 23 by Benjamin Barber, is that the optimal form is *strong* democracy. In strong democracy, decisions are made not by persons acting on behalf of the citizens but by the citizens themselves; and these decisions reflect not the fixed will of the community considered as an organic whole, but the outcome of a fluid, dynamic process in which many individuals interact. Citizens who take part in this process retain full authority over their own destiny: they surrender it neither to other people who represent them nor to such "independent grounds" for decision as abstract rights, economic markets, or the will of the community. When each citizen actively participates, the community "creates public ends where there were none before."

As Barber understands democratic participation, it encompasses a range of activities that includes "agenda-setting, deliberation, legislation, and policy implementation (in the form of 'common work')." By contrast, Amy Gutmann and Dennis Thompson also defend democratic participation in reading 24, but they stress a form of it that consists mainly of discussion and debate. Gutmann and Thomson argue that the case for deferring to a majority may depend on how thoughtful or well-informed its members are, so in addition to being fair and respecting rights, any fully adequate form of democracy must make provision for public debate of all relevant issues—including, prominently, all relevant *moral* issues. This form of democracy, they contend, is more likely than others to yield decisions that are acceptable even to those who fail to get what they want; and it can lead all citizens to take the claims of others more seriously. In addition, participating in public deliberation can help citizens understand what is morally at stake, and can increase the chances that they will recognize and learn from their mistakes.

When citizens debate, they debate the relevant factual and moral considerations. But which considerations are these, and to what restrictions, if any, should they be subject? In reading 25, Bruce Ackerman proposes a set of constraints on the reasons that can be given to justify the exercise of power. An allegiance to these constraints, he argues, is precisely what defines the liberal outlook. The constraints require, most fundamentally, that each agent be prepared to give reasons for exercising power as he proposes to do. They require, as well, that the reasons a person gives in one context be consistent with the reasons he gives in another, and that no one's reasons assert either that "his conception of the good is better than that asserted by any of his fellow citizens" or that "regardless of his conception of the good, he is intrinsically superior to one or more of his fellow citizens." In Ackerman's view, no exercise of state (or individual) power is legitimate unless it can be justified through a dialogue that

conforms to these rules. Which existing practices and institutions can be justified in this way, and what should replace any that cannot, are for Ackerman
genuinely open questions.

One obvious question about Ackerman's view is why the reasons for exercising political power *cannot* include appeals to particular conceptions of the
good. Why, if someone really believes that a given way of living is best, should
he *not* invoke its superiority to justify a policy that promotes it? In a brief but
suggestive passage, Ackerman mentions several possible answers, among them
that no one can know which way of living is best, that no one can be forced to
live a good life, and that even if someone can be forced to live a good life, the
wrong people may end up doing the forcing. However, for a more extensive
treatment of this issue, we must turn to John Rawls's discussion in reading 26.

Rawls takes as his starting point the fact that in any modern constitutional democracy, citizens are bound to hold incommensurable and conflicting
conceptions of the good. Given this fundamental fact, the challenge is to formulate an account of social justice that can be accepted by persons with radically different philosophical and religious views. To meet this challenge, we
cannot base our account on any single conception of the good, but must appeal, instead, to the "shared fund of implicitly recognized basic ideas and principles" that is embodied in our political institutions and culture. We must
appeal to these ideas and principles not because they are true—that itself
would be a controversial claim—but rather because they are widely accepted.
As Rawls develops them, the basic shared ideas include, first, an idea of persons
as free and equal—that is, as equally able to act on principles of justice and to
form, revise, and pursue conceptions of the good—and a related idea of society as a system of fair cooperation between such persons. These ideas, Rawls
says, are the basis of the theory that he advanced in his book *A Theory of Justice* (excerpted in reading 40).

Echoing Rawls, Joshua Cohen and Joel Rogers propose a "principle of
democratic legitimacy" which requires that "individuals be free and equal in
determining the conditions of their own association." They argue in reading 27
that this principle commits us not only to the familiar requirements that individual freedoms be secured by law and that any economic inequalities improve
the condition of the worst-off, but also to the further requirements that competitive political parties be subsidized, that investment decisions be subject to
democratic oversight and control, and that work be reorganized to give each
worker a chance to exercise his capacity for self-governance. Although these
requirements are quite diverse, Cohen and Rogers argue that each can be traced
to the single idea that members of the political order must "together determine
the institutions, rules, and conditions of their own association."

There is, however, an unresolved question about how this ideal can be realized in societies containing persistent minorities; and Lani Guinier returns
to this question in reading 28. She points out that the problem of persistent
minorities—that they are always outvoted so their interests are never represented—arises only in democracies in which the winner gets everything and

the loser nothing. This leads Guinier to seek an alternative in which a group's interests can be represented in proportion to its number of members. One such system is cumulative voting. Under cumulative voting, each person has as many votes as there are seats to be filled, and each can either "spend" all his votes on a single candidate or distribute them more widely. Such a system helps persistent minorities because it allows them to concentrate all their votes on a few candidates whom they favor. If a minority chooses to do this, it cannot be denied representation.

Although persistent minorities pose especially difficult problems, democracies can also mistreat minorities that are *not* persistent; and a final question is how to prevent this. Are there some decisions that democracies simply should not be allowed to make? If so, which decisions are these, and what justifies drawing the line just here? And how are violations to be detected and enforced? The final three readings discuss these questions. In doing so, they make special reference to the limitations imposed upon majoritarian decision making by the United States Constitution.

In reading 29, John Hart Ely proposes an answer that he sees as implicit in the legal and political tradition of the United States. On Ely's account, the main reason for constraining the democratic process is not to protect any independently defensible set of values or rights, but rather to ensure that all citizens are represented when decisions are made. This interpretation, he argues, illuminates both the body of our Constitution and many of its amendments. To cite just one example, it construes the Fifth Amendment's requirement that private property not be taken without compensation as protecting a particular minority—those whose property could be put to public use—from the decisions of the majority. Although Ely concedes that his interpretation does not account for every feature of the Constitution, he argues that it makes more sense of that document than any competing interpretation. He argues, as well, that if he is right about the constraints to which democracies ought to be subjected, then appointed judges, who stand outside the political process, are the persons best suited to interpret and enforce them.

Ronald Dworkin (reading 30) offers a very different account of the constraints on democratic decision making. According to Dworkin, the point of those constraints is precisely to protect moral rights. While many profess not to understand such rights, Dworkin suggests that they are easily explained. In his view, a person "has a moral right against the state if for some reason the state would do wrong to treat him in a certain way, even though it would be in the general interest to do so."

Dworkin also proposes an account of how judges should decide which rights the Constitution protects. Their decisions, he says, should be based on a "scheme of abstract and concrete principles that provides a coherent justification for all common law precedents and, so far as these are to be justified on principle, constitutional and statutory provisions as well." To arrive at such a scheme, a judge must not only decide which principles best justify each provision of the Constitution, but must square his view of what justifies each provision with his view of what justifies each other provision. He must also square all this with the precedents established by other judges. Given the magnitude of this task, it is no wonder that Dworkin calls his ideal judge "Hercules."

Finally, in reading 31, Bruce Ackerman suggests a view that stands somewhere between the theories of Ely and Dworkin. According to Ackerman, the most characteristic feature of the American political system is that it embodies two distinct levels of democratic decision making. At one level, we find the ordinary decisions that are the stuff of elections, legislative deliberation, and the like; but at another, we find a form of "higher lawmaking" that occurs only at times of crisis and that is accompanied by an extraordinary mobilization of the people's attention and will. Two examples of such higher lawmaking are, first, the deliberations that led to the adoption of the Constitution itself, and, second, the abolition of slavery. Given their special status, these extraordinary decisions must be protected from repeal through ordinary legislation, and in our system, the task of preserving them falls to the Supreme Court. By offering this defense of judicial review, Ackerman goes beyond Ely's "participation-oriented, representation-reinforcing approach" without embracing Dworkin's commitment to independent moral rights.

PART

IV

JUSTIFICATIONS OF MAJORITARIAN DECISION MAKING

19.
Utilitarian Ethics and
Democratic Government
JONATHAN RILEY

INTRODUCTION

John Hart Ely suggests that "democracy is a sort of applied utilitarianism—unfortunately possessing utilitarianism's weaknesses as well as its strengths—an institutional way of determining the happiness of the greatest number."[1] A similar suggestion is offered by Alexis de Tocqueville: "Democratic laws generally tend to promote the welfare of the greatest possible number; for they emanate from the majority of the citizens, who are subject to error, but who cannot have an interest opposed to their own advantage. . . . The advantage of democracy does not consist . . . in favoring the prosperity of all, but simply in contributing to the well-being of the greatest number."[2] This putative link between utilitarian ethics and democratic government is also taken for granted by classical English utilitarians, including Jeremy Bentham, James Mill, and (with suitable caveats) even John Stuart Mill.[3] Moreover, all of the foregoing writers use America to exemplify their thesis. Ely's remarks more or less reflect the general tenor of the discussion: "What is important to an attempt to understand the seemingly inexorable appeal of democracy in America is that whether we admit it or not . . . we are all, at least as regards the beginnings of our analysis of proposed governmental policy, utilitarians. There may be, indeed there must be, further steps, but the formation of public policy, at least in this country, begins with the questions how many are helped, how many hurt, and by how much."[4]

But are democracy and utilitarianism so closely related? Surely this is open to serious doubt. A familiar objection, for example, is that aggregate utility maximization might imply a highly unequal distribution of personal satisfaction such that a privileged elite enjoys great happiness while the majority

---

[1] John Hart Ely, "Constitutional Interpretivism: Its Allure and Impossibility," *Indiana Law Journal* 53 (1978): 407.

[2] Alexis de Tocqueville, *Democracy in America,* ed. P. Bradley (1835: New York: Vintage Books, 1945), vol. 1. pp. 247–49.

[3] See, e.g., Jeremy Bentham, *Fragment on Government* (London: Payne,1776), *Constitutional Code,* in *Works of Jeremy Bentham,* ed. J. Bowring (Edinburgh: Dent, 1838–43), vol. 9; James Mill, "Essay on Government" (1820), in *Utilitarian Logic and Politics,* ed. J. Lively and J. Rees (Oxford: Oxford Universtity Press, 1978); John Stuart Mill, "De Tocqueville on Democracy in America" (1835–40) and "Considerations on Representative Government" (1861), in *Collected Works of J. S. Mill,* ed. J. Robson (Toronto and London: University of Toronto Press and Routledge & Kegan Paul, 1977), vols. 18 and 19.

[4] Ely, "Constitutional Interpretivism," p. 407.

grovels in relative misery. Utilitarian ethics and democratic government hardly look like two sides of the same coin in that instance. Nevertheless, my intention is to show that utilitarian procedural norms really are equivalent to democratic norms under certain conditions, specifically, when interpersonal utility comparisons are impractical or impossible. The equivalence is independent of any particular interpretation of utility. Moreover, this common set of procedural norms (which I will denote "procedural equality") can be used as a test for any given decision-making procedure. As it turns out, procedural equality is satisfied by some well-known democratic voting methods and may be of some guidance in suggesting reforms to contemporary political systems. The fact that democracy and utilitarianism are so closely related in principle should give pause for thought to the many recent writers who combine their apparent faith in democracy with a rather strident anti-utilitarianism.

• • •

It is worth stressing at the outset three important features of my argument. First, I am not insisting that utilitarianism is the only conceivable ethical foundation for democracy. Democrats need not be utilitarians. But utilitarian ethics are sufficient for democratic government if interpersonal utility comparisons are ruled out.

Second, I am making a logical, not an empirical, claim. Utilitarians are necessarily democrats in the absence of interpersonal comparability. That claim is not contingent on any further cost/benefit calculation employed to compare democracy to other forms of government such as anarchy, monarchy, or a Leninist dictatorship. If utility information is really so poor that interpersonal comparisons cannot be made, then any such further calculation is rendered superfluous. The point is that a utilitarian calculus faced with such impoverished utility information already implies that the consequences of democratic government must be optimal. Democracy is necessary to utilitarianism under those circumstances.

Third, I say nothing about what I regard as a distinct question, that is, How will democracy be institutionalized by rational economic agents choosing in a strategic manner? My concern is with a logical link between utilitarian and democratic values, not with the practical implementation of democracy per se.

• • •

DEMOCRACY AND PROCEDURAL EQUALITY

Recall that utilitarianism properly relies on rich cardinal comparable personal utility information. It is important to recognize that this rich informational condition is a factual assumption rather than an ethical assumption.

• • •

Consider a version of Condition PE limited to noncomparable personal preference orderings.*

• • •

Since we cannot retrieve any information about any person's happiness beyond his preference ordering, each person's happiness receives the same total weight as any other person's happiness in social decision-making procedures. In effect, when limited to such imprecise information about each citizen's happiness, utilitarians prescribe "equal treatment and respect" for each person's preferences because utility information is simply too poor to permit comparisons of marginal units of utility. But equal treatment and respect for each citizen's preferences arguably corresponds to the usual democratic idea of procedural equality. This is not to claim that either utilitarian or democratic notions of procedural equality are adequate to characterize fair treatment and respect for each citizen's dignity. It may well be true that various substantive moral principles must somehow be integrated with the norm of procedural equality to produce credible versions of utilitarianism and democracy. Rather, my claim is a much weaker one, that ordinalist-utilitarian procedures correspond to democratic procedures. Before discussing some of the implications of ordinalist-utilitarian values for a democratic government, however, it is necessary to clarify why utilitarians themselves might recommend democratic institutions rather than a full-blown utilitarian calculus for making social choices.

FROM UTILITARIAN ETHICS TO DEMOCRATIC POLITICS

Even if we accept the argument that ordinalist-utilitarian values are democratic values, what sort of version of utilitarianism is it that recommends abandonment of the utilitarian calculus (with its reliance on cardinal comparable utility information) in favor of democratic procedures (with their reliance on purely ordinal utility information)? It seems that some sort of "indirect" version of utilitarianism is required, one that uses democratic institutions as indirect

---

* Elsewhere in the text, the author states Condition PE this way:

"*Condition PE* (procedural equality): For any given domain of admissible sets of personal utility functions, procedural equality is equivalent to the combination of strong anonymity, strong neutrality, strong Pareto principle, and strong monotonicity." He offers the following definitions of the terms used in Condition PE: "Strong anonymity requires the calculus to ignore personal identities per se. Strong neutrality requires the calculus to yield social judgments solely on the basis of the given personal utility information (whether crudely subjective or ethical). Nonutility information is strictly irrelevant. Strong Pareto principle requires the calculus to positively reflect a consensus should it happen to exist over any pair of alternatives x and y. And strong monotonicity requires the calculus to respond positively to changes in any person's utility values, ceteris paribus: if even one person alters his utility values in favor of x vis-à-vis y while everyone else's values remain unchanged between x and y, then the weight of x should increase vis-à-vis the weight of y for the social choice between x and y."–eds.

means of calculating the general welfare. But why would utilitarians prescribe democratic procedures rather than make direct use of the familiar utilitarian calculus itself?

A possible rationale appears once we take account of the economic costs involved in setting up and operating the utilitarian calculus. In this regard, it seems fair to suggest that utilitarian philosophers generally ignore such transaction costs to focus attention on how (their version of) utilitarianism works in principle. As such, it is characteristic of the broad philosophical approach to locate procedurally egalitarian social judgments in some hypothetical individual, say, an ideal observer who sets up and operates the utilitarian calculus at no cost. But utilitarians do have the option of discarding this fiction of an ideal observer in order to take seriously the costs of running a utilitarian society. Once we recognize that utilitarianism (like any other ethical doctrine) is costly for any society to implement, utilitarians can admit that procedurally egalitarian social judgments must for all practical purposes be located in social institutions whose operation consumes significant quantities of scarce resources. Kenneth Arrow, for example, asserts that "the location of welfare judgements in any individual, while logically possible, does not appear to be very interesting."[5] It is more interesting, he thinks, to locate social judgments in social institutions.[6]

Assume, then, that utilitarians are trying to judge which kinds of social institutions to put in place to implement the utilitarian calculus in the absence of an ideal observer. This problem of constitutional design is a rather extraordinary one for utilitarians to consider and requires us to transcend all views that reduce utilitarianism to a crude doctrine such as straightforward preference utilitarianism. In this regard, if the acquisition and use of any utility information richer than purely ordinal utility information involves more costs than benefits to society in at least some situations, then utilitarianism itself properly recommends reliance on purely ordinalist decision-making procedures rather than a full-blown utilitarian calculus in those situations. My central hypothesis is that these purely ordinalist utilitarian institutions can be seen as democratic institutions. Utilitarianism recommends democracy in this case because there is no ideal agent to perform without cost the many tasks implicit in the notion of the utilitarian calculus. Democratic government is seen as a set of procedures for calculating the general welfare in environments where a full-blown utilitarian calculus is too costly to establish and run. In particular, democratic decision making takes account of the fact that personal utility information is initially dispersed and costly to retrieve, compare, and aggregate.

It should be clear that I am not making a positive argument that the costs of rich utility information actually do outweigh its benefits for society. Rather, my point is that *if* this positive argument is true for all utility information beyond purely ordinal information, then utilitarianism prescribes democracy. In this

---

[5] Kenneth Arrow, *Social Choice and Individual Values,* 2nd ed. (New York: Wiley, 1963), p.106.
[6] Ibid., pp. 106–7.

regard, a widespread opinion exists in the literature that meaningful interpersonal utility comparisons are impossible.[7] If this opinion is well grounded (I do not say that it is), then infinite costs can be interpreted to negate whatever putative benefits are provided by comparable utility values in terms of more informed social judgments. Moreover, once comparability is rejected, it is well known that "the only information about individual values that can be used in the context of social choice is ordinal information."[8] That is, if interpersonal comparisons are impossible, then the extra information conveyed by, say, a cardinal utility measure becomes useless, and society might as well assume "that individual values are represented by preference orderings."[9]

Evidently, if interpersonal utility comparisons are meaningless, then any utilitarian society is for all practical purposes confined to purely ordinal utility information. This could be one explanation for why utilitarians become democrats: they are forced to do so by informational constraints beyond man's capacity to modify. Even if interpersonal comparisons are held to be possible, however, utilitarians will choose to become democrats if the costs of making comparisons outweigh their benefits for social choice. Again, without making the positive argument, this might plausibly be the case at least in some contexts, for example, large-scale elections where the issues to be decided are matters of mere general expedience rather than justice and fundamental individual rights. If the issue merely concerns which particular slate of candidates will serve as elected representatives in the legislature, for example, then perhaps the social benefits of a true utilitarian judgment are little different from those of a purely ordinalist-utilitarian judgment. In any case, if we accept that aggregate welfare can be increased by replacing a full-blown utilitarian calculus with purely ordinalist utilitarian procedures in at least some contexts, then utilitarians will properly become democrats in those contexts.

● ● ●

REPRESENTATIVE DEMOCRACY

For a large-scale society in which direct democracy is arguably not feasible, ordinalist-utilitarians must design a two-stage democratic voting rule involving popular election of representatives at the first stage and voting by elected representatives at the second stage. The two-stage voting rule ideally should satisfy

[7] For a recent discussion of the possibility of comparable utility information, see Amartya K. Sen, "Interpersonal Comparisons of Welfare." in *Economics and Human Welfare,* ed. M. Boskin (New York: Academic Press, 1979); Y. K. Ng. "Some Fundamental Issues in Social Welfare," in *Issues in Contemporary Microeconomics and Welfare,* ed. G. Feiwel (Albany: State University of New York Press, 1985): and J. Ortuno-Ortin and J. Roemer, "Deducing Interpersonal Comparability," Working Paper no. 293 (University of California, Davis, Department of Economics, 1987).

[8] P. Gardenfors, "On the Information about Individual Utilities Used in Social Choice," *Mathematical Social Sciences* 4 (1983): 219. See his theorem 1, pp. 221–22.

[9] Ibid. p. 222.

procedural equality in a purely ordinalist information setting. But procedural equality must have a somewhat different connotation in the representative context. Given that all citizens cannot participate directly in social decisions over policy alternatives, each citizen A might be said to participate in representative government if A's vote helps to elect some representative B (possibly B = A). Person A then participates "indirectly" or perhaps "virtually" when her representative B participates directly in policy-making decisions. This extended idea of participation is notoriously unsatisfactory to direct democrats in the tradition of Jean-Jacques Rousseau, of course. Without necessarily dismissing such objections, it remains interesting to speculate how each citizen can have an equal opportunity to participate in the representative context. In this regard, the representative version of purely ordinalist Condition PE is conveniently analyzed as two sets of conditions, one set imposed at the first stage, involving election of representatives by citizens, and a second set imposed at the second stage, involving decision making by elected representatives themselves.

As it turns out, this representative version of Condition PE cannot be satisfied by requiring procedural equality at each of the two stages. Two-stage majority voting (i.e., majority rule used twice over, first to elect representatives on the basis of citizens' preferences and then to arrive at decisions on the basis of representatives' preferences) is the only voting rule which satisfies purely ordinalist procedural equality at each stage, and it does not satisfy the representative version of Condition PE overall. (Technically, two-stage majority voting violates strong monotonicity.)[10] It might seem paradoxical that two-stage majority rule violates a norm which is satisfied by simple majority rule and utilitarianism. But the violation of procedural equality occurs precisely because personal representatives are assigned to merely a majority of citizens (i.e., the votes of remaining citizens are simply wasted in the sense that they do not help to elect any representative) so that majority voting by the elected representatives themselves is often representative of only a minority (a majority of a majority) of citizens. In other words, the two-stage majority rule is procedurally inegalitarian because it denies minority groups the right even to be heard (however indirectly) in the deliberations of elected representatives. As John Stuart Mill argues, if representation itself is determined by majority vote, there is a serious danger of "false democracy" in which a minority of citizens is erected into a "ruling class": "Democracy, thus constituted, does not even attain its ostensible object, that of giving the powers of government in all cases to the numerical majority. It does something very different: it gives them to a majority of the majority; who may be, and often are, but a minority of the whole."[11] Even if citizens are divided into electoral districts of equal population size, it is possible that political decisions may be taken by an elected assembly which represents little more than 25 percent of citizens, if representatives are elected from the

[10] See, e.g., J. Smith. "Aggregation of Preferences and Variable Electorate," *Econometrica* 41 (1973): 1027–41; and G. Doron and R. Kronick, "Single Transferable Vote: An Example of a Perverse Social Choice Function," *American Journal of Political Science* 21 (1977): 303–11.

[11] J. S. Mill, "Considerations on Representative Government," p.449.

districts by majority vote and political decisions require approval of a majority in the elected assembly.

To satisfy the representative version of Condition PE, procedural equality must actually be sacrificed at one of the two stages of decision making involved. More specifically, it seems clear that the system of representation itself must sacrifice procedural equality in order to enable (to the maximum extent possible) each citizen to cast a vote that helps elect a personal representative to the assembly.

20.

Representative Government

JOHN STUART MILL

Thus stands the case as regards present well-being; the good management of the affairs of the existing generation. If we now pass to the influence of the form of government upon character, we shall find the superiority of popular government over every other to be, if possible, still more decided and indisputable.

This question really depends upon a still more fundamental one, viz., which of two common types of character, for the general good of humanity, it is most desirable should predominate—the active, or the passive type; that which struggles against evils, or that which endures them; that which bends to circumstances, or that which endeavors to make circumstances bend to itself.

The commonplaces of moralists, and the general sympathies of mankind, are in favor of the passive type. Energetic characters may be admired, but the acquiescent and submissive are those which most men personally prefer. The passiveness of our neighbors increases our sense of security, and plays into the hands of our willfulness. Passive characters, if we do not happen to need their activity, seem an obstruction the less in our own path. A contented character is not a dangerous rival. Yet nothing is more certain than that improvement in human affairs is wholly the work of the uncontented characters; and, moreover, that it is much easier for an active mind to acquire the virtues of patience than for a passive one to assume those of energy.

Of the three varieties of mental excellence, intellectual, practical, and moral, there never could be any doubt in regard to the first two which side had the advantage. All intellectual superiority is the fruit of active effort. Enterprise, the desire to keep moving, to be trying and accomplishing new things for our own benefit or that of others, is the parent even of speculative, and much more of practical, talent. The intellectual culture compatible with the other type is of that feeble and vague description which belongs to a mind that stops at amusement, or at simple contemplation. The test of real and vigorous thinking, the thinking which ascertains truths instead of dreaming dreams, is successful application to practice. Where that purpose does not exist, to give definiteness, precision, and an intelligible meaning to thought, it generates nothing better than the mystical metaphysics of the Pythagoreans or the Vedas. With respect to practical improvement, the case is still more evident. The character which improves human life is that which struggles with natural powers and tendencies, not that which gives way to them. The self-benefiting qualities are all on the side of the active and energetic character: and the habits and conduct which promote the advantage of each individual member of the community must be at least a part of those which conduce most in the end to the advancement of the community as a whole.

But on the point of moral preferablitiy, there seems at first sight to be room for doubt. I am not referring to the religious feeling which has so generally existed in favor of the inactive character, as being more in harmony with the submission due to the divine will. Christianity as well as other religions has fostered this sentiment; but it is the prerogative of Christianity, as regards this and many other perversions, that it is able to throw them off. Abstractedly from religious considerations, a passive character, which yields to obstacles instead of striving to overcome them, may not indeed be very useful to others, no more than to itself, but it might be expected to be at least inoffensive. Contentment is always counted among the moral virtues. But it is a complete error to suppose that contentment is necessarily or naturally attendant on passivity of character; and useless it is, the moral consequences are mischievous. Where there exists a desire for advantages not possessed, the mind which does not potentially possess them by means of its own energies is apt to look with hatred and malice on those who do. The person bestirring himself with hopeful prospects to improve his circumstances is the one who feels good-will towards others engaged in, or who have succeeded in, the same pursuit. And where the majority are so engaged, those who do not attain the object have had the tone given to their feelings by the general habit of the country, and ascribe their failure to want of effort or opportunity, or to their personal ill luck. But those who, while desiring what others possess, put no energy into striving for it, are either incessantly grumbling that fortune does not do for them what they do not attempt to do for themselves, or overflowing with envy and ill-will towards those who possess what they would like to have.

• • •

The great mass of seeming contentment is real discontent, combined with indolence or self-indulgence, which, while taking no legitimate means of raising itself, delights in bringing others down to its own level. And if we look narrowly even at the cases of innocent contentment, we perceive that they only win our admiration when the indifference is solely to improvement in outward circumstances, and there is a striving for perpetual advancement in spiritual worth, or at least a disinterested zeal to benefit others. The contented man, or the contented family, who have no ambition to make any one else happier, to promote the good of their country or their neighborhood, or to improve themselves in moral excellence, excite in us neither admiration nor approval. We rightly ascribe this sort of contentment to mere unmanliness and want of spirit. The content which we approve is an ability to do cheerfully without what cannot be had, a just appreciation of the comparative value of different objects of desire, and a willing renunciation of the less when incompatible with the greater. These, however, are excellences more natural to the character, in proportion as it is actively engaged in the attempt to improve its own or some other lot. He who is continually measuring his energy against difficulties learns what are the difficulties insuperable to him, and what are those which, though he might overcome, the success is not worth the cost. He whose thoughts and activities are all needed for, and habitually employed in, practicable and useful enterprises, is the person of all others least likely to let his mind dwell with the brooding discontent upon things either not worth attaining, or which are not so to him. Thus the active, self-helping character is not only intrinsically the best, but is the likeliest to acquire all that is really excellent or desirable in the opposite type.

The striving, go-ahead character of England and the United States is only a fit subject of disapproving criticism on account of the very secondary objects on which it commonly expends its strength. In itself it is the foundation of the best hopes for the general improvement of mankind. It has been acutely re-marked that whenever anything goes amiss the habitual impulses of French people is to say, "Il faut de la patience;" and of English people, "What a shame." The people who think it a shame when anything goes wrong—who rush to the conclusion that the evil could and ought to have been prevented, are those who, in the long run, do most to make the world better. If the desires are low placed, if they extend to little beyond physical comfort, and the show of riches, the immediate results of the energy will not be much more than the con-tinual extension of man's power over material objects; but even this makes room, and prepares the mechanical appliances, for the greatest intellectual and social achievements; and while the energy is there, some persons will apply it, and it will be applied more and more, to the perfecting not of outward circumstances alone, but of man's inward nature. Inactivity, unaspiringness, ab-sence of desire, are a more fatal hindrance to improvement than any misdirec-tion of energy; and are that through which alone, when existing in the mass, any very formidable misdirection by an energetic few becomes possible. It is this, mainly, which retains in a savage or semi-savage state the great majority of the human race.

Now there can be no kind of doubt that the passive type of character is fa-vored by the government of one or a few, and the active self-helping type by that of the Many. Irresponsible rulers need the quiescence of the ruled more than they need any activity but that which they can compel. Submissiveness to the prescriptions of men as necessities of nature is the lesson inculcated by all governments upon those who are wholly without participation in them. The will of superiors, and the law as the will of the superiors, must be passively yielded to. But no men are mere instruments or materials in the hands of their rulers who have will or spirit or a spring of internal activity in the rest of their proceedings: and any manifestation of these qualities, instead of receiving en-couragement from despots, has to get itself forgiven by them. Even when ir-responsible rulers are not sufficiently conscious of danger from the mental activity of their subjects to be desirous of repressing it, the position itself is a re-pression. Endeavor is even more effectually restrained by the certainty of its im-potence than by any positive discouragement. Between subjection to the will of others, and the virtues of self-help and self-government, there is a natural in-compatability. This is more or less complete, according as the bondage is strained or relaxed. Rulers differ very much in the length to which they carry the con-trol of the free agency of their subjects, or the supersession of it by managing their business for them. But the difference is in degree, not in principle; and the best despots often go the greatest lengths in chaining up the free agency of their subjects. A bad despot, when his own personal indulgences have been provided for, may sometimes be willing to let the people alone; but a good despot insists on doing them good, by making them do their own business in a better way than they themselves know of. The regulations which restricted to fixed processes all the leading branches of French manufactures were the work of the great Colbert.

Very different is the state of the human faculties where a human being feels himself under no other external restraint than the necessities of nature, or mandates of society which he has his share of imposing, and which it is open to him, if he thinks them wrong, publicly to dissent from, and exert himself actively to get altered. No doubt, under a government partially popular, this freedom may be exercised even by those who are not partakers in the full privileges of citizenship. But it is a great additional stimulus to any one's self-help and self-reliance when he starts from even ground, and has not to feel that his success depends on the impression he can make upon the sentiments and dispositions of a body of whom he is not one. It is a great discouragement to an individual, and a still greater one to a class, to be left out of the constitution; to be reduced to plead from outside the door to the arbiters of their destiny, not taken into consultation within. The maximum of the invigorating effect of freedom upon the character is only obtained when the person acted on either is, or is looking forward to becoming, a citizen as fully privileged as any other. What is still more important than even this matter of feeling is the practical discipline which the character obtains from the occasional demand made upon the citizens to exercise, for a time and in their turn, some social function. It is not sufficiently considered how little there is in most men's ordinary life to give any largeness either to their conceptions or to their sentiments. Their work is a routine; not a labor of love, but of self-interest in the most elementary form, the satisfaction of daily wants; neither the thing done, nor the process of doing it, introduces the mind to thoughts or feelings extending beyond individuals; if instructive books are within their reach, there is no stimulus to read them; and in most cases the individual has no access to any person of cultivation much superior to his own. Giving him something to do for the public, supplies, in a measure, all these deficiencies. If circumstances allow the amount of public duty assigned him to be considerable, it makes him an educated man. Notwithstanding the defects of the social system and moral ideas of antiquity, the practice of the dicastery and the ecclesia raised the intellectual standard of an average Athenian citizen far beyond anything of which there is yet an example in any other mass of men, ancient or modern. The proofs of this are apparent in every page of our great historian of Greece; but we need scarcely look further than to the high quality of the addresses which their great orators deemed best calculated to act with effect on their understanding and will. A benefit of the same kind, though far less in degree, is produced on Englishmen of the lower middle class by their liability to be placed on juries and to serve parish offices; which, though it does not occur to so many, nor is so continuous, nor introduces them to so great a variety of elevated considerations, as to admit of comparison with the public education which every citizen of Athens obtained from her democratic institutions, must make them nevertheless very different beings, in range of ideas and development of faculties, from those who have done nothing in their lives but drive a quill, or sell goods over a counter. Still more salutary is the moral part of the instruction afforded by the participation of the private citizen, if even rarely, in public functions. He is called upon, while so engaged, to weigh interests not his own; to be guided, in case of conflicting claims, by another rule than his private partialities; to apply, at every turn, principles and maxims which have for their reason of existence the common good: and he usually finds associated with him in the same work minds more familiarized than his own with these ideas and operations, whose study it will be to supply reasons to his understanding, and stimulation to his feeling for the general interest. He is made to feel himself one of the public, and whatever is for their benefit to be for his benefit. Where this school of public spirit does not exist, scarcely any sense is entertained that private persons, in no eminent social situation, owe any duties to society, except to obey the laws and submit to the government. There is no unselfish sentiment of identification with the public. Every thought or feeling, either of interest or of duty, is absorbed in the individual and in the family. The man never thinks of any collective interest, of any objects to be pursued jointly with others, but only in competition with them, and in some measure at their expense. A neighbor, not being an ally or an associate, since he is never engaged in any common undertaking for joint benefit, is therefore only a rival. Thus even private morality suffers, while public is actually extinct. Were this the universal and only possible state of things, the utmost aspirations of the lawgiver or the moralist could only stretch to make the bulk of the community a flock of sheep innocently nibbling the grass side by side.

From these accumulated considerations it is evident that the only government which can fully satisfy all the exigencies of the social state is one in which the whole people participate; that any participation, even in the smallest public function, is useful; that the participation should everywhere be as great as the general degree of improvement of the community will allow; and that nothing less can be ultimately desirable than the admission of all to a share in the sovereign power of the state. But since all cannot, in a community exceeding a single small town, participate personally in any but some very minor portions of the public business, it follows that the ideal type of a perfect government must be representative.

21.
Political Equality and Majority Rule

PETER JONES

Disputes concerning democracy often seem fruitless exercises in assertion and counterassertion. Given the favorable connotations that now attach to the adjective "democratic," it is not surprising that politicians have manipulated its meaning as suits their purposes. Political theorists have neither the same need to exploit, nor therefore the same excuse for exploiting, the rhetorical potentialities of the term. Yet they seem no more agreed upon what democracy is, nor any less keen to defend their preferred definitions. Argument over the correct usage of "democracy" and "democratic" is not entirely pointless since there are criteria by which some uses can be judged more justified than others and by which still others can be dismissed as misuses. But these criteria still leave scope for disagreement and they do not tell us what, if anything, is so special about democracy.

Whatever democracy is, it is not self-justifying. If someone declared himself "against justice," we would infer either that he intended some sort of irony or else that he had no understanding of what justice meant. There is nothing similarly puzzling, let alone incomprehensible, about someone's declaring himself "against democracy." Even those of us who are "for" democracy may not be so unreservedly; we may believe it to be the right or best decision procedure for some sorts of decision but not for others. Democracy then is something that can be argued both for and against and, when it is argued for, quite different sorts of argument can be offered in its support. Granted this, instead of dealing with disputes over democracy as though they were mere battles of definition, it is more profitable to establish people's reasons for preferring the decision procedure that they deem "democratic" so that the argument can become one about those reasons and what they imply. Even where different reasons are offered in support of the same general conception of democracy, they may still imply differences of detail and emphasis.

It is with how different justifications bear upon one prominent "detail" of democracy, its decision rule, that I shall be concerned in this paper. More particularly, my concern is with the status of the majority principle and with the issues raised by "persistent minorities," that is, by groups of individuals who invariably find themselves on the losing side. Although I shall have to engage in a good deal of preliminary skirmishing, the issue I shall eventually confront is whether persistent minorities should regard their position as unfair or merely unfortunate.

When I use the term "democracy" I shall have in mind a very simple and, I hope, uncontroversial model: an association of people who enjoy equal rights of participation in their decision procedure and who vote directly upon issues. By the "majority principle" or "majority rule" I shall mean simply the rule that a proposal should be adopted if it receives the support of at least 50 percent +1 of the votes cast. My excuse for using this simple model is that the general principle of what I have to say is unaffected by the complexities and modifications exhibited by actual "democratic" political systems and there is no point in complicating the argument unnecessarily. Moreover, the argument I develop applies not only to the state but also to other associations for which democracy is thought the right or desirable form of decision procedure, and my simple model is less far removed from the reality of many such non-state associations.

I

Why should democracy be regarded as the right or desirable decision procedure for some, if not all, associations? One sort of answer is consequentialist in character. It posits a condition as desirable and then commends democracy because it is the decision procedure which is guaranteed to produce that desirable condition or which is more likely to do so than any alternative decision procedure. Thus democracy has been defended because it results in wise policies, a just society, a free society, decisions which promote the public interest or the common good, which respect individual rights, which promote science and intellectual activity, and so on. The list is limited only by one's resourcefulness in enumerating the good things of life and the conviction with which one is able to argue that democracy will promote them.[1] Each of these justifications can also be urged in defence of the majority principle. Why should the vote of the majority be decisive? Because it will promote, or is most likely to promote, this or that desirable result.

Consequentialist justifications of the type I have instanced focus upon the intrinsic quality of democratic decisions. However, there is another type of consequentialist justification in which the appeal is not to the desirable content of democratic decisions but to the benefits that flow from the way in which those decisions are reached. Perhaps the most widely used justification of this sort is that particularly associated with J. S. Mill: the argument that, in participating in the decisions that are to govern his life, an individual is improved both intellectually and morally.[2] Claims that people are more ready to respect decisions reached democratically and that democracy has an integrative effect upon a community are also examples of this second type of consequentialist justification.

It is less easy to relate this second sort of consequentialist justification to any specific decision rule such as the majority principle. Clearly it implies widespread participation and participation implies the possibility of having an influence upon decisions. That, however, need not be of any specific type. Mill,

---

[1] For (an) example of justifications of this kind, see Carl Cohen. *Democracy* (Athens: University of Georgia Press, 1971), ch. 14.

[2] J. S. Mill, *Utilitarianism, Liberty and Representative Government* (London: Dent, 1910), pp. 202–18. See also Carole Pateman, *Participation and Democratic Theory* (Cambridge: Cambridge University Press, 1970).

for example, thought that his arguments for participation did not necessarily entail that participants should be granted equal voting rights.

Consequentialist justifications of democracy have an obvious rationale. It would be surprising if one's approval or disapproval of a form of government took no account of the quality of government that one could expect from it. Nevertheless there are a number of reasons why one might be less than wholly satisfied with justifying democracy in this way. (These reasons apply with less force to one sort of consequentialist justification: the utilitarian justification of democracy in terms of the maximization of happiness or want-satisfaction. I shall deal with utilitarianism later.) Firstly, consequentialist justifications are contingent in character. They involve empirical assertions which may or may not hold true. For example, whether a society which respects certain sorts of individual right is a "good" society is not an empirical question: whether a democratic system of government will ensure such a society most definitely is. The simple confidence with which some writers are prepared to make such empirical assertions in justifying democracy is, to say the least, quite remarkable. Moreover, given that consequentialist justifications have this contingent character, they do not constitute principled commitments to democracy as such. If it turned out that the desired result would be better achieved by a non-democratic system of government, then we should abandon democracy.

Secondly, and relatedly, consequentialist justifications fail to account for our sense that democracy constitutes a fair decision procedure. That is, they do not accommodate the idea that, irrespective of what decisions are made, a democratic system constitutes a fairer way of making decisions than one in which some are excluded from the process of decision-making and others are accorded a privileged status. More particularly, consequentialist justifications cannot provide a satisfactory account of the idea of an equal *right* of participation. The assertion of a right makes the focus of concern the well-being of the individual right-holder. Thus the assertion of a right to vote entails construing a vote as of benefit to the individual voter and the removal of that right as a disbenefit to him. In consequentialist justifications of democracy, the establishment of equal voting rights is justified simply as a means to a desirable collective end. If that collective end required unequal or selective voting rights there could be no ground for complaint. Even where the attainment of a collective end did require equal voting rights, the removal of those rights from an individual or group of individuals would be construed as a harm to society at large (because it endangered the attainment of the collective end) rather than as an injustice to the disenfranchised individuals. Yet the arbitrary disenfranchisement of a group of individuals is typically thought of as an infringement of *their* (pre-legal) rights, as an injustice to them in particular rather than merely a harm to society in general.

Thirdly, of less significance but still worth mentioning, democracy is a form of decision procedure thought appropriate to many associations other than the state. Several of the consequentialist justifications offered in support of democracy have little or no relevance to these non-state associations. For example, if a gardening club or a rambling association or a film society has a democratic constitution, it is unlikely to apologize for this by appeals to the promotion of justice or freedom. It may regard its democratic constitution as *embodying* ideas of justice and freedom but that is a different matter.

How else then might democracy be justified? The answer is clearly implied in the shortcomings of consequentialist justification. The alternative is to appeal to a principle which entails that democracy is the inherently right or fair way of making decisions. Here there is not a prospective appeal to a desirable consequence but a retrospective appeal to a principle which predicates the intrinsic rightness or fairness of the democratic process itself. When equality is appealed to not merely as a feature of democratic institutions but as a reason for having those institutions, democracy is being justified in this way. It is to the justification of democracy by way of equality that I shall give most of my attention. It is not the only form of non-consequentialist justification of democracy that there can be. If one believed that democracy was the divinely approved form of government (as some have believed in the past and, for all I know, as some may still believe now) that would clearly afford a non-consequentialist justification of democracy. Justifications which stress "self-determination" will also usually be of this type. However, the appeal to equality is perhaps more frequently heard than any other.

II

In a moment, I want to look at what sort of principle of equality can justify political equality. But since my interest is ultimately in the decision rule that a democracy should adopt, let me first of all indicate the very simple way in which the majority principle is often justified by way of equality. Political equality entails that each should have an equal right of participation and, in particular, that each should have a vote and that each vote should count equally. If there is a clash of preferences and if each vote is to count equally, then the proposal preferred by the majority must be adopted. To allow the will of the minority to prevail would be to give greater weight to the vote of each member of the minority than to the vote of each member of the majority, thus violating political equality. This argument can be used not only in defence of absolute majorities but also in defence of relative majorities if, for some reason, an absolute majority is unattainable.

If we accept the spirit of this argument, does it require our unqualified acceptance of the majority principle? There are two widely canvassed limitations upon the majority principle which must be mentioned, though I mention them largely to emphasize their separateness from a third sort of limitation upon which I shall dwell.

1. People often want to assert individual or minority rights as restrictions upon the scope of majority preference. Is this compatible with the argument from equality?

In answering this we need to distinguish between democratic and non-democratic rights. By "democratic rights" I understand those rights which are integral to the democratic process. Obviously these include the right to vote but also rights such as freedom of expression and freedom of association in so far as these are essential for an individual's participation in the democratic process. Anyone committed to democracy and to the rule of the majority of a pre-defined demos must require the maintenance of those rights. One reason is that those rights are sanctioned by the principle of equality which sanctions the majority principle itself. Another is that a majority which removes democratic rights of part of a demos impairs the claim of future majorities to be majorities of that demos.

The case of non-democratic rights is perhaps more contentious. Rights such as the right of freedom of worship or the right to a fair trial rest upon some ground other than their being essential to the democratic process and are intended to limit the scope of that process. These rights are often called minority rights but that is misleading since they are usually rights ascribed to every individual in a community and not only to a specific minority. Presumably they are labelled minority rights because they are conceived as safeguards against possible ravages of the majority. As long as these rights are universal to each member of a demos, I cannot see how they can be impugned on grounds of equality. It is sometimes implied that the inhibition of majority preference by individual rights constitutes an inequality in favor of a minority. But the inequality involved in universal rights is not an inequality of persons, but an inequality in the status attributed to certain goods and is an inequality enjoyed by everyone.

This is not to say that democracy requires that such rights be recognized or respected. On the contrary, there would be nothing "undemocratic" about their denial, removal, or infringement, although these might well be objectionable on other grounds. I am holding only that a society which restricts the scope of the democratic process, and therefore the will of the majority, by the institution of individuals rights cannot be faulted on grounds of equality alone.

2. A second complication in moving from political equality to majority rule concerns intensity of preference. It is often considered a defect of the majority principle that it merely counts preferences and takes no account of the different intensities with which those preferences are held. It is not obviously right or desirable that the very mild preferences of a 52 percent "apathetic majority" should prevail over the strongly held preferences of a 48 percent "intense minority." Certainly any justification of democracy in terms of maximizing satisfactions implies that account should be taken of the intensity as well as the number of preferences. Nor would it be difficult to argue that equality allows, if it does not require, that account be taken of intensity of preference. If individuals are treated equally in respect of the criterion of intensity, the egalitarian *qua* egalitarian has no reason to complain.

There are large problems in devising procedures which take reliable account of intensity of preference and much disagreement about the sensitivity of

Western representative democracies to differing intensities of preference. But, for the moment, my concern is only with whether it is right, in principle, to take account of intensity of preference. A feature of this criterion which may make one hesitate about it at this level is its subjectivity. Some people seem to feel more strongly than others about almost everything. Some become excited without good reason; others fail to become excited when they have good reason. Taking account of intensity of preference may therefore favor over-sensitive busybodies to the disadvantage of long-suffering stoics. The point here is not that recognized by Dahl: that overt behavior may not always be a reliable indicator of individuals' states of mind. Rather it is that, even if X undoubtedly feels more strongly than Y, it is not clear that X should get his way if his strength of feeling seems "unreasonable." This element of subjectivity can be avoided by reformulating the principle in terms of interests, so that ideally a decision procedure would take account of the extent to which individuals' interests were affected beneficially or adversely even when this did not coincide with the sensitivities manifested by the individuals themselves. Certainly if the principle upon which political equality rests is that of an equal claim to the promotion of one's interests (as I shall argue), that implies that interests should be weighed as well as heads counted.

A further point of principle is that the case for taking account of intensity depends upon how the democratic process is conceived. If one thinks of it as computing wants or interests, there is a case for weighing as well as counting these. If, on the other hand, one takes a consequentialist view of democracy in which votes represent judgements rather than preferences, intensity may be irrelevant. As Rawls points out, those who have stronger feelings on an issue may do so because of their ignorance or prejudice, while those who have weaker feelings may do so because of their better appreciation of the complexities of the issue.[3] In other words, intensity of feeling is not a reliable indicator of quality of judgement.

However, having made these qualifications, there is clearly a strong case for allowing considerations of intensity to modify the majority principle (in so far as this is practicable), and a case which has more rather than less to be said for it in terms of equality of treatment.

III

Before taking up a third and more radical qualification of the majority principle, I want to return to the issue of equality itself and the principle which underlies a commitment to political equality.

Since democracy is a decision procedure, it may seem that the principle of equality relevant to democracy must be one concerning people's capacities as decision-makers. And, indeed, there are writers who assert or imply that

[3] John Rawls, *A Theory of Justice* (Cambridge, MA: Harvard University Press, 1971). pp. 230–1, 361.

adherence to democracy entails a presumption of the equality of competence of individuals on political matters. This presumption can be more or less strong. In its strongest form, the claim would be simply that people *are* equally competent to make political decisions. A slightly weaker claim would be that, although there are differences in competence between individuals, those differences are too slight to matter. A still weaker claim would be that, although some are more competent than others, those differences are insufficiently obvious for there to be agreement on who is more competent than whom and that therefore we have to treat people as if they were equally competent, even though they are not. Thus Singer suggests that the reason for rejecting Mill's proposal for plural votes for those with superior education and intelligence "is not that it would be obviously unfair to give more votes to better qualified people, but rather that it would be impossible to get everyone to agree on who was to have the extra votes." Thus, "one person, one vote," represents a sort of practical compromise.[4]

One reason, possibly the main reason, why people have been induced to make these claims is that, historically, the most common objection to democracy has been the alleged incompetence of the many. This objection implies that the right to govern is dependent upon one's competence and, if the democrat accepts that implied premiss, he has to make his case in those terms. Nevertheless, this is an unpromising and unnecessary line of argument for a democrat to pursue. Firstly, the assertion of equality of political competence is an empirical one and one that it is difficult to find convincing. Secondly, it is not usually accepted that competence is a quality which, of itself, generates rights. Consider, for example, how we distinguish between being *in* authority and being *an* authority. To be in authority is to possess a right to determine the conduct of others. To be an authority is to be distinguished by one's competence on a matter but not therefore to be *in* a position of authority on that matter; that is, it does not give you an automatic right to decide on behalf of others. Others may be well advised to heed you, but you have no right to control their conduct and they have no duty to conform to your injunctions merely in virtue of your superior wisdom. Thirdly, if equality of competence were to figure at all in a justification of democracy, it would seem that it could figure only as an empirical presumption in a consequential justification and not as an autonomous justificatory principle.

The argument from equality is much more plausible if it focuses not upon people's qualities as *producers* of decisions but on their qualities as *consumers* of decisions.[5] The members of an association are each subject to the decisions of the association. They therefore each have an interest in the decisions that the association makes. Moreover, it is often, though not always, true that each member is equally interested in the decisions of the association. This can be true whether the members of the association are pursuing some collective purpose through the association or (as may be the case in a political association) simply

---

[4] Peter Singer, *Democracy and Disobedience* (Oxford: Oxford University Press, 1973), pp. 34–5.

[5] The argument of the next few paragraphs is similar in many repects to the more detailed argument of Carl Cohen, *Democracy,* ch. 15.

making rules which provide a framework within which they can pursue their individual purposes. Even then, it may not be that each member is equally affected by each and every decision; a particular decision may affect some more than others and that is why it may be appropriate to weigh individuals' interests or to measure the intensities of their preferences. But we may still be able to say that, taking all decisions in the round, taking the "set" of all decisions, any member is as interested in the outcomes of the decision procedure as any other. In particular it would seem reasonable to say this of individuals as members of states.

This account of the position of individuals as members of associations is partly analytic and partly empirical. It is not, or not obviously, moral. To derive a prescription for an egalitarian decision procedure we have to introduce an egalitarian principle. However, that principle need not be a particular specific or strong principle of equality—simply one that entails that, *ceteris paribus,* the well-being of one person is to be valued as much as that of another. A principle such as the principle of equal human worth as elaborated by Gregory Vlastos would fit the bill.[6] For Vlastos an individual's worth is not the same as his merit. "Merit" takes in all of those qualities by which we grade people. By contrast individuals' "worth" is "the value which persons have simply because they are persons." It is because we attribute worth equally to persons *qua* persons that we hold that "one man's well-being is as valuable as any other's."[7] Following a principle such as this we may say that, where individuals' interests or wants are equally at stake (and that is the only relevant consideration), each has an equal claim to have his interests promoted or his wants satisfied. This, in turn, implies that a decision procedure should be structured so that it respects the equal claim of each to have his interests promoted or his wants satisfied. ("His" here is, of course, meant to be sexless.) Thus a decision procedure is fair in so far as it respects equally this equal claim of each; unfair in so far as it does not.

The presumption that people's interests *are* equally at stake in the decision arena is as important to this conclusion as a principle of equal human worth. If some people's interests were more greatly at stake than others, then the principle of equal human worth would not merely allow but would require that account should be taken of those differences of interest. There are cases where the members of an association have different degrees of interest in the association, where the decision procedure reflects those differences, and where that arrangement seems perfectly acceptable. For example, in general terms, there is nothing unfair or otherwise objectionable about the shareholders of a company holding votes in proportion to the number of shares that they hold.

Even now, the argument for democracy is not entirely complete. Given that each individual is equally interested in the decisions of an association, that interest may be interpreted as no more than that decisions should be, as far as possible, what he wants them to be. In that case we can move straight to the

[6] Gregory Vlastos, "Justice and Equality" in Richard B. Brandt (ed.), *Social Justice* (Englewood Cliffs, N.J.: Prentice-Hall, 1962). pp. 31–72.

[7] Ibid., pp. 48, 51.

inference that the decision procedure should afford an equal opportunity for the expression of wants and take equal account of those wants. Alternatively, acknowledging the conceptual distinction between interests and wants (even if an individual's interests have, ultimately, to connect with his wants), one might argue entirely in terms of the interests of individuals. The democrat would then have to confront the well-worn objection that a benevolent and informed despotism could promote the interests of a people as well, if not better than, a democracy. The usual reply to that objection is that we may presume that each individual is the best judge of his own interests. In fact the more relevant presumption is that each is the best promoter or, in Mill's words, the best "guardian" of his interest since it benefits him nothing if his interest is better judged by another but then ignored. However, this is not the only strategy open to the democrat. He might argue that whatever an individual's competence as judge of his own interests, he and he alone has the right to be the final arbiter of that interest. I shall not assess the merits of either argument, partly because that would be a lengthy and probably inconclusive business, but mainly because that assessment is at some distance from my chief concern: the limits of majoritarianism. I shall simply presume that the care of each individual's interest is properly left in his own hands.

IV

From the principles and presumptions that I have outlined we can derive the characteristic features of democracy, at least in its simple form: an equal right to vote, to participate in discussion, to place items on the agenda, and so on. Some might argue that this equalitarian position requires not only that these rights should be formally available to all, but also that socio-economic conditions should be adjusted to ensure that these rights constitute genuinely equal opportunities rather than merely formal entitlements. In addition it might be supposed that we can derive the majority principle in the way that I have already indicated. Individuals' interests or wants are to count equally, therefore votes are to count equally; if votes count equally and if there is a conflict of votes, then the votes of the majority must prevail. But is such an inference valid? Consider the following example.

There is a street whose residents control and pay for the amenities of the street and who decide democratically what those amenities shall be. Each resident has a vote and the vote of the majority is always decisive. They have three issues to decide upon, each of which they reckon equally important.

1. Whether to have asphalt or paved sidewalks. Asphalt is ugly but cheap. Paving stones are pleasant but more expensive.
2. Whether to keep the existing gas lighting which is picturesque and in keeping with the character of the street or to replace it with electric street-lighting which would be garish but provide the same amount of lighting more cheaply.
3. Whether to improve the appearance of the street by planting trees or to save money and plant no trees.

Two-thirds of the residents are economizers; one-third are aesthetes. Thus when each vote is taken the economizers win, the aesthetes lose. The street has asphalt instead of paved sidewalks, electric instead of gas lighting, and no trees. Is that result satisfactory?

If we took any decision in isolation the answer would be yes both for an orthodox utilitarian and for someone who adhered to the principle of equality that I have outlined. Utility has been maximized and each individual's wants or interests have been valued equally. But consider the decisions as a group. Again the utilitarian would find nothing to object to particularly if we assume, as seems reasonable in the example I have given, that successive wins do not have a declining marginal utility for the winning majority. Provided social utility has been maximized, it is of no concern to the utilitarian that, in each decision, it is the same individuals who have had their utilities promoted and the same individuals who have not.

However, this must be of concern to the democrat who is a democrat because he adheres to the principle of equality that I have outlined. He cannot be satisfied that the interests or wants of the members of a community are consistently opposed in a ratio of 2:1 but consistently satisfied in a ratio of 3:0. Those individuals who make up the persistent minority can properly complain that repeated applications of the majority principle are not consistent with their equal entitlement as individuals to want-satisfaction or interest promotion. If that entitlement were respected the aesthetes would get their way on one of the three issues.

It might be objected that there is no justification for treating the three decisions as a group. Each is an independent decision, each individually meets the requirements of equality, and it should be accepted as merely fortuitous that the same people win or lose in each of the three decisions. That objection cannot be sustained. What links the three decisions is that each is part of a process of want-satisfaction or interest-promotion. Want-satisfaction or interest-promotion is a good and a good capable of different distributions which, in turn, can be examined in the light of distributive principles. The democratic process allocates that good and it is quite legitimate to assess the overall distribution of the good even though that distribution is made by way of a number of separate decisions. If, having made such an assessment, we discover that some individuals have received all of that good and others have received none, we have good reason to doubt that the equal claim of each individual to the promotion of his interests has been respected.[8]

This, of course, relates to an essential and oft-noted difference between principles such as equality or fairness on the one hand and utilitarianism on the other. Equality and fairness are distributive principles, whereas the maximization of social utility is an aggregative principle to which distributive considerations are

---

[8] I say only "good reason to doubt" to allow for the possibility that this result could be the outcome of the sort of lottery that I consider in the next section. Another objection to my argument here might be that what I have presented as three separate issues could be equally well regarded as a single issue: should the street have the cheapest or the most pleasant amenities? However, part of the thrust of the argument I develop here is that, wherever it is practicable to divide up issues so that a fairer satisfaction of preferences becomes possible, this should be done.

entirely subordinate. It is true that utilitarians would generally follow Bentham's injunction that each should count for one and no more than one. But that is no more than a working assumption to be followed in maximizing aggregate utility and, at most, yields a principle of impersonality or "anonymity." Maximizing social utility may entail taking equal account of each individual's interest, but that does not make it the same exercise as distributing satisfactions fairly.

It is for this reason that I have avoided a formula that is often presented in discussions of this sort: that each person is entitled to equal consideration or, more specifically, that each person's interest should be considered equally. The trouble with this formula is that it is not clear what it requires. Dahl, for example, gives the following as a principle which a procedure must satisfy to be "democratic."

> *Equal Consideration for all members:* No distribution of socially allocated entities, whether actions, forbearances, or objects, is acceptable if it violates the principle that the good or interest of each member is entitled to equal consideration.[9]

But how demanding is this principle supposed to be? If "equal consideration" requires merely "taking equally into account," the utilitarian can claim to consider interests equally in maximizing social utility. If, on the other hand, "equal consideration" means that equal claims of interests should be equally met, the principle sets a test which the utilitarian cannot pass—except in those few cases where, by a happy chance, maximizing utility coincides with meeting equal claims equally. Elsewhere in the same essay, Dahl enunciates another principle that is fundamental to procedural democracy: "equally valid claims justify equal shares."[10] He apparently thinks that "this elementary principle of fairness" amounts to very little—"it falls just short of a tautology." But it is just such an "elementary" principle that a utilitarian cannot acknowledge. He can claim to consider interests equally in respect of the goal of maximum social utility; what he cannot do is to acknowledge the equal satisfaction of equal claims as a goal in its own right, for maximizing aggregate utility is not guaranteed to redeem each individual's equal claim to interest-promotion.

V

A possible counter to my argument against majoritarianism is that a system in which people have equal chances or opportunities is compatible with the egalitarian principle I have outlined, and that decision by majority vote constitutes a system of equal chance or opportunity. I would accept the first proposition but not the second.

---

[9]   Robert A. Dahl, "Procedural Democracy" in Peter Laslett and Jams Fishkin (eds.), *Philosophy, Politics and Society,* 5th series (Oxford: Basil Blackwell, 1979), p.125. See also Stanley I. Benn, "Egalitarianism and the Equal Consideration of Interests" in J. Roland Pennock and John W. Chapman (eds.), *Nomos IX: Equality* (New York: Atherton Press, 1967).

[10] Dahl, "Procedural Democracy." p. 99. Dahl himself refrains from deriving any specific decision rule from either principle of equality: ibid., pp. 101–2.

Suppose a group of individuals agreed to make the decisions which applied to them collectively by way of a lottery. For every issue there would be a lottery in which each individual held one and only one ticket. The individual who held the winning ticket for a particular issue would have the right to decide on that issue on behalf of the whole group. Thus, for any issue, each individual *qua* individual would have an equal chance of being the decider. The odds in favor of any particular proposal being adopted would be proportionate to the number of individuals who favored that alternative in the total group. However, the fairness of the lottery system would not depend upon its tendency, over time, to produce decisions roughly in proportion to the wishes of different sections of the population. Rather the procedure could be said to be inherently fair; it would be an example of what Rawls calls "pure procedural justice." [11] The mere fact that each individual's ticket counts for one and no more than one can be regarded as enough to satisfy the equal claim of each to want-satisfaction.

However, decision by majority vote cannot properly be represented as a lottery of this sort. When individuals enter the decision arena they may be ignorant of one another's preferences and therefore ignorant of whether they will be in the majority or the minority. In addition, they may be ignorant of one another's preferences on future issues. Indeed, they are likely to be ignorant of their own preferences on future issues since they will not know what all of those issues will be and therefore will not yet have formed preferences on them. But ignorance is not randomness; it is merely ignorance. That people are ignorant of the total configuration of preferences on all future issues, and therefore ignorant of how often they will find themselves in the majority or minority, does not mean that decision by majority vote amounts to a lottery in which people have equal chances of winning.

This may seem too short a way with majoritarianism. Have I not overlooked an important equality commonly claimed for majoritarian democracy: the equal opportunity of each to persuade the majority to his point of view? If the entitlement of each individual to that opportunity is respected, should that not remove our reservations about majoritarianism? There are at least three reasons why it should not. Firstly, a majority may simply be intransigent and not open to persuasion. Secondly, there are many issues—particularly those which arise from conflicting interests or wants—which are not really matters for persuasion. I do not know how the aesthetes in my street example could produce reasons which would "persuade" the economizers to change their preferences. (Issues which arise from conflicting judgements are a different matter which I shall consider separately in a moment.) Thirdly, this sort of equality presupposes what is at issue: the majority principle. Persuading the majority is simply set as the condition of a competition in which people have an equal opportunity to participate. That people have an equal right to participate in that competition does nothing to establish that the competition is itself satisfactory, that persuading the majority ought always to be the condition of promoting interests or satisfying wants.

[11] Rawls, *Theory of Justice,* p. 86.

What if people consent to majority rule, if not directly then indirectly by joining an association in which the majority principle is already an established part of the constitution? Does that not render majority rule fair? The problems involved in holding that people "consent" to be members of states are well known. However, I have said that my reservations about majority rule apply equally to many non-state associations and we would normally have no qualms about describing membership of most of those associations as "voluntary." That people have consented to a form of government rather than having it imposed upon them must count for something. Nevertheless, it is still possible to assess the fairness of an argument independently of whether it has received the consent of those to whom it applies. Consider, for example, a lottery in which there are two sorts of ticket—one for Blacks, the other for Whites. All tickets are sold at the same price but those sold to Blacks carry half the chance of winning as those sold to Whites. All are aware of this and no one is obliged to buy a ticket, so that when a Black buys a ticket he does so freely and is therefore a "consenting" participant in the lottery. Even so, it seems quite reasonable to say that, as far as Black participants are concerned, the lottery is unfair. Notice that if consent were a sufficient condition of fairness, we would have to describe as fair not just majority rule but *any* arrangement to which people consented no matter how morally grotesque it might be. Thus, even where people have consented to be governed according to the majority principle, we may still say that that principle can work unfairly, though we may also feel that there is little reason to protest on behalf of a persistent minority that has, more or less wittingly, consented to the position in which it finds itself.

VI

The conclusion that I wish to draw from all that I have said will be obvious: where majority rule results in persistent minorities those minorities have reason to complain that they are being treated unfairly. This is a simple and perhaps unsurprising statement but it is one that democratic theorists have been remarkably reluctant to make. The common assumption seems to be that a democratic minority can legitimately complain only in two sorts of circumstance: (1) if its rights are infringed or if in some other way it is persecuted, oppressed, or exploited; (2) if its special interests are overridden by an "apathetic majority." If a minority is persistently on the losing side, but can make neither of these complaints, its position is usually regarded as merely unfortunate rather than unfair.

Certainly persistent minorities are thought to be "bad" or "unhealthy" for a democracy. For one thing, persistent minorities are likely to become increasingly reluctant to bend to the majority's will. For another, persistent majorities, it is said,[12] are likely to abuse their position. Where there are fluctuating majorities, the individual who is in the majority today knows that he will be in the

[12] e.g. by Madison in *The Federalist*, No. 10 and by Cohen, *Democracy*, pp. 71–4.

minority tomorrow. He therefore has an incentive not to abuse his majority position lest he, in turn, is abused when he is in the minority. The members of a persistent majority have no such incentive to play fair by the minority. However, neither of these points questions the fairness of majoritarianism itself. Both are simply empirical assertions about the way in which persistent majorities and minorities endanger the satisfactory working of democratic institutions, whereas I have tried to argue that a persistent minority has reason to complain in terms of the very principle of equality that underlies democracy.

22.

The Market and the Forum: Three Varieties of Political Theory

JON ELSTER

I want to compare three views of politics generally, and of the democratic system more specifically. I shall first look at social choice theory, as an instance of a wider class of theories with certain common features. In particular, they share the conception that the political process is instrumental rather than an end in itself, and the view that the decisive political act is a private rather than a public action, viz. the individual and secret vote. With these usually goes the idea that the goal of politics is the optimal compromise between given, and irreducibly opposed, private interests. The other two views arise when one denies, first, the private character of political behavior and then, secondly, goes on also to deny the instrumental nature of politics. According to the theory of Jürgen Habermas, the goal of politics should be rational agreement rather than compromise, and the decisive political act is that of engaging in public debate with a view to the emergence of a consensus. According to the theorists of participatory democracy, from John Stuart Mill to Carole Pateman, the goal of politics is the transformation and education of the participants. Politics, on this view, is an end in itself—indeed many have argued that it represents the good life for man. I shall discuss these views in the order indicated. I shall present them in a somewhat stylized form, but my critical comments will not I hope, be directed to strawmen.

I

Politics, it is usually agreed, is concerned with the common good, and notably with the cases in which it cannot be realized as the aggregate outcome of individuals pursuing their private interests. In particular, uncoordinated private choices may lead to outcomes that are worse for all than some other outcome that could have been attained by coordination. Political institutions are set up to remedy such *market failures*, a phrase that can be taken either in the static sense of an inability to provide public goods or in the more dynamic sense of a breakdown of the self-regulating properties usually ascribed to the market mechanism.[1] In addition there is the redistributive task of politics—moving along the Pareto-optimal frontier once it has been reached.[2] According to the

---

[1] Elster (1978, Ch. 5) refers to these two varieties of market failure as *suboptimality* and *counterfinality* respectively, linking them both to collective action.

[2] This is a simplification. First, as argued in Samuelson (1950), there may be political constraints that prevent one from attaining the Pareto-efficient frontier. Secondly, the very existence of sev-

238

first view of politics, this task is inherently one of interest struggle and compromise. The obstacle to agreement is not only that most individuals want redistribution to be in their favor, or at least not in their disfavor.[3] More basically consensus is blocked because there is no reason to expect that individuals will converge in their views on what constitutes a just redistribution.

I shall consider social choice theory as representative of the private-instrumental view of politics, because it brings out supremely well the logic as well as the limits of that approach. Other varieties, such as the Schumpeterian or neo-Schumpeterian theories, are closer to the actual political process, but for that reason also less suited to my purpose. For instance, Schumpeter's insistence that voter preferences are shaped and manipulated by politicians[4] tends to blur the distinction, central to my analysis, between politics as the aggregation of given preferences and politics as the transformation of preferences through rational discussion. And although the neo-Schumpeterians are right in emphasizing the role of the political parties in the preference-aggregation process,[5] I am not here concerned with such mediating mechanisms. In any case, political problems also arise within the political parties, and so my discussion may be taken to apply to such lower-level political processes. In fact, much of what I shall say makes better sense for politics on a rather small scale—within the firm, the organization or the local community—than for nationwide political systems.

In very broad outline, the structure of social choice theory is as follows.[6] (1) We begin with a *given* set of agents, so that the issue of a normative justification of political boundaries does not arise. (2) We assume that the agents confront a *given* set of alternatives, so that for instance the issue of agenda manipulation does not arise. (3) The agents are supposed to be endowed with preferences that are similarly *given* and not subject to change in the course of the political process. They are, moreover, assumed to be causally independent of the set of alternatives. (4) In the standard version, which is so far the only operational version of the theory, preferences are assumed to be purely ordinal, so that it is not possible for an individual to express the intensity of his preferences, nor for an outside observer to compare preference intensities across individuals. (5) The individual preferences are assumed to be defined over all pairs of individuals, i.e. to be complete, and to have the formal property of transitivity, so that preference for A over B and for B over C implies preference for A over C.

eral points that are Pareto-superior to the *status quo*, yet involve differential benefits to the participants, may block the realization of any of them.

[3] Hammond (1976) offers a useful analysis of the consequences of selfish preferences over income distributions, showing that "without interpersonal comparisons of some kind, any social preference ordering over the space of possible income distributions must be dictatorial."

[4] Schumpeter (1961, p. 263): "the will of the people is the product and not the motive power of the political process." One should not, however, conclude (as does Lively 1975, p. 38) that Schumpeter thereby abandons the market analogy, since on his view (Schumpeter 1939, p. 73) consumer preferences are no less manipulable (with some qualifications stated in Elster 1983a, Ch. 5).

[5] Seen in particular Downs (1957).

[6] For fuller statements, see Arrow (1963), Sen (1970), and Kelly (1978), as well as the contribution of Aanund Hylland to the present volume.

Given this setting, the task of social choice theory is to arrive at a social preference ordering of the alternatives. This might appear to require more than is needed: why not define the goal as one of arriving at the choice of one alternative? There is, however, usually some uncertainty as to which alternatives are really feasible, and so it is useful to have an ordering if the top-ranked alternative proves unavailable. The ordering should satisfy the following criteria. (6) Like the individual preferences, it should be complete and transitive. (7) It should be Pareto-optimal, in the sense of never having one option socially preferred to another which is individually preferred by everybody. (8) The social choice between two given options should depend only on how the individuals rank these two options, and thus not be sensitive to changes in their preferences concerning other options. (9) The social preference ordering should respect and reflect individual preferences, over and above the condition of Pareto-optimality. This idea covers a variety of notions, the most important of which are *anonymity* (all individuals should count equally), *non-dictatorship* (*a fortiori* no single individual should dictate the social choice), *liberalism* (all individuals should have some private domain within which their preferences are decisive), and *strategy-proofness* (it should not pay to express false preferences).

The substance of social choice theory is given in a series of impossibility and uniqueness theorems, stating either that a given subset of these conditions is incapable of simultaneous satisfaction or that they uniquely describe a specific method for aggregating preferences. Much attention has been given to the impossibility theorems, yet from the present point of view these are not of decisive importance. They stem largely from the paucity of allowable information about the preferences, i.e. the exclusive focus on ordinal preferences.[7] True, at present we do not quite know how to go beyond ordinality. Log-rolling and vote-trading may capture some of the cardinal aspects of the preferences, but at some cost.[8] Yet even should the conceptual and technical obstacles to intra- and inter-individual comparison of preference intensity be overcome,[9] many objections to the social choice approach would remain. I shall discuss two sets of objections, both related to the assumption of given preferences. I shall argue, first, that the preferences people choose to express may not be a good guide to what they really prefer; and secondly that what they really prefer may in any case be a fragile foundation for social choice.

In actual fact, preference are never "given," in the sense of being directly observable. If they are to serve as inputs to the social choice process, they must somehow be *expressed* by the individuals. The expression of preferences is an action, which presumably is guided by these very same preferences.[10] It is then far from obvious that the individually rational action is to express these preferences as they are. Some methods for aggregating preferences are such that

[7] Cf. d'Aspremont and Gevers (1977).

[8] Riker and Ordeshook (1973, pp. 112–13).

[9] Cf. the contribution of Donald Davidson and Allan Gibbard to the present volume.

[10] Presumably, but not obviously, since the agent might have several preference orderings and rely on higher-order preferences to determine which of the first-order preferences to express, as suggested for instance by Sen (1976).

it may pay the individual to express false preferences, i.e. the outcome may in some cases be better according to his real preferences if he chooses not to express them truthfully. The condition for strategy-proofness for social choice mechanisms was designed expressly to exclude this possibility. It turns out, however, that the systems in which honesty always pays are rather unattractive in other respects.[11] We then have to face the possibility that even if we require that the social preferences be Pareto-optimal with respect to the expressed preferences, they might not be so with respect to the real ones. Strategy-proofness and collective rationality, therefore, stand and fall together. Since it appears that the first must fall, so must the second. It then becomes very difficult indeed to defend the idea that the outcome of the social choice mechanism represents the common good, since there is a chance that everybody might prefer some other outcome.

Amos Tversky has pointed to another reason why choices—or expressed preferences—cannot be assumed to represent the real preferences in all case.[12] According to his "concealed preference hypothesis," choices often conceal rather than reveal underlying preferences. This is especially so in two sorts of cases. First, there are the cases of anticipated regret associated with a risky decision. Consider the following example (from Tversky):

> On her twelfth birthday, Judy was offered a choice between spending the weekend with her aunt in the city (C), or having a party for all her friends. The party could take place either in the garden (GP) or inside the house (HP). A garden party would be much more enjoyable, but there is always the possibility of rain, in which case an inside party would be more sensible. In evaluating the consequences of the three options, Judy notes that the weather condition does not have a significant effect on C. If she chooses the party, however, the situation is different. A garden party will be a lot of fun if the weather is good, but quite disastrous if it rains, in which case an inside party will be acceptable. The trouble is that Judy expects to have a lot of regret if the party is to be held inside and the weather is very nice.
>
> Now, let us suppose that for some reason it is no longer possible to have an outside party. In this situation, there is no longer any regret associated with holding an inside party in good weather because (in this case) Judy has no other place for holding the party. Hence, the elimination of an available course of action (holding the party outside) removes the regret associated with an inside party, and increases its overall utility. It stands to reason, in this case, that if Judy was indifferent between C and HP, in the presence of GP, she will prefer HP to C when GP is eliminated.

What we observe here is the violation of condition (8) above, the so-called "independence of irrelevant alternatives." The expressed preferences depend causally on the set of alternatives. We may assume that the real preferences,

---

[11] Pattanaik (1978) offers a survey of the known results. The only strategy-proof mechanisms for social choice turn out to be the dictatorial one (the dictator has no incentive to misrepresent his preferences) and the randomizing one of getting the probability that a given option will be chosen equal to the proportion of voters that have it as their first choice.

[12] Tversky (1981).

defined over the set of possible outcomes, remain constant, contrary to the case to be discussed below. Yet the preferences over the *pairs* (choice, outcome) depend on the set of available choices, because the "costs of responsibility" differentially associated with various such pairs depend on what else one "could have done." Although Judy could not have escaped her predicament by deliberately making it physically impossible to have an outside party,[13] she might well have welcomed an event outside her control with the same consequence.

The second class of cases in which Tversky would want to distinguish the expressed preferences from the real preferences concerns decisions that are unpleasant rather than risky. For instance, "society may prefer to save the life of one person rather than another, and yet be unable to make this choice." In fact, losing both lives through inaction may be preferred to losing only one life by deliberate action. Such examples are closely related to the problems involved in act utilitarianism versus outcome utilitarianism.[14] One may well judge that it would be a good thing if state *A* came about, and yet not want to be the person by whose agency it comes about. The reasons for not wanting to be that person may be quite respectable, or they may not. The latter would be the case if one were afraid of being blamed by the relatives of the person who was deliberately allowed to die, or if one simply confused the causal and the moral notions of responsibility. In such cases the expressed preferences might lead to a choice that in a clear sense goes against the real preferences of the people concerned.

A second, perhaps more basic, difficulty is that the real preferences themselves might well depend causally on the feasible set. One instance is graphically provided by the fable of the fox and the sour grapes.[15] For the "ordinal utilitarian," as Arrow for instance calls himself,[16] there would be no welfare loss if the fox were excluded from consumption of the grapes, since he thought them sour anyway. But of course the cause of his holding them to be sour was his conviction that he would in any case be excluded from consuming them, and then it is difficult to justify the allocation by invoking his preferences. Conversely, the phenomenon of "counter-adaptive preferences"—the grass is always greener on the other side of the fence, and the forbidden fruit always sweeter— is also baffling for the social choice theorist, since it implies that such preferences, if respected, would not be satisfied—and yet the whole point of respecting them would be to give them a chance of satisfaction.

Adaptive and counter-adaptive preferences are only special cases of a more general class of desires, those which fail to satisfy some substantive criterion for acceptable preferences, as opposed to the purely formal criterion of transitivity. I shall discuss these under two headings: autonomy and morality.

---

[13] Cf. Elster (1979, Ch. II) or Schelling (1980) for the idea of deliberately restricting one's feasible set to make certain undesirable behavior impossible at a later time. The reason this does not work here is that the regret would not be eliminated.

[14] Cf. for instance Williams (1973) or Sen (1979).

[15] Cf. Elster (1983b, Ch. III) for a discussion of this notion.

[16] Arrow (1973).

Autonomy characterizes the way in which preferences are shaped rather than their actual content. Unfortunately I find myself unable to give a positive characterization of autonomous preferences, so I shall have to rely on two indirect approaches. First, autonomy is for desires what judgment is for belief. The notion of judgment is also difficult to define formally, but at least we know that there are persons who have this quality to a higher degree than others: people who are able to take account of vast and diffuse evidence that more or less clearly bears on the problem at hand, in such a way that no element is given undue importance. In such people the process of belief formation is not disturbed by defective cognitive processing, nor distorted by wishful thinking and the like. Similarly, autonomous preferences are those that have not been shaped by irrelevant causal processes—a singularly unhelpful explanation. To improve somewhat on it, consider, secondly, a short list of such irrelevant causal processes. They include adaptive and counter-adaptive preferences, conformity and anti-conformity, the obsession with novelty and the equally unreasonable resistance to novelty. In other words, preferences may be shaped by adaptation to what is possible, to what other people do or to what one has been doing in the past—or they may be shaped by the desire to differ as much as possible from these. In all of these cases the source of preference change is not in the person, but outside him—detracting from his autonomy.

Morality, it goes without saying, is if anything even more controversial. (Within the Kantian tradition it would also be questioned whether it can be distinguished at all from autonomy.) Preferences are moral or immoral by virtue of their content, not by virtue of the way in which they have been shaped. Fairly uncontroversial examples of unethical preferences are spiteful and sadistic desires, and arguably also the desire for positional goods, i.e. goods such that it is logically impossible for more than a few to possess them.[17] The desire for an income twice the average can lead to less welfare for everybody, so that such preferences fail to pass the Kantian generalization test.[18] Also they are closely linked to spite, since one way of getting more than others is to take care that they get less—indeed this may often be a more efficient method than trying to excel.[19]

To see how the lack of autonomy may be distinguished from the lack of moral worth, let me use *conformity* as a technical term for a desire caused by a drive to be like other people, and *conformism* for a desire to be like other people, with anti-conformity and anti-conformism similarly defined. Conformity implies that other people's desires enter into the causation of my own, conformism that they enter irreducibly into the description of the object of my desires. Conformity may bring about conformism, but it may also lead to

---

[17] Hirsch (1976).

[18] Haavelmo (1970) offers a model in which everybody may suffer a loss of welfare by trying to keep up with the neighbors.

[19] One may take the achievements of others as a parameter and one's own as the control variable, or conversely try to manipulate the achievements of others so that they fall short of one's own. The first of these ways of realizing positional goods is clearly less objectionable than the second, but still less pure than the non-comparative desire for a certain standard of excellence.

anti-conformism, as in Theodore Zeldin's comment that among the French peasantry "prestige is to a great extent obtained from conformity with traditions (so that the son of a non-conformist might be expected to be one too)."[20] Clearly, conformity may bring about desires that are morally laudable, yet lacking in autonomy. Conversely, I do not see how one could rule out on *a priori* grounds the possibility of autonomous spite, although I would welcome a proof that autonomy is incompatible not only with anti-conformity, but also with anti-conformism.

We can now state the objection to the political view underlying social choice theory. It is, basically, that it embodies a confusion between the kind of behavior that is appropriate in the market place and that which is appropriate in the forum. The notion of consumer sovereignty is acceptable because, and to the extent that, the consumer chooses between courses of action that differ only in the way they affect him. In political choice situations, however, the citizen is asked to express his preference over states that also differ in the way in which they affect other people. This means that there is no similar justification for the corresponding notion of the citizen's sovereignty, since other people may legitimately object to social choice governed by preferences that are defective in some of the ways I have mentioned. A social choice mechanism is capable of resolving the market failures that would result from unbridled consumer sovereignty, but as a way of redistributing welfare it is hopelessly inadequate. If people affected each other only by tripping over each other's feet, or by dumping their garbage into one another's backyards, a social choice mechanism might cope. But the task of politics is not only to eliminate inefficiency, but also to create justice—a goal to which the aggregation of prepolitical preferences is a quite incongruous means.

This suggests that the principles of the forum must differ from those of the market. A long-standing tradition from the Greek *polis* onwards suggests that politics must be an open and public activity, as distinct from the isolated and private expression of preferences that occurs in buying and selling. In the following sections I look at two different conceptions of public politics, increasingly removed from the market theory of politics. Before I go on to this, however, I should briefly consider an objection that the social choice theorist might well make to what has just been said. He could argue that the only alternative to the aggregation of given preferences is some kind of censorship or paternalism. He might agree that spiteful and adaptive preferences are undesirable, but he would add that any institutional mechanism for eliminating them would be misused and harnessed to the private purposes of power-seeking individuals. Any remedy, in fact, would be worse than the disease. This objection assumes (i) that the only alternative to aggregation of given preferences is censorship, and (ii) that censorship is always objectionable. Robert Goodin, in his contribution to this volume, challenges the second assumption, by arguing that laundering or filtering of preferences by self-censorship is an acceptable alternative to aggregation. I shall now discuss a challenge to the first

---

[20] Zeldin (1973, p. 134).

assumption, viz. the idea of a *transformation* of preferences through public and rational discussion.

II

Today this view is especially associated with the writings of Jürgen Habermas on "the ethics of discourse" and "the ideal speech situation." As mentioned above, I shall present a somewhat stylized version of his views, although I hope they bear some resemblance to the original.[21] The core of the theory, then, is that rather than aggregating or filtering preferences, the political system should be set up with a view to changing them by public debate and confrontation. The input to the social choice mechanism would then not be the raw, quite possibly selfish or irrational, preferences that operate in the market, but informed and other-regarding preferences. Or rather, there would not be any need for an aggregating mechanism, since a rational discussion would tend to produce unanimous preferences. When the private and idiosyncratic wants have been shaped and purged in public discussion about the public good, uniquely determined rational desires would emerge. Not optimal compromise, but unanimous agreement is the goal of politics on this view.

There appear to be two main premises underlying this theory. The first is that there are certain arguments that simply cannot be stated publicly. In a political debate it is pragmatically impossible to argue that a given solution should be chosen just because it is good for oneself. By the very act of engaging in a public debate—by arguing rather than bargaining—one has ruled out the possibility of invoking such reasons.[22] To engage in discussion can in fact be seen as one kind of self-censorship, a pre-commitment to the idea of rational decision. Now, it might well be thought that this conclusion is too strong. The first argument only shows that in public debate one has to pay some lipservice to the common good. An additional premise states that over time one will in fact come to be swayed by considerations about the common good. One cannot indefinitely praise the common good "du bout des lèvres," for—as argued by Pascal in the context of the wager—one will end up having the preferences that initially one was faking.[23] This is a psychological, not a conceptual premise. To explain why going through the motions of rational discussion should tend to bring about the real thing, one might argue that people tend to bring what they mean into line with what they say in order to reduce dissonance, but this is a dangerous argument to employ in the present context. Dissonance reduction does not tend to generate autonomous preferences. Rather one would have to invoke the power of reason to break down prejudice and selfishness. By speaking with the voice of reason, one is also exposing oneself to reason.

---

[21] I rely mainly on Habermas (1982). I also thank Helge Høibraaten, Rune Slagstad, and Gunnar Skirbekk for having patiently explained to me various aspects of Habermas's work.

[22] Midgaard (1980).

[23] For Pascal's argument, cf. Elster (1979, Ch. II. 3).

To sum up, the conceptual impossibility of expressing selfish arguments in a debate about the public good, and the psychological difficulty of expressing other-regarding preferences without ultimately coming to acquire them, jointly bring it about that public discussion tends to promote the common good. The *volonté générale*, then, will not simply be the Pareto-optimal realization of given (or expressed) preferences,[24] but the outcome of preferences that are themselves shaped by a concern for the common good. For instance, by mere aggregation of given preferences one would be able to take account of some negative externalities, but not of those affecting future generations. A social choice mechanism might prevent persons now living from dumping their garbage into one another's backyards, but not from dumping it in the future. Moreover, considerations of distributive justice within the Pareto constraint would now have a more solid foundation, especially as one would also be able to avoid the problem of strategy-proofness. By one stroke one would achieve more rational preferences, as well as the guarantee that they will in fact be expressed.

I now want to set out a series of objections—seven altogether—to the view stated above. I should explain that the goal of this criticism is not to demolish the theory, but to locate some points that need to be fortified. I am, in fact, largely in sympathy with the fundamental tenets of the view, yet fear that it might be dismissed as Utopian, both in the sense of ignoring the problem of getting from here to there, and in the sense of neglecting some elementary facts of human psychology.

The *first objection* involves a reconsideration of the issues of paternalism. Would it not, in fact, be unwarranted interference to impose on the citizens the obligation to participate in political discussion? One might answer that there is a link between the right to vote and the obligation to participate in discussion, just as rights and duties are correlative in other cases. To acquire the right to vote, one has to perform certain civic duties that go beyond pushing the voting button on the television set. There would appear to be two different ideas underlying this answer. First, only those should have the right to vote who are sufficiently *concerned* about politics to be willing to devote some of their resources—time in particular—to it. Secondly, one should try to favor *informed* preferences as inputs to the voting process. The first argument favors participation and discussion as a sign of interest, but does not give it an instrumental value in itself. It would do just as well, for the purpose of this argument, to demand that people should pay for the right to vote. The second argument favors discussion as a means to improvement—it will not only select the right people, but actually make them more qualified to participate.

These arguments might have some validity in a near-ideal world, in which the concern for politics was evenly distributed across all relevant dimensions, but in the context of contemporary politics they miss the point. The people who survive a high threshold for participation are disproportionately found in a privileged part of the population. At best this could lead to paternalism, at worst the high ideals of rational discussion could create a self-elected elite

---

[24] As suggested by Runciman and Sen (1965).

whose members spend time on politics because they want power, not out of concern for the issues. As in other cases, to be discussed later, the best can be the enemy of the good. I am not saying that it is impossible to modify the ideal in a way that allows both for rational discussion and for low-profile partici- pation, only that any institutional design must respect the trade-off between the two.

My *second objection* is that even assuming unlimited time for discussion, unanimous and rational agreement might not necessarily ensue. Could there not be legitimate and unresolvable differences of opinions over the nature of the common good? Could there not even be a plurality of ultimate values?

I am not going to discuss this objection, since it is in any case preempted by the *third objection*. Since there are in fact always time constraints on discus- sions—often the stronger the more important the issues—unanimity will rarely emerge. For any constellation of preferences short of unanimity, how- ever, one would need a social choice mechanism to aggregate them. One can discuss only for so long, and then one has to make a decision, even if strong dif- ferences of opinion should remain. This objection, then, goes to show that the transformation of preferences can never do more than supplement the aggre- gation of preferences, never replace it altogether.

This much would no doubt be granted by most proponents of the theory. True, they would say, even if the ideal speech situation can never be fully real- ized, it will nevertheless improve the outcome of the political process if one goes some way towards it. The *fourth objection* questions the validity of this reply. In some cases a little discussion can be a dangerous thing, worse in fact than no discussion at all, viz. if it makes some but not all persons align themselves on the common good. The following story provides an illustration:

> Once upon a time two boys found a cake. One of them said, "Splendid! I will eat the cake." The other one said, "No, that is not fair! We found the cake to- gether, and we should share and share alike, half for you and half for me." The first boy said, "No, I should have the whole cake!" Along came an adult who said, "Gentlemen, you shouldn't fight about this: you should *compro- mise*. Give him three quarters of the cake." [25]

What creates the difficulty here is that the first boy's preferences are allowed to count twice in the social choice mechanism suggested by the adult: once in his expression of them and then again in the other boy's internalized ethic of shar- ing. And one can argue that the outcome is socially inferior to that which would have emerged had they both stuck to their selfish preferences. When Adam Smith wrote that he had never known much good done by those who affected to trade for the public good, he may only have had in mind the harm that can be done by *unilateral* attempts to act morally. The categorical imperative itself may be badly served by people acting unilaterally on it.[26] Also, an inferior out- come may result if discussion brings about partial adherence to morality in all

[25] Smullyan (1980, p. 56).
[26] Sobel (1967).

participants rather than full adherence in some and none in others, as in the story of the two boys. Thus Serge Kolm argues that economies with moderately altruistic agents tend to work less well than economies where either everybody is selfish or everybody is altruistic.[27]

A *fifth objection* is to question the implicit assumption that the body politic as a whole is better or wiser than the sum of its parts. Could it not rather be the case that people are made more, not less, selfish and irrational by interacting politically? The cognitive analogy suggests that the rationality of beliefs may be positively as well as negatively affected by interaction. On the one hand there is what Irving Janis has called "group-think," i.e. mutually reinforcing bias.[28] On the other hand there certainly are many ways in which people can, and do, pool their opinions and supplement each other to arrive at a better estimate.[29] Similarly autonomy and morality could be enhanced as well as undermined by interaction. Against the pessimistic view of Reinhold Niebuhr that individuals in a group show more unrestrained egoism than in their personal relationships,[30] we may set Hannah Arendt's optimistic view:

> American faith was not all based on a semireligious faith in human nature, but on the contrary, on the possibility of checking human nature in its singularity, by virtue of human bonds and mutual promises. The hope for man in his singularity lay in the fact that not man but men inhabit the earth and form a world between them. It is human worldliness that will save men from the pitfalls of human nature.[31]

Niebuhr's argument suggests an aristocratic disdain of the *mass*, which transforms individually decent people—to use a characteristically condescending phrase—into an unthinking horde. While rejecting this as a general view, one should equally avoid the other extreme, suggested by Arendt. Neither the Greek nor the American assemblies were the paradigms of discursive reason that she makes them out to be. The Greeks were well aware that they might be tempted by demagogues, and in fact took extensive precautions against this tendency.[32] The American town surely has not always been the incarnation of collective freedom, since on occasion it could also serve as the springboard for witch hunts. The mere decision to engage in rational discussion does not ensure that the transactions will in fact be conducted rationally, since much depends on the structure and the framework of the proceedings. The random errors of selfish and private preferences may to some extent cancel each other out and thus be less to be feared than the massive and coordinated errors that may arise through group-think. On the other hand, it would be excessively stupid to rely on mutually compensating vices to bring about public benefits as a general rule.

[27] Kolm (1981a, b).

[28] Janis (1972).

[29] Cf. Hogarth (1977) and Lehrer (1978).

[30] Niebuhr (1932, p. 11).

[31] Arendt (1973, p. 174).

[32] Finley (1973); see also Elster (1979, Ch. II.8).

I am not arguing against the need for public discussion, only for the need to take the question of institutional and constitutional design very seriously.

A *sixth objection* is that unanimity, were it to be realized, might easily be due to conformity rather than to rational agreement. I would in fact tend to have more confidence in the outcome of a democratic decision if there was a minority that voted against it, than if it was unanimous. I am not here referring to people expressing the majority preferences against their real ones, since I am assuming that something like the secret ballot would prevent this. I have in mind that people may come to change their real preferences, as a result of seeing which way the majority goes. Social psychology has amply shown the strength of this bandwagon effect,[33] which in political theory is also known as the "chameleon" problem.[34] It will not do to argue that the majority to which the conformist adapts his view is likely to pass the test of rationality even if his adherence to it does not, since the majority could well be made up of conformists each of whom would have broken out had there been a minority he could have espoused.

To bring the point home, consider a parallel case of non-autonomous preference formation. We are tempted to say that a man is free if he can get or do whatever it is that he wants to get or do. But then we are immediately faced with the objection that perhaps he only wants what he can get, as the result of some such mechanism as "sour grapes."[35] We may then add that, other things being equal, the person is freer the more things he wants to do which he is not free to do, since these show that his wants are not in general shaped by adaptation to his possibilities. Clearly, there is an air of paradox over the statement that a man's freedom is greater the more of his desires he is not free to realize, but on reflection the paradox embodies a valid argument. Similarly, it is possible to dissolve the air of paradox attached to the view that a collective decision is more trustworthy if it is less than unanimous.

My *seventh objection* amounts to a denial of the view that the need to couch one's argument in terms of the common good will purge the desires of all selfish arguments. There are in general many ways of realizing the common good, if by that phrase we now only mean some arrangement that is Pareto-superior to uncoordinated individual decisions. Each such arrangement will, in addition to promoting the general interest, bring an extra premium to some specific group, which will then have a strong interest in that particular arrangement.[36] The group may then come to prefer the arrangement because of that premium, although it will argue for it in terms of the common good. Typically the arrangement will be justified by a causal theory—an account, say, of how the economy works—that shows it to be not only *a* way, but the only way of promoting the common good. The economic theories underlying the early Reagan administration provide an example. I am not imputing insincerity to the proponents of

[33] Asch (1956) is a classic study.

[34] See Goldman (1972) for discussion and further references.

[35] Berlin (1969, p. xxxviii); cf. also Elster (1983b, Ch. III.3).

[36] Schotter (1981, pp. 26 ff., pp. 43 ff.) has a good discussion of this predicament.

these views, but there may well be an element of wishful thinking. Since social scientists disagree so strongly among themselves as to how societies work, what could be more human than to pick on a theory that uniquely justifies the arrangement from which one stands to profit? The opposition between general interest and special interests is too simplistic, since the private benefits may causally determine the way in which one conceives of the common good.

These objections have been concerned to bring out two main ideas. First, one cannot assume that one will in fact approach the good society by acting as if one had already arrived there. The fallacy inherent in this "approximation assumption"[37] was exposed a long time ago in the economic "theory of the second best":

> It is *not* true that a situation in which more, but not all, of the optimum conditions are fulfilled is necessarily, or is even likely to be, superior to a situation in which fewer are fulfilled. It follows, therefore, that in a situation in which there exist many constraints which prevent the fulfillment of the Paretian optimum conditions, the removal of any one constraint may affect welfare or efficiency either by raising it, by lowering it or by leaving it unchanged.[38]

The ethical analogue is not the familiar idea that some moral obligations may be suspended when other people act non-morally.[39] Rather it is that the nature of the moral obligation is changed in a non-moral environment. When others act non-morally, there may be an obligation to deviate not only from what they do, but also from the behavior that would have been optimal if adopted by everybody.[40] In particular, a little discussion, like a little rationality or a little socialism, may be a dangerous thing.[41] If, as suggested by Habermas, free and rational discussion will only be possible in a society that has abolished political and economic domination, it is by no means obvious that abolition can be brought about by rational argumentation. I do not want to suggest that it could occur by force—since the use of force to end the use of force is open to obvious objections. Yet something like irony, eloquence or propaganda might be needed, involving less respect for the interlocutor than what would prevail in the ideal speech situation.

As will be clear from these remarks, there is a strong tension between two ways of looking at the relation between political ends and means. On the one hand, the means should partake of the nature of the ends, since otherwise the use of unsuitable means might tend to corrupt the end. On the other hand, there are dangers involved in choosing means immediately derived from the goal to

---

[37] Margalit (1983).

[38] Lipsey and Lancaster (1956–7, p. 12).

[39] This is the point emphasized in Lyons (1965).

[40] Cf. Hansson (1970) as well as Føllesdal and Hilpinen (1971) for discussions of "conditional obligations" within the framework of deontic logic. It does not appear, however, that the framework can easily accommodate the kind of dilemma I am concerned with here.

[41] Cf. for instance Kolm (1977) concerning the dangers of a piecemeal introduction of socialism— also mentioned by Margalit (1983) as an objection to Popper's strategy for piecemeal social engineering.

be realized, since in a non-ideal situation these might take us away from the end rather than towards it. A delicate balance will have to be struck between these two, opposing considerations. It is in fact an open question whether there exists a ridge along which we can move to the good society, and if so whether it is like a knife-edge or more like a plateau.

The second general idea that emerges from the discussion is that even in the good society, should we hit upon it, the process of rational discussion could be fragile, and vulnerable to adaptive preferences, conformity, wishful thinking and the like. To ensure stability and robustness there is a need for structures— political institutions or constitutions—that could easily reintroduce an element of domination. We would in fact be confronted, at the political level, with a perennial dilemma of individual behavior. How is it possible to ensure at the same time that one is bound by rules that protect one from irrational or unethical behavior—and that these rules do not turn into prisons from which it is not possible to break out even when it would be rational to do so?[42]

III

It is clear from Habermas's theory, I believe, that rational political discussion has an *object* in terms of which it makes sense.[43] Politics is concerned with substantive decision-making, and is to that extent instrumental. True, the idea of instrumental politics might also be taken in a more narrow sense, as implying that the political process is one in which individuals pursue their selfish interests, but more broadly understood it implies only that political action is primarily a means to a non-political end, only secondarily, if at all, an end in itself. In this section I shall consider theories that suggest a reversal of this priority, and that find the main point of politics in the educative or otherwise beneficial effects on the participants. And I shall try to show that this view tends to be internally incoherent, or self-defeating. The benefits of participation are by-products of political activity. Moreover, they are *essentially* by-products, in the sense that any attempt to turn them into the main purpose of such activity would make them evaporate.[44] It can indeed be highly satisfactory to engage in political work, but only on the condition that the work is defined by a serious purpose which goes beyond that of achieving this satisfaction. If that condition is not fulfilled, we get a narcissistic view of politics—corresponding to various consciousness-raising activities familiar from the last decade or so.

My concern, however, is with political theory rather than with political activism. I shall argue that certain types of arguments for political institutions and constitutions are self-defeating, since they justify the arrangement in question

---

[42] Cf. Ainslie (1982) and Elster (1979, Ch. II.9).

[43] Indeed, Habermas (1982) is largely concerned with maxims for *action*, not with the evaluation of states of affairs.

[44] Cf. Elster (1983b, Ch. III) for a discussion of the notion that some psychological or social states are essentially by-products of actions undertaken for some other purpose.

by effects that are essentially by-products. Here an initial and important distinction must be drawn between the task of justifying a constitution *ex ante* and that of evaluating it *ex post* and at a distance. I argue below that Tocqueville, when assessing the American democracy, praised it for consequences that are indeed by-products. In his case, this made perfectly good sense as an analytical attitude adopted after the fact and at some distance from the system he was examining. The incoherence arises when one invokes the same arguments before the fact, in public discussion. Although the constitution-makers may secretly have such side effects in mind, they cannot coherently invoke them in public.

Kant proposed a *transcendental formula of public right:* "All actions affecting the rights of other human beings are wrong if their maxim is not compatible with their being made public."[45] Since Kant's illustrations of the principle are obscure, let me turn instead to John Rawls, who imposes a similar condition of publicity as a constraint on what the parties can choose in the original position.[46] He argues, moreover, that this condition tends to favor his own conception of justice, as compared to that of the utilitarians.[47] If utilitarian principles of justice were openly adopted, they would entail some loss of self-esteem, since people would feel that they were not fully being treated as ends in themselves. Other things being equal, this would also lead to a loss in average utility. It is then conceivable that public adoption of Rawls's two principles of justice would bring about a higher average utility than public adoption of utilitarianism, although a lower average than under a secret utilitarian constitution introduced from above. The latter possibility, however, is ruled out by the publicity constraint. A utilitarian could not then advocate Rawls's two principles on utilitarian grounds, although he might well applaud them on such grounds. The fact that the two principles maximize utility would essentially be a by-product, and if chosen on the grounds that they are utility-maximizing they would no longer be so. Utilitarianism, therefore, is self-defeating in Kant's sense: "it essentially lacks openness."[48]

Derek Parfit has raised a similar objection to act consequentialism (AC) and suggested how it could be met:

> This gives to all one common aim: the best possible outcome. If we try to achieve this, we may often fail. Even when we succeed, the fact that we are disposed to try might make the outcome worse. AC might thus be indirectly self-defeating. What does this show? A consequentialist might say: "It shows that AC should be only one part of our moral theory. It should be the part that covers successful acts. When we are certain to succeed, we should aim for the best possible outcome. Our wider theory should be this: we should have the aim and dispositions having which would make the outcome best. This wider theory would not be self-defeating. So the objection has been met."[49]

---

[45] Kant (1795, p. 126).

[46] Rawls (1971, p. 133).

[47] Rawls (1971, pp. 177 ff., esp. p. 181).

[48] Williams (1973, p. 123).

[49] Parfit (1981, p. 554).

Yet there is an ambiguity in the word "should" in the penultimate sentence, since it is not clear whether we are told that it is good to have certain aims and dispositions, or that we should aim at having them. The latter answer immediately raises the problem that having certain aims and dispositions—i.e. being a certain kind of person—is essentially a by-product. When instrumental rationality is self-defeating, we cannot decide on instrumentalist grounds to take leave of it—no more than we can fall asleep by deciding not to try to fall asleep. Although spontaneity may be highly valuable on utilitarian grounds, "you cannot both genuinely possess this kind of quality and also reassure yourself that while it is free and creative and uncalculative, it is also acting for the best." [50]

Tocqueville, in a seeming paradox, suggested that democracies are less suited than aristocracies to deal with long-term planning, and yet are superior in the long-run to the latter. The paradox dissolves once it is seen that the first statement involves time at the level of the actors, the second at the level of the observer. On the one hand, "a democracy finds it difficult to coordinate the details of a great undertaking and to fix on some plan and carry it through with determination in spite of obstacles. It has little capacity for combining measures in secret and waiting patiently for the result." [51] On the other hand, "in the long run government by democracy should increase the real forces of a society, but it cannot immediately assemble at one point and at a given time, forces as great as those at the disposal of an aristocratic government." [52] The latter view is further elaborated in a passage from the chapter on "The Real Advantages Derived by American Society from Democratic Government":

> That constantly renewed agitation introduced by democratic government into political life passes, then, into civil society. Perhaps, taking everything into consideration, that is the greatest advantage of democratic government, and I praise it much more on account of what it causes to be done than for what it does. It is incontestable that the people often manage public affairs very badly, but their concern therewith is bound to extend their mental horizon and to shake them out of the rut of ordinary routine. . . . Democracy does not provide a people with the most skillful of governments, but it does that which the most skillful government often cannot do: it spreads throughout the body social a restless activity, super-abundant force, and energy never found elsewhere, which, however little favoured by circumstances, can do wonders. Those are its true advantages. [53]

The advantages of democracies, in other words, are mainly and essentially by-products. The avowed aim of democracy is to be a good system of government, but Tocqueville argues that it is inferior in this respect to aristocracy, viewed purely as a decision-making apparatus. Yet the very activity of governing democratically has as a by-product a certain energy and restlessness that benefits industry and generates prosperity. Assuming the soundness of this observation,

---

[50] Williams (1973, p. 131); also Elster (1983b, Ch. II.3).

[51] Tocqueville (1969, p. 229).

[52] Tocqueville (1969, p. 224).

[53] Tocqueville (1969, pp. 243–4).

could it ever serve as a public justification for introducing democracy in a nation that had not yet acquired it? The question is somewhat more complex than one might be led to think from what I have said so far, since the quality of the decisions is not the only consideration that is relevant for the choice of a political system. The argument from *justice* could also be decisive. Yet the following conclusion seems inescapable: if the system has no inherent advantage in terms of justice or efficiency, one cannot coherently and publicly advocate its introduction because of the side effects that would follow in its wake. There must be a *point* in democracy as such. If people are motivated by such inherent advantages to throw themselves into the system, other benefits may ensue—but the latter cannot by themselves be the motivating force. If the democratic method is introduced in a society solely because of the side effects on economic prosperity, and no one believes in it on any other ground, it will not produce them.

Tocqueville, however, did not argue that political activity is an end in itself. The justification for democracy is found in its effects, although not in the intended ones, as the strictly instrumental view would have it. More to the point is Tocqueville's argument for the jury system: "I do not know whether a jury is useful to the litigants, but I am sure that it is very good for those who have to decide the case. I regard it as one of the most effective means of popular education at society's disposal." [54] This is still an instrumental view, but the gap between the means and the end is smaller. Tocqueville never argued that the effect of democracy was to make politicians prosperous, only that it was conducive to general prosperity. By contrast, the justification of the jury system is found in the effect on the jurors themselves. And, as above, that effect would be spoilt if they believed that the impact on their own civic spirit was the main point of the proceedings.

John Stuart Mill not only applauded but advocated democracy on the ground of such educative effects on the participants. In current discussion he stands out both as an opponent of the purely instrumental view of politics, that of his father James Mill,[55] and as a forerunner of the theory of participatory democracy.[56] In his theory the gap between means and ends in politics is even narrower, since he saw political activity not only as a means to self-improvement, but also as a source of satisfaction and thus a good in itself. As noted by Albert Hirschman, this implies that "the benefit of collective action for an individual is not the difference between the hoped-for result and the effort furnished by him or her, but the *sum* of these two magnitudes." [57] Yet this very way of paraphrasing Mill's view also points to a difficulty. Could it really be the case that participation would yield a benefit even when the hoped-for results are nil, as

[54] Tocqueville (1969, p. 275).

[55] Cf. Ryan (1972). His contrast between "two concepts of democracy" corresponds in part to the distinction between the first and the second of the theories discussed here, in part to the distinction between the first and the third, as he does not clearly separate the public conception of politics from the non-instrumental one.

[56] Pateman (1970, p. 29).

[57] Hirschman (1982, p. 82).

suggested by Hirschman's formula? Is it not rather true that the effort is itself a function of the hoped-for result, so that in the end the latter is the only independent variable? When Mill refers, critically, to the limitations of Bentham, whose philosophy "can teach the means of organizing and regulating the merely *business* part of the social arrangement,"[58] he seems to be putting the cart before the horse. The non-business part of politics may be the more valuable, but the value is contingent on the importance of the business part.

For a fully developed version of the non-instrumental theory of politics, we may go to the work of Hannah Arendt. Writing about the distinction between the private and the public realm in ancient Greece, she argues that:

> Without mastering the necessities of life in the household, neither life not the "good life" is possible, but politics is never for the sake of life. As far as the members of the *polis* are concerned, household life exists for the sake of the "good life" in the *polis*.[59]
>
> The public realm . . . was reserved for individuality; it was the only place where men could show who they really and inexchangeably were. It was for the sake of this chance, and out of love for a body politic that it made it possible to them all, that each was more or less willing to share in the burden of jurisdiction, defence and administration of public affairs.[60]

Against this we may set the view of Greek politics found in the work of M. I. Finley. Asking why the Athenian people claimed the right of every citizen to speak and make proposals in the Assembly, yet left its exercise to a few, he finds that "one part of the answer is that the *demos* recognized the instrumental role of political rights and were more concerned in the end with the substantive decisions, were content with their power to select, dismiss and punish their political leaders."[61] Elsewhere he writes, even more explicitly: "Then, as now, politics was instrumental for most people, not an interest or an end in itself."[62] Contrary to what Arendt suggests, the possession or the possibility of exercising a political right may be more important than the actual exercise. Moreover, even the exercise derives its value from the decisions to be taken. Writing about the American town assemblies, Arendt argues that the citizens participated "neither exclusively because of duty nor, and even less, to serve their own interests but most of all because they enjoyed the discussions, the deliberations, and the making of decisions."[63] This, while not putting the cart before the horse, at least places them alongside each other. Although discussion and deliberation in other contexts may be independent sources of enjoyment, the satisfaction one derives from *political* discussion is parasitic on decision-making. Political debate is about what to *do*—not about what ought to be the case. It is defined by this practical purpose, not by its subject-matter.

[58] Mill (1859, p. 105).

[59] Arendt (1958, p. 37).

[60] Arendt (1958, p. 41).

[61] Finley (1976, p. 83).

[62] Finley (1981, p. 31).

[63] Arendt (1973, p. 119).

Politics in this respect is on a par with other activities such as art, science, athletics or chess. To engage in them may be deeply satisfactory, if you have an independently defined goal such as "getting it right" or "beating the opposition." A chess player who asserted that he played not to win, but for the sheer elegance of the game, would be in narcissistic bad faith—since there is no such thing as an elegant way of losing, only elegant and inelegant ways of winning. When the artist comes to believe that the process and not the end result is his real purpose, and that defects and irregularities are valuable as reminders of the struggle of creation, he similarly forfeits any claim to our interest. The same holds for E. P. Thompson, who, when asked whether he really believed that a certain rally in Trafalgar Square would have any impact at all, answered: "That's not really the point, is it? The point is, it shows that democracy's alive. . . . A rally like that gives us self-respect. Chartism was terribly good for the Chartists, although they never got the Charter."[64] Surely, the Chartists, if asked whether they thought they would ever get the Charter, would not have answered: "That's not really the point, is it?" It was because they believed they might get the Charter that they engaged in the struggle for it with the seriousness of purpose that also brought them self-respect as a side effect.[65]

IV

I have been discussing three views concerning the relation between economics and politics, between the market and the forum. One extreme is "the economic theory of democracy," most outrageously stated by Schumpeter, but in essence also underlying social choice theory. It is a market theory of politics, in the sense that the act of voting is a private act similar to that of buying and selling. I cannot accept, therefore, Alan Ryan's argument that "On any possible view of the distinction between private and public life, voting is an element in one's public life."[66] The very distinction between the secret and the open ballot shows that there is room for a private–public distinction within politics. The economic theory of democracy, therefore, rests on the idea that the forum should be like the market, in its purpose as well as in its mode of functioning. The purpose is defined in economic terms, and the mode of functioning is that of aggregating individual decisions.

At the other extreme there is the view that the forum should be completely divorced from the market, in purpose as well as in institutional arrangement. The forum should be more than the distributive totality of individuals queuing up for the election booth. Citizenship is a quality that can only be realized in public, i.e. in a collective joined for a common purpose. This purpose, moreover, is not to facilitate life in the material sense. The political process is an end in itself, a good or even the supreme good for those who participate in it. It may

[64] *Sunday Times,* 2 November 1980.

[65] Cf. also Barry (1978, p. 47).

[66] Ryan (1972, p. 105).

be applauded because of the educative effects on the participants, but the benefits do not cease once the education has been completed. On the contrary, the education of the citizen leads to a preference for public life as an end in itself. Politics on this view is not *about* anything. It is the agonistic display of excellence,[67] or the collective display of solidarity, divorced from decision-making and the exercise of influence on events.

In between these extremes is the view I find most attractive. One can argue that the forum should differ from the market in its mode of functioning, yet be concerned with decisions that ultimately deal with economic matters. Even higher-order political decisions concern lower-level rules that are directly related to economic matters. Hence constitutional arguments about how laws can be made and changed, constantly invoke the impact of legal stability and change on economic affairs. It is the concern with substantive decisions that lends the urgency to political debates. The ever-present constraint of *time* creates a need for focus and concentration that cannot be assimilated to the leisurely style of philosophical argument in which it may be better to travel hopefully than to arrive. Yet within these constraints arguments form the core of the political process. If thus defined as public in nature, and instrumental in purpose, politics assumes what I believe to be its proper place in society.

REFERENCES

Ainslie, G. "A behavioral economic approach to the defense mechanisms," *Social Science Information* 21 (1982): 735–80.

Arendt, H. *The Human Condition.* (Chicago: University of Chicago Press, 1958).

———. *On Revolution.* (Harmondsworth: Pelican Books, 1973).

Arrow, K. *Social Choice and Individual Values.* (New York: Wiley, 1963).

———. "Some ordinal-utilitarian notes on Rawls's theory of justice," *Journal of Philosophy* 70 (1973): 245–63.

Asch, S. "Studies of independence and conformity: I. A minority of one against a unanimous majority." *Psychology Monographs* 70 (1956).

Barry, B. "Comment," in *Political Participation,* S. Benn *et al.* (eds.) (Canberra: Australian National University Press, 1978), pp. 37–48.

Berlin, I. *Two Concepts of Liberty.* (Oxford: Oxford University Press, 1969).

d'Aspremont, C. and Gevers, L. "Equity and the informational basis of collective choice," *Review of Economic Studies* 44 (1977): 199–210.

Downs, A. *An Economic Theory of Democracy.* (New York: Harper, 1957).

Elster, J. *Logic and Society.* (Chichester: Wiley, 1978).

———. *Ulysses and the Sirens.* (Cambridge: Cambridge University Press, 1979).

———. *Explaining Technical Change.* (Cambridge: Cambridge University Press; Oslo: Universitetforlaget, 1983a).

———. *Sour Grapes.* (Cambridge: Cambridge University Press, 1983b).

---

[67] Veyne (1976) makes a brilliant statement of this non-instrumental attitude among the elite of the Ancient World.

Finley, M. I. *Democracy: Ancient and Modern.* (London: Chatto and Windus, 1973).

———. "The freedom of the citizen in the Greek world." (1976) reprinted as Ch. 5 in M. I. Finley, *Economy and Society in Ancient Greece,* (London: Chatto and Windus, 1981).

———. "Politics," in *The Legacy of Greece,* M. I. Finley (ed.) (Oxford: Oxford University Press, 1981), pp. 22–36.

Føllesdal, D. and Hilpinen, R. (1971) "Deontic logic: an introduction," in *Deontic Logic: Introductory and Systematic Readings.* R. Hilpinen (ed.) (Dordrecht: Reidel, 1971), pp. 1–35.

Goldman, A. "Toward a theory of social power," *Philosophical Studies* 23 (1972): 221–68.

Haavelmo, T. "Some observations on welfare and economic growth," in *Induction, Growth and Trade: Essays in Honour of Sir Roy Harrod,* W. A. Eltis, M. Scott and N. Wolfe (eds.) (Oxford: Oxford University Press, 1970), pp. 65–75.

Habermas, J. Diskursethik—notizen zu einem Begründingsprogram. (1982) Mimeographed.

Hammond, P. "Why ethical measures need interpersonal comparison," *Theory and Decision* 7 (1976): 263–74.

Hansson, B. "An analysis of some deontic logics," *Nous* 3 (1970): 373–98.

Hirsch, F. *Social Limits to Growth.* (Cambridge, Mass.: Harvard University Press, 1976).

Hirschman, A. *Shifting Involvements.* (Princeton: Princeton University Press, 1982).

Hogarth, R. M. "Methods for aggregating opinions," in *Decision Making and Change in Human Affairs,* H. Jungermann and G. de Zeeuw (eds.) (Dordrecht: Reidel, 1977), pp. 231–56.

Janis, I. *Victims of Group-Think.* (Boston: Houghton Mifflin, 1972).

Kant, I. *Perpetual Peace,* in *Kant's Political Writings,* H. Reiss (ed.) (Cambridge: Cambridge University Press, 1995).

Kelly, J. *Arrow Impossibility Theorems.* (New York: Academic Press, 1978).

Kolm, S. C. *La transition socialiste.* (Paris: Editions du Cerf, 1977).

———. "Altruismes et efficacités," *Social Science Information* 20 (1981a): 293–354.

———. "Efficacité et altruisme," *Revue Economique* 32, (1981b): 5–31.

Lehrer, K. "Consensus and comparison. A theory of social rationality," in *Foundations and Applications of Decision Theory.* Vol. 1: *Theoretical Foundations,* C. A. Hooker, J. J. Leach and E. F. McClennen (eds.), (Dordrecht: Reidel, 1978) pp. 283–310.

Lipsey, R. G. and Lancaster, K. "The general theory of the second-best," *Review of Economic Studies* 24 (1956–7): 11–32.

Lively, J. *Democracy.* (Oxford: Blackwell, 1975).

Lyons, D. *Forms and Limits of Utilitarianism.* (Oxford, Oxford University Press, 1965)

Margalit, A. (1983) "Ideals and second bests," in *Philosophy for Education,* S. Fox (ed.), (Jerusalem: Van Leer Foundation, 1983), pp. 77–90.

Midgaard, K. (1980) "On the significance of language and a richer concept of rationality," in *Politics as Rational Action,* L. Lewin and E. Vedung (eds.) (Dordrecht: Reidel, 1980, pp. 83–97.

Mill, J. S. (1859) "Bentham" in *Utilitarianism*. J. S. Mill, (London: Fontana Books 1962), pp. 78–125.

Niebuhr, R. *Moral Man and Immoral Society*. (New York: Scribner's, 1932).

Parfit, D. "Prudence, morality and the prisoner's dilemma." *Proceedings of the British Academy*. (Oxford: Oxford University Press, 1981).

Pateman, C. *Participation and Democratic Theory*. (Cambridge: Cambridge University Press, 1970).

Pattanaik, P. *Strategy and Group Choice*. (Amsterdam: North–Holland, 1978).

Rawls, J. *A Theory of Justice*. (Cambridge. Mass.: Harvard University Press, 1971).

Riker, W. and Ordeshook, P. C. *An Introduction to Positive Political Theory*. (Englewood Cliffs, N. J.: Prentice Hall, 1973).

Runciman, W. G. and Sen, A. "Games, justice and the general will," *Mind* 74 (1965): 554–62.

Ryan, A. "Two concepts of politics and democracy: James and John Stuart Mill," in *Machiavelli and the Nature of Political Thought*, M. Fleisher (ed.) (London: Croom Helm, 1972), pp. 76–113.

Samuelson, P. "The evaluation of real national income," *Oxford Economic Papers* 2 (1950): 1–29.

Schelling, T. C. "The intimate contest for self-command," *The Public Interest* 60 (1980): 94–118.

Schotter, A. *The Economic Theory of Social Institutions*. (Cambridge: Cambridge University Press, 1981).

Schumpeter, J. *Business Cycles* (New York: McGraw-Hill, 1939).

———. *Capitalism, Socialism and Democracy*. (London: Allen and Unwin, 1961).

Sen, A. K. *Collective Choice and Social Welfare*. (San Francisco: Holden–Day, 1970).

———. (1976) "Liberty, unanimity and rights," *Economica* 43, (1976): 217–45.

———. "Utilitarianism and welfarism," *Journal of Philosophy* 76, (1979): 463–88.

Sobel, J. H. (1967) "'Everyone,' consequences and generalization arguments." *Inquiry* 10 (1967): 373–404.

Smullyan, R. *This Book Needs No Title*. (Englewood Cliffs, N.J.: Prentice Hall, 1980).

Tocqueville, A. de *Democracy in America*. (New York: Anchor Books, 1969).

Tversky, A. "Choice, preference and welfare: some psychological observations," (1981) paper presented at a colloquium on "Foundations of social choice theory," Ustaoset (Norway).

William, B. A. O. "A critique of utilitarianism," in *Utilitarianism: For and Against* J. J. C. Smart and B. A. O. Williams, (Cambridge: Cambridge University Press, 1973), pp. 77–150.

Veyne, P. *Le pain et le cirque* (Paris: Seuil, 1976).

Zeldin. T. *France 1848–1945*, Vol. 1. (Oxford: Oxford University Press, 1973).

V

FORMS OF MAJORITARIAN DECISION MAKING

23.

Strong Democracy

BENJAMIN BARBER

Strong democracy is one of several democratic responses to the political condition.[1] The typology offered here distinguishes strong democracy both from the several kinds of thin or representative democracy and from unitary democracy, with which it is often confounded. The three variations on representative democracy are the authoritative, the juridical, and the pluralist, which are related to the dispositions explored in Part I but are by no means identical with them. The two more direct forms are the unitary and the strong; the former of which turns out to have certain characteristics in common with thin forms of democracy, despite its appearance as a variation on communitarianism.

All five forms are ideal types in two important senses. First, they are distinguished by features that are abstract and ideal: no actual regimes correspond perfectly with the types. Second, these forms are presented separately, yet most actual regimes are composite and combine features from each type. The three thin forms are in fact part of a single democratic praxis typical of American (and to a lesser degree, European) political experience. We can describe each of the five alternative democratic forms as follows.

Authoritative Democracy. The authoritative model of democracy is defined by the deployment of power by a centralized executive on behalf of security and order, which are among its chief justifying norms. Authoritative democracy relies on a deferential citizenry and the excellence of a governing elite, although it is still representative in that it remains accountable to the people or to the "masses" who select it. Considered as a response to the dilemmas of the political condition, as laid out in the previous chapter, authoritative democracy can be given this formal definition: *democracy in the authoritative mode resolves conflict in the absence of an independent ground through deferring to a representative executive elite that employs authority (power plus wisdom) in pursuit of the aggregate interests of its electoral constituency.*

Burke's ideal English constitution and America under the imperial presidency are possible examples of democracy operating in a predominantly authoritative mode. The government posture is centralized and active, and the citizen posture is deferential but unified (by the elite's interpretation of the citizens' interests). The institutional bias favors executive power, although the executive in

---

[1] A complete typology would have to include both democratic and nondemocratic regimes. However, the nondemocratic response to conflict in the absence of independent grounds is incoherent in relation to the conditions of politics discussed in the previous chapter: nondemocratic regimes would "solve" the political problem by eliminating politics. This places such regimes outside of the categories with which we are concerned here.

authoritative systems tends to play a prominent legislative role as well (in the New Deal or the Great Society, for example).

We can summarize some of the criticisms that were leveled at representative democracy . . . in terms of our typology here. Authoritative democracy, then, is deficient because it tends toward hegemony, is incompletely egalitarian, and has a weak view of citizenship (which is limited to the selection of elites).[2] It is also deficient because of two greater difficulties that it shares with each of the other weak forms of democracy: its dependence on representation and its reintroduction into the domain of politics, under the camouflage of "wisdom," an independent ground that becomes a surrogate for autonomous politics. The virtue of politicians thus comes to replace the activity of politics, and the excellence (*areté*) of policy is made to do the work of an engaged citizenry.

Juridical Democracy. The juridical model of democracy is defined by the arbitration, adjudication, and protection of right (its chief justifying norm) by a representative but independent judiciary that governs indirectly by placing limits and constraints on the explicit organs of government.[3] Like the authoritative model, the juridical relies on a deferential citizenry that considers the courts an institution capable of mediating and enforcing basic (i.e., nonpolitical) norms that justify civil society and limit the scope and purposes of all governmental activity.

Considered as a response to the dilemmas of the political condition, juridical democracy can be given the following formal definition: *democracy in the juridical mode resolves conflict in the absence of an independent ground through deferring to a representative juridical elite that, with the guidance of constitutional and preconstitutional norms, arbitrates differences and enforces constitutional rights and duties.* Philosophical jurisprudence of the kind practiced so persuasively by John Rawls, Ronald Dworkin, and most recently Bruce Ackerman typifies the theory of juridical democracy.[4] The American Supreme

---

[2] Joseph Schumpeter's definition of democracy illustrates these weaknesses: "The democratic method is that institutional arrangement for arriving at political decisions in which individuals acquire the power to decide by means of a competitive struggle for the people's vote" (*Capitalism, Socialism, and Democracy* [London: Allen and Unwin, 1943], p. 269).

[3] Franz Neumann first used the phrase "juridical liberty" to describe a political order in which law is used to protect the abstract freedom of individuals from governmental infringement. See "The Concept of Political Freedom," in *The Democratic and Authoritarian State* (Glencoe, Ill.: Free Press, 1957), pp. 162–63 et passim.

More recently, Theodore J. Lowl has offered "juridical democracy" as an alternative to "interest group liberalism." He argues that the former, which he labels "the rule of law operating in institutions," "is the only dependable defense the powerless have against the powerful" (*The End of Liberalism,* 2d ed. [New York: Norton, 1979], p. 298).

My definition draws on the legalism of these prior uses but is not otherwise intended to reflect them.

[4] See John Rawls, *A Theory of Justice* (Cambridge, Mass.: Harvard University Press, 1971); Ronald Dworkin, *Taking Rights Seriously* (Cambridge, Mass.: Harvard University Press, 1976); and Bruce Ackerman, *Social Justice in the Liberal State* (New Haven: Yale University Press,

Court in its activist phases and, in a quite exotic fashion, the legalists of the Han dynasty exemplify a potential juridical praxis.

The governmental posture here is centralized but more limited than in the authoritative mode. The citizenry is deferential but, in keeping with the atomistic character of rights, more often fragmented than unified. The institutional bias is juridical, even though the judiciary often comes to usurp and to exercise what might otherwise be perceived as legislative functions.

Juridical democracy is deficient because it subverts the legislative process and has a corrosive impact on citizen activity and also because it is dependent on representative principles and reintroduces independent grounds into the political realm—in this case disguised as natural right, higher law, and the constitution.

Pluralist Democracy. The pluralist model of democracy is defined by the resolution of conflict through bargaining and exchange in "free markets" under the governance of a "social contract" that makes promises binding. Liberty is both the operating principle of markets and their chief objective, making it the chief justifying norm of politics in the market mode. Unlike authoritative and juridical democracy, the pluralist model relies on an engaged and active citizenry that, fragmented into individuals, groups, and parties (political and otherwise), formulates and aggressively pursues private interests within a framework of competitive legislative bargaining.

Considered as a response to the dilemmas of the political condition, pluralist democracy can be given the following formal definition: *pluralist democracy resolves public conflict in the absence of an independent ground through bargaining and exchange among free and equal individuals and groups, which pursue their private interests in a market setting governed by the social contract.*

Examples of pluralist democratic theory include the economic and interest-group theories of democracy advanced by Anthony Downs or Mancur Olson, Robert Dahl's "polyarchy" model, and the pluralism of mainstream American political science.[5] Laissez-faire England in the nineteenth century (if there was

---

1980). Useful antidotes to this jurisprudential perspective can be found in John Hart Ely, *Democracy and Distrust* (Cambridge, Mass.: Harvard University Press, 1980) and Michael Walzer, *Radical Principles* (New York: Basic Books, 1980), as well as in Walzer's review of Ackerman in *The New Republic,* 25 October 1980.

[5] The modern locus classicus for the pluralist model is David B. Truman, *The Governmental Process* (New York: Knopf, 1957). In its more recent incarnation, the theory has been assimilated by economic modeling and rational-decision theory. See for example Anthony Downs, *An Economic Theory of Democracy* (New York: Harper Bros., 1957); Mancur Olson, Jr., *The Logic of Collective Action* (Cambridge, Mass.: Harvard University Press, 1965); and Kenneth J. Arrow, *Social Choice and Individual Values,* 2d ed. (New Haven: Yale University Press, 1963).

Two recent defenses of traditional pluralism are in William H. Riker, *Liberalism against Populism* (San Francisco: Freeman, 1982), which also contains a vigorous attack on participatory democracy; and Robert A. Dahl, *Dilemmas of Pluralist Democracy: Autonomy versus Control* (New Haven: Yale University Press, 1982). Dahl, however, has begun to question the capacity of pluralism (which he calls *polyarchy*) to deal with questions of economic and social justice—hence the "dilemma," which did not appear in his earlier *A Preface to Democratic Theory* (Chicago: University of Chicago Press, 1956).

such a thing) and pluralist America before the New Deal (if there was such a thing) are usually taken as examples of the praxis. To the extent that the market is a real thing (which is a controversial claim, as we have seen), the market model is the freest of the three variations on representative democracy: the government is decentralized (often federal) and though active, also deferential to a citizenry that, if fragmented, is much more active than in the other two cases. The institutional bias is toward legislation, although legislation is more an output of the dominant system of bargaining and exchange than an input into it.

Pluralist democracy is deficient because it relies on the fictions of the free market and of the putative freedom and equality of bargaining agents; because it cannot generate public thinking or public ends of any kind; because it is innocent about the real world of power; and (as with the first two models) because it uses the representative principle and reintroduces into politics a covert independent ground—namely, the illusions of the free market and of the invisible hand and the simplistic utilitarianism (Mandeville, Smith, and Bentham) by which the pursuit of private interests is miraculously made to yield the public good.

• • •

Before we move on to examine the direct democratic alternatives to liberalism, it may be useful for us to pause and review in summary form the two weaknesses that, I have asserted, are shared by all three modes of liberal democracy: namely, representation and the reintroduction into supposedly autonomous politics of surreptitious independent grounds.

A well-known adage has it that under a representative government the voter is free only on the day he casts his ballot. Yet even this act may be of dubious consequence in a system where citizens use the franchise only to select an executive or judicial or legislative elite that in turn exercises every other duty of civic importance. To exercise the franchise is unhappily also to renounce it. The representative principle steals from individuals the ultimate responsibility for their values, beliefs, and actions. And it is far less hospitable to such primary Western values as freedom, equality, and social justice than weak democrats might wish.

Representation is incompatible with freedom because it delegates and thus alienates political will at the cost of genuine self-government and autonomy. As Rousseau warned, "The instant a people allows itself to be represented it loses its freedom."[6] Freedom and citizenship are correlates; each sustains and gives life to the other. Men and women who are not directly responsible through common deliberation, common decision, and common action for the policies

---

[6] Jean-Jacques Rousseau, *The Social Contract*, book 3, chap. 15. A later philosopher writing in the same vein insists upon "the logical impossibility of the 'representative' system." Since "the will of the people is not transferable, nor even the will of the single individual, the first appearance of professional leadership marks the beginning of the end" (Robert Michels, *Political Parties: A Sociological Study of the Oligarchical Tendencies of Modern Democracy* [Glencoe, Ill.: Free Press, 1915; reprinted, 1949], pp. 33–34).

that determine their common lives are not really free at all, however much they enjoy security, private rights, and freedom from interference.

Representation is incompatible with equality because, in the astute words of the nineteenth-century French Catholic writer Louis Veuillot, "when I vote my equality falls into the box with my ballot—they disappear together."[7] Equality, construed exclusively in terms of abstract personhood or of legal and electoral equity, omits the crucial economic and social determinants that shape its real-life incarnation. In the absence of community, equality is a fiction that not merely divides as easily as it unites but that raises the specter of a mass society made up of indistinguishable consumer clones.

Representation, finally, is incompatible with social justice because it encroaches on the personal autonomy and self-sufficiency that every political order demands, because it impairs the community's ability to function as a regulating instrument of justice, and because it precludes the evolution of a participating public in which the idea of justice might take root.[8]

Freedom, equality, and justice are in fact all *political* values that depend for their theoretical coherence and their practical efficacy on self-government and citizenship. They cannot be apprehended or practiced except in the setting of citizenship. They are not coterminous with the condition of politics, they are aspects of a satisfactory response to the condition of politics. They cannot be externally defined and then appropriated for political use; rather, they must be generated and conditioned by politics.

This point relates directly to the problem of the independent ground. In each of the three versions of weak democracy, the banished independent ground (in whose place a mode of politics is supposed to operate) is covertly reintroduced in the guise of such notions as noblesse oblige (the wisdom of an authoritative elite), or the free market (the absolute autonomy of the individual as an irrefutable premise of pluralist market and contract relations). Yet the definition of the political condition developed above would suggest that it is precisely such notions as "wisdom," "rights," and "freedom" that need to be given meaning and significance within the setting of democratic politics. These terms and others like them are essentially contestable: their meaning is subject to controversy at a fundamental level and cannot be discovered by abstract reasoning or by an appeal to external authority.[9] This is why they become the focus of discourse in democratic politics: they do not define but are defined by politics.

[7] Cited by Michels, *Political Parties*, p. 39; my translation. Victor Considerant, a forerunner of Michels, commented on the central principle of representative government, delegation, that "in delegating its sovereignty, a people abdicate it. Such a people no longer governs itself but is governed. . . . Turning Saturn on his head, the principle of sovereignty ends up being devoured by its daughter, the principle of delegation" (*La Solution, ou le gouvernement direct du peuple* [Paris: Librairie Phalansterie, 1850], pp. 13–15; my translation).

[8] Court-ordered busing programs, which are "right" by every legal standard, nonetheless manage to remedy the effects of public prejudice only by destroying public responsibility and activity in a realm (schooling) that is traditionally associated with vigorous neighborhood civic activity. Here the principle of right collides with the principle of participation, and the damage done to the latter imperils, in the long run, the possibility of sustaining the former by democratic means.

[9] The idea of "essential contestability," first developed in a philosophical setting by W. B. Gallie, has been given an illuminating political context by William Connolly in *The Terms of Political Discourse* (Lexington, Mass.: Heath, 1974).

Representative democracy suffers, then, both from its reliance on the representative principle and from its vulnerability to seduction by an illicit rationalism—from the illusion that metaphysics can establish the meaning of debatable political terms. By permitting, even encouraging, the reintroduction of independent grounds, representative modes of democracy subvert the very political process that was supposed to meet and overcome the absence of such grounds. By subordinating the will and judgment of citizens to abstract norms about which there can be no real consensus, these modes demean citizenship itself and diminish correspondingly the capacities of a people to govern itself. And by allowing heteronomous notions of right to creep into the politics of self-legislation, they fatally undermine the autonomy on which all real political freedom depends. Citizens become subject to laws they did not truly participate in making; they become the passive constituents of representatives who, far from reconstituting the citizens' aims and interests, usurp their civic functions and deflect their civic energies.

To the extent that these criticisms apply, thin democracy is not very democratic, nor even convincingly political. For all the talk about politics in Western democratic regimes, it is hard to find in all the daily activities of bureaucratic administration, judicial legislation, executive leadership, and party policy-making anything that resembles citizen engagement in the creation of civic communities and in the forging of public ends. Politics has become what politicians do; what citizens do (when they do anything) is vote for the politicians.

Two alternative forms of democracy seem to hold out some hope that these difficulties can be alleviated through the activation of citizenship and community. The first, which I call *unitary democracy,* is motivated by the need for consensus but ultimately betrays the democratic impulse—particularly when it is separated from the small-scale institutions out of which it arose. The second, *strong democracy,* seems able to remedy a number of the shortcomings of weak democracy without falling prey to the excesses of unitary democracy. It is the argument of this book that the strong form of democracy is the only form that is genuinely and completely democratic. It may also be the only one capable of preserving and advancing the political form of human freedom in a modern world that grows ever more hostile to traditional liberal democracy.

Unitary Democracy. The unitary form of democracy is defined by politics in the consensual mode and seems at first glance to eschew representation (if not politics itself) in pursuit of its central norm, unity. It calls for all divisive issues to be settled unanimously through the organic will of a homogeneous or even monolithic community—often identified symbolically as a race or nation or people or communal will. The government posture here is centralized and active, while the posture of the citizenry is ambiguous, since the individual citizen achieves his civic identity through merging his self with the collectivity, that is to say, through self-abandonment. Although this surrender assures a certain equality (another characteristic norm of unitary and strong democracy), it is obviously corrupting to autonomy and thus ultimately to citizenship itself.

The institutional bias of unitary democracy is symbolic, i.e., government is associated with the symbolic entity in which the community will is embodied.

In subordinating participation in a greater whole to identification with that whole and autonomy and self-legislation to unity and group self-realization, unitary democracy becomes conformist, collectivist, and often even coercive. In small face-to-face communities it is relatively benign, and it has historically served both equality and citizenship reasonably well in places where they might otherwise not have been served at all.[10] In such settings, unitary democracy relies on voluntary self-identification with the group, peer pressure, social conformism, and a willing acceptance of group norms—mechanisms that, to be sure, have their own perils but that are for the most part well immunized against the virulent modern strains of infectious totalism.[11]

In larger settings, however, where the community becomes an impersonal abstraction and individuals relate anonymously and anomically with masses of strangers, unitary democracy can turn malevolent, can be perilous to freedom and citizenship and ruinous to democracy. In its final phase, the French Revolution seemed to aspire to the unitary ideal in its most obnoxious form. Thus Hippolyte Castille glorified the reign of terror in these startling words: "The most perfect community would be where tyranny was an affair of the whole community. That proves fundamentally that the most perfect society would be one where there is the least freedom in the satanic [i.e., individualist] meaning of this word."[12] It is this unitary perversion of "direct" democracy that has aroused so many liberals to condemn participation and community as well as the arguments for "political freedom" with which their proponents justify these ideals.

To bring it into our typology, we may give unitary democracy, considered as a response to the dilemmas of the political condition, the following formal definition: *democracy in the unitary mode resolves conflict in the absence of an independent ground through community consensus as defined by the identification of individuals and their interests with a symbolic collectivity and its interests.*

As I have suggested, whether the consensual community is large and abstract (as in the case of fascism in its pure, national form) or small and face-to-face (as in the case of the homogeneous eighteenth-century New England town or the rural Swiss commune) will determine whether unitary democracy becomes vicious or merely irrelevant.[13] But in neither case is it consistently participatory (since it undermines self-legislation) or genuinely political (since it "wills" away conflict). For the identification of individual with collectivity—which permits

---

[10] Peter Laslett provides the "face-to-face" society with a sociology and a history in his seminal work *The World We Have Lost* (London: Methuen, 1965).

[11] I have tried to give an account of the strengths and the dangers of face-to-face democracy in the Swiss German Alps in my *The Death of Communal Liberty* (Princeton: Princeton University Press, 1974). Readers may refer to this work for a fuller discussion.

[12] Hippolyte Castille, *History of the Second Republic,* cited by Edouard Bernstein, *Evolutionary Socialism,* ed. Sidney Hook (New York: Schocken Books, 1961).

[13] Even in such benign settings as the Vermont town meeting or an urban crisis cooperative, direct democracy can be problematic. See for example Jane J. Mansbridge's sociologically astute study *Beyond Adversary Democracy* (New York: Basic Books, 1980).

a government in the unitary mode to speak not only for but *as* "The People"—conceals and obscures the representative relationship that actually obtains between citizens and governing organs. Moreover, the symbolic collectivity denoted by such abstract terms as *the nation* or *the Aryan Race* or *the communal will*—since it is no longer circumscribed by the actual wills (or choices) of individual citizens acting in concert—usually turns out to be a cipher for some surreptitious set of substantive norms. It turns out, in other words, to be camouflage for the reintroduction of independent grounds, a stalking horse for Truth in the midst of politics, a Trojan Horse carrying Philosophers, Legislators, and other seekers of Absolute Certainty into the very inner sanctum of democracy's citadel. And so, in the place where we expect finally to hear the voices of active citizens determining their own common destiny through discourse and deliberation, we hear instead the banished voice of hubris, of would-be-truth and of could-be-right, which were unable to get a hearing on their own merits. Had they done so, the occasion for politics, democratic or otherwise, would never have arisen.

Thus does the promise of unitary democracy fade: unable to escape weak democracy's dependency on representation and the covert independent ground, it adds to them all the grave risks of monism, conformism, and coercive consensualism. No wonder that liberal democrats cringe at the prospect of "benevolent" direct democratic alternatives. With the perils of unitary democracy in mind, they justifiably fear the remedy for representation more than its ills.

The central question for the future of democracy thus becomes: Is there an alternative to liberal democracy that does not resort to the subterfuges of unitary democracy? In the absence of a safe alternative, it is the better part of prudence to stick by the representative forms of democracy, deficiencies and all.

STRONG DEMOCRACY:
POLITICS IN THE PARTICIPATORY MODE

The future of democracy lies with strong democracy—with the revitalization of a form of community that is not collectivistic, a form of public reasoning that is not conformist, and a set of civic institutions that is compatible with modern society. Strong democracy is defined by politics in the participatory mode: literally, it is self-government by citizens rather than representative government in the name of citizens. Active citizens govern themselves directly here, not necessarily at every level and in every instance, but frequently enough and in particular when basic policies are being decided and when significant power is being deployed. Self-government is carried on through institutions designed to facilitate ongoing civic participation in agenda-setting, deliberation, legislation, and policy implementation (in the form of "common work"). Strong democracy does not place endless faith in the capacity of individuals to govern themselves, but it affirms with Machiavelli that the multitude will on the whole be as wise as or even wiser than princes and with Theodore Roosevelt that "the majority of the plain people will day in and day out make fewer mistakes in governing themselves than any smaller body of men will make in trying to govern them."[14]

Considered as a response to the dilemmas of the political condition, strong democracy can be given the following formal definition: *strong democracy in the participatory mode resolves conflict in the absence of an independent ground through a participatory process of ongoing, proximate self-legislation and the creation of a political community capable of transforming dependent private individuals into free citizens and partial and private interests into public goods.*

The crucial terms in this strong formulation of democracy are *activity, process, self-legislation, creation,* and *transformation.* Where weak democracy eliminates conflict (the anarchist disposition), represses it (the realist disposition), or tolerates it (the minimalist disposition), strong democracy *transforms conflict.* It turns dissensus into an occasion for mutualism and private interest into an epistemological tool of public thinking.

Participatory politics deals with public disputes and conflicts of interest by subjecting them to a never-ending process of deliberation, decision, and action. Each step in the process is a flexible part of ongoing procedures that are embedded in concrete historical conditions and in social and economic actualities. In place of the search for a prepolitical independent ground or for an immutable rational plan, strong democracy relies on participation in an evolving problem-solving community that creates public ends where there were none before by means of its own activity and of its own existence as a focal point of the quest for mutual solutions. In such communities, public ends are neither extrapolated from absolutes nor "discovered" in a preexisting "hidden consensus." They are literally forged through the act of public participation, created through common deliberation and common action and the effect that deliberation and action have on interests, which change shape and direction when subjected to these participatory processes.

Strong democracy, then, seems potentially capable of transcending the limitations of representation and the reliance on surreptitious independent grounds without giving up such defining democratic values as liberty, equality, and social justice. Indeed, these values take on richer and fuller meanings than they can ever have in the instrumentalist setting of liberal democracy. For the strong democratic solution to the political condition issues out of a self-sustaining dialectic of participatory civic activity and continuous community-building in which freedom and equality are nourished and given political being. Community grows out of participation and at the same time makes participation possible; civic activity educates individuals how to think publicly as citizens even as citizenship informs civic activity with the required sense of publicness and justice. Politics becomes its own university, citizenship its own training ground, and participation its own tutor. Freedom is what comes out of this process, not

---

[14] "The People are wiser and more constant than Princes," writes Machiavelli in his *Discourses on Livy,* book 1, chap. 58. Roosevelt is cited in R. A. Allen, "The National Initiative Proposal: A Preliminary Analysis," *Nebraska Law Review* 58, 4 (1979): 1011.

what goes into it. Liberal and representative modes of democracy make politics an activity of specialists and experts whose only distinctive qualification, however, turns out to be simply that they engage in politics—that they encounter others in a setting that requires action and where they have to find a way to act in concert. Strong democracy is the politics of amateurs, where every man is compelled to encounter every other man without the intermediary of expertise.

This universality of participation—every citizen his own politician—is essential, because the "Other" is a construct that becomes real to an individual only when he encounters it directly in the political arena. He may confront it as an obstacle or approach it as an ally, but it is an inescapable reality in the way of and on the way to common decision and common action. We also remains an abstraction when individuals are represented either by politicians or as symbolic wholes. The term acquires a sense of concreteness and simple reality only when individuals redefine themselves as citizens and come together directly to resolve a conflict or achieve a purpose or implement a decision. Strong democracy creates the very citizens it depends upon *because* it depends upon them, because it permits the representation neither of *me* nor of *we,* because it mandates a permanent confrontation between the *me* as citizen and the "Other" as citizen, forcing *us* to think in common and act in common. The citizen is by definition a *we*-thinker, and to think of the *we* is always to transform how interests are perceived and goods defined.

This progression suggests how intimate the ties are that bind participation to community. Citizenship is not a mask to be assumed or shed at will. It lacks the self-conscious mutability of a modern social "role" as Goffman might construe it. In strong democratic politics, participation is a way of defining the self, just as citizenship is a way of living. The old liberal notion, shared even by radical democrats such as Tom Paine, was that a society is "composed of distinct, unconnected individuals [who are] continually meeting, crossing, uniting, opposing, and separating from each other, as accident, interest, and circumstances shall direct." [15] Such a conception repeats the Hobbesian error of setting participation and civic activity apart from community. Yet participation without community, participation in the face of deracination, participation by victims or bondsmen or clients or subjects, participation that is uninformed by an evolving idea of a "public" and unconcerned with the nurturing of self-responsibility, participation that is fragmentary, part-time, half-hearted, or impetuous—these are all finally sham, and their failure proves nothing.

It has in fact become a habit of the shrewder defenders of representative democracy to chide participationists and communitarians with the argument that enlarged public participation in politics produces no great results. Once empowered, the masses do little more than push private interests, pursue selfish ambitions, and bargain for personal gain, the liberal critics assert. Such participation is the work of prudent beasts and is often less efficient than the ministrations of representatives who have a better sense of the public's appetites than

[15] Tom Paine, "Dissertation on First Principles of Government," in *Writings,* ed. N. D. Conway (New York: G. P. Putnam's Sons, 1894–1896, 8 vols.), vol. 3, p. 268.

does the public itself. But such a course in truth merely gives the people all the insignia and none of the tools of citizenship and then convicts them of incompetence.[16] Social scientists and political elites have all too often indulged themselves in this form of hypocrisy. They throw referenda at the people without providing adequate information, full debate, or prudent insulation from money and media pressures and then pillory them for their lack of judgment. They overwhelm the people with the least tractable problems of mass society—busing, inflation, tax structures, nuclear safety, right-to-work legislation, industrial waste disposal, environmental protection (all of which the representative elites themselves have utterly failed to deal with)—and then carp at their uncertainty or indecisiveness or the simple-mindedness with which they muddle through to a decision. But what general would shove rifles into the hands of civilians, hurry them off to battle, and then call them cowards when they are overrun by the enemy?

Strong democracy is not government by "the people" or government by "the masses," because a people are not yet a citizenry and masses are only nominal freemen who do not in fact govern themselves. Nor is participation to be understood as random activity by maverick cattle caught up in the same stampede or as minnow-school movement by clones who wiggle in unison. As with so many central political terms, the idea of participation has an intrinsically normative dimension—a dimension that is circumscribed by citizenship. Masses make noise, citizens deliberate; masses behave, citizens act; masses collide and intersect, citizens engage, share, and contribute. At the moment when "masses" start deliberating, acting, sharing, and contributing, they cease to be masses and become citizens. Only then do they "participate."

Or, to come at it from the other direction, to be a citizen *is* to participate in a certain conscious fashion that presumes awareness of and engagement in activity with others. This consciousness alters attitudes and lends to participation that sense of the *we* I have associated with community. To participate *is* to create a community that governs itself, and to create a self-governing community *is* to participate. Indeed, from the perspective of strong democracy, the two terms *participation* and *community* are aspects of one single mode of social being: citizenship. Community without participation first breeds unreflected

---

[16] Ironically, as many leftists as conservatives have criticized populist democracy. See for example Peter Bachrach, "Testimony before the Subcommittee on the Constitution," *Committee on the Judiciary,* on S. J. Res. 67, 95th Congress, 1st session, 13–14 December 1977. Robert Michels anticipated this antipopulism of the left when he wrote:

Where party life is concerned, the socialists for the most part reject . . . practical applications of democracy, using against them conservative arguments such as we are otherwise accustomed to hear only from the opponents of socialism. In articles written by socialist leaders it is ironically asked whether it would be a good thing to hand over the leadership of the party to the ignorant masses simply for love of an abstract democratic principle. (Michels, *Political Parties,* p. 336)

Marxists have nurtured the concept of "false consciousness," by which they generally mean the unwillingness of the people to do as the scientific laws of history dictate they ought to. People are thus trusted in the abstract but disenfranchised concretely in favor of elites and vanguards who have a better grasp of what history requires.

consensus and uniformity, then nourishes coercive conformity, and finally engenders unitary collectivism of a kind that stifles citizenship and the autonomy on which political activity depends. Participation without community breeds mindless enterprise and undirected, competitive interest-mongering. Community without participation merely rationalizes collectivism, giving it an aura of legitimacy. Participation without community merely rationalizes individualism, giving it the aura of democracy.

This is not to say that the dialectic between participation and community is easily institutionalized. Individual civic activity (participation) and the public association formed through civic activity (the community) call up two strikingly different worlds. The former is the world of autonomy, individualism, and agency; the latter is the world of sociability, community, and interaction. The world views of individualism and communalism remain at odds; and institutions that can facilitate the search for common ends without sabotaging the individuality of the searchers, and that can acknowledge pluralism and conflict as starting points of the political process without abdicating the quest for a world of common ends, may be much more difficult to come by than a pretty paragraph about the dialectical interplay between individual participation and community. Yet it is just this dialectical balance that strong democracy claims to strike.

24.
Democracy and Disagreement
AMY GUTMANN AND DENNIS THOMPSON

DEMOCRATIC RESPONSES

There are better and worse ways of living with moral disagreement, and among the better is political democracy. Democracy seems a natural and reasonable way since it is a conception of government that accords equal respect to the moral claims of each citizen, and is therefore morally justifiable from the perspective of each citizen. If we have to disagree morally about public policy, it is better to do so in a democracy that as far as possible respects the moral status of each of us.

But what conception of democracy is most defensible? We should not expect to find a complete resolution of conflicts about these conceptions any more than we can find a complete resolution of more particular conflicts about policies. Nevertheless, we should be able to determine how well different conceptions of democracy deal with the general problem of moral disagreement. We can ask how well each provides a perspective that can be accepted by people who are mutually motivated to find fair terms of social cooperation among political equals.

Both procedural and constitutional democrats go some distance toward providing such a perspective. Both are committed to the basic democratic value of political equality, and therefore in principle are also committed to finding terms of cooperation that each citizen can accept. But they disagree about what those terms should be, and their disagreement can be provisionally resolved only by supplementing their conceptions with that of deliberative democracy.

Procedural democrats call attention to the importance of establishing a fair or legitimate process for making decisions about controversial moral issues. They defend majority rule as the default procedure because, other things being equal, it realizes popular rule. Proceduralists also defend those individual rights that are necessary to create a fair democratic process. Constitutional democrats add another set of rights to those that have priority over the democratic process, rights whose primary purpose is to produce justified outcomes. Procedural and constitutional democrats therefore disagree about what rights have priority over the democratic process, even though they both agree that some rights should have that priority.

Breaking the deadlock between proceduralists and constitutionalists about which rights have priority is part of the promise of deliberative democracy.[1] Procedural and constitutional democrats agree that their disagreement turns on

---

[1] Compare Jürgen Habermas, who makes a similar point about the capacity of deliberative democracy to integrate what he calls the "liberal" and "republican" views of democracy ("Three Normative Models of Democracy," *Constellations*, 1 [April 1994], esp. p. 6). See also his

the question whether democratic procedures have priority over just outcomes or just outcomes have priority over democratic procedures. Deliberative democracy rejects this dichotomy. It sees deliberation as an outcome-oriented process; citizens deliberate with the aim of justifying their collective decisions to one another as best they can. As we shall show, neither the principles that define the process of deliberation nor the principles that constitute its content have priority in deliberative democracy. Both interact dynamically in ways that overcome the dichotomy between procedure and outcome.

Procedural Democracy

Procedural democrats defend popular rule as the fairest way of resolving moral conflicts.[2] They maintain that the only alternative, rule by only some part of the citizenry, violates the democratic value of respecting citizens as political equals. If political equals disagree on moral matters, then the greater rather than the lesser number should rule. The alternative imposes the claims of the minority on the majority, and this seems to assume that some citizens' moral convictions count for more than those of others. The most straightforward form of popular rule is majoritarianism: members of a sovereign society agree to be governed by the will of a majority or their accountable representatives. The decision of a majority at any particular time is provisional, since it may always be revised by subsequent majorities. Also, some provisions are usually built into proceduralism to protect permanent minorities; most proceduralists would, for example, allow special protections for "discrete and insular minorities."[3] But what the

---

"Remarks on Discourse Ethics," in *Justification and Application*, trans. Ciaran P. Cronin (Cambridge, Mass.: MIT Press, 1993), pp. 19–111. Nonetheless, our conception of deliberative democracy should not be identified with the "discourse theory" as criticized by Frederick Schauer for assuming that deliberation is "self-evidently desirable" or an "unqualified human good" ("Discourse and Its Discontents," Working Paper no. 94-2, Joan Shorenstein Barone Center on the Press, Politics, and Public Policy, Cambridge, Mass., September 1994, p. 1). Deliberative democracy, in our view, is not purely procedural, and deliberation is an imperfect procedure. Unlike some discourse theories, deliberative democracy, as we develop it, has the capacity to criticize deliberative outcomes even in a "procedurally perfect" society.

2   We take Robert Dahl as a paradigmatic procedural democrat, in part because his subtle form of proceduralism recognizes that "the democratic process is . . . itself a rich bundle of substantive goods" (*Democracy and its Critics* [New Haven: Yale University Press, 1989], p. 175). Other proceduralists who specifically defend majority rule include Elaine Spitz, *Majority Rule* (Chatham, N.J.: Chatham House, 1984); and Douglas Rae, "Decision Rules and Individual Values in Constitutional Choice," *American Political Science Review*, 63 (March 1969): 40–56. More generally, the pluralist tradition in American political science, beginning most notably with the work of David Truman, provides numerous examples of proceduralism. Our criticism is not directed against those understandings of procedural democracy that reject the claim that popular rule is the fairest way to resolve moral conflicts.

3   In a famous footnote to his opinion for the Supreme Court in *United States v. Carolene Products Co.*, Justice Harlan Stone wrote that "prejudice against discrete and insular minorities may be a special condition, which tends seriously to curtail the operation of those political processes ordinarily to be relied upon to protect minorities, and . . . may call for a correspondingly more searching judicial inquiry." 304 U.S. 144, 152–153n.4 (1938). Precisely who constitutes a "discrete and insular" minority is a complex matter, especially for constitutional law, but we need not enter into these complexities here to recognize that disadvantaged minorities who are the targets of prejudice are not treated fairly by a simple majoritarian procedure.

majority decides resolves the moral conflict as a matter of policy at that time and for all citizens.

Procedural democrats do not claim that majority rule always resolves the substance of a moral conflict. Members of the losing minority can accept majoritarianism as a fair procedure even when it yields incorrect results because it respects their status as political equals. The results of majority rule are legitimate because the procedure is fair, not because the results are right. Of course, majorities may believe that their political views are right, but the proceduralist defense of majoritarianism (or any of its variations such as plurality rule) does not presuppose the truth of that belief. Numerical might does not make a decision morally right. Majorities have a moral right to govern only because minorities do not.

Some procedural democrats go further in their defense and deny that there are any correct substantive moral conclusions in politics. They argue that there are no "fundamental values" that should be shared by all citizens.[4] But the defense of procedural democracy does not require this moral skepticism, and indeed it would undermine the defense. If there is no reason to believe that any moral claim is valid, then there is no reason to count anyone's moral claim at all, and no reason, therefore, to defer to the claims of the greatest number.[5] The strongest justification for majoritarianism does not rest on moral skepticism. It assumes only that citizens cannot collectively agree on the solutions to many moral conflicts, and (in light of the sources of moral conflict) should not be expected to do so. The value of political equality stands behind this assumption. Thus, the very basis for establishing that the disagreement cannot be resolved—our collective incapacity to find a conclusion justifiable to each citizen who is bound by it—presupposes that the conflicting moral claims of each citizen deserve respect.

If proceduralism presumes this substantive value, then we must ask whether majority rule adequately protects it. The answer, as a simple example will make clear, is that it does not. Proceduralists need to qualify their majoritarianism in ways that move procedural democracy in the direction of constitutional democracy. (Constitutionalists, as we suggest later, need to qualify their claims in ways that move constitutional democracy in the direction of deliberative democracy.)

Imagine a new director of Arizona's health system who is faced with the rapidly increasing costs of organ transplants in the state's health care budget. Suppose further that the director calls on five citizens, chosen at random from the state's jury lists, to decide whether or not to impose a tax surcharge, which most citizens will have to pay, in order to continue providing organ transplants to terminally ill citizens like Dianna Brown. After selecting the jurors, the director simply asks them to vote, yes or no, on whether to continue funding

---

[4] A prominent example is John Hart Ely, *Democracy and Distrust* (Cambridge, Mass.: Harvard University Press, 1981).

[5] For critiques of procedural democrats such as Ely, see Ronald Dworkin, *A Matter of Principle* (Cambridge, Mass.: Harvard University Press, 1985), pp. 57–65; Frederick Schauer, *Free Speech: A Philosophical Inquiry* (Cambridge: Cambridge University Press, 1982), pp. 15–34.

organ transplants. Since he and his staff are divided about what to recommend, and so is the state legislature, the jury's decision is likely to be decisive.

All four of our sources of moral disagreement manifest themselves in this case: scarcity (the state's budget is under pressure), limited generosity (the citizens of Arizona are not altruists), incomplete understanding (the jury cannot know all the risks and benefits of the options at issue, or what the indisputably correct moral judgment should be under the circumstances), and incompatible values (some who may need an organ transplant in the future will believe that the certainty of having more expendable income is preferable to a lower risk of dying prematurely). How should the conflict be resolved by the jury?

Since citizens could offer good reasons in favor of either option, majority rule seems a natural choice. As Brian Barry shows, "the existence of relevant principles does not seem to offer a sound basis for resistance to a majority decision." [6] To strengthen the case for majority rule, Barry asks us to imagine someone claiming the right to decide the question "on the basis either of his social position or . . . of his presumptive expertise in casuistry." If his claim is accepted by all the other citizens, then no decision-making problem arises because there is agreement. If some of the citizens reject his claim to moral authority, it is again difficult to see how the question can be settled except by a vote. If the assertive citizen finds himself in the minority, it must be because he has failed to convince enough of his fellow citizens that he is right, or at least that he has the right to decide. He may continue to insist that this view should have been accepted, but in the face of actual rejection of the minority views, the case for deferring to the majority still looks strong.[7]

The defense of majority rule is not so simple if we fill in more detail in the case, however. Suppose that the first juror assumes, contrary to fact, that liver transplants like the one denied to Dianna Brown do not save lives. Out of ignorance he thinks that such transplants are a waste of taxpayers' money and he therefore votes against funding. The second and third jurors join him in voting against funding for a different reason. They believe one should prefer the satisfaction of greater disposable income to the security of a lower risk of premature death. They have this preference themselves even though, like Dianna Brown, they are at risk of premature death if the government does not fund organ transplants for people who are or who may become poor. Their preference would go against funding organ transplants no matter how effective they may be in extending life. These jurors also believe that voting one's personal preferences is the most democratic way of making the decision. The fourth and fifth jurors think that it is wrong for any democracy to deny any citizen life-saving medical care so long as the cost is not prohibitive. The fourth juror is uncertain about both the costs and the efficacy of organ transplants. The fifth juror knows

---

[6] Brian Barry, "Is Democracy Special?," in *Democracy, Power and Justice: Essays in Political Theory* (Oxford: Clarendon Press, 1989), pp. 29–30, citing his early discussion in Brian Barry, *Political Argument* (London: Routledge and Kegan Paul, 1965), p. 312. The example in the text is similar in structure to the example that Barry uses—five passengers trying to decide whether to permit smoking in a railway car.

[7] Barry, "Is Democracy Special?," p. 30.

a lot about the medical issues in question but little about the perspective of her fellow citizens. The vote is taken, and paying for organ transplants loses by a vote of 3 to 2.

Does the case for deferring to the majority look as strong as before? Whether it does surely depends in part on the cost of organ transplants and their efficacy in enabling people to live normal lives. If we assume that organ transplants are prohibitively expensive and ineffective in saving lives, then the case for accepting what the majority decided in this case still looks strong. But if we assume that the life-saving potential of organ transplants is great and the cost to individual taxpayers small, then the majority's decision looks less justifiable. Our confidence in the results of a majority decision against transplants declines as our confidence increases in the cost-effectiveness of transplants in enabling citizens to secure basic opportunities of life.

This inverse relationship reveals the most significant of several background conditions that we implicitly take for granted when we accept majority rule as the best way to deal with a particular moral conflict.[8] A majority vote alone cannot legitimate an outcome when the basic liberties or opportunities of an individual are at stake. Here the basic opportunity to live a normal life is at stake for people who, like Dianna Brown, will die young if they are denied access to an organ transplant.[9] If all the majority can say is, "We represent the popular will, and therefore our decision is legitimate, whatever its basis," then they have not said nearly enough to justify their decision to people like Dianna Brown.

The procedural defense of majority rule as the manifestation of popular will does not satisfy even the most minimal understanding of reciprocity. Dianna Brown and people like her have much more than their self-interest to invoke in reply: decisions violating the basic liberty or opportunity of any person cannot be justified simply because they result from majority rule or, for that matter, from any other generally acceptable voting procedure.[10] As we suggest later, it is plausible to claim that the chance to live a normal life by having access to organ transplants is a basic opportunity, provided that their funding is compatible with securing other basic liberties and opportunities of individuals. This constraint on proceduralism should be acceptable to all citizens since its purpose is to respect and protect each citizen's basic liberty and opportunity. Of

---

[8] In addition to the protection of "discrete and insular minorities" for which proceduralists explicitly provide, two other background conditions of cases in which majority rule seems an appropriate solution are worth noting: first, when only one question is the subject of decision; and second, when the question offers only two, dichotomous alternatives (such as "funding organ transplants" or "not funding"). When there are multiple decisions to be made, or more than two alternatives, as there almost always are in political life, then there are also likely to be procedures other than simple majority rule that are reasonable ways of resolving the controversies. Plurality rule, for example, may be a reasonable way of resolving disagreements with more than two alternatives. See Barry, "Is Democracy Special?"

[9] Cf. ibid., p. 37.

[10] Ibid., p. 38.

course, the claims of liberty and opportunity also have their limits, but all the reasonable limits entail rejecting the proceduralist claim that majority rule is legitimate, whatever its outcome.[11]

Most procedural democrats accept that procedures should be constrained by some substantive values, but they try to restrict those values to those that are necessary to preserve the democratic process itself. They agree that the majority must respect politically relevant rights such as freedoms of speech, the press, and association, the rule of law, and universal adult suffrage. But if the aim is to find a reciprocal perspective for resolving moral conflict, why limit ourselves to these procedural constraints? The simple example of the jury suggests that some decisions consistent with these constraints—such as denying life-saving health care to some people for the sake of satisfying majority preferences—cannot be justified merely by majority rule. The substance of the moral conflict affects the justifiability of the procedure and its results. If majoritarianism must be qualified by values internal to the democratic process, then why should it not also be qualified by values external to the process, especially if those values include a basic liberty or opportunity of individuals?

• • •

Constitutional Democracy

Constitutional and procedural democracy both protect individual rights against majority rule, but constitutional democrats give some rights priority over majority rule that procedural democrats do not. Procedural democrats recognize two kinds of rights that limit majoritarianism: rights such as voting equality that are *integral* to democratic procedures; and rights such as subsistence that, though *external* to the democratic process, are necessary for its fair functioning.[12] They take notice of a third kind of right but deny it priority over majority rule: rights such as protection against cruel and unusual punishment that are *external* to the democratic process and (at least arguably) not necessary for its fair functioning.[13] The view that this third kind of right should constrain democratic procedure is what distinguishes constitutional from procedural

---

[11] Deliberative democracy also rejects the claim, which is sometimes associated with constitutional democracy, that decisions can be fully just without being legitimately arrived at. For an important discussion of democratic legitimacy, see Arthur Isak Applbaum, "Democratic Legitimacy and Official Discretion," *Philosophy & Public Affairs,* 21 (1992): 240–274.

[12] Dahl, *Democracy and Its Critics,* p. 167. For a more extensive discussion of how procedural democrats can recognize rights, see Amy Gutmann, "How Liberal Is Democracy?," in *Liberalism Reconsidered,* ed. Douglas MacLean and Claudia Mills (Totowa, N.J.: Rowman and Allanheld, 1983), pp. 25–50. For a valuable discussion of why these internal and preconditional constraints on popular rule are inadequate to an understanding of democracy, see Ronald Dworkin, "Equality, Democracy, and Constitution: We the People in Court," *Alberta Law Review* 28 (Winter 1990): 324–346.

[13] Dahl, *Democracy and Its Critics,* p. 167. In "Equality, Democracy, and Constitution," Dworkin makes a similar distinction between his own view and that of John Hart Ely (pp. 328, 343).

democrats.[14] Proceduralists give priority only to rights whose primary purpose is to make the democratic process fair, whereas constitutionalists give priority to some rights whose primary purpose is to produce justified outcomes by protecting the vital interests of individuals.

We have already seen the intuitive appeal of constitutional democracy. A basic opportunity was arguably at issue in the citizen jury's decision to deny organ transplants to individuals. It is true that the opportunity for an organ transplant is not typical of those that many Americans associate with constitutional democracy. But precisely for that reason the example reinforces the point that one main purpose of constitutionalism—to limit majoritarianism by moral constraints based on nonprocedural considerations—does not necessarily depend on a written constitution and judicial review. The "adjudicated constitution" is not the same as the "full constitution."[15] Some basic liberties and opportunities (as well as outcome-oriented rights) may be better protected by deliberative majorities themselves. As we suggest in the next section, courts are not the only or necessarily the primary province of deliberation.

By considering cases in which majority rule (or any other purely procedural rule) threatens basic liberties and opportunities, we come to recognize that outcomes of fair procedures are not justified unless they respect basic liberties and opportunities. A reciprocal perspective for resolving moral conflicts must make room for moral judgments not only of procedures but also of their results. Constitutional democrats are therefore right to broaden the search for substantive values that can resolve moral disagreements in politics.

Broadening the search in this way, however, creates difficulties for constitutional democrats parallel to the difficulties faced by their procedural rivals. One difficulty is the same for both. Constitutionalists no less than proceduralists insist that citizens need morally justified procedures for arriving at politically binding decisions. Constitutionalists also often turn to majority rule in some form to meet this need. John Rawls, whose theory we take as an exemplar of constitutional democracy, writes: "Some form of majority rule is justified as the best available way of insuring just and effective legislation. It is compatible with equal liberty and possesses a certain naturalness; for if minority rule is allowed, there is no obvious criterion to select which one is to decide and equality is violated."[16] Constitutionalists also have to decide what *form* of majority rule is the most justifiable way of securing just legislation. To decide what form majority

---

[14] John Rawls is widely taken to be the paradigmatic constitutional democrat because he provides the most comprehensive theoretical rationale for constitutionalism. His theory is also compelling in so many ways that it is important for us to distinguish our own view from his. Other important views of constitutional democracy that we do not discuss in detail include Laurence Tribe, *American Constitutional Law* (Mineola, N.Y.: Foundation Press, 1978); and Ronald Dworkin, *Taking Rights Seriously* (Cambridge, Mass.: Harvard University Press, 1977), *Law's Empire* (Cambridge, Mass.: Harvard University Press, 1986), and *A Matter of Principle*.

[15] For a related argument on the scope of constitutional law, see Lawrence G. Sager, "Justice in Plain Clothes: Reflections on the Thinness of Constitutional Law," *Northwestern Law Review* 88 (Fall 1993): 410–435 (quote at 435). Compare Dworkin, "Equality, Democracy, and Constitution," pp. 343–346.

[16] Rawls, *A Theory of Justice* (Cambridge, MA: Harvard University Press, 1971), p. 356.

rule should take, constitutionalism in this respect moves, just as proceduralism does, in the direction of deliberative democracy.

Constitutional democrats face an additional difficulty. Because constitutional democrats go further than procedural democrats in constraining democratic processes by substantive standards, the moral perspective they propose to resolve disagreements becomes even more contestable. Constitutional standards seem compelling when stated abstractly: few would deny that majorities should not violate the basic liberty of their fellow citizens. But abstraction purchases agreement on principles at the price of disagreement about their interpretation. The more abstract the constitutional standard, the more contestable its interpretation. For resolving moral conflict in politics, the interpretation matters just as much as the principle. It is therefore necessary to find a way to deal with these interpretive disagreements before the role of constitutional standards in both the theory and practice of democratic politics can be secure.

Rawls does not offer his theory as a solution to moral disagreements in what we call middle democracy. By focusing on the basic structure of society and proposing principles for a nearly just society, he avoids confronting the apparent indeterminacy of many moral conflicts that arise in contemporary politics. But Rawls no less than other constitutional democrats recognizes that conflicts over issues such as abortion, preferential hiring, and health care are central to the question of justice in democratic societies as we now know them. The task of interpretation therefore remains—to determine whether and how a theory of constitutional democracy can inform our political practice in a way that helps resolve the moral conflicts that are left open by abstract principles of liberty and opportunity designed with a nearly just society in mind.

To illustrate the difficulties of interpretation, consider the constitutionalist search for principles to govern social and economic inequalities. What policies would satisfy, for example, Rawls's principle of "fair equality of opportunity" or his "difference principle"? Does fair equality of opportunity—which requires that all members of society have an adequate chance of attaining offices and positions—permit (or demand) preferential hiring for blacks and women in the United States today? Does the difference principle—which stipulates that social inequalities be to "the greatest benefit of the least advantaged"[17]—require universal access to health care? Constitutional democrats who use these or similar principles to constrain the democratic process need to provide answers to such questions, and at a level of specificity sufficient to resolve the conflicts they manifest, or else they need to admit more deliberation into their conception of how moral disagreements should be resolved in a democracy. To fulfill the promise of constitutional democracy in resolving moral disagreements, absent an explicit commitment to deliberation, the answers must show that outcome-oriented principles in some meaningful sense take priority over a deliberative democratic process. This seems a more than Herculean task.[18]

[17] Ibid., p. 83.

[18] Ronald Dworkin is a constitutional democrat who directly confronts the challenge of finding principled resolutions to moral conflicts over politically relevant issues such as legalizing

In his later writings, Rawls in effect addresses this difficulty by suggesting that fair equality of opportunity and the difference principle are not among the morally necessary elements of what he calls the constitutional essentials and basic justice, which take priority over the results of the democratic process.[19] "These matters are nearly always open to wide differences of reasonable opinion," he writes, and they "rest on complicated inferences and intuitive judgments that require us to assess complex social and economic information about topics poorly understood."[20] He concludes that "freedom of movement and free choice of occupation and a social minimum covering citizens' basic needs count as constitutional essentials while the principle of fair opportunity and the difference principle do not."[21]

Rawls thus escapes this problem of interpretation in the cases of fair equality of opportunity and the difference principle because he gives up these principles as constitutional essentials or matters of basic justice. But a "social minimum covering citizens' basic needs" remains a constitutional constraint on democratic decision making, and therefore raises a similar issue of interpretation. Furthermore, many, perhaps most, of the large moral conflicts in contemporary politics fall within the territory that would be governed by the principle of fair equality of opportunity and the difference principle. The question therefore persists, on what basis should moral conflicts about these issues be resolved? Rawls relies on "established political procedures [being] reasonably regarded as fair" to resolve these substantive disagreements.[22] If we follow him, we find ourselves either back at the door of proceduralism, with all its attendant problems, or, alternatively, driven to make more room for deliberation.

If we take the first route, back to proceduralism, the problem of resolving moral conflicts over social and economic inequalities again becomes the problem of justifying a set of political procedures. Yet neither constitutional nor procedural democrats suggest how this can be done, or why we should even think it desirable to resolve all the remaining substantive disagreements over social and economic inequalities merely by procedural means, which may neglect the need for moral deliberation about the merits of the issues involved.

The second route leads to deliberative democracy. Rawls himself argues cogently for the value of citizenship and participation in politics. In the spirit of

---

abortion, pornography, and preferential hiring. Our conception of deliberative democracy, however, seeks to avoid Dworkin's overwhelming concentration on the judicial interpretation and enforcement of constitutional values, as we explain in the final section of this chapter.

[19] In some respects our notion of a deliberative perspective resembles Rawls's "overlapping consensus" (*Political Liberalism* [New York: Columbia University Press, 1993], pp. 132–172). Both are intended to provide a standpoint from which to judge competing moral claims as far as possible independently of any popular comprehensive moral views. But we argue that a deliberative perspective can be fully established at any given time and place only through actual deliberation, and we also admit more competing claims that may be part of a comprehensive moral view into the public forum as legitimate grounds for legislation. See Amy Gutmann and Dennis Thompson, "Moral Conflict and Political Consensus," *Ethics* 101 (October 1990): 64–88.

[20] Rawls, *Political Liberalism*, p. 229.

[21] Ibid., p. 230.

[22] Ibid.

John Stuart Mill, he writes that democratic self-government enhances "the sense of political competence of the average citizen." Citizens are expected to vote and therefore "to have political opinions." He echoes Mill in declaring that the democratic citizen is "called upon to weigh interests other than his own, and to be guided by some conception of justice and the public good rather than by his own inclinations." Citizens must "appeal to principles that others can accept." Political liberty "is not solely a means" but also a valued way of life for citizens.[23] All of this suggests a morally robust political process.

Yet, like many proceduralists and other constitutional democrats, Rawls stops short of arguing that a well-ordered democracy requires extensive deliberation to resolve moral disagreements. This is puzzling. If democratic citizens are to value political liberty not merely as a means of pursuing their self-interest or group interest, if they are to weigh the interests of others and to guide their actions by a sense of justice, then democratic societies must encourage the give-and-take of moral argument about the substance of controversial political issues, of which there are bound to be many. Forums for deliberation should abound. Citizens and their accountable representatives should continually confront their moral conflicts together, in collective efforts to find justifiable ways of resolving their political disagreements. The lack of these forums in both theory and practice—the deliberative deficit it reveals—should be a matter of great concern to constitutional democrats.

When Rawls considers how to make the principles of justice more specific, he does not propose that citizens or their representatives discuss moral disagreements about these principles in public forums. Although his theory of constitutional democracy leaves room for such discussion, it emphasizes instead a solitary process of reflection, a kind of private deliberation. He suggests that each of us alone perform an intricate thought experiment in which a veil of ignorance obscures our own personal interests, including our conception of the good life, and compels us to judge on a more impersonal basis.

Here is how the solitary deliberation goes, as each of us alone tries to develop a reciprocal perspective by making the principles more specific.[24] Having agreed on the Rawlsian principles of justice, we first enter a constitutional mode of thinking. We imagine ourselves as delegates at a constitutional convention trying to design institutions and procedures that will yield results in accord with the principles of justice. Having created the best possible constitution for our social circumstances, we recognize that it does not address most of the controversial issues in contemporary politics. Lifting the veil of ignorance further so that we can know more about the current circumstances of society, we move to a legislative mode of thinking and try to decide what laws and policies would be just for our society. Even after we have gone through all the stages of thinking in this solitary process, we are likely to find that "this test is often

---

[23] Rawls, *A Theory of Justice,* p. 234.

[24] The process we describe is a simplified version of the constitutional and legislative stages of the "four-stage sequence" in Rawls, *A Theory of Justice,* pp. 195–201. The scheme Rawls outlines is intricate and somewhat elusive. We are less concerned with its details than with the general strategy it represents for resolving specific moral conflicts.

indeterminate. . . . When this is so, justice is to that extent likewise indeterminate. Institutions within the permitted range are equally just, meaning that they could be chosen; they are compatible with all the constraints of the theory. . . . This indeterminacy in the theory of justice is not in itself a defect. It is what we should expect." [25]

To take Rawls's theory (or any other theory of constitutional democracy) down a more deliberative road, one must reject the idea that the indeterminacy of justice begins just where the determinacy of our solitary philosophical reflection leaves off. Deliberative democrats also rely on solitary reflection in two ways. First, solitary philosophical reflection should inform the deliberation that in turn helps resolve moral disagreements in democratic politics. Second, it should help produce a defense of deliberative democracy itself. But deliberative democracy rejects the idea that the indeterminacy of justice begins where the determinacy of solitary reflection leaves off. Solitary reflection supplements rather than substitutes for deliberation.

Rawls is surely right to say that we should expect considerable indeterminacy in any theory of justice. He is also right to suggest that we should think through principles of justice on our own as best we can before we enter into public deliberations. But the point at which our solitary thinking about justice becomes indeterminate does not mark the point at which our ability to find a reciprocal perspective to resolve moral disagreements about social justice becomes incapacitated. This is so even if social justice is understood to refer only to constitutional essentials or the basic structure of society. If we are to increase our chances of resolving moral disagreements, we must not check our deliberative dispositions at the door to the public forum.

This conclusion is more compatible with the requirement of Rawls's own theory that democratic citizens and their representatives achieve a high degree of moral and political competence and maintain a stable commitment to principles of justice. Such competence and commitment are not likely to be sustained without extensive deliberation in public forums about the meaning of constitutional principles and their implications for specific decisions of government. Even if we cannot philosophically establish principles specific enough to determine justifiable policies, we should not dismiss the possibility of developing more conclusive moral reasons through public discussions in a process informed not only by the facts of political life but also by conceptions of the good life, and inspired by the ideals of deliberation. "Discussion," Rawls recognizes, "is a way of combining information and enlarging the range of arguments. At least in the course of time, the effects of common deliberation seem bound to improve matters." [26] In his later writings, Rawls moves significantly further toward deliberative democracy by emphasizing the role of reciprocity as a guiding principle of public discussion. His idea of public reason now includes all moral arguments that in due course can be shown to be consistent with reciprocity, even if those arguments express comprehensive moral philosophies

[25] Rawls, *A Theory of Justice*, p. 201.
[26] Rawls, *A Theory of Justice*, p. 359.

rather than distinctively political conceptions of justice.[27] His theory remains constitutionalist, however, in the priority it gives to principles of justice over processes of deliberation. It also says little about the role of actual deliberation in non-ideal conditions. Although Rawls implies that deliberation is important, he does not pursue the implication.[28] In the next chapter we develop a principle of reciprocity that welcomes a wider range of moral arguments and at the same time imposes obligations on citizens to seek moral accommodation when their comprehensive conceptions differ.

THE NEED FOR MORAL DELIBERATION

How far, then, do procedural and constitutional democracy move toward a deliberative perspective for resolving moral disagreements in politics? Both procedural and constitutional democrats rightly agree that the fundamental values of democratic institutions, such as equal political liberty, must be justified by moral arguments that are at least in principle acceptable to citizens who are bound by them. Both seek to show that democratic institutions protect the equal right of citizens to participate in political processes and to enjoy basic freedoms. The justifications typically appeal to a moral conception of the person. Constitutionalists and proceduralists agree that individual citizens should be regarded as moral agents who deserve equal respect in any justifications of the basic structure of government. For both, fundamental moral ideals that are or should be widely shared in contemporary democracies thus lie at the foundation of democratic institutions.

Procedural and constitutional democrats also agree that democratic institutions are not justified unless they generally yield morally acceptable results. Democratic institutions that produce policies that deny some citizens freedom of speech or others the basic opportunity to live a decent life should be rejected on moral grounds. The precise content of the criticisms that proceduralists and constitutionalists make against such results may differ, but both have ample resources at their disposal to sustain a substantial moral appraisal of the public policies that emerge at the end of democratic processes.

Moral argument thus plays an important role in warranting both the foundations and the conclusions of these leading conceptions of democracy. Although

[27] Rawls's move toward deliberative democracy is evident throughout Lecture 6 ("The Idea of Public Reason") in *Political Liberalism,* but he still permits comprehensive moral reasons to be introduced in public deliberation only in an unjust society (as when slavery exists), and only if there is reason to believe that appealing to such reasons would help make society more just. In Section 5 of the new introduction to the paperback edition of the book (New York: Columbia University Press, 1996), he explicitly revises this view: reasonable comprehensive doctrines may be introduced in public reason at any time to support a law or policy, provided that in due course reasons consistent with reciprocity are presented to support the same law or policy.

[28] In this respect, Rawls's comment about deliberation in *A Theory of Justice,* p. 359, still stands: "Thus we arrive at the problem of trying to formulate an ideal constitution of public deliberation in matters of justice, a set of rules well-designed to bring to bear the greater knowledge and reasoning powers of the group so as best to approximate if not to reach the correct judgment. I shall not, however, pursue this question."

such argument dominates both the beginning and the end of the democratic process, these theories assign it at best a small role within the ongoing processes of everyday politics—in middle democracy. If moral arguments are essential to justify the foundations and results of democracy, then why should they not also be essential within the ongoing processes of democracy? On this question—the place of moral argument within democratic politics—both procedural and constitutional democrats are surprisingly silent.[29] This is puzzling in a way that has not been sufficiently appreciated. If democracy must be moral at its foundations and in its outcomes, then should it not also be moral within its everyday processes?

It is in middle democracy that much of the moral life of a democracy, for good or ill, is to be found. This is the land of everyday politics, where legislators, executives, administrators, and judges make and apply policies and laws, sometimes arguing among themselves, sometimes explaining themselves and listening to citizens, other times not. Middle democracy is also the land of interest groups, civic associations, and schools, in which adults and children develop political understandings, sometimes arguing among themselves and listening to people with differing points of view, other times not. It is a land that democrats can scarcely afford to bypass. A democratic theory that is to remain faithful to its moral premises and aspirations for justice must take seriously the need for moral argument within these processes and appreciate the moral potential of such deliberation.

Given the limited generosity and incomplete understanding of both officials and citizens, what goes on in these processes generally falls far short of what our moral ideal would call for. Perhaps that is why so many democratic theorists seem to ignore the possibility, or downplay the significance, of principled moral argument within the democratic process. The everyday operation of the democratic process is imperfect, to be sure, but so are its structures and so are its outcomes. It is hard to see how we gain anything, morally speaking, by limiting ourselves to only some of its imperfect parts. It is more likely that neglecting the possibility of moral argument in any part will only multiply the imperfections in the whole. Amorality is rarely the weapon of choice in the battle against immorality. The amorality of a political process is surely more troubling than its imperfection. Imperfection is endemic to the human condition; amorality need not be.

Democratic deliberation addresses the problem of moral disagreement directly on its own terms. It offers a moral response to moral conflict. It thus

---

[29] An interesting exception is the constitutional theorist Bruce Ackerman, who explicitly argues for taking "the moral ideals that divide us off the conversational agenda of the liberal state." He calls this "the path of conversational restraint" and admits that "doubtless the exercise of conversational restraint will prove extremely frustrating—for it will prevent each of us from justifying our political actions by appealing to many of the things we hold to be among the deepest and most revealing truths known to humanity." Yet he claims that this mutual restraint brings a "priceless advantage" of not obliging any of us "to say something in liberal conversation that seems affirmatively false." Bruce Ackerman, "Why Dialogue?," *Journal of Philosophy* 86 (January 1989): 16–17. The path of deliberation that we defend here does not require citizens to affirm anything that they know to be false, but neither does it require them to be silent in politics about their moral ideals or the most revealing truths.

seems the natural and appropriate response, one that could be part of a recip-rocal perspective in politics. But exactly why is it desirable in democratic poli-tics to respond morally to a moral problem?

The case for deliberation is best made by looking at its application to specific issues, seeing how it works in practice and how it might work better. That is what we undertake in the rest of this book. But four general reasons in favor of deliberative democracy are worth emphasizing at the outset. Together they pro-vide a rationale for extending the domain of deliberation within the democratic process. This rationale justifies granting deliberation the authority to deal with the moral conflicts that procedural democracy and constitutional democracy fail to resolve. It also justifies rejecting the assumption shared by constitutional and procedural democrats that we must give priority either to process or to sub-stance. The four reasons parallel the sources of moral conflict that we identified earlier. Each points to a way in which deliberation deals with an important aspect of moral conflict.

The first reason corresponds to the first source of moral disagreement, the problem of scarce resources. Deliberation contributes to the legitimacy of deci-sions made under conditions of scarcity. Some citizens will not get what they want, or even what they need, and sometimes none will. The hard choices that democratic governments make in these circumstances should be more accept-able even to those who receive less than they deserve if everyone's claims have been considered on their merits rather than on the basis of wealth, status, or power. Even with regard to political decisions with which they disagree, citi-zens are likely to take a different attitude toward those that are adopted after careful consideration of the relevant conflicting moral claims and those that are adopted only after calculation of the relative strength of the competing politi-cal interests. Moral justifications do not of course make up for the material re-sources that citizens fail to receive. But they help sustain the political legitimacy that makes possible collective efforts to secure more of those resources in the future, and to live with one another civilly in the meantime.

Creating more deliberative forums brings previously excluded voices into politics. This is one cause of the risk of intensified conflict that greater deliber-ation may bring. But the positive face of this risk is that deliberation also brings into the open legitimate moral dissatisfactions that would be suppressed by other ways of dealing with disagreement. Deliberative democracy seeks not consensus for its own sake but rather a morally justified consensus. Citizens strive for a consensus that represents a genuinely moral perspective, one they can accept on reciprocal terms. They usually continue to disagree, often in-tensely, on many politically relevant matters. A deliberative consensus can never be complete, and perhaps never completely justified.

The second reason for valuing deliberation takes into account the second source of moral disagreement in politics, limited generosity. Deliberation re-sponds to this problem by creating forums in which citizens are encouraged to take a broader perspective on questions of public policy than they might oth-erwise take. John Stuart Mill presented one of the earliest and still most cogent accounts of such a deliberative process. He argued that by participating in political discussion, a citizen is "called upon . . . to weigh interests not his own; to be guided, in case of conflicting claims, by another rule than his private partialities; to apply, at every turn, principles and maxims which have for their reason of existence the common good." [30] We do not need to make the optimistic assumption that most citizens will suddenly become public-spirited when they find themselves deliberating in the public forum. Much depends on the background conditions: the level of political competence (how well informed citizens are), the distribution of resources (how equally situated they are), and the nature of the political culture (what kind of arguments are taken seriously). All we need to assume is that citizens and their representatives are more likely to take a broader view of issues, and to consider the claims of more of their fellows citizens, in a process in which moral arguments are taken seriously than in a process in which assertions of political power prevail.

The third reason for encouraging deliberation confronts the third source of moral disagreement: incompatible moral values. Deliberation can clarify the nature of a moral conflict, helping to distinguish among the moral, the amoral, and the immoral, and between compatible and incompatible values. Citizens are more likely to recognize what is morally at stake in a dispute if they employ moral reasoning in trying to resolve it. Deliberation helps sort out self-interested claims from public-spirited ones. Among the latter, deliberation helps identify those that have greater weight. Through this kind of deliberative process citizens can begin to isolate those conflicts that embody genuinely moral and incompatible values on both sides. Those that do not may then turn out to be more easily resolvable: citizens might discover that a conflict is the result of misunderstanding or lack of information, or they might come to see ways to settle a conflict by bargaining, negotiation, and compromise. In this way, deliberation can put bargaining in its place in a democratic society.

For those moral conflicts for which there is no deliberative agreement at present, ongoing deliberation can help citizens better understand the moral seriousness of the views they continue to oppose, and better cooperate with their fellow citizens who hold these views. Deliberation promotes an economy of moral disagreement in which citizens manifest mutual respect as they continue to disagree about morally important issues in politics.

The fourth reason for conceiving of democracy deliberatively responds to the incomplete understanding that characterizes moral conflict in politics. Compared to other methods of decision making, deliberation increases the chances of arriving at justifiable policies. More than other kinds of political processes, deliberative democracy contains the means of its own correction. Through the give-and-take of argument, citizens and their accountable representatives can learn from one another, come to recognize their individual and collective mistakes, and develop new views and policies that are more widely

---

[30] John Stuart Mill, *Considerations on Representative Government*, in *Collected Writings*, vol. 19, ed. J. M. Robson (Toronto: University of Toronto Press, 1977), chap. 3, p. 68. For discussion of empirical evidence that supports Mill, see Thompson, *John Stuart Mill and Representative Government* (Princeton: Princeton University Press, 1976), pp. 38–43, 49–53.

justifiable. When individuals and groups bargain and negotiate, they may learn how better to get what they want. But unless they also deliberate with one another, they are not likely to learn that they should not try to get what they want. When they deliberate, they move beyond the conventional patterns of group politics that characterize the standard conceptions of interest group bargaining.

The main sources of movement in middle democracy as conventionally portrayed are not changes of mind but shifts in power, as groups and individuals bargain and negotiate on the basis of preferences and self-interests. Power shifts may bring improvement, but only accidentally. Changes of mind are responsive to reasons that at least direct our attention toward improvement. When majorities are obligated to offer reasons to dissenting minorities, they expose their position to criticism and give minorities their most effective and fairest chance of persuading majorities of the justice of their position. Encouraged by both Aristotle and Mill, one may hope that views better than those held by either the majority or the minority will emerge from such a process. But even when deliberation fails to produce a satisfactory resolution of a moral conflict at any particular time, its self-correcting capacity remains the only consistently democratic hope for discovering such a resolution in the future.

It may be feared that extending the domain of deliberation has the risk of creating even greater conflict than it is intended to resolve. Once the moral sensibilities of citizens and officials are engaged, they may be less willing to compromise than before. More issues come to be seen by more citizens as matters of principle, creating occasions for high-minded statements, unyielding stands, and no-holds-barred opposition. There are moral fanatics as well as moral sages, and in politics the former are likely to be more vocal than the latter.

These are real risks. Moral sensitivity may sometimes make necessary political compromises more difficult, but its absence also makes unjustifiable compromises more common. Moral argument can arouse moral fanatics, but it can also combat their claims on their own terms. Extending the domain of deliberation may be the only democratic way to deal with moral conflict without suppressing it. No democratic political process can completely avoid the risks of intensifying moral conflict. It is a hollow hope that any one particular institution, even the Supreme Court, could be relied on to reach the right conclusion, and to convert that conclusion into effective political action, were it to do all our deliberating for us.

Other common ways of dealing with moral conflict are clearly worse. Some of the extremists in the abortion debate turn to violence outside the political process. Others try to manipulate citizens into supporting their cause rather than reasoning with them. Moral extremists must assume that they already know what constitutes the best resolution of a moral conflict without deliberating with their fellow citizens who will be bound by the resolution. In the land of middle democracy, the assumption that we know the political truth can rarely if ever be justified before we deliberate with others who have something to say about issues that affect their lives as well as ours. By refusing to give deliberation a chance, moral extremists forsake the most defensible moral ground for an uncompromising position.

Many constitutional democrats focus on the importance of extensive moral deliberation within one of our democratic institutions—the Supreme Court.[31] They argue that judges cannot interpret constitutional principles without engaging in deliberation, not least for the purpose of constructing a coherent view out of the many moral values that our constitutional tradition expresses. The fact that this process itself is imperfect—that judges disagree morally, even about the relevance of morality in the process—is not thought to be a reason to diminish the role of deliberation. On the contrary, the failures of moral argument in the judicial process are rightly thought to make the quest for successes all the more important.

Deliberative democracy extends this recognition to the rest of the democratic process. It calls into question the contrast between the principled decision making of courts and the prudential lawmaking of legislatures in which a judge seeks to "give meaning to our constitutional values . . . perhaps even [is] force[d] to be objective—not to express his preferences or personal beliefs, or those of the citizenry, as to what is right or just. . . . Legislatures . . . see their primary function in terms of registering the actual, occurrent preferences of the people—what they want and what they believe should be done." This contrast is problematic both empirically and normatively.

Empirical evidence about the behavior of judges and legislators is almost never offered to support the contrast. The argument proceeds entirely by way of a kind of deductive institutionalism, relying on certain incentives of presumed self-interest. Because of the incentives built into the legislative role (such as the necessity of standing for election), legislators, it is assumed, will consider only the preferences of their constituents. Because of the incentives built into the judicial role (such as the need for professional respect), judges will have more regard for well-reasoned principles that are capable of discounting morally suspect preferences.

The trouble with such arguments, even in their a priori form, is that institutional incentives have a way of canceling out one another. Because legislators must defend their policies to many different groups, they may be forced to

---

[31] See, e.g., Dworkin, *A Matter of Principle*, pp. 9–71, and *Law's Empire*, pp. 355–399. Although the court system is the focus of his writing, Dworkin also expects legislatures and other public forums to consider matters of principle: "Political debate . . . include[s] argument over principle not only when a case comes to the Court but also long before and long after." Yet public officials "would not be so sensitive to principle without the legal and political culture of which judicial review is the heart." Judicial review provides "the national argument of principle." Dworkin views it as the leading institution that "calls some issues from the battleground of power politics to the forum of principle" (*A Matter of Principle*, pp. 70–71). Even if this were descriptively accurate of existing democracies, it would still be important for democratic theory to emphasize that democracies work best when courts are not the primary forum of principle against a "battleground of power politics." In "Equality, Democracy, and Constitution," Dworkin defends a more extensive realm of deliberation when he writes that "an attractive political community wishes its citizens to engage in politics out of a shared and intense concern for the justice and rightness of the results" (p. 334); see also *Law's Empire*, pp. 217–219. But Dworkin does not take it to be his project to pursue the implications of this insight for extending the deliberative forums of society beyond the judiciary.

formulate generally acceptable policies, and justify them by general principles. Because judges must resolve particular cases, they may lose sight of the larger social implications of their decisions and frame their principles too narrowly, fitting only the facts of the instant case. Without much more empirical analysis than anyone has yet undertaken, no one can say, even if the contrast exists in some form, whether either the motives or the decisions of legislators are more or less principled than the motives or decisions of judges. It is true of course that courts usually give reasons for their decisions, and legislatures do not, but that difference does not take the contrast very far. Individual legislators can and do give reasons for their decisions, and would be expected to do so more often if they and other citizens were not under the influence of democratic conceptions that downplay deliberation outside the judicial process.

The normative basis of the contrast between judges and legislators is even more questionable. The implication is that legislators need not, and perhaps even should not, justify their decisions on the basis of principle. Their *ideal* function is, like that of Benthamite calculators, to aggregate the preferences of citizens, correcting them where necessary to promote social utility. Since laws sometimes *should* reflect preferences in this way, it is useful to have institutions that can perform this function. But to prescribe that legislatures should be assigned this task exclusively is to press the idea of the separation of powers beyond its legitimate purposes. If citizens ought to make political decisions on the basis of reasons and principles that they can mutually affirm, then all those who govern in the name of the citizens—legislators as well as judges—also ought to give reasons and principles for the policies that they support.[32]

To relegate principled politics to the judiciary would be to leave most of politics unprincipled. Judges review only a small proportion of public policy, and much of what they do consider they accept mostly in the form that it was made by legislators and administrators. Furthermore, the moral reasons and principles to which judges defer do not stand above those of other members of society. Judges find their principles in the experience of their own society, and they must justify those principles to other members of their society. If citizens and their representatives deal only or even primarily in preferences, judges sooner or later will find themselves doing the same, or defending principles that no one else shares.

[32] Deliberation also has an important place in the executive branch in the inner councils of government when advisers present their views to agency heads, cabinet officers, and even the president. The process of "multiple advocacy," in which advisers present diverse views in a structured setting designed to give each view its due, promotes deliberation insofar as it includes relevant moral as well as empirical arguments, and insofar as it encourages a similar debate in a wider public. See Alexander L. George, "The Case for Multiple Advocacy in Making Foreign Policy," *American Political Science Review* 66 (September 1972): 751–785; and John P. Burke and Fred I. Greenstein, *How Presidents Test Reality* (New York: Russell Sage Foundation, 1989), pp. 286–289.

25.
Constraints on Reasons for Exercising Power

BRUCE ACKERMAN

1. THE STRUGGLE FOR POWER

So long as we live, there can be no escape from the struggle for power. Each of us must control his body and the world around it. However modest these personal claims, they are forever at risk in a world of scarce resources. Someone, somewhere, will—if given the chance—take the food that sustains or the heart that beats within. Nor need such acts be attempted for frivolous reasons—perhaps my heart is the only thing that will save a great woman's life, my food sufficient to feed five starving men. No one can afford to remain passive while competitors stake their claims. Nothing will be left to reward such self-restraint. Only death can purchase immunity from hostile claims to the power I seek to exercise.

Not that all life is power lust. Social institutions may permit us to turn to better things—deterring the thief and killer while our attention is diverted. Even when our power is relatively secure, however, it is never beyond challenge in a world where total demand outstrips supply. And it is this challenge that concerns us here. Imagine someone stepping forward to claim control over resources you now take for granted. According to her, it is she, not you, who has the better right to claim them. Why, she insists on knowing, do you think otherwise? How can you justify the powers you have so comfortably exercised in the past?

A first response mixes annoyance with fear. Rather than justifying my claims to power, the urge is strong to suppress the questioner. There can be no question that her question is threatening: As soon as I begin to play the game of justification, I run the risk of defeat. I may not find it so easy to justify the powers I so thoughtlessly command. Perhaps the conversation will reveal that it is not she, but I, who is more properly called the thief in this affair. And if this is so, is it not better to suppress the conversation before it begins? This is no ordinary game; it may reveal that my deepest hopes for myself cannot be realized without denying the rights of others. If I succeed in suppressing the questioner, I may hope to live as if my power had never been challenged at all.

It is a tempting prospect which becomes more seductive as my effective power increases. Power corrupts: the more power I have, the more I can lose by trying to answer the question of legitimacy; the more power I have, the greater the chance that my effort at suppression will succeed—at least for the time that remains before I die. Yet this is not the path I mean to follow; I hope to take the question of legitimacy seriously: What would our social world look like if no one ever suppressed another's question of legitimacy, where every questioner met with a conscientious attempt at an answer?

2. CULTURE AND RIGHT

And so we come to our first principle:

Rationality: Whenever anybody questions the legitimacy of another's power, the power holder must respond not by suppressing the questioner but by giving a reason that explains why he is more entitled to the resource than the questioner is.

The first thing to notice about this formula is its generality. No form of power is immune from the question of legitimacy. By framing the Rationality requirement in this way, I hope to avoid the familiar errors of partial critique: the blindness of the partisan of laissez faire who fails to recognize that the private-property owner must legitimate his power no less than the government bureaucrat; the blindness of the communist who avoids this first mistake only to insulate the power of Party leaders from the test of dialogue.

Nor are the institutions of property and government the only means by which some people get what others want. Each person comes into the world with a set of genetic abilities that helps determine his relative power position; each is born into a particular system of education, communication, and exchange that gives some great advantages over others. Finally, there is the tremendous fact of temporal priority: one generation can transform the cultural and material possibilities available to its successors—can deny them life itself. None of these power structures can be accorded the immense privilege of invisibility; *each* person must be prepared[1] to answer the question of legitimacy when *any* of his powers is challenged by *anyone* disadvantaged by their exercise.

This comprehensive insistence on dialogue forces a break with one of the great myths of philosophy—the idea of a "state of nature." While the myth takes many forms, it always tells a story in which actors acquire "rights" that are prior to, and independent of, their social interaction. How this trick takes place is a matter of some dispute—some say by a silent act of unchallenged appropriation, others merely stipulate the "rights" their actors possess when they "first" encounter one another in a social situation. The important point, though, is the myth's assertion that people have "rights" even before they confront the harsh fact of the struggle for power.

---

[1] Is it enough to be *prepared* to answer the question of legitimacy? Must we drop everything and *actually engage* in a conversation whenever anybody challenges any of our claims to power? It would be silly to spend our entire lives in a discussion of the single question of legitimacy—at the expense of all talk and action on behalf of our personal ideals. Nonetheless, I cannot be permitted to evade questioning to such an extent that others are uncertain whether they have the power to call me to account at mutually convenient times and places.

In contrast, the Rationality principle supposes that rights have a reality only *after* people confront the fact of scarcity and begin to argue its normative implications. If you were completely confident that no one would ever question your control over X, you would never think of claiming a "right" over it; you'd simply use it without a second thought. If you were transported to an alien planet peopled by entities whose symbolic code (if it existed) you could not crack, there would be no point in claiming "rights" in regulating your dealings with them. Instead, brute force would remain the only option open.[2] Rights are not the kinds of things that grow on trees—to be plucked, when ripe, by an invisible hand. The only context in which a claim of right has a point is one where you anticipate the possibility of conversation with some potential competitor. Not that this conversation always in fact arises—brute force also remains a potent way of resolving disputes. Rights talk presupposes only the *conceptual* possibility of an alternative way of regulating the struggle for power—one where claims to scarce resources are established through a patterned cultural activity in which the question of legitimacy is countered by an effort at justification.

Since the principle of Rationality conceives this dialogue as the foundation of all claims of right, it requires a subtler, but no less decisive, break with a second familiar myth—the idea of "social contract."[3] Although the parties to a social contract must speak to one another while negotiating its terms, this conversation is understood in instrumental terms only. It does not constitute the ground of the rights that emerge from the bargaining process but simply serves as a means to induce the parties to give their consent to the contract terms. Indeed, the most compelling versions of the contract myth try to cut through the chatter of precontractual negotiation by designing a bargaining situation in which no rational actor has any sensible choice but to sign on the dotted line. Protracted discussion about contract terms at the founding convention is often positively harmful—it can reveal strategic possibilities for bluffing and coalition formation that may make the terms of the contract indeterminate. And it is only each party's promise to abide by the contract that constitutes the basis of his social rights and duties—not the talk that precedes or follows the magic moment of promising.

In contrast, Rationality does not refer to some privileged moment of promising—existing apart from ordinary social life—as the foundation of everyday claims of right. It points instead to an ongoing social practice—the dialogue engendered by the question of legitimacy—as itself the constituting matrix for

---

[2] Of course, if the aliens were triumphant, you might try to warn earth that they did not recognize any "rights"—but that is plainly a derivative use of the term.

[3] While "state of nature" and "social contract" are commonly joined in familiar classics, it is not obvious that this is a necessary connection. Thus, Rawls tries to free contract from the fallacies of the state of nature, while Nozick returns the compliment by rescuing the state of nature from contract. Since I shall be rejecting both myths on their merits, I need not consider the extent to which, as a conceptual matter, they are indissolubly tied together. John Rawls, *A Theory of Justice* (Cambridge, MA: Harvard University Press, 1971); Robert Nozick, *Anarchy, State, and Utopia* (New York: Basic Books, 1974).

any particular claim of right. At a later point, I shall defend this view at greater length. For now, though, it is enough to state the essence of my proposal: Rather than linking liberalism to ideas of natural right or imaginary contract, *we must learn to think of liberalism as a way of talking about power, a form of political culture.*

But there is another face to Rationality; one that deals with substance, not method. Consider, for example, the Nazi who answers the Jew's question of legitimacy by saying, "Jews are an intrinsically worthless people whose very existence is an insult to the morally superior races." While it is tempting to exclude such responses as ir-Rational under the first principle, I mean resolutely to resist. Rather than isolating the distinctive features of liberalism all by itself, Rationality simply points the would-be liberal in the general direction in which such a discovery is to be found: *If* there is anything distinctive about liberalism, it must be in the *kinds of reasons* liberals rely on to legitimate their claims to scarce resources. Nazis are not liberals because there is *something* about the reasons they give in support of their claims that is inconsistent with the organizing principles of liberal power talk. And what might that something be?

Before I try to answer this question, permit me a single preliminary move that is, substantively speaking, even emptier than the last. As a second principle in my model of legitimacy, I insist that like cases be treated alike.

> *Consistency.* The reason advanced by a power wielder on one occasion must not be inconsistent with the reasons he advances to justify his other claims to power.

Throughout the book, I shall remain content with an unanalyzed understanding of this second principle. The critical thing is that a power holder cannot justify his claim to X by saying, "Because Aryans are better than Jews" and then turn around and justify his claim to Y by announcing, "All men are created equal." Of course, Consistency simply requires the power wielder to resolve this tension in one way or another; it does not demand that he give up his nazism. Thus, when standing alone, Consistency hardly has an obvious claim to its preeminence—a state that killed all Jews is more illegitimate than one that muddled its way to saving some. But Consistency does not stand alone. Its function is to safeguard the intelligibility of the dialogue demanded by Rationality. When a Jew is told that he is being killed because "Jews are intrinsically vicious beasts," he will be appalled by the answer he has received, *but he will find no difficulty understanding it.* This is true, however, only because the Jew decodes the utterance with the aid of the interpretive assumption that the Nazi would not knowingly contradict himself. If the Nazi's assertion were set against the background of an equally emphatic declaration that "Jews are as good as the rest of us," it would be wrenched into a context that puts its status as a reason into question. When a person is willing to assert R and $\bar{R}$ simultaneously, he has not given two reasons for his action. He has provided some noise that adds up to no argument at all.

3. CONSTRAINED POWER TALK

The first two principles do one important thing—establish the centrality of reason giving to the concept of right. Whenever nothing intelligible can be said in justification of a power, its exercise is illegitimate. A sustained silence or a stream of self-contradictory noises are decisive signs that something very wrong is going on.

All this, it may be said, is very true but very weak stuff. Yet appearances are deceiving; with the addition of one final ingredient, we may brew a political solution with enormous resolving power. The missing idea is that particular kinds of conversation are often constrained by special rules restricting what may be appropriately said within them. We could hardly run our everyday lives if every utterance opened us up to an all-consuming conversation about everything under the sun. Even the most egregious boor recognizes that a conversation with the telephone operator is not a suitable vehicle for a blow-by-blow account of his life. It is this familiar sense of conversational constraint[4] that I mean to put to a new use. Just as there are constraints imposed in other conversations, I also want to constrain the dialogues in which people talk to one another about their claims to power. Not that I wish to constrain power talk by appealing to social etiquette. Notions of conventional propriety presuppose the legitimacy of the power structure, rather than vice versa. The question, instead, is whether fundamental philosophical arguments can be advanced to justify one or another constraint on power talk.

Suppose, for a moment, that the answer is Yes. Suppose that I can convince you that no argument of type Z should be permitted to count as a good argument in conversations about power. Given this achievement, it is easy to see how my first two principles can be transformed into a mighty philosophical engine. While it is a safe bet that *some* reason can be found to justify *any* power relationship, P_i, all bets are off once the propriety of a conversational constraint, Z, is conceded. For it might then turn out that the *only* reasons that can be advanced in support of P_i are among those eliminated by Z. Thus, once Z has done its work of exclusion, *all that may be left is silence*. And once a claimant to a scarce resource has been reduced to silence, Rationality requires him to recognize that his claim to power is illegitimate. In short, I propose to demonstrate the illegitimacy of a wide variety of power structures by reducing their proponents to silence. Call this way of delegitimating a power structure the method of *constrained silence*.

Now if this method can be deployed as a powerful engine of political appraisal, everything will depend on the choice of Z. To serve its purpose, Z must be designed with two ends in mind. First, the more reasons Z excludes, the more likely it is that at least some power structures will be unmasked as indefensible within the constraint it imposes. Ceteris paribus, the bigger the Z, the better. But this concern with quantity is worthless without an assessment of Z's

---

[4] Elaborated illuminatingly by H. P. Grice, "Logic and Conversation," in Donald Davidson and Gilbert Harman, eds., *The Logic of Grammar* (Encino, Calif.: Dickinson, 1975), pp. 64–153.

quality. Thus, we will get nowhere with constraints of the form "*Only* reasons of Z type are good reasons in this conversation." For when the proponent of such a Z is asked to justify this constraint, he will be obliged to explain why Z is better than all competing substantive principles. Yet it is just this conversation which the constraint sought to avoid in the first place.

Things get more interesting if the constraint does not pretend to specify both necessary and sufficient conditions for a good reason but contents itself with stipulating only necessary conditions: "*No* Z is a good reason" rather than "*Only* Z is a good reason." When framed in this way, a conversational constraint may seem plausible to many different people who bitterly disagree about lots of other things. For example, both communists and liberals may agree that nazi arguments (defined in some clear way by Z) are bad reasons, though they reach this judgment by means of very different arguments—call them [c] and [l], respectively. Even more striking, the arguments contained in [c] may be logically inconsistent with those contained in [l]. Nonetheless, *both groups will converge on Z by a process of argument that makes sense to them.*

Of course, the proposed "anti-Fascist" constraint is not, on its merits, a terribly incisive idea. Hitler may not have been smart enough to think of all the arguments for genocide. So if Z were carefully framed to exclude only the particular claims made by Hitler and his henchmen, our Z might not prevent someone from coming up with a new reason for genocide. If we are to hope for success from the method of constrained silence, we cannot frame our Z with a particular historical experience in mind but must proceed from more general philosophical considerations. Only in this way can we formulate a conversational constraint of such breadth that the proponents of particular power structures will find themselves speechless when called upon to defend their legitimacy.

But there are transparent dangers in broadening the constraints. The broader the Z, the harder it will be to frame a principle that will seem plausible to people with otherwise different views of the world. Nonetheless, the effort is not obviously hopeless; indeed, my object is to persuade you that the liberal tradition is best understood as precisely such an effort to define and justify broad constraints on power talk. Thus, I do not wish to claim any great novelty for the Z that will preoccupy us. To the contrary, constraints similar to mine can be found in any writer working within the historical liberal tradition.[5] The novelty is simply my claim that the notion of constrained conversation should serve as *the* organizing principle of liberal thought. When others have sought to give liberalism systematic form, they have turned to other ideas—most notably contract or utility—to serve as their organizing principle. In contrast, I hope to convince you that the idea of constrained conversation provides a far more satisfactory key to the liberal enterprise. And once the lock is turned, the liberal

[5] Moreover, there are encouraging signs of a renewed appreciation of these constraints in recent liberal theorizing, see, e.g., Ronald Dworkin, "Liberalism," in *Public and Private Morality,* Stuart Hampshire, ed. (Cambridge: Cambridge Univ. Press, 1978) pp. 113–43. No less encouraging is the emphasis upon conversational legitimation prevailing among the most creative workers in the Marxist tradition. See, e.g., Jurgen Habermas, *Legitimation Crisis* (Boston: Beacon Press, 1975).

tradition will reveal unsuspected resources of methodological rigor and substantive depth.

4. NEUTRALITY AND CONVERGENCE

My particular Z taps the liberal's opposition to paternalism. The germ of the idea is that nobody has the right to vindicate political authority by asserting a privileged insight into the moral universe which is denied the rest of us. A power structure is illegitimate if it can be justified only through a conversation in which some person (or group) must assert that he is (or they are) the privileged moral authority:

> *Neutrality.* No reason is a good reason if it requires the power holder to assert:
>
> (a) that his conception of the good is better than that asserted by any of his fellow citizens, *or*
>
> (b) that, regardless of his conception of the good, he is intrinsically superior to one or more of his fellow citizens.

I will defer important questions of interpretation to emphasize the main point—which is the way Neutrality promises to satisfy the two conditions we require for a potent Z. Since the breadth of the exclusion imposed by Neutrality is obvious, the critical question is whether the formulation suffers the defects of this virtue: Does its very breadth make it impossible to generate arguments that will justify its acceptance as a fundamental constraint on power talk?

Not at all. It is downright easy to think of several weighty arguments in support of Neutrality. The first is a skeptical argument: While everybody has an opinion about the good life, none can be known to be superior to any other. It follows that anyone who asserts that either he or his aims are intrinsically superior doesn't know what he's talking about. Yet this is precisely the move barred by Neutrality.

But there is no need to be a skeptic before you can reason your way to Neutrality. Even if you think you can *know* something about the good life, there are several good reasons for imposing liberal constraints on political conversation. Most obviously, you might think that you can only learn anything true about the good when you are free to experience in life without some authoritative teacher intervening whenever he thinks you're going wrong. And if you think this, Neutrality seems made to order. But, once again, this view is only one of many that will provide a plausible path to Neutrality. Even if you don't think you need to experiment, you may adopt a conception of the good that gives a central place to autonomous deliberation and deny that it is possible to *force* a person to be good. On this view, the intrusion of non-Neutral argument into power talk will seem self-defeating at best—since it threatens to divert people from the true means of cultivating a truly good life. Assume, finally, that you think you know what the good life is and that it is of a kind that can be forced on others; then the only question is whether the right people will be doing the forcing. A single glance at the world suggests that this is no trivial problem.

People adept in gaining power are hardly known for their depth of moral insight; the very effort to engross power corrupts—at least if your theory of the good embraces any number of familiar moral ideals.

Not that it is absolutely impossible to reason yourself to a rejection of Neutrality. Plato began systematic political philosophy with such a dream; medieval churchmen thought there were good reasons to confide ultimate secular authority to the pope. Only they recognized—as modern totalitarians do not—the depth of the reconceptualization required before a breach of Neutrality can be given a coherent justification. It is not enough to reject one or another of the basic arguments that lead to a reasoned commitment to Neutrality; one must reject *all* of them. And to do this does not require a superficial change of political opinions but a transformation of one's entire view of the world—both as to the nature of human values and the extent to which the powerful can be trusted to lead their brethren to the promised land.

In proposing Neutrality, then, I do not imagine I am defending an embattled citadel on the fringe of modern civilization. Instead, I am pointing to a place well within the cultural interior that can be reached by countless pathways of argument coming from very different directions. As time passes, some paths are abandoned while others are worn smooth; yet the exciting work on the frontier cannot blind us to the hold that the center has upon us.

5. IS LIBERALISM CONSISTENT?

By the time we complete our journey, I will investigate the conceptual routes to Neutrality with greater care. Before we engage in extensive road repair, however, simple prudence requires us to attend to sober guides who warn us that all these highways lead nowhere. According to them,[6] liberalism is incapable of formulating a self-consistent response to the struggle for power. It is doomed instead to lurch from one self-contradiction to another in a vain effort to save the myth of Neutrality. Rather than making the same mistakes again, we must have the courage to discard the myth of Neutrality and search for a Something whose nature can only be glimpsed darkly through the gray mist that liberalism has bequeathed us. And though this Something is certainly elusive, yet surely it is better than the self-contradictory Nothing that liberalism provides. On then, into the darkness—for only there will we find our hidden Humanity.

Now I take this argument seriously. Yet, like all arguments, this one can be no better than its premises. The choice is between an obscure Something and a self-contradictory Nothing only if it is conceded that liberalism is intellectually bankrupt, that it can propose no self-consistent way of resolving power conflict. And this is something that liberalism's critics are more apt to assert than prove. Not that I blame them: it is hard to prove a negative, and given their intimations of bankruptcy, they understandably prefer to spend their time on more constructive activities. For us, however, the case stands otherwise. There

---

[6] See, e.g., Roberto Mangabeira Unger, *Knowledge and Politics* (New York, Free Press: 1976); Robert Paul Wolff, *In Defense of Anarchism* (New York: Harper & Row, 1970).

is a simple way to establish, once and for all, that the accusation of bankruptcy is wrong. And that is to provide a single example of a liberal theory equal to the conceptual task of providing a Neutral order to the struggle for power. In terms of our model of legitimacy, all we need propose is a single system for regulating power conflicts that can be justified by:

1. a self-consistent set of reasons (principles one and two) that
2. do *not* violate each branch of the Neutrality principle.

If there is even one such system of power relations, P_i, then the claim that liberalism is bankrupt is simply wrong. Of course, it may well turn out that any P_i that supports a thoroughgoing Neutral dialogue looks very different from the power structures within which we live our lives. But this means that liberalism, properly understood, requires a more sweeping critique of the existing power structure than is sometimes supposed. Rather than an empty bankrupt, liberalism emerges as a coherent set of ideals of enormous critical force.

Indeed, I may make an even stronger claim if the critics are only 99.99 percent right in their accusations of bankruptcy. Assume, for example, that a complete survey of the millions of possible reasons for claiming power reveals that *all but one* of them involved the claimant saying that he was intrinsically better than the next guy or that his ends in life were especially worthwhile. The discovery of such a unique reason, R, would have just the opposite consequences of bankruptcy. As we have seen, people may be persuaded by any number of very different reasons to embrace the ideal of Neutral discourse. Since R happens to be the *only* reason that passes the test of Neutral dialogue, anybody who has been convinced (for whatever reason) to accept my three principles of legitimacy has *no choice* but to accept R.[7] Thus, we may glimpse the old liberal dream of a philosopher's stone by which a commitment to a particular procedure of dispute resolution—here, the process of constrained conversation— can be transformed into a commitment to particular substantive outcomes.

Not that such a demonstration would induce instant conversion among those who would lead us to authoritarianism in the name of Humanity. Yet there would no longer be any hope of a cheap victory over some pitiful blob of self-contradiction. Instead, the partisans of authority will confront at least one well-specified power structure, P_i, that can be rationally defended within the conversational constraints imposed by liberal principles. Before they can reject

---

[7] The style of argument is similar to Kenneth Arrow's in his *Social Choice and Individual Values* (New Haven: Yale University Press, 2d ed., 1963). Like him, I propose to constrain collective choice by a set of principles each of which, taken individually, seems relatively uncontroversial. Given these constraints, I then inquire whether any principle for collective decision can be found that does not violate at least one of them. Unlike Arrow, however, I shall conclude that there is at least one R that does satisfy all constraints.

This conclusion, however, is not inconsistent with the famous negative result derived by Arrow's General Impossibility Theorem. Arrow works within the voluntarist tradition and is concerned with the problem of aggregating individual *preferences* into a consistent collective choice; I am working within the rationalist tradition and want to determine whether any of the *reasons* that can be given in defense of power survive plausible conversational constraints. If anything, Arrow's impossibility result can only invigorate inquiries of the kind attempted here. For if, as Arrow suggests, individual *preferences* cannot be aggregated in an uncontroversial way to legitimate social choice, it is even more important to isolate the kinds of *reasons* that may best legitimate the collective choices that must be made in the course of social life.

P_i, they must proceed to do battle on far more difficult terrain—where success requires them to free themselves from the complex web of argument that binds them to Neutrality and Rationality.

But, alas, there is no a priori reason to think that things will work out so neatly. While the constraints imposed by Neutrality are broad, they may nonetheless permit more than one R to break the conversational barrier. Rather than pointing to a single kind of substantive discourse, liberalism would then be the name of a family of different substantive arguments that may lead to very different substantive conclusions concerning the right way to resolve one or another power conflict. Nonetheless, while the P_is may differ substantively, they all will share one family resemblance: all can be fathered by a rational conversation within Neutral constraints. Of course, the fact of common paternity will not then suffice to satisfy all the requirements of political evaluation. We would then be required to reach a new stage of liberal theory and articulate criteria for choosing the most promising child within the liberal family.

Before liberalisms can multiply, however, we must first establish that the ground yields any fruit whatever. Thus, most of this book will try to show how one particular R can be articulated in a way that is conceptually equal to the task of regulating all important forms of power struggle. While I do not claim that mine is the only R that will turn the trick, I can report that my own searches among the universe of possible reasons has not turned up a competitor. Unless somebody develops a formal proof of my R's uniqueness, however, the search for alternative liberal rationales must continue apace.

6. LIBERALISM AND EQUAL RESPECT

Imagine that somebody finds that your claim to some resource interferes with his effort to pursue his good. Any resource will do—your questioner may challenge your right to use your body or some natural object or some cultural artifact or whatever. Anyway, he wants it and issues a conversational challenge:

Q: I want X.
A: So do I! And if I have my way, I'll use force to stop you from taking X.
Q: What gives you the right to do this? Do you think you're better than I am?
A: Not at all. But I think I'm just as good.
Q: And how is that a reason for your use of power?
A: Because you *already* have an X that's at least as good as mine is. If you take this X as well, you'd be better off than I am. And that's not right. Since I'm at least as good as you are, I should have power over an X that is at least as good as yours is.
Q: But haven't you just violated Neutrality?
A: Not at all. Neutrality forbids me from saying that I'm any better than you are; it doesn't prevent me from saying that I'm at least as good.
Q: But if I don't get this extra X, I won't achieve my ends in life.
A: That's not a good reason for your getting X, because the reason I'm claiming X is that I too want it to achieve my ends in life. And do you

imagine that it is intrinsically more important for you to achieve your ends in life than it is for me?

Q: I can't say that within the constraints imposed by Neutrality.

A: So, then, what *can* you say in defense of your effort to get a better X than I have?

Q: And if I can't answer that?

A: Then you must recognize that I've given you a Neutral answer to your question of legitimacy, while you have backed up your power play with nothing that looks like a reason.

My purpose in producing this script must be kept clearly in mind. For the present, I do not care what you think of the *merits* of A's argument. Perhaps, upon finding out more facts about A, you will deny that he's as good as Q; perhaps, on thinking further, you will reject the idea that a person's assertion of *moral equality* implies a right to equality in *worldly possessions*. No such objection, however, defeats my purpose in presenting the script for your inspection. To pass the Neutrality test, I do not need to claim that A has presented a *convincing* argument for initial equality; instead, I need only establish that A has presented an *intelligible* argument on behalf of initial equality while keeping within Neutral ground rules. Even if you *disagree* with A when he says, "Since I'm at least as good as you are, I should have an X that is at least as good as yours is," there is something intelligible here with which to disagree. The only thing, then, that I want to say on behalf of my script is that *it can be said*.

And this, my reader, you already know to be true. For you've just read the dialogue and found no difficulty understanding it.

Yet this small concession is larger than it seems. It places the burden of articulation squarely upon those who seek an inegalitarian distribution of worldly advantage. While they may have all sorts of premonitions of superiority, they cannot engross a greater share of power within a liberal state unless they justify their claims in a way that passes the Neutrality constraint. And if they fail to articulate a Neutral justification, they can only succeed in the conversation over power by justifying a change in the conversational ground rules—explaining how they have reasoned their way free of all the arguments that lead to Neutrality. And if they fail in that, they will have no choice but to attack Rationality, joining with Nietzsche in celebrating the power of the powerful to transcend all talk of good and evil.

And if they do declare themselves supermen, they surely will understand me when I say that I'm willing to fight for my rival understanding of the world.

7. FINISHING THE CONVERSATION

But I have gotten ahead of myself. There is lots of work to do before the stakes can get so high as this. To see why, consider two ways in which the first script is incomplete. First, the dialogue does not end with an unconditional conversational victory by A, but simply establishes that Q cannot expect to win his claim so long as he remains silent. There is, however, no certainty that Q will remain silent. Instead, he can respond in one of two ways. On the one hand, he may reject A's claim that Q's X is at least as good as A's is. On the other hand, Q may accept A's characterization of their power relation and try to frame a Neutral reason why his X *ought* to be better than A's. If Q succeeds in either conversational move, the burden of conversational initiative will shift back to A—obliging him to explain, consistently with Neutrality, why he finds Q's reason unpersuasive; and so on, back and forth, until somebody fails to meet his conversational burden. It is only when this occurs that the silenced party's claim has been unmasked as illegitimate in a liberal state. To use a helpful legalism, our initial script merely describes a way that A might establish a prima facie case in support of the legitimacy of his power over X. A complete theory, however, must move beyond this first, prima facie stage of the conversation and describe the kinds of power structures that would be legitimated in a dialogue in which the parties are free to talk until they have nothing more to say.[8]

As this dialogue unfolds, I hope to show that it resolves a central ambivalence that has greatly weakened the liberal analysis of power. The ambiguity concerns the place of equality in a just society. On the one hand, certain forms of equal treatment—say, formal equality in the administration of justice—have been central to the liberal tradition. On the other hand, there has been a recurrent fear of a nightmare world where all human diversity has been destroyed in the name of an equality that levels everyone to the lowest common denominator. Haunted by these fears, liberals have too often accustomed themselves to an awkward position on the slippery slope, unable to explain what in principle distinguishes the equalities they cherish from those they detest. My thesis is that an extended conversation is precisely the therapy required to dispel this nightmare equality from our vision. While, as we have seen, Neutral dialogue begins with the affirmation of a right to equal shares, subsequent conversational moves will define a liberal conception of equality that is compatible with a social order rich in diversity of talents, personal ideals, and forms of community. The articulation of this distinctive conception of equality—I shall call it *undominated* equality—will be one of my major purposes.

---

[8] An essay by H. L. A. Hart was important in suggesting to me the potential fruitfulness of this line of development. See his "The Ascription of Responsibility and Rights" in *Logic and Language,* First Series, Anthony Flew, ed. (New York: Philosophical Library, 1951), pp. 145–66 in which the notion of a prima facie case is discussed in terms of "defeasible concepts." Unfortunately, Hart presented his analysis of defeasibility as part of a more ambitious—and much criticized—analysis of the nature of human action. See Peter Geach, "Ascriptivisim," *Philosophical Review* 69 (1960): 221; George Pitcher, "Hart on Action and Responsibility," ibid., p. 226. With characteristic thoughtfulness, Hart responded to these critics by abandoning his larger claims about human action. Nonetheless, even his critics recognize that Hart's point about defeasibility "seems to be true in one type of case, namely, that in which the action is bad and, in addition, is designated by a condemnatory verb" (p. 232). This is precisely the sort of case we are dealing with here. Q is condemning A's power play as illegitimate and A is trying to defend himself by asserting some reason in defense of his power.

For thoughtful efforts to save something of Hart's analysis, see Richard Epstein, "Pleadings and Presumptions," *University of Chicago Law Review* 40 (1974): 556; Joel Feinberg *Doing and Deserving* (Princeton: Princeton Univ. Press, 1970), pp. 119–51.

To accomplish it, however, will require a remedy for a second kind of incompleteness in the initial script. Here the concern is not with the prima facie character of the text but with the dim background against which Q and A recite their lines. The stage directions simply describe two citizens struggling over some scarce resource, X, which both of them desire. But in the world as we know it, the struggle occurs over more concrete resources and takes many different forms: assailant versus victim; trespasser versus property owner; dissident versus bureaucrat; child versus parent; handicapped versus talented; and so forth. To understand the practical implications of liberal conversation, we must grasp the way it can discipline the concrete power struggle of our everyday lives.

In bringing the script down to earth, moreover, we must be careful about the way we fill in the dialogic background. While it is impossible to analyze every concrete institution that regulates the struggle for power, we must resist the temptation of a grossly simplified account. This is, perhaps, the most common mistake made by partisans of the liberal tradition. Time and again, these people speak as if the only significant power in society comes out of the smoking typewriter of a government bureaucrat. While they are tireless in their efforts to constrain this power by exacting standards of Neutrality, they often react with shocked surprise at the very idea of subjecting the powers of "private" citizens to an identical scrutiny. Yet, first of all, we live in a world in which the powers of government are routinely called upon to enforce (as well as define) all of these "private" entitlements. Without this reinforcement, there is no reason to think that those presently advantaged by the distribution of "private" rights would remain so. Second, even if something like the status quo could be maintained without a central government, Q could still ask A to justify his possession of "private" powers that Q also wants to exercise. And unless A can frame a Neutral answer, the three principles require him to recognize that his "private" power is illegitimate. Of course, in the absence of a central government, A might find it very easy to suppress Q and maintain control over "private" powers he cannot justify. But this merely shows that a decentralized system of "private" power can be just as illegitimate as one in which a tyrannical central government holds sway. The task, then, is to deny *any* fundamental power structure the priceless advantage of invisibility—to define a world where *all* power is distributed so that each person might defend his share in a conversation that begins (but does not end) with the move: "because I'm at least as good as you are."

8. TECHNOLOGIES OF JUSTICE

It is one thing to count the ways our initial script is unfinished, quite another to "complete" the text. Indeed, since a single book can only supply a fragment of the required conversation, it is almost fatuous to ask what a *complete* script might look like. Yet it is only by asking this question that we can glimpse the relationship between the fragment presented here and other fragments provided elsewhere.

Consider, then, that a complete liberal analysis of power would contain two different parts. First, there would be an exhausting empirical exercise that would not only describe the power structure, P_s, into which people are presently born but every other power structure, $[P_a \ldots P_n]$ into which P_s might be transformed through collective action. Then, having specified the "feasibility set," we could move to an equally exhausting normative exercise. Here we would consider each power structure separately to determine whether it would support a thoroughgoing Neutral dialogue. So far as the status quo, P_s, is concerned, this could be determined by considering the kind of power talk that actually takes place, noting especially whether questions of legitimacy are ever systematically suppressed or ignored or answered in a patently illiberal way. But so far as the other $[P_a \ldots P_n]$ in the feasibility set are concerned, we must instead imagine what people would say if they had a set of powers different from the ones they presently exercise. The only way to do this, of course, is to write imaginary dialogues between the incumbents of the various power positions specified by the particular P_i. If it *is* possible to write Neutral scripts for the various A's when they are confronted by the relevant Q's, then P_i would be legitimated as a liberal state operating under the three principles; if not, not.

There is, as I have already noted, no a priori reason to expect that one, and only one, P_i would pass this dialogic test. Instead, the discipline of Neutral script writing would sort the entire feasibility set into two distinct subsets. On the one hand, there would be a *legitimacy subset,* containing those P_is (if any exist) that support a comprehensive Neutral dialogue of justification. On the other hand, the *illegitimacy subset* would contain all the other feasible power structures. For those convinced of the merits of Neutrality and Rationality, *all* P_is in the first subset will seem superior to *any* P_i in the second. It is the class of power structures that fall within the legitimacy subset that I mean to call liberal states.

26.
Justice as Fairness:
Political not Metaphysical

JOHN RAWLS

In this discussion I shall make some general remarks about how I now understand the conception of justice that I have called "justice as fairness" (presented
in my book *A Theory of Justice*).[1] I do this because it may seem that this conception depends on philosophical claims I should like to avoid, for example,
claims to universal truth, or claims about the essential nature and identity of
persons. My aim is to explain why it does not. I shall first discuss what I regard
as the task of political philosophy at the present time and then briefly survey how
the basic intuitive ideas drawn upon in justice as fairness are combined into a
political conception of justice for a constitutional democracy. Doing this will
bring out how and why this conception of justice avoids certain philosophical
and metaphysical claims. Briefly, the idea is that in a constitutional democracy
the public conception of justice should be, so far as possible, independent of
controversial philosophical and religious doctrines. Thus, to formulate such a
conception, we apply the principle of toleration to philosophy itself: the public
conception of justice is to be political, not metaphysical. Hence the title.

I want to put aside the question whether the text of *A Theory of Justice* supports different readings than the one I sketch here. Certainly on a number of
points I have changed my views, and there are no doubt others on which my
views have changed in ways that I am unaware of. I recognize further that certain faults of exposition as well as obscure and ambiguous passages in *A Theory of Justice* invite misunderstanding; but I think these matters need not
concern us and I shan't pursue them beyond a few footnote indications. For our
purposes here, it suffices first, to show how a conception of justice with the
structure and content of justice as fairness can be understood as political and
not metaphysical, and second, to explain why we should look for such a conception of justice in a democratic society.

I

One thing I failed to say in *A Theory of Justice,* or failed to stress sufficiently,
is that justice as fairness is intended as a political conception of justice. While
a political conception of justice is, of course, a moral conception, it is a moral
conception worked out for a specific kind of subject, namely, for political,
social, and economic institutions. In particular, justice as fairness is framed to

---

[1] Cambridge, MA: Harvard University Press, 1971.

apply to what I have called the "basic structure" of a modern constitutional democracy. (I shall use "constitutional democracy" and "democratic regime," and similar phrases interchangeably.) By this structure I mean such a society's main political, social, and economic institutions, and how they fit together into one unified system of social cooperation. Whether justice as fairness can be extended to a general political conception for different kinds of societies existing under different historical and social conditions, or whether it can be extended to a general moral conception, or a significant part thereof, are altogether separate questions. I avoid prejudging these larger questions one way or the other.

It should also be stressed that justice as fairness is not intended as the application of a general moral conception to the basic structure of society, as if this structure were simply another case to which that general moral conception is applied.[2] In this respect justice as fairness differs from traditional moral doctrines, for these are widely regarded as such general conceptions. Utilitarianism is a familiar example, since the principle of utility, however it is formulated, is usually said to hold for all kinds of subjects ranging from the actions of individuals to the law of nations. The essential point is this: as a practical political matter no general moral conception can provide a publicly recognized basis for a conception of justice in a modern democratic state. The social and historical conditions of such a state have their origins in the Wars of Religion following the Reformation and the subsequent development of the principle of toleration, and in the growth of constitutional government and the institutions of large industrial market economies. These conditions profoundly affect the requirements of a workable conception of political justice: such a conception must allow for a diversity of doctrines and the plurality of conflicting, and indeed incommensurable, conceptions of the good affirmed by the members of existing democratic societies.

Finally, to conclude these introductory remarks, since justice as fairness is intended as a political conception of justice for a democratic society, it tries to draw solely upon basic intuitive ideas that are embedded in the political institutions of a constitutional democratic regime and the public traditions of their interpretation. Justice as fairness is a political conception in part because it starts from within a certain political tradition. We hope that this political conception of justice may at least be supported by what we may call an "overlapping consensus," that is, by a consensus that includes all the opposing philosophical and religious doctrines likely to persist and to gain adherents in a more or less just constitutional democratic society.

II

There are, of course, many ways in which political philosophy may be understood, and writers at different times, faced with different political and social

---

[2] See "The Basic Structure as Subject," in *Values and Morals,* eds. Alvin Goldman and Jaegwon Kim (Dordrecht: Reidel, 1978), pp. 47–71.

circumstances, understand their work differently. Justice as fairness I would now understand as a reasonably systematic and practicable conception of justice for a constitutional democracy, a conception that offers an alternative to the dominant utilitarianism of our tradition of political thought. Its first task is to provide a more secure and acceptable basis for constitutional principles and basic rights and liberties than utilitarianism seems to allow. The need for such a political conception arises in the following way.

There are periods, sometimes long periods, in the history of any society during which certain fundamental questions give rise to sharp and divisive political controversy, and it seems difficult, if not impossible, to find any shared basis of political agreement. Indeed, certain questions may prove intractable and may never be fully settled. One task of political philosophy in a democratic society is to focus on such questions and to examine whether some underlying basis of agreement can be uncovered and a mutually acceptable way of resolving these questions publicly established. Or if these questions cannot be fully settled, as may well be the case, perhaps the divergence of opinion can be narrowed sufficiently so that political cooperation on a basis of mutual respect can still be maintained.

The course of democratic thought over the past two centuries or so makes plain that there is no agreement on the way basic institutions of a constitutional democracy should be arranged if they are to specify and secure the basic rights and liberties of citizens and answer to the claims of democratic equality when citizens are conceived as free and equal persons (as explained in the last three paragraphs of Section III). A deep disagreement exists as to how the values of liberty and equality are best realized in the basic structure of society. To simplify, we may think of this disagreement as a conflict within the tradition of democratic thought itself, between the tradition associated with Locke, which gives greater weight to what Constant called "the liberties of the moderns," freedom of thought and conscience, certain basic rights of the person and of property, and the rule of law, and the tradition associated with Rousseau, which gives greater weight to what Constant called "the liberties of the ancients," the equal political liberties and the values of public life. This is a stylized contrast and historically inaccurate, but it serves to fix ideas.

Justice as fairness tries to adjudicate between these contending traditions first, by proposing two principles of justice to serve as guidelines for how basic institutions are to realize the values of liberty and equality, and second, by specifying a point of view from which these principles can be seen as more appropriate than other familiar principles of justice to the nature of democratic citizens viewed as free and equal persons. What it means to view citizens as free and equal persons is, of course, a fundamental question and is discussed in the following sections. What must be shown is that a certain arrangement of the basic structure, certain institutional forms, are more appropriate for realizing the values of liberty and equality when citizens are conceived as such persons, that is (very briefly), as having the requisite powers of moral personality that enable them to participate in society viewed as a system of fair cooperation for mutual advantage. So to continue, the two principles of justice (mentioned above) read as follows:

1. Each person has an equal right to a fully adequate scheme of equal basic rights and liberties, which scheme is compatible with a similar scheme for all.
2. Social and economic inequalities are to satisfy two conditions: first, they must be attached to offices and positions open to all under conditions of fair equality of opportunity; and second, they must be to the greatest benefit of the least advantaged members of society.

Each of these principles applies to a different part of the basic structure; and both are concerned not only with basic rights, liberties, and opportunities, but also with the claims of equality; while the second part of the second principle underwrites the worth of these institutional guarantees. The two principles together, when the first is given priority over the second, regulate the basic institutions which realize these values. But these details, although important, are not our concern here.

We must now ask: how might political philosophy find a shared basis for settling such a fundamental question as that of the most appropriate institutional forms for liberty and equality? Of course, it is likely that the most that can be done is to narrow the range of public disagreement. Yet even firmly held convictions gradually change: religious toleration is now accepted, and arguments for persecution are no longer openly professed; similarly, slavery is rejected as inherently unjust, and however much the aftermath of slavery may persist in social practices and unavowed attitudes, no one is willing to defend it. We collect such settled convictions as the belief in religious toleration and the rejection of slavery and try to organize the basic ideas and principles implicit in these convictions into a coherent conception of justice. We can regard these convictions as provisional fixed points which any conception of justice must account for if it is to be reasonable for us. We look, then, to our public political culture itself, including its main institutions and the historical traditions of their interpretation, as the shared fund of implicitly recognized basic ideas and principles. The hope is that these ideas and principles can be formulated clearly enough to be combined into a conception of political justice congenial to our most firmly held convictions. We express this by saying that a political conception of justice, to be acceptable, must be in accordance with our considered convictions, at all levels of generality, on due reflection (or in what I have called "reflective equilibrium").

The public political culture may be of two minds even at a very deep level. Indeed, this must be so with such an enduring controversy as that concerning the most appropriate institutional forms to realize the values of liberty and equality. This suggests that if we are to succeed in finding a basis of public agreement, we must find a new way of organizing familiar ideas and principles into a conception of political justice so that the claims in conflict, as previously understood, are seen in another light. A political conception need not be an original creation but may only articulate familiar intuitive ideas and principles so that they can be recognized as fitting together in a somewhat different way than before. Such a conception may, however, go further than this: it may organize these familiar ideas and principles by means of a more fundamental intuitive idea within the complex structure of which the other familiar intuitive ideas are then systematically connected and related. In justice as fairness, as we shall see in the next section, this more fundamental idea is that of society as a system of fair social cooperation between free and equal persons. The concern of this section is how we might find a public basis of political agreement. The point is that a conception of justice will only be able to achieve this aim if it provides a reasonable way of shaping into one coherent view the deeper bases of agreement embedded in the public political culture of a constitutional regime and acceptable to its most firmly held considered convictions.

Now suppose justice as fairness were to achieve its aim and a publicly acceptable political conception of justice is found. Then this conception provides a publicly recognized point of view from which all citizens can examine before one another whether or not their political and social institutions are just. It enables them to do this by citing what are recognized among them as valid and sufficient reasons singled out by that conception itself. Society's main institutions and how they fit together into one scheme of social cooperation can be examined on the same basis by each citizen, whatever that citizen's social position or more particular interests. It should be observed that, on this view, justification is not regarded simply as valid argument from listed premises, even should these premises be true. Rather, justification is addressed to others who disagree with us, and therefore it must always proceed from some consensus, that is, from premises that we and others publicly recognize as true; or better, publicly recognize as acceptable to us for the purpose of establishing a working agreement on the fundamental questions of political justice. It goes without saying that this agreement must be informed and uncoerced, and reached by citizens in ways consistent with their being viewed as free and equal persons.[3]

Thus, the aim of justice as fairness as a political conception is practical, and not metaphysical or epistemological. That is, it presents itself not as a conception of justice that is true, but one that can serve as a basis of informed and willing political agreement between citizens viewed as free and equal persons. This agreement when securely founded in public political and social attitudes sustains the goods of all persons and associations within a just democratic regime. To secure this agreement we try, so far as we can, to avoid disputed philosophical, as well as disputed moral and religious, questions. We do this not because these questions are unimportant or regarded with indifference,[4] but because we think them too important and recognize that there is no way to resolve them politically. The only alternative to a principle of toleration is the autocratic use of state power. Thus, justice as fairness deliberately stays on the surface, philosophically speaking. Given the profound differences in belief and conceptions

---

[3] *Theory,* pp. 580–83.

[4] Ibid., pp. 214f.

of the good at least since the Reformation, we must recognize that, just as on questions of religious and moral doctrine, public agreement on the basic questions of philosophy cannot be obtained without the state's infringement of basic liberties. Philosophy as the search for truth about an independent metaphysical and moral order cannot, I believe, provide a workable and shared basis for a political conception of justice in a democratic society.

We try, then, to leave aside philosophical controversies whenever possible, and look for ways to avoid philosophy's longstanding problems. Thus, in what I have called "Kantian constructivism," we try to avoid the problem of truth and the controversy between realism and subjectivism about the status of moral and political values. This form of constructivism neither asserts nor denies these doctrines. Rather, it recasts ideas from the tradition of the social contract to achieve a practicable conception of objectivity and justification founded on public agreement in judgment on due reflection. The aim is free agreement, reconciliation through public reason. And similarly, as we shall see (in Section V), a conception of the person in a political view, for example, the conception of citizens as free and equal persons, need not involve, so I believe, questions of philosophical psychology or a metaphysical doctrine of the nature of the self. No political view that depends on these deep and unresolved matters can serve as a public conception of justice in a constitutional democratic state. As I have said, we must apply the principle of toleration to philosophy itself. The hope is that, by this method of avoidance, as we might call it, existing differences between contending political views can at least be moderated, even if not entirely removed, so that social cooperation on the basis of mutual respect can be maintained. Or if this is expecting too much, this method may enable us to conceive how, given a desire for free and uncoerced agreement, a public understanding could arise consistent with the historical conditions and constraints of our social world. Until we bring ourselves to conceive how this could happen, it can't happen.

III

Let's now survey briefly some of the basic ideas that make up justice as fairness in order to show that these ideas belong to a political conception of justice. As I have indicated, the overarching fundamental intuitive idea, within which other basic intuitive ideas are systematically connected, is that of society as a fair system of cooperation between free and equal persons. Justice as fairness starts from this idea as one of the basic intuitive ideas which we take to be implicit in the public culture of a democratic society.[5] In their political thought, and in the context of public discussion of political questions, citizens do not view the social order as a fixed natural order, or as an institutional hierarchy

---

[5] Although *Theory* uses this idea from the outset (it is introduced on p. 4), it does not emphasize, as I do here and in "Kantian Constructivism in Moral Theory," *Journal of Philosophy* 77 (September 1980), that the basic ideas of justice as fairness are regarded as implicit or latent in the public culture of a democratic society.

justified by religious or aristocratic values. Here it is important to stress that from other points of view, for example, from the point of view of personal morality, or from the point of view of members of an association, or of one's religious or philosophical doctrine, various aspects of the world and one's relation to it, may be regarded in a different way. But these other points of view are not to be introduced into political discussion.

We can make the idea of social cooperation more specific by noting three of its elements:

1. Cooperation is distinct from merely socially coordinated activity, for example, from activity coordinated by orders issued by some central authority. Cooperation is guided by publicly recognized rules and procedures which those who are cooperating accept and regard as properly regulating their conduct.
2. Cooperation involves the idea of fair terms of cooperation: these are terms that each participant may reasonably accept, provided that everyone else likewise accepts them. Fair terms of cooperation specify an idea of reciprocity or mutuality: all who are engaged in cooperation and who do their part as the rules and procedures require, are to benefit in some appropriate way as assessed by a suitable benchmark of comparison. A conception of political justice characterizes the fair terms of social cooperation. Since the primary subject of justice is the basic structure of society, this is accomplished in justice as fairness by formulating principles that specify basic rights and duties within the main institutions of society, and by regulating the institutions of background justice over time so that the benefits produced by everyone's efforts are fairly acquired and divided from one generation to the next.
3. The idea of social cooperation requires an idea of each participant's rational advantage, or good. This idea of good specifies what those who are engaged in cooperation, whether individuals, families, or associations, or even nation-states, are trying to achieve, when the scheme is viewed from their own standpoint.

Now consider the idea of the person.[6] There are, of course, many aspects of human nature that can be singled out as especially significant depending on our point of view. This is witnessed by such expressions as *homo politicus, homo oeconomicus, homo faber,* and the like. Justice as fairness starts from the idea that society is to be conceived as a fair system of cooperation and so it adopts a conception of the person to go with this idea. Since Greek times, both in

---

[6] It should be emphasized that a conception of the person, as I understand it here, is a normative conception, whether legal, political, or moral, or indeed also philosophical or religious, depending on the overall view to which it belongs. In this case the conception of the person is a moral conception, one that begins from our everyday conception of persons as the basic units of thought, deliberation and responsibility, and adapted to a political conception of justice and not to a comprehensive moral doctrine. It is in effect a political conception of the person, and given the aims of justice as fairness, a conception of citizens. Thus, a conception of the person is to be distinguished from an account of human nature given by natural science or social theory. On this point, see "Kantian Constructivism," p. 534f.

philosophy and law, the concept of the person has been understood as the concept of someone who can take part in, or who can play a role in, social life, and hence exercise and respect its various rights and duties. Thus, we say that a person is someone who can be a citizen, that is, a fully cooperating member of society over a complete life. We add the phrase "over a complete life" because a society is viewed as a more or less complete and self-sufficient scheme of cooperation, making room within itself for all the necessities and activities of life, from birth until death. A society is not an association for more limited purposes; citizens do not join society voluntarily but are born into it, where, for our aims here, we assume they are to lead their lives.

Since we start within the tradition of democratic thought, we also think of citizens as free and equal persons. The basic intuitive idea is that in virtue of what we may call their moral powers, and the powers of reason, thought, and judgment connected with those powers, we say that persons are free. And in virtue of their having these powers to the requisite degree to be fully cooperating members of society, we say that persons are equal.[7] We can elaborate this conception of the person as follows. Since persons can be full participants in a fair system of social cooperation, we ascribe to them the two moral powers connected with the elements in the idea of social cooperation noted above: namely, a capacity for a sense of justice and a capacity for a conception of the good. A sense of justice is the capacity to understand, to apply, and to act from the public conception of justice which characterizes the fair terms of social cooperation. The capacity for a conception of the good is the capacity to form, to revise, and rationally to pursue a conception of one's rational advantage, or good. In the case of social cooperation, this good must not be understood narrowly but rather as a conception of what is valuable in human life. Thus, a conception of the good normally consists of a more or less determinate scheme of final ends, that is, ends we want to realize for their own sake, as well as of attachments to other persons and loyalties to various groups and associations. These attachments and loyalties give rise to affections and devotions, and therefore the flourishing of the persons and associations who are the objects of these sentiments is also part of our conception of the good. Moreover, we must also include in such a conception a view of our relation to the world—religious, philosophical, or moral—by reference to which the value and significance of our ends and attachments are understood.

In addition to having the two moral powers, the capacities for a sense of justice and a conception of the good, persons also have at any given time a particular conception of the good that they try to achieve. Since we wish to start from the idea of society as a fair system of cooperation, we assume that persons as citizens have all the capacities that enable them to be normal and fully cooperating members of society. This does not imply that no one ever suffers from illness or accident; such misfortunes are to be expected in the ordinary course of human life; and provision for these contingencies must be made. But for our

[7] *Theory,* Sec. 77.

purposes here I leave aside permanent physical disabilities or mental disorders so severe as to prevent persons from being normal and fully cooperating members of society in the usual sense.

Now the conception of persons as having the two moral powers, and therefore as free and equal, is also a basic intuitive idea assumed to be implicit in the public culture of a democratic society. Note, however, that it is formed by idealizing and simplifying in various ways. This is done to achieve a clear and uncluttered view of what for us is the fundamental question of political justice: namely, what is the most appropriate conception of justice for specifying the terms of social cooperation between citizens regarded as free and equal persons, and as normal and fully cooperating members of society over a complete life? It is this question that has been the focus of the liberal critique of aristocracy, of the socialist critique of liberal constitutional democracy, and of the conflict between liberals and conservatives at the present time over the claims of private property and the legitimacy (in contrast to the effectiveness) of social policies associated with the so-called welfare state.

IV

I now take up the idea of the original position.[8] This idea is introduced in order to work out which traditional conception of justice, or which variant of one of those conceptions, specifies the most appropriate principles for realizing liberty and equality once society is viewed as a system of cooperation between free and equal persons. Assuming we had this purpose in mind, let's see why we would introduce the idea of the original position and how it serves its purpose.

Consider again the idea of social cooperation. Let's ask: how are the fair terms of cooperation to be determined? Are they simply laid down by some outside agency distinct from the persons cooperating? Are they, for example, laid down by God's law? Or are these terms to be recognized by these persons as fair by reference to their knowledge of a prior and independent moral order? For example, are they regarded as required by natural law, or by a realm of values known by rational intuition? Or are these terms to be established by an undertaking among these persons themselves in the light of what they regard as their mutual advantage? Depending on which answer we give, we get a different conception of cooperation.

Since justice as fairness recasts the doctrine of the social contract, it adopts a form of the last answer: the fair terms of social cooperation are conceived as agreed to by those engaged in it, that is, by free and equal persons as citizens who are born into the society in which they lead their lives. But their agreement, like any other valid agreement, must be entered into under appropriate conditions. In particular, these conditions must situate free and equal persons fairly and must not allow some persons greater bargaining advantages than

---

[8] Ibid., Sec. 4, Ch. 3, and the index.

others. Further, threats of force and coercion, deception and fraud, and so on, must be excluded.

So far so good. The foregoing considerations are familiar from everyday life. But agreements in everyday life are made in some more or less clearly specified situation embedded within the background institutions of the basic structure. Our task, however, is to extend the idea of agreement to this background framework itself. Here we face a difficulty for any political conception of justice that uses the idea of a contract, whether social or otherwise. The difficulty is this: we must find some point of view, removed from and not distorted by the particular features and circumstances of the all-encompassing background framework, from which a fair agreement between free and equal persons can be reached. The original position, with the feature I have called "the veil of ignorance," is this point of view.[9] And the reason why the original position must abstract from and not be affected by the contingencies of the social world is that the conditions for a fair agreement on the principles of political justice between free and equal persons must eliminate the bargaining advantages which inevitably arise within background institutions of any society as the result of cumulative social, historical, and natural tendencies. These contingent advantages and accidental influences from the past should not influence an agreement on the principles which are to regulate the institutions of the basic structure itself from the present into the future.

• • •

Both of the above mentioned difficulties, then, are overcome by viewing the original position as a device of representation: that is, this position models what we regard as fair conditions under which the representatives of free and equal persons are to specify the terms of social cooperation in the case of the basic structure of society; and since it also models what, for this case, we regard as acceptable restrictions on reasons available to the parties for favoring one agreement rather than another, the conception of justice the parties would adopt identifies the conception we regard—*here* and *now*—as fair and supported by the best reasons. We try to model restrictions on reasons in such a way that it is perfectly evident which agreement would be made by the parties in the original position as citizens' representatives. Even if there should be, as surely there will be, reasons for and against each conception of justice available, there may be an overall balance of reasons plainly favoring one conception over the rest. As a device of representation the idea of the original position serves as a means of public reflection and self-clarification. We can use it to help us work out what we now think, once we are able to take a clear and uncluttered view of what justice requires when society is conceived as a scheme of cooperation between free and equal persons over time from one generation to the next. The original position serves as a unifying idea by which our considered convictions

[9] On the veil of ignorance, see ibid., Sec. 24, and the index.

at all levels of generality are brought to bear on one another so as to achieve greater mutual agreement and self-understanding.

To conclude: we introduce an idea like that of the original position because there is no better way to elaborate a political conception of justice for the basic structure from the fundamental intuitive idea of society as a fair system of cooperation between citizens as free and equal persons. There are, however, certain hazards. As a device of representation the original position is likely to seem somewhat abstract and hence open to misunderstanding. The description of the parties may seem to presuppose some metaphysical conception of the person, for example, that the essential nature of persons is independent of and prior to their contingent attributes, including their final ends and attachments, and indeed, their character as a whole. But this is an illusion caused by not seeing the original position as a device of representation. The veil of ignorance, to mention one prominent feature of that position, has no metaphysical implications concerning the nature of the self; it does not imply that the self is ontologically prior to the facts about persons that the parties are excluded from knowing. We can, as it were, enter this position any time simply by reasoning for principles of justice in accordance with the enumerated restrictions. When, in this way, we simulate being in this position, our reasoning no more commits us to a metaphysical doctrine about the nature of the self than our playing a game like Monopoly commits us to thinking that we are landlords engaged in a desperate rivalry, winner take all.[10] We must keep in mind that we are trying to show how the idea of society as a fair system of social cooperation can be unfolded so as to specify the most appropriate principles for realizing the institutions of liberty and equality when citizens are regarded as free and equal persons.

---

[10] *Theory*, pp. 138f., 147. The parties in the original position are said (p. 147) to be theoretically defined individuals whose motivations are specified by the account of that position and not by a psychological view about how human beings are actually motivated. This is also part of what is meant by saying (p. 121) that the acceptance of the particular principles of justice is not conjectured as a psychological law or probability but rather follows from the full description of the original position. Although the aim cannot be perfectly achieved, we want the argument to be deductive, "a kind of moral geometry." In "Kantian Constructivism" (p. 532) the parties are described as merely artificial agents who inhabit a construction. Thus I think R. B. Brandt mistaken in objecting that the argument from the original position is based on defective psychology. See his *A Theory of the Good and the Right* (Oxford: Clarendon Press, 1979), pp. 239–42. Of course, one might object to the original position that it models the conception of the person and the deliberations of the parties in ways that are unsuitable for the purposes of a political conception of justice; but for these purposes psychological theory is not directly relevant. On the other hand, psychological theory is relevant for the account of the stability of a conception of justice, as discussed in *Theory*, Pt. III. Similarly, I think Michael Sandel mistaken in supposing that the original position involves a conception of the self ". . . shorn of all its contingently-given attributes," a self that "assumes a kind of supra-empirical status, . . . and given prior to its ends, a pure subject of agency and possession, ultimately thin." See *Liberalism and the Limits of Justice* (Cambridge: Cambridge University Press, 1982), pp. 93–95. I cannot discuss these criticisms in any detail. The essential point (as suggested in the introductory remarks) is not whether certain passages in *Theory* call for such an interpretation (I doubt that they do), but whether the conception of justice as fairness presented therein can be understood in the light of the interpretation I sketch in this article and in the earlier lectures on constructivism, as I believe it can be.

V

I just remarked that the idea of the original position and the description of the parties may tempt us to think that a metaphysical doctrine of the person is presupposed. While I said that this interpretation is mistaken, it is not enough simply to disavow reliance on metaphysical doctrines, for despite one's intent they may still be involved. To rebut claims of this nature requires discussing them in detail and showing that they have no foothold. I cannot do that here.[11]

I can, however, sketch a positive account of the political conception of the person, that is, the conception of the person as citizen (discussed in Section III), involved in the original position as a device of representation. To explain what is meant by describing a conception of the person as political, let's consider how citizens are represented in the original position as free persons. The representation of their freedom seems to be one source of the idea that some metaphysical doctrine is presupposed. I have said elsewhere that citizens view themselves as free in three respects, so let's survey each of these briefly and indicate the way in which the conception of the person used is political.[12]

First, citizens are free in that they conceive of themselves and of one another as having the moral power to have a conception of the good. This is not to say that, as part of their political conception of themselves, they view themselves as inevitably tied to the pursuit of the particular conception of the good which they affirm at any given time. Instead, as citizens, they are regarded as capable of revising and changing this conception on reasonable and rational grounds,

---

[11] Part of the difficulty is that there is no accepted understanding of what a metaphysical doctrine is. One might say, as Paul Hoffman has suggested to me, that to develop a political conception of justice without presupposing, or explicitly using, a metaphysical doctrine, for example, some particular metaphysical conception of the person, is already to presuppose a metaphysical thesis: namely, that no particular metaphysical doctrine is required for this purpose. One might also say that our everyday conception of persons as the basic units of deliberation and responsibility presupposes, or in some way involves, certain metaphysical theses about the nature of persons as moral or political agents. Following the method of avoidance, I should not want to deny these claims. What should be said is the following. If we look at the presentation of justice as fairness and note how it is set up, and note the ideas and conceptions it uses, no particular metaphysical doctrine about the nature of persons, distinctive and opposed to other metaphysical doctrines, appears among its premises, or seems required by its argument. If metaphysical presuppositions are involved, perhaps they are so general that they would not distinguish between the distinctive metaphysical views—Cartesian, Leibnizian, or Kantian: realist, idealist, or materialist—with which philosophy traditionally has been concerned. In this case, they would not appear to be relevant for the structure and content of a political conception of justice one way or the other. I am grateful to Daniel Brudney and Paul Hoffman for discussion of these matters.

[12] For the first two respects, see "Kantian Constructivism," pp. 544f. (For the third respect, see footnote 15 below.) The account of the first two respects found in those lectures is further developed in the text above and I am more explicit on the distinction between what I call here our "public" versus our "nonpublic or moral identity." The point of the term "moral" in the latter phrase is to indicate that persons' conceptions of the (complete) good are normally an essential element in characterizing their nonpublic (or nonpolitical) identity, and these conceptions are understood as normally containing important moral elements, although they include other elements as well, philosophical and religious. The term "moral" should be thought of as a stand-in for all these possibilities. I am indebted to Elizabeth Anderson for discussion and clarification of this distinction.

and they may do this if they so desire. Thus, as free persons, citizens claim the right to view their persons as independent from and as not identified with any particular conception of the good, or scheme of final ends. Given their moral power to form, to revise, and rationally to pursue a conception of the good, their public identity as free persons is not affected by changes over time in their conception of the good. For example, when citizens convert from one religion to another, or no longer affirm an established religious faith, they do not cease to be, for questions of political justice, the same persons they were before. There is no loss of what we may call their public identity, their identity as a matter of basic law. In general, they still have the same basic rights and duties; they own the same property and can make the same claims as before, except insofar as these claims were connected with their previous religious affiliation. We can imagine a society (indeed, history offers numerous examples) in which basic rights and recognized claims depend on religious affiliation, social class, and so on. Such a society has a different political conception of the person. It may not have a conception of citizenship at all; for this conception, as we are using it, goes with the conception of society as a fair system of cooperation for mutual advantage between free and equal persons.

It is essential to stress that citizens in their personal affairs, or in the internal life of associations to which they belong, may regard their final ends and attachments in a way very different from the way the political conception involves. Citizens may have, and normally do have at any given time, affections, devotions, and loyalties that they believe they would not, and indeed could and should not, stand apart from and objectively evaluate from the point of view of their purely rational good. They may regard it as simply unthinkable to view themselves apart from certain religious, philosophical, and moral convictions, or from certain enduring attachments and loyalties. These convictions and attachments are part of what we may call their "nonpublic identity." These convictions and attachments help to organize and give shape to a person's way of life, what one sees oneself as doing and trying to accomplish in one's social world. We think that if we were suddenly without these particular convictions and attachments we would be disoriented and unable to carry on. In fact, there would be, we might think, no point in carrying on. But our conceptions of the good may and often do change over time, usually slowly but sometimes rather suddenly. When these changes are sudden, we are particularly likely to say that we are no longer the same person. We know what this means: we refer to a profound and pervasive shift, or reversal, in our final ends and character; we refer to our different nonpublic, and possibly moral or religious, identity. On the road to Damascus Saul of Tarsus becomes Paul the Apostle. There is no change in our public or political identity, nor in our personal identity as this concept is understood by some writers in the philosophy of mind.[13]

---

[13] Here I assume that an answer to the problem of personal identity tries to specify the various criteria (for example, psychological continuity of memories and physical continuity of body, or some part thereof) in accordance with which two different psychological states, or actions (or whatever), which occur at two different times may be said to be states or actions of the same person who endures over time; and it also tries to specify how this enduring person is to be

The second respect in which citizens view themselves as free is that they regard themselves as self-originating sources of valid claims. They think their claims have weight apart from being derived from duties or obligations specified by the political conception of justice, for example, from duties and obligations owed to society. Claims that citizens regard as founded on duties and obligations based on their conception of the good and the moral doctrine they affirm in their own life are also, for our purposes here, to be counted as self-originating. Doing this is reasonable in a political conception of justice for a constitutional democracy; for provided the conceptions of the good and the moral doctrines citizens affirm are compatible with the public conception of justice, these duties and obligations are self-originating from the political point of view.

When we describe a way in which citizens regard themselves as free, we are describing how citizens actually think of themselves in a democratic society should questions of justice arise. In our conception of a constitutional regime, this is an aspect of how citizens regard themselves. That this aspect of their freedom belongs to a particular political conception is clear from the contrast with a different political conception in which the members of society are not viewed as self-originating sources of valid claims. Rather, their claims have no weight except insofar as they can be derived from their duties and obligations owed to society, or from their ascribed roles in the social hierarchy justified by religious or aristocratic values. Or to take an extreme case, slaves are human beings who are not counted as sources of claims, not even claims based on social duties or obligations, for slaves are not counted as capable of having duties or obligations. Laws that prohibit the abuse and maltreatment of slaves are not founded on claims made by slaves on their own behalf, but on claims originating either from slaveholders, or from the general interests of society (which does not include the interests of slaves). Slaves are, so to speak, socially dead: they are not publicly recognized as persons at all.[14] Thus, the contrast with a political conception which allows slavery makes clear why conceiving of citizens as free persons in virtue of their moral powers and their having a conception of the good, goes with a particular political conception of the person. This conception of

---

conceived, whether as a Cartesian or a Leibnizian substance, or as a Kantian transcendental ego, or as a continuant of some other kind, for example, bodily or physical. See the collection of essays edited by John Perry, *Personal Identity* (Berkeley, CA: University of California Press, 1975), especially Perry's introduction, pp. 3–30; and Sydney Shoemaker's essay in *Personal Identity* (Oxford: Basil Blackwell, 1984), both of which consider a number of views. Sometimes in discussions of this problem, continuity of fundamental aims and aspirations is largely ignored, for example, in views like H. P. Grice's (included in Perry's collection) which emphasizes continuity of memory. Of course, once continuity of fundamental aims and aspirations is brought in, as in Derek Parfit's *Reasons and Persons* (Oxford: Clarendon Press, 1984), Pt. III, there is no sharp distinction between the problem of persons' nonpublic or moral identity and the problem of their personal identity. This latter problem raises profound questions on which past and current philosophical views widely differ, and surely will continue to differ. For this reason it is important to try to develop a political conception of justice which avoids this problem as far as possible.

[14] For the idea of social death, see Orlando Patterson, *Slavery and Social Death* (Cambridge, MA: Harvard University Press, 1982), esp. pp. 5–9, 38–45, 337. This idea is interestingly developed in this book and has a central place in the author's comparative study of slavery.

persons fits into a political conception of justice founded on the idea of society as a system of cooperation between its members conceived as free and equal.

The third respect in which citizens are regarded as free is that they are regarded as capable of taking responsibility for their ends and this affects how their various claims are assessed.[15] Very roughly, the idea is that, given just background institutions and given for each person a fair index of primary goods (as required by the principles of justice), citizens are thought to be capable of adjusting their aims and aspirations in the light of what they can reasonably expect to provide for. Moreover, they are regarded as capable of restricting their claims in matters of justice to the kinds of things the principles of justice allow. Thus, citizens are to recognize that the weight of their claims is not given by the strength and psychological intensity of their wants and desires (as opposed to their needs and requirements as citizens), even when their wants and desires are rational from their point of view. I cannot pursue these matters here. But the procedure is the same as before: we start with the basic intuitive idea of society as a system of social cooperation. When this idea is developed into a conception of political justice, it implies that, viewing ourselves as persons who can engage in social cooperation over a complete life, we can also take responsibility for our ends, that is, that we can adjust our ends so that they can be pursued by the means we can reasonably expect to acquire given our prospects and situation in society. The idea of responsibility for ends is implicit in the public political culture and discernible in its practices. A political conception of the person articulates this idea and fits it into the idea of society as a system of social cooperation over a complete life.

To sum up, I recapitulate three main points of this and the preceding two sections:

First, in Section III persons were regarded as free and equal in virtue of their possessing to the requisite degree the two powers of moral personality (and the powers of reason, thought, and judgment connected with these powers), namely, the capacity for a sense of justice and the capacity for a conception of the good. These powers we associated with two main elements of the idea of cooperation, the idea of fair terms of cooperation and the idea of each participant's rational advantage, or good.

Second, in this section (Section V), we have briefly surveyed three respects in which persons are regarded as free, and we have noted that in the public political culture of a constitutional democratic regime citizens conceive of themselves as free in these respects.

Third, since the question of which conception of political justice is most appropriate for realizing in basic institutions the value of liberty and equality has long been deeply controversial within the very democratic tradition in which citizens are regarded as free and equal persons, the aim of justice as fairness is to try to resolve this question by starting from the basic intuitive idea of society as a fair system of social cooperation in which the fair terms of cooperation

---

[15] See "Social Unity and Primary Goods," in *Utilitarianism and Beyond,* eds. Amartya Sen and Bernard Williams (Cambridge: Cambridge University Press, 1982), Sec. IV, pp. 167–70.

are agreed upon by citizens themselves so conceived. In Section IV, we saw why this approach leads to the idea of the original position as a device of representation.

VI

I now take up a point essential to thinking of justice as fairness as a liberal view. Although this conception is a moral conception, it is not, as I have said, intended as a comprehensive moral doctrine. The conception of the citizen as a free and equal person is not a moral ideal to govern all of life, but is rather an ideal belonging to a conception of political justice which is to apply to the basic structure. I emphasize this point because to think otherwise would be incompatible with liberalism as a political doctrine. Recall that as such a doctrine, liberalism assumes that in a constitutional democratic state under modern conditions there are bound to exist conflicting and incommensurable conceptions of the good. This feature characterizes modern culture since the Reformation. Any viable political conception of justice that is not to rely on the autocratic use of state power must recognize this fundamental social fact. This does not mean, of course, that such a conception cannot impose constraints on individuals and associations, but that when it does so, these constraints are accounted for, directly or indirectly, by the requirements of political justice for the basic structure.[16]

Given this fact, we adopt a conception of the person framed as part of, and restricted to, an explicitly political conception of justice. In this sense, the conception of the person is a political one. As I stressed in the previous section, persons can accept this conception of themselves as citizens and use it when discussing questions of political justice without being committed in other parts of their life to comprehensive moral ideals often associated with liberalism, for example, the ideals of autonomy and individuality. The absence of commitment to these ideals, and indeed to any particular comprehensive ideal, is essential to liberalism as a political doctrine. The reason is that any such ideal, when pursued as a comprehensive ideal, is incompatible with other conceptions of the good, with forms of personal, moral, and religious life consistent with justice and which, therefore, have a proper place in a democratic society. As comprehensive moral ideals, autonomy and individuality are unsuited for a political conception of justice. As found in Kant and J. S. Mill, these comprehensive ideals, despite their very great importance in liberal thought, are extended too far when presented as the only appropriate foundation for a

---

[16] For example, churches are constrained by the principle of equal liberty of conscience and must conform to the principle of toleration, universities by what may be required to maintain fair equality of opportunity, and the rights of parents by what is necessary to maintain their children's physical well-being and to assure the adequate development of their intellectual and moral powers. Because churches, universities, and parents exercise their authority within the basic structure, they are to recognize the requirements this structure imposes to maintain background justice.

constitutional regime.[17] So understood, liberalism becomes but another sectarian doctrine.

This conclusion requires comment: it does not mean, of course, that the liberalisms of Kant and Mill are not appropriate moral conceptions from which we can be led to affirm democratic institutions. But they are only two such conceptions among others, and so but two of the philosophical doctrines likely to persist and gain adherents in a reasonably just democratic regime. In such a regime the comprehensive moral views which support its basic institutions may include the liberalisms of individuality and autonomy; and possibly these liberalisms are among the more prominent doctrines in an overlapping consensus, that is, in a consensus in which, as noted earlier, different and even conflicting doctrines affirm the publicly shared basis of political arrangements. The liberalisms of Kant and Mill have a certain historical preeminence as among the first and most important philosophical views to espouse modern constitutional democracy and to develop its underlying ideas in an influential way; and it may even turn out that societies in which the ideals of autonomy and individuality are widely accepted are among the most well-governed and harmonious.[18]

By contrast with liberalism as a comprehensive moral doctrine, justice as fairness tries to present a conception of political justice rooted in the basic intuitive ideas found in the public culture of a constitutional democracy. We conjecture that these ideas are likely to be affirmed by each of the opposing comprehensive moral doctrines influential in a reasonably just democratic society. Thus justice as fairness seeks to identify the kernel of an overlapping consensus, that is, the shared intuitive ideas which when worked up into a political conception of justice turn out to be sufficient to underwrite a just constitutional regime. This is the most we can expect, nor do we need more.[19] We must note, however, that when justice as fairness is fully realized in a well-ordered society, the value of full autonomy is likewise realized. In this way justice as fairness is indeed similar to the liberalisms of Kant and Mill; but in contrast with them, the value of full autonomy is here specified by a political conception of justice, and not by a comprehensive moral doctrine.

It may appear that, so understood, the public acceptance of justice as fairness is no more than prudential; that is, that those who affirm this conception do so simply as a *modus vivendi* which allows the groups in the overlapping consensus to pursue their own good subject to certain constraints which each thinks to be for its advantage given existing circumstances. The idea of an overlapping consensus may seem essentially Hobbesian. But against this, two remarks: first, justice as fairness is a moral conception: it has conceptions of

[17] For Kant, see *The Foundations of the Metaphysics of Morals* and *The Critique of Practical Reason*. For Mill, see *On Liberty*, particularly Ch. 3 where the ideal of individuality is most fully discussed.

[18] This point has been made with respect to the liberalisms of Kant and Mill, but for American culture one should mention the important conceptions of democratic individuality expressed in the works of Emerson, Thoreau, and Whitman. These are instructively discussed by George Kateb in his "Democratic Individuality and the Claims of Politics," *Political Theory* 12 (August 1984).

[19] For the idea of the kernel of an overlapping consensus (mentioned above), see *Theory*, last par. of Sec. 35, pp. 220f. For the idea of full autonomy, see "Kantian Constructivism," pp. 528ff.

person and society, and concepts of right and fairness, as well as principles of justice with their complement of the virtues through which those principles are embodied in human character and regulate political and social life. This conception of justice provides an account of the cooperative virtues suitable for a political doctrine in view of the conditions and requirements of a constitutional regime. It is no less a moral conception because it is restricted to the basic structure of society, since this restriction is what enables it to serve as a political conception of justice given our present circumstances. Thus, in an overlapping consensus (as understood here), the conception of justice as fairness is not regarded merely as a *modus vivendi*.

Second, in such a consensus each of the comprehensive philosophical, religious, and moral doctrines accepts justices as fairness in its own way; that is, each comprehensive doctrine, from within its own point of view, is led to accept the public reasons of justice specified by justice as fairness. We might say that they recognize its concepts, principles, and virtues as theorems, as it were, at which their several views coincide. But this does not make these points of coincidence any less moral or reduce them to mere means. For, in general, these concepts, principles, and virtues are accepted by each as belonging to a more comprehensive philosophical, religious, or moral doctrine. Some may even affirm justice as fairness as a natural moral conception that can stand on its own feet. They accept this conception of justice as a reasonable basis for political and social cooperation, and hold that it is as natural and fundamental as the concepts and principles of honesty and mutual trust, and the virtues of cooperation in everyday life. The doctrines in an overlapping consensus differ in how far they maintain a further foundation is necessary and on what that further foundation should be. These differences, however, are compatible with a consensus on justice as fairness as a political conception of justice.

VII

I shall conclude by considering the way in which social unity and stability may be understood by liberalism as a political doctrine (as opposed to a comprehensive moral conception).[20]

One of the deepest distinctions between political conceptions of justice is between those that allow for a plurality of opposing and even incommensurable conceptions of the good and those that hold that there is but one conception of the good which is to be recognized by all persons, so far as they are fully rational. Conceptions of justice which fall on opposite sides of this divide are distinct in many fundamental ways. Plato and Aristotle, and the Christian tradition as represented by Augustine and Aquinas, fall on the side of the one rational good. Such views tend to be teleological and to hold that institutions are just to the extent that they effectively promote this good. Indeed, since classical

---

[20] This account of social unity is found in "Social Unity and Primary Goods," referred to in footnote 15 above. See esp. pp. 160f., 170–73, 183f.

times the dominant tradition seems to have been that there is but one rational conception of the good, and that the aim of moral philosophy, together with theology and metaphysics, is to determine its nature. Classical utilitarianism belongs to this dominant tradition. By contrast, liberalism as a political doctrine supposes that there are many conflicting and incommensurable conceptions of the good, each compatible with the full rationality of human persons, so far as we can ascertain within a workable political conception of justice. As a consequence of this supposition, liberalism assumes that it is a characteristic feature of a free democratic culture that a plurality of conflicting and incommensurable conceptions of the good are affirmed by its citizens. Liberalism as a political doctrine holds that the question the dominant tradition has tried to answer has no practicable answer; that is, it has no answer suitable for a political conception of justice for a democratic society. In such a society a teleological political conception is out of the question: public agreement on the requisite conception of the good cannot be obtained.

As I have remarked, the historical origin of this liberal supposition is the Reformation and its consequences. Until the Wars of Religion in the sixteenth and seventeenth centuries, the fair terms of social cooperation were narrowly drawn: social cooperation on the basis of mutual respect was regarded as impossible with persons of a different faith; or (in the terminology I have used) with persons who affirm a fundamentally different conception of the good. Thus one of the historical roots of liberalism was the development of various doctrines urging religious toleration. One theme in justice as fairness is to recognize the social conditions that give rise to these doctrines as among the so-called subjective circumstances of justice and then to spell out the implications of the principle of toleration.[21] As liberalism is stated by Constant, de Tocqueville, and Mill in the nineteenth century, it accepts the plurality of incommensurable conceptions of the good as a fact of modern democratic culture, provided, of course, these conceptions respect the limits specified by the appropriate principles of justice. One task of liberalism as a political doctrine is to answer the question: how is social unity to be understood, given that there can be no public agreement on the one rational good, and a plurality of opposing and incommensurable conceptions must be taken as given? And granted that social unity is conceivable in some definite way, under what conditions is it actually possible?

In justice as fairness, social unity is understood by starting with the conception of society as a system of cooperation between free and equal persons. Social unity and the allegiance of citizens to their common institutions are not founded on their all affirming the same conception of the good, but on their publicly accepting a political conception of justice to regulate the basic structure of society. The concept of justice is independent from and prior to the

---

[21] The distinction between the objective and the subjective circumstances of justice is made in *Theory*, pp. 126ff. The importance of the role of the subjective circumstances is emphasized in "Kantian Constructivism," pp. 540–42.

concept of goodness in the sense that its principles limit the conceptions of the good which are permissible. A just basic structure and its background institutions establish a framework within which permissible conceptions can be advanced. Elsewhere I have called this relation between a conception of justice and conceptions of the good the priority of right (since the just falls under the right). I believe this priority is characteristic of liberalism as a political doctrine and something like it seems essential to any conception of justice reasonable for a democratic state. Thus to understand how social unity is possible given the historical conditions of a democratic society, we start with our basic intuitive idea of social cooperation, an idea present in the public culture of a democratic society, and proceed from there to a public conception of justice as the basis of social unity in the way I have sketched.

As for the question of whether this unity is stable, this importantly depends on the content of the religious, philosophical, and moral doctrines available to constitute an overlapping consensus. For example, assuming the public political conception to be justice as fairness, imagine citizens to affirm one of three views: the first view affirms justice as fairness because its religious beliefs and understanding of faith lead to a principle of toleration and underwrite the fundamental idea of society as a scheme of social cooperation between free and equal persons; the second view affirms it as a consequence of a comprehensive liberal moral conception such as those of Kant and Mill; while the third affirms justice as fairness not as a consequence of any wider doctrine but as in itself sufficient to express values that normally outweigh whatever other values might oppose them, at least under reasonably favorable conditions. This overlapping consensus appears far more stable than one founded on views that express skepticism and indifference to religious, philosophical, and moral values, or that regard the acceptance of the principles of justice simply as a prudent *modus vivendi* given the existing balance of social forces. Of course, there are many other possibilities.

The strength of a conception like justice as fairness may prove to be that the more comprehensive doctrines that persist and gain adherents in a democratic society regulated by its principles are likely to cohere together into a more or less stable overlapping consensus. But obviously all this is highly speculative and raises questions which are little understood, since doctrines which persist and gain adherents depend in part on social conditions, and in particular, on these conditions when regulated by the public conception of justice. Thus we are forced to consider at some point the effects of the social conditions required by a conception of political justice on the acceptance of that conception itself. Other things equal, a conception will be more or less stable depending on how far the conditions to which it leads support comprehensive religious, philosophical, and moral doctrines which can constitute a stable overlapping consensus. These questions of stability I cannot discuss here. It suffices to remark that in a society marked by deep divisions between opposing and incommensurable conceptions of the good, justice as fairness enables us at least to conceive how social unity can be both possible and stable.

27.

The Principle of Democratic Legitimacy

JOSHUA COHEN AND JOEL ROGERS

. . . Our elaboration of the democratic order must satisfy three major conditions. The principles of that order must be clarified by describing more fully the idea of democracy, at least in its most fundamental aspects. Some indication must then be given of a set of institutional requirements rooted in those principles. And an account must be offered of the motivations that might plausibly lead people to struggle to create such institutions under conditions in which they do not yet exist. In describing the democratic order, we consider these three conditions in turn.

The first condition has already been met implicitly in our previous discussion, but we can make it more explicit here. A democratic society is an ongoing order characterized in the first instance by a certain principle of justification, or principle of democratic legitimacy (PDL).[1] The PDL requires that individuals be free and equal in determining the conditions of their own association. In part the PDL articulates a claim about the nature of sovereignty in a democratic order. That members of the order together determine the institutions, rules, and conditions of their own association means that they themselves are sovereign. This sovereignty is *freely* exercised in the sense that participants in the order have, and are recognized as having, the capacity to form reasoned judgments about the ends of social life; that they are constrained in making those judgments only by the conditions necessary to preserve reasoned public deliberation; and that nothing actually determines the ends of social life other than the judgments arrived at by the members of the order. Sovereignty is *equally* exercised in the sense that the views of each member of the democratic order are accorded equal weight in public deliberation.

The PDL thus cannot be satisfied merely through a proper arrangement of formal arenas of politics, if those arenas remain prey to the intrusions of private power. As indicated in our discussion of capitalist democracy, the power of formal guarantees of freedom and equality is severely limited if political activities within those formal arenas are constrained by material inequalities in resource allocation and control. Satisfaction of the PDL's requirement of equal freedom thus requires attention to such background constraints on formal freedom. It requires that the conditions of equal freedom be satisfied in the arrangement of all social arenas that bear on the conditions of public deliberation.

---

[1] On the idea of democratic legitimacy see Jean-Jacques Rousseau, *The Social Contract,* ed. Roger D. Masters, trans. Judith R. Masters (New York: St. Martin's Press, 1978), Book 1, chs. 6 and 7; Book 2, chs. 1–4; and Book 4, chs. 1–2; Jürgen Habermas, *Legitimation Crisis,* trans. Thomas McCarthy (Boston: Beacon Press, 1975), Part 3, ch. 2; and idem. *Communication and the Evolution of Society,* trans. Thomas McCarthy (Boston: Beacon Press, 1979), pp. 184–88.

For the PDL to serve as a principle of public justification, the satisfaction of the PDL must, like the satisfaction of any principle of legitimacy (e.g. the process of orderly elections), be *manifest* or clearly visible to members of the order in the actual workings of its institutions. The institutions of the democratic order must in other words be organized in such a way that they not only in fact satisfy the requirement of equal freedom and reasoned deliberation, but do so in such a way that members of the order recognize this satisfaction as having been achieved. Such manifest satisfaction of the PDL in turn provides a plausible basis for the *stability* of the democratic order over time, that is, for the ability of the order to remain democratic. In seeing that the institutions of the democratic order satisfy the announced principle of legitimacy of that order, members of the democratic society have plausible grounds for loyalty to that society and its arrangements. While the stability of capitalist democracy rests upon its ability to satisfy the interest in short-term material gain which it systematically generates, the stability of the democratic order rests upon the respect for individuals as free and equal that is expressed in its basic institutions, and upon the recognition of that respect by its members.[2]

Finally, this general conception of democratic society has consequences for the sorts of claims that members of a democratic order can make on one another. There are many such claims that can be made by free and equal participants in the exercise of sovereignty, but of particular importance is the claim to *autonomy*. Autonomy consists in the exercise of self-governing capacities, such as the capacities of understanding, imagining, reasoning, valuing, and desiring. Free persons have and are recognized as having such capacities, and in a political order centrally dedicated to securing the conditions of free deliberation for its members, those members can legitimately expect of that order that it not only permit but also encourage the exercise of such capacities, that is, that it permit and encourage autonomy. But since the basis of the claim to autonomy is the claim to the status of an equal member of a free association, to claim autonomy for oneself is to recognize the perfectly reciprocal and equally legitimate claims to autonomy by others. Thus the claim to individual autonomy is really a claim about how the social order should be constructed. It effectively

[2] The idea of manifestness and its relation to stability has been expressed in many different ways. See John Rawls, *A Theory of Justice* (Cambridge: Harvard University Press, 1971), §29 (on publicity and stability); and his more recent Dewey Lectures, "Kantian Constructivism in Moral Theory," *Journal of Philosophy*, vol. 57, no. 9 (September 1980), pp. 537–49; Habermas, *Communication and the Evolution of Society*, p. 186 (on "finding arrangements which can ground the presumption"); G. W. F. Hegel, *The Philosophy of Right*, trans. T. M. Knox (Oxford: Oxford University Press, 1952); and Karl Marx, *Capital*, vol. 1, trans. Ben Fowkes (Middlesex: Penguin, 1976), especially paras. 142–56 (on the role of self-consciousness in Ethical Life); paras. 211–28 (on the right of self-consciousness and the rule of law); and paras. 298–320 (on the role of the legislative body in relation to "the subjective moment in universal freedom"); and Marx, *Capital*, p. 173 (on the removal of the "veil . . . from the countenance of the social life-process"). Rousseau does not expressly state a requirement of manifestness or publicity, though it is natural to interpret his conception of the "general will" and his views about direct (non-representative) democracy as presupposing this idea. On the relationship between the general will, direct democracy, and stability, see Rousseau, *Social Contract*, Book 3, chs. 12–15.

consists in the acknowledgment of and accession to a social structure of *mutually* recognized autonomy.

The PDL thus requires an ongoing order of mutually assured and encouraged *autonomy* in which political decisions are *manifestly* based on the judgments of the members as *free* and *equal* persons. It requires that the expression of self-governing capacities operate both within the formal institutions of politics and in the affairs of daily life. And it requires that the democratic order *stably* satisfy the conditions of equal freedom and autonomy that give it definition.

Taken together, these conditions provide the basis for considering the more specific institutional requirements of the democratic order. Elaborating these requirements comprises the second element in our discussion of the democratic conception. That elaboration can proceed only in general outline. Like other political conceptions, the democratic conception states a broad framework of social cooperation. How exactly that framework will be expressed institutionally will vary under different conditions. In outlining the democratic conception our aim is to anticipate neither the details of such varied institutional expression nor the variety of conditions under which democratic institutions might arise. Our aim is only to state the basic requirements of a democratic political order, and in some cases to try to clarify the content of those requirements by outlining what they would imply under current conditions. In describing the institutional requirements of the democratic order, our discussion must therefore remain somewhat abstract and provisional. But it is worth underscoring that such abstract specification of basic institutional principles is a precondition for pursuing the important but subordinate task of providing a more detailed specification of institutions themselves. And however abstract and provisional the discussion here may be, it is worth underscoring as well that the various requirements on institutions within the democratic order do comprise a system, an interrelated set of constraints and conditions which together define a distinct social structure of coordination and power. They thus require one another for interpretation and justification, and this fact is reflected in our presentation here. While we take up various elements separately, as the presentation proceeds there will be need for reference back to the basic framework of principle, and for cross-reference among the different institutional conditions. Finally, the order in which the conditions are presented does not indicate any priority among them. Since they comprise a system, no such priority can be assigned.

With these provisos, the institutional requirements of the democratic order follow immediately:

1. Formal guarantee of the individual freedoms necessary to autonomy and reasoned public deliberation must be secured. Thus the basic liberties of thought, speech, association, assembly, and participation that might ordinarily be exercised by free individuals must be inviolate. By themselves, formal public liberties are notoriously incapable of addressing the distortions of politics by private advantage. But that plainly provides no argument for their destruction. Within the democratic order, politics would continue. There would still be

debate and disagreement over the direction of public policy and the proper ends of social life. For the free deliberative process among equals that lies at the core of the democratic order to proceed, individual expression and participation must be absolutely protected activities. And for the PDL's requirement of manifestness to be satisfied, it is important that the protections afforded such activities be part of the visible framework of social regulation—that is, that they assume the form of law.

It is worth emphasizing that such protection must extend significantly beyond traditional "political" liberties. Free public deliberation follows upon and itself requires the exercise of individual self-governing capacities in arenas that are not commonly recognized as political. That exercise in turn depends on the protection of freedom of expression, speech, belief, and thought within those arenas. Autonomy thus requires not only explicit political liberties and protections, but more personal ones as well. As a means of guaranteeing the exercise of autonomy, the scope of such protections must of course conform to the requirement that autonomy be recognized as mutual. Individual exercise of such self-governing capacities would not be protected at or beyond the point at which it constrains the autonomy of others. But within the democratic order, the fact that some forms of private activity or expression are offensive to the tastes and sensibilities of others within that order does not by itself provide any argument for curbing that activity or expression.[3]

2. While such protections of individual autonomy are a necessary condition for the social exercise of deliberative capacities, they are not sufficient. The democratic conception requires as well that the organized expression of political debate be recognized as a goal of a democratic order and be conducted in a manner attentive to the PDL's more general requirement of manifest equal freedom. Public assumption of the costs of competition among multiple political parties would be a natural way to provide such recognition consistent with the PDL's background requirements.

That the costs of group political activity should be publicly assumed follows from the requirement that the institutions of the democratic order *manifestly* respect the condition of equal freedom. As our discussion of capitalist democracy indicated, there are many reasons to believe that in the absence of public funding, both political activity and the results of that activity will reflect the distribution of private resources among individuals in the political system. Some guarantee against such distortion is needed if the democratic order is to be one in which political outcomes are to reflect the judgments of its members. But in a democratic order it is not enough that political outcomes *in fact* reflect the political judgments of its members. It is also crucial, as the condition of

---

[3] For a classic treatment, see John Stuart Mill's *On Liberty* in John Stuart Mill, *Utilitarianism, On Liberty, and Considerations on Representative Government*, ed. H. B. Acton (New York: E. P. Dutton, 1972), especially chs. 2–3. For more recent considerations of the scope and rationale of individual liberties, see John Hart Ely, *Democracy and Distrust: A Theory of Judicial Review* (Cambridge: Harvard University Press, 1980); and especially Ronald Dworkin, *Taking Rights Seriously* (Cambridge: Harvard University Press, 1977), in particular ch. 12.

manifestness emphasizes, that this fact be *evident* to the participants in the order. The organization of the political arena must itself be a source of confidence
in the satisfaction of the requirement of political equality. Public assumption of
the costs of deliberation is needed to secure this confidence, although it is not
sufficient on its own.

The second aspect of meeting this requirement, that such public assumption
of the costs of deliberation take the specific form of a subsidy to *competitive political parties,* is also based on the PDL. As indicated already, the achievement
of a democratic order does not imply the end of politics. Disagreement over the
ends of social life continues, and it would be expected that questions about the
proper level of current savings, the rate of economic growth, and the allocation
of public resources to different ends would still be objects of social concern and
public debate. In helping to shape that concern into coherent public debate, the
role of competitive political parties is crucial, although not for the reasons commonly offered. In one especially important traditional view of party competition, such competition is necessary to the winnowing out of "bad" or "untrue"
political views. Here the aims of the political order are defined as the achievement of the "best" policy outcomes, and the value of political party competition is understood in terms of the value of achieving those aims.

But as indicated by the examples of possible disagreement within the democratic order, under democratic conditions the "truth" of different policy views
is a notion without clear content. It is not clear, for example, that there is a
single "correct" level of current savings or economic growth that should be
sought or achieved, or that there is a "correct" pattern of allocation of social
resources between education and health. Even if there were "correct" solutions
to such problems, it is not clear what sort of political arrangement, if any, could
guarantee their achievement. And even if there were some arrangement that
could guarantee their achievement, that arrangement might very well be unacceptably oppressive.

While not relying on a view of party competition as necessary for producing
"correct" policy outcomes, the democratic conception nevertheless supports
such competition as an expression of a democratic order's commitment to the
enhancement of deliberative capacities in public arenas. Satisfying the conditions of reasonable deliberation requires that public discussion proceed against
a background of alternative coherent views. The presentation of such views
comprises one function of political parties. Within the democratic conception,
the coherent statement of alternative policy choices is thus not taken as an end
in itself, nor as a means to guaranteeing correct choices, but as a precondition
for public deliberation. Political parties and their competition are required
not to discover the "truth" of correct policy, but for the exercise of autonomy
itself.

The third aspect of the requirement regarding political parties, that the
democratic order provide for the competition of a multiplicity of such parties,
follows directly from this conception of their role. The subsidy of one party
alone would, of course, make a mockery of the commitment of a democratic order to an equal consideration of views, since the views of the single party would

in any case determine the outcome of such consideration. But the existence of several parties is important for another reason as well. Just as the total absence of political parties would for most citizens effectively block the consideration of many issues of public concern, so too the existence of only a single party—even one with a highly coherent program and set of views—would impair the process of comparing and evaluating alternative policy choices that is required for reasoned political judgment.[4]

As a public expression of the principle of free deliberation, public funding of party costs would logically be tied to allegiance to that principle. It would violate the principles of the democratic order to divert the monies of that order to groups actively opposed to its very existence. But this in no way precludes the legal existence of such groups, and indeed the legality of their existence at the level of expression and peaceful participation would have to be assured. Thus, the existence for example of a fascist party would be permitted, but would not be subsidized with public funds.

Additional limitations on the collective assumption of the costs of party competition might be built into the democratic order through political judgments on the aggregate number of parties to enjoy such subsidy, the level of subsidy, and the requirements of achieving "public" party status. Such judgments would in turn have to be the products of social deliberation.

Within a democratic order, meeting the condition of free competition would finally require the elimination of any formal barriers to equal participation and representation. The participation requirement is effectively met through the guarantee of formal liberties of expression and participation already noted.

---

[4] The point about the relationship between diversity and reasoned judgment is made powerfully in Mill's *On Liberty:* "But it is not the minds of heretics that are deteriorated most by the ban placed on all inquiry which does not end in the orthodox conclusions. The greatest harm done is to those who are not heretics, and whose whole mental development is cramped, and their reason cowed, by fear of heresy. Who can compute what the world loses in the multitude of promising intellects combined with timid characters, who dare not follow out any bold, vigorous, independent train of thought, lest it should land them in something which would admit of being considered irreligious or immoral? . . . Not that it is solely, or chiefly, to form great thinkers, that free thinking is required. On the contrary, it is as much and even more indispensable to enable average human beings to attain the mental stature which they are capable of. There have been, and may again be, great individual thinkers in a general atmosphere of mental slavery. But there never has been, nor ever will be, in that atmosphere an intellectually active people" (p. 94). For more recent discussion specifically attentive to the function of parties, see Ernest Mandel, *From Stalinism to Eurocommunism: The Bitter Fruits of "Socialism in One Country,"* trans. Jon Rothschild (London: New Left Books, 1978). Mandel comments: "But under these conditions, the essential function of the state in post-capitalist society is to determine *which* priorities and preferences should orient the plan. There are only two possible institutional variants. Either the selection of these priorities is imposed on the producer-consumers by forces outside themselves . . . or else they are made democratically by the mass of citizens, the producer-consumers themselves. Since there is no material possibility for this mass to choose among 10,000 variants of the plan (nor, for that matter, is there any possibility of their elaborating 10,000 different and coherent general plans each year), the real content of socialist democracy is indissolubly linked to the possibility of their choosing among *certain* coherent alternatives for the general plan. . . . The formulation of such alternatives presupposes precisely a multi-party system, with free access to the mass media and free debate by the mass of the population. It is only under these conditions that the enormous potential for creative initiative that exists among a highly skilled and cultivated proletariat can be fully liberated" (pp. 123–24).

Under conditions of representative democracy, the representation requirement might be achieved through the establishment of a system of proportional representation.[5] While other systems of representation may plausibly claim to meet the requirement as well, proportional representation has the merit of manifestly satisfying the requirement that the views of individual members of the political order be given equal weight. In addition, the exercise of deliberative capacities in social arenas is enhanced by the ability to judge as far as possible the capacity of different parties to act as responsible agents of representation. Since proportional representation ensures that parties with significant support actually have the opportunity to participate in government, it helps to ensure that deliberation over support for those parties is more fully informed.

3. Since the absence of material deprivation is a precondition for free and unconstrained deliberation, a basic level of material satisfaction, which would be more precisely specified through a free process of deliberation, would be required for all members of the political order. This might at first be satisfied through the achievement of full employment, but since the goal is not employment per se but the absence of material deprivation, the democratic order might soon devote itself, within conditions of full employment, to the reduction of the labor time necessary to secure an acceptable level of material well-being for all. Such reduction would in obvious ways enhance the conditions of individual autonomy and social deliberation by increasing the availability of free time within conditions of basic material satisfaction.[6]

[5] A system of proportional representation (PR) is a system in which the votes of participating citizens are directly reflected in the composition of legislative bodies. Such a system can be clarified by its contrast with the "winner take all" balloting and representation procedure of the United States. In the United States, for example, if 50 percent of the participating electorate vote for a Democratic candidate for the House of Representatives, 40 percent vote for a Republican, and the remaining 10 percent divide their votes among a variety of lesser parties, then the Democratic candidate wins the seat. The winner takes all. If the results above were consistent across districts, a Democrat would win in each district, and the composition of the House would be 100 percent Democratic. If the same pattern of voting obtained within a pure PR system, on the other hand, then the composition of the legislative body would be 50 percent Democratic and 40 percent Republican, with 10 percent of the seats divided among the lesser parties. The overall pattern of voting would thus actually be reflected in the composition of the legislature. It is common for states to impose minimal barriers to representation within PR schemes. The Federal Republic of Germany, for example, has a "5 percent rule," meaning that to have any representation within the Bundestag a party must garner at least 5 percent of the national vote. Even on such modified plans, however, what distinguishes PR systems of representation from "winner take all" systems is the way in which the votes of participating citizens are aggregated to social decisions. Within "winner take all" systems like that featured in the United States, the final distribution of representation (Democrats versus Republicans versus other parties) may not and usually does not reflect the aggregate levels of support for different representing parties. Within a PR system, the procedure for allocating seats comes closer to providing the basis for a distribution of representation that does reflect these aggregate levels of support. By providing representation for political parties that do not win majorities in any single district, a PR system removes a formidable obstacle to the formation of "third parties," and thus helps to ensure representation of minority views.

[6] See Karl Marx, *Capital,* vol. 3 (Moscow: Progress Publishers, 1971). Marx comments: "In fact, the realm of freedom actually begins only where labour which is determined by necessity and mundane considerations ceases; thus in the very nature of things it lies beyond the sphere of

Material inequalities are not inconsistent with such a requirement of basic material satisfaction for all. But as noted repeatedly, material inequalities can subvert a structure of free and equal public deliberation by translating into sharply unequal capacities for political action. This is especially a problem in view of the requirement of full formal political freedom (requirements 1 and 2 above). Since the democratic conception prohibits restrictions on political expression, it must set limits on the material background of that expression. Thus the democratic order would have to discriminate between those inequalities that were consistent with the conditions of the order and those that were not. The discrimination between different material inequalities would have to take the form of permitting those material inequalities that contribute to the material well-being of those least well-off.[7] It is worth emphasizing that the operation of such a principle of distributive equity does not disturb the requirement of providing basic levels of material satisfaction for all members of the democratic order. Nor, surely, does it mandate the proliferation of inequalities within that order. Rather, it comes into play as a restrictive control on inequalities, a control that is itself attentive to the requirements of the PDL. This may be clarified by briefly indicating the sorts of conditions under which the principle might come into play, and then indicating its rationale within the democratic order.

Take the example of material incentives. If attracting people to some sorts of work requires special material incentives, the PDL does not provide an absolute and general bar to their use. It does, however, require some evident connection between the existence of such incentives and the material well-being of those who do not receive them. The point of such incentives in a democratic order is not per se to reward the skilled or the talented, but to encourage contributions to the overall level of material satisfaction. For incentives to be justified, it must be shown that the material inequalities they generate contribute to the material well-being of the least well-off. That is, it must be demonstrated that they would be even less well-off, in absolute terms, under a scheme that did not feature the particular incentives or material inequalities whose justification is sought.

The rationale for limiting inequalities in this particular way follows from the democratic conception's requirement of a manifest structure of equal freedom. Requiring that incentives contribute to the well-being of the least well-off respects the equal status of the least well-off within the political order. It does so by taking improvements in their material position as a necessary precondition for justifying the existence of any kind of material inequality.

---

actual material production. . . . Beyond it [the sphere of material production] begins that development of human energy which is an end in itself, the true realm of freedom, which, however, can blossom forth only with this realm of necessity as its basis. The shortening of the working day is its basic prerequisite" (p. 820).

[7] As stated, our second principle of distributional equality is very nearly identical to Rawls's "Difference Principle." Rawls states this principle as follows: "Social and economic inequalities are to be arranged so that they are . . . to the greatest benefit of the least advantaged." Rawls, *Theory of Justice*, p. 302. Our use of the principle is constrained by conditions 4 and 5 of the democratic order (i.e. public control of investment and workplace democracy). It is also limited in its application to material goods.

Such stringent requirements on distributional equality may be controversial. As such, they provide occasion for anticipating what may be a recurring objection to the democratic conception outlined here, namely, that instead of enhancing the exercise of democratic judgment, such a conception actually constrains it. Thus the requirement of distributive equity might be thought inconsistent with the general concerns of the democratic conception, since it may appear to "constrain" the exercise of democratic judgment in the area of material equality. Suppose that members of the democratic order wanted to allow greater material inequalities. Does it not violate the idea of a democratic order to constrain such desires by insisting on the satisfaction of the requirement of distributive equity?

In responding to this concern, it might be useful to notice first how such a question could be generalized to any of the institutional requirements presented thus far. Thus it could equally well be argued that it violates the idea of a democratic order to require that there be protection of individual political liberties. After all, could it not be decided "democratically" that some minority group should be excluded from the protections of those liberties? No, it could not.

The PDL does not specify an initial starting point from which any departures are legitimate if they are made from that point according, for example, to a requirement of majority rule. It specifies a *standing requirement* of an ongoing order, and thus requires that democratic conditions be preserved over time. Insofar as the PDL requires political liberties, it requires that those liberties be preserved. If they are not preserved, then the order is no longer democratic, and therefore the denial of such liberties is itself undemocratic, since such denial violates the very principles which make the existing procedures of social choice legitimate. Once the principle of individual liberties is violated, then individuals no longer retain their status as participants in an order of equal freedom.

The same may be said of the requirement of distributional equity. It too is a standing requirement of the ongoing democratic order. It too is not merely a condition to be secured at some starting point of social deliberation. And its violation, like the violation of political liberties, cannot therefore be accorded legitimacy as a "democratic" act. A genuinely democratic order sets requirements on the structure of formal arenas of social deliberation, and on the material background of those formal arenas. Both sorts of requirement must continue to be satisfied if the order is to continue to express in its manifest structure the conditions of equal freedom and autonomy that give it definition.

4. As indicated already, the democratic conception requires the maintenance of conditions of formal political equality, but it requires as well attention to the material background of such formal structuring of political arenas. In part this attention is provided in the stipulation of public funding of party competition and the distributional measures just discussed. But as our previous discussion of capitalist democracy indicated, such measures are not adequate to address the structural constraints on political decision-making that accompany any system in which investment decisions remain in private hands. Investment is effectively the only guarantee of a society's future. If that future is not available as a

subject of social deliberation, then social deliberations are fundamentally constrained and incomplete. It was this point that provided a central focus in our discussion of capitalist democracy, and it is this point which must be directly addressed by the democratic order. That order cannot proceed under free and equal conditions if some of its members have a restrictive monopoly on decisions over the disposition of social surplus. The democratic conception therefore requires that formal political freedom, public funding of party competition, and distributional measures of the sort described be accompanied by public control of investment.

Such public control of the investment function must not in turn provide another occasion for removing control over the economy from arenas of democratic deliberation. Investment decisions must be made by a body either subject to control by a democratic legislative body or itself subject to direct democratic accountability. They cannot be the exclusive purview of some unaccountable administrative or police elite. For decisions over social surplus to be "public" means that those decisions are centralized and subject to national political debate, but it means as well that that debate cannot itself be constrained by other structures of decision-making or authority that members of the order do not enter as free and equal. Here again the role of political parties and the existence of grounds for debate within the political order are highlighted. There may well be serious disagreements as to the direction of investment—disagreements over the pattern and rates of growth, over the correct manner of "signaling" from firm to public authority, over the level of present surplus extraction necessary to sustain future growth, over the extent of present obligations to future generations. It is the task of the political arena to present these disagreements and the probable consequences of different policies in as coherent a fashion as possible, and thus facilitate reasoned choice and deliberation by the members of the order.[8]

Public control over investment does not imply a new principle of workers' sovereignty, embodied for example in a system of councils rooted in the workplace. A potential problem with councilist organization is that producers' interests are, as such, particular interests, and representation of interests organized exclusively on this basis may tend to select out those social interests (such as those of communities or those of consumers) not easily organized from the standpoint of the workplace. This problem may be susceptible to resolution within the framework of democratic legitimacy. Organizational experimentation would be needed to determine specific forms of coordination between decisions of particular enterprises and broader political judgments of the system as a whole. The objection to a workplace-based form of council democracy is not one of principle, but of political judgment. But the objection indicates that the defense of this particular form should not itself be made a matter of principle.[9]

---

[8] See remarks of Ernest Mandel cited in note 4 above.

[9] A similar point is made in Rudolf Bahro, *The Alternative in Eastern Europe,* trans. David Fernbach (London: New Left Books, 1978), p. 441. See as well related discussion in Poulantzas,

5. To qualify this idea of council democracy, however, is not at all to qualify the signal importance of workplace democracy for the democratic conception. Rather than serving as the organizational basis of a democratic order, however, worker-controlled enterprises are seen here as elements *within* that order, and their place and importance are interpreted in terms of the good of autonomy.

A minimal condition required for the satisfaction of mutual autonomy within the individual enterprise is the abolition of all positions which by their very definition preclude the exercise of self-governing capacities. This requirement of autonomy is not satisfied by the mere availability of choice of jobs, since that choice may range over alternatives which themselves involve subordination or the performance of relatively mechanical tasks. Rather, the principle requires the redefinition and reorganization of work in a way that offers to each participating individual the opportunity to exercise self-governing capacities. What this requires in detail would be expected to vary between different sorts of work. But at the level of general principle, autonomy within the workplace demands the elimination of traditional hierarchical forms of control of the labor process, most centrally the distinction between the planning and execution of production tasks. A structure of workplace democracy directly satisfies this requirement. It ensures that there are no positions which by their very specification deny the exercise of self-governing capacities, since all positions include participation in the functions of controlling the workplace itself. In such a structure of decision-making, the autonomy of some individuals is not realized at the expense of others. Workplace democracy thus extends the PDL's requirement of an order of mutually assured autonomy, and helps to satisfy the condition that such autonomy be expressed within important arenas of everyday life, as well as within the formal arenas of politics.[10]

Such an argument for the centrality of workplace democracy to a democratic conception should be distinguished from an argument that less hierarchical forms of work organization are desirable because they contribute to the material productivity of social systems. Such productivist claims have some plausibility. Less hierarchically organized work might be expected to generate greater enthusiasm among workers, and in any case would draw on the creative power

---

State, Power, Socialism, Part 5. For an opposing view, see Mandel, *From Stalinism to Eurocommunism,* particularly pp. 158–78. For a summary of debate on this point, see Perry Anderson, *Arguments Within English Marxism* (London: New Left Books, 1980), ch. 7.

[10] The need for producer control of the instruments of production is associated most squarely with Marx. See Karl Marx, *Grundrisse: Foundations of the Critique of Political Economy,* trans. Martin Nicolaus (New York: Random House, 1973), pp. 611–12 and 705–12 for particularly important statements of the argument that express concerns close to those we note. For a more recent Marxist view on the subject also analogous to our own, see Mihailo Markovic´, *The Contemporary Marx: Essays on Humanist Communism* (Bristol: Spokesman Books, 1974), especially ch. 12. For a version of the point as made within the liberal tradition, see John Stuart Mill, *Principles of Political Economy* (London and Toronto: University of Toronto Press, 1965). Mill comments: "The form of association, however, which if mankind continue to improve, must be expected in the end to predominate, is not that which can exist between a capitalist as chief, and workpeople without a voice in the management, but the association of the labourers themselves on terms of equality, collectively owning the capital with which they carry on their operations, and working under managers elected and removable by themselves." See generally Book 4, ch. 7, §6.

of a broader pool of individuals than does traditionally organized and relatively mechanical work. But the importance of workplace democracy to the democratic conception does not depend on the truth of such speculations. It can freely acknowledge that as people shift among different types of work and spend time debating the problems facing a particular workplace and the relationship between that workplace and the democratic order, there may in fact be some loss of potential output (even if total output were growing). If there were such a loss, by conventional criteria workplace democracy could be regarded as "inefficient," but that is because those criteria apply only to losses or gains in material output, and not to losses or gains in human autonomy. The defense of workplace democracy provided by the democratic conception no more rests upon its being the most materially productive form of social order than the familiar defenses of capitalism as preferable to slavery depend for their force on judgments about the relative productivity of wage labor and slave labor.

The PDL's requirement of workplace democracy may be further clarified by noting its relation to received understandings of "meaningful work." It is sometimes said that work must be made "meaningful," but the idea is an ambiguous one, both because there are many grounds for finding meaning in work and because there is no final way of ensuring against alienation. Work may be regarded as meaningful in view of its contribution to some overall social good, or because it furthers the realization of divine purpose in the mundane world. The democratic conception respects these sources of meaning. Members of the democratic order may for example regard their work as contributing to the preservation of that order, and those who are religious may continue to see their activity as expressing a divine plan. But the conception also recognizes another source of meaningfulness, namely, that many find activities meaningful not because they contribute to a broader purpose, but because they draw on distinctively human capacities for thought, judgment, imagination, and reasoning. In its requirement of workplace democracy, the democratic conception is institutionally attentive to these other sources of meaning.

Finally it should be noted that the existence of workplace democracy does not violate the requirement of public control over investment decisions. Decisions at the level of the individual workplace are made *within* the framework provided by that broader social judgment, although they may of course contribute to the formation of that judgment. In a capitalist economy, decisions over the disposition of the social surplus and decisions about the organization of the production process are both subject to the control of capitalists. Property as control of the surplus and property as control of production are united in such systems. In the democratic order these two aspects of property are kept separate from one another. Investment decisions are subject to public debate and administration. Control over the organization of work is subject to workplace democracy.

6. Even when coupled with the requirements of distributive equity, the removal of institutional barriers to free deliberation within the polity or the economy does not ensure that individuals might not come to such arenas with clear

prior disabilities resulting from material inequality. The democratic conception requires a commitment to a principle of "equal opportunity" in the sense that it requires commitment to the social removal of all such materially based disabilities. These commitments follow from the PDL's basic framework of equal freedom, a framework requiring that the absence of prior claims of advantage be manifest in the institutions of a democratic order.

This principle of equal opportunity has, at the minimum, two consequences.

The first is that education must be freely available under such conditions that residual material inequalities in the democratic order would not determine individual life chances. This not only means that free public education must be available up to a level sufficient to assure that the deliberative capacities of individuals can be exercised in public arenas. It requires as well that any sorts of special training that are a precondition for better paying jobs also be available without cost to the trainee.

The second consequence that follows is the required availability of child care. The conditions of the democratic order as an order of mutual autonomy are violated if the preparation or education of individuals for the free exercise of deliberative capacities in public itself imposes special barriers to the autonomous activities of any select subgroup of adult members of the order. Attention to the distribution of child-rearing costs is required in view of the historic division of labor within the household, where women have traditionally assumed the major burden of child care and nurture.[11] Insofar as the household is itself an arena for the exercise of autonomy, public authority cannot be permitted to undermine or intrude directly in that arena. But barriers to simultaneously raising children and maintaining public autonomy must be removed so far as possible. To ensure against a double burden for women, the costs of child care at a commonly determined level sufficient to assure the minimal conditions of public life for responsible parents would have to be collectively assumed. Equal opportunity for all members of the political order to participate actively in the order would thus be sought as a shared general social principle, but with due attention to the historical conditions that have imposed de facto limits on women's participation. Such attention to the dangers that traditional constraints on women pose to their status as equal members of the political order reflects the general commitment of the democratic conception of equal freedom to address informal noninstitutional barriers to the exercise of that freedom, as well as formal institutional ones.

---

[11] For useful recent discussions of this problem see Michèle Barrett, *Women's Oppression Today: Problems in Marxist Feminist Analysis* (London: New Left Books, 1980); and Maxine Molyneux, "Socialist Societies Old and New: Progress Toward Women's Emancipation?," *Monthly Review*, vol. 34, no. 3 (July–August 1982), pp. 56–100.

28.

Persistent Minorities and Fairness

LANI GUINIER

I have always wanted to be a civil rights lawyer. This lifelong ambition is based on a deep-seated commitment to democratic fair play—to playing by the rules as long as the rules are fair. When the rules seem unfair, I have worked to change them, not subvert them. When I was eight years old, I was a Brownie. I was especially proud of my uniform, which represented a commitment to good citizenship and good deeds. But one day, when my Brownie group staged a hat-making contest, I realized that uniforms are only as honorable as the people who wear them. The contest was rigged. The winner was assisted by her milliner mother, who actually made the winning entry in full view of all the participants. At the time, I was too young to be able to change the rules, but I was old enough to resign, which I promptly did.

To me, fair play means that the rules encourage everyone to play. They should reward those who win, but they must be acceptable to those who lose. The central theme of my academic writing is that not all rules lead to elemental fair play. Some even commonplace rules work against it.

The professional milliner competing with amateur Brownies stands as an example of rules that are patently rigged or patently subverted. Yet, sometimes, even when rules are perfectly fair in form, they serve in practice to exclude particular groups from meaningful participation. When they do not encourage everyone to play, or when, over the long haul, they do not make the losers feel as good about the outcomes as the winners, they can seem as unfair as the milliner who makes the winning hat for her daughter.

Sometimes, too, we construct rules that force us to be divided into winners and losers when we might have otherwise joined together. This idea was cogently expressed by my son, Nikolas, when he was four years old, far exceeding the thoughtfulness of his mother when she was an eight-year-old Brownie. While I was writing one of my law journal articles, Nikolas and I had a conversation about voting prompted by a *Sesame Street Magazine* exercise. The magazine pictured six children: four children had raised their hands because they wanted to play tag; two had their hands down because they wanted to play hide-and-seek. The magazine asked its readers to count the number of children whose hands were raised and then decide what game the children would play.

Nikolas quite realistically replied, "They will play both. First they will play tag. Then they will play hide-and-seek." Despite the magazine's "rules," he was right. To children, it is natural to take turns. The winner may get to play first or more often, but even the "loser" gets something. His was a positive-sum solution that many adult rule-makers ignore.

The traditional answer to the magazine's problem would have been a zero-sum solution: "The children—all the children—will play tag, and only tag." As a zero-sum solution, everything is seen in terms of "I win; you lose." The conventional answer relies on winner-take-all majority rule, in which the tag players, as the majority, win the right to decide for all the children what game to play. The hide-and-seek preference becomes irrelevant. The numerically more powerful majority choice simply subsumes minority preferences.

In the conventional case, the majority that rules gains all the power and the minority that loses gets none. For example, two years ago Brother Rice High School in Chicago held two senior proms. It was not planned that way. The prom committee at Brother Rice, a boys' Catholic high school, expected just one prom when it hired a disc jockey, picked a rock band, and selected music for the prom by consulting student preferences. Each senior was asked to list his three favorite songs, and the band would play the songs that appeared most frequently on the lists.

Seems attractively democratic. But Brother Rice is predominantly white, and the prom committee was all white. That's how they got two proms. The black seniors at Brother Rice felt so shut out by the "democratic process" that they organized their own prom. As one black student put it: "For every vote we had, there were eight votes for what they wanted. . . . [W]ith us being in the minority we're always outvoted. It's as if we don't count."

Some embittered white seniors saw things differently. They complained that the black students should have gone along with the majority: "The majority makes a decision. That's the way it works."

In a way, both groups were right. From the white students' perspective, this was ordinary decisionmaking. To the black students, majority rule sent the message: "we don't count" is the "way it works" for minorities. In a racially divided society, majority rule may be perceived as majority tyranny.

That is a large claim, and I do not rest my case for it solely on the actions of the prom committee in one Chicago high school. To expand the range of the argument, I first consider the ideal of majority rule itself, particularly as reflected in the writings of James Madison and other founding members of our Republic. These early democrats explored the relationship between majority rule and democracy. James Madison warned, "If a majority be united by a common interest, the rights of the minority will be insecure." The tyranny of the majority, according to Madison, requires safeguards to protect "one part of the society against the injustice of the other part."

For Madison, majority tyranny represented the great danger to our early constitutional democracy. Although the American revolution was fought against the tyranny of the British monarch, it soon became clear that there was another tyranny to be avoided. The accumulations of all powers in the same hands, Madison warned, "whether of one, a few, or many, and whether hereditary, self-appointed, or elective, may justly be pronounced the very definition of tyranny."

As another colonist suggested in papers published in Philadelphia, "We have been so long habituated to a jealousy of tyranny from monarchy and aristocracy, that we have yet to learn the dangers of it from democracy." Despotism had to be opposed "whether it came from Kings, Lords or the people."

The debate about majority tyranny reflected Madison's concern that the majority may not represent the whole. In a homogeneous society, the interest of the majority would likely be that of the minority also. But in a heterogeneous community, the majority may not represent all competing interests. The majority is likely to be self-interested and ignorant or indifferent to the concerns of the minority. In such case, Madison observed, the assumption that the majority represents the minority is "altogether fictitious."

Yet even a self-interested majority can govern fairly if it cooperates with the minority. One reason for such cooperation is that the self-interested majority values the principle of reciprocity. The self-interested majority worries that the minority may attract defectors from the majority and become the next governing majority. The Golden Rule principle of reciprocity functions to check the tendency of a self-interested majority to act tyrannically.

So the argument for the majority principle connects it with the value of reciprocity: You cooperate when you lose in part because members of the current majority will cooperate when they lose. The conventional case for the fairness of majority rule is that it is not really the rule of a fixed group—The Majority—on all issues; instead it is the rule of shifting majorities, as the losers at one time or on one issue join with others and become part of the governing coalition at another time or on another issue. The result will be a fair system of mutually beneficial cooperation. I call a majority that rules but does not dominate a Madisonian Majority.

The problem of majority tyranny arises, however, when the self-interested majority does not need to worry about defectors. When the majority is fixed and permanent, there are no checks on its ability to be overbearing. A majority that does not worry about defectors is a majority with total power.

In such a case, Madison's concern about majority tyranny arises. In a heterogeneous community, any faction with total power might subject "the minority to the caprice and arbitrary decisions of the majority, who instead of consulting the interest of the whole community collectively, attend sometimes to partial and local advantages."

"What remedy can be found in a republican Government, where the majority must ultimately decide," argued Madison, but to ensure "that no one common interest or passion will be likely to unite a majority of the whole number in an unjust pursuit." The answer was to disaggregate the majority to ensure checks and balances or fluid, rotating interests. The minority needed protection against an overbearing majority, so that "a common sentiment is less likely to be felt, and the requisite concern less likely to be formed, by a majority of the whole."

Political struggles would not be simply a contest between rulers and people; the political struggles would be among the people themselves. The work of government was not to transcend different interests but to reconcile them. In an ideal democracy, the people would rule, but the minorities would also be protected against the power of majorities. Again, where the rules of decisionmaking protect the minority, the Madisonian Majority rules without dominating.

But if a group is unfairly treated, for example, when it forms a racial minority, *and* if the problems of unfairness are not cured by conventional assumptions about majority rule, then what is to be done? The answer is that we may need an *alternative* to winner-take-all majoritarianism. . . . I describe the alternative, which, with Nikolas's help, I now call the "principle of taking turns." In a racially divided society, this principle does better than simple majority rule if it accommodates the values of self-government, fairness, deliberation, compromise, and consensus that lie at the heart of the democratic ideal.

In my legal writing, I follow the caveat of James Madison and other early American democrats. I explore decisionmaking rules that might work in a multi-racial society to ensure that majority rule does not become majority tyranny. I pursue voting systems that might disaggregate The Majority so that it does not exercise power unfairly or tyrannically. I aspire to a more cooperative political style of decisionmaking to enable all of the students at Brother Rice to feel comfortable attending the same prom. In looking to create Madisonian Majorities, I pursue a positive-sum, taking-turns solution.

Structuring decisionmaking to allow the minority "a turn" may be necessary to restore the reciprocity ideal when a fixed majority refuses to cooperate with the minority. If the fixed majority loses its incentive to follow the Golden Rule principle of shifting majorities, the minority never gets to take a turn. Giving the minority a turn does not mean the minority gets to rule; what it does mean is that the minority gets to influence decisionmaking and the majority rules more legitimately.

Instead of automatically rewarding the preferences of the monolithic majority, a taking-turns approach anticipates that the majority rules, but is not overbearing. Because those with 51 percent of the votes are not assured 100 percent of the power, the majority cooperates with, or at least does not tyrannize, the minority.

The sports analogy of "I win; you lose" competition within a political hierarchy makes sense when only one team can win; Nikolas's intuition that it is often possible to take turns suggests an alternative approach. Take family decisionmaking, for example. It utilizes a taking-turns approach. When parents sit around the kitchen table deciding on a vacation destination or activities for a rainy day, often they do not simply rely on a show of hands, especially if that means that the older children always prevail or if affinity groups among the children (those who prefer movies to video games, or those who prefer baseball to playing cards) never get to play their activity of choice. Instead of allowing the majority simply to rule, the parents may propose that everyone take turns, going to the movies one night and playing video games the next. Or as Nikolas proposes, they might do both on a given night.

Taking turns attempts to build consensus while recognizing political or social differences, and it encourages everyone to play. The taking-turns approach gives those with the most support more turns, but it also legitimates the outcome from each individual's perspective, including those whose views are shared only by a minority.

In the end, I do not believe that democracy should encourage rule by the powerful—even a powerful majority. Instead, the ideal of democracy promises a fair discussion among self-defined equals about how to achieve our common aspirations. To redeem that promise, we need to put the idea of taking turns and disaggregating the majority at the center of our conception of representation. Particularly as we move into the twenty-first century as a more highly diversified citizenry, it is essential that we consider the ways in which voting and representational systems succeed or fail at encouraging Madisonian Majorities.

To use Nikolas's terminology, "it is no fair" if a fixed, tyrannical majority excludes or alienates the minority. It is no fair if a fixed, tyrannical majority monopolizes all the power all the time. It is no fair if we engage in the periodic ritual of elections, but only the permanent majority gets to choose who is elected. Where we have tyranny by The Majority, we do not have genuine democracy.

My life's work, with the essential assistance of people like Nikolas, has been to try to find the rules that can best bring us together as a democratic society. Some of my ideas about democratic fair play were grossly mischaracterized in the controversy over my nomination to be Assistant Attorney General for Civil Rights. Trying to find rules to encourage fundamental fairness inevitably raises the question posed by Harvard Professor Randall Kennedy in a summary of this controversy: "What is required to create political institutions that address the needs and aspirations of all Americans, not simply whites, who have long enjoyed racial privilege, but people of color who have long suffered racial exclusion from policymaking forums?" My answer, as Professor Kennedy suggests, varies by situation. But I have a predisposition, reflected in my son's yearning for a positive-sum solution, to seek an integrated body politic in which all perspectives are represented and in which all people work together to find common ground. I advocate empowering voters and their representatives in ways that give even minority voters a chance to influence legislative outcomes.

But those in the majority do not lose; they simply learn to take turns. This is a positive-sum solution that allows all voters to feel that they participate meaningfully in the decisionmaking process. This is a positive-sum solution that makes legislative outcomes more legitimate.

• • •

I struggle to conceptualize the representatives' relationship with voters to make that relationship more dynamic and interactive.

It is in the course of this struggle that I made my much maligned references to "the authenticity assumption." Authenticity is a concept I describe within my general criticism of conventional empowerment strategies. The Voting Rights Act expressly provides that black and Latino voters must be afforded an equal opportunity "to participate in the political process and to elect representatives of their choice." The question is: which candidates are the representatives of choice of black or Latino voters?

Authenticity subsumes two related but competing views to answer that question. The first version of authenticity seeks information from election results to learn how the voters perceive elected officials. In this view, voting behavior is key. Authentic representatives are simply those truly chosen by the people. The second authenticity assumption is that voters trust elected officials who "look like" or act like the voters themselves. In this view, authenticity refers to a candidate who shares common physical or cultural traits with constituents. In this aspect of authenticity, the nominally cultural becomes political.

Despite the importance of voter choice in assessing minority preferred or minority sponsored candidates, those who support the second authenticity assumption substitute the concept of presumptive or descriptive representativeness in which candidates who look like their constituents are on that basis alone presumed to be representative. In the name of authenticity, these observers have argued that the current voting rights litigation model is effective because it provides blacks or Latinos an opportunity to elect physically black or culturally Latino representatives. This is an understandable position, and I present it as such, but it is not *my* position. Indeed, I term it "a limited empowerment concept."

My preference is for the first view of authenticity, the one that focuses on the voter, not the candidate. In *Thornburg v. Gingles,* a 1986 Supreme Court opinion, Justice William Brennan stressed that it is the "status of the candidate as the chosen representative of a particular racial group, not the race of the candidate, that is important."

This leads to two complementary conclusions that are firmly embedded in the caselaw and the literature. First, white candidates can legitimately represent nonwhite voters if those voters elected them. I state this explicitly in my Michigan Law Review article, reproduced here in chapter 3. And second, the election of a black or Latino candidate or two will not defeat a voting rights lawsuit, especially if those black or Latino elected officials did not receive electoral support from their community. Just because a candidate is black does not mean that he or she is the candidate of choice of the black community.

Borrowing from the language of the statute, I say voters, not politicians, should count. And voters count most when voters can exercise a real choice based on what the candidates think and do rather than what the candidates look like.

• • •

Concern over majority tyranny has typically focused on the need to monitor and constrain the substantive policy outputs of the decisionmaking process. In my articles, however, I look at the *procedural* rules by which preferences are identified and counted. Procedural rules govern the process by which outcomes are decided. They are the rules by which the game is played.

I have been roundly, and falsely, criticized for focusing on outcomes. Outcomes are indeed relevant, but *not* because I seek to advance particular ends, such as whether the children play tag or hide-and-seek, or whether the band at Brother Rice plays rock music or rap. Rather, I look to outcomes as *evidence* of whether all the children—or all the high school seniors—feel that their choice is represented and considered. The purpose is not to guarantee "equal legislative outcomes"; equal opportunity to *influence* legislative outcomes regardless of race is more like it.

For these reasons, I sometimes explore alternatives to simple, winner-take-all majority rule. I do not advocate any one procedural rule as a universal panacea for unfairness. Nor do I propose these remedies primarily as judicial solutions. They can be adopted only in the context of litigation after the court first finds a legal violation.

Outside of litigation, I propose these approaches as political solutions if, depending on the local context, they better approximate the goals of democratic fair play. One such decisionmaking alternative is called cumulative voting, which could give all the students at Brother Rice multiple votes and allow them to distribute their votes in any combination of their choice. If each student could vote for ten songs, the students could plump or aggregate their votes to reflect the intensity of their preferences. They could put ten votes on one song; they could put five votes on two songs. If a tenth of the students opted to "cumulate" or plump all their votes for one song, they would be able to select one of every ten or so songs played at the prom. The black seniors could have done this if they chose to, but so could any other cohesive group of sufficient size. In this way, the songs preferred by a majority would be played most often, but the songs the minority enjoyed would also show up on the play list.

Under cumulative voting, voters get the same number of votes as there are seats or options to vote for, and they can then distribute their votes in any combination to reflect their preferences. Like-minded voters can vote as a solid bloc or, instead, form strategic, cross-racial coalitions to gain mutual benefits. This system is emphatically not racially based; it allows voters to organize themselves on whatever basis they wish.

Corporations use this system to ensure representation of minority shareholders on corporate boards of directors. Similarly, some local municipal and county governments have adopted cumulative voting to ensure representation of minority voters. Instead of awarding political power to geographic units called districts, cumulative voting allows voters to cast ballots based on what they think rather than where they live.

Cumulative voting is based on the principle of one person–one vote because each voter gets the same total number of votes. Everyone's preferences are counted equally. It is not a particularly radical idea; thirty states either require or permit corporations to use this election system. Cumulative voting is certainly not antidemocratic because it emphasizes the importance of voter choice in selecting public or social policy. And it is neither liberal nor conservative. Both the Reagan and Bush administrations approved cumulative voting schemes pursuant to the Voting Rights Act to protect the rights of racial- and language-minority voters.

But, as in Chilton County, Alabama, which now uses cumulative voting to elect both the school board and the county commission, any politically cohesive group can vote strategically to win representation. Groups of voters win representation depending on the exclusion threshold, meaning the percentage of votes needed to win one seat or have the band play one song. That threshold can be set case by case, jurisdiction by jurisdiction, based on the size of minority groups that make compelling claims for representation.

Normally the exclusion threshold in a head-to-head contest is 50 percent, which means that only groups that can organize a majority can get elected. But if multiple seats (or multiple songs) are considered simultaneously, the exclusion threshold is considerably reduced. For example, in Chilton County, with seven seats elected simultaneously on each governing body, the threshold of exclusion is now one-eighth. Any group with the solid support of one-eighth the voting population cannot be denied representation. This is because any self-identified minority can plump or cumulate all its votes for one candidate. Again, minorities are not defined solely in racial terms.

As it turned out in Chilton County, both blacks and Republicans benefited from this new system. The school board and commission now each have three white Democrats, three white Republicans, and one black Democrat. Previously, when each seat was decided in a head-to-head contest, the majority not only ruled but monopolized. Only white Democrats were elected at every prior election during this century.

Similarly, if the black and white students at Brother Rice have very different musical taste, cumulative voting permits a positive-sum solution to enable both groups to enjoy one prom. The majority's preferences would be respected in that their songs would be played most often, but the black students could express the intensity of their preferences too. If the black students chose to plump all their votes on a few songs, their minority preferences would be recognized and played. Essentially, cumulative voting structures the band's repertoire to enable the students to take turns.

As a solution that permits voters to self-select their identities, cumulative voting also encourages cross-racial coalition building. No one is locked into a minority identity. Nor is anyone necessarily isolated by the identity they choose. Voters can strengthen their influence by forming coalitions to elect more than one representative or to select a range of music more compatible with the entire student body's preferences.

Women too can use cumulative voting to gain greater representation. Indeed, in other countries with similar, alternative voting systems, women are more likely to be represented in the national legislature. For example, in some Western European democracies, the national legislatures have as many as 37 percent female members compared to a little more than 5 percent in our Congress.

There is a final benefit from cumulative voting. It eliminates gerrymandering. By denying protected incumbents safe seats in gerrymandered districts, cumulative voting might encourage more voter participation. With greater interest-based electoral competition, cumulative voting could promote the political turnover sought by advocates of term limits. In this way, cumulative voting serves many of the same ends as periodic elections or rotation in office, a solution that Madison and others advocated as a means of protecting against permanent majority factions.

VI

CONSTITUTIONAL LIMITS ON MAJORITARIAN DECISION MAKING

29.

Judicial Review and the Representation of Interests

JOHN HART ELY

. . . My main point in using the examples has been to suggest a way in which what are sometimes characterized as two conflicting American ideals—the protection of popular government on the one hand, and the protection of minorities from denials of equal concern and respect on the other—in fact can be understood as arising from a common duty of representation. Once again, Madison said it early and well:

> I will add, as a fifth circumstance in the situation of the House of Representatives, restraining them from oppressive measures, that they can make no law which will not have its full operation on themselves and their friends, as well as on the great mass of society . . . If it be asked, what is to restrain the House of Representatives from making legal discriminations in favor of themselves and a particular class of the society? I answer: the genius of the whole system; the nature of just and constitutional laws; and above all, the vigilant and manly spirit which actuates the people of America . . .[1]

The remainder of this chapter will comprise three arguments in favor of a participation-oriented, representation-reinforcing approach to judicial review. The first will take longer than the others, since it will necessitate a tour, albeit brisk, of the Constitution itself. What this tour will reveal, contrary to the standard characterization of the Constitution as "an enduring but evolving statement of general values,"[2] is that in fact the selection and accommodation of substantive values is left almost entirely to the political process and instead the document is overwhelmingly concerned, on the one hand, with procedural fairness in the resolution of individual disputes (process writ small), and on the other, with what might capaciously be designated process writ large—with ensuring broad participation in the processes and distributions of government.[3]

---

[1] James Madison, *The Federalist* no. 57, at 385 (B. Wright ed. 1961).

[2] D. Wright, "The Role of the Judiciary: From *Marbury* to *Anderson*," 60 *Calif. L. Rev.* 1262, 1268 (1972). See also, e.g., Sandalow, "Judicial Protection of Minorities," 75 *Mich. L. Rev.* 1162, 1178 (1977); J. S. Wright, "Professor Bickel, the Scholarly Tradition, and the Supreme Court," 84 *Harv. L. Rev.* 769, 784 (1971); Murphy, "Constitutional Interpretation: The Art of the Historian, Magician, or Statesman?" 87 *Yale L. J.* 1752, 1764 (1978).

[3] I suppose one might argue that the reason so few values are singled out by the document for special substantive protection is that the various framers and ratifiers were assuming that that was a function the Supreme Court could be counted on to perform. This argument seems plainly fallacious. Judicial review was not even a clearly contemplated feature of the original Constitution (though it is certainly a bona fide feature of today's). Neither could anyone acquainted with the data argue that prior to Reconstruction the Court had been in the business of value definition long or clearly enough to suppose that the framers of the Fourteenth Amendment were framing against the assumption that that was its job.

An argument by way of *ejusdem generis* seems particularly justified in this case, since the constitutional provisions for which we are attempting to identify modes of supplying content, such as the Ninth Amendment and the Privileges or Immunities Clause, seem to have been included in a "we must have missed something here, so let's trust our successors to add what we missed" spirit. On my more expansive days, therefore, I am tempted to claim that the mode of review developed here represents the ultimate interpretivism.[4] Our review will tell us something else that may be even more relevant to the issue before us — that the few attempts the various framers *have* made to freeze substantive values by designating them for special protection in the document have been ill-fated, normally resulting in repeal, either officially or by interpretative pretense. This suggests a conclusion with important implications for the task of giving content to the document's more open-ended provisions, that preserving fundamental values is not an appropriate constitutional task.

The other two arguments are susceptible to briefer statement but are not less important. The first is that a representation-reinforcing approach to judicial review, unlike its rival value-protecting approach, is not inconsistent with, but on the contrary (and quite by design) entirely supportive of, the underlying premises of the American system of representative democracy. The second is that such an approach, again in contradistinction to its rival, involves tasks that courts, as experts on process and (more important) as political outsiders, can sensibly claim to be better qualified and situated to perform than political officials.

THE NATURE OF THE UNITED STATES CONSTITUTION

"In the United States the basic charter of the law-making process is found in a written constitution . . . [W]e should resist the temptation to clutter up that document with amendments relating to substantive matters . . . [Such attempts] involve the obvious unwisdom of trying to solve tomorrow's problems today. But their more insidious danger lies in the weakening effect they would have on the moral force of the Constitution itself."

—*Lon Fuller*[5]

---

[4] As I've indicated, I don't think this terminological question is either entirely coherent or especially important. Obviously the approach recommended is neither "interpretivist" in the usual sense (of treating constitutional clauses as self-contained units) nor "noninterpretivist" in the usual sense (of seeking the principal stuff of constitutional judgment in one's rendition of society's fundamental values rather than in the document's broader themes). What counts is not whether it is "really" a broad interpretivism or rather a position that does not fall entirely in either camp, but whether it is capable of keeping faith with the document's promise in a way I have argued that a clause-bound interpretivism is not, and capable at the same time of avoiding the objections to a value-laden form of noninterpretivism, objections rooted most importantly in democratic theory. In that regard the two arguments that close this chapter, those addressed explicitly to consistency with democratic theory and the relative institutional capacities of legislatures and courts, seem at least as important as the argument from the nature of the Constitution (which given the complexity of the document must be a qualified one in any event).

[5] Fuller, "American Legal Philosophy at Mid-Century," 6 *J. Leg. Educ.* 457, 463–64 (1954).

Many of our colonial forebears' complaints against British rule were phrased in "constitutional" terms. Seldom, however, was the claim one of deprivation of some treasured good or substantive right: the American colonists, at least the white males, were among the freest and best-off people in the history of the world, and by and large they knew it. "Constitutional" claims thus were often jurisdictional—that Parliament lacked authority, say, to regulate the colonies' "internal commerce"—the foundation for the claim being generally that we were not represented in Parliament. (Obviously the colonists weren't any crazier about being taxed than anyone else is, but what they damned as tyrannical was taxation *without representation*.) Or they were arguments of inequality: claims of entitlement to "the rights of Englishmen" had an occasional natural law flavor, but the more common meaning was that suggested by the words, a claim for equality of treatment with those living in England. Thus the colonists' "constitutional" arguments drew on the two participational themes we have been considering: that (1) their input into the process by which they were governed was insufficient, and that (partly as a consequence) (2) they were being denied what others were receiving. The American version of revolution, wrote Hannah Arendt, "actually proclaims no more than the necessity of civilized government for all mankind; the French version . . . proclaims the existence of rights independent of and outside the body public . . ."[6]

The theme that justice and happiness are best assured not by trying to define them for all time, but rather by attending to the governmental processes by which their dimensions would be specified over time, carried over into our critical constitutional documents. Even our foremost "natural law" statement, the Declaration of Independence, after adverting to some admirable but assuredly open-ended goals—made more so by using "the pursuit of happiness" in place of the already broad Lockean reference to "property"[7]—signals its appreciation of the critical role of (democratic) process:

> We hold these truths to be self-evident, that all men are created equal, that they are endowed by their creator with certain unalienable rights; that among these are life, liberty, and the pursuit of happiness; that *to secure these rights governments are instituted among men, deriving their just powers from the consent of the governed* . . .

The Constitution, less surprisingly, begins on the same note, not one of trying to set forth some governing ideology—the values mentioned in the Preamble could hardly be more pliable—but rather one of ensuring a durable structure for the ongoing resolution of policy disputes:

> We the People of the United States, in Order to form a more perfect Union, establish Justice, insure domestic Tranquility, provide for the common defence, promote the general Welfare, and secure the Blessings of Liberty to ourselves

[6] Hannah Arendt, *On Revolution* (New York: Viking Press, 1963), p. 147.

[7] See Kenyon, "Republicanism and Radicalism in the American Revolution: An Old-Fashioned Interpretation," 19 *Wm and M. Q.* 153, 168–78 (1962).

and our Posterity, do ordain and establish this Constitution for the United States of America.

I don't suppose it will surprise anyone to learn that the body of the original Constitution is devoted almost entirely to structure, explaining who among the various actors—federal government, state government; Congress, executive, judiciary—has authority to do what, and going on to fill in a good bit of detail about how these persons are to be selected and to conduct their business. Even provisions that at first glance might seem primarily designed to assure or preclude certain substantive results seem on reflection to be principally concerned with process. Thus, for example, the provision that treason "shall consist only in levying War against [the United States], or in adhering to their Enemies, giving them Aid and Comfort," appears at least in substantial measure to have been a precursor of the First Amendment, reacting to the recognition that persons in power can disable their detractors by charging disagreement as treason. The prohibitions against granting titles of nobility seem rather plainly to have been designed to buttress the democratic ideal that all are equals in government. The Ex Post Facto and Bill of Attainder Clauses prove on analysis to be separation of powers provisions, enjoining the legislature to act prospectively and by general rule (just as the judiciary is implicitly enjoined by Article III to act retrospectively and by specific decree). And we have seen that the Privileges and Immunities Clause of Article IV, and at least in one aspect—the other being a grant of congressional power—the Commerce Clause as well, function as equality provisions, guaranteeing virtual representation to the politically powerless.

During most of this century the Obligation of Contracts Clause has not played a significant role. Powerful arguments have been made that the clause was intended importantly to limit the extent to which state governments could control the subjects and terms of private contracts. Early in the nineteenth century the Supreme Court rejected this broad interpretation, however, holding that the clause affected only the extent to which the legislature could alter or overrule the terms of contracts in existence at the time the statute was passed, and thus did not affect what legislation could say about future contracts. What's more, though there have been signs of stiffening in the past two years, the Court in general has not been very energetic about protecting existing contracts either, holding in essence that legislatures can alter them so long as they do so reasonably (which virtually denudes the clause of any independent function). It is tempting to conclude that the Court's long-standing interpretation of the clause as protecting only existing contracts reduces it to just another hedge against retroactive legislation and thus, like the Ex Post Facto Clause, essentially a separation of powers provision. That conclusion, however, is a little quick. Legislation effectively overruling the terms of an existing contract is not really "retroactive" in the ex post facto sense of attaching untoward consequences to an act performed before it was enacted; rather it refuses to recognize a prior act (the making of the contract) as a defense to or exemption from a legal regime the legislature now wishes to impose. Thus both interpretations of the clause recognize the existence of a contract as a special shield against legislative regulation of future behavior, though on the long-accepted narrow interpretation only contracts already in existence can serve thus.

At this point another temptation arises, to characterize the Contracts Clause as serving an institutional or "separation of powers" function of cordoning off an extragovernmental enclave, in this case an enclave of decision via contract, to serve as a counterpoise to governmental authority. The problem with this account is not that it does not fit, but rather that it will *always* fit: it is difficult to imagine any purported constitutional right that cannot be described as creating a private space where actions antithetical to the wishes of our elected representatives can be taken. For this reason the account seems incapable of serving as a meaningful explanation (or as a basis from which broader constitutional themes can responsibly be extrapolated).[8] Thus whichever interpretation of the clause was in fact intended, it is difficult to avoid the conclusion that in the Contracts Clause the framers and ratifiers meant to single out for special protection from the political processes—though note that in this case it is only the *state* political processes—a substantive value that is not wholly susceptible to convincing rationalization in terms of either the processes of government or procedure more narrowly conceived. On the broad and rejected interpretation, that value is contract, the ability to arrive at binding agreements. On the narrower and received interpretation, applying the clause only to contracts in existence at the time of the legislation which I should reiterate is an interpretation the Court has not, at least until very recently, pursued very enthusiastically either—what is protected is a somewhat narrower reliance interest, an assurance that by entering into a contract one can render oneself immune from future shifts in the identity or thinking of one's elected representatives.

This needn't throw us into a tailspin: my claim is only that the original Constitution was principally, indeed I would say overwhelmingly, dedicated to concerns of process and structure and not to the identification and preservation of specific substantive values. Any claim that it was exclusively so conceived would be ridiculous (as would any comparable claim about any comparably complicated human undertaking). And indeed there are other provisions in the original document that seem almost entirely value-oriented, though my point, of course, is that they are few and far between.[9] Thus "corruption of blood" is forbidden as a punishment for treason. Punishing people for their parents'

---

8 I hesitate to give up on this entirely, since it arises from an appropriately "constitutional" concern with the fractionalization of decision-making authority. Unless it can be responsibly qualified, however, it yields a sort of anarchy that is at entire odds with our constitutional order, and all I can see as plausible limiting strategies—aside, of course, from the all-too-popular strategy of invoking the idea when one likes the substantive outcome and either neglecting it or announcing that it "goes too far" when one doesn't—are strategies geared on the one hand to "traditionally recognized" alternative decision centers, and on the other to those alternative decision centers that are mentioned in the Constitution. Since the former is notoriously susceptible to manipulation and played straight would protect precisely those who least need protection, it seems clearly unacceptable. That leaves the option of protecting those alternative power centers mentioned in the Constitution—the church, the press, arguably contract and property (though on the face of the document the special constitutional protection of at least the latter is limited substantially.)

9 I realize that by stressing the few occasions on which values *were* singled out for protection, I run the risk of conveying the impression that that is the character of much of the Constitution.

transgressions is outlawed as a substantively unfair outcome: it just can't be done, irrespective of procedures and also irrespective of whether it is done to the children of all offenders. The federal government, along with the states, is precluded from taxing articles exported from any state. Here too an outcome is simply precluded; what might be styled a value, the economic value of free trade among the states, is protected. This short list, however, covers just about all the values protected in the original Constitution—save one. And a big one it was. Although an understandable squeamishness kept the word out of the document, *slavery* must be counted a substantive value to which the original Constitution meant to extend unusual protection from the ordinary legislative process, at least temporarily. Prior to 1808, Congress was forbidden to prohibit the slave trade into any state that wanted it,[10] and the states were obliged to return escaping slaves to their "homes."

The idea of a bill of rights was not even brought up until close to the end of the Constitutional Convention, at which time it was rejected. The reason is not that the framers were unconcerned with liberty, but rather that by their lights a bill of rights did not belong in a constitution, at least not in the one they had drafted. As Hamilton explained in *Federalist* 84, "a minute detail of particular rights is certainly far less applicable to a Constitution like that under consideration, which is merely intended to regulate the general political interests of the nation . . ."[11] Moreover, the very point of all that had been wrought had been, in large measure, to preserve the liberties of individuals. "The truth is, after all the declamations we have heard, that the Constitution is itself, in every rational sense, and to every useful purpose, *a Bill of Rights*."[12] "The additional securities to republican government, to liberty, and to property, to be derived from the adoption of the plan under consideration, consist chiefly in the restraints which the preservation of the Union will impose on local factions . . . in the prevention of extensive military establishments . . . in the express guarantee of a republican form of government to each [state]; in the absolute and universal exclusion of titles of nobility . . ."[13]

Of course a number of the state ratifying conventions remained apprehensive, and a bill of rights did emerge. Here too, however, the data are unruly. The

---

My point of course is quite the opposite, but I'm not sufficiently sadistic to list all the provisions that are obviously concerned only with process. If you find yourself thinking I'm not making my case here, please read a few pages of the Constitution to assure yourself that I could.

[10] Technically this is a federalism provision, since the states were left free to prohibit the importation of slaves. Since the authority was so pointedly excluded from what would otherwise have been the sweep of federal power, however, it seems fair to read the clause as what history teaches it was, an attempt to forestall a certain substantive result, the abolition of slavery in the South. I'm not prepared to fight very strenuously for this point, however, since disagreement here is only further agreement with my overall thesis.

[11] *The Federalist* no. 84, at 534 (B. Wright ed. 1961) (Hamilton). See also, e.g., J. Pole, *Foundations of American Independence: 1763–1815*, at 196 (1972); J. Goebel, *Antecedents and Beginnings to 1801*, vol. I of *History of the Supreme Court of the United States* 249 (P. Freund ed. 1971).

[12] *The Federalist* no. 84, at 536 (B. Wright ed. 1961) (Hamilton).

[13] *The Federalist* no. 85, at 542 (B. Wright ed. 1961) (Hamilton). See also id. no. 9, at 125 (Hamilton).

expression-related provisions of the first Amendment—"Congress shall make no law . . . abridging the freedom of speech, or of the press; or the right of the people peaceably to assemble, and to petition the Government for a redress of grievances"—were centrally intended to help make our governmental processes work, to ensure the open and informed discussion of political issues, and to check our government when it gets out of bounds. We can attribute other functions to freedom of expression, and some of them must have played a role, but the exercise has the smell of the lamp about it: the view that free expression per se, without regard to what it means to the process of government, is our preeminent right has a highly elitist cast. Positive law has its claims, and I am not suggesting that such other purposes as are plausibly attributable to the language should not be attributed: the amendment's language is not limited to political speech and it should not be so limited by construction (even assuming someone could come up with a determinate definition of "political"). But we are at present engaged in an exploration of what sort of document our forebears thought they were putting together, and in that regard the linking of the politically oriented protections of speech, press, assembly, and petition is highly informative.

The first Amendment's religious clauses—"Congress shall make no law respecting an establishment of religion, or prohibiting the free exercise thereof"— are a different matter. Obviously part of the point of combining these crosscutting commands was to make sure the church and the government gave each other breathing space: the provision thus performs a structural or separation of powers function. But we must not infer that because one account fits the data it must be the only appropriate account, and here the obvious cannot be blinked: part of the explanation of the Free Exercise Clause has to be that for the framers religion was an important substantive value they wanted to put significantly beyond the reach of at least the federal legislature.

The Second Amendment, protecting "the right of the people to keep and bear Arms," seems (at least if that's all you read) calculated simply to set beyond congressional control another "important" value, the right to carry a gun. It hasn't been construed that way, however, and instead has been interpreted as protecting only the right of state governments to keep militias (National Guards) and to arm them. The rationalization for this narrow construction has ordinarily been historical, that the purpose the framers talked most about was maintaining state militias. However, a provision cannot responsibly be restricted to less than its language indicates simply because a particular purpose received more attention than others (and in fact that favored purpose of today's firearms enthusiasts, the right of *individual* self-protection, was mentioned more than a couple of times). Arguments can be right for the wrong reasons, however, and though the point is debatable, the conclusion here is probably correct. The Second Amendment has its own little preamble: "A well regulated Militia, being necessary to the security of a free State, the right of the people to keep and bear Arms, shall not be infringed." Thus here, as almost nowhere else, the framers and ratifiers apparently opted against leaving to the future the attribution of purposes, choosing instead explicitly to legislate the goal in terms of which the provision was to be interpreted.

The Third Amendment, undoubtedly another of your favorites, forbids the nonconsensual peacetime quartering of troops. Like the Establishment of Religion Clause, it grew largely out of fear of an undue influence, this time by the military: in that aspect it can be counted a "separation of powers" provision. Again, however, one cannot responsibly stop there. Other provisions provide for civilian control of the military, and although that is surely one of the purposes here, there is obviously something else at stake, a desire to protect the privacy of the home from prying government eyes, to say nothing of the annoyance of uninvited guests. Both process and value seem to be involved here.

Amendments five through eight tend to become relevant only during lawsuits, and we tend therefore to think of them as procedural—instrumental provisions calculated to enhance the fairness and efficiency of the litigation process. That's exactly what most of them are: the importance of the guarantees of grand juries, criminal and civil petit juries, information of the charge, the right of confrontation, compulsory process, and even the assistance of counsel inheres mainly in their tendency to ensure a reliable determination. Unconcerned with the substance of government regulation, they refer instead to the ways in which regulations can be enforced against those they cover. Once again, however, that is not the whole story. The Fifth Amendment's privilege against self-incrimination surely has a lot to do with wanting to find the truth: coerced confessions are less likely to be reliable. But at least as interpreted, the privilege needs further rationalization than that: the argument runs that there is simply something immoral—though it has proved tricky pinning down exactly what it is—about the state's asking somebody whether he committed a crime and expecting him to answer. The same amendment's guarantee against double jeopardy gets complicated. Insofar as it forbids retrial after acquittal, it seems a largely procedural protection, designed to guard against the conviction of innocent persons. But insofar as it forbids additional prosecution after conviction or added punishment after sentence, it performs the quite different (and substantive) function, which obviously is present in the acquittal situation too, of guaranteeing a sense of repose, an assurance that at some definable point the defendant can assume the ordeal is over, its consequences known.

The Fourth Amendment provides: "The right of the people to be secure in their persons, houses, papers, and effects, against unreasonable searches and seizures, shall not be violated, and no Warrants shall issue, but upon probable cause, supported by Oath or affirmation, and particularly describing the place to be searched, and the persons or things to be seized." This provision most often becomes relevant when a criminal defendant tries to suppress evidence seized as the fruit of an illegal search or arrest, but it would be a mistake to infer from that that it is a purely procedural provision. In fact (as thus enforced by the exclusionary rule) it *thwarts* the procedural goal of accurately determining the facts, in order to serve one or more other goals felt to be more important. The standard line is that that other, more important goal is privacy, and surely privacy is sometimes implicated.[14] But the language of the amendment reaches further—so for that matter did the customs abuses we know had a lot to do with its inclusion—and when it is read in its entirety the notion of "privacy" proves inadequate as an explanation. The amendment covers seizures of goods and arrests ("seizures of the person") along with searches, and it does not distinguish public episodes from private: a completely open arrest or seizure of goods is as illegal as a search of a private area if it is effected without probable cause. It thus "protects individual privacy against certain kinds of governmental intrusion, but its protections go further, and often have nothing to do with privacy at all."[15]

A major point of the amendment, obviously, was to keep the government from disrupting our lives without at least moderately convincing justification. That rationale intertwines with another—and the historic customs abuses are relevant here too—namely, a fear of official discretion. In deciding whose lives to disrupt in the ways the amendment indicates—that is, whom to search or arrest or whose goods to seize—law enforcement officials will necessarily have a good deal of low visibility discretion. In addition they are likely in such situations to be sensitive to social station and other factors that should not bear on the decision. The amendment thus requires not simply a certain quantum of probability but also when possible, via the warrant requirement, the judgment of a "neutral and detached magistrate." From this perspective, which obviously is only one of several, the Fourth Amendment can be seen as another harbinger of the Equal Protection Clause, concerned with avoiding indefensible inequities in treatment. The Eighth Amendment's ban on "cruel and unusual punishments" is even more obviously amenable to this account. Apparently part of the point was to outlaw certain understood and abhorred forms of torture, but the decision to use open-ended language can hardly have been inadvertent. It is possible that part of the point also was to ban punishments that were unusually severe in relation to the crimes for which they were being imposed. But much of it surely had to do with a realization that in the context of imposing penalties too there is tremendous potential for the arbitrary or invidious infliction of "unusually" severe punishments on persons of various classes other than "our own."

On first reading, the Fifth Amendment's requirement that private property not be taken for public use without just compensation may appear simply to mark the substantive value of private property for special protection from the political process (though, on the face of the document, from only the state political process). Again, though, we must ask why. Because property was regarded as unusually important? That may be part of the explanation, but note that property is not shielded from condemnation by this provision. On the

---

[14] In light of the recent, though mercifully declining, vogue for using "privacy" to include personal autonomy, it may be well explicitly to note that the sort of privacy the Fourth Amendment appears in part to have been designed to protect is privacy properly so called, the ability to keep private information one would rather not disseminate.

[15] *Katz v. United States,* 389 U.S. 347, 350 (1967). See also *Griswold v. Connecticut,* 381 U.S. 479, 509 (1965) (Black, J., dissenting), quoted in *Katz v. United States,* 389 U.S. 347, 350 n.4 (1967).

contrary, the amendment assumes that property will sometimes be taken and provides instead for compensation. Read through it thus emerges—and this account fits the historical situation like a glove—as yet another protection of the few against the many, "a limit on government's power to isolate particular individuals for sacrifice to the general good." [16] Its point is to "spread the cost of operating the governmental apparatus throughout the society rather than imposing it upon some small segment of it." [17] If we want a highway or a park we can have it, but we're all going to have to share the cost rather than imposing it on some isolated individual or group.[18]

With one important exception, the Reconstruction Amendments do not designate substantive values for protection from the political process.[19] The Fourteenth Amendment's Due Process Clause, we have seen, is concerned with process writ small, the processes by which regulations are enforced against individuals. Its Privileges or Immunities Clause is quite inscrutable, indicating only that there should exist some set of constitutional entitlements not explicitly enumerated in the document: it is one of the provisions for which we are seeking guides to construction. The Equal Protection Clause is also unforthcoming with details, though it at least gives us a clue: by its explicit concern with equality among the persons within a state's jurisdiction it constitutes the document's clearest, though not sole, recognition that technical access to the process may not always be sufficient to guarantee good-faith representation of all those putatively represented. The Fifteenth Amendment, forbidding abridgment of the right to vote on account of race, opens the process to persons who had previously been excluded and thus by another strategy seeks to enforce the representative's duty of equal concern and respect. The exception, of course, involves a value I have mentioned before, slavery. The Thirteenth Amendment can be forced into a "process" mold—slaves don't participate effectively in the political process—and it surely significantly reflects a concern with equality as

---

[16] L. Tribe, *American Constitutional Law* 452 (1978), p. 463.

[17] J. Sax, "Takings and the Police Power," 74 *Yale L. J.* 36, 75–76 (1964). See also id. at 64–65; Sax, "Takings, Private Property and Public Rights," 81 *Yale L. J.* 149, 169–70 (1971); B. Ackerman, *Private Property and the Constitution* (New Haven: Yale University Press, 1977), pp. 52–53, 68, 79–80.

[18] This view of the clause is also of some assistance in deciding whether a given government action should be counted a taking in the first place as opposed to, say, a regulation or a tax. In recent discussions of this issue the Court has begun to ask whether the measure under review singles out a minority for unusually harsh treatment or rather affects a class sufficiently generalized to have a fair shot at protecting itself politically. E.g., *Penn Central Transp. Co. v. New York City*, 438 U.S. 104, 132 (1978).

[19] The Ninth Amendment is one of the open-ended provisions for which we are seeking guides to construction, at present by exploring the nature of the rest of the document. The Tenth Amendment is a federalism provision, underscoring the reservation of nonenumerated powers to the states. The Eleventh and Twelfth Amendments both are concerned with the mechanics of government. Even a decision to extend sovereign immunity to the states would obviously have been generated by a concern for the machinery of government rather than by a substantive decision to place the costs on the injured party rather than spread them among the population. In any event the better view seems to be that the Eleventh Amendment was intended merely to make clear that Article III did not by itself grant federal courts jurisdiction in cases where states were defendants, not to bar Congress from creating such jurisdiction.

well. Just as surely, however, it embodies a substantive judgment that human slavery is simply not morally tolerable. Thus at no point has the Constitution been neutral on this subject. Slavery was one of the few values the original document singled out for protection from the political branches; *non*slavery is one of the few values it singles out for protection now.

What has happened to the Constitution in the second century of our nationhood, though ground less frequently plowed, is most instructive on the subject of what jobs we have learned our basic document is suited to. There were no amendments between 1870 and 1913, but there have been eleven since. Five of them have extended the franchise: the Seventeenth extends to all of us the right to vote for our Senators directly, the Twenty-Fourth abolishes the poll tax as a condition of voting in federal elections, the Nineteenth extends the vote to women, the Twenty-Third to residents of the District of Columbia, and the Twenty-Sixth to eighteen-year-olds. Extension of the franchise to groups previously excluded has therefore been the dominant theme of our constitutional development since the Fourteenth Amendment, and it pursues both of the broad constitutional themes we have observed from the beginning: the achievement of a political process open to all on an equal basis and a consequent enforcement of the representative's duty of equal concern and respect to minorities and majorities alike. Three other amendments—the Twentieth, Twenty-Second, and Twenty-Fifth—involve Presidential eligibility and succession. The Sixteenth, permitting a federal income tax, adds another power to the list of those that had previously been assigned to the central government.[20] That's it, save two, and indeed one of those two did place a substantive value beyond the reach of the political process. The amendment was the Eighteenth, and the value shielded was temperance. It was, of course, repealed fourteen years later by the Twenty-First Amendment, precisely, I suggest, because such attempts to freeze substantive values do not belong in a constitution. In 1919 temperance obviously seemed like a fundamental value; in 1933 it obviously did not.

What has happened to the Constitution's other value-enshrining provisions is similar, and similarly instructive. Some surely have survived, but typically because they are so obscure that they don't become issues (corruption of blood, quartering of troops) or so interlaced with procedural concerns they seem appropriate in a constitution (self-incrimination, double jeopardy). Those sufficiently conspicuous and precise to be controvertible have not survived.[21] The most dramatic examples, of course, were slavery and prohibition. Both were removed by repeal, in one case a repeal requiring unprecedented carnage. Two other substantive values that at least arguably were placed beyond the reach of

---

[20] Moreover, the amendment most likely (though perhaps not likely enough) to become the Twenty-Seventh, the Equal Rights Amendment, is a guarantor of fair distribution akin to the Equal Protection Clause: it does not designate any substantive values as worthy of constitutional protection.

[21] *Judicial* attempts to cement fundamental values in the Constitution have for similar reasons met similar fates. That *Dred Scott v. Sandford* did not prove durable is the grisliest of understatements. Neither, though not so dramatically, did *Lochner v. New York,* and even as I write, the Supreme Court is backing away, in a quite discriminatory way at that, from *Roe v. Wade.*

the political process by the Constitution have been "repealed" by judicial construction—the right of individuals to bear arms, and freedom to set contract terms without significant state regulation. Maybe in fact our forebears did not intend very seriously to protect those values, but the fact that the Court, in the face of what must be counted at least plausible contrary arguments, so readily read these values out of the Constitution is itself instructive of American expectations of a constitution. Finally, there is the value of religion, still protected by the Free Exercise Clause. Something different has happened here. In recent years that clause has functioned primarily to protect what must be counted as discrete and insular minorities, such as the Amish, Seventh Day Adventists, and Jehovah's Witnesses. Whatever the original conception of the Free Exercise Clause, its function during essentially all of its effective life has been one akin to the Equal Protection Clause and thus entirely appropriate to a constitution.

Don't get me wrong: our Constitution has always been substantially concerned with preserving liberty. If it weren't, it would hardly be worth fighting for. The question that is relevant to our inquiry here, however, is how that concern has been pursued. The principal answers to that, we have seen, are by a quite extensive set of procedural protections, and by a still more elaborate scheme designed to ensure that in the making of substantive choices the decision process will be open to all on something approaching an equal basis, with the decision-makers held to a duty to take into account the interests of all those their decisions affect. (Most often the document has proceeded on the assumption that assuring access is the best way of assuring that someone's interests will be considered, and so in fact it usually is. Other provisions, however—centrally but not exclusively the Equal Protection Clause—reflect a realization that access will not always be sufficient.) The general strategy has therefore not been to root in the document a set of substantive rights entitled to permanent protection. The Constitution has instead proceeded from the quite sensible assumption that an effective majority will not inordinately threaten its own rights, and has sought to assure that such a majority not systematically treat others less well than it treats itself—by structuring decision processes at all levels to try to ensure, first, that everyone's interests will be actually or virtually represented (usually both) at the point of substantive decision, and second, that the processes of individual application will not be manipulated so as to reintroduce in practice the sort of discrimination that is impermissible in theory. We have noted a few provisions that do not comfortably conform to this pattern. But they're an odd assortment, the understandable products of particular historical circumstances—guns, religion, contract, and so on—and in any event they are few and far between. To represent them as a dominant theme of our constitutional document one would have to concentrate quite single-mindedly on hopping from stone to stone and averting one's eyes from the mainstream.

The American Constitution has thus by and large remained a constitution properly so called, concerned with constitutive questions. What has distinguished it, and indeed the United States itself, has been a process of government, not a governing ideology. Justice Linde has written: "As a charter of government a constitution must prescribe legitimate processes, not legitimate outcomes, if like ours (and unlike more ideological documents elsewhere) it is to serve many generations through changing times."

DEMOCRACY AND DISTRUST

As I have tried to be scrupulous about indicating, the argument from the general contours of the Constitution is necessarily a qualified one. In fact the documentary dictation of particular substantive outcomes has been rare (and generally unsuccessful), but our Constitution is too complex a document to lie still for *any* pat characterization. Beyond that, the premise of the argument, that aids to construing the more open-ended provisions are appropriately found in the nature of the surrounding document, though it is a premise that seems to find acceptance on all sides, is not one with which it is impossible to disagree. Thus the two arguments that follow, each overtly normative, are if anything more important than the one I have just reviewed. The first is entirely obvious by now, that unlike an approach geared to the judicial imposition of "fundamental values," the representation-reinforcing orientation whose contours I have sketched and will develop further is not inconsistent with, but on the contrary is entirely supportive of, the American system of representative democracy. It recognizes the unacceptability of the claim that appointed and life-tenured judges are better reflectors of conventional values than elected representatives, devoting itself instead to policing the mechanisms by which the system seeks to ensure that our elected representatives will actually represent. There may be an illusion of circularity here: my approach is more consistent with representative democracy because that's the way it was planned. But of course it isn't any more circular than setting out to build an airplane and ending up with something that flies.

The final point worth serious mention is that (again unlike a fundamental-values approach) a representation-reinforcing approach assigns judges a role they are conspicuously well situated to fill.[22] My reference here is not principally to expertise. Lawyers *are* experts on process writ small, the processes by which facts are found and contending parties are allowed to present their claims. And to a degree they are experts on process writ larger, the processes by which issues of public policy are fairly determined: lawyers do seem genuinely to have a feel, indeed it is hard to see what other special value they have, for ways of insuring that everyone gets his or her fair say. But too much

---

[22] For reasons that are currently obscure, I went through a period of worrying that the orientation here recommended might mean less protection for civil liberties. (Of course it would deny the opportunity to create rights out of whole cloth: that is much of its point and strength. What I had in mind was the possibility that the *same* freedoms might systematically come out thinner if derived from a participational orientation than they would if protected on the ground that they are "good.") Reflection has convinced me that just the opposite is true, that freedoms are more secure to the extent that they find foundation in the theory that supports our entire government, rather than gaining protection because the judge deciding the case thinks they're important. Cf. C. Black, *Structure and Relationship in Constitutional Law* (Baton Rouge: Louisiana State University Press, 1969), p. 29–30. Indeed, the only remotely systematic "Carolene Products" Court we have had was also clearly the most protective of civil liberties.

shouldn't be made of this. Others, particularly the full-time participants, can also claim expertise on how the political process allocates voice and power. And of course many legislators are lawyers themselves. So the point isn't so much one of expertise as it is one of perspective.

The approach to constitutional adjudication recommended here is akin to what might be called an "antitrust" as opposed to a "regulatory" orientation to economic affairs—rather than dictate substantive results it intervenes only when the "market," in our case the political market, is systemically malfunctioning. (A referee analogy is also not far off: the referee is to intervene only when one team is gaining unfair advantage, not because the "wrong" team has scored.) Our government cannot fairly be said to be "malfunctioning" simply because it sometimes generates outcomes with which we disagree, however strongly (and claims that it is reaching results with which "the people" really disagree—or would "if they understood"—are likely to be little more than self-deluding projections). In a representative democracy value determinations are to be made by our elected representatives, and if in fact most of us disapprove we can vote them out of office. Malfunction occurs when the *process* is undeserving of trust, when (1) the ins are choking off the channels of political change to ensure that they will stay in and the outs will stay out, or (2) though no one is actually denied a voice or a vote, representatives beholden to an effective majority are systematically disadvantaging some minority out of simple hostility or a prejudiced refusal to recognize commonalities of interest, and thereby denying that minority the protection afforded other groups by a representative system.

Obviously our elected representatives are the last persons we should trust with identification of either of these situations. Appointed judges, however, are comparative outsiders in our governmental system, and need worry about continuance in office only very obliquely. This does not give them some special pipeline to the genuine values of the American people: in fact it goes far to ensure that they won't have one. It does, however, put them in a position objectively to assess claims—though no one could suppose the evaluation won't be full of judgment calls—that either by clogging the channels of change or by acting as accessories to majority tyranny, our elected representatives in fact are not representing the interests of those whom the system presupposes they are.

Before embarking on his career-long quest for a satisfactory approach to constitutional adjudication, Alexander Bickel described the challenge thus:

> The search must be for a function . . . which is peculiarly suited to the capabilities of the courts; which will not likely be performed elsewhere if the courts do not assume it; which can be so exercised as to be acceptable in a society that generally shares Judge Hand's satisfaction in a "sense of common venture"; which will be effective when needed; and whose discharge by the courts will not lower the quality of the other departments' performance by denuding them of the dignity and burden of their own responsibility.[23]

---

[23] A. Bickel, *The Least Dangerous Branch* (New Haven: Yale University Press, 1986), p. 24.

As quoted, it's a remarkably appropriate set of specifications, one that fits the orientation suggested here precisely. Unfortunately, by adding one more specification (where I have put the elipsis) and thereby committing himself to a value orientation—"which might (indeed must) involve the making of policy, yet which differs from the legislative and executive functions"—he built in an inescapable contradiction and thereby ensured the failure of his enterprise.

30.
Taking Rights Seriously
RONALD DWORKIN

I. HARD CASES

5. Legal Rights

A. *Legislation*

· · ·

We might therefore do well to consider how a philosophical judge might develop, in appropriate cases, theories of what legislative purpose and legal principles require. We shall find that he would construct these theories in the same manner as a philosophical referee would construct the character of a game. I have invented, for this purpose, a lawyer of superhuman skill, learning, patience and acumen, whom I shall call Hercules. I suppose that Hercules is a judge in some representative American jurisdiction. I assume that he accepts the main uncontroversial constitutive and regulative rules of the law in his jurisdiction. He accepts, that is, that statutes have the general power to create and extinguish legal rights, and that judges have the general duty to follow earlier decisions of their court or higher courts whose rationale, as lawyers say, extends to the case at bar.

1. The constitution. Suppose there is a written constitution in Hercules' jurisdiction which provides that no law shall be valid if it establishes a religion. The legislature passes a law purporting to grant free busing to children in parochial schools. Does the grant establish a religion? The words of the constitutional provision might support either view. Hercules must nevertheless decide whether the child who appears before him has a right to her bus ride.

He might begin by asking why the constitution has any power at all to create or destroy rights. If citizens have a background right to salvation through an established church, as many believe they do, then this must be an important right. Why does the fact that a group of men voted otherwise several centuries ago prevent this background right from being made a legal right as well? His answer must take some form such as this. The constitution sets out a general political scheme that is sufficiently just to be taken as settled for reasons of fairness. Citizens take the benefit of living in a society whose institutions are arranged and governed in accordance with that scheme, and they must take the burdens as well, at least until a new scheme is put into force either by discrete amendment or general revolution. But Hercules must then ask just what scheme of principles has been settled. He must construct, that is, a constitutional theory; since he is Hercules we may suppose that he can develop a full political theory that justifies the constitution as a whole. It must be a scheme that fits the particular rules of this constitution, of course. It cannot include a powerful background right to an established church. But more than one fully specified theory may fit the specific provision about religion sufficiently well. One theory might provide, for example, that it is wrong for the government to enact any legislation that will cause great social tension or disorder; so that since the establishment of a church will have that effect, it is wrong to empower the legislature to establish one. Another theory will provide a background right to religious liberty, and therefore argue that an established church is wrong, not because it will be socially disruptive, but because it violates that background right. In that case Hercules must turn to the remaining constitutional rules and settled practices under these rules to see which of these two theories provides a smoother fit with the constitutional scheme as a whole.

But the theory that is superior under this test will nevertheless be insufficiently concrete to decide some cases. Suppose Hercules decides that the establishment provision is justified by a right to religious liberty rather than any goal of social order. It remains to ask what, more precisely, religious liberty is. Does a right to religious liberty include the right not to have one's taxes used for any purpose that helps a religion to survive? Or simply not to have one's taxes used to benefit one religion at the expense of another? If the former, then the free transportation legislation violates that right, but if the latter it does not. The institutional structure of rules and practice may not be sufficiently detailed to rule out either of these two conceptions of religious liberty, or to make one a plainly superior justification of that structure. At some point in his career Hercules must therefore consider the question not just as an issue of fit between a theory and the rules of the institution, but as an issue of political philosophy as well. He must decide which conception is a more satisfactory elaboration of the general idea of religious liberty. He must decide that question because he cannot otherwise carry far enough the project he began. He cannot answer in sufficient detail the question of what political scheme the constitution establishes.

So Hercules is driven, by this project, to a process of reasoning that is much like the process of the self-conscious chess referee. He must develop a theory of the constitution, in the shape of a complex set of principles and policies that justify that scheme of government, just as the chess referee is driven to develop a theory about the character of his game. He must develop that theory by referring alternately to political philosophy and institutional detail. He must generate possible theories justifying different aspects of the scheme and test the theories against the broader institution. When the discriminating power of that test is exhausted, he must elaborate the contested concepts that the successful theory employs.

2. *Statutes.* A statute in Hercules' jurisdiction provides that it is a federal crime for someone knowingly to transport in interstate commerce "any person who shall have been unlawfully seized, confined, inveigled, decoyed, kidnapped, abducted, or carried away by any means whatsoever. . . ." Hercules

is asked to decide whether this statute makes a federal criminal of a man who persuaded a young girl that it was her religious duty to run away with him, in violation of a court order, to consummate what he called a celestial marriage. The statute had been passed after a famous kidnapping case, in order to enable federal authorities to join in the pursuit of kidnappers. But its words are sufficiently broad to apply to this case, and there is nothing in the legislative record or accompanying committee reports that says they do not.

Do they apply? Hercules might himself despise celestial marriage, or abhor the corruption of minors, or celebrate the obedience of children to their parents. The groom nevertheless has a right to his liberty, unless the statute properly understood deprives him of that right; it is inconsistent with any plausible theory of the constitution that judges have the power retroactively to make conduct criminal. Does the statute deprive him of that right? Hercules must begin by asking why any statute has the power to alter legal rights. He will find the answer in his constitutional theory: this might provide, for example, that a democratically elected legislature is the appropriate body to make collective decisions about the conduct that shall be criminal. But that same constitutional theory will impose on the legislature certain responsibilities: it will impose not only constraints reflecting individual rights, but also some general duty to pursue collective goals defining the public welfare. That fact provides a useful test for Hercules in this hard case. He might ask which interpretation more satisfactorily ties the language the legislature used to its constitutional responsibilities. That is, like the referee's question about the character of a game. It calls for the construction, not of some hypothesis about the mental state of particular legislators, but of a special political theory that justifies this statute, in the light of the legislature's more general responsibilities, better than any alternative theory.

• • •

B. *The common law*

1. Precedent. One day lawyers will present a hard case to Hercules that does not turn upon any statute; they will argue whether earlier common law decisions of Hercules' court, properly understood, provide some party with a right to a decision in his favor. *Spartan Steel* was such a case. The plaintiff did not argue that any statute provided it a right to recover its economic damages; it pointed instead to certain earlier judicial decisions that awarded recovery for other sorts of damage, and argued that the principle behind these cases required a decision for it as well.

Hercules must begin by asking why arguments of that form are ever, even in principle, sound. He will find that he has available no quick or obvious answer. When he asked himself the parallel question about legislation he found, in general democratic theory, a ready reply. But the details of the practices of precedent he must now justify resist any comparably simple theory.

• • •

The gravitational force of precedent cannot be captured by any theory that takes the full force of precedent to be its enactment force as a piece of legislation. But the inadequacy of that approach suggests a superior theory. The gravitational force of a precedent may be explained by appeal, not to the wisdom of enforcing enactments, but to the fairness of treating like cases alike. A precedent is the report of an earlier political decision; the very fact of that decision, as a piece of political history, provides some reason for deciding other cases in a similar way in the future. This general explanation of the gravitational force of precedent accounts for the feature that defeated the enactment theory, which is that the force of a precedent escapes the language of its opinion. If the government of a community has forced the manufacturer of defective motor cars to pay damages to a woman who was injured because of the defect, then that historical fact must offer some reason, at least, why the same government should require a contractor who has caused economic damage through the defective work of his employees to make good that loss. We may test the weight of that reason, not by asking whether the language of the earlier decision, suitably interpreted, requires the contractor to pay damages, but by asking the different question whether it is fair for the government, having intervened in the way it did in the first case, to refuse its aid in the second.

Hercules will conclude that this doctrine of fairness offers the only adequate account of the full practice of precedent. He will draw certain further conclusions about his own responsibilities when deciding hard cases. The most important of these is that he must limit the gravitational force of earlier decisions to the extension of the arguments of principle necessary to justify those decisions. If an earlier decision were taken to be entirely justified by some argument of policy, it would have no gravitational force. Its value as a precedent would be limited to its enactment force, that is, to further cases captured by some particular words of the opinion. The distributional force of a collective goal, as we noticed earlier, is a matter of contingent fact and general legislative strategy. If the government intervened on behalf of Mrs MacPherson, not because she had any right to its intervention, but only because wise strategy suggested that means of pursuing some collective goal like economic efficiency, there can be no effective argument of fairness that it therefore ought to intervene for the plaintiff in *Spartan Steel*.

We must remind ourselves, in order to see why this is so, of the slight demands we make upon legislatures in the name of consistency when their decisions are generated by arguments of policy. Suppose the legislature wishes to stimulate the economy and might do so, with roughly the same efficiency, either by subsidizing housing or by increasing direct government spending for new roads. Road construction companies have no right that the legislature choose road construction; if it does, then home construction firms have no right, on any principle of consistency, that the legislature subsidize housing as well. The legislature may decide that the road construction program has stimulated the economy just enough, and that no further programs are needed. It may decide this even if it now concedes that subsidized housing would have been the more efficient decision in the first place. Or it might concede even that more stimulation of the economy is needed, but decide that it wishes to wait for more evidence—perhaps evidence about the success of the road program—to see whether subsidies provide an effective stimulation. It might even say that it does not now wish to commit more of its time and energy to economic policy. There is, perhaps, some limit to the arbitrariness of the distinctions the legislature may make in its pursuit of collective goals. Even if it is efficient to build all ship-yards in southern California, it might be thought unfair, as well as politically unwise, to do so. But these weak requirements, which prohibit grossly unfair distributions, are plainly compatible with providing sizeable incremental bene-fits to one group that are withheld from others.

There can be, therefore, no general argument of fairness that a government which serves a collective goal in one way on one occasion must serve it that way, or even serve the same goal, whenever a parallel opportunity arises. I do not mean simply that the government may change its mind, and regret either the goal or the means of its earlier decision. I mean that a responsible gov-ernment may serve different goals in a piecemeal and occasional fashion, so that even though it does not regret, but continues to enforce, one rule designed to serve a particular goal, it may reject other rules that would serve that same goal just as well. It might legislate the rule that manufacturers are responsible for damages flowing from defects in their cars, for example, and yet properly refuse to legislate the same rule for manufacturers of washing machines, let alone contractors who cause economic damage like the damage of *Spartan Steel*. Government must, of course, be rational and fair; it must make decisions that overall serve a justifiable mix of collective goals and nevertheless respect whatever rights citizens have. But that general requirement would not sup-port anything like the gravitational force that the judicial decision in favor of Mrs MacPherson was in fact taken to have.

So Hercules, when he defines the gravitational force of a particular prece-dent, must take into account only the arguments of principle that justify that precedent. If the decision in favor of Mrs MacPherson supposes that she has a right to damages, and not simply that a rule in her favor supports some collec-tive goal, then the argument of fairness, on which the practice of precedent re-lies, takes hold. It does not follow, of course, that anyone injured in any way by the negligence of another must have the same concrete right to recover that she has. It may be that competing rights require a compromise in the later case that they did not require in hers. But it might well follow that the plaintiff in the later case has the same abstract right, and if that is so then some special argument citing the competing rights will be required to show that a contrary decision in the later case would be fair.

2. *The seamless web*. Hercules' first conclusion, that the gravitational force of a precedent is defined by the arguments of principle that support the prece-dent, suggests a second. Since judicial practice in his community assumes that earlier cases have a *general* gravitational force, then he can justify that judicial practice only by supposing that the rights thesis holds in his community. It is never taken to be a satisfactory argument against the gravitational force of

some precedent that the goal that precedent served has now been served sufficiently, or that the courts would now be better occupied in serving some other goal that has been relatively neglected, possibly returning to the goal the precedent served on some other occasion. The practices of precedent do not suppose that the *rationales* that recommend judicial decisions can be served piecemeal in that way. If it is acknowledged that a particular precedent is justified for a particular reason; if that reason would also recommend a particular result in the case at bar; if the earlier decision has not been recanted or in some other way taken as a matter of institutional regret; then that decision must be reached in the later case.

Hercules must suppose that it is understood in his community, though perhaps not explicitly recognized, that judicial decisions must be taken to be justified by arguments of principle rather than arguments of policy. He now sees that the familiar concept used by judges to explain their reasoning from precedent, the concept of certain principles that underlie or are embedded in the common law, is itself only a metaphorical statement of the rights thesis. He may henceforth use that concept in his decisions of hard common law cases. It provides a general test for deciding such cases that is like the chess referee's concept of the character of a game, and like his own concept of a legislative purpose. It provides a question—What set of principles best justifies the precedents?—that builds a bridge between the general justification of the practice of precedent, which is fairness, and his own decision about what that general justification requires in some particular hard case.

Hercules must now develop his concept of principles that underlie the common law by assigning to each of the relevant precedents some scheme of principle that justifies the decision of that precedent. He will now discover a further important difference between this concept and the concept of statutory purpose that he used in statutory interpretation. In the case of statutes, he found it necessary to choose some theory about the purpose of the particular statute in question, looking to other acts of the legislature only insofar as these might help to select between theories that fit the statute about equally well. But if the gravitational force of precedent rests on the idea that fairness requires the consistent enforcement of rights, then Hercules must discover principles that fit, not only the particular precedent to which some litigant directs his attention, but all other judicial decisions within his general jurisdiction and, indeed, statutes as well, so far as these must be seen to be generated by principle rather than policy. He does not satisfy his duty to show that his decision is consistent with established principles, and therefore fair, if the principles he cites as established are themselves inconsistent with other decisions that his court also proposes to uphold.

Suppose, for example, that he can justify Cardozo's decision in favor of Mrs MacPherson by citing some abstract principle of equality, which argues that whenever an accident occurs then the richest of the various persons whose acts might have contributed to the accident must bear the loss. He nevertheless cannot show that that principle has been respected in other accident cases, or, even if he could, that it has been respected in other branches of the law, like contract, in which it would also have great impact if it were recognized at all.

If he decides against a future accident plaintiff who is richer than the defendant, by appealing to this alleged right of equality, that plaintiff may properly complain that the decision is just as inconsistent with the government's behavior in other cases as if *MacPherson* itself had been ignored. The law may not be a seamless web; but the plaintiff is entitled to ask Hercules to treat it as if it were.

You will now see why I called our judge Hercules. He must construct a scheme of abstract and concrete principles that provides a coherent justification for all common law precedents and, so far as these are to be justified on principle, constitutional and statutory provisions as well. We may grasp the magnitude of this enterprise by distinguishing, within the vast material of legal decisions that Hercules must justify, a vertical and a horizontal ordering. The vertical ordering is provided by distinguishing layers of authority; that is, layers at which official decisions might be taken to be controlling over decisions made at lower levels. In the United States the rough character of the vertical ordering is apparent. The constitutional structure occupies the highest level, the decisions of the Supreme Court and perhaps other courts interpreting that structure the next, enactments of the various legislatures the next and decisions of the various courts developing the common law different levels below that. Hercules must arrange justification of principle at each of these levels so that the justification is consistent with principles taken to provide the justification of higher levels. The horizontal ordering simply requires that the principles taken to justify a decision at one level must also be consistent with the justification offered for other decisions at that level.

Suppose Hercules, taking advantage of his unusual skills, proposed to work out this entire scheme in advance, so that he would be ready to confront litigants with an entire theory of law should this be necessary to justify any particular decision. He would begin, deferring to vertical ordering, by setting out and refining the constitutional theory he has already used. That constitutional theory would be more or less different from the theory that a different judge would develop, because a constitutional theory requires judgments about complex issues of institutional fit, as well as judgments about political and moral philosophy, and Hercules' judgments will inevitably differ from those other judges would make. These differences at a high level of vertical ordering will exercise considerable force on the scheme each judge would propose at lower levels. Hercules might think, for example, that certain substantive constitutional constraints on legislative power are best justified by postulating an abstract right to privacy against the state, because he believes that such a right is a consequence of the even more abstract right to liberty that the constitution guarantees. If so, he would regard the failure of the law of tort to recognize a parallel abstract right to privacy against fellow citizens, in some concrete form, as an inconsistency. If another judge did not share his beliefs about the connection between privacy and liberty, and so did not accept his constitutional interpretation as persuasive, that judge would also disagree about the proper development of tort.

So the impact of Hercules' own judgments will be pervasive, even though some of these will be controversial. But they will not enter his calculations in such a way that different parts of the theory he constructs can be attributed to his independent convictions rather than to the body of law that he must justify. He will not follow those classical theories of adjudication I mentioned earlier, which suppose that a judge follows statutes or precedent until the clear direction of these runs out, after which he is free to strike out on his own. His theory is rather a theory about what the statute or the precedent itself requires, and though he will, of course, reflect his own intellectual and philosophical convictions in making that judgment, that is a very different matter from supposing that those convictions have some independent force in his argument just because they are his.

II. CONSTITUTIONAL CASES

2.

The constitutional theory on which our government rests is not a simple majoritarian theory. The Constitution, and particularly the Bill of Rights, is designed to protect individual citizens and groups against certain decisions that a majority of citizens might want to make, even when that majority acts in what it takes to be the general or common interest. Some of these constitutional restraints take the form of fairly precise rules, like the rule that requires a jury trial in federal criminal proceedings or, perhaps, the rule that forbids the national Congress to abridge freedom of speech. But other constraints take the form of what are often called "vague" standards, for example, the provision that the government shall not deny men due process of law, or equal protection of the laws.

This interference with democratic practice requires a justification. The draftsmen of the Constitution assumed that these restraints could be justified by appeal to moral rights which individuals possess against the majority, and which the constitutional provisions, both "vague" and precise, might be said to recognize and protect.

The "vague" standards were chosen deliberately, by the men who drafted and adopted them, in place of the more specific and limited rules that they might have enacted. But their decision to use the language they did has caused a great deal of legal and political controversy, because even reasonable men of good will differ when they try to elaborate, for example, the moral rights that the due process clause or the equal protection clause brings into the law. They also differ when they try to apply these rights, however defined, to complex matters of political administration, like the educational practices that were the subject of the segregation cases.

The practice has developed of referring to a "strict" and a "liberal" side to these controversies, so that the Supreme Court might be said to have taken the "liberal" side in the segregation cases and its critics the "strict" side. Nixon has this distinction in mind when he calls himself a "strict constructionist." But the distinction is in fact confusing, because it runs together two different issues that must be separated. Any case that arises under the "vague" constitutional guarantees can be seen as posing two questions: (1) Which decision is required by strict, that is to say faithful, adherence to the text of the Constitution or to the intention of those who adopted that text? (2) Which decision is required by a political philosophy that takes a strict, that is to say narrow, view of the moral rights that individuals have against society? Once these questions are distinguished, it is plain that they may have different answers. The text of the First Amendment, for example, says that Congress shall make *no* law abridging the freedom of speech, but a narrow view of individual rights would permit many such laws, ranging from libel and obscenity laws to the Smith Act.

In the case of the "vague" provisions, however, like the due process and equal protection clauses, lawyers have run the two questions together because they have relied, largely without recognizing it, on a theory of meaning that might be put this way: If the framers of the Constitution used vague language, as they did when they condemned violations of "due process of law," then what they "said" or "meant" is limited to the instances of official action that they had in mind as violations, or, at least, to those instances that they would have thought were violations if they had had them in mind. If those who were responsible for adding the due process clause to the Constitution believed that it was fundamentally unjust to provide separate education for different races, or had detailed views about justice that entailed that conclusion, then the segregation decisions might be defended as an application of the principle they had laid down. Otherwise they could not be defended in this way, but instead would show that the judges had substituted their own ideas of justice for those the constitutional drafters meant to lay down.

This theory makes a strict interpretation of the text yield a narrow view of constitutional rights, because it limits such rights to those recognized by a limited group of people at a fixed date of history. It forces those who favor a more liberal set of rights to concede that they are departing from strict legal authority, a departure they must then seek to justify by appealing only to the desirability of the results they reach.

But the theory of meaning on which this argument depends is far too crude; it ignores a distinction that philosophers have made but lawyers have not yet appreciated. Suppose I tell my children simply that I expect them not to treat others unfairly. I no doubt have in mind examples of the conduct I mean to discourage, but I would not accept that my "meaning" was limited to these examples, for two reasons. First I would expect my children to apply my instructions to situations I had not and could not have thought about. Second, I stand ready to admit that some particular act I had thought was fair when I spoke was in fact unfair, or vice versa, if one of my children is able to convince me of that later; in that case I should want to say that my instructions covered the case he cited, not that I had changed my instructions. I might say that I meant the family to be guided by the *concept* of fairness, not by any specific *conception* of fairness I might have had in mind.

This is a crucial distinction which it is worth pausing to explore. Suppose a group believes in common that acts may suffer from a special moral defect which they call unfairness, and which consists in a wrongful division of benefits and burdens, or a wrongful attribution of praise or blame. Suppose also that they agree on a great number of standard cases of unfairness and use these as benchmarks against which to test other, more controversial cases. In that case, the group has a concept of unfairness, and its members may appeal to that concept in moral instruction or argument. But members of that group may nevertheless differ over a large number of these controversial cases, in a way that suggests that each either has or acts on a different theory of *why* the standard cases are acts of unfairness. They may differ, that is, on which more fundamental principles must be relied upon to show that a particular division or attribution is unfair. In that case, the members have different conceptions of fairness.

If so, then members of this community who give instructions or set standards in the name of fairness may be doing two different things. First they may be appealing to the concept of fairness, simply by instructing others to act fairly; in this case they charge those whom they instruct with the responsibility of developing and applying their own conception of fairness as controversial cases arise. That is not the same thing, of course, as granting them a discretion to act as they like; it sets a standard which they must try—and may fail—to meet, because it assumes that one conception is superior to another. The man who appeals to the concept in this way may have his own conception, as I did when I told my children to act fairly; but he holds this conception only as his own theory of how the standard he set must be met, so that when he changes his theory he has not changed that standard.

On the other hand, the members may be laying down a particular conception of fairness; I would have done this, for example, if I had listed my wishes with respect to controversial examples or if, even less likely, I had specified some controversial and explicit theory of fairness, as if I had said to decide hard cases by applying the utilitarian ethics of Jeremy Bentham. The difference is a difference not just in the *detail* of the instructions given but in the *kind* of instructions given. When I appeal to the concept of fairness I appeal to what fairness means, and I give my views on that issue no special standing. When I lay down a conception of fairness, I lay down what I mean by fairness, and my view is therefore the heart of the matter. When I appeal to fairness I pose a moral issue; when I lay down my conception of fairness I try to answer it.

Once this distinction is made it seems obvious that we must take what I have been calling "vague" constitutional clauses as representing appeals to the concepts they employ, like legality, equality, and cruelty. The Supreme Court may soon decide, for example, whether capital punishment is "cruel" within the meaning of the constitutional clause that prohibits "cruel and unusual punishment." It would be a mistake for the Court to be much influenced by the fact that when the clause was adopted capital punishment was standard and unquestioned. That would be decisive if the framers of the clause had meant to lay down a particular conception of cruelty, because it would show that the conception did not extend so far. But it is not decisive of the different question the Court now faces, which is this: Can the Court, responding to the framers' appeal to the concept of cruelty, now defend a conception that does not make death cruel?

Those who ignore the distinction between concepts and conceptions, but who believe that the Court ought to make a fresh determination of whether the death penalty is cruel, are forced to argue in a vulnerable way. They say that ideas of cruelty change over time, and that the Court must be free to reject out-of-date conceptions; this suggests that the Court must change what the Constitution enacted. But in fact the Court can enforce what the Constitution says only by making up its own mind about what is cruel, just as my children, in my example, can do what I said only by making up their own minds about what is fair. If those who enacted the broad clauses had meant to lay down particular conceptions, they would have found the sort of language conventionally used to do this, that is, they would have offered particular theories of the concepts in question.

Indeed the very practice of calling these clauses "vague," in which I have joined, can now be seen to involve a mistake. The clauses are vague only if we take them to be botched or incomplete or schematic attempts to lay down particular conceptions. If we take them as appeals to moral concepts they could not be made more precise by being more detailed.[1]

The confusion I mentioned between the two senses of "strict construction" is therefore very misleading indeed. If courts try to be faithful to the text of the Constitution, they will for that very reason be forced to decide between competing conceptions of political morality. So it is wrong to attack the Warren Court, for example, on the ground that it failed to treat the Constitution as a binding text. On the contrary, if we wish to treat fidelity to that text as an over-riding requirement of constitutional interpretation, then it is the conservative critics of the Warren Court who are at fault, because their philosophy ignores the direction to face issues of moral principle that the logic of the text demands.

I put the matter in a guarded way because we may *not* want to accept fidelity to the spirit of the text as an overriding principle of constitutional adjudication. It may be more important for courts to decide constitutional cases in a manner that respects the judgments of other institutions of government, for example. Or it may be more important for courts to protect established legal doctrines, so that citizens and the government can have confidence that the courts will hold to what they have said before. But it is crucial to recognize that these other policies compete with the principle that the Constitution is the fundamental and imperative source of constitutional law. They are not, as the "strict constructionists" suppose, simply consequences of that principle.

---

[1] It is less misleading to say that the broad clauses of the Constitution "delegate" power to the Court to enforce its own conceptions of political morality. But even this is inaccurate if it suggests that the Court need not justify its conception by arguments showing the connections between its conception and standard cases, as described in the text. If the Court finds that the death penalty is cruel, it must do so on the basis of some principles or groups of principles that unite the death penalty with the thumbscrew and the rack.

3.

Once the matter is put in this light, moreover, we are able to assess these competing claims of policy, free from the confusion imposed by the popular notion of "strict construction." For this purpose I want now to compare and contrast two very general philosophies of how the courts should decide difficult or controversial constitutional issues. I shall call these two philosophies by the names they are given in the legal literature—the programs of "judicial activism" and "judicial restraint"—though it will be plain that these names are in certain ways misleading.

The program of judicial activism holds that courts should accept the directions of the so-called vague constitutional provisions in the spirit I described, in spite of competing reasons of the sort I mentioned. They should work out principles of legality, equality, and the rest, revise these principles from time to time in the light of what seems to the Court fresh moral insight, and judge the acts of Congress, the states, and the President accordingly. (This puts the program in its strongest form; in fact its supporters generally qualify it in ways I shall ignore for the present.)

The program of judicial restraint, on the contrary, argues that courts should allow the decisions of other branches of government to stand, even when they offend the judges' own sense of the principles required by the broad constitutional doctrines, except when these decisions are so offensive to political morality that they would violate the provisions on any plausible interpretation, or, perhaps, when a contrary decision is required by clear precedent. (Again, this put the program in a stark form; those who profess the policy qualify it in different ways.)

The Supreme Court followed the policy of activism rather than restraint in cases like the segregation cases because the words of the equal protection clause left it open whether the various educational practices of the states concerned should be taken to violate the Constitution, no clear precedent held that they did, and reasonable men might differ on the moral issues involved. If the Court had followed the program of judicial restraint, it would therefore have held in favor of the North Carolina statute in *Swann,* not against it. But the program of restraint would not always act to provide decisions that would please political conservatives. In the early days of the New Deal, as critics of the Warren Court are quick to point out, it was the liberals who objected to Court decisions that struck down acts of Congress in the name of the due process clause.

It may seem, therefore, that if Nixon has a legal theory it depends crucially on some theory of judicial restraint. We must now, however, notice a distinction between two forms of judicial restraint, for there are two different, and indeed incompatible, grounds on which that policy might be based.

The first is a theory of political *skepticism* that might be described in this way. The policy of judicial activism presupposes a certain objectivity of moral principle; in particular it presupposes that citizens do have certain moral rights against the state, like a moral right to equality of public education or to fair treatment by the police. Only if such moral rights exist in some sense can activism be justified as a program based on something beyond the judge's personal preferences. The skeptical theory attacks activism at its roots; it argues that in fact individuals have no such moral rights against the state. They have only such *legal* rights as the Constitution grants them, and these are limited to the plain and uncontroversial violations of public morality that the framers must have had actually in mind, or that have since been established in a line of precedent.

The alternative ground of a program of restraint is a theory of judicial *deference*. Contrary to the skeptical theory, this assumes that citizens do have moral rights against the state beyond what the law expressly grants them, but it points out that the character and strength of these rights are debatable and argues that political institutions other than courts are responsible for deciding which rights are to be recognized.

This is an important distinction, even though the literature of constitutional law does not draw it with any clarity. The skeptical theory and the theory of deference differ dramatically in the kind of justification they assume, and in their implications for the more general moral theories of the men who profess to hold them. These theories are so different that most American politicians can consistently accept the second, but not the first.

A skeptic takes the view, as I have said, that men have no moral rights against the state and only such legal rights as the law expressly provides. But what does this mean, and what sort of argument might the skeptic make for his view? There is, of course, a very lively dispute in moral philosophy about the nature and standing of moral rights, and considerable disagreement about what they are, if they are anything at all. I shall rely, in trying to answer these questions, on a low-keyed theory of moral rights against the state . . . . Under that theory, a man has a moral right against the state if for some reason the state would do wrong to treat him in a certain way, even though it would be in the general interest to do so. So a black child has a moral right to an equal education, for example, if it is wrong for the state not to provide that education, even if the community as a whole suffers thereby.

I want to say a word about the virtues of this way of looking at moral rights against the state. A great many lawyers are wary of talking about moral rights, even though they find it easy to talk about what is right or wrong for government to do, because they suppose that rights, if they exist at all, are spooky sorts of things that men and women have in much the same way as they have non-spooky things like tonsils. But the sense of rights I propose to use does not make ontological assumptions of that sort: it simply shows a claim of right to be a special, in the sense of a restricted, sort of judgment about what is right or wrong for governments to do.

Moreover, this way of looking at rights avoids some of the notorious puzzles associated with the concept. It allows us to say, with no sense of strangeness, that rights may vary in strength and character from case to case, and from point to point in history. If we think of rights as things, these metamorphoses seem strange, but we are used to the idea that moral judgments about what it is right or wrong to do are complex and are affected by considerations that are relative and that change.

The skeptic who wants to argue against the very possibility of rights against the state of this sort has a difficult brief. He must rely, I think, on one of three general positions: (a) He might display a more pervasive moral skepticism, which holds that even to speak of an act being morally right or wrong makes no sense. If no act is morally wrong, then the government of North Carolina cannot be wrong to refuse to bus school children. (b) He might hold a stark form of utilitarianism, which assumes that the only reason we ever have for re-garding an act as right or wrong is its impact on the general interest. Under that theory, to say that busing may be morally required even though it does not benefit the community generally would be inconsistent. (c) He might accept some form of totalitarian theory, which merges the interests of the individual in the good of the general community, and so denies that the two can conflict.

Very few American politicians would be able to accept any of these three grounds. Nixon, for example, could not, because he presents himself as a moral fundamentalist who knows in his heart that pornography is wicked and that some of the people of South Vietnam have rights of self-determination in the name of which they and we may properly kill many others.

I do not want to suggest, however, that no one would in fact argue for ju-dicial restraint on grounds of skepticism; on the contrary, some of the best known advocates of restraint have pitched their arguments entirely on skepti-cal grounds. In 1957, for example, the great judge Learned Hand delivered the Oliver Wendell Holmes lectures at Harvard. Hand was a student of Santayana and a disciple of Holmes, and skepticism in morals was his only religion. He argued for judicial restraint, and said that the Supreme Court had done wrong to declare school segregation illegal in the *Brown* case. It is wrong to suppose, he said, that claims about moral rights express anything more than the speak-ers' preferences. If the Supreme Court justifies its decisions by making such claims, rather than by relying on positive law, it is usurping the place of the leg-islature, for the job of the legislature, representing the majority, is to decide whose preferences shall govern.

This simple appeal to democracy is successful if one accepts the skeptical premise. Of course, if men have no rights against the majority, if political deci-sion is simply a matter of whose preferences shall prevail, then democracy does provide a good reason for leaving that decision to more democratic institutions than courts, even when these institutions make choices that the judges them-selves hate. But a very different, and much more vulnerable, argument from de-mocracy is needed to support judicial restraint if it is based not on skepticism but on deference, as I shall try to show.

4.

If Nixon holds a coherent constitutional theory, it is a theory of restraint based not on skepticism but on deference. He believes that courts ought not to decide controversial issues of political morality because they ought to leave such decisions to other departments of government. If we ascribe this policy to Nixon, we can make sense of his charge that the Warren Court "twisted and bent" the law. He would mean that they twisted and bent the principle of judicial deference, which is an understatement, because he would be more accurate if he said that they ignored it. But are there any good reasons for holding this policy of deference? If the policy is in fact unsound, then Nixon's jurisprudence is undermined, and he ought to be dissuaded from urging further Supreme Court appointments, or encouraging Congress to oppose the Court, in its name.

There is one very popular argument in favor of the policy of deference, which might be called the argument from democracy. It is at least debatable, according to this argument, whether a sound conception of equality forbids segregated education or requires measures like busing to break it down. Who ought to decide these debatable issues of moral and political theory? Should it be a majority of a court in Washington, whose members are appointed for life and are not politically responsible to the public whose lives will be affected by the decision? Or should it be the elected and responsible state or national legislators? A democrat, so this argument supposes, can accept only the second answer.

But the argument from democracy is weaker than it might first appear. The argument assumes, for one thing, that state legislatures are in fact responsible to the people in the way that democratic theory assumes. But in all the states, though in different degrees and for different reasons, that is not the case. In some states it is very far from the case. I want to pass that point, however, because it does not so much undermine the argument from democracy as call for more democracy, and that is a different matter. I want to fix attention on the issue of whether the appeal to democracy in this respect is even right in principle.

The argument assumes that in a democracy all unsettled issues, including issues of moral and political principle, must be resolved only by institutions that are politically responsible in the way that courts are not. Why should we accept that view of democracy? To say that that is what democracy means does no good, because it is wrong to suppose that the word, as a word, has anything like so precise a meaning. Even if it did, we should then have to rephrase our question to ask why we should have democracy, if we assume that is what it means. Nor is it better to say that that view of democracy is established in the American Constitution, or so entrenched in our political tradition that we are committed to it. We cannot argue that the Constitution, which provides no rule limiting judicial review to clear cases, establishes a theory of democracy that excludes wider review, nor can we say that our courts have in fact consistently accepted such a restriction. The burden of Nixon's argument is that they have.

So the argument from democracy is not an argument to which we are committed either by our words or our past. We must accept it, if at all, on the strength of its own logic. In order to examine the arguments more closely, however, we must make a further distinction. The argument as I have set it out might be continued in two different ways: one might argue that judicial deference is required because democratic institutions, like legislatures, are in fact likely to make *sounder* decisions than courts about the underlying issues that constitutional cases raise, that is, about the nature of an individual's moral rights against the state.

Or one might argue that it is for some reason *fairer* that a democratic institution rather than a court should decide such issues, even though there is no reason to believe that the institution will reach a sounder decision. The distinction between these two arguments would make no sense to a skeptic, who would not admit that someone could do a better or worse job at identifying moral rights against the state, any more than someone could do a better or worse job of identifying ghosts. But a lawyer who believes in judicial deference rather than skepticism must acknowledge the distinction, though he can argue both sides if he wishes.

I shall start with the second argument, that legislatures and other democratic institutions have some special title to make constitutional decisions, apart from their ability to make better decisions. One might say that the nature of this title is obvious, because it is always fairer to allow a majority to decide any issue than a minority. But that, as has often been pointed out, ignores the fact that decisions about rights against the majority are not issues that in fairness ought to be left to the majority. Constitutionalism—the theory that the majority must be restrained to protect individual rights—may be a good or bad political theory, but the United States has adopted that theory, and to make the majority judge in its own cause seems inconsistent and unjust. So principles of fairness seem to speak against, not for, the argument from democracy.

Chief Justice Marshall recognized this in his decision in *Marbury v. Madison,* the famous case in which the Supreme Court first claimed the power to review legislative decisions against constitutional standards. He argued that since the Constitution provides that the Constitution shall be the supreme law of the land, the courts in general, and the Supreme Court in the end, must have power to declare statutes void that offend that Constitution. Many legal scholars regard his argument as a *non sequitur,* because, they say, although constitutional constraints are part of the law, the courts, rather than the legislature itself, have not necessarily been given authority to decide whether in particular cases that law has been violated.[2] But the argument is not a *non sequitur* if we take the principle that no man should be judge in his own cause to be so fundamental a part of the idea of legality that Marshall would have been entitled to disregard it only if the Constitution had expressly denied judicial review.

Some might object that it is simple-minded to say that a policy of deference leaves the majority to judge its own cause. Political decisions are made, in the

---

[2] I distinguish this objection to Marshall's argument from the different objection, not here relevant, that the Constitution should be interpreted to impose a legal *duty* on Congress not, for example, to pass laws abridging freedom of speech, but it should not be interpreted to detract from the legal *power* of Congress to make such a law valid if it breaks its duty. In this view, Congress is in the legal position of a thief who has a legal duty not to sell stolen goods, but retains legal power to make a valid transfer if he does. This interpretation has little to recommend it since Congress, unlike the thief, cannot be disciplined except by denying validity to its wrongful acts, at least in a way that will offer protection to the individuals the Constitution is designed to protect.

United States, not by one stable majority but by many different political institutions each representing a different constituency which itself changes its composition over time. The decision of one branch of government may well be reviewed by another branch that is also politically responsible, but to a larger or different constituency. The acts of the Arizona police which the Court held unconstitutional in *Miranda,* for example, were in fact subject to review by various executive boards and municipal and state legislatures of Arizona, as well as by the national Congress. It would be naïve to suppose that all of these political institutions are dedicated to the same policies and interests, so it is wrong to suppose that if the Court had not intervened the Arizona police would have been free to judge themselves.

But this objection is itself too glib, because it ignores the special character of disputes about individual moral rights as distinct from other kinds of political disputes. Different institutions do have different constituencies when, for example, labor or trade or welfare issues are involved, and the nation often divides sectionally on such issues. But this is not generally the case when individual constitutional rights, like the rights of accused criminals, are at issue. It has been typical of these disputes that the interests of those in political control of the various institutions of the government have been both homogeneous and hostile. Indeed that is why political theorists have conceived of constitutional rights as rights against the "state" or the "majority" as such, rather than against any particular body or branch of government.

The early segregation cases are perhaps exceptions to that generality, for one might argue that the only people who wanted *de jure* segregation were white Southerners. But the fact remains that the national Congress had not in fact checked segregation, either because it believed it did not have the legal power to do so or because it did not want to; in either case the example hardly argues that the political process provides an effective check on even local violations of the rights of politically ineffective minorities. In the dispute over busing, moreover, the white majority mindful of its own interests has proved to be both national and powerful. And of course decisions of the national government, like executive decisions to wage war or congressional attempts to define proper police policy, as in the Crime Control Act of 1968, are subject to no review if not court review.

It does seem fair to say, therefore, that the argument from democracy asks that those in political power be invited to be the sole judge of their own decisions, to see whether they have the right to do what they have decided they want to do. That is not a final proof that a policy of judicial activism is superior to a program of deference. Judicial activism involves risks of tyranny; certainly in the stark and simple form I set out. It might even be shown that these risks override the unfairness of asking the majority to be judge in its own cause. But the point does undermine the argument that the majority, in fairness, must be allowed to decide the limits of its own power.

We must therefore turn to the other continuation of the argument from democracy, which holds that democratic institutions, like legislatures, are likely to reach *sounder* results about the moral rights of individuals than would

courts. In 1969 the late Professor Alexander Bickel of the Yale Law School delivered his Holmes lectures at Harvard and argued for the program of judicial
restraint in a novel and ingenious way. He allowed himself to suppose, for purposes of argument, that the Warren Court's program of activism could be
justified if in fact it produced desirable results.[3] He appeared, therefore, to be
testing the policy of activism on its own grounds, because he took activism to
be precisely the claim that the courts have the moral right to improve the future, whatever legal theory may say. Learned Hand and other opponents of activism had challenged that claim. Bickel accepted it, at least provisionally, but
he argued that activism fails its own test.

The future that the Warren Court sought has already begun not to work,
Bickel said. The philosophy of racial integration it adopted was too crude, for
example, and has already been rejected by the more imaginative leaders of the
black community. Its thesis of simple and radical equality has proved unwork-
able in many other ways as well; its simple formula of one-man-one-vote for
passing on the fairness of election districting, for instance, has produced neither sense nor fairness.

Why should a radical Court that aims at improving society fail even on its
own terms? Bickel has this answer: Courts, including the Supreme Court, must
decide blocks of cases on principle, rather than responding in a piecemeal way
to a shifting set of political pressures. They must do so not simply because their
institutional morality requires it, but because their institutional structure provides no means by which they might gauge political forces even if they wanted
to. But government by principle is an inefficient and in the long run fatal form
of government, no matter how able and honest the statesmen who try to administer it. For there is a limit to the complexity that any principle can contain
and remain a recognizable principle, and this limit falls short of the complexity of social organization.

The Supreme Court's reapportionment decisions, in Bickel's view, were not
mistaken just because the Court chose the wrong principle. One-man-one-vote
is too simple, but the Court could not have found a better, more sophisticated
principle that would have served as a successful test for election districting
across the country, or across the years, because successful districting depends
upon accommodation with thousands of facts of political life, and can be
reached, if at all, only by the chaotic and unprincipled development of history.
Judicial activism cannot work as well as government by the more-or-less democratic institutions, not because democracy is required by principle, but, on the
contrary, because democracy works without principle, forming institutions and
compromises as a river forms a bed on its way to the sea.

---

[3] Professor Bickel also argued, with his usual very great skill, that many of the Warren Court's ma-
jor decisions could not even be justified on conventional grounds, that is, by the arguments the
Court advanced in its opinions. His criticism of these opinions is often persuasive, but the
Court's failures of craftsmanship do not affect the argument I consider in the text. (His Holmes
lectures were amplified in his book *The Supreme Court and the Idea of Progress* (New York:
Harper & Row, 1970).

What are we to make of Bickel's argument? His account of recent history can be, and has been, challenged. It is by no means plain, certainly not yet, that racial integration will fail as a long-term strategy; and he is wrong if he thinks that black Americans, of whom more still belong to the NAACP than to more militant organizations, have rejected it. No doubt the nation's sense of how to deal with the curse of racism swings back and forth as the complexity and size of the problem become more apparent, but Bickel may have written at a high point of one arc of the pendulum.

He is also wrong to judge the Supreme Court's effect on history as if the Court were the only institution at work, or to suppose that if the Court's goal has not been achieved the country is worse off than if it had not tried. Since 1954, when the Court laid down the principle that equality before the law requires integrated education, we have not had, except for a few years of the Johnson Administration, a national executive willing to accept that principle as an imperative. For the past several years we have had a national executive that seems determined to undermine it. Nor do we have much basis for supposing that the racial situation in America would now be more satisfactory, on balance, if the Court had not intervened, in 1954 and later, in the way that it did.

But there is a very different, and for my purpose much more important, objection to take to Bickel's theory. His theory is novel because it appears to concede an issue of principle to judicial activism, namely, that the Court is entitled to intervene if its intervention produces socially desirable results. But the concession is an illusion, because his sense of what is socially desirable is inconsistent with the presupposition of activism that individuals have moral rights against the state. In fact, Bickel's argument cannot succeed, even if we grant his facts and his view of history, except on a basis of a skepticism about rights as profound as Learned Hand's.

I presented Bickel's theory as an example of one form of the argument from democracy, the argument that since men disagree about rights, it is safer to leave the final decision about rights to the political process, safer in the sense that the results are likely to be sounder. Bickel suggests a reason why the political process is safer. He argues that the endurance of a political settlement about rights is some evidence of the political morality of that settlement. He argues that this evidence is better than the sorts of argument from principle that judges might deploy if the decision were left to them.

There is a weak version of this claim, which cannot be part of Bickel's argument. This version argues that no political principle establishing rights can be sound, whatever abstract arguments might be made in its favor, unless it meets the test of social acceptance in the long run; so that, for example, the Supreme Court cannot be right in its views about the rights of black children, or criminal suspects, or atheists, if the community in the end will not be persuaded to recognize these rights.

This weak version may seem plausible for different reasons. It will appeal, for instance, to those who believe both in the fact and in the strength of the ordinary man's moral sense, and in his willingness to entertain appeals to that sense. But it does not argue for judicial restraint except in the very long run. On the contrary, it supposes what lawyers are fond of calling a dialogue between the judges and the nation, in which the Supreme Court is to present and defend its reflective view of what the citizen's rights are, much as the Warren Court tried to do, in the hope that the people will in the end agree.

We must turn, therefore, to the strong version of the claim. This argues that the organic political process will secure the genuine rights of men more certainly if it is not hindered by the artificial and rationalistic intrusion of the courts. On this view, the rights of blacks, suspects, and atheists will emerge through the process of political institutions responding to political pressures in the normal way. If a claim of right cannot succeed in this way, then for that reason it is, or in any event it is likely to be, an improper claim of right. But this bizarre proposition is only a disguised form of the skeptical point that there are in fact no rights against the state.

Perhaps, as Burke and his modern followers argue, a society will produce the institutions that best suit it only by evolution and never by radical reform. But rights against the state are claims that, if accepted, require society to settle for institutions that may not suit it so comfortably. The nerve of a claim of right, even on the demythologized analysis of rights I am using, is that an individual is entitled to protection against the majority even at the cost of the general interest. Of course the comfort of the majority will require some accommodation for minorities but only to the extent necessary to preserve order; and that is usually an accommodation that falls short of recognizing their rights.

Indeed the suggestion that rights can be demonstrated by a process of history rather than by an appeal to principle shows either a confusion or no real concern about what rights are. A claim of right presupposes a moral argument and can be established in no other way. Bickel paints the judicial activists (and even some of the heroes of judicial restraint, like Brandeis and Frankfurter, who had their lapses) as eighteenth-century philosophers who appeal to principle because they hold the optimistic view that a blueprint may be cut for progress. But this picture confuses two grounds for the appeal to principle and reform, and two senses of progress.

It is one thing to appeal to moral principle in the silly faith that ethics as well as economics moves by an invisible hand, so that individual rights and the general good will coalesce, and law based on principle will move the nation to a frictionless utopia where everyone is better off than he was before. Bickel attacks that vision by his appeal to history, and by his other arguments against government by principle. But it is quite another matter to appeal to principle *as* principle, to show, for example, that it is unjust to force black children to take their public education in black schools, even if a great many people *will* be worse off if the state adopt the measures needed to prevent this.

This is a different version of progress. It is moral progress, and though history may show how difficult it is to decide where moral progress lies, and how difficult to persuade others once one has decided, it cannot follow from this that those who govern us have no responsibility to face that decision or to attempt that persuasion.

31.
Dualist Democracy
BRUCE ACKERMAN

. . . If I am right, the present moment is characterized by a remarkable breach between constitutional theory and constitutional practice. While our civic practice remains rooted in the distinctive patterns of the American past, sophisticated constitutional thought has increasingly elaborated the genius of American institutions with theories fabricated elsewhere—to the point where these rivals are more familiar than the framework I shall be developing. It seems wise, then, to begin by comparing these familiar academic competitors to a model that is better designed to capture the distinctive spirit of the American Constitution. I shall call this the model of *dualist democracy*.

THE BASIC IDEA

Above all else, a dualist Constitution seeks to distinguish between two different decisions that may be made in a democracy. The first is a decision by the American people; the second, by their government.

Decisions by the People occur rarely, and under special constitutional conditions. Before gaining the authority to make supreme law in the name of the People, a movement's political partisans must, first, convince an extraordinary number of their fellow citizens to take their proposed initiative with a seriousness that they do not normally accord to politics; second, they must allow their opponents a fair opportunity to organize their own forces; third, they must convince a majority of their fellow Americans to support their initiative as its merits are discussed, time and again, in the deliberative fora provided for "higher lawmaking." It is only then that a political movement earns the enhanced legitimacy the dualist Constitution accords to decisions made by the People.

Decisions made by the government occur daily, and also under special conditions. Most importantly, key officials must be held accountable regularly at the ballot box. In addition, they must be given incentives to take a broad view of the public interest without the undue influence of narrow interest groups. Even when this system of "normal lawmaking" is operating well, however, the dualist Constitution prevents elected politicians from exaggerating their authority. They are not to assert that a normal electoral victory has given them a mandate to enact an ordinary statute that overturns the considered judgments previously reached by the People. If they wish to claim this higher form of democratic legitimacy, they must take to the specially onerous obstacle course provided by a dualist Constitution for purposes of higher lawmaking. Only if they succeed in mobilizing their fellow citizens and gaining their repeated support in response to their opponents' counterattacks may they finally earn the authority to proclaim that *the People* have changed their mind and have given their government new marching orders.

Such a brief statement raises many more questions than answers. One set involves issues of institutional design. First, we must consider the design of a good higher lawmaking system: How to organize a process that will reliably mark out the rare occasions when a political movement rightly earns the special recognition accorded the outcomes of mobilized deliberation made in the name of We the People? Second, there is the question of normal lawmaking: How to create incentives for regularly elected officials to engage in public-spirited deliberation despite the pressures of special interests? Third, there is the design of preservation mechanisms: How to preserve the considered judgments of the mobilized People from illegitimate erosion by the statutory decisions of normal government?

And then there are the ultimate issues that transcend institutional mechanics: Is dualist democracy a good form of government for America? The best? If not, what's better?

This chapter does not aim for final answers. It simply describes how the very questions provoked by dualist democracy suggest inquiries different from those now dominant in the academy. Although each academic competitor differs from dualism in a different way, it may help to begin with the one thing they have in common. For all their luxuriant variety, they ignore the special importance dualists place upon *constitutional politics:* the series of political movements that have, from the Founding onward, called upon their fellow Americans to engage in acts of citizenship that, when successful, culminate in the proclamation of higher law in the name of We the People.

But let me be more specific.

MONISTIC DEMOCRACY

Of the modern schools, the monistic democrats have the most impressive pedigree: Woodrow Wilson,[1] James Thayer,[2] Charles Beard,[3] Oliver Wendell Holmes,[4] Robert Jackson,[5] Alexander Bickel,[6] John Ely.[7] These, and many

---

[1] Woodrow Wilson, *Congressional Government* (New York: Houghton Mifflin, 1913). Woodrow Wilson, *Constitutional Government in the United States* (New York: Columbia University Press, 1911).

[2] James Thayer, "The Origin and Scope of the American Doctrine of Constitutional Law," 7 *Harv. L. Rev.* 129 (1893).

[3] Charles Beard, *An Economic Interpretation of the Constitution of the United States* (New York: Macmillan, 1961).

[4] Lochner v. New York, 198 U.S. 45, 74 (1905) (Holmes, J., dissenting).

[5] Robert Jackson, *The Struggle for Judicial Supremacy* (New York: A. A. Knopf, 1941); Railway Express Co. v. New York, 336 U.S. 106, 111 (Jackson, J., concurring).

[6] Alexander Bickel, *The Least Dangerous Branch* (New Haven: Yale University Press, 1986).

[7] John Ely, *Democracy and Distrust: A Theory of Judicial Review* (Cambridge, MA: Harvard University Press, 1980).

other distinguished thinkers and doers, have made monism dominant amongst serious constitutionalists over the course of the last century. As with all received opinions, complexities abound.[8] But, at its root, monism is very simple: Democracy requires the grant of plenary lawmaking authority to the winners of the last general election—so long, at least, as the election was conducted under free and fair ground rules and the winners don't try to prevent the next scheduled round of electoral challenges.

This idea motivates, in turn, a critical institutional conclusion: during the period between elections, all institutional checks upon the electoral victors are presumptively antidemocratic. For sophisticated monists, this is only a presumption. Perhaps certain constitutional checks may prevent the victors from abrogating the next scheduled election; perhaps others might be justified once one considers the deeper ways normal elections fail to satisfy our ideals of electoral fairness. While these exceptions may have great practical importance, monists refuse to let them obscure the main point: when the Supreme Court, or anybody else, invalidates a statute, it suffers from a "countermajoritarian difficulty"[9] which must be overcome before a good democrat can profess satisfaction with this extraordinary action.

In the work of this school, the brooding omnipresence is (an idealized version of) British parliamentary practice. For more than a century now, the Prime Minister has won her office after a relatively fair and square election, and except in truly exceptional circumstances the House of Commons has given its unswerving support to the proposals of Her Majesty's Government. If the people of Great Britain don't like what's going on, they will return the Opposition at the next election. Until that time, neither the House of Lords, nor the Queen, nor the courts seriously undermine the legislative decisions made by a majority of the Commons.

So far as the monist is concerned, the British design captures the essence of democracy. The problem posed by America is its failure to follow the trans-Atlantic model. Rather than granting a power monopoly to a single, popularly elected House of Representatives, Americans tolerate a great deal of insubordination from branches whose electoral connection is suspect or nonexistent. While the Senate gets its share of the lumps, the principal object is the Supreme Court. Whoever gave Nine Old Lawyers authority to overrule the judgments of democratically elected politicians?

There are monistic answers to this question—which try to reconcile judicial review with the fundamental premises of monistic democracy. Thus, constitutional conservatives like Alexander Bickel,[10] centrists like John Ely,[11] and progressives like Richard Parker[12] have proposed roles for the Supreme Court that

---

[8] For a balanced statement see Jesse Choper, *Judicial Review and the National Political Process* (Chicago: University of Chicago Press, 1980), ch. 1.

[9] For the classic statement, see Alexander Bickel, supra n. 6, at 16–23.

[10] See Alexander Bickel, supra n. 6; Alexander Bickel, *The Supreme Court and the Idea of Progress* (1970).

[11] John Ely, supra n. 7.

[12] Richard Parker, "The Past of Constitutional Theory—And Its Future," 42 *Ohio St. L.J.* 223 (1981).

operate within monistic premises. For present purposes, it is the monistic question, not the proliferating number of answers, that needs critical scrutiny.

The monist begs a big question when he asserts that the winner of a fair and open election is entitled to rule with the full authority of We the People. It is much better, of course, for electoral winners to take office rather than suffer an authoritarian putsch by the losers. But it does not follow that all statutes gaining the support of a legislative majority in Washington, D.C., represent the considered judgment of a mobilized majority of American citizens. Instead, the dualist sees a profoundly democratic point to many of the distinctive practices that baffle the monist. For her, they express our Constitution's effort to require elected politicians to operate within a two-track system. If politicians hope to win normal democratic legitimacy for an initiative, they are directed down the normal lawmaking path and told to gain the assent of the House, Senate, and President in the usual ways. If they hope for higher lawmaking authority, they are directed down a specially onerous lawmaking path—whose character and historical development will be the subject of the next chapter. Only if a political movement successfully negotiates the special challenges of the higher lawmaking system can it rightfully claim that its initiative represents the constitutional judgment of We the People.

Once the two-track character of the system is recognized, the Supreme Court appears in a different light. Consider that all the time and effort required to push an initiative down the higher lawmaking track would be wasted unless the Constitution prevented future normal politicians from enacting statutes that ignored the movement's higher law achievement. If future politicians could so easily ignore established higher law, why would any mass movement take the trouble to overcome the special hurdles placed on the higher lawmaking track?

To maintain the integrity of higher lawmaking, all dualist constitutions must provide for one or more institutions to discharge a preservationist function. These institutions must effectively block efforts to repeal established constitutional principles by the simple expedient of passing a normal statute and force the reigning group of elected politicians to move onto the higher lawmaking track if they wish to question the judgments previously made by We the People. Only after negotiating this more arduous obstacle course can a political elite earn the authority to say that We the People have changed our mind.

It follows, then, that the dualist will view the Supreme Court from a very different perspective than the monist. The monist treats every act of judicial review as presumptively antidemocratic and strains to save the Supreme Court from the "countermajoritarian difficulty" by one or another ingenious argument. In contrast, the dualist sees the discharge of the preservationist function by the courts as an essential part of a well-ordered democratic regime. Rather than threatening democracy by frustrating the statutory demands of the political elite in Washington, the courts serve democracy by protecting the hard-won principles of a mobilized citizenry against erosion by political elites who have failed to gain broad and deep popular support for their innovations.

This is not to say that any particular decision by the modern Supreme Court can be justified in preservationist terms. The key point is that dualists cannot dismiss a good-faith effort by the Court to interpret the Constitution as "anti-democratic" simply because it leads to the invalidation of normal statutes; this ongoing judicial effort to look backward and interpret the meaning of the great achievements of the past is an indispensable part of the larger project of distinguishing the will of We the People from the acts of We the Politicians.

RIGHTS FOUNDATIONALISTS

In confronting monism, the dualist's main object is to break the tight link monists construct between two distinct ideas: "democracy" on the one hand and "parliamentary sovereignty" on the other. Like monists, dualists are democrats—they believe that the People are the ultimate authority in America. They disagree only about the easy way in which normally elected politicians claim to legislate with the full authority of the People.

In contrast, the primacy of popular sovereignty is challenged by a second modern school. While none of these theorists completely denies a place for democratic principles, their populist enthusiasms are constrained by deeper commitments to fundamental rights. Unsurprisingly, members of this school differ when it comes to identifying the rights that are fundamental. Conservatives like Richard Epstein emphasize the foundational role of property rights;[13] liberals like Ronald Dworkin emphasize the right to equal concern and respect;[14] collectivists like Owen Fiss, the rights of disadvantaged groups.[15] These transparent differences should not blind us to the idea that binds them together. Whatever rights are Right, all agree that the American constitution is concerned, first and foremost, with their protection. Indeed, the whole point of having rights is to trump decisions rendered by democratic institutions that may otherwise legislate for the collective welfare. To emphasize this common thread, I shall group these thinkers together by calling them *rights foundationalists*.

As with the monists, this school is hardly a trendy creation of yesterday. There is, however, an interesting difference in the intellectual lineage they construct for themselves. While monists refer to a series of Americans from Wilson and Thayer to Frankfurter and Bickel, foundationalists favor philosophical writers further removed in time and space—with Kant (via Rawls)[16] and Locke (via Nozick)[17] presently serving as the most important sources of inspiration. Right now, I am not interested in these internal debates. My aim is to describe how foundationalists as a group differ from more democratic schools.

[13] Richard Epstein, *Takings: Private Property and the Power of Eminent Domain* (Cambridge, MA: Harvard University Press, 1985).

[14] Ronald Dworkin, *Taking Rights Seriously* (Cambridge, MA: Harvard University Press, 1977), chapter 5; Ronald Dworkin, *Law's Empire*, (Cambridge, MA: Belknap Press, 1986), chapters 10–11.

[15] Owen Fiss, "Groups and the Equal Protection Clause," 5 *J. Phil. & Pub. Aff.* 107 (1976).

[16] John Rawls, "Kantian Constructivism in Moral Theory," 77 *J. Phil.* 515 (1980).

[17] Robert Nozick, *Anarchy, State, and Utopia* (New York: Basic Books, 1974).

Begin with the monists. It is fair to say that they are hostile to rights, at least as foundationalists understand them. Indeed, it is just when the Supreme Court begins to invalidate statutes in the name of fundamental rights that the monist begins to worry about the "countermajoritarian difficulty" that renders judicial review presumptively illegitimate.[18]

This "difficulty" does not seem so formidable to the foundationalist. Instead, she is more impressed by the fact that a democratic legislature might endorse any number of oppressive actions—establish a religion, or authorize torture, or . . . When such violations occur, the foundationalist demands judicial intervention despite the breach of democratic principle. Rights trump democracy—provided, of course, that they're the Right rights.

And there's the rub. Indeed, it is their anxiety over the arbitrary definition of rights that induces thoughtful foundationalists to recur to great philosophers like Kant and Locke in an effort to understand the Constitution. If judges are to avoid arbitrariness in defining fundamental rights, shouldn't they take advantage of the most profound reflections on the subject available in the Western tradition?

For the monist, this turn to the Great Books is yet another symptom of the foundationalist's antidemocratic disease. Whatever its philosophical merits, the foundationalist's discourse is invariably esoteric—involving encounters with authors and doctrines that most college-educated people successfully avoided during their most academic moments. This exalted talk of Kant and Locke only emphasizes the elitism involved in removing fundamental questions from the democratic process.

These objections hardly convince the foundationalist. They serve only to generate further anxieties about the ease with which monistic democracy can be swept by demagogic irrationality. And so the debate proceeds, with the two sides talking past one another: democracy versus rights versus democracy versus—point and counterpoint, with all the talk changing few minds.

How does the introduction of dualism change the shape of this familiar conversational field? By offering a framework which allows both sides to accommodate some—if not all—of their concerns. The basic mediating device is the dualist's two-track system of democratic lawmaking. It allows an important place for the foundationalist's view of "rights as trumps" without violating the monist's deeper commitment to the primacy of democracy. To grasp the logic of accommodation, suppose that a rights-oriented movement took to the higher lawmaking track and successfully mobilized the People to endorse one or another Bill of Rights. Given this achievement, the dualist can readily endorse the judicial invalidation of later statutes that undermine these rights, even when they concern matters, like the protection of personal freedom or privacy, that have nothing much to do with the integrity of the electoral process so central

---

[18] Not that monists necessarily oppose all exercises of judicial review. As I have suggested, the school has been quite ingenious in justifying the judicial protection of one or another right as instrumental for the ongoing democratic functioning of the regime. See authors cited at nn. 6, 7, 12, supra.

to monistic democrats. As we have seen, the dualist believes that the Court furthers the cause of democracy when it preserves constitutional rights against erosion by politically ascendant elites who have yet to mobilize the People to support the repeal of previous higher lawmaking principles. Thus, unlike the monist, she will have no trouble supporting the idea that rights can properly trump the conclusions of normal democratic politics. She can do so, moreover, without the need for non-democratic principles of the kinds proffered by the rights foundationalist. Thus, the dualist can offer a deeper reconciliation of democracy and rights to those who find a certain amount of truth in both sides of the debate.

This reconciliation will not, of course, prove satisfactory to all members of the previously contending schools. The problem for the committed foundationalist, unsurprisingly, is the insufficiently deep foundations the dualist has built for the protection of rights. Granted, concedes the foundationalist, the dualist will applaud the judicial protection of rights if a warrant can be found in prior higher lawmaking activity. But that is an awfully big "if." What if the People have not adopted the right Bill of Rights? Should the Constitution then be construed in ways that allow the statutory perpetration of injustice?

It is their different answers to this question that continue to distinguish dualist from committed foundationalist. For the dualist, judicial protection of rights does depend on a prior democratic affirmation on the higher lawmaking track. In this sense, the dualist's Constitution is democratic first, rights-protecting second. The committed foundationalist reverses this priority: the Constitution is first concerned with protecting rights; only then does it authorize the People to work their will on other matters. Having isolated this disagreement, we must next see whether it can be resolved. Are there very general arguments that indicate whether the American Constitution has been built on dualist or foundationalist lines?

My answer is yes. Once again, the decisive consideration is drawn from the distinctive character of two-track lawmaking. My argument against foundationalism focuses on the fact that our Constitution has never (with two exceptions I will consider shortly) explicitly entrenched existing higher law against subsequent revision by the People. While the original Constitution gave higher law protection to slavery, at least it did not try to make it unconstitutional for Americans of later generations to reconsider the question; similarly, when Americans of the early twentieth century enacted Prohibition into higher law, they did not seek to make the amendment unamendable. In these two cases, of course, the People have exercised their right to change their mind. And few among us would say that we were the worse for repeal. Foundationalists, however, must acknowledge the general availability of repeal with embarrassment. For this open-ended practice allows constitutional amendments of a kind that most modern foundationalists would consider morally disastrous.

A hypothetical case: Suppose that the religious revival now prominent in the Islamic world is the first wave of a Great Awakening that envelops the Christian West. A general revulsion against godless materialism yields mass political mobilization that finally results in a successful campaign for partial repeal of the first Amendment. With the dawn of the new millennium, Amendment XXVII is proclaimed throughout the land:

> Christianity is established as the state religion of the American people, and the public worship of other gods is hereby forbidden.

This enactment would inaugurate a deep transformation of our higher law heritage—on more or less the same order, though of a very different kind, as those achieved by Reconstruction Republicans and New Deal Democrats in earlier generations. Moreover, such an amendment would deeply offend my own commitment to freedom of conscience. Nonetheless, if I were then so unlucky as to be a Justice of the Supreme Court (serving as a holdover from the last secular Administration), I would have no doubt about my judicial responsibility. While I hope that I would stick to my conviction that this Christianity amendment was terribly wrong, I would uphold it as a fundamental part of the American Constitution: if some diehard brought a lawsuit in 2001 seeking to convince the Supreme Court to declare the Christianity amendment unconstitutional, I would join my colleagues in summarily rejecting the petition—or resign my office and join in a campaign to convince the American people to change their mind.

But I wouldn't take the course suggested by foundationalism: stay on the bench and write a dissent denying that the First Amendment had been validly amended. I doubt, moreover, that one may find many American lawyers who seriously disagree—even among those who presently wrap themselves up in foundationalist rhetoric.[19]

Judicial dissent would not be preposterous in other countries, most notably modern Germany. In the aftermath of Nazism, the new West German constitution explicitly declared that a long list of fundamental human rights *cannot* constitutionally be revised, regardless of the extent to which a majority of Germans support repeal. Given this self-conscious act of entrenchment, it would be absolutely right for the German constitutional court to issue an opinion, absurd in the American context, striking down an amendment blatantly violating freedom of conscience. Under this foundationalist constitution, judges would be within their rights to continue resisting: if the dominant political majority insisted on repeal, it would be obliged to replace the entire constitution with a new one in its grim determination to destroy fundamental rights.

But this only makes it clear how far dualist America is from foundationalist Germany at the present time. Insofar as America has had constitutional experience with German-style entrenchment, the lessons have been very negative. The Founders were perfectly aware of entrenchment in 1787, but they did not use the device to serve the cause of human freedom. They used it to entrench the African slave trade—explicitly forbidding the American people from

---

[19] The recent flap over President Bush's proposed flag-burning amendment illustrates this point. No serious opponent suggested that the First Amendment could not be validly revised, even though the Bush initiative went to the very heart of the amendment's concerns with free political expression. Instead, opponents trusted to the good sense of the American people and successfully persuaded them to reject this flag-waving assault on their heritage of freedom.

enacting an amendment barring the practice before the year 1808. This history suggests that the foundationalist interpretation is inconsistent with the existing premises of the American higher lawmaking system. In America, in contrast to Germany, it is the People who are the source of rights; the Constitution does not spell out rights that the People must accept (or settle for).[20]

Speaking as a citizen, I don't take much joy from this discovery. I myself think it would be a good idea to entrench the Bill of Rights against subsequent revision by some future American majority caught up in some awful neo-Nazi paroxysm. But this, in a way, only makes my point—which is to clarify the spirit of the Constitution as it is, not as it may (or may not) become. Unless and until a political movement does succeed in entrenching a modern Bill of Rights, dualism describes the ambition of the American enterprise better than any foundationalist interpretation. The Constitution puts democracy first, though not in the simple way that monists suppose.

HISTORICISM

The clash between monists and foundationalists dominates the present field of constitutional debate and has moved beyond the classroom to the courtroom. The sharp split between the two schools mimics the split between plaintiff and defendant in the typical lawsuits—the plaintiff insisting that a statute has violated her fundamental rights, the defendant responding that courts should defer to the democratic authority of Congress. Little wonder that thoughtful judges and citizens are drawn to reflections about democracy and rights—creating an audience for the work of the two competing schools.

Dualism expresses a more hopeful possibility. Perhaps the conflict between plaintiff and defendant is not a sign of unremitting conflict between the

---

[20] My hypothetical Christianity amendment involves a right that most foundationalists would consider fundamental but that almost all lawyers—and all dualists—would immediately recognize as repealable. While this example suffices to distinguish dualism from foundationalism, the hypothetical does not allow us to consider whether dualist theory allows any conceptual room at all for entrenchment.

To test this question, imagine that a religious movement managed to ratify a second amendment along with the one hypothesized in the text: "Any American advocating the repeal of Amendment XXVII is hereby declared guilty of treason and subject to capital punishment upon conviction." This amendment, in contrast to the first, aims to make it impossible for the People to reconsider its commitment to Christianity, and so amounts to the repeal of dualist democracy itself. Would it therefore be constitutionally appropriate for judges to invalidate it? Or would it simply be best for all decent people to quit the regime and struggle to overthrow it?

Such questions are best left to the dark day they arise. For now, it is enough to beware easy answers. In particular, I do not believe that judges would be justified in asserting a general authority to protect the fundamental principles of dualist democracy against repudiation by the People. Suppose, for example, that the next round of our constitutional politics were dominated by a mobilized coalition of liberals who sought to entrench a modernized version of the Bill of Rights, guaranteeing a right to a minimum income along with other new rights unknown to our eighteenth-century Founders. *This* act of entrenchment, no less than the second Christianity amendment, would be inconsistent with the principles of dualist democracy, since it makes it impossible for the People to change their mind about certain constitutional values. Yet would the judges have the constitutional authority to force the People to keep *these* possibilities open?

democratic and rights-oriented aspects of our tradition. Instead, both the enactment of normal statutes *and* the judicial protection of constitutional rights
are part of a larger practice of dualist democracy. This abstract synthesis, of
course, is hardly enough to decide concrete cases. But it points in a particular
direction—toward a reflective study of the past to determine when the People
have spoken and what they have said during their historic moments of successful constitutional politics.

The Paradoxes of American "Burkeanism"

This historicizing tendency allows the dualist to make contact with a third
strand of constitutional thought. I will call it Burkean, since it has yet to find
its modern spokesman who is Burke's equal.[21] While one can isolate Burkean
aspects of recent theoretical work,[22] this tendency is far more pronounced
amongst practicing lawyers and judges.

These professionals do not require brilliant theorists to convince them to
cultivate Burkean sensibilities. They are already deeply immersed in a common
law tradition that demands the very skills and sensitivities that self-conscious
Burkeans commend. What counts for the common lawyer is not some fancy
theory but the patterns of concrete decision built up by courts and other practical decision-makers over decades, generations, centuries. Slowly, often in a
half-conscious and circuitous fashion, these decisions build upon one another
to yield the constitutional rights that modern Americans take for granted, just
as they slowly generate precedents that the President and Congress may use to
claim new grants of constitutional authority. The task of the Burkean lawyer or
judge is to master these precedents, thereby gaining a sense of their hidden po-
tentials for growth and decay.

This basic conception can be elaborated in conservative or reformist directions. Reformist incrementalists will try to keep the precedents abreast with the
"evolving moral sense of the country"; more conservative types may be more
open to the incremental development of new Presidential powers than new constitutional rights. As always, it is more important to focus upon the point that
all these common lawyers have in common—which is an emphasis on the ongoing cultivation of a concrete historical tradition that is sorely missing from
the talk of the "high theorists" of either the monistic or the foundationalist
persuasion.

So far as these Burkeans are concerned, there is more wisdom in the gradual
accretion of concrete decisions than in the abstract speculations of our most
brilliant academics. The only "theory" with any real value is found in the
opinions of judges responding to the facts of particular cases. And even these

---

[21] Although Alexander Bickel became an eloquent spokesman, he died before he had a fair chance
to develop his evolving views. But see, Alexander Bickel, *The Morality of Consent* (New Haven:
Yale University Press, 1975), pp. 1–30.

[22] See, for example, Anthony Kronman, "Alexander Bickel's Philosophy of Prudence," 94 *Yale
L. J.* 1567 (1985); Charles Fried, "The Artificial Reason of the Law or: What Lawyers Know,"
60 *Tex. L. Rev.* 31 (1981).

theories should not be taken too seriously. They will take on different meanings as they are tested over the generations by different judges confronting different cases. The Constitution simply cannot be understood by speculative theorists who have failed to immerse themselves in the historical practice of concrete decision, and hence have been unable to cultivate the prudent sense of statecraft necessary for wise constitutional development.

Such sentiments contain important insights—but they should not be confused with the whole truth. To put the Burkean sensibility in its place, I begin with the aspect of dualist constitutionalism it entirely ignores. Only then will it be possible to isolate important points of convergence.

The common lawyers' blind side can be summarized in two words: constitutional politics. Indeed, on those occasions that Burkeanism reaches self-consciousness—as in the work of the later Bickel[23]—constitutional politics is aggressively disparaged. All that Burkeans see in popular political movements are the charismatic, but unscrupulous, leaders; the loud, but hopelessly ambiguous, pronunciamentos; the excited, but ignorant, masses. They recoil from the scene of mass mobilization in disgust. At best, eruptions of collective irrationality will quickly disintegrate amid clouds of factional recrimination. Otherwise, a government seized by utopian rhetoric can degenerate into unspeakable tyranny with bewildering speed. Given this nightmare, could anyone of sound mind support any regime in which the sober and sensible Burkean did not have the final say?

The dualist responds by rejecting the Burkean's self-congratulatory statement of the alternatives. While only a fool fails to recognize the dangers of mass demagogy, the dualist refuses to forget a very different possibility. Here a political leadership challenges the traditional wisdom on behalf of principles which, though inevitably open-ended, do have rational content. While these transformative initiatives inspire mass involvement, passionate commitment, great sacrifice, the result is not some unspeakable tyranny but a deepening dialogue between leaders and masses within a democratic structure that finally succeeds in generating broad popular consent for a sharp break with the status quo. Finally, the dualist challenges the Burkeans' suggestion to constitutional lawyers that they forget, as quickly as possible, the results of these nightmarish popular eruptions. To the contrary: most Americans identify our great popular struggles as culminating in the nation's greatest constitutional achievements. Thus, the original Constitution codified the Revolutionary generation's defeat of monarchy on behalf of republican self-government; the Civil War amendments codified the struggle of an entire generation to repudiate slavery on behalf of a new constitutional ideal of equality; and so forth. Rather than forgetting such popular achievements, *our* Constitution seeks to protect them against erosion during more normal times, when the People are less involved in affairs of state.

---

[23] See Alexander Bickel, supra n. 23. For eloquent spokesmen in allied disciplines, see, Friedrich Hayek, *Law, Legislation and Liberty* (London: Routledge & Kegan Paul, 1982); Samuel Huntington, *American Politics: The Promise of Disharmony* (Cambridge, MA: Belknap Press, 1985); Michael Oakeshott, *On Human Conduct* (Oxford: Clarendon Press, 1975).

This dualist conclusion challenges the standard Burkean sensibility in four ways. first, it undermines its commitment to incrementalism. Although gradual adaptation is an important part of the story, the Constitution cannot be understood without recognizing that Americans have, time and again, successfully repudiated large chunks of their past and transformed their higher law to express deep changes in their political identities. Perhaps these changes do not seem radical to those who long for a total revolution that (vainly) seeks to obliterate every trace of the old regime. But, when judged by any other standard, they were hardly incremental. If a label will clarify matters, American history has been punctuated by successful exercises in *revolutionary reform*—in which protagonists struggled over basic questions of principle that had ramifying implications for the conduct of large areas of American life.

Which leads to a second challenge from the dualist. The Burkean is suspicious not only of big breaks but of the self-conscious appeals to abstract principles that accompany them. He prides himself in avoiding loose talk of Freedom, Equality, or Democracy. Even more modest theories dealing with "free speech" or "equal protection" seem impossibly vague to him. The dualist, in contrast, finds an encounter with abstract ideals an inescapable part of the American past. Whatever else may be said about the Founders, they were hardly content with the Burkean arts of muddling through crises. They were children of the Enlightenment, eager to use the best political science of their time to prove to a doubting world that republican self-government was no utopian dream.[24] Otherwise they would never have tried to write a Constitution whose few thousand words contained a host of untried ideas and institutions. If abstract ideals were important to the Founders and their successors in constitutional politics, how can we pretend to understand our legacy without confronting them?

But there is a particular abstraction that gives the Burkean special trouble. And that is rule by the People. The People rule best, the Burkean says with a broad wink, when they leave the business of government to a well-trained elite immersed in the nation's concrete constitutional tradition. Slowly but surely, this elite will sense the drift of popular sentiment and take the countless small steps needed to keep the tradition responsive to the present's half-articulate sense of its special needs. For the Burkean, however, the public dialogue accompanying such ongoing adaptation is best kept to relatively small elites— judges talking to one another about the relationship of past decisions to present problems, statesmen telling one another that their constituents haven't given them a mandate to accomplish particular goals but have selected them for their prudent capacity to make sensible public policy.

Once again, it is not necessary for the dualist to belittle the importance of this ongoing enterprise in normal political adaptation. She refuses, however, to allow this elite conversation to obscure the even greater importance of a different dialogue—one through which mobilized masses of ordinary citizens may

---

[24] See Paul Kahn, "Reason and Will in the Origins of American Constitutionalism," 98 *Yale L. J.* 449, 453–73 (1989).

finally organize their political will with sufficient clarity to lay down the law to those who speak in their name on a daily basis in Washington, D.C. While competing elites play a critical role in this higher lawmaking dialectic, the process typically involves a conflictual kind of ideological politics that Burkeans disdain. This disdain is all the more unfortunate because successful higher lawmaking also requires prudence and statesmanship—to which Burkeans might otherwise make important contributions.

To sum up the dualist critique in a fourth point that presupposes the first three: the Burkean fails to recognize that he can easily become part of the problem, rather than its solution. The problem is how to prevent normal government from departing from the great principles of higher law validated by the People during their relatively rare successes in constitutional politics. Burkeans threaten to make this problem worse by taking advantage of the citizenry's weak involvement in·normal politics to embrace "statesmanly" solutions that undercut fundamental principles previously affirmed by the People. In these cases, Burkean "prudence" degenerates, in dualist eyes, into obscurantist elitism that prides itself on ignoring the greatest constitutional achievements of the American people.

THREE

BEYOND THE STATE

In the modern world, the dominant political unit is the nation-state—a political entity whose boundaries can span a vast geographic area, and whose citizens can include members of many cultural, ethnic, and religious groups. Because nations are large and powerful, they provide more security than smaller political units can; but because their populations are diverse, they often must cope with tensions among their constituent groups. When group relations are sufficiently troubled—when, for example, there is persistent religious strife, or one ethnic group oppresses another—a group that is in the minority may find secession appealing. But when, if ever, does a group that is a minority within one state have a right to form a new state within which it is a majority?

As Allen Buchanan argues in reading 32, there are two basic classes of theories about when secession is legitimate: *remedial right only theories,* which assert that groups only have a right to secede when they have suffered serious injustice that can be remedied in no other way, and *primary right theories,* which assert that groups with certain characteristics have a right to secede whether or not their members have been treated unjustly. According to some primary right theories, the relevant characteristic is sharing a common culture, language, or history, while according to others, it is simply having chosen to form an independent state.

Buchanan offers several arguments against primary right theories. These theories, he contends, are unrealistic: they are unlikely to be acted on because their implementation would seriously threaten many existing states. Moreover, those who support the integrity of territorial boundaries are right to do so; for these boundaries define the jurisdiction that any political authority must have to enforce its laws effectively. In this way, fixed boundaries both enhance security and give us the stability that we need to plan. In addition, acknowledging a primary right to secede would create perverse incentives for states that wished to block the formation of secessionist groups; for these states would have reason both to restrict immigration and to prevent groups and regions from developing the sorts of political and economic structures that might enable them to become independent.

Unlike Buchanan, Avishai Margalit and Joseph Raz (reading 33) defend a primary right theory. The crux of their argument is that there are certain groups whose prosperity profoundly affects the well-being of their members. These groups, which Margalit and Raz call *encompassing groups,* tend to be large and anonymous, to have a common culture that determines the outlook and options of those who grow up within them, and to supply both the terms in which others identify their members and the terms in which their members identify themselves. Because the well-being of these groups and the well-being of their members is so closely intertwined, Margalit and Raz argue that the groups have a right to determine the course of their own affairs when there is no other way for them to prosper. And while persecution is indeed one factor that can prevent an encompassing group from prospering, it is not the only such factor. A group may also suffer as the result "of neglect or ignorance or of indifference to the prosperity of a minority group by the majority."

According to Margalit and Raz, the links between group membership and individual well-being show that national boundaries should sometimes be redrawn. But in reading 34, Will Kymlicka invokes a similar linkage to support a very different conclusion. He points out that "freedom involves making choices amongst various options, and our societal culture not only provides these options, but also makes them meaningful to us"; and he infers that if people need the freedom to choose their own ways of living, then nations must protect the cultures of any minorities they contain. Because abolishing national boundaries would allow existing cultures to be swamped by newcomers, protecting minority cultures does not require a policy of open borders; but because relinquishing one's culture is so difficult, nations also must not allow minority cultures to decay and be replaced by a single cosmopolitan culture. Instead, the best policy is to preserve both national boundaries and the cultures of any minorities that exist within them.

So far, the question has been how cultural differences should affect national boundaries. But cultural differences also raise other problems, and some of these are discussed by Charles Taylor in reading 35. Taylor's theme is the tension between the traditional liberal "politics of equal recognition"—the idea that all individuals should be treated the same and be accorded the same rights—and a "politics of difference" which insists that we recognize "the unique identity of this individual or group, their distinctness from everyone else." Although these approaches to politics may seem diametrically opposed, Taylor argues that the demand for group recognition is itself a version of the demand for equal treatment—a version which reflects the idea that each person's identity is conferred by his group. Nevertheless, despite this connection, there remains an important difference between treating everyone the same and treating people differently on the basis of group membership.

Given this difference, which approach should we adopt? Taylor's answer is mixed: he accepts the liberal view that there are many rights which must be accorded to everyone, but also agrees with Kymlicka that uniform treatment is sometimes less important than cultural survival. In addition, Taylor distinguishes two versions of the claim that all cultures are owed equal respect. One version requires only that we presume "that all human cultures that have animated whole societies over some considerable stretch of time have something important to say to all human beings"; while the other imposes the more stringent demand that we judge all cultures to *be* of equal worth. Although Taylor accepts the claim's first version, he rejects the second on the grounds that anyone who insisted that every culture had to be as good as every other would not be making a *judgment* about different cultures at all. To withhold judgment in this way, he argues, is not respectful, but merely condescending.

Unlike the authors of the three preceding selections, all of whom express at least some sympathy for the idea that retaining one's native culture plays an important role in determining one's well-being, Jeremy Waldron (reading 36) is an unabashed cosmopolitan. Although Waldron agrees with Kymlicka that a person's options are determined by his cultural context, he does not agree that a person has fewer options, or worse options, if his cultural context consists of a melange of diverse influences. Moreover, any attempt to insulate a minority culture from change would require preventing group members from learning about alternative cultures—an effort which, if successful, would inhibit rather than facilitate choice. Because we all derive our identity from a variety of sources, and because a politics of group membership "can be blinding, dangerous, and disruptive in the real world, where . . . communal allegiances are as much ancient hatreds of one's neighbor as immemorial traditions of culture," Waldron urges that we embrace, rather than resist, the complexity of the modern self.

VII

NATIONAL
SELF-DETERMINATION
AND SECESSION

32.
Theories of Secession
ALLEN BUCHANAN

II. TWO TYPES OF NORMATIVE THEORIES OF SECESSION

All theories of the right to secede either understand the right as a *remedial* right only or also recognize a *primary* right to secede. By a right in this context is meant a *general,* not a *special,* right (one generated through promising, contract, or some special relationship). Remedial Right Only Theories assert that a group has a general right to secede if and only if it has suffered certain injustices, for which secession is the appropriate remedy of last resort.[1] Different Remedial Right Only Theories identify different injustices as warranting the remedy of secession.

Primary Right Theories, in contrast, assert that certain groups can have a (general) right to secede in the absence of any injustice. They do not limit legitimate secession to being a means of remedying an injustice. Different Primary Right Theories pick out different conditions that groups must satisfy to have a right to secede in the absence of injustices.

Remedial Right Only Theories. According to this first type of theory, the (general) right to secede is in important respects similar to the right to revolution, as the latter is understood in what may be called the mainstream of normative theories of revolution. The latter are typified by John Locke's theory, according to which the people have the right to overthrow the government if and only if their fundamental rights are violated, and more peaceful means have been to no avail.[2]

The chief difference between the right to secede and the right to revolution, according to Remedial Right Only Theories, is that the right to secede accrues to a portion of the citizenry, concentrated in a part of the territory of the state. The object of the exercise of the right to secede is not to overthrow the government, but only to sever the government's control over that portion of the territory.

The recognition of a remedial right to secede can be seen as supplementing Locke's theory of revolution and theories like it. Locke tends to focus on cases

---

[1] Some versions of Remedial Right Only Theory, including the one considered below, add another necessary condition: the *proviso* that the new state makes credible guarantees that it will respect the human rights of all those who reside in it.

[2] John Locke, *Second Treatise of Civil Government* (Hackett Publishing Co., 1980), pp. 100–124. Strictly speaking, it may be incorrect to say that Locke affirms a right to revolution if by revolution is meant an attempt to overthrow the existing political authority. Locke's point is that if the government acts in ways that are not within the scope of the authority granted to it by the people's consent, then governmental authority ceases to exist. In that sense, instead of a Lockean right to revolution it would be more accurate to speak of the right of the people to constitute a new governmental authority.

where the government perpetrates injustices against "the people," not a particular group within the state, and seems to assume that the issue of revolution arises usually only when there has been a persistent pattern of abuses affecting large numbers of people throughout the state. This picture of legitimate revolution is conveniently simple: When the people suffer prolonged and serious injustices, the people will rise.

In some cases however, the grosser injustices are perpetrated, not against the citizenry at large, but against a particular group, concentrated in a region of the state. (Consider, for example, Iraq's genocidal policies against Kurds in northern Iraq.) Secession may be justified, and may be feasible, as a response to selective tyranny, when revolution is not a practical prospect.

If the only effective remedy against selective tyranny is to oppose the government, then a strategy of opposition that stops short of attempting to overthrow the government (revolution), but merely seeks to remove one's group and the territory it occupies from the control of the state (secession), seems both morally unexceptionable and, relatively speaking, moderate. For this reason, a Remedial Right Only approach to the right to secede can be seen as a valuable complement to the Lockean approach to the right to revolution understood as a remedial right. In both the case of revolution and that of secession, the right is understood as the right of persons subject to a political authority to defend themselves from serious injustices, as a remedy of last resort.

It was noted earlier that Remedial Right Only Theories hold that the *general* right to secession exists only where the group in question has suffered injustices. This qualification is critical. Remedial Right Only Theories allow that there can be *special* rights to secede if (1) the state grants a right to secede (as with the secession of Norway from Sweden in 1905), or if (2) the constitution of the state includes a right to secede (as does the 1993 Ethiopian Constitution), or perhaps if (3) the agreement by which the state was initially created out of previously independent political units included the implicit or explicit assumption that secession at a later point was permissible (as some American Southerners argued was true of the states of the Union). If any of these three conditions obtain, we can speak of a *special* right to secede. The point of Remedial Right Only Theories is not to deny that there can be special rights to secede in the absence of injustices. Rather, it is to deny that there is a *general* right to secede that is not a remedial right.

Because they allow for special rights to secede, Remedial Right Only Theories are not as restrictive as they might first appear. They do *not* limit permissible secession to cases where the seceding group has suffered injustices. They *do* restrict the general (as opposed to special) right to secede to such cases.

Depending upon which injustices they recognize as grievances sufficient to justify secession, Remedial Right Theories may be more liberal or more restrictive. What all Remedial Right Only Theories have in common is the thesis that there is no (general) right to secede from a just state.

A Remedial Right Only Theory. For purposes of comparison with the other basic type of theory, Primary Right Theories, I will take as a representative of Remedial Right Only Theories the particular version of this latter type of theory that I have argued for at length elsewhere.[3] According to this version, a group has a right to secede only if:

1. The physical survival of its members is threatened by actions of the state (as with the policy of the Iraqi government toward Kurds in Iraq) or it suffers violations of other basic human rights (as with the East Pakistanis who seceded to create Bangladesh in 1970), *or*
2. Its previously sovereign territory was unjustly taken by the state (as with the Baltic Republics).

I have also argued that other conditions ought to be satisfied if a group that suffers any of these injustices is to be recognized through international law or international political practice as having the right to secede.[4] Chief among these is that there be credible guarantees that the new state will respect the human rights of all of its citizens and that it will cooperate in the project of securing other *just terms* of secession.[5] (In addition to the protection of minority and human rights, the just terms of secession include a fair division of the national debt; a negotiated determination of new boundaries; arrangements for continuing, renegotiating, or terminating treaty obligations; and provisions for defense and security.) This bare sketch of the theory will suffice for the comparisons that follow.

Primary Right Theories. Primary Right Theories fall into two main classes: *Ascriptive Group Theories* and *Associative Group Theories.* Theories that include the Nationalist Principle (according to which every nation or people is entitled to its own state) fall under the first heading. Those that confer the right to secede on groups that can muster a majority in favor of independence in a plebiscite fall under the second.

Ascriptive Group Theories. According to Ascriptive Group versions of Primary Right Theories, it is groups whose memberships are defined by what are sometimes called ascriptive characteristics that have the right to secede (even in the absence of injustices). Ascriptive characteristics exist independently of any actual political association that the members of the group may have forged. In other words, according to Ascriptive Group Theories of secession, it is first and foremost certain *nonpolitical* characteristics of groups that ground the group's right to an independent political association.

Being a nation or people is an ascriptive characteristic. What makes a group a nation or people is the fact that it has a common culture, history, language, a

---

[3] Allen Buchanan, *Secession* (Boulder: Westview Press, 1991), pp. 27–80.

[4] Allen Buchanan, "Self-Determination, Secession, and the Rule of International Law," in *The Morality of Nationalism*, Robert McKim and Jeffrey McMahan, eds. (Oxford: Oxford University Press, 1997).

[5] This proviso warrants elaboration. For one thing, virtually no existing state is without some infringements of human rights. Therefore, requiring credible guarantees that a new state will avoid all infringements of human rights seems excessive. Some might argue, instead, that the new state must simply do a better job of respecting human rights than the state from which it secedes. It can be argued, however, that the international community has a legitimate interest in requiring somewhat higher standards for recognizing new states as legitimate members of the system of states.

sense of its own distinctiveness, and perhaps a shared aspiration for constituting its own political unit. No actual political organization of the group, nor any
actual collective choice to form a political association, is necessary for the
group to be a nation or people.

Thus Margalit and Raz appear to embrace the Nationalist Principle when
they ascribe the right to secede to what they call "encompassing cultures,"
defined as large-scale, anonymous (rather than small-scale, face-to-face) groups
that have a common culture and character that encompasses many important
aspects of life and which marks the character of the life of its members,
where membership in the group is in part a matter of mutual recognition and
is important for one's self-identification and is a matter of belonging, not of
achievement.[6]

Associative Group Theories. In contrast, Associative Group versions of Primary Right Theories do not require that a group have any ascriptive characteristic in common such as ethnicity or an encompassing culture, even as a
necessary condition for having a right to secede. The members of the group
need not even believe that they share any characteristics other than the desire
to have their own state. Instead, Associative Group Theorists focus on the *voluntary political choice* of the members of a group (or the majority of them),
their decision to form their own independent political unit. Any group, no matter how heterogeneous, can qualify for the right to secede. Nor need the seces-
sionists have any common connection, historical or imagined, to the territory
they wish to make into their own state. All that matters is that the members of
the group voluntarily choose to associate together in an independent political
unit of their own. Associative Group Theories, then, assert that there is a right
to secede that is, or is an instance of, *the right of political association.*

The simplest version of Associative Group Primary Right Theory is what I
have referred to elsewhere as the *pure plebiscite theory* of the right to secede.[7]
According to this theory, any group that can constitute a majority (or, on some
accounts, a "substantial" majority) in favor of secession within a portion of the
state has the right to secede. It is difficult to find unambiguous instances of the
pure plebiscite theory, but there are several accounts which begin with the
plebiscite condition and then add weaker or stronger *provisos.*

One such variant is offered by Harry Beran.[8] On his account, any group is
justified in seceding if (1) it constitutes a substantial majority in its portion of
the state, wishes to secede, and (2) will be able to marshal the resources necessary for a viable independent state.[9] Beran grounds his theory of the right to secede in a *consent theory of political obligation.* According to Beran, actual (not
"hypothetical" or "ideal contractarian") consent of the governed is a necessary

---

[6] Avishai Margalit and Joseph Raz, "National Self-Determination," *Journal of Philosophy* 87
(September 1990): 445–47.

[7] Allen Buchanan, "Self-Determination, Secession, and the Rule of International Law."

[8] Harry Beran, *The Consent Theory of Political Obligation* (New York: Croom Helm, 1987),
p. 42.

[9] Beran, *ibid.,* p. 42, adds another condition: that the secession not harm the remainder state's essential military, economic, or cultural interests.

condition for political obligation, and consent cannot be assured unless those who wish to secede are allowed to do so.

Christopher Wellman has more recently advanced another variant of plebiscite theory.[10] According to his theory, there is a primary right of political association, or, as he also calls it, of political self-determination. Like Beran's right, it is primary in the sense that it is not a remedial right, derived from the violation of other, independently characterizable rights. Wellman's right of political association is the right of any group that resides in a territory to form its own state if (1) that group constitutes a majority in that territory; if (2) the state it forms will be able to carry out effectively what was referred to earlier as the legitimating functions of a state (preeminently the provision of justice and security); and if (3) its severing the territory from the existing state will not impair the latter's ability to carry out effectively those same legitimating functions.

Like Beran's theory, Wellman's is an Associative Group, rather than an Ascriptive Group variant of Primary Right Theory, because any group that satisfies these three criteria, not just those with ascriptive properties (such as nations, peoples, ethnic groups, cultural groups, or encompassing groups) is said to have the right to secede. Both Beran and Wellman acknowledge that there can also be a right to secede grounded in the need to remedy injustices, but both are chiefly concerned to argue for a Primary Right, and thus to argue *against* all Remedial Right Only Theories.

According to Primary Right Theories, a group can have a (general) right to secede even if it suffers no injustices, and hence it may have a (general) right to secede from a perfectly just state. Ascriptive characteristics, such as being a people or nation, do not imply that the groups in question have suffered injustices. Similarly, according to Associative Group Theories, what confers the right to secede on a group is the voluntary choice of members of the group to form an independent state; no grievances are necessary.

Indeed, as we shall see, existing Primary Right Theories go so far as to recognize a right to secede even under conditions in which the state is effectively, indeed flawlessly, performing all of what are usually taken to be the *legitimating functions* of the state. As noted above in the description of Wellman's view, these functions consist chiefly, if not exclusively, in the provision of justice (the establishment and protection of rights) and of security.

Notice that in the statement that Primary Right Theories recognize a right to secede from perfectly just states the term "just" must be understood in what might be called the uncontroversial or standard or theory-neutral sense. In other words, a perfectly just state here is one that does not violate relatively uncontroversial individual moral rights, including above all human rights, and which does not engage in uncontroversially discriminatory policies toward minorities. This conception of justice is a neutral or relatively uncontroversial one in this sense: We may assume that it is acknowledged both by Remedial Right Only Theories and Primary Right Only Theorists—that both types of theorists

[10] Christopher Wellman, "A Defense of Secession and Self-Determination," 24 *Philosophy and Public Affairs* 2 (Spring 1995): 161.

recognize these sorts of actions as injustices, though they may disagree in other ways as to the scope of justice. In contrast, to understand the term "just" here in such a fashion that a state is assumed to be *unjust* simply because it contains a minority people or nation (which lacks its own state) or simply because it includes a majority that seeks to secede but has not been permitted to do so, would be to employ a conception of the justice that begs the question in this context, because it includes elements that are denied by one of the parties to the debate, namely Remedial Right Only Theorists. To repeat: the point is that Primary Right Theories are committed to the view that there is a right to secede even from a state that is perfectly just in the standard and uncontroversial, and hence theory-neutral sense.[11]

• • •

IV. COMPARING THE TWO TYPES OF THEORIES

Remedial Right Only Theories have several substantial attractions. First, a Remedial Right Only Theory places significant constraints on the right to secede, while not ruling out secession entirely. No group has a (general) right to secede unless that group suffers what are uncontroversially regarded as injustices and has no reasonable prospect of relief short of secession. Given that the majority of secessions have resulted in considerable violence, with attendant large-scale violations of human rights and massive destruction of resources, common sense urges that secession should not be taken lightly.

Furthermore, there is good reason to believe that secession may in fact exacerbate the ethnic conflicts which often give rise to secessionist movements, for two reasons. First, in the real world, though not perhaps in the world of some normative theorists, many, perhaps most, secessions are by ethnic minorities. But when an ethnic minority secedes, the result is often that another ethnic group becomes a minority within the new state. All too often, the formerly persecuted become the persecutors. Second, in most cases, not all members of the seceding group lie within the seceding area, and the result is that those who do not become an even smaller minority and hence even more vulnerable to the discrimination and persecution that fueled the drive for secession in the first place.[12] Requiring serious grievances as a condition for legitimate secession creates a significant hurdle that reflects the gravity of state-breaking in our world and the fact that secession often does perpetuate and sometimes exacerbate the ethnic conflicts that give rise to it.

---

[11] It is advisable at this point to forestall a misunderstanding about the contrast between the two types of theories. Remedial Right Only Theories, as the name implies, recognize a (general) right to secede only as a remedy for injustice, but Primary Right Theories need not, and usually do not, deny that there is a remedial right to secede. They only deny that the right to secede is only a remedial right. Thus a Primary Right Theory is not necessarily a Primary Right Only Theory.

[12] Donald Horowitz, "Self-Determination: Politics, Philosophy, and Law," *NOMOS XXXIX*, pp. 421–463.

Minimal Realism. Remedial Right Only Theories score much better on the condition of minimal realism than Primary Right Theories. Other things being equal, proposals for international institutional responses to secessionist claims that do not pose pervasive threats to the territorial integrity of existing states are more likely to be adopted by the primary makers of international law—that is, states—than those which do.

Primary Right theories are not likely to be adopted by the makers of international law because they authorize the dismemberment of states even when those states are perfectly performing what are generally recognized as the legitimating functions of states. Thus Primary Right Theories represent a direct and profound threat to the territorial integrity of states—even just states. Because Remedial Right Only Theories advance a much more restricted right to secede, they are less of a threat to the territorial integrity of existing states; hence, other things being equal, they are more likely to be incorporated into international law.

At this point it might be objected that the fact that states would be unlikely to incorporate Primary Right Theories into international law is of little significance, because their interest in resisting such a change is itself not morally legitimate. Of course, states will not be eager to endanger their own existence. Similarly, the fact that a ruling class of slaveholders would be unlikely to enact a law abolishing slavery would not be a very telling objection to a moral theory that says people have the right not to be enslaved.[13]

This objection would sap some of the force of the charge that Primary Right Theories score badly on the minimal realism requirement *if* states had no morally legitimate interest in resisting dismemberment. However, it is not just the self-interest of states that encourages them to reject theories of the right to secede that makes their control over territory much more fragile. States have a *morally legitimate interest* in maintaining their territorial integrity. The qualifier "morally legitimate" is crucial here. The nature of his morally legitimate interest will become clearer as we apply the next criterion to our comparative evaluation of the two types of theories.

Consistency with Well-Entrenched, Morally Progressive Principles of International Law. Unlike Primary Right Theories, Remedial Right Only Theories are consistent with, rather than in direct opposition to, a morally progressive interpretation of what is generally regarded as the single most fundamental principle of international law: the principle of the territorial integrity of existing states.

It is a mistake to view this principle simply as a monument to the self-interest of states in their own survival. Instead, I shall argue, it is a principle that serves some of the most basic morally legitimate interests of *individuals*.

The interest that existing states have in continuing to support the principle of territorial integrity is a morally legitimate interest because the recognition of that principle in international law and political practice promotes two morally

---

[13] This example is drawn from Christopher Wellman, "Political Self-Determination," unpublished manuscript.

important goals: (1) the protection of individuals' physical security, the preservation of their rights, and the stability of their expectations; and (2) an incentive structure in which it is reasonable for individuals and groups to invest themselves in participating in the fundamental processes of government in a conscientious and cooperative fashion over time. Each of these benefits of the maintenance of the principle of territorial integrity warrants explanation in detail.

Individuals' rights, the stability of individuals' expectations, and ultimately their physical security, depend upon the effective enforcement of a legal order. Effective enforcement requires effective *jurisdiction,* and this in turn requires a clearly bounded territory that is recognized to be the domain of an identified political authority. Even if political authority strictly speaking is exercised only over persons, not land, the effective exercise of political authority over persons depends, ultimately upon the establishment and maintenance of jurisdiction in the territorial sense. This fact rests upon an obvious but deep truth about human beings: They have bodies that occupy space, and the materials for living upon which they depend do so as well. Furthermore, if an effective legal order is to be possible, both the boundaries that define the jurisdiction and the identified political authority whose jurisdiction it is must persist over time.

So by making effective jurisdiction possible, observance of the principle of territorial integrity facilitates the functioning of a legal order and the creation of the benefits that only a legal order can bring. Compliance with the principle of territorial integrity, then, does not merely serve the self-interest of states in ensuring their own survival; it furthers the most basic morally legitimate interests of the individuals and groups that states are empowered to serve, their interest in the preservation of their rights, the security of their persons, and the stability of their expectations.

For this reason, states have a morally legitimate interest in maintaining the principle of territorial integrity. Indeed, that is to indulge in understatement: states, so far as their authority rests on their ability to serve the basic interests of individuals, have an *obligatory* interest in maintaining territorial integrity.

The principle of territorial integrity not only contributes to the possibility of maintaining an enforceable legal order and all the benefits that depend on it; it also gives citizens an incentive to invest themselves sincerely and cooperatively in the existing political processes. Where the principle of territorial integrity is supported, citizens can generally proceed on the assumption that they and their children and perhaps their children's children will be subject to laws that are made through the same processes to which they are now subject—and whose quality they can influence by the character of their participation.

For it to be reasonable for individuals and groups to so invest themselves in participating in political processes there must be considerable stability both in the effective jurisdiction of the laws that the processes create and in the membership of the state. Recognition of the principle of the territorial integrity of existing states contributes to both.

In Albert Hirschman's celebrated terminology, where exit is too easy, there is little incentive for voice—for sincere and constructive criticism and, more generally, for committed and conscientious political participation.[14] Citizens can exit the domain of the existing political authority in different ways. To take an example pertinent to our investigation of secession, if a minority could escape the authority of laws whose enactment it did not support by unilaterally redrawing political boundaries, it would have little incentive to submit to the majority's will, or to reason with the majority to change its mind.[15]

Of course, there are other ways to escape the reach of a political authority, emigration being the most obvious. But emigration is usually not a feasible option for minority groups and even where feasible is not likely to be attractive, since it will only involve trading minority status in one state for minority status in another. Staying where one is and attempting to transfer control over where one is to another, more congenial political authority is a much more attractive alternative, if one can manage it.

Moreover, in order to subvert democratic processes it is not even necessary that a group actually exit when the majority decision goes against it. All that may be needed is to issue a credible threat of exit, which can serve as a *de facto* minority veto.[16] However, in a system of states in which the principle of territorial integrity is given significant weight, the costs of exit are thereby increased, and the ability to use the threat of exit as a strategic bargaining tool is correspondingly decreased.

In addition, the ability of representative institutions to approximate the ideal of deliberative democracy, in which citizens strive together in the ongoing articulation of a conception of the public interest, also depends, in part, upon stable control over a definite territory, and thereby the effective exercise of political authority over those within it. This stability is essential if it is to be reasonable for citizens to invest themselves in cultivating and practicing the demanding virtues of deliberative democracy.

All citizens have a morally legitimate interest in the integrity of political participation. To the extent that the principle of territorial integrity helps to support the integrity of political participation, the legitimacy of this second interest adds moral weight to the principle.

To summarize: Adherence to the principle of territorial integrity serves two fundamental morally legitimate interests: the interest in the protection of individual security, rights, and expectations, and the interest in the integrity of political participation.

We can now see that this point is extremely significant for our earlier application of the criterion of minimal realism to the comparison of the two types of theories of secession. If the sole source of support for the principle of territorial integrity—and hence the sole source of states' resistance to implementing Primary Right Theories in international law—were the selfish or evil motives

---

[14] Albert O. Hirschman, *Exit, Voice, and Loyalty* (Cambridge, Mass.: Harvard University Press, 1970).

[15] Cass R. Sunstein, "Constitutionalism and Secession," *University of Chicago Law Review* 58 (1991): 633–70.

[16] Allen Buchanan, *Secession*, pp. 98–100.

of states, then the fact that such theories have scant prospect of being incorporated into international law would be of little significance. For in that case the Primary Right Theorist could simply reply that the criterion of minimal realism gives undue weight to the interests of states in their own preservation.

That reply, however, rests on a misunderstanding of my argument. My point is that it is a strike against Primary Right Theories that they have little prospect of implementation even when states are motivated solely or primarily by interests that are among the most morally legitimate interests that states can have. Thus my application of the minimal realism requirement cannot be countered by objecting that it gives undue weight to the interests of states in their own preservation.

Before turning to the application of the third criterion, my argument that the principle of the territorial integrity of existing states serves morally legitimate interests requires an important qualification. That principle can be abused; it has often been invoked to shore up a morally defective status quo. However, some interpretations of the principle of territorial integrity are less likely to be misused to perpetuate injustices and more likely to promote moral progress, however.

The Morally Progressive Interpretation of the Principle of Territorial Integrity. What might be called the *absolutist* interpretation of the principle of the territorial integrity of existing states makes no distinction between legitimate and illegitimate states, extending protection to all existing states. *Any* theory that recognizes a (general) right to secede, whether remedial only, or primary as well as remedial, is inconsistent with the absolutist interpretation, since any such theory permits the nonconsensual breakup of existing states under certain conditions. This first, absolutist interpretation has little to recommend it, however. For it is inconsistent with there being *any* circumstances in which other states, whether acting alone or collectively, may rightly intervene in the affairs of an existing state, even for the purpose of preventing the most serious human-rights abuses, including genocide.

According to the *progressive* interpretation, the principle that the territorial integrity of existing states is not to be violated applies only to *legitimate* states—and not all existing states are legitimate. There is, of course, room for disagreement about how stringent the relevant notion of legitimacy is. However, recent international law provides some guidance: States are *not* legitimate if they (1) threaten the lives of significant portions of their populations by a policy of ethnic or religious persecution, or if they (2) exhibit institutional racism that deprives a substantial proportion of the population of basic economic and political rights.

The most obvious case in which the organs of international law have treated an existing state as illegitimate was that of Apartheid South Africa (which satisfied condition [2]). The United Nations as well as various member states signaled this lack of legitimacy not only by various economic sanctions, but by refusing even to use the phrase "The Republic of South Africa" in public documents and pronouncements. More recently, the Iraqi government's genocidal actions toward Kurds within its borders (condition [1]) was accepted as a justification for infringing Iraq's territorial sovereignty in order to establish a "safe zone" in the North for the Kurds. To the extent that the injustices cited by a Remedial Right Only Theory are of the sort that international law regards as depriving a state of legitimacy, the right to secede is consistent with the principle of the territorial integrity of existing (legitimate) states.

Here, too, it is important to emphasize that the relevance of actual international law is conditional upon the moral legitimacy of the interests that the law, or in this case, changes in the law, serves. The key point is that the shift in international law away from the absolutist interpretation of the principle of territorial integrity toward the progressive interpretation serves morally legitimate interests and reflects a superior normative stance. So it is not mere conformity to existing law, but consonance with morally progressive developments in law, which speaks here in favor of Remedial Right Only Theories. Moreover, as I argued earlier, the principle that is undergoing a progressive interpretation, the principle of territorial integrity, is one that serves basic moral interests of individuals and groups, not just the interests of states.

In contrast, any theory of secession that recognizes a primary right to secede for any group within a state, in the absence of injustices that serve to delegitimize the state, directly contradicts the principle of the territorial integrity of existing states, *on its progressive interpretation.*[17] Accordingly, Remedial Right Only Theories have a singular advantage: Unlike Primary Right Theories, they are consistent with, rather than in direct opposition to, one of the most deeply entrenched principles of international law on its morally progressive interpretation. This point strengthens our contention that according to our second criterion Remedial Right Only Theories are superior to Primary Right Theories.

So far, the comparisons drawn have not relied upon the particulars of the various versions of the two types of theories. This has been intentional, since my main project is to compare the two basic *types* of theories. Further assessments become possible, as we examine the details of various Primary Right Theories.

V. PRIMARY RIGHT THEORIES

Avoiding Perverse Incentives. Remedial Right Only Theories also enjoy a third advantage: If incorporated into international law, they would create laudable

---

[17] Here it is important to repeat a qualification noted earlier: the progressive interpretation of the principle of territorial integrity operates within the limits of what I have called the relatively uncontroversial, standard, or theory-neutral conception of justice, as applied to the threshold condition that states must be minimally just in order to be legitimate and so to fall within the scope of the principle of territorial integrity. Therefore, it will not do for the Primary Right Theorist to reply that his theory is compatible with the progressive interpretation of the principle of territorial integrity because on his view a state that does not allow peoples or nations to secede or does not allow the secession of majorities that desire independent statehood is unjust. The problem with this reply is that it operates with a conception of justice that goes far beyond the normative basis of the progressive interpretation and in such a way as to beg the question by employing an understanding of the rights of groups that is not acknowledged by both parties to the theoretical debate.

incentives, while Primary Right Theories would engender very destructive ones (criterion 3).

A regime of international law that limits the right to secede to groups that suffer serious and persistent injustices at the hands of the state, when no other recourse is available to them, would provide protection and support to just states, by unambiguously sheltering them under the umbrella of the principle of the territorial integrity of existing (legitimate) states. States, therefore, would have an incentive to improve their records concerning the relevant injustices in order to reap the protection from dismemberment that they would enjoy as legitimate, rights-respecting states. States that persisted in treating groups of their citizens unjustly would suffer the consequences of international disapprobation and possibly more tangible sanctions as well. Furthermore, such states would be unable to appeal to international law to support them in attempts to preserve their territories intact.

In contrast, a regime of international law that recognized a right to secede in the absence of any injustices would encourage even just states to act in ways that would prevent groups from becoming claimants to the right to secede, and this might lead to the perpetration of injustices. For example, according to Wellman's version of Primary Right Theory, any group that becomes capable of having a functioning state of its own in the territory it occupies is a potential subject of the right to secede. Clearly, any state that seeks to avoid its own dissolution would have an incentive to implement policies designed to prevent groups from becoming prosperous enough and politically well-organized enough to satisfy this condition.

In other words, states would have an incentive to prevent regions within their borders from developing economic and political institutions that might eventually become capable of performing the legitimating functions of a state. In short, Wellman's version of Primary Right Theory gives the state incentives for fostering economic and political dependency. Notice that here, too, one need not attribute evil motives to states to generate the problem of perverse incentives. That problem arises even if states act only from the morally legitimate interest in preserving their territories.

In addition, a theory such as Wellman's, if used as a guide for international legal reform, would run directly contrary to what many view as the most promising response to the problems that can result in secessionist conflicts. I refer here to the proposal, alluded to earlier and increasingly endorsed by international legal experts, that every effort be made to accommodate aspirations for autonomy of groups *within* the state, by exploring the possibilities for various forms of decentralization, including federalism.

Wellman might reply that the fact that the implementation of his theory would hinder efforts at decentralization is no objection, since on his account there is no reason to believe that decentralization is superior to secession. There are two reasons, however, why this reply is inadequate.

First, as we saw earlier, decentralization can be the best way to promote morally legitimate interests (in more efficient administration, and in avoiding excessive concentrations of power) in many contexts in which secession is not even an issue. Hence, any theory of secession whose general acceptance and in-stitutionalization would inhibit decentralization is deficient, other things being equal. Second, and more importantly, according to our second criterion for evaluating proposals for international legal reform, other things being equal, a theory is superior if it is consonant with the most well-entrenched, fundamen-tal principles of international law on their morally progressive interpretations. The principle of territorial integrity, understood as conferring protection on le-gitimate states (roughly, those that respect basic rights) fits that description, and that principle favors first attempting to address groups' demands for autonomy be decentralization, since this is compatible with maintaining the territorial in-tegrity of existing states. It follows that the Primary Right Theorists cannot reply that the presumption in favor of decentralization as opposed to secession gives too much moral weight to the interests of *states* and that there is no reason to prefer decentralization to secession. The point, rather, is that decentralization has its own moral attractions and in addition is favored by a well-entrenched, fundamental principle of international law that serves basic, morally legitimate interests of individuals (and groups).

Even if Wellman's view were never formally incorporated into international law, but merely endorsed and supported by major powers such as the United States, the predictable result would be to make centralized states even less re-sponsive to demands for autonomy within them than they are now. Allowing groups within the state to develop their own local institutions of government and to achieve a degree of control over regional economic resources would run the risk of transforming them into successful claimants for the right to secede. Beran's version of Primary Right Theory suffers the same flaw, because it too gives states incentives to avoid decentralization in order to prevent secessionist majorities from forming in viable regions.

If either Wellman's or Beran's theories were implemented, the incentives re-garding *immigration* would be equally perverse. States wishing to preserve their territory would have incentives to prevent potential secessionist majorities from concentrating in economically viable regions. The predictable result would be restrictions designed to prevent ethnic, cultural, or political groups who might become local majorities from moving into such regions, whether from other parts of the state or from other states. Similarly, groups that wished to create their own states would have an incentive to try to concentrate in economically viable regions in which they can *become* majorities—and to displace members of other groups from those regions.

There is a general lesson here. Theories according to which majorities in re-gions of the state are automatically legitimate candidates for a right to secede (in the absence of having suffered injustices) look more plausible if one assumes that populations are fixed. Once it is seen that acceptance of these theories would create incentives for population shifts and for the state to attempt to pre-vent them, they look much less plausible.

The same objections just noted in regard to the Primary Right Theories of Wellman and Beran also afflict that of Margalit and Raz, although it is an Ascriptive Group, rather than an Associative Group, variant. On Margalit and Raz's view, it is "encompassing groups" that have the right to secede.

Like the other Primary Right Theories already discussed, this one scores badly on the criteria of minimal realism and consistency with deeply entrenched, morally progressive principles of international law. Also, if incorporated in international law, it would create perverse incentives.

First, it is clear that no principle which identifies all "encompassing groups" as bearers of the right of self-determination, where this is understood to include the right to secede from any existing state, would have much of a chance of being accepted in international law, even when states' actions were determined primarily by the pursuit of morally legitimate interests. The reason is straightforward: most, if not all, existing states include two or more encompassing groups; hence acceptance of Margalit and Raz's principle would authorize their own dismemberment. Second, the right to independent statehood, as Margalit and Raz understand it, is possessed by every encompassing group even in the absence of any injustices. Consequently, it too runs directly contrary to the principle of the territorial integrity of existing states on its most progressive interpretation (according to which just states are entitled to the protection the principle provides).

Third, if accepted as a matter of international law, the right endorsed by Margalit and Raz would give states incentives to embark on (or continue) all-too-familiar "nation-building" programs designed to obliterate minority group identities—to eliminate all "encompassing groups," within their borders save the one they favor for constituting "the nation" and to prevent new "encompassing groups" from emerging. Instead of encouraging states to support ethnic and cultural pluralism within their borders, Margalit and Raz's proposal would feed the reaction against pluralism.

Moral Accessibility. The last of the four criteria for assessment, moral accessibility, is perhaps the most difficult to apply. None of the accounts of the right to secede under consideration (with the possible exception of the Nationalist Principle in its cruder formulations) clearly fails the test of moral accessibility. Therefore, it may be that the comparative assessment of the rival theories must focus mainly on the other criteria, as I have done.

Nevertheless, it can be argued that Remedial Right Only Theories have a significant advantage, so far as moral accessibility is concerned. They restrict the right to secede to cases in which the most serious and widely recognized sorts of moral wrongs have been perpetrated against a group, namely violations of human rights and the unjust conquest of a sovereign state. That these are injustices is widely recognized. Hence if anything can justify secession, surely these injustices can. Whether other conditions also justify secession is more controversial, across the wide spectrum of moral and political views.

Recall that according to all Primary Right Theories, a group has the right to form its own state from a part of an existing state, even if the state is flawlessly performing what are generally taken to be the legitimating functions of states—even if perfect justice to all citizens and perfect security for all prevail. Presumably the intuitive moral appeal of this proposition is somewhat less than that of the thesis that the most serious injustices can justify secession.

33.
National Self-Determination*

AVISHAI MARGALIT AND JOSEPH RAZ

In the controversy-ridden fields of international law and international relations, the widespread recognition of the existence of national rights to self-determination provides a welcome point of agreement. Needless to say, the core consensus is but the eye of a raging storm concerning the precise definition of the right, its content, its bearers, and the proper means for its implementation. This paper will not address such questions, though indirectly it may help with their investigation. Its concern is with the moral justification of the case for national self-determination. Its purpose is critical and evaluative, its subject lies within the morality of international relations rather than within international law and international relations proper.

It is assumed throughout that states and international law should recognize such a right only if there is a sound moral case for it. This does not mean that international law should mirror morality. Its concern is with setting standards that enjoy the sort of clarity required to make them the foundations of international relations between states and fit for recognition and enforcement through international organs. These concerns give rise to special considerations that should be fully recognized in the subtle process of applying moral principles to the law. The derivation of legal principles from moral premises is never a matter of copying morality into law. Still, the justification of the law rests ultimately on moral considerations, and therefore those considerations should also help shape the contours of legal principles. That is why the conclusions of this paper bear on controversies concerning the proper way in which the law on this subject should develop, even though such issues are not here discussed directly.

Moral inquiry is sometimes understood in a utopian manner, i.e., as an inquiry into the principles that should prevail in an ideal world. It is doubtful whether this is a meaningful enterprise, but it is certainly not the one we are engaged in here. We assume that things are roughly as they are, especially that our world is a world of states and of a variety of ethnic, national, tribal, and other groups.[1] We do not question the justification for this state of affairs. Rather, we ask whether, given that this is how things are and for as long as they remain the same, a moral case can be made in support of national self-determination.

---

* This reading is excerpted from an essay which also includes, among other things, a section on the right to self-determination which is omitted here—eds.

[1] This fact is doubly relevant. It is a natural fact about our world that it is a populated world with no unappropriated lands. It is a social and a moral fact that it is a world of nations, tribes, peoples, etc., that is, that people's perception of themselves and of others and their judgments of the opportunities and the responsibilities of life are shaped, to an extent, by the existence of such groups and their membership in them. It may be meaningful to claim that our views regarding national self-determination apply only to a populated world like ours. One may point to

1. ISOLATING THE ISSUE

The core content of the claim to be examined is that there is a right to determine whether a certain territory shall become, or remain, a separate state (and possibly also whether it should enjoy autonomy within a large state). The idea of national self-determination or (as we shall refer to it in order to avoid confusion) the idea of self-government encompasses much more. The value of national self-government is the value of entrusting the general political power over a group and its members to the group. If self-government is valuable then it is valuable that whatever is a proper matter for political decision should be subject to the political decision of the group in all matters concerning the group and its members. The idea of national self-government, in other words, speaks of groups determining the character of their social and economic environment, their fortunes, the course of their development, and the fortunes of their members by their own actions, i.e., by the action of those groups, in as much as these are matters which are properly within the realm of political action.[2] Given the current international state system, in which political power rests, in the main, with sovereign states,[3] the right to determine whether a territory should be an independent state is quite naturally regarded as the main instrument for realizing the ideal of self-determination. Consideration of this right usually dominates all discussions of national self-determination. To examine the justification of the right is the ultimate purpose of this article. But we shall continuously draw attention to the fact that, as we shall try to show, the right of self-determination so understood is not ultimate, but is grounded in the wider value of national self-government, which is itself to be only instrumentally justified.

The next section deals with the nature of the groups that might be the subject of such a right. Section III considers what value, if any, is served by the enjoyment of political independence by such groups. Section IV examines the case for conceding that there is a moral right to self-determination. This examination may lead to revising our understanding of the content of the right. It may reveal that moral considerations justify only a narrower right, or that the argument that justifies the right warrants giving it a wider scope. But the

---

different principles that would prevail in a world with vast unoccupied fertile lands. Such speculation is utopian but it may serve to highlight some of the reasons for the principles that apply in our condition. To speculate concerning a reality different from ours in its basic social and moral constitution is pointless in a deeper way. Such social facts are constitutive of morality. Their absence undercuts morality's very foundations. We could say that under such changed conditions people will have normative beliefs and will be guided by some values. But they are not ones for which we can claim any validity.

[2] This qualification is to take account of the fact that, according to doctrines of limited government, certain matters are outside the realm of politics, and no political action regarding them may be undertaken.

[3] Among the exceptions to this rule are the slowly growing importance of supernational, especially regional, associations such as the European Community, the growth of a doctrine of sovereignty limited by respect for fundamental human rights, and the continuing (usually thinly veiled) claims of some states that they are not bound by the international law regarding the sovereignty of states.

core as identified here will provide the working base from which to launch the inquiry.

• • •

2. GROUPS

Assuming that self-determination is enjoyed by groups, what groups qualify? Given that the right is normally attributed to peoples or nations, it is tempting to give that as the answer and concentrate on characterizing "peoples" or "nations." The drawbacks of this approach are two: it assumes too much and it poses problems that may not require a solution.

It is far from clear that peoples or nations rather than tribes, ethnic groups, linguistic, religious, or geographical groups are the relevant reference group. What is it that makes peoples particularly suited to self-determination? The right concerns determination whether a certain territory shall be self-governing or not. It appears to affect most directly the residents of a territory, and their neighbors. If anyone, then residents of geographical regions seem intuitively to be the proper bearers of the right. Saying this does not get us very far. It does not help in identifying the residents of which regions should qualify. To be sure, this is the crucial question. But even posing it in this way shows that the answer, "the largest regions inhabited by one people or nation," is far from being the obvious answer.

We have some understanding of the benefits self-government might bring. We need to rely on this in looking for the characteristics that make groups suitable recipients of those benefits. We want, in other words, to identify groups by those characteristics which are relevant to the justification of the right. If it turns out that those do not apply to peoples or nations, we shall have shown that the right to self-determination is misconceived and, as recognized in international law, unjustified. Alternatively, the groups identified may encompass peoples (or some peoples) as well as other groups. This will provide a powerful case for redrawing the boundaries of the right. Either way we shall be saved much argument concerning the characterization of nations which, interesting as it is in itself, is irrelevant to our purpose.

Having said that, it may be useful to take nations and peoples as the obvious candidates for the right. We need not worry about their defining characteristics. But we may gain insight by comparing them with groups, e.g., the fiction-reading public, or Tottenham Football Club supporters, which obviously do not enjoy such a right. Reflection on such examples suggests six characteristics that in combination are relevant to a case for self-determination.

1. The group has a common character and a common culture that encompass many, varied and important aspects of life, a culture that defines or marks a variety of forms or styles of life, types of activities, occupations, pursuits, and

relationships. With national groups we expect to find national cuisines, distinctive architectural styles, a common language, distinctive literary and artistic traditions, national music, customs, dress, ceremonies and holidays, etc. None of these is necessary. They are but typical examples of the features that characterize peoples and other groups that are serious candidates for the right to self-determination. They have pervasive cultures, and their identity is determined at least in part by their culture. They possess cultural traditions that penetrate beyond a single or a few areas of human life, and display themselves in a whole range of areas, including many which are of great importance for the well-being of individuals.

2. The correlative of the first feature is that people growing up among members of the group will acquire the group culture, will be marked by its character. Their tastes and their options will be affected by that culture to a significant degree. The types of careers open to one, the leisure activities one learned to appreciate and is therefore able to choose from, the customs and habits that define and color relations with strangers and with friends, patterns of expectations and attitudes between spouses and among other members of the family, features of lifestyles with which one is capable of empathizing and for which one may therefore develop a taste—all these will be marked by the group culture.

They need not be indelibly marked. People may migrate to other environments, shed their previous culture, and acquire a new one. It is a painful and slow process, success in which is rarely complete. But it is possible, just as it is possible that socialization will fail and one will fail to be marked by the culture of one's environment, except negatively, to reject it. The point made is merely the modest one that, given the pervasive nature of the culture of the groups we are seeking to identify, their influence on individuals who grow up in their midst is profound and far-reaching. The point needs to be made in order to connect concern with the prosperity of the group with concern for the well-being of individuals. This tie between the individual and the collective is at the heart of the case for self-determination.

As one would expect, the tie does not necessarily extend to all members of the group, the failure of socialization is not the only reason. The group culture affects those who grow up among its members, be they members or not. But to say this is no more than to point to various anomalies and dilemmas that may arise. Most people live in groups of these kinds, so that those who belong to none are denied full access to the opportunities that are shaped in part by the group's culture. They are made to feel estranged and their chances to have a rewarding life are seriously damaged. The same is true of people who grow up among members of a group so that they absorb its culture, but are then denied access to it because they are denied full membership in the group.

Nothing in the above presupposes that groups of the kind we are exploring are geographically concentrated, let alone that their members are the only inhabitants of any region. Rather, by drawing on the transmission of the group culture through the socialization of the young, these comments emphasize the historical nature of the groups with which we are concerned. Given that they are identified by a common culture, at least in part, they also share a history, for it is through a shared history that cultures develop and are transmitted.

3. Membership in the group is, in part, a matter of mutual recognition. Typically, one belongs to such groups if, among other conditions, one is recognized by other members of the group as belonging to it. The other conditions (which may be the accident of birth or the sharing of the group culture, etc.) are normally the grounds cited as reasons for such recognition. But those who meet those other conditions and are yet rejected by the group are at best marginal or problematic members of it. The groups concerned are not formal institutionalized groups, with formal procedures of admission. Membership in them is a matter of informal acknowledgment of belonging by others generally, and by other members specifically. The fiction-reading public fails our previous tests. It is not identified by its sharing a wide-ranging pervasive culture. It also fails the third test. To belong to the fiction-reading public all we have to do is to read fiction. It does not matter whether others recognize us as fiction-reading.[4]

4. The third feature prepares the way for, and usually goes hand in hand with, the importance of membership for one's self-identification. Consider the fiction-reading public again. It is a historically significant group. Historians may study the evolution of the fiction-reading public, how it spread from women to men, from one class to others, from reading aloud in small groups to silent reading, from reliance on libraries to book buying, etc.; how it is regarded as important to one's qualification as a cultured person in one country, but not in another; how it furnishes a common topic of conversation in some classes but not in others; how belonging to the group is a mark of political awareness in some countries, while being a sign of escapist retreat from social concerns in another.

Such studies will show, however, that it is only in some societies that the existence of these features of the fiction-reading public is widely known. For the most part, one can belong to the group without being aware that one is a typical reader, that one's profile is that of most readers. Sometimes this is a result of a mistaken group image's being current in that society. Our concern is rather with those cases where the society lacks any very distinct image of that group. This indicates that, in such societies, membership of that group does not have a highly visible social profile. It is not one of the facts by which people pigeonhole each other. One need not be aware who, among people one knows, friends, acquaintances, shopkeepers one patronizes, one's doctor, etc., shares the habit. In such societies, membership of the fiction-reading public is not highly visible, that is, it is not one of the things one will normally know about

---

[4] The fiction-reading public can take the character of a literary elite with mutual recognition as part of its identity. The importance of "acceptability" in such groups has often been noted and analyzed.

people one has contact with, one of the things that identify "who they are." But it happens in some countries that membership of the reading public becomes a highly visible mark of belonging to a social group, to the intelligentsia, etc. In such countries, talk of the recently published novel becomes a means of mutual recognition.

One of the most significant facts differentiating various football cultures is whether they are cultures of self-recognition: whether identification as a fan or supporter of this club or that is one of the features that are among the main markers of people in the society. The same is true of occupational groups. In some countries, membership is highly visible and is among the primary means of pigeon-holing people, of establishing "who they are"; in others, it is not.

Our concern is with groups, membership of which has a high social profile, that is, groups, membership of which is one of the primary facts by which people are identified, and which form expectations as to what they are like, groups, membership of which is one of the primary clues for people generally in interpreting the conduct of others. Since our perceptions of ourselves are in large measure determined by how we expect others to perceive us, it follows that membership of such groups is an important identifying feature for each about himself. These are groups, members of which are aware of their membership and typically regard it as an important clue in understanding who they are, in interpreting their actions and reactions, in understanding their tastes and their manner.

5. Membership is a matter of belonging, not of achievement. One does not have to prove oneself, or to excel in anything, in order to belong and to be accepted as a full member. To the extent that membership normally involves recognition by others as a member, that recognition is not conditional on meeting qualifications that indicate any accomplishment. To be a good Irishman, it is true, is an achievement. But to be an Irishman is not. Qualification for membership is usually determined by nonvoluntary criteria. One cannot choose to belong. One belongs because of who one is. One can come to belong to such groups, but only by changing, e.g., by adopting their culture, changing one's tastes and habits accordingly—a very slow process indeed. The fact that these are groups, membership of which is a matter of belonging and not of accomplishment, makes them suitable for their role as primary foci of identification. Identification is more secure, less liable to be threatened, if it does not depend on accomplishment. Although accomplishments play their role in people's sense of their own identity, it would seem that at the most fundamental level our sense of our own identity depends on criteria of belonging rather than on those of accomplishment. Secure identification at that level is particularly important to one's well-being.

6. The groups concerned are not small face-to-face groups, members of which are generally known to all other members. They are anonymous groups where mutual recognition is secured by the possession of general characteristics.

The exclusion of small groups from consideration is not merely *ad hoc*. Small groups that are based on personal familiarity of all with all are markedly different in the character of their relationships and interactions from anonymous groups. For example, given the importance of mutual recognition to members of these groups, they tend to develop conventional means of identification, such as the use of symbolic objects, participation in group ceremonies, special group manners, or special vocabulary, which help quickly to identify who is "one of us" and who is not.

The various features we listed do not entail each other but they tend to go together. It is not surprising that groups with pervasive cultures will be important in determining the main options and opportunities of their members, or that they will become focal points of identification, etc. The way things are in our world, just about everyone belongs to such a group, and not necessarily to one only. Membership is not exclusive and many people belong to several groups that answer to our description. Some of them are rather like national groups, e.g., tribes or ethnic groups. Others are very different. Some religious groups meet our conditions, as do social classes, and some racial groups. Not all religious or racial groups did develop rich and pervasive cultures. But some did and those qualify.

3. THE VALUE OF SELF-GOVERNMENT

(A) *The Value of Encompassing Groups.* The description of the relevant groups in the preceding section may well disappoint the reader. Some will be disappointed by the imprecise nature of the criteria provided. This would be unjustified. The criteria are not meant to provide operational legal definitions. As such they clearly would not do. Their purpose is to pick on the features of groups which may explain the value of self-determination. As already mentioned, the key to the explanation is in the importance of these groups to the well-being of their members. This thought guided the selection of the features. They are meant to assist in identifying that link. It is not really surprising that they are all vague matters of degree, admitting of many variants and many nuances. One is tempted to say "that's life." It does not come in neatly parceled parts. While striving to identify the features that matter, we have to recognize that they come in many shapes, in many shades, and in many degrees rife with impurities in their concrete mixing.

A more justified source of disappointment is the suspicion that we have cast the net too wide. Social classes clearly do not have a right to self-determination. If they meet the above conditions then those conditions are at best incomplete. Here we can only crave the reader's patience. We tried to identify the features of groups which help explain the value of self-determination. These may apply not only beyond the sphere in which the right is commonly recognized. They may apply to groups that really should not possess it for other reasons yet to be explored.

The defining properties of the groups we identified are of two kinds. On the one hand, they pick out groups with pervasive cultures; on the other, they focus on groups, membership in which is important to one's self-identity. This combination makes such groups suitable candidates for self-rule. Let us call groups manifesting the six features *encompassing groups*. Individuals find in them a culture which shapes to a large degree their tastes and opportunities, and which provides an anchor for their self-identification and the safety of effortless secure belonging.

Individual well-being depends on the successful pursuit of worthwhile goals and relationships. Goals and relationships are culturally determined. Being social animals means not merely that the means for the satisfaction of people's goals are more readily available within society. More crucially it means that those goals themselves are (when one reaches beyond what is strictly necessary for biological survival) the creatures of society, the products of culture. Family relations, all other social relations between people, careers, leisure activities, the arts, sciences, and other obvious products of "high culture" are the fruits of society. They all depend for their existence on the sharing of patterns of expectations, on traditions preserving implicit knowledge of how to do what, of tacit conventions regarding what is part of this or that enterprise and what is not, what is appropriate and what is not, what is valuable and what is not. Familiarity with a culture determines the boundaries of the imaginable. Sharing in a culture, being part of it, determines the limits of the feasible.

It may be no more than a brute fact that our world is organized in a large measure around groups with pervasive cultures. But it is a fact with far-reaching consequences. It means, in the first place, that membership in such groups is of great importance to individual well-being, for it greatly affects one's opportunities, one's ability to engage in the relationships and pursuits marked by the culture. Secondly, it means that the prosperity of the culture is important to the well-being of its members. If the culture is decaying, or if it is persecuted or discriminated against, the options and opportunities open to its members will shrink, become less attractive, and their pursuit less likely to be successful.

It may be no more than a brute fact that people's sense of their own identity is bound up with their sense of belonging to encompassing groups and that their self-respect is affected by the esteem in which these groups are held. But these facts, too, have important consequences. They mean that individual dignity and self-respect require that the groups, membership in which contributes to one's sense of identity, be generally respected and not be made a subject of ridicule, hatred, discrimination, or persecution.

All this is mere common sense, and is meant to be hedged and qualified in the way our common understanding of these matters is. Of course, strangers can participate in activities marked by a culture. They are handicapped, but not always very seriously. Of course, there are other determinants of one's opportunities, and of one's sense of self-respect. Membership in an encompassing group is but one factor. Finally, one should mention that groups and their culture may be pernicious, based on exploitation of people, be they their members or not, or on the denigration and persecution of other groups. If so, then the case for their protection and flourishing is weakened, and may disappear altogether.

Having regard for this reservation, the case for holding the prosperity of encompassing groups as vital for the prosperity of their members is a powerful one. Group interests cannot be reduced to individual interests. It makes sense to talk of a group's prospering or declining, of actions and policies as serving the group's interest or of harming it, without having to cash in on this in terms of individual interests. The group may flourish if its culture prospers, but this need not mean that the lot of its members or of anyone else has improved. It is in the interest of the group to be held in high regard by others, but it does not follow that, if an American moon landing increases the world's admiration for the United States, Americans necessarily benefit from this. Group interests are conceptually connected to the interests of their members but such connections are nonreductive and generally indirect. For example, it is possible that what enhances the interest of the group provides opportunities for improvement for its members, or that it increases the chance that they will benefit.

This relative independence of group interest is compatible with the view that informs this article: that the moral importance of the group's interest depends on its value to individuals. A large decline in the fortunes of the group may, e.g., be of little consequence to its members. There is no a priori way of correlating group interest with that of its members or of other individuals. It depends on the circumstances of different groups at different times. One clear consequence of the fact that the moral significance of a group's interest is in its service to individuals is the fact that it will depend, in part, on the size of the group. The fortunes of a larger group may be material to the well-being of a larger number of people. Other things being equal, numbers matter.

(B) *The Instrumental Case.* Does the interest of members in the prosperity of the group establish a right to self-determination? Certainly not, at least not yet, not without further argument. For one thing we have yet to see any connection between the prosperity of encompassing groups and their political independence. The easiest connection to establish under certain conditions is an instrumental one. Sometimes the prosperity of the group and its self-respect are aided by, sometimes they may be impossible to secure without, the group's enjoying political sovereignty over its own affairs. Sovereignty enables the group to conduct its own affairs in a way conducive to its prosperity.[5] There is no need to elaborate the point. It depends on historical conditions. Hence the prominence of a history of persecution in most debates concerning self-determination. But a history of persecution is neither a necessary nor a sufficient condition for the instrumental case for self-government. It is not a necessary condition, because persecution is not the only reason why the groups may suffer without independence. Suffering can be the result of neglect or ignorance of or indifference

---

[5] This is not meant to suggest that there are not often drawbacks to self-rule. They will be considered below.

to the prosperity of a minority group by the majority. Such attitudes may be so well entrenched that there is no realistic prospect of changing them.

Persecution is not a sufficient condition, for there may be other ways to fight and overcome persecution and because whatever the advantages of independence it may, in the circumstances, lead to economic decline, cultural decay, or social disorder, which only make their members worse off. Besides, as mentioned above, pernicious groups may not deserve protection, especially if it will help them to pursue repressive practices with impunity. Finally, there are the interests of nonmembers to be considered. In short, the instrumental argument (as well as others) for self-government is sensitive to counterarguments pointing to its drawbacks, its cost in terms of human well-being, possible violations of human rights, etc.

We shall return to these issues below. First, let us consider the claim that the instrumental argument trivializes the case for self-government by overlooking its intrinsic value. Of the various arguments for the intrinsic value of self-government which have been and can be advanced, we examine one which seems the most promising.

(C) *An Argument for the Intrinsic Value of Self-government.* The argument is based on an extension of individual autonomy or of self-expression (if that is regarded as independently valuable). The argument unravels in stages: (1) people's membership of encompassing groups is an important aspect of their personality, and their well-being depends on giving it full expression; (2) expression of membership essentially includes manifestation of membership in the open, public life of the community; (3) this requires expressing one's membership in political activities within the community. The political is an essential arena of community life, and consequently of individual well-being; (4) therefore, self-government is inherently valuable, it is required to provide the group with a political dimension.

The first premise is unexceptionable. So is the second, though an ambiguity might be detected in the way it is often understood. Two elements need separating. First, given the importance of membership to one's well-being, it is vital that the dignity of the group be preserved. This depends, in part, on public manifestations of respect for the group and its culture, and on the absence of ridicule of the group, etc., from the public life of the society of which one is a member. One should not have to identify with or feel loyalty to a group that denigrates an encompassing group to which one belongs. Indeed, one should not have to live in an environment in which such attitudes are part of the common culture. Second, an aspect of well-being is an ability to express publicly one's identification with the group and to participate openly in its public culture. An encompassing group is centered on mutual recognition and is inevitably a group with a public culture. One cannot enjoy the benefits of membership without participation in its public culture, without public participation in its culture.

Both elements are of great importance. Both indicate the vital role played by public manifestations of group culture and group membership among the conditions of individual well-being. To the extent that a person's well-being is bound up with his identity as a member of an encompassing group it has an important public dimension. But that dimension is not necessarily political in the conventional narrow sense of the term. Even where it is, its political expression does not require a political organization whose boundaries coincide with those of the group. One may be politically active in a multinational, multicultural polity.

Here supporters of the argument for the intrinsic value of self-government may protest. The expression of membership in the political life of the community, they will say, involves more than its public expression. It involves the possibility of members of an encompassing group participating in the political life of their state, and fighting in the name of group interests in the political arena. Such actions, they will insist, may be not only instrumentally valuable to the group, but intrinsically important to its politically active members. They are valuable avenues of self-fullfilment. These points, too, have to be readily admitted. There is no reason to think that everyone must take part in politics, or else his or her development is stunted and personality or life are deficient. In normal times, politics is but an option that people may choose to take or to leave alone. Although its availability is important, for its absence deprives people of valuable opportunities, its use is strictly optional. Even if it is possible to argue that one's personal well-being requires some involvement with larger groups, and the avoidance of exclusive preoccupation with one's own affairs and those of one's close relations or friends, that involvement can take nonpolitical forms, such as activity in a social club, interest in the fortunes of the arts in one's region, etc.

Politics is no more than an option, though this is true in normal times only. In times of political crises that have moral dimensions, it may well be the duty of everyone to stand up and be counted. In Weimar, Germans had a moral duty to become politically involved to oppose Nazism. There are many other situations where an apolitical attitude is not morally acceptable. But all of them are marked by moral crises. In the absence of crisis there is nothing wrong in being nonpolitical.

Having said this, we must repeat that the option of politics must remain open, and with it the option of fighting politically for causes to do with the interests of one's encompassing groups. But there is nothing here to suggest that this should be done in a political framework exclusive to one's group or dominated by it. There is nothing wrong with multinational states, in which members of the different communities compete in the political arena for public resources for their communities. Admittedly, prejudice, national fanaticism, etc., sometimes make such peaceful and equitable sharing of the political arena impossible. They may lead to friction and persecution. This may constitute a good argument for the value of self-government, but it is an instrumental argument of the kind canvassed above. There is nothing in the need for a public or even a political expression of one's membership of an encompassing group which points to an intrinsic value of self-government.

(D) *The Subjective Element.* In an indirect way, the attempt to argue for the intrinsic value of self-government does point to the danger of misinterpreting the instrumental approach to the question. First, the argument does not deny the intrinsic value of the existence of the political option as a venue for activity and self-expression to all (adult) members of society. We are not advocating a purely instrumentalist view of politics generally. The intrinsic value to individuals of the political option does not require expression in polities whose boundaries coincide with those of encompassing groups. That is the only point argued for above.

Second, the pragmatic, instrumentalist character of the approach advocated here should not be identified with an aggregating impersonal consequentialism. Some people tend to associate any instrumentalist approach with images of a bureaucracy trading off the interest of one person against that of another on the basis of some cost-benefit analysis designed to maximize overall satisfaction; a bureaucracy, moreover, in charge of determining for people what is really good for them, regardless of their own views of the matter. Nothing of the kind should be countenanced. Of course, conflicts among people's interests do arise, and call for rational resolution that is likely to involve sacrificing some interests of some people for the sake of others. Such conflicts, however, admit of a large degree of indeterminacy, and many alternative resolutions may be plausible or rational. In such contexts, talking of maximization, with its connotations of comparability of all options, is entirely out of place.

Furthermore, nothing in the instrumentalist and pragmatic nature of our approach should be allowed to disguise its sensitivity to subjective elements, its responsiveness to the perceptions and sensibilities of the people concerned. To a considerable extent, what matters is how well people feel in their environment: Do they feel at home in it or are they alienated from it? Do they feel respected or humiliated? etc. This leads to a delicate balance between "objective" factors and subjective perceptions. On the one hand, when prospects for the future are concerned, subjective perceptions of danger and likely persecution, etc., are not necessarily to be trusted. These are objective issues on which the opinion of independent spectators may be more reliable than that of those directly involved. On the other hand, the actual issue facing the independent spectators is how people will respond to their conditions, what will be their perceptions, their attitudes to their environment, to their neighbors, etc. Even a group that is not persecuted may suffer many of the ills of real persecution if it feels persecuted. That its perceptions are mistaken or exaggerated is important in pointing to the possibility of a different cure: removing the mistaken perception. But that is not always possible, and up to a point in matters of respect, identification, and dignity, subjective responses, justified or not, are the ultimate reality so far as the well-being of those who have them is concerned.

VIII

COSMOPOLITANISM, MULTICULTURALISM, AND COMMUNITY

34.
Cultural Membership and Choice

WILL KYMLICKA

2. LIBERALISM AND INDIVIDUAL FREEDOM

I believe that societal cultures are important to people's freedom, and that liberals should therefore take an interest in the viability of societal cultures. To show this, however, I need briefly to consider the nature of freedom, as it is conceived within the liberal tradition.

The defining feature of liberalism is that it ascribes certain fundamental freedoms to each individual. In particular, it grants people a very wide freedom of choice in terms of how they lead their lives. It allows people to choose a conception of the good life, and then allows them to reconsider that decision, and adopt a new and hopefully better plan of life.

Why should people be free to choose their own plan of life? After all, we know that some people will make imprudent decisions, wasting their time on hopeless or trivial pursuits. Why then should the government not intervene to protect us from making mistakes, and to compel us to lead the truly good life? There are a variety of reasons why this is not a good idea: governments may not be trustworthy; some individuals have idiosyncratic needs which are difficult for even a well-intentioned government to take into account; supporting controversial conceptions of the good may lead to civil strife. Moreover, paternalistic restrictions on liberty often simply do not work—lives do not go better by being led from the outside, in accordance with values the person does not endorse. Dworkin calls this the "endorsement constraint," and argues that "no component contributes to the value of a life without endorsement . . . it is implausible to think that someone can lead a better life against the grain of his profound ethical convictions than at peace with them" (Dworkin, 1989: 486).

However, the fact that we can get it wrong is important, because (paradoxically) it provides another argument for liberty. Since we can be wrong about the worth or value of what we are currently doing, and since no one wants to lead a life based on false beliefs about its worth, it is of fundamental importance that we be able rationally to assess our conceptions of the good in the light of new information or experiences, and to revise them if they are not worthy of our continued allegiance.

This assumption that our beliefs about the good life are fallible and revisable is widely endorsed in the liberal tradition—from John Stuart Mill to the most prominent contemporary American liberals, such as John Rawls and Ronald Dworkin. (Because of their prominence, I will rely heavily on the works of Rawls and Dworkin in the rest of this chapter.) As Rawls puts it, individuals "do not view themselves as inevitably tied to the pursuit of the particular conception of the good and its final ends which they espouse at any given time."

Instead, they are "capable of revising and changing this conception." They can "stand back" from their current ends to "survey and assess" their worthiness (Rawls 1980: 544; cf. Mill 1982: 122; Dworkin 1983).

So we have two preconditions for leading a good life. The first is that we lead our life from the inside, in accordance with our beliefs about what gives value to life. Individuals must therefore have the resources and liberties needed to lead their lives in accordance with their beliefs about value, without fear of discrimination or punishment. Hence the traditional liberal concern with individual privacy, and opposition to "the enforcement of morals." The second precondition is that we be free to question those beliefs, to examine them in light of whatever information, examples, and arguments our culture can provide. Individuals must therefore have the conditions necessary to acquire an awareness of different views about the good life, and an ability to examine these views intelligently. Hence the equally traditional liberal concern for education, and freedom of expression and association. These liberties enable us to judge what is valuable, and to learn about other ways of life.

It is important to stress that a liberal society is concerned with both of these preconditions, the second as much as the first. It is all too easy to reduce individual liberty to the freedom to pursue one's conception of the good. But in fact much of what is distinctive to a liberal state concerns the forming and revising of people's conceptions of the good, rather than the pursuit of those conceptions once chosen.

Consider the case of religion. A liberal society not only allows individuals the freedom to pursue their existing faith, but it also allows them to seek new adherents for their faith (proselytization is allowed), or to question the doctrine of their church (heresy is allowed), or to renounce their faith entirely and convert to another faith or to atheism (apostasy is allowed). It is quite conceivable to have the freedom to pursue one's current faith without having any of these latter freedoms. There are many examples of this within the Islamic world. Islam has a long tradition of tolerating other monotheistic religions, so that Christians and Jews can worship in peace. But proselytization, heresy, and apostasy are generally prohibited. This was true, for example, of the "millet system" of the Ottoman Empire. Indeed, some Islamic states have said the freedom of conscience guaranteed in the Universal Declaration of Human Rights should not include the freedom to change religion (Lerner 1991: 79–80). Similarly, the clause in the Egyptian constitution guaranteeing freedom of conscience has been interpreted so as to exclude freedom of apostasy (Peters and de Vries 1976: 23). In such a system, freedom of conscience means there is no forced conversion, but nor is there voluntary conversion.

A liberal society, by contrast, not only allows people to pursue their current way of life, but also gives them access to information about other ways of life (through freedom of expression), and indeed requires children to learn about other ways of life (through mandatory education), and makes it possible for people to engage in radical revision of their ends (including apostasy) without legal penalty. These aspects of a liberal society only make sense on the assumption that revising one's ends is possible, and sometimes desirable, because one's current ends are not always worthy of allegiance. A liberal society does not compel such questioning and revision, but it does make it a genuine possibility.

3. SOCIETAL CULTURES AS CONTEXT OF CHOICE

I have just outlined what I take to be the predominant liberal conception of individual freedom. But how does this relate to membership in societal cultures? Put simply, freedom involves making choices amongst various options, and our societal culture not only provides these options, but also makes them meaningful to us.

People make choices about the social practices around them, based on their beliefs about the value of these practices (beliefs which, I have noted, may be wrong). And to have a belief about the value of a practice is, in the first instance, a matter of understanding the meanings attached to it by our culture.

I noted earlier that societal cultures involve "a shared vocabulary of tradition and convention" which underlies a full range of social practices and institutions (Dworkin 1985: 231). To understand the meaning of a social practice, therefore, requires understanding this "shared vocabulary"—that is, understanding the language and history which constitute that vocabulary. Whether or not a course of action has any significance for us depends on whether, and how, our language renders vivid to us the point of that activity. And the way in which language renders vivid these activities is shaped by our history, our "traditions and conventions." Understanding these cultural narratives is a precondition of making intelligent judgements about how to lead our lives. In this sense, our culture not only provides options, it also "provides the spectacles through which we identify experiences as valuable" (Dworkin 1985: 228).

What follows from this? According to Dworkin, we must protect our societal culture from "structural debasement or decay" (1985: 230). The survival of a culture is not guaranteed, and, where it is threatened with debasement or decay, we must act to protect it. Cultures are valuable, not in and of themselves, but because it is only through having access to a societal culture that people have access to a range of meaningful options. Dworkin concludes his discussion by saying, "We inherited a cultural structure, and we have some duty, out of simple justice, to leave that structure at least as rich as we found it" (1985: 232–3).

In this passage and elsewhere, Dworkin talks about "cultural structures." This is a potentially misleading term, since it suggests an overly formal and rigid picture of what (as I discuss below) is a very diffuse and open-ended phenomenon. Cultures do not have fixed centres or precise boundaries. But his main point is, I think, sound enough. The availability of meaningful options depends on access to a societal culture, and on understanding the history and language of that culture—its "shared vocabulary of tradition and convention" (Dworkin 1985: 228, 231).

This argument about the connection between individual choice and culture provides the first step towards a distinctively liberal defence of certain group-differentiated rights. For meaningful individual choice to be possible, individuals need not only access to information, the capacity to reflectively evaluate it, and freedom of expression and association. They also need access to a societal culture. Group-differentiated measures that secure and promote this access may, therefore, have a legitimate role to play in a liberal theory of justice.

Of course, many details remain to be filled in, and many objections need to be answered. In particular, this connection between individual choice and societal cultures raises three obvious questions: (1) is individual choice tied to membership in one's *own* culture, or is it sufficient for people to have access to some or other culture? (2) if (as I will argue) people have a deep bond to their own culture, should immigrant groups be given the rights and resources necessary to recreate their own societal cultures? and (3) what if a culture is organized so as to preclude individual choice—for example, if it assigns people a specific role or way of life, and prohibits any questioning or revising of that role? I will start answering these questions in the rest of the chapter, although a full answer will only emerge in later chapters.

4. THE VALUE OF CULTURAL MEMBERSHIP

I have tried to show that people's capacity to make meaningful choices depends on access to a cultural structure. But why do the members of a national minority need access to their *own* culture? Why not let minority cultures disintegrate, so long as we ensure their members have access to the majority culture (e.g. by teaching them the majority language and history)? This latter option would involve a cost to minorities, but governments could subsidize it. For example, governments could pay for the members of national minorities to learn about the majority language and history.

This sort of proposal treats the loss of one's culture as similar to the loss of one's job. Language training for members of a threatened culture would be like worker retraining programmes for employees of a dying industry. We do not feel obliged to keep uncompetitive industries afloat in perpetuity, so long as we help employees to find employment elsewhere, so why feel obliged to protect minority cultures, so long as we help their members to find another culture?

This is an important question. It would be implausible to say that people are never able to switch cultures. After all, many immigrants function well in their new country (although others flounder, and many return home). Waldron thinks that these examples of successful "cosmopolitan" people who move between cultures disprove the claim that people are connected to their own culture in any deep way. Suppose, he says, that

> a freewheeling cosmopolitan life, lived in a kaleidoscope of cultures, is both possible and fulfilling. . . . Immediately, one argument for the protection of minority cultures is undercut. It can no longer be said that all people need their rootedness in the particular culture in which they and their ancestors were reared in the way that they need food, clothing, and shelter . . . Such

immersion may be something that particular people like and enjoy. But they no longer can claim that it is something that they need. . . . The collapse of the Herderian argument based on distinctively human *need* seriously undercuts any claim that minority cultures might have to special support or assistance or to extraordinary provision or forbearance. At best, it leaves the right to culture roughly on the same footing as the right to religious freedom. (Waldron 1992a: 762)

Because people do not need their own culture, minority cultures can ("at best") claim the same negative rights as religious groups—that is, the right to non-interference, but not to state support.

I think Waldron is seriously overstating the case here. For one thing, he vastly overestimates the extent to which people do in fact move between cultures, because (as I discuss below) he assumes that cultures are based on ethnic descent. On his view, an Irish-American who eats Chinese food and reads her child *Grimms' Fairy-Tales* is thereby "living in a kaleidoscope of cultures" (e.g. Waldron 1992a: 754). But this is not moving between societal cultures. Rather it is enjoying the opportunities provided by the diverse societal culture which characterizes the anglophone society of the United States.

Of course, people do genuinely move between cultures. But this is rarer, and more difficult. In some cases, where the differences in social organization and technological development are vast, successful integration may be almost impossible for some members of the minority. (This seems to be true of the initial period of contact between European cultures and indigenous peoples in some parts of the world.)

But even where successful integration is possible, it is rarely easy. It is a costly process, and there is a legitimate question whether people should be required to pay those costs unless they voluntarily choose to do so. These costs vary, depending on the gradualness of the process, the age of the person, and the extent to which the two cultures are similar in language and history. But even where the obstacles to integration are smallest, the desire of national minorities to retain their cultural membership remains very strong (just as the members of the majority culture typically value their cultural membership).

In this sense, the choice to leave one's culture can be seen as analogous to the choice to take a vow of perpetual poverty and enter a religious order. It is not impossible to live in poverty. But it does not follow that a liberal theory of justice should therefore view the desire for a level of material resources above bare subsistence simply as "something that particular people like and enjoy" but which "they no longer can claim is something that they need" (Waldron 1992a: 762). Liberals rightly assume that the desire for nonsubsistence resources is so normal—and the costs of forgoing them so high for most people's way of life— that people cannot reasonably be *expected* to go without such resources, even if a few people voluntarily choose to do so. For the purposes of determining people's claims of justice, material resources are something that people can be assumed to want, whatever their particular conception of the good. Although a small number of people may choose to forgo non-subsistence resources, this is seen as forgoing something to which they are entitled.

Similarly, I believe that, in developing a theory of justice, we should treat access to one's culture as something that people can be expected to want, whatever their more particular conception of the good. Leaving one's culture, while possible, is best seen as renouncing something to which one is reasonably entitled. This is a claim, not about the limits of human possibility, but about reasonable expectations.

I think that most liberals have implicitly accepted this claim about people's legitimate expectation to remain in their culture. Consider Rawls's argument about why the right to emigrate does not make political authority voluntary:

> normally leaving one's country is a grave step: it involves leaving the society and culture in which we have been raised, the society and culture whose language we use in speech and thought to express and understand ourselves, our aims, goals, and values; the society and culture whose history, customs, and conventions we depend on to find our place in the social world. In large part, we affirm our society and culture, and have an intimate and inexpressible knowledge of it, even though much of it we may question, if not reject. The government's authority cannot, then, be freely accepted in the sense that the bonds of society and culture, of history and social place of origin, begin so early to shape our life and are normally so strong that the right of emigration (suitably qualified) does not suffice to make accepting its authority free, politically speaking, in the way that liberty of conscience suffices to make accepting ecclesiastical authority free. (Rawls 1993a: 222)

Because of these bonds to the "language we use in speech and thought to express and understand ourselves," cultural ties "are normally too strong to be given up, and this fact is not to be deplored." Hence, for the purposes of developing a theory of justice, we should assume that "people are born and are expected to lead a complete life" within the same "society and culture" (Rawls 1993a: 277).

I agree with Rawls's view about the difficulty of leaving one's culture. Yet his argument has implications beyond those which he himself draws. Rawls presents this as an argument about the difficulty of leaving one's political community. But his argument does not rest on the value of specifically political ties (e.g. the bonds to one's government and fellow citizens). Rather it rests on the value of cultural ties (e.g. bonds to one's language and history). And cultural boundaries may not coincide with political boundaries. For example, someone leaving East Germany for West Germany in 1950 would not be breaking the ties of language and culture which Rawls emphasizes, even though she would be crossing state borders. But a francophone leaving Quebec City for Toronto, or a Puerto Rican leaving San Juan for Chicago, would be breaking those ties, even though she is remaining within the same country.

According to Rawls, then, the ties to one's culture are normally too strong to give up, and this is not to be regretted. We cannot be expected or required to make such a sacrifice, even if some people voluntarily do so. It is an interesting question why the bonds of language and culture are so strong for most people. It seems particularly puzzling that people would have a strong attachment to a liberalized culture. After all, as a culture is liberalized—and so allows members to question and reject traditional ways of life—the resulting cultural identity becomes both "thinner" and less distinctive. That is, as a culture becomes more liberal, the members are less and less likely to share the same substantive conception of the good life, and more and more likely to share basic values with people in other liberal cultures.

The Québécois provide a nice illustration of this process. Before the Quiet Revolution, the Québécois generally shared a rural, Catholic, conservative, and patriarchal conception of the good. Today, after a rapid period of liberalization, most people have abandoned this traditional way of life, and Québécois society now exhibits all the diversity that any modern society contains—e.g. atheists and Catholics, gays and heterosexuals, urban yuppies and rural farmers, socialists and conservatives, etc. To be a "Québécois" today, therefore, simply means being a participant in the francophone society of Quebec. And francophones in Quebec no more agree about conceptions of the good than anglophones in the United States. So being a "Québécois" seems to be a very thin form of identity.

Moreover, the process of liberalization has also meant that the Québécois have become much more like English Canadians in their basic values. Liberalization in Quebec over the last thirty years has been accompanied by a pronounced convergence in personal and political values between English- and French-speaking Canadians, so that it would now be "difficult to identify consistent differences in attitudes on issues such as moral values, prestige ranking of professions, role of the government, workers' rights, aboriginal rights, equality between the sexes and races, and conception of authority" (Dion 1992: 99; cf. Dion 1991: 301; Taylor 1991: 54).

In short, liberalization in Quebec has meant both an increase in differences amongst the Québécois, in terms of their conceptions of the good, and a reduction in differences between the Québécois and the members of other liberal cultures. This is not unique to Quebec. The same process is at work throughout Europe. The modernization and liberalization of Western Europe has resulted both in fewer commonalities within each of the national cultures, and greater commonalities across these cultures. As Spain has liberalized, it has become both more pluralistic internally, and more like France or Germany in terms of its modern, secular, industrialized, democratic, and consumerist civilization.

This perhaps explains why so many theorists have assumed that liberalization and modernization would displace any strong sense of national identity. As cultures liberalize, people share less and less with their fellow members of the national group, in terms of traditional customs or conceptions of the good life, and become more and more like the members of other nations, in terms of sharing a common civilization. Why then would anyone feel strongly attached to their own nation? Such an attachment seems, to many commentators, like the "narcissism of minor differences" (Ignatieff 1993: 21; Dion 1991).

Yet the evidence is overwhelming that the members of liberal cultures *do* value their cultural membership. Far from displacing national identity, liberalization has in fact gone hand in hand with an increased sense of nationhood.

Many of the liberal reformers in Quebec have been staunch nationalists, and the nationalist movement grew in strength throughout the Quiet Revolution and afterwards. The same combination of liberalization and a strengthened national identity can be found in many other countries. For example, in Belgium, the liberalization of Flemish society has been accompanied by a sharp rise in nationalist sentiment (Peterson 1975: 208). The fact that their culture has become tolerant and pluralistic has in no way diminished the pervasiveness or intensity of people's desire to live and work in their own culture. Indeed, Walker Connor goes so far as to suggest that few if any examples exist of recognized national groups in this century having voluntarily assimilated to another culture, even though many have had significant economic incentives and political pressures to do so (Connor 1972: 350–1; 1973: 20).

Why are the bonds of language and culture so strong for most people? Commentators offer a number of reasons. Margalit and Raz argue that membership in a societal culture (what they call a "pervasive culture") is crucial to people's well-being for two reasons. The first reason is the one I have discussed above—namely, that cultural membership provides meaningful options, in the sense that "familiarity with a culture determines the boundaries of the imaginable." Hence if a culture is decaying or discriminated against, "the options and opportunities open to its members will shrink, become less attractive, and their pursuit less likely to be successful" (Margalit and Raz 1990: 449).

But why cannot the members of a decaying culture simply integrate into another culture? According to Margalit and Raz, this is difficult, not only because it is "a very slow process indeed," but also because of the role of cultural membership in people's self-identity. Cultural membership has a "high social profile," in the sense that it affects how others perceive and respond to us, which in turn shapes our self-identity. Moreover, national identity is particularly suited to serving as the "primary foci of identification," because it is based on belonging, not accomplishment:

> Identification is more secure, less liable to be threatened, if it does not depend on accomplishment. Although accomplishments play their role in people's sense of their own identity, it would seem that at the most fundamental level our sense of our own identity depends on criteria of belonging rather than on those of accomplishment. Secure identification at that level is particularly important to one's well-being.

Hence cultural identity provides an "anchor for [people's] self-identification and the safety of effortless secure belonging." But this in turn means that people's self-respect is bound up with the esteem in which their national group is held. If a culture is not generally respected, then the dignity and self-respect of its members will also be threatened (Margalit and Raz 1990: 447–9). Similar arguments about the role of respect for national membership in supporting dignity and self-identity are given by Charles Taylor (1992a) and Yael Tamir (1993: 41, 71–3).

Tamir also emphasizes the extent to which cultural membership adds an "additional meaning" to our actions, which become not only acts of individual accomplishment, but also "part of a continuous creative effort whereby culture is made and remade." And she argues that, where institutions are "informed by a culture [people] find understandable and meaningful," this "allows a certain degree of transparency that facilitates their participation in public affairs." This in turn promotes a sense of belonging and relationships of mutual recognition and mutual responsibility (Tamir 1993: 72, 85–6). Other commentators make the related point that the mutual intelligibility which comes from shared national identity promotes relationships of solidarity and trust (Miller 1993; Barry 1991: 174–5). James Nickel emphasizes the potential harm to valuable intergenerational bonds when parents are unable to pass on their culture to their children and grandchildren (Nickel 1995). Benedict Anderson emphasizes the way national identity enables us to transcend our mortality, by linking us to something whose existence seems to extend back into time immemorial, and forward into the indefinite future (Anderson 1983).

No doubt all of these factors play a role in explaining people's bond to their own culture. I suspect that the causes of this attachment lie deep in the human condition, tied up with the way humans as cultural creatures need to make sense of their world, and that a full explanation would involve aspects of psychology, sociology, linguistics, the philosophy of mind, and even neurology (Laponce 1987).

But whatever the explanation, this bond does seem to be a fact, and, like Rawls, I see no reason to regret it. I should emphasize, again, that I am only dealing with general trends. Some people seem most at home leading a truly cosmopolitan life, moving freely between different societal cultures. Others have difficulty making sense of the cultural meanings within their own culture. But most people, most of the time, have a deep bond to their own culture.

It may seem paradoxical for liberals like Rawls to claim that the bonds to one's culture are "normally too strong to be given up." What has happened to the much vaunted liberal freedom of choice? But Rawls's view is in fact common within the liberal tradition. The freedom which liberals demand for individuals is not primarily the freedom to go beyond one's language and history, but rather the freedom to move around within one's societal culture, to distance oneself from particular cultural roles, to choose which features of the culture are most worth developing, and which are without value.

This may sound like a rather "communitarian" view of the self. I do not think this is an accurate label. One prominent theme in recent communitarian writing is the rejection of the liberal view about the importance of being free to revise one's ends. Communitarians deny that we can "stand apart" from (some of) our ends. According to Michael Sandel, a leading American communitarian, some of our ends are "constitutive" ends, in the sense that they define our sense of personal identity (Sandel 1982: 150–65; cf. MacIntyre 1981: ch. 15; Bell 1993: 24–54). It makes no sense, on his view, to say that my ends might not be worthy of my allegiance, for they define who I am. Whereas Rawls claims that individuals "do not regard themselves as inevitably bound to, or identical with, the pursuit of any particular complex of fundamental interests that they may have at any given moment" (1974: 641), Sandel responds that we are in fact "identical with" at least some of our final ends. Since these ends are constitutive of people's identity, there is no reason why the state should not re- inforce people's allegiance to those ends, and limit their ability to question and revise these ends.

I believe that this communitarian conception of the self is mistaken. It is not easy or enjoyable to revise one's deepest ends, but it is possible, and sometimes a regrettable necessity. New experiences or circumstances may reveal that our earlier beliefs about the good are mistaken. No end is immune from such po- tential revision. As Dworkin puts it, it is true that "no one can put everything about himself in question all at once," but it "hardly follows that for each person there is some one connection or association so fundamental that it cannot be detached for inspection while holding others in place" (Dworkin 1989: 489).

Some people may think of themselves as being incapable of questioning or revising their ends, but in fact "our conceptions of the good may and often do change over time, usually slowly but sometimes rather suddenly," even for those people who think of themselves as having constitutive ends (Rawls 1985: 242). No matter how confident we are about our ends at a particular moment, new circumstances or experiences may arise, often in unpredictable ways, that cause us to re-evaluate them. There is no way to predict in advance when the need for such a reconsideration will arise. As I noted earlier, a liberal society does not compel people to revise their commitments—and many people will go years without having any reason to question their basic commitments—but it does recognize that the freedom of choice is not a one-shot affair, and that ear- lier choices sometimes need to be revisited.

Since our judgements about the good are fallible in this way, we have an in- terest, not only in pursuing our existing conception of the good, but also in be- ing able to assess and potentially revise that conception. Our current ends are not always worthy of our continued allegiance, and exposure to other ways of life helps us make informed judgements about what is truly valuable.

The view I am defending is quite different, therefore, from the communitar- ian one, although both views claim that we have a deep bond to a particular sort of social group. The difference is partly a matter of scope. Communitari- ans typically talk about our attachment to subnational groups—churches, neighbourhoods, family, unions, etc.—rather than to the larger society which encompasses these sub-groups. But this difference in scope reflects an even deeper divergence. Communitarians are looking for groups which are defined by a shared conception of the good. They seek to promote a "politics of the common good," in which groups can promote a shared conception of the good, even if this limits the ability of individual members to revise their ends. They believe that members have a "constitutive" bond to the group's values, and so no harm is done by limiting individual rights in order to promote shared values.

As most communitarians admit, this "politics of the common good" cannot apply at the national level. As Sandel puts it, "the nation proved too vast a scale across which to cultivate the shared self-understandings necessary to commu- nity in the . . . constitutive sense" (Sandel 1984: 93; cf. MacIntyre 1981: 221;

Miller 1988–9: 60–7). The members of a nation rarely share moral values or traditional ways of life. They share a language and history, but often disagree fundamentally about the ultimate ends in life. A common national identity, therefore, is not a useful basis for communitarian politics, which can only exist at a more local level.

The liberal view I am defending insists that people can stand back and assess moral values and traditional ways of life, and should be given not only the legal right to do so, but also the social conditions which enhance this capacity (e.g. a liberal education). So I object to communitarian politics at the subnational level. To inhibit people from questioning their inherited social roles can condemn them to unsatisfying, even oppressive, lives. And at the national level, the very fact which makes national identity so inappropriate for communitarian politics—namely, that it does not rest on shared values—is precisely what makes it an appropriate basis for liberal politics. The national culture provides a meaningful context of choice for people, without limiting their ability to question and revise particular values or beliefs.

Put another way, the liberal ideal is a society of free and equal individuals. But what is the relevant "society"? For most people it seems to be their nation. The sort of freedom and equality they most value, and can make most use of, is freedom and equality within their own societal culture. And they are willing to forgo a wider freedom and equality to ensure the continued existence of their nation.

For example, few people favour a system of open borders, where people could freely cross borders and settle, work, and vote in whatever country they desired. Such a system would dramatically increase the domain within which people would be treated as free and equal citizens. Yet open borders would also make it more likely that people's own national community would be overrun by settlers from other cultures, and that they would be unable to ensure their survival as a distinct national culture. So we have a choice between, on the one hand, increased mobility and an expanded domain within which people are free and equal individuals, and, on the other hand, decreased mobility but a greater assurance that people can continue to be free and equal members of their own national culture. Most people in liberal democracies clearly favour the latter. They would rather be free and equal within their own nation, even if this means they have less freedom to work and vote elsewhere, than be free and equal citizens of the world, if this means they are less likely to be able to live and work in their own language and culture.

And most theorists in the liberal tradition have implicitly agreed with this. Few major liberal theorists have endorsed open borders, or even seriously considered it. They have generally accepted—indeed, simply taken for granted—that the sort of freedom and equality which matters most to people is freedom and equality within one's societal culture. Like Rawls, they assume that "people are born and are expected to lead a complete life" within the same "society and culture," and that this defines the scope within which people must be free and equal (Rawls 1993a: 277).

In short, liberal theorists have generally, if implicitly, accepted that cultures or nations are basic units of liberal political theory. In this sense, as Yael Tamir puts it, "most liberals are liberal nationalists" (1993: 139)—that is, liberal goals are achieved in and through a liberalized societal culture or nation.

REFERENCES

Anderson, Benedict. *Imagined Communities: Reflections on the Origin and Spread of Nationalism.* London: New Left Books, 1983.

Barry, Brian. "Self-Government Revisited." In *Democracy and Power: Essays in Political Theory,* i, 156–86. Oxford: Oxford University Press, 1991.

Bell, Daniel. *Communitarianism and its Critics.* Oxford: Oxford University Press, 1993.

Connor, Walker. "Nation-Building or Nation-Destroying." *World Politics* 24 (1972): 319–55.

———. "The Politics of Ethnonationalism." *Journal of International Affairs* 27/1 (1973): 1–21.

Dion, Stéphane. "Le Nationalisme dans la convergence culturelle." In *L'Engagement intellectuel: mélanges en l'honneur de Léon Dion,* edited by R. Hudon and R. Pelletier, 291–311. Sainte-Foy: Les Presses de l'Université Laval, 1991.

———. "Explaining Quebec Nationalism." In *The Collapse of Canada?,* edited by R. Kent Weaver. Washington, D.C.: Brookings Institute, 1992.

Dworkin, Ronald. "In Defense of Equality." *Social Philosophy and Policy* 1/1 (1983): 24–40.

———. *A Matter of Principle.* London: Harvard University Press, 1985.

———. "Liberal Community." *California Law Review* 77/3 (1989): 479–504.

Ignatieff, Michael. *Blood and Belonging: Journeys into the New Nationalism.* New York: Farrar, Straus & Giroux, 1993.

Laponce, J. A. *Languages and their Territories.* Toronto: University of Toronto Press, 1987.

Lerner, Natan. *Group Rights and Discrimination in International Law.* Dordrecht: Martinus Nijhoff, 1991.

MacIntyre, Alasdair. *After Virtue: A Study in Moral Theory.* London: Duckworth, 1981.

Margalit, Avishai, and Halbertal, Moshe. "Liberalism and the Right to Culture." *Social Research* 61/3 (1994): 491–510.

Mill, J. S. *On Liberty,* edited by G. Himmelfarb. Harmondsworth: Penguin, 1982.

Miller, David. "In What Sense Must Socialism Be Communitarian?" *Social Philosophy and Policy* 6/2 (1988–9): 51–73.

———. "In Defense of Nationality." *Journal of Applied Philosophy* 10/1 (1993): 3–16.

Nickel, James. "The Value of Cultural Belonging: Expanding Kymlicka's Theory." *Dialogue* 33/4 (1995): 635–42.

Peters, R. and de Vries, G. "Apostasy in Islam." *Die Welt des Islams* 17 (1976): 1–25.

Peterson, William. "On the Subnations of Europe." In *Ethnicity: Theory and Experience,* edited by N. Glazer and D. Moynihan, 117–208. Cambridge, MA: Harvard University Press, 1975.

Rawls, John. "Reply to Alexander and Musgrave." *Quarterly Journal of Economics* 88/4 (1974): 633–55.

———. "Kantian Constructivism in Moral Theory." *Journal of Philosophy* 77/9 (1980): 515–72.

———. "Justice as Fairness: Political not Metaphysical." *Philosophy and Public Affairs* 14/3 (1985): 223–51.

———. *Political Liberalism.* New York: Columbia University Press, 1993a.

Sandel, Michael. *Liberalism and the Limits of Justice.* Cambridge: Cambridge University Press, 1982.

———. "The Procedural Republic and the Unencumbered Self." *Political Theory* 12/1 (1984): 81–96.

Tamir, Yael. *Liberal Nationalism.* Princeton, NJ: Princeton University Press, 1993.

Taylor, Charles. "Shared and Divergent Values." In *Options for a New Canada,* edited by Ronald Watts and D. Brown, 53–76. Toronto: University of Toronto Press, 1991.

———. "The Politics of Recognition." In *Multiculturalism and the 'Politics of Recognition,'* edited by Amy Gutmann, 25–73. Princeton, NJ: Princeton University Press, 1992a.

Waldron, Jeremy. "Minority Cultures and the Cosmopolitan Alternative." *University of Michigan Journal of Law Reform* 25/3 (1992a): 751–93.

35.
The Politics of Recognition
CHARLES TAYLOR

I

A number of strands in contemporary politics turn on the need, sometimes the demand, for *recognition*. The need, it can be argued, is one of the driving forces behind nationalist movements in politics. And the demand comes to the fore in a number of ways in today's politics, on behalf of minority or "subaltern" groups, in some forms of feminism and in what is today called the politics of "multiculturalism."

The demand for recognition in these latter cases is given urgency by the supposed links between recognition and identity, where this latter term designates something like a person's understanding of who they are, of their fundamental defining characteristics as a human being. The thesis is that our identity is partly shaped by recognition or its absence, often by the *mis*recognition of others, and so a person or group of people can suffer real damage, real distortion, if the people or society around them mirror back to them a confining or demeaning or contemptible picture of themselves. Nonrecognition or misrecognition can inflict harm, can be a form of oppression, imprisoning someone in a false, distorted, and reduced mode of being.

Thus some feminists have argued that women in patriarchal societies have been induced to adopt a depreciatory image of themselves. They have internalized a picture of their own inferiority, so that even when some of the objective obstacles to their advancement fall away, they may be incapable of taking advantage of the new opportunities. And beyond this, they are condemned to suffer the pain of low self-esteem. An analogous point has been made in relation to blacks: that white society has for generations projected a demeaning image of them, which some of them have been unable to resist adopting. Their own self-depreciation, on this view, becomes one of the most potent instruments of their own oppression. Their first task ought to be to purge themselves of this imposed and destructive identity. Recently, a similar point has been made in relation to indigenous and colonized people in general. It is held that since 1492 Europeans have projected an image of such people as somehow inferior, "uncivilized," and through the force of conquest have often been able to impose this image on the conquered. The figure of Caliban has been held to epitomize this crushing portrait of contempt of New World aboriginals.

Within these perspectives, misrecognition shows not just a lack of due respect. It can inflict a grievous wound, saddling its victims with a crippling self-hatred. Due recognition is not just a courtesy we owe people. It is a vital human need.

• • •

The discourse of recognition has become familiar to us, on two levels: First, in the intimate sphere, where we understand the formation of identity and the self as taking place in a continuing dialogue and struggle with significant others. And then in the public sphere, where a politics of equal recognition has come to play a bigger and bigger role. Certain feminist theories have tried to show the links between the two spheres.[1]

I want to concentrate here on the public sphere, and try to work out what a politics of equal recognition has meant and could mean.

In fact, it has come to mean two rather different things, connected, respectively, with the two major changes I have been describing. With the move from honor to dignity has come a politics of universalism, emphasizing the equal dignity of all citizens, and the content of this politics has been the equalization of rights and entitlements. What is to be avoided at all costs is the existence of "first-class" and "second-class" citizens. Naturally, the actual detailed measures justified by this principle have varied greatly, and have often been controversial. For some, equalization has affected only civil rights and voting rights; for others, it has extended into the socioeconomic sphere. People who are systematically handicapped by poverty from making the most of their citizenship rights are deemed on this view to have been relegated to second-class status, necessitating remedial action through equalization. But through all the differences of interpretation, the principle of equal citizenship has come to be universally accepted. Every position, no matter how reactionary, is now defended under the colors of this principle. Its greatest, most recent victory was won by the civil rights movement of the 1960s in the United States. It is worth noting that even the adversaries of extending voting rights to blacks in the southern states found some pretext consistent with universalism, such as "tests" to be administered to would-be voters at the time of registration.

By contrast, the second change, the development of the modern notion of identity, has given rise to a politics of difference. There is, of course, a universalist basis to this as well, making for the overlap and confusion between the two. *Everyone* should be recognized for his or her unique identity. But recognition here means something else. With the politics of equal dignity, what is established is meant to be universally the same, an identical basket of rights and immunities; with the politics of difference, what we are asked to recognize is the unique identity of this individual or group, their distinctness from everyone else. The idea is that it is precisely this distinctness that has been ignored, glossed over, assimilated to a dominant or majority identity. And this assimilation is the cardinal sin against the ideal of authenticity.[2]

[1] There are a number of strands that have linked these two levels, but perhaps special prominence in recent years has been given to a psychoanalytically oriented feminism, which roots social inequalities in the early upbringing of men and women. See, for instance, Nancy Chodorow, *Feminism and Psychoanalytic Theory* (New Haven: Yale University Press, 1989); and Jessica Benjamin, *Bonds of Love: Psychoanalysis, Feminism and the Problem of Domination* (New York: Pantheon, 1988).

[2] A prime example of this charge from a feminist perspective is Carol Gilligan's critique of Lawrence Kohlberg's theory of moral development, for presenting a view of human development

Now underlying the demand is a principle of universal equality. The politics of difference is full of denunciations of discrimination and refusals of second-class citizenship. This gives the principle of universal equality a point of entry within the politics of dignity. But once inside, as it were, its demands are hard to assimilate to that politics. For it asks that we give acknowledgment and status to something that is not universally shared. Or, otherwise put, we give due acknowledgment only to what is universally present—everyone has an identity—through recognizing what is peculiar to each. The universal demand powers an acknowledgment of specificity.

The politics of difference grows organically out of the politics of universal dignity through one of those shifts with which we are long familiar, where a new understanding of the human social condition imparts a radically new meaning to an old principle. Just as a view of human beings as conditioned by their socioeconomic plight changed the understanding of second-class citizenship, so that this category came to include, for example, people in inherited poverty traps, so here the understanding of identity as formed in interchange, and as possibly so malformed, introduces a new form of second-class status into our purview. As in the present case, the socioeconomic redefinition justified social programs that were highly controversial. For those who had not gone along with this changed definition of equal status, the various redistributive programs and special opportunities offered to certain populations seemed a form of undue favoritism.

Similar conflicts arise today around the politics of difference. Where the politics of universal dignity fought for forms of nondiscrimination that were quite "blind" to the ways in which citizens differ, the politics of difference often redefines nondiscrimination as requiring that we make these distinctions the basis of differential treatment. So members of aboriginal bands will get certain rights and powers not enjoyed by other Canadians, if the demands for native self-government are finally agreed on, and certain minorities will get the right to exclude others in order to preserve their cultural integrity, and so on.

To proponents of the original politics of dignity, this can seem like a reversal, a betrayal, a simple negation of their cherished principle. Attempts are therefore made to mediate, to show how some of these measures meant to accommodate minorities can after all be justified on the original basis of dignity. These arguments can be successful up to a point. For instance, some of the (apparently) most flagrant departures from "difference-blindness" are reverse discrimination measures, affording people from previously unfavored groups a competitive advantage for jobs or places in universities. This practice has been justified on the grounds that historical discrimination has created a pattern within which the unfavored struggle at a disadvantage. Reverse discrimination is defended as a temporary measure that will eventually level the playing field and allow the old "blind" rules to come back into force in a way that doesn't disadvantage anyone. This argument seems cogent enough—wherever

---

that privileges only one facet of moral reasoning, precisely the one that tends to predominate in boys rather than girls. See Gilligan, *In a Different Voice* (Cambridge, Mass.: Harvard University Press, 1982).

its factual basis is sound. But it won't justify some of the measures now urged on the grounds of difference, the goal of which is not to bring us back to an eventual "difference-blind" social space but, on the contrary, to maintain and cherish distinctness, not just now but forever. After all, if we're concerned with identity, then what is more legitimate than one's aspiration that it never be lost?[3]

So even though one politics springs from the other, by one of those shifts in the definition of key terms with which we're familiar, the two diverge quite seriously from each other. One basis for the divergence comes out even more clearly when we go beyond what each requires that we acknowledge—certain universal rights in one case, a particular identity on the other—and look at the underlying intuitions of value.

The politics of equal dignity is based on the idea that all humans are equally worthy of respect. It is underpinned by a notion of what in human beings commands respect, however we may try to shy away from this "metaphysical" background. For Kant, whose use of the term *dignity* was one of the earliest influential evocations of this idea, what commanded respect in us was our status as rational agents, capable of directing our lives through principles.[4] Something like this has been the basis for our intuitions of equal dignity ever since, though the detailed definition of it may have changed.

Thus, what is picked out as of worth here is a *universal human potential*, a capacity that all humans share. This potential, rather than anything a person may have made of it, is what ensures that each person deserves respect. Indeed, our sense of the importance of potentiality reaches so far that we extend this protection even to people who through some circumstance that has befallen them are incapable of realizing their potential in the normal way—handicapped people, or those in a coma, for instance.

In the case of the politics of difference, we might also say that a universal potential is at its basis, namely, the potential for forming and defining one's own identity, as an individual, and also as a culture. This potentiality must be respected equally in everyone. But at least in the intercultural context, a stronger

---

[3] Will Kymlicka, in his very interesting and tightly argued book *Liberalism, Community and Culture* (Oxford: Clarendon Press, 1989), tries to argue for a kind of politics of difference, notably in relation to aboriginal rights in Canada, but from a basis that is firmly within a theory of liberal neutrality. He wants to argue on the basis of certain cultural needs—minimally, the need for an integral and undamaged cultural language with which one can define and pursue his or her own conception of the good life. In certain circumstances, with disadvantaged populations, the integrity of the culture may require that we accord them more resources or rights than others. The argument is quite parallel to that made in relation to socioeconomic inequalities that I mentioned above.

But where Kymlicka's interesting argument fails to recapture the actual demands made by the groups concerned—say Indian bands in Canada, or French-speaking Canadians—is with respect to their goal of survival. Kymlicka's reasoning is valid (perhaps) for *existing* people who find themselves trapped within a culture under pressure, and can flourish within it or not at all. But it doesn't justify measures designed to ensure survival through indefinite future generations. For the populations concerned, however, that is what is at stake. We need only think of the historical resonance of "la survivance" among French Canadians.

[4] See Kant, *Grundlegung der Metaphysik der Sitten* (Berlin: Gruyter, 1968; reprint of the Berlin Academy edition), p. 434.

demand has recently arisen: that one accord equal respect to actually evolved cultures. Critiques of European or white domination, to the effect that they have not only suppressed but failed to appreciate other cultures, consider these depreciatory judgments not only factually mistaken but somehow morally wrong. When Saul Bellow is famously quoted as saying something like, "When the Zulus produce a Tolstoy we will read him," [5] this is taken as a quintessential statement of European arrogance, not just because Bellow is allegedly being *de facto* insensitive to the value of Zulu culture, but frequently also because it is seen to reflect a denial in principle of human equality. The possibility that the Zulus, while having the same potential for culture formation as anyone else, might nevertheless have come up with a culture that is less valuable than others is ruled out from the start. Even to entertain this possibility is to deny human equality. Bellow's error here, then, would not be a (possibly insensitive) particular mistake in evaluation, but a denial of a fundamental principle.

To the extent that this stronger reproach is in play, the demand for equal recognition extends beyond an acknowledgment of the equal value of all humans potentially, and comes to include the equal value of what they have made of this potential in fact. This creates a serious problem, as we shall see below.

These two modes of politics, then, both based on the notion of equal respect, come into conflict. For one, the principle of equal respect requires that we treat people in a difference-blind fashion. The fundamental intuition that humans command this respect focuses on what is the same in all. For the other, we have to recognize and even foster particularity. The reproach the first makes to the second is just that it violates the principle of nondiscrimination. The reproach the second makes to the first is that it negates identity by forcing people into a homogeneous mold that is untrue to them. This would be bad enough if the mold were itself neutral—nobody's mold in particular. But the complaint generally goes further. The claim is that the supposedly neutral set of difference-blind principles of the politics of equal dignity is in fact a reflection of one hegemonic culture. As it turns out, then, only the minority or suppressed cultures are being forced to take alien form. Consequently, the supposedly fair and difference-blind society is not only inhuman (because suppressing identities) but also, in a subtle and unconscious way, itself highly discriminatory.[6]

This last attack is the cruelest and most upsetting of all. The liberalism of equal dignity seems to have to assume that there are some universal, difference-

---

[5] I have no idea whether this statement was actually made in this form by Saul Bellow, or by anyone else. I report it only because it captures a widespread attitude, which is, of course, why the story had currency in the first place.

[6] One hears both kinds of reproach today. In the context of some modes of feminism and multiculturalism, the claim is the strong one, that the hegemonic culture discriminates. In the Soviet Union, however, alongside a similar reproach leveled at the hegemonic Great Russian culture, one also hears the complaint that Marxist-Leninist communism has been an alien imposition on all equally, even on Russia itself. The communist mold, on this view, has been truly nobody's. Solzhenitsyn has made this claim, but it is voiced by Russians of a great many different persuasions today, and has something to do with the extraordinary phenomenon of an empire that has broken apart through the quasi-secession of its metropolitan society.

blind principles. Even though we may not have defined them yet, the project of defining them remains alive and essential. Different theories may be put forward and contested—and a number have been proposed in our day[7]—but the shared assumption of the different theories is that one such theory is right.

The charge leveled by the most radical forms of the politics of difference is that "blind" liberalisms are themselves the reflection of particular cultures. And the worrying thought is that this bias might not just be a contingent weakness of all hitherto proposed theories, that the very idea of such a liberalism may be a kind of pragmatic contradiction, a particularism masquerading as the universal.

• • •

IV

There is a form of the politics of equal respect, as enshrined in a liberalism of rights, that is inhospitable to difference, because (a) it insists on uniform application of the rules defining these rights, without exception, and (b) it is suspicious of collective goals. Of course, this doesn't mean that this model seeks to abolish cultural differences. This would be an absurd accusation. But I call it inhospitable to difference because it can't accommodate what the members of distinct societies really aspire to, which is survival. This is (b) a collective goal, which (a) almost inevitably will call for some variations in the kinds of law we deem permissible from one cultural context to another, as the Quebec case clearly shows.

I think this form of liberalism is guilty as charged by the proponents of a politics of difference. Fortunately, however, there are other models of liberal society that take a different line on (a) and (b). These forms do call for the invariant defense of *certain* rights, of course. There would be no question of cultural differences determining the application of *habeas corpus,* for example. But they distinguish these fundamental rights from the broad range of immunities and presumptions of uniform treatment that have sprung up in modern cultures of judicial review. They are willing to weigh the importance of certain forms of uniform treatment against the importance of cultural survival, and opt sometimes in favor of the latter. They are thus in the end not procedural models of liberalism, but are grounded very much on judgments about what makes a good life—judgments in which the integrity of cultures has an important place.

Although I cannot argue it here, obviously I would endorse this kind of model. Indisputably, though, more and more societies today are turning out to be multicultural, in the sense of including more than one cultural community

---

[7] See John Rawls, *A Theory of Justice* (Cambridge, Mass.: Harvard University Press, 1971); Ronald Dworkin, *Taking Rights Seriously* (London: Duckworth, 1977) and *A Matter of Principle* (Cambridge, Mass.: Harvard University Press, 1985); and Jürgen Habermas, *Theorie des kommunikativen Handelns* (Frankfurt: Suhrkamp, 1981).

that wants to survive. The rigidities of procedural liberalism may rapidly become impractical in tomorrow's world.

V

The politics of equal respect, then, at least in this more hospitable variant, can be cleared of the charge of homogenizing difference. But there is another way of formulating the charge that is harder to rebut. In this form, however, it perhaps ought not to be rebutted, or so I want to argue.

The charge I'm thinking of here is provoked by the claim sometimes made on behalf of "difference-blind" liberalism that it can offer a neutral ground on which people of all cultures can meet and coexist. On this view, it is necessary to make a certain number of distinctions—between what is public and what is private, for instance, or between politics and religion—and only then can one relegate the contentious differences to a sphere that does not impinge on the political.

But a controversy like that over Salman Rushdie's *Satanic Verses* shows how wrong this view is. For mainstream Islam, there is no question of separating politics and religion the way we have come to expect in Western liberal society. Liberalism is not a possible meeting ground for all cultures, but is the political expression of one range of cultures, and quite incompatible with other ranges. Moreover, as many Muslims are well aware, Western liberalism is not so much an expression of the secular, postreligious outlook that happens to be popular among liberal *intellectuals* as a more organic outgrowth of Christianity—at least as seen from the alternative vantage point of Islam. The division of church and state goes back to the earliest days of Christian civilization. The early forms of the separation were very different from ours, but the basis was laid for modern developments. The very term *secular* was originally part of the Christian vocabulary.[8]

All this is to say that liberalism can't and shouldn't claim complete cultural neutrality. Liberalism is also a fighting creed. The hospitable variant I espouse, as well as the most rigid forms, has to draw the line. There will be variations when it comes to applying the schedule of rights, but not where incitement to assassination is concerned. But this should not be seen as a contradiction. Substantive distinctions of this kind are inescapable in politics, and at least the nonprocedural liberalism I was describing is fully ready to accept this.

But the controversy is nevertheless disturbing. It is so for the reason I mentioned above: that all societies are becoming increasingly multicultural, while at the same time becoming more porous. Indeed, these two developments go together. Their porousness means that they are more open to multinational migration; more of their members live the life of diaspora, whose center is

---

[8] The point is well argued in Larry Siedentop, "Liberalism: the Christian Connection," *Times Literary Supplement,* 24–30 March 1989, p. 308. I have also discussed these issues in "The Rushdie Controversy," in *Public Culture* 2, no. 1 (Fall 1989): 118–22.

elsewhere. In these circumstances, there is something awkward about replying simply, "This is how we do things here." This reply must be made in cases like the Rushdie controversy, where "how we do things" covers issues such as the right to life and to freedom of speech. The awkwardness arises from the fact that there are substantial numbers of people who are citizens and also belong to the culture that calls into question our philosophical boundaries. The challenge is to deal with their sense of marginalization without compromising our basic political principles.

This brings us to the issue of multiculturalism as it is often debated today, which has a lot to do with the imposition of some cultures on others, and with the assumed superiority that powers this imposition. Western liberal societies are thought to be supremely guilty in this regard, partly because of their colonial past, and partly because of their marginalization of segments of their populations that stem from other cultures. It is in this context that the reply "this is how we do things here" can seem crude and insensitive. Even if, in the nature of things, compromise is close to impossible here—one either forbids murder or allows it—the attitude presumed by the reply is seen as one of contempt. Often, in fact, this presumption is correct. Thus we arrive again at the issue of recognition.

Recognition of equal value was not what was at stake—at least in a strong sense—in the preceding section. There it was a question of whether cultural survival will be acknowledged as a legitimate goal, whether collective ends will be allowed as legitimate considerations in judicial review, or for other purposes of major social policy. The demand there was that we let cultures defend themselves, within reasonable bounds. But the further demand we are looking at here is that we all *recognize* the equal value of different cultures; that we not only let them survive, but acknowledge their *worth*.

What sense can be made of this demand? In a way, it has been operative in an unformulated state for some time. The politics of nationalism has been powered for well over a century in part by the sense that people have had of being despised or respected by others around them. Multinational societies can break up, in large part because of a lack of (perceived) recognition of the equal worth of one group by another. This is at present, I believe, the case in Canada— though my diagnosis will certainly be challenged by some. On the international scene, the tremendous sensitivity of certain supposedly closed societies to world opinion—as shown in their reactions to findings of, say, Amnesty International, or in their attempts through UNESCO to build a new world information order— attests to the importance of external recognition.

But all this is still *an sich*, not *für sich*, to use Hegelian jargon. The actors themselves are often the first to deny that they are moved by such considerations, and plead other factors, like inequality, exploitation, and injustice, as their motives. Very few Quebec independentists, for instance, can accept that what is mainly winning them their fight is a lack of recognition on the part of English Canada.

What is new, therefore, is that the demand for recognition is now explicit. And it has been made explicit, in the way I indicated above, by the spread of the idea that we are formed by recognition. We could say that, thanks to this idea, misrecognition has now graduated to the rank of a harm that can be hardheadedly enumerated along with the ones mentioned in the previous paragraph.

One of the key authors in this transition is undoubtedly the late Frantz Fanon, whose influential *Les Damnés de la Terre (The Wretched of the Earth)*[9] argued that the major weapon of the colonizers was the imposition of their image of the colonized on the subjugated people. These latter, in order to be free, must first of all purge themselves of these depreciating self-images. Fanon recommended violence as the way to this freedom, matching the original violence of the alien imposition. Not all those who have drawn from Fanon have followed him in this, but the notion that there is a struggle for a changed self-image, which takes place both within the subjugated and against the dominator, has been very widely applied. The idea has become crucial to certain strands of feminism, and is also a very important element in the contemporary debate about multiculturalism.

The main locus of this debate is the world of education in a broad sense. One important focus is university humanities departments, where demands are made to alter, enlarge, or scrap the "canon" of accredited authors on the grounds that the one presently favored consists almost entirely of "dead white males." A greater place ought to be made for women, and for people of non-European races and cultures. A second focus is the secondary schools, where an attempt is being made, for instance, to develop Afrocentric curricula for pupils in mainly black schools.

The reason for these proposed changes is not, or not mainly, that all students may be missing something important through the exclusion of a certain gender or certain races or cultures, but rather that women and students from the excluded groups are given, either directly or by omission, a demeaning picture of themselves, as though all creativity and worth inhered in males of European provenance. Enlarging and changing the curriculum is therefore essential not so much in the name of a broader culture for everyone as in order to give due recognition to the hitherto excluded. The background premise of these demands is that recognition forges identity, particularly in its Fanonist application: dominant groups tend to entrench their hegemony by inculcating an image of inferiority in the subjugated. The struggle for freedom and equality must therefore pass through a revision of these images. Multicultural curricula are meant to help in this process of revision.

Although it is not often stated clearly, the logic behind some of these demands seems to depend upon a premise that we owe equal respect to all cultures. This emerges from the nature of the reproach made to the designers of traditional curricula. The claim is that the judgments of worth on which these latter were supposedly based were in fact corrupt, were marred by narrowness or insensitivity or, even worse, a desire to downgrade the excluded. The implication seems to be that absent these distorting factors, true judgments of value

[9] (Paris: Maspero, 1961).

of different works would place all cultures more or less on the same footing. Of course, the attack could come from a more radical, neo-Nietzschean stand-point, which questions the very status of judgments of worth as such, but short of this extreme step (whose coherence I doubt), the presumption seems to be of equal worth.

I would like to maintain that there is something valid in this presumption, but that the presumption is by no means unproblematic, and involves something like an act of faith. As a presumption, the claim is that all human cultures that have animated whole societies over some considerable stretch of time have something important to say to all human beings. I have worded it in this way to exclude partial cultural milieux within a society, as well as short phases of a major culture. There is no reason to believe that, for instance, the different art forms of a given culture should all be of equal, or even of considerable, value; and every culture can go through phases of decadence.

But when I call this claim a "presumption," I mean that it is a starting hy-pothesis with which we ought to approach the study of any other culture. The validity of the claim has to be demonstrated concretely in the actual study of the culture. Indeed, for a culture sufficiently different from our own, we may have only the foggiest idea *ex ante* of in what its valuable contribution might consist. Because, for a sufficiently different culture, the very understanding of what it is to be of worth will be strange and unfamiliar to us. To approach, say, a raga with the presumptions of value implicit in the well-tempered clavier would be forever to miss the point. What has to happen is what Gadamer has called a "fusion of horizons." [10] We learn to move in a broader horizon, within which what we have formerly taken for granted as the background to valuation can be situated as one possibility alongside the different background of the for-merly unfamiliar culture. The "fusion of horizons" operates through our de-veloping new vocabularies of comparison, by means of which we can articulate these contrasts.[11] So that if and when we ultimately find substantive support for our initial presumption, it is on the basis of an understanding of what consti-tutes worth that we couldn't possibly have had at the beginning. We have reached the judgment partly through transforming our standards.

We might want to argue that we owe all cultures a presumption of this kind. I will explain later on what I think this claim might be based. From this point of view, withholding the presumption might be seen as the fruit merely of prejudice or of ill-will. It might even be tantamount to a denial of equal status. Something like this might lie behind the accusation leveled by supporters of multiculturalism against defenders of the traditional canon. Supposing that their reluctance to enlarge the canon comes from a mixture of prejudice and ill-will, the multiculturalists charge them with the arrogance of assuming their own superiority over formerly subject peoples.

[10] *Wahrheit und Methode* (Tübingen: Mohr, 1975), pp. 289–90.

[11] I have discussed what is involved here at greater length in "Comparison, History, Truth," in *Myth and Philosophy*, ed. Frank Reynolds and David Tracy (Albany: State University of New York Press, 1990); and in "Understanding and Ethnocentricity," in *Philosophy and the Human Sciences* (Cambridge: Cambridge University Press, 1985).

This presumption would help explain why the demands of multiculturalism build on the already established principles of the politics of equal respect. If withholding the presumption is tantamount to a denial of equality, and if important consequences flow for people's identity from the absence of recognition, then a case can be made for insisting on the universalization of the presumption as a logical extension of the politics of dignity. Just as all must have equal civil rights, and equal voting rights, regardless of race or culture, so all should enjoy the presumption that their traditional culture has value. This extension, however logically it may seem to flow from the accepted norms of equal dignity, fits uneasily within them, as described in Section II, because it challenges the "difference-blindness" that was central to them. Yet it does indeed seem to flow from them, albeit uneasily.

I am not sure about the validity of demanding this presumption as a right. But we can leave this issue aside, because the demand made seems to be much stronger. The claim seems to be that a proper respect for equality requires more than a presumption that further study will make us see things this way, but actual judgments of equal worth applied to the customs and creations of these different cultures. Such judgments seem to be implicit in the demand that certain works be included in the canon, and in the implication that these works have not been included earlier only because of prejudice or ill-will or the desire to dominate. (Of course, the demand for inclusion is logically separable from a claim of equal worth. The demand could be: Include these because they're ours, even though they may well be inferior. But this is not how the people making the demand talk.)

But there is something very wrong with the demand in this form. It makes sense to demand as a matter of right that we approach the study of certain cultures with a presumption of their value, as described above. But it can't make sense to demand as a matter of right that we come up with a final concluding judgment that their value is great, or equal to others'. That is, if the judgment of value is to register something independent of our own wills and desires, it cannot be dictated by a principle of ethics. On examination, either we will find something of great value in culture C, or we will not. But it makes no more sense to demand that we do so than it does to demand that we find the earth round or flat, the temperature of the air hot or cold.

I have stated this rather flatly, when as everyone knows there is a vigorous controversy over the "objectivity" of judgments in this field, and whether there is a "truth of the matter" here, as there seems to be in natural science, or indeed, whether even in natural science "objectivity" is a mirage. I do not have space to address this here. I have discussed it somewhat elsewhere.[12] I don't have much sympathy for these forms of subjectivism, which I think are shot through with confusion. But there seems to be some special confusion in invoking them in this context. The moral and political thrust of the complaint concerns unjustified judgments of inferior status allegedly made of nonhegemonic cultures. But if those judgments are ultimately a question of the human

---

[12] See part 1 of [my] *Sources of the Self,* (Cambridge, MA: Harvard University Press, 1989).

will, then the issue of justification falls away. One doesn't, properly speaking, make judgments that can be right or wrong; one expresses liking or dislike, one endorses or rejects another culture. But then the complaint must shift to address the refusal to endorse, and the validity or invalidity of judgments here has nothing to do with it.

Then, however, the act of declaring another culture's creations to be of worth and the act of declaring oneself on their side, even if their creations aren't all that impressive, become indistinguishable. The difference is only in the packaging. Yet the first is normally understood as a genuine expression of respect, the second often as unsufferable patronizing. The supposed beneficiaries of the politics of recognition, the people who might actually benefit from acknowledgment, make a crucial distinction between the two acts. They know that they want respect, not condescension. Any theory that wipes out the distinction seems at least *prima facie* to be distorting crucial facets of the reality it purports to deal with.

In fact, subjectivist, half-baked neo-Nietzschean theories are quite often invoked in this debate. Deriving frequently from Foucault or Derrida, they claim that all judgments of worth are based on standards that are ultimately imposed by and further entrench structures of power. It should be clear why these theories proliferate here. A favorable judgment on demand is nonsense, unless some such theories are valid. Moreover, the giving of such a judgment on demand is an act of breathtaking condescension. No one can really mean it as a genuine act of respect. It is more in the nature of a pretend act of respect given on the insistence of its supposed beneficiary. Objectively, such an act involves contempt for the latter's intelligence. To be an object of such an act of respect demeans. The proponents of neo-Nietzschean theories hope to escape this whole nexus of hypocrisy by turning the entire issue into one of power and counterpower. Then the question is no more one of respect, but of taking sides, of solidarity. But this is hardly a satisfactory solution, because in taking sides they miss the driving force of this kind of politics, which is precisely the search for recognition and respect.

Moreover, even if one could demand it of them, the last thing one wants at this stage from Eurocentered intellectuals is positive judgments of the worth of cultures that they have not intensively studied. For real judgments of worth suppose a fused horizon of standards, as we have seen; they suppose that we have been transformed by the study of the other, so that we are not simply judging by our original familiar standards. A favorable judgment made prematurely would be not only condescending but ethnocentric. It would praise the other for being like us.

Here is another severe problem with much of the politics of multiculturalism. The peremptory demand for favorable judgments of worth is paradoxically—perhaps one should say tragically—homogenizing. For it implies that we already have the standards to make such judgments. The standards we have, however, are those of North Atlantic civilization. And so the judgments implicitly and unconsciously will cram the others into our categories. For instance, we will think of their "artists" as creating "works," which we then can include in our canon. By implicitly invoking our standards to judge all civilizations and cultures, the politics of difference can end up making everyone the same.[13]

In this form, the demand for equal recognition is unacceptable. But the story doesn't simply end there. The enemies of multiculturalism in the American academy have perceived this weakness, and have used this as an excuse to turn their backs on the problem. But this won't do. A response like that attributed to Bellow which I quoted above, to the effect that we will be glad to read the Zulu Tolstoy when he comes along, shows the depths of ethnocentricity. First, there is the implicit assumption that excellence has to take forms familiar to us: the Zulus should produce a *Tolstoy*. Second, we are assuming that their contribution is yet to be made (*when* the Zulus produce a Tolstoy . . .). These two assumptions obviously go hand in hand. If they have to produce our kind of excellence, then obviously their only hope lies in the future. Roger Kimball puts it more crudely: "The multiculturalists notwithstanding, the choice facing us today is not between a 'repressive' Western culture and a multicultural paradise, but between culture and barbarism. Civilization is not a gift, it is an achievement—a fragile achievement that needs constantly to be shored up and defended from besiegers inside and out."[14]

There must be something midway between the inauthentic and homogenizing demand for recognition of equal worth, on the one hand, and the self-immurement within ethnocentric standards, on the other. There are other cultures, and we have to live together more and more, both on a world scale and commingled in each individual society.

What there is in the presumption of equal worth I described above: a stance we take in embarking on the study of the other. Perhaps we don't need to ask whether it's something that others can demand from us as a right. We might simply ask whether this is the way we ought to approach others.

Well, is it? How can this presumption be grounded? One ground that has been proposed is a religious one. Herder, for instance, had a view of divine providence, according to which all this variety of culture was not a mere accident but was meant to bring about a greater harmony. I can't rule out such a view. But merely on the human level, one could argue that it is reasonable to suppose that cultures that have provided the horizon of meaning for large numbers of human beings, of diverse characters and temperaments, over a long period of time—that have, in other words, articulated their sense of the good, the holy, the admirable—are almost certain to have something that deserves our admiration and respect, even if it is accompanied by much that we have to

---

[13] The same homogenizing assumptions underlie the negative reaction that many people have to claims to superiority in some definite respect on behalf of Western civilization, say in regard to natural science. But it is absurd to cavil at such claims in principle. If all cultures have made a contribution of worth, it cannot be that these are identical, or even embody the same kind of worth. To expect this would be to vastly underestimate the differences. In the end, the presumption of worth imagines a universe in which different cultures complement each other with quite different kinds of contribution. This picture not only is compatible with, but demands judgments of, superiority-in-a-certain-respect.

[14] "Tenured Radicals," *New Criterion*, January 1991, p. 13.

abhor and reject. Perhaps one could put it another way: it would take a supreme arrogance to discount this possibility *a priori.*

There is perhaps after all a moral issue here. We only need a sense of our own limited part in the whole human story to accept the presumption. It is only arrogance, or some analogous moral failing, that can deprive us of this. But what the presumption requires of us is not peremptory and inauthentic judgments of equal value, but a willingness to be open to comparative cultural study of the kind that must displace our horizons in the resulting fusions. What it requires above all is an admission that we are very far away from that ultimate horizon from which the relative worth of different cultures might be evident. This would mean breaking with an illusion that still holds many "multiculturalists"—as well as their most bitter opponents—in its grip.[15]

---

[15] There is a very interesting critique of both extreme camps, from which I have borrowed in this discussion, in Benjamin Lee, "Towards a Critical Internationalism" (forthcoming).

36.
Minority Cultures and the Cosmopolitan Alternative

JEREMY WALDRON

If it were appropriate to make dedications, this Article would be for Salman Rushdie, who a few months ago celebrated his one-thousandth day in hiding in Britain under police protection from the sentence of death passed upon him in Tehran in 1988. I want to begin with an extended quotation from an essay entitled *In Good Faith,* which Rushdie wrote in 1990 in defense of his execrated book *The Satanic Verses:*

> If *The Satanic Verses* is anything, it is a migrant's-eye view of the world. It is written from the very experience of uprooting, disjuncture and metamorphosis (slow or rapid, painful or pleasurable) that is the migrant condition, and from which, I believe, can be derived a metaphor for all humanity.
>
> Standing at the centre of the novel is a group of characters most of whom are British Muslims, or not particularly religious persons of Muslim background, struggling with just the sort of great problems that have arisen to surround the book, problems of hybridization and ghettoization, of reconciling the old and the new. Those who oppose the novel most vociferously today are of the opinion that intermingling with a different culture will inevitably weaken and ruin their own. I am of the opposite opinion. *The Satanic Verses* celebrates hybridity, impurity, intermingling, the transformation that comes of new and unexpected combinations of human beings, cultures, ideas, politics, movies, songs. It rejoices in mongrelization and fears the absolutism of the Pure. *Mélange,* hotchpotch, a bit of this and a bit of that is *how newness enters the world.* It is the great possibility that mass migration gives the world, and I have tried to embrace it. *The Satanic Verses* is for change-by-fusion, change-by-conjoining. It is a love-song to our mongrel selves . . .
>
> I was born an Indian, and not only an Indian, but a Bombayite—Bombay, most cosmopolitan, most hybrid, most hotchpotch of Indian cities. My writing and thought have therefore been as deeply influenced by Hindu myths and attitudes as Muslim ones. . . . Nor is the West absent from Bombay. I was already a mongrel self, history's bastard, before London aggravated the condition.[1]

It is not my intention here to contribute further to the discussion of *The Satanic Verses* or of the price its author has paid for its publication. Instead, I want to take the comments that I have just quoted as a point of departure to explore the vision of life, agency, and responsibility that is implicit in this affirmation of

---

[1] Salman Rushdie, 'In Good Faith', in *Imaginary Homelands* 393, 394, 404 (1991).

cosmopolitanism. I want to explore the tension between that vision and the more familiar views with which we are concerned in this Symposium—views that locate the coherence and meaning of human life in each person's immersion in the culture and ethnicity of a particular community.

1. COMMUNITARIANISM

What follows is in part a contribution to the debate between liberals and communitarians, though those labels are becoming rather tattered in the modern discussion.

Although there is a rough correlation between the liberty claimed by Rushdie and the ideal of liberal freedom, the life sketched out by Rushdie really does not answer to the more earnest or high-minded characterizations of the liberal individual in modern political philosophy. Modern liberal theorists place great stress on the importance of an autonomous individual leading his life according to a chosen plan; his autonomy is evinced in the formulation and execution of a life-plan and the adoption of ground-projects, and his rights are the liberties and protections that he needs in order to do this. Liberals stress the importance of each individual's adoption of a particular conception of the good, a view about what makes life worth living, and again a person's rights are the protections he needs in order to be able to choose and follow such values on equal terms with others who are engaged in a similar enterprise. The approach to life sketched out by Rushdie has little in common with this, apart from the elements of freedom and decision. It has none of the ethical unity that the autonomous Kantian individual is supposed to confer on his life; it is a life of kaleidoscopic tension and variety. It is not the pursuit of a chosen conception of goodness along lines indicated by Ronald Dworkin; nor does its individuality consist, in Rawls's words, in "a human life lived according to a plan."[2] Instead, it rightly challenges the rather compulsive rigidity of the traditional liberal picture. If there is liberal autonomy in Rushdie's vision, it is choice running rampant, and pluralism internalized from the relations *between* individuals to the chaotic coexistence of projects, pursuits, ideas, images, and snatches of culture *within* an individual.

If I knew what the term meant, I would say it was a "postmodern" vision of the self. But, as I do not, let me just call it "cosmopolitan," although this term is not supposed to indicate that the practitioner of the ethos in question is necessarily a migrant (like Rushdie), a perpetual refugee (like, for example, Jean-Jacques Rousseau), or a frequent flyer (like myself). The cosmopolitan may live all his life in one city and maintain the same citizenship throughout. But he refuses to think of himself as *defined* by his location or his ancestry or his citizenship or his language. Though he may live in San Francisco and be of Irish ancestry, he does not take his identity to be compromised when he learns Spanish, eats Chinese, wears clothes made in Korea, listens to arias by Verdi sung by

---

[2] John Rawls, *A Theory of Justice,* (Cambridge, MA: Harvard University Press, 1971), p. 408.

a Maori princess on Japanese equipment, follows Ukrainian politics, and practices Buddhist meditation techniques. He is a creature of modernity, conscious of living in a mixed-up world and having a mixed-up self.

I want to use the opportunity provided by Rushdie's sketch of such a life to challenge the claims that are made by modern communitarians about the need people have for involvement in the substantive life of a particular community as a source of meaning, integrity, and character. One of the things that we are going to find, as we proceed with this exploration, is the importance of pressing the communitarian on the meaning of the term "community." Many of us have been puzzled and frustrated by the absence of a clear understanding of this concept in some of the assertions made by communitarians like Alasdair MacIntyre, Michael Sandel, Charles Taylor, and Michael Walzer. I do not mean the absence of a precise definition. I mean the absence of any settled sense about the *scope* and *scale* of the social entity that they have in mind.

When they say that the modern individual is a creation of community, or that each of us owes her identity to the community in which she is brought up, or that our choices necessarily are framed in the context of a community, or that we must not think of ourselves as holding rights against the community, or that communities must have boundaries, or that justice is fidelity to shared understandings within a community, what scale of entity are we talking about? Is "community" supposed to denote things as small as villages and neighborhoods, social relations that can sustain *gemeinschaft*-type solidarity and face-to-face friendships? What is the relation between the community and the political system? Is "community" supposed to do work comparable to "civil society," picking out the social infrastructure of whatever state or political entity we are talking about? If, as John Dunn recently has argued, the concept of *the state* no longer picks out a natural kind, denoting as it does political entities as small as Fiji and as large as the United States, as tight as Singapore and as loose as the Commonwealth of Independent States (C.I.S.), is there any sense in supposing that for every state there is just one community or society to which individuals owe their being and allegiance?

Should we even suppose that communities are no bigger than states? If each of us is a product of a community, is that heritage limited to national boundaries, or is it as wide (as *world*wide) as the language, literature, and civilization that sustain us? Are we talking about particular communities, at the level of self-contained ethnic groups, or are we talking about the common culture and civilization that makes it possible for a New Zealander trained at Oxford to write for a symposium in the *University of Michigan Journal of Law Reform?*[3]

I suspect that the popularity of modern communitarianism has depended on *not* giving unequivocal answers to these questions. I suspect that it depends on using premises that evoke community on one scale (usually large) to support conclusions requiring allegiance to community on quite a different scale (usually small).

---

[3] Jeremy Waldron, "Particular Values and Critical Morality," 77 *Cal. L. Rev.* 561, 582 (1989).

For the purposes of this Article, I want to single out one meaning of the term as worthy of special attention. It is "community" in the sense of *ethnic* community: a particular people sharing a heritage of custom, ritual, and way of life that is in some real or imagined sense immemorial, being referred back to a shared history and shared provenance or homeland. This is the sense of "community" implicated in nineteenth- and twentieth-century nationalism. I shall use community in this sense as a sort of counterpoint to my exploration of Rushdie's cosmopolitan ideal. I want to pin down the communitarian critique of the cosmopolitan style of life to something like the claim, made by the German historian Johann Gottfried Von Herder, that (in Isaiah Berlin's paraphrase) "among elementary human needs—as basic as those for food, shelter, security, procreation, communication—is the need to belong to a particular group, united by some common links—especially language, collective memories, continuous life upon the same soil," and perhaps "race, blood, religion, a sense of common mission, and the like." [4]

Some will protest that it is unfair to pin matters down in this way. Michael Sandel, they will say, is not Johann Gottfried Von Herder. But the aim is not to underestimate the subtlety of any particular philosopher's position. From time to time, it is important for us not only to read the ordinary ambiguous literature of communitarianism, but also to see how much substance there would be if various *determinate* communitarian claims were taken one by one, and their proponents were forced to abandon any reliance on vagueness and equivocation. In the end, that is the best way to evaluate the array of different meanings that are evoked in this literature. This Article is certainly not a complete execution of that task, but it is intended as a substantial beginning.

2. MINORITY CULTURE AS A HUMAN RIGHT

There is an additional reason for being interested in social entities on this scale. In modern discussions of human rights, we are presented with the claim that particular cultures, communities, and ethnic traditions have a right to exist and a right to be protected from decay, assimilation, and desuetude. The claim is presented, in a rather modest form, in Article 27 of the International Covenant on Civil and Political Rights:

> In those States in which ethnic, religious or linguistic minorities exist, persons belonging to such minorities shall not be denied the right, in community with the other members of their group, to enjoy their own culture, to profess and practise their own religion, or to use their own language. [5]

Now, as it stands, this provision leaves quite unclear what is to count as the enjoyment of one's culture, the profession of one's religion, and the use of one's

---

[4] Isaiah Berlin, "Benjamin Disraeli, Karl Marx and the Search for Identity," in *Against the Current,* 252, 257 (Henry Hardy ed., 1980).

[5] *International Covenant on Civil and Political Rights,* adopted Dec. 19, 1966, art. 27, 999 U.N.T.S. 172, 179.

language. Are these goods secured when a dwindling band of demoralized individuals continues, against all odds, to meet occasionally to wear their national costume, recall snatches of their common history, practice their religious and ethnic rituals, and speak what they can remember of what was once a flourishing tongue? Is that the *enjoyment* of their culture? Or does enjoyment require more along the lines of the active flourishing of the culture on its own terms, in something approximating the conditions under which it originally developed?

Many have thought that respect for minority cultures does require more. A recent United Nations report rejected the view that Article 27 is nothing but a nondiscrimination provision: it insisted that special measures for minority cultures (such as some form of affirmative action) are required and that such measures are as important as nondiscrimination in defending fundamental human rights in this area. Such affirmative measures may include subsidies from the wider society. But they also may involve the recognition that minority cultures are entitled to protect themselves by placing limits on the incursion of outsiders and limits on their own members' choices about career, family, lifestyle, loyalty, and exit—limits that might be unpalatable in the wider liberal context.

It is not my intention to get involved in a detailed debate about the interpretation of Article 27. Instead, I want to examine the implicit claim about human life that lies behind provisions like this. For, once again, we are dealing with the Herderian claim that there is a human yearning or need to belong: a need that is in danger of being miserably frustrated—for example in the case of North American aboriginal groups. This is the need that scholars appeal to when they criticize or defend various interpretations of the right of cultural preservation.

3. A THIN THEORY OF THE GOOD

So there are two visions to be considered—the cosmopolitan vision intimated by Salman Rushdie and the vision of belonging and immersion in the life and culture of a particular community espoused by the proponents of Article 27.

It is important to see that these are not merely different lifestyles of the sort that old-fashioned liberalism could comfortably accommodate in a pluralistic world—some like campfires, some like opera; some are Catholics, some are Methodists—that sort of thing. Instead, we are talking, as I indicated earlier, about the background view of life, agency, and responsibility that is presupposed already by any account of what it is for lifestyles to be diverse or for diversity to be tolerated.

This contrast between lifestyle and background assumptions is worth explaining a little further. Any political theory, *including* a theory of toleration or liberal neutrality, must be predicated on some view of what human life is like. This is true even if it is only what philosophers call a "thin" theory—that is, a theory giving us the bare framework for conceptualizing choice and agency but leaving the specific content of choices to be filled in by individuals. We need a thin theory to tell us what goods should be at stake in a theory of justice, what liberties and rights are going to be called for, and, more broadly, what the skeletal outlines of human lives can be expected to be so that we can have some sense of how everything will fit together. For example, a liberal theory of rights needs to be able to say that religious choices and matters of conscience are very important to people (and so worthy of special protection) without begging any questions about what the content of those choices should be. A thin theory is also necessary in order to work out a subject-matter for a theory of justice: What is a just distribution ultimately a distribution of? Should we be interested in the just distribution of happiness, the just distribution of material resources, or the just distribution of human abilities and capacities? Each society must share some consensus at this level, no matter what plurality it envisages on some other level.

Above all, we need a thin theory of choice, agency, and responsibility so that we can say something about the shape of individual lives in relation to matters like society, community, politics, and justice. We need to have some skeletal sense of how things are to fit together. Are we envisaging a society of *individuals* in some strong sense, or a community of persons bound together in some organic common life? Are we envisaging a society of equals, so that each person's claims against others are to be matched by others' reciprocal claims against him? Or are we envisaging a hierarchy, oriented functionally towards some nonegalitarian end?

We cannot make any progress at all in political philosophy unless we tie ourselves down to some extent here; certainly a liberal theory of neutrality that purports to be neutral about *everything* in this area quickly falls apart into fatuous incoherence. Critics of liberalism are fond of uncovering the assumptions made at this level, as if that were a way of discrediting the neutrality of the liberal ideal. But every political theory must take some stand on what authentic human agency is like and how that relates to the fact of our location in society. The tensions that I intend to explore—between the cosmopolitan and communitarian account of human life and activities—are not merely disagreements at the level of comfortably competing lifestyles. They are not to be thought of as liberal bedfellows who have already settled the basic terms and conceptions of their association. They are tensions at a deep philosophical level.

4. OPPOSITION AND AUTHENTICITY

But are the two visions of human life that we are discussing really antagonists? It may seem odd to oppose them this starkly. Salman Rushdie is not noted as an opponent of aboriginal rights, nor are the Native American tribes particularly interested in *The Satanic Verses*. The defenders of Article 27 may frown on cultural impurity, but they are not proposing exactly to limit the freedom of those who, like Rushdie, choose to entangle their roots with foreign grafts. Not *exactly*, but the fact that one of the charges for which Rushdie was sentenced to death was apostasy is a sobering reminder of what it really may mean to insist that people must keep faith with their roots.

Nor are the citizens of the world, the modernist dreamers of cosmopolis, proposing exactly to destroy minority cultures. Their apartments are quite likely to be decorated with Inuit artifacts or Maori carvings. Still, we know that a world in which deracinated cosmopolitanism flourishes is not a safe place for minority communities. Our experience has been that they wither and die in the harsh glare of modern life, and that the custodians of these dying traditions live out their lives in misery and demoralization.

We are dealing, in other words, with conceptions of man and society which, if not actually inconsistent, certainly are opposed in some important sense. Each envisions an environment in which the other is, to a certain extent, in danger.

It is also true that, although these two conceptions are not formally inconsistent, still the best case that can be made in favor of each of them tends to cast doubt upon the best case that can be made for the other.

Suppose first, that a freewheeling cosmopolitan life, lived in a kaleidoscope of cultures, is both possible and fulfilling. Suppose such a life turns out to be rich and creative, and with no more unhappiness than one expects to find anywhere in human existence. Immediately, one argument for the protection of minority cultures is undercut. It can no longer be said that all people *need* their rootedness in the particular culture in which they and their ancestors were reared in the way that they need food, clothing, and shelter. People used to think they *needed* red meat in their diet. It turns out not to be true: vegetarian alternatives are available. Now some still may prefer and enjoy a carnivorous diet, but it is no longer a matter of necessity. The same—if the cosmopolitan alternative can be sustained—is true for immersion in the culture of a particular community. Such immersion may be something that particular people like and enjoy. But they no longer can claim that it is something that they need.

Of course, it does not follow from this that we are entitled to crush and destroy minority cultures. But the collapse of the Herderian argument based on distinctively human *need* seriously undercuts any claim that minority cultures might have to special support or assistance or to extraordinary provision or forbearance. At best, it leaves the right to culture roughly on the same footing as the right to religious freedom. We no longer think it true that everyone needs some religious faith or that everyone must be sustained in the faith in which he was brought up. A secular lifestyle is evidently viable, as is conversion from one church to another. Few would think it right to try to extirpate religious belief in consequence of these possibilities. But equally, few would think it right to subsidize religious sects merely in order to preserve them. If a particular church is dying out because its members are drifting away, no longer convinced by its theology or attracted by its ceremonies, that is just the way of the world. It is like the death of a fashion or a hobby, not the demise of anything that people really need.

So the sheer existence and vitality of the cosmopolitan alternative is enough to undercut an important part of the case for the preservation of minority cultures. Sometimes the cosmopolitan argument goes further. The stronger claim that Salman Rushdie suggests, in the passage we began with, is that the hybrid lifestyle of the true cosmopolitan is in fact the only appropriate response to the modern world in which we live. We live in a world formed by technology and trade; by economic, religious, and political imperialism and their offspring; by mass migration and the dispersion of cultural influences. In this context, to immerse oneself in the traditional practices of, say, an aboriginal culture might be a fascinating anthropological experiment, but it involves an artificial dislocation from what actually is going on in the world. That it is an artifice is evidenced by the fact that such immersion often requires special subsidization and extraordinary provision by those who live in the real world, where cultures and practices are not so sealed off from one another. The charge, in other words, is one of *inauthenticity*.

Let me state it provocatively. From a cosmopolitan point of view, immersion in the traditions of a particular community in the modern world is like living in Disneyland and thinking that one's surroundings epitomize what it is for a culture really to exist. Worse still, it is like demanding the funds to live in Disneyland and the protection of modern society for the boundaries of Disneyland, while still managing to convince oneself that what happens inside Disneyland is all there is to an adequate and fulfilling life. It is like thinking that what every person most deeply needs is for one of the Magic Kingdoms to provide a framework for her choices and her beliefs, completely neglecting the fact that the framework of Disneyland depends on commitments, structures, and infrastructures that far outstrip the character of any particular facade. It is to imagine that one could belong to Disneyland while professing complete indifference towards, or even disdain for, Los Angeles.

That is the case from one side. Suppose, on the other hand, that we accept what defenders of minority culture often say—that there is a universal human need for rootedness in the life of a particular community and that this communal belonging confers character and depth on our choices and our actions. Then the freedom that Rushdie claims looks deviant and marginal, an odd or eccentric exercise of license rather than a consummation of human liberty. It sometimes is said that claims of freedom must be made with respect to actions that make sense and that unintelligibility rather than hostility is the first obstacle to toleration. If anything like this is correct, then the more credence that we give to the communitarian thesis, the less intelligible the claim to cosmopolitan freedom becomes.

From the point of view of community, the cosmopolitan freedom that Rushdie extols—the freedom to renounce his heritage and just play with it, mixing it with imagery and movies and jokes and obscenities—is like the freedom claimed by any other oddball: the freedom to sail the Atlantic in a bathtub or the freedom to steer one's way through a bewildering series of marriages and divorces. Those who hop from one community to another, merging their roots and never settling down into any stable practices and traditions may, like the bathtub sailor or the matrimonial athlete, excite our sneaking admiration.

But when things go wrong for them, our pitying response will be, "Well, what did you expect?"

A moment ago, we considered the view that immersion in the life of a minority culture is like hiding in Disneyland and that it is an inauthentic way of evading the complex actualities of the world as it is. But the charge of inauthenticity is likely to be returned with interest by the proponents of minority culture. From their point of view, it is the Rushdian life of shifting and tangled attachments that is the shallow and inauthentic way of living in the world. The cosmopolitan ideal, they will say, embodies all the worst aspects of classic liberalism—atomism, abstraction, alienation from one's roots, vacuity of commitment, indeterminacy of character, and ambivalence towards the good. The accusation is implicit in the undertones of words like "deracinated" and "alienated" or in the terminology that Rushdie turns bravely to his own purposes in the passage quoted earlier: "hybrid," "impurity," "hotchpotch," "*mélange*," and "mongrelization." [6] It is no accident that these terms, which so accurately describe the cosmopolitan ideal, are fraught with negative and cautionary connotations. This is the case that must be answered if the cosmopolitan vision is to be sustained.

7. OUR DEBT TO GLOBAL COMMUNITY

One advantage of our focus on the cosmopolitan vision is that it forces us to think a little more grandly about the scale on which community and friendship are available for the constitution of the individual and the sustenance of friendship and interdependence. Talk of community is the nostalgic first-person plural of belonging, is, as I have said, apt to evoke images of small-scale community, neighborhood, or intimacy—the aboriginal hunting band, the Athenian city-state, or the misty dawn in a Germanic village.

Think honestly, however, of the real communities to which many of us owe our allegiance and in which we pursue our values and live large parts of our lives: the international community of scholars (defined in terms of some shared specialization), the scientific community, the human rights community, the artistic community, the feminist movement, what's left of international socialism, and so on. These structures of action and interaction, dependence and interdependence, effortlessly transcend national and ethnic boundaries and allow men and women the opportunity to pursue common and important projects under conditions of goodwill, cooperation, and exchange throughout the world. Of course, one should not paint too rosy a picture of this interaction. Such groupings exhibit rivalry, suspicion, and divisive controversy as well; but no more than any common enterprise and certainly no more than the gossip or backbiting one finds in smaller, more localized entities. It is community on this global scale which is the modern realization of Aristotelean friendship: equals

[6] *See supra* text accompanying note 1.

who are good at orienting themselves in common to the pursuit of virtue. This form of community is quite missed by those who lament the loss of true friendship in modern life.

Once we recognize this, the simple Herderian picture of the constitution of an individual through his belonging to a homogeneous group begins to fall apart. Think how much we owe in history and heritage—in the culture, or the cultures that have formed us—to the international communities that have existed among merchants, clerics, lawyers, agitators, scholars, scientists, writers, and diplomats. We are not the self-made atoms of liberal fantasy, certainly, but neither are we exclusively products or artifacts of single national or ethnic communities. We are made by our languages, our literature, our cultures, our science, our religions, our civilization—and these are human entities that go far beyond national boundaries and exist, if they exist anywhere, simply *in the world*. If, as the communitarians insist, we owe a debt of provenance to the social structures that have formed us, then we owe a debt to the world and to the global community and civilization, as well as whatever we owe to any particular region, country, nation, or tribe.

The argument that we must not think of our individuality as self-made, but that we must own up to the role that society has played in the constitution of our selves and cultivate a sense of allegiance and obligation that is appropriate to that social provenance has been a staple of modern communitarian thought. It finds its most eloquent recent expression in a paper by Charles Taylor, entitled *Atomism,* though I fear that in that article Taylor is guilty of exactly the equivocation I mentioned earlier: tracing our debt to society, in the sense of a whole civilization, and inferring an obligation to society, in the sense of a particular nation-state.

Be that as it may, Taylor's argument is one that can be turned as easily against the partisans of small-scale community as against the advocates of atomistic individualism. For just as the allegedly self-made individual needs to be brought to a proper awareness of her dependence on social, communal, and cultural structures, so too in the modern world particular cultures and national communities have an obligation to recognize their dependence on the wider social, political, international, and civilizational structures that sustain them.

This is obvious in the case of indigenous communities in countries like the United States, Canada, Australia, and New Zealand. Indigenous communities make their claims for special provision and for the autonomous direction of their own affairs in the context of the wider political life of the countries where they are situated, and by the logic of Taylor's argument they must accept some responsibility to participate in and sustain this wider life. They are not entitled to accept the benefits of its protection and subsidization and at the same time disparage and neglect the structures, institutions, and activities that make it possible for indigenous communities to secure the aid, toleration, and forbearance of the large numbers of other citizens and other small communities by which they are surrounded.

Indigenous communities of course will lament that they are thus at the mercy of larger polities and that they have to make a case for the existence of their culture to fellow citizens who do not necessarily share their ethnic allegiance. They may yearn for the days of their own self-sufficiency, the days when the question of sharing their lands with anyone else simply did not arise. They have that in common, I think, with Nozickian individualists who yearn for the days when the individual person was not so much at the mercy of the community and did not owe so much to the state, and who resent the processes that have brought them to this point. Yet here we all are. Our lives or practices, whether individual or communal, are in fact no longer self-sufficient. We may pretend to be self-sufficient atoms, and behave as we are supposed to behave in the fantasies of individualistic economics; but the pretense easily is exposed by the reality of our communal life. And similarly—though we may drape ourselves in the distinctive costumes of our ethnic heritage and immure ourselves in an environment designed to minimize our sense of relation to the outside world—no honest account of our being will be complete without an account of our dependence on larger social and political structures that goes far beyond the particular community with which we pretend to identify ourselves.

If this is true of the relation of indigenous minorities to the larger state, it applies also to the relation of particular cultures and nations to the world order as a whole. The point is evident enough from the ironies of Article 27 of the International Covenant on Civil and Political Rights, quoted earlier, which claims the integrity of indigenous cultures as a matter of human rights. One hardly can maintain that immersion in a particular community is all that people need in the way of connection with others when the very form in which that claim is couched—the twenty-seventh article of one of a succession of human rights charters administered and scrutinized by international agencies from Ottawa to Geneva—indicates an organized social context that already takes us far beyond a specific nation, community, or ethnicity. The point is not that we should all therefore abandon our tribal allegiances and realign ourselves under the flag of the United Nations. The theoretical point is simply that it ill behoves the partisans of a particular community to sneer at and to disparage those whose cosmopolitan commitments make possible the lives that they are seeking to lead. The activity of these international organizations does not happen by magic; it presupposes large numbers of men and women who are prepared to devote themselves to issues of human and communal values *in general* and who are prepared to pursue that commitment in abstraction from the details of their own particular heritage.

So far as I have developed the *instrumental* side of Taylor's argument: just as individuals need communal structures in order to develop and exercise the capacities that their rights protect, so minority communities need larger political and international structures to protect and to sustain the cultural goods that they pursue. But Taylor's critique of individualist atomism also goes deeper than this. The very idea of individuality and autonomy, he argues, is a social artifact, a way of thinking about and managing the self that is sustained in a particular social and historical context. I am sure that he is right about that. But we must not assume, simply because individuality is an artifact, that the social structures that are said to produce it are necessarily natural. Certainly there is nothing natural about communitarian, ethnic, or nationalist ideas. The idea of a small-scale national community is as much a product (and indeed a quite recent product) of civilization, growing and flourishing as the convergence of a number of disparate currents under particular conditions in a particular era, as is the idea of the autonomous individual. Certainly, ethnic nationality is an idea which postulates or dreams its own naturalness, its own antiquity, its immemorial cultivation of a certain patch of soil. Each national community, in Benedict Anderson's phrase, *imagines* itself as something that can be traced to the misty dawn of time. But so did *individuals* dream themselves, as the natural units of mankind, in the heyday of atomistic philosophy. The claim that we always have belonged to specific, defined, and culturally homogeneous peoples— the staple claim of modern nationalism—needs to be treated with the same caution as individualist fantasies about the state of nature: useful, perhaps, as a hypothesis for some theoretical purpose, but entirely misleading for others.

8. KYMLICKA'S VIEW OF THE SOCIAL WORLD

A. The Importance of Cultural Membership

In all of this, the cosmopolitan strategy is not to deny the role of culture in the constitution of human life, but to question, first, the assumption that the social world divides up neatly into particular distinct cultures, one to every community, and, secondly, the assumption that what everyone needs is just *one* of these entities—a single, coherent culture—to give shape and meaning to his life.

That assumption, I am afraid, pervades Will Kymlicka's recent book on community and culture,[7] and it is to his argument that I now want to turn. Kymlicka's aim is to show that liberal theorists, such as John Rawls and Ronald Dworkin, have underestimated radically the importance of culture as a primary good for the self-constitution of individual lives. He wants to fill that gap and to enlist liberal theories in the cause of the preservation of minority cultures.

Thus, Kymlicka's starting point is not so much the Herderian urge to belong, but a Rawlsian conviction about the importance to people of the freedom to form, reform, and revise their individual beliefs about what makes life worth living. To sustain that freedom, one needs a certain amount of self-respect, and one needs the familiar protections, guarantees, opportunities, and access to the means of life—all the things that figure already on Rawls's list of the primary goods to be governed by a theory of justice. In order to make the case that culture is also one of these primary goods, Kymlicka argues that people cannot choose a conception of the good for themselves in isolation, but that they need a clear sense of an established range of options to choose from.

> In deciding how to lead our lives, we do not start *de novo,* but rather we examine "definite ideals and forms of life that have been developed and tested by innumerable individuals, sometimes for generations." The decision about

---

[7]   Will Kymlicka, *Liberalism, Community, and Culture* (Oxford: Oxford University Press, 1989), p. 165.

how to lead our lives must ultimately be ours alone, but this decision is always a matter of selecting what we believe to be most valuable from the various options available, selecting from a context of choice which provides us with different ways of life.[8]

Kymlicka elaborates the point by insisting that what we choose among are not ways of life understood simply as different physical patterns of behavior.

> The physical movements only have meaning to us because they are identified as having significance by our culture, because they fit into some pattern of activities which is culturally recognized as a way of leading one's life. We learn about these patterns of activity through their presence in stories we've heard about the lives, real or imaginary, of others. . . . We decide how to lead our lives by situating ourselves in these cultural narratives, by adopting roles that have struck us as worthwhile ones, as ones worth living (which may, of course, include the roles we were brought up to occupy).[9]

"What follows from this?" Kymlicka asks.

> Liberals should be concerned with the fate of cultural structures, not because they have some moral status of their own, but because it's only through having a rich and secure cultural structure that people can become aware, in a vivid way, of the options available to them, and intelligently examine their value.[10]

On the face of it, the argument is a convincing one. Of course, choice takes place in a cultural context, among options that have culturally defined meanings. But in developing his case, Kymlicka is guilty of something like the fallacy of composition. From the fact that each option must have a cultural meaning, it does not follow that there must be one cultural framework in which each available option is assigned a meaning. Meaningful options may come to us as items or fragments from a variety of cultural sources. Kymlicka is moving too quickly when he says that each item is given its significance by some entity called "our culture," and he is not entitled to infer from that that there are things called "cultural structures" whose integrity must be guaranteed in order for people to have meaningful choices. His argument shows that people need cultural materials; it does not show that what people need is "a rich and secure cultural structure." It shows the importance of access to a variety of stories and roles; but it does not, as he claims, show the importance of something called *membership* in a culture.

Kymlicka's claim about the difference between physically and culturally defined options was an echo of an argument made earlier by Alasdair MacIntyre, and it may reinforce my point to discuss that argument as well. According to MacIntyre:

> We enter human society . . . with one or more imputed characters—roles into which we have been drafted—and we have to learn what they are in order to

[8] Ibid. at 164.
[9] Ibid. at 165.
[10] Ibid.

be able to understand how others respond to us and how our responses to them are apt to be construed. It is through hearing stories about wicked step-mothers, lost children, good but misguided kings, wolves that suckle twin boys, youngest sons who receive no inheritance but must make their own way in the world and eldest sons who waste their inheritance on riotous living and go into exile to live with the swine, that children learn or mislearn both what a child and what a parent is, what the cost of characters may be in the drama into which they have been born and what the ways of the world are. Deprive children of stories and you leave them unscripted, anxious stutterers in their actions as in their words.[11]

Again, it is important to see that these are heterogenous characters drawn from a variety of disparate cultural sources: from first-century Palestine, from the heritage of Germanic folklore, and from the mythology of the Roman Republic. They do not come from some *thing* called "the structure of our culture." They are familiar to us because of the immense variety of cultural materials, various in their provenance as well as their character, that are in fact available to us. But neither their familiarity nor their availability constitute them as part of a single cultural matrix. Indeed, if we were to insist that they are all part of the same matrix because they are all available to us, we would trivialize the individuation of cultures beyond any sociological interest. Any array of materials would count as part of a single culture whenever they were familiar to one and the same person. It would then be *logically* impossible for an individual to have access to more than one cultural framework.

Someone may object to the picture of cultural heterogeneity I am painting: "Doesn't each item take its full character from the integrity of the surrounding cultural context, so that it is a distortion to isolate it from that context and juxtapose it with disparate materials?" Maybe that is true, for certain purposes. If we were making an anthropological study of each item, we *would* want to explore the detail of its context and provenance; we would look at the tale of the prodigal son in the context of Aramaic storytelling, and we would confine the children lost in the wood to the Germanic villages from which the Grimm brothers drew their collection of folklore. But that is absurd as an account of how cultural materials enter into the lives and choices of ordinary people. For that purpose, the materials are simply *available,* from all corners of the world, as more or less meaningful fragments, images, and snatches of stories. Their significance for each person consists in large part in the countless occasions on which they have been (from the anthropological purist's point of view) misread and misinterpreted, wrenched from a wider context and juxtaposed to other fragments with which they may have very little in common. Since this in fact is the way in which cultural meanings enter people's lives, Salman Rushdie's description of a life lived in the shadow of Hindu gods, Muslim film stars, Kipling, Christ, Nabokov, and the *Mahabharata* is at least as authentic as Kymlicka's insistence on the purity of a particular cultural heritage.

---

[11] Alasdair MacIntyre, *After Virtue* (Notre Dame, IN: University of Notre Dame Press, 1981), p. 216.

If all this is correct, then membership in a particular community, defined by its identification with a single cultural frame or matrix, has none of the importance that Kymlicka claims it does. We need cultural meanings, but we do not need homogeneous culture frameworks. We need to understand our choices in the contexts in which they make sense, but we do not need any single context to structure all our choices. To put it crudely, we need culture, but we do not need cultural integrity. Since none of us needs a homogenous cultural framework or the integrity of a particular set of meanings, none of us needs to be immersed in one of the small-scale communities which, according to Kymlicka and others, are alone capable of securing this integrity and homogeneity. Some, of course, still may prefer such immersion, and welcome the social subsidization of their preference. But it is not, as Kymlicka maintained, a necessary presupposition of rational and meaningful choice.

B. Evaluation and Cultural Security

In addition to the claim (which I have just criticized) that each person needs to be a member of a particular cultural community, Kymlicka also argues that each person needs some assurance of the *security* of the cultural framework or frameworks from which she makes her choices. This seems to me a self-defeating claim.

Kymlicka's liberal individual is supposed to be making not just a choice, but an evaluation: "Which of the roles presented to me by the cultural materials at hand is a good role or an attractive one (for me)?" Now evaluation is a practical and, in part, a comparative matter. I choose role A because it seems a better way of living and relating to others than role B. It is difficult to see how one can make these comparisons without the ability to take a role, defined by a given culture, and compare it with what one might term loosely other ways of doing roughly the same sort of thing. For example, a traditional culture may define the role of *male elder,* a patriarchal position of tribal power, as a source of authority and the embodiment of tradition. Is this something for a young man to aspire to? One thing he may want to know is that the politics of patriarchal authority have, in almost all other social contexts, come under fierce challenge, and that people have developed other means of authoritative governance that do not embody male power and fatherhood in the same way. But to the extent that our young man can know this, he is not choosing from a cultural framework which is secure, in Kymlicka's sense. He only can make his choice a genuine *evaluation* to the extent that the culture he is scrutinizing is vulnerable to challenge and comparison from the outside. Unless the culture is vulnerable to his evaluation (and other evaluations like it), his evaluation will have no practical effect; and unless it has been vulnerable in this way in the past, he will have no basis for an informed and sensible choice.

To preserve a culture—to insist that it must be *secure,* come what may—is to insulate it from the very forces and tendencies that allow it to operate in a context of genuine choice. How does one tell, for example, whether the gender roles defined in a given culture structure have value? One way is to see whether the culture erodes and collapses as a way of life in a world once different ways of doing things are perceived. The possibility of the erosion of allegiance, or of the need to compromise a culture beyond all recognition in order to retain allegiance and prevent mass exodus, is the key to cultural evaluation. It is what cultures do, under pressure, as contexts of genuine choice. But if that is so, we cannot *guarantee* at the same time the integrity of a given community and say that its culture (or the fate of its culture) can *tell* people about the value and viability of this particular way of life. Either people learn about value from the dynamics of their culture and its interactions with others or their culture can operate for them at most as a museum display on which they can pride themselves. There is, I suppose, nothing wrong with such fierce nostalgic pride, but it certainly should not be confused with genuine choice and evaluation. To confer meaning on one's life is to take risks with one's culture, and these are risks that dismay those whose interest is the preservation of some sort of cultural purity.[12]

In general, there is something artificial about a commitment to *preserve* minority cultures. Cultures live and grow, change and sometimes wither away; they amalgamate with other cultures, or they adapt themselves to geographical or demographic necessity. To *preserve* a culture is often to take a favored "snapshot" version of it, and insist that this version must persist at all costs, in its defined purity, irrespective of the surrounding social, economic, and political circumstances. But the *stasis* envisaged by such preservation is seldom itself a feature of the society in question, or if it is, it is itself a circumstantial feature. A society may have remained static for centuries precisely because it did not come into contact with the influence from which now people are proposed to protect it. If stasis is not an inherent feature, it may be important to consider, as part of *that very culture,* the ability it has to adapt to changes in circumstances. To preserve or protect it, or some favored version of it, artificially, in the face of that change, is precisely to cripple the mechanisms of adaptation and compromise (from warfare to commerce to amalgamation) with which all societies confront the outside world. It is to preserve part of the culture, but not what many would regard as its most fascinating feature: its ability to generate *a history.*

---

[12] I think what this shows, by the way, is that Kymlicka's strategy (arguing from liberal premises) is simply a dangerous one for the proponents of cultural preservation to adopt. The liberal conception of autonomous choice evokes a spirit of discernment, restlessness, and comparison. It is, I think, simply antithetical to the idea that certain structures of community are to be *preserved* in their integral character. As long as cultures depend for their existence on people's allegiance and support, their use as frameworks of choice for individual lives is always liable to cut across the interest we have in preserving them.

SOCIAL
PHILOSOPHY

FOUR

SOCIAL IDEALS

In this section of the book, we will examine a number of important social ideals including justice, equality, liberty, rights, property and self-ownership. As we shall see, different philosophers have offered different interpretations of these ideals, both in and of themselves and in relation to each other. They have also ascribed to each of them greater or lesser significance in relationship to each other. As a result, while the section is structured to analyze many of these ideals separately, we shall see that they are usually closely interrelated with each other, although the interrelationships differ according to different analyses.

We begin with the ideal of justice. Many traditional formulas (or canons) of distributive justice exist, each claiming that justice requires that goods be distributed according to some characteristic (with each canon identifying a different characteristic). In reading 37, Rescher argues that all of these canons are mistaken because they are monistic—recognizing only one characteristic which generates claims that justice must recognize. Rescher believes that we need a pluralistic theory of justice which recognizes the legitimacy of a wide variety of claims which involve different characteristics. In different contexts, he believes, different claims will be relevant. Like most pluralistic theorists, Rescher does not clearly specify which claims are legitimate in which settings and about how to prioritize several legitimate claims in one setting. The difficulties raised by these questions are part of what has motivated many philosophers to promote monistic theories as more plausible than the pluralistic canons.

Mill's utilitarian theory of justice (reading 38) is one such monistic theory. Justice, for Mill, consists in recognizing those claims which society ought to defend because of the general utility of their possession. The person whose claim should be defended has a right to the thing in question. In an important passage, Mill uses this formula to discuss how people ought to be rewarded for their labor and what theory of taxation should be adopted, highlighting issues concerning the distribution of property which have become central to the discussion of justice. He recognizes that different conclusions might be supported by different reasonable arguments, and that it might therefore be difficult to come to any definite conclusions about the justice of social arrangements. He believes that the appeal to general utility offers the best hope of resolving these issues. The concern that utility appeals might not be adequate in resolving disputes is one of the reasons why many philosophers have rejected this theory and offered in its place other monistic theories.

One such theory is Nozick's entitlement theory of justice (reading 39). This theory is based upon principles of justice in the acquisition of property and in the transfer of property. It says that any distribution of property is just which arose from just initial acquisitions or by just transfers. Alternatively, the distribution can be just if it is in accord with appropriate rectifications of injustices (as defined by the principles of justice in acquisition and transfer). Therefore, Nozick classifies his theory as a *historical theory of justice*—one which assesses justice by how a distribution came about and not by a resulting structural pattern of the distribution. This distinguishes his theory from most other monistic theories. Nozick illustrates a historical theory by referring to John Locke's theory of just acquisitions of property, which leads him to introduce a proviso that might be thought to limit the applicability of his theory of justice. Nozick feels that this proviso is theoretically sound, yet it has few practical implications. While some have criticized that aspect of his discussion, most have been critical instead of its purely historical character, believing that justice has implications for the pattern of the distribution of goods. Those who have raised this criticism have usually believed that the pattern demanded by justice involves considerable equality in the distribution of goods. Among the theorists who support the demand for greater equality are Rawls, Roemer, and Cohen in readings 40–42.

The egalitarian component of Rawls's theory of justice as fairness is clear in the statement of its two basic principles. The first is an egalitarian principle that basic rights should be distributed equally (and they should be maximized to the extent compatible with this equal distribution). The second principle, while not egalitarian, allows for social and economic inequalities only if their existence is beneficial for everyone, and only if the advantages are open to all. This is in sharp contrast to the utilitarian who would allow for these inequalities so long as their existence promoted the general good, even if their existence harmed some. Rawls justifies his two principles at least in part by the claim that they would be chosen by rational individuals in a situation he describes as the original situation, using a mode of reasoning (the maximin rule) that Rawls thinks is appropriate for choosing principles of justice.

The egalitarianism in Roemer's theory of justice comes in indirectly, through his use of the concept of exploitation which had been so central to classical Marxist thought. Roemer first defines a non-normative concept of exploitation, in which some workers are exploited when they must work more time than is socially necessary for them to earn the goods they consume. The crucial technical issue involved is defining the socially necessary time of work. Exploitation, according to Roemer, results from the differential ownership of capital stock, together with its relative scarcity. Roemer argues that when this differential ownership is due to an unjust initial distribution of assets (resulting from such forces as robbery and plunder), the resulting exploitation is an unjust exploitation. In this respect, Roemer's theory of justice, like Nozick's, contains a historical component, since the justice of a distribution is at least in part a function of its history. But since this unjust exploitation can only be remedied by producing a pattern in which we have equalized the work effort of the various parties, Roemer's theory has a patterned egalitarian component as well. Roemer then considers, but rejects, a variety of capitalist defenses of the unequal initial distribution of capital stock.

Egalitarian theories of justice are often criticized on the grounds that differential rewards for differential contributions are necessary as an incentive to encourage productive efforts. Mill had raised that issue in his utilitarian analysis. Cohen confronts that question and argues, in opposition, that egalitarian societies have the capacity to produce people whose incentives for productive labor are more generous than the market motives of greed and fear. It remains, as Cohen recognizes, an open question whether these alternative motives can work.

As one reviews the readings on justice, it is clear that one of the central questions is the relation between justice and equality. Much as there are alternative conceptions of justice, there are alternative conceptions of equality. Equality has, moreover, been treated as a social ideal independent of, even if in relation to, the ideal of justice. We turn therefore to an examination of the alternative theories of equality. The theories of equality which we will examine parallel in many ways the theories of justice.

Walzer, in reading 43, offers a pluralistic theory of equality which in many ways resembles Rescher's pluralistic theory of justice. Walzer believes that there are different goods which define different distributive spheres and which must be distributed according to different criteria. For example, medical care should be distributed in accord with sickness. His concern is less with limiting inequalities in each sphere of distribution (the breakup of monopolies), and more with ensuring that inequalities in one sphere do not result in inequalities in all other spheres (the reduction of dominance). This would result in a special type of egalitarian society, one in which there will be many inequalities in different spheres without a single overall pattern of inequality.

Most theories of equality, like most theories of justice, are monistic rather than pluralistic theories. Singer, as a utilitarian thinker, offers in reading 44 a monistic account of equality which only requires that the interests of each be considered equally. As he points out, this principle of the equal consideration of interests is presupposed in all utilitarian assessments and rules out racism, sexism, and other ideologies that disregard or discount the interests of members of discriminated-against groups. If, moreover, we believe in the declining marginal utility of goods (the principle that any good means less to someone who has more of the good in question than it would to someone who has less), then we are likely as a result of equally considering interests to favor more equal distributions of goods. Still, it remains an empirical issue which distribution of goods is best from a utilitarian perspective, and various conflicting factual arguments can be offered. Not surprisingly, utilitarian theories of equality suffer from the same indeterminancy of conclusion as utilitarian theories of justice.

Hayek, in reading 45, offers a theory of equality which is very similar to Nozick's theory of justice. This theory of equality requires no pattern in the distribution of material goods. Instead, it requires only that everyone be treated equally under the law. Hayek's main argument in support of this notion of equality is that it is the only conception of equality compatible with a free society. Other theories of equality, in opposition to Hayek, insist that equality requires some degree of equal distribution of material goods. Among these theories are those proposed by Dworkin, Sen, and Arneson in readings 46–48.

Dworkin distinguishes two approaches to equality in the distribution of material goods—equality of welfare (subjective well-being) and equality of resources. The former requires transfer of resources among people until no further transfer would leave them more equal in welfare. The latter requires transfers until no further transfer would leave them more equal in resources. After explaining some of the differences between the two, Dworkin develops the latter theory. A certain type of auction results in an initial distribution of resources that meets the demands of equality (recall the significance of initial distributions in Roemer's theory). This auction is supplemented by a compulsory insurance market to cover inequalities due to handicaps. Furthermore, to deal with later inequalities (since Dworkin's theory of equality requires more than an initial equality of opportunity in terms of resources), a periodic redistribution of resources through taxation is adopted. Dworkin argues that the resulting scheme captures the idea of equality as an independent social ideal.

Sen begins his essay by making the crucial observation that all plausible social philosophies are committed to some belief in equality; if they were not, then they would fail to have the impartiality required for making them credible to all. The crucial difference among social philosophies then becomes the difference between what they propose to distribute equally. Sen thinks that the answer cannot be particular goods, such as the goods covered in Rawls's second principle of justice. The crucial point is that no distribution of goods can take into account the capacities of differing people to use those goods because of their varying abilities and handicaps. Sen proposes instead that the demands of equality require that goods be distributed to produce an equality in basic capabilities, admitting that there are serious cultural dependencies in that notion. It is important to note that both Sen and Dworkin are motivated to modify their understanding of the demands of equality to deal with the problem of equality for the handicapped, a problem that is not solved by a mere equal distribution of resources. It is important to carefully compare and evaluate their two responses to this problem.

Arneson points out that Dworkin's discussion has really raised two separate issues about equality: the first is the issue of equality of welfare versus equality of resources, while the second is the issue of equality versus equality of opportunity. In opposition to Dworkin's position, Arneson advocates a distribution of material goods to produce equality of opportunity for welfare. He argues for equality of opportunity (thereby opposing Dworkin's later tax scheme) because he thinks that it is morally preferable that individuals receive the foreseeable consequences of their choices. He argues for equality of welfare to avoid one of the consequences of Dworkin's approach, that the talents of the talented must be included among the resources to be redistributed in the initial equal distribution of resources.

As one reviews the monistic theories of justice and of equality, it becomes clear that they divide between those which impose considerable demands of equality on the distribution of material goods, either in the name of maximizing utility or in the name of independent ideals of justice or equality, and those which do not. Nozick's theory of justice and Hayek's theory of equality are our prime examples of theories which do not. In Part 3 of this section, we look at a number of additional ideals which have been mentioned as providing support for accounts of justice and equality that do not require the equal distribution of material goods. Among them are the ideals of the right to liberty, to self-ownership, and to property.

The discussion of the varied meanings of liberty, and of their implications for other social ideals, has been greatly influenced by Berlin's distinction between negative and positive freedoms developed in reading 49. For Berlin, negative freedom consists in noninterference by others. Different theories of negative freedom emphasize different spheres of life that ought to be free in this way. For Berlin, positive freedom consists of self-mastery, an ideal often transformed into mastery of others by ideals of equality and justice. Berlin argues for the superiority of negative freedom and against any of these other ideals.

Berlin's framework structures the debate between Lomasky and Shue in readings 50 and 51. Lomasky distinguishes two types of liberals—*classical liberals* who emphasize the liberty rights which are necessary for the attainment of items of value, and *welfare liberals* who emphasize positive rights which are jointly sufficient to obtain the items of value. The former emphasize negative freedoms while the latter emphasize positive freedoms. All of the above-surveyed egalitarians of material goods are welfare liberals. Lomasky argues for the primacy of these negative liberty rights of noninterference on the grounds that noninterference by others can only be provided by others, unlike material goods which the individual may obtain by himself. By contrast, Shue argues for the primacy of the positive liberty right to basic subsistence on the grounds that the enjoyment of basic subsistence is necessary for the enjoyment of any rights. He also argues that the distinction between the negative and the positive rights is misleading.

This debate is continued in readings 52 and 53, by Nozick and Cohen. It is important to remember, in reading that debate, that Nozick is defending his entitlement theory of justice, while Cohen is responding to Nozick's arguments in defense of the form of egalitarianism advocated by Cohen in his discussion of justice. Nozick offers two arguments: the first, developed by use of his Wilt

Chamberlain example, is the claim that noninterference with people's liberty of contract inevitably results in upsetting any pattern imposed in the name of justice. Consequently, only a nonpatterned theory of justice is compatible with our negative liberties. The second is the argument that the redistribution required to maintain any patterned principle of distribution (e.g., Dworkin's tax scheme) is analogous to the servitude of forced labor and is incompatible with the classical liberal ideal of self-ownership.

Cohen responds separately to each of these arguments. He agrees that even in the most egalitarian societies, there will be legitimate gifts and transfers, and that people have a right to make those transfers without social interference. However, there is no reason to accept an unlimited right of freedom to transfer, particularly when the transfers in question, as in Nozick's case, may result in great concentrations of wealth and resulting unacceptable concentrations of power over others. More generally, he rejects the notion that negative liberty rights of noninterference should have the moral priority that would prohibit society from interfering with transfers to accomplish other important social ideals. And if, he argues, these other social ideals contain non-contractual obligations to serve other people, the use of redistributive taxation to meet those obligations involves no illegitimate denial of self-ownership. In fact, argues Cohen, even Nozick's limited state designed to secure basic negative rights involves some element of this redistributive taxation.

One other social ideal, the right to own private property, is often invoked in the discussions of justice and equality. The claim is advanced that this right is violated by the redistributive programs required by patterned conceptions of justice and by conceptions of equality involving egalitarian distribution of material goods. Those claims form the background to the readings by Becker and Waldron. The reader should not, however, neglect the preliminary conceptual analysis of property rights provided by Honore in reading 54.

Becker, in reading 55, begins with a summary of four arguments, some utilitarian and some not, which he believes justify the institution of private property. He recognizes that there are concerns which may undercut these arguments in particular cases: duties to others (also stressed by Cohen), exhaustion or excessive accumulation of vital resources, and harmful uses of property. But subject to these limitations, Becker believes that the four arguments provide a presumption in favor of systems which allow individuals as much ownership as they want and can legitimately obtain. Such a presumption could be used to ground the objection to redistributive programs which take away some of the owned property.

A very different approach to the distributive implications of property is found in the selection from Waldron (reading 56). Waldron sees arguments of the sort advocated by Becker as special rights (SR) arguments supporting rights to property had by particular individuals because of what they have done. By contrast, Waldron supports a general rights (GR) approach to private property in which the right to property is had by all individuals because it is required for recognizing them as free moral agents. Since there are many individuals who do not own this property, a recognition of this approach to property rights supports, rather than challenges, redistributive programs.

Taylor, in reading 57, challenges the emphasis on individual rights found in so many of the selections in Part 3. Taylor believes that this emphasis represents an atomistic conception of human nature which fails to do justice to humanity's social nature. For Taylor, the ascription of a right (e.g., noninterference with autonomous choices) presupposes a positive evaluation of the moral worth of certain characteristics or capacities associated with that right (e.g., autonomy). But then we must be committed to a social order which protects and nourishes those capacities for others. This means, for Taylor, that the affirmation of these individual rights merely as constraints on social action is unacceptable.

IX

JUSTICE

37.
A Pluralistic Conception of Justice

NICHOLAS RESCHER

1. THE CANONS OF DISTRIBUTIVE JUSTICE

In the course of the long history of discussions on the subject, distributive justice has been held to consist, wholly or primarily, in the treatment of all people:

1. as equals (except possibly in the case of certain "negative" distributions such as punishments).
2. according to their needs.
3. according to their ability or merit or achievements.
4. according to their efforts and sacrifices.
5. according to their actual productive contribution.
6. according to the requirements of the common good, or the public interest, or the welfare of mankind, or the greater good of a greater number.
7. according to a valuation of their socially useful services in terms of their scarcity in the essentially economic terms of supply and demand.

Correspondingly, seven "canons" of distributive justice result, depending upon which of these factors is taken as the ultimate or primary determinant of individual claims, namely, the canons of equality, need, ability, effort, productivity, public utility, and supply and demand. Brief consideration must be given to each of these proposed conceptions of justice.[1]

2. THE CANON OF EQUALITY

This canon holds that justice consists in the treatment of people as equals. Here we have the *egalitarian* criterion of (idealistic) democratic theorists. The shortcomings of this canon have already been canvassed in considerable detail . . . , to the effect that the principle is oblivious to the reality of differential claims and desert. It is vulnerable to all the same lines of objection which hold against the type of just-wage principle advocated by G. B. Shaw—to let all who contribute to the production of the social-economic product share in it equally.[2] Moreover, the specification of the exact way in which equality is to be understood is

---

[1] All of these canons except number 3 (the Canon of Ability) are competently and instructively discussed from an essentially economic point of view—from the special angle of the idea of a just wage or income—in ch. 14 of John A. Ryan, *Distributive Justice* (3rd edn., New York: Macmillan, 1942).

[2] Ryan, *Distributive Justice* (3rd edn.), pp. 180–181: "According to the rule of arithmetical equality, all persons who contribute to the product should receive the same amount of remuneration. With the exception of Bernard Shaw, no important writer defends this rule to-day. It is unjust

by no means so simple and straightforward as it seems on first view. Is one, for example, to think of the type of fixed constant equality that is at issue in a sales tax, or the "equal burden" type of differential equality at issue in a graduated income tax; and more generally, is the "equality" at issue strict equality, equality of sacrifice, equality of opportunity-and-risk, equality of rights, or equality of "consideration," etc.?[3]

A rule of strict equality violates the most elemental requisites of the concept of justice itself: justice not only requires the equal treatment of equals, as the canon at issue would certainly assure, but also under various circumstances requires the converse, the (appropriately measured) unequal treatment of unequals, a requisite which the canon violates blatantly. In any distribution among individuals whose legitimate claims with respect to this distribution are diverse, the treatment of people as equals without reference to their differential claims outrages rather than implements our sense of justice.

3. THE CANON OF NEED

This canon holds that justice consists in the treatment of people according to their needs. Here we have the *socialistic* principle of the idealistic socialistic and communist theoreticians: "to each according to his needs."[4] Basically this principle is closely allied with the preceding one, and is, like it, one of *rectification*: recognizing that as things stand, men come into the world with different possessions and opportunities as well as differences in natural endowments, the principle professes to treat them, not equally, but so as to *make* them as equal as possible.

Regarding this principle, it has been said:

If the task of distribution were entirely independent of the process of production, this rule would be ideal [from the standpoint of justice]; for it would treat men as equal in those respects in which they are equal; namely as beings

---

because it would treat unequals equally. Although men are equal as moral entities, as human persons, they are unequal in desires, capacities, and powers. An income that would fully satisfy the needs of one man would meet only 75 per cent., or 50 per cent., of the capacities of another. To allot them equal amounts of income would be to treat them unequally with regard to the requisites of life and self development. To treat them unequally in these matters would be to treat them unequally as regards the real and only purpose of property rights. That purpose is welfare. Hence the equal moral claims of men which admittedly arise out of their moral equality must be construed as claims to equal degrees of welfare, not to equal amounts of external goods . . . Moreover, the rule of equal incomes is socially impracticable. It would deter the great majority of the more efficient from putting forth their best efforts and turning out their maximum product. As a consequence, the total volume of product would be so diminished as to render the share of the great majority of persons smaller than it would have been under a rational plan of unequal distribution."

[3]   Regarding these problems, see S. I. Benn and R. S. Peters, *Social Principles and the Democratic State* (London: Allen & Unwin, 1959), ch. 5, "Justice and Equality."

[4]   The formula "From each according to his abilities; to each according to his needs" was first advanced by the early French socialists of the Utopian school, and was officially adopted by German socialists in the Gotha Program of 1875.

endowed with the dignity and the potencies of personality; and it would treat them as unequal in those respects in which they are unequal; that is, in their desires and capacities.[5]

This limitation of the rule is of itself too narrow. The principle does recognize inequalities, but it recognizes only one sort; it rides roughshod not only over the matter of productive contributions but over all other ways of grounding legitimate claims (e.g., those based on kinship, on [nonproductive] services rendered, on contracts and compacts, etc.) that make for relevant differences, i.e., inequalities, among the potential recipients of a distribution. Nor, for that matter, is the principle as clear-cut as it seems on first view: by the time anything like an adequate analysis of "need" has been provided, the principle covers a wide-ranging area.[6] For example, are we to interpret the "needs" at issue as *real* needs or as *felt* needs?

4. THE CANON OF ABILITY AND/OR ACHIEVEMENT

This canon holds that justice consists in the treatment of people according to their abilities. Here we have the *meritarian* criterion going back to Aristotle and echoed by the (Jeffersonian) theorists of a "natural aristocracy of ability." Natural ability, however, is a latent quality which subsists in the mode of potentiality. It represents natural endowments that can be cultivated to varying degrees and may or may not become operative and actually put to work. To allocate rewards with reference solely to innate ability, unqualified by considerations of how the abilities in question are used or abused, would be to act in a way that is patently unjust. Moreover, a question can validly be raised as to the propriety of having natural ability—which is, after all, wholly a "gift of the gods" and in no way a matter of desert—count as the sole or even the primary basis of claims.[7]

This objection might be countered by granting that it may hold for *natural* (or innate) ability, but that it fails to be applicable when the "ability" at issue is an *acquired* ability, or perhaps even more aptly, a *demonstrated* ability of the persons at issue, as determined by their achievements. This is the criterion naturally used in giving grades to students and prizes to tennis players (where need, for instance, and effort are deliberately discounted). But in this case the canon becomes transformed, in its essentials, into the Canon of Productivity, which will be dealt with below.

---

[5] Ryan, *Distributive Justice* (3rd edn.), p. 181.

[6] See Benn and Peters, *Social Principles and the Democratic State*, pp. 141–148.

[7] "That part of a man's income which he owes to the possession of extraordinary natural abilities is a free boon to him; and from an abstract point of view bears some resemblance to the rent of other free gifts of nature. . . ." A. Marshall, *Principles of Economics* (8th edn., London: Macmillan, 1920), p. 664. The receipt of such "rents" is surely a matter of capitalizing on public necessity rather than one of obtaining the just reward due to individual desert.

5. THE CANON OF EFFORT

This canon holds that justice consists in the treatment of people according to their efforts and sacrifices on their own behalves, or perhaps on behalf of their group (family, society, fellowmen). Here we have the *puritanical* principle espoused by theorists of a "Puritan ethic," who hold that God helps (and men should help) those who help themselves. Burke lauded the "natural society" in which "it is an invariable law that a man's acquisitions are in proportion to his labors."[8] Think also of the historic discussions of a just wage and the traditional justification of differential wage scales. On the question of wages, classical socialists such as Fourier and St. Simon argued that the wage should be inversely proportioned to the intrinsic pleasantness (interest, appeal, prestige) of the task. (Presumably, thus, the policeman walking the beat shall receive more than the captain sitting at headquarters.) But the difficulties of this standpoint lie on the surface, e.g., the difficulty of maintaining morale and discipline in a setting in which the claims of ability and responsibility go unrecognized.

Moreover, the principle ignores the fact that effort is of its very nature a many-sided thing: it can be either fruitful or vain, well-directed or misguided, properly applied or misapplied, availing or unavailing, etc. To allocate rewards by effort as such without reference to its nature and direction is to ignore a key facet of just procedure—to fail to make a distinction that makes a difference. Also, to reward by effort rather than achievement is socially undesirable: it weakens incentive and encourages the inefficient, the untalented, the incompetent.

6. THE CANON OF PRODUCTIVITY

This canon holds that justice consists in the treatment of people according to their actual productive contribution to their group.[9] Here we have the essentially economic principle of the social-welfare-minded *capitalistic* theoreticians. The claim-bases at issue here are primarily those traditionally considered in economics: services rendered, capital advanced, risks run, and the like. Much is to be said on behalf of this principle as a *restricted* rule, governing the division of proceeds and profits resulting from a common productive enterprise; but it is clearly defective as a general principle of distributive justice, simply because it is an overly limited single-factor criterion. The principle is prepared to put aside all considerations not only of unmerited claims in general, but also of merited claims when merited through extra-productive factors such as need and effort.

---

[8] Edmund Burke, *Vindication of a Natural Society,* cited by E. Halévy in *The Growth of Philosophic Radicalism,* tr. Mary Morris, p. 216.

[9] Two alternative constructions of the principle arise, according as the "productive contribution" at issue is construed as the *total* contribution, or as solely the *net* contribution, i.e., the part that is available for consumption by others after deletion of the producers' own share.

Yet one cannot fail to be impressed by the appeal to justice of such an argument as the following:

> When men of equal productive power are performing the same kind of labour, superior amounts of product do represent superior amounts of effort. . . . If men are unequal in productive power their products are obviously not in proportion to their efforts. Consider two men whose natural physical abilities are so unequal that they can handle with equal effort shovels differing in capacity by fifty per cent. Instances of this kind are innumerable in industry. If these two men are rewarded according to productivity, one will get fifty per cent more compensation than the other. Yet the surplus received by the more fortunate man does not represent any action or quality for which he is personally responsible. It corresponds to no larger output of personal effort, no superior exercise of will, no greater personal desert.[10]

Note here the criticism of a (restricted) purely economic application of the principle by an appeal to one's sense of justice. If such an appeal is to be given but the slightest (even if not ultimately decisive) weight, as I think it must, then the canon in question must *a fortiori* be at once abandoned as an exclusive and exhaustive general principle of distributive justice.

7. THE CANON OF SOCIAL UTILITY

This canon holds that justice consists in the treatment of people according to the best prospects for advancing the common good, or the public interest, or the welfare of mankind, or the greater good of a greater number. The theory has two basic variants, according as one resorts to a distinction between the common good of men considered *collectively,* as constituting a social group with some sort of life of its own, or merely *distributively,* as an aggregation of separate individuals. In the former case we have the "public interest," expedientialist variant of the canon with roots going back to Hebraic theology, Stoic philosophy, and Roman jurisprudence (*pro bono publico*). In the second case we have the *utilitarian* and more modern, individualistic version of the canon.

The same fundamental criticism (already dwelt upon at considerable length in our preceding discussion) can be deployed against both versions of the theory: an individual's *proper share viewed from the angle of the general good* cannot be equated with his *just share* pure and simple, because there is no "pre-established harmony" to guarantee that all of the individual's legitimate claims (the authoritative determinants of his just share) be recognized and acceded to when "the *general* good" becomes the decisive criterion. And insofar as these legitimate claims are disallowed—or *could* be disallowed—in a patently unjust (though socially advantageous) way, the principle of the primary of the general good exhibits a feature which precludes its acceptance as a principle of justice.

---

[10] Ryan, *Distributive Justice* (3rd edn.), pp. 183–184.

8. THE CANON OF SUPPLY AND DEMAND

This canon holds that justice consists in the treatment of people according to a valuation of their socially useful—or perhaps merely desired—contributions, these being evaluated not on the basis of the value of the product (as with the Canon of Productivity above), but on the basis of relative scarcity of the service. Here we have the essentially economic principle of the more hard-boiled "play of the market" school of laissez-faire theoreticians. The train dispatcher would thus deserve a larger part of the proceeds of the joint operation than the conductor, the general manager more than the section foreman, the buyer more than the salesgirl, because—while in each case both kinds of contribution are alike essential to the enterprise—the former type of labor calls for skills that are relatively scarcer, being less plentifully diffused throughout the working population. Such valuation then rests not upon the relative extent or intrinsic merit of the contribution made, but upon the fact that that contribution is viewed by the community as necessary or desirable, and can either be made successfully by fewer people, or else involves such expenditures, risks, hardships, or hazards that fewer people are willing to undertake the task. (Throughout recent years successful entertainers have been remunerated more highly than successful physicians—and on this principle, justly so.)

As a criterion of justice, this canon suffers from the same general defects as does the Canon of Productivity which it seeks to qualify. Not only does it put aside any accommodation of unmerited claims, but also any claims based upon factors (such as individual need and expenditure of effort) which have no basis in the making of a productive contribution to felt social needs.

9. OUR OWN POSITION: THE CANON OF CLAIMS

One and the same shortcoming runs through all of the above canons of distributive justice: they are all *monistic*. They all recognize but one solitary, homogeneous mode of claim production (be it need, effort, productivity, or whatever), to the exclusion of all others. A single specific ground of claim establishment is canonized as uniquely authoritative, and all the others dismissed. As a result, these canons all suffer the aristocratic fault of hyperexclusiveness. As we see it, they err not so much in commission as in omission.

To correct this failing requires that we go from a concept of claim establishment that is monistic and homogeneous to one that is pluralistic and heterogeneous. To do so we put forward, as representing (in essentials) our own position on the issue of distributive justice, the CANON OF CLAIMS: Distributive justice consists in the treatment of people *according to their legitimate claims, positive and negative.* This canon shifts the burden to—and thus its implementation hinges crucially upon—the question of the nature of legitimate claims, and of the machinery for their mutual accommodation in cases of plurality, and their reconciliation in cases of conflict. To say this is not a criticism of the principle, but simply the recognition of an inevitable difficulty which must be encountered by any theory of distributive justice at the penalty of showing itself grossly inadequate.

The Canon of Claims plainly avoids the fault of overrestrictiveness: indeed, it reaches out to embrace all the other canons. From its perspective each canon represents one particular sort of ground (need, effort, productivity, etc.) on whose basis certain legitimate claims—upon whose accommodation it insists—can be advanced. The evaluation of these claims in context, and their due recognition under the circumstances, is in our view the key element of distributive justice.

We must be prepared to take such a multifaceted approach to claims because of the propriety of recognizing different kinds of claim-grounds as appropriate types of distribution. Our society inclines to the view that in the case of wages, desert is to be measured according to productivity of contribution qualified by supply-and-demand considerations; in the case of property income, by productivity considerations; in public-welfare distributions, by need qualified to avoid the demoralization inherent in certain types of means-tests; and in the negative distributions of taxation, by ability-to-pay qualified by social-utility considerations. The list could be extended and refined at great length but is already extensive enough to lend support to our pluralistic view of claims.

38.

A Utilitarian Theory of Justice

JOHN STUART MILL

ON THE CONNECTION BETWEEN JUSTICE AND UTILITY

In all ages of speculation, one of the strongest obstacles to the reception of the doctrine that Utility or Happiness is the criterion of right and wrong, has been drawn from the idea of Justice. The powerful sentiment, and apparently clear perception, which that word recalls with a rapidity and certainty resembling an instinct, have seemed to the majority of thinkers to point to an inherent quality in things; to show that the Just must have an existence in Nature as something absolute, generically distinct from every variety of the Expedient, and, in idea, opposed to it, though (as is commonly acknowledged) never, in the long run, disjoined from it in fact.

In the case of this, as of our other moral sentiments, there is no necessary connection between the question of its origin, and that of its binding force. That a feeling is bestowed on us by Nature, does not necessarily legitimate all its promptings. The feeling of justice might be a peculiar instinct, and might yet require, like our other instincts, to be controlled and enlightened by a higher reason. If we have intellectual instincts, leading us to judge in a particular way, as well as animal instincts that prompts us to act in a particular way, there is no necessity that the former should be more infallible in their sphere than the latter in theirs: it may as well happen that wrong judgments are occasionally suggested by those, as wrong actions by these. But though it is one thing to believe that we have natural feelings of justice, and another to acknowledge them as an ultimate criterion of conduct, these two opinions are very closely connected in point of fact. Mankind are always predisposed to believe that any subjective feeling, not otherwise accounted for, is a revelation of some objective reality. Our present object is to determine whether the reality, to which the feeling of justice corresponds, is one which needs any such special revelation; whether the justice or injustice of an action is a thing intrinsically peculiar, and distinct from all its other qualities, or only a combination of certain of those qualities, presented under a peculiar aspect. For the purpose of this inquiry it is practically important to consider whether the feeling itself, of justice and injustice, is *sui generis* like our sensations of color and taste, or a derivative feeling, formed by a combination of others. And this it is the more essential to examine, as people are in general willing enough to allow, that objectively the dictates of Justice coincide with a part of the field of General Expediency; but inasmuch as the subjective mental feeling of Justice is different from that which commonly attaches to simple expediency, and except in the extreme cases of the latter, is far more imperative in its demands, people find it difficult to see, in Justice, only a particular kind or branch of general utility, and think that its superior binding force requires a totally different origin.

To throw light upon this question, it is necessary to attempt to ascertain what is the distinguishing character of justice, or of injustice: what is the quality, or whether there is any quality, attributed in common to all modes of conduct designated as unjust (for justice, like many other moral attributes, is best defined by its opposite), and distinguishing them from such modes of conduct as are disapproved, but without having that particular epithet of disapprobation applied to them. If in everything which men are accustomed to characterize as just or unjust, some one common attribute or collection of attributes is always present, we may judge whether this particular attribute or combination of attributes would be capable of gathering round it a sentiment of that peculiar character and intensity by virtue of the general laws of our emotional constitution, or whether the sentiment is inexplicable, and requires to be regarded as a special provision of Nature. If we find the former to be the case, we shall, in resolving this question, have resolved also the main problem: if the latter, we shall have to seek for some other mode of investigating it.

To find the common attributes of a variety of objects, it is necessary to begin by surveying the objects themselves in the concrete. Let us therefore advert successively to the various modes of action, and arrangements of human affairs, which are classed, by universal or widely spread opinion, as Just or as Unjust. The things well known to excite the sentiments associated with those names are of a very multifarious character. I shall pass them rapidly in review, without studying any particular arrangement.

In the first place, it is mostly considered unjust to deprive any one of his personal liberty, his property, or any other thing which belongs to him by law. Here, therefore, is one instance of the application of the terms just and unjust in a perfectly definite sense, namely, that it is just to respect, unjust to violate, the *legal rights* of any one. But this judgment admits of several exceptions, arising from the other forms in which the notions of justice and injustice present themselves. For example, the person who suffers the deprivation may (as the phrase is) have *forfeited* the rights which he is so deprived of: a case to which we shall return presently. But also,

Secondly, the legal rights of which he is deprived, may be rights which *ought* not to have belonged to him; in other words, the law which confers on him these rights, may be a bad law. When it is so, or when (which is the same thing for our purpose) it is supposed to be so, opinions will differ as to the justice or injustice of infringing it. Some maintain that no law, however bad, ought to be disobeyed by an individual citizen; that his opposition to it, if shown at all, should only be shown in endeavoring to get it altered by competent authority. This opinion (which condemns many of the most illustrious benefactors of mankind, and would often protect pernicious institutions against the only weapons which, in the state of things existing at the time, have any chance of succeeding against them) is defended, by those who hold it, on grounds of expediency; principally on that of the importance, to the common interest of mankind, of maintaining inviolate the sentiment of submission to law. Other persons, again, hold the directly contrary opinion, that any law, judged to be bad, may blamelessly be disobeyed, even though it be not judged to be unjust, but only inexpedient; while others would confine the license of disobedience to the case of unjust laws; but again, some say, that all laws which are inexpedient are unjust; since every law imposes some restriction on the natural liberty of mankind, which restriction is an injustice, unless legitimated by tending to their good. Among these diversities of opinion, it seems to be universally admitted that there may be unjust laws, and that law, consequently, is not the ultimate criterion of justice, but may give to one person a benefit, or impose on another an evil, which justice condemns. When, however, a law is thought to be unjust, it seems always to be regarded as being so in the same way in which a breach of law is unjust, namely, by infringing somebody's right; which, as it cannot in this case be a legal right, receives a different appellation, and is called a moral right. We may say, therefore, that a second case of injustice consists in taking or withholding from any person that to which he has a *moral right.*

Thirdly, it is universally considered just that each person should obtain that (whether good or evil) which he *deserves;* and unjust that he should obtain a good, or be made to undergo an evil, which he does not deserve. This is, perhaps, the clearest and most emphatic form in which the idea of justice is conceived by the general mind. As it involves the notion of desert, the question arises, what constitutes desert? Speaking in a general way, a person is understood to deserve good if he does right, evil if he does wrong; and in a more particular sense, to deserve good from those to whom he does or has done good, and evil from those to whom he does or has done evil. The precept of returning good for evil has never been regarded as a case of the fulfilment of justice, but as one in which the claims of justice are waived, in obedience to other considerations.

Fourthly, it is confessedly unjust to *break faith* with any one: to violate an engagement, either express or implied, or disappoint expectations raised by our own conduct, at least if we have raised those expectations knowingly and voluntarily. Like the other obligations of justice already spoken of, this one is not regarded as absolute, but as capable of being overruled by a stronger obligation of justice on the other side; or by such conduct on the part of the person concerned as is deemed to absolve us from our obligation to him, and to constitute a *forfeiture* of the benefit which he has been led to expect.

Fifthly, it is, by universal admission, inconsistent with justice to be *partial;* to show favor or preference to one person over another, in matters to which favor and preference do not properly apply. Impartiality, however, does not seem to be regarded as a duty in itself, but rather as instrumental to some other duty; for it is admitted that favor and preference are not always censurable, and indeed the cases in which they are condemned are rather the exception than the rule. A person would be more likely to be blamed than applauded for giving his family or friends no superiority in good offices over strangers, when he could do so without violating any other duty; and no one thinks it unjust to seek one person in preference to another as a friend, connection, or companion. Impartiality where rights are concerned is of course obligatory, but this is involved in the more general obligation of giving to every one his right. A tribunal, for example, must be impartial, because it is bound to award, without regard to any other consideration, a disputed object to the one of two parties who has the right to it. There are other cases in which impartiality means, being solely influenced by desert; as with those who, in the capacity of judges, preceptors, or parents, administer reward and punishment as such. There are cases, again, in which it means, being solely influenced by consideration for the public interest; as in making a selection among candidates for a government employment. Impartiality, in short, as an obligation of justice, may be said to mean, being exclusively influenced by the considerations which it is supposed ought to influence the particular case in hand; and resisting the solicitation of any motives which prompt to conduct different from what those considerations would dictate.

Nearly allied to the idea of impartiality is that of *equality;* which often enters as a component part both into the conception of justice and into the practice of it, and, in the eyes of many persons, constitutes its essence. But in this, still more than in any other case, the notion of justice varies in different persons, and always conforms in its variations to their notion of utility. Each person maintains that equality is the dictate of justice, except where he thinks that expediency requires inequality. The justice of giving equal protection to the rights of all, is maintained by those who support the most outrageous inequality in the rights themselves. Even in slave countries it is theoretically admitted that the rights of the slave, such as they are, ought to be as sacred as those of the master; and that a tribunal which fails to enforce them with equal strictness is wanting in justice; while, at the same time, institutions which leave to the slave scarcely any rights to enforce, are not deemed unjust, because they are not deemed inexpedient. Those who think that utility requires distinctions of rank, do not consider it unjust that riches and social privileges should be unequally dispensed; but those who think this inequality inexpedient, think it unjust also. Whoever thinks that government is necessary, sees no injustice in as much inequality as is constituted by giving to the magistrate powers not granted to other people. Even among those who hold levelling doctrines, there are as many questions of justice as there are differences of opinion about expediency. Some Communists consider it unjust that the produce of the labor of the community should be shared on any other principle than that of exact equality; others think it just that those should receive most whose wants are greatest; while others hold that those who work harder, or who produce more, or whose services are more valuable to the community, may justly claim a larger quota in the division of the produce. And the sense of natural justice may be plausibly appealed to in behalf of every one of these opinions.

Among so many diverse applications of the term Justice, which yet is not regarded as ambiguous, it is a matter of some difficulty to seize the mental link which holds them together, and on which the moral sentiment adhering to the term essentially depends. Perhaps, in this embarrassment, some help may be derived from the history of the word, as indicated by its etymology.

In most, if not in all, languages, the etymology of the word which corresponds to Just, points distinctly to an origin connected with the ordinances of law. *Justum* is a form of *jussum*, that which has been ordered. *Dikaion* comes directly from *dike*, a suit at law. *Recht*, from which came *right* and *righteous*, is synonymous with law. The courts of justice, the administration of justice, are the courts and the administration of law. *La justice*, in French, is the established term for judicature. I am not committing the fallacy imputed with some show of truth to Horne Tooke, of assuming that a word must still continue to mean what it originally meant. Etymology is slight evidence of what the idea now signified is, but the very best evidence of how it sprang up. There can, I think, be no doubt that the *idée mère*, the primitive element, in the formation of the notion of justice, was conformity to law. It constituted the entire idea among the Hebrews, up to the birth of Christianity; as might be expected in the case of a people whose laws attempted to embrace all subjects on which precepts were required, and who believed those laws to be a direct emanation from the Supreme Being. But other nations, and in particular the Greeks and Romans, who knew that their laws had been made originally, and still continued to be made, by men, were not afraid to admit that those men might make bad laws; might do, by law, the same things, and from the same motives, which if done by individuals without the sanction of law, would be called unjust. And hence the sentiment of injustice came to be attached, not to all violations of law, but only to violations of such laws as *ought* to exist, including such as ought to exist, but do not; and to laws themselves, if supposed to be contrary to what ought to be law. In this manner the idea of law and of its injunctions was still predominant in the notion of justice, even when the laws actually in force ceased to be accepted as the standard of it.

It is true that mankind consider the idea of justice and its obligations as applicable to many things which neither are, nor is it desired that they should be, regulated by law. Nobody desires that laws should interfere with the whole detail of private life; yet every one allows that in all daily conduct a person may and does show himself to be either just or unjust. But even here, the idea of the breach of what ought to be law, still lingers in a modified shape. It would always give us pleasure, and chime in with our feelings of fitness, that acts which we deem unjust should be punished, though we do not always think it expedient that this should be done by the tribunals. We forego that gratification on account of incidental inconveniences. We should be glad to see just conduct enforced and injustice repressed, even in the minutest details, if we were not, with reason, afraid of trusting the magistrate with so unlimited an amount of power over individuals. When we think that a person is bound in justice to do a thing, it is an ordinary form of language to say, that he ought to be compelled to do it. We should be gratified to see the obligation enforced by anybody who had the power. If we see that its enforcement by law would be inexpedient, we lament the impossibility, we consider the impunity given to injustice as an evil, and strive to make amends for it by bringing a strong expression of our own and the public disapprobation to bear upon the offender. Thus the idea of legal constraint is still the generating idea of the notion of justice, though undergoing several transformations before that notion, as it exists in an advanced state of society, becomes complete.

The above is, I think, a true account, as far as it goes, of the origin and progressive growth of the idea of justice. But we must observe, that it contains, as yet, nothing to distinguish that obligation from moral obligation in general. For the truth is, that the idea of penal sanction, which is the essence of law, enters not only into the conception of injustice, but into that of any kind of wrong. We do not call anything wrong, unless we mean to imply that a person ought to be punished in some way or other for doing it; if not by law, by the opinion of his fellow creatures; if not by opinion, by the reproaches of his own conscience. This seems the real turning point of the distinction between morality and simple expediency. It is a part of the notion of Duty in every one of its forms, that a person may rightfully be compelled to fulfil it. Duty is a thing which may be *exacted* from a person, as one exacts a debt. Unless we think that it may be exacted from him, we do not call it his duty. Reasons of prudence, or the interest of other people, may militate against actually exacting it; but the person himself, it is clearly understood, would not be entitled to complain. There are other things, on the contrary, which we wish that people should do, which we like or admire them for doing, perhaps dislike or despise them for not doing, but yet admit that they are not bound to do; it is not a case of moral obligation; we do not blame them, that is, we do not think that they are proper objects of punishment. How we come by these ideas of deserving and not deserving punishment, will appear, perhaps, in the sequel; but I think there is no doubt that this distinction lies at the bottom of the notions of right and wrong; that we call any conduct wrong, or employ, instead, some other term of dislike or disparagement, according as we think that the person ought, or ought not, to be punished for it; and we say, it would be right to do so and so, or merely that it would be desirable or laudable, according as we would wish to see the person whom it concerns, compelled, or only persuaded and exhorted, to act in that manner.

This, therefore, being the characteristic difference which marks off, not justice, but morality in general, from the remaining provinces of Expediency and Worthiness; the character is still to be sought which distinguishes justice from other branches of morality. Now it is known that ethical writers divide moral duties into two classes, denoted by the ill-chosen expressions, duties of perfect and of imperfect obligation; the latter being those in which, though the act is obligatory, the particular occasions of performing it are left to our choice; as in the case of charity or beneficence, which we are indeed bound to practice, but not towards any definite person, nor at any prescribed time. In the more precise language of philosophic jurists, duties of perfect obligation are those duties in virtue of which a correlative *right* resides in some person or persons; duties of imperfect obligation are those moral obligations which do not give birth to any right. I think it will be found that this distinction exactly coincides with that which exists between justice and the other obligations of morality. In our survey of the various popular acceptations of justice, the term appeared generally to involve the idea of a personal right—a claim on the part of one or more individuals, like that which the law gives when it confers a proprietary or other legal right. Whether the injustice consists in depriving a person of a possession, or in breaking faith with him, or in treating him worse than he deserves, or worse than other people who have no greater claims, in each case the supposition implies two things—a wrong done, and some assignable person who is wronged. Injustice may also be done by treating a person better than others; but the wrong in this case is to his competitors, who are also assignable persons.

It seems to me that this feature in the case—a right in some person, correlative to the moral obligation—constitutes the specific difference between justice, and generosity or beneficence. Justice implies something which it is not only right to do, and wrong not to do, but which some individual person can claim from us as his moral right. No one has a moral right to our generosity or beneficence, because we are not morally bound to practise those virtues towards any given individual. And it will be found with respect to this as to every correct definition, that the instances which seem to conflict with it are those which most confirm it. For if a moralist attempts, as some have done, to make out that mankind generally, though not any given individual, have a right to all the good we can do them, he at once, by that thesis, includes generosity and beneficence within the category of justice. He is obliged to say, that our utmost exertions are *due* to our fellow creatures, thus assimilating them to a debt; or that nothing less can be a sufficient *return* for what society does for us, thus classing the case as one of gratitude; both of which are acknowledged cases of justice. Wherever there is a right, the case is one of justice, and not of the virtue of beneficence: and whoever does not place the distinction between justice and morality in general, where we have now placed it, will be found to make no distinction between them at all, but to merge all morality in justice.

Having thus endeavoured to determine the distinctive elements which enter into the composition of the idea of justice, we are ready to enter on the inquiry, whether the feeling, which accompanies the idea, is attached to it by a special dispensation of nature, or whether it could have grown up, by any known laws, out of the idea itself; and in particular, whether it can have originated in considerations of general expediency.

I conceive that the sentiment itself does not arise from anything which would commonly, or correctly, be termed an idea of expediency; but that though the sentiment does not, whatever is moral in it does.

We have seen that the two essential ingredients in the sentiment of justice are, the desire to punish a person who has done harm, and the knowledge or belief that there is some definite individual or individuals to whom harm has been done.

Now it appears to me, that the desire to punish a person who has done harm to some individual is a spontaneous outgrowth from two sentiments, both in the highest degree natural, and which either are or resemble instincts; the impulse of self-defense, and the feeling of sympathy.

It is natural to resent, and to repel or retaliate, any harm done or attempted against ourselves, or against those with whom we sympathize. The origin of this sentiment it is not necessary here to discuss. Whether it be an instinct or a result of intelligence, it is, we know, common to all animal nature; for every animal tries to hurt those who have hurt, or who it thinks are about to hurt, itself or its young. Human beings, on this point, only differ from other animals in two particulars. First, in being capable of sympathizing, not solely with their offspring, or, like some of the more noble animals, with some superior animal who is kind to them, but with all human, and even with all sentient, beings. Secondly, in having a more developed intelligence, which gives a wider range to the whole of their sentiments, whether self-regarding or sympathetic. By virtue of his superior intelligence, even apart from his superior range of sympathy, a human being is capable of apprehending a community of interest between himself and the human society of which he forms a part, such that any conduct which threatens the security of the society generally, is threatening to his own, and calls forth his instinct (if instinct it be) of self-defence. The same superiority of intelligence, joined to the power of sympathizing with human beings generally, enables him to attach himself to the collective idea of his tribe, his country, or mankind, in such a manner that any act hurtful to them, raises his instinct of sympathy, and urges him to resistance.

The sentiment of justice, in that one of its elements which consists of the desire to punish, is thus, I conceive, the natural feeling of retaliation or vengeance, rendered by intellect and sympathy applicable to those injuries, that is, to those hurts, which wound us through, or in common with, society at large. This sentiment, in itself, has nothing moral in it; what is moral is, the exclusive subordination of it to the social sympathies, so as to wait on and obey their call. For the natural feeling would make us resent indiscriminately whatever any one does that is disagreeable to us; but when moralized by the social feeling, it only acts in the directions conformable to the general good: just persons resenting a hurt to society, though not otherwise a hurt to themselves, and not resenting a hurt to themselves, however painful, unless it be of the kind which society has a common interest with them in the repression of.

It is no objection against this doctrine to say, that when we feel our sentiment of justice outraged, we are not thinking of society at large, or of any collective interest, but only of the individual case. It is common enough certainly, though the reverse of commendable, to feel resentment merely because we have suffered pain; but a person whose resentment is really a moral feeling, that is, who considers whether an act is blamable before he allows himself to resent it—such a person, though he may not say expressly to himself that he is standing up for the interest of society, certainly does feel that he is asserting a rule which is for the benefit of others as well as for his own. If he is not feeling this— if he is regarding the act solely as it affects him individually—he is not consciously just; he is not concerning himself about the justice of his actions. This is admitted even by anti-utilitarian moralists. When Kant (as before remarked) propounds as the fundamental principle of morals, "So act, that thy rule of conduct might be adopted as a law by all rational beings," he virtually acknowledges that the interest of mankind collectively, or at least of mankind indiscriminately, must be in the mind of the agent when conscientiously deciding on the morality of the act. Otherwise he uses words without a meaning: for, that a rule even of utter selfishness could not *possibly* be adopted by all rational beings—that there is any insuperable obstacle in the nature of things to its adoption—cannot be even plausibly maintained. To give any meaning to Kant's principle, the sense put upon it must be, that we ought to shape our conduct by a rule which all rational beings might adopt *with benefit to their collective interest.*

To recapitulate: the idea of justice supposes two things; a rule of conduct, and a sentiment which sanctions the rule. The first must be supposed common to all mankind, and intended for their good. The other (the sentiment) is a desire that punishment may be suffered by those who infringe the rule. There is involved, in addition, the conception of some definite person who suffers by the infringement; whose rights (to use the expression appropriated to the case) are violated by it. And the sentiment of justice appears to me to be, the animal desire to repel or retaliate a hurt or damage to oneself, or to those with whom one sympathizes, widened so as to include all persons, by the human capacity of enlarged sympathy, and the human conception of intelligent self-interest. From the latter elements, the feeling derives its morality; from the former, its peculiar impressiveness, and energy of self-assertion.

I have, throughout, treated the idea of a *right* residing in the injured person, and violated by the injury, not as a separate element in the composition of the idea and sentiment, but as one of the forms in which the other two elements clothe themselves. These elements are, a hurt to some assignable person or persons on the one hand, and a demand for punishment on the other. An examination of our own minds, I think, will show, that these two things include all that we mean when we speak of violation of a right. When we call anything a person's right, we mean that he has a valid claim on society to protect him in the possession of it, either by the force of law, or by that of education and opinion. If he has what we consider a sufficient claim, on whatever account, to have something guaranteed to him by society, we say that he has a right to it. If we desire to prove that anything does not belong to him by right, we think this done as soon as it is admitted that society ought not to take measures for securing it to him, but should leave him to chance, or to his own exertions. Thus, a person is said to have a right to what he can earn in fair professional competition; because society ought not to allow any other person to hinder him from endeavoring to earn in that manner as much as he can. But he has not a right to three hundred a-year, though he may happen to be earning it; because society is not called on to provide that he shall earn that sum. On the contrary, if he owns ten thousand pounds three percent stock, he *has* a right to three hundred a-year; because society has come under an obligation to provide him with an income of that amount.

To have a right, then, is, I conceive, to have something which society ought to defend me in the possession of. If the objector goes on to ask, why it ought? I can give him no other reason than general utility. If that expression does not seem to convey a sufficient feeling of the strength of the obligation, nor to account for the peculiar energy of the feeling, it is because there goes to the composition of the sentiment, not a rational only, but also an animal element, the thirst for retaliation; and this thirst derives its intensity, as well as its moral justification, from the extraordinarily important and impressive kind of utility which is concerned. The interest involved is that of security, to every one's feelings the most vital of all interests. All other earthly benefits are needed by one person, not needed by another; and many of them can, if necessary, be cheerfully foregone, or replaced by something else; but security no human being can possibly do without; on it we depend for all our immunity from evil, and for the whole value of all and every good, beyond the passing moment; since nothing but the gratification of the instant could be of any worth to us, if we could be deprived of anything the next instant by whoever was momentarily stronger than ourselves. Now this most indispensable of all necessaries, after physical nutriment, cannot be had, unless the machinery for providing it is kept unintermittedly in active play. Our notion, therefore, of the claim we have on our fellow-creatures to join in making safe for us the very groundwork of our existence, gathers feelings around it so much more intense than those concerned in any of the more common cases of utility, that the difference in degree (as is often the case in psychology) becomes a real difference in kind. The claim assumes that character of absoluteness, that apparent infinity, and incommensurability with all other considerations, which constitute the distinction between the feeling of right and wrong and that of ordinary expediency and inexpediency. The feelings concerned are so powerful, and we count so positively on finding a responsive feeling in others (all being alike interested), that *ought* and *should* grow into *must,* and recognized indispensability becomes a moral necessity, analogous to physical, and often not inferior to it in binding force.

If the preceding analysis, or something resembling it, be not the correct account of the notion of justice; if justice be totally independent of utility, and be a standard *per se,* which the mind can recognize by simple introspection of itself; it is hard to understand why that internal oracle is so ambiguous, and why so many things appear either just or unjust, according to the light in which they are regarded.

• • •

To take another example from a subject already once referred to. In a co-operative industrial association, is it just or not that talent or skill should give a title to superior remuneration? On the negative side of the question it is argued, that whoever does the best he can, deserves equally well, and ought not in justice to be put in a position of inferiority for no fault of his own; that superior abilities have already advantages more than enough, in the admiration they excite, the personal influence they command, and the internal sources of satisfaction attending them, without adding to these a superior share of the world's goods; and that society is bound in justice rather to make compensation to the less favored, for this unmerited inequality of advantages, than to aggravate it. On the contrary side it is contended, that society receives more from the more efficient laborer; that his services being more useful, society owes him a larger return for them; that a greater share of the joint result is actually his work, and not to allow his claim to it is a kind of robbery; that if he is only to receive as much as others, he can only be justly required to produce as much, and to give a smaller amount of time and exertion, proportioned to his superior efficiency. Who shall decide between these appeals to conflicting principles of justice? Justice has in this case two sides to it, which it is impossible to bring into harmony, and the two disputants have chosen opposite sides; the one looks to what it is just that the individual should receive, the other to what it is just that the community should give. Each, from his own point of view, is unanswerable; and any choice between them, on grounds of justice, must be perfectly arbitrary. Social utility alone can decide the preference.

How many, again, and how irreconcilable, are the standards of justice to which reference is made in discussing the repartition of taxation. One opinion is, that payment to the State should be in numerical proportion to pecuniary means. Others think that justice dictates what they term graduated taxation; taking a higher percentage from those who have more to spare. In point of natural justice a strong case might be made for disregarding means altogether, and taking the same absolute sum (whenever it could be got) from every one: as the subscribers to a mess, or to a club, all pay the same sum for the same privileges, whether they can all equally afford it or not. Since the protection (it might be said) of law and government is afforded to, and is equally required by all, there is no injustice in making all buy it at the same price. It is reckoned justice, not injustice, that a dealer should charge to all customers the same price for the same article, not a price varying according to their means of payment. This doctrine, as applied to taxation, finds no advocates, because it conflicts so strongly with man's feelings of humanity and social expediency; but the principle of justice which it invokes is as true and as binding as those which can be appealed to against it. Accordingly it exerts a tacit influence on the line of defense employed for other modes of assessing taxation. People feel obliged to argue that the State does more for the rich than for the poor, as a justification for its taking more from them: though this is in reality not true, for the rich would be far better able to protect themselves, in the absence of law or government, than the poor, and indeed would probably be successful in converting the poor into their slaves. Others, again, so far defer to the same conception of justice, as to maintain that all should pay an equal capitation tax for the protection of their persons (these being of equal value to all), and an unequal tax for the protection of their property, which is unequal. To this others reply, that the all of one man is as valuable to him as the all of another. From these confusions there is no other mode of extrication than the utilitarian.

Is, then, the difference between the Just and the Expedient a merely imaginary distinction? Have mankind been under a delusion in thinking that justice is a more sacred thing than policy, and that the latter ought only to be listened to after the former has been satisfied? By no means. The exposition we have given of the nature and origin of the sentiment, recognizes a real distinction;

and no one of those who profess the most sublime contempt for the consequences of actions as an element in their morality, attaches more importance to
the distinction than I do. While I dispute the pretensions of any theory which
sets up an imaginary standard of justice not grounded on utility, I account the
justice which is grounded on utility to be the chief part, and incomparably the
most sacred and binding part, of all morality. Justice is a name for certain
classes of moral rules, which concern the essentials of human well-being more
nearly, and are therefore of more absolute obligation, than any other rules for
the guidance of life; and the notion which we have found to be of the essence
of the idea of justice, that of a right residing in an individual, implies and
testifies to this more binding obligation.

39.
An Entitlement Theory of Justice
ROBERT NOZICK

THE ENTITLEMENT THEORY

The subject of justice in holdings consists of three major topics. The first is the *original acquisition of holdings,* the appropriation of unheld things. This includes the issues of how unheld things may come to be held, the process, or processes, by which unheld things may come to be held, the things that may come to be held by these processes, the extent of what comes to be held by a particular process, and so on. We shall refer to the complicated truth about this topic, which we shall not formulate here, as the principle of justice in acquisition. The second topic concerns the *transfer of holdings* from one person to another. By what processes may a person transfer holdings to another? How may a person acquire a holding from another who holds it? Under this topic come general descriptions of voluntary exchange, and gift and (on the other hand) fraud, as well as reference to particular conventional details fixed upon in a given society. The complicated truth about this subject (with placeholders for conventional details) we shall call the principle of justice in transfer. (And we shall suppose it also includes principles governing how a person may divest himself of a holding, passing it into an unheld state.)

If the world were wholly just, the following inductive definition would exhaustively cover the subject of justice in holdings.

1. A person who acquires a holding in accordance with the principle of justice in acquisition is entitled to that holding.
2. A person who acquires a holding in accordance with the principle of justice in transfer, from someone else entitled to the holding, is entitled to the holding.
3. No one is entitled to a holding except by (repeated) applications of 1 and 2.

The complete principle of distributive justice would say simply that a distribution is just if everyone is entitled to the holdings they possess under the distribution.

A distribution is just if it arises from another just distribution by legitimate means. The legitimate means of moving from one distribution to another are specified by the principle of justice in transfer. The legitimate first "moves" are specified by the principle of justice in acquisition.[1] Whatever arises from a just

---

[1] Applications of the principle of justice in acquisition may also occur as part of the move from one distribution to another. You may find an unheld thing now and appropriate it. Acquisitions also are to be understood as included when, to simplify, I speak only of transitions by transfers.

situation by just steps is itself just. The means of change specified by the principle of justice in transfer preserve justice. As correct rules of inference are truth-preserving, and any conclusion deduced via repeated application of such rules from only true premises is itself true, so the means of transition from one situation to another specified by the principle of justice in transfer are justice-preserving, and any situation actually arising from repeated transitions in accordance with the principle from a just situation is itself just. The parallel between justice-preserving transformations and truth-preserving transformations illuminates where it fails as well as where it holds. That a conclusion could have been deduced by truth-preserving means from premises that are true suffices to show its truth. That from a just situation a situation *could* have arisen via justice-preserving means does *not* suffice to show its justice. The fact that a thief's victims voluntarily *could* have presented him with gifts does not entitle the thief to his ill-gotten gains. Justice in holdings is historical; it depends upon what actually has happened. We shall return to this point later.

Not all actual situations are generated in accordance with the two principles of justice in holdings: the principle of justice in acquisition and the principle of justice in transfer. Some people steal from others, or defraud them, or enslave them, seizing their product and preventing them from living as they choose, or forcibly exclude others from competing in exchanges. None of these are permissible modes of transition from one situation to another. And some persons acquire holdings by means not sanctioned by the principle of justice in acquisition. The existence of past injustice (previous violations of the first two principles of justice in holdings) raises the third major topic under justice in holdings: the rectification of injustice in holdings. If past injustice has shaped present holdings in various ways, some identifiable and some not, what now, if anything, ought to be done to rectify these injustices? What obligations do the performers of injustice have toward those whose position is worse than it would have been had the injustice not been done? Or, than it would have been had compensation been paid promptly? How, if at all, do things change if the beneficiaries and those made worse off are not the direct parties in the act of injustice, but, for example, their descendants? Is an injustice done to someone whose holding was itself based upon an unrectified injustice? How far back must one go in wiping clean the historical slate of injustices? What may victims of injustice permissibly do in order to rectify the injustices being done to them, including the many injustices done by persons acting through their government? I do not know of a thorough or theoretically sophisticated treatment of such issues.[2] Idealizing greatly, let us suppose theoretical investigation will produce a principle of rectification. This principle uses historical information about previous situations and injustices done in them (as defined by the first two principles of justice and rights against interference), and information about the actual course of events that flowed from these injustices, until the present, and it yields a description (or descriptions) of holdings in the society. The

---

[2] See, however, the useful book by Boris Bittker, *The Case for Black Reparations* (New York: Random House, 1973).

principle of rectification presumably will make use of its best estimate of sub-junctive information about what would have occurred (or a probability distri-bution over what might have occurred, using the expected value) if the injustice had not taken place. If the actual description of holdings turn out not to be one of the descriptions yielded by the principle, then one of the descriptions yielded must be realized.[3]

The general outlines of the theory of justice in holdings are that the holdings of a person are just if he is entitled to them by the principles of justice in ac-quisition and transfer, or by the principle of rectification of injustice (as speci-fied by the first two principles). If each person's holdings are just, then the total set (distribution) of holdings is just. To turn these general outlines into a specific theory we would have to specify the details of each of the three principles of jus-tice in holdings: the principle of acquisition of holdings, the principle of trans-fer of holdings, and the principle of rectification of violations of the first two principles. I shall not attempt that task here. (Locke's principle of justice in acquisition is discussed below.)

HISTORICAL PRINCIPLES AND END-RESULT PRINCIPLES

The general outlines of the entitlement theory illuminate the nature and defects of other conceptions of distributive justice. The entitlement theory of justice in distribution is *historical;* whether a distribution is just depends upon how it came about. In contrast, *current time-slice principles* of justice hold that the jus-tice of a distribution is determined by how things are distributed (who has what) as judged by some *structural* principle(s) of just distribution. A utilitar-ian who judges between any two distributions by seeing which has the greater sum of utility and, if the sums tie, applies some fixed equality criterion to choose the more equal distribution, would hold a current time-slice principle of justice. As would someone who had a fixed schedule of trade-offs between the sum of happiness and equality. According to a current time-slice principle, all that needs to be looked at, in judging the justice of a distribution, is who ends up with what; in comparing any two distributions one need look only at the matrix presenting the distributions. No further information need be fed into a principle of justice. It is a consequence of such principles of justice that any two structurally identical distributions are equally just. (Two distributions are structurally identical if they present the same profile, but perhaps have differ-ent persons occupying the particular slots. My having ten and your having five, and my having five and your having ten are structurally identical distributions.) Welfare economics is the theory of current time-slice principles of justice. The

---

[3] If the principle of rectification of violations of the first two principles yields more than one de-scription of holdings, then some choice must be made as to which of these is to be realized. Per-haps the sort of considerations about distributive justice and equality that I argue against play a legitimate role in *this* subsidiary choice. Similarly, there may be room for such considerations in deciding which otherwise arbitrary features a statute will embody, when such features are un-avoidable because other considerations do not specify a precise line; yet a line must be drawn.

subject is conceived as operating on matrices representing only current information about distribution. This, as well as some of the usual conditions (for example, the choice of distribution is invariant under relabeling of columns), guarantees that welfare economics will be a current time-slice theory, with all of its inadequacies.

Most persons do not accept current time-slice principles as constituting the whole story about distributive shares. They think it relevant in assessing the justice of a situation to consider not only the distribution it embodies, but also how that distribution came about. If some persons are in prison for murder or war crimes, we do not say that to assess the justice of the distribution in the society we must look only at what this person has, and that person has, and that person has, . . . at the current time. We think it relevant to ask whether someone did something so that he *deserved* to be punished, deserved to have a lower share. Most will agree to the relevance of further information with regard to punishments and penalties. Consider also desired things. One traditional socialist view is that workers are entitled to the product and full fruits of their labor; they have earned it; a distribution is unjust if it does not give the workers what they are entitled to. Such entitlements are based upon some past history. No socialist holding this view would find it comforting to be told that because the actual distribution A happens to coincide structurally with the one he desires D, A therefore is no less just than D; it differs only in that the "parasitic" owners of capital receive under A what the workers are entitled to under D, and the workers receive under A what the owners are entitled to under D, namely very little. This socialist rightly, in my view, holds onto the notions of earning, producing, entitlement, desert, and so forth, and he rejects current time-slice principles that look only to the structure of the resulting set of holdings. (The set of holdings resulting from what? Isn't it implausible that how holdings are produced and come to exist has no effect at all on who should hold what?) His mistake lies in his view of what entitlements arise out of what sorts of productive processes.

We construe the position we discuss too narrowly by speaking of *current* time-slice principles. Nothing is changed if structural principles operate upon a time sequence of current time-slice profiles and, for example, give someone more now to counterbalance the less he has had earlier. A utilitarian or an egalitarian or any mixture of the two over time will inherit the difficulties of his more myopic comrades. He is not helped by the fact that *some* of the information others consider relevant in assessing a distribution is reflected, unrecoverably, in past matrices. Henceforth, we shall refer to such unhistorical principles of distributive justice, including the current time-slice principles, as *end-result principles* or *end-state principles.*

In contrast to end-result principles of justice, *historical principles* of justice hold that past circumstances or actions of people can create differential entitlements or differential deserts to things. An injustice can be worked by moving from one distribution to another structurally identical one, for the second, in profile the same, may violate people's entitlements or deserts; it may not fit the actual history.

PATTERNING

The entitlement principles of justice in holdings that we have sketched are historical principles of justice. To better understand their precise character, we shall distinguish them from another subclass of the historical principles. Consider, as an example, the principle of distribution according to moral merit. This principle requires that total distributive shares vary directly with moral merit; no person should have a greater share than anyone whose moral merit is greater. (If moral merit could be not merely ordered but measured on an interval or ratio scale, stronger principles could be formulated.) Or consider the principle that results by substituting "usefulness to society" for "moral merit" in the previous principle. Or instead of "distribute according to moral merit," or "distribute according to usefulness to society," we might consider "distribute according to the weighted sum of moral merit, usefulness to society, and need," with the weights of the different dimensions equal. Let us call a principle of distribution *patterned* if it specifies that a distribution is to vary along with some natural dimension, weighted sum of natural dimensions, or lexicographic ordering of natural dimensions. And let us say a distribution is patterned if it accords with some patterned principle. (I speak of natural dimensions, admittedly without a general criterion for them, because for any set of holdings some artificial dimensions can be gimmicked up to vary along with the distribution of the set.) The principle of distribution in accordance with moral merit is a patterned historical principle, which specifies a patterned distribution. "Distribute according to I.Q." is a patterned principle that looks to information not contained in distributional matrices. It is not historical, however, in that it does not look to any past actions creating differential entitlements to evaluate a distribution; it requires only distributional matrices whose columns are labeled by I.Q. scores. The distribution in a society, however, may be composed of such simple patterned distributions, without itself being simply patterned. Different sectors may operate different patterns, or some combination of patterns may operate in different proportions across a society. A distribution composed in this manner, from a small number of patterned distributions, we also shall term "patterned." And we extend the use of "pattern" to include the overall designs put forth by combinations of end-state principles.

Almost every suggested principle of distributive justice is patterned: to each according to his moral merit, or needs, or marginal product, or how hard he tries, or the weighted sum of the foregoing, and so on. The principle of entitlement we have sketched is *not* patterned.[4] There is no one natural dimension or weighted sum or combination of a small number of natural dimensions that yields the distributions generated in accordance with the principle of entitlement. The set of holdings that results when some persons receive their marginal

---

[4] One might try to squeeze a patterned conception of distributive justice into the framework of the entitlement conception, by formulating a gimmicky obligatory "principle of transfer" that would lead to the pattern. For example, the principle that if one has more than the mean income one must transfer everything one holds above the mean to persons below the mean so as to bring them up to (but not over) the mean. We can formulate a criterion for a "principle of transfer" to

products, others win at gambling, others receive a share of their mate's income, others receive gifts from foundations, others receive interest on loans, others receive gifts from admirers, others receive returns on investment, others make for themselves much of what they have, others find things, and so on, will not be patterned. Heavy strands of patterns will run through it; significant portions of the variance in holdings will be accounted for by pattern-variables. If most people most of the time choose to transfer some of their entitlements to others only in exchange for something from them, then a large part of what many people hold will vary with what they held that others wanted. More details are provided by the theory of marginal productivity. But gifts to relatives, charitable donations, bequests to children, and the like, are not best conceived, in the first instance, in this manner. Ignoring the strands of pattern, let us suppose for the moment that a distribution actually arrived at by the operation of the principle of entitlement is random with respect to any pattern. Though the resulting set of holdings will be unpatterned, it will not be incomprehensible, for it can be seen as arising from the operation of a small number of principles. These principles specify how an initial distribution may arise (the principle of acquisition of holdings) and how distributions may be transformed into others (the principle of transfer of holdings). The process whereby the set of holdings is generated will be intelligible, though the set of holdings itself that results from this process will be unpatterned.

The writings of F. A. Hayek focus less than is usually done upon what patterning distributive justice requires. Hayek argues that we cannot know enough about each person's situation to distribute to each according to his moral merit (but would justice demand we do so if we did have this knowledge?); and he goes on to say, "our objection is against all attempts to impress upon society a deliberately chosen pattern of distribution, whether it be an order of equality or of inequality." [5] However, Hayek concludes that in a free society there will be distribution in accordance with value rather than moral merit; that is, in accordance with the perceived value of a person's actions and services to others. Despite his rejection of a patterned conception of distributive justice, Hayek himself suggests a pattern he thinks justifiable: distribution in accordance with the perceived benefits given to others, leaving room for the complaint that a free society does not realize exactly this pattern. Stating this patterned strand of a free capitalist society more precisely, we get "To each according to how much he benefits others who have the resources for benefiting those who benefit them." This will seem arbitrary unless some acceptable initial set of holdings is specified, or unless it is held that the operation of the system over time washes

---

rule out such obligatory transfers, or we can say that no correct principle of transfer, no principle of transfer in a free society will be like this. The former is probably the better course, though the latter also is true.

  Alternatively, one might think to make the entitlement conception instantiate a pattern, by using matrix entries that express the relative strength of a person's entitlements as measured by some real-valued function. But even if the limitation to natural dimensions failed to exclude this function, the resulting edifice would *not* capture our system of entitlements to *particular* things.

[5] F. A. Hayek, *The Constitution of Liberty* (Chicago: University of Chicago Press, 1960), p. 87.

out any significant effects from the initial set of holdings. As an example of the latter, if almost anyone would have bought a car from Henry Ford, the supposition that it was an arbitrary matter who held the money then (and so bought) would not place Henry Ford's earnings under a cloud. In any event, *his* coming to hold it is not arbitrary. Distribution according to benefits to others *is* a major patterned strand in a free capitalist society, as Hayek correctly points out, but it is only a strand and does not constitute the whole pattern of a system of entitlements (namely, inheritance, gifts for arbitrary reasons, charity, and so on) or a standard that one should insist a society fit. Will people tolerate for long a system yielding distributions that they believe are unpatterned?[6] No doubt people will not long accept a distribution they believe is *unjust*. People want their society to be and to look just. But must the look of justice reside in a resulting pattern rather than in the underlying generating principles? We are in no position to conclude that the inhabitants of a society embodying an entitlement conception of justice in holdings will find it unacceptable. Still, it must be granted that were people's reasons for transferring some of their holdings to others always irrational or arbitrary, we would find this disturbing. (Suppose people always determined what holdings they would transfer, and to whom, by using a random device.) We feel more comfortable upholding the justice of an entitlement system if most of the transfers under it are done for reasons. This does not mean necessarily that all deserve what holdings they receive. It means only that there is a purpose or point to someone's transferring a holding to one person rather than to another; that usually we can see what the transferrer thinks he's gaining, what cause he thinks he's serving, what goals he thinks he's helping to achieve, and so forth. Since in a capitalist society people often transfer holdings to others in accordance with how much they perceive these others benefiting them, the fabric constituted by the individual transactions and transfers is largely reasonable and intelligible.[7] (Gifts to loved ones, bequests to children, charity to the needy also are nonarbitrary components of the fabric.) In stressing the large strand of distribution in accordance with benefit to others, Hayek shows the point of many transfers, and so shows that the system of transfer of entitlements is not just spinning its gears aimlessly. The system of

---

[6] This question does not imply that they will tolerate any and every patterned distribution. In discussing Hayek's views, Irving Kristol has recently speculated that people will not long tolerate a system that yields distributions patterned in accordance with value rather than merit. (" 'When Virtue Loses All Her Loveliness'—Some Reflections on Capitalism and 'The Free Society,' " *The Public Interest*, Fall 1970, pp. 3–15.) Kristol, following some remarks of Hayek's, equates the merit system with justice. Since some case can be made for the external standard of distribution in accordance with benefit to others, we ask about a weaker (and therefore more plausible) hypothesis.

[7] We certainly benefit because great economic incentives operate to get others to spend much time and energy to figure out how to serve us by providing things we will want to pay for. It is not mere paradox mongering to wonder whether capitalism should be criticized for most rewarding and hence encouraging, not individualists like Thoreau who go about their own lives, but people who are occupied with serving others and winning them as customers. But to defend capitalism one need not think businessmen are the finest human types. (I do not mean to join here the general maligning of businessmen, either.) Those who think the finest should acquire the most can try to convince their fellows to transfer resources in accordance with *that* principle.

entitlements is defensible when constituted by the individual aims of individual transactions. No overarching aim is needed, no distributional pattern is required.

To think that the task of a theory of distributive justice is to fill in the blank in "to each according to his _____" is to be predisposed to search for a pattern; and the separate treatment of "from each according to his _____" treats production and distribution as two separate and independent issues. On an entitlement view these are *not* two separate questions. Whoever makes something, having bought or contracted for all other held resources used in the process (transferring some of his holdings for these cooperating factors), is entitled to it. The situation is *not* one of something's getting made, and there being an open question of who is to get it. Things come into the world already attached to people having entitlements over them. From the point of view of the historical entitlement conception of justice in holdings, those who start afresh to complete "to each according to his _____" treat objects as if they appeared from nowhere, out of nothing. A complete theory of justice might cover this limit case as well; perhaps here is a use for the usual conceptions of distributive justice.[8]

So entrenched are maxims of the usual form that perhaps we should present the entitlement conception as a competitor. Ignoring acquisition and rectification, we might say:

> From each according to what he chooses to do, to each according to what he makes for himself (perhaps with the contracted aid of others) and what others choose to do for him and choose to give him of what they've been given previously (under this maxim) and haven't yet expended or transferred.

This, the discerning reader will have noticed, has its defects as a slogan. So as a summary and great simplification (and not as a maxim with any independent meaning) we have:

> *From each as they choose, to each as they are chosen.*

• • •

LOCKE'S THEORY OF ACQUISITION

Before we turn to consider other theories of justice in detail, we must introduce an additional bit of complexity into the structure of the entitlement theory. This is best approached by considering Locke's attempt to specify a principle of justice in acquisition. Locke views property rights in an unowned object as originating through someone's mixing his labor with it. This gives rise to many questions. What are the boundaries of what labor is mixed with? If a private

---

[8] Varying situations continuously from that limit situation to our own would force us to make explicit the underlying rationale of entitlements and to consider whether entitlement considerations lexicographically precede the considerations of the usual theories of distributive justice, so that the *slightest* strand of entitlement outweighs the considerations of the usual theories of distributive justice.

astronaut clears a place on Mars, has he mixed his labor with (so that he comes to own) the whole planet, the whole uninhabited universe, or just a particular plot? Which plot does an act bring under ownership? The minimal (possibly disconnected) area such that an act decreases entropy in that area, and not else-where? Can virgin land (for the purposes of ecological investigation by high-flying airplane) come under ownership by a Lockean process? Building a fence around a territory presumably would make one the owner of only the fence (and the land immediately underneath it).

Why does mixing one's labor with something make one the owner of it? Per-haps because one owns one's labor, and so one comes to own a previously un-owned thing that becomes permeated with what one owns. Ownership seeps over into the rest. But why isn't mixing what I own with what I don't own a way of losing what I own rather than a way of gaining what I don't? If I own a can of tomato juice and spill it in the sea so that its molecules (made radio-active, so I can check this) mingle evenly throughout the sea, do I thereby come to own the sea, or have I foolishly dissipated my tomato juice? Perhaps the idea, instead, is that laboring on something improves it and makes it more valuable; and anyone is entitled to own a thing whose value he has created. (Reinforcing this, perhaps, is the view that laboring is unpleasant. If some people made things effortlessly, as the cartoon characters in *The Yellow Submarine* trail flowers in their wake, would they have lesser claim to their own products whose making didn't *cost* them anything?) Ignore the fact that laboring on something may make it less valuable (spraying pink enamel paint on a piece of driftwood that you have found). Why should one's entitlement extend to the whole object rather than just to the *added value* one's labor has produced? (Such reference to value might also serve to delimit the extent of ownership; for example, sub-stitute "increases the value of" for "decreases entropy in" in the above entropy criterion.) No workable or coherent value-added property scheme has yet been devised, and any such scheme presumably would fall to objections (similar to those) that fell the theory of Henry George.

It will be implausible to view improving an object as giving full ownership to it, if the stock of unowned objects that might be improved is limited. For an object's coming under one person's ownership changes the situation of all others. Whereas previously they were at liberty (in Hohfeld's sense) to use the object, they now no longer are. This change in the situation of others (by re-moving their liberty to act on a previously unowned object) need not worsen their situation. If I appropriate a grain of sand from Coney Island, no one else may now do as they will with *that* grain of sand. But there are plenty of other grains of sand left for them to do the same with. Or if not grains of sand, then other things. Alternatively, the things I do with the grain of sand I appropriate might improve the position of others, counterbalancing their loss of the liberty to use that grain. The crucial point is whether appropriation of an unowned object worsens the situation of others.

Locke's proviso that there be "enough and as good left in common for oth-ers" (sect. 27)* is meant to ensure that the situation of others is not worsened.

---

* The reference is to Locke's *Second Treatise of Government*—eds.

(If this proviso is met is there any motivation for his further condition of non-waste?) It is often said that this proviso once held but now no longer does. But there appears to be an argument for the conclusion that if the proviso no longer holds, then it cannot ever have held so as to yield permanent and inheritable property rights. Consider the first person Z for whom there is not enough and as good left to appropriate. The last person Y to appropriate left Z without his previous liberty to act on an object, and so worsened Z's situation. So Y's appropriation is not allowed under Locke's proviso. Therefore the next to last person X to appropriate left Y in a worse position, for X's act ended permissible appropriation. Therefore X's appropriation wasn't permissible. But then the appropriator two from last, W, ended permissible appropriation and so, since it worsened X's position, W's appropriation wasn't permissible. And so on back to the first person A to appropriate a permanent property right.

This argument, however, proceeds too quickly. Someone may be made worse off by another's appropriation in two ways: first, by losing the opportunity to improve his situation by a particular appropriation or any one; and second, by no longer being able to use freely (without appropriation) what he previously could. A *stringent* requirement that another not be made worse off by an appropriation would exclude the first way if nothing else counterbalances the diminution in opportunity, as well as the second. A *weaker* requirement would exclude the second way, though not the first. With the weaker requirement, we cannot zip back so quickly from Z to A, as in the above argument; for though person Z can no longer *appropriate,* there may remain some for him to *use* as before. In this case Y's appropriation would not violate the weaker Lockean condition. (With less remaining that people are at liberty to use, users might face more inconvenience, crowding, and so on; in that way the situation of others might be worsened, unless appropriation stopped far short of such a point.) It is arguable that no one legitimately can complain if the weaker provision is satisfied. However, since this is less clear than in the case of the more stringent proviso, Locke may have intended this stringent proviso by "enough and as good" remaining, and perhaps he meant the nonwaste condition to delay the end point from which the argument zips back.

Is the situation of persons who are unable to appropriate (there being no more accessible and useful unowned objects) worsened by a system allowing appropriation and permanent property? Here enter the various familiar social considerations favoring private property: it increases the social product by putting means of production in the hands of those who can use them most efficiently (profitably); experimentation is encouraged, because with separate persons controlling resources, there is no one person or small group whom someone with a new idea must convince to try it out; private property enables people to decide on the pattern and types of risks they wish to bear, leading to specialized types of risk bearing; private property protects future persons by leading some to hold back resources from current consumption for future markets; it provides alternate sources of employment for unpopular persons who don't have to convince any one person or small group to hire them, and so on. These considerations enter a Lockean theory to support the claim that appropriation of private property satisfies the intent behind the "enough and as good left over" proviso, *not* as a utilitarian justification of property. They enter to rebut the claim that because the proviso is violated no natural right to private property can arise by a Lockean process. The difficulty in working such an argument to show that the proviso is satisfied is in fixing the appropriate base line for comparison. Lockean appropriation makes people no worse off than they would be *how*?[9] This question of fixing the baseline needs more detailed investigation than we are able to give it here. It would be desirable to have an estimate of the general economic importance of original appropriation in order to see how much leeway there is for differing theories of appropriation and of the location of the baseline. Perhaps this importance can be measured by the percentage of all income that is based upon untransformed raw materials and given resources (rather than upon human actions), mainly rental income representing the unimproved value of land, and the price of raw material *in situ*, and by the percentage of current wealth which represents such income in the past.[10]

We should note that it is not only persons favoring *private* property who need a theory of how property rights legitimately originate. Those believing in collective property, for example those believing that a group of persons living in an area jointly own the territory, or its mineral resources, also must provide a theory of how such property rights arise; they must show why the persons living there have rights to determine what is done with the land and resources there that persons living elsewhere don't have (with regard to the same land and resources).

THE PROVISO

Whether or not Locke's particular theory of appropriation can be spelled out so as to handle various difficulties, I assume that any adequate theory of justice in acquisition will contain a proviso similar to the weaker of the ones we have attributed to Locke. A process normally giving rise to a permanent bequeathable property right in a previously unowned thing will not do so if the position of others no longer at liberty to use the thing is thereby worsened. It is important to specify *this* particular mode of worsening the situation of others, for the proviso does not encompass other modes. It does not include the worsening due to more limited opportunities to appropriate (the first way above, corresponding to the more stringent condition), and it does not include how I "worsen" a seller's position if I appropriate materials to make some of what he is selling,

---

[9] Compare this with Robert Paul Wolff's "A Refutation of Rawls' Theorem on Justice," *Journal of Philosophy*, March 31, 1966, sect. 2. Wolff's criticism does not apply to Rawls' conception under which the baseline is fixed by the difference principle.

[10] I have not seen a precise estimate. David Friedman, *The Machinery of Freedom* (N.Y.: Harper & Row, 1973), pp. xiv, xv, discusses this issue and suggests 5 percent of U.S. national income as an upper limit for the first two factors mentioned. However he does not attempt to estimate the percentage of current wealth which is based upon such income in the past. (The vague notion of "based upon" merely indicates a topic needing investigation.)

and then enter into competition with him. Someone whose appropriation otherwise would violate the proviso still may appropriate provided he compensates the others so that their situation is not thereby worsened; unless he does compensate these others, his appropriation will violate the proviso of the principle of justice in acquisition and will be an illegitimate one.[11] A theory of appropriation incorporating this Lockean proviso will handle correctly the cases (objections to the theory lacking the proviso) where someone appropriates the total supply of something necessary for life.[12]

A theory which includes this proviso in its principle of justice in acquisition must also contain a more complex principle of justice in transfer. Some reflection of the proviso about appropriation constrains later actions. If my appropriating all of a certain substance violates the Lockean proviso, then so does my appropriating some and purchasing all the rest from others who obtained it without otherwise violating the Lockean proviso. If the proviso excludes someone's appropriating all the drinkable water in the world, it also excludes his purchasing it all. (More weakly, and messily, it may exclude his charging certain prices for some of his supply.) This proviso (almost?) never will come into effect; the more someone acquires of a scarce substance which others want, the higher the price of the rest will go, and the more difficult it will become for him to acquire it all. But still, we can imagine, at least, that something like this occurs: someone makes simultaneous secret bids to the separate owners of a substance, each of whom sells assuming he can easily purchase more from the other owners; or some natural catastrophe destroys all of the supply of something except that in one person's possession. The total supply could not be permissibly appropriated by one person at the beginning. His later acquisition of it all does not show that the original appropriation violated the proviso (even by a reverse argument similar to the one above that tried to zip back from Z to A). Rather,

---

[11] Fourier held that since the process of civilization had deprived the members of society of certain liberties (to gather, pasture, engage in the chase), a socially guaranteed minimum provision for persons was justified as compensation for the loss (Alexander Gray, *The Socialist Tradition* (New York: Harper & Row, 1968), p. 188). But this puts the point too strongly. This compensation would be due those persons, if any, for whom the process of civilization was a *net loss*, for whom the benefits of civilization did not counterbalance being deprived of these particular liberties.

[12] For example, Rashdall's case of someone who comes upon the only water in the desert several miles ahead of others who also will come to it and appropriates it all. Hastings Rashdall, "The Philosophical Theory of Property," in *Property, its Duties and Rights* (London: MacMillan, 1915).

We should note Ayn Rand's theory of property rights ("Man's Rights" in *The Virtue of Selfishness* (New York: New American Library, 1964), p. 94), wherein these follow from the right to life, since people need physical things to live. But a right to life is not a right to whatever one needs to live; other people may have rights over these other things. . . . At most, a right to life would be a right to have or strive for whatever one needs to live, provided that having it does not violate anyone else's rights. With regard to material things, the question is whether having it does violate any right of others. (Would appropriation of all unowned things do so? Would appropriating the water hole in Rashdall's example?) Since special considerations (such as the Lockean proviso) may enter with regard to material property, one *first* needs a theory of property rights before one can apply any supposed right to life (as amended above). Therefore the right to life cannot provide the foundation for a theory of property rights.

it is the combination of the original appropriation *plus* all the later transfers and actions that violates the Lockean proviso.

Each owner's title to his holding includes the historical shadow of the Lockean proviso on appropriation. This excludes his transferring it into an agglomeration that does violate the Lockean proviso and excludes his using it in a way, in coordination with others or independently of them, so as to violate the proviso by making the situation of others worse than their baseline situation. Once it is known that someone's ownership runs afoul of the Lockean proviso, there are stringent limits on what he may do with (what it is difficult any longer unreservedly to call) "his property." Thus a person may not appropriate the only water hole in a desert and charge what he will. Nor may he charge what he will if he possesses one, and unfortunately it happens that all the water holes in the desert dry up, except for his. This unfortunate circumstance, admittedly no fault of his, brings into operation the Lockean proviso and limits his property rights.[13] Similarly, an owner's property right in the only island in an area does not allow him to order a castaway from a shipwreck off his island as a trespasser, for this would violate the Lockean proviso.

Notice that the theory does not say that owners do have these rights, but that the rights are overridden to avoid some catastrophe. (Overridden rights do not disappear; they leave a trace of a sort absent in the cases under discussion.)[14] There is no such external (and *ad hoc?*) overriding. Considerations internal to the theory of property itself, to its theory of acquisition and appropriation, provide the means for handling such cases. The results, however, may be coextensive with some condition about catastrophe, since the baseline for comparison is so low as compared to the productiveness of a society with private appropriation that the question of the Lockean proviso being violated arises only in the case of catastrophe (or a desert-island situation).

The fact that someone owns the total supply of something necessary for others to stay alive does *not* entail that his (or anyone's) appropriation of anything left some people (immediately or later) in a situation worse than the baseline one. A medical researcher who synthesizes a new substance that effectively treats a certain disease and who refuses to sell except on his terms does not worsen the situation of others by depriving them of whatever he has appropriated. The others easily can possess the same materials he appropriated; the researcher's appropriation or purchase of chemicals didn't make those chemicals scarce in a way so as to violate the Lockean proviso. Nor would someone else's purchasing the total supply of the synthesized substance from the medical researcher. The fact that the medical researcher uses easily available chemicals to synthesize the drug no more violates the Lockean proviso than does the fact

---

[13] The situation would be different if his water hole didn't dry up, due to special precautions he took to prevent this. Compare our discussion of the case in the text with Hayek, *The Constitution of Liberty*, p. 136; and also with Ronald Hamowy, "Hayek's Concept of Freedom; a Critique," *New Individualist Review*, April 1961, pp. 28–31.

[14] I discuss overriding and its moral traces in "Moral Complications and Moral Structures," *Natural Law Forum*, 1968, pp. 1–50.

that the only surgeon able to perform a particular operation eats easily obtainable food in order to stay alive and to have the energy to work. This shows that the Lockean proviso is not an "end-state principle"; it focuses on a particular way that appropriative actions affect others, and not on the structure of the situation that results.

Intermediate between someone who takes all of the public supply and someone who makes the total supply out of easily obtainable substances is someone who appropriates the total supply of something in a way that does not deprive the others of it. For example, someone finds a new substance in an out-of-the-way place. He discovers that it effectively treats a certain disease and appropriates the total supply. He does not worsen the situation of others; if he did not stumble upon the substance no one else would have, and the others would remain without it. However, as time passes, the likelihood increases that others would have come across the substance; upon this fact might be based a limit to his property right in the substance so that others are not below their baseline position; for example, its bequest might be limited. The theme of someone worsening another's situation by depriving him of something he otherwise would possess may also illuminate the example of patents. An inventor's patent does not deprive others of an object which would not exist if not for the inventor. Yet patents would have this effect on others who independently invent the object. Therefore, these independent inventors, upon whom the burden of proving independent discovery may rest, should not be excluded from utilizing their own invention as they wish (including selling it to others). Furthermore, a known inventor drastically lessens the chances of actual independent invention. For persons who know of an invention usually will not try to reinvent it, and the notion of independent discovery here would be murky at best. Yet we may assume that in the absence of the original invention, sometime later someone else would have come up with it. This suggests placing a time limit on patents, as a rough rule of thumb to approximate how long it would have taken, in the absence of knowledge of the invention, for independent discovery.

I believe that the free operation of a market system will not actually run afoul of the Lockean proviso. (Recall that crucial to our story in Part I of how a protective agency becomes dominant and a *de facto* monopoly is the fact that it wields force in situations of conflict, and is not merely in competition, with other agencies. A similar tale cannot be told about other businesses.) If this is correct, the proviso will not play a very important role in the activities of protective agencies and will not provide a significant opportunity for future state action. Indeed, were it not for the effects of previous *illegitimate* state action, people would not think the possibility of the proviso's being violated as of more interest than any other logical possibility. (Here I make an empirical historical claim; as does someone who disagrees with this.) This completes our indication of the complication in the entitlement theory introduced by the Lockean proviso.

40.
Justice as Fairness

JOHN RAWLS

THE SUBJECT OF JUSTICE

Many different kinds of things are said to be just and unjust: not only laws, institutions, and social systems, but also particular actions of many kinds, including decisions, judgments, and imputations. We also call the attitudes and dispositions of persons, and persons themselves, just and unjust. Our topic, however, is that of social justice. For us the primary subject of justice is the basic structure of society, or more exactly, the way in which the major social institutions distribute fundamental rights and duties and determine the division of advantages from social cooperation. By major institutions I understand the political constitution and the principal economic and social arrangements. Thus the legal protection of freedom of thought and liberty of conscience, competitive markets, private property in the means of production, and the monogamous family are examples of major social institutions. Taken together as one scheme, the major institutions define men's rights and duties and influence their life-prospects, what they can expect to be and how well they can hope to do. The basic structure is the primary subject of justice because its effects are so profound and present from the start. The intuitive notion here is that this structure contains various social positions and that men born into different positions have different expectations of life determined, in part, by the political system as well as by economic and social circumstances. In this way the institutions of society favor certain starting places over others. These are especially deep inequalities. Not only are they pervasive, but they affect men's initial chances in life; yet they cannot possibly be justified by an appeal to the notions of merit or desert. It is these inequalities, presumably inevitable in the basic structure of any society, to which the principles of social justice must in the first instance apply. These principles, then, regulate the choice of a political constitution and the main elements of the economic and social system. The justice of a social scheme depends essentially on how fundamental rights and duties are assigned and on the economic opportunities and social conditions in the various sectors of society.

• • •

THE MAIN IDEA OF THE THEORY OF JUSTICE

My aim is to present a conception of justice which generalizes and carries to a higher level of abstraction the familiar theory of the social contract as found, say, in Locke, Rousseau, and Kant.[1] In order to do this we are not to think of the original contract as one to enter a particular society or to set up a particular form of government. Rather, the guiding idea is that the principles of justice for the basic structure of society are the object of the original agreement. They are the principles that free and rational persons concerned to further their own interests would accept in an initial position of equality as defining the fundamental terms of their association. These principles are to regulate all further agreements; they specify the kinds of social cooperation that can be entered into and the forms of government that can be established. This way of regarding the principles of justice I shall call justice as fairness.

Thus we are to imagine that those who engage in social cooperation choose together, in one joint act, the principles which are to assign basic rights and duties and to determine the division of social benefits. Men are to decide in advance how they are to regulate their claims against one another and what is to be the foundation charter of their society. Just as each person must decide by rational reflection what constitutes his good, that is, the system of ends which it is rational for him to pursue, so a group of persons must decide once and for all what is to count among them as just and unjust. The choice which rational men would make in this hypothetical situation of equal liberty, assuming for the present that this choice problem has a solution, determines the principles of justice.

In justice as fairness the original position of equality corresponds to the state of nature in the traditional theory of the social contract. This original position is not, of course, thought of as an actual historical state of affairs, much less as a primitive condition of culture. It is understood as a purely hypothetical situation characterized so as to lead to a certain conception of justice.[2] Among the essential features of this situation is that no one knows his place in society, his class position or social status, nor does any one know his fortune in the distribution of natural assets and abilities, his intelligence, strength, and the like. I shall even assume that the parties do not know their conceptions of the good or their special psychological propensities. The principles of justice are chosen behind a veil of ignorance. This ensures that no one is advantaged or disadvantaged in the choice of principles by the outcome of natural chance or the

---

[1] As the text suggests, I shall regard Locke's *Second Treatise of Government,* Rousseau's *The Social Contract,* and Kant's ethical works beginning with *The Foundations of the Metaphysics of Morals* as definitive of the contract tradition. For all of its greatness, Hobbes's *Leviathan* raises special problems. A general historical survey is provided by J. W. Gough, *The Social Contract,* 2nd ed. (Oxford, The Clarendon Press, 1957), and Otto Gierke, *Natural Law and the Theory of Society,* trans. with an introduction by Ernest Barker (Cambridge, The University Press, 1934). A presentation of the contract view as primarily an ethical theory is to be found in G. R. Grice, *The Grounds of Moral Judgment* (Cambridge, The University Press, 1967). . . .

[2] Kant is clear that the original agreement is hypothetical. See *The Metaphysics of Morals,* pt. I (*Rechtslehre*), especially §§47, 52; and pt. II of the essay "Concerning the Common Saying: This May Be True in Theory but It Does Not Apply in Practice," in *Kant's Political Writings,* ed. Hans Reiss and trans. by H. B. Nisbet (Cambridge, The University Press, 1970), pp. 73–87. See Georges Vlachos, *La Pensée politique de Kant* (Paris, Presses Universitaires de France, 1962), pp. 326–335; and J. G. Murphy, *Kant: The Philosophy of Right* (London, Macmillan, 1970), pp. 109–112, 133–136, for a further discussion.

contingency of social circumstances. Since all are similarly situated and no one is able to design principles to favor his particular condition, the principles of justice are the result of a fair agreement or bargain. For given the circumstances of the original position, the symmetry of everyone's relations to each other, this initial situation is fair between individuals as moral persons, that is, as rational beings with their own ends and capable, I shall assume, of a sense of justice. The original position is, one might say, the appropriate initial status quo, and thus the fundamental agreements reached in it are fair. This explains the propriety of the name "justice as fairness": it conveys the idea that the principles of justice are agreed to in an initial situation that is fair. The name does not mean that the concepts of justice and fairness are the same, any more than the phrase "poetry as metaphor" means that the concepts of poetry and metaphor are the same.

Justice as fairness begins, as I have said, with one of the most general of all choices which persons might make together, namely, with the choice of the first principles of a conception of justice which is to regulate all subsequent criticism and reform of institutions. Then, having chosen a conception of justice, we can suppose that they are to choose a constitution and a legislature to enact laws, and so on, all in accordance with the principles of justice initially agreed upon. Our social situation is just if it is such that by this sequence of hypothetical agreements we would have contracted into the general system of rules which defines it. Moreover, assuming that the original position does determine a set of principles (that is, that a particular conception of justice would be chosen), it will then be true that whenever social institutions satisfy these principles those engaged in them can say to one another that they are cooperating on terms to which they would agree if they were free and equal persons whose relations with respect to one another were fair. They could all view their arrangements as meeting the stipulations which they would acknowledge in an initial situation that embodies widely accepted and reasonable constraints on the choice of principles. The general recognition of this fact would provide the basis for a public acceptance of the corresponding principles of justice. No society can, of course, be a scheme of cooperation which men enter voluntarily in a literal sense; each person finds himself placed at birth in some particular position in some particular society, and the nature of this position materially affects his life prospects. Yet a society satisfying the principles of justice as fairness comes as close as a society can to being a voluntary scheme, for it meets the principles which free and equal persons would assent to under circumstances that are fair. In this sense its members are autonomous and the obligations they recognize self-imposed.

One feature of justice as fairness is to think of the parties in the initial situation as rational and mutually disinterested. This does not mean that the parties are egoists, that is, individuals with only certain kinds of interests, say in wealth, prestige, and domination. But they are conceived as not taking an interest in one another's interests. They are to presume that even their spiritual aims may be opposed, in the way that the aims of those of different religions may be opposed. Moreover, the concept of rationality must be interpreted as far as possible in the narrow sense, standard in economic theory, of taking the most effective means to given ends. I shall modify this concept to some extent, as explained later (§25), but one must try to avoid introducing into it any controversial ethical elements. The initial situation must be characterized by stipulations that are widely accepted.

In working out the conception of justice as fairness one main task clearly is to determine which principles of justice would be chosen in the original position. To do this we must describe this situation in some detail and formulate with care the problem of choice which it presents. These matters I shall take up in the immediately succeeding chapters. It may be observed, however, that once the principles of justice are thought of as arising from an original agreement in a situation of equality, it is an open question whether the principle of utility would be acknowledged. Offhand it hardly seems likely that persons who view themselves as equals, entitled to press their claims upon one another, would agree to a principle which may require lesser life prospects for some simply for the sake of a greater sum of advantages enjoyed by others. Since each desires to protect his interests, his capacity to advance his conception of the good, no one has a reason to acquiesce in an enduring loss for himself in order to bring about a greater net balance of satisfaction. In the absence of strong and lasting benevolent impulses, a rational man would not accept a basic structure merely because it maximized the algebraic sum of advantages irrespective of its permanent effects on his own basic rights and interests. Thus it seems that the principle of utility is incompatible with the conception of social cooperation among equals for mutual advantage. It appears to be inconsistent with the idea of reciprocity implicit in the notion of a well-ordered society. Or, at any rate, so I shall argue.

I shall maintain instead that the persons in the initial situation would choose two rather different principles: the first requires equality in the assignment of basic rights and duties, while the second holds that social and economic inequalities, for example inequalities of wealth and authority, are just only if they result in compensating benefits for everyone, and in particular for the least advantaged members of society. These principles rule out justifying institutions on the grounds that the hardships of some are offset by a greater good in the aggregate. It may be expedient but it is not just that some should have less in order that others may prosper. But there is no injustice in the greater benefits earned by a few provided that the situation of persons not so fortunate is thereby improved. The intuitive idea is that since everyone's well-being depends upon a scheme of cooperation without which no one could have a satisfactory life, the division of advantages should be such as to draw forth the willing cooperation of everyone taking part in it, including those less well situated. Yet this can be expected only if reasonable terms are proposed. The two principles mentioned seem to be a fair agreement on the basis of which those better endowed, or more fortunate in their social position, neither of which we can be said to deserve, could expect the willing cooperation of others when some workable scheme is a necessary condition of the welfare of all.[3] Once we decide

---

[3] For the formulation of this intuitive idea I am indebted to Allan Gibbard.

to look for a conception of justice that nullifies the accidents of natural endowment and the contingencies of social circumstance as counters in quest for political and economic advantage, we are led to these principles. They express the result of leaving aside those aspects of the social world that seem arbitrary from a moral point of view.

The problem of the choice of principles, however, is extremely difficult. I do not expect the answer I shall suggest to be convincing to everyone. It is, therefore, worth noting from the outset that justice as fairness, like other contract views, consists of two parts: (1) an interpretation of the initial situation and of the problem of choice posed there, and (2) a set of principles which, it is argued, would be agreed to. One may accept the first part of the theory (or some variant thereof), but not the other, and conversely. The concept of the initial contractual situation may seem reasonable although the particular principles proposed are rejected. To be sure, I want to maintain that the most appropriate conception of this situation does lead to principles of justice contrary to utilitarianism and perfectionism, and therefore that the contract doctrine provides an alternative to these views. Still, one may dispute this contention even though one grants that the contractarian method is a useful way of studying ethical theories and of setting forth their underlying assumptions.

Justice as fairness is an example of what I have called a contract theory. Now there may be an objection to the term "contract" and related expressions, but I think it will serve reasonably well. Many words have misleading connotations which at first are likely to confuse. The terms "utility" and "utilitarianism" are surely no exception. They too have unfortunate suggestions which hostile critics have been willing to exploit; yet they are clear enough for those prepared to study utilitarian doctrine. The same should be true of the term "contract" applied to moral theories. As I have mentioned, to understand it one has to keep in mind that it implies a certain level of abstraction. In particular, the content of the relevant agreement is not to enter a given society or to adopt a given form of government, but to accept certain moral principles. Moreover, the undertakings referred to are purely hypothetical: a contract view holds that certain principles would be accepted in a well-defined initial situation.

The merit of the contract terminology is that it conveys the idea that principles of justice may be conceived as principles that would be chosen by rational persons, and that in this way conceptions of justice may be explained and justified. The theory of justice is a part, perhaps the most significant part, of the theory of rational choice. Furthermore, principles of justice deal with conflicting claims upon the advantages won by social cooperation; they apply to the relations among several persons or groups. The word "contract" suggests this plurality as well as the condition that the appropriate division of advantages must be in accordance with principles acceptable to all parties. The condition of publicity for principles of justice is also connoted by the contract phraseology. Thus, if these principles are the outcome of an agreement, citizens have a knowledge of the principles that others follow. It is characteristic of contract theories to stress the public nature of political principles. Finally there is the long tradition of the contract doctrine. Expressing the tie with this line of thought helps to define ideas and accords with natural piety. There are then several advantages in the use of the term "contract." With due precautions taken, it should not be misleading.

A final remark. Justice as fairness is not a complete contract theory. For it is clear that the contractarian idea can be extended to the choice of more or less an entire ethical system, that is, to a system including principles for all the virtues and not only for justice. Now for the most part I shall consider only principles of justice and others closely related to them; I make no attempt to discuss the virtues in a systematic way. Obviously if justice as fairness succeeds reasonably well, a next step would be to study the more general view suggested by the name "rightness as fairness." But even this wider theory fails to embrace all moral relationships, since it would seem to include only our relations with other persons and to leave out of account how we are to conduct ourselves toward animals and the rest of nature. I do not contend that the contract notion offers a way to approach these questions which are certainly of the first importance; and I shall have to put them aside. We must recognize the limited scope of justice as fairness and of the general type of view that it exemplifies. How far its conclusions must be revised once these other matters are understood cannot be decided in advance.

• • •

TWO PRINCIPLES OF JUSTICE

I shall now state in a provisional form the two principles of justice that I believe would be chosen in the original position. In this section I wish to make only the most general comments, and therefore the first formulation of these principles is tentative. As we go on I shall run through several formulations and approximate step by step the final statement to be given much later. I believe that doing this allows the exposition to proceed in a natural way.

The first statement of the two principles reads as follows.

First: each person is to have an equal right to the most extensive basic liberty compatible with a similar liberty for others.

Second: social and economic inequalities are to be arranged so that they are both (a) reasonably expected to be to everyone's advantage, and (b) attached to positions and offices open to all.

• • •

By way of general comment, these principles primarily apply, as I have said, to the basic structure of society. They are to govern the assignment of rights and duties and to regulate the distribution of social and economic advantages. As their formulation suggests, these principles presuppose that the social structure can be divided into two more or less distinct parts, the first principle applying to the one, the second to the other. They distinguish between those aspects of the social system that define and secure the equal liberties of citizenship and those that specify and establish social and economic inequalities. The basic liberties of citizens are, roughly speaking, political liberty (the right to vote and to be eligible for public office) together with freedom of speech and assembly; liberty of conscience and freedom of thought; freedom of the person along with the right to hold (personal) property; and freedom from arbitrary arrest and seizure as defined by the concept of the rule of law. These liberties are all required to be equal by the first principle, since citizens of a just society are to have the same basic rights.

The second principle applies, in the first approximation, to the distribution of income and wealth and to the design of organizations that make use of differences in authority and responsibility, or chains of command. While the distribution of wealth and income need not be equal, it must be to everyone's advantage, and at the same time, positions of authority and offices of command must be accessible to all. One applies the second principle by holding positions open, and then, subject to this constraint, arranges social and economic inequalities so that everyone benefits.

These principles are to be arranged in a serial order with the first principle prior to the second. This ordering means that a departure from the institutions of equal liberty required by the first principle cannot be justified by, or compensated for, by greater social and economic advantages. The distribution of wealth and income, and the hierarchies of authority, must be consistent with both the liberties of equal citizenship and equality of opportunity.

It is clear that these principles are rather specific in their content, and their acceptance rests on certain assumptions that I must eventually try to explain and justify. A theory of justice depends upon a theory of society in ways that will become evident as we proceed. For the present, it should be observed that the two principles (and this holds for all formulations) are a special case of a more general conception of justice that can be expressed as follows.

> All social values—liberty and opportunity, income and wealth, and the bases of self-respect—are to be distributed equally unless an unequal distribution of any, or all, of these values is to everyone's advantage.

Injustice, then, is simply inequalities that are not to the benefit of all. Of course, this conception is extremely vague and requires interpretation.

As a first step, suppose that the basic structure of society distributes certain primary goods, that is, things that every rational man is presumed to want. These goods normally have a use whatever a person's rational plan of life. For simplicity, assume that the chief primary goods at the disposition of society are rights and liberties, powers and opportunities, income and wealth. . . . These are the social primary goods. Other primary goods such as health and vigor, intelligence and imagination, are natural goods; although their possession is influenced by the basic structure, they are not so directly under its control. Imagine, then, a hypothetical initial arrangement in which all the social primary goods are equally distributed: everyone has similar rights and duties, and income and wealth are evenly shared. This state of affairs provides a benchmark for judging improvements. If certain inequalities of wealth and organizational powers would make everyone better off than in this hypothetical starting situation, then they accord with the general conception.

Now it is possible, at least theoretically, that by giving up some of their fundamental liberties men are sufficiently compensated by the resulting social and economic gains. The general conception of justice imposes no restrictions on what sort of inequalities are permissible; it only requires that everyone's position be improved. We need not suppose anything so drastic as consenting to a condition of slavery. Imagine instead that men forego certain political rights when the economic returns are significant and their capacity to influence the course of policy by the exercise of these rights would be marginal in any case. It is this kind of exchange which the two principles as stated rule out; being arranged in serial order they do not permit exchanges between basic liberties and economic and social gains. The serial ordering of principles expresses an underlying preference among primary social goods. When this preference is rational so likewise is the choice of these principles in this order.

In developing justice as fairness I shall, for the most part, leave aside the general conception of justice and examine instead the special case of the two principles in serial order. The advantage of this procedure is that from the first the matter of priorities is recognized and an effort made to find principles to deal with it. One is led to attend throughout to the conditions under which the acknowledgment of the absolute weight of liberty with respect to social and economic advantages, as defined by the lexical order of the two principles, would be reasonable. Offhand, this ranking appears extreme and too special a case to be of much interest; but there is more justification for it than would appear at first sight. Or at any rate, so I shall maintain . . . . Furthermore, the distinction between fundamental rights and liberties and economic and social benefits marks a difference among primary social goods that one should try to exploit. It suggests an important division in the social system. Of course, the distinctions drawn and the ordering proposed are bound to be at best only approximations. There are surely circumstances in which they fail. But it is essential to depict clearly the main lines of a reasonable conception of justice; and under many conditions anyway, the two principles in serial order may serve well enough. When necessary we can fall back on the more general conception.

The fact that the two principles apply to institutions has certain consequences. Several points illustrate this. First of all, the rights and liberties referred to by these principles are those which are defined by the public rules of the basic structure. Whether men are free is determined by the rights and duties established by the major institutions of society. Liberty is a certain pattern of social forms. The first principle simply requires that certain sorts of rules, those defining basic liberties, apply to everyone equally and that they allow the most extensive liberty compatible with a like liberty for all. The only reason for circumscribing the rights defining liberty and making men's freedom less extensive than it might otherwise be is that these equal rights as institutionally defined would interfere with one another.

Another thing to bear in mind is that when principles mention persons, or require that everyone gain from an inequality, the reference is to representative persons holding the various social positions, or offices, or whatever, established by the basic structure. Thus in applying the second principle I assume that it is possible to assign an expectation of well-being to representative individuals holding these positions. This expectation indicates their life prospects as viewed from their social station. In general, the expectations of representative persons depend upon the distribution of rights and duties throughout the basic structure. When this changes, expectations change. I assume, then, that expectations are connected: by raising the prospects of the representative man in one position we presumably increase or decrease the prospects of representative men in other positions. Since it applies to institutional forms, the second principle (or rather the first part of it) refers to the expectations of representative individuals. As I shall discuss below, neither principle applies to distributions of particular goods to particular individuals who may be identified by their proper names. The situation where someone is considering how to allocate certain commodities to needy persons who are known to him is not within the scope of the principles. They are meant to regulate basic institutional arrangements. We must not assume that there is much similarity from the standpoint of justice between an administrative allotment of goods to specific persons and the appropriate design of society. Our common sense intuitions for the former may be a poor guide to the latter.

Now the second principle insists that each person benefit from permissible inequalities in the basic structure. This means that it must be reasonable for each relevant representative man defined by this structure, when he views it as a going concern, to prefer his prospects with the inequality to his prospects without it. One is not allowed to justify differences in income or organizational powers on the ground that the disadvantages of those in one position are outweighed by the greater advantages of those in another. Much less can infringements of liberty be counterbalanced in this way. Applied to the basic structure, the principle of utility would have us maximize the sum of expectations of representative men (weighted by the number of persons they represent, on the classical view); and this would permit us to compensate for the losses of some by the gains of others. Instead, the two principles require that everyone benefit from economic and social inequalities.

• • •

DEMOCRATIC EQUALITY AND THE DIFFERENCE PRINCIPLE

. . . To illustrate the difference principle, consider the distribution of income among social classes. Let us suppose that the various income groups correlate with representative individuals by reference to whose expectations we can judge the distribution. Now those starting out as members of the entrepreneurial class in property-owning democracy, say, have a better prospect than those who begin in the class of unskilled laborers. It seems likely that this will be true even when the social injustices which now exist are removed. What, then, can possibly justify this kind of initial inequality in life prospects? According to the difference principle, it is justifiable only if the difference in expectation is to the advantage of the representative man who is worse off, in this case the representative unskilled worker. The inequality in expectation is permissible only if lowering it would make the working class even more worse off. Supposedly, given the rider in the second principle concerning open positions, and the principle of liberty generally, the greater expectations allowed to entrepreneurs encourages them to do things which raise the long-term prospects of the laboring class. Their better prospects act as incentives so that the economic process is more efficient, innovation proceeds at a faster pace, and so on. Eventually the resulting material benefits spread throughout the system and to the least advantaged. I shall not consider how far these things are true. The point is that something of this kind must be argued if these inequalities are to be just by the difference principle.

FAIR EQUALITY OF OPPORTUNITY
AND PURE PROCEDURAL JUSTICE

. . . Now I have said that the basic structure is the primary subject of justice. This means, as we have seen, that the first distributive problem is the assignment of fundamental rights and duties and the regulation of social and economic inequalities and of the legitimate expectations founded on these. Of course, any ethical theory recognizes the importance of the basic structure as a subject of justice, but not all theories regard its importance in the same way. In justice as fairness society is interpreted as a cooperative venture for mutual advantage. The basic structure is a public system of rules defining a scheme of activities that leads men to act together so as to produce a greater sum of benefits and assigns to each certain recognized claims to a share in the proceeds. What a person does depends upon what the public rules say he will be entitled to, and what a person is entitled to depends on what he does. The distribution which results is arrived at by honoring the claims determined by what persons undertake to do in the light of these legitimate expectations.

These considerations suggest the idea of treating the question of distributive shares as a matter of pure procedural justice.[4] The intuitive idea is to design the social system so that the outcome is just whatever it happens to be, at least so long as it is within a certain range. The notion of pure procedural justice is best understood by a comparison with perfect and imperfect procedural justice. To

[4] For a general discussion of procedural justice, see Brian Barry, *Political Argument* (London, Routledge and Kegan Paul, 1965), ch. VI. On the problem of fair division, see R. D. Luce and Howard Raiffa, *Games and Decisions* (New York, John Wiley and Sons, Inc., 1957), pp. 363–368; and Hugo Steinhaus, "The Problem of Fair Division," *Econometrica*, vol. 16 (1948).

illustrate the former, consider the simplest case of fair division. A number of men are to divide a cake: assuming that the fair division is an equal one, which procedure, if any, will give this outcome? Technicalities aside, the obvious solution is to have one man divide the cake and get the last piece, the others being allowed their pick before him. He will divide the cake equally, since in this way he assures for himself the largest share possible. This example illustrates the two characteristic features of perfect procedural justice. First, there is an independent criterion for what is a fair division, a criterion defined separately from and prior to the procedure which is to be followed. And second, it is possible to devise a procedure that is sure to give the desired outcome. Of course, certain assumptions are made here, such as that the man selected can divide the cake equally, wants as large a piece as he can get, and so on. But we can ignore these details. The essential thing is that there is an independent standard for deciding which outcome is just and a procedure guaranteed to lead to it. Pretty clearly, perfect procedural justice is rare, if not impossible, in cases of much practical interest.

Imperfect procedural justice is exemplified by a criminal trial. The desired outcome is that the defendant should be declared guilty if and only if he has committed the offense with which he is charged. The trial procedure is framed to search for and to establish the truth in this regard. But it seems impossible to design the legal rules so that they always lead to the correct result. The theory of trials examines which procedures and rules of evidence, and the like, are best calculated to advance this purpose consistent with the other ends of the law. Different arrangements for hearing cases may reasonably be expected in different circumstances to yield the right results, not always but at least most of the time. A trial, then, is an instance of imperfect procedural justice. Even though the law is carefully followed, and the proceedings fairly and properly conducted, it may reach the wrong outcome. An innocent man may be found guilty, a guilty man may be set free. In such cases we speak of a miscarriage of justice: the injustice springs from no human fault but from a fortuitous combination of circumstances which defeats the purpose of the legal rules. The characteristic mark of imperfect procedural justice is that while there is an independent criterion for the correct outcome, there is no feasible procedure which is sure to lead to it.

By contrast, pure procedural justice obtains when there is no independent criterion for the right result: instead there is a correct or fair procedure such that the outcome is likewise correct or fair, whatever it is, provided that the procedure has been properly followed. This situation is illustrated by gambling. If a number of persons engage in a series of fair bets, the distribution of cash after the last bet is fair, or at least not unfair, whatever this distribution is. I assume here that fair bets are those having a zero expectation of gain, that the bets are made voluntarily, that no one cheats, and so on. The betting procedure is fair and freely entered into under conditions that are fair. Thus the background circumstances define a fair procedure. Now any distribution of cash summing to the initial stock held by all individuals could result from a series of fair bets. In this sense all of these particular distributions are equally fair. A

distinctive feature of pure procedural justice is that the procedure for determining the just result must actually be carried out; for in these cases there is no
independent criterion by reference to which a definite outcome can be known
to be just. Clearly we cannot say that a particular state of affairs is just because
it could have been reached by following a fair procedure. This would permit far
too much and would lead to absurdly unjust consequences. It would allow one
to say that almost any distribution of goods is just, or fair, since it could have
come about as a result of fair gambles. What makes the final outcome of betting fair, or not unfair, is that it is the one which has arisen after a series of fair
gambles. A fair procedure translates its fairness to the outcome only when it is
actually carried out.

In order, therefore, to apply the notion of pure procedural justice to distributive shares it is necessary to set up and to administer impartially a just system
of institutions. Only against the background of a just basic structure, including
a just political constitution and a just arrangement of economic and social institutions, can one say that the requisite just procedure exists. . . . I shall describe in some detail a basic structure that has the necessary features. Its various
institutions are explained and connected with the two principles of justice. The
intuitive idea is familiar. Suppose that law and government act effectively to
keep markets competitive, resources fully employed, property and wealth (especially if private ownership of the means of production is allowed) widely distributed by the appropriate forms of taxation, or whatever, and to guarantee a
reasonable social minimum. Assume also that there is fair equality of opportunity underwritten by education for all; and that the other equal liberties are secured. Then it would appear that the resulting distribution of income and the
pattern of expectations will tend to satisfy the difference principle. In this complex of institutions, which we think of as establishing social justice in the modern state, the advantages of the better situated improve the condition of the least
favored. Or when they do not, they can be adjusted to do so, for example, by
setting the social minimum at the appropriate level. As these institutions
presently exist they are riddled with grave injustices. But there presumably are
ways of running them compatible with their basic design and intention so that
the difference principle is satisfied consistent with the demands of liberty and
fair equality of opportunity. It is this fact which underlies our assurance that
these arrangements can be made just.

• • •

THE TENDENCY TO EQUALITY

. . . We see then that the difference principle represents, in effect, an agreement
to regard the distribution of natural talents as a common asset and to share
in the benefits of this distribution whatever it turns out to be. Those who
have been favored by nature, whoever they are, may gain from their good fortune only on terms that improve the situation of those who have lost out. The
naturally advantaged are not to gain merely because they are more gifted, but

only to cover the costs of training and education and for using their endowments in ways that help the less fortunate as well. No one deserves his greater natural capacity nor merits a more favorable starting place in society. But it does not follow that one should eliminate these distinctions. There is another way to deal with them. The basic structure can be arranged so that these contingencies work for the good of the least fortunate. Thus we are led to the difference principle if we wish to set up the social system so that no one gains or loses from his arbitrary place in the distribution of natural assets or his initial position in society without giving or receiving compensating advantages in return.

In view of these remarks we may reject the contention that the ordering of institutions is always defective because the distribution of natural talents and the contingencies of social circumstance are unjust, and this injustice must inevitably carry over to human arrangements. Occasionally this reflection is offered as an excuse for ignoring injustice, as if the refusal to acquiesce in injustice is on a par with being unable to accept death. The natural distribution is neither just nor unjust; nor is it unjust that persons are born into society at some particular position. These are simply natural facts. What is just and unjust is the way that institutions deal with these facts. Aristocratic and caste societies are unjust because they make these contingencies the ascriptive basis for belonging to more or less enclosed and privileged social classes. The basic structure of these societies incorporates the arbitrariness found in nature. But there is no necessity for men to resign themselves to these contingencies. The social system is not an unchangeable order beyond human control but a pattern of human action. In justice as fairness men agree to share one another's fate. In designing institutions they undertake to avail themselves of the accidents of nature and social circumstances only when doing so is for the common benefit. The two principles are a fair way of meeting the arbitrariness of fortune; and while no doubt imperfect in other ways, the institutions which satisfy these principles are just.

A further point is that the difference principle expresses a conception of reciprocity. It is a principle of mutual benefit. We have seen that, at least when chain connection holds, each representative man can accept the basic structure as designed to advance his interests. The social order can be justified to everyone, and in particular to those who are least favored; and in this sense it is egalitarian. But it seems necessary to consider in an intuitive way how the condition of mutual benefit is satisfied. Consider any two representative men A and B, and let B be the one who is less favored. Actually, since we are most interested in the comparison with the least favored man, let us assume that B is this individual. Now B can accept A's being better off since A's advantages have been gained in ways that improve B's prospects. If A were not allowed his better position, B would be even worse off than he is. The difficulty is to show that A has no grounds for complaint. Perhaps he is required to have less than he might since his having more would result in some loss to B. Now what can be said to the more favored man? To begin with, it is clear that the well-being of each depends on a scheme of social cooperation without which no one could have a satisfactory life. Secondly, we can ask for the willing cooperation of everyone only if the terms of the scheme are reasonable. The difference principle, then, seems to be a fair basis on which those better endowed, or more fortunate in their social circumstances, could expect others to collaborate with them when some workable arrangement is a necessary condition of the good of all.

There is a natural inclination to object that those better situated deserve their greater advantages whether or not they are to the benefit of others. At this point it is necessary to be clear about the notion of desert. It is perfectly true that given a just system of cooperation as a scheme of public rules and the expectations set up by it, those who, with the prospect of improving their condition, have done what the system announces that it will reward are entitled to their advantages. In this sense the more fortunate have a claim to their better situation; their claims are legitimate expectations established by social institutions, and the community is obligated to meet them. But this sense of desert presupposes the existence of the cooperative scheme; it is irrelevant to the question whether in the first place the scheme is to be designed in accordance with the difference principle or some other criterion.

Perhaps some will think that the person with greater natural endowments deserves those assets and the superior character that made their development possible. Because he is more worthy in this sense, he deserves the greater advantages that he could achieve with them. This view, however, is surely incorrect. It seems to be one of the fixed points of our considered judgments that no one deserves his place in the distribution of native endowments, any more than one deserves one's initial starting place in society. The assertion that a man deserves the superior character that enables him to make the effort to cultivate his abilities is equally problematic; for his character depends in large part upon fortunate family and social circumstances for which he can claim no credit. The notion of desert seems not to apply to these cases. Thus the more advantaged representative man cannot say that he deserves and therefore has a right to a scheme of cooperation in which he is permitted to acquire benefits in ways that do not contribute to the welfare of others. There is no basis for his making this claim. From the standpoint of common sense, then, the difference principle appears to be acceptable both to the more advantaged and to the less advantaged individual. Of course, none of this is strictly speaking an argument for the principle, since in a contract theory arguments are made from the point of view of the original position. But these intuitive considerations help to clarify the nature of the principle and the sense in which it is egalitarian.

$$\bullet \quad \bullet \quad \bullet$$

THE REASONING LEADING
TO THE TWO PRINCIPLES OF JUSTICE

. . . It seems clear . . . that the two principles are at least a plausible conception of justice. The question, though, is how one is to argue for them more systematically. Now there are several things to do. One can work out their consequences for institutions and note their implications for fundamental social policy. In this way they are tested by a comparison with our considered judgments of justice. . . . But one can also try to find arguments in their favor that are decisive from the standpoint of the original position. In order to see how this might be done, it is useful as a heuristic device to think of the two principles as the maximin solution to the problem of social justice. There is an analogy between the two principles and the maximin rule for choice under uncertainty.[5] This is evident from the fact that the two principles are those a person would choose for the design of a society in which his enemy is to assign him his place. The maximin rule tells us to rank alternatives by their worst possible outcomes: we are to adopt the alternative the worst outcome of which is superior to the worst outcomes of the others. The persons in the original position do not, of course, assume that their initial place in society is decided by a malevolent opponent. As I note below, they should not reason from false premises. The veil of ignorance does not violate this idea, since an absence of information is not misinformation. But that the two principles of justice would be chosen if the parties were forced to protect themselves against such a contingency explains the sense in which this conception is the maximin solution. And this analogy suggests that if the original position has been described so that it is rational for the parties to adopt the conservative attitude expressed by this rule, a conclusive argument can indeed be constructed for these principles. Clearly the maximin rule is not, in general, a suitable guide for choices under uncertainty. But it is attractive in situations marked by certain special features. My aim, then, is to show that a good case can be made for the two principles based on the fact that the original position manifests these features to the fullest possible degree, carrying them to the limit, so to speak.

· · ·

Now there appear to be three chief features of situations that give plausibility to this unusual rule.[6] First, since the rule takes no account of the likelihoods of the possible circumstances, there must be some reason for sharply discounting estimates of these probabilities. Offhand, the most natural rule of choice would seem to be to compute the expectation of monetary gain for each decision and then to adopt the course of action with the highest prospect. (This expectation is defined as follows: let us suppose that g_{ij} represent the numbers in the gain-and-loss table, where i is the row index and j is the column index; and let p_j, $j = 1, 2, 3$, be the likelihoods of the circumstances, with $\Sigma p_j = 1$. Then the expectation for the ith decision is equal to $\Sigma p_j g_{ij}$.) Thus it must be, for example, that the situation is one in which a knowledge of likelihoods is

---

[5] An accessible discussion of this and other rules of choice under uncertainty can be found in W. J. Baumol, *Economic Theory and Operations Analysis,* 2nd ed. (Englewood Cliffs, NJ, Prentice-Hall, Inc., 1965), ch. 24. Baumol gives a geometric interpretation of these rules, including the diagram used in §13 to illustrate the difference principle. See pp. 558–562. See also R. D. Luce and Howard Raiffa, *Games and Decisions* (New York, John Wiley and Sons, Inc., 1957), ch. XIII, for a fuller account.

[6] Here I borrow from William Fellner, *Probability and Profit* (Homewood, IL, R. D. Irwin, Inc., 1965), pp. 140–142, where these features are noted.

impossible, or at best extremely insecure. In this case it is unreasonable not to be skeptical of probabilistic calculations unless there is no other way out, particularly if the decision is a fundamental one that needs to be justified to others.

The second feature that suggests the maximin rule is the following: the person choosing has a conception of the good such that he cares very little, if anything, for what he might gain above the minimum stipend that he can, in fact, be sure of by following the maximin rule. It is not worthwhile for him to take a chance for the sake of a further advantage, especially when it may turn out that he loses much that is important to him. This last provision brings in the third feature, namely, that the rejected alternatives have outcomes that one can hardly accept. The situation involves grave risks. Of course these features work most effectively in combination. The paradigm situation for following the maximin rule is when all three features are realized to the highest degree. This rule does not, then, generally apply, nor of course is it self-evident. Rather, it is a maxim, a rule of thumb, that comes into its own in special circumstances. Its application depends upon the qualitative structure of the possible gains and losses in relation to one's conception of the good, all this against a background in which it is reasonable to discount conjectural estimates of likelihoods.

• • •

Now, as I have suggested, the original position has been defined so that it is a situation in which the maximin rule applies. In order to see this, let us review briefly the nature of this situation with these three special features in mind. To begin with, the veil of ignorance excludes all but the vaguest knowledge of likelihoods. The parties have no basis for determining the probable nature of their society, or their place in it. Thus they have strong reasons for being wary of probability calculations if any other course is open to them. They must also take into account the fact that their choice of principles should seem reasonable to others, in particular their descendants, whose rights will be deeply affected by it. There are further grounds for discounting that I shall mention as we go along. For the present it suffices to note that these considerations are strengthened by the fact that the parties know very little about the gain-and-loss table. Not only are they unable to conjecture the likelihood of the various possible circumstances, they cannot say much about what the possible circumstances are, much less enumerate them and foresee the outcome of each alternative available. Those deciding are much more in the dark than the illustration by a numerical table suggests. It is for this reason that I have spoken of an analogy with the maximin rule.

Several kinds of arguments for the two principles of justice illustrate the second feature. Thus, if we can maintain that these principles provide a workable theory of social justice, and that they are compatible with reasonable demands of efficiency, then this conception guarantees a satisfactory minimum. There may be, on reflection, little reason for trying to do better. Thus much of the argument . . . is to show, by their application to the main questions of social justice, that the two principles are a satisfactory conception. These details have a philosophical purpose. Moreover, this line of thought is practically decisive if we can establish the priority of liberty, the lexical ordering of the two principles. For this priority implies that the persons in the original position have no desire to try for greater gains at the expense of the equal liberties. The minimum assured by the two principles in lexical order is not one that the parties wish to jeopardize for the sake of greater economic and social advantages. . . .

Finally, the third feature holds if we can assume that other conceptions of justice may lead to institutions that the parties would find intolerable. For example, it has sometimes been held that under some conditions the utility principle (in either form) justifies, if not slavery or serfdom, at any rate serious infractions of liberty for the sake of greater social benefits. We need not consider here the truth of this claim, or the likelihood that the requisite conditions obtain. For the moment, this contention is only to illustrate the way in which conceptions of justice may allow for outcomes which the parties may not be able to accept. And having the ready alternative of the two principles of justice which secure a satisfactory minimum, it seems unwise, if not irrational, for them to take a chance that these outcomes are not realized.

41.
Justice and Exploitation
JOHN ROEMER

THE ORIGIN OF EXPLOITATION

Exploitation has a technical definition that must be distinguished from its colloquial one. When Marxists say that workers are exploited by capitalists, they mean—colloquially—that an economic relation of exploitation exists between workers and capitalists (that workers are used by capitalists) and that capitalists take unfair advantage of workers (that workers are used by capitalists in an ethically indefensible way). In this chapter I will define exploitation in a technical sense, using a simple model of an economy that produces only one good. In Chapter 5, I will discuss when technical exploitation should be considered as unfair treatment of workers by capitalists.

2.1 An Egalitarian Distribution of Capital

Imagine a society consisting of 1,000 members. There is one produced good, corn, which all like to consume. Corn is produced from inputs of labor and seed corn. All members of this society are equally skilled and productive, and all have knowledge of the technologies that exist for producing corn. Each person is assumed to have *subsistence preferences:* each needs to consume 1 unit of corn per week (to survive, let us say); after having done so he prefers to take leisure rather than to work more and consume more corn. There is one additional condition: each agent desires to reproduce the stock of seed corn, if any, with which he began. He does not want to begin the next week with a smaller corn stock, which is the only kind of capital in this model. Thus, a person's utility, or welfare level, is a function of corn consumed and labor expended—or corn consumed and leisure consumed. The particular preferences I have posited are easy to analyze, because the trade-offs between corn and leisure are very simple: to get 1 unit of corn, a person is willing to do anything, and after that he is willing to do nothing.

Suppose there is a total initial capital stock of 500 units of corn ($K = 500$). Further, assume that in this society there are two ways of producing corn, or two techniques of production, which are called the Farm and the Factory:

Farm	3 days labor + 0 units of seed corn	→	1 unit of corn
Factory	1 day labor + 1 unit of seed corn	→	2 units of corn, gross, or 1 unit of corn, net

The production period for both the Farm and the Factory techniques is 1 week (7 days); that is, seed corn is tied up in the ground that long before it produces a harvest, even though it may take only 1 day to plant, as in the Factory technology.

Thus far, no distribution of the means of production, or of the capital stock, which in this model is just seed corn, has been assumed. Now assume that there is an egalitarian distribution of capital stock. Each agent owns 1/2 unit of corn—the aggregate capital stock is divided equally among all. Given the technologies described, the preferences of the agents, and the distribution of assets, what is the equilibrium in this economy?

The equilibrium solution is that each agent works a total of 2 days: 1/2 day in the Factory and 1-1/2 days on the Farm. Assume that a person can switch costlessly and instantaneously between one technology and the other. In the 1/2 day a woman works in the Factory technology, she plants her 1/2 unit of seed corn, which at the end of the week will yield for her 1 unit of corn, gross. Her capital stock is tied up in the ground for that week. The 1 unit of corn, gross, she gets in this process is sufficient to replace her original seed corn stock and leave her 1/2 unit of corn to consume. She must somewhere produce another 1/2 unit of corn for consumption; and to do so she moves to the Farm, where in 1-1/2 days she can produce 1/2 unit of corn, with no capital stock.

One might ask what type of technology can produce corn using labor alone. Perhaps the Farm technology involves going to the forest and hunting around for wild corn, which grows there: this labor-intensive process yields corn but requires much more labor than is needed to produce an equivalent amount of corn using the Factory process. But the specific technologies of production are irrelevant. The important assumption is that there are two ways of surviving in the economy. One way is to engage in a production process that uses capital, that is, some scarce nonlabor input, which in this model is seed corn. The alternative way is one everyone can engage in whether or not he has access to capital—in this model, the Farm technology.

The solution I have outlined is autarkic—there is no trade. Each person works only for herself; she neither sells nor hires labor, nor does anyone sell corn to anyone else. The solution is clearly egalitarian. Each person works 2 days and consumes 1 unit of corn. No one can do any better, and the corn stock is reproduced for the beginning of the next week. A careful definition of the term *equilibrium* is not necessary; simply notice that this is the natural solution to the problem that people face in this economy—of producing the corn they require subject to the constraints determined by their capital stock and the technology. Given the subsistence preferences that have been posited, no one will work any longer, for after consuming 1 unit of corn, these people prefer only to take leisure.

From this solution I can define the *socially necessary labor time* (SNLT) for this society to reproduce itself. Given the technologies, the capital stock, and the consumption requirement, the socially necessary labor time required to produce 1,000 units of corn is 2,000 days; or, from the vantage point of an individual, the labor socially necessary to produce 1 unit of corn is 2 days. Each producer works, in this equilibrium, precisely socially necessary labor time. More generally, the labor time socially necessary to produce a certain amount of corn is the amount of labor that is needed to produce that corn and to re-produce the seed corn used up in the process. Society will use all its capital stock first in the Factory process, which in 1 week will produce 500 units of corn, net, with 500 days of labor; in the meantime the remaining 500 units of corn will be produced by working a total of 1,500 days on the Farm.

• • •

Return, now, to the initial subsistence preferences, in which each person needs or wants to consume 1 unit of corn per week, in which case the amount of labor time socially necessary to produce society's requirement is 2 days per unit of corn per individual (or 2,000 days in total). I can also say that 2 days is the labor embodied in 1 unit of corn. In other words, the *labor embodied* in a unit of corn is the amount of labor required to produce that commodity and to reproduce the inputs used in producing it, given the technologies and capital stock available. Socially necessary labor time is the labor embodied in the corn consumption bundle required by the population.

There is, however, an ambiguity in this definition that I wish to point out. If I ask, Given the technologies, how much labor is required to produce 1 unit of corn, net? the answer is 1 day. (Just use 1 unit of seed corn in the Factory.) This, however, cannot be done on an economy-wide scale—that is, this society cannot produce 1,000 units of corn in 1,000 days. When I speak of the labor embodied in a unit of corn, that should be understood to mean the average amount of social labor time required to produce that unit, given the total amount of corn produced. Thus, the labor embodied in 1 unit of corn is 2 days in this economy, because at equilibrium 1,000 units of corn, net, are produced with 2,000 days of labor.

The particular equilibrium solution I have discussed above is autarkic, but there are other ways of arranging an equilibrium in this economy that do involve trading among members—in particular, when some persons hire the labor of others. Suppose there are two groups of agents, called H (for hirers of labor) and S (for sellers of labor). Any 750 agents may constitute the H group and the remaining 250 will constitute the S group. Those in the S group are going to sell their labor for a wage to those in the H group. Each person in the S group first works up her own capital stock using the Factory technology. That requires 1/2 day of labor and generates for her 1/2 unit of corn, net, by the end of the week. She needs to earn another 1/2 unit of corn to consume. Instead of going to the Farm to produce that corn, she offers to sell her labor to someone, or to several members, of the H group. What real wage will prevail in this economy to make this offer of labor attractive to both hirers and sellers on the labor market?

The answer is that members of H will offer to hire members of S to work on their (H's) capital stock at a wage rate of 3 days labor for 1 unit of corn, or a real wage of 1/3 unit of corn per day's labor. Why? First, observe that at this wage rate a member of S can work up the capital stock of 3 members of H, expending a total of 1-1/2 days of labor, and she will earn as a total wage precisely 1/2 unit of corn. Combining the labor traded with that she has already done for herself, she will have worked a total of 2 days—partly for herself and mainly for others—earned exactly 1 unit of corn, and reproduced her original seed stock, as required. So a member of S is willing to accept this wage: she is indifferent between this proposal and working autarkically in the Factory and then on the Farm, as in the first equilibrium solution described. Now from the viewpoint of a member of H, he will have his 1/2 unit of corn capital worked up by some member of S, producing 1 unit of corn, gross. Out of that, 1/2 unit reproduces his capital and he pays a wage of 1/3 unit of corn/day × 1/2 day = 1/6 unit of corn, which leaves a profit for him of 1/3 unit of corn. He must go elsewhere to produce the other 2/3 units of corn he needs, for his capital stock is tied up. To earn the additional corn he requires, he uses the Farm technology and works for 2 days, producing 2/3 units of corn. Thus, he, too, ends up working exactly 2 days, reproducing his capital stock and having 1 unit of corn left for consumption.

The second equilibrium is exactly the same with regard to the labor–corn allocation as the first one. Each person works 2 days, reproduces his or her capital stock, and consumes 1 unit of corn. But the *class structure* differs from that of the first equilibrium. Every producer just works for himself in the first equilibrium; there is only one class of self-employed producers and no division of labor. In the second equilibrium there are two classes—H and S—and there is a complete *social division of labor*. Some work only on the Farm and some only in the Factory.

What is a *class?* That is best seen from the model. It is a group of people, all of whom relate to the labor market in the same way. In the first equilibrium each person is a self-employed peasant, or artisan. In the second equilibrium 250 people are sellers of labor power (and also work for themselves part time) and 750 people are hirers of labor power (and also work for themselves part time).

• • •

Note that in both of these equilibria each person works just socially necessary labor time. Indeed, given the preferences of agents in this model, no one has any reason to prefer one equilibrium over the other. For in each equilibrium each person works 2 days and consumes 1 unit of corn. This indifference between the equilibria follows because the only arguments of the utility function of people in this society are leisure and corn. No person has any preference for rural life over urban life or vice versa. Nor does anyone care whether she works for herself or for a boss. But suppose that working for a boss is a source of disutility; that is, labor performed for hire is more unpleasant than labor performed for oneself. In that case it would no longer be correct to say people cared just about corn and leisure: they would care about corn and the various types of labor they expend—labor expended on one's own account being of a different type from labor expended for someone else. Were this the case, the second equilibrium outlined would not be an equilibrium, because members of

S would prefer to work autarkically, as in the first equilibrium, rather than work for a boss. Given this preference, would it still be possible to arrange an equilibrium involving the two classes H and S? The wage rate would have to be higher than 1/3 unit of corn per day to compensate a member of S for expending labor under a boss, an activity that she now finds relatively distasteful. But if that were so, the hirer's profits would fall, and he would have to work longer than 2 days on the Farm to get all the corn he needs. What would entice him to do that? Nothing—unless, perversely, he receives utility from being a boss over someone, or unless he has a preference for rural life over urban life. If hirers have preferences of this sort, then indeed one could have an equilibrium with a complete social division of labor, but with slightly different outcomes than those described in the second equilibrium above.

Conditions other than disutilities involving types of labor expended can motivate a social division of labor. Suppose there are *set-up costs* in moving from the Farm to the Factory, because it takes time to move. Then, in fact, the autarkic equilibrium discussed above is not achievable, for when each person moves from Farm to Factory, he uses up some time. It would require 2 days plus set-up time to produce 1 unit of corn by oneself. If these set-up costs exist, it would be to the advantage of society to minimize them, by having one group work only in the Factory and the other only on the Farm. This is, in fact, what the second equilibrium accomplishes. With set-up costs, one would observe *only* the second equilibrium, because the autarkic solution would not be Pareto optimal: everyone could be rendered better off by the social division of labor, because only by specializing could each person acquire 1 unit of corn for consumption for 2 days of labor. Thus, despite the class structure of this equilibrium, the result is completely egalitarian in terms of the corn consumed and the labor expended by members of the society. So a class structure is not ipso facto associated with inequality of final welfare.

2.2 The Technical Definition of Exploitation

Exploitation is said to exist if in a given economy some agents must work more time than is socially necessary (longer than the socially necessary labor time) to earn their consumption bundles and others work less time than is socially necessary to earn their bundles. Exploitation does not exist in the economy described in Section 2.1, because everyone works precisely socially necessary labor time. Nevertheless, it is noteworthy that *class differentiation* can emerge without exploitation, at least at this level of theoretical abstraction. That is the lesson of the second equilibrium, which has the two classes H and S. However, without the kind of set-up costs referred to above, the class structure is rather ephemeral: it is not forced into existence, for society could just as well organize itself as it does in the autarkic equilibrium, that is, in an undifferentiated way. Class structure becomes interesting, and conforms more to Marxist expectation, when there is no other way for society to organize itself to achieve an equilibrium.

2.3 Unequal Ownership of the Capital Stock

What happens when a society is organized with unequal ownership of the capital stock (in this model, capital stock is the seed corn)? Instead of the equal distribution posited in Section 2.1, suppose that each of 10 agents (call them rich agents 1, 2, 3, . . . , 10) owns 50 units of corn and the other 990 own none. The only productive asset these last own is their labor power, the capacity to work. This economy also differs from that described in Section 2.1 in another way, namely, that each person's utility function is strictly increasing in corn. In other words, if he can get more corn without expending additional labor, then he wishes to do so. A person having subsistence preferences is not indifferent to getting more than 1 unit of corn, he simply is not willing to expend more of his own time to get more corn. Should more corn come his way for nothing, he is happy to accept it. Otherwise, all features of the economy (preferences for leisure time and technologies) are the same as before.

What is the equilibrium in this economy with the skewed initial distribution of seed corn? First I will try the obvious autarkic arrangement. Each of the propertyless agents (I will call them peasants) works 3 days on the Farm, to get 1 unit of corn. Each of the propertied agents works up to 1 unit of corn of his capital stock, producing 1 unit of corn, net, at the end of the week, which he consumes. Thus, each of the rich agents 1, 2, . . . , 10 works 1 day and each of the other 990 agents works 3 days. This arrangement would be a case of exploitation, but it is not an equilibrium. There is exploitation in this society because the socially necessary labor time for this society is 2 days of labor. That calculation does not change as the distribution of corn changes, because the calculation of socially necessary labor time is independent of the distribution of assets. It depends only on total consumption, technology, and the total amount of capital and labor available. (If the needs of people, or their demands, were to change with the redistribution of wealth, the story would be more complicated.)

But this arrangement is not an equilibrium. The rich agents can do better for themselves, without the poor ones doing any worse. Using a labor market, a deal can be struck. Each rich agent can become a capitalist and offer to hire labor. As before, the rich agents constitute the class H. Each rich agent has a lot of unused seed corn in the preceding solution. Suppose each rich person offers to hire peasants to work up his capital stock in the Factory technology—at a wage rate of 2 days of labor for 1 unit of corn (that is, 1/2 unit of corn per day). Then all 990 peasants will flock to the Factory gates to work, for that is a better deal than working on the Farm, at a rate of 3 days of labor for 1 unit of corn. Each peasant will wish to supply 2 days of labor (and thereby earn his needed 1 unit of corn). But, to put this supply of labor to work in the Factory requires $2 \times 990 = 1{,}980$ units of seed corn, an amount that is not available. Thus, at the wage rate just proposed, the supply of labor far exceeds the demand for the labor by the capitalists. Hence, 1/2 unit of corn per day is not an equilibrium wage. The capitalists can lower the wage from 1/2 unit of corn per day, because the supply of labor exceeds the demand for labor at that proposed wage.

How far will they lower it? The alternative for a peasant is to work at a real wage of 1/3 unit of corn per day on the Farm. So long as the Factory wage is higher than that, all peasants will flock to the Factory. But there is not enough capital stock to produce the subsistence needs of this population using only the Factory. Therefore, no wage higher than 1/3 unit of corn per day can be sustained. Furthermore, no wage lower than 1/3 unit of corn per day can be sustained, for at a wage lower than 1/3 unit of corn per day no labor will be offered; all peasants will prefer to stay peasants, earning their livelihood on the Farm. Hence, the only possible wage that can clear the labor market is 1/3 unit of corn per day (3 days of labor for 1 unit of corn).

At this wage each peasant is indifferent to working on the Farm or in the Factory, because the real wage is the same in both places. Hence, the labor supplied at the wage 1/3 unit of corn per day is anything between 0 days and $3 \times 990 = 2{,}970$ days. That is, each peasant, and there are 990 of them, is willing to work any amount of labor from 0 to 3 days for a capitalist at the wage of 1/3 unit of corn per day. Figure 2.1 shows the supply and demand curves of labor in this economy. An equilibrium can be arranged as follows. The capitalists hire exactly the number of peasants required to utilize fully their capital stock. This requires 500 days of labor, or 500/3 peasants, each of whom becomes a "factory worker" and earns 1 unit of corn for 3 days of labor. The other 823.33 (990 − 500/3) peasants stay as peasants on the Farm and earn their subsistence bundle of corn there. The capitalists, as a class, work 0 days; the workers in their factories produce 1,000 units of corn, of which 500 units replace the seed stock, 500/3 units is paid out as wages, and the remaining $2/3 \times 500 = 333.33$ units of corn are profits. Thus, each capitalist gets 33.3 units of corn as profit in this equilibrium, and does not work at all. He can certainly consume his needed 1 unit of corn, or even much more than that. Or he can accumulate corn.

In the equilibrium in this model, there are three classes: capitalists, who do not work but only hire others and reap profits; workers, who work for capitalists and earn a subsistence wage; and peasants, who do not work for capitalists and earn a subsistence wage. Each worker and peasant works for 3 days to earn 1 unit of corn. But I concluded earlier that the amount of *labor embodied* in 1 unit of corn is 2 days, given the demands of this society. So exploitation has emerged in this model, because capitalists work less than socially necessary labor time, whereas the workers and the peasants work more than socially necessary labor time.

2.4 The Causes of Exploitation

What are the features of the economy described in the preceding section that have caused exploitation to emerge? Two are worthy of mention: the scarcity of capital relative to the labor available for it to employ; and differential ownership of the capital stock. The second feature has already been emphasized by the comparison of the models of Sections 2.1 and 2.3; exploitation has emerged with the differential ownership of the capital stock. But what effect does scarcity of capital have?

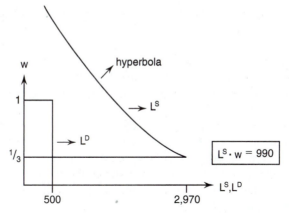

Figure 2.1
Equilibrium in the peasant economy. L^S, labor supply (days); L^D, labor demand (days); w, wage (units of corn per day).

Capital is relatively scarce in the economy described in Section 2.3. By this I mean that it is impossible for the society to "reproduce itself economically" (that is, to produce 1,000 units of corn, net, in a week) using only the Factory technology, because it lacks the necessary capital stock to do so. Suppose, on the other hand, that capital is abundant—say, the total endowment of capital is 5,000 units of corn instead of 500, and that each capitalist owns 500 units of seed corn. What would happen when the wage rate offered is 3 days of labor for 1 unit of corn? I have computed that at most $3 \times 990 = 2,970$ days of labor will be offered, which can be used in conjunction with 2,970 units of seed corn in the Factory, but there is much more seed corn lying around. Capitalists will start to compete with each other; one thinks that if he raises the real wage a bit, he will attract more labor, thereby using all his capital stock and reaping much more profit than he currently gets. Hence, the real wage rate will rise, essentially to the point where profits are zero. It will rise to the rate of 1 unit of corn per day's labor, at which rate the capitalists make zero profits, and no one works on the Farm. (In fact, this is a simplification; it will rise to some value a bit less than 1 unit of corn per day, so that the capitalists can earn at least some of their own consumption bundle. But this is a detail that is not important for my story.)

If capital is sufficiently abundant relative to the labor available for it to employ, then the profit rate drops and exploitation virtually disappears. Of course, socially necessary labor time decreases in this economy as the capital to labor ratio rises, because it becomes possible to produce 1,000 units of corn with much less labor. With $K = 5,000$, socially necessary labor time per individual is 1 day of labor, because society does not need to use the Farm at all.

The essential aspect of capital is that it is an input to production that cannot be instantaneously produced. It must already exist in order to be used in the present. Thus, either it was produced in the past (as I assumed the seed corn was) or it is a nonproduced factor (like land or some natural resource). (The incomes that accrue to owners of capital that was produced in the past are often called profits, whereas the incomes to owners of natural resources that were never produced are called rents.) When capital (whether it was produced in the past or is an appropriated natural resource) becomes private property and is distributed in an inegalitarian manner, differentiation and exploitation arise, through the market process.

Recall that the sense in which the exploitation that occurs here is a technical, but not obviously an ethical, one. It is not clear that the factory workers who are exploited in the equilibrium described in this section are being unfairly taken advantage of (or being exploited in the colloquial sense) unless one had some reason to believe that the initial unequal distribution of the capital stock that gave rise to that exploitation is unfair.

• • •

THE MORALITY OF EXPLOITATION

5.2 The Initial Distribution

If the exploitation of the worker is an important concept, it is so for normative reasons—because it is indicative of some injustice and not because the exploitability of labor power is the unique source of profits. In the model in Section 2.3, exploitation emerged because of the inequality of ownership of the capital stock. If the exploitation of the worker seems unfair, it is because one thinks the initial distribution of capital stock, which gives rise to it, is unfair.

I will elucidate this claim. Imagine the following situation, in which exploitation emerges as a consequence of an initial distribution of resources that one thinks of as fair. (Note that I use the term *exploitation* in its technical sense throughout this chapter.) Suppose that there are two agents, Adam and Karl. They have different preferences for corn and leisure and will live for many weeks. Assume that a week is the length of time required for corn to grow and that Karl and Adam have available the same technologies used in the models of Chapter 2:

| Farm | 3 days labor | $\rightarrow$ | 1 unit of corn |
| Factory | 1 day labor
+ 1 unit of corn | $\rightarrow$ | 2 units of corn, gross |

Adam and Karl each start with 1/2 unit of corn. Karl is highly averse to performing work in the present: he desires only to consume 1 unit of corn per week, subject to the requirement that he not run down his seed stock. In the first week, he therefore works 1/2 day in the Factory (fully utilizing his seed corn) and 1-1/2 days on the Farm, producing a total of 1-1/2 units of corn, 1 of which he consumes at harvest time, leaving him with 1/2 unit to start with in week 2. Adam accumulates during the first week; he works 1/2 day in the Factory, utilizing his seed corn, and 4-1/2 days on the Farm, producing 2-1/2

Table 5.1   Work patterns of Karl and Adam

Week	Amount of Adam's labor expended (days)	Amount of Karl's labor expended (days)	Units of corn consumed by each individual
1	5	2	1
2	0	2	1
3	0	2	1
4	0	2	1

units of corn, gross. After consuming 1 unit of corn, he has 1-1/2 units left with which to start week 2. In week 2, Karl works up his own seed stock in 1/2 day in the Factory, producing 1 unit of corn; then, instead of going to the Farm, Karl borrows or rents Adam's 1-1/2 units of seed corn and works it up in the Factory. This takes Karl precisely 1-1/2 days and he produces 3 units of corn, gross, in the process. Of the 3 units of corn, he keeps 1/2 unit of corn and returns 2-1/2 units of corn to Adam (Adam's principal of 1-1/2 units of corn plus interest of 1 unit of corn). Indeed, Karl is quite content with this arrangement, for he has worked for a total of 2 days and received 1-1/2 units of corn, just as in week 1, when he had to use the inferior Farm technology. This means the rate of interest that Adam has charged him (66.6%) is just the rate at which he is indifferent between borrowing from Adam and working on the Farm. (One can see that if there are many people like Karl and only a few like Adam, then competition will drive the interest rate to this value. Thus, the competitors for access to Adam's capital will have bid away any advantage they might have derived from borrowing from Adam rather than working on the Farm. The equilibrium interest rate is the competitive interest rate in a world where there are many people with Karl's preferences and relatively few with Adam's.) Adam, on the other hand, receives a profit of 1 unit of corn from Karl's labor, which he consumes, and is left again to begin week 3 with 1-1/2 units of corn. He has not worked at all in week 2. This arrangement can continue forever, with Karl working 2 days and consuming 1 unit of corn each week, and Adam consuming 1 unit of corn each week but working 5 days during the first week and 0 days thereafter (Table 5.1).

Clearly there is exploitation in all weeks after the first in this arrangement. Adam does not work but lives off the interest he receives from lending his capital to Karl. Alternatively, I could have had Adam hire Karl to work on his capital stock in the Factory, paying him a wage of 1/3 unit of corn per day. The interest rate, like the wage that Karl will settle for, is determined by his next best opportunity on the Farm, and if there are many Karls and a few Adams, the competitive wage is 1/3 unit of corn per day.

But is there anything wrong with this exploitation? Karl and Adam (or the Karls and the Adams) started out with equal endowments of corn. Is there any sense in which Adam has taken unfair advantage of Karl? None is apparent, unless one views Karl's preference for leisure today as a kind of handicap, which gives him the right to some kind of protection from Adam's offer. Or, perhaps, Karl (but not Adam) was incapacitated in some way and thereby prevented from working more than 3 days a week. In this case one might decide that they faced unequal opportunities at the beginning, which would surely prejudice the judgment that the outcome was fair.

Karl is said to have a high rate of time preference, as he is relatively unwilling to forestall present consumption for the sake of greater consumption in the future. Adam has a low rate of time preference. In this case, the commodity whose consumption over time is at issue is leisure. Suppose Karl's high rate of time preference is due to impatience rather than to some physical handicap that prevents him from working as long as Adam does during the first week. If one were to forbid transactions of lending or hiring between Adam and Karl, then Karl still would be no better off (he would continue to work, as he did in week 1, in both Factory and Farm for a total of 2 days to produce his 1 unit of corn, net), but Adam would be worse off. Would it not, therefore, be spiteful to forbid these trades between them? Forbidding these transactions would only give rise to a Pareto suboptimal allocation of streams of corn and leisure over the lives of Adam and Karl. If Adam could not deal with Karl, then he would have to work every period himself, while Karl would work no less. Now suppose— to make the argument stronger—that there are set-up costs in moving from the Factory to the Farm. Then, when Karl works in both places, as in week 1, he would have to expend more than 2 days of labor to get 1 unit of corn. In week 2, when he borrows from Adam, he uses only the Factory, and so he works just the 2 days. Thus, with set-up costs, both Karl and Adam strictly gain by virtue of Adam's accumulation in week 1. (It is not clear precisely how the interest rate would be set when set-up costs exist, but that is a matter of second-order concern.) For a socialist society to prevent such exploitation, it "would have to forbid capitalist acts between consenting adults." [1]

There may be reasons to forbid such transactions, but they are not visible at the level of simplicity of this model. Yet even at this level exploitation unquestionably obtains. The conclusion to be drawn from the example, then, is this: when exploitation is an injustice, it is not because it is exploitation as such, but because the distribution of labor expended and income received in an exploitative situation are consequences of an initial distribution of assets that is unjust. The injustice of an exploitative allocation depends upon the injustice of the initial distribution. In the example, the initial distribution of equal seed corn endowment was taken to be just, and I was consequently hard put to identify the ensuing exploitation as evidence of anything nasty.

What, then, might be the cause of a highly unequal initial distribution of the means of production, and what are our attitudes toward such causes? Should the exploitation that will arise from an unequal distribution, variously caused, in a system of private property be considered morally bad?

5.2.1 Robbery and Plunder

If the initial distribution is highly unequal because some agents robbed and plundered, then clearly there are grounds for viewing the ensuing exploitation as bad. This is the case Marx made against European capitalism, particularly

---

[1] Nozick, Robert. *Anarchy, State, and Utopia* (New York: Basic Books, 1974), p. 163.

English capitalism. Part VIII of the first volume of *Capital* is entitled "The So-Called Primitive Accumulation." In this section Marx relates the history of the concentration of wealth by the English gentry through the enclosure movement and other forms of robbery. The appropriate folk rhyme, popular at the time is:

> The law locks up the man or woman
> Who steals the goose from off the common,
> But leaves the greater villain loose
> Who steals the common from the goose.[2]

The unequal distribution of land that the enclosure movement accomplished not only created a wealthy class but also created a potential proletariat by dis-enfranchising peasants of all means of production except their labor power. Before the enclosure movement the yeoman peasant had access to the commons and a small herd, and perhaps a small plot of land of his own; therefore, he had no need to sell his labor power to survive. The enclosure movement made it impossible for large numbers of disenfranchised peasants to survive without selling labor power. Thus, proletarianization of a population is often a by-product, intended or otherwise, of the concentration of land or capital. The newly formed class of propertied agents thus becomes wealthy, not only by virtue of the land it has acquired, but also because, in the process of that acquisition, it has "liberated" a mass of producers from their means of production, thus making them available as a labor force for hire. Without the existence of a class willing to sell its labor power (or to be enslaved or enserfed), large land holdings would do their owners no good.

In the Marxist account, the enclosure movement in England was a clear case of robbery and plunder, although that interpretation is not unchallenged. A contemporary analogue to enclosure was accomplished in the mid-twentieth century by the green revolution, during which new varieties of seed (for example, wheat) that were vastly more productive than old varieties were developed. Use of the new seed, however, required capital investment in irrigation, insecticides, and fertilizers (as well as knowledge), which small peasants could not undertake. Large landholders, by virtue of their wealth, were able to make the transition to the new technology, which created an increase in wheat yield and a decrease in the price of wheat. Small peasants who had survived by selling wheat on the market could no longer survive under these competitive pressures. They had to sell their land and become either landless laborers or urban proletarians. (The amount they could get for their small plots was too little to enable them to become petty capitalists, in part because the big landlord to whom a peasant sold his land was in a monopsonistic position.) It is argued that this process of proletarianization contributed to the rapid growth of Mexico City and the massive unemployment accompanying it. Even though the long-term consequence of technological change has been to increase the income of society, including that of its proletarians, in the short-run technological changes of certain kinds, like the green revolution, can proletarianize large

[2] Cheyney, Edward P. *An Introduction to the Industrial and Social History of England* (New York: Macmillan, 1923), p. 188.

masses of people, who become unemployed and poor. This example is not precisely a case of robbery or plunder, but it underscores the point that the concentration of capital (a process leading to unequal distribution of capital) is often accompanied by the proletarianization of a mass of people, and, hence, benefits the propertied class in a double sense. (For further discussion of the green revolution, see the book by Hewitt de Alcantara.)[3]

•   •   •

Most historical episodes of rapid concentration of land in the hands of a few are accomplished either by direct force or at least by deals in which political power is used in unprincipled ways. The history of capitalism is replete with examples of the accumulation of wealth through clearly unethical means, so it is not very difficult, on these grounds, to condemn the present distribution of wealth. But the question I am investigating is whether all possible causes of an unequal distribution of capital are condemnable.

5.2.2 Differential Rates of Time Preference

If agents have differential rates of time preference, then exploitation will quickly be generated, as it was in the story of Karl and Adam. Whether one views such exploitation as bad depends upon the view one takes toward the genesis of the different rates of time preference of these agents. Suppose the different rates came about as a consequence of exposure to different environments—say, families with different habits and different wealths. Adam, with a low rate of time preference, learned to save because he grew up in a well-off family that taught him the virtues of delayed gratification, whereas Karl's impatient preferences are the consequence of never having been taught by his parents to think about tomorrow. Perhaps, in such a situation, one could say that the differential rates of time preference that brought about the exploitation were themselves the consequence of a prior injustice—the different wealths of Karl's and Adam's families, which gave rise to their attitudes. More generally, the different attitudes toward saving of Karl and Adam may be the consequence of different external opportunities that one deems to be unfair.

Suppose, on the other hand, that Karl's and Adam's external opportunities were identical but that they were born with different rates of time preference. To condemn the ensuing exploitation, in this case, involves construing a high rate of time preference as a handicap. (This is the kind of value judgment that economists are loath to make.) Even if Karl's rate of time preference is so high that he does not take proper care of himself, does one have some objective basis for interfering with the deals he might make? (One might want to interfere because Karl's behavior eventually imposes costs on the minimally benevolent society that insists upon hospitalizing him, and paying for it, when he deteriorates as a result of his own neglect. But that is an issue quite different from the one of exploitation, which I am currently discussing.)

[3] Hewitt de Alcantara, Cynthia. *Modernizing Mexican Agriculture: Socioeconomic Implications of Technological Change 1940–1970.* Geneva: United Nations Research Institute for Social Development, 1976.

Suppose that Karl and Adam have different rates of time preference because of their prior exposure to different external opportunities. It is not necessarily the case that the preferences either one of them has are irrational. In fact, it may be that their rates of time preference are adapted to the environments in which they expect to live. Suppose that there are many Karls, each of whom expects to live only two weeks, and a small number of Adams, each of whom expects to live for many weeks. Except insofar as their different expectations about the lengths of their lives may influence their choices, the Karls and Adams all have the same attitudes about consumption of corn and leisure over time. If a Karl only expects to live two weeks, it is rational for him to enjoy life this week, as well as next week; and so he chooses to work, each week, just long enough to produce his subsistence requirement (and not run down his stock of corn, which he wants to pass on to his child, who will survive him). An Adam, however, is willing to work exceedingly hard during the first week, knowing that he can reap the benefits of leisure postponed to later periods by hiring the Karl types, an option that Karl does not have. Hence, to say that Karl and Adam have different rates of time preference by virtue of their different environments does not imply that one of them is behaving irrationally—against his self-interest, calculated by his best estimate. Each chooses a pattern of work and consumption based on his life expectancy. In this case, one might have grounds to condemn the exploitation of Karl by Adam, not because of the exploitation as such, but because the cause of their differential life expectancies may be proximately related to an injustice. One cannot, in this example, say that the cause of Karl's low life expectancy is his poverty, because by assumption Karl and Adam each began with the same wealth in corn. But perhaps Karl came from a poor family or a poor country (whereas Adam did not) and his attitudes about life expectancy were formed in that environment.

It might seem silly to discuss these possibilities, but an important justification for capitalism, which Marx attacked, was the theory that capital was the reward for abstinence from consumption: some people abstain from present consumption and provide a benefit to everyone as a consequence, as does Adam in the example. The "surplus labor" that others perform is the premium they pay to those who provide the socially useful function of abstinence from present consumption of leisure or corn, which produces a capital stock for tomorrow. Marx's answer to the abstinence defense of capitalist inequality was that the primitive accumulation of capital did not come about that way. Doubtless that is true. The original capitalists, by and large, both saved and consumed at prodigious rates. Nevertheless, even in modern capitalism, it is quite clear that some people become moderately well-off by virtue of extremely hard but unskilled work, such as small shopkeepers who are willing to work 80 to 90 hours a week. The argument, for example, is made that in England East Indians are willing to set up shops and work those hours; eventually, they become moderately well-off, in consequence of having chosen a path the native English worker is unwilling to take, even though the capital requirements and skills are within his means. East Indian immigrants have created, for the first time, a British dream.

Although one does observe different rates of time preference, it is a mistake to consider those differences to be a consequence of autonomous choices that people have made. Neoclassical economists tend to treat the rate of time preference as an aspect of a person's nature, something that the person should therefore bear the consequences of. But I think this is a myopic view. Attitudes toward saving are shaped by culture, and cultures are formed by the objective conditions that their populations face. If the East Indians work hard and build up small businesses while the native British workers do not, then that outcome is due to the history of the societies in which those populations formerly lived, societies that inculcated them with different values. Their differential success in capitalist enterprise is itself a consequence of past experience with capitalism, which in the one case demoralized the worker and in the other engendered in him a certain degree of ambition. When one sees patterns of behavior that characterize whole populations or classes, one must look for factors of social origin. If there is very little movement out of the working class in Britain, but more in the United States, that difference is due not to an innate enterprising spirit among American workers but to the differences between institutions and cultures in the two countries.

Marxists and left-liberals view rates of time preference as socially determined. Therefore in their view it is not possible to justify exploitation and inequality by appealing to differential rates of time preference, for those differences arose from prior conditions of inequality and oppression. Conservatives generally view the rate of time preference as innate. But even if one grants that the trait is innate, it does not follow that a person should bear the responsibility for that trait. In the 1960s, a number of conservative writers, such as Arthur Jensen[4] and Richard Herrnstein[5], argued that blacks were innately inferior to whites, as measured by IQ tests, and that a high rate of time preference was linked to low intelligence. The evidence for an innate difference in IQs between blacks and whites has now been thoroughly discredited, but in the mid-1980s a new version of the argument surfaced. James Q. Wilson and Richard Herrnstein[6] argue that the consumption of tobacco and alcohol by poor and, particularly, black pregnant women creates brain damage in fetuses and results in a population of black children who lack the capacity to think about tomorrow. In their provocatively titled book, *Crime and Human Nature*, they claim that much inner city crime is explained by this population of black youth with pathologically high rates of time preference. The evidence for this position has been sharply challenged by Leon Kamin,[7] the same psychologist who exposed the concocted data that was used to advance the racist IQ theories of the 1960s.

Thus, ideological positions are fought over in an apparently scientific way. The origin of differential rates of time preference is an important case in point,

4 Jensen, Arthur. How much can we boost IQ and scholastic achievement? *Harvard Educational Review* 33: 1–33, 1969.

5 Herrnstein, Richard. IQ. *Atlantic Monthly,* September: 43–64, 1971.

6 Wilson, James Q., and Richard Herrnstein. *Crime and Human Nature.* New York: Simon and Schuster, 1985.

7 Kamin, Leon J. *The Science and Politics of IQ.* Potomac, Md.: Lawrence Erlbaum Associates, 1974.

because the view that wealth is a return to abstinence and saving has a long history. If people can be shown to "deserve" their rates of time preference, perhaps because a preference for planning and saving is a constituent of a person's personality or character, then an argument will have been established to justify inequality. It is important to recall the structure of the counterargument. First, the initial conditions of differential ownership were established, in all capitalist societies, by processes of theft and brute power. Second, to the extent that people do have different rates of time preference, and succeed differentially in capitalist society on that account, those differences are largely due to the process by which they are formed, namely, as a reaction to conditions of inequality and oppression. It is incorrect to argue that differential rates of time preference are the primal cause of unequal wealths if the genesis of those differences is due to a prior history of inequality. Third, even if there are some genetic or innate differences in rates of time preference, why should people benefit or lose on that account? If having a high rate of time preference is a handicap in a society with minimal social insurance, then should not those with that handicap receive social compensation?

5.2.3 Entrepreneurship

It is often argued in defense of capitalist inequality that profits are a return to entrepreneurial ability. People with this ability see ways of organizing labor and producing commodities that others do not see, and this scarce factor is rewarded with profits. Entrepreneurial ability plays the role in this explanation that a low rate of time preference played in the explanation in Section 5.2.2. Two questions concerning entrepreneurial ability can be raised: Is it a factor that is necessarily scarce, or is it scarce because most people in a capitalist system do not have the opportunities to develop their entrepreneurial abilities? Even if entrepreneurial ability is really scarce, is it appropriate for it to be rewarded as it is, with the accumulation of capital? I cannot answer the first question. With respect to the second, the argument can be made that entrepreneurs will continue to exercise their scarce talents even without the tremendous rewards that accrue to them in a capitalist system, so the capital stock that they (under assumption) accumulate need not be personally accumulated by them in order for their talents to be available to society. Perhaps the salary society would have to pay an entrepreneur is considerably less than he gets in a free enterprise system. By virtue of the private property rights, the entrepreneur who organizes and hires other factors of production is the claimant who gets what is left after wages and other costs are paid. But one can argue that a good part of that residual is a surplus that the entrepreneur neither needs (to perform his productive function) nor is entitled to.

Why might he not be entitled to it? Because his entrepreneurial skill could be considered to be the consequence of environmental or genetic factors from which he does not deserve to benefit. Suppose, to invoke an example already given, he acquired those entrepreneurial skills by virtue of growing up in a family in which he learned them by example. The proletarian had no such luck. The advantage accruing to the entrepreneur over that accruing to the proletarian is then a consequence of an unequal opportunity and is perhaps one a society committed to equality of opportunity should not condone. Granted, the entrepreneur performs a socially beneficial function, but in this case he should be paid only what is required to get him to do so. Indeed, various capitalist societies do take this position to different degrees, because they tax profits and managerial salaries at very different rates. In Japan the managers of big corporations are paid much less than their counterparts in the United States. But apparently they perform their entrepreneurial and organizational functions at least as well. Some argue that managers are not entrepreneurs but hired labor. But many entrepreneurial functions are performed by managers, and the popular justification of high managerial salaries in the United States is based on a belief in the scarcity of entrepreneurial talent.

Suppose that entrepreneurs do not learn their talents but are born with them, or, more realistically, that some people are born with the capacity to acquire entrepreneurial skills and others are not. In this case, people face different opportunities, but of a genetic sort. There may appear to be more reason to allow these natural entrepreneurs to keep the capital they accumulate, if one holds to a principle of *self-ownership,* which claims that a person ought to be entitled to the income that can be earned by the traits coming with his person. This principle can be challenged. First, do not such genetic dispositions constitute unequal opportunities, and what is our attitude toward such inequality? Perhaps the entrepreneur will derive sufficient pleasure from exercising his entrepreneurship, a pleasure unexperienced by the ordinary person, to draw forth his scarce talent. Is it necessarily the case that he should be repaid, as well, with the accumulation of a large capital stock? Even if one endorses self-ownership, it does not obviously require that degree of accumulation. Second, the entrepreneur may be perfectly willing to exercise his organizational talent without the accumulation of capital that attends its exercise under capitalism. In that case, there would be no reason from a social point of view to reward him in this way.

Thus far, I have taken the position that entrepreneurship is a talent. In reality, much of that "talent" may consist in having the right connections, something that is clearly associated with growing up with a certain class background. There may be an element of the feudal lord in the modern entrepreneur: somebody has to be one, but almost anyone could be, and so the positions go to those with family connections. Joseph Schumpeter[8] argued that in early capitalism entrepreneurship was scarce and that capitalism served the function of bringing it to the fore. But now the requisite entrepreneurial skill can be taught to managers of socialist enterprises in business schools. It is available to many, regardless of connections and background.

Neoclassical economists tend to argue, in various ways, that each factor receives its appropriate return. Sometimes, in cruder versions of the neoclassical theory, appropriate return is translated as "just return." But, usually, appropriate return is taken to mean "that return required to make the factor contribute its services." This hardly seems to be the case, however, given the large variation in remuneration to talent that exists in different capitalist societies. The Marxist position is that each factor requires some remuneration to be

[8] Schumpeter, Joseph. *Can Capitalism Survive?* New York: Harper & Row, 1978.

reproduced and for it to be offered for productive service. What is left over after the payment of these necessary remunerations is an economic surplus, and there is considerable leeway in the manner in which society may distribute this surplus. In a laissez-faire system, there is some bargaining over the surplus (between workers and capitalists, for example), but there is no guarantee that the agreement reached is just or that it reflects a socially necessary pattern of remuneration. Thus, one need not deny the existence of a scarce talent called entrepreneurship to deny the justice of the vast inequalities that may be attributable to it in a capitalist system. Moreover, it is incorrect to assume that entrepreneurship is a resource that would only be forthcoming in a private property system. Even without the remuneration to entrepreneurship available in a capitalist system, there would in all likelihood be many people who would learn and would like to exercise the entrepreneurial skill that society needs.

5.2.4 Risk Propensity
The third category of scarce and valuable attributes that capitalism rightly (it is said) remunerates with profits is the willingness to take risks. This factor, again, is not captured in the models presented thus far. In reality investment is a risky business. Suppose there are two kinds of people: those willing to take risks and those not willing to take risks. Among the risk takers, many go bankrupt (and perhaps become proletarians or people of modest income) and some become capitalists. Proletarians are those who are not willing to take risks or those who have taken them and failed. Their surplus labor, accruing to the capitalists as profits, is the insurance premium they pay to capitalists to take risks for them. The worker is guaranteed his steady wage and sleeps well at night, paying the capitalist to gamble for him.

I find this story extremely implausible. I believe that many workers would like to have the opportunity to become capitalists; they would love to take those risks. But they cannot, either because of lack of access to capital markets or because of lack of some aspect of entrepreneurial ability (which might include having the right connections). Second, it cannot be seriously maintained that a worker's life involves less risk than a capitalist's. Workers face the risk of occupational disease, unemployment, and an impoverished retirement, which capitalists and managers do not face. Failing as a capitalist does not usually mean becoming destitute. I do not know of any sociological studies that verify my belief, but I think that the "American dream" encourages most young American white workers to try to escape from the working class, in one way or another, by taking various kinds of financial risks. If they fail, it is not for lack of trying but for lack of something else, most likely access to capital of a sufficient amount to escape the perils of small business.

5.2.5 Luck
Some argue[9] that luck is a legitimate means of acquiring assets and that this factor could justify an initial distribution of capital that is highly unequal. Here I am not referring to luck that is the consequence of having taken a gamble: that

---

[9] Nozick, for example, in *Anarchy, State, and Utopia.*

would be covered under risk propensity. The kind of luck I am referring to is that which is not the outcome of choice under uncertainty on the part of the agent but is completely unanticipated; it is sometimes called brute luck. Perhaps the most important kind of luck by which people may acquire differential ownership of capital stock is inheritance.

Inheritance can be looked at from the point of view of the giver or the receiver. If one agrees that the giver has property rights in the wealth that she has legitimately earned and saved by virtue of her labor, skills, rate of time preference, and propensity toward risk, then it would seem that she should be entitled to dispose of that wealth as she pleases, and that would include giving it away to whatever heir she chooses. But from the point of view of the next generation—the group of potential receivers—inheritance constitutes perhaps the grossest of unequal opportunities. Does not everyone in the next generation have the right to begin with the same opportunities, including those determined by access to capital? This, after all, is a particularly easy kind of opportunity to equalize, unlike the differential opportunities that exist naturally by virtue of the fact that people grow up in different families.

Rights must be circumscribed in many ways, because a complete set of rights one might like to specify cannot simultaneously be satisfied. It seems to me that the right of the generation of givers must be constrained by the unequal opportunities it creates for the receivers. From an ethical viewpoint, I do not think it is so difficult to argue against the right to inheritance. But there is an efficiency issue that must be faced in advocating stiff inheritance taxes, and it is of the same nature as the efficiency question discussed under entrepreneurship. If inheritance of physical assets is forbidden, will that restriction act as a disincentive for people to save? The answer to this question is unclear; we do not have enough experience with the enforcement of stiff inheritance taxes in capitalist countries to know. Alfred Nobel created the trust that finances the prizes bearing his name instead of giving his accumulated wealth to his children, for he felt that they should earn it the hard way, as he did. One might allow an estate to escape taxes if the donor gave it for some specific purpose, such as building a hospital, or buying a piece of land for a park, or financing an opera company, each of which could bear her name. Means by which her contribution to society would be publicly recognized could easily be created. These alternatives to passing wealth down to individuals might both be socially more useful than the individual alternative and create as much incentive to save as the present inheritance laws do. The efficiency argument for individualized inheritance is not convincing; such a claim would have to be established empirically.

In a recent paper, D. W. Haslett[10] argues for purifying capitalism, a system that he otherwise likes, by abolishing inheritance. He regards inheritance as an institution inconsistent with the equality of opportunity that capitalism champions. Haslett, like Alfred Nobel, believes that virtuous incentive effects would be generated by abolishing inheritance. He offers the following analogy. If two runners start a race with one far behind the other, will the second runner

[10] Haslett, D. W. Is inheritance justified? *Philosophy and Public Affairs* 15: 122–155, 1986.

try hard to win? Indeed, how fast will the leader run? Contrast this with how hard each of them will run if they begin the race together. The analogy implies that everyone will work harder if the members of each generation begin with the same level of wealth, assuming people have the usual desires to excel materialistically.

It is worth noting the degree to which inheritance is responsible for differential wealth in the United States. The wealthiest 1 to 2% of American families own 20 to 30% of the net family wealth in the United States. The wealthiest 20% own 80% of the wealth, whereas the poorest 20% own just 0.2% of the wealth. Inequality of wealth is far more severe than inequality of income: the top 20% of families in the income distribution earned 57% of the total family income in the mid-1970s. In a study published in 1978, John Brittain[11] showed that 67% of the largest fortunes in the United States are derived from inheritance, not present earnings. Even while nominal inheritance taxes were fairly high (before 1981, when the Reagan administration started reducing them), the actual taxes paid on large estates were incredibly small. The average tax rate on estates was 0.2%, and on estates of over $500,000 it was a mere 0.8%. Thus it is said that the inheritance tax is a voluntary one, or a tax on poor planning. Given these facts about the origins of current American wealth, it is hard to countenance the conservative position that the position of people in American society is due to their hard or skillful work. The family into which a person is born is much more important in determining her fortune than are any voluntary choices she makes.

On grounds of equal opportunity, I think there is a strong argument against luck as a legitimate means for acquiring material assets. One might better argue that those assets which materialize because of luck belong to everyone, not to the person on whom they just happen to fall. Why should the point in time at which opportunities are declared to be equal be before Lady Luck has thrown the dice, and not after? After all, by definition, no one has done anything to earn the fruits of luck, and the motivation for equality of opportunity is that each is entitled to what he earns from a starting point of equality. (This statement applies to luck that is not the outcome of a calculated gamble, which, as I said, is a case excluded here but included under considerations of the rights to earn differentially from differential risk propensities.)

Whether the argument of the preceding paragraph also makes a case against allowing individuals to reap the fruits of genetic luck is a more difficult question. Do I have the moral right to the income stream that my inborn talent enables me to earn?

5.3 Justification of Unequal Distribution

A normative justification for measuring exploitation lies in the meaning of the colloquial definition of exploitation: "to take unfair advantage of." Because

---

[11] Brittain, John. *Inheritance and the Inequality of National Wealth*. Washington, D.C.: Brookings Institution, 1978.

exploitation is the consequence of inequality in the initial distribution of physical assets, it would seem that its existence indicates unfairness only if the initial unequal distribution of assets is unfair. Marxists argue that all capitalist societies established the take-off point of unequal capital ownership by processes akin to robbery, slavery, and plunder. If this argument is accepted, the case for unfairness is then clearly made, the unfair nature of the exploitative allocation being inherited, as it were, from the initial unjust distribution. But ideologues of capitalism have argued that the initial distribution of unequal ownership could have arisen (even if actually it did not) in morally respectable ways: as a result of differences in the rates of time preference, or in risk propensities, or in entrepreneurial abilities and skills, or as a result of unanticipated luck. Such a clean beginning would establish the cogency of capitalism as a system against which there is, so they say, no principled ethical argument—although there may be specific arguments against specific historical instances of capitalism. Capitalist ideologues argue from two fronts: that it is necessary to recognize and reward these differential attributes of people differentially in order for the good attributes to emerge and be available for society, and that the holders of these attributes deserve the fruits that thereby accrue to them in a private ownership system. These arguments are not consistent either with economic theory or with the history of developed capitalism, a history replete with the establishment of fortunes by wars, or through the exercise of monopoly power, or as the consequence of market imperfections.

42.

Egalitarianism with Changed Motivation

GERALD COHEN

Marx was no friend of the market, even in its socialist form. The communist society which he envisaged proclaimed the slogan "From each according to his ability, to each according to his needs." One might ask what it means for each to give according to his ability, and to get according to his needs. But, for our purposes, the unambiguous message of the communist slogan is that what you get is *not* a function of what you give, that contribution and reward are entirely separate matters. You do not get more because you produce more, and you do not get less because you are not good at producing. Accordingly, the ideal flourished in the communist slogan represents a complete rejection of the logic of the market.

Marx also described a second best to full communism, which he called "the first phase of communist society,"[1] a phase transitional to the final one in which the just-discussed principle of distribution is sovereign. Because of later Marxist verbal usage, the two phases are more familiarly known under the titles "socialism" and "communism." And although Marxist socialism is not a market socialism, Marx's criticism of that transitional form of society also bears against market socialism.

Marxist socialism, the lower phase of communism, is a non-market society in which remuneration is supposed to reward labor contribution. That is the import of its ruling slogan, which says: To each according to his contribution. If, as David Miller thinks, contribution establishes desert and rewarding desert suffices for justice, then Marxist socialism would possess the virtue that it rewards desert and is, therefore, just: perhaps, indeed, more just than any market socialism could be.

That last speculation is, however, a pretty idle one, since measuring contribution in a non-market society requires questionable assignments of product to heterogenous labors, and to labors of different skill levels; and while a market society assigns salaries to labor in an automatic process free of the application of contestable criteria, it is impossible to treat those salaries as measures of *contribution,* influenced as they are by vagaries of bargaining power and other accidental market circumstances. It is, accordingly, difficult to compare the relative merits of the two forms of socialism as devices for rewarding producers according to their contribution.

But let us here set aside the question of whether Marx was right to prefer a non-market socialism to a market one, and also the problem of how labor contributions are to be measured. Of greater present relevance is that Marx's

---

[1] Karl Marx, *Critique of the Gotha Programme in Marx/Engels: Selected Works in One Volume* (London: 1968) p. 324.

strictures against the principle of reward to contribution expose the anti-socialist (because bourgeois) character of market socialism's reward structure. While pointing out that first-stage communism abolishes capitalist exploitation, since differential access to means of production is gone, and no one now consumes more labor value than he produces, Marx criticized the principle of reward for contribution because of the (unjust)[2] inequality that it generates. For Marx, it is indeed a recommendation of low-stage communism that the bourgeois principle of reward for contribution is in this society not just invoked as ideological rationalization but actually instituted, so that "principle and practice are no longer at loggerheads." But he did not doubt that reward for contribution *is* a bourgeois principle, one which treats a person's talents "as a natural privilege."[3] Reward for contribution honours the principle of self-ownership. Nothing is more bourgeois than that principle—it is, indeed, *the* principle of the bourgeois revolution—and the Gotha Critique lesson for market socialism is that, while market socialism may remove the income injustice caused by differential ownership of capital, it preserves the income injustice caused by differential ownership of endowments of personal capacity.

Before we settle for market socialism, let us recall why socialists in the past rejected the market. Some of their reasons were better than others, and here I shall review what I take to be the four principal criticisms of the market in the socialist tradition, starting with two that I consider misplaced, and ending with two that I consider sound. The market was judged (1) inefficient, (2) anarchic, (3) unjust in its results, and (4) mean in its motivational presuppositions.

(1) To say that the market is inefficient is to criticize it in its allocative as opposed to in its distributive function, where allocation concerns the assignment of resources to different productive uses (so much steel to housing and so much to automobiles and so many engineers to each and so on) and distribution concerns the assignment of income to persons. Manifestly, allocation and distribution are in intimate causal relationship, but the bottom line of this first criticism relates to allocation alone: it is that the market is wasteful, variously over- and under-productive, and here the question of who in particular suffers from that waste is set to one side. And the reason for the wastefulness, so the criticism goes, is that a market economy is unplanned.

We now know that the traditional socialist view about the market's lack of planning was misconceived. It failed to acknowledge how remarkably well the unplanned market organizes information, and, indeed, how difficult it is for a planning center to possess itself of the information about preferences and production possibilities dispersed through the market in a non-planning system. Even if the planner's computer could do wonders with that information, there would remain the problem that there are systematic obstacles to gathering it: to that extent, Von Mises and Hayek were right. And the traditional socialist

---

[2] The adjective has to go in parentheses because Marx disparaged the notion of justice, and, so I have claimed, did not realize that he believed passionately in it: see my review of Allen Wood's *Karl Marx*, in *Mind*, 92, 1983.

[3] *The Critique of the Gotha Programme*, p. 324.

critique also failed to appreciate the degree to which it would prove possible to correct for market inefficiencies through an external regulation which falls far short of comprehensive planning.

(2) There was, however, in the traditional socialist objection to the market, a separate emphasis that the market's generation of massive unplanned outcomes are deplorable as such (that is, apart from the particular disbenefits and injustices of those outcomes). They are deplorable *just* because they are unplanned, since the fact that they are not planned means that society is not in control of its own destiny. Marx and Engels did not favor planning solely because of the particular advantageous economic consequences that they thought it would have, but also because of the significance of planning as a realization of the idea, derived no doubt from the Hegelian legacy under which they labored, of humanity rising to consciousness of and control over itself. The advent of the planned society was seen as "the ascent of man from the kingdom of necessity to the kingdom of freedom . . . Man, at last the master of his own form of social organization, becomes at the same time the lord over Nature, his own master—free." [4]

In my view, that idea is entirely misplaced. Individual self-direction, a person's determining the course of his own life, may have value *per se,* but collective self-direction does not.[5]

· · ·

There is harm to no one in the *mere* fact that social purpose is lacking, although society-wide decision-making is of course required for instrumental reasons, such as, sometimes, to promote individual freedom, and in order to suppress or control the evil aspects of the market, two of which relate to two traditional criticisms of the market which seem to me to be unanswerable.

Those criticisms are (3) that the market distributes in unjustly unequal amounts, about which enough has been said above, and (4) that it motivates productive contribution not on the basis of commitment to one's fellow human beings, but on the basis of impersonal cash reward. The immediate motive to productive activity in a market society is typically[6] some mixture of greed and fear, in proportions that vary with the details of a person's market position and personal character. In greed, other people are seen as possible sources of enrichment, and in fear they are seen as threats. These are horrible ways of seeing other people, however much we have become habituated and inured to them, as a result of centuries of capitalist development.

---

[4] Friedrich Engels, *Socialism: Utopian and Scientific* (London) 1892, pp. 82, 86.

[5] Except in the here totally irrelevant sense of non-subjection to another collective. Not wanting your society's course to be determined from without does not imply wanting it to be deliberately determined from within.

[6] People can operate under a sense of service even in a market society, but in so far as they do so, what makes the market work is not what makes them work. Their discipline is not market discipline.

In (at least one kind of) non-market motivation I produce because I desire to serve my fellow human beings while being served by them. Such motivation embodies an expectation of reciprocation, but it nevertheless differs critically from market motivation. The marketeer is willing to serve, but only in order to be served. He does not desire the conjunction (serve-and-be-served) as such, for he would not serve if doing so were not a means to get service. The difference is expressed in the lack of fine tuning that attends non-market motivation. Contrast taking turns in a loose way with respect to who buys the drinks with keeping a record of who has paid what for them. In the former procedure, we distance ourselves from the rules of the market.

Now, the history of the twentieth century encourages the thought that the easiest way to generate productivity in a modern society is by nourishing the motives of greed and fear, in a hierarchy of unequal income. But that does not make them attractive motives. Who would propose running a society on such motives, and thereby promoting the psychology to which they belong, if they were not known to be effective, did they not have the instrumental value which is the only value that they have? In the famous statement in which Adam Smith justified market relations, he pointed out that we place our faith not in the butcher's generosity but on his self-interest when we rely on him to provision us. Smith thereby propounded a wholly extrinsic justification of market motivation, in face of what he acknowledged to be its unattractive intrinsic character. Traditional socialists have often ignored Smith's point, in a moralistic condemnation of market motivation which fails to address its extrinsic justification. Certain contemporary over-enthusiastic market socialists tend, contrariwise, to forget that the market is intrinsically repugnant, because they are blinded by their belated discovery of the market's extrinsic value. The genius of the market is that it recruits shabby motives to desirable ends, and, in a balanced view, both sides of that proposition must be kept in focus.

Both self-interest and generosity exist in everyone. We know how to make an economic system work on the basis of self-interest. We do not know how to make it work on the basis of generosity. But that does not mean that we should forget generosity: we should still confine the sway of self-interest as much as we can. We do that, for example, when we tax, redistributively, the unequalizing results of market activity. The extent to which we can do that without defeating our aim (of making the badly off better off) varies inversely with the extent to which self-interest has been allowed to triumph in private and public consciousness. (To the extent that it has triumphed, heavily progressive taxation drives high earners abroad, or causes them to decide to reduce their labor input, or induces in them a morose attitude which makes their previous input hard or impossible to sustain.)

The fact that the first great experiment in running a modern economy without relying on avarice and anxiety has failed, disastrously, is not a good reason for giving up the attempt, forever. Philosophers least of all should join the contemporary choruses of dirge and hosanna whose common refrain is that the socialist project is over. I am sure that it has a long way to go yet, and it is part of the mission of philosophy to explore unanticipated possibilities.

What is true and, as the interest in market socialism shows, widely appreciated, is that different ways forward must now be tried. And in the light of the
misallocating propensity of comprehensive planning on the one hand and of the
injustice of market results and the moral shabbiness of market motivation on
the other, it is natural to ask whether it might be possible to preserve the allocative function of the market, to continue to get the benefits it provides of
information generation and processing, while extinguishing its normal motivational presuppositions and distributive consequences.

EQUALITY

43.
Multidimensional Equality

MICHAEL WALZER

In the matter of distributive justice, history displays a great variety of arrangements and ideologies. But the first impulse of the philosopher is to resist the displays of history, the world of appearances, and to search for some underlying unity: a short list of basic goods, quickly abstracted to a single good; a single distributive criterion or an interconnected set; and the philosopher himself standing, symbolically at least, at a single decision point. I shall argue that to search for unity is to misunderstand the subject matter of distributive justice. Nevertheless, in some sense the philosophical impulse is unavoidable. Even if we choose pluralism, as I shall do, that choice still requires a coherent defense. There must be principles that justify the choice and set limits to it, for pluralism does not require us to endorse every proposed distributive criteria or to accept every would-be agent. Conceivably, there is a single principle and a single legitimate kind of pluralism. But this would still be a pluralism that encompassed a wide range of distributions. By contrast, the deepest assumption of most of the philosophers who have written about justice, from Plato onward, is that there is one, and only one, distributive system that philosophy can rightly encompass.

Today this system is commonly described as the one that ideally rational men and women would choose if they were forced to choose impartially, knowing nothing of their own situation, barred from making particularist claims, confronting an abstract set of goods.[1] If these constraints on knowing and claiming are suitably shaped, and if the goods are suitably defined, it is probably true that a singular conclusion can be produced. Rational men and women, constrained this way or that, will choose one, and only one, distributive system. But the force of that singular conclusion is not easy to measure. It is surely doubtful that those same men and women, if they were transformed into ordinary people, with a firm sense of their own identity, with their own goods in their hands, caught up in everyday troubles, would reiterate their hypothetical choice or even recognize it as their own. The problem is not, most importantly, with the particularism of interest, which philosophers have always assumed they could safely—that is, uncontroversially—set aside. Ordinary people can do that too, for the sake, say, of the public interest. The greater problem is with the particularism of history, culture, and membership. Even if they are committed to impartiality, the question most likely to arise in the minds of the members of a political community is not, What would rational individuals choose under universalizing conditions of such-and-such a sort? But rather, What

---

[1] See John Rawls, *A Theory of Justice* (Cambridge, Mass., 1971); Jürgen Habermas, *Legitimation Crisis,* trans. Thomas McCarthy (Boston, 1975), esp. p. 113; Bruce Ackerman, *Social Justice in the Liberal State* (New Haven, 1980).

would individuals like us choose, who are situated as we are, who share a culture and are determined to go on sharing it? And this is a question that is readily transformed into, What choices have we already made in the course of our common life? What understandings do we (really) share?

Justice is a human construction, and it is doubtful that it can be made in only one way. At any rate, I shall begin by doubting, and more than doubting, this standard philosophical assumption. The questions posed by the theory of distributive justice admit of a range of answers, and there is room within the range for cultural diversity and political choice. It's not only a matter of implementing some singular principle or set of principles in different historical settings. No one would deny that there is a range of morally permissible implementations. I want to argue for more than this: that the principles of justice are themselves pluralistic in form; that different social goods ought to be distributed for different reasons, in accordance with different procedures, by different agents; and that all these differences derive from different understandings of the social goods themselves—the inevitable product of historical and cultural particularism.

A THEORY OF GOODS

Theories of distributive justice focus on a social process commonly described as if it had this form:

People distribute goods to (other) people.

Here, "distribute" means give, allocate, exchange, and so on, and the focus is on the individuals who stand at either end of these actions: not on producers and consumers, but on distributive agents and recipients of goods. We are as always interested in ourselves, but, in this case, in a special and limited version of ourselves, as people who give and take. What is our nature? What are our rights? What do we need, want, deserve? What are we entitled to? What would we accept under ideal conditions? Answers to these questions are turned into distributive principles, which are supposed to control the movement of goods. The goods, defined by abstraction, are taken to be movable in any direction.

But this is too simple an understanding of what actually happens, and it forces us too quickly to make large assertions about human nature and moral agency—assertions unlikely, ever, to command general agreement. I want to propose a more precise and complex description of the central process:

People conceive and create goods, which they then distribute among themselves.

Here, the conception and creation precede and control the distribution. Goods don't just appear in the hands of distributive agents who do with them as they like or give them out in accordance with some general principle.[2] Rather, goods

---

[2] Robert Nozick makes a similar argument in *Anarchy, State, and Utopia* (New York, 1974), pp. 149–50, but with radically individualistic conclusions that seem to me to miss the social character of production.

with their meanings—because of their meanings—are the crucial medium of social relations; they come into people's minds before they come into their hands; distributions are patterned in accordance with shared conceptions of what the goods are and what they are for. Distributive agents are constrained by the goods they hold; one might almost say that goods distribute themselves among people.

> Things are in the saddle
> And ride mankind.[3]

But these are always particular things and particular groups of men and women. And, of course, we make the things—even the saddle. I don't want to deny the importance of human agency, only to shift our attention from distribution itself to conception and creation: the naming of the goods, and the giving of meaning, and the collective making. What we need to explain and limit the pluralism of distributive possibilities is a theory of goods. For our immediate purposes, that theory can be summed up in six propositions.

1. All the goods with which distributive justice is concerned are social goods. They are not and they cannot be idiosyncratically valued. I am not sure that there are any other kinds of goods; I mean to leave the question open. Some domestic objects are cherished for private and sentimental reasons, but only in cultures where sentiment regularly attaches to such objects. A beautiful sunset, the smell of new-mown hay, the excitement of an urban vista: these perhaps are privately valued goods, though they are also, and more obviously, the objects of cultural assessment. Even new inventions are not valued in accordance with the ideas of their inventors; they are subject to a wider process of conception and creation. God's goods, to be sure, are exempt from this rule—as in the first chapter of Genesis: "and God saw every thing that He had made, and, behold, it was very good" (1:31). That evaluation doesn't require the agreement of mankind (who might be doubtful), or of a majority of men and women, or of any group of men and women meeting under ideal conditions (though Adam and Eve in Eden would probably endorse it). But I can't think of any other exemptions. Goods in the world have shared meanings because conception and creation are social processes. For the same reason, goods have different meanings in different societies. The same "thing" is valued for different reasons, or it is valued here and disvalued there. John Stuart Mill once complained that "people like in crowds," but I know of no other way to like or to dislike social goods.[4] A solitary person could hardly understand the meaning of the goods or figure out the reasons for taking them as likable or dislikable. Once people like in crowds, it becomes possible for individuals to break away, pointing to latent or subversive meanings, aiming at alternative values—including the values, for

---

[3] Ralph Waldo Emerson, "Ode," in *The Complete Essays and Other Writings*, ed. Brooks Atkinson (New York, 1940), p. 770.

[4] John Stuart Mill, *On Liberty*, in *The Philosophy of John Stuart Mill*, ed. Marshall Cohen (New York, 1961), p. 255. For an anthropological account of liking and not liking social goods, see Mary Douglas and Baron Isherwood, *The World of Goods* (New York, 1979).

example, of notoriety and eccentricity. An easy eccentricity has sometimes been one of the privileges of the aristocracy: it is a social good like any other.

2. Men and women take on concrete identities because of the way they conceive and create, and then possess and employ social goods. "The line between what is me and mine," wrote William James, "is very hard to draw." [5] Distributions cannot be understood as the acts of men and women who do not yet have particular goods in their minds or in their hands. In fact, people already stand in a relation to a set of goods; they have a history of transactions, not only with one another but also with the moral and material world in which they live. Without such a history, which begins at birth, they wouldn't be men and women in any recognizable sense, and they wouldn't have the first notion of how to go about the business of giving, allocating, and exchanging goods.

3. There is no single set of primary or basic goods conceivable across all moral and material worlds—or, any such set would have to be conceived in terms so abstract that they would be of little use in thinking about particular distributions. Even the range of necessities, if we take into account moral as well as physical necessities, is very wide, and the rank orderings are very different. A single necessary good, and one that is always necessary—food, for example—carries different meanings in different places. Bread is the staff of life, the body of Christ, the symbol of the Sabbath, the means of hospitality, and so on. Conceivably, there is a limited sense in which the first of these is primary, so that if there were twenty people in the world and just enough bread to feed the twenty, the primacy of bread-as-staff-of-life would yield a sufficient distributive principle. But that is the only circumstance in which it would do so; and even there, we can't be sure. If the religious uses of bread were to conflict with its nutritional uses—if the gods demanded that bread be baked and burned rather than eaten—it is by no means clear which use would be primary. How, then, is bread to be incorporated into the universal list? The question is even harder to answer, the conventional answers less plausible, as we pass from necessities to opportunities, powers, reputations, and so on. These can be incorporated only if they are abstracted from every particular meaning—hence, for all practical purposes, rendered meaningless.

4. But it is the meaning of goods that determines their movement. Distributive criteria and arrangements are intrinsic not to the good-in-itself but to the social good. If we understand what it is, what it means to those for whom it is a good, we understand how, by whom, and for what reasons it ought to be distributed. All distributions are just or unjust relative to the social meanings of the goods at stake. This is in obvious ways a principle of legitimation, but it is also a critical principle. When medieval Christians, for example, condemned the sin of simony, they were claiming that the meaning of a particular social good, ecclesiastical office, excluded its sale and purchase. Given the Christian understanding of office, it followed—I am inclined to say, it necessarily followed—that office holders should be chosen for their knowledge and piety and

---

[5] William James, quoted in C. R. Snyder and Howard Fromkin, *Uniqueness: The Human Pursuit of Difference* (New York, 1980), p. 108.

not for their wealth. There are presumably things that money can buy, but not this thing. Similarly, the words *prostitution* and *bribery,* like *simony,* describe the sale and purchase of goods that, given certain understandings of their meanings, ought never to be sold or purchased.

5. Social meanings are historical in character; and so distributions, and just and unjust distributions, change over time. To be sure, certain key goods have what we might think of as characteristic normative structures, reiterated across the lines (but not all the lines) of time and space. It is because of this reiteration that the British philosopher Bernard Williams is able to argue that goods should always be distributed for "relevant reasons"—where relevance seems to connect to essential rather than to social meanings.[6] The idea that offices, for example, should go to qualified candidates—though not the only idea that has been held about offices—is plainly visible in very different societies where simony and nepotism, under different names, have similarly been thought sinful or unjust. (But there has been a wide divergence of views about what sorts of position and place are properly called "offices.") Again, punishment has been widely understood as a negative good that ought to go to people who are judged to deserve it on the basis of a verdict, not of a political decision. (But what constitutes a verdict? Who is to deliver it? How, in short, is justice to be done to accused men and women? About these questions there has been significant disagreement.) These examples invite empirical investigation. There is no merely intuitive or speculative procedure for seizing upon relevant reasons.

6. When meanings are distinct, distributions must be autonomous. Every social good or set of goods constitutes, as it were, a distributive sphere within which only certain criteria and arrangements are appropriate. Money is inappropriate in the sphere of ecclesiastical office; it is an intrusion from another sphere. And piety should make for no advantage in the marketplace, as the marketplace has commonly been understood. Whatever can rightly be sold ought to be sold to pious men and women and also to profane, heretical, and sinful men and women (else no one would do much business). The market is open to all comers; the church is not. In no society, of course, are social meanings entirely distinct. What happens in one distributive sphere affects what happens in the others; we can look, at most, for relative autonomy. But relative autonomy, like social meaning, is a critical principle—indeed, as I shall be arguing throughout this book, a radical principle. It is radical even though it doesn't point to a single standard against which all distributions are to be measured. There is no single standard. But there are standards (roughly knowable even when they are also controversial) for every social good and every distributive sphere in every particular society; and these standards are often violated, the goods usurped, the spheres invaded, by powerful men and women.

[6] Bernard Williams, *Problems of the Self: Philosophical Papers, 1956–1972* (Cambridge, England, 1973), pp. 230–49 ("The Idea of Equality"). This essay is one of the starting points of my own thinking about distributive justice. See also the critique of Williams's argument (and of an earlier essay of my own) in Amy Gutmann, *Liberal Equality* (Cambridge, England, 1980), chap. 4.

DOMINANCE AND MONOPOLY

In fact, the violations are systematic. Autonomy is a matter of social meaning and shared values, but it is more likely to make for occasional reformation and rebellion than for everyday enforcement. For all the complexity of their distributive arrangements, most societies are organized on what we might think of as a social version of the gold standard: one good or one set of goods is dominant and determinative of value in all the spheres of distribution. And that good or set of goods is commonly monopolized, its value upheld by the strength and cohesion of its owners. I call a good dominant if the individuals who have it, because they have it, can command a wide range of other goods. It is monopolized whenever a single man or woman, a monarch in the world of value—or a group of men and women, oligarchs—successfully hold it against all rivals. Dominance describes a way of using social goods that isn't limited by their intrinsic meanings or that shapes those meanings in its own image. Monopoly describes a way of owning or controlling social goods in order to exploit their dominance. When goods are scarce and widely needed, like water in the desert, monopoly itself will make them dominant. Mostly, however, dominance is a more elaborate social creation, the work of many hands, mixing reality and symbol. Physical strength, familial reputation, religious or political office, landed wealth, capital, technical knowledge: each of these, in different historical periods, has been dominant; and each of them has been monopolized by some group of men and women. And then all good things come to those who have the one best thing. Possess that one, and the others come in train. Or, to change the metaphor, a dominant good is converted into another good, into many others, in accordance with what often appears to be a natural process but is in fact magical, a kind of social alchemy.

No social good ever entirely dominates the range of goods; no monopoly is ever perfect. I mean to describe tendencies only, but crucial tendencies. For we can characterize whole societies in terms of the patterns of conversion that are established within them. Some characterizations are simple: in a capitalist society, capital is dominant and readily converted into prestige and power; in a technocracy, technical knowledge plays the same part. But it isn't difficult to imagine, or to find, more complex social arrangements. Indeed, capitalism and technocracy are more complex than their names imply, even if the names do convey real information about the most important forms of sharing, dividing, and exchanging. Monopolistic control of a dominant good makes a ruling class, whose members stand atop the distributive system—much as philosophers, claiming to have the wisdom they love, might like to do. But since dominance is always incomplete and monopoly imperfect, the rule of every ruling class is unstable. It is continually challenged by other groups in the name of alternative patterns of conversion.

Distribution is what social conflict is all about. Marx's heavy emphasis on productive processes should not conceal from us the simple truth that the struggle for control of the means of production is a distributive struggle. Land and capital are at stake, and these are goods that can be shared, divided, exchanged, and endlessly converted. But land and capital are not the only dominant goods; it is possible (it has historically been possible) to come to them by way of other goods—military or political power, religious office and charisma, and so on. History reveals no single dominant good and no naturally dominant good, but only different kinds of magic and competing bands of magicians.

The claim to monopolize a dominant good—when worked up for public purposes—constitutes an ideology. Its standard form is to connect legitimate possession with some set of personal qualities through the medium of a philosophical principle. So aristocracy, or the rule of the best, is the principle of those who lay claim to breeding and intelligence: they are commonly the monopolists of landed wealth and familial reputation. Divine supremacy is the principle of those who claim to know the word of God: they are the monopolists of grace and office. Meritocracy, or the career open to talents, is the principle of those who claim to be talented: they are most often the monopolists of education. Free exchange is the principle of those who are ready, or who tell us they are ready, to put their money at risk: they are the monopolists of movable wealth. These groups—and others, too, similarly marked off by their principles and possessions—compete with one another, struggling for supremacy. One group wins, and then a different one; or coalitions are worked out, and supremacy is uneasily shared. There is no final victory, nor should there be. But that is not to say that the claims of the different groups are necessarily wrong, or that the principles they invoke are of no value as distributive criteria; the principles are often exactly right within the limits of a particular sphere. Ideologies are readily corrupted, but their corruption is not the most interesting thing about them.

It is in the study of these struggles that I have sought the guiding thread of my own argument. The struggles have, I think, a paradigmatic form. Some group of men and women—class, caste, strata, estate, alliance, or social formation—comes to enjoy a monopoly or a near monopoly of some dominant good; or, a coalition of groups comes to enjoy, and so on. This dominant good is more or less systematically converted into all sorts of other things—opportunities, powers, and reputations. So wealth is seized by the strong, honor by the wellborn, office by the well educated. Perhaps the ideology that justifies the seizure is widely believed to be true. But resentment and resistance are (almost) as pervasive as belief. There are always some people, and after a time there are a great many, who think the seizure is not justice but usurpation. The ruling group does not possess, or does not uniquely possess, the qualities it claims; the conversion process violates the common understanding of the goods at stake. Social conflict is intermittent, or it is endemic; at some point, counterclaims are put forward. Though these are of many different sorts, three general sorts are especially important:

1. The claim that the dominant good, whatever it is, should be redistributed so that it can be equally or at least more widely shared: this amounts to saying that monopoly is unjust.
2. The claim that the way should be opened for the autonomous distribution of all social goods: this amounts to saying that dominance is unjust.

3. The claim that some new good, monopolized by some new group, should replace the currently dominant good: this amounts to saying that the existing pattern of dominance and monopoly is unjust.

The third claim is, in Marx's view, the model of every revolutionary ideology—except, perhaps, the proletarian or last ideology. Thus, the French Revolution in Marxist theory: the dominance of noble birth and blood and of feudal landholding is ended, and bourgeois wealth is established in its stead. The original situation is reproduced with different subjects and objects (this is never unimportant), and then the class war is immediately renewed. It is not my purpose here to endorse or to criticize Marx's view. I suspect, in fact, that there is something of all three claims in every revolutionary ideology, but that, too, is not a position that I shall try to defend here. Whatever its sociological significance, the third claim is not philosophically interesting—unless one believes that there is a naturally dominant good, such that its possessors could legitimately claim to rule the rest of us. In a sense, Marx believed exactly that. The means of production is the dominant good throughout history, and Marxism is a historicist doctrine insofar as it suggests that whoever controls the prevailing means legitimately rules.[7] After the communist revolution, we shall all control the means of production: at that point, the third claim collapses into the first. Meanwhile, Marx's model is a program for ongoing distributive struggle. It will matter, of course, who wins at this or that moment, but we won't know why or how it matters if we attend only to the successive assertions of dominance and monopoly.

SIMPLE EQUALITY

It is with the first two claims that I shall be concerned, and ultimately with the second alone, for that one seems to me to capture best the plurality of social meanings and the real complexity of distributive systems. But the first is the more common among philosophers; it matches their own search for unity and singularity; and I shall need to explain its difficulties at some length.

Men and women who make the first claim challenge the monopoly but not the dominance of a particular social good. This is also a challenge to monopoly in general; for if wealth, for example, is dominant and widely shared, no other good can possibly be monopolized. Imagine a society in which everything is up for sale and every citizen has as much money as every other. I shall call this the "regime of simple equality." Equality is multiplied through the conversion process, until it extends across the full range of social goods. The regime of simple equality won't last for long, because the further progress of conversion, free exchange in the market, is certain to bring inequalities in its train. If one wanted to sustain simple equality over time, one would require a

---

[7] See Alan W. Wood, "The Marxian Critique of Justice," *Philosophy and Public Affairs* 1 (1972): 244–82.

"monetary law" like the agrarian laws of ancient times or the Hebrew sabbatical, providing for a periodic return to the original condition. Only a centralized and activist state would be strong enough to force such a return; and it isn't clear that state officials would actually be able or willing to do that, if money were the dominant good. In any case, the original condition is unstable in another way. It's not only that monopoly will reappear, but also that dominance will disappear.

In practice, breaking the monopoly of money neutralizes its dominance. Other goods come into play, and inequality takes on new forms. Consider again the regime of simple equality. Everything is up for sale, and everyone has the same amount of money. So everyone has, say, an equal ability to buy an education for his children. Some do that, and others don't. It turns out to be a good investment: other social goods are, increasingly, offered for sale only to people with educational certificates. Soon everyone invests in education; or, more likely, the purchase is universalized through the tax system. But then the school is turned into a competitive world within which money is no longer dominant. Natural talent or family upbringing or skill in writing examinations is dominant instead, and educational success and certification are monopolized by some new group. Let's call them (what they call themselves) the "group of the talented." Eventually the members of this group claim that the good they control should be dominant outside the school: offices, titles, prerogatives, wealth too, should all be possessed by themselves. This is the career open to talents, equal opportunity, and so on. This is what fairness requires; talent will out; and in any case, talented men and women will enlarge the resources available to everyone else. So Michael Young's meritocracy is born, with all its attendant inequalities.[8]

What should we do now? It is possible to set limits to the new conversion patterns, to recognize but constrain the monopoly power of the talented. I take this to be the purpose of John Rawls's difference principle, according to which inequalities are justified only if they are designed to bring, and actually do bring, the greatest possible benefit to the least advantaged social class.[9] More specifically, the difference principle is a constraint imposed on talented men and women, once the monopoly of wealth has been broken. It works in this way: Imagine a surgeon who claims more than his equal share of wealth on the basis of the skills he has learned and the certificates he has won in the harsh competitive struggles of college and medical school. We will grant the claim if, and only if, granting it is beneficial in the stipulated ways. At the same time, we will act to limit and regulate the sale of surgery—that is, the direct conversion of surgical skill into wealth.

This regulation will necessarily be the work of the state, just as monetary laws and agrarian laws are the work of the state. Simple equality would require continual state intervention to break up or constrain incipient monopolies and

---

[8] Michael Young, *The Rise of the Meritocracy, 1870–2033* (Hammondsworth, England, 1961)—a brilliant piece of social science fiction.

[9] Rawls, *Theory of Justice* [1], pp. 75ff.

to repress new forms of dominance. But then state power itself will become the central object of competitive struggles. Groups of men and women will seek to monopolize and then to use the state in order to consolidate their control of other social goods. Or, the state will be monopolized by its own agents in accordance with the iron law of oligarchy. Politics is always the most direct path to dominance, and political power (rather than the means of production) is probably the most important, and certainly the most dangerous, good in human history. Hence the need to constrain the agents of constraint, to establish constitutional checks and balances. These are limits imposed on political monopoly, and they are all the more important once the various social and economic monopolies have been broken.

One way of limiting political power is to distribute it widely. This may not work, given the well-canvassed dangers of majority tyranny; but these dangers are probably less acute than they are often made out to be. The greater danger of democratic government is that it will be weak to cope with re-emerging monopolies in society at large, with the social strength of plutocrats, bureaucrats, technocrats, meritocrats, and so on. In theory, political power is the dominant good in a democracy, and it is convertible in any way the citizens choose. But in practice, again, breaking the monopoly of power neutralizes its dominance. Political power cannot be widely shared without being subjected to the pull of all the other goods that the citizens already have or hope to have. Hence democracy is, as Marx recognized, essentially a reflective system, mirroring the prevailing and emerging distribution of social goods.[10] Democratic decision making will be shaped by the cultural conceptions that determine or underwrite the new monopolies. To prevail against these monopolies, power will have to be centralized, perhaps itself monopolized. Once again, the state must be very powerful if it is to fulfill the purposes assigned to it by the difference principle or by any similarly interventionist rule.

Still, the regime of simple equality might work. One can imagine a more or less stable tension between emerging monopolies and political constraints, between the claim to privilege put forward by the talented, say, and the enforcement of the difference principle, and then between the agents of enforcement and the democratic constitution. But I suspect that difficulties will recur, and that at many points in time the only remedy for private privilege will be statism, and the only escape from statism will be private privilege. We will mobilize power to check monopoly, then look for some way of checking the power we have mobilized. But there is no way that doesn't open opportunities for strategically placed men and women to seize and exploit important social goods.

These problems derive from treating monopoly, and not dominance, as the central issue in distributive justice. It is not difficult, of course, to understand why philosophers (and political activists, too) have focused on monopoly. The

---

[10] See Marx's comment, in his "Critique of the Gotha Program," that the democratic republic is the "form of state" within which the class struggle will be fought to a conclusion: the struggle is immediately and without distortion reflected in political life (Marx and Engels, *Selected Works* [Moscow, 1951], vol. II, p. 31).

distributive struggles of the modern age begin with a war against the aristocracy's singular hold on land, office, and honor. This seems an especially pernicious monopoly because it rests upon birth and blood, with which the individual has nothing to do, rather than upon wealth, or power, or education, all of which—at least in principle—can be earned. And when every man and woman becomes, as it were, a smallholder in the sphere of birth and blood, an important victory is indeed won. Birthright ceases to be a dominant good; henceforth, it purchases very little; wealth, power, and education come to the fore. With regard to these latter goods, however, simple equality cannot be sustained at all, or it can only be sustained subject to the vicissitudes I have just described. Within their own spheres, as they are currently understood, these three tend to generate natural monopolies that can be repressed only if state power is itself dominant and if it is monopolized by officials committed to the repression. But there is, I think, another path to another kind of equality.

TYRANNY AND COMPLEX EQUALITY

I want to argue that we should focus on the reduction of dominance—not, or not primarily, on the break-up or the constraint of monopoly. We should consider what it might mean to narrow the range within which particular goods are convertible and to vindicate the autonomy of distributive spheres. But this line of argument, though it is not uncommon historically, has never fully emerged in philosophical writing. Philosophers have tended to criticize (or to justify) existing or emerging monopolies of wealth, power, and education. Or, they have criticized (or justified) particular conversions—of wealth into education or of office into wealth. And all this, most often, in the nature of some radically simplified distributive system. The critique of dominance will suggest instead a way of reshaping and then living with the actual complexity of distributions.

Imagine now a society in which different social goods are monopolistically held—as they are in fact and always will be, barring continual state intervention—but in which no particular good is generally convertible. As I go along, I shall try to define the precise limits on convertibility, but for now the general description will suffice. This is a complex egalitarian society. Though there will be many small inequalities, inequality will not be multiplied through the conversion process. Nor will it be summed across different goods, because the autonomy of distributions will tend to produce a variety of local monopolies, held by different groups of men and women. I don't want to claim that complex equality would necessarily be more stable than simple equality, but I am inclined to think that it would open the way for more diffused and particularized forms of social conflict. And the resistance to convertibility would be maintained, in large degree, by ordinary men and women within their own spheres of competence and control, without large-scale state action.

This is, I think, an attractive picture, but I have not yet explained just why it is attractive. The argument for complex equality begins from our understanding—I mean, our actual, concrete, positive, and particular understanding—of the various social goods. And then it moves on to an account of the way we relate to one another through those goods. Simple equality is a simple distributive condition, so that if I have fourteen hats and you have fourteen hats, we are equal. And it is all to the good if hats are dominant, for then our equality is extended through all the spheres of social life. On the view that I shall take here, however, we simply have the same number of hats, and it is unlikely that hats will be dominant for long. Equality is a complex relation of persons, mediated by the goods we make, share, and divide among ourselves; it is not an identity of possessions. It requires then, a diversity of distributive criteria that mirrors the diversity of social goods.

The argument for complex equality has been beautifully put by Pascal in one of his *Pensées*.

> The nature of tyranny is to desire power over the whole world and outside its own sphere.
>
> There are different companies—the strong, the handsome, the intelligent, the devout—and each man reigns in his own, not elsewhere. But sometimes they meet, and the strong and the handsome fight for mastery—foolishly, for their mastery is of different kinds. They misunderstand one another, and make the mistake of each aiming at universal dominion. Nothing can win this, not even strength, for it is powerless in the kingdom of the wise. . . .
>
> *Tyranny.* The following statements, therefore, are false and tyrannical: "Because I am handsome, so I should command respect." "I am strong, therefore men should love me. . . ." "I am . . . et cetera."
>
> Tyranny is the wish to obtain by one means what can only be had by another. We owe different duties to different qualities: love is the proper response to charm, fear to strength, and belief to learning.[11]

Marx made a similar argument in his early manuscripts; perhaps he had this *pensée* in mind:

> Let us assume man to be man, and his relation to the world to be a human one. Then love can only be exchanged for love, trust for trust, etc. If you wish to enjoy art you must be an artistically cultivated person; if you wish to influence other people, you must be a person who really has a stimulating and encouraging effect upon others. . . . If you love without evoking love in return, i.e., if you are not able, by the manifestation of yourself as a loving person, to make yourself a beloved person—then your love is impotent and a misfortune.[12]

These are not easy arguments, and most of my book is simply an exposition of their meaning. But here I shall attempt something more simple and schematic: a translation of the arguments into the terms I have already been using.

[11] Blaise Pascal, *The Pensées,* trans. J. M. Cohen (Hammondsworth, England, 1961), p. 96 (no. 244).

[12] Karl Marx, *Economic and Philosophical Manuscripts,* in *Early Writings,* ed. T. B. Bottomore (London, 1963), pp. 193–94. It is interesting to note an earlier echo of Pascal's argument in

The first claim of Pascal and Marx is that personal qualities and social goods have their own spheres of operation, where they work their effects freely, spontaneously, and legitimately. There are ready or natural conversions that follow from, and are intuitively plausible because of, the social meaning of particular goods. The appeal is to our ordinary understanding and, at the same time, against our common acquiescence in illegitimate conversion patterns. Or, it is an appeal from our acquiescence to our resentment. There is something wrong, Pascal suggests, with the conversion of strength into belief. In political terms, Pascal means that no ruler can rightly command my opinions merely because of the power he wields. Nor can he, Marx adds, rightly claim to influence my actions: if a ruler wants to do that, he must be persuasive, helpful, encouraging, and so on. These arguments depend for their force on some shared understanding of knowledge, influence, and power. Social goods have social meaning, and we find our way to distributive justice through an interpretation of those meanings. We search for principles internal to each distributive sphere.

The second claim is that the disregard of these principles is tyranny. To convert one good into another, when there is no intrinsic connection between the two, is to invade the sphere where another company of men and women properly rules. Monopoly is not inappropriate within the spheres. There is nothing wrong, for example, with the grip that persuasive and helpful men and women (politicians) establish on political power. But the use of political power to gain access to other goods is a tyrannical use. Thus, an old description of tyranny is generalized: princes become tyrants, according to medieval writers, when they seize the property or invade the family of their subjects.[13] In political life—but more widely, too—the dominance of goods makes for the domination of people.

The regime of complex equality is the opposite of tyranny. It establishes a set of relationships such that domination is impossible. In formal terms, complex equality means that no citizen's standing in one sphere or with regard to one social good can be undercut by his standing in some other sphere, with regard to some other good. Thus, citizen X may be chosen over citizen Y for political office, and then the two of them will be unequal in the sphere of politics. But they will not be unequal generally so long as X's office gives him no advantages over Y in any other sphere—superior medical care, access to better schools for his children, entrepreneurial opportunities, and so on. So long as office is not a dominant good, is not generally convertible, office holders will stand, or at least can stand, in a relation of equality to the men and women they govern.

But what if dominance were eliminated, the autonomy of the spheres established—and the same people were successful in one sphere after another, triumphant in every company, piling up goods without the need for illegitimate

---

Adam Smith's *Theory of Moral Sentiment* (Edinburgh, 1813), vol. I, pp. 378–79; but Smith seems to have believed that distribution in his own society actually conformed to this view of appropriateness—a mistake neither Pascal nor Marx ever made.

[13] See the summary account in Jean Bodin, *Six Books of a Commonweale,* ed. Kenneth Douglas McRae (Cambridge, Mass., 1962), pp. 210–18.

conversions? This would certainly make for an inegalitarian society, but it would also suggest in the strongest way that a society of equals was not a lively possibility. I doubt that any egalitarian argument could survive in the face of such evidence. Here is a person whom we have freely chosen (without reference to his family ties or personal wealth) as our political representative. He is also a bold and inventive entrepreneur. When he was younger, he studied science, scored amazingly high grades in every exam, and made important discoveries. In war, he is surpassingly brave and wins the highest honors. Himself compassionate and compelling, he is loved by all who know him. Are there such people? Maybe so, but I have my doubts. We tell stories like the one I have just told, but the stories are fiction, the conversion of power or money or academic talent into legendary fame. In any case, there aren't enough such people to constitute a ruling class and dominate the rest of us. Nor can they be successful in every distributive sphere, for there are some spheres to which the idea of success doesn't pertain. Nor are their children likely, under conditions of complex equality, to inherit their success. By and large, the most accomplished politicians, entrepreneurs, scientists, soldiers, and lovers will be different people; and so long as the goods they possess don't bring other goods in train, we have no reason to fear their accomplishments.

The critique of dominance and domination points toward an open-ended distributive principle. *No social good x should be distributed to men and women who possess some other good y merely because they possess y and without regard to the meaning of x.* This is a principle that has probably been reiterated, at one time or another, for every y that has ever been dominant. But it has not often been stated in general terms. Pascal and Marx have suggested the application of the principle against all possible y's, and I shall attempt to work out that application. I shall be looking, then, not at the members of Pascal's companies—the strong or the weak, the handsome or the plain—but at the goods they share and divide. The purpose of the principle is to focus our attention; it doesn't determine the shares or the division. The principle directs us to study the meaning of social goods, to examine the different distributive spheres from the inside.

44.

Equality of Interests

PETER SINGER

. . . When I make an ethical judgment I must go beyond a personal or sectional point of view and take into account the interests of all those affected. This means that we weigh up interests, considered simply as interests and not as my interests, or the interests of Australians, or of people of European descent. This provides us with a basic principle of equality: the principle of equal consideration of interests.

The essence of the principle of equal consideration of interests is that we give equal weight in our moral deliberations to the like interests of all those affected by our actions. This means that if only X and Y would be affected by a possible act, and if X stands to lose more than Y stands to gain, it is better not to do the act. We cannot, if we accept the principle of equal consideration of interests, say that doing the act is better, despite the facts described, because we are more concerned about Y than we are about X. What the principle really amounts to is this: *an interest is an interest, whoever's interest it may be.*

We can make this more concrete by considering a particular interest, say the interest we have in the relief of pain. Then the principle says that the ultimate moral reason for relieving pain is simply the undesirability of pain as such, and not the undesirability of X's pain, which might be different from the undesirability of Y's pain. Of course, X's pain might be more undesirable than Y's pain because it is more painful, and then the principle of equal consideration would give greater weight to the relief of X's pain. Again, even where the pains are equal, other factors might be relevant, especially if others are affected. If there has been an earthquake we might give priority to the relief of a doctor's pain so she can treat other victims. But the doctor's pain itself counts only once, and with no added weighting. The principle of equal consideration of interests acts like a pair of scales, weighing interests impartially. True scales favor the side where the interest is stronger or where several interests combine to outweigh a smaller number of similar interests; but they take no account of whose interests they are weighing.

From this point of view race is irrelevant to the consideration of interests; for all that counts are the interests themselves. To give less consideration to a specified amount of pain because that pain was experienced by a member of a particular race would be to make an arbitrary distinction. Why pick on race? Why not on whether a person was born in a leap year? Or whether there is more than one vowel in her surname? All these characteristics are equally ir-relevant to the undesirability of pain from the universal point of view. Hence the principle of equal consideration of interests shows straightforwardly why the most blatant forms of racism, like that of the Nazis, are wrong. For the

Nazis were concerned only for the welfare of members of the "Aryan" race, and the sufferings of Jews, Gypsies, and Slavs were of no concern to them.

The principle of equal consideration of interests is sometimes thought to be a purely formal principle, lacking in substance and too weak to exclude any inegalitarian practice. We have already seen, however, that it does exclude racism and sexism, at least in their most blatant forms. If we look at the impact of the principle on the imaginary hierarchial society based on intelligence tests we can see that it is strong enough to provide a basis for rejecting this more sophisticated form of inegalitarianism, too.

The principle of equal consideration of interests prohibits making our readiness to consider the interests of others depend on their abilities or other characteristics, apart from the characteristic of having interests. It is true that we cannot know where equal consideration of interests will lead us until we know what interests people have, and this may vary according to their abilities or other characteristics. Consideration of the interests of mathematically gifted children may lead us to teach them advanced mathematics at an early age, which for different children might be entirely pointless or positively harmful. But the basic element, the taking into account of the person's interests, whatever they may be, must apply to everyone, irrespective of race, sex, or scores on an intelligence test. Enslaving those who score below a certain line on an intelligence test would not—barring extraordinary and implausible beliefs about human nature—be compatible with equal consideration. Intelligence has nothing to do with many important interests that humans have, like the interest in avoiding pain, in developing one's abilities, in satisfying basic needs for food and shelter, in enjoying friendly and loving relations with others, and in being free to pursue one's projects without unnecessary interference from others. Slavery prevents the slaves from satisfying these interests as they would want to; and the benefits it confers on the slave-owners are hardly comparable in importance to the harm it does to the slaves.

So the principle of equal consideration of interests is strong enough to rule out an intelligence-based slave society as well as cruder forms of racism and sexism. It also rules out discrimination on the grounds of disability, whether intellectual or physical, in so far as the disability is not relevant to the interests under consideration (as, for example, severe intellectual disability might be if we are considering a person's interest in voting in an election). The principle of equal consideration of interests therefore may be a defensible form of the principle that all humans are equal, a form that we can use in discussing more controversial issues about equality. Before we go on to these topics, however, it will be useful to say a little more about the nature of the principle.

Equal consideration of interests is a minimal principle of equality in the sense that it does not dictate equal treatment. Take a relatively straightforward example of an interest, the interest in having physical pain relieved. Imagine that after an earthquake I come across two victims, one with a crushed leg, in agony, and one with a gashed thigh, in slight pain. I have only two shots of morphine left. Equal treatment would suggest that I give one to each injured person, but one shot would not do much to relieve the pain of the person with the crushed leg. She would still be in much more pain than the other victim, and even after I have given her one shot, giving her the second shot would bring greater relief than giving a shot to the person in slight pain. Hence equal consideration of interests in this situation leads to what some may consider an inegalitarian result: two shots of morphine for one person, and none for the other.

There is a still more controversial inegalitarian implication of the principle of equal consideration of interests. In the case above, although equal consideration of interests leads to unequal treatment, this unequal treatment is an attempt to produce a more egalitarian result. By giving the double dose to the more seriously injured person, we bring about a situation in which there is less difference in the degree of suffering felt by the two victims than there would be if we gave one dose to each. Instead of ending up with one person in considerable pain and one in no pain, we end up with two people in slight pain. This is in line with the principle of declining marginal utility, a principle well-known to economists, which states that for a given individual, a set amount of something is more useful when people have little of it than when they have a lot. If I am struggling to survive on 200 grams of rice a day, and you provide me with an extra fifty grams per day, you have improved my position significantly; but if I already have a kilo of rice per day, I won't care much about the extra fifty grams. When marginal utility is taken into account the principle of equal consideration of interests inclines us towards an equal distribution of income, and to that extent the egalitarian will endorse its conclusions. What is likely to trouble the egalitarian about the principle of equal consideration of interests is that there are circumstances in which the principle of declining marginal utility does not hold or is overridden by countervailing factors.

We can vary the example of the earthquake victims to illustrate this point. Let us say, again, that there are two victims, one more severely injured than the other, but this time we shall say that the more severely injured victim, A, has lost a leg and is in danger of losing a toe from her remaining leg; while the less severely injured victim, B, has an injury to her leg, but the limb can be saved. We have medical supplies for only one person. If we use them on the more severely injured victim the most we can do is save her toe, whereas if we use them on the less severely injured victim we can save her leg. In other words, we assume that the situation is as follows: without medical treatment, A loses a leg and a toe, while B loses only a leg; if we give the treatment to A, A loses a leg and B loses a leg; if we give the treatment to B, A loses a leg and a toe, while B loses nothing.

Assuming that it is worse to lose a leg than it is to lose a toe (even when that toe is on one's sole remaining foot) the principle of declining marginal utility does not suffice to give us the right answer in this situation. We will do more to further the interests, impartially considered, of those affected by our actions if we use our limited resources on the less seriously injured victim than on the more seriously injured one. Therefore this is what the principle of equal consideration of interests leads us to do. Thus equal consideration of interests can, in special cases, widen rather than narrow the gap between two people at different levels of welfare. It is for this reason that the principle is a minimal principle of equality, rather than a thoroughgoing egalitarian principle. A more thoroughgoing form of egalitarianism would, however, be difficult to justify, both in general terms and in its application to special cases of the kind just described.

45.

Formal Legal Equality

F. A. HAYEK

1. The great aim of the struggle for liberty has been equality before the law. This equality under the rules which the state enforces may be supplemented by a similar equality of the rules that men voluntarily obey in their relations with one another. This extension of the principle of equality to the rules of moral and social conduct is the chief expression of what is commonly called the democratic spirit—and probably that aspect of it that does most to make inoffensive the inequalities that liberty necessarily produces.

Equality of the general rules of law and conduct, however, is the only kind of equality conducive to liberty and the only equality which we can secure without destroying liberty. Not only has liberty nothing to do with any other sort of equality, but it is even bound to produce inequality in many respects. This is the necessary result and part of the justification of individual liberty: if the result of individual liberty did not demonstrate that some manners of living are more successful than others, much of the case for it would vanish.

It is neither because it assumes that people are in fact equal nor because it attempts to make them equal that the argument for liberty demands that government treat them equally. This argument not only recognizes that individuals are very different but in a great measure rests on that assumption. It insists that these individual differences provide no justification for government to treat them differently. And it objects to the differences in treatment by the state that would be necessary if persons who are in fact very different were to be assured equal positions in life.

Modern advocates of a more far-reaching material equality usually deny that their demands are based on any assumption of the factual equality of all men.[1] It is nevertheless still widely believed that this is the main justification for such demands. Nothing, however, is more damaging to the demand for equal treatment than to base it on so obviously untrue an assumption as that of the factual equality of all men. To rest the case for equal treatment of national or racial minorities on the assertion that they do not differ from other men is implicitly to admit that factual inequality would justify unequal treatment; and the proof that some differences do, in fact, exist would not be long in forthcoming. It is of the essence of the demand for equality before the law that people should be treated alike in spite of the fact that they are different.

2. The boundless variety of human nature—the wide range of differences in individual capacities and potentialities—is one of the most distinctive facts about the human species. Its evolution has made it probably the most variable

---

[1] See, e.g., R. H. Tawney, *Equality* (London, 1931), p. 47.

among all kinds of creatures. It has been well said that "biology, with variability as its cornerstone, confers on every human individual a unique set of attributes which give him a dignity he could not otherwise possess. Every newborn baby is an unknown quantity so far as potentialities are concerned because there are many thousands of unknown interrelated genes and gene-patterns which contribute to his makeup. As a result of nature and nurture the newborn infant may become one of the greatest of men or women ever to have lived. In every case he or she has the making of a distinctive individual. . . . If the differences are not very important, then freedom is not very important and the idea of individual worth is not very important."[2] The writer justly adds that the widely held uniformity theory of human nature, "which on the surface appears to accord with democracy . . . would in time undermine the very basic ideals of freedom and individual worth and render life as we know it meaningless."[3]

It has been the fashion in modern times to minimize the importance of congenital differences between men and to ascribe all the important differences to the influence of environment.[4] However important the latter may be, we must not overlook the fact that individuals are very different from the outset. The importance of individual differences would hardly be less if all people were brought up in very similar environments. As a statement of fact, it just is not true that "all men are born equal." We may continue to use this hallowed phrase to express the ideal that legally and morally all men ought to be treated alike. But if we want to understand what this ideal of equality can or should mean, the first requirement is that we free ourselves from the belief in factual equality.

From the fact that people are very different it follows that, if we treat them equally, the result must be inequality in their actual position,[5] and that the only way to place them in an equal position would be to treat them differently. Equality before the law and material equality are therefore not only different but are in conflict with each other; and we can achieve either the one or the other, but not both at the same time. The equality before the law which freedom requires leads to material inequality. Our argument will be that, though where the state must use coercion for other reasons, it should treat all people alike, the desire of making people more alike in their condition cannot be accepted in a free society as a justification for further and discriminatory coercion.

We do not object to equality as such. It merely happens to be the case that a demand for equality is the professed motive of most of those who desire to impose upon society a preconceived pattern of distribution. Our objection is against all attempts to impress upon society a deliberately chosen pattern of

[2] Roger J. Williams, *Free and Unequal: The Biological Basis of Individual Liberty* (Austin: University of Texas Press, 1953), pp. 23 and 70; cf. also J. B. S. Haldane, *The Inequality of Man* (London, 1932), and P. B. Medawar, *The Uniqueness of the Individual* (London, 1957).

[3] Williams, op. cit., p. 152.

[4] See the description of this fashionable view in H. M. Kallen's article "Behaviorism," *E.S.S.,* II, 498: "At birth human infants, regardless of their heredity, are as equal as Fords."

[5] Cf. Plato *Laws* vi. 757A: "To unequals equals become unequal."

distribution, whether it be an order of equality or of inequality. We shall indeed see that many of those who demand an extension of equality do not really demand equality but a distribution that conforms more closely to human conceptions of individual merit and that their desires are as irreconcilable with freedom as the more strictly egalitarian demands.

If one objects to the use of coercion in order to bring about a more even or a more just distribution, this does not mean that one does not regard these as desirable. But if we wish to preserve a free society, it is essential that we recognize that the desirability of a particular object is not sufficient justification for the use of coercion. One may well feel attracted to a community in which there are no extreme contrasts between rich and poor and may welcome the fact that the general increase in wealth seems gradually to reduce those differences. I fully share these feelings and certainly regard the degree of social equality that the United States has achieved as wholly admirable.

There also seems no reason why these widely felt preferences should not guide policy in some respects. Wherever there is a legitimate need for government action and we have to choose between different methods of satisfying such a need, those that incidentally also reduce inequality may well be preferable. If, for example, in the law of intestate succession one kind of provision will be more conducive to equality than another, this may be a strong argument in its favor. It is a different matter, however, if it is demanded that, in order to produce substantive equality, we should abandon the basic postulate of a free society, namely, the limitation of all coercion by equal law. Against this we shall hold that economic inequality is not one of the evils which justify our resorting to discriminatory coercion or privilege as a remedy.

46.
Equality of Resources

RONALD DWORKIN

I shall consider two general theories of distributional equality. The first (which I shall call equality of welfare) holds that a distributional scheme treats people as equals when it distributes or transfers resources among them until no further transfer would leave them more equal in welfare. The second (equality of resources) holds that it treats them as equals when it distributes or transfers so that no further transfer would leave their shares of the total resources more equal. Each of these two theories, as I have just stated them, is very abstract because, as we shall see, there are many different interpretations of what welfare is, and also different theories about what would count as equality of resources. Nevertheless, even in this abstract form, it should be plain that the two theories will offer different advice in many concrete cases.

Suppose, for example, that a man of some wealth has several children, one of whom is blind, another a playboy with expensive tastes, a third a prospective politician with expensive ambitions, another a poet with humble needs, another a sculptor who works in expensive material, and so forth. How shall he draw his will? If he takes equality of welfare as his goal, then he will take these differences among his children into account, so that he will not leave them equal shares. Of course he will have to decide on some interpretation of welfare and whether, for example, expensive tastes should figure in his calculations in the same way as handicaps or expensive ambitions. But if, on the contrary, he takes equality of resources as his goal then, assuming his children have roughly equal wealth already, he may well decide that his goal requires an equal division of his wealth. In any case the questions he will put to himself will then be very different.

It is true that the distinction between the two abstract theories will be less clear-cut in an ordinary political context, particularly when officials have very little information about the actual tastes and ambitions of particular citizens. If a welfare-egalitarian knows nothing of this sort about a large group of citizens, he may sensibly decide that his best strategy for securing equality of welfare would be to establish equality of income. But the theoretical difference between the two abstract theories of equality nevertheless remains important in politics, for a variety of reasons. Officials often do have sufficient general information about the distribution of tastes and handicaps to justify general adjustments to equality of resource (for example by special tax allowances) if their goal is equality of welfare. Even when they do not, some economic structures they might devise would be antecedently better calculated to reduce inequality of welfare, under conditions of uncertainty, and others to reduce inequality of resources. But the main importance of the issue I now raise is theoretical. Egalitarians must decide whether the equality they seek is equality of resource of welfare, or some combination or something very different, in order plausibly to argue that equality is worth having at all.

• • •

I argue that an equal division of resources presupposes an economic market of some form, mainly as an analytical device but also, to a certain extent, as an actual political institution. That claim may seem sufficiently paradoxical to justify the following preliminary comments. The idea of a market for goods has figured in political and economic theory, since the eighteenth century, in two rather different ways. It has been celebrated, first, as a device for both defining and achieving certain community-wide goals variously described as prosperity, efficiency, and overall utility. It has been hailed, second, as a necessary condition of individual liberty, the condition under which free men and women may exercise individual initiative and choice so that their fates lie in their own hands. The market, that is, has been defended both through arguments of policy, appealing to the overall, community-wide gains it produces, and arguments of principle that appeal instead to some supposed right to liberty.

But the economic market, whether defended in either or both of these ways, has during this same period come to be regarded as the enemy of equality, largely because the forms of economic market systems developed and enforced in industrial countries have permitted and indeed encouraged vast inequality in property. Both political philosophers and ordinary citizens have therefore pictured equality as the antagonist or victim of the values of efficiency and liberty supposedly served by the market, so that wise and moderate politics consists in striking some balance or trade-off between equality and these other values, either by imposing constraints on the market as an economic environment, or by replacing it, in part or altogether, with a different economic system.

I shall try to suggest, on the contrary, that the idea of an economic market, as a device for setting prices for a vast variety of goods and services, must be at the center of an attractive theoretical development of equality of resources. The main point can be shown most quickly by constructing a reasonably simple exercise in equality of resources, deliberately artificial so as to abstract from problems we shall later have to face. Suppose a number of shipwreck survivors are washed up on a desert island which has abundant resources and no native population, and any likely rescue is many years away. These immigrants accept the principle that no one is antecedently entitled to any of these resources, but that they shall instead be divided equally among them. (They do not yet realize, let us say, that it might be wise to keep some resources as owned in common by any state they might create.) They also accept (at least provisionally) the following test of an equal division of resources, which I shall call the envy test. No division of resources is an equal division if, once the division is complete, any immigrant would prefer someone else's bundle of resources to his own bundle.[1]

---

[1] D. Foley, "Resource Allocation and the Public Sector," *Yale Economic Essays* 7 (Spring 1967); H. Varian, "Equity, Energy and Efficiency, *Journal of Economic Theory* (Sept. 1974): 63–91.

Now suppose some one immigrant is elected to achieve the division according to that principle. It is unlikely that he can succeed simply by physically dividing the resources of the island into n identical bundles of resources. The number of each kind of the nondivisible resources, like milking cows, might not be an exact multiple of n, and even in the case of divisible resources, like arable land, some land would be better than others, and some better for one use than another. Suppose, however, that by a great deal of trial and error and care the divider could create n bundles of resources, each of which was somewhat different from the others, but was nevertheless such that he could assign one to each immigrant and no one would in fact envy anyone else's bundle.

The distribution might still fail to satisfy the immigrants as an equal distribution, for a reason that is not caught by the envy test. Suppose (to put the point in a dramatic way) the divider achieved his result by transforming all the available resources into a very large stock of plovers' eggs and pre-phylloxera claret (either by magic or trade with a neighboring island that enters the story only for that reason) and divides this glut into identical bundles of baskets and bottles. Many of the immigrants—let us say all but one—are delighted. But if that one hates plovers' eggs and pre-phylloxera claret he will feel that he has not been treated as an equal in the division of resources. The envy test is met—he does not prefer any one's bundle to his own—but he prefers what he would have had under some fairer treatment of the initially available resources.

A similar, though less dramatic, piece of unfairness might be produced even without magic or bizarre trades. For the combination of resources that composes each bundle the divider creates will favor some tastes over others, compared with different combinations he might have composed. That is, different sets of n bundles might be created by trial and error, each of which would pass the envy test, so that for any such set that the divider chooses, someone will prefer that he had chosen a different set, even though that person would not prefer a different bundle within that set. Trades after the initial distribution may, of course, improve that person's position. But they will be unlikely to bring him to the position he would have had under the set of bundles he would have preferred, because some others will begin with a bundle they prefer to the bundle they would have had in that set, and so will have no reason to trade to that bundle.

So the divider needs a device that will attack two distinct foci of arbitrariness and possible unfairness. The envy test cannot be satisfied by any simple mechanical division of resources. If any more complex division can be found that will satisfy it, many such might be found, so that the choice amongst these would be arbitrary. The same solution will now have occurred to all readers. The divider needs some form of auction or other market procedure in order to respond to these problems. I shall describe a reasonably straightforward procedure that would seem acceptable if it could be made to work, though as I shall describe it it will be impossibly expensive of time. Suppose the divider hands each of the immigrants an equal and large number of clamshells, which are sufficiently numerous and in themselves valued by no one, to use as counters in a market of the following sort. Each distinct item on the island (not

including the immigrants themselves) is listed as a lot to be sold, unless someone notifies the auctioneer (as the divider has now become) of his or her desire
to bid for some part of an item, including part, for example, of some piece of
land, in which case that part becomes itself a distinct lot. The auctioneer then
proposes a set of prices for each lot and discovers whether that set of prices
clears all markets, that is, whether there is only one purchaser at that price and
all lots are sold. If not, then the auctioneer adjusts his prices until he reaches a
set that does clear the markets.[2] But the process does not stop then, because
each of the immigrants remains free to change his bids even when an initially
market-clearing set of prices is reached, or even to propose different lots. But
let us suppose that in time even this leisurely process comes to an end, everyone
declares himself satisfied, and goods are distributed accordingly.[3]

Now the envy test will have been met. No one will envy another's set of purchases because, by hypothesis, he could have purchased that bundle with his
clamshells instead of his own bundle. Nor is the choice of sets of bundles arbitrary. Many people will be able to imagine a different set of bundles meeting the
no-envy test that might have been established, but the actual set of bundles has
the merit that each person played, through his purchases against an initially
equal stock of counters, an equal role in determining the set of bundles actually
chosen. No one is in the position of the person in our earlier example who
found himself with nothing but what he hated. Of course, luck plays a certain
role in determining how satisfied anyone is with the outcome, against other
possibilities he might envision. If plovers' eggs and old claret were the only resources to auction, then the person who hated these would be as badly off as in
our earlier example. He would be unlucky that the immigrants had not washed
up on an island with more of what he wanted (though lucky, of course, that
it did not have even less). But he could not complain that the division of the
actual resources they found was unequal.

He might think himself lucky or unlucky in other ways as well. It would be a
matter of luck, for example, how many others shared various of his tastes. If his
tastes or ambitions proved relatively popular, this might work in his favor in the
auction, if there were economies of scale in the production of what he wanted.
Or against him, if what he wanted was scarce. If the immigrants had decided to
establish a regime of equality of welfare, instead of equality of resources, then
these various pieces of good or bad luck would be shared with others, because
distribution would be based, not on any auction of the sort I described, in which
luck plays this role, but on a strategy of evening out differences in whatever

---

[2] I mean to describe a Walrasian auction in which all productive resources are sold. I do not assume that the immigrants enter into complete forward contingent claims contracts, but only that
markets will remain open and will clear in a Walrasian fashion once the auction of productive
resources is completed. I make all the assumptions about production and preferences made in
G. Debreu, *Theory of Value* (New Haven: Yale University Press, 1959). In fact the auction I describe here will become more complex in virtue of a tax scheme discussed later.

[3] The process does not guarantee that the auction will come to an end in this way, because there
may be various equilibria. I am supposing that people will come to understand that they cannot
do better by further runs of the auction, and will for practical reasons settle on one equilibrium.
If I am wrong, then this fact provides one of the aspects of incompleteness I describe in the next
section.

concept of welfare had been chosen. Equality of resources, however, offers no similar reason for correcting for the contingencies that determine how expensive or frustrating someone's preferences turn out to be.[4]

Under equality of welfare, people are meant to decide what sorts of lives they want independently of information relevant to determining how much their choices will reduce or enhance the ability of others to have what they want.[5] That sort of information becomes relevant only at a second, political level at which administrators then gather all the choices made at the first level to see what distribution will give each of these choices equal success under some concept of welfare taken as the correct dimension of success. Under equality of resources, however, people decide what sorts of lives to pursue against a background of information about the actual cost their choices impose on other people and hence on the total stock of resources that may fairly be used by them. The information left to an independent political level under equality of welfare is therefore brought into the initial level of individual choice under equality of resources. The elements of luck in the auction we have just described are in fact pieces of information of a crucial sort; information that is acquired and used in that process of choice.

So the contingent facts of raw material and the distribution of tastes are not grounds on which someone might challenge a distribution as unequal. They are rather background facts that determine what equality of resources, in these circumstances, is. Under equality of resources, no test for calculating what equality requires can be abstracted from these background facts and used to test them. The market character of the auction is not simply a convenient or ad hoc device for resolving technical problems that arise for equality of resources in very simple exercises like our desert island case. It is an institutionalized form of the process of discovery and adaptation that is at the center of the ethics of that ideal. Equality of resources supposes that the resources devoted to each person's life should be equal. That goal needs a metric. The auction proposes what the envy test in fact assumes, that the true measure of the social resources devoted to the life of one person is fixed by asking how important, in fact, that resource is for others. It insists that the cost, measured in that way, figure in each person's sense of what is rightly his and in each person's judgment of what life he should lead, given that command of justice. Anyone who insists that equality is violated by any particular profile of initial tastes, therefore, must reject equality of resources, and fall back on equality of welfare.

• • •

If the auction is successful as described, then equality of resources holds for the moment among the immigrants. But perhaps only for the moment, because if

---

[4] See, however, the discussion of handicaps below, which recognizes that certain kinds of preferences, which people wish they did not have, may call for compensation as handicaps.

[5] See Part I of this essay (*Philosophy & Public Affairs* 10, no. 3 [Summer 1981]) for a discussion of whether equality of welfare can be modified so as to make an exception here for "expensive tastes" deliberately cultivated. I argue that it cannot.

they are left alone, once the auction is completed, to produce and trade as they wish, then the envy test will shortly fail. Some may be more skillful than others at producing what others want and will trade to get. Some may like to work, or to work in a way that will produce more to trade, while others like not to work or prefer to work at what will bring them less. Some will stay healthy while others fall sick, or lightning will strike the farms of others but avoid theirs. For any of these and dozens of other reasons some people will prefer the bundle others have in say, five years, to their own.

We must ask whether (or rather how far) such developments are consistent with equality of resources, and I shall begin by considering the character and impact of luck on the immigrants' post-auction fortunes. I shall distinguish, at least for the moment, between two kinds of luck. Option luck is a matter of how deliberate and calculated gambles turn out—whether someone gains or loses through accepting an isolated risk he or she should have anticipated and might have declined. Brute luck is a matter of how risks fall out that are not in that sense deliberate gambles. If I buy a stock on the exchange that rises, then my option luck is good. If I am hit by a falling meteorite whose course could not have been predicted, then my bad luck is brute (even though I could have moved just before it struck if I had any reason to know where it would strike). Obviously the difference between these two forms of luck can be represented as a matter of degree, and we may be uncertain how to describe a particular piece of bad luck. If someone develops cancer in the course of a normal life, and there is no particular decision to which we can point as a gamble risking the disease, then we will say that he has suffered brute bad luck. But if he smoked cigarettes heavily then we may prefer to say that he took an unsuccessful gamble.

Insurance, so far as it is available, provides a link between brute and option luck, because the decision to buy or reject catastrophe insurance is a calculated gamble. Of course, insurance does not erase the distinction. Someone who buys medical insurance and is hit by an unexpected meteorite still suffers brute bad luck, because he is worse off than if he had bought insurance and not needed it. But he has had better option luck than if he had not bought the insurance, because his situation is better in virtue of his not having run the gamble of refusing to insure.

Is it consistent with equality of resources that people should have different income or wealth in virtue of differing option luck? Suppose some of the immigrants plant valuable but risky crops while others play it safer, and that some of the former buy insurance against uncongenial weather while others do not. Skill will play a part in determining which of these various programs succeed, of course, and we shall consider the problems this raises later. But option luck will also play a part. Does its role threaten or invade equality of resources?

Consider, first, the differences in wealth between those who play it safe and those who gamble and succeed. Some people enjoy, while others hate, risks; but this particular difference in personality is comprehended in a more general difference between the kinds of lives that different people wish to lead. The life chosen by someone who gambles contains, as an element, the factor of risk; someone who chooses not to gamble has decided that he prefers a safer life. We have already decided that people should pay the price of the life they have decided to lead, measured in what others give up in order that they can do so. That was the point of the auction as a device to establish initial equality of resources. But the price of a safer life, measured in this way, is precisely forgoing any chance of the gains whose prospect induces others to gamble. So we have no reason to object, against the background of our earlier decisions, to a result in which those who decline to gamble have less than some of those who do not.

But we must also compare the situation of those who gamble and win with that of those who gamble and lose. We cannot say that the latter have chosen a different life and must sacrifice gains accordingly; for they have chosen the same lives as those who won. But we can say that the possibility of loss was part of the life they chose—that it was the fair price of the possibility of gain. For we might have designed our initial auction so that people could purchase (for example) lottery tickets with their clamshells. But the price of those tickets would have been some amount of other resources (fixed by the odds and the gambling preferences of others) that the shells would otherwise have bought, and which will be wholly forgone if the ticket does not win.

The same point can be made by considering the arguments for redistribution from winners to losers after the event. If winners were made to share their winnings with losers, then no one would gamble, as individuals, and the kind of life preferred by both those who in the end win and those who lose would be unavailable. Of course, it is not a good argument, against someone who urges redistribution in order to achieve equality of resources, that redistribution would make some forms of life less attractive or even impossible. For the demands of equality (we assume in this essay) are prior to other desiderata, including variety in the kinds of life available to people. (Equality will in any case make certain kinds of lives—a life of economic and political domination of others, for example—impossible.) In the present case, however, the difference is apparent. For the effect of redistribution from winners to losers in gambles would be to deprive both of lives they prefer, which indicates, not simply that this would produce an unwanted curtailment of available forms of life, but that it would deprive them of an equal voice in the construction of lots to be auctioned, like the man who hated both plovers' eggs and claret but was confronted only with bundles of both. They both want gambles to be in the mix, either originally or as represented by resources with which they can take risks later, and the chance of losing is the correct price, measured on the metric we have been using, of a life that includes gambles with a chance of gain.

We may, of course, have special reasons for forbidding certain forms of gambles. We may have paternalistic reasons for limiting how much any individual may risk, for example. We may also have reasons based in a theory of political equality for forbidding someone to gamble with his freedom or his religious or political rights. The present point is more limited. We have no general reason for forbidding gambles altogether in the bare fact that in the event winners will control more resources than losers, any more than in the fact that winners will have more than those who do not gamble at all. Our initial principle, that equality of resources requires that people pay the true cost of the lives that they lead, warrants rather than condemns these differences.

We may (if we wish) adjust our envy test to record that conclusion. We may say that in computing the extent of someone's resources over his life, for the purpose of asking whether anyone else envies those resources, any resources gained through a successful gamble should be represented by the opportunity to take the gamble at the odds in force, and comparable adjustments made to the resources of those who have lost through gambles. The main point of this artificial construction of the envy test, however, would be to remind us that the argument in favor of allowing differences in option luck to affect income and wealth assumes that everyone has in principle the same gambles available to him. Someone who never had the opportunity to run a similar risk, and would have taken the opportunity had it been available, will still envy some of those who did have it.

Nor does the argument yet confront the case of brute bad luck. If two people lead roughly the same lives, but one goes suddenly blind, then we cannot explain the resulting differences in their incomes either by saying that one took risks that the other chose not to take, or that we could not redistribute without denying both the lives they prefer. For the accident has (we assume) nothing to do with choices in the pertinent sense. It is not necessary to the life either has chosen that he run the risk of going blind without redistribution of funds from the other. This is a fortiori so if one is born blind and the other sighted.

But the possibility of insurance provides, as I suggested, a link between the two kinds of luck. For suppose insurance against blindness is available, in the initial auction, at whatever level of coverage the policy holder chooses to buy. And also suppose that two sighted people have, at the time of the auction, equal chance of suffering an accident that will blind them, and know that they have. Now if one chooses to spend part of his initial resources for such insurance and the other does not, or if one buys more coverage than the other, then this difference will reflect their different opinions about the relative value of different forms or components of their prospective lives. It may reflect the fact that one puts more value on sight than the other. Or, differently, that one would count monetary compensation for the loss of his sight as worthless in the face of such a tragedy while the other, more practical, would fix his mind on the aids and special training that such money might buy. Or simply that one minds or values risk differently from the other, and would, for example, rather try for a brilliant life that would collapse under catastrophe than a life guarded at the cost of resources necessary to make it brilliant.

But in any case the bare idea of equality of resources, apart from any paternalistic additions, would not argue for redistribution from the person who had insured to the person who had not if, horribly, they were both blinded in the same accident. For the availability of insurance would mean that, though they had both had brute bad luck, the difference between them was a matter of option luck, and the arguments we entertained against disturbing the results of option luck under conditions of equal antecedent risk hold here as well. But then the situation cannot be different if the person who decided not to insure is the only one to be blinded. For once again the difference is a difference in option luck against a background of equal opportunity to insure or not. If neither had been blinded, the man who had insured against blindness would have been the loser. His option luck would have been bad—though it seems bizarre to put it this way—because he spent resources that, as things turned out, would have been better spent otherwise. But he would have no claim, in that event, from the man who did not insure and also survived unhurt.

So if the condition just stated were met—if everyone had an equal risk of suffering some catastrophe that would leave him or her handicapped, and everyone knew roughly what the odds were and had ample opportunity to insure—then handicaps would pose no special problem for equality of resources. But of course that condition is not met. Some people are born with handicaps, or develop them before they have either sufficient knowledge or funds to insure on their own behalf. They cannot buy insurance after the event. Even handicaps that develop later in life, against which people do have the opportunity to insure, are not randomly distributed through the population, but follow genetic tracks, so that sophisticated insurers would charge some people higher premiums for the same coverage before the event. Nevertheless the idea of a market in insurance provides a counterfactual guide through which equality of resources might face the problem of handicaps in the real world.

Suppose we can make sense of and even give a rough answer to the following question. If (contrary to fact) everyone had at the appropriate age the same risk of developing physical or mental handicaps in the future (which assumes that no one has developed these yet) but that the total number of handicaps remained what it is, how much insurance coverage against these handicaps would the average member of the community purchase? We might then say that but for (uninsurable) brute luck that has altered these equal odds, the average person would have purchased insurance at that level, and compensate those who do develop handicaps accordingly, out of some fund collected by taxation or other compulsory process but designed to match the fund that would have been provided through premiums if the odds had been equal. Those who develop handicaps will then have more resources at their command than others, but the extent of their extra resources will be fixed by the market decisions that people would supposedly have made if circumstances had been more equal than they are. Of course, this argument does involve the fictitious assumption that everyone who suffers handicaps would have bought the average amount of insurance, and we may wish to refine the argument and the strategy so that that no longer holds.[6] But it does not seem an unreasonable assumption for this purpose as it stands.

• • •

It might be wise (if for no other reason than as a convenient summary of the argument from time to time) to bring our story of the immigrants up to date.

---

[6] The averaging assumption is a simplifying assumption only, made to provide a result in the absence of the detailed (and perhaps, for reasons described in the text, indeterminate) information that would enable us to decide how much each handicapped person would have purchased in the hypothetical market. If we had such full information, so that we could tailor compensation to what a particular individual in fact would have bought, the accuracy of the program would be improved. But in the absence of such information averaging is second best, or in any case better than nothing.

By way of supplement to the auction, they now establish a hypothetical insurance market which they effectuate through compulsory insurance at a fixed premium for everyone based on speculations about what the average immigrant would have purchased by way of insurance had the antecedent risk of various handicaps been equal. (We choose for them, that is, one of the simpler possible forms of instituting the hypothetical insurance market. We shall see, when we discuss the problem of skills, that they might well choose a more complex scheme of the sort discussed there.)

But now a question arises. Does this decision place too much weight on the distinction between handicaps, which the immigrants treat in this compensatory way, and accidents touching preferences and ambitions (like the accident of what material resources are in fact available, and of how many other people share a particular person's taste)? The latter will also affect welfare, but they are not matters for compensation under our scheme. Would it not now be fair to treat as handicaps eccentric tastes, or tastes that are expensive or impossible to satisfy because of scarcity of some good that might have been common? We might compensate those who have these tastes by supposing that everyone had an equal chance of being in that position and then establishing a hypothetical insurance market against that possibility.

A short answer is available. Someone who is born with a serious handicap faces his life with what we concede to be fewer resources, just on that account, than others do. This justifies compensation, under a scheme devoted to equality of resources, and though the hypothetical insurance market does not right the balance—nothing can—it seeks to remedy one aspect of the resulting unfairness. But we cannot say that the person whose tastes are expensive, for whatever reason, therefore has fewer resources at his command. For we cannot state (without falling back on some version of equality of welfare) what equality in the distribution of tastes and preferences would be. Why is there less equality of resources when someone has an eccentric taste that makes goods cheaper for others, than when he shares a popular taste and so makes goods more expensive for them? The auction, bringing to bear information about the resources that actually exist and the competing preferences actually in play, is the only true measure of whether any particular person commands equal resources. If the auction has in fact been an equal auction, then the man of eccentric tastes has no less than equal material resources, and the argument that justifies a compensatory hypothetical auction in the case of handicaps has no occasion even to begin. It is true that this argument produces a certain view of the distinction between a person and his circumstances, and assigns his tastes and ambitions to his person, and his physical and mental powers to his circumstances. That is the view of a person I sketched in the introductory section, of someone who forms his ambitions with a sense of their cost to others against some presumed initial equality of economic power, and though this is different from the picture assumed by equality of welfare, it is a picture at the center of equality of resources.

• • •

Equality of resources, once established by the auction, and corrected to provide for handicaps, would be disturbed by production and trade. If one of the immigrants, for example, was specially proficient at producing tomatoes, he might trade his surplus for more than anyone else could acquire, in which case others would begin to envy his bundle of resources. Suppose we wished to create a society in which the division of resources would be continuously equal, in spite of different kinds and degrees of production and trade. Can we adapt our auction so as to produce such a society?

We should begin by considering a different sequence after which people would envy each other's resources, and the division might be thought no longer to be equal. Suppose all the immigrants are in fact sufficiently equal in talent at the few modes of production that the resources allow so that each could produce roughly the same goods from the same set of resources. Nevertheless they wish to lead their lives in different ways, and they in fact acquire different bundles of resources in the initial auction and use them differently thereafter. Adrian chooses resources and works them with the single-minded ambition of producing as much of what others value as possible; and so, at the end of a year, his total stock of goods is larger than anyone else's. Each of the other immigrants would now prefer Adrian's stock to his own; but by hypothesis none of them would have been willing to lead his life so as to produce them. If we look for envy at particular points in time, then each envies Adrian's resources at the end of the year, and the division is therefore not equal. But if we look at envy differently, as a matter of resources over an entire life, and we include a person's occupation as part of the bundle of his goods, then no one envies Adrian's bundle, and the distribution cannot be said to be unequal on that account.

Surely we should take the second, synoptic, point of view. Our final aim is that an equal share of resources should be devoted to the lives of each person, and we have chosen the auction as the right way to measure the value of what is made available to a person, through his decision, for that purpose. If Bruce chooses to acquire land for use as a tennis court, then the question is raised how much his account should be charged, in the reckoning whether an equal share has been put to his use, in virtue of that choice, and it is right that his account should be charged the amount that others would have been willing to pay had the land been devoted to their purposes instead. The appeal of the auction, as a device for picturing equality of resources, is precisely that it enforces that metric. But this scheme will fail, and the device disappoints us, unless Adrian is able to bid a price for the same land that reflects his intention to work rather than play on it and so to acquire whatever gain would prompt him to make that decision. For unless this is permitted, those who want tomatoes and would pay Adrian his price for them will not be able to bid indirectly, through Adrian's decision, against Bruce, who will then secure his tennis court at a price that, because it is too low, defeats equality of resources. This is not, I should add, an argument from efficiency as distinct from fairness; but rather an argument that in the circumstances described, in which talents are equal, efficiency simply is fairness, at least as fairness is conceived under equality of resources. If Adrian is willing to spend his life at drudgery, in return for the profit he will make at prices that others will pay for what he produces, then the land on which he would drudge should not be used for a tennis court instead, unless its value as a tennis court is greater as measured by someone's willingness to invade an initially equal stock of abstract resources.

Now this is to look at the matter entirely from the standpoint of those who want Adrian's tomatoes, a standpoint that treats Adrian only as a means. But we reach the same conclusion if we look at the matter from his point of view as well. If someone chooses to have something inexpensive in his life, under a regime of equality of resources, then he will have more left over for the rest of what he wants. Someone who accepts Algerian wine may use it to wash down plovers' eggs. But a decision to produce one thing rather than another with land, or to use the land for leisure rather than production, is also the choice of something for one's life, and this may be inexpensive as well. Suppose Adrian is desperate for plovers' eggs but would rather work hard at tilling his land than settle for less than champagne. The total may be no more expensive, measured in terms of what his decisions cost others, than a life of leisure and grape juice. If he earns enough by working hard, or by working at work that no one else wants to do, to satisfy all his expensive tastes, then his choice for his own life costs the rest of the community no more than if his tastes were simpler and his industry less. So we have no more reason to deny him hard work and high consumption than less work and frugality. The choice should be indifferent under equality of resources, so long as no one envies the total package of work plus consumption that he chooses. So long as no one envies, that is, his life as a whole. Of course, Adrian might actually enjoy his hard work, so that he makes no sacrifice. He prefers working hard to anything else. But this cannot provide any argument, under equality of resources, that he should gain less in money or other goods by his work than if he hated every minute of it, any more than it argues against charging someone a low price for lettuce, which he actually prefers to truffles.

So we must apply the envy test diachronically: it requires that no one envy the bundle of occupation and resources at the disposal of anyone else over time, though someone may envy another's bundle at any particular time. It would therefore violate equality of resources if the community were to redistribute Adrian's wealth, say, at the end of each year. If everyone had equal talents (as we have been assuming just now), the initial auction would produce continuing equality of resources even though bank-account wealth became more and more unequal as years passed.

Is that unlikely condition—that everyone has equal talent—absolutely necessary to that conclusion? Would the auction produce continuing equality of resources if (as in the real world) talents for production differed sharply from person to person? Now the envy test would fail, even interpreted diachronically. Claude (who likes farming but has a black thumb) would not bid enough for farming land to take that land from Adrian. Or, if he did, he would have to settle for less in the rest of his life. But he would then envy the package of Adrian's occupation and wealth. If we interpret occupation in a manner sensitive to the joys of craft, then Adrian's occupation, which must then be described as skillful, craftsmanlike farming, is simply unavailable to Claude. If we interpret occupation in a more census-like fashion, then Claude may undertake Adrian's occupation, but he cannot have the further resources that Adrian has along with it. So if we continue to insist that the envy test is a necessary condition of equality of resources, then our initial auction will not insure continuing equality, in the real world of unequal talents for production.

But it may now be objected that we should not insist on the envy test at this point, even in principle, for the following reason. We are moving too close to a requirement that people must not envy each other, which is different from the requirement that they must not envy each other's bundles of resources. People may envy each other for a variety of reasons: some are physically more attractive, some more easily satisfied with their condition, some better liked by others, some more intelligent or able in different ways, and so on. Of course, under a regime of equality of welfare each of these differences would be taken into account, and transfers made to erase their welfare consequences so far as possible or feasible. But the point of equality of resources is fundamentally different: it is that people should have the same external resources at their command to make of them what, given these various features and talents, they can. That point is satisfied by an initial auction, but since people are different it is neither necessary nor desirable that resources should remain equal thereafter, and quite impossible that all envy should be eliminated by political distribution. If one person, by dint of superior effort or talent, uses his equal share to create more than another, he is entitled to profit thereby, because his gain is not made at the expense of someone else who does less with his share. We recognized that, just now, when we conceded that superior industry should be rewarded, so that Adrian, who worked hard, should be allowed to keep the rewards of his effort.

Now this objection harbors many mistakes, but they all come to this: it confuses equality of resources with the fundamentally different idea sometimes called equality of opportunity. It is not true, in the first place, that someone who does more with his initial share does not, in so doing, lessen the value of what others have. If Adrian were not so successful at agriculture, then Claude's own efforts would be rewarded more, because people would buy his inferior produce having no better alternative. If Adrian were not so successful and hence so rich he would not be able to pay so much for wine, and Claude, with his smaller fortune, would be able to buy more at a cheaper price. These are simply the most obvious consequences of the fact that the immigrants form one economy, after the initial auction, rather than a set of distinct economies. Of course these consequences also follow from the situation we discussed a moment ago. If Adrian and Bruce have the same talents, but Adrian chooses to work harder or differently and acquires more money, then this may also decrease the value of Claude's share to him. The difference between these two circumstances, if there is one, lies elsewhere; but it is important to reject the claim, instinct in some arguments for equality of opportunity, that if people start with equal shares the prosperity of one does no damage to the other.

Nor is it true that if we aim at a result in which those with less talent do not envy the circumstances of those with more talent we have destroyed the distinction between envying others and envying what they have. For Adrian has two things that Claude would prefer to have which belong to Adrian's circumstances rather than his person. The desires and needs of other people provide Adrian but not Claude with a satisfying occupation, and Adrian has more money than Claude can have. Perhaps nothing can be done, by way of political structure or distribution, to erase these differences and remove the envy entirely. We cannot, for example, alter the tastes of other people by electrical means so as to make them value what Claude can produce more and what Adrian can produce less. But this provides no argument against other schemes, like schemes of education that would allow Claude to find satisfaction in his work or of taxation that would redistribute some of Adrian's wealth to him, and we could fairly describe these schemes as aiming to remove Claude's envy of what Adrian has rather than of what Adrian is.

Important as these points are, it is more important still to identify and correct another mistake that the present objection makes. It misunderstands our earlier conclusion, that when talents are roughly equal the auction provides continuing equality of resources, and so misses the important distinction between that case and the present argument. The objection supposes that we reached that conclusion because we accept, as the basis of equality of resources, what we might call the starting-gate theory of fairness: that if people start in the same circumstances, and do not cheat or steal from one another, then it is fair that people keep what they gain through their own skill. But the starting-gate theory of fairness is very far from equality of resources. Indeed it is hardly a coherent political theory at all.

The starting-gate theory holds that justice requires equal initial resources. But it also holds that justice requires laissez-faire thereafter, in accordance, presumably, with some version of the Lockean theory that people acquire property by mixing their labor with goods or something of that sort. But these two principles cannot live comfortably together. Equality can have no greater force in justifying initial equal holdings when the immigrants land—against the competing that all property should be available for Lockean acquisition at that time—than later in justifying redistributions when wealth becomes unequal because people's productive talents are different. The same point may be put the other way around. The theory of Lockean acquisition (or whatever other theory of justice in acquisition is supposed to justify the laissez-faire component in a starting-gate theory) can have no less force in governing the initial distribution than it has in justifying title through talent and effort later. If the theory is sound later, then why does it not command a Lockean process of acquisition in the first instance, rather than an equal distribution of all there is? The moment when the immigrants first land is, after all, an arbitrary point in their lives at which to locate any one-shot requirement that they each have an equal share of any available resources. If that requirement holds then, it must also hold on the tenth anniversary of that date, which is, in the words of the banal and important cliché, the first day in the rest of their lives. So if justice requires an equal auction when they land, it must require a fresh, equal auction from time to time thereafter; and if justice requires laissez-faire thereafter, it must require it when they land.

Suppose someone replies that there is an important difference between the initial distribution of resources and any later redistribution. When the immigrants land, no one owns any of the resources, and the principle of equality therefore dictates equal initial shares. But later, after the initial resources have been auctioned, they are each owned in some way by someone, so that the principle of equality is superceded by respect for people's rights in property or something of that sort. This reply begs the question straightway. For we are considering precisely the question whether a system of ownership should be established in the first instance that has that consequence, or, rather, whether a different system of ownership should be chosen that explicitly makes any acquisition subject to schemes of redistribution later. If the latter sort of system is chosen, at the outset, then no one can later complain that redistribution is ruled out by his property rights alone. I do not mean that no theory of justice can consistently distinguish between justice in initial acquisition and justice in transfer on the ground that anyone may do what he wants with property that is already his. Nozick's theory, for example, does just that. This is consistent, because his theory of justice in initial acquisition purports to justify a system of property rights which have that consequence: justice in transfer, that is, flows from the rights the theory of acquisition claims are acquired in acquiring property. But the theory of initial acquisition on which the starting-gate theory relies, which is equality of resources, does not even purport to justify a characterization of property that necessarily includes absolute control without limit of time thereafter.

So the starting-gate theory, that the immigrants should start off equal in resources but grow prosperous or lean through their own efforts thereafter, is an indefensible combination of very different theories of justice. Something like that combination makes sense in games, such as Monopoly, whose point is to allow luck and skill to play a highly circumscribed and, in the last analysis, arbitrary, role; but it cannot hold together a political theory. Our own principle, that if people of equal talent choose different lives it is unfair to redistribute halfway through those lives, makes no appeal to the starting-gate theory at all. It is based on the very different idea that the equality in question is equality of resources devoted to whole lives. This principle offers a clear answer to the question that embarrasses the present objection. Our theory does not suppose that an equal division of resources is appropriate at one moment in someone's life but not at any other. It argues only that resources available to him at any moment must be a function of resources available or consumed by him at others, so that the explanation of why someone has less money now may be that he has consumed expensive leisure earlier. Nothing like that explanation is available to explain why Claude, who has worked as hard and in the same way as Adrian, should have less in virtue of the fact that he is less skillful.

So we must reject the starting-gate theory, and recognize that the requirements of equality (in the real world at least) pull in opposite directions. On the

one hand we must, on pain of violating equality, allow the distribution of resources at any particular moment to be (as we might say) ambition-sensitive. It
must, that is, reflect the cost or benefit to others of the choices people make so
that, for example, those who choose to invest rather than consume, or to consume less expensively rather than more, or to work in more rather than less
profitable ways, must be permitted to retain the gains that flow from these decisions in an equal auction followed by free trade. But on the other hand, we
must not allow the distribution of resources at any moment to be endowment-
sensitive, that is, to be affected by differences in ability of the sort that produce
income differences in a laissez-faire economy among people with the same ambitions. Can we devise some formula that offers a practical, or even a theoretical, compromise between these two, apparently competing, requirements?

•   •   •

We should turn, therefore, to a more familiar idea: the periodic redistribution of resources through some form of income tax.[7] We want to develop a
scheme of redistribution, so far as we are able, that will neutralize the effects of
differential talents, yet preserve the consequences of one person choosing an occupation, in response to his sense of what he wants to do with his life, that is
more expensive for the community than the choice another makes. An income
tax is a plausible device for this purpose because it leaves intact the possibility
of choosing a life in which sacrifices are constantly made and discipline steadily
imposed for the sake of financial success and the further resources it brings,
though of course it neither endorses nor condemns that choice. But it also recognizes the role of genetic luck in such a life. The accommodation it makes is a
compromise; but it is a compromise of two requirements of equality, in the face
of both practical and conceptual uncertainty how to satisfy these requirements,
not a compromise of equality for the sake of some independent value such as
efficiency.

But of course the appeal of a tax depends on our ability to fix rates of taxation that will make that compromise accurately. It might be helpful, in that aim,
if we were able to find some way of identifying, in any person's wealth at any
particular time, the component traceable to differential talents as distinguished
from differential ambitions. We might then try to devise a tax that would

---

[7] Notice that our analysis of the problem that differential talents presents to equality of resources
calls for an income tax, rather than either a wealth or a consumption tax. If people begin with
equal resources, then we wish to tax to adjust for different skills so far as these produce different income, because it is only in that way that they threaten equality of resources. Someone's decision to spend rather than save what he has earned is precisely the kind of decision whose
impact should be determined by the market uncorrected for tax under this analysis. Of course,
there might be technical or other reasons why a society dedicated to equality of welfare would
introduce taxes other than income taxes. Such a society might want to encourage savings, for
example. But these taxes would not be responses to the problem now under consideration.
Should unearned (investment) income be taxed under the present argument? I assume that unearned income reflects skill in investment as well as preferences for later consumption, in which
case that argument would extend to taxing such income. Since I am not considering, in this essay, the problem of later generations, I do not consider inheritance or estate taxes at all.

recapture, for redistribution, just this component. But we cannot hope to identify such a component, even given perfect information about people's personalities. For we will be thwarted by the reciprocal influence that talents and ambitions exercise on each other. Talents are nurtured and developed, not discovered full-blown, and people choose which talents to develop in response to their beliefs about what sort of person it is best to be. But people also wish to develop and use the talents they have, not simply because they prefer a life of relative success, but because the exercise of talent is enjoyable and perhaps also out of a sense that an unused talent is a waste. Someone with a good eye or a skilled hand conceives a picture of what would make his life valuable that someone more clumsy would not.

So we cannot hope to fix the rates of our income tax so as to redistribute exactly that part of each person's income that is attributable to his talent as distinguished from his ambitions. Talents and ambitions are too closely intertwined. Can we do better by proceeding on a slightly different tack? Can we aim to fix rates so as to leave each person with the income he would have had if, counterfactually, talents for production had all been equal? No, because it is impossible to say, in any relevant way, what sort of world that would be. We should have to decide what sort and level of talent everyone would have equally, and then what income people exploiting those talents to different degrees of effort would reach. Should we stipulate that in that world everyone would have the talents that the most talented people in the real world now have? Do we mean, by "the most talented people," the people who are able to earn the most money in the actual world if they work single-mindedly for money? But in a world in which everyone could hit a high inside pitch, or play sexy roles in films, with equal authority, there would probably be no baseball or films; in any case no one would be paid much for exercising such talents. Nor would any other description of the talents everyone would be supposed to have in equal degree be any more help.

But though this crude counterfactual exercise must fail, it suggests a more promising exercise. Let us review our situation. We want to find some way to distinguish fair from unfair differences in wealth generated by differences in occupation. Unfair differences are those traceable to genetic luck, to talents that make some people prosperous but are denied to others who would exploit them to the full if they had them. But if this is right, then the problem of differential talents is in certain ways like the problem of handicaps we have already considered.

• • •

Though skills are different from handicaps, the difference can be understood as one of degree: we may say that someone who cannot play basketball like Wilt Chamberlain, paint like Piero, or make money like Geneen, suffers from an (especially common) handicap. This description emphasizes one aspect of skills, which is their genetic and, hence, luck component, at the expense of hiding the more intimate and reciprocal play we noticed between skills and ambitions. But it also points to one theoretical solution to the problem of identifying at least the minimum requirements of a fair redistribution policy responding to differences in skill. We may capitalize on the similarities between handicaps and relative lack of skill to propose that the level of compensation for the latter be fixed, in principle, by asking how much insurance someone would have bought, in an insurance sub-auction with initially equal resources, against the possibility of not having a particular level of some skill.

Of course, there is no actual insurance market against lack of what we ordinarily take to be skill, as there is an insurance market against catastrophes that result in handicap. For one thing, a person's level of skills is sufficiently fixed and known, at least roughly, before that person enters the insurance market, so that lack of skill is primarily a matter of history rather than future contingency. (There are other reasons as well, which we shall have to identify in a moment.) But let us nevertheless try to frame a hypothetical question something like the question we asked in the case of handicaps. Suppose an imaginary world in which, though the distribution of skills over the community were in the aggregate what it actually is, people for some reason all had the same antecedent chance of suffering the consequences of lacking any particular set of these skills, and were all in a position to buy insurance against these consequences at the same premium structure. How much insurance would each buy at what cost? If we can make sense of that question, and answer it even by fixing rough lower limits on average, then we shall have a device for fixing at least the lower bounds of a tax-and-redistribution program satisfying the demands of equality of resources.

• • •

But we must now state and consider the important argument that the hypothetical insurance market is altogether the wrong approach to the problem of reconciling these two requirements, because it undervalues the transfer payments that those whose talents are not in great demand should receive. The hypothetical insurance market approach aims to put such people in the position they would have been in had the risk of their fate been subjectively equally shared. But it does not make them as well-off in the end as those whose talents are in more demand, or those with similar talents lucky enough to find more profitable employment. Some people (movie stars and captains of industry and first basemen) in fact earn at a rate far beyond the rate of coverage any reasonable person would choose in an insurance market, as our inspection showed. The hypothetical insurance market approach is beside the point (it might be said) exactly because it provides no answer to someone who is unable to find a job, points to the movie star and declares, perfectly accurately, that he would do that work for that pay if asked. The fact that no one would buy coverage at a movie-star level in an equal insurance market simply underscores the injustice. The movie star had no need to buy that insurance. He won his life of luxury and glamor without it. The brute fact remains that some people have much more than others of what both desire, through no reason connected with choice. The envy test we once seemed to respect has been decisively defeated, and no defensible conception of equality can argue that equality recommends that result.

This is a powerful complaint, and there is no answer, I think, but to summarize and restate our earlier arguments to see if they can still persuade with that complaint ringing in our ears. Let us return to the immigrants. Claude cannot argue, on grounds of equality, for a world in which he has the movie star's income. The immigrants cannot create a world in which everyone who would be willing to work movie-star hours can have movie-star pay. If Claude is unhappy with his situation, even after the tax scheme is put into play, he must propose a world in which no one will have such an income and his income will be relatively (and perhaps absolutely) higher in consequence. But whichever such world he proposes will be changed not only for those who under our scheme would have more than he does, but for everyone else as well, including those who for one reason or another, including their preferences for work, leisure, and consumption, will have less. If, for example, no one can earn movie-star wages, people who wish to watch movies may perhaps find very different fare available which, rightly or wrongly, they will not regard as highly as what they now have. It is, of course, impossible to say in advance just what the consequences of any profound change in an economic system would be, and who would gain or lose in the long run. These changes could not be properly charted along any one simple dimension. They could not be measured simply in the funds or other "primary goods" available to one or another economic class, for example. For they also affect the prices and scarcity of different goods and opportunities that members of any particular class, even economic class, will value very differently from one another. That is exactly why the immigrants chose an auction, sensitive to what people in fact wanted for their lives, as their primary engine for achieving equality.

So though Claude may truly say that the difference between him and the movie star does not reflect any differences in tastes or ambitions or theories of the good, and so does not in itself implicate our first, ambition-sensitive requirement of equality in wage structure, he could not recommend any general change in relative economic positions that would not wreak wholesale and dramatic changes in the positions of others, changes which do implicate that requirement. Of course, this fact does not in itself rule out any changes that Claude might propose. On the contrary, the status quo achieved by laissez-faire production and trade from an equal start has no natural or privileged status, as I have been at pains to emphasize, particularly my argument against the "starting-gate" theory of equality. If Claude can show that a proper conception of equality of resources recommends some change, the fact that many people from all ranks would be then worse-off, given their particular tastes and ambitions, provides no objection, any more than the fact that Claude is worse-off without some change in itself provides an argument in favor of that change. I mean to emphasize only that Claude needs some argument in favor of the change he recommends which is independent of his own relative position. It is not enough for him to point to people, even those of the same ambitions and tastes as himself, who do better as things are.

• • •

But it is nevertheless important to try to discover arguments showing that equality of resources, as a distinct ideal, would recommend erasing even those wealth differentials that the hypothetical insurance argument would permit, and this project is not threatened by my uncertainty whether we should feel dismayed, or find our intuitions undermined, if we did not in fact discover any. I do not doubt that such arguments can be found, and it is part of my purpose to provoke them. But it is worth mentioning certain arguments that do not seem promising. It might be said, for example, that equality of resources would approve a different world still, in which people had in fact equal talents for production, more than either of the other two I described, so that we ought to strive to create a system in which wealth differences traceable to occupation were no greater than they would be in that world. There is an important point locked in that claim, which is that an egalitarian society ought, just in the name of equality, to devote special resources to training those whose talents, as things fall out, place them lower on the income scale. That is part of the larger question of an egalitarian theory of education, which I have not even attempted to take up here. But the more general point suffers from the fact that we could not even begin to replicate the wealth distribution that would hold in that different world without making assumptions about the mix of talents that everyone in that world would share in equal abundance, and no specification of the mix could be neutral amongst the various ambitions and tastes in the real world in which we attempt that replication.

Suppose someone says simply (and with creditable impatience) that equality of resources just *must* prefer a world in which people have more nearly equal wealth than they are likely to have in a world of free trade, even against a background of equal initial wealth and even as corrected by the hypothetical insurance market. To deny that (it might be said) is simply to prefer other values of equality, not to state an acceptable conception of equality itself. That is, of course, exactly what my arguments have been meant to challenge. Once we understand the importance, under equality of resources, of the requirement that any theory of distribution must be ambition-sensitive, and understand the wholesale effects of any scheme of distribution or redistribution on the lives which almost everyone in the community will want and be permitted to lead, we must regard with suspicion any flat statement that equality of resources just must be defined in a way that ignores these facts. Equality of resources is a complex ideal. It is probably (as the various arguments we have canvassed in this essay suggest) an indeterminate ideal that accepts, within a certain range, a variety of different distributions. But this much seems clear: any defensible conception of that ideal must attend to its different dimensions, and not reject out of hand the requirement that it be sensitive to the cost of one person's life to other people. The present suggestion, that genuine theories of equality must be concerned only with the quantity of disposable goods or liquid assets people command at a particular time, is a piece of pre-analytic dogma that does not, in fact, protect the boundaries of the concept of equality from confusion with other concepts, but rather thwarts the attempt to picture equality as an independent and powerful political ideal.

47.
Equality of Capacity

AMARTYA SEN

WHY EQUALITY? WHAT EQUALITY?

Two central issues for ethical analysis of equality are: (1) Why equality? (2) Equality of what? The two questions are distinct but thoroughly inter-dependent. We cannot begin to defend or criticize equality without knowing what on earth we are talking about, i.e. equality of what features (e.g., incomes, wealths, opportunities, achievements, freedoms, rights)? We cannot possibly answer the first question without addressing the second. That seems obvious enough.

But if we *do* answer question (2), do we still *need* to address question (1)? If we have successfully argued in favor of equality of x (whatever that x is—some outcome, some right, some freedom, some respect, or some something else), then we have already argued for equality in *that* form, with x as the standard of comparison. Similarly, if we have rebutted the claim to equality of x, then we have already argued against equality in that form, with x as the standard of comparison. There is, in this view, no "further," no "deeper," question to be answered about why—or why not—"equality." Question (1), in this analysis, looks very much like the poor man's question (2).

There is some sense in seeing the matter in this way, but there is also a more interesting substantive issue here. It relates to the fact that every normative theory of social arrangement that has at all stood the test of time seems to demand equality of *something*—something that is regarded as particularly important in that theory. The theories involved are diverse and frequently at war with each other, but they still seem to have that common feature. In the contemporary disputes in political philosophy, equality does, of course, figure prominently in the contributions of John Rawls (equal liberty and equality in the distribution of "primary goods"), Ronald Dworkin ("treatment as equals," "equality of resources"), Thomas Nagel ("economic equality"), Thomas Scanlon ("equality"), and others generally associated with a "pro equality" view. But equality in some space seems to be demanded even by those who are typically seen as having disputed the "case for equality" or for "distributive justice." For example, Robert Nozick may not demand equality of utility or equality of holdings of primary goods, but he does demand equality of libertarian rights—no one has any more right to liberty than anyone else. James Buchanan builds equal legal and political treatment—indeed a great deal more—into his view of a good society. In each theory, equality *is* sought in some space—a space that is seen as having a central role in that theory.

But what about utilitarianism? Surely, utilitarians do not, in general, want the equality of the total utilities enjoyed by different people. The utilitarian formula requires the maximization of the sum-total of the utilities of all people *taken together*, and that is, in an obvious sense, not particularly egalitarian. In fact, the equality that utilitarianism seeks takes the form of equal treatment of human beings in the space of *gains and losses of utilities*. There is an insistence on equal weights on everyone's utility gains in the utilitarian objective function.

This diagnosis of "hidden" egalitarianism in utilitarian philosophy might well be resisted on the ground that utilitarianism really involves a sum-total maximizing approach, and it might be thought that, as a result, any egalitarian feature of utilitarianism cannot be more than accidental. But this reasoning is deceptive. The utilitarian approach is undoubtedly a *maximizing* one, but the real question is what is the nature of the objective function it maximizes. That objective function could have been quite inegalitarian, e.g. giving much more weight to the utilities of some than to those of others. Instead, utilitarianism attaches exactly the same importance to the utilities of all people in the objective function, and that feature—coupled with the maximizing format—guarantees that everyone's utility gains get the same weight in the maximizing exercise. The egalitarian foundation is, thus, quite central to the entire utilitarian exercise. Indeed, it is precisely this egalitarian feature that relates to the foundational principle of utilitarianism of "giving equal weight to the equal interests of all the parties"[1] or to "always assign the same weight to all individuals' interests."[2]

What do we conclude from this fact? One obvious conclusion is that being egalitarian (i.e. egalitarian in *some space or other* to which great importance is attached) is not really a "uniting" feature. Indeed, it is precisely because there are such substantive differences between the endorsement of different spaces in which equality is recommended by different authors that the basic similarity between them (in the form of wanting equality in *some* space that is seen as important) can be far from transparent. This is especially so when the term "equality" is defined—typically implicitly—as equality in a *particular* space.

●   ●   ●

Wanting equality of *something*—something seen as *important*—is undoubtedly a similarity of some kind, but that similarity does not put the warring camps on the same side. It only shows that the battle is not, in an important sense, about "why equality?", but about "equality of what?".

Since some spaces are traditionally associated with claims of "equality" in political or social or economic philosophy, it is equality in one of those spaces (e.g. incomes, wealths, utilities) that tend to go under the heading "egalitarianism." I am *not* arguing against the continued use of the term "egalitarianism" in one of those senses; there is no harm in that practice if it is understood to be a claim about equality in a specific space (and by implication, *against* equality

---

[1] R. M. Hare. *Moral Thinking: Its Levels, Methods and Point* (Oxford: Clarendon Press, 1981), p. 26.

[2] J. C. Harsanyi. "Morality and the Theory of Rational Behavior," in *Utilitarianism and Beyond*, A. Sen and B. Williams, eds. (Cambridge: Cambridge University Press, 1982), p. 47.

in other spaces). But it is important to recognize the limited reach of that usage, and also the fact that demanding equality in one space—no matter how hallowed by tradition—can lead one to be anti-egalitarian in some other space, the comparative importance of which in the overall assessment has to be critically assessed.

IMPARTIALITY AND EQUALITY

The analysis in the last section pointed to the partisan character of the usual interpretations of the question "why equality?". That question, I have argued, has to be faced, just as much, even by those who are seen—by themselves and by others—as "anti-egalitarian," for they too are egalitarian in *some* space that is important in their theory. But it was not, of course, argued that the question "why equality?" was, in any sense, pointless. We may be persuaded that the basic disputations are likely to be about "equality of what?", but it might still be asked whether there *need be* a demand for equality in *some* important space or other. Even if it turns out that every substantive theory of social arrangements in vogue *is,* in fact, egalitarian in some space—a space seen as central in that theory—there is still the need to explain and defend that general characteristic in each case. The shared practice—even if it were universally shared—would still need some defense.

The issue to address is not so much whether there *must* be *for strictly formal reasons* (such as the discipline of "the language of morals"), equal consideration for all, at some level, in all ethical theories of social arrangement. That is an interesting and hard question, but one I need not address in the present context; the answer to it is, in my judgment, by no means clear. I am more concerned with the question whether ethical theories must have this basic feature of equality to have substantive plausibility in the world in which we live.

It may be useful to ask *why* it is that so many altogether different substantive theories of the ethics of social arrangements have the common feature of demanding equality of *something*—something important. It is, I believe, arguable that to have any kind of plausibility, ethical reasoning on social matters must involve elementary equal consideration for all at *some* level that is seen as critical. The absence of such equality would make a theory arbitrarily discriminating and hard to defend. A theory may accept—indeed demand—inequality in terms of many variables, but in defending those inequalities it would be hard to duck the need to relate them, ultimately, to equal consideration for all in some adequately substantial way.

Perhaps this feature relates to the requirement that ethical reasoning, especially about social arrangements, has to be, in some sense, credible from the viewpoint of others—potentially *all* others. The question "why this system?" has to be answered, as it were, for all the participants in that system. There are some Kantian elements in this line of reasoning, even though the equality demanded need not have a strictly Kantian structure.

Recently Thomas Scanlon[3] has analysed the relevance and power of the requirement that one should "be able to justify one's actions to others on grounds that they could not reasonably reject." The requirement of "fairness" on which Rawls[4] builds his theory of justice can be seen as providing a specific structure for determining what one can or cannot reasonably reject. Similarly, the demands of "impartiality"—and some substantively exacting forms of "universalizability"—invoked as general requirements have that feature of equal concern in some major way. Reasoning of this general type certainly has much to do with the foundations of ethics, and has cropped up in different forms in the methodological underpinning of substantive ethical proposals.

The need to defend one's theories, judgements, and claims to others who may be—directly or indirectly—involved, makes equality of consideration at some level a hard requirement to avoid. There are interesting methodological questions regarding the status of this condition, in particular: whether it is a logical requirement or a substantive demand, and whether it is connected with the need for "objectivity" in ethics. I shall not pursue these questions further here, since the main concerns of this monograph do not turn on our answers to these questions.

What is of direct interest is the plausibility of claiming that equal consideration at some level—a level that is seen as important—is a demand that cannot be easily escaped in presenting a political or ethical theory of social arrangements. It is also of considerable pragmatic interest to note that impartiality and equal concern, in some form or other, provide a shared background to all the major ethical and political proposals in this field that continue to receive argued support and reasoned defence. One consequence of all this is the acceptance—often implicit—of the need to justify disparate advantages of different individuals in things that matter. That justification frequently takes the form of showing the integral connection of that inequality with equality in some *other* important—allegedly *more* important—space.

Indeed, it is equality in that more important space that may then be seen as contributing to the contingent demands for *inequality* in the other spaces. The justification of inequality in some features is made to rest on the equality of some other feature, taken to be more basic in that ethical system. Equality in what is seen as the "base" is invoked for a reasoned defence of the resulting inequalities in the far-flung "peripheries."

•   •   •

[3] Thomas Scanlon. "Contractualism and Utilitarianism," in *Utilitarianism and Beyond*. Amartya Sen and Bernard Williams, eds. (Cambridge: Cambridge University Press, 1982).

[4] John Rawls. *A Theory of Justice* (Cambridge, MA: Harvard University Press, 1971).

RAWLSIAN EQUALITY

Rawls's "two principles of justice" characterize the need for equality in terms of—what he has called—"primary social goods."[5] These are "things that every rational man is presumed to want," including "rights, liberties and opportunities, income and wealth, and the social bases of self-respect." Basic liberties are separated out as having priority over other primary goods, and thus priority is given to the principle of liberty which demands that "each person is to have an equal right to the most extensive basic liberty compatible with a similar liberty for others." The second principle supplements this, demanding efficiency and equality, judging advantage in terms of an index of primary goods. Inequalities are condemned unless they work out to everyone's advantage. This incorporates the "Difference Principle" in which priority is given to furthering the interests of the worst-off. And that leads to maximin, or to leximin, defined not on individual utilities but on the index of primary goods. But given the priority of the liberty principle, no trade-offs are permitted between basic liberties and economic and social gain.

Herbert Hart has persuasively disputed Rawls's arguments for the priority of liberty, but with that question I shall not be concerned in this lecture. What is crucial for the problem under discussion is the concentration on bundles of primary social goods. Some of the difficulties with welfarism that I tried to discuss will not apply to the pursuit of Rawlsian equality. Objective criteria of well-being can be directly accommodated within the index of primary goods. So can be Mill's denial of the parity between pleasures from different sources, since the sources can be discriminated on the basis of the nature of the goods. Furthermore, while the Difference Principle is egalitarian in a way similar to leximin, it avoids the much-criticised feature of leximin of giving more income to people who are hard to please and who have to be deluged in champagne and buried in caviar to bring them to a normal level of utility, which you and I get from a sandwich and beer. Since advantage is judged not in terms of utilities at all, but through the index of primary goods, expensive tastes cease to provide a ground for getting more income. Rawls justifies this in terms of a person's responsibility for his own ends.

But what about the cripple with utility disadvantage, whom we discussed earlier?* Leximin will give him more income in a pure distribution problem. Utilitarianism, I had complained, will give him *less*. The Difference Principle will give him neither more nor less on grounds of his being a cripple. His utility disadvantage will be irrelevant to the Difference Principle. This may seem hard, and I think it is. Rawls justifies this by pointing out that "hard cases" can "distract our moral perception by leading us to think of people distant from us whose fate arouses pity and anxiety.[6] This can be so, but hard cases do exist,

---

* This is an individual whose disabilities mean that he can obtain less utility than others from a given set of resources—Eds.

[5] Ibid., pp. 60–5.

[6] John Rawls, "A Kantian Concept of Equality" *Cambridge Review* (February 1975), p. 96.

and to take disabilities, or special health needs, or physical or mental defects, as morally irrelevant, or to leave them out for fear of making a mistake, may guarantee that the *opposite* mistake will be made.

And the problem does not end with hard cases. The primary goods approach seems to take little note of the diversity of human beings. In the context of assessing utilitarian equality, it was argued that if people were fundamentally similar in terms of utility functions, then the utilitarian concern with maximizing the sum-total of utilities would push us simultaneously also in the direction of equality of utility levels. Thus utilitarianism could be rendered vastly more attractive if people really were similar. A corresponding remark can be made about the Rawlsian Difference Principle. If people were basically very similar, then an index of primary goods might be quite a good way of judging advantage. But, in fact, people seem to have very different needs varying with health, longevity, climatic conditions, location, work conditions, temperament, and even body size (affecting food and clothing requirements). So what is involved is not merely ignoring a few hard cases, but overlooking very widespread and real differences. Judging advantage purely in terms of primary goods leads to a partially blind morality.

Indeed, it can be argued that there is, in fact, an element of "fetishism" in the Rawlsian framework. Rawls takes primary goods as the embodiment of advantage, rather than taking advantage to be a *relationship* between persons and goods. Utilitarianism, or leximin, or—more generally—welfarism does not have this fetishism, since utilities are reflections of one type of relation between persons and goods. For example, income and wealth are not valued under utilitarianism as physical units, but in terms of their capacity to create human happiness or to satisfy human desires. Even if utility is not thought to be the right focus for the person–good relationship, to have an entirely good-oriented framework provides a peculiar way of judging advantage.

It can also be argued that while utility in the form of happiness or desire-fulfilment may be an *inadequate* guide to urgency, the Rawlsian framework asserts it to be *irrelevant* to urgency, which is, of course, a much stronger claim. The distinction was discussed earlier in the context of assessing welfarism, and it was pointed out that a rejection of welfarism need not take us to the point in which utility is given no role whatsoever. That a person's interest should have nothing directly to do with his happiness or desire-fulfilment seems difficult to justify. Even in terms of the prior-principle of prudential acceptability in the "original position," it is not at all clear why people in that primordial state should be taken to be so indifferent to the joys and sufferings in occupying particular positions, or if they are not, why their concern about these joys and sufferings should be taken to be morally irrelevant.

BASIC CAPABILITY EQUALITY

This leads to the further question: Can we not construct an adequate theory of equality on the *combined* grounds of Rawlsian equality and equality under the two welfarist conceptions, with some trade-offs among them. I would now like to argue briefly why I believe this too may prove to be informationally short. This can, of course, easily be asserted *if* claims arising from considerations other than well-being were acknowledged to be legitimate. Non-exploitation, or non-discrimination, requires the use of information not fully captured either by utility or by primary goods. Other conceptions of entitlements can also be brought in going beyond concern with personal well-being only. But in what follows I shall not introduce these concepts. My contention is that *even* the concept of *needs* does not get adequate coverage through the information on primary goods and utility.

I shall use a case-implication argument. Take the cripple again with marginal utility disadvantage. We saw that utilitarianism would do nothing for him; in fact it will give him *less* income than to the physically fit. Nor would the Difference Principle help him; it will leave his physical disadvantage severely alone. He did, however, get preferential treatment under leximin, and more generally, under criteria fostering total equality. His low level of total utility was the basis of his claim. But now suppose that he is no worse off than others in utility terms despite his physical handicap because of certain other utility features. This could be because he has a jolly disposition. Or because he has a low aspiration level and his heart leaps up whenever he sees a rainbow in the sky. Or because he is religious and feels that he will be rewarded in after-life, or cheerfully accepts what he takes to be just penalty for misdeeds in a past incarnation. The important point is that despite his marginal utility disadvantage, he has no longer a total utility deprivation. Now not even leximin—or any other notion of equality focussing on total utility—will do much for him. If we still think that he has needs as a cripple that should be catered to, then the basis of that claim clearly rests neither in high marginal utility, nor in low total utility, nor—of course—in deprivation in terms of primary goods.

It is arguable that what is missing in all this framework is some notion of "basic capabilities": a person being able to do certain basic things. The ability to move about is the relevant one here, but one can consider others, e.g., the ability to meet one's nutritional requirements, the wherewithal to be clothed and sheltered, the power to participate in the social life of the community. The notion of urgency related to this is not fully captured by either utility or primary goods, or any combination of the two. Primary goods suffers from fetishist handicap in being concerned with goods, and even though the list of goods is specified in a broad and inclusive way, encompassing rights, liberties, opportunities, income, wealth, and the social basis of self-respect, it still is concerned with good things rather than with what these good things *do* to human beings. Utility, on the other hand, *is* concerned with what these things do to human beings, but uses a metric that focusses not on the person's capabilities but on his mental reaction. There is something still missing in the combined list of primary goods and utilities. If it is argued that resources should be devoted to remove or substantially reduce the handicap of the cripple despite there being no marginal utility argument (because it is expensive), despite there being no total utility argument (because he is so contented), and despite there being no primary goods deprivation (because he has the goods that others have), the case must rest on something else. I believe what is at issue is the interpretation of needs in the form of basic capabilities. This interpretation of needs and interests is often implicit in the demand for equality. This type of equality I shall call "basic capability equality."

The focus on basic capabilities can be seen as a natural extension of Rawls's concern with primary goods, shifting attention from goods to what goods do to human beings. Rawls himself motivates judging advantage in terms of primary goods by referring to capabilities, even though his criteria end up focussing on goods as such: on income rather than on what income does, on the "social bases of self-respect" rather than on self-respect itself, and so on. If human beings were very like each other, this would not have mattered a great deal, but there is evidence that the conversion of goods to capabilities varies from person to person substantially, and the equality of the former may still be far from the equality of the latter.

There are, of course, many difficulties with the notion of "basic capability equality." In particular, the problem of indexing the basic capability bundles is a serious one. It is, in many ways, a problem comparable with the indexing of primary good bundles in the context of Rawlsian equality. This is not the occasion to go into the technical issues involved in such an indexing, but it is clear that whatever partial ordering can be done on the basis of broad uniformity of personal preferences must be supplemented by certain established conventions of relative importance.

The ideas of relative importance are, of course, conditional on the nature of the society. The notion of the equality of basic capabilities is a very general one, but any application of it must be rather culture-dependent, especially in the weighting of different capabilities. While Rawlsian equality has the characteristic of being both culture-dependent and fetishist, basic capability equality avoids fetishism, but remains culture-dependent. Indeed, basic capability equality can be seen as essentially an extension of the Rawlsian approach in a non-fetishist direction.

48.
Equality of Opportunity for Welfare

RICHARD ARNESON

Insofar as we care for equality as a distributive ideal, what is it exactly that we prize? Many persons are troubled by the gap between the living standards of rich people and poor people in modern societies or by the gap between the average standard of living in rich societies and that prevalent in poor societies. To some extent at any rate it is the gap itself that is troublesome, not just the low absolute level of the standard of living of the poor. But it is not easy to decide what measure of the "standard of living" it is appropriate to employ to give content to the ideal of distributive equality. Recent discussions by John Rawls[1] and Ronald Dworkin[2] have debated the merits of versions of equality of welfare and equality of resources taken as interpretations of the egalitarian ideal. In this paper I shall argue that the idea of equal opportunity for welfare is the best interpretation of the ideal of distributive equality.

Consider a distributive agency that has at its disposal a stock of goods that individuals want to own and use. We need not assume that each good is useful for every person, just that each good is useful for someone. Each good is homogeneous in quality and can be divided as finely as you choose. The problem to be considered is: How to divide the goods in order to meet an appropriate standard of equality. This discussion assumes that some goods are legitimately available for distribution in this fashion, hence that the entitlements and deserts of individuals do not predetermine the proper ownership of all resources. No argument is provided for this assumption, so in this sense my article is addressed to egalitarians, not their opponents.

I. EQUALITY OF RESOURCES

The norm of equality of resources stipulates that to achieve equality the agency ought to give everybody a share of goods that is exactly identical to everyone else's and that exhausts all available resources to be distributed. A straightforward objection to equality of resources so understood is that if Smith and Jones have similar tastes and abilities except that Smith has a severe physical handicap remediable with the help of expensive crutches, then if the two are accorded equal resources, Smith must spend the bulk of his resources on crutches

---

[1] John Rawls, "Social Unity and Primary Goods," in Amartya Sen and Bernard Williams, eds., *Utilitarianism and Beyond* (Cambridge: Cambridge University Press, 1982), pp. 159–185.

[2] Ronald Dworkin, "What Is Equality? Part 1: Equality of Welfare," *Philosophy and Public Affairs* 10 (1981): 185–246; and "What Is Equality? Part 2: Equality of Resources," *Philosophy and Public Affairs* 10 (1981): 283–345. See also Thomas Scanlon, "Preference and Urgency," *Journal of Philosophy* 72 (1975): 655–669.

whereas Jones can use his resource share to fulfill his aims to a far greater extent. It seems forced to claim that any notion of equality of condition that is worth caring about prevails between Smith and Jones in this case.

At least two responses to this objection are worth noting. One, pursued by Dworkin,[3] is that in the example the cut between the individual and the resources at his disposal was made at the wrong place. Smith's defective legs and Jones's healthy legs should be considered among their resources, so that only if Smith is assigned a gadget that renders his legs fully serviceable in addition to a resource share that is otherwise identical with Jones's can we say that equality of resources prevails. The example then suggests that an equality of resources ethic should count personal talents among the resources to be distributed. This line of response swiftly encounters difficulties. It is impossible for a distributive agency to supply educational and technological aid that will offset inborn differences of talent so that all persons are blessed with the same talents. Nor is it obvious how much compensation is owed to those who are disadvantaged by low talent. The worth to individuals of their talents varies depending on the nature of their life plans. An heroic resolution of this difficulty is to assign every individual an equal share of ownership of everybody's talents in the distribution of resources.[4] Under this procedure each of the N persons in society begins adult life owning a tradeable 1/N share of everybody's talents. We can regard this share as amounting to ownership of a block of time during which the owner can dictate how the partially owned person is to deploy his talent. Dworkin himself has noticed a flaw in this proposal, which he has aptly named "the slavery of the talented."[5] The flaw is that under this equal distribution of talent scheme the person with high talent is put at a disadvantage relative to her low-talent fellows. If we assume that each person strongly wants liberty in the sense of ownership over his own time (that is, ownership over his own body for his entire lifetime), the high-talent person finds that his taste for liberty is very expensive, as his time is socially valuable and very much in demand, whereas the low-talent person finds that his taste for liberty is cheap, as his time is less valuable and less in demand. Under this version of equality of resources, if two persons are identical in all respects except that one is more talented than the other, the more talented will find she is far less able to achieve her life plan than her less talented counterpart. Again, once its implications are exhibited, equality of resources appears an unattractive interpretation of the ideal of equality.

A second response asserts that given an equal distribution of resources, persons should be held responsible for forming and perhaps reforming their own preferences, in the light of their resource share and their personal characteristics and likely circumstances.[6] The level of overall preference satisfaction that

---

[3] Dworkin, "Equality of Resources."

[4] Hal Varian discusses this mechanism of equal distribution, followed by trade to equilibrium, in "Equity, Envy, and Efficiency," *Journal of Economic Theory* 9 (1974): 63–91. See also John Roemer, "Equality of Talent," *Economics and Philosophy* 1 (1985): 151–186; and "Equality of Resources Implies Equality of Welfare," *Quarterly Journal of Economics* 101 (1986): 751–784.

[5] Dworkin, "Equality of Resources," p. 312.

[6] Rawls, "Social Unity and Primary Goods," pp. 167–170.

each person attains is then a matter of individual responsibility, not a social problem. That I have nil singing talent is a given, but that I have developed an aspiration to become a professional opera singer and have formed my life around this ambition is a further development that was to some extent within my control and for which I must bear responsibility.

The difficulty with this response is that even if it is accepted it falls short of defending equality of resources. Surely social and biological factors influence preference formation, so if we can properly be held responsible only for what lies within our control, then we can at most be held to be partially responsible for our preferences. For instance, it would be wildly implausible to claim that a person without the use of his legs should be held responsible for developing a full set of aims and values toward the satisfaction of which leglessness is no hindrance. Acceptance of the claim that we are sometimes to an extent responsible for our preferences leaves the initial objection against equality of resources fully intact. For if we are sometimes responsible we are sometimes not responsible.

The claim that "we are responsible for our preferences" is ambiguous. It could mean that our preferences have developed to their present state due to factors that lay entirely within our control. Alternatively, it could mean that our present preferences, even if they have arisen through processes largely beyond our power to control, are now within our control in the sense that we could now undertake actions, at greater or less cost, that would change our preferences in ways that we can foresee. If responsibility for preferences on the first construal held true, this would indeed defeat the presumption that our resource share should be augmented because it satisfies our preferences to a lesser extent than the resource shares of others permit them to satisfy their preferences. However, on the first construal, the claim that we are responsible for our preferences is certainly always false. But on the second, weaker construal, the claim that we are responsible for our preferences is compatible with the claim that an appropriate norm of equal distribution should compensate people for their hard-to-satisfy preferences at least up to the point at which by taking appropriate adaptive measures now, people could reach the same preference satisfaction level as others.

The defense of equality of resources by appeal to the claim that persons are responsible for their preferences admits of yet another interpretation. Without claiming that people have caused their preferences to become what they are or that people could cause their preferences to change, we might hold that people can take responsibility for their fundamental preferences in the sense of identifying with them and regarding these preferences as their own, not as alien intrusions on the self. T. M. Scanlon has suggested the example of religious preferences in this spirit.[7] That a person was raised in one religious tradition rather than another may predictably affect his lifetime expectation of preference satisfaction. Yet we would regard it as absurd to insist upon compensation

[7] Thomas Scanlon, "Equality of Resources and Equality of Welfare: A Forced Marriage?", *Ethics* 97 (1986): 111–118; see esp. pp. 115–117.

in the name of distributive equality for having been raised fundamentalist Protestant rather than atheist or Catholic (a matter that of course does not lie within the individual's power to control). Provided that a fair (equal) distribution of the resources of religious liberty is maintained, the amount of utility that individuals can expect from their religious upbringings is "specifically not an object of public policy." [8]

The example of compensation for religious preferences is complex, and I will return to it in section II below. Here it suffices to note that even if in some cases we do deem it inappropriate to insist on such compensation in the name of equality, it does not follow that equality of resources is an adequate rendering of the egalitarian ideal. Differences among people including sometimes differences in their upbringing may render resource equality nugatory. For example, a person raised in a closed fundamentalist community such as the Amish who then loses his faith and moves to the city may feel at a loss as to how to satisfy ordinary secular preferences, so that equal treatment of this rube and city sophisticates may require extra compensation for the rube beyond resource equality. Had the person's fundamental values not altered, such compensation would not be in order. I am not proposing compensation as a feasible government policy, merely pointing out that the fact that people might in some cases regard it as crass to ask for indemnification of their satisfaction-reducing upbringing does not show that in principle it makes sense for people to assume responsibility (act as though they were responsible) for what does not lie within their control. Any policy that attempted to ameliorate these discrepancies would predictably inflict wounds on innocent parents and guardians far out of proportion to any gain that could be realized for the norm of distributive equality. So even if we all agree that in such cases a policy of compensation is inappropriate, all things considered, it does not follow that so far as distributive equality is concerned (one among the several values we cherish), compensation should not be forthcoming.

Finally, it is far from clear why assuming responsibility for one's preferences and values in the sense of affirming them and identifying them as essential to one's self precludes demanding or accepting compensation for these preferences in the name of distributive equality. Suppose the government has accepted an obligation to subsidize the members of two native tribes who are badly off, low in welfare. The two tribes happen to be identical except that one is strongly committed to traditional religious ceremonies involving a psychedelic made from the peyote cactus while the other tribe is similarly committed to its traditional rituals involving an alcoholic drink made from a different cactus. If the market price of the psychedelic should suddenly rise dramatically while the price of the cactus drink stays cheap, members of the first tribe might well claim that equity requires an increase in their subsidy to compensate for the greatly increased price of the wherewithal for their ceremonies. Advancing such a claim, so far as I can see, is fully compatible with continuing to affirm and identify with one's preferences and in this sense to take personal responsibility for them.

[8] Scanlon, "Equality of Resources and Equality of Welfare," p. 116.

In practice, many laws and other public policies differentiate roughly between preferences that we think are deeply entrenched in people, alterable if at all only at great personal cost, and very widespread in the population, versus preferences that for most of us are alterable at moderate cost should we choose to try to change them and thinly and erratically spread throughout the population. Laws and public policies commonly take account of the former and ignore the latter. For example, the law caters to people's deeply felt aversion to public nudity but does not cater to people's aversion to the sight of tastelessly dressed strollers in public spaces. Of course, current American laws and policies are not designed to achieve any strongly egalitarian ideal, whether resource-based or not. But in appealing to common sense as embodied in current practises in order to determine what sort of equality we care about insofar as we do care about equality, one would go badly astray in claiming support in these practises for the contention that equality of resources captures the ideal of equality. We need to search further.

II. EQUALITY OF WELFARE

According to equality of welfare, goods are distributed equally among a group of persons to the degree that the distribution brings it about that each person enjoys the same welfare. (The norm thus presupposes the possibility of cardinal interpersonal welfare comparisons.) The considerations mentioned seven paragraphs back already dispose of the idea that the distributive equality worth caring about is equality of welfare. To bring this point home more must be said to clarify what "welfare" means in this context.

I take welfare to be preference satisfaction. The more an individual's preferences are satisfied, as weighted by their importance to that very individual, the higher her welfare. The preferences that figure in the calculation of a person's welfare are limited to self-interested preferences—what the individual prefers insofar as she seeks her own advantage. One may prefer something for its own sake or as a means to further ends; this discussion is confined to preferences of the former sort.

The preferences that most plausibly serve as the measure of the individual's welfare are hypothetical preferences. Consider this familiar account: The extent to which a person's life goes well is the degree to which his ideally considered preferences are satisfied.[9] My ideally considered preferences are those I would have if I were to engage in thoroughgoing deliberation about my preferences with full pertinent information, in a calm mood, while thinking clearly and making no reasoning errors. (We can also call these ideally considered preferences "rational preferences.")

---

[9] See, e.g., John Rawls, *A Theory of Justice* (Cambridge, MA: Harvard University Press, 1971), pp. 416–424; Richard Brandt, *A Theory of the Good and the Right* (Oxford: Oxford University Press, 1979), pp. 110–129; David Gauthier, *Morals by Agreement* (Oxford: Oxford University Press, 1986), pp. 29–38; and Derek Parfit, *Reasons and Persons* (Oxford: Oxford University Press, 1984), pp. 493–499.

To avoid a difficulty, we should think of the full information that is pertinent to ideally considered preferences as split into two stages corresponding to "first-best" and "second-best" rational preferences. At the first stage one is imagined to be considering full information relevant to choice on the assumption that the results of this ideal deliberation process can costlessly correct one's actual preferences. At the second stage one is imagined to be considering also information regarding (a) one's actual resistance to advice regarding the rationality of one's preferences, (b) the costs of an educational program that would break down this resistance, and (c) the likelihood that anything approaching this educational program will actually be implemented in one's lifetime. What it is reasonable to prefer is then refigured in the light of these costs. For example, suppose that low-life preferences for cheap thrills have a large place in my actual conception of the good, but no place in my first-best rational preferences. But suppose it is certain that these lowlife preferences are firmly fixed in my character. Then my second-best preferences are those I would have if I were to deliberate in ideal fashion about my preferences in the light of full knowledge about my actual preferences and their resistance to change. If you are giving me a birthday present, and your sole goal is to advance my welfare as much as possible, you are probably advised to give me, say, a bottle of jug wine rather than a volume of Shelley's poetry even though it is the poetry experience that would satisfy my first-best rational preference.[10]

On this understanding of welfare, equality of welfare is a poor ideal. Individuals can arrive at different welfare levels due to choices they make for which they alone should be held responsible. A simple example would be to imagine two persons of identical tastes and abilities who are assigned equal resources by an agency charged to maintain distributive equality. The two then voluntarily engage in highstakes gambling, from which one emerges rich (with high expectation of welfare) and the other poor (with low welfare expectation). For another example, consider two persons similarly situated, so they could attain identical welfare levels with the same effort, but one chooses to pursue personal welfare zealously while the other pursues an aspirational preference (e.g., saving the whales), and so attains lesser fulfillment of self-interested preferences. In a third example, one person may voluntarily cultivate an expensive preference (not cognitively superior to the preference it supplants), while another person does not. In all three examples it would be inappropriate to insist upon equality of welfare when welfare inequality arises through the voluntary choice of the person who gets lesser welfare. Notice that in all three examples as described, there need be no grounds for finding fault with any aims or actions of any of the individuals mentioned. No imperative of practical reason commands us to devote our lives to the maximal pursuit of (self-interested) preference satisfaction. Divergence from equality of welfare arising in these ways need not signal any fault imputable to individuals or to "society" understood as responsible for maintaining distributive equality.

[10] In this paragraph I attempt to solve a difficulty noted by James Griffin in "Modern Utilitarianism," *Revue Internationale de Philosophie* 36 (1982): 331–375; esp. pp. 334–335. See also Amartya Sen and Bernard Williams, "Introduction" to *Utilitarianism and Beyond*, p. 10.

This line of thought suggests taking equal opportunity for welfare to be the appropriate norm of distributive equality.

In the light of the foregoing discussion, consider again the example of compensation for one's religious upbringing regarded as affecting one's lifetime preference satisfaction expectation. This example is urged as a reductio ad absurdum of the norm of equality of welfare, which may seem to yield the counterintuitive implication that such differences do constitute legitimate grounds for redistributing people's resource shares, in the name of distributive equality. As I mentioned, the example is tricky; we should not allow it to stampede us toward resource-based construals of distributive equality. Two comments on the example indicate something of its trickiness.

First, if a person changes her values in the light of deliberation that bring her closer to the ideal of deliberative rationality, we should credit the person's conviction that satisfying the new values counts for more than satisfying the old ones, now discarded. The old values should be counted at a discount due to their presumed greater distance from deliberative rationality. So if I was a Buddhist, then become a Hindu, and correctly regard the new religious preference as cognitively superior to the old, it is not the case that a straight equality of welfare standard must register my welfare as declining even if my new religious values are less easily achievable than the ones they supplant.

Secondly, the example might motivate acceptance of equal opportunity for welfare over straight equality of welfare rather than rejection of subjectivist conceptions of equality altogether. If equal opportunity for welfare obtains between Smith and Jones, and Jones subsequently undergoes religious conversion that lowers his welfare prospects, it may be that we will take Jones's conversion either to be a voluntarily chosen act or a prudentially negligent act for which he should be held responsible. (Consider the norm: Other things equal, it is bad if some people are worse off than others through no voluntary choice or fault of their own.) This train of thought also motivates an examination of equal opportunity for welfare.

III. EQUAL OPPORTUNITY FOR WELFARE

An opportunity is a chance of getting a good if one seeks it. For equal opportunity for welfare to obtain among a number of persons, each must face an array of options that is equivalent to every other person's in terms of the prospects for preference satisfaction it offers. The preferences involved in this calculation are ideally considered secondbest preferences (where these differ from first-best preferences). Think of two persons entering their majority and facing various life choices, each action one might choose being associated with its possible outcomes. In the simplest case, imagine that we know the probability of each outcome conditional on the agent's choice of an action that might lead to it. Given that one or another choice is made and one or another outcome realized, the agent would then face another array of choices, then another, and so on. We construct a decision tree that gives an individual's possible complete life-histories. We then add up the preference satisfaction expectation for each possible life history. In doing this we take into account the preferences that people have regarding being confronted with the particular range of options given at each decision point. Equal opportunity for welfare obtains among persons when all of them face equivalent decision trees—the expected value of each person's best (= most prudent[11]) choice of options, second-best, . . . nth-best is the same. The opportunities persons encounter are ranked by the prospects for welfare they afford.

The criterion for equal opportunity for welfare stated above is incomplete. People might face an equivalent array of options, as above, yet differ in their awareness of these options, their ability to choose reasonably among them, and the strength of character that enables a person to persist in carrying out a chosen option. Further conditions are needed. We can summarize these conditions by stipulating that a number of persons face *effectively* equivalent options just in case one of the following is true: (1) the options are equivalent and the persons are on a par in their ability to "negotiate" these options, or (2) the options are nonequivalent in such a way as to counterbalance exactly any inequalities in people's negotiating abilities, or (3) the options are equivalent and any inequalities in people's negotiating abilities are due to causes for which it is proper to hold the individuals themselves personally responsible. Equal opportunity for welfare obtains when all persons face effectively equivalent arrays of options.

• • •

IV. STRAIGHT EQUALITY VERSUS EQUAL OPPORTUNITY; WELFARE VERSUS RESOURCES

The discussion to this point has explored two independent distinctions: (1) straight equality versus equal opportunity and (2) welfare versus resources as the appropriate basis for measuring distributive shares. Hence there are four positions to consider. On the issue of whether an egalitarian should regard welfare or resources as the appropriate standard of distributive equality, it is important to compare like with like, rather than, for instance, just to compare equal opportunity for resources with straight equality of welfare. (In my opinion Ronald Dworkin's otherwise magisterial treatment of the issue in his two-part discussion of "What Is Equality?" is marred by a failure to bring these four distinct positions clearly into focus.[12])

---

[11] Here the most prudent choice cannot be identified with the choice that maximizes lifelong expected preference satisfaction, due to complications arising from the phenomenon of preference change. The prudent choice as I conceive it is tied to one's actual preferences in ways I will not try to describe here.

[12] See the articles cited in note 2. Dworkin's account of equality of resources is complex, but without entering into its detail I can observe that Dworkin is discussing a version of what I call "equal opportunity for resources." By itself, the name chosen matters not a bit. But confusion enters because Dworkin neglects altogether the rival doctrine of equal opportunity for welfare. For a criticism of Dworkin's objections against a welfarist conception of equality that do not depend on this confusion, see my "Liberalism, Distributive Subjectivism, and Equal Opportunity for Welfare."

The argument for equal opportunity rather than straight equality is simply that it is morally fitting to hold individuals responsible for the foreseeable consequences of their voluntary choices, and in particular for that portion of these consequences that involves their own achievement of welfare or gain or loss of resources. If accepted, this argument leaves it entirely open whether we as egalitarians ought to support equal opportunity for welfare or equal opportunity for resources.

For equal opportunity for resources to obtain among a number of persons, the range of lotteries with resources as prizes available to each of them must be effectively the same. The range of lotteries available to two persons is effectively the same whenever it is the case that, for any lottery the first can gain access to, there is an identical lottery that the second person can gain access to by comparable effort. (So if Smith can gain access to a lucrative lottery by walking across the street, and Jones cannot gain access to a similar lottery except by a long hard trek across a desert, to this extent their opportunities for resources are unequal.) We may say that equal opportunity for resources in an extended sense obtains among a number of persons just in case there is a time at which their opportunities are equal and any later inequalities in the resource opportunities they face are due to voluntary choices or differentially negligent behavior on their part for which they are rightly deemed personally responsible.

I would not claim that the interpretation of equal opportunity for resources presented here is the only plausible construal of the concept. However, on any plausible construal, the norm of equal opportunity for resources is vulnerable to the "slavery of the talented" problem that proved troublesome for equality of resources. Supposing that personal talents should be included among the resources to be distributed (for reasons given in section I), we find that moving from a regime of equality of resources to a regime that enforces equal opportunity for resources does not change the fact that a resource-based approach causes the person of high talent to be predictably and (it would seem) unfairly worse off in welfare prospects than her counterpart with lesser talent.[13] If opportunities for resources are equally distributed among more and less talented persons, then each person regardless of her native talent endowment will have comparable access to identical lotteries for resources that include time slices of the labor power of all persons. Each person's expected ownership of talent, should he seek it, will be the same. Other things equal, if all persons strongly desire personal liberty or initial ownership of one's own lifetime labor power, this good will turn out to be a luxury commodity for the talented, and a cheap bargain for the untalented.

A possible objection to the foregoing reasoning is that it relies on a vaguely specified idea of how to measure resource shares that is shown to be dubious by the very fact that it leads back to the slavery of the talented problem. Perhaps by taking personal liberty as a separate resource this result can be avoided. But waiving any other difficulties with this objection, we note that the

[13] Roemer notes that the person with high talent is cursed with an involuntary expensive preference for personal liberty. See Roemer, "Equality of Talent."

assumption that any measure of resource equality must be unacceptable if applying it leads to unacceptable results for the distribution of welfare amounts to smuggling in a welfarist standard by the back door.

Notice that the welfare distribution implications of equal opportunity for resources will count as intuitively unacceptable only on the assumption that people cannot be deemed to have chosen voluntarily the preferences that are frustrated or satisfied by the talent pooling that a resourcist interpretation of equal opportunity enforces. Of course it is strictly nonvoluntary that one is born with a particular body and cannot be separated from it, so if others hold ownership rights in one's labor power one's individual liberty is thereby curtailed. But in principle one's self-interested preferences could be concerned no more with what happens to one's own body than with what happens to the bodies of others. To the extent that you have strong self-interested hankerings that your neighbors try their hand at, say, farming, and less intense desires regarding the occupations you yourself pursue, to that extent the fact that under talent pooling your own labor power is a luxury commodity will not adversely affect your welfare. As an empirical matter, I submit that it is just false to hold that in modern society whether any given individual does or does not care about retaining her own personal liberty is due to that person's voluntarily choosing one or the other preference. The expensive preference of the talented person for personal liberty cannot be assimilated to the class of expensive preferences that people might voluntarily cultivate.[14] On plausible empirical assumptions, equal opportunity for welfare will often find tastes compensable, including the talented person's taste for the personal liberty to command her own labor power. Being born with high talent cannot then be a curse under equal opportunity for welfare (it cannot be a blessing either).

---

[14] As Rawls writes, ". . . those with less expensive tastes have presumably adjusted their likes and dislikes over the course of their lives to the income and wealth they could reasonably expect; and it is regarded as unfair that they now should have less in order to spare others from the consequences of their lack of foresight or self-discipline." See "Social Unity and Primary Goods," p. 169.

XI

LIBERTY, RIGHTS, PROPERTY, AND SELF-OWNERSHIP

49.
Two Concepts of Liberty
ISAIAH BERLIN

To coerce a man is to deprive him of freedom—freedom from what? Almost every moralist in human history has praised freedom. Like happiness and goodness, like nature and reality, the meaning of this term is so porous that there is little interpretation that it seems able to resist. I do not propose to discuss either the history or the more than two hundred senses of this protean word recorded by historians of ideas. I propose to examine no more than two of these senses—but those central ones, with a great deal of human history behind them, and, I dare say, still to come. The first of these political senses of freedom or liberty (I shall use both words to mean the same), which (following much precedent) I shall call the "negative" sense, is involved in the answer to the question "What is the area within which the subject—a person or group of persons—is or should be left to do or be what he is able to do or be, without interference by other persons?" The second, which I shall call the positive sense, is involved in the answer to the question, "What, or who, is the source of control or interference that can determine someone to do, or be, this rather than that?" The two questions are clearly different, even though the answers to them may overlap.

THE NOTION OF "NEGATIVE" FREEDOM

I am normally said to be free to the degree to which no man or body of men interferes with my activity. Political liberty in this sense is simply the area within which a man can act unobstructed by others. If I am prevented by others from doing what I could otherwise do, I am to that degree unfree; and if this area is contracted by other men beyond a certain minimum, I can be described as being coerced, or, it may be, enslaved. Coercion is not, however, a term that covers every form of inability. If I say that I am unable to jump more than ten feet in the air, or cannot read because I am blind, or cannot understand the darker pages of Hegel, it would be eccentric to say that I am to that degree enslaved or coerced. Coercion implies the deliberate interference of other human beings within the area in which I could otherwise act. You lack political liberty or freedom only if you are prevented from attaining a goal by human beings.[1] Mere incapacity to attain a goal is not lack of political freedom.[2] This is brought out

---

[1] I do not, of course, mean to imply the truth of the converse.

[2] Helvétius made this point very clearly: "The free man is the man who is not in irons, nor imprisoned in a gaol, nor terrorized like a slave by the fear of punishment . . . it is not lack of freedom not to fly like an eagle or swim like a whale."

by the use of such modern expressions as "economic freedom" and its counterpart, "economic slavery." It is argued, very plausibly, that if a man is too poor to afford something on which there is no legal ban—a loaf of bread, a journey round the world, recourse to the law courts—he is as little free to have it as he would be if it were forbidden him by law. If my poverty were a kind of disease, which prevented me from buying bread, or paying for the journey round the world or getting my case heard, as lameness prevents me from running, this inability would not naturally be described as a lack of freedom, least of all political freedom. It is only because I believe that my inability to get a given thing is due to the fact that other human beings have made arrangements whereby I am, whereas others are not, prevented from having enough money with which to pay for it, that I think myself a victim of coercion or slavery. In other words, this use of the term depends on a particular social and economic theory about the causes of my poverty or weakness. If my lack of material means is due to my lack of mental or physical capacity, then I begin to speak of being deprived of freedom (and not simply about poverty) only if I accept the theory.[3] If, in addition, I believe that I am being kept in want by a specific arrangement which I consider unjust or unfair, I speak of economic slavery or oppression. "The nature of things does not madden us, only ill will does," said Rousseau. The criterion of oppression is the part that I believe to be played by other human beings, directly or indirectly, with or without the intention of doing so, in frustrating my wishes. By being free in this sense I mean not being interfered with by others. The wider the area of non-interference the wider my freedom.

This is what the classical English political philosophers meant when they used this word.[4] They disagreed about how wide the area could or should be. They supposed that it could not, as things were, be unlimited, because if it were, it would entail a state in which all men could boundlessly interfere with all other men; and this kind of "natural" freedom would lead to social chaos in which men's minimum needs would not be satisfied; or else the liberties of the weak would be suppressed by the strong. Because they perceived that human purposes and activities do not automatically harmonize with one another, and because (whatever their official doctrines) they put high value on other goals, such as justice, or happiness, or culture, or security, or varying degrees of equality, they were prepared to curtail freedom in the interests of other values and, indeed, of freedom itself. For, without this, it was impossible to create the kind of association that they thought desirable. Consequently, it is assumed by these thinkers that the area of men's free action must be limited by law. But equally it is assumed, especially by such libertarians as Locke and Mill in England, and Constant and Tocqueville in France, that there ought to exist a certain minimum

---

[3] The Marxist conception of social laws is, of course, the best-known version of this theory, but it forms a large element in some Christian and utilitarian, and all socialist, doctrines.

[4] "A free man," said Hobbes, "is he that . . . is not hindered to do what he hath the will to do." Law is always a "fetter," even if it protects you from being bound in chains that are heavier than those of the law, say, some more repressive law or custom, or arbitrary despotism or chaos. Bentham says much the same.

area of personal freedom which must on no account be violated; for if it is over-stepped, the individual will find himself in an area too narrow for even that minimum development of his natural faculties which alone makes it possible to pursue, and even to conceive, the various ends which men hold good or right or sacred. It follows that a frontier must be drawn between the area of private life and that of public authority. Where it is to be drawn is a matter of argument, indeed of haggling. Men are largely interdependent, and no man's activity is so completely private as never to obstruct the lives of others in any way. "Freedom for the pike is death for the minnows"; the liberty of some must depend on the restraint of others. "Freedom for an Oxford don," others have been known to add, "is a very different thing from freedom for an Egyptian peasant."

This proposition derives its force from something that is both true and important, but the phrase itself remains a piece of political claptrap. It is true that to offer political rights, or safeguards against intervention by the state, to men who are half-naked, illiterate, underfed, and diseased is to mock their condition; they need medical help or education before they can understand, or make use of, an increase in their freedom. What is freedom to those who cannot make use of it? Without adequate conditions for the use of freedom, what is the value of freedom? First things come first: there are situations, as a nineteenth-century Russian radical writer declared, in which boots are superior to the works of Shakespeare; individual freedom is not everyone's primary need. For freedom is not the mere absence of frustration of whatever kind; this would inflate the meaning of the word until it meant too much or too little. The Egyptian peasant needs clothes or medicine before, and more than, personal liberty, but the minimum freedom that he needs today, and the greater degree of freedom that he may need tomorrow, is not some species of freedom peculiar to him, but identical with that of professors, artists, and millionaires.

What troubles the consciences of Western liberals is not, I think, the belief that the freedom that men seek differs according to their social or economic conditions, but that the minority who possess it have gained it by exploiting, or, at least, averting their gaze from, the vast majority who do not. They believe, with good reason, that if individual liberty is an ultimate end for human beings, none should be deprived of it by others; least of all that some should enjoy it at the expense of others. Equality of liberty; not to treat others as I should not wish them to treat me; repayment of my debt to those who alone have made possible my liberty or prosperity or enlightenment; justice, in its simplest and most universal sense—these are the foundations of liberal morality. Liberty is not the only goal of men. I can, like the Russian critic Belinsky, say that if others are to be deprived of it—if my brothers are to remain in poverty, squalor, and chains—then I do not want it for myself, I reject it with both hands and infinitely prefer to share their fate. But nothing is gained by a confusion of terms. To avoid glaring inequality or widespread misery I am ready to sacrifice some, or all, of my freedom: I may do so willingly and freely: but it is freedom that I am giving up for the sake of justice or equality or the love of my fellow men. I should be guilt-stricken, and rightly so, if I were not, in some circumstances, ready to make this sacrifice. But a sacrifice is not an increase in what is being sacrificed, namely freedom, however great the moral need or the compensation for it. Everything is what it is: liberty is liberty, not equality or fairness or justice or culture, or human happiness or a quiet conscience. If the liberty of myself or my class or nation depends on the misery of a number of other human beings, the system which promotes this is unjust and immoral. But if I curtail or lose my freedom, in order to lessen the shame of such inequality, and do not thereby materially increase the individual liberty of others, an absolute loss of liberty occurs. This may be compensated for by a gain in justice or in happiness or in peace, but the loss remains, and it is a confusion of values to say that although my "liberal," individual freedom may go by the board, some other kind of freedom—"social" or "economic"—is increased. Yet it remains true that the freedom of some must at times be curtailed to secure the freedom of others. Upon what principle should this be done? If freedom is a sacred, untouchable value, there can be no such principle. One or other of these conflicting rules or principles must, at any rate in practice, yield: not always for reasons which can be clearly stated, let alone generalized into rules or universal maxims. Still, a practical compromise has to be found.

Philosophers with an optimistic view of human nature and a belief in the possibility of harmonizing human interests, such as Locke or Adam Smith and, in some moods, Mill, believed that social harmony and progress were compatible with reserving a large area for private life over which neither the state nor any other authority must be allowed to trespass. Hobbes, and those who agreed with him, especially conservative or reactionary thinkers, argued that if men were to be prevented from destroying one another and making social life a jungle or a wilderness, greater safeguards must be instituted to keep them in their places; he wished correspondingly to increase the area of centralized control and decrease that of the individual. But both sides agreed that some portion of human existence must remain independent of the sphere of social control. To invade that preserve, however small, would be despotism. The most eloquent of all defenders of freedom and privacy, Benjamin Constant, who had not forgotten the Jacobin dictatorship, declared that at the very least the liberty of religion, opinion, expression, property, must be guaranteed against arbitrary invasion. Jefferson, Burke, Paine, Mill, compiled different catalogues of individual liberties, but the argument for keeping authority at bay is always substantially the same. We must preserve a minimum area of personal freedom if we are not to "degrade or deny our nature." We cannot remain absolutely free, and must give up some of our liberty to preserve the rest. But total self-surrender is self-defeating. What then must the minimum be? That which a man cannot give up without offending against the essence of his human nature. What is this essence? What are the standards which it entails? This has been, and perhaps always will be, a matter of infinite debate. But whatever the principle in terms of which the area of non-interference is to be drawn, whether it is that of natural law or natural rights, or of utility or the pronouncements of a categorical imperative, or the sanctity of the social contract, or any other concept with which men have sought to clarify and justify their convictions, liberty in this sense means liberty *from;* absence of interference beyond the shifting, but always recognizable, frontier. "The only freedom which deserves the name is that of pursuing our own good in our own way," said the most celebrated of its champions. If this is so, is compulsion ever justified? Mill had no doubt that it was. Since justice demands that all individuals be entitled to a minimum of freedom, all other individuals were of necessity to be restrained, if need be by force, from depriving anyone of it. Indeed, the whole function of law was the prevention of just such collisions: the state was reduced to what Lassalle contemptuously described as the functions of a night-watchman or traffic policeman.

• • •

Liberty in this sense is not incompatible with some kinds of autocracy, or at any rate with the absence of self-government. Liberty in this sense is principally concerned with the area of control, not with its source. Just as a democracy may, in fact, deprive the individual citizen of a great many liberties which he might have in some other form of society, so it is perfectly conceivable that a liberal-minded despot would allow his subjects a large measure of personal freedom. The despot who leaves his subjects a wide area of liberty may be unjust, or encourage the wildest inequalities, care little for order, or virtue, or knowledge; but provided he does not curb their liberty, or at least curbs it less than many other régimes, he meets with Mill's specification.[5] Freedom in this sense is not, at any rate logically, connected with democracy or self-government. Self-government may, on the whole, provide a better guarantee of the preservation of civil liberties than other régimes, and has been defended as such by libertarians. But there is no necessary connexion between individual liberty and democratic rule. The answer to the question "Who governs me?" is logically distinct from the question "How far does government interfere with me?" It is in this difference that the great contrast between the two concepts of negative and positive liberty, in the end, consists.[6] For the "positive" sense of liberty

---

[5] Indeed, it is arguable that in the Prussia of Frederick the Great or in the Austria of Josef II men of imagination, originality, and creative genius, and, indeed, minorities of all kinds, were less persecuted and felt the pressure, both of institutions and custom, less heavy upon them than in many an earlier or later democracy.

[6] "Negative liberty" is something the extent of which, in a given case, it is difficult to estimate. It might, prima facie, seem to depend simply on the power to choose between at any rate two alternatives. Nevertheless, not all choices are equally free, or free at all. If in a totalitarian state I betray my friend under threat of torture, perhaps even if I act from fear of losing my job, I can reasonably say that I did not act freely. Nevertheless, I did, of course, make a choice, and could, at any rate in theory, have chosen to be killed or tortured or imprisoned. The mere existence of alternatives is not, therefore, enough to make my action free (although it may be voluntary) in the normal sense of the word. The extent of my freedom seems to depend on (a) how many possibilities are open to me (although the method of counting these can never be more than impressionistic. Possibilities of action are not discrete entities like apples, which can be exhaustively enumerated); (b) how easy or difficult each of these possibilities is to actualize; (c) how important in my plan of life, given my character and circumstances, these possibilities are when compared with each other; (d) how far they are closed and opened by deliberate human acts; (e) what value not merely the agent, but the general sentiment of the society in which he lives, puts on the various possibilities. All these magnitudes must be "integrated," and a conclusion, necessarily never precise, or indisputable, drawn from this process. It may well be that there are many incommensurable kinds and degrees of freedom, and that they cannot be drawn up on any single scale of magnitude. Moreover, in the case of societies, we are faced by such (logically absurd)

comes to light if we try to answer the question, not "What am I free to do or be?," but "By whom am I ruled?" or "Who is to say what I am, and what I am not, to be or do?" The connexion between democracy and individual liberty is a good deal more tenuous than it seemed to many advocates of both. The desire to be governed by myself, or at any rate to participate in the process by which my life is to be controlled, may be as deep a wish as that of a free area for action, and perhaps historically older. But it is not a desire for the same thing. So different is it, indeed, as to have led in the end to the great clash of ideologies that dominates our world. For it is this—the "positive" conception of liberty: not freedom from, but freedom to—to lead one prescribed form of life—which the adherents of the "negative" notion represent as being, at times, no better than a specious disguise for brutal tyranny.

THE NOTION OF POSITIVE FREEDOM

The "positive" sense of the word "liberty" derives from the wish on the part of the individual to be his own master. I wish my life and decisions to depend on myself, not on external forces of whatever kind. I wish to be the instrument of my own, not of other men's, acts of will. I wish to be a subject, not an object; to be moved by reasons, by conscious purposes, which are my own, not by causes which affect me, as it were, from outside. I wish to be somebody, not nobody; a doer—deciding, not being decided for, self-directed and not acted upon by external nature or by other men as if I were a thing, or an animal, or a slave incapable of playing a human role, that is, of conceiving goals and policies of my own and realizing them. This is at least part of what I mean when I say that I am rational, and that it is my reason that distinguishes me as a human being from the rest of the world. I wish, above all, to be conscious of myself as a thinking, willing, active being, bearing responsibility for my choices and able to explain them by references to my own ideas and purposes. I feel free to the degree that I believe this to be true, and enslaved to the degree that I am made to realize that it is not.

The freedom which consists in being one's own master, and the freedom which consists in not being prevented from choosing as I do by other men, may, on the face of it, seem concepts at no great logical distance from each other— no more than negative and positive ways of saying much the same thing. Yet the "positive" and "negative" notions of freedom historically developed in divergent

---

questions as "Would arrangement X increase the liberty of Mr. A more than it would that of Messrs. B, C, and D between them, added together?" The same difficulties arise in applying utilitarian criteria. Nevertheless, provided we do not demand precise measurement, we can give valid reasons for saying that the average subject of the King of Sweden is, on the whole, a good deal freer today than the average citizen of Spain or Albania. Total patterns of life must be compared directly as wholes, although the method by which we make the comparison, and the truth of the conclusions, are difficult or impossible to demonstrate. But the vagueness of the concepts, and the multiplicity of the criteria involved, is an attribute of the subject-matter itself, not of our imperfect methods of measurement, or incapacity for precise thought.

directions not always by logically reputable steps, until, in the end, they came into direct conflict with each other.

One way of making this clear is in terms of the independent momentum which the, initially perhaps quite harmless, metaphor of self-mastery acquired. "I am my own master"; "I am slave to no man"; but may I not (as Platonists or Hegelians tend to say) be a slave to nature? Or to my own "unbridled" passions? Are these not so many species of the identical genus "slave"—some political or legal, others moral or spiritual? Have not men had the experience of liberating themselves from spiritual slavery, or slavery to nature, and do they not in the course of it become aware, on the one hand, of a self which dominates, and, on the other, of something in them which is brought to heel? This dominant self is then variously identified with reason, with my "higher nature," with the self which calculates and aims at what will satisfy it in the long run, with my "real," or "ideal," or "autonomous" self, or with my self "at its best"; which is then contrasted with irrational impulse, uncontrolled desires, my "lower" nature, the pursuit of immediate pleasures, my "empirical" or "heteronomous" self, swept by every gust of desire and passion, needing to be rigidly disciplined if it is ever to rise to the full height of its "real" nature. Presently the two selves may be represented as divided by an even larger gap: the real self may be conceived as something wider than the individual (as the term is normally understood), as a social "whole" of which the individual is an element or aspect: a tribe, a race, a church, a state, the great society of the living and the dead and the yet unborn. This entity is then identified as being the "true" self which, by imposing its collective, or "organic," single will upon its recalcitrant "members," achieves its own, and therefore their, "higher" freedom. The perils of using organic metaphors to justify the coercion of some men by others in order to raise them to a "higher" level of freedom have often been pointed out. But what gives such plausibility as it has to this kind of language is that we recognize that it is possible, and at times justifiable, to coerce men in the name of some goal (let us say, justice or public health) which they would, if they were more enlightened, themselves pursue, but do not, because they are blind or ignorant or corrupt. This renders it easy for me to conceive of myself as coercing others for their own sake, in their, not my, interest. I am then claiming that I know what they truly need better than they know it themselves. What, at most, this entails is that they would not resist me if they were rational and as wise as I and understood their interests as I do. But I may go on to claim a good deal more than this. I may declare that they are actually aiming at what in their benighted state they consciously resist, because there exists within them an occult entity—their latent rational will, or their "true" purpose—and that this entity, although it is belied by all that they overtly feel and do and say, is their "real" self, of which the poor empirical self in space and time may know nothing or little; and that this inner spirit is the only self that deserves to have its wishes taken into account.[7] Once I take this view, I am in a position to ignore the

---

[7] "The ideal of true freedom is the maximum of power for all the members of human society alike to make the best of themselves," said T. H. Green in 1881. Apart from the confusion of freedom with equality, this entails that if a man chose some immediate pleasure—which (in whose view?)

actual wishes of men or societies, to bully, oppress, torture them in the name, and on behalf, of their "real" selves, in the secure knowledge that whatever is the true goal of man (happiness, performance of duty, wisdom, a just society, self-fulfilment) must be identical with his freedom—the free choice of his "true," albeit often submerged and inarticulate, self.

This paradox has been often exposed. It is one thing to say that I know what is good for X, while he himself does not; and even to ignore his wishes for its— and his—sake; and a very different one to say that he has *eo ipso* chosen it, not indeed consciously, not as he seems in everyday life, but in his role as a rational self which his empirical self may not know—the "real" self which discerns the good, and cannot help choosing it once it is revealed. This monstrous impersonation, which consists in equating what X would choose if he were something he is not, or at least not yet, with what X actually seeks and chooses, is at the heart of all political theories of self-realization. It is one thing to say that I may be coerced for my own good which I am too blind to see: this may, on occasion, be for my benefit; indeed it may enlarge the scope of my liberty. It is another to say that if it is my good, then I am not being coerced, for I have willed it, whether I know this or not, and am free (or "truly" free) even while my poor earthly body and foolish mind bitterly reject it, and struggle against those who seek however benevolently to impose it, with the greatest desperation.

This magical transformation, or sleight of hand (for which William James so justly mocked the Hegelians), can no doubt be perpetrated just as easily with the "negative" concept of freedom, where the self that should not be interfered with is no longer the individual with his actual wishes and needs as they are normally conceived, but the "real" man within, identified with the pursuit of some ideal purpose not dreamed of by his empirical self. And, as in the case of the "positively" free self, this entity may be inflated into some super-personal entity—a state, a class, a nation, or the march of history itself, regarded as a more "real" subject of attributes than the empirical self. But the "positive" conception of freedom as self-mastery, with its suggestion of a man divided against himself, has, in fact, and as a matter of history, of doctrine and of practice, lent itself more easily to this splitting of personality into two: the transcendent, dominant controller, and the empirical bundle of desires and passions to be disciplined and brought to heel. It is this historical fact that has been influential. This demonstrates (if demonstration of so obvious a truth is needed) that conceptions of freedom directly derive from views of what constitutes a self, a person, a man. Enough manipulation with the definition of man, and freedom can be made to mean whatever the manipulator wishes. Recent history has made it only too clear that the issue is not merely academic.

• • •

One belief, more than any other, is responsible for the slaughter of individuals on the altars of the great historical ideals—justice or progress or the happiness

---

would not enable him to make the best of himself (what self?)—what he was exercising was not "true" freedom: and if deprived of it, would not lose anything that mattered. Green was a genuine liberal: but many a tyrant could use this formula to justify his worst acts of oppression.

of future generations, or the sacred mission or emancipation of a nation or race or class, or even liberty itself, which demands the sacrifice of individuals for the freedom of society. This is the belief that somewhere, in the past or in the future, in divine revelation or in the mind of an individual thinker, in the pronouncements of history or science, or in the simple heart of an uncorrupted good man, there is a final solution. This ancient faith rests on the conviction that all the positive values in which men have believed must, in the end, be compatible, and perhaps even entail one another. "Nature binds truth, happiness, and virtue together as by an indissoluble chain," said one of the best men who ever lived, and spoke in similar terms of liberty, equality, and justice.[8] But is this true? It is a commonplace that neither political equality nor efficient organization nor social justice is compatible with more than a modicum of individual liberty, and certainly not with unrestricted *laissez-faire;* that justice and generosity, public and private loyalties, the demands of genius and the claims of society, can conflict violently with each other. And it is no great way from that to the generalization that not all good things are compatible, still less all the ideals of mankind. But somewhere, we shall be told, and in some way, it must be possible for all these values to live together, for unless this is so, the universe is not a cosmos, not a harmony; unless this is so, conflicts of values may be an intrinsic, irremovable element in human life. To admit that the fulfilment of some of our ideals may in principle make the fulfilment of others impossible is to say that the notion of total human fulfilment is a formal contradiction, a metaphysical chimaera. For every rationalist metaphysician, from Plato to the last disciples of Hegel or Marx, this abandonment of the notion of a final harmony in which all riddles are solved, all contradictions reconciled, is a piece of crude empiricism, abdication before brute facts, intolerable bankruptcy of reason before things as they are, failure to explain and to justify, to reduce everything to a system, which "reason" indignantly rejects. But if we are not armed with an *a priori* guarantee of the proposition that a total harmony of true values is somewhere to be found—perhaps in some ideal realm the characteristics of which we can, in our final state, not so much as conceive—we must fall back on the ordinary resources of empirical observation and ordinary human knowledge. And these certainly give us no warrant for supposing (or even understanding what would be meant by saying) that all good things, or all bad things for that matter, are reconcilable with each other. The world that we encounter in ordinary experience is one in which we are faced with choices between ends equally ultimate, and claims equally absolute, the realization of some of which must inevitably involve the sacrifice of others. Indeed, it is because this is their

---

[8] Condorcet, from whose *Esquisse* these words are quoted, declares that the task of social science is to show "by what bonds Nature has united the progress of enlightenment with that of liberty, virtue, and respect for the natural rights of man; how these ideals, which alone are truly good, yet so often separated from each other that they are even believed to be incompatible, should, on the contrary, become inseparable, as soon as enlightenment has reached a certain level simultaneously among a large number of nations." He goes on to say that: "Men still preserve the errors of their childhood, of their country, and of their age long after having recognized all the truths needed for destroying them." Ironically enough, his belief in the need and possibility of uniting all good things may well be precisely the kind of error he himself so well described.

situation that men place such immense value upon the freedom to choose; for if they had assurance that in some perfect state, realizable by men on earth, no ends pursued by them would ever be in conflict, the necessity and agony of choice would disappear, and with it the central importance of the freedom to choose. Any method of bringing this final state nearer would then seem fully justified, no matter how much freedom were sacrificed to forward its advance. It is, I have no doubt, some such dogmatic certainty that has been responsible for the deep, serene, unshakeable conviction in the minds of some of the most merciless tyrants and persecutors in history that what they did was fully justified by its purpose. I do not say that the ideal of self-perfection—whether for individuals or nations or churches or classes—is to be condemned in itself, or that the language which was used in its defence was in all cases the result of a confused or fraudulent use of words, or of moral or intellectual perversity. Indeed, I have tried to show that it is the notion of freedom in its "positive" sense that is at the heart of the demands for national or social self-direction which animate the most powerful and morally just public movements of our time, and that not to recognize this is to misunderstand the most vital facts and ideas of our age. But equally it seems to me that the belief that some single formula can in principle be found whereby all the diverse ends of men can be harmoniously realized is demonstrably false. If, as I believe, the ends of men are many, and not all of them are in principle compatible with each other, then the possibility of conflict—and of tragedy—can never wholly be eliminated from human life, either personal or social. The necessity of choosing between absolute claims is then an inescapable characteristic of the human condition. This gives its value to freedom as Acton had conceived of it—as an end in itself, and not as a temporary need, arising out of our confused notions and irrational and disordered lives, a predicament which a panacea could one day put right.

I do not wish to say that individual freedom is, even in the most liberal societies, the sole, or even the dominant, criterion of social action. We compel children to be educated, and we forbid public executions. These are certainly curbs to freedom. We justify them on the ground that ignorance, or a barbarian upbringing, or cruel pleasures and excitements are worse for us than the amount of restraint needed to repress them. This judgment in turn depends on how we determine good and evil, that is to say, on our moral, religious, intellectual, economic, and aesthetic values; which are, in their turn, bound up with our conception of man, and of the basic demands of his nature. In other words, our solution of such problems is based on our vision, by which we are consciously or unconsciously guided, of what constitutes a fulfilled human life, as contrasted with Mill's "cramped and warped," "pinched and hidebound" natures. To protest against the laws governing censorship or personal morals as intolerable infringements of personal liberty presupposes a belief that the activities which such laws forbid are fundamental needs of men as men, in a good (or, indeed, any) society. To defend such laws is to hold that these needs are not essential, or that they cannot be satisfied without sacrificing other values which come higher—satisfy deeper needs—than individual freedom, determined by some standard that is not merely subjective, a standard for which some objective status—empirical or *a priori*—is claimed.

The extent of a man's, or a people's, liberty to choose to live as they desire must be weighed against the claims of many other values, of which equality, or justice, or happiness, or security, or public order are perhaps the most obvious examples. For this reason, it cannot be unlimited. We are rightly reminded by R. H. Tawney that the liberty of the strong, whether their strength is physical or economic, must be restrained. This maxim claims respect, not as a consequence of some *a priori* rule, whereby the respect for the liberty of one man logically entails respect for the liberty of others like him; but simply because respect for the principles of justice, or shame at gross inequality of treatment, is as basic in men as the desire for liberty. That we cannot have everything is a necessary, not a contingent, truth. Burke's plea for the constant need to compensate, to reconcile, to balance; Mill's plea for novel "experiments in living" with their permanent possibility of error, the knowledge that it is not merely in practice but in principle impossible to reach clear-cut and certain answers, even in an ideal world of wholly good and rational men and wholly clear ideas—may madden those who seek for final solutions and single, all-embracing systems, guaranteed to be eternal. Nevertheless, it is a conclusion that cannot be escaped by those who, with Kant, have learnt the truth that out of the crooked timber of humanity no straight thing was ever made.

There is little need to stress the fact that monism, and faith in a single criterion, has always proved a deep source of satisfaction both to the intellect and to the emotions. Whether the standard of judgment derives from the vision of some future perfection, as in the minds of the *philosophes* in the eighteenth century and their technocratic successors in our own day, or is rooted in the past—*la terre et les morts*—as maintained by German historicists or French theocrats, or neo-Conservatives in English-speaking countries, it is bound, provided it is inflexible enough, to encounter some unforeseen and unforeseeable human development, which it will not fit; and will then be used to justify the *a priori* barbarities of Procrustes—the vivisection of actual human societies into some fixed pattern dictated by our fallible understanding of a largely imaginary past or a wholly imaginary future. To preserve our absolute categories or ideals at the expense of human lives offends equally against the principles of science and of history; it is an attitude found in equal measure on the right and left wings in our days, and is not reconcilable with the principles accepted by those who respect the facts.

Pluralism, with the measure of "negative" liberty that it entails, seems to me a truer and more humane ideal than the goals of those who seek in the great, disciplined, authoritarian structures the ideal of "positive" self-mastery by classes, or peoples, or the whole of mankind. It is truer, because it does, at least, recognize the fact that human goals are many, not all of them commensurable, and in perpetual rivalry with one another. To assume that all values can be graded on one scale, so that it is a mere matter of inspection to determine the highest, seems to me to falsify our knowledge that men are free agents, to represent moral decision as an operation which a slide-rule could, in principle, perform. To say that in some ultimate, all-reconciling, yet realizable synthesis, duty *is* interest, or individual freedom *is* pure democracy or an authoritarian state, is to throw a metaphysical blanket over either self-deceit or deliberate hypocrisy. It is more humane because it does not (as the system builders do) deprive men, in the name of some remote, or incoherent, ideal, of much that they have found to be indispensable to their life as unpredictably self-transforming human beings.[9] In the end, men choose between ultimate values; they choose as they do, because their life and thought are determined by fundamental moral categories and concepts that are, at any rate over large stretches of time and space, a part of their being and thought and sense of their own identity; part of what makes them human.

It may be that the ideal of freedom to choose ends without claiming eternal validity for them, and the pluralism of values connected with this, is only the late fruit of our declining capitalist civilization: an ideal which remote ages and primitive societies have not recognized, and one which posterity will regard with curiosity, even sympathy, but little comprehension. This may be so; but no sceptical conclusions seem to me to follow. Principles are not less sacred because their duration cannot be guaranteed. Indeed, the very desire for guarantees that our values are eternal and secure in some objective heaven is perhaps only a craving for the certainties of childhood or the absolute values of our primitive past. "To realise the relative validity of one's convictions," said an admirable writer of our time, "and yet stand for them unflinchingly, is what distinguishes a civilised man from a barbarian." To demand more than this is perhaps a deep and incurable metaphysical need; but to allow it to determine one's practice is a symptom of an equally deep, and more dangerous, moral and political immaturity.

[9] On this also Bentham seems to me to have spoken well: "Individual interests are the only real interests . . . can it be conceived that there are men so absurd as to . . . prefer the man who is not to him who is; to torment the living, under pretence of promoting the happiness of them who are not born, and who may never be born?" This is one of the infrequent occasions when Burke agrees with Bentham; for this passage is at the heart of the empirical, as against the metaphysical, view of politics.

50.

A Defense of the Primacy of Liberty Rights

LOREN LOMASKY

What, then, are the basic rights that project pursuers possess? It has been argued that they amount to minimal demands on the forbearance of others, but is it *exclusively* forbearance that individuals can demand from one another as a matter of basic right or should claims to recipience of goods be acknowledged as well? A familiar way to phrase this distinction is as a contrast between "liberty" rights and "welfare" rights. Alternatively, rights are spoken of as "negative" (entailing noninterference with an activity) or "positive" (entailing the provision by some individual or institution of a valued item).

Liberalism has bifurcated into two distinctive variants in its response to the question of whether persons possess positive or welfare rights along with negative or liberty rights. *Classical liberalism,* a modern form of which is libertarianism, maintains that all rights individuals possess (or: a vastly preponderant share of the rights that individuals possess[1]) are negative in character. *Welfare liberalism* maintains that individuals possess extensive positive claims on others, and that these positive claims are on a par with negative claims not only with respect to their prominence on the moral landscape but also with respect to their justification. That is, whatever reasons we have to acknowledge that individuals may not be interfered with are also reasons for holding that individuals are entitled to aid from others. If it is *need* that validates claims to noninterference, then it is also need that confers a right to be provided the requisites for a satisfactory life. Or if it is alleged that individuals would *contract* amongst themselves in a suitably described setting, perhaps the Rawlsian original position, to respect each other's liberties, then they would similarly contract to guarantee to each other some specified level of welfare goods.

The argument to rights by way of project pursuit resides thoroughly within a liberal tradition. It is based on the proposition that individuals can and do commit themselves to long-terms ends which they have primary reason to advance. These ends are directive in that they determine what will count as a potential item of value for that individual. Individuals therefore are to be understood as project pursuers. That status is not to be assigned to units more encompassing than individual persons such as tribes, nations, economic classes,

---

[1] Classical liberalism typically does affirm the existence of a few select rights that entail positive performances on the part of others. These include the right to be defended against aggression upon one's person or property, the right to participate by voting and other means in the making of political determinations, and the right to be afforded a fair trial in the event that criminal charges are lodged. Although these may in toto impose very limited demands of a positive sort, they are significant as an entering wedge for those intent to expand the scope of liberalism. If even an austerely classical liberalism will admit that positive rights have some legitimacy within the overall structure of basic rights, then the argument between alternative varieties of liberalism becomes one of degree, not of basic principle. Or so it seems. . . .

or all of humanity; neither is it assigned at the subindividual level to particular genes,[2] the left and right lobes of the brain,[3] or time-slices of persons.[4] Those who pursue projects thereby have reason to value their own ability to be project pursuers and so have reason to try to establish conditions of reciprocal recognition and respect for the interest each has in being able to pursue his personal ends. These conditions are provided by rights—liberal rights.

Persons require noninterference from others, metaphorically described as "moral space," to be able to pursue their own designs. Therefore, it is initially plausible to insist that basic rights be understood as negative or liberty rights that forbid coercive encroachment. However, it is also the case that individuals need more than liberty in order to carve out for themselves satisfactory lives. Conditions of minimal well-being are also needed, and these typically depend on having means of access to economic goods. Because project pursuers have reason to value both the liberty to promote their own ends and the material means to secure those ends, it may seem that the argument to this point tips decisively to the side of welfare liberalism.

THE ARGUMENT FROM NEED

Although it may be the case that basic rights afford protection to those interests of individuals which are especially important, which individuals *need,* it does not follow that everything which individuals find important will justifiably be theirs as a matter of right. Importance is at most a necessary condition for being the object of a right, not both necessary and sufficient. Therefore, it is invalid to argue, as does D. D. Raphael:

> One cannot exercise the initiative of a human being (which is what the rights of liberty are intended to protect), or indeed remain a human being at all, unless the basic needs of life are satisfied, and if a man is not in a position to do this for himself, it seems to me reasonable to say that he has a right, as a human being, to the assistance of others in meeting these needs.[5]

It is important to see why this argument, representative of a prominent strand in the case for welfare liberalism, fails. There are at least three respects in which it is defective.

---

2 Richard Dawkins, *The Selfish Gene* (New York: Oxford University Press, 1976).

3 Thomas Nagel, "Brain Bisection and the Unity of Consciousness," in his *Mortal Questions* (Cambridge: Cambridge University Press, 1979), pp. 147–164.

4 Most energetically explored by Derek Parfit. See his *Reasons and Persons* (Oxford: Clarendon Press, 1984). This important book crossed my desk while I was preparing final revisions of *Persons, Rights, and the Moral Community.* It engages many of the themes contained herein and does so with the author's characteristic verve and imagination. I have not been able to take up the challenges presented in *Reasons and Persons* but commend it to the reader as a significant work in the foundations of moral theory.

5 D. D. Raphael, "Human Rights, Old and New," in D. D. Raphael, ed., *Political Theory and the Rights of Man* (Bloomington: Indiana University Press, 1967), p. 64.

First, even if some item is a vital component of a worthwhile human life, there will be no presumption whatsoever that one has a right to it if it is not the case that others are able to provide it. The impossibility of provision can be either causal or conceptual. An example of the former is a needed transplantable organ when no spare organs are at hand. The latter sort of impossibility is more difficult to specify but of considerable moral significance in that it stakes out the boundaries between self and others in the sphere of practical activity. It is reasonable to maintain that no satisfactory life, viewed either externally or internally, can be lived by someone who lacks altogether a conception of a good that is directive for his activities. The complete cynic, for whom no end is worthy of pursuit, not even the development and defense of his own cynicism, is a pitiable figure. But the propriety of pity does not carry over into a justifiable claim on others to provide that which the cynic sorely lacks; a conception of the good is something that individuals must provide by themselves and for themselves if they are to have it at all.

Similarly, persons require motivational energy to propel themselves actively to realize that which they hold valuable. They require sufficient fixity of purpose to hold to plans of activity over extended periods of time such that they are not subject to diversion by every passing whim or caprice if their lives are to exhibit coherence and fixed identity. Persons also require flexibility of response so that previously held conceptions of value worthy of pursuit can be modified in the light of new information and evolving structures of attachment. All of these can justifiably be regarded as basic needs of human beings, yet they are not moral commodities that those who are well supplied can be asked to donate to those whose stock is low.

John Rawls writes, "Perhaps the most important primary good is that of self-respect." [6] Note that self-respect is yet another good that, though of inordinate value, cannot be conferred on one by some other person or by some set of institutions. At most, these external agencies can provide conditions within which individuals are rendered able to develop and act on a conception of a good that, in turn, promotes a sturdy sense of self-worth. But the primary good of self-respect is not one that is amenable to external provision. The Rawlsian theory of justice involves principles for the allocation of liberties, opportunities, and economic goods to persons; yet Rawls is careful to say that "justice as fairness *gives more support* to self-esteem than other principles." [7] It does not and cannot mandate the provision of self-respect.

The point concerning the impossibility of provision of some highly valued good needs little more than to be stated in order to gain acceptability. However, though evident, it is not innocuous, for what it reveals is the limits of a welfare liberalism. There are components of the good for man that cannot be provided. Society can arrange itself so that individuals are *not impeded* in producing and sustaining these goods, can provide channels through which *support and encouragement* by others is directed toward persons whose capacity for achieving these goods will thereby be enhanced, but it cannot offer these goods to all

[6] *A Theory of Justice* (Cambridge, Mass.: Harvard University Press, 1971), p. 440.
[7] Ibid. (Emphasis added.)

who are in need of them as a matter of right. Classical liberalism can be understood as recognizing, at least implicitly, this limit. For by promoting an ideal of thorough-going liberty within which persons can develop coherent life schemes, and thus a firm sense of self-worth, classical liberalism stands opposed to the placing of obstacles in the way of individuals' cultivation of moral commodities that, in the last analysis, must be internally generated.

A second defect of Raphael's argument is that it takes into account only the magnitude of the need a potential recipient has for a good without giving corresponding attention to the magnitude of sacrifice that must be exacted from others in order to provide that good. In other words, it is entirely oriented toward *demand* and ignores factors concerning *supply*. It may appear intuitively plausible to suggest that persons have a right to some good that they very much need when it is the case that others can easily supply it at little cost to themselves. But when the demand side of the equation is held constant and the supply side allowed steadily to increase, there comes a point at which it is no longer obvious, or even credible, that there is any right of recipience to the good and thus a correlative duty to provide it.

A strict utilitarian will concur with this judgment but will claim that this point is reached only when the equation is exactly balanced: when the marginal cost to the provider of supplying one more unit of the good is equal to the marginal value of that unit to the recipient. That utilitarian cost-benefit equilibrium rests on the presupposition that there exists an impersonal standard of value (in this case, the standard of overall utility) to which all agents have reason to adhere, and in terms of which the ends of all persons are commensurable. In Chapter 2 it was argued that this presupposition merits rejection, that individuals rather have reason to subscribe to a personal (at least partly) standard of value. The individual called on to be a donor is not rationally obliged to weigh impartially his own ends and those of the would-be recipient. He acts rationally if he assigns special value—personal value, value-for-himself—to his own ends simply in virtue of their being his. Therefore, there can be no general obligation to give up that which is of considerable instrumental value to the pursuit of one's own projects on the grounds that someone else has pressing need for those items.

Our moral intuitions seems to support this theoretical position. Suppose that the population of the Indian subcontinent could be brought up to a level of tolerable material subsistence, however that be measured, if the United States were to divert some 70% of its gross national product toward that end. Few persons (or is it "few persons in the United States"?) would take that fact to confer a right upon hundreds of millions of Asians to receive that sum.[8] The need is certainly genuine, and the ability to alleviate it present at least in large measure, but the inference to a welfare right is highly dubious.

---

[8] Probably most Americans would deny that they are *morally required* to provide *any amount* of relief to foreign nationals. That claim is more arguable; perhaps intuitions are mixed. However, to the extent that even the minimal welfare right can be rendered persuasive, it would be by way of arguing that a *relatively trivial* sacrifice by Americans would provide *extremely great* benefits to the recipients.

Cases yielding the same conclusion can also be adduced at the micro level. The autocratic father may urgently require that his adult daughter remain at home with him as companion, captive audience, domestic servant, and token of his capacity to command respectful deference. She would prefer a life of her own with far more independence and self-direction than the paternal roost affords, but the father would be devastated should the daughter "abandon" him. Is there then a case to be made for a right on his part to her perpetual servility?

You have two good corneas and I have none. No other source of bodily parts is at hand. Do I then have a right to one cornea? (I'll generously leave to you the choice of which one to give up.) The operation will be a bit painful to you, although not otherwise demanding, and afterwards you will have trouble hitting a major league curveball, should baseball be a preferred activity of yours. However, it is undeniably the case that my being totally blind is a much graver hardship than would be your loss of sight in one eye. It is unlikely, though, that any such consideration will persuade you that I have a right to one of your corneas.

It is not being denied that the recognition by A that B lacks some crucial good which it is in the power of A to provide (though at some substantial cost to A) is a reason for A to provide that good to B. We might very well want to say that Americans *should* donate some appreciable share of their income to impoverished Asians, that it would be *morally praiseworthy* for them to do so, or that you would be acting wonderfully well if you choose to give up one of your eyes so that I could see. These judgments of moral approbation, though, do not imply a right on the part of the beneficiary. That it would be *outstandingly good* for A to provide some good to B, or even that A *ought to* provide the good to B, is not equivalent to the judgment that A *must* provide B with the good. All arguments that needs as such confer rights are flawed in this respect.

A third defect of Raphael's argument, related to the preceding one, is that it fails to distinguish between that which is held to be needed and the manner in which there is an obligation to respond to the need. Suppose that B needs, with the relevant degree of urgency, good G. The extent to which B's need entails on the part of A some obligation toward B ranges from *not at all* to its being *mandatory* for A that he bring about conditions sufficient for B's attainment of G.

The argument from need to rights characteristically rests on the claim that the former of these extremes is implausible. To hold that need is entirely irrelevant to the moral relationships in which persons stand toward each other is to plump for a desiccated view of the moral realm. Of what account would morality be if it were unresponsive to undeniably pressing constraints on individuals' abilities to make a start at constructing for themselves minimally satisfactory lives? If morality is to be *practical* in its traditional sense, to hazard judgments concerning how men ought to conduct themselves in a world in which they are vulnerable to circumstance, then it must address the ways in which vulnerabilities can be rectified through the concerted action of persons within a moral order. Accordingly, it is asserted that need *does* confer rights, and that others must (subject to a few complicating qualifications such as knowledge of the need, ability to meet it, no greater unmet need resulting as a consequence, and so on) provide that which would otherwise be lacking.

But this is too quick. Even if it be admitted that B's need does figure within the moral calculus such that it is not in every respect a matter of moral indifference for A whether B secures G or not, it does not follow that A must do whatever will suffice to bring it about that B have G. There are ways of construing A's obligation toward B with respect to G that lie between the two extremes. At least two deserve mention.

First, it may be held that A need not go as far as providing G to B but must *assist* in the provision of G. This is a natural way to construe the obligations on individuals engendered by most of the positive rights put forth by welfare liberalism. Suppose that what B needs is income, or a job that will generate income. If there are many other persons besides A who have the capacity to provide B with income or employment, then it is arbitrary to maintain that A alone is required to make provision to B. And it would seem a case of conspicuous overkill to maintain that each of the *n* persons who is able to aid B has the obligation to do so in full; B does not need *n* jobs or *n* streams of income. Rather, the phrasing that suggests itself is that B's right to G creates a *shared* or *social* obligation. Each of the other parties can be called upon to contribute a fair share to the maintenance of B's well-being, such that their acting together will be sufficient to bring about B's having G.[9] It will be the case then for welfare liberalism that the obligation actually to provide G falls on the state; individuals will be obligated to contribute their suitably defined share to governmental institutions.

But there is a second way in which individuals can be required to be responsive to a need without it being the case that any one of them must supply that which is needed—or without the collectivity as a whole being obligated to do so. A takes account of B's need for G if A intentionally brings about a condition *necessary* for B's attainment of G, even though that condition is not simultaneously sufficient. If B needs clean water to drink, A may walk down to the stream, fill up a quart jug, and carefully carry it back to B. Alternatively, A may respond to B's need by refraining from dumping raw sewage into the stream (which, for purposes of simplicity, can be supposed to be the only source of potable water available to B). In the former case, A *provides* B with drinking water; in the latter, A *refrains from preventing* B from having the water. The argument from need will not be morally impotent if it generates rights to treatment of the latter sort, rights, however, that fall short of mandating provision of the good G.

It is clear from preceding stages of the discussion that there are some needs to which no right of provision can correspond. Self-respect is one such good. No one can provide another with the day's ration of self-respect as one can a quantity of water. Self-respect, if it is to be attained at all, must in the last resort be internally generated. "The last resort": the phrase is to signify that how others act is not altogether inconsequential for one's ability to develop self-respect. To be treated contemptuously by others as a pariah whose conception of the good merits scorn and denigration will predictably cause all but the

---

[9] For those goods which no one party has the means to produce it will be the case that only a shared obligation could ensure their distribution. Most public goods will be of this sort.

hardiest egos to waver or capitulate. Although no one can confer this good on anyone else, it is certainly the case that others can act to impede its realization.

Accordingly, were we to acknowledge a right to self-respect, it logically could not take the form of a right to provision. There is, however, no logical bar to arguing for a right to certain conditions necessary for the development of self-respect. Persons would thereby be placed under an obligation not to degrade others or render them servile in a manner that would obliterate chances for respect of one's own ends and one's status as a moral agent. Admittedly, there would be complications, perhaps insuperable, in applying a right to self-respect so generally stated. Suppose that Jones sets for himself the life task of squaring the circle; he would be absolutely bereft and hold his life to be devoid of meaning were he to be led to believe that he is unable to attain this goal. Would Smith be violating Jones' right if she sent him clippings from a geometry text? Or if she refrained from encouraging Jones to continue his quest in spite of the fact that the first hundred dozen attempts had failed? We might say that only those conditions *typically* necessary for self-respect, those that a vast majority of human beings find essential, must be afforded as a matter of right. But that would seem to be too weak a protection: members of a small racial or religious minority M could then permissibly be degraded in virtue of their inclusion within M because most persons do not require respect for M-members. These, though, are digressions; the intent of the example was not to argue for the existence of a right to (the conditions necessary for the attainment and maintenance of) self-respect. Rather, the argument was conditional: *if* there is a right to self-respect, it can *only* be a right to certain necessary conditions and not to sufficient conditions.

The distinction between classical liberalism and welfare liberalism is often misleadingly characterized as revolving around which needs or, more generally, which interests are to be accorded primary moral status and, therefore, to be safeguarded by ascriptions of rights. Classical liberalism, it is said, recognizes that persons require security in person and possessions, and so it posits the familiar Lockean triumvirate of rights to life, liberty, and estate. No one may properly intrude on the enjoyment of these, where intrusion is understood as coercive interference.

Welfare liberals agree with classical liberals that individuals have a strong interest in not being interfered with, but emphasize that noninterference hardly exhausts persons' vital interests. The liberty to untrammeled use of one's estate will be of little value to the beggar who has no estate; his primary concern is the acquisition of material goods in the first place. The proclaimed right to life will ring hollow to the man who lacks the means to procure medical care necessary for his survival. Welfare liberalism claims to be consistently carrying out the unfinished program of classical liberalism. Rather than restricting attention to a *select* class of human needs, it maintains that *all* needs possess moral weight in virtue of their being needs, and therefore they create rights. It is not only liberty that is generally valuable but also health care, housing, employment, education, recreation, and so on. If there are liberty rights, then there are also rights to these welfare goods.

This way of putting the contrast between classical and welfare liberalism trades on a fundamental confusion. It is mistaken to say that one version is responsive to a narrow array of interests while the other ascribes moral weight to a much wider range of interests. The difference is almost not at all with regard to *which interests merit moral protection* but rather with the *manner in which moral protection is afforded*. Classical liberalism recognizes rights to conditions *necessary* for the attainment of valued items, while welfare liberalism is concerned to bring about *sufficient* conditions for their attainment. If the older version of liberalism is myopic, it is not because it is blind to the value of things like employment and medical care. If it is to be faulted, it will be because the degree of moral response to these interests is held to be inadequate, and not because the interest itself is dismissed.

Consider the status of an alleged right to employment (or, more grandly, a right to "meaningful and productive employment"). It is tempting to classify this as one of the "new rights," one unknown to the liberalism of an earlier century. That classification would be importantly mistaken. Whether or not classical liberals used the term "right to employment," they clearly believed that there was such a right, and that it was violated whenever private parties, or more commonly, state institutions acted to restrict the liberty of persons to engage in chosen occupations. The feudalism that tied a serf to the manor and the patriarchy that sought to restrict women to a domestic existence as the appendage of husband or father were both, at different historical stages of the career of liberalism, condemned. So, too, were grants of patent and monopoly that restricted access to various lines of work. If people need employment, then they need the liberty to contract for whatever employment is available. The liberty right vouchsafed by classical liberalism is a moral response to this need and therefore fully deserves to be accorded recognition as a right to employment.

That is not, of course, to maintain that classical liberalism anticipated the welfare right to employment. In its recent incarnation the right to employment does not merely uphold a condition necessary for the securing of employment, but one that is sufficient. The government is called upon to provide jobs to all those not employed by the private sector. In theory this is to strengthen the classical liberal's right to employment by recognizing additional obligations toward the unemployed; alongside the liberty right of free contract are positive rights to the provision of a job. Nothing is taken away, but something is added.

Practice, however, significantly diverges from theory. Welfare liberalism in fact has largely acceded to major erosions in the liberty right to employment. Minimum wage laws tend to receive strong support from contemporary versions of liberalism,[10] but these laws restrict persons' freedom to secure employment without in any way providing additional sources of jobs. Moreover, the persons who are inconvenienced will almost always be those for whom the

---

[10] With a few exceptions. Lester Thurow, an economist of impeccable welfare liberal credentials, endorses a governmental guaranteed employment program but favors abolishment of minimum wage laws. This represents a more consistent version of welfare liberalism than is usually espoused. See *The Zero-Sum Society* (New York: Basic Books, 1980), p. 145.

securing of any employment at all is difficult. Brain surgeons and master carpenters will rarely be touched by the existence of minimum wage laws, but seventeen-year-old black high school dropouts will often be guaranteed an absence of work opportunities. Occupational licensure laws also restrict access to employment, and these too are typically sanctioned by welfare liberalism. Therefore, it is not at all obvious that the right to employment espoused by welfare liberalism is stronger or more encompassing than the version set forth by classical liberals.

The two varieties of liberalism do not differ essentially in the interests they hold worthy of protection but rather in the nature of the protection that is to be accorded. The decision between them will have to be made on grounds of which response is the more adequate in doing justice to the gravity of the interests at stake. And these are grounds on which the case for welfare liberalism seems especially strong. It can be put in the following terms:

> To judge an interest *important* is to judge that it should be *met*. Simply to eliminate a group of obstacles to its attainment will be of value only when those are the only obstacles. It is small comfort to a person who lacks some vitally important good G to be informed that he has complete liberty to pursue G if possession of that liberty is insufficient to ensure his attainment of G. Liberties that are unaccompanied by the ability to make effective use of the liberty are of negligible value. What should be of preeminent moral concern is not how many or how few conditions necessary for the securing of G are satisfied, but whether in fact the need for G will be met. To take seriously an interest is to bring it about that the interest will, if possible, be satisfied. Only the recognition of positive rights entails an obligation of *provision*.

This argument is presumptively strong because it links the theory of rights to a theory of personal value. If rights are to be the hard currency of moral exchange rather than counterfeit coin, rights must be something that persons have reason to value. They will value a right to the extent that it enhances their ability to act successfully on their conception of the good. (A right to an equal share of aluminum mined on the moon will be assigned little value by its holders.) If possession of a right is fully sufficient to guarantee the attainment of some valued component of a person's good, then the person has reason to value that right. But if a right to G will predictably fail to lead to the securing of G because it protects only some of the conditions necessary for G, others of which will remain unsatisfied, it becomes mysterious on what grounds such a right could be held to be of value. Insofar, then, as the rights espoused by classical liberalism fall short of ensuring the enjoyment of goods, their lofty position in the moral pantheon is in jeopardy.

That is not to claim that liberty rights are altogether insignificant. Rather, it is to specify with some precision for whom they will be of value: individuals who need nothing more than liberty of the relevant sort in order to pursue G with a high probability of success. They will be persons for whom the other necessary conditions have antecedently been satisfied. Typically, this classification will include members of the upper and middle economic and social classes and will exclude those whose economic and social position is marginal. Marxist theoreticians have found it entirely unsurprising that the staunchest upholders of liberty rights come from the classes that will be most advanced by their recognition; "bourgeois rights" are advocated by the bourgeoisie because they are, in a very direct sense, *for* the bourgeoisie. Welfare liberals decline to embrace the full Marxist critique of a liberal order, but they go along with the Marxists in asserting the moral indefensibility of a class-biased scheme of rights, where "class bias" is defined in terms of de facto differential advantage. Their preferred way of surmounting this bias is to buttress a structure of negative rights with a collection of positive rights such that they are jointly sufficient to guarantee to all persons the various goods which are held to be objects of rights.

If a cogent case is to be made for classical liberalism, it will have to meet the charge that assigning favored status to liberty rights is morally arbitrary. It will require arguing either (1) that liberty of action is a more valuable moral possession than are other necessary conditions for achievement of one's ends or (2) that the provision of welfare goods carries liabilities that do not similarly attach to the provision of liberty. The two prongs are complementary; each aims at showing that liberty is, in some sense, unique and that liberty rights inherit this uniqueness. To the extent that such a case can be developed, the presumptively powerful argument supportive of welfare liberalism will be defused.

THE LIBERAL IDEAL: NONINTERFERENCE OR AID?

Because rights generate correlative obligations of compliance, the justification of an alleged right necessarily displays two aspects. It must ground the object of the right in some compelling interest of the potential right holder, and it must also demonstrate that those who transact with the potential right holder have reason to acknowledge and respect the interest in question. If either is absent, the justification fails. That is why an argument that proceeds directly from needs to rights is, at best, incomplete. The fact that B needs G may afford A no reason whatsoever to act in a way that enhances B's likelihood of securing G. Or, less arguably, it may have some bearing on A's choice of activity without mandating that A provide G to B. The more onerous the demands placed on A, the less reason that A has, *ceteris paribus,* to accede to those demands.

A requirement of noninterference with the liberty of persons to pursue some good will typically be less costly than a requirement of provision. For that reason, an argument for a liberty right can go through in circumstances where the argument for a corresponding welfare right does not. Specifically, that will be so when a bona fide interest has been established but where

$$C_L^G < I^G < C_W^G$$

C_L being the cost to a representative individual of acknowledging a liberty right to G, C_W the cost of acknowledging a welfare right to G, and I^G the moral weight of the interest in G.

It is intuitively plausible to suppose that, for many I^G, the inequality holds. Consider two cases cited above. It is undeniable that impoverished Asians have a strong interest in securing means of subsistence, yet few will argue that this fact imposes an obligation on Americans to ship abroad 70% of their GNP. However, it is very persuasive to maintain that Americans (and others) are obliged *not to interfere* with the efforts of Asians to secure economic sufficiency. It would therefore be impermissible to send a flotilla to commandeer a share of the none-too-bulging Bangladesh granary, or to forbid by governmental edict relief agencies from sending cash or commodities to that country. It is also morally impermissible to enact protectionist legislation that in any way interferes with the liberty of foreign nationals to trade with whomsoever they choose in order to secure income. (If this implication of a right to noninterference seems more questionable than the other two, it may be because our familiarity with protectionist practices lends them a veneer of respectability. A century ago imperialistic exactions enjoyed similar familiarity, as did the practice of slavery a century before that. Surely there is more than a little inconsistency exemplified by those who argue for protectionism coupled with foreign aid.) If Asians possess any rights against Americans for subsistence, then they at least possess a liberty right.

Similarly, my interest in acquiring a serviceable cornea imposes on others at least the duty not to prevent my getting the part from a willing donor. If someone chooses to give me an eye, bequeath it in his will, or sell it for an agreed sum, then it would be a violation of my liberty right should a private individual or the state act to impede such a transaction. The acknowledgment of a liberty right to secure the cornea does not, of course, entail that, should no donor be forthcoming, you are morally required to turn over to me one of your two good corneas.

The criticism of classical liberalism was that the rights it sets forth are too modest to correspond adequately to the gravity of interests at stake. But what the preceding discussion shows is that modesty is a virtue. Because C_L^G is typically much less than C_W^G, individuals will often have reason to acknowledge liberty rights, though not welfare rights. Welfare liberalism claims to take seriously the interests on which rights are founded; perhaps it does. But it fails to attend with equal attention to the rational motivation of persons to accede to a rights claim. By insisting that a right to G worthy of the name must entail the provision of G, welfare liberalism jeopardizes the underpinnings of a structure of basic rights. Rights are moral claims with which others *must* comply. Because the demand for compliance is (maximally) strong, an interpersonally acceptable structure of rights has to restrict the area over which compliance is mandatory. Otherwise individuals will find that they have no rational stake in the maintenance of a regime of rights.[11] . . . It can now be seen that classical liberalism is

---

[11] By way of contrast, an *ethic of supererogation* need not display a similarly restricted scope. Individuals inclined to pursue a path of heroism or sainthood may be asked to assume burdens that are almost too heavy for a man to bear. The point, though, is that they are free to *decline* to take this path. If living an extraordinarily good life is perceived to be too difficult a task, then one can

concerned *both* to recognize rights that correspond to grave interests *and* to ensure that all members of the moral community have a stake in securing for themselves and others the rights so defined.

It may be objected that this line of argument is question-begging. It has been argued that moral demands which are stringent must therefore not be excessive. But what is to count as "excessive"? Unless this preliminary question is answered, it will be impossible to determine whether welfare liberalism requires too much of persons—or classical liberalism too little. After all, the surest way to avoid excess imposition is to demand nothing at all of anyone. Such a retreat into Hobbesian anarchy is not what any liberal defends. Let it be granted that obligations corresponding to rights lie on an Aristotelian continuum between deficiency and excess. Until the mean is specified, it is impossible to determine the extent to which negative rights should properly be augmented by positive rights.

A second line of objection is to demur at the equation of positive rights with severe impositions. The critic can admit that some positive rights will fall heavily on others: e.g., those very carefully selected as examples for this chapter. However, the critic will be prepared to respond with his own examples in which the balance of benefits and burdens is quite different.

> 1. A small child has slipped into a swimming pool and is in danger of drowning. One person is sitting by the side of the pool doing the Sunday *New York Times* crossword puzzle. By getting out of his chair, walking a few steps, and reaching into the pool, he could save the child. That, though, would mean abandoning the crossword puzzle for a minute or two. Does the child have a right against this man to be saved? Is there a positive obligation to save the child or no more than an obligation not to prevent anyone else who wishes to do so from saving the child?
>
> 2. Persons who lack the means to purchase antibiotics will suffer from diseases that are easily curable. Thousands of impoverished individuals will live longer and happier lives if the rest of us are taxed a few pennies each, the proceeds to go toward supplying needed drugs. Do the indigent have a right to medical relief that is inexpensive and easily tendered, yet which has great therapeutic benefits?

These are cases in which it seems entirely persuasive to maintain that I^G exceeds C^G_W, and that therefore a welfare right to G should be admitted. It is barely, if at all, more inconvenient directly to provide the good than to pledge noninterference with respect to attainment of the good. (Won't it disturb one's concentration if rescuers are scurrying around the sides of the pool?) If important needs support a structure of minimally imposing *liberty* rights, then they should equally well support minimally imposing *welfare* rights. There is no presumption that all and only welfare rights are very burdensome on others or that all and only liberty rights embody suitable moderation in demands placed on

---

choose instead to display no more than minimal goodness. The structure of rights is what provides the standard of minimal goodness.

others. Therefore, it cannot be concluded that a rationally defensible version of liberalism will be one in which liberty rights are dominant.

Both strands of objection implicitly concede that the direct argument from needs to rights is defective. Because that argument is so prominently deployed as a chief prop for welfare liberalism, the concession is significant. It implies that if there are welfare rights, then they must be like liberty rights with respect to the degree of burdensomeness imposed. The welfare liberalism that could emerge from such a basis would be a modest extension of classical liberalism rather than a sharply revisionary view of what rights people have.

Classical liberalism does not, however, rest merely on the claim that liberty is more easily provided than many other things individuals require. Rather, it insists that liberty is unique among goods necessary for project pursuit in that it *must be provided by others* if it is to be enjoyed at all. The conditions necessary for an agent to lead a successful life may be divided into three mutually exclusive categories. In the first are those items which only the agent himself can generate. These include motivational energy and self-respect. If they are lacking, then no one else can provide them.

In Category 2 are goods of which the agent may avail himself through his own efforts or which may be provided to him by others. Food, clothing, shelter, and most other economic goods fall within this classification. It is, of course, the case that individuals who "provide themselves" with these goods typically do so within a framework of institutions involving the voluntary cooperation of others. To purchase one's food at a grocery store requires the cooperation of others in a way that solitary berry-picking does not; do-it-yourself neurosurgery is not likely to be as successful as the services involving the efforts of thousands of persons provided at a major medical center. The division of labor in complex modern societies leads to more efficient provision of some goods and to the very availability of others. Without in any way wishing to downplay the significance of specialization within the social order, there is still a point to saying that individuals who command resources that can predictably be transformed into or exchanged for desired goods and services provide those goods and services for themselves. As it were, the social levers are already there waiting to be pulled. By way of contrast, a person who commands no appreciable stock of resources may yet receive valued items, but the levers then must be pulled by others. The distinction is between the ability to purchase or secure an item through one's labor and securing that item as a gift or through coercive extraction.

Category 3 includes those conditions which the agent cannot bring about for himself but which others can provide. These include fame, adulation, friendship, and other services that make essential reference to others. Paramount, though, among these is *noninterference*. Whatever it is that one desires to do, one requires the absence of interference by others. Noninterference is thus a good that is both *universal* and *general*: it is universal in the sense that it is of value to every project pursuer and is general in that it is valued irrespective of the nature of the ends that one endeavors to advance. Moreover, it is needed *from everyone.* Of course, not everyone is in fact able to intrude on one's pursuit of ends, and so there will be no point to insisting on the noninterference of someone who totally lacks the power to affect one's designs. But that is to say that a Benign Nature is arrayed so as to limit possibilities of interference, and is not to deny that such noninterference is needed. Should *anyone* interfere with A's pursuit of end E_1, then A is thereby harmed.

Among the members of Category 3, noninterference is unique. Unlike, say, fame, it is of basic value to everyone irrespective of the particular nature of the ends to which one commits oneself. And even if it be argued that friendship is also a good that must be present for a life to be minimally satisfactory, it is not a good that must be supplied by everyone. One or several friends will satisfy the condition quite nicely. Perhaps—though this is arguable—more friends, all else equal, are always better than fewer; and perhaps a community exemplifying universal mutual affection is the best of all possible moral orders—if it be possible at all. However, it cannot be *demanded* of persons that they contribute a full share to the maintenance of a superlatively good social design, both because such a contribution is supererogatory rather than a matter of duty, and also because goods such as friendship cannot be procured via edict. Friendship (or affection, or solidarity, or fraternity) presupposes an antecedent regard for persons and their ends. To be a friend is voluntarily to enroll oneself in the projects of another, to regard his good as one's own simply because it is his good and not because there happens to be a coincidence of aims. Noninterference entails no such presupposition. It involves the recognition of other persons as distinct individuals committed to their distinct projects, but assumes no sympathy with person or project. No aid for a design that is not one's own (and to which one may be indifferent or antipathetic) is required, only the avoidance of instrusion.

What these considerations seem to indicate is that classical liberalism is not myopic in its strong emphasis on liberty rights. The moral theory that it puts forth is continuous with the account of practical reason as responsive to personal value that was sketched out in Chapter 2. If E_1 is A's end, then there is reason-for-the-promotion-of-E_1-by-A that is not similarly reason-for-B. If C is a condition necessary for A's attainment of E_1, then A has reason to bring it about that C obtain. B, though, does not possess equivalent reason to bring it about that C obtain. If C falls into Category 2 (i.e., C is a condition which either A or B could satisfy), then it is A on whom the practical necessity of satisfying C primarily falls. However, should A have a right against B that B provide for the satisfaction of C, then it would be B and not A for whom reasons to provide C would be maximally weighty (or they would face reasons of equal weightiness). To posit the existence of such a right, then, is at odds with the essentially individuated character of practical reason. Classical liberalism is quite properly hesitant in acknowledging the existence of such rights.

Because liberty falls within Category 3, its provision is a very different matter. B's noninterference with A's pursuit of E_1 is something that A cannot provide for himself; it must be tendered by B. Unlike the previous case, the responsibility for providing the good is necessarily external to the recipient of the good. To demand liberty as a right is not in conflict with the recognition of the separateness of persons and their projects. Rather, it is responsive to such separateness: because persons are separate beings individuated in part by virtue of the particular projects to which they commit themselves, they are rationally entitled to insist that they be let alone to pursue their own designs and not be enlisted as adjuncts to the projects of others. Classical liberalism is the moral endorsement of persons' individuality.

Reference was made in the previous chapter to Kantian formulations of liberal individualism. It is now possible to spell out in somewhat more detail how thoroughly consonant with the structure of a Kantian ethic is the preeminence of liberty rights. Kant insists that universality and generality are formal properties of all binding ethical principles. We have now seen that a moral requirement of respect for persons' liberty satisfies the generality criterion in that the value of liberty is not dependent on individuals' particular choice of projects. It doubly satisfies the universality criterion: every project pursuer needs liberty, and liberty is needed from everyone. The formulation of Kant's Categorical Imperative that enjoins one to treat all persons as ends in themselves and not merely as means can be read as requiring the recognition that each project pursuer is a being who accords to his own projects a special personal value, and that respect for persons entails that they not be precluded from acting as project pursuers.

It is open to the welfare liberal to identify other goods that are like liberty in being capable of provision only by others, and that are general and universal in the relevant senses. These goods, once identified, may serve to ground rights in as deep a theoretical base of individuated practical reason as are liberty rights. This course is open to the welfare liberal—if there are any such goods to be discovered. Prospects, though, seem dim. It is clear that the usual listing of interests that are to be satisfied by individual or, more commonly, political provision does not come close to qualifying. Most of these interests are in Category 2, not Category 3. Those in the third category lack either generality or universality or both. One can, then, with some confidence, predict that future development of the theory of welfare liberalism is unlikely to shake the primacy of liberty and liberty rights.

It would be too abrupt, however, to proceed from the *primacy* of liberty rights to an extreme libertarian stance that countenances *only* liberty rights, whatever the circumstances in which human beings find themselves. It has been argued that noninterference is requisite for successful civility. Therefore, individuals have reason to supply noninterference to others conditional upon the like receipt of noninterference from them. It has not been argued nor, I believe, can it be that no acts of positive performance are such that persons can claim them as their rightful due. . . . Even were that so for advanced capitalistic liberal democracies, itself a highly debatable point, it would be parochial to extend by fiat that recipe to all settings for social existence. Respect for the individuality of persons as project pursuers with their own lives to lead is compatible with the acknowledgment of dependency relations that validate positive claims on others.[12] Moral theory, including the theory of rights, must be chary of prescribing for all times and all places in an apodictic voice. Principles derived from philosophical anthropology and the a priori form of practical reason admit of widely varying applications. Morality is not a Procrustean bed into which, willy-nilly, social existence can be trimmed to fit.

---

[12] Anthropological findings could be exhibited in support of this modest defense of a place for positive rights. One need not, however, range very far afield to find plausible instances of warranted claims involving more than noninterference. The moral status of *children* is of special interest in this connection. Even staunchly classical liberals will assign to children positive rights of provision, rights held both against private individuals—parents—and against the state. It will not do to condemn as inconsistent this departure from a strict standard of noninterference. Children *are* a special case of non–project pursuers who are engaged in the process of becoming full-fledged project pursuers, and it is not a defect of moral theory but a virtue that special cases be accorded special treatment.

51.
Basic Positive Subsistence Rights
HENRY SHUE

BASIC RIGHTS

Nietzsche, who holds strong title to being the most misunderstood and most underrated philosopher of the last century, considered much of conventional morality—and not conceptions of rights only—to be an attempt by the powerless to restrain the powerful: an enormous net of fine mesh busily woven around the strong by the masses of the weak.[1] And he was disgusted by it, as if fleas were pestering a magnificent leopard or ordinary ivy were weighing down a soaring oak. In recoiling from Nietzsche's *assessment* of morality, many have dismissed too quickly his insightful *analysis* of morality. Moral systems obviously serve more than one purpose, and different specific systems serve some purposes more fully or better than others, as of course Nietzsche himself also recognized. But one of the chief purposes of morality in general, and certainly of conceptions of rights, and of basic rights above all, is indeed to provide some minimal protection against utter helplessness to those too weak to protect themselves. Basic rights are a shield for the defenseless against at least some of the more devastating and more common of life's threats, which include, as we shall see, loss of security and loss of subsistence. Basic rights are a restraint upon economic and political forces that would otherwise be too strong to be resisted. They are social guarantees against actual and threatened deprivations of at least some basic needs. Basic rights are an attempt to give to the powerless a veto over some of the forces that would otherwise harm them the most.

Basic rights are the morality of the depths. They specify the line beneath which no one is to be allowed to sink. This is part of the reason that basic rights are tied as closely to self-respect as Feinberg indicates legal claim-rights are.[2] And this helps to explain why Nietzsche found moral rights repugnant. His eye was on the heights, and he wanted to talk about how far some might soar, not about how to prevent the rest from sinking lower. It is not clear that we cannot do both.[3]

And it is not surprising that what is in an important respect the essentially negative goal of preventing or alleviating helplessness is a central purpose of

[1] For his clearest single presentation of this analysis, see Friedrich Nietzsche, *On the Genealogy of Morals,* edited by Walter Kaufmann and translated by Walter Kaufmann and R. J. Hollingdale (New York: Vintage Books, 1967). Much, but not all, of what is interesting in Nietzsche's account was put into the mouth of Callicles in Plato's *Gorgias.*

[2] Many legal claim-rights make little or no contribution to self-respect, but moral claim-rights (and the legal claim-rights based upon them) surely do.

[3] Nietzsche was also conflating a number of different kinds of power/weakness. Many of today's politically powerful, against whom people need protection, totally lack the kind of dignified power Nietzsche most admired and would certainly have incurred his cordial disgust.

something as important as conceptions of basic rights. For everyone healthy adulthood is bordered on each side by helplessness, and it is vulnerable to interruption by helplessness, temporary or permanent, at any time. And many of the people in the world now have very little control over their fates, even over such urgent matters as whether their own children live through infancy.[4] Nor is it surprising that although the goal is negative, the duties correlative to rights will turn out to include positive actions. The infant and the aged do not need to be assaulted in order to be deprived of health, life, or the capacity to enjoy active rights. The classic liberal's main prescription for the good life—do not interfere with thy neighbor—is the only poison they need. To be helpless they need only to be left alone. This is why avoiding the infliction of deprivation will turn out . . . not to be the only kind of duty correlative to basic rights.

Basic rights, then, are everyone's minimum reasonable demands upon the rest of humanity.[5] They are the rational basis for justified demands the denial of which no self-respecting person can reasonably be expected to accept. Why should anything be so important? The reason is that rights are basic in the sense used here only if enjoyment of them is essential to the enjoyment of all other rights. This is what is distinctive about a basic right. When a right is genuinely basic, any attempt to enjoy any other right by sacrificing the basic right would be quite literally self-defeating, cutting the ground from beneath itself. Therefore, if a right is basic, other, non-basic rights may be sacrificed, if necessary, in order to secure the basic right. But the protection of a basic right may not be sacrificed in order to secure the enjoyment of a non-basic right. It may not be sacrificed because it cannot be sacrificed successfully. If the right sacrificed is indeed basic, then no right for which it might be sacrificed can actually be enjoyed in the absence of the basic right. The sacrifice would have proven self-defeating.[6]

In practice, what this priority for basic rights usually means is that basic rights need to be established securely before other rights can be secured. The point is that people should be able to *enjoy,* or *exercise,* their other rights. The point is simple but vital. It is not merely that people should "have" their other rights in some merely legalistic or otherwise abstract sense compatible with being unable to make any use of the substance of the right. For example, if people have rights to free association, they ought not merely to "have" the rights to free association but also to enjoy their free association itself. Their freedom of association ought to be provided for by the relevant social institutions. This

---

[4] Anyone not familiar with the real meaning of what gets called "infant mortality rates" might consider the significance of the fact that in nearby Mexico seven out of every 100 babies fail to survive infancy—see United States, Department of State, *Background Notes: Mexico,* Revised February 1979 (Washington: Government Printing Office, 1979), p. 1. . . .

[5] It is controversial whether rights are claims only upon members of one's own society or upon other persons generally. . . .

[6] Since the enjoyment of a basic right is necessary for the enjoyment of all other rights, it is basic not only to non-basic rights but to other basic rights as well. Thus the enjoyment of the basic rights is an all-or-nothing matter. Each is necessary to the other basic ones as well as to all non-basic ones. Every right, including every basic right, can be enjoyed only if all basic rights are enjoyed. . . .

distinction between merely having a right and actually enjoying a right may seem a fine point, but it turns out later to be critical.

What is not meant by saying that a right is basic is that the right is more valuable or intrinsically more satisfying to enjoy than some other rights. For example, I shall soon suggest that rights to physical security, such as the right not to be assaulted, are basic, and I shall not include the right to publicly supported education as basic. But I do not mean by this to deny that enjoyment of the right to education is much greater and richer—more distinctively human, perhaps— than merely going through life without ever being assaulted. I mean only that, if a choice must be made, the prevention of assault ought to supersede the provision of education. Whether a right is basic is independent of whether its enjoyment is also valuable in itself. Intrinsically valuable rights may or may not also be basic rights, but intrinsically valuable rights can be enjoyed only when basic rights are enjoyed. Clearly few rights could be basic in this precise sense.

SECURITY RIGHTS

Our first project will be to see why people have a basic right to physical security—a right that is basic not to be subjected to murder, torture, mayhem, rape, or assault. The purpose in raising the questions why there are rights to physical security and why they are basic is not that very many people would seriously doubt either that there are rights to physical security or that they are basic. Although it is not unusual in practice for members of at least one ethnic group in a society to be physically insecure—to be, for example, much more likely than other people to be beaten by the police if arrested—few, if any, people would be prepared to defend in principle the contention that anyone lacks a basic right to physical security. Nevertheless, it can be valuable to formulate explicitly the presuppositions of even one's most firmly held beliefs, especially because these presuppositions may turn out to be general principles that will provide guidance in other areas where convictions are less firm. Precisely because we have no real doubt that rights to physical security are basic, it can be useful to see why we may properly think so.[7]

If we had to justify our belief that people have a basic right to physical security to someone who challenged this fundamental conviction, we could in

---

[7] It is odd that the list of "primary goods" in Rawlsian theory does not mention physical security as such. See John Rawls, *A Theory of Justice* (Cambridge, Mass.: The Belknap Press of Harvard University Press, 1971), p. 62 and p. 303. The explanation seems to be that security is lumped in with political participation and a number of civil liberties, including freedom of thought, of speech, of press, et al. To do this is to use "liberty" in a confusingly broad sense. One can speak intelligibly of "freedom from" almost anything bad: the child was free from fear, the cabin was free from snakes, the picnic was free from rain. Similarly, it is natural to speak of being free from assault, free from the threat of rape, etc., but this does not turn all these absences of evils into liberties. Freedom from assault, for example, is a kind of security or safety, not a kind of liberty. It may of course be a necessary condition for the exercise of any liberties, which is exactly what I shall now be arguing, but a necessary condition for the exercise of a liberty may be many things other than another kind of liberty. . . .

fact give a strong argument that shows that if there are any rights (basic or not basic) at all, there are basic rights to physical security.

No one can fully enjoy any right that is supposedly protected by society if someone can credibly threaten him or her with murder, rape, beating, etc., when he or she tries to enjoy the alleged right. Such threats to physical security are among the most serious and—in much of the world—the most widespread hindrances to the enjoyment of any right. If any right is to be exercised except at great risk, physical security must be protected. In the absence of physical security people are unable to use any other rights that society may be said to be protecting without being liable to encounter many of the worst dangers they would encounter if society were not protecting the rights.

A right to full physical security belongs, then, among the basic rights— not because the enjoyment of it would be more satisfying to someone who was also enjoying a full range of other rights, but because its absence would leave available extremely effective means for others, including the government, to interfere with or prevent the actual exercise of any other rights that were supposedly protected. Regardless of whether the enjoyment of physical security is also desirable for its own sake, it is desirable as part of the enjoyment of every other right. No rights other than a right to physical security can in fact be enjoyed if a right to physical security is not protected. Being physically secure is a necessary condition for the exercise of any other right, and guaranteeing physical security must be part of guaranteeing anything else as a right.

A person could, of course, always try to enjoy some other right even if no social provision were made to protect his or her physical safety during attempts to exercise the right. Suppose there is a right to peaceful assembly but it is not unusual for peaceful assemblies to be broken up and some of the participants beaten. Whether any given assembly is actually broken up depends largely on whether anyone else (in or out of government) is sufficiently opposed to it to bother to arrange an attack. People could still try to assemble, and they might sometimes assemble safely. But it would obviously be misleading to say that they are protected in their right to assemble if they are as vulnerable as ever to one of the most serious and general threats to enjoyment of the right, namely physical violence by other people. If they are as helpless against physical threats with the right "protected" as they would have been without the supposed protection, society is not actually protecting their exercise of the right to assembly.

So anyone who is entitled to anything as a right must be entitled to physical security as a basic right so that threats to his or her physical security cannot be used to thwart the enjoyment of the other right. This argument has two critical premises. The first is that everyone is entitled to enjoy something as a right.[8]

---

[8] At considerable risk of encouraging unflattering comparisons I might as well note myself that in its general structure the argument here has the same form as the argument in H. L. A. Hart's classic, "Are There Any Natural Rights?" *Philosophical Review,* 64:2 (April 1955), pp. 175–191.

The second, which further explains the first, is that everyone is entitled to the removal of the most serious and general conditions that would prevent or severely interfere with the exercise of whatever rights the person has. I take this second premise to be part of what is meant in saying that everyone is entitled to enjoy something as a right, as explained in the opening section of this chapter. Since this argument applies to everyone, it establishes a right that is universal.

SUBSISTENCE RIGHTS

The main reason for discussing security rights, which are not very controversial, was to make explicit the basic assumptions that support the usual judgment that security rights are basic rights. Now that we have available an argument that supports them, we are in a position to consider whether matters other than physical security should, according to the same argument, also be basic rights. It will emerge that subsistence, or minimal economic security, which is more controversial than physical security, can also be shown to be as well justified for treatment as a basic right as physical security is—and for the same reasons.

By minimal economic security, or subsistence, I mean unpolluted air, unpolluted water, adequate food, adequate clothing, adequate shelter, and minimal preventive public health care. Many complications about exactly how to specify the boundaries of what is necessary for subsistence would be interesting to explore. But the basic idea is to have available for consumption what is needed for a decent chance at a reasonably healthy and active life of more or less normal length, barring tragic interventions. This central idea is clear enough to work with, even though disputes can occur over exactly where to draw its outer boundaries. A right to subsistence would not mean, at one extreme, that every baby born with a need for open-heart surgery has a right to have it, but it also would not count as adequate food a diet that produces a life expectancy of 35 years of fever-laden, parasite-ridden listlessness.

By a "right to subsistence" I shall always mean a right to at least subsistence. People may or may not have economic rights that go beyond subsistence rights, and I do not want to prejudge that question here. But people may have rights to subsistence even if they do not have any strict rights to economic well-being extending beyond subsistence. Subsistence rights and broader economic rights are separate questions, and I want to focus here on subsistence.

I also do not want to prejudge the issue of whether healthy adults are entitled to be provided with subsistence *only* if they cannot provide subsistence for themselves. Most of the world's malnourished, for example, are probably also

---

That is, Hart can be summarized as maintaining: if there are any rights, there are rights to liberty. I am saying: if there are any rights, there are rights to security—and to subsistence. The finer structures of the arguments are of course quite different. I find Hart's inference considerably less obvious than he did. So, evidently, do many thoughtful people in the Third and Fourth Worlds, which counts against its obviousness but not necessarily against its validity. . . .

diseased, since malnutrition lowers resistance to disease, and hunger and infestation normally form a tight vicious circle. Hundreds of millions of the malnourished are very young children. A large percentage of the adults, besides being ill and hungry, are also chronically unemployed, so the issue of policy toward healthy adults who refuse to work is largely irrelevant. By a "right to subsistence," then, I shall mean a right to subsistence that includes the provision of subsistence at least to those who cannot provide for themselves. I do not assume that no one else is also entitled to receive subsistence—I simply do not discuss cases of healthy adults who could support themselves but refuse to do so. If there is a right to subsistence in the sense discussed here, at least the people who cannot provide for themselves, including the children, are entitled to receive at least subsistence. Nothing follows one way or the other about anyone else.

It makes no difference whether the legally enforced system of property where a given person lives is private, state, communal, or one of the many more typical mixtures and variants. Under all systems of property people are prohibited from simply taking even what they need for survival. Whatever the property institutions and the economic system are, the question about rights to subsistence remains: if persons are forbidden by law from taking what they need to survive and they are unable within existing economic institutions and policies to provide for their own survival (and the survival of dependents for whose welfare they are responsible), are they entitled, as a last resort, to receive the essentials for survival from the remainder of humanity whose lives are not threatened?

The same considerations that support the conclusion that physical security is a basic right support the conclusion that subsistence is a basic right. Since the argument is now familiar, it can be given fairly briefly.

It is quite obvious why, if we still assume that there are some rights that society ought to protect and still mean by this the removal of the most serious and general hindrances to the actual enjoyment of the rights, subsistence ought to be protected as a basic right:

> No one can fully, if at all, enjoy any right that is supposedly protected by society if he or she lacks the essentials for a reasonably healthy and active life. Deficiencies in the means of subsistence can be just as fatal, incapacitating, or painful as violations of physical security. The resulting damage or death can at least as decisively prevent the enjoyment of any right as can the effects of security violations. Any form of malnutrition, or fever due to exposure, that causes severe and irreversible brain damage, for example, can effectively prevent the exercise of any right requiring clear thought and may, like brain injuries caused by assault, profoundly disturb personality. And, obviously, any fatal deficiencies end all possibility of the enjoyment of rights as firmly as an arbitrary execution.
>
> Indeed, prevention of deficiencies in the essentials for survival is, if anything, more basic than prevention of violations of physical security. People who lack protection against violations of their physical security can, if they are free, fight back against their attackers or flee, but people who lack essentials,

such as food, because of forces beyond their control, often can do nothing and are on their own utterly helpless.[9]

The scope of subsistence rights must not be taken to be broader than it is. In particular, this step of the argument does not make the following absurd claim: since death and serious illness prevent or interfere with the enjoyment of rights, everyone has a basic right not to be allowed to die or to be seriously ill. Many causes of death and illness are outside the control of society, and many deaths and illnesses are the result or very particular conjunctions of circumstances that general social policies cannot control. But it is not impractical to expect some level of social organization to protect the minimal cleanliness of air and water and to oversee the adequate production, or import, and the proper distribution of minimal food, clothing, shelter, and elementary health care. It is not impractical, in short, to expect effective management, when necessary, of the supplies of the essentials of life. So the argument is: when death and serious illness could be prevented by different social policies regarding the essentials of life, the protection of any human right involves avoidance of fatal or debilitating deficiencies in these essential commodities. And this means fulfilling subsistence rights as basic rights. This is society's business because the problems are serious and general. This is a basic right because failure to deal with it would hinder the enjoyment of all other rights.

Thus, the same considerations that establish that security rights are basic for everyone also support the conclusion that subsistence rights are basic for everyone. It is not being claimed or assumed that security and subsistence are parallel in all, or even very many, respects. The only parallel being relied upon is that guarantees of security and guarantees of subsistence are equally essential to providing for the actual exercise of any other rights. As long as security and subsistence are parallel in this respect, the argument applies equally to both cases, and other respects in which security and subsistence are not parallel are irrelevant.

It is not enough that people merely happen to be secure or happen to be subsisting. They must have a right to security and a right to subsistence—the continued enjoyment of the security and the subsistence must be socially guaranteed. Otherwise a person is readily open to coercion and intimidation through threats of the deprivation of one or the other, and credible threats can

---

[9] In originally formulating this argument for treating both security and subsistence as basic rights I was not consciously following any philosopher but attempting instead to distill contemporary common sense. As many people have noted, today's common sense tends to be yesterday's philosophy. I was amused to notice recently the following passage from Mill, who not only gives a similar argument for security but notices and then backs away from the parallel with subsistence: "The interest involved is that of security, to everyone's feelings the most vital of all interests. All other earthly benefits are needed by one person, not needed by another; and many of them can, if necessary, be cheerfully foregone or replaced by something else; but security no human being can possibly do without; on it we depend for all our immunity from evil and for the whole value of all and every good, beyond the passing moment, since nothing but the gratification of the instant could be of any worth to us if we could be deprived of everything the next instant by whoever was momentarily stronger than ourselves. Now this most indispensable of all necessaries, after physical nutriment, cannot be had unless. . . ." John Stuart Mill, *Utilitarianism* (Indianapolis: Bobbs-Merrill Co., 1957), p. 67 (chapter V, 14th paragraph from the end).

paralyze a person and prevent the exercise of any other right as surely as actual beatings and actual protein/calorie deficiencies can. Credible threats can be reduced only by the actual establishment of social arrangements that will bring assistance to those confronted by forces that they themselves cannot handle.

Consequently the guaranteed security and guaranteed subsistence are what we might initially be tempted to call "simultaneous necessities" for the exercise of any other right. They must be present at any time that any other right is to be exercised, or people can be prevented from enjoying the other right by deprivations or threatened deprivations of security or of subsistence. But to think in terms of simultaneity would be largely to miss the point. A better label, if any is needed, would be "inherent necessities." For it is not that security from beatings, for instance, is separate from freedom of peaceful assembly but that it always needs to accompany it. Being secure from beatings if one chooses to hold a meeting is part of being free to assemble. If one cannot safely assemble, one is not free to assemble. One is, on the contrary, being coerced not to assemble by the threat of the beatings.

• • •

CORRELATIVE DUTIES

Many Americans would probably be initially inclined to think that rights to subsistence are at least slightly less important than rights to physical security, even though subsistence is at least as essential to survival as security is and even though questions of security do not even arise when subsistence fails. Much official U.S. government rhetoric routinely treats all "economic rights," among which basic subsistence rights are buried amidst many non-basic rights, as secondary and deferrable, although the fundamental enunciation of policy concerning human rights by the then Secretary of State did appear to represent an attempt to correct the habitual imbalance. Now that the same argument in favor of basic rights to both aspects of personal survival, subsistence and security, is before us, we can examine critically some of the reasons why it sometimes appears that although people have basic security rights, the right, if any, to even the physical necessities of existence like minimal health care, food, clothing, shelter, unpolluted water, and unpolluted air is somehow less urgent or less basic.

Frequently it is asserted or assumed that a highly significant difference between rights to physical security and rights to subsistence is that they are respectively "negative" rights and "positive" rights.[10] This position, which I will

---

[10] For a forceful re-affirmation of this view in the current political context (and further references), see Hugo Adam Bedau, "Human Rights and Foreign Assistance Programs," in *Human Rights and U.S. Foreign Policy,* ed. by Peter G. Brown and Douglas MacLean (Lexington, Mass: Lexington Books, 1979), pp. 29–44. Also see Charles Frankel, *Human Rights and Foreign Policy,* Headline Series No. 241 (New York: Foreign Policy Association, 1978), especially pp. 36–49, where Frankel advanced a "modest list of fundamental rights" that explicitly excluded

now try to refute, is considerably more complex than it at first appears. I will sometimes refer to it as the position that subsistence rights are *positive* and *therefore secondary*. Obviously taking the position involves holding that subsistence rights are positive in some respect in which security rights are negative and further claiming that this difference concerning positive/negative is a good enough reason to assign priority to negative rights over positive rights. I will turn shortly to the explanation of this assumed positive/negative distinction. But first I want to lay out all the premises actually needed by the position that subsistence rights are positive and therefore secondary, although I need to undercut only some—strictly speaking, only one—of them in order to cast serious doubt upon the position's conclusions.

The alleged lack of priority for subsistence rights compared to security rights assumes:

1. The distinction between subsistence rights and security rights is (a) sharp and (b) significant.[11]
2. The distinction between positive rights and negative rights is (a) sharp and (b) significant.
3. Subsistence rights are positive.
4. Security rights are negative.

---

economic rights as "dangerously utopian." A version of the general distinction has recently been re-affirmed by Thomas Nagel—see "Equality," in *Mortal Questions* (New York: Cambridge University Press, 1979), pp. 114–115. An utterly unrealistic but frequently invoked version of the distinction is in Maurice Cranston, *What Are Human Rights?* (London: The Bodley Head, 1973), chapter VIII. An interesting attempt to show that the positive/negative distinction is compatible with economic rights is John Langan, "Defining Human Rights: A Revision of the Liberal Tradition," Working Paper (Washington: Woodstock Theological Center, 1979). For a provocative and relevant discussion of "negative responsibility" (responsibility for what one fails to prevent), see Bernard Williams, "A Critique of Utilitarianism," in *Utilitarianism: For & Against* (New York: Cambridge University Press, 1973), pp. 93 ff.

11 Naturally my use of the same argument for the basic status of both security and subsistence is at least an indirect challenge to (1) (b). No question is raised here, however, about (1) (a): the thesis that subsistence and security are sharply distinguishable. People who should be generally sympathetic to my fundamental thesis that subsistence rights are basic rights, do sometimes try to reach the same conclusion by the much shorter seeming route of denying that security and subsistence are importantly different from each other. For example, it is correctly observed that both security and subsistence are needed for survival and then maintained that both are included in a right to survival, or right to life. Though I am by no means hostile to this approach, it does have three difficulties that I believe can be avoided by my admittedly somewhat more circuitous path of argument. First, it is simply not correct that one cannot maintain a clear and useful distinction between security and subsistence, as, in fact, I hope to have done up to this point. Second, arguments for a general right to life that includes subsistence rights appear to need some premise to the effect that the right to life entails rights to at least some of the means of life. Thus, they . . . [strain] credulity by implying more than most people are likely to be able to believe. . . . A right-to-the-means-of-life argument might be able to skirt the problem equally well by using a notion of a standard threat to life, analogous to our notion of a standard threat to the enjoyment of rights, but this alternative tack seems, at best, no better off. Third, the concept of a right to life is now deeply infected with ambiguities concerning whether it is a purely negative right, a purely positive right, or, as I shall soon be maintaining with regard to both security and subsistence, an inseparable mixture of positive and negative elements. The appeal for many people of a right to life seems to depend, however, upon its being taken to be essentially negative, while it can fully include subsistence rights only if it has major positive elements.

I am not suggesting that anyone has ever laid out this argument in all the steps it actually needs. On the contrary, a full statement of the argument is the beginning of its refutation—this is an example of the philosophical analogue of the principle that sunlight is the best antiseptic.[12]

In this chapter I will concentrate on establishing that premises 3 and 4 are both misleading. Then I will suggest a set of distinctions among duties that accurately transmits the insight distorted by 3 and 4. Insofar as 3 and 4 are inaccurate, considerable doubt is cast upon 2, although it remains possible that someone can specify some sharply contrasting pair of rights that actually are examples of 2.[13] I will not directly attack premise 1.[14]

Now the basic idea behind the general suggestion that there are positive rights and negative rights seems to have been that one kind of rights (the positive ones) require other people to act positively—to "do something"—whereas another kind of rights (the negative ones) require other people merely to refrain from acting in certain ways—to do nothing that violates the rights. For example, according to this picture, a right to subsistence would be positive because it would require other people, in the last resort, to supply food or clean air to those unable to find, produce, or buy their own; a right to security would be negative because it would require other people merely to refrain from murdering or otherwise assaulting those with the right. The underlying distinction, then, is between acting and refraining from acting; and positive rights are those with correlative duties to act in certain ways and negative rights are those with correlative duties to refrain from acting in certain ways. Therefore, the moral significance, if any, of the distinction between positive rights and negative rights depends upon the moral significance, if any, of the distinction between action and omission of action.[15]

The ordinarily implicit argument for considering rights to subsistence to be secondary would, then, appear to be basically this. Since subsistence rights are positive and require other people to do more than negative rights require—perhaps more than people can actually do—negative rights, such as those to security, should be fully guaranteed first. Then, any remaining resources could be devoted, as long as they lasted, to the positive—and perhaps impossible—task

[12] I think one can often show the implausibility of an argument by an exhaustive statement of all the assumptions it needs. I have previously attempted this in the case of one of John Rawls's arguments for the priority of liberty—see "Liberty and Self-Respect," *Ethics*, 85:3 (April 1975), pp. 195–203.

[13] I have given a summary of the argument against 3 and arguments against thinking that either the right to a fair trail or the right not to be tortured are negative rights in "Rights in the Light of Duties," in Brown and MacLean, pp. 65–81. I have also argued directly against what is here called 2b and briefly introduced the account of duties presented in the final sections of this chapter. My goal, which I have no illusions about having attained, has been to do as definitive a job on positive and negative rights as Gerald C. MacCallum, Jr. did on positive and negative liberty in his splendid article, "Negative and Positive Freedom," *Philosophical Review*, 76:3 (July 1967), pp. 312–334.

[14] See note 11 above.

[15] Elsewhere I have briefly queried the moral significance of the action/omission distinction—see the essay cited in note 13 above. For a fuller discussion, see Judith Lichtenberg, "On Being Obligated to Give Aid: Moral and Political Arguments," Diss., City University of New York, 1978.

of providing for subsistence. Unfortunately for this argument, neither rights to physical security nor rights to subsistence fit neatly into their assigned sides of the simplistic positive/negative dichotomy. We must consider whether security rights are purely negative and then whether subsistence rights are purely positive. I will try to show (1) that security rights are more "positive" than they are often said to be, (2) that subsistence rights are more "negative" than they are often said to be, and, given (1) and (2), (3) that the distinctions between security rights and subsistence rights, though not entirely illusory, are too fine to support any weighty conclusions, especially the very weighty conclusion that security rights are basic and subsistence rights are not.

In the case of rights to physical security, it may be possible *to avoid violating* someone's rights to physical security yourself by merely refraining from acting in any of the ways that would constitute violations. But it is impossible to *protect* anyone's rights to physical security without taking, or making payments toward the taking of, a wide range of positive actions. For example, at the very least the protection of rights to physical security necessitates police forces; criminal courts; penitentiaries; schools for training police, lawyers, and guards; and taxes to support an enormous system for the prevention, detection, and punishment of violations of personal security.[16] All these activities and institutions are attempts at providing social guarantees for individuals' security so that they are not left to face alone forces that they cannot handle on their own. How much more than these expenditures one thinks would be necessary in order for people actually to be reasonably secure (as distinguished from merely having the cold comfort of knowing that the occasional criminal is punished after someone's security has already been violated) depends on one's theory of violent crime, but it is not unreasonable to believe that it would involve extremely expensive, "positive" programs. Probably no one knows how much positive action would have to be taken in a contemporary society like the United States significantly to reduce the levels of muggings, rapes, murders, and other assaults that violate personal security, and in fact to make people reasonably secure.

Someone might suggest that this blurs rights to physical security with some other type of rights, which might be called rights-to-be-protected-against-assaults-upon-physical-security. According to this distinction, rights to physical security are negative, requiring others only to refrain from assaults, while rights-to-be-protected-against-assaults-upon-physical-security are positive, requiring others to take positive steps to prevent assaults.

Perhaps if one were dealing with some wilderness situation in which individuals' encounters with each other were infrequent and irregular, there might

---

[16] In FY 1975 in the United States the cost of the "criminal justice system" was $17 billion, or $71 per capita, *New York Times,* July 21, 1977, p. A3. In several countries that year the total annual income was less than $71 per capita. Obviously such isolated statistics prove nothing, but they are suggestive. One thing they suggest is that adequate provisions for this supposedly negative right would not necessarily be less costly than adequate provisions for some rights supposed to be positive. Nor is it evident that physical security does any better on what Frankel called the test of being "realistically deliverable" (45) and Cranston called "the test of practicability" (66). . . .

be some point in noting to someone: I am not asking you to cooperate with a system of guarantees to protect me from third parties, but only to refrain from attacking me yourself. But in an organized society, insofar as there were any such things as rights to physical security that were distinguishable from some other rights-to-be-protected-from-assaults-upon-physical-security, no one would have much interest in the bare rights to physical security. What people want and need, as even Mill partly recognized, is the protection of their rights.[17] Insofar as this frail distinction holds up, it is the rights-to-be-protected-against-assaults that any reasonable person would demand from society. A demand for physical security is not normally a demand simply to be left alone, but a demand to be protected against harm.[18] It is a demand for positive action, or, in the words of our initial account of a right, a demand for social guarantees against at least the standard threats.

So it would be very misleading to say simply that physical security is a negative matter of other people's refraining from violations. Ordinarily it is instead a matter of some people refraining from violations and of third parties being prevented from violations by the positive steps taken by first and second parties. The "negative" refraining may in a given case be less significant than the "positive" preventing—it is almost never the whole story. The end-result of the positive preventative steps taken is of course an enforced refraining from violations, not the performance of any positive action. The central core of the right is a right that others not act in certain ways. But the mere core of the right indicates little about the social institutions needed to secure it, and the core of the right does not contain its whole structure. The protection of "negative rights" requires positive measures, and therefore their actual enjoyment requires positive measures. In any imperfect society enjoyment of a right will depend to some extent upon protection against those who do not choose not to violate it.

Rights to subsistence too are in their own way considerably more complex than simply labeling them "positive" begins to indicate. In fact, their fulfillment involves at least two significantly different types of action. On the one hand, rights to subsistence sometimes do involve correlative duties on the part of others to provide the needed commodities when those in need are helpless to secure a supply for themselves, as, for example, the affluent may have a duty to finance food supplies and transportation and distribution facilities in the case of famine. Even the satisfaction of subsistence rights by such positive action,

[17] "To have a right, then, is, I conceive, to have something which society ought to defend me in the possession of"—John Stuart Mill, *Utilitarianism* (Indianapolis: Bobbs-Merrill Co., 1957), p. 66 (chapter V, 14th paragraph from the end).

[18] This is not a point about ordinary language, in which there is obviously a significant difference between "leave me alone" and "protect me against people who will not leave me alone." My thesis is that people who are not already grinding axes for minimal government will naturally and reasonably think in terms of enjoying a considerable degree of security, will want to have done whatever within reason is necessary, and will recognize that more is necessary than refraining campaigns—campaigns urging self-restraint upon would-be murderers, muggers, rapists, et al. I am of course not assuming that existing police and penal institutions are the best forms of social guarantees for security; I am assuming only that more effective institutions would probably be at least equally complex and expensive.

however, need not be any more expensive or involve any more complex governmental programs than the effective protection of security rights would. A
food stamp program, for example, could be cheaper or more expensive than,
say, an anti-drug program aimed at reducing muggings and murders by addicts.
Which program was more costly or more complicated would depend upon the
relative dimensions of the respective problems and would be unaffected by any
respect in which security is "negative" and subsistence is "positive." Insofar as
any argument for giving priority to the fulfillment of "negative rights" rests on
the assumption that actually securing "negative rights" is usually cheaper or
simpler than securing "positive rights," the argument rests on an empirical
speculation of dubious generality.

The other type of action needed to fulfill subsistence rights is even more
difficult to distinguish sharply from the action needed to fulfill security rights.
Rights to physical subsistence often can be completely satisfied without the provision by others of any commodities to those whose rights are in question. All
that is sometimes necessary is to protect the persons whose subsistence is
threatened from the individuals and institutions that will otherwise intentionally or unintentionally harm them. A demand for the fulfillment of rights to
subsistence may involve not a demand to be provided with grants of commodities but merely a demand to be provided some opportunity for supporting
oneself.[19] The request is not to be supported but to be allowed to be self-supporting on the basis of one's own hard work.

What is striking is the similarity between protection against the destruction
of the basis for supporting oneself and protection against assaults upon one's
physical security. We can turn now to some examples that clearly illustrate that
the honoring of subsistence rights sometimes involves action no more positive
than the honoring of security rights does. Some cases in which all that is asked
is protection from harm that would destroy the capacity to be self-supporting
involve threats to subsistence of a complexity that is not usually noticed with
regard to security, although the adequate protection of security would involve
analyses and measures more complex than a preoccupation with police and
prisons. The complexity of the circumstances of subsistence should not, however, be allowed to obscure the basic fact that essentially all that is being asked
in the name of subsistence rights in these examples is protection from destructive acts by other people.

• • •

The choice of examples for use in an essentially theoretical discussion that does
nevertheless have implications for public policy presents an intractable dilemma.
Hypothetical cases and actual cases each have advantages and disadvantages
that are mirror images of each other's. A description of an actual case has the

---

[19] Therefore, as we shall see below, the complete fulfillment of a subsistence right may involve not
the actual provision of any aid at all but only the performance of duties to avoid depriving and
to protect against deprivation.

obvious advantage that it is less susceptible to being tailored to suit the theoretical point it is adduced to support, especially if the description is taken from the work of someone other than the proponent of the theoretical point. Its disadvantage is that if the description is in fact an inaccurate account of the case in question, the mistake about what is happening in that case may appear to undercut the theoretical point that is actually independent of what is happening in any single case. Thus the argument about the theoretical point may become entangled in arguments about an individual instance that was at most only one supposed illustration of the more general point.

Hypothetical cases are immune to disputes about whether they accurately depict an independent event, since, being explicitly hypothetical, they are not asserted to correspond to any one real case. But precisely because they are not constrained by the need to remain close to an independent event, they may be open to the suspicion of having been streamlined precisely in order to fit the theoretical point they illustrate and having thereby become atypical of actual cases.

The only solution I can see is to offer, when a point is crucial, an example of each kind. It is vital to the argument of this book to establish that many people's lack of the substance of their subsistence rights—of, that is, the means of subsistence like food—is a deprivation caused by standard kinds of threats that could be controlled by some combination of the mere restraint of second parties and the maintenance of protective institutions by first and third parties, just as the standard threats that deprive people of their physical security could be controlled by restraint and protection against non-restraint. So I will start with a hypothetical case in order to clarify the theoretical point before introducing the partly extraneous complexity of actual events, and then I will quote a description of some actual current economic policies that deprive people of subsistence. The hypothetical case is at the level of a single peasant village, and the actual case concerns long-term national economic strategies. Anyone familiar with the causes of malnutrition in underdeveloped countries today will recognize that the following hypothetical case is in no way unusual.

Suppose the largest tract of land in the village was the property of the descendant of a family that had held title to the land for as many generations back as anyone could remember. By absolute standards this peasant was by no means rich, but his land was the richest in the small area that constituted the universe for the inhabitants of this village. He grew, as his father and grandfather had, mainly the black beans that are the staple (and chief—and adequate—source of protein) in the regional diet. His crop usually constituted about a quarter of the black beans marketed in the village. Practically every family grew part of what they needed, and the six men he hired during the seasons requiring extra labor held the only paid jobs in the village—everyone else just worked his own little plot.

One day a man from the capital offered this peasant a contract that not only guaranteed him annual payments for a 10-year lease on his land but also guaranteed him a salary (regardless of how the weather, and therefore the crops, turned out—a great increase in his financial security) to be the foreman for a

new kind of production on his land. The contract required him to grow flowers for export and also offered him the opportunity, which was highly recommended, to purchase through the company, with payments in installments,
equipment that would enable him to need to hire only two men. The same contract was offered to, and accepted by, most of the other larger landowners in
the general region to which the village belonged.

Soon, with the sharp reduction in supply, the price of black beans soared.
Some people could grow all they needed (in years of good weather) on their
own land, but the families that needed to supplement their own crop with purchases had to cut back their consumption. In particular, the children in the four
families headed by the laborers who lost their seasonal employment suffered severe malnutrition, especially since the parents had originally worked as laborers only because their own land was too poor or too small to feed their families.

Now, the story contains no implication that the man from the capital or the
peasants-turned-foremen were malicious or intended to do anything worse
than single-mindedly pursue their own respective interests. But the outsider's
offer of the contract was one causal factor, and the peasant's acceptance of the
contract was another causal factor, in producing the malnutrition that would
probably persist, barring protective intervention, for at least the decade the
contract was to be honored. If the families in the village had rights to subsistence, their rights were being violated. Society, acting presumably by way of the
government, ought to protect them from a severe type of active harm that eliminates their ability even to feed themselves.

But was anyone actually harming the villagers, or were they simply suffering
a regrettable decline in their fortunes? If someone was violating their rights,
who exactly was the violator? Against whom specifically should the government be protecting them? For, we normally make a distinction between violating someone's rights and allowing someone's rights to be violated while simply
minding our own business. It makes a considerable difference—to take an example from another set of basic rights—whether I myself assault someone or I
merely carry on with my own affairs while allowing a third person to assault
someone when I could protect the victim and end the assault. Now, I may have
a duty not to allow assaults that I can without great danger to myself prevent
or stop, as well as a duty not to assault people myself, but there are clearly two
separable issues here. And it is perfectly conceivable that I might have the one
duty (to avoid harming) and not the other (to protect from harm by third parties), because they involve two different types of action.[20]

The switch in land-use within the story might then be described as follows.
Even if one were willing to grant tentatively that the villagers all seemed to have
rights to subsistence, some of which were violated by the malnutrition that some
suffered after the switch in crops, no individual or organization can be identified as the violator: not the peasant-turned-foreman, for example, because—let

---

[20] That is, they are conceptually distinct; whether this distinction makes any moral difference is another matter. See above, note 15, and the distinctions at the beginning of this chapter.

us assume—he did not foresee the "systemic" effects of his individual choice; not the business representative from the capital because—let us assume—although he was knowledgeable enough to know what would probably happen, it would be unrealistically moralistic to expect him to forgo honest gains for himself and the company he represented because the gains had undesired, even perhaps regretted, "side-effects"; not any particular member of the governmental bureaucracy because—let us assume—no one had been assigned responsibility for maintaining adequate nutrition in this particular village. The local peasant and the business representative were both minding their own business in the village, and no one in the government had any business with this village. The peasant and the representative may have attended to their own affairs while harm befell less fortunate villagers, but allowing harm to occur without preventing it is not the same as directly inflicting it yourself. The malnutrition was just, literally, unfortunate: bad luck, for which no one could fairly be blamed. The malnutrition was, in effect, a natural disaster—was, in the obnoxious language of insurance law, an act of God. Perhaps the village was, after all, becoming overpopulated.[21]

But, of course, the malnutrition resulting from the new choice of crop was not a natural disaster. The comforting analogy does not hold. The malnutrition was a social disaster. The malnutrition was the product of specific human decisions permitted by the presence of specific social institutions and the absence of others, in the context of the natural circumstances, especially the scarcity of land upon which to grow food, that were already given before the decisions were made. The harm in question, the malnutrition, was not merely allowed to happen by the parties to the flower-growing contract. The harm was partly caused by the requirement in the contract for a switch away from food, by the legality of the contract, and by the performance of the required switch in crops. If there had been no contract or if the contract had not required a switch away from food for local consumption, there would have been no malnutrition as things were going.[22] In general, when persons take an action that is sufficient in some given natural and social circumstances to bring about an undesirable effect, especially one that there is no particular reason to think would otherwise have occurred, it is perfectly normal to consider their action to be one active cause of the harm. The parties to the contract partly caused the malnutrition.

But the society could have protected the villagers by countering the initiative of the contracting parties in any one of a number of ways that altered the circumstances, and the absence of the appropriate social guarantees is another cause of the malnutrition. Such contracts could, for example, have already been made illegal. Or they could have been allowed but managed or taxed in order to compensate those who would otherwise predictably be damaged by them.

---

[21] The increasingly frequent and facile appeal to "overpopulation" as a reason not to prevent preventable starvation is considered in chapter 4.

[22] This much of the analysis is derived from the following important article: Onora O'Neill, "Lifeboat Earth," in *World Hunger and Moral Obligation,* edited by William Aiken and Hugh La Follette (Englewood Cliffs: Prentice-Hall, Inc., 1977), pp. 140–164.

Exactly what was done would be, *for the most part,* an economic and political question.[23] But it is possible to have social guarantees against the malnutrition that is repeatedly caused in such standard, predictable ways.

Is a right to subsistence in such a case, then, a positive right in any important ways that a right to security is not? Do we actually find a contrast of major significance? No. As in the cases of the threats to physical security that we normally consider, the threat to subsistence is human activity with largely predictable effects.[24] Even if, as we tend to assume, the motives for deprivations of security tend to be vicious while the motives for deprivations of subsistence tend to be callous, the people affected usually need protection all the same. The design, building, and maintenance of institutions and practices that protect people's subsistence against the callous—and even the merely over-energetic— is no more and no less positive than the conception and execution of programs to control violent crimes against the person. It is not obvious which, if either, it is more realistic to hope for or more economical to pursue. It is conceivable, although I doubt if anyone really knows, that the two are more effectively and efficiently pursued together. Neither looks simple, cheap, or "negative."

This example of the flower contract is important in part because, at a very simple level, it is in fact typical of much of what is happening today among the majority of the people in the world, who are poor and rural, and are threatened by forms of "economic development" that lower their own standard of living. But it is also important because, once again in a very simple way, it illustrates the single most critical fact about rights to subsistence; where subsistence depends upon tight supplies of essential commodities (like food), a change in supply can have, often by way of intermediate price effects, an indirect but predictable and devastating effect on people's ability to survive. A change in supply can transport self-supporting people into helplessness and, if no protection

---

[23] For example, land-use laws might prohibit removing prime agricultural land from food production. Alternatively, land might be allowed to be used in the manner most beneficial to the national balance of payments with tax laws designed to guarantee compensating transfers to increase the purchasing power of the villagers (e.g., food stamps), etc. . . .

[24] There are of course non-human threats to both security and subsistence, like floods, as well. And we expect a minimally adequate society also to make arrangements to prevent, to control, or to minimize the ill effects of floods and other destructive natural forces. However, for an appreciation of the extent to which supposedly natural famines are the result of inadequate social arrangements, see Richard G. Robbins, *Famine in Russia 1891–92* (New York: Columbia University Press, 1975); and Michael F. Lofchie, "Political and Economic Origins of African Hunger," *Journal of Modern African Studies,* 13:4 (December 1975), pp. 551–567. As Lofchie says: "The point of departure for a political understanding of African hunger is so obvious it is almost always overlooked: the distinction between drought and famine. . . . To the extent that there is a connection between drought and famine, it is mediated by the political and economic arrangements of a society. These can either minimize the human consequences of drought or accentuate its effects" (533). For a demonstration that the weather and other natural factors actually played fairly minor roles in the Great Bengal Famine, see the analysis by Amartya Sen, "Starvation and Exchange Entitlements: A General Approach and its Application to the Great Bengal Famine," *Cambridge Journal of Economics,* 1:1 (1977), pp. 35–39. To treat the *absence* of adequate social arrangements as a cause of a famine precipitated by a natural event like a drought or a flood, as these writers and I do, is to assume that it is reasonable to have expected the absent arrangements to have been present.

against the change is provided, into malnutrition or death. Severe harm to some people's ability to maintain themselves can be caused by changes in the use to which other people put vital resources (like land) they control. In such cases even someone who denied that individuals or organizations have duties to supply commodities to people who are helpless to obtain them for themselves, might grant that the government ought to execute the society's duty of protecting people from having their ability to maintain their own survival destroyed by the actions of others. If this protection is provided, there will be much less need later to provide commodities themselves to compensate for deprivations.

What transmits the effect in such cases is the local scarcity of the vital commodity. Someone might switch thousands of acres from food to flowers without having any effect on the diet of anyone else where the supply of food was adequate to prevent a significant price rise in response to the cut in supply. And it goes without saying that the price rises are vitally important only if the income and wealth of at least some people is severely limited, as of course it is in every society, often for the rural majority. It is as if an abundant supply sometimes functions as a sponge to absorb the otherwise significant effect on other people, but a tight supply (against a background of limited income and wealth) sometimes functions as a conductor to transmit effects to others, who feel them sharply.

It is extremely difficult merely to mind one's own business amidst a scarcity of vital commodities. It is illusory to think that this first commandment of liberalism can always be obeyed. The very scarcity draws people into contact with each other, destroys almost all area for individual maneuver, and forces people to elbow each other in order to move forward. The tragedy of scarcity, beyond the deprivations necessitated by the scarcity itself, is that scarcity tends to make each one's gain someone else's loss. One can act for oneself only by acting against others, since there is not enough for all. Amidst abundance of food a decision to grow flowers can be at worst a harmless act and quite likely a socially beneficial one. But amidst a scarcity of food, due partly to a scarcity of fertile land, an unmalicious decision to grow flowers can cause death—unless there are social guarantees for adequate nutrition. A call for social guarantees for subsistence in situations of scarcity is not a call for intervention in what were formerly private affairs.

52.
The Importance of Liberty and Self-Ownership

ROBERT NOZICK

HOW LIBERTY UPSETS PATTERNS

It is not clear how those holding alternative conceptions of distributive justice can reject the entitlement conception of justice in holdings. For suppose a distribution favored by one of these nonentitlement conceptions is realized. Let us suppose it is your favorite one and let us call this distribution D_1; perhaps everyone has an equal share, perhaps shares vary in accordance with some dimension you treasure. Now suppose that Wilt Chamberlain is greatly in demand by basketball teams, being a great gate attraction. (Also suppose contracts run only for a year, with players being free agents.) He signs the following sort of contract with a team: In each home game, twenty-five cents from the price of each ticket of admission goes to him. (We ignore the question of whether he is "gouging" the owners, letting them look out for themselves.) The season starts, and people cheerfully attend his team's games; they buy their tickets, each time dropping a separate twenty-five cents of their admission price into a special box with Chamberlain's name on it. They are excited about seeing him play; it is worth the total admission price to them. Let us suppose that in one season one million persons attend his home games, and Wilt Chamberlain winds up with $250,000, a much larger sum than the average income and larger even than anyone else has. Is he entitled to this income? Is this new distribution D_2, unjust? If so, why? There is *no* question about whether each of the people was entitled to the control over the resources they held in D_1; because that was the distribution (your favorite) that (for the purposes of argument) we assumed was acceptable. Each of these persons *chose* to give twenty-five cents of their money to Chamberlain. They could have spent it on going to the movies, or on candy bars, or on copies of *Dissent* magazine, or of *Monthly Review*. But they all, at least one million of them, converged on giving it to Wilt Chamberlain in exchange for watching him play basketball. If D_1 was a just distribution, and people voluntarily moved from it to D_2, transferring parts of their shares they were given under D_1 (what was it for if not to do something with?), isn't D_2 also just? If the people were entitled to dispose of the resources to which they were entitled (under D_1), didn't this include their being entitled to give it to, or exchange it with, Wilt Chamberlain? Can anyone else complain on grounds of justice? Each other person already has his legitimate share under D_1. Under D_1, there is nothing that anyone has that anyone else has a claim of justice against. After someone transfers something to Wilt Chamberlain, third parties will *still* have their legitimate shares; *their* shares are not changed. By what process could such a transfer among two persons give rise to a legitimate claim of distributive justice on a portion of what was transferred, by a third party who had no claim of justice on any holding of the others *before* the transfer?[1] To cut off objections irrelevant here, we might imagine the exchanges occurring in a socialist society, after hours. After playing whatever basketball he does in his daily work, or doing whatever other daily work he does, Wilt Chamberlain decides to put in *overtime* to earn additional money. (First his work quota is set; he works time over that.) Or imagine it is a skilled juggler people like to see, who puts on shows after hours.

Why might someone work overtime in a society in which it is assumed their needs are satisfied? Perhaps because they care about things other than needs. I like to write in books that I read, and to have easy access to books for browsing at odd hours. It would be very pleasant and convenient to have the resources of Widener Library in my back yard. No society, I assume, will provide such resources close to each person who would like them as part of his regular allotment (under D_1). Thus, persons either must do without some extra things that they want, or be allowed to do something extra to get some of these things. On what basis could the inequalities that would eventuate be forbidden? Notice also that small factories would spring up in a socialist society, unless forbidden. I melt down some of my personal possessions (under D_1) and build a machine out of the material. I offer you, and others, a philosophy lecture once a week in exchange for your cranking the handle on my machine, whose products I exchange for yet other things, and so on. (The raw materials used by the machine are given to me by others who possess them under D_1, in exchange for hearing lectures.) Each person might participate to gain things over and above their allotment under D_1. Some persons even might want to leave their job in socialist industry and work full time in this private sector. I shall say something more about these issues in the next chapter. Here I wish merely to note how private property even in means of production would occur in a socialist society that did not forbid people to use as they wished some of the resources they are given under the socialist distribution D_1.[2] The socialist society would have to forbid capitalist acts between consenting adults.

---

[1] Might not a transfer have instrumental effects on a third party, changing his feasible options? (But what if the two parties to the transfer independently had used their holdings in this fashion?) I discuss this question below, but note here that this question concedes the point for distributions of ultimate intrinsic noninstrumental goods (pure utility experiences, so to speak) that are transferable. It also might be objected that the transfer might make a third party more envious because it worsens his position relative to someone else. I find it incomprehensible how this can be thought to involve a claim of justice.

   Here and elsewhere in this chapter, a theory which incorporates elements of pure procedural justice might find what I say acceptable, *if* kept in its proper place; that is, if background institutions exist to ensure the satisfaction of certain conditions on distributive shares. But if these institutions are not themselves the sum of invisible-hand result of people's voluntary (nonaggressive) actions, the constraints they impose require justification. At no point does *our* argument assume any background institutions more extensive than those of the minimal night-watchman state, a state limited to protecting persons against murder, assault, theft, fraud, and so forth.

[2] See the selection from John Henry MacKay's novel, *The Anarchists,* reprinted in Leonard Krimmerman and Lewis Perry, eds., *Patterns of Anarchy* (New York: Doubleday Anchor Books,

The general point illustrated by the Wilt Chamberlain example and the example of the entrepreneur in a socialist society is that no end-state principle or distributional patterned principle of justice can be continuously realized without continuous interference with people's lives. Any favored pattern would be transformed into one unfavored by the principle, by people choosing to act in various ways; for example, by people exchanging goods and services with other people, or giving things to other people, things the transferrers are entitled to under the favored distributional pattern. To maintain a pattern one must either continually interfere to stop people from transferring resources as they wish to, or continually (or periodically) interfere to take from some persons resources that others for some reason chose to transfer to them. (But if some time limit is to be set on how long people may keep resources others voluntarily transfer to them, why let them keep these resources for *any* period of time? Why not have immediate confiscation?) It might be objected that all persons voluntarily will choose to refrain from actions which would upset the pattern. This presupposes unrealistically (1) that all will most want to maintain the pattern (are those who don't, to be "reeducated" or forced to undergo "self-criticism"?), (2) that each can gather enough information about his own actions and the ongoing activities of others to discover which of his actions will upset the pattern, and (3) that diverse and far-flung persons can coordinate their actions to dovetail into the pattern. Compare the manner in which the market is neutral among persons' desires, as it reflects and transmits widely scattered information via prices, and coordinates persons' activities.

It puts things perhaps a bit too strongly to say that every patterned (or end-state) principle is liable to be thwarted by the voluntary actions of the individual parties transferring some of their shares they receive under the principle. For perhaps some *very* weak patterns are not so thwarted.[3] Any distributional

1966), in which an individualist anarchist presses upon a communist anarchist the following question: "Would you, in the system of society which you call 'free Communism' prevent individuals from exchanging their labor among themselves by means of their own medium of exchange? And further: Would you prevent them from occupying land for the purpose of personal use?" The novel continues: "[the] question was not to be escaped." If he answered 'Yes!' he admitted that society had the right of control over the individual and threw overboard the autonomy of the individual which he had always zealously defended; if on the other hand, he answered 'No!' he admitted the right of private property which he had just denied so emphatically. . . . Then he answered 'In Anarchy any number of men must have the right of forming a voluntary association, and so realizing their ideas in practice. Nor can I understand how any one could justly be driven from the land and house which he uses and occupies . . . every serious man must declare himself: for Socialism, and thereby for force and against liberty, or for Anarchism, and thereby for liberty and against force.'" In contrast, we find Noam Chomsky writing, "Any consistent anarchist must oppose private ownership of the means of production," "the consistent anarchist then . . . will be a socialist . . . of a particular sort." Introduction to Daniel Guerin, *Anarchism: From Theory to Practice* (New York: Monthly Review Press, 1970), pages xiii, xv.

3 Is the patterned principle stable that requires merely that a distribution be Pareto-optimal? One person might give another a gift or bequest that the second could exchange with a third to their mutual benefit. Before the second makes this exchange, there is not Pareto-optimality. Is a stable pattern presented by a principle choosing that among the Pareto-optimal positions that satisfies some further condition *C*? It may seem that there cannot be a counterexample, for won't any voluntary exchange made away from a situation show that the first situation wasn't Pareto-optimal? (Ignore the implausibility of this last claim for the case of bequests.) But principles are

pattern with any egalitarian component is overturnable by the voluntary actions of individual persons over time; as is every patterned condition with sufficient content so as actually to have been proposed as presenting the central core of distributive justice. Still, given, the possibility that some weak conditions or patterns may not be unstable in this way, it would be better to formulate an explicit description of the kind of interesting and contentful patterns under discussion, and to prove a theorem about their instability. Since the weaker the patterning, the more likely it is that the entitlement system itself satisfies it, a plausible conjecture is that any patterning either is unstable or is satisfied by the entitlement system.

• • •

REDISTRIBUTION AND PROPERTY RIGHTS

Proponents of patterned principles of distributive justice focus upon criteria for determining who is to receive holdings; they consider the reasons for which someone should have something, and also the total picture of holdings. Whether or not it is better to give than to receive, proponents of patterned principles ignore giving altogether. In considering the distribution of goods, income, and so forth, their theories are theories of recipient justice; they completely ignore any right a person might have to give something to someone. Even in exchanges where each party is simultaneously giver and recipient, patterned principles of justice focus only upon the recipient role and its supposed rights. Thus discussions tend to focus on whether people (should) have a right to inherit, rather than on whether people (should) have a right to bequeath or on whether persons who have a right to hold also have a right to choose that others hold in their place. I lack a good explanation of why the usual theories of distributive justice are so recipient oriented; ignoring givers and transferrers and their rights is of a piece with ignoring producers and their entitlements. But why is it *all* ignored?

Patterned principles of distributive justice necessitate *re*distributive activities. The likelihood is small that any actual freely-arrived-at set of holdings fits a given pattern; and the likelihood is nil that it will continue to fit the pattern as people exchange and give. From the point of view of an entitlement theory, redistribution is a serious matter indeed, involving, as it does, the violation of people's rights. (An exception is those takings that fall under the principle of the rectification of injustices.) From other points of view, also, it is serious.

---

to be satisfied over time, during which new possibilities arise. A distribution that at one time satisfies the criterion of Pareto-optimality might not do so when some new possibilities arise (Wilt Chamberlain grows up and starts playing basketball); and though people's activities will tend to move then to a new Pareto-optimal position, *this* new one need not satisfy the contentful condition C. Continual interference will be needed to insure the continual satisfaction of C. (The theoretical possibility of a pattern's being maintained by some invisible-hand process that brings it back to an equilibrium that fits the pattern when deviations occur should be investigated.)

Taxation of earnings from labor is on a par with forced labor.[4] Some persons find this claim obviously true: taking the earnings of *n* hours labor is like taking *n* hours from the person; it is like forcing the person to work *n* hours for another's purpose. Others find the claim absurd. But even these, *if* they object to forced labor, would oppose forcing unemployed hippies to work for the benefit of the needy. And they would also object to forcing each person to work five extra hours each week for the benefit of the needy. But a system that takes five hours' wages in taxes does not seem to them like one that forces someone to work five hours, since it offers the person forced a wider range of choice in activities than does taxation in kind with the particular labor specified. (But we can imagine a gradation of systems of forced labor, from one that specifies a particular activity, to one that gives a choice among two activities, to . . . ; and so on up.) Furthermore, people envisage a system with something like a proportional tax on everything above the amount necessary for basic needs. Some think this does not force someone to work extra hours, since there is no fixed number of extra hours he is forced to work, and since he can avoid the tax entirely by earning only enough to cover his basic needs. This is a very uncharacteristic view of forcing for those who *also* think people are forced to do something *whenever* the alternatives they face are considerably worse. However, *neither* view is correct. The fact that others intentionally intervene, in violation of a side constraint against aggression, to threaten force to limit the alternatives, in this case to paying taxes or (presumably the worse alternative) bare subsistence, makes the taxation system one of forced labor and distinguishes it from other cases of limited choices which are not forcings.[5]

The man who chooses to work longer to gain an income more than sufficient for his basic needs prefers some extra goods or services to the leisure and activities he could perform during the possible nonworking hours; whereas the man who chooses not to work the extra time prefers the leisure activities to the extra goods or services he could acquire by working more. Given this, if it would be illegitimate for a tax system to seize some of a man's leisure (forced labor) for the purpose of serving the needy, how can it be legitimate for a tax system to seize some of a man's goods for that purpose? Why should we treat the man whose happiness requires certain material goods or services differently from the man whose preferences and desires make such goods unnecessary for his happiness? Why should the man who prefers seeing a movie (and who has to earn money for a ticket) be open to the required call to aid the needy, while the person who prefers looking at a sunset (and hence need earn no extra money) is not? Indeed, isn't it surprising that redistributionists choose to ignore

---

[4] I am unsure as to whether the arguments I present below show that such taxation merely *is* forced labor; so that "is on a par with" means "is one kind of." Or alternatively, whether the arguments emphasize the great similarities between such taxation and forced labor, to show it is plausible and illuminating to view such taxation in the light of forced labor. This latter approach would remind one of how John Wisdom conceives of the claims of metaphysicians.

[5] Further details which this statement should include are contained in my essay "Coercion," in *Philosophy, Science, and Method,* ed. S. Morgenbesser, P. Suppes, and M. White (New York: St. Martin, 1969).

the man whose pleasures are so easily attainable without extra labor, while adding yet another burden to the poor unfortunate who must work for his pleasures? If anything, one would have expected the reverse. Why is the person with the nonmaterial or nonconsumption desire allowed to proceed unimpeded to his most favored feasible alternative, whereas the man whose pleasures or desires involve material things and who must work for extra money (thereby serving whomever considers his activities valuable enough to pay him) is constrained in what he can realize? Perhaps there is no difference in principle. And perhaps some think the answer concerns merely administrative convenience. (These questions and issues will not disturb those who think that forced labor to serve the needy or to realize some favored end-state pattern is acceptable.) In a fuller discussion we would have (and want) to extend our argument to include interest, entrepreneurial profits, and so on. Those who doubt that this extension can be carried through, and who draw the line here at taxation of income from labor, will have to state rather complicated patterned *historical* principles of distributive justice, since end-state principles would not distinguish *sources* of income in any way. It is enough for now to get away from end-state principles and to make clear how various patterned principles are dependent upon particular views about the sources or the illegitimacy or the lesser legitimacy of profits, interest, and so on; which particular views may well be mistaken.

What sort of right over others does a legally institutionalized end-state pattern give one? The central core of the notion of a property right in X, relative to which other parts of the notion are to be explained, is the right to determine what shall be done with X; the right to choose which of the constrained set of options concerning X shall be realized or attempted. The constraints are set by other principles or laws operating in the society; in our theory, by the Lockean rights people possess (under the minimal state). My property rights in my knife allow me to leave it where I will, but not in your chest. I may choose which of the acceptable options involving the knife is to be realized. This notion of property helps us to understand why earlier theorists spoke of people as having property in themselves and their labor. They viewed each person as having a right to decide what would become of himself and what he would do, and as having a right to reap the benefits of what he did.

This right of selecting the alternative to be realized from the constrained set of alternatives may be held by an *individual* or by a *group* with some procedure for reaching a joint decision; or the right may be passed back and forth, so that one year I decide what's to become of X, and the next year you do (with the alternative of destruction, perhaps, being excluded). Or, during the same time period, some types of decisions about X may be made by me, and others by you. And so on. We lack an adequate, fruitful, analytical apparatus for classifying the *types* of constraints on the set of options among which choices are to be made, and the *types* of ways decision powers can be held, divided, and amalgamated. A *theory* of property would, among other things, contain such a classification of constraints and decision modes, and from a small number of principles would follow a host of interesting statements about the *consequences* and effects of certain combinations of constraints and modes of decision.

When end-result principles of distributive justice are built into the legal structure of a society, they (as do most patterned principles) give each citizen an enforceable claim to some portion of the total social product; that is, to some portion of the sum total of the individually and jointly made products. This total product is produced by individuals laboring, using means of production others have saved to bring into existence, by people organizing production or creating means to produce new things or things in a new way. It is on this batch of individual activities that patterned distributional principles give each individual an enforceable claim. Each person has a claim to the activities and the products of other persons, independently of whether the other persons enter into particular relationships that give rise to these claims, and independently of whether they voluntarily take these claims upon themselves, in charity or in exchange for something.

Whether it is done through taxation on wages or on wages over a certain amount, or through seizure of profits, or through there being a big *social pot* so that it's not clear what's coming from where and what's going where, patterned principles of distributive justice involve appropriating the actions of other persons. Seizing the results of someone's labor is equivalent to seizing hours from him and directing him to carry on various activities. If people force you to do certain work, or unrewarded work, for a certain period of time, they decide what you are to do and what purposes your work is to serve apart from your decisions. This process whereby they take this decision from you makes them a *part-owner* of you; it gives them a property right in you. Just as having such partial control and power of decision, by right, over an animal or inanimate object would be to have a property right in it.

End-state and most patterned principles of distributive justice institute (partial) ownership by others of people and their actions and labor. These principles involve a shift from the classical liberals' notion of self-ownership to a notion of (partial) property rights in *other* people.

53.
Reevaluating Liberty of Contract and Self-Ownership

GERALD COHEN

I. HOW PATTERNS PRESERVE LIBERTY

1. Nozick's case against socialism can be taken in two ways. He proposes a definition of justice in terms of liberty, and on that basis he argues that what socialists consider just is not in fact just. But even if his definition of justice is wrong, so that the basis of his critique, taken in this first way, is faulty, he would still press a claim against socialism, namely, that, however *just* it may or may not be, it is incompatible with *liberty*. Even if Nozick is mistaken about what justice is, he might still be right that the cost in loss of liberty imposed by what socialists regard as just is intolerably high. (Hence the title of the section of the book on which we shall focus: "How Liberty Upsets Patterns"—patterns being distributions answering to, for example, a socialist principle of justice.) So it is not enough, in defending socialism against Nozick, to prove that he has not shown that it is unjust. It must also be proved that he has not shown that it frustrates liberty.

2. A full definition of socialism is not required for our purposes. All we need suppose is that a socialist society upholds some principle of equality in the distribution of benefits enjoyed and burdens borne by its members. The principle need not be specified further, since Nozick's argument is against the institution of *any* such principle.

   Let us now imagine that such an egalitarian principle is instituted, and that it leads to a distribution of goods and bads which, following Nozick, we shall call D1. Then Nozick argues by example that D1 can be maintained only at the price of tyranny and injustice. The example concerns the best basketball player in the imagined society.

> . . . suppose that Wilt Chamberlain is greatly in demand by basketball teams, being a great gate attraction . . . He signs the following sort of contract with a team: In each home game, twenty-five cents from the price of each ticket of admission goes to him . . . The season starts, and people cheerfully attend his team's games; they buy their tickets, each time dropping a separate twenty-five cents of their admission price into a special box with Chamberlain's name on it. They are excited about seeing him play; it is worth the total admission price to them. Let us suppose that in one season one million persons attend his home games, and Wilt Chamberlain winds up with $250,000, a much larger sum than the average income . . . Is he entitled to this income? Is this

new distribution D2, unjust? If so, why? There is *no* question about whether each of the people was entitled to the control over the resources they held in D1; because that was the distribution . . . that (for the purposes of argument) we assumed was acceptable. Each of these persons *chose* to give twenty-five cents of their money to Chamberlain. They could have spent it on going to the movies, or on candy bars, or on copies of *Dissent* magazine, or of *Monthly Review*. But they all, at least one million of them, converged on giving it to Wilt Chamberlain in exchange for watching him play basketball. If D1 was a just distribution, and people voluntarily moved from it to D2, transferring parts of their shares they were given under D1 (what was it for if not to do something with?), isn't D2 also just? If the people were entitled to dispose of the resources to which they were entitled (under D1), didn't this include their being entitled to give it to, or exchange it with, Wilt Chamberlain? Can anyone else complain on grounds of justice? Each other person already has his legitimate share under D1. Under D1, there is nothing that anyone has that anyone else has a claim of justice against. After someone transfers something to Wilt Chamberlain, third parties *still* have their legitimate shares; *their* shares are not changed. By what process could such a transfer among two persons give rise to a legitimate claim of distributive justice on a portion of what was transferred, by a third party who had no claim of justice on any holding of the others *before* the transfer?[1]

According to Nozick

(1) "Whatever arises from a just situation by just steps is itself just."[2]

Nozick holds that *steps* are just if they are free of injustice, and that they are free of injustice if they are fully voluntary on the part of all the agents who take them. We can therefore spell (1) out as follows:

(2) Whatever arises from a just situation as a result of fully voluntary transactions on the part of all the transacting agents it itself just.

So convinced is Nozick that (2) is true that he thinks that it must be accepted by people attached to a doctrine of justice which in other respects differs from his own. This is why he feels able to rely on (2) in the Chamberlain parable, despite having granted, for the sake of argument, the justice of an initial situation patterned by an egalitarian principle.

Even if (2) is true, it does not follow that pattern D1 can be maintained only at the price of injustice, for people might simply *fail* to use their liberty in a pattern-subverting manner. But that is not an interesting possibility. A more interesting one is that they deliberately *refuse* to use their liberty subversively. Reasons for refusing will be adduced shortly. But is (2) true? Does liberty always preserve justice?

---

[1]　Robert Nozick. *Anarchy, State, and Utopia* (New York: Basic Books, 1974), pp. 161–2.

[2]　Ibid., p. 151.

A standard way of testing the claim would be to look for states of affairs which would be accounted unjust but which might be generated by the route (2) endorses. Perhaps the strongest counter-example of this form would be slavery. We might then say: voluntary self-enslavement is possible. But slavery is unjust. Therefore (2) is false. Yet whatever may be the merits of that argument, we know that Nozick is not moved by it. For he thinks that there is no injustice in a slavery that arises out of the approved process.

Though Nozick accepts slavery with an appropriate genesis, there is a restriction, derived from (2) itself, on the kind of slavery he accepts: (2) does not allow slave status to be inherited by offspring of the self-enslaved, for then a concerned party's situation would be decided for him, independently of his will. "Some things individuals may choose for themselves no one may choose for another."[3] Let us remember this when we come to scrutinize the Wilt Chamberlain transaction, for widespread contracting of the kind which occurs in the parable might have the effect of seriously modifying, for the worse, the situation of members of future generations.

Should we say that in Nozick's conception of justice in a slave society need be no less just than one where people are free? That would be a tendentious formulation. For Nozick can claim that rational persons in an initially just situation are unlikely to contract into slavery, except, indeed, where circumstances are so special that it would be wrong to forbid them to do so. This diminishes the danger that (2) can be used to stamp approval on morally repellent social arrangements.

I attribute some such response to Nozick on the basis, *inter alia,* of this passage:

> it must be granted that were people's reasons for transferring some of their holdings to others always irrational or arbitrary, we would find this *disturbing* . . . We feel more comfortable upholding the justice of an entitlement system if most of the transfers under it are done for reasons. This does not mean necessarily that all deserve what holdings they receive. It means only that there is a purpose or point to someone's transferring a holding to one person rather than to another; that usually we can see what the transferrer thinks he's gaining, what cause he *thinks* he's serving, what goals he *thinks* he's helping to achieve, and so forth. Since in a capitalist society people often transfer holdings to others in accordance with how much they *perceive* these others benefiting them, the fabric constituted by the individual transactions and transfers is largely reasonable and intelligible.[4]

Accordingly, Nozick emphasizes the motives people have when they pay to watch Chamberlain, instead of stipulating that they do so freely and leaving us to guess why. It is important to the persuasive allure of the example that we should consider what the fans are doing not only voluntary but sensible: transactions

---

[3] Ibid., p. 331.

[4] Ibid., p. 159, my emphasis.

are disturbing (even though they are entirely just?) when we cannot see what the (or some of the) contracting parties *think* they are gaining by them.

Yet we should surely also be disturbed if we can indeed see what the agent *thinks* he is gaining, but we know that what he *will* gain is not that, but something he thinks less valuable; or that what results is not only the gain he expects but also unforeseen consequences which render negative the net value, according to his preferences and standards, of the transaction. We should not be content if what he *thinks* he is getting is good, but what he actually gets is bad, by his own lights. I shall assume that Nozick would accept this plausible extension of his concession. It is hard to see how he could resist it.

Accordingly, if we can show that Chamberlain's fans get not only the pleasure of watching him minus twenty-five cents, but also uncontemplated disbenefits of a significant order, then, even if, for Nozick, the outcome remains just, it should, even to Nozick, be disturbing. We shall need to ask whether we do not find Chamberlain's fans insufficiently reflective, when we think through, as they do not, the *full* consequences of what they are doing.

But now we can go further. For, in the light of the considerations just reviewed, (2) appears very probably false. Nozick says that a transaction is free of injustice if every transacting agent agrees to it. Perhaps that is so. But transactional justice, so characterized, is supposed—given an initially just situation—to confer justice on what results from it. (That is why (2) is supposed to follow them (1).) And that is questionable. Of each person who agrees to a transaction we may ask: *would he have agreed to it had he known what its outcome would be?* Since the answer may be negative, it is far from evident that transactional justice, as described, transmits justice to its results.

Perhaps the desired transmission occurs when the answer to the italicized question is positive. Perhaps, in other words, we can accept (3), which increases the requirements for steps to be justice-preserving:

(3) Whatever arises from a just situation as a result of fully voluntary transactions which all transacting agents would still have agreed to if they had known what the results of so transacting were to be is itself just.

(3) looks plausible, but its power to endorse market-generated states of affairs is, while not nil, very weak. Stronger principles may also be plausible, but (2), Nozick's principle, is certainly too strong to be accepted without much more defense than he provides.

3. Let us now apply this critique of Nozick's principles to the parable which is supposed to secure (or reveal) our allegiance to them.

Before describing the Chamberlain transaction, Nozick says: "It is not clear how those holding alternative conceptions of distributive justice can reject the entitlement conception of justice in holdings." [5] There follows the Chamberlain story, where we assume that D1 is just, and are then, supposedly, constrained to admit that D2, into which it is converted, must also be just; an admission,

---

[5] Ibid., p. 160.

according to Nozick, which is tantamount to accepting the entitlement conception. But how much of it must we accept if we endorse D2 as just? At most that there is *a* role for the entitlement principle. For what the transaction subverts is the original pattern, not the principle governing it, *taken as a principle conjoinable with others to form a total theory of just or legitimate holdings.* The example, even if successful, does not defeat the initial assumption that D1 is just. Rather, it exploits that assumption to argue that D2, though it breaks D1's pattern, must also be just. The Chamberlain story, even when we take it at its face value, impugns not the original distribution, but the *exclusive* rightness of the principle mandating it.

Now Nozick is certainly right to this extent, even if we do not accept everything he says about the Chamberlain story: there must be *a* role for entitlement in determining acceptable holdings. For unless the just society forbids gifts, it must allow transfers which do not answer to a patterning principle. This is compatible with placing restraints on the scope of gift, and we shall shortly see why an egalitarian society might be justified in doing so. But the present point is that assigning a certain role to unregulated transactions in the determination of holdings is compatible with using an egalitarian principle to decide the major distribution of goods and to limit, for example by taxation, how much more or less than what he would get under that principle alone a person may come to have in virtue of transactions which escape its writ. I think socialists do well to concede that an egalitarian principle should not be the only guide to the justice of holdings, or that, if it is, then justice should not be the only guide to policy with respect to holdings.

Among the reasons for limiting how much an individual may hold, regardless of how he came to hold it, is to prevent him from acquiring, through his holdings, an unacceptable amount of power over others: the Chamberlain transaction looks less harmless when we focus on that consideration.

The fans "are excited about seeing him play; it is worth the total admission price to them." The idea is that they see him play if and only if they pay, and seeing him play is worth more to them than anything else they can get for twenty-five cents. So it may be, but this fails to cover everything in the outcome which is relevant. For, once Chamberlain has received the payments, he is in a very special position of power in what was previously an egalitarian society. The fans' access to resources might now be prejudiced by the disproportionate access Chamberlain's wealth gives him, and the consequent power over others that he now has. *For all that Nozick shows,* a socialist may claim that this is not a bargain informed people in an egalitarian society will be apt to make: they will refrain from so contracting as to upset the equality they prize, and they will be especially averse to doing so because the resulting changes would profoundly affect their children. (This may seem an hysterical projection of the effect of the Chamberlain transaction, but I take it that we have to consider the upshot of general performance of transactions of that kind, and then the projection is entirely realistic.)

It is easy to think carelessly about the example. How we feel about people like Chamberlain getting a lot of money *as things are* is a poor index of how people would feel in the imagined situation. Among us the ranks of the rich and the powerful exist, and it can be pleasing, given that they do, when a figure like Chamberlain joins them. Who better and more innocently deserves to be among them? But the case before us is a society of equality in danger of losing its essential character. Reflective people would have to consider not only the joy of watching Chamberlain and its immediate money price but also the fact, which socialists say that they would deplore, that their society would be set on the road to class division. In presenting the Chamberlain fable Nozick ignores the commitment people may have to living in a society of a particular kind, and the rhetorical power of the illustration depends on that omission. At a later stage, Nozick takes up this point, but, so I argue in section 4 below, he says nothing interesting about it.

Nozick tacitly supposes that a person willing to pay twenty-five cents to watch Wilt play, is *ipso facto* a person willing to pay *Wilt* twenty-five cents to watch him play. It is no doubt true that in our society people rarely care who gets the money they forgo to obtain goods. But the tacit supposition is false, and the common unconcern is irrational. Nozick exploits our familiarity with this unconcern. Yet a person might welcome a world in which he and a million others watch Wilt play, at a cost of twenty-five cents to each, and consistently disfavor one in which, in addition, Wilt rakes in a cool quarter million.

Accordingly, if a citizen of the D1 society joins with others in paying twenty-five cents to Wilt to watch Wilt play, without thinking about the effect on Wilt's power, then the result may be deemed "disturbing" in the sense of p. 159 of *Anarchy*. Of course a single person's paying a quarter makes no appreciable difference if the rest are anyway going to do so. But a convention might evolve not to make such payments, or, more simply, there could be a democratically authorized taxation system which maintains wealth differentials within acceptable limits. Whether Wilt would then still play is a further question on which I shall not comment, except to say that anyone who thinks it obvious that he would not play misunderstands human nature, or basketball, or both.

4. In defending the justice of the Chamberlain transaction, Nozick glances at the position of persons not directly party to it: "After someone transfers something to Wilt Chamberlain, third parties *still* have their legitimate shares; *their* shares are not changed.[6] That is false, in one relevant sense. For a person's effective share depends on what he can do with what he has, and that depends not only on how much he has but on what others have and on how what others have is distributed. If it is distributed equally among them he will often be better placed than if some have especially large shares. Third parties, including the as yet unborn, may therefore have an interest against the contract. It is roughly the same interest as the fans themselves may have in not making it. (But, unlike third parties, a fan gets the compensation of watching Wilt play, which—I have not ruled this out—might be worth a whole lot of inequality, as far as a particular individual fan is concerned.)

[6] Ibid., p. 161.

Nozick addresses this issue in a footnote:

> Might not a transfer have instrumental effects on a third party, changing his feasible options? (But what if the two parties to a transfer independently had used their holdings in this fashion?)[7]

He promises further treatment of the problem later, and, although he does not say where it will come, he presumably has in mind his section on "Voluntary Exchange," which I shall address . . . below. Here I respond to Nozick's parenthetical rhetorical question.

First, there are some upshots of transfers of holdings, some effects on the options of the other parties, which will not occur as effects of the unconcerted use of dispersed holdings by individuals, because those individuals could not, or would not, use them in that way. The Chamberlain fans, acting independently, are less likely than Chamberlain is to buy a set of houses and leave them unoccupied, with speculative intent. Sometimes, though, a set of fans, acting independently, could indeed bring about effects inimical to the interests of others, of just the kind one may fear Chamberlain might cause. But whoever worries about Chamberlain doing so will probably also be concerned about the case where it results from the independent action of many. The rhetorical second question in the Nozick passage should not silence those who ask the first one.[8]

As an argument about *justice* the Chamberlain story is either question-begging or uncompelling. Nozick asks:

> If the people were entitled to dispose of the resources to which they were entitled (under D1), didn't this include their being entitled to give it to, or exchange it with, Wilt Chamberlain?[9]

If this interrogative is intended as a vivid way of asserting the corresponding indicative, then Nozick is telling us that the rights in shares with which people were vested are violated unless they are allowed to contract as described. If so, he begs the question. For it will be clear that their rights are violated only if the entitlement they received was of the absolute Nozickian sort, and this cannot be assumed. Whatever principles underlie D1 will generate restrictions on the use of what is distributed in accordance with them.

The other way of taking the quoted question is not as an assertion but as an appeal. Nozick is then asking us whether we do not agree that any restrictions which would forbid the Chamberlain transaction must be unjustified. So construed the argument is not question-begging, but it is inconclusive. For

[7] Ibid., p. 162.

[8] The purpose of the second question, so I take it, is to suggest this argument:

1. The fans might have so used their several quarters with the same effect on third parties that one asks the first question fears Wilt's use of his quarter million might have.
2. No one could object to the fans so using their quarters.
3. No one can object to what Wilt does with his quarter million.

Whether or not the stated premises imply that argument's conclusion, the present point is that an alert rejecter of its conclusion will also reject its second premiss.

[9] Op. cit., p. 161.

considerations which might justify restrictions on transactions are not canvassed. It is easy to think that what happens afterwards is that Chamberlain eats lots of chocolate, sees lots of movies and buys lots of subscriptions to expensive socialist journals. But, as I have insisted, we must remember the considerable power that he can now exercise over others. In general, holdings are not only sources of enjoyment but, in certain distributions, sources of power. Transfers which look unexceptionable come to seem otherwise when we bring into relief the aspect neglected in "libertarian" apologetic.

5. Let us turn, now, from justice to liberty: is it true that a "socialist society would have to forbid capitalist acts between consenting adults"?[10] Socialism perishes if there are too many such acts, but it does not follow that it must forbid them. In traditional socialist doctrine capitalist action wanes not primarily because it is illegal, but because the impulse behind it atrophies, or, less Utopianly, because other impulses become stronger, or because people believe that capitalistic exchange is unfair. *Such expectation rests on a conception of human nature, and so does its denial.* Nozick has a different conception, for which he does not argue, one that fits many twentieth-century Americans, which is no reason for concluding that it is universally true. The people in Nozick's state of nature are intelligible only as well-socialized products of a market society. In the contrary socialist conception, human beings have and may develop further a (noninstrumental) desire for community, a relish of cooperation, and an aversion to being on either side of a master/servant relationship. No one should assume without argument, or take it on trust from the socialist tradition, that this conception is sound. But *if* it is sound, then there will be no need for incessant invigilation against "capitalist acts," and Nozick does not *argue* that it is unsound. Hence he has not shown that socialism conflicts with freedom, even if his unargued premiss that its citizens will want to perform capitalist acts attracts the assent of the majority of his readers.

How much equality would conflict with liberty in given circumstances depends on how much people would value equality in those circumstances. If life in a cooperative commonwealth appeals to them, they do not have to sacrifice liberty to belong to it.

This banal point relates to the first of what Nozick says are the three "unrealistic" presuppositions of the moral and practical possibility of socialism:

(5) that all will most want to maintain the [socialist] pattern
(6) that each can gather enough information about his own actions and the ongoing activities of others to discover which of his actions will upset the pattern
(7) that diverse and far-flung persons can coordinate their actions to dovetail into the pattern.[11]

---

[10] Ibid., p. 163.
[11] Ibid., p. 163.

Something like the first presupposition is made by socialists in the light of the idea of human nature which informs their tradition. It is, of course, controversial, but its dismissal as "unrealistic" contributes nothing to the controversy.

Socialists presuppose only something *like* (5), because they need not think that everyone will have socialist sentiments, but only a preponderant majority, especially in the nascency of socialism. If (5) itself is unrealistic, three possibilities present themselves: very few would lack enthusiasm for socialism; very many would; some intermediate proportion would. What I mean by these magnitudes emerges immediately.

In the first possibility, there remain a few capitalistically minded persons, meaning by "a few" that their capitalist acts would not undermine the basic socialist structure. No sane socialist should commit himself to the suppression of capitalist activity on the stated scale. (It might even be desirable to allocate to capitalistophiles a territory in which they can bargain with and hire one another.)

Suppose, though, that the disposition to perform capitalist acts is strong and widespread, so that socialism is possible only with tyranny. What socialist favours socialism in such circumstances? What socialist denies that there are such circumstances? Certainly Marx insisted that it would be folly to attempt an institution of socialism except under the propitious conditions he was confident capitalism would create. A socialist believes that propitious conditions are accessible. He need not proclaim the superiority of socialism regardless of circumstances.

Could a socialist society contain an amount of inclination to capitalism of such a size that unless it were coercively checked socialism would be subverted, yet sufficiently small that, in socialist judgement, socialism, with the required coercion, would still be worthwhile? Marxian socialists believe so, and that does commit them to prohibiting capitalist acts between consenting adults in certain circumstances, notably those which follow a successful revolution. But why should they flinch from that prohibition? They can defend it by reference to the social good and widened freedom that it promotes. Nozick would object that the prohibition violates moral "side constraints": certain freedoms, for example of contract, ought never to be infringed, whatever the consequences of allowing their exercise may be. We shall look at side constraints in the next section.

But first we must treat presuppositions (6) and (7). Unlike (5), these are red herrings. At most, they are preconditions of realizing socialist justice *perfectly*. But justice is not the only virtue of social orders (and it is not even "the first virtue" of socialism, for most socialists). Even if we identify justice with equality, as socialists, broadly speaking, do, we may tolerate deviations from equality consequent on perturbations caused by gift, small-scale market transactions, and so on. Considerations of privacy, acquired expectations, the moral and economic costs of surveillance, etc. declare against attempting a realization of justice in the high degree that would be possible if (6) and (7) were satisfied. We let justice remain rough, in deference to other values.

Accordingly, socialism tolerates gift-giving, and "loving behavior" is not "forbidden." Gift is possible under a system which limits how much anyone may have and what he may do with it. Relatively well-endowed persons will sometimes not be fit recipients of gifts, but we are assuming a socialist psychology whose natural tendency is not to give to them that hath. And the notion that the institutions we are contemplating fetter the expression of love is too multiply bizarre to require comment.

6. Any but the most utopian socialist must be willing under certain conditions to restrict the liberty of a few for the sake of the liberty of many. But, so Nozick would charge, such a socialist would thereby violate "moral side constraints" that apply to all human action. For Nozick thinks that we may never restrict one person's freedom in order to enhance the welfare or the freedom of very many others, or even of everyone, that person included (where we know that the restriction will redound to his benefit).

If children are undernourished in our society, we are not allowed to tax millionaires in order to finance a subsidy on the price of milk to poor families, for we would be violating the rights, and the "dignity" of the millionaires. We cannot appeal that the effective liberty of the children (and the adults they will become) would be greatly enhanced at little expense to the millionaires' freedom, for Nozick forbids any act which restricts freedom: he does not call for its maximization. (This means that if it were true that certain exercises of freedom would lead to totalitarianism, Nozick would still protect them. Market freedom itself would be sacrificed by Nozick if the only way to preserve it were by limiting it.)

If Nozick argues for this position, he does so in the section called "Why Side Constraints?," which begins as follows:

> Isn't it *irrational* to accept a side constraint C, rather than a view that directs minimizing the violation of C? . . . If nonviolation of C is so important, shouldn't that be the goal? How can a concern for the nonviolation of C lead to the refusal to violate C even when this would prevent other more extensive violations of C? What is the rationale for placing the nonviolation of rights as a side constraint upon action instead of including it solely as a goal of one's actions?
>
> Side constraints upon action reflect the underlying Kantian principle that individuals are ends and not merely means; they may not be sacrificed or used for the achieving of other ends without their consent. Individuals are inviolable.[12]

The second paragraph is lame as a response to the questions of the first, for they obviously reassert themselves: if such sacrifice and violation are so horrendous, why should we not be concerned to minimize their occurrence? There is more appearance of argument in the final paragraph of the section:

> Side constraints express the inviolability of other persons. But why may not one violate persons for the greater social good? Individually, we each

---

[12] Ibid., pp. 30–1.

sometimes choose to undergo some pain or sacrifice for a greater benefit or to avoid a greater harm . . . Why not, *similarly*, hold that some persons have to bear some costs that benefit other persons more, for the sake of the overall social good? But there is no *social entity* with a good that undergoes some sacrifice for its own good. There are only individual people, different individual people, with their own individual lives. Using one of these people for the benefit of others, uses him and benefits the others. Nothing more. What happens is that something is done to him for the sake of others. Talk of an overall social good covers this up . . .[13]

This passage is hard to construe. In one interpretation what is says is correct but ineffectual, in the other what is says is pertinent, but wrong, and anyone who is impressed has probably failed to spot the ambiguity. For it is unclear whether Nozick is only arguing *against* one who puts redistribution across lives on a moral par with a person's sacrificing something for his own greater benefit, or arguing *for* the moral impermissibility of redistribution. In other words, is Nozick simply rejecting argument A, or is he (also) propounding argument B?

A since   persons compose a social entity relevantly akin to the entity a single person is (p), redistribution across persons is morally permissible (q).

B since   it is false that p, it is false that q.

If Nozick is just rejecting argument A, then I agree with him, but side constraints remain unjustified. Unless we take Nozick to be propounding argument B, there is no case to answer. And then the answer is that the truth of p is not a necessary condition of the truth of q. A redistributor does not have to believe in a social entity.

According to Nozick, the redistributive attitude ignores the separateness of persons. But what does it mean to say in a normative tone of voice (for it is uncontroversial, descriptively speaking) that persons are separate? Either it means that who gets what is morally relevant, or it means that it is morally forbidden to redistribute across persons. If the first (moral relevance) is what is meant, then all patterned principles (as opposed to, for example, the unpatterned end-state principle of utilitarianism) embody the requirement, and even an unpatterned egalitarianism manifestly presupposes the moral separateness of persons. If the second (prohibition on redistribution) is what is meant, then the separateness of persons is no *argument* against redistribution.

Side constraints remain unjustified, and socialists need not apologize for being willing to restrict freedom in order to expand it.

II. SELF-OWNERSHIP

The central form of rejection of the thesis of self-ownership is in the affirmation of non-contractual obligations to serve other people. According to Robert

[13] Ibid., pp. 32–3.

Nozick, principles that impose non-contractual obligations "institute (partial) ownership by others of people and their actions and labor. These principles involve a shift from the classical liberals' notion of self-ownership to a notion of (partial) property rights in other people." [14] I take the quoted passage to be an *argument* against the obligation-imposing principles, rather than a characterization of them which even their proponents can be expected to accept. The argument I discern exploits an aversion to property rights in other people, which is to say, an aversion to slavery, an aversion that need not reflect an antecedent commitment to the principle of self-ownership itself. The purpose of the argument is to convert non-believers in self-ownership by showing them that rejection of self-ownership is tantamount to endorsement of slavery.

The polemically operative sequence in the argument runs, I think as follows:

(1) If *X* is non-contractually obliged to do *A* for *Y*, then *Y* has a right of disposal over *X*'s labor of the sort that a slave-owner has.
(2) If *Y* has a right of disposal over *X*'s labor of the sort that a slave-owner has, then *X* is, *pro tanto,* *Y*'s slave.
(3) It is morally intolerable for anyone to be, in any degree, another's slave. Therefore
(4) It is morally intolerable for *X* to be non-contractually obliged to do *A* for Y.

The argument, as reconstructed above, is valid. Accordingly, opposition to it must fix on one or more of its three premises. A clever person might find subtle reasons for rejecting premiss (2), but I do not think that it would be profitable to speculate about that. The interesting premisses are (1) and (3), and I shall begin with (3), since what I have to say about (1) is rather complicated, and what I have to say about (3) is not.

An objection to (3) might be developed as follows. Consider, for a moment, a condition different from (though also partly similar to) slavery, to wit, the condition of imprisonment. Suppose that you are an innocent person and that I forcibly detain you in a room for five minutes. Then, indeed, I forcibly detain you, albeit for only five minutes. Now, whether or not such brief detention should qualify as short-term *imprisonment,* whether or not to call it "imprisonment" would be a preposterous exaggeration, there is a massive *normative* difference between this brief detention and life-long imprisonment. Brief detention of an innocent person might be justified by, for example, temporary needs of social order, even if life-long imprisonment of an innocent person could never be justified. And, similarly, even if premiss (1) in the argument under examination is true, so that redistributive taxation does mean, as Nozick insists, slavery-like forced labor, a limited dose of forced labor is massively different, normatively, from the life-long forced labor that characterizes a slave.

I turn, now, to premiss (1), and to a way of resisting Nozick's argument that was put to me by Joseph Raz. Raz argued that, when *X* is non-contractually

---

[14] Ibid., p. 172, and see, further, the associated passage which forms the epigraph of this chapter.

obliged to *Y*, it does not follow that anyone has a slave-owner-like right to dispose over *X*'s labor. Raz resisted (1) by pressing the following example: although I might be obliged to assist my mother if she falls ill, she might have no right to absolve me from that obligation, and, therefore, no more right than I have to decide whether my capacity to assist, in this respect, is or is not exercised. Even if, moreover, my mother does have the right to absolve me from that particular obligation, it remains untrue that she has unrestricted disposal, of the kind a slave-owner has, over the personal power that I must use to discharge the obligation. She cannot tell me to do with my power whatever she happens to want me to do with it.

Three progressively weaker claims might be made about the rights-entailments of my obligation with respect to my mother, and the third and weakest claim, and, therefore, the hardest one to deny, suffices to show that my obligation to her need not reflect a right of the sort that a slave-holder has—which is the sort of right Nozick needs for his argument.

First, it might be said that my having an obligation to her need not mean that my mother has any right against me at all. But the notion of a right against someone is not so clear that one can expect everyone to agree with that first claim. Some will find it very difficult to separate in their minds the idea that I have an obligation to my mother from the idea that she has a corresponding right against me. (I would defend the separation by saying that, if I fail in my obligation, then it might be that she has no stronger basis for complaining about my failure than others have.)

The second, weaker, claim is that, although my mother may indeed have a right against me, although it may be she and no one else who has a grievance if I do not fulfil my obligation, she may yet lack the right to absolve me of my obligation, and therefore lack the sort of right that a slave-holder has.

Finally, even if my mother does have the right to absolve me of the obligation, or even to forbid me to carry it out, it does not follow that she has the slave-holder-like right to tell me to do whatever she chooses with whatever resource I would use to carry out the stated obligation.

The general point is that the question of how, in certain conditions, I am entitled to use my power to assist might be settled not by anyone's exercise of a right, but by the existence of a relevant obligation, or, in the weakest claim, by truths about rights which are consistent with gaps in the space of rights, gaps which mean that "nobody" is the answer to some questions of the form: who has the right to decide whether or not I do *A*? And this defeats Nozick's claim that, to the extent that I do not own myself, I am a slave. Slavery is characterized by non-contractual obligation, and, when I lack a right with respect to some aspect of my power or activity, then that may indeed be because I have such an obligation. But it does not follow that I am then a slave, for it does not follow that another then has the right that I lack. Accordingly, absences of self-ownership need not be presences *pro tanto* of slavery.

Some will object that this excursus about my obligation to my mother is beside the point. They will say that the thesis of self-ownership does not exclude moral obligations, but only legally enforceable obligations. Only those obligations betoken slavery, and my obligation to my mother would not normally be regarded as legally enforceable. Call that the "enforcement objection."

One way of resisting the enforcement objection is to question the consistency of self-ownership and (even) non-enforceable obligations to others. And that style of resistance certainly appears in the anti-libertarian polemical literature. But, even if such resistance is correct, the consequent conceptual gain—that self-ownership is inconsistent with intuitively evident moral obligations of a non-enslaving sort—is not matched by victory at the level of political philosophy. For the libertarian bottom line in political philosophy is not, indeed, that we are self-owners but that the state has no right to impose or enforce non-contractual obligations on us, and the line of resistance canvassed here leaves that claim intact. It is, moreover, unclear that even a conceptual victory is available on this front. For it is not clearly inconsistent to say both that I am the unambiguous full owner of this tract of land and that I have a moral obligation to let my neighbor peacefully traverse it when he desperately needs to get water from the brook to which he has no other means of access. It is not obviously false that all that relevantly follows from my unambiguous full ownership of the land is that I have a right to exclude him (which I might be morally obliged not to exercise) and that he has no right to traverse it.

So the nettle must be grasped, we need a different way of meeting the enforcement objection, which says that Raz invokes the wrong sort of obligation against premiss (1) in the Nozick argument. Let us, then, suppose that, whether or not I would otherwise have any kind of obligation to her, the state imposes on me a legal obligation to serve my mother, or the needy in general. Does this not, indeed, show that it arrogates to itself the sort of right over my labor that a slave-holder has?

It does not, for points similar to those made above about my mother's not relating to me as a slave-owner in the original example can now be made about the state. Thus one might believe that the state has no right to absolve me from this obligation, that it has a duty to tax me, and, consequently, no right to decide whether or not I should transfer income to the needy. The state therefore lacks the relevant right to dispose over my labor even if it has the right to direct this particular other-assisting use of it. Nor do my mother, or the needy, now have slave-holder-like rights over me, by virtue of the enforcement by the state of whatever rights they do have against me. The reasons offered previously against saying that they are my partial owners remain intact.

A defender of the enforcement objection might now say that the state simply cannot have the particular right here attributed to it unless it has the comprehensive right over me that betokens slavery. But that is just not true. The socialist constitution requires the state to tax redistributively; the Nozick constitution forbids it to do so. It is equally false in each case that the state is thereby vested with a right to decide whether or not some will serve others. Of course, and this could confuse the issue in the minds of some, the redistributive state may have the *de facto* power to do something forbidden by its constitution. But that is also true of Nozick's state, and it is therefore irrelevant.

In sum, we could all have enforceable obligations to one another which imply no slave-owner-like rights of disposal in anyone over anyone's labor. Indeed, such obligations form the normative substance of a redistributive state. In that state, there are no self-ownership rights with respect to certain dimensions of the capacity to assist, but there are also no slave-owner/slave relations.

The objection to Raz, that his case against Nozick's argument collapses when we turn to obligations of the relevant enforceable kind, does not succeed. But, even if Raz has refuted premiss (1) of Nozick's argument, there is a broader objection to his response to Nozick which seems to me correct, although the objection also shows, ironically, that Nozick somewhat mis-states his own case in the passage quoted at the beginning of this section.

Here is the broad objection. Suppose that I am obliged to spend a stretch of time carrying out a task for you that no one has the right to absolve me from performing and that it is so precisely specified that there are only trivially different ways in which it might be performed. Then, for the Razian reasons articulated . . . above, my being weighted with this task does not mean that anyone is my short-term slave-holder or partial owner. But, for all that, my own condition, so far as I am concerned, is not in every important way different from that of a short-term or partial slave. For *I* have no more right to decide what to do with my faculties within the given frame of task and time than I would have if my obligation had been whimfully imposed by an arbitrary master. What matters to an agent is not only whether he is subject to the comprehensive concentrated control of a single alien will but whether what he does is subject to his own will. Accordingly, and here I turn this strategic objection to Raz against Nozick's own formulations, he, Nozick, should not have brought forth the motif of partial ownership rights in other people, but emphasized, instead, the predicament of lack of full ownership rights in oneself. Mere absence of self-ownership turns out, ironically, to be a more robust objection to enforced obligation than the ownership by another that was supposed to point up the awfulness of absence of self-ownership.

Does the indicated re-orientation of Nozick's argument make it safe? No, because there are two decisive objections to it, each of which turns on Nozick's own theoretical commitments. In two ways, those commitments disentitle him to say that welfare state redistribution is to be rejected because it makes the citizen's condition like that of a slave.

The first point is that citizens in the minimal state whose coercion Nozick regards as legitimate are obliged to pay taxes which support that state's coercive apparatus whether or not they want the protection they get in exchange. It is impossible to argue that an hour's labor that ends up as part of somebody's welfare payment is like slavery, while an hour's labor that ends up as part of a policeman's salary is not, when focus is on the condition of the putative slave himself. To be sure, and this is not here denied, if Nozick is right, then taxation for policemen is justified and taxation for the poor is not, because the principle of self-ownership, through a complicated argument to do with self-defence, licenses the first taxation and forbids the second. But the principle of self-ownership cannot here be invoked to distinguish the cases, nor, in particular, to show that one case is like slavery and the other is not, since the slavery consideration is here supposed to be an argument *for* the principle of self-ownership.

And a second internally based criticism of the suggested re-orientated form of the slavery argument (away from other-ownership and pivoting, now, on non-self-ownership) is also powerful. Nozick needs to distinguish between contractual obligations, which do not, in general, constitute slavery, and non-contractual obligations, which, so he says, do. Now, Nozick allows that a person might, in certain circumstances, voluntarily contract into full and, because contractually based, legitimate slavery: he would not say that what the contemplated person enters is not slavery because he enters it voluntarily. To be sure, this is not logically inconsistent with his further view that it distinguishes non-contractual obligations that they always betoken (at least partial) slavery, since that view is that they are sufficient, not necessary, for slavery. But Nozick must nevertheless explain why there is more slavery in every non-contractual obligation than there is in any contractual obligation (short of full slavery) regardless of why it was entered, and however close that contractual obligation comes to completely binding over all of a person's labor power. Pending further argument, it seems entirely arbitrary to rule that there cannot be a contractually based partial slavery, when there can be contractually based complete slavery.

54.
An Analysis of Ownership of Property*
A. M. HONORÉ

Ownership is one of the characteristic institutions of human society. A people to whom ownership was unknown, or who accorded it a minor place in their arrangements, who meant by *meum* and *tuum* no more than "what I (or you) presently hold" would live in a world that is not our world. Yet to see why their world would be different, and to assess the plausibility of vaguely conceived schemes to replace "ownership" by "public administration," or of vaguely stated claims that the importance of ownership has declined or its character changed in the twentieth century, we need first to have a clear idea of what ownership is.

I propose, therefore, to begin by giving an account of the standard incidents of ownership: *i.e.* those legal rights, duties and other incidents which apply, in the ordinary case, to the person who has the greatest interest in a thing admitted by a mature legal system. To do so will be to analyse the concept of ownership, by which I mean the "liberal" concept of "full" individual ownership, rather than any more restricted notion to which the same label may be attached in certain contexts.

• • •

If ownership is provisionally defined as the *greatest possible interest in a thing which a mature system of law recognizes,* then it follows that, since all mature systems admit the existence of "interests" in "things," all mature systems have, in a sense, a concept of ownership. Indeed, even primitive systems, like that of the Trobriand islanders, have rules by which certain persons, such as the "owners" of canoes, have greater interests in certain things than anyone else.

For mature legal systems it is possible to make a larger claim. In them certain important legal incidents are found, which are common to different systems. If it were not so, "He owns that umbrella," said in a purely English context, would mean something different from "He owns that umbrella," proferred as a translation of "Ce parapluie est à lui." Yet, as we know, they mean the same. There is indeed, a substantial similarity in the position of one who "owns" an umbrella in England, France, Russia, China, and any other modern country one may care to mention. Everywhere the "owner" can, in the simple uncomplicated case, in which no other person has an interest in the thing, use it, stop others using it, lend it, sell it or leave it by will. Nowhere may he use it to poke his neighbor in the ribs or to knock over his vase. Ownership,

*A slightly revised version of this essay was published in Tony Honoré, *Making Law Bind: Essays Legal and Philosophical* (Oxford: Oxford University Press, 1987). —eds.

dominium, propriété, Eigentum and similar words stand not merely for the greatest interest in things in particular systems but for a type of interest with common features transcending particular systems. It must surely be important to know what these common features are?

• • •

Nor must the present thesis be confused with the claim that all systems attach an equal importance to ownership (in the full, liberal sense) or regard the same things as capable of being owned. The latter claim would be patently false. In the Soviet Union, for instance, important assets such as land, businesses and collective farms are in general withdrawn from "personal ownership" (*viz.* the liberal type of ownership) and subjected to "government" or "collective" ownership, which is a different, though related institution. The notion of things "outside commerce," not subject to private ownership but to special regulation by the state or public authorities, is an ancient one and has retained its importance in modern continental law. Again, there is a case for saying that, in the early middle ages, land in England could not plausibly be said to be "owned" because the standard incidents of which I shall speak were so divided between lord and tenant that the position of neither presented a sufficient analogy with the paradigm case of owning a thing.

• • •

THE STANDARD INCIDENTS

I now list what appear to be the standard incidents of ownership. They may be regarded as necessary ingredients in the notion of ownership, in the sense that, if a system did not admit them, and did not provide for them to be united in a single person, we would conclude that it did not know the liberal concept of ownership, though it might still have a modified version of ownership, either of a primitive or sophisticated sort. But the listed incidents are not individually necessary, though they may be together sufficient, conditions for the person of inherence to be designated "owner" of a particular thing in a given system. As we have seen, the use of "owner" will extend to cases in which not all the listed incidents are present.

Ownership comprises the right to possess, the right to use, the right to manage, the right to the income of the thing, the right to the capital, the right to security, the rights or incidents of transmissibility and absence of term, the prohibition of harmful use, liability to execution, and the incident of residuarity: this makes eleven leading incidents. Obviously, there are alternative ways of classifying the incidents; moreover, it is fashionable to speak of ownership as if it were just a bundle of rights, in which case at least two items in the list would have to be omitted.

No doubt the concentration in the same person of the right (liberty) of using as one wishes, the right to exclude others, the power of alienating and an immunity from expropriation is a cardinal feature of the institution. Yet it would be a distortion—and one of which the eighteenth century, with its over-emphasis on subjective rights, was patently guilty—to speak as if this concentration of patiently garnered rights was the only legally or socially important characteristic of the owner's position. The present analysis, by emphasizing that the owner is subject to characteristic prohibitions and limitations, and that ownership comprises at least one important incident independent of the owner's choice, is an attempt to redress the balance.

(1) The right to possess

The right to possess, *viz.* to have exclusive physical control of a thing, or to have such control as the nature of the thing admits, is the foundation on which the whole superstructure of ownership rests. It may be divided into two aspects, the right (claim) to be put in exclusive control of a thing and the right to remain in control, *viz.* the claim that others should not without permission, interfere. Unless a legal system provides some rules and procedures for attaining these ends it cannot be said to protect ownership.

It is of the essence of the right to possess that it is *in rem* in the sense of availing against persons generally. This does not, of course, mean that an owner is necessarily entitled to exclude everyone from his property. We happily speak of the ownership of land, yet a largish number of officials have the right of entering on private land without the owner's consent, for some limited period and purpose. On the other hand, a general licence so to enter on the "property" of others would put an end to the institution of landowning as we now know it.

The protection of the right to possess (still using "possess" in the convenient, though over-simple, sense of "have exclusive physical control") should be sharply marked off from the protection of mere present possession. To exclude others from what one presently holds is an instinct found in babies and even, as Holmes points out, in animals, of which the seal gives a striking example. To sustain this instinct by legal rules is to protect possession but not, as such, to protect the right to possess and so not to protect ownership. If dispossession without the possessor's consent is, in general, forbidden, the possessor is given a right *in rem*, valid against persons generally, to remain undisturbed, but he has no *right to possess in rem* unless he is entitled to recover from persons generally what he has lost or had taken from him, and to obtain from them what is due to him but not yet handed over. Admittedly there may be borderline cases in which the right to possess is partially recognized, *e.g.* where a thief is entitled to recover from those who oust him and all claiming under them, but not from others.

The protection of the right to possess, and so of one essential element in ownership, is achieved only when there are rules allotting exclusive physical control to one person rather than another, and that not merely on the basis that the person who has such control at the moment is entitled to continue in control. When children understand that Christmas presents go not to the finder but to the child whose name is written on the outside of the parcel, when a primitive tribe has a rule that a dead man's things go not to the first taker but to his son or his sister's son, we know that they have at least an embryonic idea of ownership.

To have worked out the notion of "having a right to" as distinct from merely "having," or, if that is too subjective a way of putting it, of rules allocating things to people as opposed to rules merely forbidding forcible taking, was a major intellectual achievement. Without it society would have been impossible. Yet the distinction is apt to be overlooked by English lawyers, who are accustomed to the rule that every adverse possession is a root of title, *i.e.* gives rise to a right to possess, or at least that "*de facto* possession is *prima facie* evidence of seisin in fee and right to possession."[1]

The owner, then, has characteristically a battery of remedies in order to obtain, keep and, if necessary, get back the thing owned. Remedies such as the actions for ejectment and wrongful detention and the *vindicatio* are designed to enable the plaintiff either to obtain or to get back a thing, or at least to put some pressure on the defendant to hand it over. Others, such as the actions for trespass to land and goods, the Roman possessory interdicts and their modern counterparts are primarily directed towards enabling a present possessor to keep possession. Few of the remedies mentioned are confined to the owner; most of them are available also to persons with a right to possess falling short of ownership, and some to mere possessors. Conversely, there will be cases in which they are not available to the owner, for instance because he has voluntarily parted with possession for a temporary purpose, as by hiring the thing out. The availability of such remedies is clearly not a necessary and sufficient condition of owning a thing; what is necessary, in order that there may be ownership of things at all, is that such remedies shall be available to the owner in the usual case in which no other person has a right to exclude him from the thing.

(2) The right to use

The present incident and the next two overlap. On a wide interpretation of "use," management and income fall within use. On a narrow interpretation, "use" refers to the owner's personal use and enjoyment of the thing owned. On this interpretation it excludes management and income.

The right (liberty) to use at one's discretion has rightly been recognized as a cardinal feature of ownership, and the fact that, as we shall see, certain limitations on use also fall within the standard incidents of ownership does not detract from its importance, since the standard limitations are, in general, rather precisely defined, while the permissible types of use constitute an open list.

(3) The right to manage

The right to manage is the right to decide how and by whom the thing owned shall be used. This right depends, legally, on a cluster of powers, chiefly powers

---

[1] *N.R.M.A. Insurance, Ltd. v. B. & B. Shipping and Marine Salvage Co. (Pty.), Ltd.* (1947), 47 S.C.R. (N.S.W.) 273.

of licensing acts which would otherwise be unlawful and powers of contracting: the power to admit others to one's land, to permit others to use one's things, to define the limits of such permission, and to contract effectively in regard to the use (in the literal sense) and exploitation of the thing owned. An owner may not merely sit in his own deck chair but may validly license others to sit in it, lend it, impose conditions on the borrower, direct how it is to be painted or cleaned, contract for it to be mended in a particular way. This is the sphere of management in relation to a simple object like a deck chair. When we consider more complex cases, like the ownership of a business, the complex of powers which make up the right to manage seems still more prominent. The power to direct how resources are to be used and exploited is one of the cardinal types of economic and political power; the owner's legal powers of management are one, but only one possible basis for it. Many observers have drawn attention to the growth of managerial power divorced from legal ownership; in such cases it may be that we should speak of split ownership or redefine our notion of the thing owned. This does not affect the fact that the right to manage is an important element in the notion of ownership; indeed, the fact that we feel doubts in these cases whether the "legal owner" *really* owns is a testimony to its importance.

Management often takes the form of making contracts relating to the thing owned, whether with servants or agents or independent contractors. This fact, and the growing relative importance of management in comparison with personal use, at least in regard to some types of thing such as businesses, has led some observers to the neat conclusion that, over a wide sphere, *obligatio* has swallowed up *res*. Even if the contrast were an apt one (and, after all, an *obligatio* is a *res*, a chose in action a chose) the sentiment would be exaggerated because many powers of management are exercised otherwise than by way of contract, not to mention powers of alienation. The point would be better made by saying that, in the owner's battery of rights, powers have increased in calibre while liberties have declined.

(4) The right to the income

To use or occupy a thing may be regarded as the simplest way of deriving an income from it, of enjoying it. It is, for instance, expressly contemplated by the English income tax legislation that the rent-free use or occupation of a house is a form of income, and only the inconvenience of assessing and collecting the tax presumably prevents the extension of this principle to movables.

Income in the more ordinary sense (fruits, rents, profits) may be thought of as a surrogate of use, a benefit derived from forgoing personal use of a thing and allowing others to use it for reward; as a reward for work done in exploiting the thing; or as the brute product of a thing, made by nature or by other persons. Obviously the line to be drawn between the earned and unearned income from a thing cannot be firmly drawn.

The owner's right to the income, which has always, under one name or another, bulked large in an analysis of his rights, has assumed still greater significance with the increased importance of income relative to capital. Legally it takes the form of a claim sometimes *in rem,* sometimes *in personam* to the income. When the latter is in the form of money, the claim before receipt of the money is *in personam;* and since the income from many forms of property, such as shares and trust funds, is in this form, there is another opportunity for introducing the apophthegm that *obligatio* has swallowed up *res.*

(5) The right to the capital

The right to the capital consists in the power to alienate the thing and the liberty to consume, waste or destroy the whole or part of it: clearly it has an important economic aspect. The latter liberty need not be regarded as unrestricted; but a general provision requiring things to be conserved in the public interest, so far as not consumed by use in the ordinary way, would perhaps be inconsistent with the liberal idea of ownership.

Most people do not wilfully destroy permanent assets; hence the power of alienation is the more important aspect of the owner's right to the capital of the thing owned. This comprises the power to alienate during life or on death, by way of sale, mortgage, gift or other mode, to alienate a part of the thing and partially to alienate it. The power to alienate may be subdivided into the power to make a valid disposition of the thing and the power to transfer the holder's title (or occasionally a better title) to it. The two usually concur but may be separated. as when *A* has a power of appointment over property held by *B* in trust. Again, in some systems, a sale, mortgage, bequest, etc. may be regarded as valid though the seller or mortgagor cannot give a good title. By giving a good title is meant transferring to the transferee the rights of the owner including his power of alienation.

An owner normally has both the power of disposition and the power of transferring title. Disposition on death is not permitted in many primitive societies but seems to form an essential element in the mature notion of ownership. The tenacity of the right of testation once it has been recognized is shown by the Soviet experience. The earliest writers were hostile to inheritance, but gradually Soviet law has come to admit that citizens may dispose freely of their "personal property" on death, subject to limits not unlike those known elsewhere.

(6) The right to security

An important aspect of the owner's position is that he should be able to look forward to remaining owner indefinitely if he so chooses and he remains solvent. His right to do so may be called the right to security. Legally, this is in effect an immunity from expropriation, based on rules which provide that, apart from bankruptcy and execution for debt, the transmission of ownership is consensual.

However, a general right to security, availing against others, is consistent with the existence of a power to expropriate or divest in the state or public authorities. From the point of view of security of property, it is important that when expropriation takes place, adequate compensation should be paid; but a general power to expropriate subject to paying compensation would be fatal to the institution of ownership as we know it. Holmes' paradox, that where specific restitution of goods is not a normal remedy, expropriation and wrongful conversion are equivalent, obscures the vital distinction between acts which a legal system permits as rightful and those which it reprobates as wrongful: but if wrongful conversion were general and went unchecked, ownership as we know it would disappear, though damages were regularly paid.

In some systems, as (*semble*) English law, a private individual may destroy another's property without compensation when this is necessary in order to protect his own person or property from a greater danger. Such a rule is consistent with security of property only because of its exceptional character. Again, the state's (or local authority's) power of expropriation is usually limited to certain classes of thing and certain limited purposes. A general power to expropriate any property for any purpose would be inconsistent with the institution of ownership. If, under such a system, compensation were regularly paid, we might say either that ownership was not recognized in that system, or that money alone could be owned, "money" here meaning a strictly fungible claim on the resources on the community. As we shall see, "ownership" of such claims is not identical with the ownership of material objects and simple claims.

(7) The incident of transmissibility

It is often said that one of the main characteristics of the owner's interest is its "duration." In England, at least, the doctrine of estates made lawyers familiar with the notion of the "duration" of an interest and Maitland, in a luminous metaphor, spoke of estates as "projected upon the plane of time."[2]

Yet this notion is by no means as simple as it seems. What is called "unlimited" duration (*perpétuité*) comprises at least two elements (i) that the interest can be transmitted to the holder's successors and so on *ad infinitum* (The fact that in medieval land law all interests were considered "temporary" is one reason why the terminology of ownership failed to take root, with consequences which have endured long after the cause has disappeared); (ii) that it is not certain to determine at a future date. These two elements may be called "transmissibility" and "absence of term" respectively. We are here concerned with the former.

No one, as Austin points out, can enjoy a thing after he is dead (except vicariously) so that, in a sense, no interest can outlast death. But an interest which is transmissible to the holder's successors (persons designated by or closely related to the holder who obtain the property after him) is more valuable than one which stops with his death. This is so both because on alienation the alienee or, if transmissibility is generally recognized, the alienee's successors, are thereby enabled to enjoy the thing after the alienor's death so that a better price can be obtained for the thing, and because, even if alienation were not

[2] Pollock and Maitland, *History of English Law to 1290*, Vol. II, p. 10.

recognized, the present holder would by the very fact of transmissibility be dispensed *pro tanto* from making provision for his intestate heirs. Hence, for example, the moment when the tenant in fee acquired a heritable (though not yet fully alienable) right was a crucial moment in the evolution of the fee simple. Heritability by the state would not, of course, amount to transmissibility in the present sense: it is assumed that the transmission is in some sense *advantageous* to the transmitter.

Transmissibility can, of course, be admitted, yet stop short at the first, second or third generation of transmittees. The owner's interest is characterized by *indefinite* transmissibility, no limit being placed on the possible number of transmissions, though the nature of the thing may well limit the actual number.

In deference to the conventional view that the exercise of a right must depend on the choice of the holder, I have refrained from calling transmissibility a right. It is, however, clearly something in which the holder has an economic interest, and it may be that the notion of a right requires revision in order to take account of incidents not depending on the holder's choice which are nevertheless of value to him.

(8) The incident of absence of term

This is the second part of what is vaguely called "duration." The rules of a legal system usually seem to provide for determinate, indeterminate and determinable interests. The first are certain to determine at a future date or on the occurence of a future event which is certain to occur. In this class come leases for however long a term, copyrights, etc. Indeterminate interests are those, such as ownership and easements, to which no term is set. Should the holder live for ever, he would, in the ordinary way, be able to continue in the enjoyment of them for ever. Since human beings are mortal, he will in practice only be able to enjoy them for a limited period, after which the fate of his interest depends on its transmissibility. Again, since human beings are mortal, interests for life, whether of the holder of another, must be regarded as determinate. The notion of an indeterminate interest, in the full sense, therefore requires the notion of transmissibility, but, if the latter were not recognized, there would still be value to the holder in the fact that his interest was not due to determine on a fixed date or on the occurence of some contingency, like a general election, which is certain to occur sooner or later.

On inspection it will be found that what I have called indeterminate interests are really determinable. The rules of legal systems always provide some contingencies such as bankruptcy, sale in execution, or state expropriation on which the holder of an interest may lose it. It is true that in most of these cases the interest is technically said to be transmitted to a successor (*e.g.,* a trustee in bankruptcy) whereas in the case of determinable interests the interest is not so transmitted. Yet the substance of the matter is that the present holder may lose his interest in certain events. It is never, therefore, certain that, if the present holder and his successors so choose, the interest will never determine as long as the thing remains in existence. The notion of indeterminate interests can only be saved by regarding the purchaser in insolvency or execution, or the state, as succeeding to the same interest as that had by the previous holder. This is an implausible way of looking at the matter, because the expropriability and executability of a thing is not an incident of value to the owner, but a restriction on the owner's rights imposed in the social interest. It seems better, therefore, to deny the existence of indeterminate interests and to classify those which are not determinate according to the number and character of the contingencies on which they will determine. This affords a justification for speaking of a "determinable fee," of "fiduciary ownership" etc., for these do not differ essentially from "full ownership," determinable on bankruptcy or expropriation.

(9) The prohibition of harmful use

An owner's liberty to use and manage the thing owned as he chooses is in mature systems of law, as in primitive systems, subject to the condition that uses harmful to other members of society are forbidden. There may, indeed, be much dispute over what is to count as "harm" and to what extent give and take demands that minor inconvenience between neighbors shall be tolerated. Nevertheless, at least for material objects, one can always point to abuses which a legal system will not allow.

I may use my car freely but not in order to run my neighbor down, or to demolish his gate, or even to go on his land if he protests; nor may I drive uninsured. I may build on my land as I choose, but not in such a way that my building collapses on my neighbor's land. I may let off fireworks on Guy Fawkes night, but not in such a way as to set fire to my neighbor's house. These and similar limitations on the use of things are so familiar and so obviously essential to the existence of an orderly community that they are not often thought of as incidents of ownership; yet, without them "ownership" would be a destructive force.

(10) Liability to execution

Of a somewhat similar character is the liability of the owner's interest to be taken away from him for debt, either by execution of a judgment debt or on insolvency. Without such a general liability the growth of credit would be impeded and ownership would, again, be an instrument by which the owner could defraud his creditors. This incident, therefore, which may be called *executability,* seems to constitute one of the standard ingredients of the liberal idea of ownership.

It is a question whether any other limitations on ownership imposed in the social interest should be regarded as among its standard incidents. A good case can certainly be made for listing *liability to tax* and *expropriability by the state* as such. Although it is often convenient to contrast taxes on property with taxes on persons, all tax must ultimately be taken from something owned, whether a material object or a fund or a chose in action. A general rule exempting the owners of things from paying tax from those things would therefore make taxation impracticable. But it may be thought that to state the matter in this way is to obliterate the useful contrast between taxes on what is owned and taxes on what is earned. Although therefore, a society could not continue to exist without taxation, and although the amount of tax is commonly dependent on what the taxpayer owns or earns, and must be paid from his assets, I should not wish to press the case for the inclusion of liability to tax as a standard incident of ownership. Much the same will hold good of expropriability; for though some state or public expropriation takes place in every society, and though it is not easy to see how administration could continue without it, it tends to be restricted to special classes of property. We are left with the thought that it is, perhaps, a characteristic of ownership that the owner's claims are ultimately postponed to the claims of the public authority, even if only indirectly, in that the thing owned may, within defined limits, be taken from the owner in order to pay the expenses of running the state or to provide it with essential facilities.

55.

The Justification of Property Rights and Some Limitations on Them

LAWRENCE BECKER

I. JUSTIFICATIONS OF PROPERTY RIGHTS

Traditional accounts—in some cases as reformulated here or by other writers—supply four sound lines of argument for a general justification of private property. Briefly, and somewhat formally put, they are as follows:

Mill's Argument From Labor

(1a) When the labor is beyond what is required, morally, that one do for others; when it produces something which would not have existed except for it; and when its product is something others lose nothing by being excluded from; then it is not wrong for producers to exclude others from the possession, use, management, and so forth of the fruits of their labors.

(1b) Whenever giving producers ownership rights in the fruits of their labors is a justifiable way of excluding others (under the conditions of (1a)), then such ownership rights are justifiable.

The limitations of this argument have been pointed out in detail. . . . In particular, for competitive situations, the "no loss" criterion is a very stringent one. And the fact that property rights (in so far as they involve claim rights for the holder) entail duties for others toward the owners, makes the no loss requirement, (1a), even harder to satisfy.

The Argument From Desert for Labor

(2a) When it is beyond what morality requires them to do for others, people deserve some benefit for the value their (morally permissible) labor produces; conversely, they deserve some penalty for the disvalue their labor produces.

(2b) The benefits and penalties deserved are those proportional to the values and disvalues produced and those fitting for the type of labor done.

(2c) When, in terms of the purposes of the labor, nothing but property rights in the things produced can be considered a fitting benefit for the labor, and when the benefit provided by such rights is proportional to the value produced by the labor, the property rights are deserved.

When, in terms of the purposes of the labor, *either* property rights in the things produced *or* something else can be considered a fitting and proportional benefit, then either the property rights or one of the acceptable alternatives is deserved.

When, in terms of the purposes of the labor, property rights in the things produced cannot be considered a fitting benefit, or when the benefit of such rights is in excess of the values produced by the labor, the rights are not deserved.

(2d) Any diminution of value produced by the labor must be assessed against the laborer as a penalty deserved for the loss produced. (Penalties must be proportional to the loss produced, and a fitting remedy for that loss—fitting with respect to the purposes in terms of which it can be considered a loss.)

The soundness of (2a) is assumed—but not arbitrarily, for it meets the criteria for a primitive moral principle. The remaining steps are deduced from the concepts of desert, fittingness, benefit, and loss.

The Argument From Utility

(3a) People need to acquire, possess, use, and consume some things in order to achieve (the means to) a reasonable degree of individual happiness and general welfare.

(3b) Insecurity in possession and use, and uncontrolled acquisition of the things people need (and want) makes achievement of (the means to) a reasonable degree of individual happiness and general welfare impossible (or very unlikely).

(3c) Security in possession and use and control of acquisition is thus necessary. But it is impossible unless enforced by an institution which amounts to the administration of a system of property rights.

(3d) Therefore, a system of property rights is necessary (or very nearly so) if people are to achieve (the means to) a reasonable degree of individual happiness and general welfare.

The crucial premise is clearly the first one. It may be argued for in the following way:

(i)   People need to use and consume and possess some things merely for *survival* (food, shelter, etc.).
(ii)   People are purposive; the satisfaction of the propensity to purposive activity (not necessarily any particular purpose) requires the consumption, possession, and use of some raw materials, and the expectation of continued use, etc.
(iii) Acquisition, possession, and use is necessary to the development of personality, self-esteem, and valued abilities, and the subsequent expression of personality, confirmation of self-esteem, and use of valued abilities.
(iv)   Acquisition, possession, and use of things by one person can be a benefit to others as well as to the one who possesses, and occasionally the general welfare requires such acquisition and use by individuals.

The second and third premises may be extrapolated from the first—as in the traditional utility argument—or be argued for on independent grounds such as used by the general forms of economic utility arguments: cost-effective management of externalities and efficiency in resource allocation.

Utility thus provides a straightforward, clear, and convincing general justification for a system of property-right-making social institutions. Attempts to rebut its premises fail, in my judgment, and the *disutility* argument put forward by anti-property theorists has force only at the specific and particular levels of justification, not the general one.

The Argument From Political Liberty

(4a) It is a fact that human beings will acquire things, try to control them, exclude others from their use, modify them, and use them as wealth.

(4b) The effective prohibition of such activities—i.e. the elimination of private property—would require a comprehensive and continuous abridgment of people's liberty which is at best unjustifiable and at worst prohibited by the existence of political liberties to which people are entitled, morally.

(4c) The regulation of acquisitive activities, by what amounts to a system of property rights, is likewise required to preserve political liberties.

(4d) Therefore, property rights are justifiable.

The crucial premise here is (4b), and the justifiability of a (minimal) system of political liberties is all that is required: a system in which liberties are at least Hohfeldian liberty rights, and in which the liberty to survive by one's own efforts is guaranteed materially as well as formally. This much can be accomplished with the familiar strategies of hypothetical-social-contract theorists or with a strategy based on the concept of natural liberty.

• • •

II. LIMITATIONS ON PROPERTY RIGHTS

Duties to Others

If it can be established that we have positive duties of care toward others—that is, if beyond our negative duties not to do harm there are positive duties to do good—then the labor theory arguments are concomitantly restricted in their applicability. Each of the two sound labor arguments is limited to cases in which the labor at issue is other than what is morally required. So communitarians have an important opening wedge here against the "as long as it does no harm" argument. If I have a *prior* moral duty to contribute positively to the welfare of my fellows, then until that duty is fulfilled (or its fulfillment is guaranteed in some way), I cannot work for myself, so to speak. That is, neither version of the labor theory will in that case provide a sound basis for claiming property rights.

But there are two interesting features of this limitation. First, the moral duty to contribute (positively) to the welfare of others must have *priority* over any moral requirements to work for one's own good. That is, it is only "*prior*" moral duties which are at issue here now. It is reasonable to suppose that no positive duties to others could have priority over a requirement (if there is one) to do the (morally permissible) work necessary for one's own survival. And certainly many people would hold that one's positive duties to others cannot have priority over even one's *liberty right* to survive. That is, they would hold that there is no moral duty of (literal) self-sacrifice. But this is controversial, as is the further issue of whether "figurative" self-sacrifice—in the form of inconvenience, expenditure of effort, etc.—is ever a moral duty in the absence of undertaking some special role (e.g. parent, physician) or making some special agreement. What is interesting is just that this important moral question is tied so directly to two important lines of argument for property rights.

The second interesting feature of this limitation on labor arguments is that some of my (positive) duties of care may be only toward a few (my family, say). Thus it may be that while the labor I perform to fulfill duties to my family does not justify the acquisition of property rights *against my family,* it may justify the acquisition of property rights *for my family* (me included) against everyone else. Thus one has a basis for holding that a child's entitlement to food, clothing, shelter, and the like is not at all weakened by the fact that the parents produced these things by their own labor.

Exhaustibility

It is unlikely that any sort of property right could be justified whose implementation entails (or makes highly probable) the exhaustion of a significant resource by a subset of the total population. Such exhaustion would very likely constitute a loss to those left out, or be subject to prohibitive penalties for the losses caused, or amount to an interference with their liberty, or produce a net disutility, or perhaps all four. Either of the last two of these circumstances would be sufficient to prohibit it, in the absence of a conflicting requirement. And the exhaustion of a significant resource certainly would not be required by any of the lines of general justification (at least, I can think of no candidate for such a requirement).

Exhaustibility therefore will be a very large consideration in specific justifications. Goods such as space (in land, sea, or air) and matter can be exhausted simply by appropriation—that is, given the requisite system of property rights, a subset of the population can come to own all that is available.[1] Goods such as clean air and global water resources are exhaustible primarily by misuse rather than simple appropriation, but this is no less important for the theory of property rights. Uses which pollute the air or sea, for example, are likely to be prohibited by the general justifications of property, thus defining

---

[1] For a recent legal writing on this topic, see Lynton K. Caldwell, "Rights of Ownership or Rights of Use?—The Need for a New Conceptual Basis for Land Use Theory," *William and Mary Law Review,* 15: 759 (1974); and Donald W. Large, "This Land is Whose Land? Changing Concepts of Land as Property," *Wisconsin Law Review,* 1039–83 (1973); and McDougall, Lasswell, Vlasic and Smith, "The Enjoyment and Acquisition of Resources in Outer Space," *University of Pennsylvania Law Review,* 111: 521 at pp. 575 ff. (1963). The last is particularly helpful.

specific limitations on the use and management rights of owners. Goods such as fertile land, fresh water, fossil fuels, and wilderness areas are exhaustible either by appropriation or by misuse, and are also likely to be hedged with restrictions to prevent both.[2]

Technology and population size are important issues here. Things which were exhaustible only in principle several centuries ago are now in imminent danger of being exhausted. Specific justifications must change with such circumstances if nothing else (e.g. population policy) does; the justifiability of full, liberal ownership of land under the social conditions which existed in seventeenth-century North America does not guarantee that such property rights can be justified now. If they cannot, then the ownership rights in land must be redefined. And the question of injustice to current owners who possess the sort of title which is now unjustifiable, is not as serious as it might seem. In most cases, one probably will only need to change the rights of bequest and transfer so that only justifiable sorts of title may be passed on. This would leave the current owner's use, possessory, management, income, and security rights unchanged. And in situations so desperate that these rights must be redefined, compensation may be paid in lieu of honoring the right.

(It may be worth noting in passing that there *are* some goods which are not exhaustible by human agency—at least not with foreseeable technology. Sunlight and related radiation, magnetic energy, and electrical energy are all in this category. Materials used to convert these things to human use are exhaustible, of course. And sunlight can be blocked out. But the things themselves are not now vulnerable to exhaustion by appropriation or misuse.)

Accumulation

Limitations on the sorts of property rights which can be justified arise when goods are exhaustible, then. But they can also come from the fact that accumulations which are prior to or much larger than the acquisitions of others can constitute a loss of competitive advantage for those others, or a restriction of their material liberty, or a serious enough, and widespread enough, frustration of human purposes to cause significant social instability.[3] This is the stuff of popular revolutions, and it is safe to say that none of the general justifications would license a system of property rights which had *all* these effects.

Clearly, however, conflicts between the prohibitions and restrictions of utility on the one hand and liberty on the other are likely. This is another juncture at which the weight of priority attached to liberty is a leading problem. If liberty has priority, in Rawls's sense, then no "balancing" of utilities and liberties

---

[2] An interesting attempt to deal with this is Frank E. Maloney *et al., A Model Water Code, With Commentary* (Gainesville, University of Florida Press, 1972). For a critique, see Frank J. Trelease, "The Model Water Code, The Wise Administrator, and the Goddam Bureaucrat," *Natural Resources Journal,* 14: 207–29 (1974).

[3] For a discussion of some aspects of the current problem here, see John W. VanDoren, "Redistributing Wealth by Curtailing Inheritance," *Florida State University Law Review,* 3: 33–63 (1975).

is possible; the demands of liberty must be satisfied first. If utility is given priority, then the situation is reversed. If liberties and utilities are weighted, however, balancing is possible (e.g. if one's liberty to smoke is much less important than one's liberty to participate in the political process, and the importance of the latter is comparable to the importance of some disutility which would be suffered by permitting the liberty to smoke, then the liberty to smoke is outweighed by its disutility).

Goods for which problems of accumulation can arise include those exhaustible by appropriation. But the problems are particularly severe, in contemporary Western society, for liquid assets and the so-called "new forms of property" (e.g. management rights to corporate shares, pension funds, and trusts).[4] Accumulations of such wealth give the owners the power to influence political and social institutions to their advantage, and such advantages tend to snowball. Manipulation of the right of bequest is virtually useless as a way of dealing with the problem since trusts (and in the case of businesses, corporate management structures) are specifically designed to avoid the consequences of such manipulation. Revision of the tax system and what might be called "personal anti-trust legislation" are the primary devices which must now be used when restrictions on the accumulation of property are called for. The details of specific and particular justification will be very complex, but at least the guidelines from the analysis of general justification are reasonably straightforward.

Harmful Use

The (Millean) labor theory will not justify any use of property which represents a loss to someone other than the owner. Liberty requires that the use owners make of their property not interfere with the liberty to which people are entitled. And utility prohibits uses which have a net disutility. The "no harmful use" element of full, liberal ownership is therefore going to be a stringent one for goods which are dangerous. Use rights allowable for guns and pesticides, for example, are likely to be sharply limited. And in the case of hand guns, if significant disutility and loss of liberty to others is entailed by extensive private possession, it may be necessary to limit possession in order to satisfy the no harmful use requirement.[5]

Many restrictions on use imposed by the general justifications are identical with those alluded to under the headings of exhaustibility and accumulation. But use restrictions go beyond those others to provide, for example, a foundation for nuisance law and public safety law in cases where no problems of exhaustion or accumulation exist. The "life before property" rule also finds a foundation here.

---

[4] *Ibid,.* p. 33, n. 2.

[5] The case law on the no harmful use doctrine is fascinating. For a start, the reader might compare *Pennsylvania Coal Co. v. Sanderson* 113 Pa. 126, 6A. 453 (1886) in which a coal mining company was given the right virtually to destroy a stream; and *Just v. Marinette County* 56 Wisc. 2nd 7, 201 N.W.2^d 761 (1972) in which an individual landowner was fined for filling in a marshy area near a lake without a permit.

III. CONCLUSION

. . . Within the limits on ownership just discussed, the arguments from labor and liberty combine to produce a presumption in favor of allowing people to acquire full ownership (or whatever other variety they choose) of as much property as they want. Disutility significant enough to outweigh the labor and liberty arguments (assuming such balancing is morally permissible) can defeat the presumption, as can other considerations. . . . But once the disutilities of exhaustibility, accumulation, and harmful use are taken care of, other disutilities serious enough to outweigh the labor and liberty arguments are likely to be rare—especially since most ownership which has an overall disutility also has some significant utility as well. Within the limits discussed, then, the general justifications support a presumption in favor of a system of private property which allows as much ownership as individuals choose to have.

56.

A General Right to Property and Its Distributional Implications

JEREMY WALDRON

I. THE CHALLENGE: NOZICK AND MARX

Could private property be the subject of a general right? Is it something we could plausibly provide *for everyone* in the way we try to provide political rights, civil liberty, health, education and welfare? Or—to put it another way—is the ideal of a "property-owning democracy" anything more than a *petit-bourgeois* utopian pipe-dream? [1]

In this final chapter, I want to consider two negative answers to these questions which amount to quite radical challenges to the idea that private property could be one of the general rights of man. The challenges come from utterly different political perspectives.

(i) Nozick

The first comes from the Right and is most lucidly expressed in an argument adapted from Nozick's work.

A principle of justice requiring private property for everyone would, if implemented, soon be frustrated by the exercise of the very property rights that were distributed. Suppose access to and control of resources were distributed so that everyone was the owner of at least the share deemed necessary for liberty or ethical development by whatever GR-based argument we favored. What would happen subsequently when someone lost his shirt in a poker game or invested his share imprudently in an enterprise that went bust? The required pattern of distribution of private property would be disrupted by these events and the GR-based case for a distribution of private property would no longer be satisfied on a universal scale. But yet that would have happened as a result of the free exercise of the rights which it was the whole point of the argument to make available. As Nozick puts it:

> Any favored pattern would be transformed into one unfavored by the principle, by people choosing to act in various ways; for example, by people exchanging goods and services with other people, or giving things to other people, things the transferrers are entitled to under the favored distributional pattern. To maintain a pattern one must either continually interfere to stop

---

[1] The idea of a property-owning democracy is found in Rawls, *Theory of Justice*, (Cambridge, MA: Harvard University Press, 1971), p. 274.

people from transferring resources as they wish to, or continually (or periodically) interfere to take from some persons resources that others for some reason chose to transfer to them. (But if some time limit is to be set on how long people may keep resources others voluntarily transfer to them, why let them keep resources for *any* period of time? Why not have immediate confiscation?)[2]

(The answer to the last question, I suppose, will refer to difficulties of administration.) The point of Nozick's challenge in the present context is that the only way to ensure that everyone has a specified amount of private property seems to involve prohibiting or frustrating the exercise of the very rights which constitute the private property that we want everybody to have.

In my view this is the only interesting interpretation of what has become known as "the Wilt Chamberlain argument" in *Anarchy, State, and Utopia*. There is no doubt that Nozick intends it to establish a lot more: he intends it to establish that any theory of justice with an end-state or patterned component built into it would be oppressive or self-defeating or both. He purports to show that since voluntary actions by individuals with the holdings assigned to them will tend to upset patterns of distribution favored on grounds of social justice, attempts effectively to implement a theory of social justice over time are bound to be oppressive. But this is not shown. It is *not* always oppressive to prohibit people from trading in holdings or in goods assigned to them: everything depends on the basis on which the goods were distributed and received in the first place. Jobs, office furniture in a university, council-house tenancies, and so on are all goods received on the explicit understanding that they are to be used exclusively by the people to whom they are assigned but not to be transferred or traded by them. *Pace* Nozick, the fact that a given distribution D of these goods has been established does *not* show that "[t]here is no question about whether each of the people was entitled to control over the resources they held in D_1"[3] if "control" is supposed to include giving it to others (such as Wilt Chamberlain) in exchange for their holdings or services. As C. C. Ryan points out:

> [F]or any set of holdings, sustaining a pattern implies coercive restrictions (restrictions on personal liberty) only if the "holdings" are private property— holders have full rights of ownership in them. . . . *Without* the assumption that private property rights extend to all present and potential economic holdings, Nozick's general contention that sustaining patterns of distribution implies the restriction of liberty simply will not hold: if each individual's holdings are not assumed to be his private property, then there is no reason to conclude that restrictions on the "free exchange" of holdings constitutes coercion.[4]

---

[2] Nozick, *Anarchy, State, and Utopia* (New York: Basic Books, Inc., 1974), p. 163.

[3] Ibid. 161.

[4] Cheyney C. Ryan, "Yours, Mine, and Ours: Property and Liberty" in *Reading Nozick: Essays on Anarchy, State, and Utopia*. Jeffrey Paul, ed. (Oxford: Basil Blackwell, 1982), pp. 330–1.

It *is* oppressive, as Bentham pointed out, for legislators to frustrate expecta-tions which they themselves have engendered.[5] But it is not necessarily oppres-sive for them to discourage certain expectations from the start in the interests of justice. The Wilt Chamberlain argument does not, therefore, have the gen-eral force that Nozick thought it had.

However, if there are *independent* reasons for distributing holdings as pri-vate property, then the argument is important. For those independent rea-sons—for example, GR-based arguments for private property—may show that it is oppressive to say to citizens even at the outset that no economic hold-ing assigned to them may be dealt with as private property. If private property is what we think people need, we must not give it to them on terms which dero-gate, as it were, from its privacy. But if private property is what we want to dis-tribute on the basis of a certain pattern, then the very nature of the rights we are distributing will make it difficult for that pattern to be sustained.

(ii) Marx

The second attack comes from the opposite direction. It is the challenge laid down by Karl Marx in a furious response to bourgeois critics of the socialist program outlined in *The Communist Manifesto:*

> You are horrified at our intending to do away with private property. But in your existing society, private property is already done away with for nine tenths of the population; its existence for the few is solely due to its nonexis-tence in the hands of these nine-tenths. You reproach us, therefore, with in-tending to do away with a form of property the necessary condition for whose existence is the nonexistence of any property for the immense majority of so-ciety. In one word, you reproach us for intending to do away with your prop-erty. Precisely so; that is just what we intend.[6]

Throughout his work, Marx is adamant that the indictment against capitalism is not merely the fact that private property happens to be distributed unequally or in a way that leaves millions without any guaranteed access to the means of production; the problem is that private ownership is a form of property that has this characteristic *necessarily.* No matter how noble your egalitarian inten-tions, the existence of any distribution of private property rights in the means of production will lead quickly to their concentration in the hands of a few. Thus egalitarian intentions, so far as private property is concerned are hope-lessly utopian, for they underestimate the dynamic tendencies of the system they are interested in: "for us the issue cannot be the alteration of private prop-erty but its annihilation."[7] GR-based arguments for private property therefore

---

[5]   Jeremy Bentham, "Principles of the Civil Code" in *Theory of Legislation,* C. K. Ogden, ed. (Lon-don: Routledge and Kegan Paul, 1931), p. 113.

[6]   Karl Marx and F. Engels, *Communist Manifesto* (Harmondsworth: Penguin Books, 1967), p. 98.

[7]   See Karl Marx, "Address to the Communist League" in *Karl Marx: Selected Writings* (Oxford: Oxford University Press, 1977), p. 280.

would stand condemned on this approach just to the extent that they have egalitarian or quasi-egalitarian implications.

This is not Marx's only criticism of private property. The main critique throughout his work is . . . private property as a form for productive relations divides man from man, disguises the underlying co-operative nature of production and economic endeavor, and thus prevents the development of conscious and rational freedom in the economic sphere—the only sphere where man can find his true self-realization.[8] If there is a moral basis to Marx's indictment of capitalism, it is not a theory of equality but, as George Brenkert and others have argued, a theory of freedom.[9]

Nevertheless, according to Marx, it is no accident that *petit-bourgeois* theories of distributive justice are hopelessly impractical. They fly in the face of the logic of the institutions they purport to be dealing with:

> The justice of transactions between agents of production rests on the fact that these arise as natural consequences out of the production relationships. . . . [The content of a transaction] is just whenever it corresponds, is appropriate, to the mode of production. It is unjust whenever it contradicts that mode. Slavery on the basis of capitalist production is unjust; likewise fraud in the quality of commodities.[10]

But accumulation and the concentration of capital in a few hands, leading to mass propertylessness, is not only "appropriate to" a capitalist mode of production; it is its inevitable result.

There is a controversy as to whether Marx offers a moral indictment of injustice of capitalism at all.[11] Certainly, in *Capital,* Marx argues that capitalist exploitation depends on proletarian propertylessness—that is, on the worker being, as Marx put it ironically, "free in the double sense that . . . he can dispose of his labor power . . . and that, on the other hand, . . . he is *free* of all objects needed for the realization of his labor power"—and that it got under-way initially on the basis of forcible and bloody expropriation.[12] The justice of this process was dubious even relative to the relations of production prevailing at the time. But those relations were pre-capitalist relations and expropriation was in those circumstances a revolutionary act by the bourgeoisie against social and political forces stifling their progressive aspirations. Relative to the capitalist relations that it ushered in, that revolutionary beginning is (retrospectively) legitimate. Certainly, on the Marxian account, there is no suggestion either of the possibility or the desirability of rectificatory redress or reversal for any putative

---

[8] For Marx's attack on private property see e.g. "On the Jewish Question" in *Nonsense Upon Stilts.* Jeremy Waldron, ed. (London: Methuen, 1987), p. 146.

[9] George C. Brenkert, *Marx's Ethics of Freedom* (London: Routledge and Kegan Paul, 1983).

[10] Karl Marx, *Capital: A Critique of Political Economy,* Vol. III, 8. Engels, ed. (Moscow: Progress Publishers, 1971), pp. 339–40.

[11] The debate is aired in *Marx, Justice and History,* Marshall Cohen, ed. (Princeton: Princeton University Press, 1980).

[12] Karl Marx, *Capital: A Critique of Political Economy,* Vol. I, translated by Ben Fowkes (Harmondsworth: Penguin Books, 1976), p. 273. For capitalist accumulation, see ibid. Chs. 27–8.

injustice that accompanied the birth of capitalism. That would be a wholly reactionary step.

Often the most Marx appears to be saying is that private property is doomed
historically, that it is obsolescent, that it will eventually, under pressure, give
way to social control. If there is an evaluative dimension, it may be nothing
more substantial than a commitment to the value of historical progress: "From
the standpoint of a higher economic form of society, private ownership of the
globe by single individuals will appear quite as absurd [*abgeschmacht*] as private ownership of one man by another." [13] From this point of view, it is wrong
to see Marx *condemning* the inevitability of propertylessness under capitalism.
Nevertheless, even on this account, Marx is always prepared to get involved in
moral polemics in a characteristic "counter-punching" sort of way. If someone
offers to *defend* private property on the sort of moral grounds that we have
been considering, then Marx (as much as Proudhon) is ready to expose the contradictions and inconsistencies in that defense. That, I think, is the context of
the challenge we are considering. (I should add that, on Marx's view of ideology, it is to be expected that the historically transient and contradictory character of a form of society like capitalism should be reflected in similar
inconsistencies in the superstructural ideas involved in its defense.) [14]

• • •

Let us concentrate now on the tighter point posed by the Nozickian and Marxian challenges. Apart from the bare possibility that private property rights
could be exercised in a way which fortuitously sustained the pattern required
for their distribution, and leaving aside the suggestion that the direction of history is bound to defeat the ideal of a property-owning democracy, is it the case
that private property rights *as such* are essentially unamenable to the sort of distributional constraints that would flow, as we saw, from a GR-based argument?
If they are, then those arguments are not just utopian but self-contradictory. In
calling for something, they are also calling for the conditions that are bound to
defeat it.

Proudhon appears to have been convinced on this score. As we have seen,
his intention to show that "every argument which has been invented in behalf
of property, *whatever it may be,* always and of necessity leads to equality; that
is, to the negation of property." [15] Later he elaborated the indictment:

> They did not foresee, these old founders of the domain of property, that the
> perpetual and absolute right to retain one's estate,—a right which seemed to
> them equitable, because it was common,—involves the right to transfer, sell,

[13] Marx, *Capital,* Vol. III, p. 776.

[14] See Marx, "Preface to Critique of Political Economy" in *Karl Marx: Selected Writings,* David
McLellan, ed. (Oxford: Oxford University Press, 1977), p. 390.

[15] Pierre-Joseph Proudhon. *What is Property?,* translated by Benjamin R. Tucker (New York:
Dover Publications, 1970), pp. 39–40.

give, gain, and lose it; that it tends, consequently, to nothing less than the destruction of that equality which they established it to maintain.[16]

Now if the right to retain control of certain resources did involve these other powers, then the Wilt Chamberlain argument would apply and the objection would be sustained. Not only would we expect equality to be destroyed in a short time, but we would expect also that before long a large number of people would have little or no private property of their own at all and certainly much less than was deemed necessary for each individual by any plausible GR-based argument for that institution.

But . . . private property is a concept of which there are many conceptions. The tight logical connection that Proudhon saw between "the right to retain one's estate" on the one hand, and "the right to transfer, sell, give, gain, and lose it," on the other, does not exist. The various rights are separable in thought and in fact, and a conception of private property is imaginable in which individuals would be assigned an exclusive right to determine what use should be made of particular resources without their necessarily having the power to transfer that right, on their own initiative, to anyone else. Such a "no-transfer" system of private property might then in effect prevent disruption of the pattern of initial distribution, at least disruption of the sort envisaged in the Wilt Chamberlain argument.

It is, however, not enough simply to say that "no-transfer" conceptions of private property are conceivable, and that we can avail ourselves of them in order to avoid the present difficulties. Although private property is a concept of which there are many conceptions, we may not simply pluck the conception that we want to use out of the air. Just because a conception would help us to avoid a certain difficulty does not mean that we are entitled to use it. Everything depends, as always, on what the upshot is of the particular *argument* for private property that we want to deploy. If the argument focuses, for example, on the importance to individuals of being able to trade freely or to exercise virtues like generosity and discrimination in gift-giving, then it is clearly an argument for private property; but it is also an argument which requires exchange and which precludes any deployment of a "no-transfer" conception of the concept. If, on the other hand, it focuses purely on the importance to individuals of making responsible decisions about how to draw subsistence over a period of time from a given stock of resources, it may not require exchange and it need not rule out a "no-transfer" conception. To repeat: the conception of private property we adopt is not a matter of independent choice; it is the upshot of the arguments we are convinced by. (The same seems true of other contestable concepts in political philosophy. For example, we cannot simply opt for one conception of harm or another in the context of Mill's famous "Harm Principle." Everything depends on the arguments used to defend the "Harm Principle": for example, one set of arguments may have as its upshot a conception

---

[16] Ibid. 78.

of harm that necessarily includes moral offense; another set of arguments may have as its upshot a conception that excludes this.[17] Since our arguments are our connection with the considerations that ultimately *matter* to us, we should take their upshot more seriously than we take the results of any independent "conceptual analysis." For if we are really worried about the "proper" analysis of the concepts we are using, we can always express our conclusions in terms of fresh concepts, even ones we have newly invented.)

The objection we are considering, then, is an embarrassment primarily to those GR-based arguments for private property that lay great importance on individuals' being able to exercise powers of transfer. These arguments cannot avoid deploying a conception of ownership that includes powers whose exercise would generate the embarrassment that Nozick's and Proudhon's arguments predict. Fortunately, as a matter of fact, few of the arguments we are considering have this feature. Hegel thought it important that individuals should be able to withdraw their will from the objects in which they had "embodied" it; but in our interpretation of his account of the ethical importance of private property, that did not play a significant role. One argument we considered, however, did attribute importance to freedom of trade and contract: it was based on an idea of respect for the individual capacity to enter into arrangements and reach accommodations in the economic sphere with other individuals without the need for overarching direction, and on the view that this required respect for the arrangements and accommodations that were actually entered into. (The underlying notion here is respect for a capacity that is as distinctively human as the capacity to plan on a communal scale.) This argument, then, is prima facie vulnerable to the objection we are considering. It makes it a matter of importance that all individuals should have the wherewithal to enter into arrangements with others on matters of economic significance, but the result of the exercise of that capacity will almost certainly be that some individuals come in time to be deprived of the wherewithal to exercise it.

Moreover, even though Proudhon is wrong in discerning a *logical* connection between private property and powers of transfer, and even though our favorite argument for private property may permit as its upshot a "no-transfer" conception of ownership, still there may be other non-logical but none the less contingently important connections between being a private owner and having the power to transfer one's holding to another. . . . most societies that face the problem of allocation will also face the problem of *reallocation* from time to time as individuals' circumstances change. It will tend to be overwhelmingly inconvenient to call in all resources and redistribute them on every occasion when such changes are deemed appropriate, for those occasions are likely to be very numerous indeed. If there is any possibility at all that transfers arranged by individuals between individuals could solve the problem of reallocation, then that will appear the more attractive solution. This then is an independent reason (arising out of the allocation problem) for including a power of transfer in any practicable conception of ownership. (It is not, by the way, a reason for

---

[17] See Jeremy Waldron. "Mill and the Value of Moral Distress," in *Political Studies,* 35 (1987), Pt. 1.

instituting such a conception of ownership as opposed to a system of collective property, since in a collective regime the problem of reallocation can be solved much more easily; but it is a reason for adopting such a conception *if* we are already well-disposed towards private property.)

These points suggest that it may not be open to us to adopt a pure "no-transfer" conception of private property. But they suggest also that there may be room for compromise in other directions. Whether or not a conception of private property includes powers of transfer is not an all-or-nothing affair. To begin with, there are several powers to be considered: gift, sale and purchase, abandonment, bequest, inheritance, and so on. It is possible that the points just made could be met by a conception which included some of these powers but not others. Many people have argued that powers of transfer *post mortem,* such as bequest and inheritance, are much more inimical to equality than powers of transfer *inter vivos* such as sale and purchase: the disruption to a favored distribution of property caused by the latter may be trivial, whereas the former may upset distributional patterns in a more significant way.[18] It is possible that the powers whose exercise threatens the pattern are not those that our argument for property requires. For example, the principle of respecting the arrangements people have entered into may be thought to apply more to arrangements *inter vivos* than to *post mortem* arrangements.[19] Similarly, if the problem of reallocation is the source of our concern that powers of transfer should be included in a conception of ownership, it may be that this concern is much less in the case of the reallocation of deceased estates than it is in the case of goods that somebody is currently holding. As Bentham argued, a general principle of escheat (and redistribution by the state) does not threaten to disrupt expectations in the way that expropriation of living proprietors would.[20]

Further, we should remember that there are a number of different ways in which any given power of transfer may be limited or curtailed. An extreme case is one in which the purported exercise of the power is given no effect in law at all: a man purports to leave his estate to his friend, but because the system does not recognize a power of bequest that exercise is null and void. A much less extreme case is one in which transactions are taxed, either as far as the transferor is concerned (e.g. death and gift duties, payroll taxes, VAT, etc.), or as far as the transferee is concerned (e.g. income tax, capital gains tax, etc.). In this case, the transfer is recognized but made subject to certain conditions: for example, no one in New Zealand may make a gift of more than $10,000 without paying a proportion of that sum to the government in gift duty; and no one in Britain may receive income of any sort from another person without paying a (rather large) proportion of that to the state in income tax. When Nozick discusses taxes of this sort, he suggests that their intention is to defeat or partially to

---

[18] For arguments to this effect, see: C. A. R. Crosland, *The Future of Socialism* (London: Jonathan Cape, 1967), Ch. 12; and A. B. Atkinson, *Unequal Shares: Wealth in Britain* (Harmondsworth: Penguin Books, 1974), Ch. 3–4 et passim.

[19] See my discussion in "Locke's Account of Inheritance," *Journal of the History of Philosophy,* 19 (1981).

[20] Jeremy Bentham, "Supply without Burthern" in *Bentham's Economic Writings,* W. Stark, ed. (London: George Allen and Unwin, 1951), esp. pp. 290–4.

defeat the transaction or the point of the transaction.[21] This may be the case but it need not be. Suppose the *point* of my transferring a large sum of money to my son is to disrupt the pattern of the equal distribution of private property. Then it is true that the point of the gift duty we are considering would be to defeat that intention. But that is because the intention, in its content, is explicitly at odds with the ideas of rights, liberty, and justice as we conceive them; it does not seem oppressive in a society committed to those ideals to set out to defeat intentions which are calculated to undermine them. But most transfers will not be motivated in this way. For those that have ordinary commercial or philanthropic motivation, our fiscal experience suggests that taxation is *not* perceived as defeating or undermining the point of a transfer. People adjust their expectations of what they can do in transferring and receiving goods to the exigencies of the fiscal regime, and seem able to carry on transferring goods freely within the constraints it imposes. Once again, whether a power of transfer constrained by taxation is sufficient for the conception of ownership yielded by a particular GR-based argument will depend on the details of the argument. But it is difficult to imagine an argument placing such great value on absolutely untrammelled transfer that it required a conception of ownership that was stronger than this.

So far the argument has concerned the powers of transfer that might be connected with particular conceptions of private ownership. Our response to the objection has been that although many of the conceptions we are dealing with will involve powers of transfer, they will seldom involve any requirement that there should be *unlimited* powers of transfer. If the powers of transfer that we recognize are qualified by a system of taxation, understood to be imposed for the express purpose of maintaining a wide distribution of the property rights in question, then that system can be used to redress any disruption of the distributional patterns favored by the arguments which have generated the conceptions of private ownership that are giving us this difficulty.

We should note, however, that Proudhon does not rest his argument against private property purely on this putative incompatibility between equality and powers of transfer. At times he seems prepared to make an even stronger claim—that the very element of exclusive and indefinite control that private property involves is incompatible with the demand for equality that the arguments he is considering give rise to. Considering questions of First Occupancy, for example, he writes:

> For, since every man, from the fact of his existence, has the right of occupation, and, in order to live, must have material for cultivation on which he may labor; and since, on the other hand, the number of occupants varies continually with the births and deaths—it follows that the quantity of material which each laborer may claim varies with the number of occupants; consequently, that occupation is always subordinate to population. Finally, that, inasmuch as possession, in right, can never remain fixed, it is impossible, in fact, that it can ever become property. . . . *All have an equal right of occupancy. The*

---

[21] Nozick, *Anarchy, State, and Utopia,* pp. 163 and 167–8.

amount occupied being measured, not by the will, but by the variable conditions of space and number, property cannot exist.[22]

The suggestion is that private property involves the idea of the allocation of a resource to the control of a single individual for an indefinite period (or for a period determined only by his own say-so). But since the population varies, the number of people whose right to property must be satisfied varies with it, and the rightful demands placed on the stock of available resources will change accordingly. An increase in population will mean that the satisfaction of a universal right to property demands a reduction in the amount of resources allocated to individuals before the increase. Since such an increase is always likely, putative proprietors must always hold themselves ready to give up some of their resources in favor of newcomers. But holding resources in this spirit, Proudhon contends, is incompatible with the idea of property as that is usually understood.

Once again, no doubt there are conceptions of private property which make this a plausible objection. On some conceptions, a man cannot be said to be the owner of a resource if his holding is subject continually or even periodically to a redistributive wealth tax. The private property rights of each individual, on these conceptions, are absolutely resistant to redistributive considerations. But it seems unlikely that any of these conceptions will be the upshot of the GR-based arguments we have been considering; that is, it seems unlikely that any of those arguments will establish that private property must be either absolute in this sense or not worth having.

Whether the ethical importance of owning property is undermined significantly by periodic taxation will depend in part on how frequent, how drastic, and how unpredictable such taxation would have to be. If the population varies greatly at irregular intervals, and if the stock of resources available for private holdings remains constant or is liable to diminution, then there is a danger that the redistribution required to ensure that everyone has private property will make it almost impossible for individuals to make medium- or long-term plans about the use of the resources assigned to them. For example, if the population of a small society is periodically increased by the influx of large numbers of refugees, then land redistribution may be so drastic that farmers are unable to follow through on their own plans for development, crop rotation, and so on. In this case, Proudhon's objection is sustained: those to whom land is initially assigned hold it not as owners but, at best, as "usufructuaries," owing a duty to society at large to keep it in a condition where it can be easily transferred to the use of others.[23] In societies not subject to such vicissitudes, however, the effect will be much less drastic. For example, in a society where the birth-rate is not overwhelmingly greater than the death rate, and where the increase in population is matched by economic growth, the need for redistribution in favor of newcomers can possibly be accommodated by a system of taxation on deceased

---

[22] Proudhon, *What is Property?*, pp. 82–3.

[23] Proudhon, *What is Property*, p. 82.

estates, and the owners of property can be confident that their holdings will not normally be subject in their lifetime to compulsory and debilitating transfers.

In all of this, we should bear in mind the possibility of approaching the problem also from the other direction. The GR-based arguments we are considering have important distributive implications, as we have noticed. But, . . . they are not implications of strict egalitarianism or anything like it; they are requirements that everyone must have private property in some significant holding, not that everyone must have at most a certain or an equal amount. There is the further point that, though a given argument may require that everyone have property, it may not necessarily require that everyone should continue to be the owner of a significant holding at all times. Indeed, in relation to some arguments, a guarantee of this sort might be counter-productive: for example, it might diminish the contribution that owning property makes to the development of prudence, thrift, and responsibility. This means that the GR-based case for private property may allow for a certain amount of flexibility in distributive patterns. Those concerned for it need not be upset by every fluctuation in the relative wealth and fortunes of individuals. What they will be on the lookout for will be tendencies towards the accumulation of enormous holdings, particularly of capital resources, on the one hand, and the accompanying development of long-term propertylessness, on the other. The danger with these trends is that they give rise to the possibility of what Marxists have called "exploitative" economic relations—relations which are unwelcome in the present context, not because of their injustice or putative coerciveness, but because of the way in which they tend to preclude the autonomous development or occurrence of the sort of transactions and relationships which could shift the distributive balance back in a more egalitarian direction. When these trends become apparent, intervention will be necessary. It does not seem to be unduly optimistic or utopian to suggest that they can be kept in check, at least in a relatively prosperous society, by action which falls considerably short of threatening the very basis of individual ownership.

• • •

3. GENERAL AND SPECIAL RIGHTS AND THE CLAIMS OF NEED

. . . I argued that no SR-based system of private property would be acceptable if it were not qualified by a principle of provision for basic human needs.* No one can be expected voluntarily to refrain from using what is putatively the property of another if that is the only way he can see to satisfy his most pressing bodily needs. Since this is so, no one can agree in advance in good faith to abide by a system of property which has, as one of its rules, that an owner's decision to withold resources from the relief of desperate need must be respected.

---

* An SR-based system of private property is one that appeals to special rights—that is, rights that individuals have as a result of specific contingent events or transactions—Eds.

Accordingly, no system which included such a rule could possibly have been the subject of an original contract or agreement for the establishment of a just society.

This argument, however, does not merely concern the case for special rights. It is quite general in its application, and applies equally to the implementation of a GR-based case for private property. So the private property rights which are justified by a GR-based argument will be subject, not only to the distributive requirements which that argument itself is likely to generate, but also to this independently-grounded principle of need. . . . we discussed briefly the possibility that these requirements might conflict under conditions of great scarcity: *if* basic needs could be provided for more efficiently under a system of collective control of resources, then we would have to decide which of these considerations—the considerations invoked in the GR-based argument for private property or the considerations involved in the principle of need—should prevail. Fortunately, however, if the situation is not one of great scarcity or if the argument about the greater efficiency of collective provision does not go through, then the two principles will not conflict, and indeed are likely to converge, in terms of their practical implications. The argument for their convergence goes as follows. As we saw in our discussion of Hegel, a GR-based argument for private property is not satisfied by the assignment of one or two trivial or useless resources to each individual; it requires the assignment to individuals of resources that they take seriously as the basis of their individual economic well-being. Thus the universal distribution of private property required by a GR-based argument is likely, as a matter of fact, to satisfy the demands of the principle of need, for in seeing to it that everyone has private property, the proponents of that argument will also in effect be seeing to it that everyone has the wherewithal to satisfy his basic needs.

There is also perhaps a more subtle point involved here. The principle of need provides an independent basis for qualifying and restricting otherwise unlimited rights of private property. So even if it is true that a given GR-based argument for private property, considered on its own, requires something like absolute rights of ownership, not limited by any possibility of a wealth tax or by restrictions on traditional powers of transfer, still, when that argument is considered in conjunction with other independent moral considerations, such as the principle of need, the upshot is likely to be a system of limited property rights. In our discussion in the previous section, we did not think it likely that very many GR-based arguments would have such extreme implications. But if any did, there would have been contradictions of the sort to which Proudhon drew our attention: these would be arguments at the same time *for* private property on a certain conception and also, in so far as they had distributive implications, *against* private property on that conception. So long as such arguments are considered in isolation, that is a problem: they appear contradictory and self-defeating. But once their force is adjusted to take account of other moral considerations, the danger that they will be self-defeating in practice will disappear. The distributive implications generated by GR-based argument will converge in fact with the implications of principles which the argument would have had to be subject to in any case.

In an SR-based system of private property, there is no such convergence. SR-based arguments do not, as we have seen, have in themselves any universal distributive implications. Those who have got hold of resources (by the specified procedures) are entitled to retain exclusive control of them; those who have not have no right to have property at all. Though SR-based theories sometimes talk of private property as one of the rights of man, it is clear that they do not mean anything like a general right to be the owner of private property. They mean at most a conditional right to-be-an-owner-*if*-certain-events-or-transactions-have-taken-place. There is no basis for any suggestion that one person can demand respect from another for his property only on condition that he respect the other's property as well. The suggestion at most would be: "You should respect my property for I would respect yours if you had any." The principle of need, then, cuts right across the SR-based case for private property in a way that it does not cut across the GR-based case.

It may be objected that we have been, till now, far more generous to GR-based arguments for private property than to SR-based ones. For the former, we have been willing to argue that there are all sorts of different conceptions of private property, and to insist that the fact that an argument does not generate anything like a case for absolute property does not deprive it of all interest for us. The argument . . . might indicate that we are likely to be much more dismissive of an SR-based argument if it does not establish the absolutist conclusions that its proponents want it to establish. The point is perhaps a fair one. Partly it is a matter of tactics. Often proponents of an SR-based approach (such as Nozick) are endeavoring explicitly to use that approach as a basis for attacking redistribution, welfare provision, and any limitation on owners' control or powers of transfer over the resources they hold.[24] It is worth pointing out in the strongest possible terms that SR-based arguments fall woefully short of adequately establishing that sort of conclusion.

Having said that, we must beware of dismissing SR-based arguments altogether simply because they do not establish the extreme positions that their proponents want to occupy. The point of stressing throughout this work that private property is a concept of which there are several conceptions is to draw attention to the contribution that an argument may make to the debate about private property even when it fails woefully to vindicate absolute *laissez-faire* capitalism. The debate about the merits of different types of property system is not a simple one. Often, in the real world, we face questions like: "How and in what direction should the property institutions of a mixed economy be modified or reformed?" A modest argument in favor of private property, under some very mild conception, may make an important contribution to answering this question even if we are sceptical about its ability to generate a justification for a pure private property system. Of course, if an argument is simply incoherent, then it makes no contribution at all: this, I have urged, is how we should treat the literal interpretation of Locke's argument about the "mixing" of labor. But arguments can be weak in other ways, and their weakness does not always mean they should be ignored altogether. For ex-

[24] Nozick, *Anarchy, State, and Utopia,* Ch. 8.

ample, . . . I argued that a desert-based argument cannot be regarded as a plausible interpretation of the Lockean case for property since, among other things, it falls far short of generating the sort of conception of private property that Locke wanted to defend. But considerations of desert may still be relevant to the case for private property, and the argument based on desert—even if it cannot sustain the burden of justifying a system of private property—should not be dismissed until we are sure that it draws to our attention nothing that we ought to consider. Or, to take another example, we found that the idea of a person's *identifying* himself with an object (regarded by Olivecrona as crucial to Locke's theory of entitlement)[25] could not lie at the basis of a theory of entitlement, or in its "infrastructure" as Nozick puts it,[26] because the psychology of identification would already presuppose the stability of a set of property rules of a certain sort. Nevertheless, when we are considering, not which property system to *institute,* but rather where to go from here—how to reform already existing property institutions—the idea of identification will have an important role to play. For once a property system gets under way, it will be wrong simply to push aside people's expectations in the interests of distributive justice, even if those expectations have been generated by unjust institutions. The idea of identification, as a broadly SR-based consideration, helps explain why.

4. CONCLUDING REMARKS

This has been an exercise in the exploration of the space for argument in favor of private property. I wanted to consider what arguments were possible on a right-based approach and, in broad terms, what the conditions of their plausibility would be. The aim was not to *argue* in favor of private property, nor was it to extol the virtues of one form of argument against another. It was rather to sketch a map of the terrain of argument in this area—a map whose necessity was indicated by the disarray and disrepute into which the suggestion that private property was one of the rights of man had fallen.

As I indicated . . . , I began with the suspicion that quite radically different claims were being put forward under the rubric of *"The Right to Property"* and that no real progress could be made in assessing these claims until those differences were brought to the surface. I hope I have shown how deep-set the differences are between SR-based and GR-based modes of right-based argument. The former, associated with Lockean political theory, sees private property as a right that someone may have rather in the way that he has certain promissory or contractual rights; he has it because of what he has done or what has happened to him. The latter, associated in the last hundred years with Hegelian political theory, sees private property as a right that all men have rather in the way they are supposed to have the right to free speech or to an elementary education; not because they have contingently acquired it, but because its recognition

[25] Karl Olivecrona, "Locke's Theory of Appropriation" *Philosophical Quarterly,* 24 (1974).
[26] Nozick, *Anarchy, State, and Utopia,* p. 238.

is part and parcel of respect for them as free moral agents. These are basic differences in the *structure* of the respective moral positions: they are not merely differences in content. As we saw . . . , the structural difference may be elucidated in different ways: perhaps it is the difference between conditional and unconditional rights, though I preferred to view it as the difference between special or contingent rights and general rights which the holders were conceived to have *ab initio*.

However they are characterized, the differences have important practical implications. A GR-based argument is *radical* in its distributive implications: even if it is not obsessively egalitarian, it generates a requirement that private property, under some conception, is something all men must have. SR-based theories *may* have radical implications: if the procedures by which wealth has been accumulated in a society are not the procedures specified by the theory, then the theory may generate quite radical requirements as a matter of rectification. But the distributional implications inherent in the arguments are not radical: there is no case for distributing private property in resources more widely than those who have legitimately appropriated them choose to do.

These differences of structure and implication are not merely of academic interest. Politicians and theorists alike often try to bring the two strands of argument together in a single case, saying for example, that those who have acquired private property ought to be able to keep it since property is an indispensable condition for the development of a sense of individual responsibility. That juxtaposition needs to be exposed as fraudulent eclecticism, aligning as it does considerations that pull in different directions from utterly different and in fact mutually incompatible theoretical perspectives. Once this has been acknowledged, it may still be the case, as I suggested at the end of the previous section, that the two strands of argument both have contributions to make to the discussion of the moral importance of private property. But that discussion is not merely a matter of *assembling*, on one list, considerations in favor of private property and, on another list, considerations against. It must be informed by an understanding of how different considerations, with different provenances can be related to one another, and by an awareness of the difficulties as well as the possibilities of fitting them together into a single case. It is to that understanding that I have tried to make a contribution in the present work.

57.

Atomism and the Primacy of Rights

CHARLES TAYLOR

Theories which assert the primacy of rights are those which take as the fundamental, or at least a fundamental, principle of their political theory the ascription of certain rights to individuals and which deny the same status to a principle of belonging or obligation, that is a principle which states our obligation as men to belong to or sustain society, or a society of a certain type, or to obey authority or an authority of a certain type. Primacy-of-right theories in other words accept a principle ascribing rights to men as binding unconditionally, binding, that is, on men as such. But they do not accept as similarly unconditional a principle of belonging or obligation. Rather our obligation to belong to or sustain a society, or to obey its authorities, is seen as derivative, as laid on us conditionally, through our consent, or through its being to our advantage. The obligation to belong is derived in certain conditions from the more fundamental principle which ascribes rights.

The paradigm of primacy-of-right theories is plainly that of Locke. But there are contemporary theories of this kind, one of the best known in recent years being that of Robert Nozick. Nozick too makes the assertion of rights to individuals fundamental and then proceeds to discuss whether and in what conditions we can legitimately demand obedience to a state.

Primacy-of-right theories have been one of the formative influences on modern political consciousness. Thus arguments like that of Nozick have at least a surface plausibility for our contemporaries and sometimes considerably more. At the very least, opponents are brought up short, and have to ponder how to meet the claims of an argument, which reaches conclusions about political obedience which lie far outside the common sense of our society; and this because the starting point in individual rights has an undeniable prima facie force for us.

This is striking because it would not always have been so. In an earlier phase of Western civilization, of course, not to speak of other civilizations, these arguments would have seemed wildly eccentric and implausible. The very idea of starting an argument whose foundation was the rights of the individual would have been strange and puzzling—about as puzzling as if I were to start with the premise that the Queen rules by divine right. You might not dismiss what I said out of hand, but you would expect that I should at least have the sense to start with some less contentious premise and argue up to divine right, not take it as my starting point.

Why do we even begin to find it reasonable to start a political theory with an assertion of individual rights and to give these primacy? I want to argue that the answer to this question lies in the hold on us of what I have called atomism. Atomism represents a view about human nature and the human condition which (among other things) makes a doctrine of the primacy of rights plausible; or to put it negatively, it is a view in the absence of which this doctrine is suspect to the point of being virtually untenable.

How can we formulate this view? Perhaps the best way is to borrow the terms of the opposed thesis—the view that man is a social animal. One of the most influential formulations of this view is Aristotle's. He puts the point in terms of the notion of self-sufficiency (*autarkeia*). Man is a social animal, indeed a political animal, because he is not self-sufficient alone, and in an important sense is not self-sufficient outside a polis. Borrowing this term then we could say that atomism affirms the self-sufficiency of man alone or, if you prefer, of the individual.

That the primacy-of-rights doctrine needs a background of this kind may appear evident to some; but it needs to be argued because it is vigorously denied by others. And generally proponents of the doctrine are among the most vigorous deniers. They will not generally admit that the assertion of rights is dependent on any particular view about the nature of man, especially one as difficult to formulate and make clear as this. And to make their political theory dependent on a thesis formulated in just this way seems to be adding insult to injury. For if atomism means that man is self-sufficient alone, then surely it is a very questionable thesis.

What then does it mean to say that men are self-sufficient alone? That they would survive outside of society? Clearly, lots of men would not. And the best and luckiest would survive only in the most austere sense that they would not succumb. It would not be living as we know it. Surely proponents of the primacy of rights do not have to deny these brute facts. Just because one would fail a survival course and not live for a week if dropped north of Great Slave Lake with only a hatchet and a box of (waterproof) matches, does one have to stop writing books arguing for the minimal state on the basis of the inviolable rights of the individual?

Under the impact of this rhetorical question, one might be tempted to conclude that the whole effort to find a background for the arguments which start from rights is misguided. They do not seem to have anything to do with any beliefs. If we take the widely held view that normative questions are autonomous and not to be adjudicated by factual considerations, then why shouldn't a normative position in which rights are the ultimate standard be combinable with any set of factual beliefs about what men can and cannot do, and what society does or does not do for them?

From this point of view it would be a matter of uninteresting historical accident that the great classical theorists of atomism also held to some strange views about the historicity of a state of nature in which men lived without society. Indeed, one could argue that even they were not committed to the self-sufficiency of man as we defined the issue in the above paragraph. It was not only Hobbes who saw man's life in the state of nature as nasty, brutish, and short. All social contract theorists stressed the great and irresistible advantages that men gained from entering society. And in the case of Locke, one could claim that even his state of nature was not one of self-sufficiency in the sense of our survivor north of Great Slave Lake; rather it was clearly a condition of exchange and fairly developed and widespread social relations, in which only political authority was lacking.

Perhaps then we should not look for a background at all, and the whole enterprise of this paper is misguided. Readers who are convinced by this argument should, of course, stop here. But I am convinced that there is a lot more to be said.

To begin with, what is at stake is not self-sufficiency in the Great Slave Lake sense, but rather something else. What has been argued in the different theories of the social nature of man is not just that men cannot physically survive alone, but much more that they only develop their characteristically human capacities in society. The claim is that living in society is a necessary condition of the development of rationality, in some sense of this property, or of becoming a moral agent in the full sense of the term, or of becoming a fully responsible, autonomous being. These variations and other similar ones represent the different forms in which a thesis about man as a social animal have been or could be couched. What they have in common is the view that outside society, or in some variants outside certain kinds of society, our distinctively human capacities could not develop. From the standpoint of this thesis, too, it is irrelevant whether an organism born from a human womb would go on living in the wilderness; what is important is that this organism could not realize its specifically human potential.

But, one might argue, all this too is irrelevant to the individual-rights argument. Such argument is as independent of any thesis about the conditions of development of human potential, whatever this is, as it is of the conditions of survival in the wilderness. The argument simply affirms that justification of political authority ought to start from a foundation of individual rights. The proof of this independence is usually taken to be this: that plainly we do not deny rights to beings born of woman who lack the fully developed human potential, for instance infants. And if one objects that these are on the way to develop to full humanity, the reply is that we accord rights to lunatics, people in a coma, people who are irreversibly senile, and so on. Plainly, in our ordinary attribution of rights, we accord them to human beings as such, quite regardless of whether they have developed such potential or not. And so why should any thesis about the conditions for developing such potential be relevant to arguments about such rights?

• • •

The claim I am trying to make could be summed up in this way. (1) To ascribe the natural (not just legal) right of X to agent A is to affirm that A commands our respect, such that we are morally bound not to interfere with A's doing or enjoying of X. This means that to ascribe the right is far more than simply to issue the injunction: don't interfere with A's doing or enjoying X. The injunction can be issued, to self or others, without grounds, should we so choose. But to affirm the right is to say that a creature such as A lays a moral claim on us not to interfere. It thus also asserts something about A: A is such that this injunction is somehow inescapable.

(2) We may probe further and try to define what it is about A which makes the injunction inescapable. We can call this, whatever it is, A's essential property or properties, E. Then it is E (in our case, the essentially human capacities) which defines not only who are the bearers of rights but what they have rights to. A has a natural right to X, if doing or enjoying X is essentially part of manifesting E (e.g., if E is being a rational life-form, then A's have a natural right to life and also to the unimpeded development of rationality); or if X is a causally necessary condition of manifesting E (e.g., the ownership of property, which has been widely believed to be a necessary safe-guard of life or freedom, or a living wage).

(3) The assertion of a natural right, while it lays on us the injunction to respect A in his doing or enjoying of X, cannot but have other moral consequences as well. For if A is such that this injunction is inescapable and he is such in virtue of E, then E is of great moral worth and ought to be fostered and developed in a host of appropriate ways, and not just interfered with.

Hence asserting a right is more than issuing an injunction. It has an essential conceptual background, in some notion of the moral worth of certain properties or capacities, without which it would not make sense. Thus, for example, our position would be incomprehensible and incoherent, if we ascribed rights to human beings in respect of the specifically human capacities (such as the right to one's own convictions or to the free choice of one's life-style or profession) while at the same time denying that these capacities ought to be developed, or if we thought it a matter of indifference whether they were realized or stifled in ourselves or others.

From this we can see that the answer to our question of a few pages ago (why do we ascribe these rights to men and not to animals, rocks, or trees?) is quite straightforward. It is because men and women are the beings who exhibit certain capacities which are worthy of respect. The fact that we ascribe rights to idiots, people in a coma, bad men who have irretrievably turned their back on the proper development of these capacities, and so on, does not show that the capacities are irrelevant. It shows only that we have a powerful sense that the status of being a creature defined by its potential for these capacities cannot be lost. This sense has been given a rational account in certain ways, such as for instance by the belief in an immortal soul. But it is interestingly enough shared even by those who have rejected all such traditional rationales. We sense that in the incurable psychotic there runs a current of human life, where the definition of "human" may be uncertain but relates to the specifically human capacities; we sense that he has feelings that only a human being, a language-using animal can have, that his dreams and fantasies are those which only a human can have. Pushed however deep, and however distorted, his humanity cannot be eradicated.

If we look at another extreme case, that of persons in a terminal but long-lasting coma, it would seem that the sense that many have that the life-support machines should be disconnected is based partly on the feeling that the patients themselves, should they *per impossibile* be able to choose, would not want to continue, precisely because the range of human life has been shrunk here to zero.

How does the notion then arise that we can assert rights outside of a context of affirming the worth of certain capacities? The answer to this question will take us deep into the issue central to modern thought of the nature of the subject. We can give but a partial account here. There clearly are a wide number of different conceptions of the characteristically human capacities and thus differences too in what are recognized as rights. I will come back to this in another connection later.

But what is relevant for our purposes here is that there are some views of the properly human which give absolutely central importance to the freedom to choose one's own mode of life. Those who hold this ultra-liberal view are chary about allowing that the assertion of right involves any affirmation about realizing certain potentialities; for they fear that the affirming of any obligations will offer a pretext for the restriction of freedom. To say that we have a right to be free to choose our life-form must be to say that any choice is equally compatible with this principle of freedom and that no choices can be judged morally better or worse by this principle—although, of course, we might want to discriminate between them on the basis of other principles.

Thus if I have a right to do what I want with my property, then any disposition I choose is equally justifiable from the point of view of this principle: I may be judged uncharitable if I hoard it to myself and won't help those in need, or uncreative if I bury it in the ground and don't engage in interesting enterprises with it. But these latter criticisms arise from our accepting other moral standards, quite independent from the view that we have a right to do what we want with our own.

But this independence from a moral obligation of self-realization cannot be made good all around. All choices are equally valid; but they must be *choices*. The view that makes freedom of choice this absolute is one that exalts choice as a human capacity. It carries with it the demand that we become beings capable of choice, that we rise to the level of self-consciousness and autonomy where we can exercise choice, that we not remain enmired through fear, sloth, ignorance, or superstition in some code imposed by tradition, society, or fate which tells us how we should dispose of what belongs to us. Ultra-liberalism can only appear unconnected with any affirmation of worth and hence obligation of self-fulfilment, where people have come to accept the utterly facile moral psychology of traditional empiricism, according to which human agents possess the full capacity of choice as a given rather than as a potential which has to be developed.

If all this is valid, then the doctrine of the primacy of rights is not as independent as its proponents want to claim from considerations about human nature and the human social condition. For the doctrine could be undermined by arguments which succeeded in showing that men were not self-sufficient in the sense of the above argument—that is, that they could not develop their characteristically human potentialities outside of society or outside of certain kinds of society. The doctrine would in this sense be dependent on an atomist thesis, which affirms this kind of self-sufficiency.

The connection I want to establish here can be made following the earlier discussion of the background of rights. If we cannot ascribe natural rights without affirming the worth of certain human capacities, and if this affirmation has other normative consequences (i.e., that we should foster and nurture these capacities in ourselves and others), then any proof that these capacities can only develop in society or in a society of a certain kind is a proof that we ought to belong to or sustain society or this kind of society. But then, provided a social (i.e., an anti-atomist) thesis of the right kind can be true, an assertion of the primacy of rights is impossible; for to assert the rights in question is to affirm the capacities, and granted the social thesis is true concerning these capacities, this commits us to an obligation to belong. This will be as fundamental as the assertion of rights, because it will be inseparable from it. So that it would be incoherent to try to assert the rights, while denying the obligation or giving it the status of optional extra which we may or may not contract; this assertion is what the primacy doctrine makes.

The normative incoherence becomes evident if we see what it would be to assert the primacy of rights in the face of such a social thesis. Let us accept, for the sake of this argument, the view that men cannot develop the fullness of moral autonomy—that is, the capacity to form independent moral convictions—outside a political culture sustained by institutions of political participation and guarantees of personal independence. In fact, I do not think this thesis is true as it stands, although I do believe that a much more complicated view, formed from this one by adding a number of significant reservations, is tenable. But for the sake of simplicity let us accept this thesis in order to see the logic of the arguments.

Now if we assert the right to one's own independent moral convictions, we cannot in the face of this social thesis go on to assert the primacy of rights, that is, claim that we are not under obligation "by nature" to belong to and sustain a society of the relevant type. We could not, for instance, unreservedly assert our right in the face of, or at the expense of, such a society; in the event of conflict we should have to acknowledge that we were legitimately pulled both ways. For in undermining such a society we should be making the activity defended by the right assertion impossible of realization. But if we are justified in asserting the right, we cannot be justified in our undermining; for the same considerations which justify the first condemn the second.

In whatever way the conflict might arise it poses a moral dilemma for us. It may be that we have already been formed in this culture and that the demise of this mode of society will not deprive us of this capacity. But in asserting our rights to the point of destroying the society, we should be depriving all those who follow after us of the exercise of the same capacity. To believe that there is a right to independent moral convictions must be to believe that the exercise of the relevant capacity is a human good. But then it cannot be right, if no over-riding considerations intervene, to act so as to make this good less available to others, even though in so doing I could not be said to be depriving them of their rights.

The incoherence of asserting primacy of rights is even clearer if we imagine another way in which the conflict could arise: that, in destroying the society, I would be undermining my own future ability to realize this capacity. For then in defending my right, I should be condemning myself to what I should have to acknowledge as a truncated mode of life, in virtue of the same considerations that make me affirm the right. And this would be a paradoxical thing to defend as an affirmation of my rights—in the same way as it would be paradoxical for me to offer to defend you against those who menace your freedom by hiding you in my deep freeze. I would have to have misunderstood what freedom is all about; and similarly in the above case, I should have lost my grasp of what affirming a right is.

We could put the point in another way. The affirmation of certain rights involves us in affirming the worth of certain capacities and thus in accepting certain standards by which a life may be judged full or truncated. We cannot then sensibly claim the morality of a truncated form of life for people on the ground of defending their rights. Would I be respecting your right to life if I agreed to leave you alive in a hospital bed, in an irreversible coma, hooked up to life-support machines? Or suppose I offered to use my new machine to erase totally your personality and memories and give you quite different ones? These questions are inescapably rhetorical. We cannot take them seriously as genuine questions because of the whole set of intuitions which surround our affirmation of the right to life. We assert this right because human life has a certain worth; but exactly wherein it has worth is negated by the appalling conditions I am offering you. That is why the offer is a sick joke, the lines of the mad scientist in a B movie.

It is the mad scientist's question, and not the question whether the person in the coma still enjoys rights, which should be decisive for the issue of whether asserting rights involves affirming the worth of certain capacities. For the latter question just probes the conditions of a right being valid; whereas the former shows us what it is to respect a right and hence what is really being asserted in a rights claim. It enables us to see what else we are committed to in asserting a right.

How would it do for the scientist to say, "Well, I have respected his right to *life*, it is other rights (free movement, exercise of his profession, etc.) which I have violated"? For the separation in this context is absurd. True, we do sometimes enumerate these and other rights. But the right to life could never have been understood as excluding all these activities, as a right just to biological non-death in a coma. It is incomprehensible how anyone could assert a right to life meaning just this. "Who calls that living?" would be the standard reaction. We could understand such an exiguous definition of life in the context of forensic medicine, for instance, but not in the affirmation of a right to life. And this is because the right-assertion is also an affirmation of worth, and this would be incomprehensible on behalf of this shadow of life.

If these arguments are valid, then the terms of the arguments are very different from what they are seen to be by most believers in the primacy of rights. Nozick, for instance, seems to feel that he can start from our intuitions that people have certain rights to dispose, say, of what they own so long as they harm no one else in doing so; and that we can build up (or fail to build up) a case for legitimate allegiance to certain forms of society and/or authority from this basis, by showing how they do not violate the rights. But he does not recognize that asserting rights itself involves acknowledging an obligation to belong. If the above considerations are valid, one cannot just baldly start with such an assertion of primacy. We would have to show that the relevant potentially mediating social theses are not valid; or, in other terms, we would have to defend a thesis of social atomism, that men are self-sufficient outside of society. We would have to establish the validity of arguing from the primacy of right.

But we can still try to resist this conclusion, in two ways. We can resist it first of all in asserting a certain schedule of rights. Suppose I make the basic right I assert that to life, on the grounds of sentience. This I understand in the broad sense that includes also other animals. Now sentience, as was said above, is not a capacity which can be realized or remain undeveloped; living things have it, and in dying they fail to have it; and there is an end to it. This is not to say that there are not conditions of severe impairment which constitute an infringement on sentient life, short of death. And clearly a right to life based on sentience would rule out accepting the mad scientist's offer just as much as any other conception of this right. But sentient life, while it can be impaired, is not a potential which we must develop and frequently fail to develop, as is the capacity to be a morally autonomous agent, or the capacity for self-determining freedom, or the capacity for the full realization of our talents.

But if we are not dealing with a capacity which can be underdeveloped in this sense, then there is no room for a thesis about the conditions of its development, whether social or otherwise. No social thesis is relevant. We are sentient beings whatever the social organization (or lack of it) of our existence; and if our basic right is to life, and the grounds of this right concern sentience (being capable of self-feeling, of desire and its satisfaction/frustration, of experiencing pain and pleasure), then surely we are beings of this kind in any society or none. In this regard we are surely self-sufficient.

I am not sure that even this is true—that is, that we really are self-sufficient even in regard to sentience. But it certainly is widely thought likely that we are. And therefore it is not surprising that the turn to theories of the primacy of rights goes along with an accentuation of the right to life which stresses life as sentience. For Hobbes our attachment to life is our desire to go on being agents of desire. The connection is not hard to understand. Social theories require a conception of the properly human life which is such that we are not assured it by simply being alive, but it must be developed and it can fail to be developed; on this basis they can argue that society or a certain form of society is the essential condition of this development. But Hobbesian nominalism involves rejecting utterly all such talk of forms or qualities of life which are properly human. Man is a being with desires, all of them on the same level. "Whatsoever is the object of any man's desire . . . that is it which he for his part calleth good." [1] At one stroke there is no further room for a social thesis; and at the same time the right to life is interpreted in terms of desire. To be alive now in the meaning of the act is to be an agent of desires.

So we can escape the whole argument about self-sufficiency, it would seem, by making our schedule of rights sparse enough. Primacy-of-rights talk tends to go with a tough-mindedness which dismisses discussion of the properly human life-form as empty and metaphysical. From within its philosophical position, it is impregnable; but this does not mean that it is not still open to objection.

For the impregnability is purchased at a high price. To affirm a right for man merely *qua* desiring being, or a being feeling pleasure and pain, is to restrict his rights to those of life, desire-fulfilment, and freedom and pain. Other widely claimed rights, like freedom, enter only as means to these basic ones. If one is a monster of (at least attempted) consistency, like Hobbes, then one will be willing to stick to this exiguous conception of rights regardless of the consequences. But even then the question will arise of what on this view is the value of human as against animal life; and of whether it really is not a violation of people's rights if we transform them, unknown to themselves, into child-like lotus-eaters, say, by injecting them with some drug.

In fact, most of those who want to affirm the primacy of rights are more interested in asserting the right of freedom, and moreover, in a sense which can only be attributed to humans, freedom to choose life plans, to dispose of possessions, to form one's own convictions and within reason act on them, and so on. But then we are dealing with capacities which do not simply belong to us in virtue of being alive—capacities which at least in some cases can fail to be properly developed; thus, the question of the proper conditions for their development arises.

We might query whether this is so with one of the freedoms mentioned above—that to dispose of one's own possessions. This is the right to property which has figured prominently with the right to life in the schedules put forward by defenders of primacy. Surely this right, while not something we can attribute to an animal, does not presuppose a capacity which could fail to be developed, at least for normal adults! We all are capable of possessing things, of knowing what we possess, and of deciding what we want to do with these possessions. This right does not seem to presuppose a capacity needing development, as does the right to profess independent convictions, for instance.

But those who assert this right almost always are affirming a capacity which we can fail to develop. And this becomes evident when we probe the reason for asserting this right. The standard answer, which comes to us from Locke, is that we need the right to property as an essential underpinning of life. But this is patently not true. Men have survived very well in communal societies all the way from paleolithic hunting clans through the Inca empire to contemporary China. And if one protests that the issue is not under what conditions one would not starve to death, but rather under what conditions one is independent

[1]   Thomas Hobbes, *Leviathan,* I, chap. 6.

enough of society not to be at its mercy for one's life, then the answer is that, if the whole point is being secure in my life, then I would be at less risk of death from agents of my own society in the contemporary Chinese commune than I would be in contemporary Chile. The property regime is hardly the only relevant variable.

But the real point is this: supposing a proponent of the right to property were to admit that the above was true—that the right to property does not as such secure life—would he change his mind? And the answer is, in the vast majority of cases, no. For what is at stake for him is not just life, but life in freedom. My life is safe in a Chinese commune, he might agree, but that is so only for so long as I keep quiet and do not profess heterodox opinions; otherwise the risks are very great. Private property is seen as essential, because it is thought to be an essential part of a life of genuine independence. But realizing a life of this form involves developing the capacity to act and choose in a genuinely independent way. And here the issue of whether a relevant social thesis is not valid can arise.

Hence this way of resisting the necessity of arguing for self-sufficiency (by scaling down one's schedules of rights to mere sentience or desire) is hardly likely to appeal to most proponents of primacy—once they understand the price they pay. For it involves sacrificing the central good of freedom, which it is their principal motive to safe-guard.

There remains another way of avoiding the issue. A proponent of primacy could admit that the question arises of the conditions for the development of the relevant capacities; he could even agree that a human being entirely alone could not possibly develop them (this is pretty hard to contest: wolf-boys are not candidates for properly human freedoms), and yet argue that society in the relevant sense was not necessary.

Certainly humans need others in order to develop as full human beings, he would agree. We must all be nurtured by others as children. We can only flourish as adults in relationship with friends, mates, children, and so on. But all this has nothing to do with any obligations to belong to political society. The argument about the state of nature should never have been taken as applying to human beings alone in the wilderness. This is a Rousseauian gloss, but is clearly not the conception of the state of nature with Locke, for instance. Rather it is clear that men must live in families (however families are constituted); that they need families even to grow up human; and that they continue to need them to express an important part of their humanity.

But what obligations to belong does this put on them? It gives us obligations in regard to our parents. But these are obligations of gratitude, and are of a different kind; for when we are ready to discharge these obligations our parents are no longer essential conditions of our human development. The corresponding obligations are to our children, to give them what we have been given; and for the rest we owe a debt to those with whom we are linked in marriage, friendship, association, and the like. But all this is perfectly acceptable to a proponent of the primacy of rights. For all obligations to other adults are freely taken on in contracting marriage, friendships, and the like; there is no natural obligation to belong. The only involuntary associations are those between generations: our obligations to our parents and those to our children (if we can think of these as involuntary associations, since no one picks his children in the process of natural generation). But these are obligations to specific people and do not necessarily involve continuing associations; and they are neither of them cases where the obligation arises in the way it does in the social thesis, viz., that we must maintain the association as a condition of our continued development.

Hence we can accommodate whatever is valid in the social thesis without any danger to the primacy of rights. Family obligations and obligations of friendship can be kept separate from any obligations to belong.

I do not think that this argument will hold. But I cannot really undertake to refute it here, not just on the usual cowardly grounds of lack of space, but because we enter here precisely on the central issue of the human condition which divides atomism from social theories. And this issue concerning as it does the human condition cannot be settled in a knockdown argument. My aim in this paper was just to show that it is an issue, and therefore has to be addressed by proponents of primacy. For this purpose I would like to lay out some considerations to which I subscribe, but of which I can do no more than sketch an outline in these pages.

The kind of freedom valued by the protagonists of the primacy of rights, and indeed by many others of us as well, is a freedom by which men are capable of conceiving alternatives and arriving at a definition of what they really want, as well as discerning what commands their adherence or their allegiance. This kind of freedom is unavailable to one whose sympathies and horizons are so narrow that he can conceive only one way of life, for whom indeed the very notion of a way of life which is *his* as against everyone's has no sense. Nor is it available to one who is riveted by fear of the unknown to one familiar life-form, or who has been so formed in suspicion and hate of outsiders that he can never put himself in their place. Moreover, this capacity to conceive alternatives must not only be available for the less important choices of one's life. The greatest bigot or the narrowest xenophobe can ponder whether to have Dover sole or Wiener schnitzel for dinner. What is truly important is that one be able to exercise autonomy in the basic issues of life, in one's most important commitments.

Now, it is very dubious whether the developed capacity for this kind of autonomy can arise simply within the family. Of course, men may learn, and perhaps in part must learn, this from those close to them. But my question is whether this kind of capacity can develop within the compass of a single family. Surely it is something which only develops within an entire civilization. Think of the developments of art, philosophy, theology, science, of the evolving practices of politics and social organization, which have contributed to the historic birth of this aspiration to freedom, to making this ideal of autonomy a comprehensible goal men can aim at—something which is in their universe of potential aspiration (and it is not yet so for all men, and may never be).

But this civilization was not only necessary for the genesis of freedom. How could successive generations discover what it is to be an autonomous agent, to have one's own way of feeling, of acting, of expression, which cannot be simply derived from authoritative models? This is an identity, a way of understanding themselves, which men are not born with. They have to acquire it. And they do not in every society; nor do they all successfully come to terms with it in ours. But how can they acquire it unless it is implicit in at least some of their common practices, in the ways that they recognize and treat each other in their common life (for instance, in the acknowledgment of certain rights), or in the manner in which they deliberate with or address each other, or in the manner in which they deliberate with or address each other, or engage in economic exchange, or in some mode of public recognition of individuality and the worth of autonomy?

Thus we live in a world in which there is such a thing as public debate about moral and political questions and other basic issues. We constantly forget how remarkable that is, how it did not have to be so, and may one day no longer be so. What would happen to our capacity to be free agents if this debate should die away, or if the more specialized debate among intellectuals who attempt to define and clarify the alternatives facing us should also cease, or if the attempts to bring the culture of the past to life again as well as the drives to cultural innovation were to fall off? What would there be left to choose between? And if the atrophy went beyond a certain point, could we speak of choice at all? How long would we go on understanding what autonomous choice was? Again, what would happen if our legal culture were not constantly sustained by a contact with our traditions of the rule of law and a confrontation with our contemporary moral institutions? Would we have as sure a grasp of what the rule of law and the defence of rights required?

In other words, the free individual or autonomous moral agent can only achieve and maintain his identity in a certain type of culture, some of whose facets and activities I have briefly referred to. But these and others of the same significance do not come into existence spontaneously each successive instant. They are carried on in institutions and associations which require stability and continuity and frequently also support from society as a whole—almost always the moral support of being commonly recognized as important, but frequently also considerable material support. These bearers of our culture include museums, symphony orchestras, universities, laboratories, political parties, law courts, representative assemblies, newspapers, publishing houses, television stations, and so on. And I have to mention also the mundane elements of infrastructure without which we could not carry on these higher activities: buildings, railroads, sewage plants, power grids, and so on. Thus requirement of a living and varied culture is also the requirement of a complex and integrated society, which is willing and able to support all these institutions.

I am arguing that the free individual of the West is only what he is by virtue of the whole society and civilization which brought him to be and which nourishes him; that our families can only form us up to this capacity and these aspirations because they are set in this civilization; and that a family alone outside of this context—the real old patriarchal family—was a quite different animal which never tended these horizons. And I want to claim finally that all this creates a significant obligation to belong for whoever would affirm the value of this freedom; this includes all those who want to assert rights either to this freedom or for its sake.

One could answer this by saying that the role of my civilization in forming me is a thing of the past; that, once adult, I have the capacity to be an autonomous being; and that I have no further obligation arising out of the exigencies of my development to sustain this civilization. I doubt whether this is in fact true; I doubt whether we could maintain our sense of ourselves as autonomous beings or whether even only a heroic few of us would succeed in doing so, if this liberal civilization of ours were to be thoroughly destroyed. I hope never to have to make the experiment. But even if we could, the considerations advanced a few pages back would be sufficient here: future generations will need this civilization to reach these aspirations; and if we affirm their worth, we have an obligation to make them available to others. This obligation is only increased if we ourselves have benefited from this civilization and have been enabled to become free agents ourselves.

But then the proponent of primacy could answer by questioning what all this has to do with political authority, with the obligation to belong to a polity or to abide by the rules of a political society. Certainly, we could accept that we are only what we are in virtue of living in a civilization and hence in a large society, since a family or clan could not sustain this. But this does not mean that we must accept allegiance to a polity.

To this there are two responses. First, there is something persuasive about this objection in that it seems to hold out the alternative of an anarchist civilization—one where we have all the benefits of wide association and none of the pains of politics. And indeed, some libertarians come close to espousing an anarchist position and express sympathy for anarchism, as does Nozick. Now it is perfectly true that there is nothing in principle which excludes anarchism in the reflection that we owe our identity as free men to our civilization. But the point is that the commitment we recognize in affirming the worth of this freedom is a commitment to this civilization whatever are the conditions of its survival. If these can be assured in conditions of anarchy, that is very fortunate. But if they can only be assured under some form of representative government to which we all would have to give allegiance, then this is the society we ought to try to create and sustain and belong to. For this is by hypothesis the condition of what we have identified as a crucial human good, by the very fact of affirming this right. (I have, of course, taken as evident that this civilization could not be assured by some tyrannical form of government, because the civilization I am talking about is that which is the essential milieu for free agency.)

The crucial point here is this: since the free individual can only maintain his identity within a society/culture of a certain kind, he has to be concerned about the shape of this society/culture as a whole. He cannot, following the libertarian anarchist model that Nozick sketched, be concerned purely with his individual choices and the associations formed from such choices to the neglect of the matrix in which such choices can be open or closed, rich or meagre. It is important to him that certain activities and institutions flourish in society. It is even of importance to him what the moral tone of the whole society is—shocking as it may be to libertarians to raise this issue—because freedom and individual diversity can only flourish in a society where there is a general recognition of their worth. They are threatened by the spread of bigotry, but also by other conceptions of life—for example, those which look on originality, innovation, and diversity as luxuries which society can ill afford given the need for efficiency, productivity, or growth, or those which in a host of other ways depreciate freedom.

Now, it is possible that a society and culture propitious for freedom might arise from the spontaneous association of anarchist communes. But it seems much more likely from the historical record that we need rather some species of political society. And if this is so then we must acknowledge an obligation to belong to this kind of society in affirming freedom. But there is more. If realizing our freedom partly depends on the society and culture in which we live, then we exercise a fuller freedom if we can help determine the shape of this society and culture. And this we can only do through instruments of common decision. This means that the political institutions in which we live may themselves be a crucial part of what is necessary to realize our identity as free beings.

This is the second answer to the last objection. In fact, men's deliberating together about what will be binding on all of them is an essential part of the exercise of freedom. It is only in this way that they can come to grips with certain basic issues in a way which will actually have an effect in their lives. Those issues, which can only be effectively decided by society as a whole and which often set the boundary and framework for our lives, can indeed be discussed freely by politically irresponsible individuals wherever they have licence to do so. But they can only be truly *deliberated* about politically. A society in which such deliberation was public and involved everyone would realize a freedom not available anywhere else or in any other mode.

Thus, always granted that an anarchist society is not an available option, it is hard to see how one can affirm the worth of freedom in this sense of the exercise of autonomous deliberation and at the same time recognize no obligation to bring about and sustain a political order of this kind.

FIVE

SOCIAL INSTITUTIONS

In the final section of this book, we will examine a number of important social institutions, including education, the family, and punishment. Philosophers have examined different aspects of these institutions from many perspectives; our primary focus will be on those examinations which seek to evaluate aspects of these institutions from the perspective of the various ideals we examined in Section 4 of this book.

One negative freedom often claimed by parents is noninterference by others (including the state) in the education of their children. Particular importance is often ascribed to the freedom of parents to educate their children about their values. At the same time, the state is often perceived as having a great interest in education of children, an education that modem states usually pay for. From the state's perspective, particular importance is often ascribed to the state's control over the values education of children, so that the state can ensure that its younger citizens adopt the values that are crucial to the social order created by the state. If the values of the parents and the social values of the state are not consonant, the potential exists for real conflict. Who should control the education of children, and about whose values should children be educated? These questions are central to the first three selections.

Gutmann in reading 58 identifies three approaches which she finds unacceptable. The first is the *family state approach,* which gives the state exclusive authority over the education of children to ensure that they are educated about the objectively correct theories of the good and the just. Gutmann believes that this approach fails to do justice to the family's claim to perpetuate its values in its children. The second is the *state of families approach,* which, in recognition of that claim, gives the family exclusive authority over the education of its children. Gutmann believes that this approach fails to do justice to the child's need to be exposed to other ways of life and to learn the value of mutual respect among people with different values. The third is the *state of individuals approach,* which would give authority to educators who will educate children to freely choose their own values. Gutmann resists this third approach on the grounds that it gives excessive emphasis to the value of individual freedom. In the end, Gutmann develops an approach—called democratic education—of shared authority over education subject to two principles, the *principle of nondiscrimination* (no educable child can be excluded from an adequate education) and the *principle of nonrepression* (no education can restrict rational deliberation about competing conceptions of the good). These principles, she argues, are particularly appropriate for a democratic society.

Galston in reading 59 sees this approach as insensitive to the extent of parental freedom, which may include the authority to educate children without exposing them to alternative value systems and without encouraging them to reflect critically about alternative conceptions of the good. The classic example of this approach to education is the education provided in such communities as the Old Order Amish. Galston agrees that there must be limits on this parental freedom; the state can insist that children be taught respect for the law, the obligation to care for oneself, the need to coexist peacefully with others, and minimal skills in democratic decision making. The further requirements imposed by the principle of nonrepression, argues Galston, represent a commitment to the value of the reflective life, a value that is not shared by all and that is not necessary for the needs of the state. They should not therefore be imposed by the state as restrictions on parental freedom of education.

Sher and Bennett in reading 60 identify a much larger set of substantive values which they take to be noncontroversial, even in a society as pluralistic as ours, and which they also take to be supportive of the value of tolerance which is central to the existence of a pluralistic society. Education supportive of those values is not, therefore, incompatible with pluralism. They also argue that directive education about these values does not violate anyone's personal autonomy; it may actually augment that autonomy. All of this leads them to the conclusion that the state may include education about such values in its educational program.

The discussion until now has focused on control of the content of education, especially of values education. Equally important, however, is the question of the control of the actual educational institutions. That crucial question is discussed in the debate between Friedman and Gutmann in readings 61 and 62.

Friedman discusses three roles the state may play in education. The first is the state's *requiring* that all children receive a certain level of education. The second is the state's *funding* that education to enable that mandate to be met by all parents, including those who lack the means to meet it on their own. Friedman accepts the legitimacy of both of these roles of the state, appealing to the concept of the neighborhood effects of schooling (that concept needs to be compared to the various theories of the legitimate functions of the state discussed earlier in this book). The third is the state's actually *providing* the education in question. Friedman rejects that function of the state, arguing that parents should be given vouchers to enable them to purchase education for their children at the school of their choice, so long as the schools in question meet minimum standards about educational content. He believes that this would both improve educational quality through competition and augment the equality of opportunity of poorer children.

Gutmann's challenge, based upon her earlier discussion of democratic education, focuses on the question of the standards which schools would have to meet. She feels that the minimum content standards which Friedman would impose are inadequate to ensure that the demands of democratic education are met. More substantive requirements would mean that there is less room for parental choice. Moreover, she feels that a voucher scheme would leave too little room for public deliberation about how the demands for democratic education should be met. All of this leads her to support the continued state role in providing public education.

Many of the theories of justice discussed in Section 4 stress the importance of equality of opportunity in the design of any just institution. Considerable attention has been paid to the question of what equality of opportunity means in the educational setting. Jencks (reading 63) distinguishes five different accounts in connection with the distribution of teacher time and attention: *democratic equality* (everyone gets equal time and attention from the teacher); *moralistic justice* (teacher time and attention is proportioned in accord with student effort); *weak humane justice* (students who have been shortchanged at home or in earlier schooling get more time and attention); *strong humane justice* (more time and attention is also given to those who are disadvantaged genetically); *utilitarianism* (time and attention should be proportioned in accord with student achievement). Jencks then develops and evaluates each of these accounts. One thing he does not consider, but which would be very worthwhile for the reader to examine, is the relation between his five accounts and the ideas about handicaps in such authors as Dworkin, Sen, and Arneson. In any case, Jencks concludes that the uncertainties raised by the existence of each of these accounts may lead to treating all of the students equally, not as a result of the adoption of democratic equality but as a result of the failure to justify the acceptance of one of the other accounts. This presupposes, of course, a presumption in favor of equality, but in light of Sen's argument in Section 4 about how all theories are egalitarian in some way or another, Jencks' argument on this crucial point may need further elaboration.

Issues about the possibility of equality of opportunity also arise as we turn to the second of the social institutions we will be examining, the family. Fishkin in reading 64 presents an argument that three often accepted assumptions are incompatible with each other. The first, the *autonomy of the family,* allows parents to substantially influence the development of their children. It is closely related to the negative liberty rights of parents which were central to our discussion of education. The second, the *principle of merit,* insists that positions should be assigned according to fair evaluations of qualifications. The third, the *principle of equality of life chances,* maintains that arbitrary native characteristics should not determine children's eventual positions. These latter two principles are Fishkin's account of equality of opportunity. His basic argument is that parental differences in a world of parental autonomy result in unequal life chances if positions are assigned in accordance with the principle of merit. At the end of his essay, he discusses various leveling-up and leveling-down strategies as well as strategies that more systematically intrude into the autonomy of families.

The other selections related to the family discuss issues of justice within the family, issues of *gender justice* and issues of *intergenerational justice*. Okin (reading 65) begins by considering the claim that justice is irrelevant to gender relations within the family because the family is characterized by affection and by shared purposes, and these are not the circumstances in which justice is a virtue. Okin's response is that justice in these circumstances provides a foundation, which is important to ensure even when the family appears to be operating harmoniously. With justice as a foundation, these other feelings enable the family to attain superior virtues. She also has a second point to make about gender and justice. Justice requires more than a Rawlsian insistence that primary goods be distributed equally without discrimination on the basis of gender. It also requires taking into account the unique perspective of women, particularly in their emphasis on relations and on identification with others, in developing the principles of justice from the initial position. These latter suggestions are, as she concedes, in need of much further development.

Another issue of justice which often arises within the family is the issue of what adult children owe to their aging parents, an issue which is of increasing importance in an aging society. Some would deal with the problem of the aging needy by imposing responsibilities on their adult children. Daniels in reading 66 objects to this privatization of what he sees as a problem of social justice, arguing that the content of these filial obligations cannot be determined, because of a lack of a homogenous tradition or a compelling philosophical account. Just institutions of social support should provide a resolution of this problem, with people pursuing their own conception of filial obligations as an addition to that basic framework of social support. Sommers (reading 67), in contrast, sees such positions as part of the failure of contemporary moral philosophy to understand special duties as independent of particular promises. But she does see these as duties justly owed, and not simply as free desires to aid one's parents. There is an important analogy here to Okin's arguments about the legitimacy of justice in family relations. None of this, however, leads her to a determinate conception of the nature and extent of filial obligations, so it is not clear that she can fully respond to Daniels's argument.

The last of the institutions we will consider is the institution of punishment. Philosophers are in fundamental disagreement about the justification of punishment. Utilitarian theorists see the infliction of punishment as an evil justified by the greater good of deterrence it produces, while retributivists see it as an act of justice which society has a right to perform. Readings 68 and 69 from Bentham and Morris present these differing position.

Bentham, after stating the fundamental utilitarian position, goes on to discuss the cases in which punishment is unjustified from a utilitarian perspective. These are cases in which punishment is *groundless* (e.g., when no unconsented act to perform mischief was performed), is *inefficacious* (e.g., punishment for ex post facto laws or for actions which could not be prevented by the threat of punishment), is *unprofitable* (e.g., too many people want mercy to be extended), or *needless* (e.g., when something else can change behavior). Bentham's discussion, while brief on each point, is a classic presentation of many of the complex issues of detail in the practice of punishment. He then goes on to discuss the utilitarian theory of the extent of punishment, emphasizing that the extent of punishment is dependent upon a number of factors, including such issues as the likelihood of being punished and the proximity between the crime and the punishment.

The selection from Morris is more concerned with articulating the foundations of the retributive justification of punishment. He asks us to contrast two ways of treating wrongdoing: *punishment* versus *control/treatment*. The former system supposes that society establishes rules that create a fair mutual distribution of benefits and burdens and that those who freely and responsibly break the rules unfairly obtain additional benefits, so it is just that they be punished to restore that fair distribution. Such a system treats humans as agents who are worthy of respect and admiration as well as shame and blame. In contrast, the latter system treats wrongdoing as the manifestation of a disease and as something which happens to the person. We then treat that disease while controlling the person's behavior. Morris finds the former way of thinking far more appropriate, and suggests that we would all want to be treated as responsible agents.

There are many who find aspects of both of these theories attractive and who have tried to combine them. One standard way of doing that is to say that *utilitarianism* explains why we have the institution of punishment, what is its goal, while *retributivism* explains particular punishment decisions. In particular, it imposes a restriction that the punishment of the criminal not be excessive, not be out of proportion to the harm caused to the victim. Goldman in reading 70 argues that this results in a paradox. After all, many criminals are not caught, so the probability of a criminal being punished may be quite modest. As Bentham already noted, this may require increasing the amount of punishment for those caught if punishment is to have a deterrent effect. But the level of punishment needed to deter may therefore be greater than that level of punishment acceptable under the retributive restrictions. So how can we deter criminals if we are not prepared to punish excessively? This is Goldman's paradox about the level of punishment.

An even more fundamental paradox about acceptable punishment is raised by Murphy (reading 71) working in the framework of a retributive theory. Murphy draws upon considerable social science data about many criminals, data relating to both the needs and deprivations that lead them to commit crimes and the characteristics (greed, selfishness) that help make these crimes acceptable to the criminals who commit them. Murphy asks whether all of this data is compatible with the picture of free agents who take advantage of a just system of distribution of burdens and benefits and who must "pay the price" for doing so? In addition to evaluating this challenge, the reader might want to consider whether the utilitarian approach is immune from the same challenge.

The selections conclude with Montague's defense in reading 72 of a new, social defense approach to punishment. Analyzing cases in which individuals, and other acting on their behalf, may use force to protect themselves, Montague develops a principle of *defensible harm* (DH) which categorizes the cases in which the blameworthy may be harmed. He argues that a properly structured system of punishment would meet the requirements of DH and that this justifies the use of such a system. He concludes by comparing this new approach to the more traditional approaches.

XII

EDUCATION

58.

Educating about Democratic Values

AMY GUTMANN

THE FAMILY STATE

Can we speak meaningfully about a good education without knowing what a just society and a virtuous person are? Socrates poses this challenge to the Sophists in the *Protagoras*. Like most of Socrates's questions, it has remained unanswered after twenty-five centuries. But it is still worth re-asking.

In his critique of the Sophists and in the *Republic,* Plato suggests that we cannot speak about a good education without knowing what justice and virtue really are, rather than what a society assumes that they are by virtue of their shared social understandings. Justice, Socrates suggests, is the concurrent realization of individual and social good. Since the good life for individuals entails contributing to the social good, there is no necessary conflict between what is good for us and what is good for our society—provided our society is just. The defining feature of the family state is that it claims exclusive educational authority as a means of establishing a harmony—one might say, a constitutive relation—between individual and social good based on knowledge. Defenders of the family state expect to create a level of like-mindedness and camaraderie among citizens that most of us expect to find only within families (and now perhaps not even there). The purpose of education in the family state is to cultivate that unity by teaching all educable children what the (sole) good life is for them and by inculcating in them a desire to pursue the good life above all inferior ones. Citizens of a well-ordered family state learn that they cannot realize their own good except by contributing to the social good, and they are also educated to desire only what is good for themselves and their society.

One need not accept Plato's view of natural human inequality to take seriously his theoretical defense of the family state. Once we discount this view, we can find in Plato the most cogent defense of the view that state authority over education is necessary for establishing a harmony between individual virtue and social justice. Unless children learn to associate their own good with the social good, a peaceful and prosperous society will be impossible. Unless the social good that they are taught is worthy of pursuit, they will grow to be unfulfilled and dissatisfied with the society that miseducated them. All states that claim less than absolute authority over the education of children will therefore degenerate out of internal disharmony.

● ● ●

The more telling criticism of the family state proceeds by accepting the possibility that someone sufficiently wise and conscientious might discover the good.

She would then try to convince the rest of us that she had discovered *the* good, not just another contestable theory of the good, and the good for *us,* not just the good appropriate to some other people. It's possible that a few of us—an unusually open-minded or uncommitted few—might be convinced, but most of us (as Plato realized) would not; and we would refuse to relinquish all authority over the education of our children to the philosopher-queen (or the state).

In order to create a just family state, the philosopher therefore must wipe the social slate clean by exiling "all those in the city who happen to be older than ten; and taking over their children, . . . rear them—far away from those dispositions they now have from their parents. . . ."[1] That is an exorbitantly high price to pay for realizing a just society. Socrates himself on behalf of the philosopher recoils from the idea, suggesting that "he won't be willing to mind the political things . . . in his fatherland unless some divine chance coincidentally comes to pass."[2]

• • •

What about a state that lets us live our less-than-objectively good lives, but that insists on educating our children so they will not face the same dilemma or create the same problem for the next generation of citizens? Here a significant variant of the previous problem arises: "Don't we also have a claim to try to perpetuate the way of life that seems good to us within our families? After all, an essential part of *our* good life is imparting an understanding of our values to our children." We can say something similar about our good as citizens: "Don't we also have a claim to participate in shaping the basic structure of our society? After all, an essential part of our good is the freedom to share in shaping the society that in turn influences our very evaluation of a family and the degree to which different kinds of families flourish. The Platonic perspective refuses to recognize the force of these claims about *our* good. Yet these claims constitute the most forceful challenge to the philosopher-queen's claim to have discovered the good for us, even if she has discovered what is objectively good for our children. The cycle of imperfection must continue,[3] not merely because the costs of realizing the family state are too great, but because our good must be counted in any claim about what constitutes a just society for us and our children.[4] Our good might conceivably be overridden by the prospects of

---

[1] *The Republic of Plato,* trans. Allan Bloom (New York: Basic Books, 1968), p. 220 (541a).

[2] Ibid., p. 274 (592a).

[3] Alternately, one might argue: If the philosopher-queen could convince us that her claims are correct, then the cycle of imperfection need not continue. But the only context in which she can be said to have convinced us (rather than to have manipulated our views by taking advantage of her monopoly on political power) is democratic. The family state therefore must become democratic to be legitimate.

[4] And, one might add, we can only know our good if our conception is uncoerced. Our conception must, to borrow a phrase from Bernard Williams, "grow from inside human life." The idea of an uncoerced conception of the good life, like the idea of an uncoerced social agreement on

achieving the objectively good life for our children, but the objectively good is likely to be the fully operative good only for a society of orphaned infants.

If she is perfectly wise, the philosopher-queen must moderate her claims. Perhaps she may claim to know what is good for our children, but surely she may not claim the right to impose that good on them without taking our good, both as parents and as citizens, into account. If we now relax the rather absurd assumption that we can find a perfectly wise philosopher-queen, we shall want some assurance from even the wisest educational authority that our good as parents and as citizens, and not just the good of our children, will be considered in designing the educational system for our society. The only acceptable form of assurance is for parents and citizens both to have a significant share of educational authority.

If one begins with a society whose members all already agree about what is good (say, an entire society of Old Order Amish), then the moral dilemmas of personal identity and transformation costs may never arise. Unlike some contemporary theorists who in their criticisms of liberalism implicitly support a family state, Plato faces up to its more troubling implications. Part of Platonic wisdom is not to assume away the problems of founding a family state, but to recognize that the process of creating social agreement on the good comes at a very high price, and to wonder whether the price is worth paying.

Yet Plato ultimately fails to recognize the moral implication of the fact that our attachments to (and disagreements over) the good run so deep, into our earliest education. Even if there is an objective ideal of the good for an imaginary society created out of orphaned infants, our good is relative to our education and the choices we are capable of making for ourselves, our children, and our communities. The objectively good life for us, we might say, must be a life that can fulfill us according to our best moral lights. This, I think, is the truth in educational relativism.[5] As long as we differ not just in our opinions but in our moral convictions about the good life, the state's educational role cannot be defined as realizing *the* good life, objectively defined, for each of its citizens. Neither can educational authorities simply claim that a good education is whatever in their opinion is best for the state.

The family state attempts to constrain our choices among ways of life and educational purposes in a way that is incompatible with our identity as parents and citizens. In its unsuccessful attempt to do so, it successfully demonstrates that we cannot ground our conception of a good education merely on personal or political preferences. Plato presents a forceful case for resting educational authority exclusively with a centralized state, a case grounded on the principle that knowledge should be translated into political power. But even the Platonic case is not sufficiently strong to override the claims of parents and citizens to

an ethical life, "implies free institutions, ones that allow not only for free inquiry but also for diversity of life and some ethical variety." See Bernard Williams, *Ethics and the Limits of Philosophy* (Cambridge, Mass.: Harvard University Press, 1985), pp. 172–73.

[5] Cf. Bernard Williams, "The Truth in Relativism," in *Moral Luck* (New York: Cambridge University Press, 1981), pp. 132–43.

share in social reproduction, claims to which I return in defending a democratic state of education.

THE STATE OF FAMILIES

States that aspire to the moral unity of families underestimate the strength and deny the legitimacy of the parental impulse to pass values on to children. Radically opposed to the family state is the state of families, which places educational authority exclusively in the hands of parents, thereby permitting parents to predispose their children, through education, to choose a way of life consistent with their familial heritage. Theorists of the state of families typically justify placing educational authority in the hands of parents on grounds either of consequences or of rights. John Locke maintained that parents are the best protectors of their children's future interests. Some Catholic theologians, following Thomas Aquinas, claim that parents have a natural right to educational authority. Many modern-day defenders of the state of families maintain both, and add another argument: if the state is committed to the freedom of individuals, then it must cede educational authority to parents whose freedom includes the right to pass their own way of life on to their children.[6] Charles Fried, for example, argues that "the right to form one's child's values, one's child's life plan and the right to lavish attention on the child are extensions of the basic right not to be interfered with in doing these things for oneself."[7] Fried bases parental rights over children on "the facts of reproduction" and the absence of a societal right to make choices for children. Fried's denial of a societal right is based on the consequentialist judgment that parents can be relied upon to pursue the best interests of their children.

Although the appeal of the state of families is apparent upon recognizing the defects of a family state, none of these theoretical arguments justifies resting educational authority exclusively—or even primarily—in the hands of parents. It is one thing to recognize the right (and responsibility) of parents to educate their children as members of a family, quite another to claim that this right of familial education extends to a right of parents to insulate their children from

---

[6] For the former justification, Milton Friedman, *Capitalism and Freedom* (Chicago: University of Chicago Press, 1962), pp. 85–107; and John E. Coons and Stephen Sugarman, *Education by Choice: The Case for Family Control* (Berkeley: University of California Press, 1978). For the latter, see Thomas Aquinas, *Supplement Summa Theologica un Divini Illius Magistri of His Holiness Pope Pius XI*, and a 1936 encyclical of the Catholic Church, where Aquinas is quoted as saying: "The child is naturally something of the father, . . . so by natural right the child before reaching the age of reason, is under the father's care. Hence it would be contrary to natural justice if any disposition were made concerning [the child] against the will of the parents." (Quoted in Francis Schrag, "The Right to Educate," *School Review,* vol. 79, no. 3 [May 1971]: 363.) Article 41 of the Irish Constitution also "recognizes the Family as the natural primary and fundamental unit group of Society, and as a moral institution, possessing inalienable and imprescriptible rights, antecedent and superior to all positive law." (Quoted in Walter F. Murphy, "An Ordering of Constitutional Values," *Southern California Law Review,* vol. 53, no. 2 [January 1980]: 739.)

[7] Charles Fried, *Right and Wrong* (Cambridge, Mass.: Harvard University Press, 1978), p. 152.

exposure to ways of life or thinking that conflict with their own. The consequentialist argument is surely unconvincing: parents cannot be counted upon to equip their children with the intellectual skills necessary for rational deliberation. Some parents, such as the Old Order Amish in America, are morally committed to shielding their children from all knowledge that might lead them to doubt and all worldly influences that might weaken their religious beliefs.[8] Many other parents, less radical in their rejection of modern society, are committed to teaching their children religious and racial intolerance.

• • •

This argument against exclusive parental authority depends neither upon parental ignorance nor upon irrationality. From the perspective of individual parents who desire above all to perpetuate their particular way of life, teaching disrespect for differing ways of life need not be irrational even if the outcome turns out to be undesirable. For many deeply religious parents, mutual respect is a public good (in the strict economic sense). As long as they have reason to believe that their religion will continue to be respected, they need not worry about teaching their children to respect other religions. But even if they can foresee a serious threat to their religion in the future, they still have no reason to believe that they can solve (or even ameliorate) the problem by teaching their children to respect the disrespectful.

American history provides an informative example. Many public schools in the mid-nineteenth century were, to say the least, disrespectful of Catholicism. Catholic children who attended these schools were often humiliated, sometimes whipped for refusing to read the King James version of the Bible. Imagine that instead of becoming more respectful, public schools had been abolished, and states had subsidized parents to send their children to the private school of their choice. Protestant parents would have sent their children to Protestant schools, Catholic parents to Catholic schools. The Protestant majority would have continued to educate their children to be disrespectful if not intolerant of Catholics. The religious prejudices of Protestant parents would have been visited on their children, and the social, economic, and political effects of those prejudices would have persisted, probably with considerably less public protest, to this very day. There may be little reason today for Catholic parents to worry that privatizing schools will reinstitutionalize bigotry against Catholics, at least in the short run. But one reason that Catholics need not worry is that a state of families today would be built on the moral capital created over almost a century by a public school system. That moral capital is just now being created for blacks and Hispanics, and even more well-established minorities might reasonably fear that returning to a state of families would eventually squander the moral capital created by public schooling.

---

[8] See *Wisconsin v. Yoder*, 406 U.S. 210–11.

Like most collective goods, the "costs" of mutual respect among citizens may have to be imposed on everyone to avoid the free-rider problem. But this virtue is a cost only to parents who do not accept its intrinsic moral worth. The state of families can overcome the free-rider problem by violating its basic premise of parental supremacy in education and requiring all parents to let schools teach their children mutual respect. For children who are not yet free (in any case) to make their own choices, teaching the lesson of mutual respect is not a cost. It is both an instrumental good and a good worth valuing on its own account. Teaching mutual respect is instrumental to assuring all children the freedom to choose in the future. It is a good in itself to all citizens who are not yet committed to a way of life that precludes respect for other ways of life.

The state of families mistakenly conflates the welfare of children with the freedom of parents when it assumes that the welfare of children is best defined or secured by the freedom of parents. But the state of families rightly recognizes, as the family state does not, the value of parental freedom, at least to the extent that such freedom does not interfere with the interests of children in becoming mutually respectful citizens of a society that sustains family life. There is no simple solution to the tension between the freedom of parents and the welfare of children. The state may not grant parents absolute authority over their children's education in the name of individual freedom, nor may it claim exclusive educational authority in the name of communal solidarity. That there is no *simple* solution, however, should not deter us from searching for a better solution than that offered by either the family state or the state of families.

The attractions of the state of families are apparent to most Americans: by letting parents educate their own children as they see fit, the state avoids all the political battles that rage over the content of public education. The state of families also appears to foster pluralism by permitting many ways of life to be perpetuated in its midst. But both these attractions are only superficial in a society where many parents would teach racism, for example, in the absence of political pressure to do otherwise. States that abdicate all educational authority to parents sacrifice their most effective and justifiable instrument for securing mutual respect among their citizens.

The "pluralism" commonly identified with the state of families is superficial because its internal variety serves as little more than an ornament for onlookers. Pluralism is an important political value insofar as social diversity enriches our lives by expanding our understanding of differing ways of life. To reap the benefits of social diversity, children must be exposed to ways of life different from their parents and—in the course of their exposure—must embrace certain values, such as mutual respect among persons, that make social diversity both possible and desirable. There is no reason to assume that placing educational authority exclusively in the hands of parents is the best way of achieving these ends, and good reason to reject the claim that, regardless of the consequences for individual citizens or for society as a whole, parents have a natural right to exclusive educational authority over their children. Children are no more the property of their parents than they are the property of the state.

THE STATE OF INDIVIDUALS

"It is in the case of children," John Stuart Mill argued, "that misapplied notions of liberty are a real obstacle to the fulfillment by the State of its duties. One would almost think that a man's children were supposed to be literally, and not metaphorically, a part of himself, so jealous is opinion of the smallest interference of law with his absolute and exclusive control over them. . . ." [9] Having exposed the central flaw in the state of families, Mill defended a more liberal conception of education. "All attempts by the State to bias the conclusions of its citizens on disputed subjects are evil," Mill argued. Some contemporary liberals extend the logic of Mill's argument to defend what I call a state of individuals.[10] They criticize all educational authorities that threaten to bias the choices of children toward some disputed or controversial ways of life and away from others. Their ideal educational authority is one that maximizes future choice without prejudicing children towards any controversial conception of the good life. The state of individuals thus responds to the weakness of both the family state and the state of families by championing the dual goals of *opportunity* for choice and *neutrality* among conceptions of the good life. A just educational authority must not bias children's choices among good lives, but it must provide every child with an opportunity to choose freely and rationally among the widest range of lives.

If neutrality is what we value, then a child must be protected from all—or at least all controversial—social prejudices. Neither parents nor states are capable of fulfilling this educational ideal. Parents are unlikely (and unwilling) to resist a strong human impulse: the desire to pass some of their particular prejudices on to their children. And even the most liberal states are bound to subvert the neutrality principle: they will try, quite understandably, to teach children to appreciate the basic (but disputed) values and the dominant (but controversial) cultural prejudices that hold their society together.[11]

Recognizing the power of these parental and political impulses, some liberals look for an educational authority more impartial than parents or public

---

[9] Mill, *On Liberty*, ch. 5, para. 12.

[10] Mill himself suggested an educational policy often associated with the state of families: the government should "leave to parents to obtain the education where and how they pleased, and content itself with helping to pay the school fees of the poorer classes of children . . ." (*On Liberty*, ch. 5, para. 13). There are, however, two significant differences between Mill's defense of private schools and that of the state of families. (1) Mill's preference for private control of schools follows not from a principled defense of parental choice but from an empirical presumption that state control of schools leads to repression ("a despotism over the mind"). Since absolute parental control over education also threatens despotism over children's minds, it is as suspect on Millean grounds. (2) Perhaps for this reason, Mill severely limits the educational authority of parents by (among other things) a system of "public examinations, extending to all children and beginning at an early age." If a child fails the examination, Mill recommends that "the father, unless he has some sufficient ground of excuse, might be subjected to a moderate fine, to be worked out, if necessary, by his labor. . . ." To insure neutrality, the knowledge tested by the examinations should "be confined to facts and positive science exclusively" (ch. 5, para. 14).

[11] I assume from here on the understanding that liberalism aims at neutrality only among disputed or controversial conceptions of the good. I therefore omit further use of the adjectives "disputed" or "controversial."

officials—"experts" or professional educators—motivated solely, or at least predominantly, by the interests of children in learning and unconstrained by parental or political authority. I suspect that were professional educators ever to rule, they would convince everyone, albeit unintentionally, that liberal neutrality is an unlivable ideal. But as long as we focus our critical attention on the detrimental effects of parental and political prejudices, we are likely to overlook the limitations of the neutrality ideal, and the tension between it and the ideal of opportunity. Children may grow to have a greater range of choice (and to live more satisfying lives) if their education is biased by those values favored by their society. Bentham and Kant both recognized this. Kant defended—as one of four essential parts of a basic education—teaching children the kind of "discretion" associated with "refinement" of manners, which "changes according to the ever-changing tastes of different ages." [12] One of the primary aims of education, according to Bentham, was to secure for children "admission into and agreeable intercourse with good company." [13]

Contemporary liberal theorists often invoke the spirit of Bentham, Kant, or Mill to defend the ideal of neutrality, overlooking both its moral limitations and the substantial qualifications that each of these theorists placed on the ideal. All sophisticated liberals recognize the practical limitation of neutrality as an educational ideal: it is, in its fullest form, unrealizable. But most fail to appreciate the value of our resistance to the ideal of unprejudiced individual freedom: the value of our desire to cultivate, and allow communities to cultivate, only a select range of choice for children, to prune and weed their desires and aspirations so they are likely to choose a worthy life and sustain a flourishing society when they mature and are free to choose for themselves. Bruce Ackerman argues:

> Such horticultural imagery has no place in a liberal theory of education. We have no right [and the state has no right] to look upon future citizens as if we were master gardeners who can tell the difference between a pernicious weed and a beautiful flower. A system of liberal education provides children with a sense of the very different lives that could be theirs.[14]

But what *kind* of sense do we want to provide? Of *which* very different lives? Ackerman, like all sensible liberals, recognizes that the capacity for rational choice requires that we place some prior limitations on children's choices. To have a rational sense of what we want to become, we need to know who we are; otherwise our choices will be endless and meaningless.[15] We learn to speak English rather than Urdu, not by choice, but by cultural determination.[16] And this

[12] Immanuel Kant. *Kant on Education,* translated by Annette Churton. (Boston: D. C. Heath & Co., 1990), p. 19.

[13] Jeremy Bentham. "Chrestomathia," in *The Works of Jeremy Bentham* (Edinburgh: 1843), p. 10.

[14] Bruce Ackerman. *Social Justice in the Liberal State* (New Haven: Yale University Press, 1980), p. 139.

[15] This insight is common to critics of liberalism. See, e.g., Michael Sandel, *Liberalism and the Limits of Justice* (New York: Cambridge University Press, 1982), esp. pp. 161–65, 168–83.

[16] Ackerman, *Social Justice,* p. 141.

cultural determination limits the range of our future choices, even if it does not uniquely determine who we become. Ackerman identifies this prior determination with the need for "cultural coherence," which he uses to justify the family and its nonneutral education. The need for cultural coherence, Ackerman argues, does not justify "adult pretensions to moral superiority." [17] Neither parents nor the state may shape the character of children on the grounds that they can distinguish between better and worse moral character, yet they may shape children's character for the sake of cultural coherence, or in order to maximize their future freedom of choice.

Why, one might ask, should parents and states be free to shape children's character and guide their choices for the sake of cultural coherence but not for the sake of their leading morally good lives? Sometimes the claim that we know better than children the difference between morally good and bad lives is not a pretension to moral superiority, but a reflection of our greater moral maturity. Why, then, should adults resist shaping children's character and guiding their choices on *moral* grounds?

The resistance of many contemporary liberals to one of our strongest moral impulses stems, I suspect, from formulating educational purposes and their justifications as a dichotomous choice.[18] Either we must educate children so that they are free to choose among the widest range of lives (given the constraints of cultural coherence) because freedom of choice is the paramount good, or we must educate children so that they will choose *the* life that we believe is best because leading a virtuous life is the paramount good. Let children define their own identity or define it for them. Give children liberty or give them virtue. Neither alternative is acceptable: we legitimately value education not just for the liberty but also for the virtue that it bestows on children; and the virtue that we value includes the ability to deliberate among competing conceptions of the good.

But precisely which virtues do "we" value? No set of virtues remains undisputed in the United States, or in any modern society that allows its members to dispute its dominant understandings. The problem in using education to bias children towards some conceptions of the good life and away from others stems not from pretense on the part of educators to moral superiority over children but from an assertion on their part to political authority over other citizens who reject their conception of virtue. Neutrality is no more acceptable a solution to this problem than the use of education to inculcate a nonneutral set of virtues. Neither choice—to teach or not to teach virtue—is uncontroversial. Neither avoids the problem of instituting an educational authority whose aims are not universally accepted among adult citizens. The decision not to teach virtue (or, more accurately, to teach only the virtues of free choice) faces opposition by citizens who can claim, quite reasonably, that freedom of choice is not

---

[17] Ibid., p. 148.

[18] The tendency to dichotomize our moral choices is not unique to advocates of liberal neutrality. What I call the "tyranny of dualisms" is also common to communitarian critics of liberalism. See my "Communitarian Critics of Liberalism," *Philosophy and Public Affairs,* vol. 14, no. 5 (Summer 1985): 316–20.

the only, or even the primary, purpose of education. Why should these citizens be forced to defer to the view that children must be educated for freedom rather than for virtue? Liberals might reply that freedom is the *correct* end of education. This reply is inadequate, because being right is neither a necessary nor a sufficient condition for claiming the right to shape the character of future citizens.

Because the educational ideal of free choice commands no *special* political legitimacy, the state of individuals poses the same problem as the family state. Even if liberals could establish that, of all disputed aims of education, neutrality is singularly right, they would still have to establish why being right is a necessary or sufficient condition for ruling. The same argument that holds against the family state holds against the state of individuals: being right is not a necessary or sufficient condition because parents and citizens have a legitimate interest (independent of their "rightness") in passing some of their most salient values on to their children.

Proponents of the state of individuals might argue that they avoid the problem of the family state by offering a principled solution morally distinct from that of the family state: authorize only those authorities whose educational techniques maximize the future freedom of children. They try, as Ackerman does and I once did,[19] to justify pruning children's desires solely on liberal paternalistic grounds: by restricting the freedom of children when they are young, we increase it over their lifetimes. Although the liberal state is often contrasted to the family state, its end of individual freedom is subject to a similar challenge. Why must freedom be the sole end of education, given that most of us value things that conflict with freedom? We value, for example, the moral sensibility that enables us to discriminate between good and bad lives, and the character that inclines us to choose good rather than bad lives.[20] A well-cultivated moral character constrains choice among lives at least as much as it expands choice. Why prevent teachers from cultivating moral character by biasing the choices of children toward good lives and, if necessary, by constraining the range of lives that children are capable of choosing when they mature?

Liberals occasionally reply that the standard of freedom supports such moral education. When teachers or parents admonish children not to be lazy, for example, the implicit purpose of their admonition is to expand the future freedom of children by encouraging them to become the kind of people who have the greatest range of choice later in life.[21] This reply begs two crucial questions: Is such an admonition easier to justify because it furthers the freedom of children rather than cultivates a virtue? Is the aim of educating children for freedom as fully compatible with teaching them virtue as this example suggests?

The answer to each question, I suspect, is "no," because both educational ends—freedom and virtue—are controversial, and neither is inclusive. To establish a privileged place for freedom as *the* aim of education, liberals would

---

[19] See Amy Gutmann, "Children, Paternalism and Education: A Liberal Argument," *Philosophy and Public Affairs*, vol. 9, no. 4 (Summer 1980): 338–58.

[20] For an excellent account of moral freedom, see Susan Wolf, "Asymmetrical Freedom," *The Journal of Philosophy* (1980): 151–66.

[21] Ackerman suggests this rationale in *Social Justice*, pp. 147–49.

have to demonstrate that freedom is the singular social good, a demonstration that cannot succeed in a society where citizens sometimes (one need not claim always) value virtue above freedom. Were freedom of choice an inclusive good such that teaching children to choose entailed teaching them virtue, then the debate between whether to educate for freedom or for virtue would be academic. It's not academic, because an education for freedom and for virtue part company in any society whose citizens are free not to act virtuously, yet it is at least as crucial to cultivate virtue in a free society as it is in one where citizens are constrained to act virtuously. The admonition not to be lazy may serve the cause of cultivating virtue rather than maximizing children's freedom in an affluent society that offers generous benefits to the unemployed, but why should it be any more suspect on this account? Neither aim of education is neutral, and each can exclude the other, at least in some instances. Assuming that some citizens value virtue, others freedom, and the two aims do not support identical pedagogical practices, the more liberal aim cannot claim a privileged political position. Educators need not be bound to maximize the future choices of children if freedom is not the only value.

By what standards then, if any, are educators bound to teach? After criticizing the liberal paternalistic standard—constrain the present freedom of children only if necessary to maximize their future freedom—we are left with the problem of finding another standard that can justify a necessarily nonneutral education in the face of social disagreement concerning what constitutes the proper aim of education. Shifting the grounds of justification from future freedom to some other substantive end—such as happiness, autonomy, intellectual excellence, salvation, or social welfare—only re-creates the same problem. None of these standards is sufficiently inclusive to solve the problem of justification in the face of dissent by citizens whose conception of the good life and the good society threatens to be undermined by the conception of a good (but necessarily nonneutral) education instituted by some (necessarily exclusive) educational authority.

• • •

A DEMOCRATIC STATE OF EDUCATION

Cultivating character is a legitimate—indeed, an inevitable—function of education. And there are many kinds of moral character—each consistent with conscious social reproduction—that a democratic state may legitimately cultivate. Who should decide what kind of character to cultivate? I have examined and rejected three popular and philosophically forceful answers to this question. Theorists of the family state rest educational authority exclusively in the hands of a centralized state in a mistaken attempt to wed knowledge of the good life with political power. Theorists of the state of families place educational authority exclusively in the hands of parents, on the unfounded assumption that they have a natural right to such authority or that they will thereby maximize the welfare of their children. Theorists of the state of individuals refuse to rest educational authority in any hands without the assurance that the choices of children will not be prejudiced in favor of some ways of life and against others—an assurance that no educator can or should be expected to provide.

If my criticisms are correct, then these three theories are wrong. None provides an adequate foundation for educational authority. Yet each contains a partial truth. States, parents, and professional educators all have important roles to play in cultivating moral character. A democratic state of education recognizes that educational authority must be shared among parents, citizens, and professional educators even though such sharing does not guarantee that power will be wedded to knowledge, that parents can successfully pass their prejudices on to their children, or that education will be neutral among competing conceptions of the good life.

If a democratic state of education does not guarantee virtue based on knowledge, or the autonomy of families, or neutrality among ways of life, what is the value of its premise of shared educational authority? The broad distribution of educational authority among citizens, parents, and professional educators supports the core value of democracy: conscious social reproduction in its most inclusive form. Unlike a family state, a democratic state recognizes the value of parental education in perpetuating particular conceptions of the good life. Unlike a state of families, a democratic state recognizes the value of professional authority in enabling children to appreciate and to evaluate ways of life other than those favored by their families. Unlike a state of individuals, a democratic state recognizes the value of political education in predisposing children to accept those ways of life that are consistent with sharing the rights and responsibilities of citizenship in a democratic society. A democratic state is therefore committed to allocating educational authority in such a way as to provide its members with an education adequate to participating in democratic politics, to choosing among (a limited range of) good lives, and to sharing in the several subcommunities, such as families, that impart identity to the lives of its citizens.

A democratic state of education constrains choice among good lives not only out of necessity but out of a concern for civic virtue. Democratic states can acknowledge two reasons for permitting communities to use education to predispose children toward some ways of life and away from others. One reason is grounded on the value of moral freedom, a value not uniquely associated with democracy. All societies of self-reflective beings must admit the moral value of enabling their members to discern the difference between good and bad ways of life. Children do not learn to discern this difference on the basis of an education that strives for neutrality among ways of life. Children are not taught that bigotry is bad, for example, by offering it as one among many competing conceptions of the good life, and then subjecting it to criticism on grounds that bigots do not admit that other people's conceptions of the good are "equally" good. Children first become the kind of people who are repelled by bigotry, and then they feel the force of the reasons for their repulsion. The liberal reasons to reject bigotry are quite impotent in the absence of such sensibilities: they offer no compelling argument to people who feel no need to treat other people as equals and are willing to live with the consequences of their disrespect. To cultivate in children the character that feels the force of right reason is an essential purpose of education in any society.

The second, more specifically democratic, reason for supporting the non-neutral education of states and families is that the good of children includes not just freedom of choice, but also identification with and participation in the good of their family and the politics of their society. The need for cultural coherence does not fully capture this democratic value, because it would not be enough for a centralized state to choose a set of parents and a coherent cultural orientation at random for children. People, quite naturally, value the specific cultural and political orientations of their society and family more than those of others, even if they cannot provide objective reasons for their preferences. The fact that these cultural orientations are theirs is an adequate (and generalizable) reason. Just as we love our (biological or adopted) children more than those of our friends because they are part of *our* family, so we differentially value the cultural orientations of our country because it is *ours*. We need not claim moral superiority (or ownership) to say any of this. We need claim only that some ways of life are better than others *for us and our children* because these orientations impart meaning to and enrich the internal life of family and society. To focus exclusively on the value of freedom, or even on the value of moral freedom, neglects the value that parents and citizens may legitimately place on *partially* prejudicing the choices of children by their familial and political heritages.

In authorizing (but not requiring) democratic states and families within them to predispose children to particular ways of life, we integrate the insights of both the family state and the state of families into a democratic theory of education. But in doing so, we do not necessarily avoid the weakness of both theories in sanctioning the imposition of a noncritical consciousness on children. To avoid this weakness, a democratic state must aid children in developing the capacity to understand and to evaluate competing conceptions of the good life and the good society. The value of critical deliberation among good lives and good societies would be neglected by a society that inculcated in children uncritical acceptance of any particular way or ways of (personal and political) life. Children might then be taught to accept uncritically the set of beliefs, say, that supports the view that the only acceptable role for women is to serve men and to raise children. A society that inculcated such a sexist set of values would be undemocratic not because sexist values are wrong (although I have no doubt that they are, at least for our society), but because that society failed to secure any space for educating children to deliberate critically among a range of good lives and good societies. To integrate the value of critical deliberation among good lives, we must defend some principled limits on political and parental authority over education, limits that in practice require parents and states to cede some educational authority to professional educators.

One limit is that of *nonrepression*. The principle of nonrepression prevents the state, and any group within it, from using education to restrict rational deliberation of competing conceptions of the good life and the good society. Nonrepression is not a principle of negative freedom. It secures freedom from interference only to the extent that it forbids using education to restrict *rational* deliberation or consideration of different ways of life. Nonrepression is therefore compatible with the use of education to inculcate those character traits, such as honesty, religious toleration, and mutual respect for persons, that serve as foundations for rational deliberation of differing ways of life. Nor is nonrepression a principle of positive liberty, as commonly understood. Although it secures more than a freedom from interference, the "freedom to" that it secures is not a freedom to pursue the singularly correct way of personal or political life, but the freedom to deliberate rationally among differing ways of life.[22] Rational deliberation should be secured, I have argued, not because it is neutral among all ways of life—even all decent ways of life. Rational deliberation makes some ways of life—such as that of the Old Order Amish—more difficult to pursue insofar as dedication to such lives depends upon resistance to rational deliberation. Rational deliberation remains the form of freedom most suitable to a democratic society in which adults must be free to deliberate and disagree but constrained to secure the intellectual grounds for deliberation and disagreement among children. Adults must therefore be prevented from using their present deliberative freedom to undermine the future deliberative freedom of children. Although nonrepression constitutes a limit on democratic authority, its defense thus derives from the primary value of democratic education. Because *conscious* social reproduction is the primary ideal of democratic education, communities must be prevented from using education to stifle rational deliberation of competing conceptions of the good life and the good society.

A second principled limit on legitimate democratic authority, which also follows from the primary value of democratic education, is *nondiscrimination*. For democratic education to support conscious *social* reproduction, all educable children must be educated. Nondiscrimination extends the logic of nonrepression, since states and families can be selectively repressive by excluding entire groups of children from schooling or by denying them an education conducive to deliberation among conceptions of the good life and the good society. Repression has commonly taken the more passive form of discrimination in schooling against racial minorities, girls, and other disfavored groups of children. The effect of discrimination is often to repress, at least temporarily, the capacity and even the desire of these groups to participate in the processes that structure choice among good lives. Nondiscrimination can thus be viewed as the distributional complement to nonrepression. In its most general application to education, nondiscrimination prevents the state, and all groups within it, from denying anyone an educational good on grounds irrelevant to the legitimate social purpose of that good. Applied to those forms of education necessary to prepare children for future citizenship (participation in conscious social reproduction), the nondiscrimination principle becomes a principle of nonexclusion. No educable child may be excluded from an education adequate to participating in the political processes that structure choice among good lives.

---

[22] For a conceptual analysis of freedom that fits my understanding of rational freedom, see Gerald C. MacCallum, Jr., "Negative and Positive Freedom," *Philosophical Review* 76 (1967): 312–24. Reprinted in Richard E. Flathman, ed., *Concepts in Social and Political Philosophy* (New York: Macmillan, 1973), pp. 294–308.

Why is a theory that accepts these two principled constraints on popular (and parental) sovereignty properly considered democratic? Democratic citizens are persons partially constituted by subcommunities (such as their family, their work, play, civic, and religious groups), yet free to choose a way of life compatible with their larger communal identity because no single subcommunity commands absolute authority over their education, and because the larger community has equipped them for deliberating and thereby participating in the democratic processes by which choice among good lives and the chance to pursue them are politically structured. The principles of nonrepression and nondiscrimination simultaneously support deliberative freedom and communal self-determination. The form of educational relativism acceptable under these principles is therefore democratic in a significant sense: all citizens must be educated so as to have a chance to share in self-consciously shaping the structure of their society. Democratic education is not neutral among conceptions of the good life, nor does its defense depend on a claim to neutrality. Democratic education is bound to restrict pursuit, although not conscious consideration, of ways of life dependent on the suppression of politically relevant knowledge. Democratic education supports choice among those ways of life that are compatible with conscious social reproduction.

Nondiscrimination requires that *all* educable children be educated adequately to participate as citizens in shaping the future structure of their society. Their democratic participation as adults, in turn, shapes the education of the next generation of children, within the constraints set by nondiscrimination and nonrepression. These principles permit families and other subcommunities to shape but not totally to determine their children's future choices, in part by preventing any single group from monopolizing educational authority and in part by permitting (indeed, obligating) professional educators to develop in children the deliberative capacity to evaluate competing conceptions of good lives and good societies. Democratic education thus appreciates the value of education as a means of creating (or re-creating) cohesive communities and of fostering deliberative choice without elevating either of these partial purposes to an absolute or overriding end.

Like the family state, a democratic state of education tries to teach virtue— not the virtue of the family state (power based upon knowledge), but what might best be called *democratic* virtue: the ability to deliberate, and hence to participate in conscious social reproduction. Like the state of families, a democratic state upholds a degree of parental authority over education, resisting the strong communitarian view that children are creatures of the state. But in recognizing that children are future citizens, the democratic state resists the view, implicit in the state of families, that children are creatures of their parents. Like the state of individuals, a democratic state defends a degree of professional authority over education—not on grounds of liberal neutrality, but to the extent necessary to provide children with the capacity to evaluate those ways of life most favored by parental and political authorities.

59.

Educating about Familial Values

WILLIAM GALSTON

Perhaps the most poignant problem raised by liberal civic education is the clash between the content of that education and the desire of parents to pass on their way of life to their children. Few parents, I suspect, are unaware of or immune to the force of this desire. What could be more natural? If you believe that you are fit to be a parent, you must also believe that at least some of the choices you have made are worthy of emulation by your children, and the freedom to pass on the fruits of those choices must be highly valued. Conversely, who can contemplate without horror totalitarian societies in which families are compelled to yield all moral authority to the state?

Still, your child is at once a future adult and a future citizen. Your authority as a parent is limited by both these facts. For example, you are not free to treat your child in a manner that impedes normal development. You may not legitimately starve or beat your child or thwart the acquisition of basic linguistic and social skills. The systematic violation of these and related norms suffices to warrant state intervention. Similarly, you are not free to impede the child's acquisition of a basic civic education—the beliefs and habits that support the polity and enable individuals to function competently in public affairs. In particular, you are not free to act in ways that will lead your child to impose significant and avoidable burdens on the community. For example, the liberal state has a right to teach all children respect for the law, and you have no opposing right as a parent to undermine that respect. Similarly, the liberal state has a right to inculcate the expectation that all normal children will become adults capable of caring for themselves and their families.

Thus far, I think, the argument is reasonably strong and uncontroversial. But how much farther may the liberal state go? Gutmann argues that children must be taught both "mutual respect among persons" and "rational deliberation among ways of life," and that parents are unlikely to do this on their own. Indeed, it is precisely because communities such as the Old Order Amish are morally committed to shielding their children from influences that might weaken their faith that the state is compelled to step in:

> The same principle that requires a state to grant adults personal and political freedom also commits it to assuring children an education that makes those freedoms both possible and meaningful in the future. A state makes choice possible by teaching its future citizens respect for opposing points of view and ways of life. It makes choice meaningful by equipping children with the intellectual skills necessary to evaluate ways of life different from that of their parents.[1]

[1] Amy Gutmann, *Democratic Education* (Princeton, NJ: Princeton University Press, 1988), pp. 30–1. Don Herzog has also advanced a version of this thesis: "Parents need to teach their

I do not believe that this argument can be sustained. In a liberal-democratic polity, to be sure, the fact of social diversity means that the willingness to co-exist peacefully with ways of life very different from one's own is essential. Furthermore, the need for public evaluation of leaders and policies means that the state has an interest in developing citizens with at least the minimal conditions of reasonable public judgment. But neither of these civic requirements entails a need for public authority to take an interest in how children think about different ways of life. Civic tolerance of deep differences is perfectly compatible with unswerving belief in the correctness of one's own way of life. It rests on the conviction that the pursuit of the better course should (and in many cases must) result from persuasion rather than coercion—a classic Lockean premise that the liberal state *does* have an interest in articulating. Civic deliberation is also compatible with unshakable personal commitments. It requires only that each citizen accept the minimal civic commitments, sketched above, without which the liberal polity cannot long endure. In short, the civic standpoint does not warrant the conclusion that the state must (or may) structure public education to foster in children skeptical reflection on ways of life inherited from parents or local communities.

It is hardly accidental, however, that Gutmann takes the argument in this direction. At the heart of much modern liberal democratic thought is a (sometimes tacit) commitment to the Socratic proposition that the unexamined life is an unworthy life, that individual freedom is incompatible with ways of life guided by unquestioned authority or unswerving faith. As philosophic conclusions, these commitments have much to recommend them. The question, though, is whether the liberal state is justified in building them into its system of public education. The answer is that it cannot do so without throwing its weight behind a conception of the human good unrelated to the functional needs of its sociopolitical institutions and at odds with the deep beliefs of many of its loyal citizens. As a political matter, liberal freedom entails the right to live unexamined as well as examined lives—a right the effective exercise of which

---

children to be critical thinkers or at least to tolerate others so teaching them. . . . [C]hildren taught the skills of questioning their own commitments are better off. They can sculpt their own identities" (*Happy Slaves: A Critique of Consent Theory* [Chicago: University of Chicago Press, 1989], p. 242). And Stephen Macedo has also endorsed such a thesis: "Liberal persons are distinguished by the possession of self-governing reflective capacities. Further developing these reflective capacities leads one toward the ideal of autonomy. . . . Striving for autonomy involves developing the self-conscious, self-critical, reflective capacities that allow one to formulate, evaluate, and revise ideals of life and character, to bring these evaluations to bear on actual choices and on the formulation of projects and commitments" (Macedo, *Liberal Virtues: Citizenship, Virtue, and Community in Liberal Constitutionalism* [Oxford: Clarendon Press, 1990], p. 269).

My objection to all these views is more or less the same: Liberalism is about the protection of diversity, not the valorization of choice. To place an ideal of autonomous choice at the core of liberalism is in fact to narrow the range of possibilities available within liberal societies. It is a drive toward a kind of uniformity, disguised in the language of liberal diversity. In this respect, at least, I agree with Charles Larmore: "The Kantian and Millian conceptions of liberalism [which rest on autonomy and individuality as specifications of the good life] are not adequate solutions to the political problem of reasonable disagreement about the good life. They have themselves become simply another part of the problem" (Larmore, "Political Liberalism," *Political Theory* 18, 3 [August 1990]: 345).

may require parental bulwarks against the corrosive influence of modernist skepticism. I might add that in practice, there is today a widespread perception that our system of public education already embodies a bias against authority and faith. This perception, in large measure, is what underlies the controversy over "secular humanism" that is so incomprehensible to liberal elites.

It is not difficult to anticipate the objections that will be raised against the argument I have just advanced. There are, after all, three parties to the educational transaction: children, their parents, and the state. Perhaps the state has no direct right to shape public education in accordance with the norms of Socratic self-examination. But doesn't liberal freedom mean that children have the right to be exposed to a range of possible ways of life? If parents thwart this right by attempting (as some would say) to "brainwash" their children, doesn't the state have a right—indeed, a duty—to step in?

The answer is no on both counts. Children do have a wide range of rights that parents are bound to respect and that government is bound to enforce against parental violation. As I argued earlier, parents may not rightly impede the normal physical, intellectual, and emotional development of their children. Nor may they impede the acquisition of civic competence and loyalty. The state may act *in loco parentis* to overcome family-based obstacles to normal development. And it may use public instrumentalities, including the system of education, to promote the attainment by all children of the basic requisites of citizenship. These are legitimate intrusive state powers. But they are limited by their own inner logic. In a liberal state, interventions that cannot be justified on this basis cannot be justified at all. That is how liberal democracies must draw the line between parental and public authority over the education of children, or (to put it less conflictually) that is the principle on the basis of which such authority must be shared.[2]

But doesn't this position evade the emotional force of the objection? Doesn't it legitimate parental brainwashing of children, and isn't that a terrible thing? Again, the answer is no, for two reasons. First, the simple fact that authority is divided means that from an early age, every child will see that he or she is answerable to institutions other than the family—institutions whose substantive requirements may well cut across the grain of parental wishes and beliefs. Some measure of reflection, or at least critical distance, is likely to result. Second, the basic features of liberal society make it virtually impossible for parents to seal their children off from knowledge of other ways of life. And as every parent knows, possibilities that are known but forbidden take on an allure out of all proportion to their intrinsic merits.

To these points I would add a basic fact of liberal sociology: The greatest threat to children in modern liberal societies is not that they will believe in something too deeply, but that they will believe in nothing very deeply at all. Even to achieve the kind of free self-reflection that many liberals prize, it is better to begin by believing something. Rational deliberation among ways of life

---

[2] For a very different way of drawing this line, see Bruce Ackerman, *Social Justice in the Liberal State* (New Haven: Yale University Press, 1980), ch. 5.

is far more meaningful if (and I am tempted to say *only* if) the stakes are mean-ingful, that is, if the deliberator has strong convictions against which compet-ing claims can be weighed. The role of parents in fostering such convictions should be welcomed, not feared.[3]

Despite the pluralism of liberal societies, it is perfectly possible to identify a core of civic commitments and competences the broad acceptance of which un-dergirds a well-ordered liberal polity. The state has a right to ensure that this core is generally and effectively disseminated, either directly, through public civic education, or indirectly, through regulation of private education. In cases of conflict, this civic core takes priority over individual or group commitments (even the demands of conscience), and the state may legitimately use coercive mechanisms to enforce this priority.

But the liberal state must not venture beyond this point. It must not throw its weight behind ideals of personal excellence outside the shared understand-ing of civic excellence, and it must not give pride of place to understandings of personal freedom outside the shared understanding of civic freedom. For if it does so, the liberal state will prescribe—as valid for, and binding on, all— a single debatable conception of how human beings should lead their lives. In the name of liberalism, it will betray its own deepest and most defensible principles.

---

[3] For a nuanced and carefully argued defense of a similar position that unfortunately came to my attention too late to have an appropriate impact on my own formulation, see Brian Crittenden, *Parents, the State and the Right to Educate* (Burwood, Victoria: Melbourne University Press, 1988), chs. 5, 7, and 8.

60.

Educating about Basic Substantive Values

GEORGE SHER AND WILLIAM J. BENNETT

It is now widely agreed that educators have no business inculcating moral views in the classroom. According to many philosophers and educational theorists, all attempts to influence students' moral behavior through exhortation and personal example are indoctrinative and should give way to more discursive efforts to guide children in developing their own values.[1] Yet although the nondirective approach to moral education has become the new orthodoxy, its philosophical underpinnings remain largely unexplored. In particular, the familiar charge that all directive moral education is indoctrinative has not been carefully defended. In this paper, we will argue that no plausible version of it *can* be defended and that adequate moral education must include both directive and discursive elements. Because the charge of indoctrination is so far clear, we will not confront it directly. Instead, we will address two closely related claims: that directive moral education (1) violates a student's autonomy, and (2) involves sectarian teaching inappropriate to a pluralistic society. If these complaints can be shown to lack substance, then the charge of indoctrination will carry little weight.

I

Before discussing the major objections to directive education, we must make clearer what such education involves. In particular, we must specify (a) the traits and principles to be taught and (b) the relevant methods of teaching them, and (c) the positive reasons for adopting such methods.

The traits and principles we have in mind are best illustrated by example. In Talawanda, Ohio, the local school district recently took the position that "the schools should help students realize the importance" of principles and traits including:

- Achieving self-discipline, defined as strength to do what we believe we should do, even when we would rather not do it.

---

[1] Thus, for example: "[I]t is . . . wrong to teach ethics by presenting and attempting to inculcate a number of rules or precepts of conduct so as to improve, or at least to alter character, dispositions, or responses. The most effective means for altering responses, and possibly character as well, are those of advertising, propaganda (is there any difference?), indoctrination and brainwashing. These are all objectionable on moral grounds, so one cannot possibly improve character by these means" [Marcus Singer, "The Teaching of Introductory Ethics," *The Monist,* LVIII, 4 (October 1974), p. 617]. "If moral education promotes a definite moral perspective, it tends to be toward indoctrination and the denial of moral autonomy. . . . The problem and the challenge of moral education in our age is to find a middle way which neither indoctrinates young people into one set of moral rules nor gives them the impression that decision making is all a matter of personal opinion" [Robert Hall, "Moral Education Today: Progress, Prospects and Problems of a Field Come of Age," *The Humanist* (November/December 1978), p, 12].

- Being trustworthy, so that when we say we will or will not do something, we can be believed.
- Telling the truth, especially when it hurts us to do so.
- Having the courage to resist group pressures to do what we believe, when alone, that we should not do.
- Using honorable means, those that respect the rights of others, in seeking our individual and collective ends.
- Conducting ourselves, where significant moral behavior is involved, in a manner which does not fear exposure.
- Having the courage to say, "I'm sorry, I was wrong."
- Treating others as we would wish to be treated; recognizing that this principle applies to persons of every class, race, nationality, and religion.
- Doing work well, whatever that work may be.
- Respecting the democratic values of free speech, a free press, freedom of assembly, freedom of religion, and due process of law. Recognizing that this principle applies to speech we abhor, groups we dislike, persons we despise.

Later, we will discuss the degree to which the Talawanda list embodies moral or ideological bias. For now, it suffices to note that the items just listed are close to noncontroversial within our society. They illustrate, but do not exhaust, the traits and principles whose directive teaching we will discuss.

What, exactly, does such teaching involve? Although a full account is again impossible, certain elements stand out. Of these, perhaps the most important is a teacher or administrator's willingness to demonstrate that he himself endorses certain principles—that he accepts them as guides in his own conduct and expects his students to do likewise. This requires that he act as an intentional model of behavior in accordance with the favored principles. It also requires that he explicitly urge his students to develop habits of acting in similar ways and that he express his disapproval, both verbally and through punishment, when his expectations are not met. It is often desirable to explain *why* one should act in the relevant ways, but efforts to influence behavior should not be confined to such explanations. Both encouragement and expressions of disapproval may persist when the proffered reasons are not grasped.

Why should morality be taught in these ways? Quite obviously, any rationale for adopting directive methods must be an instrumental one. The claim must be that, at elementary levels of development, such methods are effective ways of getting children to internalize desirable habits and behave in desirable ways and that, at more advanced levels, the previous application of these methods is necessary for the success of more discursive methods. We believe these claims are supported by recent studies of child and adolescent development and "moral psychology."[2] However, even if all empirical issues remained open, the permissibility of directive moral education would still be worth ascertaining.

[2] See especially Norman T. Feather, "Values in Adolescence," and Martin L. Hoffman, "Moral Development in Adolescence," in Joseph Adelson, ed., *The Handbook of Adolescent Psychology* (New York: Wiley, 1980), pp. 247–344.

Even those who are not convinced that such methods work must be interested in learning whether we would be morally permitted to employ them if they did.

II

Consider, first, the objection that directive moral education violates autonomy. At the core of this objection is a distinction between actions produced by non-rational causes and actions motivated by an awareness of the reasons for performing them. When a child acts to imitate a respected model or in response to exhortation or threat, he is said to be motivated only in the former way. Even if there are good reasons for his action, the very same techniques that have motivated his act could just as well have been used to motivate behavior unsupported by such reasons. Thus, his behavior is evidently *not* produced simply by his appreciation of the reasons for it. Hence, it is said to be neither fully his own nor an appropriate object of moral appraisal.

There is plainly something right about this objection. On any plausible account, an adequate moral education must produce not only a tendency to act rightly, but also a tendency to do so for the right reasons. But, despite its superficial clarity, the objection as stated is both ambiguous and incomplete. It is ambiguous because it does not specify whether the person whose autonomy is violated is the child to whom directive education is administered or the adult whom the child will later become. It is incomplete because it does not explain *how* autonomy is violated in either case.

Whose autonomy is violated by directive moral education? Of the two possible answers, the more straightforward is "the child's." But to this answer, there is a quick rejoinder. However desirable it is to appeal to a person's appreciation of reasons, it surely need not be wrong to influence his behavior in other ways when he cannot respond to reasons alone. But this is manifestly true of young children. With them, appeals to principle simply fail. We must ascend the developmental scale quite far before such appeals promise much success. According to the leading proponent of nondirective moral education, Lawrence Kohlberg, the most common motive for moral action among 13-year-olds is still a desire to avoid disapproval and dislike by others.[3] In Kohlberg's typology, this motive is three full stages away from conscientious aversion to self-reproach. Moreover, in Kohlberg's view, one cannot reach a given stage of moral development without first traversing all the lower stages. Thus, even Kohlberg must acknowledge that, before middle adolescence, most children cannot respond to unadorned appeals to moral reasons. But if so, we do not violate their autonomy when we supplement such appeals with more efficacious influences.

This reply may appear inconclusive; for the opponent of directive moral education can respond by weakening his requirements for autonomy. Instead of

---

[3] For elaboration, see Kohlberg, *The Philosophy of Moral Development* (New York: Harper & Row, 1981).

contending that moral autonomy requires that one act from moral reasons, he can assert that it requires only that one's motives be those of the highest Kohlbergian level available to one. If so, even a child who acts to satisfy an impersonally construed authority (Kohlberg's level 4) may act significantly more autonomously than one who seeks to imitate a respected elder or to avoid punishment. However, considered by itself, such denatured "autonomy" has little value. Its main significance is pretty clearly to pave the way for further moral development. Thus, the response does not really save the claim that directive techniques violate a child's autonomy. If anything, it reinforces the claim that what is violated is the autonomy of the adult whom the child will become.

Put in this second form, the objection no longer presupposes an obviously impossible ideal of autonomy. Unlike children, mature adults often do seem to respond to moral reasons. But why should the previous application of directive techniques be thought to prevent this? It is true that directive techniques use nonrational means to produce desires and character traits that will eventually influence one's adult actions. However, even if an adult *is* motivated by a desire that was originally produced by nonrational means, it still seems possible for his action to be done for good moral reasons. In particular, this still seems possible if his nonrationally produced desire is precisely to act *in accordance with* such reasons. But it is surely just this desire which the sensitive practitioner of directive moral education seeks to instill.

If moral autonomy required only action in accordance with moral reasons, this response would be decisive. However, another strain of thought construes the requirements for autonomy more strictly. On this view, genuine moral autonomy requires not only that an agent act *in accordance with* moral reasons, but also that he *be motivated by* his awareness of them. In Kantian terms, the autonomous agent must be "self-legislating." On this expanded account the effectiveness of a past directive education may again seem threatening to current autonomy. If without his past directive education the agent would not now act as he does, then it is apparently just the desires produced by that education which supply the motivational energy for his current act. But if so, that motivational energy is evidently *not* supplied by his recognition of reasons themselves. His recognition of reasons may *trigger* the motivational energy for his act; but what is triggered is still energy with an independent source. Hence, the requirements for moral autonomy still seem unsatisfied.

With this refinement, we approach the heart of the objection that directive moral education violates autonomy. But although the refinement is familiar, the resulting argument is problematical. Most obviously, it rests on both the obscure metaphor of motivational energy and the undefended requirement that autonomous acts must draw such energy from reasons themselves. But the difficulty goes deeper. Even if its premises were both intelligible and defensible, the argument would be a non sequitur. Although it purports to demonstrate that directive moral education *violates* moral autonomy, it really shows only that such education does not *contribute* to moral autonomy. Far from establishing that directive techniques are pernicious, it at best establishes that they are morally neutral.

For why *should* desires produced by nonrational techniques be thought to prevent one from being motivated by an appreciation of reasons? Is the point merely that anyone subject to nonrationally produced desires would perform his act even if he were *not* motivated by an appreciation of the moral reasons for it? If so, then the most that follows is that his act is motivationally overdetermined. Since this does not negate the motivating force of his appreciation of reasons, it does not undermine his autonomy. Is the point rather that, if one's directively induced desires are required to produce one's action, then the motivation supplied by one's appreciation of reasons is too *weak* to produce it— that the latter motivation requires supplementation? If so, then, without his directive moral education, the agent would not have performed the act at all, and so *a fortiori* would not have performed it autonomously. Here again, nothing suggests that his directive moral education has reduced or violated his autonomy.

Given these considerations, even the strengthened analysis of autonomy does not establish that directive moral education violates one's later autonomy. To show this, one would need two yet stronger premises: that (1) a single act cannot simultaneously be motivated by both the agent's recognition of reasons and a nonrationally induced desire, and (2) when motivation from both sources converges, the motivational energy supplied by the nonrationally induced desire always excludes that supplied by an appreciation of reasons. But although these premises would indeed save the argument, there is little independent basis for them. In ordinary contexts, energy from any number of sources can combine to produce a single result. Hence, given our working metaphor, we must also presume that *motivational* energy from different sources can combine. The presumption must be that the motivating force of reasons does *not* give way when other factors motivate the same act. Moreover, these presumptions are not defeated by any independent theoretical considerations; for no adequate theory of how reasons motivate has yet been proposed.

III

So far, we have argued that directive moral education need not violate anyone's present or future moral autonomy. This conclusion, if correct, suffices to rebut the first objection to directive education. But more can be said here. Even if autonomy does require motivation by moral reasons, one's past directive education may actually help such autonomy to develop and flourish.

To see how directive education can have this result, recall first that, even if one's grasp of a moral reason does supply one with some impulse to do the right thing, that impulse may be too weak to issue in action. Because of this, its effect may depend on other factors. In particular, that effect may well be increased by one's past directive education. Of course, the desires produced by such education will not contribute to one's moral autonomy if they merely add their weight to the motivation supplied by one's appreciation of reasons. However, and crucially, a past directive education may also augment one's appreciation of reasons in another way. It may neutralize or eliminate what would otherwise be a competing motive, and so may enable one's appreciation of reasons to affect one more strongly. If directive education works this way, it will indeed render the agent more autonomous. Put in terms of our guiding metaphor, its function will be not to provide an additional source of motivational energy, but rather to clear away obstacles so that the energy supplied by reasons can suffice.

How likely is it that directive moral education actually does work in this way? It is not likely to do so always or exclusively. That directive education does not *always* work by eliminating obstacles to moral reasons is shown by the fact that it motivates even very young children and can motivate adults to act immorally. That it rarely works *only* by eliminating such obstacles is suggested by the fact that one's prerational desires seem likely to persist as one matures. But even if a past directive education often affects adults in ways that do not enhance their autonomy, it may simultaneously affect them in other ways as well. Thus, the question is not whether our model is exclusively correct, but only whether it accurately reflects *one* way in which directive moral education often works.

When the question is put this way, we think its answer is clearly yes. It is a psychological commonplace that one's ability to respond to any reason depends on various external considerations. Hunger, anxiety, pain, and fear can all reduce the effect of reasons by diminishing attention to them and by supplying other motives. Thus, eliminating these distractions plainly does increase the motivating force of reasons. But if so, then eliminating other distractions seems likely to serve a similar function. Two considerations which most often distract us from moral obligations are preoccupation with our own interests and concern for our own comfort. Hence, one very natural way of increasing the motivating force of moral reasons is to reduce the impact of such distractions. But how better to prevent someone from being unduly distracted by self-interest than by causing him to acquire settled habits of honesty, fair play, and concern for others? Given these habits, one will automatically discount one's selfish interests when they conflict with one's duty. Hence, one will attach proper weight to one's moral obligations as a matter of course. Moreover, how better to ensure that someone will follow his decisions through than by causing him to acquire further habits of diligence, perseverance, and conscientiousness? Given *these* habits, one will not be sidetracked by the blandishments of comfort or inertia. Hence, one's appreciation of reasons will again be rendered more effective.

Given all of this, the traditional content of directive moral education acquires new significance. As the Talawanda list suggests, such education has long aimed at producing the habits just mentioned. These habits are often criticized as poor substitutes for self-conscious and reasoned morality, but we can now see that this criticism misses the point. Far from being alternatives to self-conscious morality, the habits are best understood as indispensible auxiliaries to it. They increase the impact of moral reasons by reducing one's tendency to be diverted. When the habits exist in persons who do not appreciate moral reasons, they may be mere facsimiles of virtue. However, when they exist in conjunction *with* an appreciation of reasons, they surely do contribute to moral autonomy.

IV

Until now, we have considered only the objection that directive moral education violates the ideal of the morally autonomous agent. However, one may also argue that it violates a related *social* ideal. There is wide agreement that our society should be both tolerant and pluralistic. Instead of stifling disagreements, it should accept and encourage diversity of opinion and should protect unpopular attitudes and beliefs. But a society that officially practices directive moral education seems not to do this. Instead of encouraging diversity, it instills in all children a single "approved" set of values. Far from being neutral, it is unabashedly partisan. Thus, such education may seem flatly incompatible with pluralism and tolerance.

This argument is narrower in scope than its predecessor; for it tells only against the use of directive techniques in public schools. Still, it does seem to animate many charges of indoctrination, and so we must examine it. To see the problems it raises, consider first the premise that society should tolerate and protect diverse values. This premise may mean either that (1) society should not coerce or persecute those who already hold unorthodox values, or (2) society should not try to induce people to acquire (or prevent people from acquiring) any values they do not yet hold. Whenever society coerces or persecutes those with unpopular values, it provides a disincentive for others to acquire those values. Hence, any violation of (1) is likely to violate (2). However, society may tolerate dissenters while trying to prevent others from acquiring their values. Hence, a violation of (2) does not necessarily violate (1).

Directive moral education neither persecutes anyone nor coerces any adults. When its techniques include punishment, it may be said to coerce children. However, (1) is generally not taken to apply to children, and punishment is in any case theoretically dispensible. Thus, directive moral education need not violate (1). It does violate (2); but that counts against it only if (2) is a proper interpretation of the pluralistic ideal. At first glance, (2) may appear to follow from a more general requirement that unorthodox views should receive a fair hearing. However, this would imply that we owe fair treatment to values as well as persons; and, as John Rawls has noted, such an obligation is highly unlikely.[4] Thus, the more promising strategy is to defend (2) less directly. To do that, one might appeal either to a societal obligation to allow persons to choose their own values or else to the undesirable consequences of inculcating official values. We will argue that neither defense succeeds.

The claim that societal attempts to inculcate values would violate an obligation to allow people to choose their own values is inherently problematical. In standard cases, people's choices are guided by their values, but here it is

---

[4] "Fairness to Goodness," *Philosophical Review*, LXXXIV, 4 (October 1975): pp. 536–554.

precisely one's basic values that are said to *be* chosen. Hence, the relevant choices cannot be grounded in any deeper values. But how, then, *are* such choices grounded? Shall we say they have no grounding, but are simply arbitrary? If so, they hardly warrant society's protection. Are they grounded in considerations outside the agent's value system, such as his recognition of independent moral reasons? If so, the complaint against inculcating values must be that it prevents people from *responding* to such reasons. But we already know this is false. The desires and habits produced by directive moral education need not diminish, but may actually enhance, the motivating force of moral reasons. Is the claim, finally, that societally induced desires and habits do allow rational choice of values when they coincide with moral reasons, but prevent it in cases of conflict? If so, the argument is not that it is wrong to inculcate values, but only that society may inculcate the wrong values. Thus construed, the argument appeals to consequences. Hence, having come this far, we may abandon the rubric of choice, and confront the consequentialist approach directly.

The *locus classicus* of consequentialist arguments for tolerance is John Stuart Mill's *On Liberty*.[5] It is true that Mill's main target is not the inculcation of values, but rather intolerance involving coercion and persecution. However, there are also passages where Mill suggests that his arguments *do* extend to education, and presumably *a fortiori* to directive education (104–106). Moreover, whatever Mill's own views, any convincing consequentialist argument for (2) is likely to rest on precisely the familiar claims that society is fallible, that genuine challenges to belief enhance understanding, and that diverse practices provide people with a variety of models and "experiments of living." Thus, it is essentially the Millian arguments that we must now consider. Do they show that society should refrain from using nonrational techniques to instill values in its citizens?

We think not. Mill is right to insist that neither anyone's subjective feeling of certainty nor the agreement of society can guarantee the truth of an opinion or the utility of its adoption. However, the warrant for accepting the values of fairness, honesty, and consideration of others is no mere feeling of conviction. Instead, there is good independent reason to believe that, if any moral propositions are true, propositions enjoining such behavior are among them. Moreover, if the issue turns on social utility, then the warrant for inculcating these values is still more obvious. There is of course a danger that, once any inculcation of values is admitted, dogmatists and fanatics will seek to inculcate values that are *not* well-grounded or useful. However, this danger, though real, is far from decisive. If we can avoid the slippery slope by insisting that *no* values be inculcated, then we can also do so by insisting that society inculcate only values that satisfy high standards of justifiability. This will of course require some exercise of judgment; but that seems unavoidable in any case. As Mill himself remarks, "there is no difficulty in proving any ethical standard whatever to work ill, if we suppose universal idiocy to be conjoined with it."[6]

---

[5] *On Liberty* (Indianapolis: Hackett, 1978).

[6] *Utilitarianism* (Indianapolis: Hackett, 1979), p. 23.

In view of this, (2) cannot be supported by appealing to human fallibility. But the other consequentialist arguments are no better. A person's comprehension of his beliefs and values may indeed be deepened by challenges posed by dissenters, but such challenges are generally not needed to promote either adequate comprehension or tenacious acceptance of moral values. The suggestion that they are is contradicted by common experience. Moreover, even if widespread challenges to moral values did bring real benefits, these would be trivial compared to the mischief done by large numbers of people uncommitted to honesty, integrity, or concern for others. Nor, similarly, is it likely that exposure to cruelty, dishonesty, and insensitivity will promote personal development or bring out traits beneficial to others.

These considerations show that directive moral education need not be condemned as incompatible with pluralism. But that point can also be made in another way. It would be self-defeating for pluralists to demand that society be completely neutral toward all values; for the general acceptance of some values is required by pluralism itself. This holds most obviously for the value of toleration, but it is no less true of other values on the Talawanda list. If people were not committed to fairness, cooperation, and trustworthiness, they could hardly maintain a framework within which the rights of the weak and unpopular were protected. This may or may not justify the coercive suppression of some views—intolerance in the name of tolerance remains a disputed question of liberalism—but it surely does call for something beyond mere neutrality. If we as a society value toleration, then we must also value the general acceptance of principles that support and further it. Hence, if there is an effective method of advancing such principles which is not otherwise objectionable, we must acknowledge a strong case for adopting it. But precisely this is true of directive moral education. Thus, at least some forms of it seem justified by our commitment to toleration itself.

V

We have now rejected several familiar arguments against directive moral education. However, in endorsing such education, we do not mean that it should be used to teach every widely accepted moral belief or that it should utilize every effective method of procuring assent. Despite the strong moral component in many issues of economic distribution, foreign policy, and religion, we believe that normative propositions about these matters should generally not be taught directively. And although we believe that fairness and honesty *should* be taught directively, we believe their teaching should not involve immoderate humiliation or pain. But if we are to make such distinctions, we face a difficult further question: why are some forms of directive moral education permissible but others not?

This question is too large for us to answer fully, but some considerations are obviously relevant. To warrant directive teaching, a moral principle must first be clearly and firmly grounded. In addition, it should be simple enough to be comprehended at an early developmental stage, general enough to apply in a variety of situations, and central rather than peripheral to our moral corpus. To be acceptable as a *method* of directive teaching, a practice must neither impair a child's later ability to respond to moral reasons nor violate his rights. In many instances, the satisfaction of these requirements is undisputed. However, if an otherwise eligible principle or method is unacceptable to a conscientious minority, then respect for that minority may itself dictate restraint in directive teaching.

With this we can confront a final objection. It is sometimes said that because directive moral education reflects the prevailing moral climate, it inevitably favors existing practices and institutions. Because it grows out of entrenched attitudes, it is said objectionably to perpetuate the status quo. But we can now see that such worries are overblown. If the principles and habits that are directively taught are strongly justified, central to our evaluative scheme, and of more than parochial application, they are not likely to ratify all aspects of the status quo. Instead, they may well generate considerable dissatisfaction with existing realities. If someone is fair, considers others' interests, and respects democratic values, then he will be highly critical of many existing practices. If he is unmoved by group pressures, he will press his criticism even when it is unpopular. If he respects the truth and disdains dishonorable means, he will abjure self-interested silence. All in all, such a person is unlikely to be passive and indiscriminately accepting. Instead, he is apt vigorously to oppose various existing practices.

This shows that directive moral education need not favor the status quo. But should it ever be used to teach principles that *do* have this effect? To see the problem here, consider some further Talawanda entries:

- Practicing good sportsmanship. Recognizing that although the will to win is important, winning is not all-important.
- Showing respect for the property of others—school property, business property, government property, everyone's property.
- Abstaining from premature sexual experience and developing sexual attitudes compatible with the values of family life.

We believe there is much to be said for each of these. However, each is closely associated with a contested social institution. The first presupposes the legitimacy of competition, the second assumes an economic system which distributes wealth unequally, and the third overtly favors marriage and the family. Alternatives to each institution have been proposed. Does this imply that these principles should not be directively taught?

We believe this question has no simple answer. To decide whether association with an existing institution disqualifies a principle, one must first clarify the nature of the association. Does the principle merely apply *only in the context of* the institution? Or does it, in addition, require that one *accept* it? If acceptance of (say) property or the family is required, must one accept only some form of the institution, or all its current details? If the details need not be accepted, the argument amounts to little. But even if a principle does require full acceptance of an existing institution, the question of its directive teaching is not settled. The main reasons for not directively teaching such principles are to permit full evaluation of alternative institutions and to display respect for persons proposing them. However, despite their relevance, these factors are not always decisive. We saw above that a major determinant of whether a principle should be directively taught is its degree of justification. But if so, then when a principle requires acceptance of a contested institution, we cannot avoid asking how reasonable it is to oppose that institution and how plausible the alternatives are. If these questions are asked, their answers may tip the balance. Hence, directive teaching of principles favoring existing institutions cannot be ruled out.

This of course says little of substance. To evaluate directive teaching about property, sexual behavior, or other matters of controversy, one must say more about a whole range of issues. But that much more must be said is precisely our point. Where directive moral education is concerned, we begin to make progress only when we abandon as sterile the notion of indoctrination and its cognates.

61.

For Vouchers and Parental Choice

MILTON FRIEDMAN

A stable and democratic society is impossible without a minimum degree of literacy and knowledge on the part of most citizens and without widespread acceptance of some common set of values. Education can contribute to both. In consequence, the gain from the education of a child accrues not only to the child or to his parents but also to other members of the society. The education of my child contributes to your welfare by promoting a stable and democratic society. It is not feasible to identify the particular individuals (or families) benefited and so to charge for the services rendered. There is therefore a significant "neighborhood effect."

What kind of governmental action is justified by this particular neighborhood effect? The most obvious is to require that each child receive a minimum amount of schooling of a specified kind. Such a requirement could be imposed upon the parents without further government action, just as owners of buildings, and frequently of automobiles, are required to adhere to specified standards to protect the safety of others. There is, however, a difference between the two cases. Individuals who cannot pay the costs of meeting the standards required for buildings or automobiles can generally divest themselves of the property by selling it. The requirement can thus generally be enforced without government subsidy. The separation of a child from a parent who cannot pay for the minimum required schooling is clearly inconsistent with our reliance on the family as the basic social unit and our belief in the freedom of the individual. Moreover, it would be very likely to detract from his education for citizenship in a free society.

If the financial burden imposed by such a schooling requirement could readily be met by the great bulk of the families in a community, it might still be both feasible and desirable to require the parents to meet the cost directly. Extreme cases could be handled by special subsidy provisions for needy families. There are many areas in the United States today where these conditions are satisfied. In these areas, it would be highly desirable to impose the costs directly on the parents. This would eliminate the governmental machinery now required to collect tax funds from all residents during the whole of their lives and then pay it back mostly to the same people during the period when their children are in school. It would reduce the likelihood that governments would also administer schools, a matter discussed further below. It would increase the likelihood that the subsidy component of school expenditures would decline as the need for such subsidies declined with increasing general levels of income. If, as now, the government pays for all or most schooling, a rise in income simply leads to a still larger circular flow of funds through the tax mechanism, and an expansion in the role of the government. Finally, but by no means least, imposing the costs on the parents would tend to equalize the social and private costs of having children and so promote a better distribution of families by size.[1]

Differences among families in resources and in number of children, plus the imposition of a standard of schooling involving very sizable costs, make such a policy hardly feasible in many parts of the United States. Both in such areas, and in areas where such a policy would be feasible, government has instead assumed the financial costs of providing schooling. It has paid, not only for the minimum amount of schooling required of all, but also for additional schooling at higher levels available to youngsters but not required of them. One argument for both steps is the "neighborhood effects" discussed above. The costs are paid because this is the only feasible means of enforcing the required minimum. Additional schooling is financed because other people benefit from the schooling of those of greater ability and interest, since this is a way of providing better social and political leadership. The gain from these measures must be balanced against the costs, and there can be much honest difference of judgment about how extensive a subsidy is justified. Most of us, however, would probably conclude that the gains are sufficiently important to justify some government subsidy.

• • •

As we have seen, both the imposition of a minimum required level of schooling and the financing of this schooling by the state can be justified by the "neighborhood effects" of schooling. A third step, namely the actual administration of educational institutions by the government, the "nationalization," as it were, of the bulk of the "education industry" is much more difficult to justify on these, or, so far as I can see, any other, grounds. The desirability of such nationalization has seldom been faced explicitly. Governments have, in the main, financed schooling by paying directly the costs of running educational institutions. Thus this step seemed required by the decision to subsidize schooling. Yet the two steps could readily be separated. Governments could require a minimum level of schooling financed by giving parents vouchers redeemable for a specified maximum sum per child per year if spent on "approved" educational services. Parents would then be free to spend this sum and any additional sum they themselves provided on purchasing educational services from an "approved" institution of their own choice. The educational services could be rendered by private enterprises operated for profit, or by non-profit institutions. The role of the government would be limited to insuring that the schools met certain minimum standards, such as the inclusion of a minimum common content in their programs, much as it now inspects restaurants to insure that they maintain minimum sanitary standards. An excellent example of a program of this sort is

---

[1] It is by no means so fantastic as may appear that such a step would noticeably affect the size of families. For example, one explanation of the lower birth rate among higher than among lower socio-economic groups may well be that children are relatively more expensive to the former, thanks in considerable measure to the higher standards of schooling they maintain, the costs of which they bear.

the United States educational program for veterans after World War II. Each veteran who qualified was given a maximum sum per year that could be spent at any institution of his choice, provided it met certain minimum standards. A more limited example is the provision in Britain whereby local authorities pay the fees of some students attending non-state schools. Another is the arrangement in France whereby the state pays part of the costs for students attending non-state schools.

One argument for nationalizing schools resting on a "neighborhood effect" is that it might otherwise be impossible to provide the common core of values deemed requisite for social stability. The imposition of minimum standards on privately conducted schools, as suggested above, might not be enough to achieve this result. The issue can be illustrated concretely in terms of schools run by different religious groups. Such schools, it can be argued, will instil sets of values that are inconsistent with one another and with those instilled in non-sectarian schools; in this way, they convert education into a divisive rather than a unifying force.

Carried to its extreme, this argument would call not only for governmentally administered schools, but also for compulsory attendance at such schools. Existing arrangements in the United States and most other Western countries are a halfway house. Governmentally administered schools are available but not compulsory. However, the link between the financing of schooling and its administration places other schools at a disadvantage: they get the benefit of little or none of the governmental funds spent on schooling—a situation that has been the source of much political dispute, particularly in France and at present in the United States. The elimination of this disadvantage might, it is feared, greatly strengthen the parochial schools and so render the problem of achieving a common core of values even more difficult.

Persuasive as this argument is, it is by no means clear that it is valid or that denationalizing schooling would have the effects suggested. On grounds of principle, it conflicts with the preservation of freedom itself. Drawing a line between providing for the common social values required for a stable society, on the one hand, and indoctrination inhibiting freedom of thought and belief, on the other is another of those vague boundaries that is easier to mention than to define.

In terms of effects, denationalizing schooling would widen the range of choice available to parents. If, as at present, parents can send their children to public schools without special payment, very few can or will send them to other schools unless they too are subsidized. Parochial schools are at a disadvantage in not getting any of the public funds devoted to schooling, but they have the compensating advantage of being run by institutions that are willing to subsidize them and can raise funds to do so. There are few other sources of subsidies for private schools. If present public expenditures on schooling were made available to parents regardless of where they send their children, a wide variety of schools would spring up to meet the demand. Parents could express their views about schools directly by withdrawing their children from one school and sending them to another, to a much greater extent than is now possible. In general, they can now take this step only at considerable cost—by sending their children to a private school or by changing their residence. For the rest, they can express their views only through cumbrous political channels. Perhaps a somewhat greater degree of freedom to choose schools could be made available in a governmentally administered system, but it would be difficult to carry this freedom very far in view of the obligation to provide every child with a place. Here, as in other fields, competitive enterprise is likely to be far more efficient in meeting consumer demand than either nationalized enterprises or enterprises run to serve other purposes. The final result may therefore be that parochial schools would decline rather than grow in importance.

A related factor working in the same direction is the understandable reluctance of parents who send their children to parochial schools to increase taxes to finance higher public school expenditures. As a result, those areas where parochial schools are important have great difficulty raising funds for public schools. Insofar as quality is related to expenditure, as to some extent it undoubtedly is, public schools tend to be of lower quality in such areas and hence parochial schools are relatively more attractive.

Another special case of the argument that governmentally conducted schools are necessary for education to be a unifying force is that private schools would tend to exacerbate class distinctions. Given greater freedom about where to send their children, parents of a kind would flock together and so prevent a healthy intermingling of children from decidedly different backgrounds. Whether or not this argument is valid in principle, it is not at all clear that the stated results would follow. Under present arrangements, stratification of residential areas effectively restricts the intermingling of children from decidedly different backgrounds. In addition, parents are not now prevented from sending their children to private schools. Only a highly limited class can or does do so, parochial schools aside, thus producing further stratification.

Indeed, this argument seems to me to point in almost the diametrically opposite direction—toward the denationalizing of schools. Ask yourself in what respect the inhabitant of a low income neighborhood, let alone of a Negro neighborhood in a large city, is most disadvantaged. If he attaches enough importance to, say, a new automobile, he can, by dint of saving, accumulate enough money to buy the same car as a resident of a high-income suburb. To do so, he need not move to that suburb. On the contrary, he can get the money partly by economizing on his living quarters. And this goes equally for clothes, or furniture, or books, or what not. But let a poor family in a slum have a gifted child and let it set such high value on his or her schooling that it is willing to scrimp and save for the purpose. Unless it can get special treatment, or scholarship assistance, at one of the very few private schools, the family is in a very difficult position. The "good" public schools are in the high income neighborhoods. The family might be willing to spend something in addition to what it pays in taxes to get better schooling for its child. But it can hardly afford simultaneously to move to the expensive neighborhood.

Our views in these respects are, I believe, still dominated by the small town which had but one school for the poor and rich residents alike. Under such circumstances, public schools may well have equalized opportunities. With the growth of urban and suburban areas, the situation has changed drastically. Our present school system, far from equalizing opportunity, very likely does the opposite. It makes it all the harder for the exceptional few—and it is they who are the hope of the future—to rise above the poverty of their initial state.

Another argument for nationalizing schooling is "technical monopoly." In small communities and rural areas, the number of children may be too small to justify more than one school of reasonable size, so that competition cannot be relied on to protect the interests of parents and children. As in other cases of technical monopoly, the alternatives are unrestricted private monopoly, state-controlled private monopoly, and public operation—a choice among evils. This argument, though clearly valid and significant, has been greatly weakened in recent decades by improvements in transportation and increasing concentration of the population in urban communities.

The arrangement that perhaps comes closest to being justified by these considerations—at least for primary and secondary education—is a combination of public and private schools. Parents who choose to send their children to private schools would be paid a sum equal to the estimated cost of educating a child in a public school, provided that at least this sum was spent on education in an approved school. This arrangement would meet the valid features of the "technical monopoly" argument. It would meet the just complaints of parents that if they send their children to private non-subsidized schools they are required to pay twice for education—once in the form of general taxes and once directly. It would permit competition to develop. The development and improvement of all schools would thus be stimulated. The injection of competition would do much to promote a healthy variety of schools. It would do much, also, to introduce flexibility into school systems.

62.

Against Vouchers and Parental Choice

AMY GUTMANN

Some critics challenge this conclusion by invoking democratic, rather than liberal or conservative, values. They claim that the fairest—and the most democratic—procedure for determining the purposes of primary education is to empower parents rather than communities to choose among schools, and thereby among educational purposes and methods for their children. We do not escape philosophizing about the purposes of primary education, therefore, when we determine that the independent philosophical justifications of amoralism, liberal neutrality, and the various types of moralism are too weak to override our disagreements. We still must wonder what constitutes a fair and democratic procedure for resolving our disagreements. Should parents or democratic communities be the primary authorities to choose among the legitimate purposes and methods of primary education?

This question presupposes what we have already argued, that democratic virtue can be taught. Now we need to know what kinds of schools should be empowered (by whom) to teach it. The United States relies primarily on local public schools, which admit all and only those school-age children residing in a particular geographical area. In the judgment of many critics of public schools, their record in teaching democratic virtue ranges from disappointing to disastrous. Critics have ample evidence to support their charges: public school systems in this country have engaged in educationally unnecessary tracking, they have presided over racial segregation in schools and classrooms, and they have instituted some of the most intellectually deadening methods of teaching American history and civics that one might imagine.

Perhaps schools with less captive clients would do better. Were all parents able to send their children to private schools, perhaps the democratic purposes of education would be better fulfilled. The idea of empowering all parents to choose among schools for their children is in this sense democratic: it increases the incentive for schools to respond to the market choices of middle-class and poor as well as rich parents. The idea may seem even more appealing when we compare the record of public and private schooling in the United States. The evidence is scanty, but it suggests that private schools may on average do better than public schools in bringing all their students up to a relatively high level of learning, in teaching American history and civics in an intellectually challenging manner, and even in racially integrating classrooms. Why not simultaneously increase the option of exiting from public schools and the incentive for all schools to respond to the critical voices of parents by providing "every set of parents with a voucher certificate redeemable for a specified maximum sum per child per year if spent on 'approved' educational services"?

To the extent that advocates of voucher plans focus on the rights of individual parents to control the schooling of their children, they rest their defense on the fundamental premise of the state of families, which we have already called into question. More sophisticated voucher plans, however, make substantial concessions to the democratic purposes of primary education by conditioning certification of voucher schools upon their meeting a set of minimal standards. The most carefully designed and defended voucher plan would constrain all schools that accepted vouchers (a) not to discriminate in their admissions policies against children on grounds of race, socio-economic status, or intelligence, (b) not to require or accept tuition payments above the level set by the vouchers, (c) not to expel students except under certain specified circumstances and then only with due process, (d) to supply a governmental information agency with detailed reports of their governance procedures and the academic achievement, socio-economic status, and racial composition of their student body, and (e) to require a minimum number of hours of instruction with a significant portion devoted to reading and mathematics.[1] This list is meant to be suggestive rather than exhaustive. The essence of the constrained voucher proposal is the following: within some predetermined set of constitutional and legislative constraints, voucher plans would empower parents to choose among schools rather than forcing them to send their children to the local public school, regardless of its quality or their preferences. The democratic virtue of parental empowerment is based on a consequentialist calculation: that schools will improve— they will better serve their democratic purposes—if the guardians of their clients are less captive.

Proponents of the constrained voucher plan put the debate over the purposes of education in a new perspective. Having rejected the claim that parents have an a priori right to control the schooling of their children, the case for a constrained voucher plan rests on an assessment of the consequences of increasing parental choice for fulfilling the purposes of education in a democratic society. John Coons and Stephen Sugarman suggest that the only way of fulfilling the democratic purposes of education is to empower parents to choose among schools that are constrained by the government to satisfy some (but by the logic of their case not all) of the purposes of democratic education. Coons and Sugarman recognize that there is no a priori reason to limit the role of government, as Milton Friedman does, "to assuring that the schools met certain minimum standards such as the inclusion of a minimum content in their programs, much as it now inspects restaurants to assure that they maintain minimum sanitary standards."[2] Based on this logic, the standards that constrain voucher schools must be "minimal" in only two senses: (1) schools should not be constrained any more than is necessary to satisfy our collective interests in primary education,

[1] John E. Coons and Stephen D. Sugarman, *Education By Choice: The Case for Family Control* (Berkeley: University of California Press, 1978), pp. 133–89.

[2] Milton Friedman, "The Role of Government in Education," in *Economics and the Public Interest*, ed. by Robert Solo (New Brunswick, N.J.: Rutgers University Press, 1955), pp. 123–45. See also Friedman, *Capitalism and Freedom*, pp. 85–107.

and (2) schools cannot be constrained to satisfy fully the democratic purposes of education, because a substantial degree of parental control over schooling is necessary to realize those purposes.

Resting as it does on a complicated consequentialist comparison, the claim of the constrained voucher plan defies easy assessment. Were citizens to agree on what consequences count (and how much to count them), it would be very difficult to predict the consequences of a thoroughgoing voucher plan versus an improved public school system. But we do not agree, nor is it likely that we shall ever agree as long as we have the freedom to disagree. On consequentialist grounds, the question of whether to institute a constrained voucher plan or to improve public schools by decentralization coupled with other similarly far-reaching reforms is inherently indeterminate. It is not surprising, therefore, that Coons and Sugarman do not argue the case for vouchers exclusively—or even primarily—on consequentialist grounds. They focus instead on the fact that we disagree over the purposes of primary education:

> If there ever was a national understanding about adult society's responsibility for the young, there is no longer. There remains, nonetheless, a general conviction that a just society makes ample provision for the formal portion of children's education and assures a measure of fairness and rationality in its distribution. But distribution of what? Given the diversity of values among American adults, in what should publicly supported education consist?[3]

Given our inability to agree on common standards, Coons and Sugarman conclude that publicly supported education should reflect the diversity of our values by imposing only a minimal set of common standards on primary schools.

But why should the fact of our disagreement over common standards favor the side that argues for minimizing our common standards? Consider Friedman's comparison of the regulation of schools to that of restaurants. The analogy implies that our common educational standards consist only of preventing schools from physically harming children or fraudulently claiming to educate them. Were our public interest in regulating schools as analogous to our interest in regulating restaurants as Friedman suggests, it would be hard to explain why we should subsidize schooling for every child. A necessary condition for justifying public subsidy of schools—but not of restaurants—is the fact that citizens have an important and common interest in educating future citizens. By labelling that interest an "externality" of education, Friedman suggests that educating citizens is a side effect, rather than a central purpose or "internality," of schooling. Although Coons and Sugarman do not use Friedman's language, they ultimately fall back upon his vision of schooling as primarily a private rather than a public concern.

To justify public support, standards to which voucher schools are held must fulfill the public purposes—the "internalities"—of primary education. In keeping with this claim, Coons and Sugarman (unlike Friedman) defend stringent

---

[3] Coons and Sugarman, *Education By Choice*, pp. 1–2.

constraints on the admissions processes of voucher schools to ensure that all children—not just white or intellectually talented or well-motivated children— have access to a good education. But are the set of constraints that Coons and Sugarman support sufficient for ensuring that voucher schools satisfy the public purposes of schooling? If a primary purpose of schools is to develop democratic character, then the externalities of education may be more extensive than even a constrained voucher plan admits. The externalities may include, among other things, how children of different intellectual abilities, races, and religions are distributed within classrooms, what subjects are taught and how they are taught, how authority in and over schools is distributed, and so on. The externalities of schooling extend beyond the admissions process, the curriculum, and the authority structure, to encompass almost every aspect of schooling, rendering indefensible the distinction between a publicly mandated "minimum" and parentally chosen standards for voucher schools.

Voucher plans attempt to avoid rather than settle our disagreements over how to develop democratic character through schooling. The attempt succeeds insofar as decisions concerning choice among schools are left to sets of parents, who are more likely to agree with one another than they are with other parents as to what constitutes a good school. The attempt fails insofar as the decisions concerning the constraints to be imposed upon voucher schools must still be collective. The most defensible voucher plans, like Coons and Sugarman's, make room for a set of centrally imposed constraints that reflect our collective interest in primary education. But having admitted the possibility—indeed, the necessity—of imposing a set of collective standards on schools, Coons and Sugarman can no longer rest the case for vouchers on the claim that such plans avoid the need for settling our disagreements over how citizens should be educated.

Minimally constrained voucher plans, like Friedman's, avoid the controversial issue of how schools should educate citizens only at the cost of denying our collective interests in democratic education. Maximally constrained voucher plans, like Coons and Sugarman's, appear to avoid the issue only by shifting our controversies over democratic education from a mixture of local, state, and national politics to a more purely centralized politics. If a voucher plan aims to increase diversity in schooling while providing citizens with more control over how schools educate children, then its effect of relegating collective interests in education to a more centralized politics is counter-productive.

In criticizing voucher plans for not recognizing the primacy of our public interest in schooling, we need not claim that society has a greater interest in the education of children than do parents. The point is rather that parents command a domain other than schools in which they can—and should—seek to educate their children, to develop their moral character and teach them religious or secular standards and skills that they value. We can therefore agree that not even the most extensive constraints upon schools can fully satisfy the democratic purposes of primary education, since parental influence over the education of their children is among those purposes. Turning public schools into a domain of parental authority is not, however, the appropriate means of satisfying this democratic purpose of education. The discretionary domain for education—particularly but not only for moral education—within the family has always been and must continue to be vast within a democratic society. And the existence of this domain of parental discretion provides a partial defense against those who claim that public schooling is a form of democratic tyranny over the mind. The risks of democratic and parental tyranny over moral education are reduced (although they can never be eliminated) by providing two substantially separate domains of control over moral education.

In recognition of our collective interest in schooling, voucher plans can incorporate regulations even more extensive than those advocated by Coons and Sugarman. The more room voucher plans make for regulation, the less room they leave for parental choice. Anyone who defends vouchers on the basis of their educational consequences rather than parental rights can defend this trade-off if necessary to fulfill the collective purposes of primary education. But advocates of vouchers cannot adequately defend the means—centralized governmental regulation—by which their plans constrain citizens to manifest their collective interests in influencing primary education. Were there a self-evident set of such regulations, then centralized governmental control over all voucher schools might be desirable. But there is no single self-evident set of regulations. Our collective interests in the moral education of future citizens might be manifest in many ways: by requiring more civics courses or restructuring schools to become more internally democratic, by increasing graduation requirements or retaining our present requirements and making promotion more difficult, by busing black and white children across district lines or dramatically improving the quality of inner-city schools. Which of these practices (if any) reflect our collective interest in influencing the shape of schooling must be determined to a large extent through democratic deliberations. If the politics of schooling does not leave room for such deliberations, we cannot say that the public constraints on schools—whether minimal or maximal—reflect our collective interests in primary education. The problem with voucher plans is not that they leave too much room for parental choice but that they leave too little room for democratic deliberation.

The appeal of vouchers to many Americans who are not otherwise committed to a state of families stems, I suspect, from three facts. One is that our public schools, especially in many of our largest cities, are so centralized and bureaucratized that parents along with other citizens actually exercise very little democratic control over local schools. The second is that only poor parents lack the option of exiting from public schools, and this seems unfair. The third, and most sweeping fact, is that the condition of many public schools today is bleak by any common-sensical standard of what democratic education ought to be.

The proper response to the first problem is to make public school systems less bureaucratic and more democratic. The best response to the second problem is to redistribute income more equitably, which would also overcome many other inequities in the ability of citizens to make use of their freedoms. Were *private* schooling an essential welfare good like health care, then the case for directly subsidizing it would be stronger. But we have already argued that public, not private, schooling is an essential welfare good for children as well as the primary means by which citizens can morally educate future citizens. We have yet to consider whether (and why), given the democratic purposes of education, a democratic society should leave room for private schooling. But based on our considerations so far, we can conclude that the welfare of children and the well-being of democracy can be supported simultaneously by improving education, especially moral education, within public schools rather than by encouraging parents to exit from them. We need not deny the third problem—that the condition of many public schools today is bleak—to recognize that we know of no more effective way, nor is there a more consistently democratic way, of trying to develop democratic character than to improve public schooling.

63.

Justice and Equality of Opportunity

CHRISTOPHER JENCKS

Americans never argue about whether educational opportunity should be equal. Egalitarians say equal opportunity is not enough. Pragmatists say it is unattainable. But no significant group defends unequal opportunity, either in education or elsewhere.

Instead of arguing about the desirability of equal educational opportunity, we argue about its meaning. We all assume that equal opportunity is comparable with our vision of a good society. Since we disagree about what such a society should be like, we usually disagree about the meaning of equal educational opportunity as well.

Everyone's conception of equal educational opportunity requires that educational institutions "treat equals equally." But we have dramatically different views about *whom* educational institutions should treat equally and whom they can legitimately treat unequally. Indeed, the enduring popularity of equal educational opportunity probably derives from the fact that we can all define it in different ways without realizing how profound our differences really are.

This paper discusses five common ways of thinking about equal educational opportunity, each of which draws on a different tradition and each of which has different practical consequences.[1] To illustrate both the differences among these five conceptions of equal opportunity and also the different ways in which each of them can be interpreted, I will focus on a single concrete example: a third-grade reading class in a small town, taught by a teacher whom I will call Ms. Higgins. Like all of us, Ms. Higgins believes in equal opportunity. Her problem—and ours—is what her belief in equal opportunity implies about the distribution of the main educational resources at her disposal, namely her time and attention.

Two features of this example deserve comment. First, the unit of analysis is small—as small as I could make it. I believe, but will not try to prove, that all the *principled* claims about how Ms. Higgins ought to allocate her time among her pupils recur in essentially the same form when we argue about how school principals, boards of education, or legislatures ought to allocate scarce resources. I recognize, however, that the *practical* arguments for various possible distributions of Ms. Higgins's time are often quite different from those that come into play when a board of education or a legislature is allocating resources.

The second distinctive feature of my "case study" is that it focuses on *young* students. As students get older, the case for paternalism grows weaker. As a

---

[1] Because this paper focuses on popular understanding of equal opportunity, I have not tried to tie my discussion to scholarly papers on the subject. Readers familiar with this literature will, however, find that it echoes many of the themes I discuss.

result, both the principled and the practical arguments for certain courses of action grow weaker too. I focus on young children because I believe that their youth dramatizes certain ambiguities in our thinking about equal opportunity, but it may obscure others.

MS. HIGGINS'S CHOICES

Before Ms. Higgins enters the classroom, she is likely to imagine that her commitment to equal opportunity implies that she should give every pupil equal time and attention. Once she starts teaching, however, she is likely to discover a number of principled reasons for deviating from this simple formula. Ms. Higgins's ruminations will, I think, eventually suggest at least five possibilities, to which I propose to attach the following labels:

1. *Democratic equality.* Democratic equality requires Ms. Higgins to give everyone equal time and attention, regardless of how well they read, how hard they try, how deprived they have been in the past, what they want, or how much they or others will benefit.
2. *Moralistic justice.* Moralistic justice requires Ms. Higgins to reward virtue and punish vice. In the classroom, virtue involves effort, and moralistic justice means rewarding those who make the most effort to learn whatever Ms. Higgins is trying to teach.
3. *Weak humane justice.* Since some students have gotten less than their proportionate share of advantages in the past, humane justice requires Ms. Higgins to compensate those students by giving them more than their proportionate share of her attention while they are in her classroom. But the "weak" variant of humane justice only requires Ms. Higgins to compensate those who have been shortchanged at home or in their earlier schooling, not those who have been shortchanged genetically.
4. *Strong humane justice.* This variant of humane justice requires Ms. Higgins to compensate those who have been shortchanged in *any* way in the past, including genetically. In practice, this means giving the most attention to the worst readers, regardless of the reasons for their illiteracy.
5. *Utilitarianism.* Most utilitarians assume that the best way to get individuals to do what we want is to make every activity, including education, a race for unequal rewards. Equal opportunity means that such races must be open to all, run on a level field, and judged solely on the basis of performance. Thus, insofar as Ms. Higgins's attention is a prize, it should go to the best readers.

Equal opportunity can therefore imply either a meritocratic distribution of resources, a compensatory distribution of resources, or an equal distribution of resources. A meritocratic conception of equal opportunity can, in turn, favor either those who try hard or those who achieve a lot, while a compensatory conception of equal opportunity can favor either those who have suffered from some sort of handicap in the past or those whose current achievement is below average.

DEMOCRATIC EQUALITY

If Ms. Higgins were a student teacher who had never thought carefully about teaching, and if we were to ask her what she thought equal opportunity implied about how she should distribute her time, she would probably answer that a commitment to equal opportunity meant giving all children equal time and attention. I refer to this view as "democratic" equality not because democracy has traditionally required it but because Americans habitually invoke the fact that they live in a democracy to justify it. We will say, for example, that our Constitution guarantees everyone "equal protection of the laws" and that this implies equal treatment. The idea of treating everyone in the same way, regardless of extenuating circumstances, certainly has a democratic ring to it.

Yet neither the Constitution of the United States nor democratic tradition requires either a board of education or Ms. Higgins to treat everyone in exactly the same way. School boards, for example, have never interpreted the democratic tradition as requiring them to spend equal sums on all pupils. They have set up programs of varying cost, especially at the secondary level, and have assumed that if they made these programs available on the basis of merit, past or current disadvantages, demand, or expected benefits, this was compatible with both equal opportunity and the equal protection clause of the Constitution.

As Ms. Higgins gains experience in the classroom she too is likely to feel dissatisfied with the idea that she must distribute her time in mathematically equal dollops to all children. Her first qualms about equal treatment are likely to arise when some of her pupils show more interest than others, and she finds herself responding to their interest with extra attention. This observation will lead her to think more seriously about moralistic justice.

THE MORALISTIC THEORY OF JUSTICE

Moralistic theories of justice assert that we should all try to reward virtue and punish vice. When students make an effort to do what Ms. Higgins asks of them, moralistic justice allows her to respond not only with praise but with extra attention as well. When students make no effort to do what she asks of them, moralistic justice tells her she need not "waste her time" on them. While she might not put it this way, moralistic justice encourages her to think of her classroom as a moral community, held together by an unwritten contract which states that "I'll do my best if you'll do yours." Those who respect the contract reap its benefits. Those who do not respect it are subject to internal exile—or to expulsion if they behave badly enough.

In principle, a moralistic view of the classroom should focus on intentions. This means that it should define virtue in terms of effort, not achievement. In practice, large institutions can seldom observe effort directly. All they can usually observe is actual achievement, which depends not only on current effort but also on ability and prior knowledge. Because large institutions habitually reward achievement rather than effort, Ms. Higgins may be tempted to do the same. But rewarding effortless achievement is not compatible with moralistic justice. Rather, it is a by-product of utilitarianism.

Moralistic justice is easy to reconcile with equal opportunity. One simply says that all students have an equal opportunity to make an effort and that all who make equal effort get equal treatment.

But moralistic justice is not likely to satisfy Ms. Higgins for long, because it treats third graders' motivation as fixed. If Ms. Higgins is at all perceptive, she will begin to ask why some children work harder than others and what she can do about this. Sooner or later such questions will force her to think about what I have called humane justice.

HUMANE THEORIES OF JUSTICE

Instead of focusing on what we deserve because of our virtues and vices, "humane" theories of justice focus on what we deserve simply because we are members of the human species. Since we are all equally human, our claims as members of the species are all equal. Such claims, based on the mere fact of being human, are commonly labeled "rights." Since there is no general agreement about the nature of these rights, there are many versions of human justice. For convenience, I will try to array them on a spectrum running from strong to weak.

In its strongest variant, humane justice asserts that all individuals have an equal claim on all of society's resources, regardless of their virtues or vices. This version of humane justice demands equal outcomes rather than equal opportunity, however, so it need not concern us here.

What I will call here the strong variant of humane justice holds that society can make an adult's claim to resources conditional on various forms of socially useful behavior, but that society must offer all children an equal chance of meeting whatever requirements it sets. If some students need special help to develop the skills or character traits society values, society must give them whatever help they need. If, for example, some children need unusually good schooling to compensate for an unusually unfavorable home environment or unusual physical handicaps, society must make sure they get it.[2]

While advocates of this position do not insist explicitly on equal outcomes, it is hard to see how they can settle for less in the educational arena. If Johnny is a worse reader than Mary, Johnny must have had fewer advantages than

---

[2] Advocates of humane justice often say they favor distributing resources on the basis of need, but the meaning of "need" is ambiguous in this context. When we say that Johnny needs a minute of Ms. Higgins's time more than Mary does, we can mean either that Johnny is a worse reader, and therefore "needs" to improve more, or that Johnny will *actually* improve more if he gets the time. The first use of "need" is analogous to its use in a phrase like "the 100 neediest cases." The second use is analogous to that in the statement "Adults need to eat more than children." Distributing resources on the basis of "need" can thus imply either humane justice or utilitarianism, depending on whether you equate need with prior deprivation or subsequent benefits. Because of this ambiguity I will focus directly on disadvantages and benefits rather than on need.

Mary. Johnny's disadvantages may have been genetic, social, or educational, but whatever their origin strong humane justice demands that Ms. Higgins compensate Johnny by giving him extra attention (or by sending him to a remedial reading teacher who may give him extra attention in a less obtrusive way).

What I will call the weak variant of humane justice has less stringent requirements. It holds only that all students have an equal lifetime claim on *educational* resources. Students have a claim to additional educational resources if they are currently disadvantaged because of some deficiency in their previous education but not if they are disadvantaged for non-educational reasons. If a student has had unusually bad schooling prior to entering Ms. Higgins's classroom, for example, she has an obligation to provide the student with extra help. If a student has incompetent parents, the case is more controversial, but since most advocates of humane justice see the home at least in part as an educational environment, most feel that Ms. Higgins owes children extra help if their parents are unable to do as much for them as a good parent should.

If students lack ability for genetic reasons, however, weak humane justice does not require Ms. Higgins to give them extra help. In effect, the weak interpretation defines equal educational opportunity as "equal opportunity for the genetically equal and unequal opportunity for the genetically unequal." The aim of such an educational system would be to create a society in which success depended entirely on "native ability," just as it did in Michael Young's meritocracy.[3]

The logic behind the weak variant of humane justice seems to be that society is responsible for the environment in which children are raised but not for the genes they inherit. This view has always baffled me. I can understand the argument that society is not responsible either for children's genes or for their upbringing. I have never seen a coherent defense of the proposition that society is responsible for one but not the other.

The most common argument for compensating children who have been raised in unfavorable home environments is that these environments are a by-product of our collective commitment to unequal socioeconomic rewards for adults. Having committed ourselves to an economic system that produces a high level of inequality among adults, we acquire an obligation to neutralize the effects of such inequality on children. Since we do not appear to have a comparable commitment to perpetuating genetic inequality among adults, we have no comparable obligation to neutralize the effects of genetic inequality on children.

But if it can be said that we have "chosen" a high level of socioeconomic inequality among parents and have thus acquired special obligation to its victims, can it not equally well be said that we have "chosen" not to limit the fertility of the genetically disadvantaged? Most people assume that restricting the right to have children is an unacceptable limit on adult liberty. As a result,

---

[3] Michael Young, *The Rise of Meritocracy* (London: Thames & Hudson, 1958).

many children are born into awful environments and many are born with unfavorable genes. Such a policy appears to create some societal obligation to the children on whom it imposes *either* genetic *or* environmental costs.

I suspect, however, that all these arguments are beside the point. The reason most of us want to limit society's responsibility for the genetically disadvantaged is prudential, not ethical. Most of us assume that it is harder to offset the effects of genetic disadvantages than environmental disadvantages. Because our genes are essentially immutable, we assume that their consequences are immutable too. Because the environment is mutable, we assume its effects are equally mutable. But there is no necessary relationship between the mutability of causes and the mutability of their effects. Two examples should suffice to dramatize this point.

First, consider two children who are deaf, one because of an early childhood disease, the other because of a genetic defect. The fact that one child's deafness was a product of heredity while the other child's deafness was environmental in origin tells us nothing about the physical character of the problem or the likelihood that it has a medical remedy. If no remedy is available, both children face the same educational problems. Whether they will develop the skills and character traits required for a "normal" life depends on their parents, their schooling, and their other characteristics, not on the initial cause of their deafness. The cost of educating them also depends on these factors, not on the origin of their disorder.

Second, consider an eager but slow-witted girl who has great difficulty mastering reading. Assume her difficulty is genetic in origin and manifests itself in a generalized inability to master skills that require her to see analogies or remember large amounts of miscellaneous information for long periods. Compare her to another girl who also has great difficulty reading because she comes from a disorganized and abusive home, is always angry at her teachers and fellow students, and cannot concentrate on any task long enough to learn much. If we ask which of these children will benefit most from a minute of Ms. Higgins's time, the answer is far from obvious. If we ask experienced teachers, some will say that they think it would be easier to teach the "slow" child, while others will say that they think it would be easier to teach the "disturbed" child. Such disagreement would probably persist if we stipulated that the slow child had been brought up in the wrong way, while the disturbed child had an inherited metabolic disorder.

For all these reasons the moral and empirical foundations of weak humane justice seem to me very shaky. Nonetheless, experience suggests that Ms. Higgins is more likely to endorse the weak interpretation of humane justice than the strong interpretation.

Another weak variant of humane justice, which I will call "moralistic humane justice," requires Ms. Higgins to pursue equal educational outcomes only when students make equal effort to do what she asks of them. Those who advocate this form of humane justice believe that society must provide all students with equal educational resources, including extra school resources to compensate for deficiencies in their home environments and perhaps even their genes, but not that society is responsible for an individual's values or character. They therefore reject the notion that Ms. Higgins must compensate children for the consequences of having the wrong values. If a parent fails to provide a child with books or gives the child very limited exposure to unusual words at home, Ms. Higgins has an obligation to provide compensatory help at school. But if a parent teaches a child that mastering unusual words is a waste of time, Ms. Higgins has no obligation to alter the child's values, even if these values will be socially and economically costly to the child in the long run.

There does not seem to be any principled reason why we should hold either Ms. Higgins or society as a whole responsible for giving all children equal educational resources but not for making sure that they learn to use these resources in ways that will promote their long-term self-interest. The argument for this view is once again strictly pragmatic. It asserts, correctly, that the only way to be sure that all children value learning equally is to make child rearing a collective rather than an individual responsibility, as the kibbutz does. This being politically unacceptable, making all children value learning equally is impractical. Equalizing access to educational resources requires less drastic institutional changes and is therefore more practical.

The argument that society is responsible for children's values also creates a "moral hazard" for the children. If children are not responsible for the consequences of their own choices, they have no incentive to make choices that are disagreeable in the short run but beneficial in the long run. If, for example, Ms. Higgins decides not to hold her working-class pupils personally responsible when they neglect their work, on the grounds that they come from homes where studying is not encouraged, their main incentive to study disappears.

While it is impossible to ensure that all children value learning equally, the way in which we organize schools can surely *reduce* the gap between students whose parents have taught them to value learning and students whose parents have not. Any theory that exonerates Ms. Higgins from all responsibility on this score is morally suspect, since it provides an excuse for doing nothing in circumstances where a lot can and should be done.

Unfortunately, it is philosophically difficult to find a middle ground between holding society completely responsible for children's values and holding children themselves completely responsible for their values. Most advocates of humane justice therefore choose to hold society responsible, at least in their public pronouncements and political arguments. But if society as a whole is responsible for an individual's preferences and values, the boundary between the individual and the larger society no longer has the moral significance that Europeans and Americans have traditionally assigned it. Indeed, the boundary almost disappears, and the notion that individuals are the proper units for moral accounting breaks down.

The assumption that society as a whole is responsible for children's values, and hence for their level of effort, inevitably changes the meaning of equal opportunity. Instead of asserting that opportunities are equal when the objective costs and benefits of various choices are equal in the eye of the average outside observer, this stance requires Ms. Higgins to take account of *all* the factors that influence an individual's choices, including subjective costs and benefits. If Johnny's parents do not praise him for reading as often as Mary's parents praise her, Johnny does not get the same subjective benefits from reading. Other things equal, Johnny will therefore make less effort to read. Most advocates of humane justice feel that under these circumstances Johnny has less opportunity to master reading than Mary has, even if he has the same books on his shelves at home and the same teacher at school.

This is not, of course, the way we usually use the term "opportunity" in everyday language. If Johnny and Mary have the same access to books and are taught in the same way, we ordinarily say that they have the same opportunity to learn. If Mary's parents encourage her to take advantage of this opportunity, while Johnny's do not, we usually say that Mary has more incentive or motivation to learn, not that she has more opportunity to do so. But in the past twenty years many have argued that this traditional linguistic distinction is sociologically and ethically meaningless and that we should read equal opportunity more broadly.

HUMANE JUSTICE AND SOCIOECONOMIC INEQUALITY

American liberals and radicals have traditionally defined equal opportunity as requiring that children from different socioeconomic backgrounds have the same probability of learning to read competently, attending good colleges, getting good jobs, and enjoying a good life. If these probabilities vary, opportunity is unequal. This is almost always a matter of definition. No evidence regarding the reasons for the difference is ordinarily required.

Most liberals and radicals also seem to assume that children from different socioeconomic backgrounds are genetically indistinguishable. This assumption persists despite the fact that there are powerful logical and empirical arguments against it. We know, for example, that genes have some influence on academic achievement.[4] We also know that academic achievement has some effect on adults' socioeconomic position, independent of everything else we have been able to measure.[5] Logic therefore suggests that a child's genes must have some influence on his or her adult socioeconomic position. If that is so, adults in different socioeconomic positions must differ genetically. It follows that their children must also differ genetically. These differences may not be large, and they may not explain much of the achievement gap between children from different backgrounds, but they must exist.[6]

---

[4] My colleagues and I summarized this evidence in Christopher Jencks et al., *Inequality* (New York: Basic Books, 1972). Subsequent work suggests that genes may have slightly more effect on test scores than *Inequality* found, but the differences are quite minor.

[5] See, e.g., James Crouse, "The Effects of Test Scores," in Christopher Jencks et al., *Who Gets Ahead?* (New York: Basic Books, 1979).

[6] For a review of empirical evidence on this point up to 1972, see Christopher Jencks et al., *Inequality*. For more recent evidence see Sandra Scarr and Richard Weinberg, "The Influence of 'Family Background' on Intellectual Attainment," *American Sociological Review* 43 (1978): 674–92.

Nonetheless, few liberals or radicals will even entertain the possibility that genes contribute to achievement differences between socioeconomic groups. This position appears to be based on political expedience: people are more likely to believe that society should try to help the environmentally disadvantaged than the genetically disadvantaged. Thus even if you believe in your heart that poor children labor under genetic as well as environmental handicaps, you are likely to think it expedient to deemphasize this possibility when you are campaigning for programs to help such children.

Some advocates of humane justice also deny that middle-class children are unusually eager to master cognitive skills. Those who take this position typically insist that working-class children enter school eager to learn and are then "turned off" by large classes, authoritarian teachers, low expectations, and a curriculum that assumes knowledge or experience they do not have. There is certainly some truth in all this. Indeed, if we were to measure effort simply by looking at the number of minutes children spent doing schoolwork, we might not find much difference between middle-class and working-class children in the early grades. But effort also includes the games children choose to play (Scrabble versus basketball), the things they think about at breakfast (childish puns versus fast cars), and a multitude of other activities that contribute in subtle ways to cognitive development. If we define effort in this comprehensive way, the claim that middle-class children value cognitive skills more than working-class children is almost surely correct, though I know no hard evidence supporting it.

If children from different socioeconomic backgrounds are to have equal chances of doing well in school, Ms. Higgins must find ways to offset the effects of whatever genetic and motivational differences now distinguish them. If poor children labor under genetic disadvantages, she must give them extra attention. If their parents value cognitive skills less than middle-class parents, Ms. Higgins must reward poor children more than middle-class children who learn the same amount. Only in this way can she make the subjective value of learning equal for working-class and middle-class children. Some socialist societies have tried to achieve something like this by making bourgeois origins an explicit obstacle to advancement. Such policies hardly conform to American notions of equal opportunity, however.

These practical difficulties do not call into question the fundamental moral premise of humane justice, namely that educational resources should go disproportionately to the disadvantaged. The practical difficulties do, however, suggest that if equal opportunity means that children raised in different families must have equal probabilities of success, we can never fully achieve it. Since most of us think of rights as goals that *can* be achieved, we must either reject the argument that equal opportunity is a right, substituting the notion that it is an ideal, or else we must reject the conventional humane definition of equal opportunity.

If advocates of humane justice concede that equal probabilities of success are unattainable, they must face another difficulty. Their theory requires Ms. Higgins to spend more time with poor readers than with good readers. But *how much* more time? The logic of a deprivation-based theory of justice seems to imply that Ms. Higgins should devote *all* her time and attention to the worst reader in her class. If the worst reader moves ahead of the next worst, she shifts her attention to the next worst. She keeps doing this until everyone reads equally well. But if the worst reader *never* catches up, what principle (other than utilitarianism) can she use to justify not devoting her life to him?

MORALISTIC VERSUS HUMANE JUSTICE

If a society can take concerted action to reward virtue and punish vice, it can usually enforce a high degree of conformity to its norms, whatever these may be. Moralistic justice has great appeal in such societies because it works. Such societies seldom have to carry out their threats.

In societies like our own, which have great difficulty taking concerted action against those who violate rules, violations are far more common. Paradoxically, as the likelihood that violations will be punished declines, the absolute amount of misery that society inflicts on those who violate its rules may well increase. When punishment is certain, violations are rare, so punishment is also rare. When punishment is less certain, violations become common, and punishment, while less likely in any individual case, may well be both more common and more severe in the society as a whole.

This paradoxical development often leads compassionate observers to discover reasons for rejecting moralistic justice. They are likely to argue that moralistic justice has "failed," without asking what would happen if we abandoned it altogether. Compassionate observers are also likely to argue that those who reject society's rules are simply reacting to the fact that society rejects them. Humane justice has considerable appeal in such societies, especially to the virtuous, who tend to assume that everyone would be as virtuous as they if everyone had the same advantages.

The tension between moralistic and humane justice is, of course, related to the old problem of free will versus determinism. The moralistic theory of justice assumes that children have free will. Parents should provide appropriate incentives for children to make the right choices, but if a child then makes a wrong choice, the child rather than the parent is expected to suffer for the mistake. The humane theory of justice assumes that the environments in which children find themselves determine their choices. As a result, those who create the environment are ultimately responsible for children's choices and are morally obligated to absorb the costs of foolish choices.

Both theories of justice are compatible with a "fair contest" theory of equal opportunity, but they assign Ms. Higgins different roles in this contest. Moralistic justice is a system for awarding prizes. It tells Ms. Higgins to act as a judge, giving different students what they deserve on the basis of their past academic effort. Humane justice focuses on preparing runners for the next contest. It tells Ms. Higgins to act as a coach, whose job is to ensure that all competitors get enough training.

Every moment in our lives is both an ending and a beginning. When we think of the moment as an ending, we apply the standards of moralistic justice. When we think of it as a beginning we apply the standards of humane justice. When we recognize that the moment is both, we find ourselves in a quandary. For this reason neither Ms. Higgins nor American society as a whole is likely to resolve the conflict between the two visions of equal opportunity that flow from these two theories of justice.

UTILITARIANISM

Utilitarian theories of resource allocation try to maximize the average level of well-being in a society rather than trying to ensure just treatment of individuals. Maximizing the well-being of a population involves two distinct problems: (1) motivating individuals to do their best to promote the general welfare and (2) allocating scarce investment resources among competing claimants. Solving each problem requires resources. Utilitarians must therefore devise some formula for dividing resources between these two activities. In economics, this is usually seen as a problem of dividing output between consumption and investment. Claims on consumption goods are used as incentives for productive activity. Claims on investment capital are allocated on the basis of expected returns.

For Ms. Higgins, the problem is to what extent she should treat her time and attention as a reward for past performance and to what extent she should take student motivation as given and allocate her time on the basis of who will benefit most from it. Settling this question is critical because the "incentive model" and the "investment model" will lead Ms. Higgins to allocate her time very differently.

If Ms. Higgins wants her students to read well, for example, most utilitarians will tell her that she should reward her best readers with prizes of various kinds. These prizes may be high letter grades, gold stars, hugs, or attention, depending on what is most effective. But since attention is usually worth more to a third grader than grades, gold stars, or even hugs, utilitarian logic suggests that Ms. Higgins may do better if she uses attention as a prize than if she uses other things. This would mean giving more attention to her best readers. In contrast, when Ms. Higgins thinks of her time as an investment good and tries to distribute it among her students in such a way as to maximize their long-term contribution to the general welfare (including their own), she may well conclude that she should spend most of her time with her worst readers. Like the choice between moralistic and humane justice, Ms. Higgins's choice between an incentive strategy and an investment strategy depends on whether she views a given moment as an ending or as a beginning.

Viewing attention as a prize that motivates students leads naturally to the idea of equal opportunity. Utilitarians espouse equal opportunity because it sets rules for the distribution of prizes that appear likely to ensure maximum effort on the part of contestants. Three rules appear crucial. First, utilitarian equal opportunity requires that the competition be open to all. No one can be excluded for "irrelevant" reasons, such as race, sex, or family background. Second, utilitarian equal opportunity requires that prizes be distributed solely on the basis of performance, not on the basis of "irrelevant" criteria. Third, and most problematic, the utilitarian conception of equal opportunity requires that the rules of the contest be set so that as many people as possible have a reasonable chance of winning. This is desirable because it is the best way to maximize effort.

This utilitarian conception of a "fair contest" is akin to moralistic justice in that it focuses on motivating students to do their best and views Ms. Higgins's attention as a reward for past performance. But the utilitarian vision of equal opportunity differs from moralistic justice in that it rewards actual performance rather than effort. This difference is a matter of expedience rather than principle, however. If effort were easy to measure, utilitarians might well reward it instead.

The utilitarian conception of resources as an investment good is akin to humane justice in that it either ignores the problem of motivation or treats motivation as fixed. Utilitarian investment theories are also similar to what I have called strong humane justice in that both are preoccupied with producing a particular distribution of reading skills. But a utilitarian calculus focuses on maximizing the mean level of welfare whereas strong humane justice focuses on minimizing variation around the mean.

The utilitarian approach to investment also differs from humane justice in that it does not ordinarily invoke the ideal of equal opportunity. Nonetheless, it has important implications for equal opportunity, since it is the principal competing theory of resource allocation.

Investment-oriented utilitarianism requires Ms. Higgins to distribute her time so as to maximize society's long-term well-being. In order to do this she needs two kinds of information. First, she must know how much different sorts of students' reading skills will improve if the students get an extra minute of her time. Second, she must know how much raising students' reading skills will enhance their contribution to the general welfare. Each of these problems deserves brief discussion.

If Ms. Higgins simply asks herself whether her time will be of more value to good or bad readers, or to highly motivated or apathetic ones, she will be able to make a plausible a priori case for almost any conceivable answer. Like most utilitarian quandaries, this one demands empirical research. Unfortunately, if Ms. Higgins consults the research literature on this question, she will not find a clear-cut answer.

If Ms. Higgins asks how raising different kinds of students' reading scores will contribute to the general welfare, she will again be able to make a plausible case for almost any conceivable answer. If she looks at the research literature she will find that nobody has even asked the question, much less answered it convincingly. If she confines herself to adults' reports of their own happiness and has a computer handy, she will be able to discover that happiness increases as vocabulary scores increase and that this relationship is much stronger in the bottom half of the test score distribution than in the top half.[7] Thus, if she

---

[7] The General Social Survey (GSS) is an annual survey of about 1,500 adults conducted by the National Opinion Research Center. In 1974, 1976, 1978, 1982, and 1984 it included a ten-item

assumes that what is good for her students is good for the country, she will probably conclude that it is more useful to help move her worst readers up to the middle of the distribution than to move middling readers to the top.

But if Ms. Higgins is a good utilitarian she must ask herself not only what will make her own students happiest but also what will contribute most to the happiness of the species. If she asks this question, she may conclude that human happiness depends primarily on the way society is organized politically, socially, and technically and that her best hope of contributing to progress in these areas is to cultivate the talents of one or two outstanding students every year.

Because Ms. Higgins has no way of knowing with confidence how much her attention will boost any particular student's reading skills, much less how it will affect the student's long-term well-being or that of others in the society, the de facto effect of treating her attention as an investment good is to force her to make decisions whose consequences she cannot predict. This can have a variety of possible consequences.

1. Ms. Higgins may succumb to the claims of those who favor moralistic or humane justice, since such people almost always insist that their version of justice is also socially efficient. Those who are eager to reward effort and punish indolence, for example, will tell her that this is not only just but also the best way to maximize her students' long-run well-being. If she finds moralistic justice attractive on ethical grounds she may well accept such empirical claims without demanding hard evidence. Conversely, if she is eager to help students who have been shortchanged in the past, she will find plenty of writers who claim these students will benefit most from her attention, and she may well believe their claims.

2. Ms. Higgins may despair of calculating the long-run benefits of distributing her attention in different ways and may decide to focus exclusively on short-term costs. If she takes this view she is likely to conclude that the most efficient distribution of her attention is the one that leaves her with the most attention to distribute. If she finds working with slow learners tiring or frustrating, she will then conclude that the most efficient way to spend her time is with the gifted. If she finds working with slow learners raises her spirits, she will conclude that this is efficient.

3. Since Ms. Higgins does not know what will maximize social welfare in the long run, she may try to minimize the likely cost to society of her mistakes. Under plausible assumptions this will lead her to devote equal time and attention to everyone.[8]

---

vocabulary test. It also included the following question: "Taken all together, how would you say things are these days—would you say that you are very happy, pretty happy, or not too happy?" The proportion who said they were "not too happy" averaged 26 percent among those with scores of 2 or 3, 14 percent among those with scores of 4 or 5, 10 percent among those with scores of 6 or 7, 8 percent among those with scores of 8 or 9, and 9 percent among those with scores of 10. For details on this survey, see James A. Davis and Tom W. Smith, *General Social Surveys, 1972–1984: Cumulative Codebook* (Storrs, Conn.: Roper Center, 1984).

[8] If one error of two units costs more than two errors of one unit, and if nothing is known about the welfare function, equal treatment will maximize the expected value of the outcomes.

EQUAL OPPORTUNITY AND THE BURDEN OF PROOF

Given all the uncertainties that arise when Ms. Higgins tries to redefine equal opportunity so as to justify an unequal distribution of her attention, she may well begin to wonder whether any of the arguments for unequal treatment is really compelling. If her principal calls her on the carpet for favoring the talented, the diligent, the poor, or the incompetent, can she really defend herself?

The principles we use to distribute things vary with the nature of the things we are distributing. We try to distribute government jobs on the basis of virtue, public housing on the basis of disadvantages, and medical care on the basis of expected benefits. If the relative weight of these distributional principles depends on what we are distributing, none can claim to be universal. Indeed, in some cases they may all be irrelevant. Ms. Higgins must therefore ask whether any of these principles really applies to her classroom. Her arguments for ignoring all three principles would presumably go something like this:

> *Virtue.* Virtue must be rewarded and vice punished in *some* way, but Ms. Higgins need not use her time and attention for this purpose. If judicious use of praise, blame, and grades ensures that most students do their best, Ms. Higgins can make her time equally available to everyone if she wishes.
>
> *Disadvantages.* While Ms. Higgins can easily see that some of her students read better than others, she cannot usually tell whether these differences derive from differences in prior schooling, home advantages, genes, or motivation. If she rewards poor motivation with extra attention, she will undermine the implied moral contract between students and teachers, reducing students' future effort.
>
> *Benefits.* While Ms. Higgins may want to take account of potential benefits when distributing her time, she may well conclude that in practice she has no way of knowing who benefits most from her time.

In the absence of any compelling argument for favoring one group over another, Ms. Higgins may conclude that her commitment to equal opportunity implies equal treatment for all. At a minimum, her commitment to equal opportunity requires her to give reasons for treating her students unequally. As we have seen, there is no general agreement about when Ms. Higgins can legitimately treat children unequally. In practice, therefore, demanding general acceptance of her reasons for distributing her time and attention unequally would force her to distribute them equally.

Ms. Higgins's reflections may, therefore, lead her full circle, back to what I initially called democratic equality. But in this incarnation, equal treatment no longer derives directly from democratic rhetoric. Instead, it derives from the fact that democracies typically put the burden of proof on those who favor unequal treatment, and in practice this burden is so heavy that the egalitarian "null hypothesis" can always carry the day.

THE POLITICS OF AMBIGUITY

If equal opportunity can mean distributing resources either equally or un-equally, if it can be compatible with inequalities that favor either the initially advantaged or the initially disadvantaged, and if the relative weight of these principles can vary from one situation to the next, it is small wonder that most Americans support the idea. A skeptic might wonder, however, whether an idea that can embrace so much means anything at all.

Because the ideal of equal opportunity seems to forbid behavior we want to minimize while blurring disagreement about what we want to maximize, it will undoubtedly continue to command broad support. It is an ideal consistent with almost every vision of a good society. For liberal lawyers intent on expanding the domain of rights, equal opportunity implies that citizens have a "right" to lots of things they want but cannot afford, ranging from better schools to wheelchair ramps in public places. For progressive social reformers who want to minimize misery, equal opportunity implies that we need new social pro-grams to help those who labor under one or another kind of disadvantage. For conservative businessmen, equal opportunity implies that the prizes for unusual success should not be tampered with in a misguided effort to achieve equal re-sults. For politicians of all persuasions equal opportunity is therefore a universal solvent, compatible with the dreams of almost every voter in a conflict-ridden constituency. This makes equal opportunity one of the few ideals a politician can safely invoke on all occasions.

Without common ideals of this sort, societies disintegrate. With them, conflict becomes a bit more muted. But the constant reiteration of such rhetoric also numbs the senses and rots the mind. This may be a price we have to pay for gluing together a complex society, but if so there is something to be said for smaller, more politically homogeneous societies, where the terms of discourse may not have to be quite so elastic. That is one reason we develop scholarly dis-ciplines. It may also be one reason why scholars tend to prefer the political dis-course of Sweden or Switzerland to that of America.

XIII

THE FAMILY

64.
Justice, Equal Opportunity, and the Family
JAMES FISHKIN

Once the role of the family is taken into account, the apparently moderate aspiration of equal opportunity produces conflicts with the private sphere of liberty—with autonomous family relations—that are nothing short of intractable. Elements that are essential to the liberal doctrine of equal opportunity come into irreconcilable conflict with the private core of the notion of liberty, the portion that touches most of our lives most directly.

These conflicts can be formulated in terms of three assumptions—two central liberal assumptions about equal opportunity, on the one hand, and our common moral assumptions about the family, on the other. The first liberal assumption might be called the *principle of merit*. According to this assumption, there should be widespread procedural fairness in the evaluation of qualifications for positions. No discrimination should be permitted on the basis of race, sex, class, ethnic origin, or other irrelevant characteristics. While there are many interesting controversies about how qualifications for positions ought to be defined, the principle of merit in some form is a basic and familiar element in the liberal credo.

The second assumption might be called equality of life chances. According to this notion, I should not be able to enter a hospital ward of healthy newborn babies and, on the basis of class, race, sex, or other arbitrary native characteristics, predict the eventual positions in society of those children. Of course, there are many different ways of evaluating their eventual positions. By whatever plausible criterion these evaluations are made, however, it should be clear that in this society, I can confidently make such predictions.[1]

These two assumptions can both be defended in terms of the basic liberal approach to equal opportunity, namely, the notion that there should be fair competition among individuals for unequal positions in society. Henceforth, I will refer to this basic notion as the *fair competition* assumption. The two principles just defined can be viewed as explications, respectively, of what might be meant by "competition" in this context and of what might be meant, in any ultimately defensible sense, by "fairness." On the one hand, the principle of merit is merely the claim that the competition should be in terms of qualifications relevant to job performance in the positions to be filled. The principle of equal life chances, on the other hand, can be viewed as the central condition that would render the competition fair. If one can predict where people will end up in the

---

[1] See, for example, Christopher Jencks et al., *Who Gets Ahead?* (New York: Basic Books, 1979), pp. 81–83. The independent cumulative effects of meritocratic sorting on the distribution of life chances are investigated by Raymond Boudon in *Education, Opportunity and Social Inequality* (New York: John Wiley & Sons, Inc., 1974).

competition merely by knowing their race or sex or family background, then the conditions under which their talents and motivations have developed must be grossly unequal. It is unfair that some persons are given every conceivable advantage while others never really have a chance, in the first place, to develop their talents. The principle of equal life chances, when combined with the principle of merit, would require equal developmental conditions for talent development.

When these two assumptions about equal opportunity are combined with a third assumption, the *autonomy of the family*—permitting parents to substantially influence the development of their children—a pattern of difficult choices emerges. This pattern takes the form of a "trilemma," a kind of dilemma with three corners. I will argue that commitment to any two of these assumptions rules out the third. Attempting to maintain all three assumptions—the principle of merit, equality of life chances, and the autonomy of the family—would be like attempting to hold up a three-cornered stool when only two legs are available. No matter which two corners one chooses to hold up, lack of the third is enough to undermine the whole structure.

• • •

The argument that follows should be thought of as a test of the coherence and viability of this liberal focus on equal opportunity. Given the commitment of liberal theory to liberty, can its reliance on equal opportunity as an ultimate strategy of legitimation for distributional questions be maintained, even under ideal conditions? Hence, my focus will be on liberal theories that are committed to equal opportunity but not to equality of outcomes. . . .

In the trilemma to be developed below, both principles of equal opportunity can be maintained only through severe sacrifice in the autonomy of families. But this argument will depend on the assumption just defined—that there are substantial social and economic inequalities in the society. If this assumption were relaxed, the conflict among our three principles would disappear. It is worth emphasizing the role of this assumption in the argument since it brings into focus a more general claim—that liberal theory, if taken seriously, must be far more radical in its implications than has been imagined by its major proponents. For it would be difficult to imagine a defensible liberal ideal of equal opportunity that was not committed to *both* of the principles defined here (merit and equal life chances). Yet any such doctrine would require either a systematic sacrifice in the autonomy of the family or a systematic achievement of equal results (rather than merely opportunities) throughout the society. Either of these two latter options would be far more radical, and far less comfortable in its implications, than any doctrine of equal opportunity seriously advocated in liberal theory. It is worth adding that I hope to subject liberal theories to this kind of critical scrutiny, not because I think liberalism is bankrupt, but because I believe that any future, viable version of liberal theory must face up to certain hard choices. The trilemma of conflicts arising for equal opportunity will provide a starting point for that kind of re-examination.

THE FIRST OPTION

Under the ground rules just specified, implementation of any two of these principles will render achievement of the remaining one virtually impossible. For example, the first and third principles rule out the second. The autonomy of the family protects parental efforts to influence the development of their children. Given background conditions of inequality, children from the higher strata will have been systematically subjected to differential developmental opportunities that can reliably be expected to advantage them in the process of meritocratic competition. Under these conditions, the principle of merit—applied to talents as they have developed under such unequal conditions—becomes a mechanism for generating unequal life chances.

It is just as if the continuing inequality of life chances in the warrior society example came about through parental influence on talent development. If the autonomy of the family protects the process whereby parents influence their children, and if the principle of merit is employed, no matter how scrupulously, to select the best warriors, these unequal conditions for talent development—when combined with equal consideration for talents as developed—produce unequal life chances. Children of the present warriors can be expected to win in the competition disproportionately.

Furthermore, if the relevant recent history involves conscientious efforts at strict compliance, then the principle of merit will itself tend to exacerbate these unequal conditions for talent development. For parents from the higher positions will be systematically distinguishable by their greater skill, their competence, and their familiarity with all the desirable characteristics that are taken to constitute "qualifications" in that society. When the process of talent development is protected by the autonomy of the family, advantaged parents can be expected to have systematically greater success inculcating these characteristics among their children.

• • •

While empirical conditions will vary from one society to the next, the general proposition is difficult to deny: children from advantaged families in a given society will have greater opportunities to develop the skills, credentials, and motivations valued in that society. If the autonomy of the family protects the process by which parents provide those greater opportunities, and if the principle of merit sorts people accurately in terms of their skills, credentials, and motivations—as developed under those unequal conditions—then systematic inequality of life chances will result.[2]

---

[2] The visibility given to extreme upward mobility should not obscure such statistical propositions. As Harold Lasswell noted in his 1936 classic, *Politics: Who Gets What, When, How* (New York: Meridian Books, 1958): "Although any bright and talkative lad in the United States may be told that one day he may be president, only eight boys made it in the last generation." (p. 14). Lasswell then goes on to note the limited numbers of persons who actually make it to other highly valued positions, despite the widely shared character of the aspiration for those positions.

THE SECOND OPTION

Suppose one were to keep the autonomy of the family in place but attempt, nevertheless, to equalize life chances? Institutionalizing the last two principles in this way would require sacrifice of the first, the principle of merit. Given background conditions of inequality, the differential developmental influences discussed in the last section produce disproportionate talents and other qualifications among children in the higher strata. If they must be assigned to positions so as to equalize life chances, then they must be assigned regardless of these differential claims. "Reverse discrimination" in favor of those from disadvantaged backgrounds would have to be applied systematically throughout the society.

By reverse discrimination, I mean any procedure of assignment that consistently places crucial weight on some characteristic other than qualifications (as defined earlier).[3] If qualifications have been appropriately defined, in a sense of sufficiently relevant to performance, then widespread assignment of those who are less qualified can be expected to have a great cost in efficiency.[4] It would also have a substantial cost in fairness. For the analogue of a competition in which skill and effort provide a sense in which people earn or merit their payoffs would no longer apply.[5]

Now the sacrifice in efficiency might be avoided if on-the-job training could make up entirely for deficiencies in earlier preparation. It is hard to believe, however, in a modern industrial society, with a complex differentiation of tasks, that qualifications that are performance-related could not be defined so as to predict better performances. Perhaps, in some actual societies, the definition of qualifications has not carried this justificatory burden. In those societies, apparently meritocratic competition has amounted to no more than an empty credentialism. That is just to say, the principle of merit has not actually been implemented in those cases,[6] for the principle required an appropriate competition in terms of qualifications—criteria that are job-related in that they fairly can be interpreted as indicators of competence or motivation for an individual's performance in a given position. To assign persons to positions regardless of qualifications in this sense is, by definition, to assign persons who are not as likely (as those more qualified) to perform well—insofar as that matter can be judged in terms of any prior indicators of talent or motivation as these might

---

[3] Such a procedure would discriminate against those who are more qualified and in favor of those from disadvantaged backgrounds.

[4] See Norman Daniels "Merit and Meritocracy," *Philosophy and Public Affairs* 7, no. 3 (Spring 1978): 202–23.

[5] For the appeal of this model of a fair competition, embodied in the ideal of pure procedural justice, see Rawls, *Theory of Justice,* sections 12, 13, 14. It is worth noting that any institutionalization of such a fair competition can be expected to leave a substantial role for luck or chance. This is not worrisome so long as luck is not systematically maldistributed by class, race, or ethnic background.

[6] For an inflated claim that this kind of credentialism has been the rule rather than the exception in apparently meritocratic assignment see George Gilder, *Wealth and Poverty* (New York: Basic Books, 1981), chapter 13.

be displayed in a suitable competition. If there is a system of significant on-the-job training, then that must be taken into account in the prior definition of qualifications. Those who are most likely to profit or improve their performance from such training have to be given correspondingly greater consideration. Demonstration that one will be more educable on the job should itself be considered a kind of qualification.

• • •

If the autonomy of families remains undisturbed, given background conditions of inequality, unequal developmental influences will produce a differential development of qualifications among those from the higher strata. These conditions force a hard choice between equality of life chances, on the one hand, and the principle of merit, on the other. The first option explored in the last section sacrificed the former. What I am calling the second option, outlined in this section, sacrifices the latter. Only a process of assignment that was applied regardless of meritocratic factors could equalize life chances despite differential talent development. Such a system of reverse discrimination,[7] systematically applied across the society, would appear inevitably to conflict with both efficiency and fairness.

We might imagine another hypothetical system that could conceivably ameliorate some of these conflicts. Suppose a nationwide lottery for job assignment were instituted not among newborns but among fully developed adults. The private sphere of liberty would remain in place with all of its effects on the unequal development of talents and other qualifications. Life chances would be equalized since the lottery would strictly randomize the process of assignment to positions. Again, the principle sacrificed would be merit since assignment would be accomplished entirely in disregard for any qualification relevant to job performance.

Even though sacrificing meritocratic processes would divorce the system of assignment from one kind of claim to fairness, instituting the lottery would introduce another. Each person would have an equal chance for any given position. No one would have a special claim, based on any contingent factors. Note that the principle of merit distinguished relevant factors (qualifications) from irrelevant ones and based its claim to fairness on insulating the system of assignment from influences by any of the irrelevant factors. In a sense, the job assignment lottery would take this argument a step further by simply considering all contingent factors—any basis for differentiating one adult from another—as irrelevant to the process of job assignment. In doing so, it precludes applicants from claiming, in any sense, that they have "earned" or "merited" their positions through skill or effort. The model of a fair competition, when supplanted by a lottery, treats all persons as indistinguishable recipients of an equal chance.

[7] ... I am using the term "reverse discrimination" more broadly than some definitions that would restrict it to preferential treatment in favor of specified groups that had previously been discriminated against. For an example of this more restrictive definition, see the "working definition" in Barry Gross, ed., *Reverse Discrimination* (Buffalo, N.Y.: Prometheus Books, 1977), p. 3.

Of course, it is likely that the sacrifice in efficiency would be severe. Perhaps it might be ameliorated through systematic on-the-job training. As noted before, however, in a modern society with complex task differentiation, it seems undeniable that there would be a substantial cost in efficiency. Even if primary training were on the job, applicants could surely be differentiated in terms of their potential educability. If the private sphere of liberty and background conditions of inequality were maintained, then differential performance in a complex variety of positions could be predicted. Therefore, compared to an alternative system of merit, this system could be expected to require a sacrifice in efficiency.

• • •

It is also worth noting that a job lottery alternative to merit would produce a conflict with liberty of a different kind. I defined the autonomy of families and the private sphere of liberty narrowly so as to clarify the role of the family in the trilemma of equal opportunity. Another kind of liberty, which falls outside the private sphere, is the liberty to seek and compete for employment. This liberty might be formulated in a strong way so that any interference with mutual consent between a potential employer and employee is unjustified. Even the principle of merit, in this view, might constitute unjustified coercion. Or the interests of competing potential applicants might be taken into account so that liberty to seek employment (and the corresponding liberty of employers to seek employees) might be constrained by requirements of fair competition like those specified by the principle of merit. This is a weak formulation of the liberty of employment.

Liberty of employment, even in this quite weak sense, conflicts sharply with the job lottery proposal. While the proposal would leave the private sphere intact in an effort to equalize life chances, it would produce conflicts with liberty in another recognizable and important sense, even when that liberty is defined modestly. If I want to be a pediatrician, yet my lottery ticket requires that I become a corporate lawyer, or if I want to be a violinist, yet my lottery ticket requires that I become an auto mechanic, my liberty of employment, indeed, my liberty to determine the basic direction of my life plan has been severely constrained.

Since my focus here has been on the private liberties involved in the family, I note this additional difficulty only in passing. Within the framework of more general discussion, the point to note about this job lottery proposal is not its sacrifice of liberty of employment, but rather, its sacrifice of the principle of merit. Like all efforts to equalize life chances while maintaining the autonomy of families intact, it would sacrifice the third, remaining principle.

THE THIRD OPTION

Suppose one were to attempt to equalize life chances while maintaining the system of meritocratic assignment. Given background conditions of inequality, it is the autonomy of families that protects the process by which advantaged families differentially affect the development of talents and other qualifications in their children. Only if this process were interfered with could both the principles of merit and of equal life chances be achieved. In other words, if equality of life chances is to be achieved through processes consistent with the principle of merit, then conditions for the development of talents and other qualifications must be equalized. Given background conditions of inequality, this can be done only through some mechanism that systematically insulates the development of each new generation from the unequal results achieved by the last. Coercive interferences with the family would be required if advantaged parents were to be prevented, systematically, from passing on cognitive, affective, cultural, and social advantages to their children. Perhaps a massive system of collectivized child-rearing could be devised to achieve such a result. Anything short of such a large-scale alternative to the autonomous nuclear family would probably provide only an imperfect barrier between the inequalities of the parental generation and the developmental processes affecting its children.

From the communal child-rearing in Plato's *Republic* to the test tube nurseries in Huxley's *Brave New World*, the replacement of the family with some alternative strategy of child-rearing has been the centerpiece of any social engineering that required complete manipulation of human development. As long as the private sphere of liberty is in place, crucial developmental factors are entrusted to the autonomous decisions of families and are, by the very fact, insulated from social control. Whether the efforts at social engineering are aimed at equalization or hierarchy, the family constitutes a crucial barrier to the manipulability of the causal factors affecting human development.

Whatever the precise institutional design, if developmental factors are to be equalized, systematic intrusion into the autonomy of families would be required. Recall that coercive interference into consensual family relations can be justified, according to the principles stated here, only to ensure the essential prerequisites for adult participation in the society—to assure a child's physical or mental health, his literacy, or his knowledge of the necessary social conventions. This principle defines a restrictive paternalistic burden that must be met if coercive interference is to be justified. This paternalistic burden is obviously not met by strategies that simply level down or equalize developmental influences in order to lessen the advantages of children in the upper strata. The interests of *those* children are not served at all by such efforts. And, provided that scarcity is not so extreme that such intrusions are necessary to ensure the essential prerequisites for children from other strata, it would have to be considered an intrusion into the autonomy of families. In other words, under the stated ground rules of ideal theory—for which we assumed only moderate scarcity—these leveling down strategies cannot be reconciled with the autonomy of families.

In the next section I will look into various strategies of intervention, by the government or other social institutions, that might "level up," rather than down, that might, in other words, increase the developmental opportunities of the lower strata, and still leave the autonomy of families intact. My general claim will be that such strategies of leveling up are either so paltry in their efficacy or so utopian in their expense that they cannot be expected to provide a solution to our problem. While there is a compelling need to pursue them as far as possible, they cannot be expected to equalize developmental opportunities to the levels offered by more advantaged families. The only strategies of intervention that might offer a hope of the required massive effects would amount to such a wholesale change in the child's environment that their obviously prohibitive expense would violate any realistic construction of the budget constraint. Hence, leveling up strategies of intervention—that leave the private sphere intact—are either prohibitive in expense or insufficient in effect. On the other hand, by making many of the children affected worse-off (those who would have been advantaged without the equalization efforts), leveling down strategies clearly violate the autonomy of families if those provisions are to be universally enforced. They do not satisfy the restrictive, paternalistic burden required to justify such interventions.

65.
Justice and Gender
SUSAN MOLLER OKIN

I. JUSTICE AND THE IDEALIZED FAMILY

The notion that justice is not an appropriate virtue for families was most clearly expressed in the past by Rousseau and Hume. It is currently important because, as we have seen, it seems to be implicit, from their sheer disregard for family life and most aspects of gender, in the work of most contemporary theories of justice. It is rarely argued explicitly these days, but such a case is presented by Michael Sandel in his critique of John Rawls's liberal theory of justice, and I shall focus on this argument here. But first, let us take a brief look at the positions of Rousseau and Hume. On this, as on some other complex issues, Rousseau argues more than one side of the issue. Some of the time, he justifies his conclusion that the governance of the family, unlike that of political society, need not be accountable to its members or regulated by principles of justice by appealing to the notion that the family, unlike the wider society, is founded upon love. Thus unlike a government, he says, the father of a family, "in order to act right, . . . has only to consult his heart." [1] Rousseau concludes that women can, without prejudice to their well-being, be both ruled within the family and denied the right to participate in the realm of politics, where their husbands will represent the interests of the family unit.

Hume argues similarly that the circumstances of family life are such that justice is not an appropriate standard to apply to them. He begins his discussion of justice by pointing out that in situations of "enlarged affections," in which every man "feels no more concern for his own interest than for that of his fellows," justice is useless, because unnecessary. He regards the family as one of the clearest instances of such enlarged affections, in which justice is inappropriate because "all distinction of property be, in a great measure, lost and confounded. . . . Between married persons, the cement of friendship is by the laws supposed so strong as to abolish all division of possessions; and has often, in reality, the force ascribed to it." [2] The message is similar to Rousseau's: the affection and unity of interests that prevail within families make standards of justice irrelevant to them.

In his critique of Rawls, Sandel explicitly takes up and builds on Hume's vision of family life, in order to make the case that there are important social

---

[1] *Discourse on Political Economy*, translated from Jean-Jacques Rousseau, *Oeuvres Complètes* (Paris: Pléiade, 1959–1969), vol. 3, pp. 241–42.

[2] David Hume, *Enquiry Concerning the Principles of Morals,* ed. L. A. Selby-Bigge from the 1777 edition (Oxford: Oxford University Press, 1975), p. 185. See also *A Treatise on Human Nature*, ed. L. A. Selby-Bigge (Oxford: Oxford University Press, 1978), pp. 493–96.

spheres in which justice is an inappropriate virtue. A central piece of his argument against Rawls, which he presents as a case against liberal accounts of justice in general, is based on a denial of Rawls's claim that justice is the primary moral virtue.[3] This claim depends on the assumption that human society is characterized by certain "circumstances of justice." These include, first, the condition of moderate scarcity of resources, and second, the fact that, while persons have some similar or complementary needs and interests, they also have "different ends and purposes, and . . . make conflicting claims on the natural and social resources available."[4] Does Rawls think the circumstances of justice apply *within* families? It seems—although he has not held consistently to this position—that he is one of the few theorists of justice who do. . . . he goes on to *assume*, rather than to *argue*, that the family "in some form" is just. But it is clear from both his statement of this assumption and his initial inclusion of the family as part of the "basic structure of society" that (in *A Theory of Justice*, at least) he does not consider the family to be outside the circumstances of justice.

Sandel, however, argues that Rawls's claim for the primacy of justice is undetermined by the existence of numerous social groupings in which the circumstances of justice do not predominate. Among such groupings, characterized by their "more or less clearly-defined common identities and shared purposes," the family "may represent an extreme case."[5] He argues that the existence of such associations refutes in two respects Rawls's claim that justice is the first or primary virtue of social institutions. First, he agrees with Hume that in such "intimate or solidaristic associations . . . the values and aims of the participants coincide closely enough that the circumstances of justice prevail to a relatively small degree." In "a more or less ideal family situation," spontaneous affection and generosity will prevail.[6] Second, not only will justice not be the prevailing virtue in such associations, but if they were to begin to operate in accordance with principles of justice, an overall moral improvement would by no means necessarily result. Instead, the loss of certain " 'nobler virtues, and more favourable blessings' " could mean that "in some cases, justice is not a virtue but a vice."[7] Given such a possibility, the moral primacy of justice is demonstrated to be unfounded. Instead of being the primary virtue, as Rawls claims, in some situations justice is "a remedial virtue," called upon to repair fallen conditions.[8]

In both its eighteenth- and its twentieth-century manifestations, the argument that human associations exemplified by the family challenge the primacy of justice rests, in two respects, on faulty foundations. It misapprehends what

---

[3] Michael Sandel. *Liberalism and the Limits of Justice* (New York: Cambridge University Press, 1982), pp. 30–35.

[4] John Rawls, *A Theory of Justice* (Cambridge: Harvard University Press, 1971), p. 127.

[5] Sandel, *Limits of Justice*, p. 31.

[6] Ibid., pp. 30–31, 33.

[7] Ibid., p. 34 (the first phrase is quoted from Hume, *A Treatise on Human Nature*).

[8] Sandel, *Limits of Justice*, p. 31.

is meant by the claim that justice is the first or primary virtue of social institutions; and it idealizes the family. When Rawls claims the primacy of justice, he does not mean that it is the highest or noblest of virtues. Rather, he means that it is the most fundamental or essential. This is implied by the simile he employs on the opening page of *A Theory of Justice:*

> Justice is the first virtue of social institutions, as truth is of systems of thought. A theory however elegant or economical must be rejected or revised if it is untrue; likewise laws and institutions no matter how efficient and well-arranged must be reformed or abolished if they are unjust.[9]

In the same way that theories can have qualities other than truth, some of which—brilliance or social utility, for example—might be more elevated than mere truth, so can social institutions have other moral qualities, some of which might be more elevated than mere justice. The point is that justice takes primacy because it is the most *essential,* not because it is the *highest,* of virtues. In fact, Rawls states explicitly his belief that there are moral principles and sentiments that are higher and nobler than justice. He refers to "supererogatory actions," such as "acts of benevolence and mercy, of heroism and self-sacrifice," as stemming from "higher-order moral sentiments that serve to bind a community of persons together." [10] He also indicates on several occasions that the members of families do commonly exhibit such higher moral virtues in relation to one another. But he considers that only saints and heroes, not ordinary persons, can *consistently* adhere to such standards of morality, which can require considerable sacrifice of self-interest, narrowly construed.[11] Furthermore, it is clear that, in Rawls's view, such moralities of supererogation, while they require *more* than the norms of right and justice, do not in any way contradict them. This is so both because their aims are continuous with these principles but extend beyond what they require and because such moralities need to rely upon the principles of justice when the claims of the goods they seek conflict.[12] Thus justice is first or primary among virtues in that such admittedly higher forms of morality depend upon it, both conceptually and in practice, in ways that it does not depend upon them.

When these points are taken into consideration, we can see that both the argument against the moral primacy of justice and that against justice as a central virtue for the family lose their force. The morality that often prevails in communities or associations that are governed in large part by affection, generosity, or other virtues morally superior to justice is a form of supererogation; individuals' narrowly construed interests give way to their concern for common ends or the ends of others they care about a great deal. Nevertheless, it is essential that such higher moral sentiments and actions, within the family as well as in society at large, be underwritten by a foundation of justice. Justice is

[9] Rawls, *Theory,* p. 3.
[10] Ibid., pp. 117, 192.
[11] Ibid., pp. 129–30, 438–39.
[12] Ibid., pp. 479, 191.

needed as the primary, meaning most fundamental, moral virtue even in social groupings in which aims are largely common and affection frequently prevails.

We can learn more about why justice is a necessary virtue for families by examining the second flaw in Sandel's argument, which is that it relies upon an idealized, even mythical, account of the family. The picture drawn is, in fact, very close to Rawls's example of a circumstance in which he too agrees that justice is superfluous: "an association of saints agreeing on a common ideal." [13] But viewed realistically, human associations, including the family, do not operate so felicitously. And a theory of justice must concern itself not with abstractions or ideals of institutions but with their realities. If we were to concern ourselves only with ideals, we might well conclude that wider human societies, as well as families, could do without justice. The ideal society would presumably need no system of criminal justice or taxation, but that does not tell us much about what we need in the world we live in.

The vision of the family as an institution far above justice pays too little attention to what happens within such groupings when, as is surely common, they fail to meet this saintly ideal. Even a brief glance at the example that Hume regards as the paradigm setting for the exercise of moral virtues nobler than justice should serve to make us less than comfortable with his and Sandel's dismissal of the need for justice in such settings. The unity of the eighteenth-century family—enshrined in the ideology of the time and revived in the 1970s by family historians [14]—was based on the legal fiction of "coverture." The *reason* that, as Hume puts it, "the laws supposed . . . the cement of friendship [between married persons] so strong as to abolish all division of possessions," was that upon marrying, women became legal nonpersons. Contrary to what Hume's words suggest, the common law did not institute the shared or common ownership of the property of spouses. Rather, it automatically transferred all of a wife's personal property—as well as control over, and the income from, her real property—into the hands of her husband. As John Stuart Mill was later to put it: "the two are called 'one person in law,' for the purpose of inferring that whatever is hers is his, but the parallel inference is never drawn that whatever is his is hers." [15] Hume and others justified coverture by reference to the "enlarged affections" and unity of the family. This same idealized vision of the family as "the place of Peace; the shelter, not only from all injury, but from all terror, doubt, and division," as John Ruskin depicted it, was central to the arguments made by the opponents of married women's rights in the nineteenth century.[16] But *we* must realize that questions of distributive justice were not

[13] Ibid., p. 129.

[14] Edward Shorter, *The Making of the Modern Family* (New York: Basic Books, 1975); Lawrence Stone, *The Family, Sex, and Marriage in England 1500–1800* (New York: Harper & Row, 1977); Randolph Trumbach, *The Rise of the Egalitarian Family* (New York: Academic Press, 1978).

[15] *The Subjection of Women*, in *The Collected Works of John Stuart Mill*, ed. John M. Robson (Toronto: University of Toronto Press, 1984), p. 284.

[16] John Ruskin, "Of Queen's Gardens," Lecture 2 of *Sesame and Lilies* (London: A. L. Burt, 1871), p. 85, quoted in Mary L. Shanley, "Marital Slavery and Friendship. John Stuart Mill's *The*

considered important in the context of this type of family because not only the wife's property but her body, her children, and her legal rights belonged to her husband. To revert in the late twentieth century to this account of family life in order to argue that the circumstances of justice are not so socially pervasive as liberals like Rawls think they are is not only grossly ahistorical. It does not allow for the fact that the account was a myth, and a far from harmless one. It served as the ideology that veiled the *in*justice called coverture.

What this example can teach us about justice and the family is that while it is quite possible for associations to appear to operate according to virtues nobler than justice, and thus to be morally preferable to those that are *just* just, we need to scrutinize them closely before we can conclude that this is really the case. In particular, we need to ask whether their members are entitled to their fair shares of whatever benefits and burdens are at issue when and insofar as the circumstances of justice arise—when interests or ends conflict and some resources are scarce (as tends to happen at least some of the time, except in communities of saints with common ends). Thus even if wives never had occasion to ask for their just share of the family property, due to the generosity and spontaneous affection of their husbands, we would be unable to assess the families in which they lived from a moral point of view unless we knew whether, if they did ask for it, they would be considered entitled to it. It is not difficult to imagine the kind of response that would have been received by most eighteenth-century wives if they had asked for their just shares of the family property! This should make us highly skeptical of reliance on the supposedly higher virtues embodied by such institutions.

It is clear from the facts that I pointed to in chapter 1, and shall later give a more thorough account of, that Sandel's argument against the primacy of justice also depends on a highly idealized view of the *contemporary* family. "Enlarged affections" are by no means the only feelings that occur, and are acted upon, in families. Since the 1970s, it has been "discovered" that a great deal of violence—much of it serious, some of it fatal—occurs within families. Our courts and police are increasingly preoccupied with family assault and with the sexual abuse of weaker family members by more powerful ones. The family is also an important sphere of distribution. In the "more or less ideal family situation," Sandel says, the appeal to fairness is "preempted by a spirit of generosity in which I am rarely inclined to claim my fair share," and "the questions of what I get and what I am due do not loom large in the overall context of this way of life."[17] The implication seems to be that there are not likely to be systematic injustices. No account is taken of the fact that the socialization and role expectations of women mean that they are generally more inclined than men not to claim their fair share, and more inclined to order their priorities in accordance with the needs of their families. The supererogation that is expected

---

Subjection of Women," Political Theory 9, no. 2 (1981): 233. See also Shanley, *Feminism, Marriage and the Law in Victorian England 1850–1890* (Princeton: Princeton University Press, in press), esp. introduction and chap. 1.

[17] Sandel, *Limits of Justice,* p. 33.

in families often occurs at women's expense, as earlier ideologists of the family were well aware; Ruskin continues his vision by exhorting women to be "enduringly incorruptibly good; instinctively infallibly wise . . . , not for self-development but for self-renunciation." [18]

In fact, many social "goods," such as time for paid work or for leisure, physical security, and access to financial resources, typically are unevenly distributed within families. Though many may be "better than just," at least most of the time, contemporary gender-structured families are *not* just. But they *need* to be just. They cannot rely upon the spirit of generosity—though they can still aspire to it—because the life chances of millions of women and children are at stake. They need to be just, too, if they are to be the first schools of moral development, the places where we first learn to develop a sense of justice. And they need to be just if we are even to begin to approach the equality of opportunity that our country claims as one of its basic ideals.

It seems to be assumed by those who have held the position I have been criticizing that justice somehow takes away from intimacy, harmony, and love. But why should we suppose that harmonious affection, indeed deep and long-lasting love, cannot co-exist with ongoing standards of justice? Why should we be forced to choose and thereby to deprecate the basic and essential virtue, justice, by playing it off against what are claimed to be higher virtues? We are surely not faced with such a choice if, viewing human groupings like the family realistically, we insist that they be constructed upon a basis of justice. For this need not mean that we cannot also hope and expect more of them. We need to recognize that associations in which we *hope* that the best of human motivations and the noblest of virtues will prevail are, in fact, morally superior to those that are *just* just only if they are firmly built on a foundation of justice, however rarely it may be invoked. Since this is so, the existence of associations like families poses no problem for the moral primacy of justice. If they normally operate in accordance with spontaneous feelings of love and generosity, but provide justice to their members when, as circumstances of justice arise, it is needed, then they are just and better than just. But if they do not provide justice when their members have reason to ask it of them, then despite their generosity and affection, they are worse.

Thus, it is only when the family is idealized and sentimentalized that it can be perceived as an institution that undermines the primacy of justice. When we recognize, as we must, that however much the members of families care about one another and share common ends, they are still discrete persons with their own particular aims and hopes, which may sometimes conflict, we must see the family as an institution to which justice is a crucial virtue. When we recognize, as we surely must, that many of the resources that are enjoyed within the sphere of family life—leisure, nurturance, money, time, and attention, to mention only a few—are by no means always abundant, we see that justice has a highly significant role to play. When we realize that women, especially, are likely to change the whole course of their lives because of their family commitments, it

[18] Ruskin, "Of Queen's Gardens," p. 86.

becomes clear that we cannot regard families as analogous to other intimate relations like friendship, however strong the affective bonding of the latter may be. And now that it cannot be assumed, as it was earlier, that marriage is for life, we must take account of the fact that the decreasing permanence of families renders issues of justice within them more critical than ever. To substitute self-sacrifice and altruism for justice in the context of a unity that may dissolve before one's very eyes, without one's consent and to the great detriment of those one cares most about, would perhaps be better labeled lack of foresight than nobility.

• • •

II. WOMEN AND JUSTICE IN THEORY AND PRACTICE

. . . while Rawls briefly rules out formal, legal discrimination on the grounds of sex (as on other grounds that he regards as "morally irrelevant"), he fails entirely to address the justice of the gender system, which—with its roots in the sex roles of the family and with its branches extending into virtually every corner of our lives—is one of the fundamental structures of our society. If, however, we read Rawls taking seriously both the notion that those behind the veil of ignorance are sexless persons, and the requirement that the family and the gender system—as basic social institutions—are to be subject to scrutiny, constructive feminist criticism of these contemporary institutions follows. So, also, do hidden difficulties for a Rawlsian theory of justice in a gendered society.

I will explain each of these points in turn. But first, both the critical perspective and the incipient problems of a feminist reading of Rawls can perhaps be illuminated by a description of a cartoon I saw a few years ago. Three elderly, robed male justices are depicted, looking down with astonishment at their very pregnant bellies. One says to the others, without further elaboration: "Perhaps we'd better reconsider that decision." This illustration points to several things. First, it graphically demonstrates the importance, in thinking about justice, of a concept like Rawls's original position, which makes us put ourselves into the positions of others—especially positions that we ourselves can never be in. Second, it suggests that those thinking in such a way might well conclude that more than formal legal equality of the sexes is required if justice is to be done. As we have seen in recent years, it is quite possible to institutionalize the formal legal equality of the sexes and at the same time to enact laws concerning pregnancy, abortion, maternity leave, and so on, that in effect discriminate against women, not as women *per se,* but as "pregnant persons." The U.S. Supreme Court decided in 1976, for example, that "an exclusion of pregnancy from a disability benefits plan . . . providing general coverage is not a gender-based discrimination at all." [19] One of the virtues of the cartoon is its suggestion that one's thinking on such matters is likely to be affected by the

[19] *General Electric vs. Gilbert,* 429, U.S. 125 (1976).

knowledge that one might become a "pregnant person." Finally, however, the illustration suggests the limits of what is possible, in terms of thinking ourselves into the original position, as long as we live in a gender-structured society. While the elderly male justices can, in a sense, imagine *themselves* pregnant, what is much more doubtful is whether, in constructing principles of justice, they can imagine themselves *women*. This raises the question whether, in fact, sex *is* a morally irrelevant and contingent human characteristic, in a society structured by gender.

Let us first assume that sex is contingent in this way, though I will later question this assumption. Let us suppose that it is possible, as Rawls clearly considers that it is, to hypothesize the moral thinking of representative human beings, ignorant of their sex and of all the other things that are hidden by the veil of ignorance. It seems clear that, while Rawls does not do this, we must consistently take the relevant positions of both sexes into account in formulating principles of justice. In particular, those in the original position must take special account of the perspective of women, since their knowledge of "the general facts about human society."[20] must include the knowledge that women have been and continue to be the less advantaged sex in a number of respects. In considering the basic institutions of society, they are more likely to pay special attention to the family than virtually to ignore it, since its unequal assigning of responsibilities and privileges to the two sexes and its socialization of children into sex roles make it, in its current form, a crucial institution for the preservation of sex inequality.

It is impossible to discuss here all the ways in which the principles of justice that Rawls arrives at are inconsistent with a gender-structured society. A general explanation of this point and three examples to illustrate it will have to suffice. The critical impact of a feminist reading of Rawls comes chiefly from his second principle, which requires that inequalities be "to the greatest benefit of the least advantaged" and "attached to offices and positions open to all."[21] This means that if any roles or positions analogous to our current sex roles, including those of husband and wife, mother and father, were to survive the demands of the first requirement, the second requirement would disallow any linkage between these roles and sex. Gender, as I have defined it in this article, with its ascriptive designation of positions and expectations of behavior in accordance with the inborn characteristic of sex, could no longer form a legitimate part of the social structure, whether inside or outside the family. Three illustrations will help to link this conclusion with specific major requirements that Rawls makes of a just or well-ordered society.

First, after the basic political liberties, one of the most essential liberties is "the important liberty of free choice of occupation."[22] It is not difficult to see that this liberty is compromised by the assumption and customary expectation, central to our gender system, that women take far greater responsibility than

---

[20] Nozick, *A Theory of Justice,* p. 137.

[21] Ibid., p. 302.

[22] Ibid., p. 274.

men for housework and child care, whether or not they also work for wages outside the home. In fact, both the assigning of these responsibilities to women—resulting in their asymmetrical economic dependency on men—and also the related responsibility of husbands to support their wives, compromise the liberty of choice of occupation of both sexes. While Rawls has no objection to some aspects of the division of labor, he asserts that, in a well-ordered society, "no one need be servilely dependent on others and made to choose between monotonous and routine occupations which are deadening to human thought and sensibility" but that work can be "meaningful for all."[23] These conditions are far more likely to be met in a society which does not assign family responsibilities in a way that makes women into a marginal sector of the paid work force and renders likely their economic dependence upon men.

Second, the abolition of gender seems essential for the fulfillment of Rawls's criteria for political justice. For he argues that not only would equal formal political liberties be espoused by those in the original position, but that any inequalities in the *worth* of these liberties (for example, the effects on them of factors like poverty and ignorance) must be justified by the difference principle. Indeed, "the constitutional process should preserve the equal representation of the original position to the degree that this is practicable."[24] While Rawls discusses this requirement in the context of class differences, stating that those who devote themselves to politics should be "drawn more or less equally from all sectors of society,"[25] it is just as clearly applicable to sex differences. And the equal political representation of women and men, especially if they are parents, is clearly inconsistent with our gender system.

Finally, Rawls argues that the rational moral persons in the original position would place a great deal of emphasis on the securing of self-respect or self-esteem. They "would wish to avoid at almost any cost the social conditions that undermine self-respect," which is "perhaps the most important" of all the primary goods.[26] In the interests of this primary value, if those in the original position did not know whether they were to be men or women, they would surely be concerned to establish a thoroughgoing social and economic equality between the sexes that would preserve either from the need to pander to or servilely provide for the pleasures of the other. They would be highly motivated, for example, to find a means of regulating pornography that did not seriously compromise freedom of speech. In general, they would be unlikely to tolerate basic social institutions that asymmetrically either forced or gave strong incentives to members of one sex to become sex objects for the other.

There is, then, implicit in Rawls's theory of justice a potential critique of gender-structured social institutions, which can be made explicit by taking seriously the fact that those formulating the principles of justice do not know their sex. At the beginning of my brief discussion of this feminist critique, however,

[23] Ibid., p. 529.

[24] Ibid., p. 222; see also pp. 202–205, 221–28.

[25] Ibid., p. 228.

[26] Ibid., pp. 440, 396; see also pp. 178–79.

I made an assumption that I said would later be questioned—that a person's sex is, as Rawls at times indicates, a contingent and morally irrelevant characteristic, such that human beings can hypothesize ignorance of this fact about them, imagining themselves as *sexless,* free and equal, rational, moral persons. First, I will explain why, unless this assumption is a reasonable one, there are likely to be further feminist ramifications for a Rawlsian theory of justice, as well as those I have just sketched out. I will then argue that the assumption is very probably not plausible in any society that is structured along the lines of gender. The conclusion I reach is that not only is the disappearance of gender necessary if social justice is to be enjoyed in practice by members of both sexes, but that the disappearance of gender is a prerequisite for the *complete* development of a nonsexist, fully human *theory* of justice.

Although Rawls is clearly aware of the effects on individuals of their different places in the social system, he regards it as possible to hypothesize free and rational moral persons in the original position who, freed from the contingencies of actual characteristics and social circumstances, will adopt the viewpoint of the "representative human being." He is under no illusions about the difficulty of this task, which requires "a great shift in perspective" from the way we think about fairness in everyday life. But with the help of the veil of ignorance, he believes that we can "take up a point of view that everyone can adopt on an equal footing," so that "we share a common standpoint along with others and do not make our judgments from a personal slant."[27] The result of this rational impartiality or objectivity, Rawls argues, is that, all being convinced by the same arguments, agreements about the basic principles of justice will be unanimous.[28] He does not mean that those in the original position will agree about *all* moral or social issues, but that complete agreement will be reached on all basic principles, or "essential understandings."[29] It is a crucial assumption of this argument for unanimity, however, that all the parties have similar motivations and psychologies (he assumes mutually disinterested rationality and an absence of envy), and that they have experienced similar patterns of moral development (they are presumed capable of a sense of justice). Rawls regards these assumptions as the kind of "weak stipulations" on which a general theory can safely be founded.[30]

The coherence of Rawls's hypothetical original position, with its unanimity of representative human beings, however, is placed in doubt if the kinds of human beings we actually become in society not only differ in respect of interests, superficial opinions, prejudices, and points of view that we can discard for the purpose of formulating principles of justice, but also differ in their basic psychologies, conceptions of self in relation to others, and experiences of moral development. A number of feminist scholars have argued in recent years that, in a gender-structured society, women's and men's different life experiences in fact

[27] Ibid., pp. 516–17.

[28] Ibid., pp. 139–41.

[29] Ibid., pp. 516–17.

[30] Ibid., p. 149.

affect their respective psychologies, modes of thinking, and patterns of moral development in significant ways.[31] Special attention has been paid to the effects on the psychological and moral development of both sexes of the fact, fundamental to our gendered society, that children of both sexes are primarily reared by women. It has been argued that the experience of individuation—of separating oneself from the nurturer with whom one is originally psychologically fused—is a very different experience for girls than for boys, leaving the members of each sex with a different perception of themselves and of their relations with others. In addition, it has been argued that the experience of being primary nurturers (and of growing up with this expectation) also affects the psychological and moral perspective of women, as does the experience of growing up in a society in which members of one's sex are in many respects subordinate to the other. Feminist theorists' scrutiny and analysis of the different experiences that we encounter as we develop, from our actual lived lives to our absorption of their ideological underpinnings, have in valuable ways filled out de Beauvoir's claim that "one is not born, but rather becomes, a woman."[32]

What is already clearly indicated by these studies, despite their incompleteness so far, is that in a gender-structured society there is such a thing as the distinct standpoint of women, and that this standpoint cannot be adequately taken into account by male philosophers doing the theoretical equivalent of the elderly male justices in the cartoon. The formative influence on small children of female parenting, especially, seems to suggest that sex difference is more likely to affect one's moral psychology, and therefore one's thinking about justice, in a gendered society than for example, racial difference in a society in which race has social significance or class difference in a class society. The notion of the standpoint of women, while not without its own problems, suggests that a fully human moral theory can be developed only when there is full participation of both sexes in the dialogue that is moral and political philosophy. This will not come to pass until women take their place with men in the enterprise in approximately equal numbers and in positions of comparable influence. In a society structured along the lines of gender, this is most unlikely to happen.

In itself, moreover, it is insufficient for the complete development of a fully human theory of justice. For if principles of justice are to be adopted unanimously by representative human beings ignorant of their particular characteristics and positions in society, they must be persons whose psychological and

---

[31] Major works contributing to this thesis are Jean Baker Miller, *Toward a New Psychology of Women* (Boston: Beacon Press, 1976); Dorothy Dinnerstein, *The Mermaid and the Minotaur* (New York: Harper and Row, 1977); Nancy Chodorow, *The Reproduction of Mothering* (Berkeley: University of California Press, 1978); Carol Gilligan, *In a Different Voice* (Cambridge, MA: Harvard University Press, 1982); Nancy Hartsock, *Money, Sex, and Power* (New York: Longmans, 1983). Two of the more important individual papers are Jane Flax, "The Conflict between Nurturance and Autonomy in Mother-Daughter Relationships and within Feminism," *Feminist Studies* 4, no. 2 (Summer 1978); Sara Ruddick, "Maternal Thinking," *Feminist Studies* 6, no. 2 (Summer 1980). A good summary and discussion of "women's standpoint" is presented in Alison Jagger, *Feminist Politics and Human Nature* (Totowa, NJ: Rowman and Allanheid, 1983), chap. 11.

[32] Simone de Beauvoir, *The Second Sex* (1949; reprint ed., London: New English Library, 1969), p. 9.

moral developments is in all essentials identical. This means that the social factors influencing the differences presently found between the sexes—from female parenting to all the manifestations of female subordination and dependence—would have to be replaced by genderless institutions and customs. Only when men participate equally in what has been principally women's realm of meeting the daily material and psychological needs of those close to them, and when women participate equally in what have been principally men's realms of larger scale production, government, and intellectual and creative life, will members of both sexes develop a more complete *human* personality than has hitherto been possible. Whereas Rawls and most other philosophers have assumed that human psychology, rationality, moral development and so on are completely represented by the males of the species, this assumption itself is revealed as a part of the male-dominated ideology of our gendered society.

It is not feasible to indicate here at any length what effect the consideration of women's standpoint might have on a theory of justice. I would suggest, however, that in the case Rawls's theory, it might place in doubt some assumptions and conclusions, while reinforcing others. For example, Rawls's discussion of rational plans of life and primary goods might be focused more on relationships and less exclusively on the complex activities that his "Aristotelian principle" values most highly, if it were to encompass the traditionally more female parts of life.[33] On the other hand, those aspects of Rawls's theory, such as the difference principle, that seem to require a greater capacity to identify with others than is normally characteristic of liberalism, might be strengthened by reference to conceptions of relations between self and others that seem in a gendered society to be more predominantly female.

---

[33] Brian Barry has made a similar, though more general, criticism of the Aristotelian principle in *The Liberal Theory of Justice* (Oxford: Oxford University Press, 1973), pp. 27–30.

66.

Justice in Place of Filial Obligations

NORMAN DANIELS

What is a just distribution of social goods between the old and the young? I have argued that this question poses a distinct problem of justice. The problem seems novel because the rapid aging of society has forced us to consider it explicitly, but it is actually not new. All societies, past and present, transfer income, wealth, and power between age groups. The justice of such transfers is always open to discussion. Indeed, traditional arrangements might be thought of as familiar, time-tested solutions to the problem. Appealing directly to certain traditional moral notions in order to solve the problem is therefore tempting.

In many earlier societies, transfers of social goods between age groups were primarily a family matter. Some people believe that, wherever possible, we should continue to treat the issue that way. Filial obligations, for example, should determine what the young owe the old. These obligations tell us what children owe their parents. This appeal to family responsibility is an attempt to turn back the clock. The trend in this century has been to make transfers of basic income support and many health-care services a social, not a family task.

We cannot turn back the clock. Specifically, we cannot solve the age-group problem by appealing to filial obligations. For such obligations to provide a determinate basis for social policy, we would have to know just what burdens they impose. We cannot, however, just appeal to traditional family values and practices to determine the content of these obligations today. Neither can we find well-established moral foundations, references to which would clarify the content of these obligations. We live in a society in which there are diverse beliefs about family responsibility, and we have neither a homogeneous tradition nor a compelling philosophical account that can overcome this diversity.

As a result, these family obligations provide a poor foundation for public policy and should not be enforced by legal sanctions. Instead, we need a solution to the problem of justice between age groups that respects the diversity. Consequently, we must first clarify our social obligations and design institutions that ensure justice between age groups. Within that framework, people can pursue their family responsibilities as their moral convictions permit. Thus it is a mistake to think we can meet social obligations by enforcing some set of individual and family obligations. We must resist this effort to "privatize" the problem of social justice.

●　●　●

JUSTICE DESPITE DIVERSITY

Social policy concerning the young and the old should rest on a solution to the problem of justice between age groups. That solution should count as a court of final appeal; it should give us a public basis for resolving disputes about policy. Some people believe that a clear understanding of what children owe their parents would give us that solution: We could then make family responsibility the basis of social policy. Unfortunately for this strategy, filial obligations remain a singularly indeterminate solution to the problem. The Traditionalist approach failed because it could find no shared heritage from which we could unequivocally extrapolate the limits of these obligations. Similarly, we have not been successful in finding well-established moral foundations for them, and thus we have no clear grasp of their limits. Both Traditionalist and philosophical approaches failed to provide us with a publicly understandable basis for producing agreement about the content of these obligations. This failure should make us leery of attempts to base social policy on appeals to these individual obligations.

The problem is not, of course, that individuals have no idea what filial obligations entail. In fact, most people have quite strong, deeply held moral convictions. Some vehemently deny that they have any such obligations at all. Most insist just as firmly that they have them, but they may disagree about what the obligations entail. Those who believe they owe their parents extensive care may insist that others, who do not so believe, are immoral shirkers of duty. Those who do not believe they have such obligations will resent believers trying to impose obligations through legal sanctions. The diversity of cultural traditions, which frustrated the Traditionalist, may explain some of this diversity in current beliefs. Similarly, the absence of well-established moral foundations for filial obligations also explains the variety of views. Whatever the explanation, this diversity is a fact of our social life and not likely to disappear.

Of course, society could make these obligations determinate by fiat, by passing laws governing family responsibility. The difficulty with doing it that way is that social policy needs to be *just* or fair as well as determinate. The obligations we specify—even by fiat—should result in a fair system of transfers between age groups. Not merely any determinate set of legal obligations to parents will do. Moreover, the rationale we offer for the transfers we consider to be fair must be one we can publicly defend. The problem we have uncovered is that we lack any persuasive way to sanction by law one uniform set of filial obligations given the disagreement in moral beliefs about them.

A fundamental point about the nature of justice is at the heart of this problem. Principles of justice must yield a framework of institutions within which people having different views about what is good and right in other regards can cooperate. In general, and especially in heterogeneous societies such as ours, individuals will have strikingly varied conceptions of how to live a good life. They will have different fundamental goals and projects in life, so their lives will achieve value or meaning in a variety of ways. We might think of the "plan of life" that connects these goals, projects, and preferences into a rational pattern of activity as defining "the good" for an individual. (The term "plan of life" derives from Mill and is given prominence in Rawls 1971.)[1] At least some aspects of individual morality, that is, some beliefs about what is right for us to do, will also vary, and these variations form part of the diversity in plans of life. Within our society, the cultural variation in beliefs about what children owe parents helps shape individual conceptions of the good life in different ways. But it is the task of a theory of justice to provide us with principles that can act as a final and publicly acceptable basis for resolving disputes about how basic social goods, such as liberties, opportunity, income and wealth should be distributed among people who disagree about many other things. Justice must provide a framework for cooperation among individuals who may nevertheless disagree about much of what is good in life and about many of the ways they treat each other as individuals.[2]

In view of the aging of society, we face both a moral and practical problem. We must justify a system of transfers of social goods between age groups that accommodates new facts about our demography. As a result, we must consider explicitly a problem of justice that has often been left to tradition. We must discover and be able to justify principles that will govern social policy concerning the young and the old, and we must do so despite the fact that people disagree about what children owe parents. This means that we need a perspective from which we can arrive at a solution to the age-group problem without having to resolve these disputes about family responsibility. We need to solve the problem of justice in a way that allows people to pursue their own moral beliefs about family responsibility. We must define what our social obligations are in the distribution of goods between age groups, and we must design institutions that meet those obligations. At the same time, these institutions must allow diversity in the pursuit of family relationships and family responsibility. The problem of social justice is primary here: We must solve it collectively whatever other variability we allow individuals in their conceptions of what their individual or family obligations are.

This general point about the relationship between justice and family responsibility does not mean that social policy should ignore the responsibilities many children feel for their parents. Even if we abandon all talk about filial *obligations* (and I do not), we need not ignore the fact that many adult children care deeply about what happens to their parents. They believe they *owe* their parents significant efforts to care for them, and they do in fact provide such care. Sociologists have, as I noted, debunked that other myth about families, namely, that the elderly are not being cared for by their children. Enormous efforts are being made by extended, multigeneration families to provide long-term care for

[1] John Rawls. *A Theory of Justice* (Cambridge, MA: Harvard University Press, 1971).

[2] This picture of the role of justice is developed by Rawls in *A Theory of Justice;* "Kantian Constructivism in Moral Theory." *Journal of Philosophy* 77 (9) 1980: 515–572; and "Justice as Fairness: Political not Metaphysical." *Philosophy and Public Affairs* 14(3) 1985: 223–251.

their elderly.[3] Moreover, this is usually a type, quantity, and quality of care that the public sector is unlikely ever to provide a substitute for. Were this supply of services to disappear or to be undermined, it would be an unmitigated disaster for the elderly. My point throughout this discussion is that it is morally wrong to protect the supply of family care by legally enforcing some set of filial obligations for which we can provide no adequate moral justification. Rather, a just health-care system should meet social obligations concerning care of the frail elderly and, at the same time, be responsive to the importance and fragility of the family's contribution to long-term care. It should include institutions designed to encourage such family care. . . .

"PRIVATIZING" VERSUS SOCIAL JUSTICE

I have portrayed the appeal to family responsibility on the part of the Traditionalist as a nostalgic effort to turn back the clock (albeit to a mythical past). In trying to solve the social problem of justice between the young and the old by appealing to individual moral obligations, in "privatizing" the problem, the Traditionalist seeks to reestablish a more robust set of "old style" family values. What the young owe the old becomes the problem of what children traditionally owe their parents. The suggestion is that we can achieve social justice through individual morality, provided we enforce it legally.

The yearning for traditional individual values actually feeds a broader movement to "privatize" the problem of justice between age groups, indeed, to "privatize" many other issues of social justice as well. For example, some critics of the Social Security system would like to replace our socially administered system of transfers between age groups with a largely private system of individual savings and annuity plans. Similarly, wherever possible, these critics want to transform the social insurance plan called Medicare into one that relies more directly on individual ability to pay for care, for example, through cost-sharing. Specific reforms in the direction of "privatizing" social transfers are defended on various grounds, but this broader movement has its roots in certain libertarian views about justice itself. It is important to see why the Traditionalist and the libertarian unite in their support for "privatizing" transfers of services to the elderly.

The libertarian is interested in "privatizing" because of basic features of this theory of justice. With the libertarian view, . . . distributions of resources are just if they have the proper pedigree or history. They must arise through free exchanges of goods by individuals who are entitled to the property they seek to exchange. Such entitlements to goods exist where individuals acquired their property "from nature" in a just fashion or through exchanges with other individuals who themselves were entitled to it. In its pure form, this theory stands

---

[3] See E. Shanas. "The Family as a Social Support System in Old Age." *The Gerontologist* 19(2) 1979: 169–174.

opposed to redistributions of property by the state, except to rectify past injustices. The pure libertarian is opposed to a state that redistributes property even to maximize the liberty of its citizens. He is also opposed to any property transfers that are undertaken to enhance the opportunity or welfare of citizens, even if some may think such transfers make the system more fair. Justice, in this view, arises through individual actions which are fair because they are freely made. Social justice is the outcome of individual, not societal activities. The libertarian opposes, then, the trend, dominant in this century, of enhancing welfare, including the welfare of the elderly, through redistributive transfers of goods.

No social obligations exist for the libertarian, except to defend the society against external interference and to protect individuals from violations of their rights to property and security. Individual morality therefore assumes considerable importance in protecting individuals from the roughness of life and in providing a sense of community and mutual responsibility. The libertarian is likely to emphasize the importance of individual charity and other individual moral virtues that preserve some fabric of interpersonal responsibility.[4] In this spirit the libertarian joins the Traditionalist in appealing to filial and other individual obligations that enhance family responsibility.

This wedding is one of convenience, however, and not necessarily one of shared commitments. The libertarian has no basic commitment to save traditional family patterns or values from eroding in the stress of modern life. In turn, the Traditionalist may not have any fundamental aversion to a state that redistributes goods to promote equality or fairness. Some libertarians may also be Traditionalists, but such convergence in faith is not the general case.

The main argument of this chapter, that filial obligations remain indeterminate in a way that makes them an inappropriate basis for social policy, affects the partners in this marriage differently. It is a greater threat to Traditionalists than to libertarians, who may not want the state to enforce these obligations by law in any case. Traditionalists, we may suppose, remain concerned that society promote justice between the young and the old and, therefore, will be motivated to abandon the appeal to filial obligations in favor of a socially workable solution. They can still promote family responsibility within a framework of institutions that guarantee justice between the old and the young. Thus Traditionalists should divorce themselves from the libertarian's quest for privatization. Unlike libertarians, they have no principled stake in dismantling the social institutions that provide transfers of goods between age groups. If I am right that traditional family values are more likely to survive when we provide a framework of just institutions, Traditionalists should disavow the libertarian commitment to privatization.

[4] See Allan Buchanan, "The Right to a Decent Minimum of Health Care." *Philosophy and Public Affairs* 13(1) 1984: 55–78. Buchanan has argued that this emphasis on individual charity may be of little consolation to those who are really worried about the needy. Individual charity tends to be inefficient for many important kinds of needs, and strictly voluntary collective charitable efforts are likely to fail because of familiar obstacles to successful collective action, such as free-rider problems, problems of assurance, and coordination problems. Because of these problems, the libertarian may have to allow the state to enforce coercively some charitable duties.

67.
In Defense of Filial Obligations
CHRISTINA HOFF SOMMERS

What rights do parents have to the special attentions of their adult children? Before this century there was no question that a filial relationship defined a natural obligation; philosophers might argue about the nature of filial obligation, but not about its reality. Today, not a few moralists dismiss it as an illusion, or give it secondary derivative status. A. John Simmons[1] expresses "doubts . . . concerning the existence of 'filial' debts," and Michael Slote[2] seeks to show that the idea of filial obedience is an illusion whose source is the false idea that one owes obedience to a divine being. Jeffrey Blustein[3] argues that parents who have done no more than their duty may be owed nothing, and Jane English[4] denies outright that there are any filial obligations not grounded in mutual friendship.

The current tendency to deny or reconstrue filial obligation is related to the more general difficulty that contemporary philosophers have when dealing with the special duties. An account of the special obligations to one's kin, friends, community or country puts considerable strain on moral theories such as Kantianism and utilitarianism, theories that seem better designed for telling us what we should be doing for everyone impartially than for explaining something like filial obligation. The moral philosopher of a utilitarian or Kantian persuasion who is concerned to show that it is permissible to give some biased vent to family feeling *may* go on to become concerned with the more serious question of accounting for what appears to be a special obligation to care for and respect one's parents—but only as an afterthought. On the whole, the question of special agent-relative duties has not seemed pressing. In what follows I shall be arguing for a strong notion of filial obligation, and more generally I shall be making a case for the special moral relations. I first present some anecdotal materials that illustrate the thesis that a filial duty to respect one's parents is not an illusion.

I. THE CONCRETE DILEMMAS

I shall be concerned with the filial duties of adult children and more particularly with the duty to honor and respect. I have chosen almost randomly three

[1] *Moral Principles and Political Obligations* (Princeton, N.J.: University Press, 1979), p. 162.
[2] "Obedience and Illusion," in Onora O'Neill and William Ruddick, eds., *Having Children* (New York: Oxford, 1979), pp. 319–325.
[3] *Parents and Children: The Ethics of the Family* (New York: Oxford, 1982).
[4] "What Do Grown Children Owe Their Parents?", in O'Neill and Ruddick, *op. cit.*, pp. 351–356.

situations each illustrating what seems to be censurable failure on the part of adult children to respect their parents or nurturers. It would not be hard to add to these cases and real life is continually adding to them.

1. An elderly man was interviewed on National Public Radio for a program on old age. This is what he said about his daughter.

> I live in a rooming house. I lost my wife about two years ago and I miss her very much. . . . My little pleasure was to go to my daughter's house in Anaheim and have a Friday night meal. . . . She would make a meal that I would enjoy. . . . So my son-in-law got angry at me one time for a little nothing and ordered me out of the house. That was about eight months ago. . . . I was back once during the day when he was working. That was about two and a half or three months ago. I stayed for about two hours and left before he came home from work. But I did not enjoy the visit very much. That was the last time I was there to see my daughter.

2. An eighty-two-year-old woman (call her Miss Tate) spent thirty years working as a live-in housekeeper and baby-sitter for a judge's family in Massachusetts. The judge and his wife left her a small pension which inflation rendered inadequate. After her employers died, she lost contact with the children whom she had virtually brought up. One day Miss Tate arranged for a friend of hers to write to the children (by then middle-aged) telling them that she was sick and would like to see them. They never got around to visiting her or helping her in any way. She died last year without having heard from them.

3. The anthropologist Barbara Meyerhoff did a study of an elderly community in Venice, California.[5] She tells about the disappointment of a group of elders whose children failed to show up at their graduation from an adult education program:

> The graduates, 26 in all, were arranged in rows flanking the head table. They wore their finest clothing bearing blue and white satin ribbons that crossed the breast from shoulder to waist. Most were solemn and flushed with excitement. . . . No one talked openly about the conspicuous absence of the elders' children (87, 104).

I believe it may be granted that the father who had dined once a week with his daughter has a legitimate complaint. And although Miss Tate was duly salaried throughout her long service with the judge's family, it seems clear that the children of that family owe her some special attention and regard for having brought them up. The graduation ceremony is yet another example of wrongful disregard and neglect. Some recent criticisms of traditional conceptions of filial duty (e.g., by Jane English and John Simmons) make much of examples involving unworthy parents. One may agree that exceptional parents can forfeit their moral claims on their children. (What, given his behavior, remains of Fyodor Karamozov's right to filial regard?) But I am here concerned with what is owed to the average parent who is neglected or whose wishes are

[5] *Number Our Days* (New York: Simon & Schuster, 1978).

disregarded when they could at some reasonable cost be respected. I assume that such filial disregard is wrong. Although the assumption is dogmatic, it can be defended—though not by any quick maneuver. Filial morality is but one topic in the morality of special relations. The attempt to understand filial morality will lead us to a synoptic look at the moral community as a whole and to an examination of the nature of the rights and obligations that bind its members.

II. SHIFTING CONCEPTIONS

Jeffrey Blustein's *Parents and Children (op. cit.)* contains an excellent historical survey of the moral issues in the child-parent relationship. For Aristotle the obligation to serve and obey one's parents is like an obligation to repay a debt. Aquinas too explains the commandment to honor one's parents as "making a return for benefits received." [6] Both Aristotle and Aquinas count life itself as the first and most important gift that the child is given.

With Locke [7] the topic of filial morality changes: the discussion shifts from a concern with the authority and power of the parent to concern with the less formal, less enforceable, right to respect. Hume [8] was emphatic on the subject of filial ingratitude, saying, "Of all the crimes that human creatures are capable, the most horrid and unnatural is ingratitude, especially when it is committed against parents." By Sidgwick's time the special duties are beginning to be seen as problematic: "The question is on what principles . . . we are to determine the nature and extent of the special claims of affection and kind services which arise out of . . . particular relations of human beings." [9] Nevertheless, Sidgwick is still traditional in maintaining that "all are agreed that there are such duties, the nonperformance of which is ground for censure," and he is himself concerned to show how "our common notion of Justice [is] applicable to these no less than to other duties." [10]

If we look at the writings of a contemporary utilitarian such as Peter Singer, [11] we find no talk of justice or duty or rights, and *a fortiori,* no talk of special duties or parental rights. Consider how Singer, applying a version of R. M. Hare's utilitarianism, approaches a case involving filial respect. He imagines himself about to dine with three friends when his father calls saying he is ill and asking him to visit. What shall he do?

> To decide impartially I must sum up the preferences for and against going to dinner with my friends, and those for and against visiting my father. Whatever action satisfies more preferences, adjusted according to the strength of the preferences, that is the action I ought to take (101).

[6] *Summa Theologiae,* vol. 34, R. J. Batten, trans. (New York: Blackfriars, 1975), 2a2ae.

[7] John Locke, *Two Treatises of Government,* P. Laslett, ed. (New York: New American Library, 1965), Treatise 1, sec. 100.

[8] David Hume, *A Treatise on Human Nature,* Bk. III, p. 1, sec. 1.

[9] Henry Sidgwick, *The Methods of Ethics* (New York: Dover, 1966), p. 242.

[10] Ibid., p. 243.

[11] *The Expanding Circle: Ethics and Sociobiology* (New York: Farrar, Straus & Giroux, 1981).

Note that the idea of a special obligation does not enter here. Nor is any weight given to the history of the filial relationship which typically includes some two decades of parental care and nurture. According to Singer, "adding and subtracting preferences in this manner" is the only rational way of reaching ethical judgment.

Utilitarian theory is not very accommodating to the special relations. And it would appear that Bernard Williams is right in finding the same true of Kantianism. According to Williams,[12] Kant's "moral point of view is specially characterized by its impartiality and its indifference to any particular relations to particular persons." In my opinion, giving no special consideration to one's kin commits what might be called the *Jellyby fallacy.* Mrs. Jellyby, a character in Charles Dickens' *Bleak House,*[13] devotes all of her considerable energies to the foreign poor to the complete neglect of her family. She is described as a "pretty diminutive woman with handsome eyes, though they had a curious habit of seeming to look a long way off. As if they could see nothing nearer than Africa" (52). Dickens clearly intends her as someone whose moral priorities are ludicrously disordered. Yet by some modern lights Mrs. Jellyby could be viewed as a paragon of impartial rectitude. In the next two sections I will try to show what is wrong with an impartialist point of view and suggest a way to repair it.

III. THE MORAL DOMAIN

By a *moral domain* I mean a domain consisting of what G. J. Warnock[14] calls "moral patients." Equivalently, it consists of beings that have what Robert Nozick[15] calls "ethical pull." A being has *ethical pull* if it is ethically "considerable"; minimally, it is a being that should not be ill treated by a moral agent and whose ill treatment directly wrongs it. The extent of the moral domain is one area of contention (Mill includes animals; Kant does not). The nature of the moral domain is another. But here we find more uniformity. Utilitarians and deontologists are in agreement in conceiving of the moral domain as constituted by beings whose ethical pull is equal on all moral agents. To simplify matters, let us consider a domain consisting only of moral patients that are also moral agents. (For Kant, this is no special stipulation.) Then it is as if we have a gravitational field in which the force of gravitation is not affected by distance and all pairs of objects have the same attraction to one another. Or, if this sort of gravitational field is odd, consider a mutual admiration society no member of which is, intrinsically, more attractive than any other member. In this group, the pull of all is the same. Suppose that Buridan's ass was not standing in the exact middle of the bridge but was closer to one of the bags of feed at either end. We should still say that he was equally attracted to both bags, but also that

[12] "Persons, Character and Morality," in *Moral Luck* (New York: Cambridge, 1982), p. 2.

[13] New York: New American Library, 1964.

[14] *The Object of Morality* (London: Methuen, 1971), p. 152.

[15] *Philosophical Explanations* (Cambridge, Mass.: Harvard, 1981), p. 451.

he naturally would choose the closer one. So too does the utilitarian or Kantian say that the ethical pull of a needy East African and that of a needy relative are the same, but we can more easily act to help the relative. This theory of equal pull but unequal response saves the appearances for impartiality while acknowledging that, in practice, charity often begins and sometimes ends at home.

This is how the principle of impartiality appears in the moral theories of Kant and Mill. Of course their conceptions of ethical pull differ. For the Kantian any being in the kingdom of ends is an embodiment of moral law whose force is uniform and unconditional. For the utilitarian, any being's desires are morally considerable, exerting equal attraction on all moral agents. Thus Kant and Mill, in their different ways, have a common view of the moral domain as a domain of moral patients exerting uniform pull on all moral agents. I shall refer to this as the *equal-pull (EP) thesis*. It is worth commenting on the underlying assumptions that led Kant and Mill to adopt this view of the moral domain.

It is a commonplace that Kant was concerned to free moral agency from its psychological or "anthropological" determinations. In doing so he offered us a conception of moral agents as rational beings which abstracts considerably from human and animal nature. It is less of a commonplace that utilitarian theory, in its modern development, tends also to be antithetical to important empirical aspects of human nature. For the Kantian, the empirical demon to be combatted and exorcized lies within the individual. For the utilitarian it is located within society and its customs, including practices that are the sociobiological inheritance of the species. According to an act utilitarian like Singer, reason frees ethical thought from the earlier moralities of kin and reciprocal altruism and opens it to the wider morality of disinterestedness and universal concern: "The principle of impartial consideration of interests . . . alone remains a rational basis for ethics" (*op. cit.,* 109). The equal-pull thesis is thus seen to be entailed by a principle of impartiality, common to Kantian and utilitarian ethics, which is seen as liberating us from the biased dictates of our psychological, biological, and socially conventional natures.[16]

IV. DIFFERENTIAL PULL

The doctrine of equal ethical pull is a modern development in the history of ethics. It is certainly not attributable to Aristotle or Aquinas, nor, arguably, to

---

[16] See Alasdair MacIntyre, *After Virtue* (Notre Dame, Ind.: University Press, 1981). When one contrasts this modern approach to morality with classical approaches that give full play to the social and biological natures of moral agents in determining the range of moral behavior, one may come to see the history of ethics in terms of a MacIntyrean Fall; MacIntyre speaks of the "crucial moral opposition between liberal individualism in some version or other and the Aristotelian tradition in some version or other" (241). For MacIntyre, the Enlightenment is a new Dark Age both because of its abstract conception of the autonomous individual and because of the neglect of parochial contexts in determining the special obligations that were once naturally understood in terms of social roles.

Locke. Kant's authority gave it common currency and made it, so to speak, foundational. It is, therefore, important to state that EP is a dogma. Why should it be assumed that ethical pull is constant regardless of circumstance, familiarity, kinship and other special relations? The accepted answer is that EP makes sense of impartiality. The proponent of the special duties must accept this as a challenge: alternative suggestions for moral ontology must show how impartiality can be consistent with differential ethical forces.

I will refer to the rival thesis as the *thesis of differential pull (DP)*. According to the DP thesis, the ethical pull of a moral patient will always partly depend on how the moral patient is related to the moral agent on whom the pull is exerted. Moreover, the "how" of relatedness will be determined in part by the social practices and institutions in which the agent and patient play their roles. This does not mean that every moral agent will be differently affected, since it may be that different moral agents stand in the same relation to different moral patients. But where the relations differ in certain relevant ways, there the pull will differ. The relevant factors that determine ethical pull are in a broad sense circumstantial, including the particular social arrangements that determine what is expected from the moral agent. How particular circumstances and conventions shape the special duties is a complex question to which we cannot here do justice. We shall, however, approach it from a foundational standpoint which rejects EP and recognizes the crucial role of conventional practice, relationships, and roles in determining the nature and force of moral obligation. The gravitational metaphor may again be suggestive. In DP morality the community of agents and patients is analogous to a gravitational field where distance counts and forces vary in accordance with local conditions.

V. FILIAL DUTY

Filial duty, unlike the duty to keep a promise, is not self-imposed. But keeping the particular promise one has made is also a special duty, and the interplay of impartiality and specific obligation is more clearly seen in the case of a promise. We do well, therefore, to look at the way special circumstances shape obligations by examining more carefully the case of promise making.

A. I. Melden[17] has gone into the morality of promise keeping rather thoroughly, and I believe that some features of his analysis apply to the more general description of the way particular circumstances determine the degree of ethical pull on a moral agent. Following Locke, Melden assumes the natural right of noninterference with one's liberty to pursue one's interests (including one's interest in the well-being of others) where such pursuit does not interfere with a like liberty for others. Let an interest be called *invasive* if it is an interest in interfering with the pursuit of someone else's interests. Then the right that every moral patient possesses is the right not to be interfered with in the

---

[17] *Rights and Persons* (Los Angeles: California UP, 1977).

pursuit of his or her noninvasive interests. (In what follows "interest" will mean noninvasive interest.)

According to Melden, a promiser "gives the promisee the action as his own." The promise-breaking failure to perform is then "tantamount to interfering with or subverting endeavours he [the promisee] has a right to pursue" (47). The promise is "as entitled to [the action] as he is, as a responsible agent, to conduct his own affairs." What is special about this analysis is the formal grounding of the special positive duty of promise keeping in the minimalist negative obligation of noninterference. The negative, general, and indiscriminate obligation not to interfere is determined by the practice of promise making as a positive, specific, and discriminate obligation to act. Note how context here shapes and directs the initial obligation of noninterference and enhances its force. Given the conventions of the practice of promise making, the moral patient has novel and legitimate expectations of performances caused by the explicit assurances given by the promiser, who, in effect, has made over these performances to the promisee. And given these legitimate expectations, the agent's nonperformance of the promised act is invasive and tantamount to active interference with the patient's rights to its performance.

It is in the spirit of this approach to make the attempt to analyze other special obligations in the same manner. We assume a DP framework and a minimal universal deontological principle (the duty to refrain from interfering in the lives of others). This negative duty is refracted by the parochial situation as a special duty which may be positive in character, calling on the moral agent to act or refrain from acting in specific ways toward specific moral patients. This view of the special obligations needs to be justified. But for the present I merely seek to state it more fully.

The presumption of a special positive obligation arises for a moral agent when two conditions obtain: (1) In a given social arrangement (or practice) there is a specific interaction or transaction between moral agent and patient, such as promising and being promised, nurturing and being nurtured, befriending and being befriended. (2) The interaction in that context gives rise to certain conventional expectations (e.g., that a promise will be kept, that a marital partner will be faithful, that a child will respect the parent). In promising, the content of the obligation is verbally explicit. But this feature is not essential to the formation of other specific duties. In the filial situation, the basic relationship is that of nurtured to nurturer, a type of relationship which is very concrete, intimate, and long-lasting and which is considered to be more morally determining than any other in shaping a variety of rights and obligations.

Here is one of Alasdair MacIntyre's descriptions of the denizens of the moral domain:

I am brother, cousin, and grandson, member of this household, that village, this tribe. These are not characteristics that belong to human beings accidentally, to be stripped away in order to discover "the real me". They are part of my substance, defining partially at least and sometimes wholly my obligations and my duties (32).

MacIntyre's description takes Aristotle's dictum that man is a social animal in a sociological direction. A social animal has a specific social role whose prerogatives and obligations characterize a particular kind of person. Being a father or mother is socially as well as biologically descriptive: it not only defines what one is; it also defines who one is and what one owes.

Because it does violence to a social role, a filial breach is more serious than a breach of promise. In the promise the performance is legitimately expected, being, as it were, explicitly made over to the promisee as "his." In the filial situation the expected behavior is implicit, and the failure to perform affects the parent in a direct and personal way. To lose one's entitlements diminishes one as a person. Literature abounds with examples of such diminishment; King Lear is perhaps the paradigm. When Lear first becomes aware of Goneril's defection, he asks his companion: "Who am I?" to which the reply is "A shadow." Causing humiliation is a prime reason why filial neglect is tantamount to active interference. One's sense of dignity varies with temperament. But dignity itself—in the context of an institution like the family—is objective, being inseparable from one's status and role in that context.

The filial duties of adult children include such things as being grateful, loyal, attentive, respectful and deferential to parents (more so than to strangers). Many adult children, of course, are respectful and attentive to their parents out of love, not duty. But, as Melden says: "The fact that, normally, there is love and affection that unites the members of the family . . . in no way undercuts the fact that there is a characteristic distribution of rights and obligations within the family circle" (67).

The mutual understanding created by a promise is simplicity itself when compared with the range of expected behavior that filial respect comprises. What is expected in the case of a promise is clearly specified by the moral agent, but with respect to most other special duties there is little that is verbally explicit. Filial obligation is thus essentially underdetermined, although there are clear cases of what counts as disrespect—as we have seen in our three cases. The complexity and nonspecificity of expected behavior which is written into the domestic arrangements do not affect what the promissory and the filial situation have in common: both may be viewed as particular contexts in which the moral agent must refrain from behavior that interferes with the normal prerogatives of the moral patient.[18]

By taking promising as a starting point in a discussion of special duties, one runs the risk of giving the impression that DP is generally to be understood as a form of social-contract theory. But a more balanced perspective considers the

---

[18] Our account of the special moral relations is concentrating on the way the universal duty to refrain from invasive interference is refracted through circumstance into a variety of positive and discriminate duties. But a particular arrangement may produce the opposite effect: it may qualify the universal obligation to refrain from invasive interference by allowing the moral agent liberties normally forbidden. A fair amount of invasive behavior is the norm in certain private and voluntary arrangements where there is an understanding that exceptional demands may be made. My particular concern with the positive (filial) obligations has led me to confine discussion to the way context obligates moral agents to perform and not with how or to what extent it may license them.

acts required by any of the special duties as naturally and implicitly "made over" within the practices and institutions that define the moral agent in his particular role as a "social animal." Within this perspective promising and other forms of contracting are themselves special cases and not paradigmatic. Indeed, the binding force of the obligation to fulfill an explicit contract is itself to be explained by the general account to be given of special duties in a DP theory.

VI. GRATEFUL DUTY

One group of contemporary moral philosophers, whom I shall tendentiously dub *sentimentalists,* has been vocal in pointing out the shortcomings of the mainstream theories in accounting for the morality of the special relations. But they would find my formal and traditional approach equally inadequate. The sentimentalists oppose deontological approaches to the morality of the parent-child relationship, arguing that *duties* of gratitude are paradoxical, that the "owing idiom" distorts the moral ideal of the parent-child relationship which should be characterized by love and mutual respect. For them, each family relationship is unique, its moral character determined by the idiosyncratic ties of its members. Carol Gilligan[19] has recently distinguished between an "ethic of care" and an "ethic of rights." The philosophers I have in mind are objecting to the aridity of the "rights perspective" and are urging moral philosophers to attend to the morality of special relations from a "care perspective." The distinction is suggestive, but the two perspectives are not necessarily exclusive. One may recognize one's duty in what one does spontaneously and generously. And just as a Kantian caricature holds one in greater esteem when one does what is right against one's inclination, so the idea of care, responsibility and personal commitment, without formal obligation, is an equally dangerous caricature.

Approaches that oppose care and friendship to rights and obligations can be shown to be sadly inadequate when applied to real-life cases. The following situation described in this letter to Ann Landers is not atypical:

Dear Ann Landers:
    We have five children, all overachievers who have studied hard and done well. Two are medical doctors and one is a banker. . . . We are broke from paying off debts for their wedding and their education. . . . We rarely hear from our children. . . . Last week my husband asked our eldest son for some financial help. He was told 'File bankruptcy and move into a small apartment.' Ann, personal feelings are no longer a factor: it is a matter of survival. Is there any law that says our children must help out?[20]

There are laws in some states that would require that these children provide some minimal support for their indigent parents. But not a few contemporary

---

[19] *In a Different Voice* (Cambridge, Mass.: Harvard, 1983).
[20] *The Boston Globe,* Thursday, March 21, 1985.

philosophers could be aptly cited by those who would advocate their repeal. A. John Simmons, Jeffrey Blustein, and Michael Slote, for example, doubt that filial duty is to be understood in terms of special moral debts *owed* to parents. Simmons offers "reasons to believe that [the] particular duty meeting conduct [of parents to children] does not generate an obligation of gratitude on the child" (*op. cit.*, 182). And Blustein opposes what he and Jane English call the "owing idiom" for services parents were obligated to perform. "If parents have any right to repayment from their children, it can only be for that which was either above and beyond the call of parental duty, or not required by parental duty at all"[21] (The "overachievers" could not agree more.) Slote finds it "difficult to believe that one has a *duty* to show gratitude for benefits one has not requested" (320). Jane English characterizes filial duty in terms of the duties one good friend owes another. "[A]fter a friendship ends, the duties of friendship end" (354, 356).

Taking a sentimentalist view of gratitude, these philosophers are concerned to remove the taint of onerous duty from what should be a spontaneous and free desire to be considerate of one's parents. One may agree with the sentimentalists that there is something morally unsatisfactory in being considerate of one's parents *merely* out of duty. The mistake lies in thinking that duty and inclination are necessarily at odds. Moreover, the *having* of certain feelings and attitudes may be necessary for carrying out one's duty. Persons who lack feeling for their parents may be morally culpable for that very lack. The sentimentalist objection that this amounts to a paradoxical duty to *feel* (grateful, loyal, etc.) ignores the extent to which people are responsible for their characters; to have failed to develop in oneself the capacity to be considerate of others is to have failed morally, if only because many duties simply cannot be carried out by a cold and unfeeling moral agent.[22] Kant himself speaks of "the universal duty which devolves upon man of so ordering his life as to be fit for the performance of all moral duties."[23] And MacIntyre, who is no Kantian, makes the same point when he says, "moral education is an 'education sentimentale'" (151).

Sentimentalism is not harmlessly false. Its moral perspective on family relationships as spontaneous, voluntary, and duty-free is simply unrealistic. Anthropological observations provide a sounder perspective on filial obligation. Thus Corinne Nydegger[24] warns of the dangers of weakening the formal constraints that ensure that obligations are met: "No society, including our own,

---

[21] Blustein, p. 182. According to Blustein, parents who are financially able are *obligated* to provide educational opportunities for children who are able to benefit from them.

[22] See Marcia Baron, "The Alleged Moral Repugnance of Acting from Duty," *Journal of Philosophy* I.XXXI, 4 (April 1984): 197–220, especially pp. 204/5. She speaks of "the importance of the attitudes and dispositions one has when one performs certain acts, especially those which are intended to express affection or concern" and suggests that these attitudes constitute "certain parameters within which satisfactory ways of acting from duty must be located."

[23] Immanuel Kant, "Proper Self-respect," from *Lectures on Ethics*, Louis Enfield, trans. (New York: Harper & Row, 1963).

[24] "Family Ties of the Aged in Cross-cultural Perspective," *The Gerontologist*, XXIII, I (1983): 30.

relies solely on . . . affection, good will and enlightened self-interest." She notes that the aged in particular "have a vested interest in the social control of obligations" (30).

It should be noted that the sentimentalist is arguing for a morality that is sensitive to special relations and personal commitment; this is in its own way a critique of EP morality. But sentimentalism ignores the extent to which the "care perspective" is itself dependent on a formal sense of what is fitting and morally proper. The ideal relationship cannot be "duty-free," if only because sentimental ties may come unraveled, often leaving one of the parties at a material disadvantage. Sentimentalism then places in a precarious position those who are not (or no longer) the fortunate beneficiaries of sincere personal commitments. If the EP moralist tends to be implausibly abstract and therefore inattentive to the morality of the special relations, the sentimentalist tends to err on the side of excessive narrowness by neglecting the impersonal "institutional" expectations and norms that qualify all special relations.

VII. DP MORALITY: SOME QUALIFICATIONS

It might be thought that the difference between EP and DP tends to disappear when either theory is applied to concrete cases, since one must in any case look at the circumstances to determine the practical response. But this is to underestimate how what one *initially* takes to be the responsibility of moral agents to patients affects the procedure one uses in making practical decisions in particular circumstances. Recall again how Peter Singer's EP procedure pits the preferences of the three friends against the preferences of the father, and contrast this with a differential-pull approach that assumes discriminate and focused obligations to the father. Similarly, the adult children of the graduating elders and the children raised by Miss Tate gave no special weight to filial obligation in planning their day's activities.

There are, then, significant practical differences between a DP and an EP approach to concrete cases. The EP moralist is a respecter of the person whom he sees as an autonomous individual but no respecter of the person as a social animal within its parochial preserve. Moreover, a DP theory that grounds duty in the minimal principle of noninterference is sensitive to the distinction between strict duty and benevolence. Behaving as one is dutybound to behave is not the whole of moral life. But duty (in the narrow sense) and benevolence are not commensurate. If I am right, the Anaheim woman is culpably disrespectful. But it would be absurd if (in the manner of Mrs. Jellyby) she were to try to compensate for excluding her father by inviting several indigent gentlemen to dine in his stead.

I am arguing for a DP approach to the morality of the special relations. Williams, Nozick, MacIntyre, and others criticize utilitarianism and Kantianism for implausible consequences in this area. I believe that their objections to much of contemporary ethics are symptomatic of a growing discontent with the EP character of the current theories. It may be possible to revise the theories to avoid some of the implausible consequences. Rule utilitarianism seems to be a move in this direction. But, as they stand, their EP character leaves them open to criticism. EP is a dogma. But so is DP. My contention is that DP moral theories more plausibly account for our preanalytic moral judgments concerning what is right and wrong in a wide variety of real cases. Having said this, I will acknowledge that the proper antidote to the malaise Williams and others are pointing to will not be effectively available until DP moral theories are given a theoretical foundation as well worked out as those of the mainstream theories. Alasdair MacIntyre is a contemporary DP moralist who has perhaps gone furthest in this direction. Nozick and Williams are at least cognizant that a "particularistic" approach is needed.[25]

The DP moral theory is in any case better able to account for the discriminate duties that correspond to specific social roles and expectations. But of course not all duties are discriminate: there are requirements that devolve on everyone. This not only includes the negative requirement to refrain from harming one's fellowman, but also, in certain circumstances, to help him when one is singularly situated to do so. I am, for example, expected to help a lost child find its parent or to feed a starving stranger at my doorstep. Failure to do so violates an understanding that characterizes the loosest social ties binding us as fellow human beings. The "solitariness" that Hobbes speaks of is a myth; we are never in a totally unrelated "state of nature." The DP moralist recognizes degrees of relatedness and graded expectations. The most general types of positive behavior expected of anyone as a moral agent obey some minimal principle of Good Samaritanism applicable to "the stranger in thy midst."

Perhaps the most serious difficulty facing the DP approach is that it appears to leave the door wide open to ethical relativism. We turn now to this problem.

VIII. DP AND ETHICAL RELATIVISM

A theory is nonrelativistic if it has the resources to pass moral judgments on whole societies. My version of DP moral theory avoids ethical relativism by adopting a deontological principle (noninterference) which may be deployed in assessing and criticizing the moral legitimacy of the traditional arrangements within which purportedly moral interactions take place. We distinguish between unjust and merely imperfect arrangements. Arrangements that are essentially invasive are unjust and do not confer moral legitimacy on what is expected of those who are party to them. To correct the abuses of an unjust institution like slavery or a practice like suttee is to destroy the institution or

---

[25] Unfortunately, Nozick's particularism is "sentimentalist": "[Some] views will countenance particularism on one level by deriving it from 'universalistic' principles that hold at some deeper level. This misconstrues the moral weight of particularistic ties it seems to me; it is a worthwhile task, one I cannot undertake explicitly here, to investigate the nature of a more consistently particularistic theory—particularistic all the way down the line" [*Philosophical Explanations* (New York: Cambridge, 1981), 456/7]. The particularistic ties Nozick has in mind are not objectively institutional but subjectively interpersonal ("valuing the particularity of the other").

practice. By contrast, an institution like marriage or the family will often contain some unjust features, but these are usually corrigible, and the institution itself is legitimate and morally determining in a straightforward sense.

In any case the DP moralist is in a position to hold that not all social arrangements impose moral imperatives. It is not clear to me that DP can avoid relativism without *some* deontological minimal ground. But conceivably a principle other than noninterference might better serve as universal ground of the special duties. What is essential to any deontologically grounded DP morality is the recognition that the universal deontological principle is differentiated and specified by local arrangements that determine what is legitimately expected of the moral agent.

It may now be clear in what sense I believe DP theories to be plausible. A moral theory is plausible to the extent that it accounts for our pretheoretical moral judgments. Such intuitive judgments are admittedly idiosyncratic and prejudicial, being conditioned by our upbringing and the traditions we live by. The EP moralist nobly courts implausibility by jettisoning prejudice and confronting moral decisions anew. By contrast, the DP moralist jettisons only those prejudices which are exposed as rooted in and conditioned by an unjust social arrangement. But for those institutions which are not unjust, our common-sense judgments of "what is expected" (from parents, from citizens, from adult children) are generally held to be reliable guides to the moral facts of life.

The version of DP that I favor accepts the Enlightenment doctrine of natural rights in the minimal form of a universal right to noninterference and the correlative duty of moral agents to respect that right. MacIntyre's version of DP is hostile to Enlightenment "modernism," abjuring all talk of universal rights or deontic principles of a universal character. It is in this sense more classical. An adequate version of DP must nevertheless avoid the kind of ethical relativism that affords the moral philosopher no way to reject some social arrangements as immoral. MacIntyre appears to suggest that this can be achieved by accepting certain teleological constraints on good societies. Pending more detail, I am not convinced that a teleological approach can by itself do the critical job that needs to be done if we are to avoid an unacceptable ethical relativism. But other nondeontic approaches are possible. David Wong[26] has argued for a Confucian condition of adequacy that grades societies as better or worse depending on how well they foster human flourishing. My own deontic approach is not opposed to teleological or Confucianist ways of judging the acceptability of social arrangements. If a given arrangement is degenerate, then that is in itself a good reason to discount its norms as morally binding. But conceivably even a flourishing society could be unjust; nevertheless its civic norms should count as morally vacuous and illegitimate. It seems to me, therefore, that MacIntyre's version of DP morality probably goes too far in its rejection of all liberal deontic principles.

I have argued that DP best explains what we intuitively accept as our moral obligations to parents and other persons who stand to us in special relations.

[26] *Moral Relativity* (Berkeley: California UP, 1984).

And though my version of DP allows for criticizing unjust social arrangements, it may still seem unacceptably relativistic. For does it not allow that what is right for a daughter or son in one society is wrong for them in another? And does this not run afoul of the condition that what is right and wrong must be so universally? It should, I think, be acknowledged that the conservatism that is a feature of the doctrine of differential pull is somewhat hospitable to ethical relativism. Put another way: differential pull makes sense of ethical relativism's large grain of truth, but it does so without losing claim to its ability to evaluate morally the norms of different societies and institutions. Institutions that allow or encourage interference with noninvasive interests are unjust, and we have noted that the adherent of differential pull is in as good a position to apply a universal principle in evaluating an institution as anyone of an EP persuasion. But application of DP will rule out some institutions while allowing *diverse* others to count as legitimate and just. Only a just institution can assign and shape a moral obligation for those who play their roles within it. However, there are many varieties of just institutions, and so, in particular, are there many ways in which filial obligations are determined within different social and cultural contexts. What counts as filial respect in one context may not count as filial respect in another context. It is a virtue of our account that it not only tolerates but shows the way to justify different moral norms.

PART

XIV

PUNISHMENT

68.

A Utilitarian Theory of Punishment

JEREMY BENTHAM

I. CASES UNMEET FOR PUNISHMENT

§ i. General View of Cases Unmeet for Punishment

1. The general object which all laws have, or ought to have, in common, is to augment the total happiness of the community; and therefore, in the first place, to exclude, as far as may be, every thing that tends to subtract from that happiness: in other words, to exclude mischief.

2. But all punishment is mischief: all punishment in itself is evil. Upon the principle of utility, if it ought at all to be admitted, it ought only to be admitted in as far as it promises to exclude some greater evil.

3. It is plain, therefore, that in the following cases punishment ought not to be inflicted.

1. Where it is *groundless;* where there is no mischief for it to prevent; the act not being mischievous upon the whole.
2. Where it must be *inefficacious;* where it cannot act so as to prevent the mischief.
3. Where it is *unprofitable,* or too *expensive;* where the mischief it would produce would be greater than what it prevented.
4. Where it is *needless;* where the mischief may be prevented, or cease of itself, without it; that is, at a cheaper rate.

§ ii. Cases in Which Punishment is Groundless

These are,

4. (1) Where there has never been any mischief: where no mischief has been produced to any body by the act in question. Of this number are those in which the act was such as might, on some occasions, be mischievous or disagreeable, but the person whose interest it concerns gave his *consent* to the performance of it. This consent, provided it be free, and fairly obtained, is the best proof that can be produced, that, to the person who gives it, no mischief, at least no immediate mischief, upon the whole, is done. For no man can be so good a judge as the man himself, what it is gives him pleasure or displeasure.

5. (2) Where the mischief was *outweighed:* although a mischief was produced by that act, yet the same act was necessary to the production of a benefit which was of greater value than the mischief. This may be the case with any thing that is done in the way of precaution against instant calamity, as also with any thing that is done in the exercise of the several sorts of powers necessary

to be established in every community, to wit, domestic, judicial, military, and supreme.

6. (3) Where there is a certainty of an adequate compensation; and that in all cases where the offense can be committed. This supposes two things: 1. That the offense is such as admits of an adequate compensation; 2. That such a compensation is sure to be forthcoming. Of these suppositions, the latter will be found to be a merely ideal one: a supposition that cannot, in the universality here given to it, be verified by fact. It cannot, therefore, in practice, be numbered amongst the grounds of absolute impunity. It may, however, be admitted as a ground for an abatement of that punishment, which other considerations, standing by themselves, would seem to dictate.

§ iii. Cases in Which Punishment Must be Inefficacious

These are,

7. (1) Where the penal provision is *not established* until after the act is done. Such are the cases, 1. Of an *ex-post-facto* law; where the legislator himself appoints not a punishment till after the act is done; 2. Of a sentence beyond the law; where the judge, of his own authority, appoints a punishment which the legislator had not appointed.

8. (2) Where the penal provision, though established, is *not conveyed* to the notice of the person on whom it seems intended that it should operate. Such is the case where the law has omitted to employ any of the expedients which are necessary, to make sure that every person whatsoever, who is within the reach of the law, be apprized of all the cases whatsoever, in which (being in the station of life he is in) he can be subjected to the penalties of the law.

9. (3) Where the penal provision, though it were conveyed to a man's notice, *could produce no effect* on him, with respect to the preventing him from engaging in any act of the *sort* in question. Such is the case, 1. In extreme *infancy;* where a man has not yet attained that state or disposition of mind in which the prospect of evils so distant as those which are held forth by the law, has the effect of influencing his conduct; 2. In *insanity;* where the person, if he has attained to that disposition, has since been deprived of it through the influence of some permanent though unseen cause; 3. In *intoxication;* where he has been deprived of it by the transient influence of a visible cause; such as the use of wine, or opium, or other drugs, that act in this manner on the nervous system; which condition is indeed neither more nor less than a temporary insanity produced by an assignable cause.

10. (4) Where the penal provision (although, being conveyed to the party's notice, it might very well prevent his engaging in acts of the sort in question, provided he knew that it related to those acts) could not have this effect, with regard to the *individual* act he is about to engage in: to wit, because he knows not that it is of the number of those to which the penal provision relates. This may happen, 1. In the case of *unintentionality;* where he intends not to engage, and thereby knows not that he is about to engage, in the *act* in which eventually

he is about to engage; 2. In the case of *unconsciousness;* where, although he may know that he is about to engage in the *act* itself, yet, from not knowing all the material *circumstances* attending it, he knows not of the *tendency* it has to produce that mischief, in contemplation of which it has been made penal in most instances; 3. In the case of *mis-supposal;* where, although he may know of the tendency the act has to produce that degree of mischief, he supposes it, though mistakenly, to be attended with some circumstances, or set of circumstances, which, if it had been attended with, it would either not have been productive of that mischief, or have been productive of such a greater degree of good, as he determined the legislator in such a case not to make it penal.

11. (5) Where, though the penal clause might exercise a full and prevailing influence, were it to act alone, yet by the *predominant* influence of some opposite cause upon the will, it must necessarily be ineffectual; because the evil which he sees himself about to undergo, in the case of his *not* engaging in the act, is so great, that the evil denounced by the penal clause, in case of his engaging in it, cannot appear greater. This may happen, 1. In the case of *physical danger;* where the evil is such as appears likely to be brought about by the unassisted powers of *nature;* 2. In the case of a *threatened mischief;* where it is such as appears likely to be brought about through the intentional and conscious agency of *man.*

12. (6) Where (though the penal clause may exert a full and prevailing influence over the *will* of the party) yet his *physical faculties* (owing to the predominant influence of some physical clause) are not in a condition to follow the determination of the will insomuch that the act is absolutely *involuntary.* Such is the case of physical *compulsion* or *restraint,* by whatever means brought about; where the man's hand, for instance, is pushed against some object which his will disposes him *not* to touch; or tied down from touching some object which his will disposes him to touch.

§ iv. Cases Where Punishment is Unprofitable

These are,

13. (1) Where, on the one hand, the nature of the offense, on the other hand, that of the punishment, are, *in the ordinary state of things,* such, that when compared together, the evil of the latter will turn out to be greater than that of the former.

14. Now the evil of the punishment divides itself into four branches, by which so many different sets of persons are affected. 1. The evil of *coercion* or *restraint;* or the pain which it gives a man not to be able to do the act, whatever it be, which by the apprehension of the punishment he is deterred from doing. This is felt by those by whom the law is *observed;* 2. The evil of *apprehension;* or the pain which a man, who has exposed himself to punishment, feels at the thoughts of undergoing it. This is felt by those by whom the law has been *broken,* and who feel themselves in *danger* of its being executed upon them; 3. The evil of *sufferance;* or the pain which a man feels, in virtue of the punishment itself, from the time when he begins to undergo it. This is felt by

those by whom the law is broken, and upon whom it comes actually to be executed; 4. The pain of sympathy, and the other *derivative* evils resulting to the persons who are in *connection* with the several classes of original sufferers just mentioned. Now of these four lots of evil, the first will be greater or less, according to the nature of the punishment which stands annexed to that offense.

15. On the other hand, as to the evil of the offense, this will also, of course, be greater or less, according to the nature of each offense. The proportion between the one evil and the other will therefore be different in the case of each particular offense. The cases, therefore, where punishment is unprofitable on this ground, can by no other means be discovered, than by an examination of each particular offense; which is what will be the business of the body of the work.

16. (2) Where, although in the *ordinary state* of things, the evil resulting from the punishment is not greater than the benefit which is likely to result from the force with which it operates, during the same space of time, towards the excluding the evil of the offense, yet it may have been rendered so by the influence of some *occasional circumstances*. In the number of these circumstances may be, 1. The multitude of delinquents at a particular juncture; being such as would increase, beyond the ordinary measure, the *quantum* of the second and third lots, and thereby also of a part of the fourth lot, in the evil of the punishment; 2. The extraordinary value of the services of some one delinquent; in the case where the effect of the punishment would be to deprive the community of the benefit of those services; 3. The displeasure of the *people;* that is, of an indefinite number of the members of the *same* community, in cases where (owing to the influence of some occasional incident) they happen to conceive, that the offense or the offender ought not to be punished at all, or at least ought not to be punished in the way in question; 4. The displeasure of *foreign powers;* that is, of the governing body, or a considerable number of the members of some *foreign* community or communities, with which the community in question, is connected.

§ v. Cases Where Punishment is Needless

These are,

17. (1) Where the purpose of putting an end to the practice may be attained as effectually at a cheaper rate; by instruction, for instance, as well as by terror; by informing the understanding, as well as by exercising an immediate influence on the will. This seems to be the case with respect to all those offenses which consist in the disseminating pernicious principles in matters of *duty;* of whatever kind the duty be; whether political, or moral, or religious. And this, whether such principles be disseminated *under,* or even *without,* a sincere persuasion of their being beneficial. I say, even *without;* for though in such a case it is not instruction that can prevent the writer from endeavoring to inculcate his principles, yet it may the readers from adopting them; without which, his endeavoring to inculcate them will do no harm. In such a case, the sovereign will commonly have little need to take an active part; if it be the interest of *one*

individual to inculcate principles that are pernicious, it will as surely be the interest of *other* individuals to expose them. But if the sovereign must needs take a part in the controversy, the pen is the proper weapon to combat error with, not the sword.

II. OF THE PROPORTION BETWEEN PUNISHMENTS AND OFFENSES

1. We have seen that the general object of all laws is to prevent mischief; that is to say, when it is worth while; but that, where there are no other means of doing this than punishment, there are four cases in which it is *not* worth while.

2. When it *is* worth while, there are four subordinate designs or objects, which, in the course of his endeavors to compass, as far as may be, that one general object, a legislator, whose views are governed by the principle of utility, comes naturally to propose to himself.

3. (1) His first, most extensive, and most eligible object, is to prevent, in as far as it is possible, and worth while, all sorts of offenses whatsoever; in other words, so to manage, that no offense whatsoever may be committed.

4. (2) But if a man must needs commit an offense of some kind or other, the next object is to induce him to commit an offense *less* mischievous, *rather* than one *more* mischievous; in other words, to choose always the *least* mischievous, of two offenses that will either of them suit his purpose.

5. (3) When a man has resolved upon a particular offense, the next object is to dispose him to do *no more* mischief than is *necessary* to his purpose; in other words, to do as little mischief as is consistent with the benefit he has in view.

6. (4) The last object is, whatever the mischief be, which it is proposed to prevent, to prevent it at as *cheap* a rate as possible.

7. Subservient to these four objects, or purposes, must be the rules or canons by which the proportion of punishments to offenses is to be governed.

8. The first object, it has been seen, is to prevent, in as far as it is worth while, all sorts of offenses; therefore,

The value of the punishment must not be less in any case than what is sufficient to outweigh that of the profit of the offense.

If it be, the offense (unless some other considerations, independent of the punishment, should intervene and operate efficaciously in the character of tutelary motives) will be sure to be committed notwithstanding; the whole lot of punishment will be thrown away; it will be altogether *inefficacious*.

9. The above rule has been often objected to, on account of its seeming harshness; but this can only have happened for want of its being properly understood. The strength of the temptation, *caeteris paribus*, is as the profit of the offense; the quantum of the punishment must rise with the profit of the offense; *caeteris paribus*, it must therefore rise with the strength of the temptation. This there is no disputing. True it is, that the stronger the temptation, the less conclusive is the indication which the act of delinquency affords of the depravity

of the offender's disposition. So far then as the absence of any aggravation, arising from extraordinary depravity of disposition, may operate, or at the utmost, so far as the presence of a ground of extenuation, resulting from the innocence or beneficence of the offender's disposition, can operate, the strength of the temptation may operate in abatement of the demand for punishment. But it can never operate so far as to indicate the propriety of making the punishment ineffectual, which it is sure to be when brought below the level of the apparent profit of the offense.

The partial benevolence which should prevail for the reduction of it below this level, would counteract as well those purposes which such a motive would actually have in view, as those more extensive purposes which benevolence ought to have in view; it would be cruelty not only to the public, but to the very persons in whose behalf it pleads; in its effects, I mean, however opposite in its intention. Cruelty to the public, that is cruelty to the innocent, by suffering them, for want of an adequate protection, to lie exposed to the mischief of the offense; cruelty even to the offender himself, by punishing him to no purpose, and without the chance of compassing that beneficial end, by which alone the introduction of the evil of punishment is to be justified.

10. But whether a given offense shall be prevented in a given degree by a given quantity of punishment, is never any thing better than a chance; for the purchasing of which, whatever punishment is employed, is so much expended in advance. However, for the sake of giving it the better chance of outweighing the profit of the offense.

The greater the mischief of the offense, the greater is the expense, which it may be worth while to be at, in the way of punishment.

11. The next object is, to induce a man to choose always the least mischievous of two offenses; therefore

Where two offenses come in competition, the punishment for the greater offense must be sufficient to induce a man to prefer the less.

12. When a man has resolved upon a particular offense, the next object is, to induce him to do no more mischief than what is necessary for his purpose; therefore

The punishment should be adjusted in such manner to each particular offense, that for every part of the mischief there may be a motive to restrain the offender from giving birth to it.

13. The last object is, whatever mischief is guarded against, to guard against it at as cheap a rate as possible; therefore

The punishment ought in no case to be more than what is necessary to bring it into conformity with the rules here given.

14. It is further to be observed, that owing to the different manners and degrees in which persons under different circumstances are affected by the same exciting cause, a punishment which is the same in name will not always either

really produce, or even so much as appear to others to produce, in two different persons the same degree of pain; therefore,

That the quantity actually inflicted on each individual offender may correspond to the quantity intended for similar offenders in general, the several circumstances influencing sensibility ought always to be taken into account.

15. Of the above rules of proportion, the four first, we may perceive, serve to mark out the limits on the side of diminution; the limits *below* which a punishment ought not to be *diminished;* the fifth, the limits on the side of increase; the limits *above* which it ought not to be *increased.* The five first are calculated to serve as guides to the legislator; the sixth is calculated, in some measure, indeed, for the same purpose; but principally for guiding the judge in his endeavors to conform, on both sides, to the intentions of the legislator.

16. Let us look back a little. The first rule, in order to render it more conveniently applicable to practice, may need perhaps to be a little more particularly unfolded. It is to be observed, then, that for the sake of accuracy, it was necessary, instead of the word *quantity* to make use of the less perspicuous term *value.* For the word *quantity* will not properly include the circumstances either of certainty or proximity; circumstances which, in estimating the value of a lot of pain or pleasure, must always be taken into the account. Now, on the one hand, a lot of punishment is a lot of pain; on the other hand, the profit of an offense is a lot of pleasure, or what is equivalent to it. But the profit of the offense *is* commonly more *certain* than the punishment, or, what comes to the same thing, *appears* so at least to the offender. It is at any rate commonly more *immediate.* It follows, therefore, that, in order to maintain its superiority over the profit of the offense, the punishment must have its value made up in some other way, in proportion to that whereby it falls short in the two points of *certainty* and *proximity.* Now there is no other way in which it can receive any addition to its *value,* but by receiving an addition in point of *magnitude.* Wherever then the value of the punishment falls short, either in point of *certainty,* or of *proximity,* of that of the profit of the offense, it must receive a proportionable addition in point of *magnitude.*

17. Yet farther, To make sure of giving the value of the punishment the superiority over that of the offense, it may be necessary, in some cases, to take into the account the profit not only of the *individual* offense to which the punishment is to be annexed, but also of such *other* offenses of the *same sort* as the offender is likely to have already committed without detection. This random mode of calculation, severe as it is, it will be impossible to avoid having recourse to, in certain cases; in such, to wit, in which the profit is pecuniary, the chance of detection very small, and the obnoxious act of such a nature as indicates a habit; for example, in the case of frauds against the coin. If it be *not* recurred to, the practice of committing the offense will be sure to be, upon the balance of the account, a gainful practice. That being the case, the legislator will be absolutely sure of *not* being able to suppress it, and the whole punishment that is bestowed upon it will be thrown away. In a word (to keep to the

same expressions we set out with) that whole quantity of punishment will be *inefficacious.*

18. These things being considered, the three following rules may be laid down by way of supplement and explanation to Rule 1.

> *To enable the value of the punishment to outweigh that of the profit of the offense, it must be increased, in point of magnitude, in proportion as it falls short in point of certainty.*

19. Punishment must be further increased in point of magnitude, in proportion as it falls short in point of proximity.

20. Where the act is conclusively indicative of a habit, such an encrease must be given to the punishment as may enable it to outweigh the profit not only of the individual offense, but of such other like offenses as are likely to have been committed with impunity by the same offender.

21. There may be a few other circumstances or considerations which may influence, in some small degree, the demand for punishment; but as the propriety of these is either not so demonstrable, or not so constant, or the application of them not so determinate, as that of the foregoing, it may be doubted whether they be worth putting on a level with the others.

22. When a punishment, which in point of quality is particularly well calculated to answer its intention, cannot exist in less than a certain quantity, it may sometimes be of use, for the sake of employing it, to stretch a little beyond that quantity which, on other accounts, would be strictly necessary.

23. In particular, this may sometimes be the case, where the punishment proposed is of such a nature as to be particularly well calculated to answer the purpose of a moral lesson.

24. The tendency of the above considerations is to dictate an augmentation in the punishment; the following rule operates in the way of diminution. There are certain cases (it has been seen) in which, by the influence of accidental circumstances, punishment may be rendered unprofitable as to a part only. Accordingly,

> *In adjusting the quantum of punishment, the circumstances, by which all punishment may be rendered unprofitable, ought to be attended to.*

25. It is to be observed, that the more various and minute any set of provisions are, the greater the chance is that any given article in them will not be borne in mind; without which, no benefit can ensue from it. Distinctions, which are more complex than what the conceptions of those whose conduct it is designed to influence can take in, will even be worse than useless. The whole system will present a confused appearance; and thus the effect, not only of the proportions established by the articles in question, but of whatever is connected with them, will be destroyed. To draw a precise line of direction in such case seems impossible. However, by way of memento, it may be of some use to subjoin the following rule.

Among provisions designed to perfect the proportion between punishments and offenses, if any occur, which, by their own particular good effects, would not make up for the harm they would do by adding to the intricacy of the Code, they should be omitted.

26. It may be remembered, that the political sanction, being that to which the sort of punishment belongs, which in this chapter is all along in view, is but one of four sanctions, which may all of them contribute their share towards producing the same effects. It may be expected, therefore, that in adjusting the quantity of political punishment, allowance should be made for the assistance it may meet with from those other controlling powers. True it is, that from each of these several sources a very powerful assistance may sometimes be derived. But the case is, that (setting aside the moral sanction, in the case where the force of it is expressly adopted into and modified by the political) the force of those other powers is never determinate enough to be depended upon. It can never be reduced, like political punishment, into exact lots, nor meted out in number, quantity, and value. The legislator is therefore obliged to provide the full complement of punishment, as if he were sure of not receiving any assistance whatever from any of those quarters. If he does, so much the better; but lest he should not, it is necessary he should, at all events, make that provision which depends upon himself.

69.

A Retributive Theory of Punishment

HERBERT MORRIS

My aim is to argue for four propositions concerning rights that will certainly strike some as not only false but preposterous: first, that we have a right to punishment; second, that this right derives from a fundamental human right to be treated as a person; third, that this fundamental right is a natural, inalienable, and absolute right; and, fourth, that the denial of this right implies the denial of all moral rights and duties. Showing the truth of one, let alone all, of these large and questionable claims, is a tall order. The attempt or, more properly speaking, the first steps in an attempt, follow.

When someone claims that there is a right to be free, we can easily imagine situations in which the right is infringed and easily imagine situations in which there is a point to asserting or claiming the right. With the right to be punished, matters are otherwise. The immediate reaction to the claim that there is such a right is puzzlement. And the reasons for this are apparent. People do not normally value pain and suffering. Punishment is associated with pain and suffering. When we think about punishment we naturally think of the strong desire most persons have to avoid it, to accept, for example, acquittal of a criminal charge with relief and eagerly, if convicted, to hope for pardon or probation. Adding, of course, to the paradoxical character of the claim of such a right is difficulty in imagining circumstances in which it would be denied one. When would one rightly demand punishment and meet with any threat of the claim being denied?

So our first task is to see when the claim of such a right would have a point. I want to approach this task by setting out two complex types of institutions both of which are designed to maintain some degree of social control. In the one a central concept is punishment for wrongdoing and in the other the central concepts are control of dangerous individuals and treatment of disease.

Let us first turn attention to the institutions in which punishment is involved. The institutions I describe will resemble those we ordinarily think of as institutions of punishment; they will have, however, additional features we associate with a system of just punishment.

Let us suppose that men are constituted roughly as they now are, with a rough equivalence in strength and abilities, a capacity to be injured by each other and to make judgments that such injury is undesirable, a limited strength of will, and a capacity to reason and to conform conduct to rules. Applying to the conduct of these men are a group of rules, ones I shall label "primary," which closely resemble the core rules of our criminal law, rules that prohibit violence and deception and compliance with which provides benefits for all persons. These benefits consist of noninterference by others with what each person values, such matters as continuance of life and bodily security. The rules define a sphere for each person then, which is immune from interference by others. Making possible this mutual benefit is the assumption by individuals of a burden. The burden consists in the exercise of self-restraint by individuals over inclinations that would, if satisfied, directly interfere or create a substantial risk of interference with others in proscribed ways. If a person fails to exercise self-restraint even though he might have and gives in to such inclinations, he renounces a burden which others have voluntarily assumed and thus gains an advantage which others, who have restrained themselves, do not possess. This system, then, is one in which the rules establish a mutuality of benefit and burden and in which the benefits of noninterference are conditional upon the assumption of burdens.

Connecting punishment with the violation of these primary rules, and making public the provision for punishment, is both reasonable and just. First, it is only reasonable that those who voluntarily comply with the rules be provided some assurance that they will not be assuming burdens which others are unprepared to assume. Their disposition to comply voluntarily will diminish as they learn that others are with impunity renouncing burdens they are assuming. Second, fairness dictates that a system in which benefits and burdens are equally distributed have a mechanism designed to prevent a maldistribution in the benefits and burdens. Thus, sanctions are attached to noncompliance with the primary rules so as to induce compliance with the primary rules among those who may be disinclined to obey. In this way the likelihood of an unfair distribution is diminished.

Third, it is just to punish those who have violated the rules and caused the unfair distribution of benefits and burdens. A person who violates the rules has something others have—the benefits of the system—but by renouncing what others have assumed, the burdens of self-restraint, he has acquired an unfair advantage. Matters are not even until this advantage is in some way erased. Another way of putting it is that he owes something to others, for he has something that does not rightfully belong to him. Justice—that is punishing such individuals—restores the equilibrium of benefits and burdens by taking from the individual what he owes, that is, exacting the debt. It is important to see that the equilibrium may be restored in another way. Forgiveness—with its legal analogue of a pardon—while not the righting of an unfair distribution by making one pay his debt is, nevertheless, a restoring of the equilibrium by forgiving the debt. Forgiveness may be viewed, at least in some types of cases, as a gift after the fact, erasing a debt, which had the gift been given before the fact, would not have created a debt. But the practice of pardoning has to proceed sensitively, for it may endanger in a way the practice of justice does not, the maintenance of an equilibrium of benefits and burdens. If all are indiscriminately pardoned less incentive is provided individuals to restrain their inclinations, thus increasing the incidence of persons taking what they do not deserve.

There are also in this system we are considering a variety of operative principles compliance with which provides some guarantee that the system of punishment does not itself promote an unfair distribution of benefits and burdens. For one thing, provision is made for a variety of defenses, each one of which can be said to have as its object diminishing the chances of forcibly depriving a person of benefits others have if that person has not derived an unfair advantage. A person has not derived an unfair advantage if he could not have restrained himself or if it is unreasonable to expect him to behave otherwise than he did. Sometimes the rules preclude punishment of classes of persons such as children. Sometimes they provide a defense if on a particular occasion a person lacked the capacity to conform his conduct to the rules. Thus, someone who in an epileptic seizure strikes another is excused. Punishment in these cases would be punishment of the innocent, punishment of those who do not voluntarily renounce a burden others have assumed. Punishment in such cases, then, would not equalize but rather cause an unfair distribution in benefits and burdens.

Along with principles providing defenses there are requirements that the rules be prospective and relatively clear so that persons have a fair opportunity to comply with the rules. There are, also, rules governing, among other matters, the burden of proof, who shall bear it and what it shall be, the prohibition on double jeopardy, and the privilege against self-incrimination. Justice requires conviction of the guilty, and requires their punishment, but in setting out to fulfill the demands of justice we may, of course, because we are not omniscient, cause injustice by convicting and punishing the innocent. The resolution arrived at in the system I am describing consists in weighing as the greater evil the punishment of the innocent. The primary function of the system of rules was to provide individuals with a sphere of interest immune from interference. Given this goal, it is determined to be a greater evil for society to interfere unjustifiably with an individual by depriving him of good than for the society to fail to punish those that have unjustifiably interfered.

Finally, because the primary rules are designed to benefit all and because the punishments prescribed for their violation are publicized and the defenses respected, there is some plausibility in the exaggerated claim that in choosing to do an act violative of the rules an individual has chosen to be punished. This way of putting matters brings to our attention the extent to which, when the system is as I have described it, the criminal "has brought the punishment upon himself" in contrast to those cases where it would be misleading to say "he has brought it upon himself," cases, for example, where one does not know the rules or is punished in the absence of fault.

To summarize, then: first, there is a group of rules guiding the behavior of individuals in the community which establish spheres of interest immune from interference by others; second, provision is made for what is generally regarded as a deprivation of some thing of value if the rules are violated; third, the deprivations visited upon any person are justified by that person's having violated the rules; fourth, the deprivation, in this just system of punishment, is linked to rules that fairly distribute benefits and burdens and to procedures that strike some balance between not punishing the guilty and punishing the innocent, a class defined as those who have not voluntarily done acts violative of the law, in which it is evident that the evil of punishing the innocent is regarded as greater than the nonpunishment of the guilty.

At the core of many actual legal systems one finds, of course, rules and procedures of the kind I have sketched. It is obvious, though, that any ongoing legal system differs in significant respects from what I have presented here, containing "pockets of injustice."

I want now to sketch an extreme version of a set of institutions of a fundamentally different kind, institutions proceeding on a conception of man which appears to be basically at odds with that operative within a system of punishment.

Rules are promulgated in this system that prohibit certain types of injuries and harms.

In this world we are now to imagine when an individual harms another his conduct is to be regarded as a symptom of some pathological condition in the way a running nose is a symptom of a cold. Actions diverging from some conception of the normal are viewed as manifestations of a disease in the way in which we might today regard the arm and leg movements of an epileptic during a seizure. Actions conforming to what is normal are assimilated to the normal and healthy functioning of bodily organs. What a person does, then, is assimilated, on this conception, to what we believe today, or at least most of us believe today, a person undergoes. We draw a distinction between the operation of the kidney and raising an arm on request. This distinction between mere events or happenings and human actions is erased in our imagined system.

There is, however, bound to be something strange in this erasing of a recognized distinction, for, as with metaphysical suggestions generally, and I take this to be one, the distinction may be reintroduced but given a different description, for example, "happenings with X type of causes" and "happenings with Y type of causes." Responses of different kinds, today legitimated by our distinction between happenings and actions may be legitimated by this new manner of description. And so there may be isomorphism between a system recognizing the distinction and one erasing it. Still, when this distinction is erased certain tendencies of thought and responses might naturally arise that would tend to affect unfavorably values respected by a system of punishment.

Let us elaborate on this assimilation of conduct of a certain kind to symptoms of a disease. First, there is something abnormal in both the case of conduct, such as killing another, and a symptom of a disease such as an irregular heart beat. Second, there are causes for this abnormality in action such that once we know of them we can explain the abnormality as we now can explain the symptoms of many physical diseases. The abnormality is looked upon as a happening with a causal explanation rather than an action for which there were reasons. Third, the causes that account for the abnormality interfere with the normal functioning of the body, or, in the case of killing with what is regarded as a normal functioning of an individual. Fourth, the abnormality is in some way a part of the individual, necessarily involving his body. A well going dry might satisfy our three foregoing conditions of disease symptoms, but it is hardly a disease or the symptom of one. Finally, and most obscure, the abnormality arises in some way from within the individual. If Jones is hit with a mallet by Smith, Jones may reel about and fall on James who may be injured. But this abnormal conduct of Jones is not regarded as a symptom of disease. Smith, not Jones, is suffering from some pathological condition.

With this view of man the institutions of social control respond, not with punishment, but with either preventive detention, in case of "carriers," or therapy in the case of those manifesting pathological symptoms. The logic of sickness implies the logic of therapy. And therapy and punishment differ widely in their implications. In bringing out some of these differences I want again to draw attention to the important fact that while the distinctions we now draw are erased in the therapy world, they may, in fact, be reintroduced but under different descriptions. To the extent they are, we really have a punishment system combined with a therapy system. I am concerned now, however, with what the implications would be were the world indeed one of therapy and not a disguised world of punishment and therapy, for I want to suggest tendencies of thought that arise when one is immersed in the ideology of disease and therapy.

First, punishment is the imposition upon a person who is believed to be at fault of something commonly believed to be a deprivation where that deprivation is justified by the person's guilty behavior. It is associated with resentment, for the guilty are those who have done what they had no right to do by failing to exercise restraint when they might have and where others have. Therapy is not a response to a person who is at fault. We respond to an individual, not because of what he has done, but because of some condition from which he is suffering. If he is no longer suffering from the condition, treatment no longer has a point. Punishment, then, focuses on the past; therapy on the present. Therapy is normally associated with compassion for what one undergoes, not resentment for what one has illegitimately done.

Second, with therapy, unlike punishment, we do not seek to deprive the person of something acknowledged as a good, but seek rather to help and to benefit the individual who is suffering by ministering to his illness in the hope that the person can be cured. The good we attempt to do is not a reward for desert. The individual suffering has not merited by his disease the good we seek to bestow upon him but has, because he is a creature that has the capacity to feel pain, a claim upon our sympathies and help.

Third, we saw with punishment that its justification was related to maintaining and restoring a fair distribution of benefits and burdens. Infliction of the prescribed punishment carries the implication, then, that one has "paid one's debt" to society, for the punishment is the taking from the person of something commonly recognized as valuable. It is this conception of "a debt owed" that may permit, as I suggested earlier, under certain conditions, the nonpunishment of the guilty, for operative within a system of punishment may be a concept analogous to forgiveness, namely pardoning. Who it is that we may pardon and under what conditions—contrition with its elements of self-punishment no doubt plays a role—I shall not go into though it is clearly a matter of the greatest practical and theoretical interest. What is clear is that the conceptions of "paying a debt" or "having a debt forgiven" or pardoning have no place in a system of therapy.

Fourth, with punishment there is an attempt at some equivalence between the advantage gained by the wrongdoer—partly based upon the seriousness of the interest invaded, partly on the state of mind with which the wrongful act was performed—and the punishment meted out. Thus, we can understand a prohibition on "cruel and unusual punishments" so that disproportionate pain and suffering are avoided. With therapy attempts at proportionality make no sense. It is perfectly plausible giving someone who kills a pill and treating for a lifetime within an institution one who has broken a dish and manifested accident proneness. We have the concept of "painful treatment." We do not have the concept of "cruel treatment." Because treatment is regarded as a benefit, though it may involve pain, it is natural that less restraint is exercised in bestowing it, than in inflicting punishment. Further, protests with respect to treatment are likely to be assimilated to the complaints of one whose leg must be amputated in order for him to live, and, thus, largely disregarded. To be sure, there is operative in the therapy world some conception of the "cure being worse than the disease," but if the disease is manifested in conduct harmful to others, and if being a normal operating human being is valued highly, there will naturally be considerable pressure to find the cure acceptable.

Fifth, the rules in our system of punishment governing conduct of individuals were rules violation of which involved either direct interference with others or the creation of a substantial risk of such interference. One could imagine adding to this system of primary rules other rules proscribing preparation to do acts violative of the primary rules and even rules proscribing thoughts. Objection to such suggestions would have many sources but a principal one would consist in its involving the infliction of punishment on too great a number of persons who would not, because of a change of mind, have violated the primary rules. Though we are interested in diminishing violations of the primary rules, we are not prepared to punish too many individuals who would never have violated the rules in order to achieve this aim. In a system motivated solely by a preventive and curative ideology there would be less reason to wait until symptoms manifest themselves in socially harmful conduct. It is understandable that we should wish at the earliest possible stage to arrest the development of the disease. In the punishment system, because we are dealing with deprivations, it is understandable that we should forbear from imposing them until we are quite sure of guilt. In the therapy system, dealing as it does with benefits, there is less reason for forbearance from treatment at an early stage.

Sixth, a variety of procedural safeguards we associate with punishment have less significance in a therapy system. To the degree objections to double jeopardy and self-incrimination are based on a wish to decrease the chances of the innocent being convicted and punished, a therapy system, unconcerned with this problem, would disregard such safeguards. When one is out to help people there is also little sense in urging that the burden of proof be on those providing the help. And there is less point to imposing the burden of proving that the conduct was pathological beyond a reasonable doubt. Further, a jury system which, within a system of justice, serves to make accommodations to the individual situation and to introduce a human element, would play no role or a minor one in a world where expertise is required in making determinations of disease and treatment.

In our system of punishment an attempt was made to maximize each individual's freedom of choice by first of all delimiting by rules certain spheres of conduct immune from interference by others. The punishment associated with these primary rules paid deference to an individual's free choice by connecting punishment to a freely chosen act violative of the rules, thus giving some plausibility to the claim, as we saw, that what a person received by way of punishment he himself had chosen. With the world of disease and therapy all this changes and the individual's free choice ceases to be a determinative factor in how others respond to him. All those principles of our own legal system that minimize the chances of punishment of those who have not chosen to do acts violative of the rules tend to lose their point in the therapy system, for how we respond in a therapy system to a person is not conditioned upon what he has chosen but rather on what symptoms he has manifested or may manifest and what the best therapy for the disease is that is suggested by the symptoms.

Now, it is clear, I think, that were we confronted with the alternatives I have sketched, between a system of just punishment and a thoroughgoing system of treatment, a system, that is, that did not reintroduce concepts appropriate to punishment, we could see the point in claiming that a person has a right to be punished, meaning by this that a person had a right to all those institutions and practices linked to punishment. For these would provide him with, among other things, a far greater ability to predict what would happen to him on the occurrence of certain events than the therapy system. There is the inestimable value to each of us of having the responses of others to us determined over a wide range of our lives by what we choose rather than what they choose. A person has a right to institutions that respect his choices. Our punishment system does; our therapy system does not.

Apart from those aspects of our therapy model which would relate to serious limitations on personal liberty, there are clearly objections of a more profound kind to the mode of thinking I have associated with the therapy model.

First, human beings pride themselves in having capacities that animals do not. A common way, for example, of arousing shame in a child is to compare the child's conduct to that of an animal. In a system where all actions are assimilated to happenings we are assimilated to creatures—indeed, it is more extreme than this—whom we have always thought possessed of less than we. Fundamental to our practice of praise and order of attainment is that one who can do more—one who is capable of more and one who does more is more worthy of respect and admiration. And we have thought of ourselves as capable where animals are not of making, of creating, among other things, ourselves. The conception of man I have outlined would provide us with a status that today, when our conduct is assimilated to it in moral criticism, we consider properly evocative of shame.

Second, if all human conduct is viewed as something men undergo, thrown into question would be the appropriateness of that extensive range of peculiarly human satisfactions that derive from a sense of achievement. For these satisfactions we shall have to substitute those mild satisfactions attendant upon a healthy well-functioning body. Contentment is our lot if we are fortunate; intense satisfaction at achievement is entirely inappropriate.

Third, in the therapy world nothing is earned and what we receive comes to us through compassion, or through a desire to control us. Resentment is out of place. We can take credit for nothing but must always regard ourselves—if there are selves left to regard once actions disappear—as fortunate recipients of benefits or unfortunate carriers of disease who must be controlled. We know that within our own world human beings who have been so regarded and who come to accept this view of themselves come to look upon themselves as worthless. When what we do is met with resentment, we are indirectly paid something of a compliment.

Fourth, attention should also be drawn to a peculiar evil that may be attendant upon regarding a man's actions as symptoms of disease. The logic of cure will push us toward forms of therapy that inevitably involve changes in the person made against his will. The evil in this would be most apparent in those cases where the agent, whose action is determined to be a manifestation of some disease, does not regard his action in this way. He believes that what he has done is, in fact, "right" but his conception of "normality" is not the therapeutically accepted one. When we treat an illness we normally treat a condition that the person is not responsible for. He is "suffering" from some disease and we treat the condition, relieving the person of something preventing his normal functioning. When we begin treating persons for actions that have been chosen, we do not lift from the person something that is interfering with his normal functioning but we change the person so that he functions in a way regarded as normal by the current therapeutic community. We have to change him and his judgments of value. In doing this we display a lack of respect for the moral status of individuals, that is, a lack of respect for the reasoning and choices of individuals. They are but animals who must be conditioned. I think we can understand and, indeed, sympathize with a man's preferring death to being forcibly turned into what he is not.

Finally, perhaps most frightening of all would be the derogation in status of all protests to treatment. If someone believes that he has done something right, and if he protests being treated and changed, the protest will itself be regarded as a sign of some pathological condition, for who would not wish to be cured of an affliction? What this leads to are questions of an important kind about the effect of this conception of man upon what we now understand by reasoning. Here what a person takes to be a reasoned defense of an act is treated, as the action was, on the model of a happening of a pathological kind. Not just a person's acts are taken from him but also his attempt at a reasoned justification for the acts. In a system of punishment a person who has committed a crime may argue that what he did was right. We make him pay the price and we respect his right to retain the judgment he has made. A conception of pathology precludes this form of respect.

70.

A Paradox about the Level of Punishment

ALAN H. GOLDMAN

The paradox of punishment is that a penal institution somewhat similar to that in use in our society seems from a moral point of view to be both required and unjustified. Usually such a statement would be a confused way of saying that the practice is a necessary evil, hence it *is* justified, all things considered. But in the case of punishment this reduction does not appear so simple.

The paradox results from the intuitive plausibility of two theses: one associated with a retributivist point of view and another associated with a utilitarian justification of the institution of punishment. Some philosophers have thought that objections to these two theories of punishment could be overcome by making both retributive and utilitarian criteria necessary for the justification of punishment. Utilitarian criteria could be used to justify the institution, and retributive to justify specific acts within it; or utilitarian to justify legislative decisions regarding punishment, and retributive to justify enforcement decisions.[1] (These distinctions in levels of justification are matters of degree, since when justifying an institution, one must consider acts within it; and when justifying legislative decisions, one must consider their applications in the judicial system.) The compromise positions, according to which punishment must be both deserved and beneficial, have considerable plausibility. But if I am right about the two theses to be assessed here, these criteria may be ultimately inconsistent. If so, then the mixed theory of justification, initially attractive, is at least as problematic as its rivals.

Let us consider the retributivist thesis first, since it is likely to be considered the more controversial. The thesis ultimately concerns the amount of punishment justifiable in particular cases. If we are to justify punishment of particular wrongdoers or lawbreakers, that is, if we are to show why *they* cannot legitimately complain of injustice done to them by the imposition of punishment, we must argue that they have forfeited those rights of which we are depriving them. We must say that by violating the rights of others in their criminal activities, they have lost or forfeited their legitimate demands that others honor all their formerly held rights. It seems clear that this is the only way we could convince criminals themselves that they are not being treated unjustly in being punished.[2] Appeal to the idea that the community benefits from a prisoner's role as an example for others would not be sufficient, in view of the severity of the impositions. Persons normally have rights not to be severely imposed upon

[1] For classic statements of these mixed positions, see John Rawls, "Two Concepts of Rules," *Philosophical Review* 64, no. 1 (1955): 3–32; H. L. A. Hart, "Prolegomenon to the Principles of Punishment," in *Punishment and Responsibility* (Oxford: Clarendon Press, 1968), pp. 1–13.

[2] Compare Herbert Morris, "Persons and Punishment," *The Monist* 52, no. 4 (1968): 475–501.

in order to benefit others. If we are justifiably to ignore these rights, it could only be when they have been forfeited or alienated. And the only way in which this can be done involuntarily is by violation of the rights of others. Since having rights generally entails having duties to honor the same rights of others, it is plausible that when these duties are not fulfilled, the rights cease to exist.

This partial justification of the right to impose punishment upon wrongdoers is retributive in spirit, but not identical to the classic theories of Kant or Hegel, nor to the well-known contemporary retributivist argument of Morris. I do not claim here that a wrongdoer wills or consents to his own punishment by wronging others; or that he would will his action universally if he were rational; or that he would rationally will consequences for himself similar to those suffered by his victim. No rational person would will any such thing; no wrongdoer would construe his action as a consent, tacit or otherwise, to his own punishment.

Nor do I view punishment, as Morris views it, as removing some benefit unfairly enjoyed by the criminal.[3] Morris's analysis in terms of balancing social burdens and benefits throughout society faces insuperable objections as well. There is first the objection that this balancing process, to be fair, would have to take account of relative burdens and benefits over each citizen's lifetime, and consider them in relation to those of every other citizen. Hence appeal to this process might not justify particular impositions of punishment for particular criminal acts. Second, this analysis would have counterintuitive implications regarding amounts of punishment for particular crimes, since crimes against property often bring more benefits to their perpetrators than do more serious crimes against persons (crimes involving violation of more precious rights). If we restrict the burden in question to that of self-restraint, and the benefit to that of enjoyment of rights through the self-restraint of others, we come closer to the justification suggested above. But then talk of an unfair advantage that criminals enjoy over others through their criminal acts is somewhat misleading, as is the suggestion that the purpose of punishment is to restore a balance. Why balance just these burdens and benefits and not others? The partial justification for particular impositions of punishment suggested above appeals more directly to the plausible claim that a condition of having specific rights is that one honors those rights of others (when one is able to do so). When a person violates rights of others, he involuntarily loses certain of his own rights, and the community acquires the right to impose a punishment, if there is social benefit to be derived from doing so.[4]

While violating the rights of others involves forfeiting rights oneself,[5] it is clear that violating specific rights of others does not entail losing *all* one's own

---

[3] Morris, "Persons and Punishment," pp. 477–478.

[4] This way of viewing criminal desert derives from W. D. Ross, *The Right and the Good* (Oxford: Clarendon Press, 1965), pp. 56–64. My position differs from his in that he sees an insuperable problem in equating amounts of punishment and degrees of wrongdoing, and I do not; and in that he sees no problem in balancing utilitarian and retributive considerations in assigning proper amounts of punishment, and I do. See below.

[5] Violation of the rights of others may be only a necessary, but not a sufficient, condition for forfeiture if there are certain inalienable rights. The concept of forfeiture is best explained here in

rights. If *A* steals fifty dollars from *B*, this does not give *B* or anyone else, official or not, the right to impose all and any conceivable harms upon *A* in return. Nor does *A* thereby become available for any use to which the community then wants to put him. Just as an innocent person can complain if forced to make severe sacrifices for the benefit of others, so a guilty person may claim that violation of any rights beyond those forfeited or alienated in order to benefit others is an injustice. And if we ask which rights are forfeited in violating rights of others, it is plausible to answer just those rights that one violates (or an equivalent set). One continues to enjoy rights only as long as one respects those rights in others: violation constitutes forfeiture. But one retains those rights which one has continued to respect in others. Since deprivation of those particular rights violated is often impracticable, we are justified in depriving a wrongdoer of some equivalent set, or in inflicting harm equivalent to that which would be suffered in losing those same rights (for example, rights to fifty dollars of one's own and not to suffer the trauma of being a victim of theft). Equivalence here is to be measured in terms of some average or normal preference scale, much like the one used by the utilitarian when comparing and equating utilities and disutilities.

It would be difficult for a wrongdoer to complain of injustice when we treat him in a way equivalent to the way in which he treated his victim, provided that we also have a good (consequentialist) reason for imposing upon him in that way. If he cannot demonstrate a morally relevant difference between himself and his victim, then he cannot claim that he must enjoy all those rights that he was willing to violate. But if we deprive him not only of these or equivalent rights, but of ones far more important, whose loss results in far greater harm, then we begin to look like serious wrongdoers ourselves in multiplying violations of rights. It is at this point that the claim that two wrongs do not make a right begins to apply. A claim of injustice or victimization by the community made by the criminal begins to have merit, although in our anger at his wrongdoing, we are often unwilling to hear it. If a person can be said to deserve only so much punishment and no more, then any excess appears to be as objectionable as an equivalent harm imposed upon an innocent person. In fact the stronger thesis concerning the degree of justified imposition can be viewed as the source of the weaker thesis that the innocent should not be punished at all. The latter is implied as a special case of the former. Philosophers have been far more concerned with the thesis as applied to innocents than with its more general application, perhaps because of a supposed difficulty in judging when punishment is equivalent to crime. When we think in terms of forfeiting those rights one violates, or an equivalent set, there is no special difficulty here. One right or set of rights is equivalent to another for these purposes when an average preference scale registers indifference between the loss of either the one or the other. There are problems facing construction of the proper preference scale—for example, the loss of fifty dollars to which one has a right will mean more to a poor person than to a rich person—but these are problems facing any moral theory

---

terms of a contract model of rights. See my "Rights, Utilities and Contracts," *Canadian Journal of Philosophy* 3, supplement (1977): 121–135.

concerned with distribution. We also need to adjust our concept of deserved punishment to focus upon intention rather than actual harm, and to allow for excuses. I leave these complications to pursue our main topic.

To this retributivist premise might be raised an objection similar to one sometimes made against utilitarian theories of punishment. It might be claimed that our argument limiting the severity of justified punishments errs in calculating harm to the guilty and that to the innocent on the same scale. But, an objector might hold, the guilty do not deserve equal consideration or equal treatment. What they have forfeited in harming others and in violating others' rights is precisely the right to have their own interests considered equally. Society therefore has the right to impose greater harm upon wrongdoers than that done to innocent victims, if it finds it necessary or beneficial to do so. This counterargument rests upon a confusion. Treatment of wrongdoers equal to or the same as rightful treatment of the innocent would demand no harm or deprivation of rights at all. We are not, as this argument suggests, counting the interests of wrongdoers equally with those of the innocent, since we impose harm upon the former but not upon the latter. The prior wrongdoing of the guilty enables us to harm them without treating them unjustly, but only to the extent of treating them as they treated their victims. If we inflict greater harm than this, we become, like them, violators of rights nor forfeited and hence wrongdoers ourselves. Their wrongdoing does not give us the right to do equal wrong, or any wrong, ourselves. It must be remembered also that punishment justly imposed is distinct from compensation owed to victims. Justice may well require wrongdoers to be liable for restoring their victims as far as possible to the level of well-being that they would have attained had no injustice occurred (compensation *is* a matter of restoring a balance or returning to a just status quo, while punishment is not). It requires *in addition* that they be made to suffer harm equivalent to that originally caused to the victims.

To bring out the paradox in the justification of punishment, we need to combine this premise regarding the limits of justly imposed punishments with one at least equally plausible from the utilitarian theory. It states that a political institution involving the administration of punishment by state officials can be justified only in terms of the goal of reducing crime and the harms caused by crime to a tolerable level. The state is not concerned to ensure that all its members receive their just positive and negative deserts in some abstract moral sense. It is concerned neither to proportion burdens to benefits in general, nor even to protect all moral rights. Certainly that someone deserves to be harmed in some way, or that he could not complain of injustice at being harmed in some way, does not in itself entail that the state ought to take it upon itself to harm him. At least one other condition is necessary for the state to be justified in adopting rules calling for such official imposition. The wrongs in question must be so grave that the social costs of official interference do not exceed the benefits in terms of reducing these wrongs. There are, for example, moral wrongs whose detection is so unsure that their official prohibition would involve costs too great to be worthwhile: betrayals of friendship, deceptions in love affairs, and so on. The social benefits from an institution of punishment must outweigh the costs, including the harms imposed, especially when these harms are unde-served (occasional punishment of the innocent and the excessive punishments of the guilty). That our penal institution does deter crime is the primary source of its justification and social necessity. The state must seek to deter viola-tions of its distributive rules if it is serious about their adoption, and it must seek to deter serious attacks upon persons; the sanctions which attach to these violations exist primarily for this deterrent effect.

Combining this justification for a social penal institution with the limit upon just impositions so that no one may be deprived of rights he has not forfeited, we derive the mixed theory of punishment advocated by Ross and Hart, and endorsed by other philosophers in recent years.[6] This theory views the social goal of punishment as deterrence, and yet recognizes that we are entitled to pur-sue this goal only when we restrict deprivation of rights to those forfeited through crime or wrongdoing. In actuality proponents of this theory usually state the limitation only as prohibiting punishment of the innocent. But, as ar-gued above, in terms of the broader principle that no one is to be deprived of rights not forfeited, excessive punishment of the guilty is on a par with punish-ment of the innocent. Thus for officially imposed punishment to be justified, the person punished must have forfeited those rights of which he is deprived, and the state must be entitled to inflict the harm by appeal to the social benefit of deterrence. (This appeal may involve the need to have a rule calling for pun-ishment of a particular type of wrongdoing and the need to apply the rule consistently.)

The problem is that while the mixed theory can avoid punishment of the in-nocent, it is doubtful that it can avoid excessive punishment of the guilty if it is to have sufficient deterrent effect to make the social costs worthwhile. In our society the chances of apprehension and punishment for almost every class of crime are well under fifty percent. Given these odds a person pursuing what he considers his maximum prospective benefit may not be deterred by the threat of an imposition of punishment equivalent to the violation of the rights of the potential victim. If threats of sanctions are not sufficient to deter such people, they would probably fail to reduce crime to a tolerable enough level to make the social costs of the penal institution worthwhile. On the other hand, in or-der to deter crime at all effectively, given reasonable assumptions about police efficiency at bearable costs, sanctions must be threatened and applied which go far beyond the equivalence relation held to be just. The limitation stipulated in our first premise then, in effect, annuls just and effective pursuit of the social goal stipulated in our second premise. And yet pursuit of this goal seems morally required and impossible without effective punitive threats. Hence the paradox, or, more strictly, the dilemma.

Caught in this dilemma, our society does not limit punishment to depri-vation of rights forfeited, that is, rights of others which have been violated by the criminal. Especially in regard to crimes against property, punishments by

---

[6] See, for example, Michael Lessnoff, "Two Justifications of Punishment," *The Philosophical Quarterly* 21, no. 83 (1971): 141–148.

imprisonment are far more severe, on the average, than the harm caused to victims of these crimes. Probably because such punishment is administered by officials of the state, cloaked in appropriate ritual and vested with authority, most of us systematically ignore its relative severity. If, however, we imagine an apolitical context, in which there is money and property, but no penal institution, would theft of several thousand dollars justify the victim's taking the perpetrator and locking him away in some small room for five to ten years? In our society such deprivation of freedom is a small portion of the harms likely to be suffered in prison as punishment for a felonious crime against property. The disproportion between violated or deprived rights of the victims and those of the criminals in these crimes is obvious.

It might be argued that we could lower penalties to make them equal to harms from crimes and yet still have a deterrent effect, since for most persons, the threat of official sanctions simply adds to internal moral sanctions against harmful or criminal acts. Furthermore, for people who enjoy a decent standard of living without turning to criminal activity, it will not be worth even minimal risk of public exposure to attempt to increase acquisitions by criminal means. For such persons, who are reasonably well-off and have much to lose if apprehended, the moral disapproval of the community might be felt as a more serious harm than an actual prison sentence or fine. The problem with these claims is that they do not apply to the typical criminal in our society, or to the potential criminal whom threats of punishment are intended to deter. We may assume the potential criminal has a fairly desperate economic situation, and therefore, at most, a neutral attitude toward risk. Thus suggestions to the community to sharply lower penalties for property crimes would be taken about as seriously as is epistemological skepticism outside philosophy classrooms and articles. Even suggestions to eliminate the more horrid aspects of prison life that are not officially part of the penalty of imprisonment are met with resistance. I am convinced that punishments, when administered at all, tend to be far more severe than harms suffered in those particular crimes against property for which these punishments are imposed. Yet, while this strikes me as seriously unjust, it does not appear that we can afford at present to lessen the deterrent force of sanctions for potential criminals to the point at which they stand to lose nothing by attempting further crimes. At stake is not only increased harm to innocent victims but our ability to put into effect those distributive rules we consider just. (Assuming that we do consider some such set of rules just, the problem that I am defining will be real.)

Others have noted conflicts between utilitarian criteria for proper amounts of punishment and what is called the retributive proportionality principle.[7] This states that more serious crimes should draw more severe penalties. It fails to match utilitarian criteria in application. This is because utilitarian criteria call for a deterrent threat sufficient to bring crimes of a given class down to a

---

[7] Michael Clark, "The Moral Gradation of Punishment," *The Philosophical Quarterly* 21, no. 83 (1971): 132–140; Alan Wertheimer, "Should the Punishment Fit the Crime?" *Social Theory & Practice* 3, no. 4 (1975): 403–423.

tolerable level; and deterrent threat varies not only with the severity of the punishment threatened but also with such factors as the comparative probability of apprehension and conviction for various types of crime, and the degree to which various crimes are normally preceded by unemotional prudential calculations. Crimes which are more difficult to prosecute call for more severe threats, while threats are wasted for crimes of passion. But these variables are irrelevant to moral rights violated and harm suffered by the victims of the crimes, the sole variables relevant according to retributive criteria of proportionality. The conflict I have noted above is, however, more fundamental, since the absolute limitation upon justified punishment in terms of equivalence to loss of rights violated is more basic than the proportionality principle. It is clear that we require absolute as well as proportionate limits, since without absolute limits all punishments might be too severe or the spread between them might be too great, even if they are arranged in correct order of severity.[8] It is plausible again, therefore, to view the proportionality principle as a particular implication of the absolute limits for various punishments, much as we viewed the prohibition against punishing the innocent. The absolute equivalence limitation, as we may call it, is the fundamental retributive principle; and it is this principle which appears to be fundamentally in conflict with the utilitarian goal of adequate deterrence.[9]

•   •   •

There are, of course, ways of increasing deterrent effects of punishments without increasing their severity. Given the variables affecting deterrence mentioned earlier, one can, for example, increase the force of threats by improving chances of detection. One can add personnel to police forces and remove procedural constraints upon detection, apprehension, and conviction efforts. But there are social costs, not the least of which include possible abuses, convictions of innocent people, and invasions of privacy, which place limits upon the justified pursuit of this course. It has been suggested also in a recent article that penalties ought to be imposed more consistently and automatically, that inconsistent application of punishment resulting from extensive discretionary powers at all levels of enforcement significantly lowers effective deterrence.[10] It is not clear, first, that even fully automatic arrest, prosecution, and sentencing would enable us to reduce penalties to fit within the equivalence limitation and still have effective deterrence against property crimes. Second, the elimination of discretion on the part of enforcement officials undoubtedly would result

---

[8] This is admitted by Wertheimer, "Should the Punishment Fit the Crime?" p. 410. But he fails to say more on this subject, again probably because he views it as impossible to calculate an equivalence between punishment and crime. See also John Kleinig, *Punishment and Desert* (The Hague: Martinus Nijhoff, 1973), pp. 118–119.

[9] The one philosopher who notes a possible conflict here is Robert Nozick, in *Anarchy, State, and Utopia* (New York: Basic Books, 1974), pp. 59–63. Nozick does not defend both premises, however.

[10] Alan Wertheimer, "Deterrence and Retribution," *Ethics* 86, no. 3 (1976): 181–199.

in more unjust punishments in many cases, punishments which ought not to be imposed at all in the particular circumstances of particular cases. Third, there is the short-term problem of overcrowded courts and prisons, and this would have to be overcome before this suggestion could be at all capable of implementation.

The final, most fundamental, and most promising alternative would be (not surprisingly) to attack the social and economic causes of crime by reducing the great inequalities in our society. I have nothing to say against this, except that the means to accomplish it short of authoritarian political mechanisms have eluded us. But even were we to progressively achieve the egalitarian program and approach a just economic and social distribution, I believe that the moral problem defined here would remain, though perhaps in less acute form. Many would still be tempted to crime, and deterrence seemingly would still be required. It would still be true that genuinely just punishment would not suffice to deter avoidable harm to innocent members of the community, or to enforce genuinely just distributive rules.

71.

A Paradox about the
Justification of Punishment

JEFFRIE G. MURPHY

. . . I believe that retributivism can be formulated in such a way that it is the only morally defensible theory of punishment. I also believe that arguments, which may be regarded as Marxist at least in spirit, can be formulated which show that social conditions as they obtain in most societies make this form of retributivism largely inapplicable within those societies. As Marx says, in those societies retributivism functions merely to provide a "transcendental sanction" for the status quo. If this is so, then the only morally defensible theory of punishment is largely inapplicable in modern societies. The consequence: modern societies largely lack the moral right to punish.[1] The upshot is that a Kantian moral theory (which in general seems to me correct) and a Marxist analysis of society (which, if properly qualified, also seems to me correct) produces a radical and not merely reformist attack not merely on the scope and manner of punishment in our society but on the institution of punishment itself. Institutions of punishment constitute what Bernard Harrison has called structural injustices[2] and are, in the absence of a major social change, to be resisted by all who take human rights to be morally serious—i.e., regard them as genuine action guides and not merely as rhetorical devices which allow people to morally sanctify institutions which in fact can only be defended on grounds of social expediency.

Stating all of this is one thing and proving it, of course, is another. Whether I can ever do this is doubtful. That I cannot do it in one brief article is certain. I cannot, for example, here defend in detail my belief that a generally Kantian outlook on moral matters is correct.[3] Thus I shall content myself for the present with attempting to render at least plausible two major claims involved in the view that I have outlined thus far: (1) that a retributive theory, in spite of the bad press that it has received, is a morally credible theory of punishment—that it can be, H. L. A. Hart to the contrary,[4] a reasonable general justifying aim of punishment; and (2) that a Marxist analysis of a society can undercut the practical applicability of that theory.

---

[1] I qualify my thesis by the word "largely" to show at this point my realization, explored in more detail later, that no single theory can account for all criminal behavior.

[2] Bernard Harrison, "Violence and the Rule of Law," in *Violence,* ed. Jerome A. Shaffer (New York, 1971), pp. 139–176.

[3] I have made a start toward such a defense in my "The Killing of the Innocent," forthcoming in *The Monist* 57, no. 4 (October 1973).

[4] H. L. A. Hart, "Prolegomenon to the Principles of Punishment," from *Punishment and Responsibility* (Oxford, 1968), pp. 1–27.

THE RIGHT OF THE STATE TO PUNISH

It is strong evidence of the influence of a utilitarian outlook in moral and legal matters that discussions of punishment no longer involve a consideration of the right of anyone to inflict it. Yet in the eighteenth and nineteenth centuries, this tended to be regarded as the central aspect of the problem meriting philosophical consideration. Kant, Hegel, Bosanquet, Green—all tended to entitle their chapters on punishment along the lines explicitly used by Green: "The Right of the State to Punish." [5] This is not just a matter of terminology but reflects, I think, something of deeper philosophical substance. These theorists, unlike the utilitarian, did not view man as primarily a maximizer of personal satisfactions—a maximizer of individual utilities. They were inclined, in various ways, to adopt a different model of man—man as a free or spontaneous creator, man as autonomous. (Marx, it may be noted, is much more in line with this tradition than with the utilitarian outlook.) [6] This being so, these theorists were inclined to view punishment (a certain kind of coercion by the state) as not merely a causal contributor to pain and suffering, but rather as presenting at least a prima facie challenge to the values of autonomy and personal dignity and self-realization—the very values which, in their view, the state existed to nurture. The problem as they saw it, therefore, was that of reconciling punishment as state coercion with the value of individual autonomy. (This is an instance of the more general problem which Robert Paul Wolff has called the central problem of political philosophy—namely, how is individual moral autonomy to be reconciled with legitimate political authority?) [7] This kind of problem, which I am inclined to agree is quite basic, cannot even be formulated intelligibly from a utilitarian perspective. Thus the utilitarian cannot even see the relevance of Marx's charge: Even if punishment has wonderful social consequences, what gives anyone the right to inflict it on me?

Now one fairly typical way in which others acquire rights over us is by our own consent. If a neighbor locks up my liquor cabinet to protect me against my tendencies to drink too heavily, I might well regard this as a presumptuous interference with my own freedom, no matter how good the result intended or accomplished. He had no right to do it and indeed violated my rights in doing it. If, on the other hand, I had asked him to do this or had given my free consent to his suggestion that he do it, the same sort of objection on my part would be quite out of order. I had given him the right to do it, and he had the right to do it. In doing it, he violated no rights of mine—even if, at the time of his doing it, I did not desire or want the action to be performed. Here then we seem

---

[5] Thomas Hill Green, *Lectures on the Principles of Political Obligation* (1885), (Ann Arbor, 1967), pp. 180–205.

[6] For an elaboration of this point, see Steven Lukes, "Alienation and Anomie," in *Philosophy, Politics and Society* (Third Series), ed. Peter Laslett and W. G. Runciman (Oxford, 1967), pp. 134–156.

[7] Robert Paul Wolff, *In Defense of Anarchism* (New York, 1970).

to have a case where my autonomy may be regarded as intact even though a desire of mine is thwarted. For there is a sense in which the thwarting of the desire can be imputed to me (my choice or decision) and not to the arbitrary intervention of another.

How does this apply to our problem? The answer, I think, is obvious. What is needed, in order to reconcile my undesired suffering of punishment at the hands of the state with my autonomy (and thus with the state's right to punish me), is a political theory which makes the state's decision to punish me in some sense my own decision. If I have willed my own punishment (consented to it, agreed to it) then—even if at the time I happen not to desire it—it can be said that my autonomy and dignity remain intact. Theories of the General Will and Social Contract theories are two such theories which attempt this reconciliation of autonomy with legitimate state authority (including the right or authority of the state to punish). Since Kant's theory happens to incorporate elements of both, it will be useful to take it for our sample.

MORAL RIGHTS AND THE RETRIBUTIVE THEORY OF PUNISHMENT

To justify government or the state is necessarily to justify at least some coercion.[8] This poses a problem for someone, like Kant, who maintains that human freedom is the ultimate or most sacred moral value. Kant's own attempt to justify the state, expressed in his doctrine of the *moral title (Befugnis)*,[9] involves an argument that coercion is justified only in so far as it is used to prevent invasions against freedom. Freedom itself is the only value which can be used to limit freedom, for the appeal to any other value (e.g., utility) would undermine the ultimate status of the value of freedom. Thus Kant attempts to establish the claim that some forms of coercion (as opposed to violence) are morally permissible because, contrary to appearance, they are really consistent with rational freedom. The argument, in broad outline, goes in the following way. Coercion may keep people from doing what they desire or want to do on a particular occasion and is thus prima facie wrong. However, such coercion can be shown to be morally justified (and thus not absolutely wrong) if it can be

---

[8] In this section, I have adapted some of my previously published material: *Kant: The Philosophy of Right* (London, 1970), pp. 109–112 and 140–144; "Three Mistakes About Retributivism," *Analysis* (April 1971): 166–169; and "Kant's Theory of Criminal Punishment," in *Proceedings of the Third International Kant Congress*, ed. Lewis White Beck (Dordrecht, 1972), pp. 434–441. I am perfectly aware that Kant's views on the issues to be considered here are often obscure and inconsistent—e.g., the analysis of "willing one's own punishment" which I shall later quote from Kant occurs in a passage the primary purpose of which is to argue that the idea of "willing one's own punishment" makes no sense! My present objective, however, is not to attempt accurate Kant scholarship. My goal is rather to build upon some remarks of Kant's which I find philosophically suggestive.

[9] Immanuel Kant, *The Metaphysical Elements of Justice* (1797), trans. John Ladd (Indianapolis, 1965), pp. 35ff.

established that the coercion is such that it could have been rationally willed even by the person whose desire is interfered with:

> Accordingly, when it is said that a creditor has a right to demand from his debtor the payment of a debt, this does not mean that he can *persuade* the debtor that his own reason itself obligates him to this performance; on the contrary, to say that he has such a right means only that the use of coercion to make anyone do this is entirely compatible with everyone's freedom, *including the freedom of the debtor,* in accordance with universal laws.[10]

Like Rousseau, Kant thinks that it is only in a context governed by social practice (particularly civil government and its Rule of Law) that this can make sense. Laws may require of a person some action that he does not desire to perform. This is not a violent invasion of his freedom, however, if it can be shown that in some antecedent position of choice (what John Rawls calls "the original position"),[11] he would have been rational to adopt a Rule of Law (and thus run the risk of having some of his desires thwarted) rather than some other alternative arrangement like the classical State of Nature. This is, indeed, the only sense that Kant is able to make of classical Social Contract theories. Such theories are to be viewed, not as historical fantasies, but as ideal models of rational decision. For what these theories actually claim is that the only coercive institutions that are morally justified are those which a group of rational beings could agree to adopt in a position of having to pick social institutions to govern their relations:

> The contract, which is called *contractus originarius,* or *pactum sociale . . .* need not be assumed to be a fact, indeed it is not [even possible as such. To suppose that would be like insisting] that before anyone would be bound to respect such a civic constitution, it be proved first of all from history that a people, whose rights and obligations we have entered into as their descendants, had *once upon a time* executed such an act and had left a reliable document or instrument, either orally or in writing, concerning this contract. Instead, this contract is a *mere idea* of reason which has undoubted practical reality; namely, to oblige every legislator to give us laws in such a manner that the laws *could* have originated from the united will of the entire people and to regard every subject in so far as he is a citizen as though he had consented to such [an expression of the general] will. This is the testing stone of the rightness of every publicly-known law, for if a law were such that it was impossible for an entire people to give consent to it (as for example a law that a certain class of subjects, by inheritance, should have the privilege of the *status of lords*), then such a law is unjust. On the other hand, if there is a mere *possibility* that a people might consent to a (certain) law, then it is a duty to consider that the law is just even though at the moment the people might be

---

[10] *Ibid.,* p. 37.

[11] John Rawls, "Justice as Fairness," *The Philosophical Review* 67 (1958): 164–194; and *A Theory of Justice* (Cambridge, Mass., 1971), especially pp. 17–22.

in such a position or have a point of view that would result in their refusing to give their consent to it if asked.[12]

The problem of organizing a state, however hard it may seem, can be solved even for a race of devils, if only they are intelligent. The problem is: "Given a multiple of rational beings requiring universal laws for their preservation, but each of whom is secretly inclined to exempt himself from them, to establish a constitution in such a way that, although their private intentions conflict, they check each other, with the result that their public conduct is the same as if they had no such intentions."[13]

Though Kant's doctrine is superficially similar to Mill's later self-protection principle, the substance is really quite different. For though Kant in some general sense argues that coercion is justified only to prevent harm to others, he understands by "harm" only certain invasions of freedom and not simply disutility. Also, his defense of the principle is not grounded, as is Mill's, on its utility. Rather it is to be regarded as a principle of justice, by which Kant means a principle that rational beings could adopt in a situation of mutual choice:

The concept [of justice] applies only to the relationship of a will to another person's will, not to his wishes or desires (or even just his needs) which are the concern of acts of benevolence and charity. . . . In applying the concept of justice we take into consideration only the form of the relationship between the wills insofar as they are regarded as free, and whether the action of one of them can be conjoined with the freedom of the other in accordance with universal law. Justice is therefore the aggregate of those conditions under which the will of one person can be conjoined with the will of another in accordance with a universal law of freedom.[14]

How does this bear specifically on punishment? Kant, as everyone knows, defends a strong form of a retributive theory of punishment. He holds that guilt merits, and is a sufficient condition for, the infliction of punishment. And this claim has been universally condemned—particularly by utilitarians—as primitive, unenlightened and barbaric.

But why is it so condemned? Typically, the charge is that infliction of punishment on such grounds is nothing but pointless vengeance. But what is meant by the claim that the infliction is "pointless"? If "pointless" is tacitly being analyzed as "disutilitarian," then the whole question is simply being begged. You cannot refute a retributive theory merely by noting that it is a retributive theory and not a utilitarian theory. This is to confuse redescription with refutation and involves an argument whose circularity is not even complicated enough to be interesting.

---

[12] Immanuel Kant, "Concerning the Common Saying: This May be True in Theory but Does Not Apply in Practice (1793)," in *The Philosophy of Kant,* ed. and trans. Carl J. Friedrich (New York, 1949), pp. 421–422.

[13] Immanuel Kant, *Perpetual Peace* (1795), trans. Lewis White Beck in the Kant anthology *On History* (Indianapolis 1963), p. 112.

[14] Immanuel Kant, *The Metaphysical Elements of Justice,* p. 34.

Why, then, might someone claim that guilt merits punishment? Such a claim might be made for either of two very different reasons. (1) Someone (e.g., a Moral Sense theorist) might maintain that the claim is a primitive and unanalyzable proposition that is morally ultimate—that we can just intuit the "fittingness" of guilt and punishment. (2) It might be maintained that the retributivist claim is demanded by a general theory of political obligation which is more plausible than any alternative theory. Such a theory will typically provide a technical analysis of such concepts as crime and punishment and will thus not regard the retributivist claim as an indisputable primitive. It will be argued for as a kind of theorem within the system.

Kant's theory is of the second sort. He does not opt for retributivism as a bit of intuitive moral knowledge. Rather he offers a theory of punishment that is based on his general view that political obligation is to be analyzed, quasi-contractually, in terms of reciprocity. If the law is to remain just, it is important to guarantee that those who disobey it will not gain an unfair advantage over those who do obey voluntarily. It is important that no man profit from his own criminal wrongdoing, and a certain kind of "profit" (i.e., not bearing the burden of self-restraint) is intrinsic to criminal wrongdoing. Criminal punishment, then, has as its object the restoration of a proper balance between benefit and obedience. The criminal himself has no complaint, because he has rationally consented to or willed his own punishment. That is, those very rules which he has broken work, when they are obeyed by others, to his own advantage as a citizen. He would have chosen such rules for himself and others in the original position of choice. And, since he derives and voluntarily accepts benefits from their operation, he owes his own obedience as a debt to his fellow-citizens for their sacrifices in maintaining them. If he chooses not to sacrifice by exercising self-restraint and obedience, this is tantamount to his choosing to sacrifice in another way—namely, by paying the prescribed penalty:

> A transgression of the public law that makes him who commits it unfit to be a citizen is called . . . a crime. . . .
>
> What kind and what degree of punishment does public legal justice adopt as its principle and standard? None other than the principle of equality (illustrated by the pointer of the scales of justice), that is, the principle of not treating one side more favorably than the other. Accordingly, any undeserved evil that you inflict on someone else among the people is one you do to yourself. If you vilify him, you vilify yourself; if you steal from him, you steal from yourself; if you kill him, you kill yourself. . . .
>
> To say, "I will to be punished if I murder someone" can mean nothing more than, "I submit myself along with everyone else to those laws which, if there are any criminals among the people, will naturally include penal laws." [15]

This analysis of punishment regards it as a debt owed to the law-abiding members of one's community; and, once paid, it allows reentry into the community of good citizens on equal status.

---

[15] *Ibid.*, pp. 99, 101, and 105, in the order quoted.

Now some of the foregoing no doubt sounds implausible or even obscurantist. Since criminals typically desire not to be punished, what can it really mean to say that they have, as rational men, really willed their own punishment? Or that, as Hegel says, they have a right to it? Perhaps a comparison of the traditional retributivist views with those of a contemporary Kantian—John Rawls—will help to make the points clearer.[16] Rawls (like Kant) does not regard the idea of the social contract as an historical fact. It is rather a model of rational decision. Respecting a man's autonomy, at least on one view, is not respecting what he now happens, however uncritically, to desire; rather it is to respect what he desires (or would desire) as a rational man. (On Rawls's view, for example, rational men are said to be unmoved by feelings of envy; and thus it is not regarded as unjust to a person or a violation of his rights, if he is placed in a situation where he will envy another's advantage or position. A rational man would object, and thus would never consent to, a practice where another might derive a benefit from a position at his expense. He would not, however, envy the position *simpliciter,* would not regard the position as itself a benefit.) Now on Kant's (and also, I think, on Rawls's) view, a man is genuinely free or autonomous only in so far as he is rational. Thus it is man's rational will that is to be respected.

Now this idea of treating people, not as they in fact say that they want to be treated, but rather in terms of how you think they would, if rational, will to be treated, has obviously dangerous (indeed Fascistic) implications. Surely we want to avoid cramming indignities down the throats of people with the offhand observation that, no matter how much they scream, they are really rationally willing every bit of it. It would be particularly ironic for such arbitrary repression to come under the mask of respecting autonomy. And yet, most of us would agree, the general principle (though subject to abuse) also has important applications—for example, preventing the suicide of a person who, in a state of psychotic depression, wants to kill himself. What we need, then, to make the general view work, is a check on its arbitrary application; and a start toward providing such a check would be in the formulation of a public, objective theory of rationality and rational willing. It is just this, according to both Kant and Rawls, which the social contract theory can provide. On this theory, a man may be said to rationally will X if, and only if, X is called for by a rule that the man would necessarily have adopted in the original position of choice—i.e., in a position of coming together with others to pick rules for the regulation of their mutual affairs. This avoids arbitrariness because, according to Kant and Rawls at any rate, the question of whether such a rule would be picked in such a position is objectively determinable given certain (in their

---

[16] In addition to the works on justice by Rawls previously cited, the reader should consult the following for Rawls's application of his general theory to the problem of political obligation: John Rawls, "Legal Obligation and the Duty of Fair Play," in *Law and Philosophy,* ed. Sidney Hook (New York, 1964), pp. 3–18. This has been reprinted in my anthology *Civil Disobedience and Violence* (Belmont, Cal., 1971), pp. 39–52. For a direct application of a similar theory to the problem of punishment, see Herbert Morris, "Persons and Punishment," *The Monist* 52, no. 4 (October 1968): 475–501.

view) noncontroversial assumptions about human nature and rational calculation. Thus I can be said to will my own punishment if, in an antecedent position of choice, I and my fellows would have chosen institutions of punishment as the most rational means of dealing with those who might break the other generally beneficial social rules that had been adopted.

Let us take an analogous example: I may not, in our actual society, desire to treat a certain person fairly—e.g., I may not desire to honor a contract I have made with him because so doing would adversely affect my own self-interest. However, if I am forced to honor the contract by the state, I cannot charge (1) that the state has no right to do this, or (2) that my rights or dignity are being violated by my being coerced into doing it. Indeed, it can be said that I rationally will it since, in the original position, I would have chosen rules of justice (rather than rules of utility) and the principle, "contracts are to be honored," follows from the rules of justice.

Coercion and autonomy are thus reconciled, at least apparently. To use Marx's language, we may say (as Marx did in the quoted passage) that one virtue of the retributive theory, at least as expounded by Kant and Hegel on lines of the General Will and Social Contract theory, is that it manifests at least a formal or abstract respect for rights, dignity, and autonomy. For it at least recognizes the importance of attempting to construe state coercion in such a way that it is a product of each man's rational will. Utilitarian deterrence theory does not even satisfy this formal demand.

The question of primary interest to Marx, of course, is whether this formal respect also involves a material respect; i.e., does the theory have application in concrete fact in the actual social world in which we live? Marx is confident that it does not, and it is to this sort of consideration that I shall now pass.

ALIENATION AND PUNISHMENT

What can the philosopher learn from Marx? This question is a part of a more general question: What can philosophy learn from social science? Philosophers, it may be thought, are concerned to offer a priori theories, theories about how certain concepts are to be analyzed and their application justified. And what can the mundane facts that are the object of behavioral science have to do with exalted theories of this sort?

The answer, I think, is that philosophical theories, though not themselves empirical, often have such a character that their intelligibility depends upon certain empirical presuppositions. For example, our moral language presupposes, as Hart has argued,[17] that we are vulnerable creatures—creatures who can harm and be harmed by each other. Also, as I have argued elsewhere,[18] our moral language presupposes that we all share certain psychological characteristics—e.g., sympathy, a sense of justice, and the capacity to feel guilt, shame,

---

[17] H. L. A. Hart, *The Concept of Law* (Oxford, 1961), pp. 189–195.

[18] Jeffrie G. Murphy, "Moral Death: A Kantian Essay on Psychopathy," *Ethics* 82, no. 4 (July 1972): 284–298.

regret, and remorse. If these facts were radically different (if, as Hart imagines for example, we all developed crustaceanlike exoskeletons and thus could not harm each other), the old moral language, and the moral theories which employ it, would lack application to the world in which we live. To use a crude example, moral prohibitions against killing presuppose that it is in fact possible for us to kill each other.

Now one of Marx's most important contributions to social philosophy, in my judgment, is simply his insight that philosophical theories are in peril if they are constructed in disregard of the nature of the empirical world to which they are supposed to apply.[19] A theory may be formally correct (i.e., coherent, or true for some possible world) but materially incorrect (i.e., inapplicable to the actual world in which we live). This insight, then, establishes the relevance of empirical research to philosophical theory and is a part, I think, of what Marx meant by "the union of theory and practice." Specifically relevant to the argument I want to develop are the following two related points:

(1) The theories of moral, social, political and legal philosophy presuppose certain empirical propositions about man and society. If these propositions are false, then the theory (even if coherent or formally correct) is materially defective and practically inapplicable. (For example, if persons tempted to engage in criminal conduct do not in fact tend to calculate carefully the consequences of their actions, this renders much of deterrence theory suspect.)

(2) Philosophical theories may put forth as a necessary truth that which is in fact merely an historically conditioned contingency. (For example, Hobbes argued that all men are necessarily selfish and competitive. It is possible, as many Marxists have argued, that Hobbes was really doing nothing more than elevating to the status of a necessary truth the contingent fact that the people around him in the capitalistic society in which he lived were in fact selfish and competitive.)[20]

In outline, then, I want to argue the following: that when Marx challenges the material adequacy of the retributive theory of punishment, he is suggesting (a) that it presupposes a certain view of man and society that is false and (b) that key concepts involved in the support of the theory (e.g., the concept of "rationality" in Social Contract theory) are given analyses which, though they purport to be necessary truths, are in fact mere reflections of certain historical circumstances.

In trying to develop this case, I shall draw primarily upon Willem Bonger's *Criminality and Economic Conditions* (1916), one of the few sustained

[19] Banal as this point may seem, it could be persuasively argued that all Enlightenment political theory (e.g., that of Hobbes, Locke and Kant) is built upon ignoring it. For example, once we have substantial empirical evidence concerning how democracies really work in fact, how sympathetic can we really be to classical theories for the justification of democracy? For more on this, see C. B. Macpherson, "The Maximization of Democracy," in *Philosophy, Politics and Society* (Third Series), ed. Peter Laslett and W. G. Runciman (Oxford, 1967), pp. 83–103. . . .

[20] This point is well developed in C. B. Macpherson, *The Political Theory of Possessive Individualism* (Oxford, 1962). In a sense, this point affects even the formal correctness of a theory. For it demonstrates an empirical source of corruption in the analyses of the very concepts in the theory.

Marxist analyses of crime and punishment.[21] Though I shall not have time here to qualify my support of Bonger in certain necessary ways, let me make clear that I am perfectly aware that his analysis is not the whole story. (No monolithic theory of anything so diverse as criminal behavior could be the whole story.) However, I am convinced that he has discovered part of the story. And my point is simply that insofar as Bonger's Marxist analysis is correct, then to that same degree is the retributive theory of punishment inapplicable in modern societies. (Let me emphasize again exactly how this objection to retributivism differs from those traditionally offered. Traditionally, retributivism has been rejected because it conflicts with the moral theory of its opponent, usually a utilitarian. This is not the kind of objection I want to develop. Indeed, with Marx, I have argued that the retributive theory of punishment grows out of the moral theory—Kantianism—which seems to me generally correct. The objection I want to pursue concerns the empirical falsity of the factual presuppositions of the theory. If the empirical presuppositions of the theory are false, this does indeed render its application immoral. But the immorality consists, not in a conflict with some other moral theory, but immorality in terms of a moral theory that is at least close in spirit to the very moral theory which generates retributivism itself—i.e., a theory of justice.)[22]

To return to Bonger. Put bluntly, his theory is as follows. Criminality has two primary sources: (1) need and deprivation on the part of disadvantaged members of society, and (2) motives of greed and selfishness that are generated and reinforced in competitive capitalistic societies. Thus criminality is economically based—either directly in the case of crimes from need, or indirectly in the case of crimes growing out of motives or psychological states that are encouraged and developed in capitalistic society. In Marx's own language, such an economic system alienates men from themselves and from each other. It alienates men from themselves by creating motives and needs that are not "truly human." It alienates men from their fellows by encouraging a kind of competitiveness that forms an obstacle to the development of genuine communities to replace mere social aggregates.[23] And in Bonger's thought, the concept of

---

[21] The writings of Willem Adriaan Bonger (1876–1940), a Dutch criminologist, have fallen into totally unjustified neglect in recent years. Anticipating contemporary sociological theories of crime, he was insisting that criminal behavior is in the province of normal psychology (though abnormal society) at a time when most other writers were viewing criminality as a symptom of psychopathology. His major works are: *Criminality and Economic Conditions* (Boston, 1916); *An Introduction to Criminology* (London, 1936); and *Race and Crime* (New York, 1943).

[22] I say "at least in spirit" to avoid begging the controversial question of whether Marx can be said to embrace a theory of justice. Though . . . much of Marx's own evaluative rhetoric seems to overlap more traditional appeals to rights and justice (and a total lack of sympathy with anything like Utilitarianism), it must be admitted that he also frequently ridicules at least the terms "rights" and "justice" because of their apparent entrenchment in bourgeois ethics. For an interesting discussion of this issue, see Allen W. Wood, "The Marxian Critique of Justice," *Philosophy & Public Affairs* 1, no. 3 (Spring 1972): 244–282.

[23] The importance of community is also, I think, recognized in Gabriel de Tarde's notion of "social similarity" as a condition of criminal responsibility. See his *Penal Philosophy* (Boston, 1912). I have drawn on de Tarde's general account in my "Moral Death: A Kantian Essay on Psychopathy."

community is central. He argues that moral relations and moral restraint are possible only in genuine communities characterized by bonds of sympathetic identification and mutual aid resting upon a perception of common humanity. All this he includes under the general rubric of reciprocity.[24] In the absence of reciprocity in this rich sense, moral relations among men will break down and criminality will increase.[25] Within bourgeois society, then, crimes are to be re-garded as normal, and not psychopathological, acts. That is, they grow out of need, greed, indifference to others, and sometimes even a sense of indigna-tion—all, alas, perfectly typical human motives.

To appreciate the force of Bonger's analysis, it is necessary to read his books and grasp the richness and detail of the evidence he provides for his claims. Here I can but quote a few passages at random to give the reader a tantalizing sample in the hope that he will be encouraged to read further into Bonger's own text:

> The abnormal element in crime is a social, not a biological, element. With the exception of a few special cases, crime lies within the boundaries of normal psychology and physiology. . . .
>
> We clearly see that [the egoistic tendencies of the present economic sys-tem and of its consequences] are very strong. Because of these tendencies the social instinct of man is not greatly developed; they have weakened the moral force in man which combats the inclination towards egoistic acts, and hence toward the crimes which are one form of these acts. . . . Compassion for the misfortunes of others inevitably becomes blunted, and a great part of moral-ity consequently disappears. . . .
>
> As a consequence of the present environment, man has become very egoistic and hence more *capable of crime,* than if the environment had devel-oped the germs of altruism. . . .
>
> There can be no doubt that one of the factors of criminality among the bourgeoisie is bad [moral] education. . . . The children—speaking of course in a general way—are brought up with the idea that they must succeed, no matter how; the aim of life is presented to them as getting money and shining in the world. . . .
>
> Poverty (taken in the sense of absolute want) kills the social sentiments in man, destroys in fact all relations between men. He who is abandoned by all can no longer have any feeling for those who have left him to his fate. . . .

[24] By "reciprocity" Bonger intends something which includes, but is much richer than, a notion of "fair trading or bargaining" that might initially be read into the term. He also has in mind such things as sympathetic identification with others and tendencies to provide mutual aid. Thus, for Bonger, reciprocity and egoism have a strong tendency to conflict. I mention this lest Bonger's notion of reciprocity be too quickly identified with the more restricted notion found in, for ex-ample, Kant and Rawls.

[25] It is interesting how greatly Bonger's analysis differs from classical deterrence theory—e.g., that of Bentham. Bentham, who views men as machines driven by desires to attain pleasure and avoid pain, tends to regard terror as the primary restraint against crime. Bonger believes that, at least in a healthy society, moral motives would function as a major restraint against crime. When an environment that destroys moral motivation is created, even terror (as statistics tend to confirm) will not eradicate crime.

[Upon perception that the system tends to legalize the egoistic actions of the bourgeoisie and to penalize those of the proletariat], the oppressed resort to means which they would otherwise scorn. As we have seen above, the basis of the social feeling is reciprocity. As soon as this is trodden under foot by the ruling class the social sentiments of the oppressed become weak towards them. . . .[26]

The essence of this theory has been summed up by Austin J. Turk. "Criminal behavior," he says, "is almost entirely attributable to the combination of egoism and an environment in which opportunities are not equitably distributed."[27]

No doubt this claim will strike many as extreme and intemperate—a sample of the old-fashioned Marxist rhetoric that sophisticated intellectuals have outgrown. Those who are inclined to react in this way might consider just one sobering fact: of the 1.3 million criminal offenders handled each day by some agency of the United States correctional system, the vast majority (80 percent on some estimates) are members of the lowest 15-percent income level—that percent which is below the "poverty level" as defined by the Social Security Administration.[28] Unless one wants to embrace the belief that all these people are poor because they are bad, it might be well to reconsider Bonger's suggestion that many of them are "bad" because they are poor.[29] At any rate, let us

---

[26] *Introduction to Criminology,* pp. 75–76, and *Criminality and Economic Conditions,* pp. 532, 402, 483–484, 436, and 407, in the order quoted. Bonger explicitly attacks Hobbes: "The adherents of [Hobbes's theory] have studied principally men who live under capitalism, or under civilization; their correct conclusion has been that egoism is the predominant characteristic of these men, and they have adopted the simplest explanation of the phenomenon and say that this trait is inborn." If Hobbists can cite Freud for modern support, Bonger can cite Darwin. For, as Darwin had argued in the *Descent of Man,* men would not have survived as a species if they had not initially had considerably greater social sentiments than Hobbes allows them.

[27] Austin J. Turk, in the Introduction to his abridged edition of Bonger's *Criminality and Economic Conditions* (Bloomington, 1969), p. 14.

[28] Statistical data on characteristics of offenders in America are drawn primarily from surveys by the Bureau of Census and the National Council on Crime and Delinquency. While there is of course wide disagreement on how such data are to be interpreted, there is no serious disagreement concerning at least the general accuracy of statistics like the one I have cited. Even government publications openly acknowledge a high correlation between crime and socio-economic disadvantages: "From arrest records, probation reports, and prison statistics a 'portrait' of the offender emerges that progressively highlights the disadvantaged character of his life. The offender at the end of the road in prison is likely to be a member of the lowest social and economic groups in the country, poorly educated and perhaps unemployed. . . . Material failure, then, in a culture firmly oriented toward material success, is the most common denominator of offenders" (*The Challenge of Crime in a Free Society, A Report by the President's Commission on Law Enforcement and Administration of Justice,* U.S. Government Printing Office, Washington, D.C., 1967, pp. 44 and 160). The Marxist implications of this admission have not gone unnoticed by prisoners. See Samuel Jorden, "Prison Reform: In Whose Interest?" *Criminal Law Bulletin* 7, no. 9 (November 1971): 779–787.

[29] There are, of course, other factors which enter into an explanation of this statistic. One of them is the fact that economically disadvantaged guilty persons are more likely to wind up arrested or in prison (and thus be reflected in this statistic) than are economically advantaged guilty persons. Thus economic conditions enter into the explanation, not just of criminal behavior, but of society's response to criminal behavior. For a general discussion on the many ways in which crime and poverty are related, see Patricia M. Wald, "Poverty and Criminal Justice," *Task Force Report: The Courts,* U.S. Government Printing Office, Washington, D.C., 1967, pp. 139–151.

suppose for purposes of discussion that Bonger's picture of the relation between crime and economic conditions is generally accurate. At what points will this challenge the credentials of the contractarian retributive theory as outlined above? I should like to organize my answer to this question around three basic topics:

1. *Rational Choice.* The model of rational choice found in Social Contract theory is egoistic—rational institutions are those that would be agreed to by calculating egoists ("devils" in Kant's more colorful terminology). The obvious question that would be raised by any Marxist is: Why give egoism this special status such that it is built, a priori, into the analysis of the concept of rationality? Is this not simply to regard as necessary that which may be only contingently found in the society around us? Starting from such an analysis, a certain result is inevitable—namely, a transcendental sanction for the status quo. Start with a bourgeois model of rationality and you will, of course, wind up defending a bourgeois theory of consent, a bourgeois theory of justice, and a bourgeois theory of punishment.

Though I cannot explore the point in detail here, it seems to me that this Marxist claim may cause some serious problems for Rawls's well-known theory of justice, a theory which I have already used to unpack some of the evaluative support for the retributive theory of punishment. One cannot help suspecting that there is a certain sterility in Rawls's entire project of providing a rational proof for the preferability of a certain conception of justice over all possible alternative evaluative principles, for the description which he gives of the rational contractors in the original position is such as to guarantee that they will come up with his two principles. This would be acceptable if the analysis of rationality presupposed were intuitively obvious or argued for on independent grounds. But it is not. Why, to take just one example, is a desire for wealth a rational trait whereas envy is not? One cannot help feeling that the desired result dictates the premises.[30]

---

[30] The idea that the principles of justice could be proved as a kind of theorem (Rawls's claim in "Justice as Fairness") seems to be absent, if I understand the work correctly, in Rawls's recent *A Theory of Justice*. In this book, Rawls seems to be content with something less than a decision procedure. He is no longer trying to pull his theory of justice up by its own bootstraps, but now seems concerned simply to *exhibit* a certain elaborate conception of justice in the belief that it will do a good job of systematizing and ordering most of our considered and reflective intuitions about moral matters. To this, of course, the Marxist will want to say something like the following: "The considered and reflective intuitions current in our society are a product of bourgeois culture, and thus any theory based upon them begs the question against us and in favor of the status quo." I am not sure that this charge cannot be answered, but I am sure that it deserves an answer. Someday Rawls may be remembered, to paraphrase Georg Lukács's description of Thomas Mann, as the last and greatest philosopher of bourgeois liberalism. The virtue of this description is that it perceives the limitations of his outlook in a way consistent with acknowledging his indisputable genius. (None of my remarks here, I should point out, are to be interpreted as denying that our civilization derived major moral benefits from the tradition of bourgeois liberalism. Just because the freedoms and procedures we associate with bourgeois liberalism—speech, press, assembly, due process of law, etc.—are not the only important freedoms and procedures, we are not to conclude with some witless radicals that these freedoms are not terribly important and that the victories of bourgeois revolutions are not worth preserving. My

2. *Justice, Benefits, and Community.* The retributive theory claims to be grounded on justice; but is it just to punish people who act out of those very motives that society encourages and reinforces? If Bonger is correct, much criminality is motivated by greed, selfishness, and indifference to one's fellows; but does not the whole society encourage motives of greed and selfishness ("making it," "getting ahead"), and does not the competitive nature of the society alienate men from each other and thereby encourage indifference—even, perhaps, what psychiatrists call psychopathy? The moral problem here is similar to one that arises with respect to some war crimes. When you have trained a man to believe that the enemy is not a genuine human person (but only a gook, or a chink), it does not seem quite fair to punish the man if, in a war situation, he kills indiscriminately. For the psychological trait you have conditioned him to have, like greed, is not one that invites fine moral and legal distinctions. There is something perverse in applying principles that presuppose a sense of community in a society which is structured to destroy genuine community.[31]

Related to this is the whole allocation of benefits in contemporary society. The retributive theory really presupposes what might be called a "gentlemen's club" picture of the relation between man and society—i.e., men are viewed as being part of a community of shared values and rules. The rules benefit all concerned and, as a kind of debt for the benefits derived, each man owes obedience to the rules. In the absence of such obedience, he deserves punishment in the sense that he owes payment for the benefits. For, as rational man, he can see that the rules benefit everyone (himself included) and that he would have selected them in the original position of choice.

Now this may not be too far off for certain kinds of criminals—e.g., business executives guilty of tax fraud. (Though even here we might regard their motives of greed to be a function of societal reinforcement.) But to think that it applies to the typical criminal, from the poorer classes, is to live in a world of social and political fantasy. Criminals typically are not members of a shared community of values with their jailers; they suffer from what Marx calls alienation. And they certainly would be hard-pressed to name the benefits for which they are supposed to owe obedience. If justice, as both Kant and Rawls suggest, is based on reciprocity, it is hard to see what these persons are supposed to reciprocate for. Bonger addresses this point in a passage quoted earlier (p. 880): "The oppressed resort to means which they would otherwise scorn. . . . The basis of social feelings is reciprocity. As soon as this is trodden under foot by the ruling class, the social sentiments of the oppressed become weak towards them."

point is much more modest and noncontroversial—namely, that even bourgeois liberalism requires a critique. It is not self-justifying and, in certain very important respects, is not justified at all.)

[31] Kant has some doubts about punishing bastard infanticide and dueling on similar grounds. Given the stigma that Kant's society attached to illegitimacy and the halo that the same society placed around military honor, it did not seem totally fair to punish those whose criminality in part grew out of such approved motives. See *Metaphysical Elements of Justice*, pp. 106–107.

3. *Voluntary Acceptance.* Central to the Social Contract idea is the claim that we owe allegiance to the law because the benefits we have derived have been voluntarily accepted. This is one place where our autonomy is supposed to come in. That is, having benefited from the Rule of Law when it was possible to leave, I have in a sense consented to it and to its consequences—even my own punishment if I violate the rules. To see how silly the factual presuppositions of this account are, we can do no better than quote a famous passage from David Hume's essay "Of the Original Contract":

> Can we seriously say that a poor peasant or artisan has a free choice to leave his country—when he knows no foreign language or manners, and lives from day to day by the small wages which he acquires? We may as well assert that a man, by remaining in a vessel, freely consents to the dominion of the master, though he was carried on board while asleep, and must leap into the ocean and perish the moment he leaves her.

A banal empirical observation, one may say. But it is through ignoring such banalities that philosophers generate theories which allow them to spread iniquity in the ignorant belief that they are spreading righteousness.

It does, then, seem as if there may be some truth in Marx's claim that the retributive theory, though formally correct, is materially inadequate. At root, the retributive theory fails to acknowledge that criminality is, to a large extent, a phenomenon of economic class. To acknowledge this is to challenge the empirical presupposition of the retributive theory—the presupposition that all men, including criminals, are voluntary participants in a reciprocal system of benefits and that the justice of this arrangement can be derived from some eternal and ahistorical concept of rationality.

The upshot of all this seems rather upsetting, as indeed it is. How can it be the case that everything we are ordinarily inclined to say about punishment (in terms of utility and retribution) can be quite beside the point? To anyone with ordinary language sympathies (one who is inclined to maintain that what is correct to say is a function of what we do say), this will seem madness. Marx will agree that there is madness, all right, but in his view the madness will lie in what we do say—what we say only because of our massive (and often self-deceiving and self-serving) factual ignorance or indifference to the circumstances of the social world in which we live. Just as our whole way of talking about mental phenomena hardened before we knew any neurophysiology—and this leads us astray, so Marx would argue that our whole way of talking about moral and political phenomena hardened before we knew any of the relevant empirical facts about man and society—and this, too, leads us astray. We all suffer from what might be called the *embourgeoisment* of language, and thus part of any revolution will be a linguistic or conceptual revolution. We have grown accustomed to modifying our language or conceptual structures under the impact of empirical discoveries in physics. There is no reason why discoveries in sociology, economics, or psychology could not and should not have the same effect on entrenched patterns of thought and speech. It is important to remember, as

Russell remarked, that our language sometimes enshrines the metaphysics of the Stone Age.

Consider one example: a man has been convicted of armed robbery. On investigation, we learn that he is an impoverished black whose whole life has been one of frustrating alienation from the prevailing socio-economic structure—no job, no transportation if he could get a job, substandard education for his children, terrible housing and inadequate health care for his whole family, condescending-tardy-inadequate welfare payments, harassment by the police but no real protection by them against the dangers in his community, and near total exclusion from the political process. Learning all this, would we still want to talk—as many do—of his suffering punishment under the rubric of "paying a debt to society"? Surely not. Debt for what? I do not, of course, pretend that all criminals can be so described. But I do think that this is a closer picture of the typical criminal than the picture that is presupposed in the retributive theory—i.e., the picture of an evil person who, of his own free will, intentionally acts against those just rules of society which he knows, as a rational man, benefit everyone including himself.

But what practical help does all this offer, one may ask. How should we design our punitive practices in the society in which we now live? This is the question we want to ask, and it does not seem to help simply to say that our society is built on deception and inequity. How can Marx help us with our real practical problem? The answer, I think, is that he cannot and obviously does not desire to do so. For Marx would say that we have not focused (as all piecemeal reform fails to focus) on what is truly the real problem. And this is changing the basic social relations. Marx is the last person from whom we can expect advice on how to make our intellectual and moral peace with bourgeois society. And this is surely his attraction and his value.

What does Bonger offer? He suggests, near the end of his book, that in a properly designed society all criminality would be a problem "for the physician rather than the judge." But this surely will not do. The therapeutic state, where prisons are called hospitals and jailers are called psychiatrists, simply raises again all the old problems about the justification of coercion and its reconciliation with autonomy that we faced in worrying about punishment. The only difference is that our coercive practices are now surrounded with a benevolent rhetoric which makes it even harder to raise the important issues. Thus the move to therapy, in my judgment, is only an illusory solution—alienation remains and the problem of reconciling coercion with autonomy remains unsolved. Indeed, if the alternative is having our personalities involuntarily restructured by some state psychiatrist, we might well want to claim the "right to be punished" that Hegel spoke of.[32]

---

[32] This point is pursued in Herbert Morris, "Persons and Punishment." Bonger did not appreciate that "mental illness," like criminality, may also be a phenomenon of social class. On this, see August B. Hollingshead and Frederick C. Redlich, *Social Class and Mental Illness* (New York, 1958). On the general issue of punishment versus therapy, see my *Punishment and Rehabilitation* (Belmont, Cal., forthcoming 1973).

Perhaps, then, we may really be forced seriously to consider a radical proposal. If we think that institutions of punishment are necessary and desirable, and if we are morally sensitive enough to want to be sure that we have the moral right to punish before we inflict it, then we had better first make sure that we have restructured society in such a way that criminals genuinely do correspond to the only model that will render punishment permissible—i.e., make sure that they are autonomous and that they do benefit in the requisite sense. Of course, if we did this then—if Marx and Bonger are right—crime itself and the need to punish would radically decrease if not disappear entirely.

72.

Punishment and Societal Defense

PHILLIP MONTAGUE

Questions concerning the justifiability of legal punishment are commonly divided into two types: those concerned with the morality of individual acts of punishment, and those concerned with the morality of legal punishment as a general practice. I shall focus here on questions of the second type and will sketch an approach to answering them based on the concept of societal defense. On this approach, the morality of adopting systems of legal punishment depends, at least in part, on the conditions under which societies are justified in establishing practices aimed at protecting their members from being wrongfully harmed.[1]

In order to understand the moral status of defensive measures taken by societies, it will be helpful first to examine the morality of defensive actions performed by individuals.[2]

Let us refer to standard defense situations as those in which wrongful harm will culpably be done to some individual (henceforth known as Victim) by another (called Aggressor) unless the latter is himself harmed. For the sake of simplicity, we can focus for now on standard defense situations in which lives are at stake—situations in which Victim will be killed unless Aggressor is.

Standard defense situations have three noteworthy characteristics:

1. In such situations, harm is unavoidable from Victim's standpoint. Assuming that he is in a position to save himself, he must choose how to distribute this unavoidable harm: On one distribution, he will lose his life; on another distribution, Aggressor will lose his. And, of course, any Third Party who can defend Victim is faced with a similar choice.

2. Victim has a *right* to defend himself, and Third Party is required (at least ceteris paribus) to do so. Victim's right is not simply the absence of a duty to forbear. Rather, it is a right in the strong sense which implies a duty on the part of all others to refrain from interfering with him if he chooses to defend himself against Aggressor.

3. Victim's right and Third Party's obligation are unaffected by the number of Aggressors who jointly threaten Victim's life, and who must all be killed to save Victim.

---

[1] Some reasons for thinking that neither retributivism nor utilitarianism is capable of dealing adequately with the concept of societal defense are implicit in the final section of this paper. I make no attempt here to argue explicitly for this point, though I think it would not be difficult to produce arguments that are quite compelling.

[2] A particularly valuable treatment of individual self-defense is provided by Judith Thomson in "Self-defense and Rights," Findley Lecture, 1976 (Lawrence, KS: University of Kansas Press, 1977). I have also discussed the subject further in "Self-defense and Choosing Between Lives," *Philosophical Studies*, 40 (1981), pp. 207–219.

Standard defense situations are, of course, not the only ones in which individuals must decide how to distribute harm which they cannot prevent. For many of these situations, however, there are no analogs of the second and third conditions. Consider innocent threat cases, for example. These are cases in which one person will die if another does not, and where neither is an aggressor and both are the innocent victims of circumstances beyond their control.[3] In such cases, a person may be *permitted* to choose in his or her own favor, but that person surely has no *right* to do so. Similarly, a third party might be permitted to save one person at the other's expense, but there is nothing in the nature of innocent threat cases that dictate which individual should be favored. Moreover, in innocent threat cases numbers are relevant in a way they are not in standard defense situations. If a choice must be made between one innocent life and many, then this fact must certainly be taken into account when attempting to determine which choice is morally correct.

A more controversial class of cases involves innocent aggressors. We might, for example, have a case like the following:

> A suffers from a serious mental illness which causes him to believe that he is constantly the object of wrongful aggression on the part of others. He attacks B in the mistaken and totally irrational conviction that B will murder him if he does not. The only way B's life can be saved is by killing A.[4]

There are those who would claim that B has a *right* to defend himself, and hence that others are required to refrain from interfering with any attempt he might make to do so. I doubt that this is true, however. If A is in fact *innocent,* then I see no reason why B should be favored over A—why a third party who is in a position to protect A from B's defensive measures should be required to refrain from doing so. To insist that B *does* have a right to defend himself against A's attack is to imply that innocent aggressor cases differ morally from innocent threat cases by virtue of the fact that aggression is involved in the former but not in the latter. It strikes me as unreasonable to regard the presence or absence of aggression as singly making this kind of moral difference.

The morally significant features of standard defense situations become apparent when we recognize that these situations can be subsumed under a broader class of cases satisfying the following conditions: (i) some individual x can escape being harmed if and only if some other individual y is himself harmed; (ii) z (who may be identical to x) is in a position to determine which of the two individuals will be harmed; (iii) it is y's fault that he and x are in a situation in which one of them will be harmed. In these situations, z must decide how to distribute harm which is unavoidable from his standpoint. It seems clear that if z is identical to x (and if certain other things are equal), he has a

---

[3] The now-familiar "runaway trolley" cases are examples of innocent threat cases. See Judith Thomson, "Killing, Letting-die, and the Trolley Problem," *The Monist* 59 (1976), pp. 204–217.

[4] For an intriguing discussion of these cases, see George P. Fletcher, "Proportionality and the Psychotic Aggressor: A Vignette in Comparative Criminal Theory," *Israeli Law Review* 6 (1973), pp. 367–390.

right to protect himself at y's expense; and if z is different from x, then he is obligated (again ceteris paribus) to choose in x's favor. Furthermore, if a choice must be made between saving x and saving several others who are jointly to blame for the danger facing them all, then x still has a right to choose in his own favor, and third parties are obligated (ceteris paribus) to do so. Consider the following case, for example:

> C is an experienced Alpine guide and D a novice climber. As a result of culpable negligence on C's part, both are trapped on an exposed ledge without adequate clothing and with no shelter. A storm is approaching and both will die if not rescued before it arrives. E has a helicopter, but it can carry only one passenger, and there is only time for one trip to the ledge before the storm hits.

This case satisfies conditions (i), (ii), and (iii) (with z different from x), and it seems clear that E has an obligation to save D rather than C. Moreover, if we modify the case so that D is trapped on the ledge with *several* guides who are jointly at fault for their predicament; and if we assume that D is very heavy and the guides very light so that E's helicopter can carry either D or the guides; then we must still conclude that E's obligation is to save D rather than the others.

It should be readily apparent, I think, that standard defense situations are special instances of the cases defined by (i), (ii), and (iii). In the former situation it is Aggressor's fault that there is harm to be distributed—harm which is unavoidable from Victim's (and perhaps Third Party's) standpoint. Because the existence of harm is Aggressor's fault, it is quite appropriate—and appropriate as a matter of justice—that the harm should befall him rather than some innocent person. Implicit in this last claim is a principle which applies to standard defense situations and to the broader class of cases described above which defense situations instantiate:

> (DH) *When unavoidable harm is being distributed among a group of individuals, and when some members of the group are to blame for the predicament of all, then justice requires (ceteris paribus) that the harm be distributed among those who are blameworthy.*

Three major ceteris paribus conditions for DH are worth mentioning at this point. The first is a proportionality condition according to which the distribution of unavoidable harm among those who are to blame for the existence of that harm must be proportional to the harm that would be suffered by innocent persons under a different distribution. It is important to recognize that this condition concerns individual rather than collective harm. If a choice must be made between distributing harm to one person or to several, and if the several are jointly to blame for the existence of that harm; then, as was noted above in connection with standard defense situations and our example of the trapped climbers, the innocent person must be favored even if the *total* harm resulting from such a distribution is much greater than that which would result from a distribution favoring those who are blameworthy. But according to the proportionality condition, the harm suffered by each blameworthy individual under a given distribution must be proportional to that which would be suffered by an innocent person under a different distribution. Returning to our example of the trapped climbers, the proportionality condition would prevent DH from being used to justify doing major harm to C (or to any number of collectively blameworthy guides) in order to save D from suffering minor harm. If the only harm possible in a given situation is the loss of life (something we assumed when discussing standard defense situations), then the proportionality condition is automatically satisfied, and questions about the quantity of harm done do not arise unless *innocent* persons are affected differently by different distributions.

The proportionality condition places a maximum on the amount of unavoidable harm that may be done to individuals according to DH. There is also a minimization condition according to which those to blame for the existence of unavoidable harm may not themselves be harmed more than is necessary in order to protect innocent persons. Turning again to our mountain climbing example, DH with this minimization condition cannot be used to justify a distribution of harm which results in C's death if another distribution is possible which saves D's life without killing C.

The third ceteris paribus condition for DH that I shall mention here concerns the harmful side effects for innocent persons that may result from distributions of harm aimed at protecting other innocent persons. The need for this condition can be illustrated by cases of the following sort: x is in a position to distribute harm that is unavoidable from his standpoint either to y or to z; it is y's fault that either he or z must be harmed; if x distributes the harm to y, then some other innocent person will be harmed; the latter will be left untouched by a distribution which harms z rather than y. For example, we might have a defense case in which Third Party can defend Victim by harming Aggressor, but if he does, then some innocent bystander will also be harmed; while if Third Party does not act in Victim's defense, the bystander will not be harmed. Under these conditions, DH does not straightforwardly imply that Third Party should defend Victim.

Let us now consider how the above remarks pertain to matters of *societal* defense. Here we shall be concerned with the conditions under which societies are justified in establishing institutions and practices aimed at defending some of their members against the wrongfully aggressive acts of others.

Imagine a society S which contains a subclass S' of individuals who will wrongfully harm innocent members of S if not directly prevented from doing so. Assume for now that S can protect its innocent members only by establishing a police force with powers of direct intervention in cases where those in S' attempt to harm innocent persons; and assume also that in some cases the police must harm those bent on wrongdoing in order to protect their intended victims. If we focus on the choice facing S as a society, then we have a situation exactly analogous to the cases of individual self- and other-defense described earlier. A certain amount of harm is unavoidable from the standpoint of S as a whole, but it can be distributed by S in different ways. Moreover, certain members of S (i.e., those in S') are to blame for the fact that there is unavoidable harm to be distributed. Thus, according to DH, justice requires (ceteris paribus) S to distribute the harm among those in S', and hence to establish a police force.

Let us now modify our example somewhat. Suppose that those in S' cannot be *prevented* from harming innocent persons no matter how large and diligent a police force S establishes, but that they can be deterred from doing so by credible threats to their own well-being. We will also assume that S can pose such threats in only one way—that is, by establishing and effectively implementing a system of legal punishment. Under these conditions harm is again unavoidable from the standpoint of S as a whole,[5] though S does have some control over how this harm is distributed. A distribution involving the use of punishment will favor innocent members of S over those in S', while a distribution not involving punishment will have the opposite result. And since those in S' are to blame for the fact that there is unavoidable harm to be distributed, DH requires S (ceteris paribus) to establish a system of legal punishment.

As is indicated here, this last condition follows only if other things are equal—that is, only if the proportionality, minimization, and side-effect conditions for DH are satisfied. These conditions must be met whether harm is being distributed by individuals among other individuals or by groups of individuals among other groups. Thus, for example, if we think of S as wishing to distribute unavoidable harm among groups of its members by establishing and implementing a system of legal punishment, then S must select a system the implementation of which results in harm to those in S' that is proportional to the wrongful harm that will be done by members of S' if the system is not implemented. In addition, S must select a system which results in the minimum harm to those in S' that is necessary to protect innocent persons, and must also be concerned with the harm that might be distributed to some innocent persons as side effects of protecting others.

If we regard S as at least approximating a real society, then the kinds of wrongful harm which those in S' do or wish to do might well include such widely varied activities as burglary, assault, and murder. If so, then the system of punishment selected by S must reflect these differences if the proportionality condition of DH is to be satisfied. Furthermore, if it is possible to deter those in S' from engaging in some category of wrongdoing by correlating with that class of wrongdoings a punishment *less* than proportionality permits, then the minimization condition of DH requires that the lesser punishment be adopted. And if implementing the punishments prescribed by a system of punishment for given offenses will have harmful side effects for innocent persons, then this must be taken into account when assessing the moral acceptability of that system. In this way, limits are placed on the kinds of punishments that may be correlated with different kinds of wrongdoing in a system of punishment. A system which stipulates the death penalty for burglary almost certainly violates the proportionality requirement; a system according to which premeditated murder

---

[5] We can assume that some members of S are bound to be punished if a system of punishment is established and implemented.

is punishable by death may satisfy the proportionality requirement, but it may fail to meet the minimization requirement. And a system of punishment which prescribes the death penalty for certain offenses may have unacceptably harmful side effects for innocent persons. Whether a society fails to meet any of these requirements when it establishes a particular system of punishment depends on what conditions obtain in that society.

Among other things implicit in these remarks is the idea that punishments must fit crimes. This idea is commonly associated with retributivism, but it can now be seen to arise from basic and very general conditions of distributive justice having nothing to do with "getting even" or with correcting moral imbalances in the universe. Punishments must fit crimes in the same way and for the same reasons that any distribution of unavoidable harm satisfying the conditions mentioned in DH must meet proportionality requirements; and retributivist considerations clearly have no general bearing on these distributions. This is not to minimize the difficulties that can arise when attempting to answer questions about proportionality in particular cases. I do think, however, that there is a tendency to exaggerate these difficulties when the relationship between punishments and offenses is at issue.

In addition to the three general ceteris paribus conditions just discussed which qualify DH no matter how it is applied, there are conditions which are relevant primarily to the use of DH in the area of legal punishment. Two such conditions are worth some brief discussion here.

Let us continue to suppose that S cannot prevent those in S′ from harming innocent members of S, but that S can deter the former from performing their wrongful acts by establishing a system of legal punishment. Although it follows (given our assumptions about S′) that S is required (ceteris paribus) to establish a system of punishment, not every system will be morally acceptable. For example, S would not be justified in adopting a system which prescribes death by slow torture for certain offenses, no matter how grave those offenses might be. That is, for the system of punishment adopted by S to be morally acceptable, it must be humane. Moreover, if we think of systems of punishment as containing sets of rules which specify certain acts as offenses (ordered according to their gravity), and which correlate with these offenses certain punishments (ordered by severity), then for a system to be morally acceptable, it must satisfy the familiar requirement of justice that relevantly similar cases be treated similarly and relevantly dissimilar cases be treated dissimilarly.[6] This requirement would clearly be violated by a system which prescribes the death penalty for both murder and petty theft, or which prescribes twenty years in jail for burglary and six months in jail for embezzlement. Although I will not take the time to do so here, it is clear enough, I think, that by specifying in more detail the characteristics of systems of punishment (in the area of procedure, for

---

[6] I have argued elsewhere that this requirement applies quite generally to what might be called "desert systems," which include systems of compensation, grading, and reward, as well as systems of punishment. See my "Comparative and Non-comparative Justice," *The Philosophical Quarterly* 30 (1980), pp. 130–140.

example), we could generate additional restrictions on the use of DH in justifying the establishment of such systems.

The use of DH in justifying legal punishment satisfies at least one intuition underlying retributivism in requiring that systems of punishment satisfy proportionality conditions. It is also tempting to link DH with retributivism by claiming that on both views it is somehow *fitting* that wrongdoers suffer, simply by virtue of their having engaged in wrongdoing. Indeed, we may wish to express this relationship in terms that are even more closely associated with retributivism: We might say that one whose fault it is that either he or some innocent person will be harmed receives his just deserts when the harm is distributed to him rather than to the innocent person. The relationship between this use of *desert* and the retributivist's is rather tenuous and at any rate unclear, but it may provide some basis for regarding DH as containing a retributivist element.

These similarities between the two positions do not go very far, however. I think H. L. A. Hart is correct in maintaining that, according to retributivists, "the justification for punishing . . . is that the return of suffering for moral evil voluntarily done, is itself just or morally good."[7] If we accept Hart's characterization, however, then we must recognize that retributivists have a problem. For even if it is good that wrongdoers suffer, there is no reason to suppose that societies should promote this good by engaging in the practice of legal punishment. In order to maintain the retributivist position we must either take as given and absolutely fundamental the requirement that societies establish practices which inflict suffering on wrongdoers; or we must say that societies should establish practices aimed at the realization of all goods; or we must regard societies as required to seek after certain goods, and we must then provide plausible criteria according to which one of the goods at which societies must aim is that which results when wrongdoers suffer. Only the third of these alternatives strikes me as reasonable; and while it might be accepted by a retributivist, doing so will almost certainly require adjustments in his position. These adjustments might well lead to a principle like DH, which *does* provide a basis for the societal requirements to engage in legal punishment under certain conditions, but which generates this requirement from considerations that are ultimately independent of retributivism. In particular, it is not possible by the use of DH (as it is by appealing to strictly retributivist considerations) to justify establishing the practice of legal punishment when doing so has no value as an instrument of societal defense and serves only to insure that wrongdoers suffer.

Because it places considerable emphasis on forward-looking considerations, DH has a certain affinity with utilitarianism. These two approaches to justifying legal punishment differ in several important respects, however. For one thing, it is unlikely that utilitarianism can comfortably accommodate criteria for determining the moral acceptability of systems of punishment—criteria such as those embodied in the requirement that relevantly similar cases be

---

[7]   H. L. A. Hart, *Punishment and Responsibility* (Oxford: Oxford University Press, 1968), p. 231. As it is being used here, "retributivism" refers to what is sometimes called "maximal" or "strong" retributivism.

treated similarly and relevantly dissimilar cases be treated dissimilarly. Presumably, utilitarians will claim that systems of punishment which do not meet such requirements have low social utility relevant to those which do; or they might maintain that the requirements are somehow contained in the very notion of a system of punishment, and are therefore met as a matter of necessity by all such systems.[8] Although I shall not argue the point here, neither of these responses strikes me as particularly plausible.

Whatever utilitarians say about the moral acceptability of systems of punishment must obviously be consistent with their basic contention that societies are justified in establishing systems of punishment only if doing so is less harmful than alternative courses of action. Assuming that the harm referred to here is *collective* harm, the implications of utilitarianism for particular cases can differ significantly from those of DH. It might happen, for example, that if society S engages in legal punishment, its members will collectively suffer more harm than they will if no system of punishment is established. Presumably, a utilitarian must then conclude that S should not engage in legal punishment. Depending on how the harm in question is distributed, however, DH might yield a very different result. In particular, if, by establishing the practice of legal punishment, S distributes unavoidable harm among those whose fault it is that harm is unavoidable, then S should engage ceteris paribus in legal punishment even if, as a society, S suffers more collective harm than it would without legal punishment.[9]

This same point can be made in somewhat different terms.

We surely want societies to distribute burdens as well as benefits in a just manner. Utilitarians will judge these distributions (and the practices within which they occur) by their results. This idea has, of course, been criticized by a host of philosophies—but almost always in connection with distributions of benefits. It is claimed that certain kinds of non-utilitarian considerations are relevant to the justice of distributing benefits among members of societies—that, for example, an individual's contribution to producing the benefits should be taken into account. DH can be viewed as implying that certain non-utilitarian considerations are relevant to the just distribution of *burdens*—that, for example, one's blameworthiness for the existence of a situation can be relevant to whether he is justly burdened in that situation.

I realize that utilitarians have attempted in various ways to incorporate certain kinds of backward-looking considerations into their theories. What utilitarians cannot consistently maintain, however, is that such considerations are

---

[8] John Rawls seems to have something of the latter sort in mind when he makes this statement: "Now, that similar particular cases, as described by a practice, should be treated similarly as they arise, is part of the very concept of a practice; it is involved in the notion of an activity in accordance with rules." ("Justice as Fairness," *The Philosophical Review,* 67 (1958), pp. 164–194.

[9] This point about societal defense appears to have been missed by a number of writers. For example, Hugo Adam Bedau claims that there is no reasonable way to compare the value of innocent lives with that of guilty lives, and concludes from this that decisions regarding the morality of capital punishment "will probably have to be made on some basis other than societal defense." ("Capital Punishment" in Tom Regan (ed.), *Matters of Life and Death* (New York: Random House, 1980), p. 173).

morally significant in and of themselves. Thus, for example, the fact that some-one is at fault for the existence of a dangerous situation cannot be regarded by a utilitarian as relevant *in itself* to whether harm should be distributed to that individual rather than to someone else. The relevance of such considerations must be indirect, by way of their relation to appropriate forward-looking con-siderations, something which is certainly not the case when appeals are made to DH.

COPYRIGHTS AND ACKNOWLEDGMENTS